The Cambridge Encyclopedia of Human Paleopathology is a
major reference work for all those interested in identification of
disease in human remains. Many diseases leave characteristic
lesions and deformities on human bones, teeth and soft tissues
that can be identified many years after death.

This comprehensive volume includes most conditions producing effects recognizable with the unaided eye. Detailed lesion
descriptions and over 300 photographs facilitate disease recognition and each condition is placed in context with discussion
of its history, antiquity, etiology, epidemiology, geography, and
natural history.

Uniquely, diseases affecting the soft tissues are also included
as these are commonly present in mummified remains.

This book will be an indispensable resource for paleopathologists, anthropologists, physicians, archaeologists, demogra-
phers, and medical historians alike.

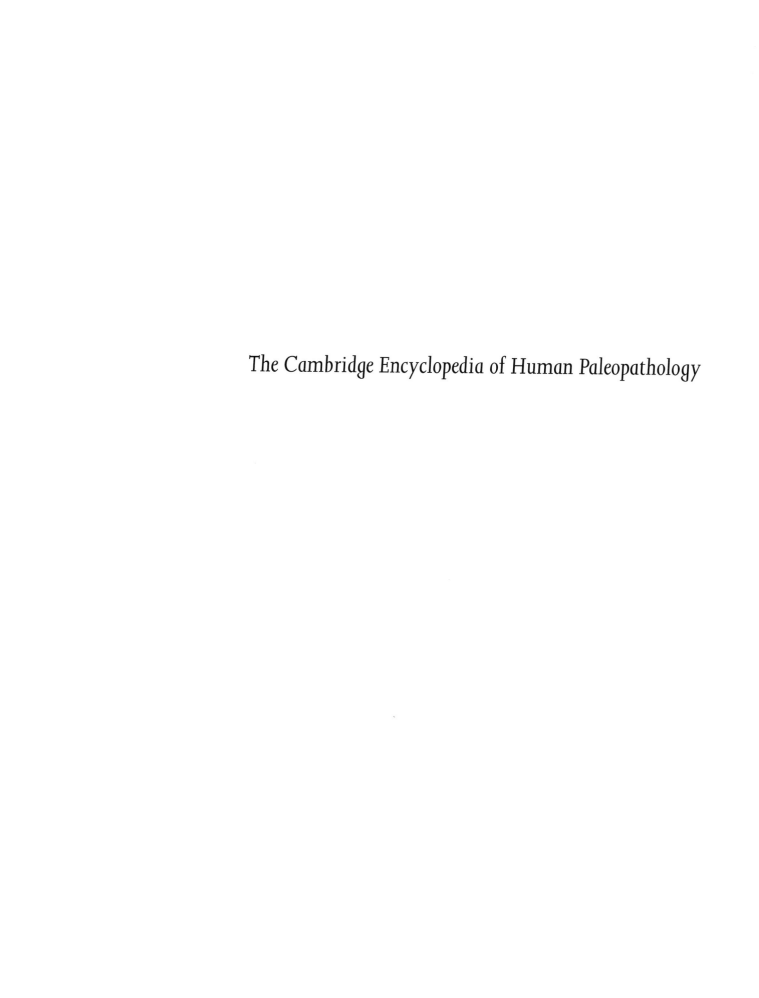

The Cambridge Encyclopedia of Human Paleopathology

The Cambridge Encyclopedia of

Human Paleopathology

by

Arthur C. Aufderheide
&
Conrado Rodríguez-Martín

including a dental chapter by

Odin Langsjoen

PUBLISHED BY THE PRESS SYNDICATE OF THE UNIVERSITY OF CAMBRIDGE
The Pitt Building, Trumpington Street, Cambridge CB2 1RP, United Kingdom

CAMBRIDGE UNIVERSITY PRESS
The Edinburgh Building, Cambridge CB2 2RU, UK http://www.cup.cam.ac.uk
40 West 20th Street, New York, NY 10011–4211, USA http://www.cup.cam.org
10 Stamford Road, Oakleigh, Melbourne 3166, Australia

First published 1998

Printed in the United Kingdom at the University Press, Cambridge

Typeset in Joanna 10.25/12.5 pt, in QuarkXpress™ [DS]

A catalogue record for this book is available from the British Library

Aufderheide, Arthur C.
The Cambridge encyclopedia of human paleopathology/by Arthur C. Aufderheide &
Conrado Rodríguez-Martín: including a dental chapter by Odin Langsjoen.

    p.   cm.
  Includes bibliographical references and index.
  ISBN 0 521 55203 6 (hardback)
   1. Paleopathology – Encyclopedias. I. Rodríguez-Martín, Conrado.
II. Langsjoen, Odin, 1923– .   III. Title.
[DNLM: 1. Paleopathology – encyclopedias.   QZ 13 A918c 1997]
R134.8.A93   1997
616.07–dc21   97-16223 CIP
DNLM/DLC
for Library of Congress

ISBN 0 521 55203 6 hardback

Contents

Part Four

Congenital anomalies 51

Part Five

Circulatory disorders 77

Preface

Human paleopathology can be defined as the study of disease in ancient populations by the examination of human remains. So defined, it has been practiced to some degree for more than a century. In the past its practitioners have come to the field with quite diverse backgrounds, though physicians and anthropologists have been the principal investigators. These two groups bring not only overlapping but also complementary skills to paleopathology. Physicians have a superb knowledge of the nature, transmission and epidemiology of disease (though not necessarily its expression in bone), while anthropologists' mastery of osteology and understanding of human behavior at the population level is unsurpassed. The field's complexity has been compounded further by the involvement of historians, molecular biologists, physicists, geochemists and those from other disciplines during the past several decades as these workers have focused their technical skills on paleopathology specimens, supplementing the morphological database with nonanatomic, often quantitative, information. Veteran paleopathologists from each group have demonstrated they can acquire many of the skills of the other, but we hope that leadership in each of these disciplines in the future will lead to joint training programs.

In this volume we have attempted to present the nature of disease expressions in skeletal and soft tissue in a manner that, to the extent possible, will meet the needs of the occasional consultant or the career investigator. Authors of a comprehensive, current paleopathology text must directly address the chimeric composition of its readership. One of the major decisions we faced was the range of topics to be included. Recognizing that gross pathology remains the core of paleopathology, we chose an anatomic approach to this question's solution: we included almost every disease that produces in human tissues an anatomic pathological change large enough to be detected by the unaided eye. Principal among our exceptions to this rule are a few (mostly infectious) conditions such as cholera that produce no gross lesions, but owe their inclusion to their epidemic nature and their often profound demographic impact on affected populations. Furthermore because one cannot diagnose a disease of whose existence one is not aware, many modern diseases are included even if no example has yet been reported in the paleopathology literature. The degree of emphasis, however, is scaled to the probability of a given disease's appearance during a paleopathological investigation.

Another controversial issue involved the question of inclusion of gross anatomic changes in preserved nonskeletal tissues. An argument could be made that only a handful of paleopathologists dissect human mummies and they are not among those who examine skeletons. The first of these assumptions was true a decade ago but is, happily, eroding rapidly, and the second never was the rule. Furthermore, many diseases affect both skeletal and nonskeletal tissues, and an understanding of such disease processes is incomplete if the paleopathologist is unaware of the soft tissue alterations. For these reasons we have included soft tissue lesions, some of which have already been reported in mummified human remains.

The distinctive feature of this text, however, is the inclusion of disease aspects not normally elaborated in paleopathology texts. The basis of their presence in this volume is our (controversial?) conviction that detailed knowledge of how lesions come to assume the form they present to the paleopathologist will be enormously helpful in the recognition of their cause. Memorization of a disease's osteological features may well be a necessity for paleopathology students but it will not, of itself, lead the reader into an appreciation of the variation in severity, morphology and frequency that characterize paleopathology lesions. Morphological expressions of various diseases overlap generously and lists of features can be threateningly confusing unless the lesions' development is understood clearly. The 'Natural History' sections are employed to present the disease as a succession of tissue events that gradually cause and shape the final form of the lesions. In this section we have tried to make it possible for the reader to create a mental image of the evolving lesions so vivid that our final listing of features will seem almost redundant. Equally important will be the reader's ability to anticipate and recognize the many variations a given disease's lesions may assume – far greater than the usually extreme examples selected for illustrations in textbooks (including ours). Since the importance of recounting the lesion's evolution will vary with its nature we have

adjusted the length of this section accordingly, perhaps least in traumatic and congenital conditions and maximal in infectious diseases.

It is also our feeling that an understanding of the state of our knowledge about the 'Antiquity, History and Epidemiology' of a disease will help maximize the integration of identified pathological conditions with information about archaeological, anthropological, cultural and other aspects of a studied ancient population. Hence, we have introduced these sections, not as topics of exhaustive depth, but hopefully adequate for the stated purpose. Certainly the information in these as well as the Natural History sections could be extracted from other, independent texts in other fields, but the latter are not necessarily written specifically for the paleopathologist's needs (e.g. the heavy emphasis on laboratory diagnostic tests and on therapy in usual medical texts). In addition we hope their ready access by inclusion in this text will result in more frequent perusal of such material by the user.

Finally, differences in readers' familiarity with medical terminology needed to be addressed. We resisted the temptation to minimize medical vocabulary, for so doing would imply that paleopathologists do not need to know it. It is true that we might maintain understanding of our text by elaborate efforts to avoid technical terms, but the simple truth is that lack of a reasonable familiarity with common medical terms will deprive the paleopathologist of the continually changing body of medical literature relevant to diseases of interest. Most directors of graduate paleopathology programs are cognizant of its importance and their students can expect to receive appropriate medical terminology training. Similarly when specific enzymes, cell membrane chemical receptors or antigens significantly affect the presence or virulence of a disease, their technical names and functions are cited and explained to enable understanding of the mechanisms. For example, the unique geographic population pattern of gene frequencies of Duffy red blood cell antigens only becomes comprehensible when the role of these antigens in the vivax malarial life cycle is understood. It is important to note that these very features are also being exploited in the evolving nonanatomic laboratory techniques for disease identification in human remains.

We hope our efforts to produce this volume will both aid diagnosis and enrich its users' experiences in this captivating field of study. The extent of acceptance of this text by its potential users may be a measure of how appropriate our assumptions are. We welcome readers' suggestions for changes in subsequent editions.

ARTHUR C. AUFDERHEIDE
CONRADO RODRIGUEZ MARTIN

Acknowledgements

In addition to the many dozens of individuals whose willingness to provide specimen photographs is acknowledged in the figure legends, we wish to call attention to several who helped us in unique ways. Mary Aufderheide not only shared both the grime and the sublime of the many field trips whose results are incorporated within this text, but her linguistic talents and personal warmth overcame the many obstacles to such field exercises. Her unfailing faith in our ultimate success provided the support necessary to endure the natural, social and military crises that seem to be an inseparable feature of global field perambulations. Elena García de Rodríguez-Martín supported the preparation of this book through her patience during the many hours her husband devoted to searching bibliographic sources and writing chapters. She also made major contributions to the preparation of the manuscripts and the final selection of the many specimens to be photographed. We also note the enormous contributions made by Sara Hammer of the Paleobiology Laboratory in the Department of Pathology at the University of Minnesota, Duluth School of Medicine. Her enthusiastic participation in and commitment to the production of this volume was clearly key to its success. Her incredible ability to find and gain access to sixteenth century documents, compulsion for accuracy in bibliographic detail, editing text that invariably improved its quality, dogged pursuit of permits for use of copyright-covered published illustrations and indefatigable efforts to meet deadlines were essential elements in bringing this manuscript to publication. We thank Drs Stanley Aschenbrenner and G. Rapp (archaeologists, University of Minnesota, Duluth) for their innumerable consultations that provided both fact and perspective necessary for our proper understanding. Also to be acknowledged is our debt to those museum curators who made their collections available to us for photography, especially Paul Sledzik and Dr Marc Micozzi of the National Museum for Health and Medicine, Gretchen Worden of the Mütter Museum, Bruce Latimer and Lyman Jellema of the Cleveland Museum of Natural History,

Dr John Gregg and photographer Glenn Malchow in the Department of Archaeology at the University of South Dakota, Dr. Jon Kramer of the Potomac Museum Group (the mammoth metatarsal with osteomyelitis) and Rose Tyson of San Diego's Museum of Man who not only provided specimens for photography, but allowed us access to the electronic paleoopathology bibliography she was developing that proved to be of great value to us. We are also very grateful to the staff at the Archaeological Museum in the University of Tarapaca in Arica, Chile for granting the opportunity to carry out so many dissections of mummified human remains under Dr. Marvin Allison's supervision and sharing their experience with us. The Guanche mummy and skeletal collection at the Museo Arqueológico de Tenerife, O.A.M.C.-Cabildo de Tenerife (Canary Islands) was especially valuable, it was made available to us by the generosity and enthusiastic support of its director Rafael Gonzáles Antón and his helpful staff. We are deeply indebted to Mrs Kenneth and Donald Erickson, Guilford and Rondi Lewis and other contributors to the Kenneth Erickson Memorial Fund for making it possible to acquire and properly process the hundreds of illustrations in this volume. Mercedes Martín, member of the Instituto Canario de Paleopatología y Bioanthropología (also belonging to the O.A.M.C.-Cabildo de Tenerife) helped in the preparation of manuscripts and in the selection of specimen photographs. The many superb photographs, as well as the skeletal paleopathology bibliography contributed by Dr Domingo Campillo (Barcelona, Spain) were extremely useful. We owe a special debt to Patrick Horne for his continuing interest and help in reviewing text (paleoparasitology) and showering us with fascinating arcane articles and photos. The reviews of other chapters by Drs Keith Manchester and S. Aaronson improved their quality enormously and deleted or modified multiple errors. Dr Bruce Ragsdale helped greatly with photographs of neoplasms as did Dr R. Elzay with examples of dental pathology. Dr Conrado Rodríguez Maffiotte, retired professor of Orthopedics and History of Medicine in the University of La Laguna (Tenerife, Canary Islands) contributed many important ancient articles on skeletal pathology and history of medicine, as well as his suggestions on both matters. He was the person who introduced me (C.R.M.) to the wonderful world of human paleopathology when I was a student in the School of Medicine of the University of La Laguna. Permission to reproduce illustrations of an ameloblastoma and that of a patient with advanced osteitis fibrosa cystica by Dr P. Slootweg and Dr Anne McNicol, respectively, allowed valuable additions. Dr Saras Aturalia and Tracy Kemp helped with critical deadline crises. The ongoing friendly and helpful photographic and art services of Mark Summers and Dan Schlies at the University of Minnesota, Duluth were invaluable to us, as were the specialized services of the staff at Custom Photo in Duluth. We thank Antonio Vela, director of the Centro de Fotografia Isla de Tenerife (O.A.M.C.-Cabildo de Tenerife) and his collaborators for their efforts in preparing illustrations of the many specimens at the Museo Arqueológico de Tenerife. We also appreciate the help provided by the World Health Organization. It was Dr E.T. Bell of the Department of Pathology at the University of Minnesota, Minneapolis who generated in me (A.C.A.) the fascination of the field of human pathology, taught me its technology and nourished in me the spirit of scientific curiosity that ultimately led to my contributions to this volume.

Finally, Dr O. Langsjoen was the author of Chapter 14 and would like to make the following acknowledgements: I express my sincere gratitude to the Archaeological Research Center in the Department of Archaeology at the University of Tarapara, Arica, Chile for providing access to their museum skeletal collection. A special thank you is also due to Mavis Langsjoen for organizing and recording the on-site data collection, Sara Hammer for innumerable secretarial services, the staff of the Educational Resources Department, University of Minnesota, Duluth School of Medicine for figures and graphics, and Dr Arthur Aufderheide for his invaluable counsel and thoughtful review of the manuscript for my chapter.

Throughout this 3-year effort, however, it was the patience and continuous support of our marriage partners, Mary, Elena and Mavis that made this production possible.

Abbreviations for photograph sources in figure legends

BM,	Briest Museum, Department of Pathology, University of Minnesota, Duluth School of Medicine, Duluth, MN.
CMNH,	Cleveland Museum of Natural History.
DMNH,	Denver Museum of Natural History.
Guanche,	Aboriginal from Tenerife, Canary Islands, Spain.
ICPB,	Instituto Canario de Paleopatalogía y Bioantropología.
MAA,	Museu Arqueologic d'Alcoi, Spain.
MAC,	Museu d'Arqueologia de Catalunya, Barcelona, Spain.
MAT,	Museo de Arqueológico de Tenerife, Canary Islands, Spain (OAMC).
MAUT,	Museo Arqueologico, Universidad de Tarapaca, Arica, Chile.
MM,	Mütter Museum, College of Physicians, Philadelphia, PA.
NMHM,	National Museum of Health and Medicine, Washington, DC.
SDUM,	School of Dentistry, University of Minnesota, Minneapolis, MN.
PBL,	Paleobiology Laboratory, University of Minnesota, Duluth School of Medicine, Duluth, MN.
UB,	Universitat de Barcelona, Spain.

PART ONE

History of paleopathology

INTRODUCTION

The evolution of a scientific discipline is usually portrayed as a chronological succession of time segments, each of which is characterized by shared concepts, methods or other features. The few, extant reviews of paleopathology's history by such writers as Jarcho (1966a) in the United States, Stroppiana (1973) in Italy and Jaén (1977) in Mexico have all used a similar format. Although there are slight differences in the parameters of the defined eras, they all identified a very early period (prior to mid-nineteenth century) in which observations of disease in fossilized animal bones were recorded. This was followed by a second interval roughly contemporaneous with the initiation and efflorescence of microbiology in the latter half of that same century, during which the focus was directed at pathological changes in <u>human</u> skeletons. The third period, occupying several decades of the early twentieth century, recorded considerable expansion of such reports and included some classification efforts. Finally, the most recent era, beginning about mid-nineteenth century, demonstrates the maturation of this field as reflected by an enormous increase in publications with more exacting definitions, criteria, systematization and an explosion of new methodology.

In this review we will follow a similar approach as outlined by Rodríguez-Martín (1989a,1990) as well as Rodríguez-Martín & Caseriego Ramírez (1991), who identified the following phases:

Antecedent phase (Renaissance to mid-nineteenth century)

Genesis of Paleopathology (mid-nineteenth century to World War I)

Interbellum Consolidation phase (1913–1945)

New Paleopathology phase (1946 to present)

The features characteristic of each of these periods are detailed in the remainder of this compendium.

ANTECEDENT PHASE (RENAISSANCE TO MID-NINETEENTH CENTURY)

During this long period most work was devoted to the study of diseases in prehistoric animals. In Europe the first reference to ancient pathology was made by the Swiss anatomist Felix Platter (1536–1614) who, in his work *De Corporis Humani Structura et Usa* incorrectly attributed several fossil elephant bones to human gigantism. The naturalist Scheuchzer (1726) confused fossilized giant salamander bones (in 1726), identifying them as a human victim of the 'universal inundation.' The German naturalist Johann Friederich Esper (1774) (Fig. 1.1) correctly diagnosed an osteosarcoma in a cave bear's femur, a feat hailed by Ubelaker (1982) as the birth of paleopathology. A Quaternary hyena's occipital skull fracture was described by George Augustus Goldfuss (1810) at the University of Bonn, and lesions from other Quaternary animals were published by the Belgian, P.C. Schmerling (1835), who also noted differential diagnosis difficulties. Though studying primarily diseases of bears and lions, the importance of knowing the antiquity of <u>human</u> diseases was emphasized by Phillip Franz von Walther (1781–1849) near the end of this period (Walther, 1825), adding that inheritance may be a major factor in disease origins.

In America, Jarcho (1966a) attributed the first paleopathology report to the Boston surgeon John Collins Warren (who also performed the first operation on an anesthetized patient) for his description of American aboriginal deformed skulls in his book *A Comparative View of the Sensorial and Nervous System in Man and Animals* in 1822. Both fractures and anthropogenic deformation were described in 1839 by Samuel George Morton in *Crania Americana* (Fig. 1.2).

The end of this period was also marked by the application of the micro-

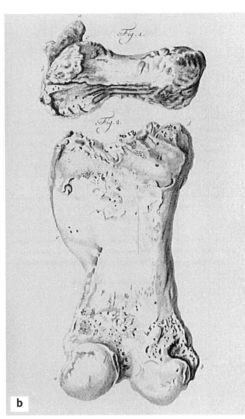

FIG. 1.1. **Femur fracture and callus of fossil cave bear.** Johann Friedrich Esper. (a) Frontispiece (portrait) and (b) Plate XIV, figure 2 from his 1774 book (see bibliography). Courtesy of Wangensteen Historical Library of Biology and Medicine, University of Minnesota, Minneapolis, MN.

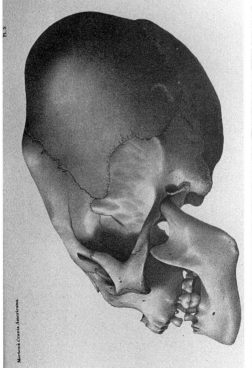
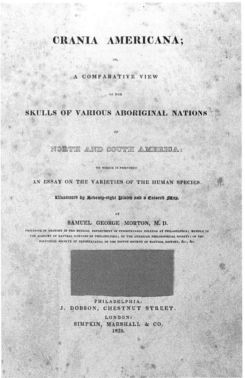

FIG. 1.2. **Cranial deformation.** Prehistoric native of site at Arica, Chile. From *Crania Americana* by Samuel George Morton (1839). Courtesy of Wangensteen Historical Library of Biology and Medicine, University of Minnesota, Minneapolis, MN.

FIG. 1.3. **Ovarian cyst.** From an Egyptian mummy dissected by Augustus Bozzi Granville. Reproduced from Granville (1825): *Philosophical Transactions of the Royal Society of London*.

scope to tissue structure. The Swiss (Neuchatel) professor Louis Agassiz studied fossilized dental microstructure between 1833–1843 as did the British anatomist Richard Owen (1804–1892), and the British gynecologist and pathologist Augustus Bozzi Granville (1783–1871) reported histological observations of samples from a twenty-seventh dynasty Egyptian mummy he dissected (Fig. 1.3).

In summary, this period's reports were isolated observations of a descriptive nature carried out mostly with little scientific precision and on specimens viewed primarily as curiosities, not as sources of medical, pathological or historical knowledge. Thus they are most appropriately viewed as antecedents to the scientific discipline of paleopathology.

FIG. 1.4. **Rudolf Virchow.** Pathologist, anthropologist, and statesman, who applied the principles of his studies on cellular pathology to ancient human remains. Reproduced from Moodie (1923a), figure 7, pp. 84. By permission, University of Chicago Press, Chicago, IL.

GENESIS OF PALEOPATHOLOGY
(MID-NINETEENTH CENTURY TO WORLD WAR I)

While a number of pioneering physicians and anthropologists clarified the medical nature of ancient skeletal pathological changes during this period, primary interest in studies of human remains remained anthropologically-focused. Archaeology can be said to have initiated in northern France when Jacques Boucher de Crevecouer de Perthes (1788–1868) found, in 1847, stone tools associated with animal bones in a canal. Subsequently the steady stream of excavated human and animal bones generated large osteological collections at museums and universities. Study of these skeletal tissues was carried out principally out of interest in their value to physical anthropology (then focused largely on racial origins). However, the incidentally observed pathological lesions in these bones did attract a number of physicians and anthropologists who were curious about the nature of the diseases that may have caused them. Their diagnostic evaluations were enhanced with application of Wilhelm Konrad Röntgen's discovery of X-rays that led to his Nobel award in 1901. While the number of publications proliferated dramatically, most were characterized by reports of individual, often spectacular cases. Few of the authors appreciated the value of those diseases' paleoepidemiology.

Among these was the German physician, pathologist and statesman Rudolph Virchow (1821–1902) (Fig. 1.4). In 1856 he examined a human skull from a Feldhofen cave (Neanderthal Man) and declared it pathological. In subsequent years he published other papers dealing with lesions

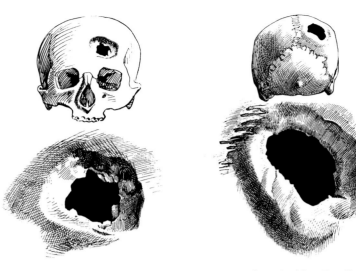

FIG. 1.6. **Cranial trepanation.** Skeletal remains of aboriginals (Guanches) from Tenerife, Canary Islands. Reproduced from Felix von Luschan (1896*a*), figures A and B. Instituto Canario de Paleopatologia y Antropologia.

FIG. 1.5. **Janos Czermak.** Czech medical scientist who performed histological studies on mummy tissues. Reproduced from Czermak (1879). Courtesy of Wangensteen Historical Library of Biology and Medicine, University of Minnesota, Minneapolis, MN.

in paleolithic and Neolithic human and animal remains (Virchow, 1895), suggesting that disease is a form of altered life and therefore is probably as old as life itself. However, Virchow's interest in these lesions remained largely medical. He had no manifest interest in the epidemiological impact of disease on culture, a view considered by most as too limited to earn him the designation of the 'Father of Paleopathology.' In addition to Virchow, others who made earlier, occasional contributions include J. N. Czermak (1879) (Fig. 1.5) (A Czech, who used histology to identify arteriosclerosis in an Egyptian mummy 50 years before Ruffer did [Strouhal & Vyhnánek, 1979]), Kovacs (1843, trepanation in Hungary), K.W. Mayer (who studied the zoopathology of the Quaternary animals) and L.A. Gosse (1861).

It was, however, the French investigators who led the paleopathology procession in the latter half of the nineteenth century. The Parisian surgeon and medical school professor Pierre Paul Broca (1824–1880) startled workers in this field when he attributed a Peruvian skull defect to antemortem surgery in 1867. He also published on congenital parietal defects in 1875. His other achievements included the study of Cro-Magnon man and establishment of the Société d' Anthropologie in 1859, the Revue d' Anthropologie in 1872 and the Ecole d' Anthropologie in 1876. His contemporary, M. Pruniéres (1874) separated the postmortem trepanations and rondelles from antemortem operations, and also described tuberculous lesions in Neolithic bones. By 1878 Just Marie Marcelin Lucas-Championniére (1833–1913) was able to write an entire book, La Trépanation, on that topic, asserting the operation was performed for both magical and therapeutic reasons, and not-

ing that the ancient surgeons prevented lethal hemorrhage from the sagittal sinus by avoiding the sagittal suture. Leonce Manouvrier (1904) had also described the 'neolithic sincipital T' type of cranial cauterization in 1895. Campillo (1983), however, feels that the general treatise *Lésions Osseuses de L'Homme Préhistorique en France et en Algérie*, written by Jules Le Baron in 1881, was a milestone both for the French workers and for the scientific field because it was a general treatise on paleopathological lesions gleaned from the thousands of bones collected at the Museé Broca and the Museé of Paris, and in which diagnosis and predicted etiology was attempted.

Among other European workers during this period, Felix von Luschan (Berlin) described trepanation and cauterization in the Canary Islands' aboriginal ('Guanche') skulls during the last years of the nineteenth century (Fig. 1.6). Similar observations were made and classified on Guanche remains curated in the university museum's Institute and Humanities School at La Plata, Argentina by Robert Lehmann-Nitsche (1904; Rodríguez-Martín, 1990), while yet another German, Detloff von Behr, published a monograph in 1908 on dental pathology of the Guanches. In addition, further reports were contributed by Djordje Jovánovic and Dragutin Gorjanovic-Kramberger in Yugoslavia, C. Engelhardt, S. Hansen (1894: 242–69), H. Kjaer and H.A. Nielson in Denmark as well as Gregorio Chil y Naranjo (1878) in Spain who was the first to identify Guanche trepanations.

In the United States the forensic specialist Joseph Jones (1833–1896) excavated and reported treponemal lesions from bones in Kentucky and Tennessee, also studied histologically. At Harvard University the work of three physicians had enormous impact on physical anthropology and related areas (Jarcho, 1966*a*). Jeffries Wyman (1814–1874), curator of Harvard's Peabody Museum in 1871 described periosteal inflammation that Jarcho thinks may have been syphilis. In 1878 Frederick W. Putnam (1839–1915) debated the possibility of syphilis described by Joseph Jones. The curator of the Warren Anatomical Museum, William F. Whitney (1850–1921), published the first American paleopathology manual *Notes on the Anomalies, Injuries and Diseases of the Bones of the Native Races of North America*, in 1886. Finally, Joseph Leidy (1823–1891), pathology professor from Philadelphia, pathologist and archaeologist Tophil Mitchell Prudden (1849–1924) as well as pathologist and archaeologist Josiah Clark Nott (1804–1873) made periodic reports of lesions, while cranial trepanation was studied in Peru by Otis T. Mason (1885), in Bolivia by A.J. Bandelier (1904) and in America by P. McGee (1894, 1897). Most of these reports, however, lack useful detail. David Matto (1886) and Antonio Lorena (1890) were contemporaneous South American scientists who reported trepanation among the Incas.

In addition to human investigators, the period is also distinguished by the formation of three institutions whose osteological collections contributed to paleopathological

studies. The U.S. Army Medical Museum (now called the National Museum of Health and Medicine) was created in 1862 to house legs amputated or other abnormal tissues extirpated on battle fields of the U.S. Civil War in the hope that their study could reduce surgical mortality. Between 1898 and 1904 it donated 3500 skeletal specimens to the National Museum of Natural History (a part of the Smithsonian Institution), keeping only the pathological specimens. In Europe the Museé de L'Homme at Paris began and continues to enlarge one of the most important osteological collections in the world, though its primary interest was normal morphology and osteometrics.

INTERBELLUM CONSOLIDATION PHASE (WORLD WAR I AND MARC ARMAND RUFFER TO WORLD WAR II)

It was during this interval that paleopathology expanded, systematically applied the methods of radiology, histology, serology, and others, and also introduced statistics into such studies. The resulting improvements in diagnosis and the concept of linking disease to culture led to the evolution of paleopathology as a scientific discipline.

The wave of Egyptomania, initiated by Bonaparte's invasion of that country and fanned by Champollion's decipherment of the Rosetta stone, led to the extensive excavations that produced a large number of mummies available for study early in the twentieth century. The British anatomist Grafton Elliot Smith & Warren Dawson (1924) (Fig. 1.7) and the chemist Alfred Lucas (1926) made major contributions to paleopathology by examining grossly these mummies and chemically analyzing natron and other substances in their tissues. But it was Marc Armand Ruffer (1859–1917) who led the way with the detailed documentation of his innovations and observations. Born in Lyon into an aristocratic family of a French baron and German mother, he acquired medical training in Germany and bacteriological expertise at the Pasteur Institute (Garrison, 1917). There he contracted diphtheria and went to Egypt in 1891 for convalescence. While a professor at the English Government School for medicine in Cairo, head of the Red Cross and president of the Sanitary, Maritime and Quarantine Council of Egypt until 1917, he recognized the wealth of potential medical knowledge that could be extracted by examination of the accumulating excavated mummies. After 1908 an uninterrupted flow of his publications about the identification of schistosome ova, atherosclerosis, osteoarthritis, congenital conditions, malaria, tuberculosis and other diseases reflected the application of his medical knowledge and techniques to mummy tissues with awareness of their epidemiological implications (Sandison, 1967a). He developed a method of rehydrating mummy soft tissues and preparing histological

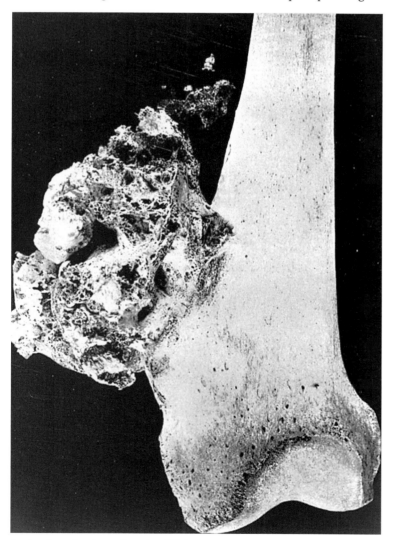

FIG. 1.7. **Osteochondroma, femur in a fifth dynasty Egyptian mummy.** This was figure 64 in Smith & Dawson's (1924) book *Egyptian Mummies*. Smith's diagnosis was osteosarcoma. With permission of Kegan Paul International (London and New York) who reprinted the original 1924 book in 1991).

slides that expanded substantially the range of diagnosable diseases. It was he that popularized the term 'paleopathology,' a designation that had been suggested earlier by the physician R.W. Shufeldt (1892–93) and that had appeared in *Funk and Wagnall's Standard Dictionary* since 1895 (Jarcho, 1966a; Ubelaker, 1982). In 1917, while returning from a public sanitation project in Greece, he died tragically when the warship on which he was a passenger was torpedoed by a German submarine. An anthology of his articles (Fig. 1.8), collected and edited by the paleontologist Roy Lee Moodie, was published in 1921 under the title *Studies in the Paleopathology of Egypt.* Oddly, after this brilliant beginning, the study of mummies faltered after his death, and paleopathologists returned to their interest in skeletal pathology.

Other French contributions during this period included the use of X-rays on ancient human remains in 1923 by M. Baudouin, a procedure that enabled him to study rheumatic diseases, hip dislocations, dental paleopathology and other conditions (Stroppiana, 1973). The military surgeon León Páles in 1930 published his treatise *Paleopathologie et Pathologie Comparative,* dealing with a lifetime of study of a broad range of diseases, and in which he noted relationships between disease, evolution and species extinction. A valuable listing of 660 paleopathology references was included in the book. Emile Guiard also published a book in 1930, *La Trépanation Craniénne chez les Néolithiques et chez les Primitifs Modernes,* in 1930 dealing with the relationship of cranial trepanation to brachiocephaly.

Neolithic cranial trepanation and nonmetric spine traits were also the focus of publications by Portugal's M.B. Barbosa Sueiro. Further Portuguese reports on paleopathological observa-

STUDIES IN THE
PALAEOPATHOLOGY
OF EGYPT

By
SIR MARC ARMAND RUFFER, Kt., C.M.G., M.D.
Late President of the Quarantine Council of Egypt; formerly Director of the British Institute of Preventive Medicine; Professor of Bacteriology in the Cairo Medical School; Member of the Indian Plague Commission, etc.

Edited by
ROY L. MOODIE, Ph.D.
Associate Professor of Anatomy in the University of Illinois

THE UNIVERSITY OF CHICAGO PRESS
CHICAGO, ILLINOIS

FIG. 1.8. **Sir Marc Armand Ruffer.** From Ruffer's collected papers published in 1921 as a book edited by his friend and colleague Roy Moodie. With permission from the University of Chicago Press, Chicago, IL.

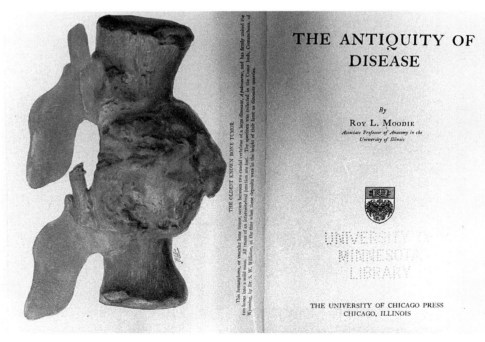

THE ANTIQUITY OF
DISEASE

By
ROY L. MOODIE
Associate Professor of Anatomy in the University of Illinois

THE UNIVERSITY OF CHICAGO PRESS
CHICAGO, ILLINOIS

FIG. 1.9. **Hemangioma in bone of dinosaur tail.** Frontispiece in Roy Moodie's (1923a) *The Antiquity of Disease.* With permission from the University of Chicago Press, Chicago, IL.

tions were contributed by the anatomist Hernani Monteiro and the medical historian Luiz de Pina (1965). In Denmark, K.M. Christopherson studied paleostomatology in the decades of the 1930s and 1940s, and K. Isager published a monograph exclusively devoted to diseases and injuries in ancient skeletal remains (Bennike, 1985). Akos Palla (Hungary), J. Petrovic (Yugoslavia), Dominik Wölfel (Germany: ancient trepanation

and cauterization), and Juan Bosch Millares (1975: Spain – Canary Islands) were numbered among other contributing European paleopathologists.

In the United States the same Roy Lee Moodie (Fig. 1.9) who edited Ruffer's anthology also published a massive tome in 1923 entitled *Paleopathology. An Introduction to the Study of Ancient Evidences of Disease* (Moodie, 1923b). Trained in anatomy and

Fig. 1.10. **Ales Hrdlicka.** He developed the Physical Anthropology Section of the Smithsonian Institution. Negative MNH 31, 513, National Anthropological Archives, the Smithsonian Institution, Washington DC.

focused on paleontology, Moodie devoted about one-third of his book to lesions in human remains, analyzed previously published reports and used about two-thirds of his volume to document disease in ancient plants and animals, many of which had been fossilized. Combining microscopy and photomicroscopy he documented the antiquity of disease in fossil plants from the early Paleozoic period and demonstrated bacteria in Carboniferous Age fossilized remains. In 1931 he again recorded the results of another major study — a radiological study of the large collection of Egyptian and Peruvian mummies at the Field Museum in Chicago. These two publications provided a major impetus to the developing field of paleopathology.

North American paleopathology experienced another major impact with the appointment of the Czechoslovakian-born Ales Hrdlicka (Fig. 1.10) to the anthropology staff of the National Museum of Natural History at the Smithsonian Institution in Washington, DC, where he created the Division of Physical Anthropology. Though his field methods may not always have resulted in random sampling, he developed large osteological collections from both North and South America that are still the objects of study today. Nevertheless, his primary focus remained physical anthropology (Hrdlicka, 1939; Ubelaker, 1982). Many of his publications concern cranial features including trepanation, ear exostoses and lesions of violence, summarized in his major opus *Anthropological Work in Peru in 1913 with Notes on the Pathology of the Ancient Peruvians* (Hrdlicka, 1914). He also denied the pre-Columbian presence of tuberculosis in America.

Hrdlicka's contemporary, Harvard's Earnest Albert Hooton introduced a demographic perspective, using a statistical, ecological and cultural approach to physical anthropology (Jarcho, 1966a; Rodríguez-Martín, 1989b), also demonstrat-

ing chronological changes in disease frequency (Ortner & Putschar, 1985). He field-tested these methods in his early studies in the Canary Islands (*The Ancient Inhabitants of the Canary Islands*, Hooton, 1925) and then applied them in a major way to his epochal work in the southwestern United States of America, published in his now famous *The Indians of Pecos Pueblo: A Study of Their Skeletal Remains* (Hooton, 1930). He also recommended the creation of a collection of modern osteological lesions of known etiology to serve for comparative paleopathology research.

Other American paleopathologists included Herbert U. Williams (1866–1938) who published a general review of paleopathology (1929), Weber (1927), Michaelis (1930) and Netman. These investigators used radiology and histology to diagnose syphilis and other lesions during the 1920s and 1930s. George Grant MacCurdy's (1923) study of human skeletal tissue from Peru's Urubamba valley is a splendid example of meticulous application of osteological methodology.

In South America, Zambaco-Pachá published a paleoepidemiological study about the antiquity of syphilis in 1897 and a similar approach was used in his study of leprosy in 1914. More well-known is the archaeologist Julio C. Tello (1880–1947), professor at Lima's Universidad Mayor de San Marcos and director of the National Museum of Anthropology. He studied artificial mummification of the head, trepanation and medical practices in Peru, and published a book (1909) on the antiquity of syphilis, alleging its pre-Columbian existence in that country.

Thus it is evident that the sporadic, hesitant and isolated paleopathological observations of the previous period were consolidated during the period between World War I and II with the introduction and gradual standardization both of new methods and new interpretive concepts, resulting in the emergence of paleopathology as a scientific discipline.

THE NEW PALEOPATHOLOGY (WORLD WAR II UP TO THE PRESENT)

A major chapter of paleopathology ended with the first fires of World War II. After this conflict, paleopathology was viewed in a different way: as an important tool for the understanding of past populations. It was during this stage of our discipline that paleopathology was related to epidemiology and demography, and when the new techniques coming from clinical and laboratory medicine allowed a much more secure diagnosis. Angel (1981) divides this new activity in paleopathology into four different areas:

1. Patterns of traits necessary to limit diagnosis.
2. Social biology or the relations between health status and society.
3. Demography and health.

4. Growth, related mainly to nutrition, including bone chemistry.

Recently the fascinating field of genetic research has been introduced to paleopathology. It is now possible to diagnose infectious diseases, such as tuberculosis and possibly treponematosis, through the extraction of ancient DNA of the bacilli from mummified tissue or archaeological bone, and its amplification by means of the polymerase chain reaction (PCR: Spigelman & Lemma, 1993; Salo *et al.*, 1994; Rogan & Lentz, 1995).

But the great impetus of paleopathology emerged during the latter part of the 1960s and especially during the decade of the 1970s. Most authors agree that the common use of modern diagnostic techniques was responsible for the scientific character of the discipline (along with the improvement of the new approaches that had appeared before World War II) that permitted the study of complete populations and not of isolated cases only. Thereafter, paleopathology ceased to be merely a curious complement to the history of disease, and became an ambitious branch of science: historical pathology endowed with true scientific rigor.

Buikstra & Cook (1980) stated that the most important advances in paleopathology are included in the following areas:

1. Major synthesis of information.
2. Disease diagnosis and paleoepidemiology.
3. Nonspecific indicators of stress.
4. Paleonutrition.
5. Investigation of mummies and mummified tissues.
6. Interdisciplinary work among the researchers interested in paleopathology.

However, as Ortner & Aufderheide (1991b) point out, it seems that inadequate attention has been given to theory in our discipline, and 'perhaps the most urgent need in paleopathology is a careful review of the methods we are using.' This fact appears clearly in different issues: meaning of disease for the individual and populations, and not only description of lesions; evolution of disease; understanding of 'what constitutes disease versus what constitutes a dysfunctional biomedical response;' relationships between population density and disease; and, finally, the impact of the cultural and social changes on human health and disease evaluation.

Ortner (1991) suggests progress of the discipline requires development of other, related scientific fields. Ortner divides the future development of paleopathology into six different stages:

1. Definition of the specific area of scientific interest.
2. Once this area is defined, the creation of the methodology to investigate it becomes necessary.
3. Creation of a 'body of descriptive data related to the subject.'
4. Development of a classification system.
5. Generation of hypotheses regarding the significance of observed phenomena.
6. Relating data and hypotheses to similar research and theory in cognate fields.

In addition to those new and important theoretical approaches, it is necessary to call attention to one of the most important events in the present development of paleopathology: the creation (in the 1970s) of the Paleopathology Association in Detroit (Michigan) by Aidan and Eve Cockburn (Fig. 1.11) as well as other scientists. The predecessor to the Association was the so-called Paleopathology Club, formed in 1973 by a group of Canadian and U.S. scientists, along with a visitor from Czechoslovakia, that met in Detroit for a symposium sponsored by the Smithsonian Institute, the Detroit Institute of Arts, and Wayne State University Medical School, and which completed a multidisciplinary autopsy on an Egyptian mummy (PUM II: Cockburn, 1994). Currently, the Paleopathology Association is an informal group of more than 500 researchers worldwide coming from different disciplines and interested in ancient diseases, and, as Cockburn (1994) states, the organization still observes the original statement of purpose: 'It has neither funds, rules, nor officials, but exists solely to provide channels of communication among workers who are active in the field.' This association holds an annual meeting in North America (U.S.A. and

Fig. 1.11. **Aidan and Eve Cockburn.** Founders of the Paleopathology Association in 1973, and pioneers of interdisciplinary approach to mummy dissections. With permission from Eve Cockburn. PBL.

Fig. 1.12. **Marvin Allison and Enrique Gerszten.** Founders of the Paleopathology Club in 1978, and pioneers of integrating biomedical, bioanthropological and archaeological findings in dissections of Peruvian and Chilean mummy populations. With permission from Drs Allison and Gerszten. PBL.

Canada) and a biennial one in Europe. The first annual meeting was held in Amherst (MA) in 1974, and the first European one in London, 2 years later. Coupled to these events in 1973 the first issue of the *Paleopathology Newsletter*, a quarterly publication, appeared as a means of communication among workers in the field.

As Campillo (1993) recalls, Allison and Gerszten (Fig. 1.12) created a Paleopathology Club in 1978 that is affiliated with the International Academy of Pathology – United States and Canadian Division, serving as a means of exchanging information about specific cases and research problems. This Club also organizes an annual companion meeting of the International Academy of Pathology. According to Buikstra & Cook (1980), the Paleopathology Club has excellent potential for 'raising awareness among medical scientists concerning the nature and importance of research in paleopathology.'

More recently, after the First World Congress on Mummy Studies that was held in Tenerife (Canary Islands, Spain) in 1992 (with the attendance of more than 350 scientists coming from all continents) the World Committee on Mummy Studies was created. This is an informal group of researchers interested in the fascinating world of mummies that is organizing this specialized field of research in which paleopathology is one of the most important aspects. The Second World Congress was held in Cartagena de Indias (Colombia) 3 years later with excellent attendance and presented improved techniques and research methodologies.

Besides the creation of specialized associations and the annual, biennial or triennial congresses, the tremendous improvement of new research techniques has permitted the development of important interdisciplinary projects with researchers coming from such different specialties as archaeology and genetics, history and paleopathology, diet and chemistry, and others. Collaboration between researchers of different disciplines is becoming more the rule than the exception. Only in this way is it possible to understand fully the way of life and death of past populations. Led by the example of PUM II and subsequent studies during the past decades, several such projects have emerged that can serve as models of interdisciplinary studies. If we consider only a few that included substantial budgets, a large number of researchers, and had widespread international impact, we can point to the *Manchester Museum Mummy Project*, developed during the 1970s on the Egyptian mummies curated in that museum under the direction of A. Rosalie David (David, 1979). The *CRONOS Project*, the *Bioanthropology of Guanche Mummies*, evolved between 1988 and 1992, targeted on the Guanche mummies and skeletal remains of the Museo Arqueológico de Tenerife, Canary Islands. Researchers from many different disciplines, and from different countries took part (González Antón et al., 1990; Aufderheide, 1995). The British study of the bog body Lindow Man and the Danish project on The Greenland Mummies are additional excellent examples (Stead et al., 1986; Hart Hanson et al., 1991). Happily, many smaller investigations are becoming increasingly popular. All of this interest has spawned many texts on paleopathology during the last 30 years. A few of them are by single authors, others are coauthored, and still others are edited. Those most widely used, listed in chronological order, include *Bones, Bodies, and Disease* (C. Wells, 1964); *Human Paleopathology* (edited by S. Jarcho, 1966b); *Diseases in Antiquity* (edited by D.R. Brothwell & A.T. Sandison, 1967); *Paleopathological Diagnosis and Interpretation* (R.T. Steinbock, 1976); *Identification of Paleopathological Conditions in Human Skeletal Remains* (D.J. Ortner & W.G.J. Putschar, 1981); *Atlas of Human Paleopathology* (M.R. Zimmerman & M.A. Kelley, 1982); *The Archaeology of Disease* (K. Manchester, 1983a); *Disease in Ancient Man* (edited by G.D. Hart, 1983); *Paleopathlogy at the Origins of Agriculture* (edited by M.N. Cohen & G.J. Armelagos, 1984a); *Human Paleopathology* (edited by D.J. Ortner & A.C. Aufderheide, 1991a); *Paleopathologie du Squelette Humaine* (J. Dastugue & V. Gervais, 1992); and *Paleopatología* (D. Campillo, 1994–95). Many excellent productions with a more restricted focus or issued in less widely employed languages are also available.

As Kerley (1976) points out, until 1975 a large fraction of the American physical anthropologists that regularly investigate ancient diseases were engaged in teaching some form of paleopathology but with varying degrees of emphasis, with different methodology, and to students of different levels. One of the most important events in the increasing interest in paleopathology during the last decades is its academic development with the organization of courses of different levels of depth. One institution that could be considered as a pioneer in this field is the Smithsonian Institution with its 'Paleopathology Program,' under the direction of Dr D.J. Ortner. Although this program is not academic *sensu strictu*, and its two major objectives are research and the development of a registry of skeletal diseases (Ortner, 1976), it was an example for the development of other courses and programs in the U.S.A. and other countries.

The example of academic organization in the field of paleopathology that many other institutions use as a model is the Calvin Wells Laboratory for Burial Archaeology now located at the University of Bradford (U.K.) which has included the discipline as a research and teaching activity since 1978.

Other institutions in different countries generate regular courses on the subject. One of the most well-known is that organized periodically by the Museum of Health and Medicine at the Armed Forces Institute of Pathology at Washington, DC. In other countries (Brazil, Spain, France, Italy, Germany, etc) other interesting courses on different aspects of this branch of science are organized with great academic and scientific success.

PART TWO

Pseudopathology

INTRODUCTION

One of the most vexing problems a paleopathologist faces is the question of whether a given tissue change is an antemortem pathological lesion or a postmortem artifact. A pseudopathological feature is a structural change in normal bone or soft tissue that resembles the lesion of some antemortem disease but is, in fact, purely the product of a postmortem process. Occasionally a normal structure will have the dimensions or appearance that is sufficiently near one end of the spectrum of the normal range to be mistaken for a disease process. Experience, of course, will enhance the certainty of the answer to that question. Some postmortem features, however, are so common that awareness of these conditions will help obviate inappropriate interpretations. It is the purpose of this section to call attention to the most prevalent of circumstances leading to pseudopathological alterations of normal tissue

Certain general principles operate to produce the appearance of excavated human remains. The different parts of bones or soft tissues vary in density, shape and size, causing differences in the extent to which these areas resist environmental influence such as acid groundwater or microbiological agents. Furthermore, antemortem lesions often render the affected tissue more susceptible to postmortem effects that may obscure or mask them (Henderson, 1987; Ortner & Putschar, 1985:44). In such examples differentiation of antemortem and postmortem effects at the same location may be a formidable and even sometimes impossible challenge.

In addition to the above, Ortner (1992) has identified several considerations he finds useful in differentiating pathology from pseudopathology. They include:

1. Integration of anatomical, radiological and microscopical data.

2. Notation of the type and the distribution pattern of the changes under consideration.

3. One's realistic expectations should include the admission that resolution of such questions is not invariably possible.

Waldron (1987b) has also called attention to the fact that a generally poor level of skeletal tissue preservation will result in loss of many antemortem lesions, inviting an erroneously low estimate of such a population's disease frequency.

The following pages note common changes in human tissues that frequently lead to inappropriate pathological diagnoses secondary to the environmental agencies of mechanical forces, chemical and microbiological agents, imprints by botanical or animal agents, excavation and laboratory handling methods as well as radiological artifacts.

SOFT TISSUE PSEUDOPATHOLOGY

Soft tissue pseudopathology can be defined as an anatomic postmortem change in soft tissues that resembles an antemortem pathological lesion. Causes can include the following mechanisms.

Pseudopathological features related to mortuary practices

Substitution of body parts

Egyptian embalmers sometimes included an additional leg, head (Notman, 1986) or other body parts. Occasionally they employed parts from multiple, different bodies, wrapped to resemble a single, intact adult body externally (Aufderheide *et al.*, 1995: Fig. 2.1). Degenerated external genitalia frequently were replaced with models using resin-saturated linen cloth. Northern Chile's ancient Chinchorro people often fit a wig of adult human hair on their mummified infants. Adolescent males of the Ecuadorian Jivaro (Shuar) natives learned the technique of shrinking human heads by practicing on sloths, producing heads with a deceptively human appearance that have appeared in the art market (Fig. 2.2). Even the label on reliquaries cannot be trusted to guarantee the modern contents of those receptacles (Zimmerman, 1993b).

Subdermal masses

Excessively tightened ropes encircling the body to fix mummy wrappings into position can cause the skin and

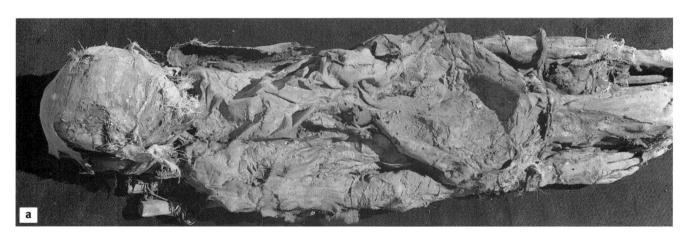

FIG. 2.1. **Composite mummy.** (a) Appears to be wrapped mummy of an intact body. (b) Reveals unwrapped contents: skeletonized head, spine and pelvis, right leg and left leg had been obtained from four different individuals. EG-2, T-15. Ptolemaic Egyptian period at Dakhleh oasis site. PBL.

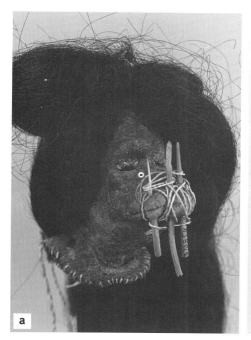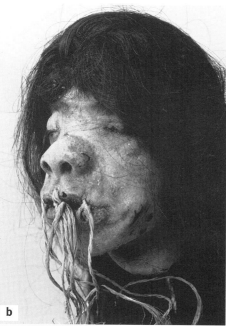

FIG. 2.2. **Shrunken head hoax.** Ecuadorian Jivaro (Shuar) natives shrank and mummified human heads of war victims (b). Similar howler monkeys' heads (a) or sloths in art market may have been prepared by tribal youths as learning or ritual experience. Photographs courtesy of David Hunt and Robert Mann, National Museum of Natural History, Smithsonian Institution.

subcutaneous tissue to bulge above the level of the cords. Postexcavation unwrapping can cause these now-desiccated, bulging masses to resemble subcutaneous tumors.

Closing body orifices

Vegetal tampons sealed the vaginal orifice of several adult Chinchorro females from northern Chile (Aufderheide & Allison, 1994). Orifice plugs were common mortuary features (ritual?) among this group's bodies, so it seems inappropriate to conclude that such crude tampons were used commonly during menstruation by these women. Similarly, the presence of oral coca leaf quids in mummified Andean bodies demonstrated no correlation with the presence of chemically identified cocaine in hair (Cartmell *et al.*, 1991), suggesting the coca leaves did not necessarily reflect antemortem leaf exposure by the specific deceased individual, but more

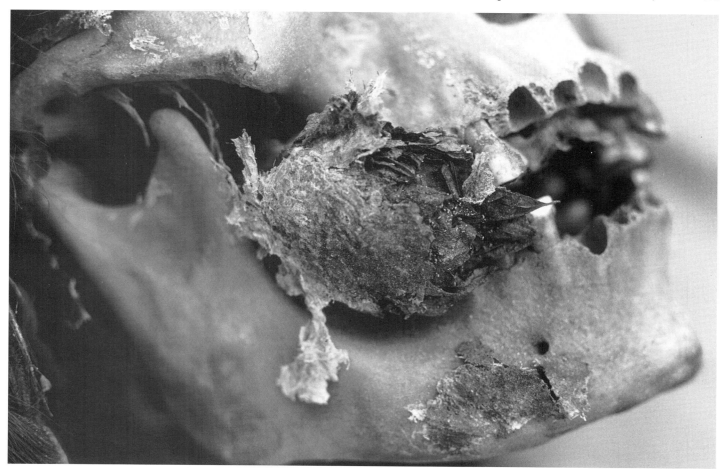

FIG. 2.3. **Coca-leaf quid in oral cavity.** Half of this Tiwanaku-related population chewed coca leaves (hair tests positive), but this body's hair was negative. Conclusion: coca quid in grave does not predict antemortem chewing (represents offering?). CHA 127. Adult female. PBL.

likely were tomb offerings placed there by those burying the deceased (Aufderheide et al., 1991: Fig. 2.3).

Heat effects

Heat 'cooks' the extremity musculature. The resulting muscle contracture flexes the upper extremities into a pugilistic posture, a postmortem mechanism that is often betrayed by the broken, dry skin where it is stretched over the elbow (Knight, 1991:35).

Embalming artifact

Alkaptonuria (ochronosis) is a rare, heritable enzyme deficiency that deposits a black, insoluble substance on the cartilage and collagen of intervertebral discs rendering them radiopaque (Rosenberg, 1991). It is discussed in detail in Chapter 9, but is mentioned here briefly because it was confused with an embalming artifact. When Egyptian mummies' radiographs frequently demonstrated radiopaque intervertebral spaces, the diagnosis of alkaptonuria was entertained seriously, particularly when dissection demonstrated black material in those spaces (Wells & Maxwell, 1962). Subsequent chemical and physico-chemical analysis of the material, however, found no evidence of the usual type of deposit in alkaptonuric individuals, but instead demonstrated the black deposit was composed of natron and resin, compounds routinely employed by Egyptian embalmers (Wallgren et al., 1986).

Pseudopathology resulting from effects arising within body tissue following interment

Changes arising from the corpse's endogenous flora, food or enzymes

Putrefaction results when anerobic, gas-forming bacilli spread through the body's veins postmortem. Soft tissues become bloated with gas that may also distend the abdomen, seep into the scrotum (resembling a hernia) and even the penis, producing a pseudoerection. Muscular necrosis progresses to tissue liquefaction, stained black by the muscle's myoglobin. Increased body cavity pressure may squeeze this foamy liquid out of the body's orifices ('purging': Knight, 1991:36), and may force protrusion of the tongue, uterus and rectum from their respective orifices (Smith & Wood Jones, 1910:219; Zumwalt & Fierro, 1990; Fig. 2.4). These effects can be misinterpreted as forms of antemortem prolapse. Even the abdominal wall, weakened by necrosis of its muscular components, may undergo dehiscence, extruding the abdominal viscera through the defect. The ragged, thinned, tissues at the defect's edges can be used to separate this postmortem artifact from an antemortem wound.

Fine, sandy soil may enter the bronchi after interment due to soil pressure and the negative pressure generated by the collapsing lungs after death. Diagnosis of pneumoconiosis due to antemortem soil inhalation can be made (Zimmerman & Smith, 1975) but requires considerable caution. Particles inhaled antemortem are seldom greater than 10 microns but soil accumulating in the lung after death contains a much greater range of size and its distribution is often recognizably within bronchi or bronchioles. The stomach's digestive juices may autodigest the gastric wall, spilling the stomach's content into the free peritoneal cavity, tempting an unwary examiner to make an incorrect diagnosis of antemortem perforated ulcer. Liquefaction decay of muscle tissue stains the muscle black. When the decay is arrested by desication, the muscle may acquire a black, glistening appearance of charring or resin application.

FIG. 2.4. **Rectal prolapse.** Right leg is disarticulated. Note patent vaginal orifice (A) beneath and behind which the large, redundant, rounded mass represents a prolapsed rectum (B). A 60 year old female, from northern Chile's 2000 B.C. Chinchorro culture. MAUT. PBL.

Finally, a comment must be added regarding facial expressions on the bodies of spontaneously mummified cadavers. The literature contains many references to these, often describing them in vivid terms as 'appearance of terror, stifling a scream,' etc. After death, muscles first undergo a period of hardening (rigor mortis) followed by autodigestive softening. Such relaxation will permit the mandible and facial muscles to sag, often asymmetrically. Wrappings and enveloping cords cause further distortion. Collectively these contortions commonly produce grotesque expressions that are independent of the countenance at time of death. Diagnostic predictions based on such facial expressions rarely have any basis in fact.

Changes arising from effects of the interment environment

Soft tissue digestion by fly larvae or by dermestid beetles may result in tissue loss of the nasal areas mimicking syphilitic or leprous processes. One of us (A.C.A.) examined a modern forensic case in which the cranial cavity was teeming with fly larvae that had destroyed the entire brain and all meninges and other soft tissues within the skull. The body had not been discovered until about 3 weeks after the murder in a house with open windows at summer temperatures, and the insects had gained access by following the track of multiple facial stab wounds that penetrated into the cranial cavity. Fulcheri *et al.* (1986) apparently identified the paleopathological equivalent of such a situation in which the larvae were visible on radiography of an Egyptian head (confirmed by dissection). The insects (identified by the authors as Hymenoptera species) had probably reached the cranial cavity via the embalmers' traditional transnasal craniotomy opening. While the forensic lieterature provides little, if any, precedence for Hymenoptera larvae in human remains, it is conceivable that the unique methods of Egyptian embalming may have made this possible. Unfortunately the authors did not document the diagnostic criteria they used for identification of the larvae, and the illustration provided is not diagnostic. These authors also found *Cryptococcus neoformans* in muscle tissue without evidence of tissue reaction, implying this was a postmortem contaminant. Horne (1993) notes the close similarity of *Ascotricha* Berk. spores and red blood cells, and describes the use of potassium hydroxide to differentiate them. Tendon stripping by vultures (Winlock, 1945:21) can be both dramatic and confusing.

Even the retraction of skin in a desiccating cadaver may produce the illusion of postmortem hair growth. Postmortem chemical changes induced by sun and soilwater can decolorize certain hair pigments, resulting in the appearance of red or blonde hair. Usually such color changes are focal, localized to areas of exposure. Conditions causing <u>all</u> of the scalp hair to change color occur only rarely.

These are only a few of the many different types of soft tissues changes that can occur after death, some of which can simulate antemortem pathology. The remaining conditions are included in discussions of the pathology of specific organs in Chapter 8. When viewing human remains, whether soft tissue or skeletal, it is useful to approach a candidate lesion by first questioning whether the tissue could have been altered by a postmortem process.

SKELETAL TISSUE PSEUDOPALEO-PATHOLOGY

Excavation skeletal artifacts

Often archaeologists first become aware of the presence of human remains when their metal excavating tools come into contact with skeletal tissue. Among unsupervised novices inappropriate force with which such tools are wielded may result in marred, perforated or fractured bones. In many (but not all) such cases the lack of patina in the fracture will betray its recent occurrence. Rough handling of excavated bones during subsequent transportation can induce further skeletal damage, especially if bones are placed unprotected into containers large enough to permit their movement. Inappropriate methods can also cause commingling of bones at time of excavation or transportation, with the potential for causing unique or incompatible patterns of pathology.

Post-excavation specimen handling

Excavated bones are especially vulnerable to commingling during laboratory examination. This is most easily avoided if the labelling of each bone is given highest priority before they are examined individually (Wells, 1967a). Other rules dealing with limitations on numbers of skeletons under examination at any one time are also useful. It is at this stage that inappropriate diagnoses are made that result from lack of awareness of the range of normal variations. For example, the phenomenon of bilateral parietal bone 'thinning' may include a completely penetrating defect. Such defects have been confused with pathological lesions including metastatic carcinoma, trepanation and other proposed causes. The sternum and olecranon fossa are other sites where similar misjudgements have been made. Another common point of confusion is differentiation of congenital vertebral fusion from the effects of trauma.

Scavenger and insect effects

Large scavengers may retrieve or at least expose shallowly-buried bodies and actually carry away major body parts.

Smaller animals such as rodents select bone areas that most conveniently fit their dentition. Thus, rodents often attack the supraorbital ridges, the created defects of which can resemble trauma, or osteitis. Still smaller gnaw marks are often obvious but at times have been mistaken for anthropogenic cut marks inflicted during postmortem defleshing procedures (Fulcheri et al., 1986), or confused with stone or metal implement marks that characterize cannibalism (White & Folkens, 1991: 394). Paleopathologists also must become acquainted with the effects of insects whose proteolytic enzyme secretions can liquefy the organic matrix of bone so that, when subsequent groundwater action solubilizes the remaining bone mineral, the localized defects can simulate disease processes. Henderson (1987), for example, recalls one of the well-known cases of pseudopathology in which several Egyptian skeletons from Naga-ed-der at the beginning of this century were reported to demonstrate cranial syphilis, when in fact the erosive patterns represented the postmortem action of beetles.

Botanical effects

Larger plant roots may invade long bone medullary cavities through biological foramina, and subsequent bone weakening may result in ultimate fracture. More commonly, however, rootlets will wrap themselves snugly around long bone diaphyses, trapping groundwater between themselves and the bone cortex. Subsequent lytic action of the groundwater and/or plant secretions can generate surface grooves that can simulate vascular impressions, though their reticulate pattern can often be recognizably different from antemortem blood vessel structures (White & Folkens, 1991: 365).

Cryogenic and thermal effects on bone

Freeze–thaw conditions may shatter a buried bone. Thawing conditions permit the accumulation of water within a bone and subsequent freezing will produce expansion by ice crystal formation to a degree that will fragment the bone structure. At sites of extreme temperature differences (e.g. Alaska) such effects on the soil can result in enormous movement of soil masses with as much as 180° rotation. Such an inverting effect can carry entire skeletons or major body parts with the soil and commingle bones from multiple bodies, producing confusing combinations of pathological lesions.

Intense heat can generate equally puzzling changes. If a body with intact soft tissue is exposed quite suddenly to very high temperatures (e.g. house fire) the brain may be vaporized while soft tissue still occludes cranial orifices. The resulting rise of intracranial pressure may be great enough to produce skull fractures or even to cause a cranium-shattering explosion. An unwary examiner may mistake such effects as being those of antemortem violence (Spitz, 1973). Lesser degrees of heat application may cause the dura to shrink with extrusion of cerebral blood into the extradural space between the cranium's inner table surface and the contracted dura. The incorrect diagnosis of antemortem traumatic extradural hematoma can be avoided by noting the absence of the most common cause of such an antemortem event: a temporal bone fracture that traverses and lacerates the middle meningeal artery.

Cremation temperatures also produce quite predictable effects on bone that result in fracture-like fragmentation of long bones into short, tubular segments. These segments also often fracture longitudinally and frequently cause a curling deformation. Lesser temperature may produce long bone bowing that can be mistaken for antemortem metabolic effects of rickets, osteomalacia or even osteogenesis imperfecta. Natural fires may stain the bones but usually don't reach temperatures high enough to simulate the changes noted at cremation temperatures.

Chemical erosion

These effects are mediated in an aqueous environment. Hence they are retarded at sites that are well-drained, subject to lesser precipitation and in temperate climates with neutral or slightly basic soil pH levels (Henderson, 1987). Acid, wet soils can extract so much bone mineral that the bones grossly resemble those with antemortem osteoporosis. Such mineral-depleted bones are also more susceptible to bowing deformation by soil pressure. If the osteolytic process reaches the marrow it may simulate the lytic effects of osteomyelitis. The absence, however, of the new bone formation that commonly accompanies antemortem osteomyelitis can aid in the recognition of the nature of the alteration.

Under other circumstances groundwater can actually deposit additional mineral in buried bone. Furthermore, while the chemical form of this is often calcium carbonate, it may be calcium phosphate in the crystalline form of hydroxyapatite. When deposited on tooth enamel, it may have the appearance of dental calculus (Flinn et al., 1987). On the other hand, such deposits on cortical surfaces of long bones may duplicate the appearance of superficial periostitis. Such deposits on the orbital roofs or skull vault may lead to an inappropriate diagnosis of cribra orbitalia or porotic hyperostosis.

Microbiological agents

Bacteria and fungi commonly gain access to the Haversian canals, generating acids capable of dissolving the bone mineral in irregular patterns suggestive of the histological changes produced by osteoclasts (Ortner & Putschar, 1985). Externally the bone surface may be eroded superficially, producing a pattern resembling periostitis.

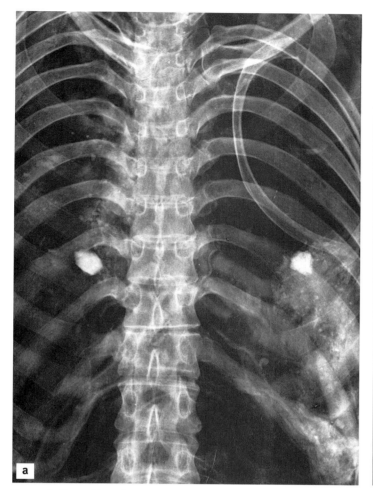 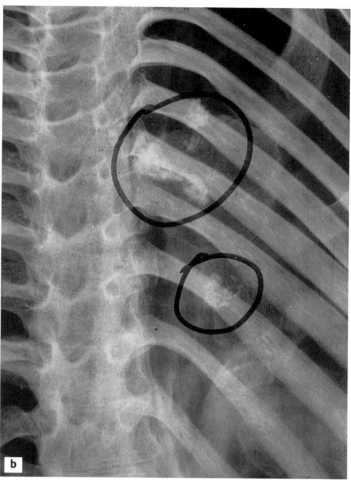

FIG. 2.5. **Radiographic artifacts in mummies.** All densities in left X-ray (a) are soil artifacts. Ringed densities in (b) were calcified lymph nodes (healed tuberculosis?).

Late pre-Spanish culture of northern Chile coast. MAUT. PBL.

Pressure effects

These forces exert their effect primarily by simple pressure, but may also erode cortical bone. Bones of varying and complex structure, such as those of the pelvis, scapula and skull, will yield to pressure deformation or actual fracture in their structurally weakest areas, while the more dense and uniformly constructed long bone diaphyses will tend to resist greater pressures (Henderson, 1987; Waldron, 1987b). Compressive effects of soil pressure frequently will flatten the hollow cranium sufficiently to simulate antemortem intentional cranial deformation, scaphocephaly or frank fracture (Wells, 1967a). Even the thick cortex of long bones can eventually yield to such mechanical forces. Such postmortem fractures are particularly common among ribs, but will also often affect the scapula, clavicle, forearm and lower leg long bones. Short tubular bones as well as the femur and humerus are more resistant (Wells, 1967a; White & Folkens, 1991: 358–9). The absence of patina at the fracture site can often exclude excavation or post-excavation effects but cannot rule out a change occurring during the *perimortem* time period.

Wells (1967a) laments the frequently mistaken diagnosis of cannibalism made on bones that have been crushed by such postmortem soil pressure. Long bones subjected to bowing deformation without fracture can also be confused with the antemortem effects of rickets. In this, as well as many of the previously mentioned circumstances the context in which these effects occur (i.e. the other bones in the skeleton or in nearby skeletons) can be the key to the resolution of the cause (White & Toth, 1991). An excellent example of exploitation of a statistical approach to such context data to resolve the antemortem/postmortem question of defects found in long bone ends is a report by Torbenson *et al.* (1992). A significant fraction of reported cranial trepanations are in actuality congenital defects or skeletal dysplasias (in addition to trauma, infections, tumors and hematopoietic disorders).

Radiological pseudopathology

Wells (1967a) notes that deceptive densities in radiology can be misleading in several ways (Fig. 2.5) including the appearance of a density resembling dental calculus that is actually due to sand located between two teeth roots; erosion of mastoid septa by postmortem processes that simulate the radiological appearance of mastoiditis; and crystal deposits in sinuses may mimic osteomas or sinusitis. In addition post-mortem silica deposits can increase the radiological density sufficiently to resemble osteopetrosis.

PART THREE

Traumatic conditions

Both accidents and certain cultural activities can lead to traumatic skeletal or soft tissue injuries. Our interest in identification of these lesions stems from our recognition that they provide important information about an ancient population's practices dealing with war, interpersonal violence, knowledge about the terrain and other aspects of daily life. However, various authors have interpreted the available evidence differently. Meiklejohn *et al.* (1984) suggest that substantial differences in the frequency of traumatic lesions between Mesolithic men and women more probably reflect differences in labor division and therefore that such lesions are of an accidental origin. Campillo (1995) feels that injuries of violence were no more frequent among the hominid australopithecines than among modern primates (other than man). However, evidence of human violence became increased detectably during the Mesolithic period while the Neolithic was characterized by an unmistakable rise in arrow or other sharp-pointed lesions that were the product of cultural practices such as war and ritual. Furthermore, Wells (1964) feels that skeletal injuries from violent blows are recognizable as early as the Paleolithic, and Dastugue & Gervais (1992) interpret the pathology among even the australopithecines and *Pithecanthropus* as well as Cro-Magnon remains as reflecting battles of extermination.

The most popular interpretations suggest that increase in population size is accompanied by competition for resources with resulting interpopulation warfare. Merbs (1989), for example, suggests that '…it is useful to look at trauma in the broader context of human behavior, such as circumstances that produce trauma, the effects on the individuals and populations, and medical efforts to heal the results of traumatic stress…' Paleopathologists are particularly interested in the changes of human trauma patterns over time (Manchester, 1983a: 11; Ortner & Putschar, 1985). Of considerable anthropologic interest also is the evidence provided (by massive healed fractures) of cooperation and support provided to the nonproductive victim during the period of immobility necessary to achieve healing (Alciati *et al.*, 1987).

SKELETAL EVIDENCE OF TRAUMA

Fracture

Definition and etiology

A fracture is a discontinuity of or crack in skeletal tissue, with or without injury to overlying soft tissues. External forces that exceed the natural strain or elasticity of the skeletal structure are applied directly or indirectly to bone.

Mechanisms

These include:

1. Flexion (bending). Force is applied perpendicular to the long axis of the bone producing angulation with a transverse or oblique fracture line beginning at the convex surface extending toward or as far as the concave.
2. Shearing. Two opposite forces perpendicular to the diaphysis resulting in a horizontal fracture line.
3. Compression. Force is applied in the axial direction, such as in a fall, resulting in crushing or impaction of skeletal tissue, characteristically in the vertebrae.
4. Rotation, twisting or torsion. Similar to shearing but in the same plane as the diaphysis, producing a spiral fracture.
5. Traction or tension. A violent muscle contraction (such as in epileptic seizure) may tear off (avulse) a small irregular fragment of bone at its tendon insertion into a bone, sometimes accompanied by joint dislocation.

Pathology

Total skeletal discontinuity characterizes complete fractures, with or without displacement of the two fragments (Fig. 3.1); both surfaces of a flat bone are involved. In incomplete fractures a bone crack does not extend the full length or thickness of the bone and hence no displacement occurs. These are common in children, especially the 'greenstick' type in which one cortical surface is buckled or crumpled. Similarly a compressive effect may involve only one side of the bone ('torus or buckling' type of fracture.) Comminuted fractures result in more than two fragments (a special 'butterfly' fragment effect may involve two bone fragments with a triangular, butterfly-shaped third fragment between them). In a closed or simple fracture the overlying soft tissues are intact while these are lacerated in a compound or open fracture. The latter obviously often becomes infected, recognizable in the paleopathological state as an area of bone surface irregularity with pitting

(Manchester, 1983a: 55). These are especially common in children. Intra-articular fracture is self-explanatory and is often complicated by subsequent degenerative joint disease. Stress or fatigue fractures are the consequence of repetitive forces generating microfractures whose cumulative effect eventually leads to complete fracture through the bone cortex (Bullough, 1992). Examples include long-distance running or long marches by soldiers. The feet (distal second metatarsal or calcaneus) are most commonly affected or the upper third of the tibia, followed less often by the femoral neck, distal femur diaphysis, pubic rami and lower fibula as well as (in children) metaphyses. In the upper limbs (usually radius or ulna), ribs and clavicles such fractures have been identified as occupationally-related to clay pigeon shooting or forking farm manure (Revell, 1986). The term 'fatigue' fractures is applied to similar but more minor, hairline fractures without displacement that are initiated by osteoclastic resorption and periosteal callus. Periosteal new bone formation in a more major stress fracture may be so exuberant that it may actually mimic a malignant neoplasm, although the presence of a fracture line can help establish the traumatic nature of the lesion (Aegerter & Kirkpatrick, 1975). Pathological fractures result from forces no greater than common, every-day stresses that are applied to an area of bone whose structural integrity has already been compromised by a local pathological process. Such local

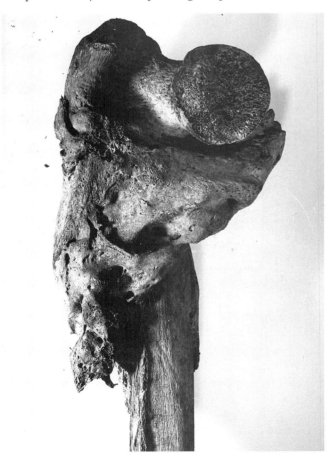

FIG. 3.1. **Fracture, femur.** Note huge callus, shortened diaphysis. Medieval adult, Catalonia, Spain, c.21. Courtesy Dr D. Campillo, MAC.

effects may be due to the lytic action of a neoplasm, osteoporosis, cysts, infection, developmental anomalies, endocrine effects (hypoparathyroidism), neurological disorders (tabes dorsalis syringomyelia) and even excessively dense but brittle bones including osteopetrosis and Paget's disease. While usually obvious, the original lesion's effects may be obscured by the healing process, making diagnosis difficult.

Fracture repair

The admirable sequence of events following fracture that results in restored function has been called a great success of nature (Bullough, 1992). It is characterized by initial hematoma formation that is organized into a fibrous mass (fibrous callus) uniting the tissues into a fragile union, with subsequent calcification and finally remodeling into normal bone. The acute hematoma at the fracture site coagulates in 6–8 hours after which an outpouring of cells (inflammatory stage) and their differentiation into fibroblasts, chondrocytes and osteoblasts together with vasculoneogenesis initiates repair at the external periosteum. The reparative stage is characterized by a fibrous union achieved by the third week which

is then calcified by mineral released from the bone fragments; cartilage is replaced by skeletal tissue. The remodeling of the callus into mature skeletal histostructure and normal anatomy is the slowest stage, requiring up to an additional 6 weeks in children or 6 months in older adults. Factors, in addition to age, that influence healing rate are adequacy of vascular supply, fracture type (horizontal heal slower than spiral fractures), bone part (tibia is slowest, metaphysis fastest), soft tissue interposition (retards), and bone nature (cancellous bone rapid, cortical bone slower, with or without external callus formation). Immobilization is paramount because mobility stimulates fibrous callus formation that requires longer healing time. Infection delays healing as does any underlying pathological process that may have led to the fracture. The complexity of the healing process requires good general health and nutrition to achieve the most rapid healing response.

Fracture complications

Acute fracture complications depend on the extent of fracture and related soft tissue injury and include shock, hemorrhage, fat embolism (liquid fat from crushed adipose tissue

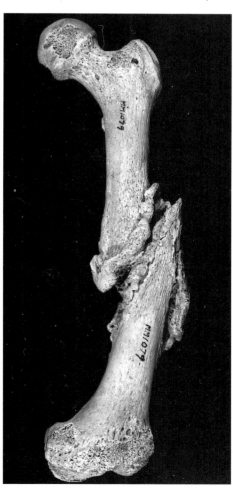

FIG. 3.2. **Pseudoarthrosis.** Interposed soft tissue probably prevented unification of callus of femur fracture ends. Modern adult. No. 3019. MM. Courtesy G. Worden.

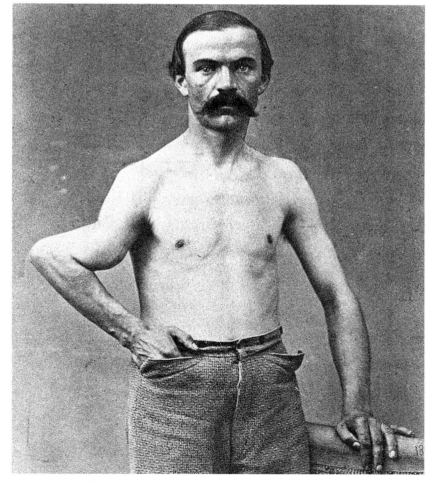

FIG. 3.3. **Pseudoarthrosis.** Ununited humerus fracture is apparent in left upper arm deformity in soldier of U.S. Civil War. Photograph 189. NMHM. Courtesy P. Sledzik.

sucked into lacerated veins), thromboembolism, secondary infection with septicemia including gas gangrene (see Chapter 7) as well as cardiac and pulmonary problems.

Local effects include the following:

1. **Delayed healing.** This term must be adjusted to expectations for the particular fracture type involved (Watson-Jones, 1980), modified by factors listed above.

2. **Pseudoarthrosis.** The bone ends are joined only by fibrous tissue and a fibrous pseudojoint envelops the bone ends (Fig. 3.2 and 3.3). Rare among children, it is most common in young adults. Factors favoring its production include interposition of soft tissue (periosteum, muscle, cartilage), excessive separation of fractured fragments, deficient blood supply and especially lack of immobilization (Watson-Jones, 1980). The fractured ends become rounded with sclerosis of the medullary cavity. Demonstration of such sclerosis is useful because it is responsible for cessation of the healing cellular response. In antiquity, nonunion was common in the proximal femur and in forearm bones (Manchester, 1983a: 57). In paleopathological specimens confusion between pseudoarthrosis and amputation may arise if the distal segment undergoes resorption (Merbs, 1989) as the fracture through the olecranon fossa of the right humerus of Shanidar I (a 60 000 year old Neanderthal skeleton from Shanidar cave in Iraq (Trinkaus, 1983)) demonstrates. Among the Guanche population of Tenerife, Rodríguez-Martín (1991) found all cases of olecranon process healed with the production of pseudoarthrosis as did half of those of the tibial malleolus. This complication is much less frequent in the radius midshaft where it is commonly related to an ulna fracture.

3. **Poor alignment.** The powerful muscles attached to the femur cause this complication to be the most common site of fracture complications observed in paleopathology. Among the Guanches all femur fractures healed in misaligned status (as did tibia and radius fractures: Fig. 3.4).

4. **Bone shortening.** Multiple causes include poor alignment with marked angulation or fragment superimposition as well as bone loss (compression, comminution) and epiphyseal growth disturbances in children (Adams, 1986). Lower limb shortening of as little as 2 cm can cause significant clinical dysfunction.

5. **Osteomyelitis.** While simple, closed fractures occasionally become infected hematogenously, post-fracture osteomyelitis is primarily associated with compound fractures. Their paucity in paleopathological reports (Ortner & Putschar, 1985) may reflect the scarcity of compound fractures in antiquity.

6. **Avascular necrosis of bone.** Insufficient blood supply can cause necrosis of the affected bone with subsequent resorption. It occurs more frequently near bone ends, such as the femur head following a femur neck fracture, the proximal end of the carpal navicular, the talus or even the entire lunate. Pseudoarthrosis or severe degenerative joint disease may be the final deformity of this complication. Traumatic interruption of blood flow in a child's growing bone can lead to bone shortening.

7. **Neuropathy.** Nerve damage leading to lack of pain sensation may encourage use and mobility of a fractured bone, retarding healing or leading to a Charcot joint (Ortner & Putschar, 1985).

8. **Articular changes.** Direct injury to joint surfaces can cause severe degenerative joint disease alterations even leading to bony ankylosis. These alterations may so closely resemble those of osteomyelitis that Morse (1978) has suggested that the presence of a fracture in the affected bone and lack of bilateral symmetry can assist in their differentiation in archaeological specimens.

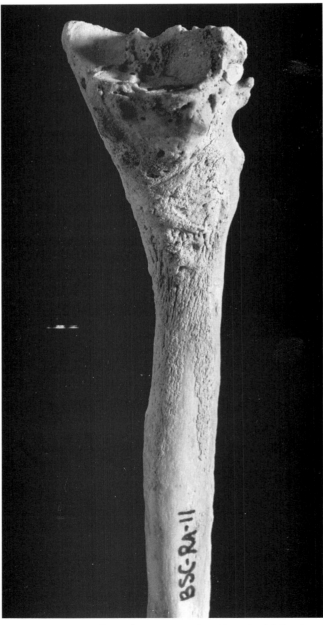

FIG. 3.4. **Fracture, wrist (Colle's).** Poorly aligned, well healed. Adult female Guanche, ca. A.D. 1000, Canary Islands. G.G.MAT, OAMC.

Paleopathologic study of fractures in dry bones

Definite evidence of healing is the most useful criterion for the determination of the antemortem or postmortem nature of a skeletal fracture. Slight rounding of the fractured edges with a polished appearance when viewed microscopically is the earliest sign of healing (Maples, 1986) but at least 7–10 days of antemortem healing are required to reach a satisfactory degree of certainty. Working with a collection of modern bones with known provenience, Mann & Murphy (1990) felt that 2 weeks is a workable minimum interval of post-fracture healing change recognition. Maples (1986) also notes that the elasticity of living bone is due to its water and protein (collagen) content and is responsible for the difference in fracture patterns among antemortem and dry bones. Greenstick and skull fractures with concentric, radiating or stellate appearance as well as depressed skull fractures are seen in bones with retained elasticity while postmortem fractures of dry skulls show smaller fragments and dry long bones show irregular edges, disappearance of small portions of bone and little beveling. Bone elasticity is, however not lost instantly at death, but is, instead, a gradual process dependent on specific taphonomic features. The 'perimortem' period during which a fracture without evidence of healing but with features suggesting the pattern found in bones with retained elasticity can range from 2 weeks before death until a varying postmortem interval of at least 2 months.

Ortner & Putschar (1985) also remind us that children's fractures may remodel so completely as to obliterate evidence of previous fracture, and that differentiation of accidental trauma from that of interpersonal violence can be very difficult, aided by location and pattern of the lesions.

Finally, while well-aligned long bone healed fractures in ancient humans are not common, Schultz (1967) found that most limb fractures in wild gibbons healed without suffi-

cient malalignment to cause dysfunction. For that reason it is probably not appropriate to credit the application of medical skills for a similar finding in an ancient human.

Skull fractures and crushing injuries

General Principles

Although scalp lacerations, cerebral contusions, and both epidural and subdural hemorrhages occurred in antiquity, these leave little certain evidence in dry bone skeletons, so the injuries of the skull in such skeletal samples are largely limited to fractures. Oddly, the correlation between the size or extent of the fracture and the degree of injury to the brain is not great. While many crushing injuries of the skull show no signs of healing, many paleopathological skull fractures demonstrate evidence of recovery. Clearly, some ancient populations developed a system of social support for such afflicted persons (Adelson, 1974).

A universally accepted classification for skull fractures has not yet been developed. While Steinbock (1976) feels that both accidental falls and blows could have been responsible for skull fractures in antiquity, and DiMaio & DiMaio (1989) group skull fractures into those acquired by blows and acceleration/deceleration injuries secondary to sudden head movements, most authors find it difficult to differentiate between these causes in dry bones. Furthermore, what evidence there is, suggests that blows are by far the most common. Thus, most studies demonstrate a substantial predominance of skull fractures in males and location of the lesions on the left side of the cranium, implying the pathology was acquired by a face-to-face encounter with a right-handed opponent. In fact Courville (1967) classifies skull injuries on the basis of the differing nature of the fractures produced by weapons of varying shape:

—Sharp-edged incisions (metal or flint axes)
—Penetrating wounds (pointed and hafted weapons)
—Linear fractures (blunt, small weapons)
—Gross crushing injuries (large stones or clubs)

Etiology, mechanisms and pathology

A sequence of events leading to a major skull fracture has been described as including (i) skull indentation without fracture, (ii) inner table fracture, (iii) both outer and inner table fracture (Fig. 3.5), (iv) depressed fracture with localized comminution and (v) outer table crushed into diploe (Gordon et al., 1988). Factors modifying the nature of the skull fracture include the physical characteristics of the impacting object (shape, size, composition), its velocity, presence and thickness of overlying soft tissues and the skull location of the impact site. In general, low velocity injuries affect a broad area and generate linear fractures while the energy of high velocity impacts is often focused on smaller

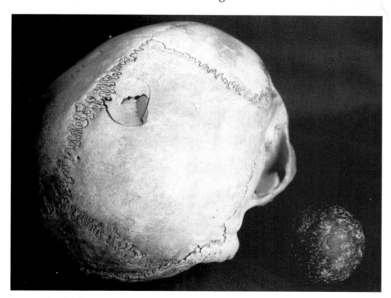

FIG. 3.5. **Cranial fracture, perimortem.** Right parietal fracture. No healing. Adult male. Guanche, ca. A.D. 1000, Canary Islands. Sling ball injury? G1. MAT, OAMC.

areas causing depressed fractures (Stewart, 1979). Local features influencing the appearance of the fracture include bone thinning to accommodate large Pacchionian granulations, aberrant veins and thickening of the diploe or tables (Gurdjan *et al.*, 1950). Fractures passing along suture lines, common in young adults, may not be easy to differentiate from postmortem bone separation (Maples, 1986).

Several types of events may complicate a fracture. The sharp-edged inner table fracture may lacerate the underlying brain causing severe intracerebral hemorrhage. Laceration only to the depth of the meninges may be followed by formation of fibrous adhesions between meninges and brain that manifest later as post-traumatic epileptiform seizures. Infection may be the direct result of introduction of contaminated skin, soil or impacting object in the event of compound skull fractures, while infection of the scalp soft tissues may extend down to the level of the fracture in other cases. If the skull fracture is comminuted, the infection may prevent consolidation of all of the fragments during healing, resulting in a defect that could be misdiagnosed as a trepanation in a dry bone skull (Adelson, 1974).

Paleopathology

Cranial fractures have been identified in *Homo erectus* and probably in *Australopithecus*. Innumerable case reports and population studies abound in the paleopathology literature. Most of them identify a high male/female ratio usually interpreted as evidence of group conflict, though Manchester (1983a: 59) has suggested that it could also reflect a division of labor with males performing the more hazardous manual labor. When a high left/right site ratio is encountered, face-to-face confrontations appear the most probable explanation. By far the most common injury is a concave indentation of the outer table. Such a healed, frontal, outer table, depressed skull fracture found in an early fourth century B.C. Samaritan has been given the sobriquet 'Goliath injury' by Bloom & Smith (1991) because of its similarity to slingshot injuries. Similar such lesions are seen so commonly in some Peruvian skull collections that they have earned the cognomen '70 caliber lesion' because their average diameter is about 70 mm and smoothed stones of that approximate diameter have been found in the area that may have been employed as sling ball ammunition (Zimmerman *et al.*, 1981). An early Etruscan body (eighth century B.C.) from the Tarquinia area is an excellent example of violence in antiquity, revealing multiple fractures of ribs, scapula, ulna and hands as well as a probably lethal massive crushing injury of the temporal bone all of which appear to have been inflicted simultaneously (Mallegni *et al.*, 1994).

Several examples of population studies also demonstrate the type of information about ancient human behavior that can be extracted from an examination of cranial fractures in an archaeological population. Rodríguez-Martín *et al.* (1993) studied skulls of Tenerife's (Canary Islands) aboriginal population (Guanches), and found cranial fractures in about 9% of those from the southern slopes but only about 2% from the island's northern side. The male/female ratio was about 2/1 and most of the lesions were in the frontal and parietal bones. The bulk of the lesions were healed and only 17% were identified within the perimortem period. The island is characterized by steep-walled, volcano-formed valleys that tended to separate the island's subpopulations. These investigators interpreted the findings as evidence of group violence, supported by ethnographic accounts of common intervalley warfare. In a similar study by Walker (1989) of Native American remains on channel islands and adjacent mainland of southern California, about 22% of the island populations showed healed, depressed fractures of the skull's outer table. While mainlander populations averaged about 3%, Walker attributed the difference to intense competition for the islands' limited resources and suggested that a subsequent decline in lesion frequency among the islanders was coincident with the introduction of the bow and arrow.

Vertebral and thoracic fractures

Etiology and pathology

Force sufficient to fracture a vertebral body may be inflicted either by a forward shearing stress associated with hyperflexion or by a vertical compressive force (e.g. toboggan injury) that can create a 'telescoping' deformity (Merbs, 1983). Although these can affect any part of the spine, the bodies of the lumbar vertebrae are most frequently affected. The shearing fractures are especially prone to compress or lacerate the spinal cord with resulting paralysis and urinary bladder infection. They also can generate a substantial hematoma with a generous quantity of callus surrounding the fracture (Fig. 3.6). The vertical compression may affect the entire vertebral body uniformly, although the additional support imparted to the posterior part of the vertebral body by the

FIG. 3.6. **Vertebra fracture.** Fifth lumbar vertebra fractured. Large callus on ventral aspect. Adult male, Chiribaya culture, coastal southern Peru, ca. A.D. 1150. PBL.

neural arch elements causes the anterior (ventral) ends of the vertebral body to be more vulnerable to compression. This results in a wedge-shaped vertebra, flattened to a greater degree anteriorly. The consequent misalignment produces a forward bending (kyphosis) of the upper trunk, the degree of which is related to the difference in compression between the anterior and posterior ends of the vertebral body. If the trabecular bone structure of the vertebral body has been weakened by a disease process such as that of osteoporosis, the degree of compression can be major and multiple vertebrae may be involved, resulting in a crippling degree of kyphotic deformity or multiple vertebral collapse ('concertina fracture'). The periosteal new bone formation is commonly of lesser degree in compression fractures and usually is limited to small nodular areas that fuse adjacent vertebrae. Since periosteum does not cover the vertebral body surface facing the intervertebral disk, reactive changes are usually found along the periphery of the disk adjoining the vertebra.

Most rib fractures are not displaced and, although painful (ribs can not be effectively splinted), usually heal uneventfully. Massive thoracic crushing injuries (e.g. steering wheel impaction in auto crashes) may displace fractured rib fragments whose sharp edges can lacerate the pleura, lung or heart with serious consequences.

Paleopathology

The telescoped type of vertebral compression fracture has been described in archaeological human remains frequently (Wells, 1964). Their high frequency in North American Inuit (Eskimo) populations has led Merbs (1983) to suggest they may have been acquired by the violent jarring to which such natives are subjected when riding their dog-powered sleds over rough ice. While massive thoracic crushing injuries carry with them a significant mortality, Wells (1964) describes an ancient skeleton whose fractured right clavicle as well as 6 right and 10 left ribs had all healed with many areas of fusion between adjacent ribs.

Dislocations (luxations)

Definition and pathology

A dislocation (luxation) consists of the complete and persistent displacement of the articular surfaces of a joint's bones with partial or complete capsular and/or ligament rupture. The term subluxation is applied to identical changes but of lesser degree. The gravity of a dislocation depends upon the joint involved, the degree of dislocation and its duration. Factors influencing the tissue changes include loss of synovial fluid with its reduction of nutrition available to the joint cartilage and impairment of blood supply to the joint elements. The trauma inducing the dislocation may also

result in soft tissue laceration sufficient to expose the joint, inviting infection. Ischemia may be severe enough to cause avascular necrosis. Persistence of the dislocation produces the more long-term changes of accelerated degenerative joint disease and bone atrophy secondary to immobilization. Force sufficient also to induce a fracture extending into the joint exaggerates the effect of these complications and may render the joint vulnerable to subsequent dislocations.

Paleopathology

Because the initial lesion of dislocation involves principally soft tissues, the diagnosis of dislocation in dry bones is dependent upon subsequent skeletal alterations that are secondary to the bone displacement. Since these require a considerable interval of time for development, the dislocation must persist to produce them. For the same reason it is probable that dislocations of lesser degree will go undetected. The dislocation sites most frequently identified in archaeological bones are the shoulder and the hip. The shoulder's dependence upon the joint capsule and ligament to attach the humeral head to the glenoid cavity makes it vulnerable to dislocation. However, it also makes it one of the easiest to reduce (i.e. to restore to normal position), thus ameliorating its effects (Merbs, 1989); it is probable that this was done frequently in antiquity. Persistence results in easily recognized changes of development of a false cavity on the scapula

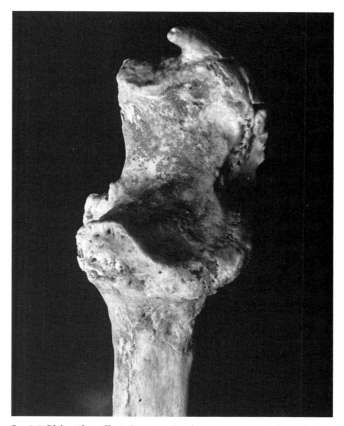

FIG. 3.7. **Dislocation, elbow.** Degenerative changes, upper articular surface, ulna. Adult male Guanche, ca. A.D. 1000, Canary Islands. G 10. MAT, OAMC.

morphological

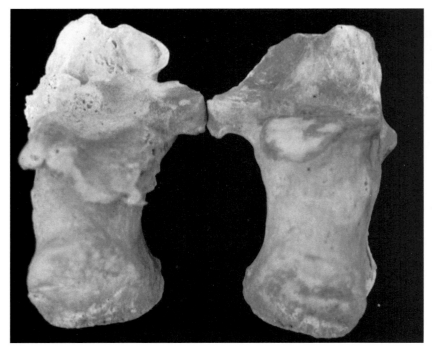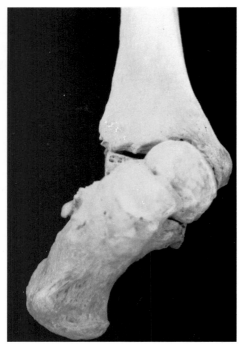

FIG. 3.8. **Dislocation, ankle.** Degeneration of talocalcaneal joint after subtalar dislocation. Young adult male Guanche, c. A.D. 1000, Canary Islands. G8. MAT, OAMC.

and distortion of the humeral head. Steinbock (1976) has identified reports of this dislocation from Neolithic France, the Early Bronze Age of Greece, Britain's Anglo-Saxon, Bronze and Medieval periods as well as late Archaic interval in Illinois and early burials in Hawaii.

Hip dislocations have also been identified repeatedly in archaeological bones. Attempts to form a false (secondary) acetabulum on the ilium are often recognizable and the femur head is commonly distorted. Because the ligamentum teres also contains blood vessels, its injury may induce sufficient ischemia to cause avascular necrosis of the femur head with its subsequent distortion of the head's morphology. Disuse atrophy of the leg bones may follow. The obvious condition from which traumatic hip dislocation must be differentiated is congenital hip dislocation. This can usually be achieved by close inspection of the acetabulum because, except for some new bone formation, this structure is normal in the cases in which trauma is responsible for the dislocation while in the congenital form the acetabulum is obviously malformed – small, shallow and triangular. Blondiaux & Millot (1991), however, feel they can detect the hip dislocations of more minor degree (subluxation) on the basis of a notched, enlarged and slightly more shallow acetabulum accompanied by femur head remodeling, since in these milder cases the femur head is not dislocated completely out of the acetabulum.

Other joints whose dislocation has been identified in ancient human skeletons include the acromioclavicular, elbow (Fig. 3.7) and ankle (Fig. 3.8) joints. Dreier (1992) reported one of the few cases of finger (fifth) dislocations in which the right first and second phalanges were dislocated,

the second and third demonstrated lateral slippage upward and backward about 10 mm upon the dorsal surface of the first phalanx with joint ankylosis.

An uncommon dislocation was identified by Rodríguez Martín (1992) in a Canary Island aboriginal (Guanche) young adult male with a left subtalar dislocation probably acquired in a fall among Tenerife's rocky, arid slopes. Osteophytosis, eburnation and porosity and pseudoarthrosis identified the presence of degenerative joint disease (DJD) in the left talus and calcaneus as well as mild changes or DJD in the distal tibial articular surface. The presence of severe spondylosis involving vertebrae from T3 to L3, probably the consequence of a limp secondary to the ankle lesion, testified to the prolonged survival following the dislocation (Fig. 3.8).

Traumatic myositis ossificans

Definition and pathology

Myositis ossificans traumatica is usually produced by avulsion of tendinous and/or muscle attachment to bone (occasionally by crushing injury of muscle against bone), generating a hematoma. Because of the proximity of hematoma to the bone's injured periosteum, the periosteum may participate in the organization of the hematoma including not only calcification but ossification as well. The resulting calcified and often ossified mass of woven bone constitutes the lesion known as myositis ossificans traumatica (Fig. 3.9). Most commonly involved sites are elbow, femur (linea aspera), shoulder and pelvis. In spite of its name, it is not a primary inflammation of muscle but is, instead, of traumatic etiology; additionally ossification is not invariable and is dependent upon its proximity to the periosteum (Watson-Jones, 1980). It should not be confused with the congenital condition termed myositis ossificans progressiva, nor with the process of heterotopic ossification.

Myositis ossificans traumatica may occur without obvious skeletal injury (Apley, 1981) and after only trivial muscle trauma. Minor muscle trauma may lead to metaplastic bony bridging of hip joints in paralyzed patients (Ortner & Putschar, 1985). Ectopic bone unattached to any bone may develop within muscle. Differential diagnosis must also separate this lesion from an osteochondroma and exostosis. The latter is usually smaller, often is related to the epiphyseal line, growing perpendicular to the plane of the diaphysis and frequently contains a rounded cap, quite unlike the irregular ossified mass of myositis ossificans traumatica. Osteochondromas are often irregular, but usually more coarsely lobular and commonly demonstrate an obvious relationship to their origin in bone. In the shoulder joint acute ossification of capsular tissues produced by hydroxyapatite crystal deposition by an inflammatory reaction can present a confusing similarity, but its restriction to the joint capsule can usually separate the possibility (Watson-Jones, 1980).

Paleopathology

Perhaps the most well-known example of this condition is that of the hypertrophic bone development on the left femur of the Java pithecanthropus, a *Homo erectus*. Ortner & Putschar (1985:70) demonstrate several well-illustrated lesions.

Localized subperiosteal thickenings

Blunt trauma, most commonly to the anterior tibial surface, the radius, fibula or ulna, will frequently generate a subperiosteal hematoma that subsequently is almost invariably ossified by the overlying periosteum (Watson-Jones, 1980). These are common in archaeological populations and can easily be differentiated from reactive changes to treponemal infection by their very sharply localized periphery and the identity of their color and texture with that of the surrounding bone (Mann & Murphy, 1990).

Skeletal injuries by weapons

Pointed and bladed weapons

As would be expected, pointed weapons generate a perforating, often conical puncture whose smooth, sharply-defined edge can be used to distinguish it from postmortem erosions if excavation tool defects can be excluded on the basis of color and patina differences. Flat-bladed instruments (knives, machetes, axes) produce elongated, V-shaped grooves, though allowance must be made for the tendency of bone elasticity to effect partial wound closure after the instrument is withdrawn (Maples, 1986). Valuable information about the inflicting weapon can be extracted from a scanning electron microscope study of an incised wound carried out either directly on the bone surface or on a resin cast of the wound.

Paleopathology

Study of Middle and Late Woodland Native American archaeological populations from Illinois revealed projectile points and fragments in 2–4% of the individuals' bones and body cavities, suggesting warfare played an active role in these groups' activities (Cook, 1984). However, the paleopathology literature contains far more case reports of these wound types than population studies (Fig. 3.10). An early Neolithic adult male skeleton from Denmark had one arrowhead in the maxilla and another in the sternum. The latter's position suggested it may have produced a fatal, exsanguinating

FIG. 3.9. Myositis ossificans traumatica. Irregular calcified masses adherent to the ilium (b) and femur (a) probably represent calcified crushed muscle. Late precontact midwestern U.S.A. aboriginal (b) and medieval adult, Spain (a). Courtesy Dr John Gregg and USDAL (b) (photograph by Glenn Malchow) and Dr D. Campillo (a), MAL.

laceration in the proximal aorta (Bennike, 1985). A wooden arrowhead was found to have penetrated a thoracic vertebra in a Canary Island aboriginal to a depth sufficient to have lacerated the spinal cord (Diego Cuscoy, 1986). A Bronze Age Basque skeleton demonstrated a silex arrowhead in the pelvis with evidence of healing (Etxeberria & Vegas, 1987). The skull of a 1100 year old Native American from Ohio revealed a projectile point had penetrated the facies infratemporalis of the maxilla, traversed the sinus and reached the anterior surface just below the infraorbital foramen; healing changes indicated the individual's survival (Sciulli et al., 1988). An Arizona Native American skeleton had a small lithic point embedded in the cuneiform bone with surrounding bone

resorption without infection, and another had a healed sinus defect suggestive of an untipped arrow wound (Merbs, 1989). An arrowhead was also found embedded in the twelfth thoracic vertebra of a Neolithic skeleton from Catalonia, Spain in a position implying it penetrated the aorta and caused fatal hemorrhage (Campillo, 1993). Four adult male skeletons from Navarra, Spain showed a healed, incised rib wound and unhealed arrowhead wounds of the maxillary sinus and right humerus as well as an arrowhead within the vertebral canal that must have macerated the spinal cord (Armendariz et al., 1994).

Gunshot wounds

A detailed description of the forensic aspects of skeletal gunshot wounds is beyond the scope of this book. Attention can be called to certain basic features (Fig. 3.11). These include the fact that entry wounds of the skull are commonly small, circular and discrete with inner table beveled edges while the exit hole is larger, irregular, often with comminution and loss of some fragments as well as outer table beveling. This is largely the consequence of transmission of the bullet's energy into intracranial pressure increase, though bullet fragmentation may modify these features and even generate more than one exit wound. Intracranial angulated bone surfaces may also cause the bullet or its fragments to deviate from its primary path. Examination of a skeletal defect radiograph with a magnifying lens may identify metal fragments that establish its gunshot nature. Castellano Arroyo (1994) points out that such other variables may produce several types of fractures and defects:

1. Incomplete fractures with radiating fissures that stop at the skull sutures;
2. Prominent, discrete holes with fissures that radiate perpendicular to the defect margin;
3. Irregular large holes typical of short distance gunshots generating an explosive intracranial pressure.

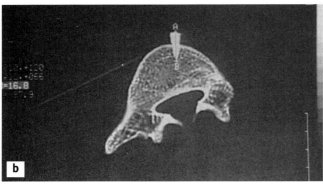

FIG. 3.10. **Arrowhead injury.** (a) Obsidian point nearly 17 mm long embedded in body of the fifth lumbar vertebra, (b) CT scan. No evidence of healing. Young adult female, (A.D. 500–1700) central California site, Ala-329. Courtesy Dr Robert Jurmain.

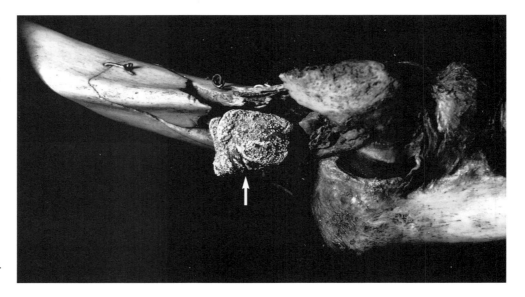

FIG. 3.11. **Gunshot fracture.** Lead musket ball (arrow) in situ at elbow fracture of U.S. Civil War soldier. MM. Courtesy G. Worden.

Paleopathology

An early twentieth century North African Bedouin male skeleton was found to have an 8 mm lead bullet that entered the skull below the left orbit and became embedded in the base of the skull adjacent to the foramen ovale near the carotid canal and jugular foramen, with changes suggesting he had survived it for at least a month (Irish *et al.*, 1993). In another body a 32 caliber bullet was embedded in a rib (Merbs, 1989) while Wells (1964) describes a Native American with a facial gunshot wound that had healed.

Decapitation

Pathology

The stigmata of decapitation are the cut marks on or through cervical vertebrae and often, but not invariably, separate burial of the skull (Merbs, 1989). Severance through any of the cervical vertebral has been reported, but the midcervical area is the most frequent transected site. Horizontal blows often include portions of the skull (especially mandible and skull base) in the transection plane (Manchester, 1983a: 60). As is true in other parts of the skeleton, it is not easy to determine whether lesions assigned to the perimortem period were inflicted premortem or postmortem. Surprisingly, expectations that the mortuary context would provide clues to the special social status of the decapitated individual frequently are not fulfilled (see below). These problems are compounded by the fact that the lesions, especially those of the skull and mandible, often mimic postmortem erosive alterations.

Paleopathology

Decapitation of an adolescent female from the Romano-British cemetery in Hertfordshire had been carried out at the level of the second cervical vertebra via six separate cuts, believed to have been performed postmortem, principally because of the absence of special mortuary treatment (McKinley, 1993). However, six bodies from the Romano-British cemetery at Cirencester (believed to represent retired legionnaires and Roman officials) all demonstrated decapitation at levels from the second to the fifth cervical vertebrae. In all, the heads had been placed in the normal anatomic position in the grave and, except for the fact that two graves each contained two decapitated bodies, no distinguishing mortuary feature unique to these burials could be identified (McWhirr *et al.*, 1982:108–9). Seven additional decapitated skeletons were found in the nearby Lankhills cemetery. Decapitation was not a common form of Roman punishment (Bush & Stirland, 1987).

An additional case from the Viking period in Denmark was probably performed by a horizontal blow at the third cervical vertebra level that also included the inferior aspect of the mandible in the transection plane. Additionally two female skulls from Denmark's Room Bog and Stidsholt Bog also reveal transection through the second and third cervical vertebrae respectively (Bennike, 1985). This author also describes the last forensic decapitation in Denmark about 200 years ago in which the head had been displayed on a stake as a public reminder.

Other decapitation examples include an Iron Age specimen from Sutton Walls (Brothwell, 1981); a 25 year old male mummy from northern Chile that also included other corporeal violence and in whom decapitation may have been performed postmortem to acquire a trophy head (Allison & Gerszten, 1983) and several New World reports from Mesoamerica (Moser, 1973) and North America (Riding, 1992).

Strangulation

Pathology

Evidence for manual strangulation in recently deceased bodies is largely limited to fractures of the hyoid bone and of calcified thyroid and cricoid cartilages as well as bruised local cervical soft tissues (Stewart, 1979; Concheiro Carro, 1994). In skeletonized bodies the cartilaginous fractures can only be detected if they are calcified, so that such a diagnosis is more apt to be made among the aged. Nonmanual (rope, rigid items) strangulation may result in cervical vertebra fracture including hairline transverse fractures on or posterior to the superior articular processes of the axis.

Paleopathology

The few paleopathological reports of strangulation are primarily in the forensic literature (Stewart, 1979). Perhaps the most well-known example is Tollund man, a bog body from Denmark who was found with a rope tied tightly around his neck (Bennike, 1985). Angel & Caldwell (1984) diagnosed death by strangulation based entirely on a fracture of the transverse process of the sixth cervical vertebra in a young, white female.

Amputation: the skeletal evidence

Methods and pathology

Circumstances under which amputations occurred in antiquity include social justice (punishment), accidental and war injuries, deliberate surgery and ritual. The latter probably was limited to finger and/or toe amputation and is discussed in the section on soft tissue injuries below. Amputation as punishment is well documented among some cultures even today and Brothwell (1967) seems sure that hand and foot removal was practiced during the Saxon Period in Britain (Fig. 3.12).

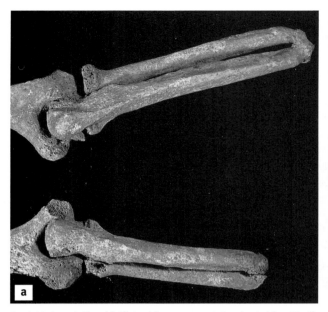

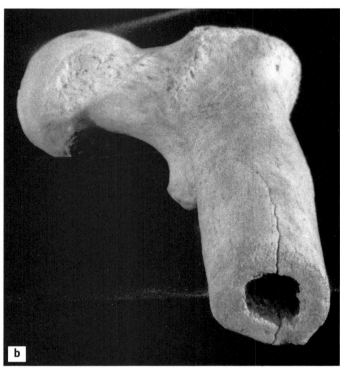

FIG. 3.12. **Amputation.** (a) Bilateral forearm amputation, healed (punitive?) (b) Midfemur amputation. Healing changes. Military wound. (a) Case 33, ca. A.D. 500, Spain. (b) Modern. (a) Courtesy D. Turbon, M. Hernandez, E. Chimenos & D. Campillo, UB. (b) CMNH.

It seems self-evident that sword and ax war injuries were capable of limb severance, though accidental amputations of major limbs must have occurred in antiquity only rarely.

An understanding of the physiological sequence of post-amputation events can be useful for the solution of the common problem facing paleopathologists in these specimens: the separation of amputations from simple pseudoarthrosis. Post-amputation survival of less than a week produces no detectable signs of healing. This is followed by vascular erosion of the bone ends and adjacent diaphysis. By the fourteenth post-amputation day an endosteal callus becomes apparent; this progresses to narrowing and finally obliteration of the medullary cavity at the bone end with rounding and smoothing of the stump. Localized osteophytes may develop and finally bone atrophy secondary to disuse may develop later.

Paleopathology

Though not really rare, archaeological examples of amputation are not abundant. The oldest case is that of a 46 000 year old Neanderthal from northern Iraq who had lost his arm. His finders postulated Neolithic surgical amputation but Majno (1975) notes that '... there were surely more lions than surgeons in the immediate neighborhood...' Punitive hand amputation is recorded in the Hammurabi Codex of about 1800 B.C. Shortened, fused distal radius and ulna of a 45 year old male in Israel dating to the Middle Bronze period 3600 years ago testify to a right hand and wrist amputation (Bloom et al., 1995). A Ptolemaic Egyptian mummy revealed amputation of a hand with a prosthesis in place that was probably added by the embalmers (Gray, 1966). Another

example of possible hand amputation in an adult male from Illinois was reported by Morse (1978); this skeleton demonstrated fusion of the distal ends of the radius and ulna. A young pre-Columbian Peruvian female body showed a well-healed amputation of a humerus (Rogers, 1985). Other reports include possible cases from medieval Denmark, seventh century Britain, Peru's Mochica period, ninth dynasty Egypt, Guatemala (900 A.D. Maya), pre-Columbian Mexico and early historic Hawaii.

Amputation: the soft tissue (finger) evidence

Both rupestrian cave art and modern ethnological studies throughout the world document the practice of amputation of human fingers. Reports of such practices during the 1930s indicate that the practice of amputation of fingers diffused to Africa from India or Indonesia, and was initially employed by Hottentot widows who buried their amputated digit in their deceased husband's grave to pacify evil spirits. Later it was extended to other threatening situations including serious illness of other family members. In focal areas especially, cultural evolution resulted in its incorporation into the judicial system as a form of punishment in some tribes. The Kyiga of eastern Central Africa amputated a vanquished foe's digit as a war trophy and with the expectation that its possession would frustrate revenge efforts. South Africa's Herero people also amputated fingers of enslaved war captives to publicize their servant status (Lagercrantz, 1935). Similar circumstances are described in Australia and Oceania (Söderström, 1938).

Undoubtedly the most commonly studied examples from antiquity are those of the Gargas cave on the western slopes of Mt. Gouret in southern France and from Tiberan cave on its eastern side. Together they display 143 handprints on the cave wall, of which many demonstrate either missing parts of digits or actually entire digits. Of these, 130 are left hands, suggesting that most ancient individuals were probably right handed. Numerous caves in the region have rupestrian handprints, but only those on Mt Gouret show mutilation changes. Janssens (1957) points out they include examples of direct imprints by a painted hand ('positive' print) as well as stenciled forms ('negative' print). Because the remainder of the hand is not distorted he also believes these are true amputations, not code messages formed by flexing various fingers. For various reasons he rejects a variety of natural diseases (atherosclerotic gangrene, frostbite, osteomyelitis, syphilis, leprosy etc) as an explanation, but is puzzled why nearby caves do not reveal the amputations if, indeed, they were of ritual origin. Janssens cites Castaret (1951) as suggesting finger amputations were a form of sacrifice, giving examples from other cultures including pygmies (sign of mourning), Hottentots (avert serious illness), Mandan Indians of North America (consecration rites), Pacific Island natives (illness or death) and Berula Kodo, India (ritual).

Janssens states that the purpose of these amputations must be resolved in medical terms, yet he does not appear to embrace any of the possible diseases he considers. Given, however, the evidence of modern ethnology, it appears to the authors of this volume that the significance of this practice is rooted in supernatural ritual with predictable cultural evolution into punitive practices in focal areas. We have been unable to identify reports of this lesion in archaeological human remains.

While there appear to be few examples of amputated digits alone in descriptions of archaeological remains, amputated feet and hands in a context suggestive of ritual have been identified quite frequently (Vreeland, 1978; Verano, 1986; Alva & Donnan, 1993).

Trephination (trepanation)

Definition

Trephination involves the production of a defect in the skull vault to create communication between the cranial cavity and the environment, whose success depends upon avoidance of injury to the meninges, brain and blood vessels.

History

Examining a pre-Columbian Peruvian skull sent him by the diplomat E.G. Squier, the French physician Pierre Paul Broca electrified the scientific community in 1867 by announcing the defect was the product of prehistoric surgery and that the 'patient' had survived the operation. This was, however, not the first reported example. In 1839 Morton had described such a skull from Pachacamac, Peru but had misdiagnosed it as accidental trauma. Another was published 4 years later from Hungary by Kovacs (in 1843). In retrospect, Wells (1964) felt that a report of a skull in 1685 from Cocherel, France was the earliest example, though its true nature was not recognized until 200 years later. The fascination with these lesions has not ceased; Majno (1975) comments dryly that the number of publications (thousands) now probably exceed the number of specimens found.

Geographical distribution

It is interesting that a procedure, seeming so exotic to us, should have such a large distribution in both time and space (Comas, 1972). In Europe and North Africa trephination can be traced to the Mesolithic in Poland, Russia, Taforalt and Morocco and was practiced in these and other areas throughout the Neolithic. In fact, Prioreschi (1991) estimates that between 6 and 10% of excavated Neolithic skulls have been trephined. Excavation of post-Neolithic sites show far fewer examples, perhaps because of the popularity of cremation during the later Bronze Age and La Tene period (Lisowski, 1967). Hippocratic authors (400 B.C.) noted its use for certain cranial wounds and the Roman Celsus (ca. A.D. 25) described it in detail. However the practice declined in Europe after the expansion of Islam and disappeared during the medieval period (Germana & Fornaciari, 1992: 164).

Nevertheless, in spite of its broad distribution, it was far from a universal practice at any time. Within a broad area, trephination seemed to flourish among certain groups. While nearly every European country has revealed some trephined skulls (Piggott, 1940), few have produced the large number excavated from sites in southern France (Dastugue, 1973). Berbers and Kabyles from northern Africa practiced trephination, as did the Guanches in the Canary Islands, the Kisii from Kenya, Tende from Tanganyika, and the Masai. A few such skulls have been found in Egypt (Shaaban, 1984; Pahl, 1987). In Oceania Polynesian islanders as well as those from Bismarck, New Britain, New Ireland, Tahiti and others also indulged in this activity but in Melanesia it was especially popular (Crump, 1901). In the New World a few specimens have been found in North America (Stone & Miles, 1990), but perhaps the highest concentration of such skulls has been found in the Andean area of South America, especially Peru and Bolivia between the fifth century B.C. to the fifth century A.D (Bandelier, 1904; Graña et al., 1954; Lastres & Cabieses, 1960; Allison & Pezzia, 1976). Such skulls have also been identified in Asia (Middle East, India, China, Japan, Pakistan, Afghanistan and southern Siberia.) Speculations regarding its spread by cultural diffusion have been difficult to support and currently popular scientific opinion views its distribution as a product of independent invention.

Purpose

Earlier literature reflects intense controversy whose views ranged from magical (release of disease spirit) to medical (therapeutics) (Courville, 1967; Margetts, 1967; Ackerknecht, 1971). Lisowski (1967) grouped the various suggestions into three views: therapeutic, magico-therapeutic and magico-ritual. Many Peruvian skulls demonstrate an intimate relationship of skull fracture lines with the trephine opening (Zimmerman *et al.*, 1981), which is cited as support for the medical therapeutic view. The magico-therapeutic concept views trephination as an attempt to release (expel?) an evil spirit causing any of a variety of different diseases originating in the head such as headache, vertigo, neuralgia, coma, delirium, meningitis, convulsions and others, even including prophylaxis (Lisowski, 1967). An example could be that of a trephined young male from the Judean desert reported by Zias & Pomeranz (1992) whose skull demonstrated three successive trephines that the authors feel were related to the onset and subsequent spread of suppurative sinusitis. A recent suggestion by Prioreschi (1991) may be a good example for support of the magico-ritual view. This author postulates that an unconscious individual was viewed as dead and his recovery (either spontaneous or assisted by

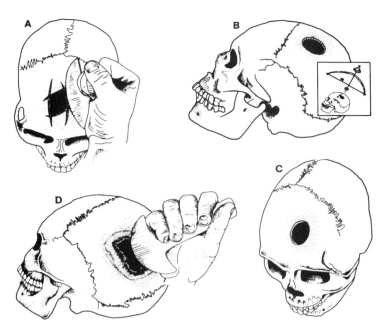

FIG. 3.13. **Trepanation methods.** Four trepanation techniques reconstructed from Peruvian skulls (see Aufderheide, 1985). Drawings by Mark Summers, reproduced here by permission of Minnesota Medicine.

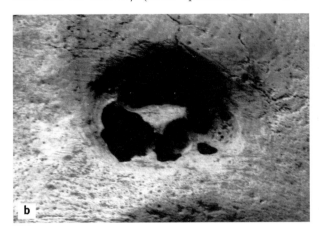

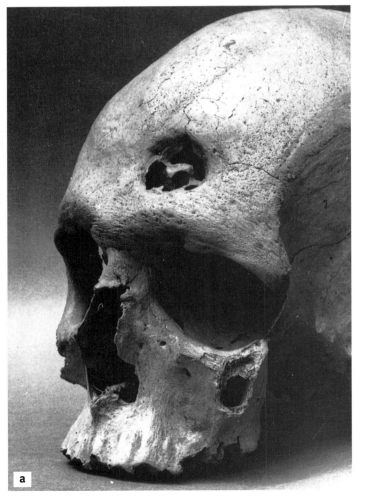

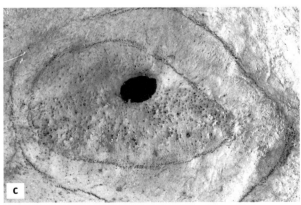

FIG. 3.14. **Trepanation.** (a) Drilled defect penetrates into frontal sinus and cranial cavity. (b) Closeup shows evidence of healing. (c) Scraping method. Case 7. Bronze age. Valencia, Spain. Courtesy Dr D. Campillo. Museu de Banyeres.

some procedure) considered as revivification (rendered 'undead'). Having established that recovery from the 'dead' state was possible, trephination may have become one of the procedures employed to bring it about. Prioreschi cites many features of trephination consistent with this interpretation. For example, unhealed trephinations could be examples of the procedure carried out on already dead persons, and incomplete trephinations may represent recovery during the procedure. To these we could add the observation that the many Neolithic examples from southern France that reveal no fracture or other pathology would also be consistent with such a magico-ritual view. In brief, all of these could have been operative among different groups in different places at different times.

Methods

At least four, distinguishable methods (Fig. 3.13) have been observed, including (Aufderheide, 1985; Brothwell, 1994):

1. Grooving: A pointed instrument inscribes a round or oval groove; repetitive tracing of this groove with pressure applied to the instrument eventually penetrates the skull. The wound edge is vertical or steeply beveled.
2. Scraping: A sharp-edged, oval stone is repeatedly scraped over a chosen area until the center penetrates the skull. The wound edges have a broad, shallow bevel. This is the most popular type used in Peru.
3. The same tool as in (2) above is used by applying the edge perpendicular to the skull surface while rocking and drawing it to and fro until a linear groove penetrates the skull. Three more grooves are produced to shape a rectangle followed by removal of the circumscribed bone. Few of this type show evidence of healing.
4. A circle of small holes are drilled through the skull, the bridges broken and the enclosed bone removed. Except for a few examples from Egypt, Palestine and France, this method was limited to Peru.

Anatomical distribution

Most trephine defects are in the left frontal (Fig. 3.14) and parietal bones (right-handed surgeons? right-handed assailants?). The occipital bone was rarely employed. Although the literature suggests most trephiners avoided the cranial sutures (and their underlying venous sinuses), outstanding exceptions have been noted (Rodríguez Maffiote, 1974a). A Neolithic skull from Sweden has a healed trephination in the middle of the sagittal suture (Persson, 1976–77). A Canary Island aboriginal skull study found half of the holes positioned on cranial sutures, most commonly the sagittal and coronal, and 80% of these demonstrated healing changes.

Most skulls have only a single trephine defect, a modest number have multiple openings and one Peruvian skull actually demonstrates seven separate defects.

Pathology

Complete trephines are those penetrating the full thickness of both tables and intervening diploe. Incomplete trephines extend a variable distance into the skull bone but do not penetrate the inner table. The latter have been viewed as a symbolic gesture (Dastugue & Gervais, 1992). Complete healing is characterized by closed, smooth-surfaced diploe but new bone formation is only rarely sufficiently abundant to close the trephine defect (Fig. 3.15). A finely granular area of osteitis surrounding the defect may indicate periosteal reflection while a more irregular, thickened surface characterizes a complication of osteomyelitis. Campillo (1991a) carried out experimental studies of trephination and cauterization in rabbits and concluded that the bone reaction to these two procedures was so similar that they were not useful for etiological predictions. The reactions were also less intense if not infected and necrotic bone sequestration and hyperostotic reactions were more marked when no sutures were applied.

Survival

Surprisingly high frequency of trephination survival is apparent in all groups studied, as are the few complications of osteomyelitis. Of 2000 trephined skulls examined by

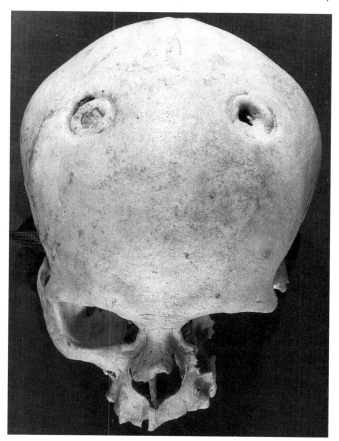

FIG. 3.15. **Trepanation, healing.** Modern skull shows healing without complete obliteration of defect 5 years after surgical trephine for draining bilateral subdural hematoma. BM.

Stewart (1958a) half revealed long-term survival (Fig. 3.14) and an additional 16% had partial healing changes. Bennike (1985) also found an 80% survival while modern operators in Kenya claim a mortality of less than 5% (Aufderheide, 1985). Factors contributing to such success include the high vascularity of the overlying soft tissues (contributing to minimizing infection), and probable relative cleanliness of the instruments (perhaps lithics created at time of use: England, 1962). Several studies based on radiological changes found similar results. Guiard (1930) noted that earliest healing changes were detectable in about 2 weeks while a dense halo of sclerotic, reactive bone around the defect was found in those with longer survival of several months and a wide zone of rarefaction was associated with survivals greater than 1 year. Similar changes using semimicroradiography were found by Lacroix (1972). These were found to correlate with expected macroscopic observations (Ortner & Putschar, 1985).

At least some of the skulls lacking healing may have been trephined postmortem – perhaps to acquire a rondelle (a round bone disc cut from the edge of a trephine defect with a central hole for purposes of suspension), a persisting, modern African practice (Merbs, 1989) or for purposes of practice surgery on cadavers. Since we can not be certain of the perimortem time of trephination, nor its purpose, Dastugue & Gervais (1992) suggest avoidance of the term trephination and suggest use of an alternative: découpage postmortem (postmortem cranial incision) (Fig. 3.16).

Differential diagnosis

Steinbock (1976) suggests that the following conditions can simulate trephination:
1. Enlarged parietal foramina ('Catlin mark') – oval and symmetrical.
2. Cranial dysraphism (sharply defined borders).
3. Tangential sword cuts (inner table defect size exceeds outer).
4. Comminuted fractures (much more irregular).
5. Metastatic carcinoma; myeloma (irregular, often multiple).
6. Bone neoplasms (benign can be similar; trauma, trephination and cauterization produce synostosis; benign tumors do not: Campillo, 1991b).
7. Infections (syphilis, tuberculosis, mycoses: irregular – Campillo, 1977).
8. Nonspecific infections (new bone response).
9. Parietal bone osteopenia (the skull depression is not sharply demarcated: Lisowski, 1967).
10. Postmortem alterations (stone abrasion, acid soils, animal effects).
11. Excavation injuries.

In addition, Steinbock (1976) notes that, if a group practiced trephination at all, usually a significant fraction of the population can be expected to demonstrate the lesion. Hence, caution

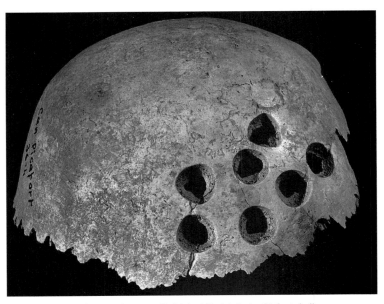

FIG. 3.16. **Trepanation, posthumous.** Multiple drilled defects of infant skull made postmortem (ritual?). Case 8, 5th century B.C. Talayotic culture, Mallorca, Spain. Courtesy Dr D. Campillo. UB.

in making the diagnosis of trephination seems advisable if only an occasional skull in an archaeological population demonstrates the defect.

Cranial deformation

Intentional deformation of the cranium has a surprising antiquity. Skulls estimated to be 45 000 years old revealing evidence of this practice have been found among Neanderthal remains in Shanidar cave; in the Andean area it can be traced back nearly 10 000 years. The Hippocratic corpus describes the practice among Crimean residents. Ancient Mayan iconography depicts it clearly. While few Egyptian skulls have been shown unequivocally to have been deformed deliberately, Egyptian sculptors have portrayed the 'heretic' pharaoh Akhenaten and his children with deformed heads (though this may be symbolic-portraiture license to emphasize his special status) (Snorrason, 1946). Indeed, evidence from the major populations throughout the world suggest a global distribution of this practice in antiquity (Weiss, 1958).

The purpose(s) of cranial deformation probably varied in time and space. Spanish chroniclers suggest that it served as a tribal marker in the New World's Andean area (Garcilaso de la Vega, [1609] 1966:485-6). Crete's Minoans used the practice as a mark of distinction for their elite members (Snorrason, 1946). Identification appears to be its most apparent function. However, the fact that Andean groups near sacred mountains deformed their heads in a manner conforming to these mountain peaks suggest a possible religious or ritual role as well.

From a pathophysiological point of view, Moss (1958) points out that the cloth deformer used to create the deformation is not, by itself, responsible for the growth stimulus, nor is the bone the immediate agent of deformation. A presently unidentified force drives and directs neural growth. When the deformer prevents its growth in a certain direction, the orientation of cerebral tissue growth is deflected. The skull growth then follows growth of the brain. The forces may be directed by the dura mater which is attached to the skull during the growth period at five fixed points. These guiding principles result in two important effects: the final volume of cerebral tissue is not different from normal, and the deformed skull does not compress or impair cerebral tissue. Björk & Björk (1964) also note that placement of the deformer is not always perfectly central, with the result that one side may be deformed more than another. Distribution of growth forces, however, is such that appropriate compensatory shortening of the mandible and cranial base occurs so that dental function is not impaired.

Cranial deformers and their use

Pressure is applied to the growing cranium by a cloth band or cord encircling the head, designed in such a way that its tension may be adjusted daily. Localization of the force is achieved by placing a substance between the scalp and the cloth band over the area of desired pressure focus. That substance may be rigid – commonly a board – if complete flattening of the area is desired. Substitution of a cloth or fur pad instead of a board results in a rounded effect (Fig. 3.17). Some of the deformers may have an additional band from occiput to the frontal area over the vertex. The usual points selected for compression are the occiput or the frontal bone. Allison et al. (1981a) have described a variety of deformers used in the Andean area, one of which contained a face mask with firm pads positioned over the malar bones. Weiss (1958) describes and illustrates one in which the infant is lashed to a palette, the deformer being stabilized by cords attached to a wood slat arching over the head. These deformers are applied soon after birth and are kept in place continually, usually removed during the third year. Growth thereafter will continue in the manner directed by the deformer during infancy. Although older children and occasionally even adults of the Andean area have been buried with a deformer in position, these may well have symbolic significance in those age groups.

The effects of these deformers have produced a bewildering array of cranial shapes. Efforts to classify these has resulted in a variety of taxonomies ranging from 2 (Hrdlicka, 1912; Moss, 1958) to 15 different groups (Allison et al., 1981a). While Moss' classification was

based on the relationship of the plane of the occiput to the Frankfurt plane as viewed on radiography, those of most others use features of a lateral cranial silhouette. The two principal influencing factors are the placement of occipital and/or frontal pressure substances and the nature of these substances (hard or soft textured). The absence of both of these pressure-localizing devices results in a uniform, tall, cylindrical deformation. Almost infinite variations can be induced by application of differing degrees of tension and by varying exact placement of the band as well as the size and location of the pressure-localizing structures. For example, excessive tension on the band may produce sufficient overlap of cranial bones so as to result in ridges and grooves in the later sutures (Fig 3.18). In fact, based on the appearance of the

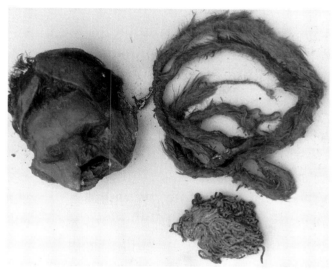

FIG. 3.17. **Cranial deformer.** Camelid hide-covered vegetal cord encircled head and held ball of cordage over occiput. M01-6, TU2. MAUT. PBL.

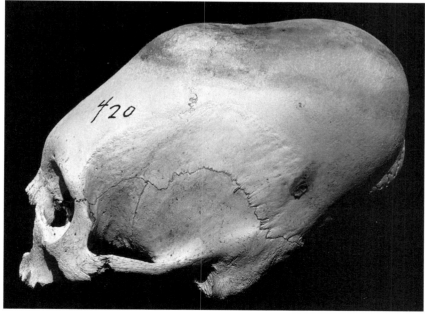

FIG. 3.18. **Intentional cranial deformation.** Placement and tension of deformer determined skull shape. Tiwanaku-related cultural group about A.D. 800–900 from northern Chile's coast. MAUT. PBL.

deformed cranium, archaeological efforts to recreate the structure of a missing deformer may mistake such a groove (produced in this manner by a simple circular band) as having been caused by an additional band over the vertex. Facial flattening is probably produced only by deformers that include a face mask with compression structures over the malar bones. Intentional cranial deformation may produce some additional minor effects. Increase in the number of wormian bones of the lambdoid sutures has been noted, but production of auditory canal exostoses, decreased cranial capacity or metopic sutures could not be confirmed in a major study of Andean skulls (Gerszten, 1993).

It is surprising that the brain, distorted by a deformer, usually functions satisfactorily, in spite of the almost astonishing degree of shape alterations that are sometimes achieved. This is probably most easily understood by reference to the previously noted observation that the growth of the brain is dominant and that of the skull will adapt and conform to it, avoiding compression. There are, however, observations that suggest the outcome is not always benign. Excessive zeal in tension adjustment may cause the occipital pad or board to exert sufficient pressure to produce necrosis of the underlying bone. More serious are occasional disasters resulting from the effects of such tension on the cranial sutures. Both the closure time and the chronological sequence of these sutures can be altered. The lambdoid usually closes before the coronal in deformed crania, opposite the normal sequence. More serious is premature closure. If a deformer deflects cerebral growth upward, few problems seem to occur as long as the vault sutures remain open. Excessive tension, however, can result in sufficient periosteal response in the affected suture to produce synostosis. Without opportunity to expand in either direction the resulting constriction of the brain may be fatal. Guillen (1992:164) has noted several examples of this in the Andean area. The reactive change at the suture may also generate a change so similar to porotic hyperostosis that it can only be differentiated from it by its distribution pattern: a band of spongy-appearing bone 1–1.5 cm wide, sharply demarcated, located immediately adjacent to the affected suture (Aufderheide, 1990; Guillen, 1992:156).

Cauterization

Thermal injury to the scalp tissues and the skull's outer table has been employed since Neolithic times until the Medieval period. The speculated purposes are similar to those expressed for trephination as discussed above. The methods of heat application varied widely and included cauterizing the scalp with smoldering ashes (Kwakiutl Indians of Canada); holding glowing ember (Yakuts) or burning wick (Central Canadian Inuit or Eskimos) or burning piece of wood (Osage Indians) or red hot stone or animal fat (Canary Island Guanches) on the scalp at the site of pain.

Sincipital T cauterization

This unique form of cauterization involved using heat, in one of the above or similar forms, applied in a linear (anterior to posterior) streak usually in the skull's midline, often (but not invariably) terminating in a shorter line at right angles to effect a T-shaped lesion. Sufficient necrosis of soft tissues and the skull's outer table is achieved to produce a permanent, depressed groove in the skull that does not penetrate the inner table. The lesion was first described in six female Neolithic skulls from southern France. Wells (1964) suggests the scalp may have been incised and boiling oil poured into the incision. In the Canarian Guanches the cauterized area is oval instead of linear. Loss of blood supply causes ischemic necrosis with bone dissolution and surrounding sclerotic response. The changes reach the level of the dura only rarely. The fact that most subjects are females and children suggests a ritual significance.

Geographical distribution

Wide distribution of such lesions have included the New World (Peru), Europe (France, Hungary, Czechoslovakia), Canary Islands (probably not as frequent as the 10% reported by Luschan, 1896a,b), Africa and central Asia. The numbers of cases, however, are far fewer than for trephination.

Differential diagnosis

Osteomyelitis can simulate this lesion. Indeed, in his experimental studies on rabbits Campillo (1977) pointed out that the skeletal response to both osteomyelitis and cauterization were qualitatively indistinguishable and were not dependent on the cause but rather on the degree of subsequent inflammation. The lesion has been confused with treponematosis and Weiss (1958) suggests using the remainder of the skeleton to exclude this infection. Occasionally senile atrophy may produce sufficient osteopenia to mimic this lesion (Ortner & Putschar, 1985).

Bloodletting

The deliberate induction of blood loss is an almost universal practice among nontechnological societies (Ackerknecht, 1971). It has been applied for almost every conceivable condition for which no other effective therapy was available. It reached the peak of its popularity in the nineteenth century: in 1883, 40 million leeches were imported into France for this purpose.

Methods varied from scarification (multiple small incisions of the skin to induce controlled bleeding) to cupping (application of a horn with negative pressure to scarified areas) to venesection (incision into a vein – popular in America, Oceania and parts of Africa) and finally to leeching

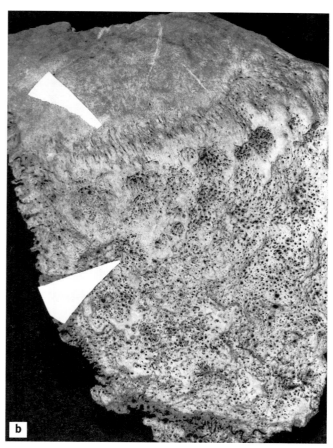

FIG. 3.19. **Scalping.** Perimortem cut marks are clear (a). Irregular new bone on outer table (b) due to osteomyelitis, indicating postscalping survival. Late precontact upper midwestern North American aboriginal. Courtesy Dr John Gregg and USDAL. Photograph by Glenn Malchow.

(the application of blood-sucking water animals to the skin or wound). The latter was rarely employed by prehistoric societies (Ackerknecht, 1971).

Scalping

Definition and Pathology

Scalping represents the excision of a variably-sized segment of scalp. While this can occur accidentally, in antiquity it was almost invariably carried out for the purpose of acquisition of a human trophy. While Hamperl & Laughlin (1959) describe the removal of the scalp with underlying periosteum, it is unlikely that areas of periosteum of significant size were removed very often because of its dense adherence to the bone and the urgency of the battle conditions that frequently prevailed. Nadeau (1944) describes the North American Indian scalping process as varying from removal of all or only part of the scalp from usually a single (occasionally multiple) area that sometimes permitted the posterior part of the avulsed scalp to hang down on a pedicle. Use of a metal knife frequently did not injure the skull bones but the irregular edges of lithic knives often incised the periosteum and underlying outer table (Hamperl & Laughlin, 1959; Steinbock, 1976).

While scalping was accompanied by substantial hemorrhage from the rich vascularization of the scalp, when death occurred it was usually due to other lethal wounds. In their absence, recovery was not uncommon. In these the bone changes were a response to the incisions and the skeletal ischemia secondary to deprivation of the scalp's blood supply with bone necrosis of the outer table, and granulation tissue separating the necrotic area from the deeper, surviving bone. New bone formation was common, resulting in a final appearance of a depressed and eventually smooth zone that can be uneven over a broad area. Moderate porosity at the margins reflects increased vascularity and inflammation. Further irregularities were superimposed by the changes induced by osteomyelitis when infection occurred (Fig. 3.19).

Geographical distribution

Although native North American scalping practices are the most well-known, it must be noted that similar procedures were practiced by ancient Scythians, Palestinés, Maccabees, as well as the Anglo-saxons, Visigoths and Franks until the ninth century A.D. Furthermore, although the practice was employed by North American aboriginals before the arrival of Europeans, it was greatly encouraged by the English, French and American governments.

Paleopathology

The paleopathological literature of the U.S.A. records numerous examples of scalping including male Arikara Indians from South Dakota, adult males from the Mississipian period in Arkansas, the middle Mississipian period in Illinois, three prehistoric and early historic skulls from Virginia, an adult female from Alabama, a prehistoric skull from Nebraska and many others. Ortner & Putschar (1985) describe an interesting example of a pre-Columbian adult female skull from Georgia (U.S.A.) with an irregular surface area on the frontal and both parietal bones without evidence of active inflammation suggesting the formation of granulation tissue without infection over this entire area and with good, complete recovery.

Allen *et al.* (1985) introduced a unique suggestion that grew out of examination of 10 Hopi Indian (Arizona) skulls with healed, depressed fractures, severe infection and unhealed injuries. In all of these the stigmata of scalping were superimposed. They suggest the purpose of the scalping incisions was to expose the underlying pathology in order to gain experience with the appearance of the tissues affected by these conditions – a primitive type of autopsy.

Crucifixion

Crucifixion was one of several methods of execution for major crimes such as treason during the Persian and Roman periods of Egyptian history. A variety of crucifixion forms was employed including the traditional + forms (with overlapping feet) as well as the X form (with legs spread). In some instances the body was tied to the cross, while in others it was nailed there. Tradition suggests that nailing of the + form involved a single nail through overlapping ankles (Lewis, 1995) (Fig. 3.20). Barbet (1953), experimenting with freshly amputated arms, concluded that suspension from hands nailed through the palms would not tolerate the body weight and these would need, in addition to the nails, to be bound to the cross with a rope. Later experiments suggested that a nail driven through the hand at the posterior end of the first and second metacarpal would, indeed, support the crucified body (Zubigwe, 1982:65-7). Alternatively, nail suspension without binding would be adequate if the nail were placed between the distal radius and ulna. Further anatomic evidence of crucifixion would be apparent through the practice of crurifragium (deliberate fracture of the long bones of the lower extremities and sometimes the upper as well). Zubigwe (1982:92), however, challenges the idea that this hastens death by causing the body to slump and impair respiration; he believes it probably induced death by shock, because his experiments with living volunteers demonstrated that respiration was impaired only if the hands were fixed above the head and not if they were spread as in crucifixion.

Crucifixion by rope suspension alone would inflict only nonspecific soft tissue lesions, while those employing nails would involve skeletal evidence. Unless nails were located precisely behind the first two metacarpals, hand nailing would abrade, traverse or shatter metacarpals while ankle nailings could be expected to involve talar bones, especially the talus and calcaneus. Furthermore, fractured long bones in the proper context can alert the examiner to this possibility, especially when crurifragium also involved the arms, suggesting a detailed search for crucifixion lesions (Redford & Lang, 1996).

Because of differing crucifixion practices (Seneca, cited in Lewis, 1995, even states some were crucified upside down), paleopathologists can expect nails to have been placed in the hands, wrists, ankles and feet (both individually and overlapping).

Paleopathology

Considering the number of crucifixions that were probably carried out, the archaeological evidence contains few examples accompanied by convincing anatomic lesions. One is that of a young adult male from a Jerusalem burial cave (Giv'at ha Mitvar:Tzaferis, 1985) in which the right calcaneus was transfixed by an 11.5 x 1 cm nail still in position, and the tibia and fibula were fractured without evidence of healing (Haas, 1970; Zias & Sekeles, 1985). The other is from Mendes harbor in the Nile delta believed to be from about A.D. 0 ± 100 years. Two adult males showed the long bone fractures characteristic of crurifragium. In addition, one of these revealed a nail hole through the distal right femur and also a nail hole suggesting the left foot overlapped the right foot at the ankle. A nail hole traversed the left ankle, the left heel and the medial side of the right heel (Redford & Lang, 1996; Patrick Horne, personal communication). Lewis (1995) suspects crucifixion evidence is being overlooked often by osteologists because the crucifixion nails, highly valued for their reputed medical therapeutic potential, were commonly salvaged after death.

Soft tissue injuries: inflicted by others

Lacerations and stab wounds

Antemortem or postmortem?

The first decision an examining paleopathologist must make is the determination whether the observed injury was inflicted before or after death. Unfortunately few reliable criteria are applicable to assist in the solution of this question even in fresh tissue, and even fewer in mummies. Of these, the most useful is hemorrhagic exudation into the wound edges, adjacent tissue or body cavity. Old hemoglobin is usually black. When present in abundance, enough molecules

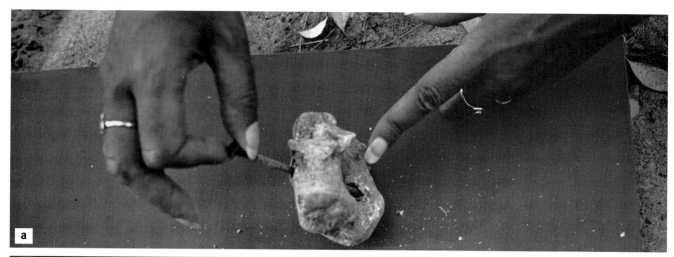

FIG. 3.20. **Crucifixion.** (a) Modern nail demonstrates calcaneus defect. (b) Crurifragium evidence (deliberate long bone fractures). Adult male, Nile delta, ca. A.D. O. Courtesy Carol Lang and Akhenaton Temple Project, Royal Ontario Museum, Toronto.

often retain their chemical composition sufficiently to react positively with commonly employed identifying chemical tests. Red blood cell preservation is rare in mummies. If the individual survived the wound for at least several days, healing changes of the wound itself (gradual rounding of the originally sharply-defined wound edge) will be valuable evidence of the wound's antemortem nature. Much less reliably, the presence of artifacts (bandages, splints, etc) relating to the apparent wound can suggest antemortem context. In addition, the paleopathologist must be alert to the possibility of a given defect being the consequence of spontaneous, postmortem changes (pseudopathology). The skin of bodies undergoing natural postmortem desiccation may become very brittle and rigid, particularly when underlying soft tissues have decayed and no longer support the dry, overlying skin. Soil pressure or even ordinary handling of the body during excavation may then split the skin in a manner suggestive of antemortem wounds. Indeed, it is our experience that far more than half of skin defects examined prove to be products of such a taphonomic process.

If the lesion is an isolated one and the paleopathologist is satisfied that it is not a pseudopathologic phenomenon, yet cannot identify evidence of its antemortem nature, the use of the term 'perimortem' may be preferable. This adjective implies the lesion was inflicted near the time of death, but could have occurred immediately before or very soon after death. On the other hand, the presence of other, clearly antemortem injuries can be useful in judging an otherwise questionable lesion. Thus, the context within which the lesion is found can supply at least circumstantial evidence of its origin.

Figure 3.21 is an example of such a quandary. The body is that of a spontaneously desiccated adult male from a cliff dwelling in southwestern U.S.A.. The right side of the anterior abdominal wall revealed a vertically-oriented defect 11.5 cm long. At its upper end the skin, muscle and peritoneum-fascia layers were all penetrated simultaneously by the cutting instrument as indicated by the fact that each layer was evident in the sharply-defined wound edges. The lower (distal) end of the wound, however, revealed all three layers arranged in a stepwise fashion, the skin being retracted the most, the muscle next and the peritoneum-fascia layer still intact beneath the muscle for a distance of several centimeters. This is precisely what would be expected if a cutting blade had stabbed the anterior abdominal wall in the right upper quadrant, and had then been forced downward (distally) to create the defect. However, after reaching the right lower quadrant the blade's downward course was apparently continued at the same time the blade was withdrawn. Thus, it left several centimeters of peritoneum and fascia intact, while continuing to lacerate the muscle layer. Further withdrawal of the blade while it continued in a distal direction lacerated an additional several centimeters of skin before its withdrawal was complete. The result is a sequential layering of the principal structural components of the anterior abdominal wall. In addition to this feature, it is also evident that the wound is not an artifact because much of the bowel had herniated through the wound and was compressed and flattened between the abdominal wall and the maximally flexed lower extremities. However, no blood could be identified. Hence, one can only declare this to be a perimortem wound, though the absence of any evidence for a tradition of a ritual involving postmortem abdominal incision ritual in this cultural group implies the wound is antemortem – a prehistoric homicide (el Najjar *et al.*, 1985).

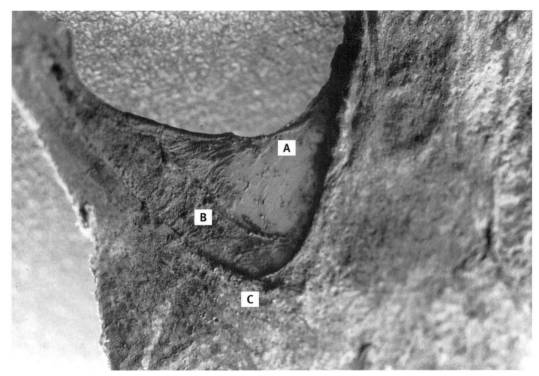

FIG. 3.21. **Stab wound.** The distal, lower end of an 11.5 x 5 cm right abdominal wall defect in which the individual layers of the abdominal wall can be defined clearly. A, peritoneum and fascia, B, muscle, C, skin. Adult male spontaneously mummified Native American from northeastern Arizona. PBL.

Another example is that of an adult female member of the Chiribaya people – a largely agricultural group occupying the lower Osmore Valley near the modern port city of Ilo in southern Peru between about A.D. 1000–1250 (Fig. 3.22). A 12 × 5 cm gaping defect in the left lower quadrant of her anterior abdominal wall was covered by wool and cotton pads. Removal of these demonstrated a 7 cm long stone (quartz) knife with knapped edges lying free in the wound. Although the wound edges demonstrated a dark stain of the skin, no definite blood product could be identified and no viscera appeared to have been removed. Clearly, this is a perimortem wound, but again it is uncertain whether it was created postmortem or antemortem. The presence of the knife suggests a postmortem ritual (Aufderheide, 1990).

Entrance or exit wound?

The usual principles of forensic pathology apply to ancient as well as to modern wounds. This is demonstrated well in the spontaneously desiccated torso of an adult male of the Chinchorros, a cultural group of mariners occupying the coast of northern Chile between 7000 and 2000 B.C. Two chest wounds completely penetrated the entire thorax. Each was about 3cm in diameter, almost exactly equal to the diameter of harpoon foreshafts commonly used by this group. Indeed, the path of each could be reconstructed by placing into these holes such harpoons that had been recovered as grave goods accompanying other Chinchorro bodies

FIG. 3.22. **Stab wound.** Lithic knife in abdominal wound with textile cover. No blood or missing viscera. Postmortem ritual? Spontaneously mummified adult female. Chiribaya culture, southern Peru coast ca. A.D. 1150. PBL.

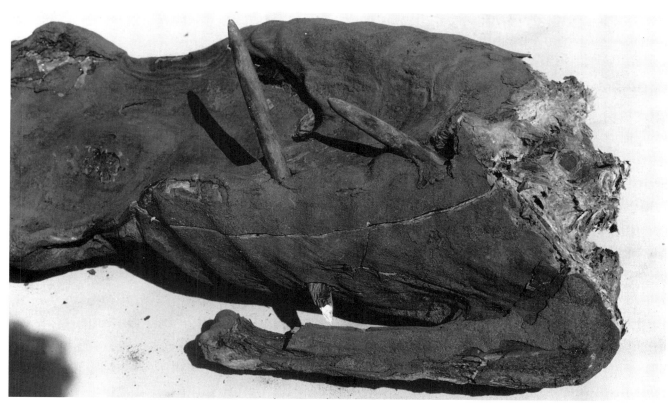

FIG. 3.23. **Stab wounds.** Stab wounds penetrating thorax of spontaneously mummified adult male body almost exactly fit harpoon foreshafts (inserted from grave artifacts to demonstrate path of the weapons). Adult male, Chinchorro culture, northern Chile, ca. 2000 B.C. MAUT. PBL.

FIG. 3.24. **Stab wound.** Intrathoracic aspect of lower chest wound shown in Fig. 3.23. Wound lips turn inward, establishing assailant faced victim. Adult male, Chinchorro culture, northern Chile, ca. 2000 B.C. MAUT. PBL.

(Fig. 3.23). On the ventral pleural surface the wound edges flared inward, into the thoracic cavity. In fact, this was so prominent that it suggests the penetrating instrument (harpoon?) may have been permitted to remain in place, retaining the soft tissues in that manner for a period of time long enough after death to dry and fix them in that position (Fig. 3.24). The skin surface of the entry wound revealed that opening had become enlarged by a skin laceration whose length was about twice the distance of the chest wall defect's diameter. Because some of the harpoons had a separate bone or stone fragment implanted in the foreshaft to act as a barb, it is conceivable that this may have been responsible for the skin laceration that enlarged the entrance wound. Multiple facial lacerations and fractures were also present (Aufderheide & Allison, 1994).

Bietak & Strouhal (1974) also demonstrated that the specific, ancient weapon inflicting a wound can sometimes be identified in a mummified body. When the seventeenth dynasty Pharaoh Seqenenre rebelled against the foreign (Hyksos) rulers of Egypt, he was killed, probably in battle. Close morphological concordance between some of the pharaoh's skin lacerations and underlying skull fractures enabled them to distinguish the bronze Hyksos war weapon as the type responsible for the injuries.

Dramatic examples of fatal projectile wounds can be seen in the illustrations accompanying Winlock's (1945) report of 60 soldiers of the eleventh dynasty Pharaoh Nebhepetre's army, whose spontaneously mummified bodies Winlock found at Deir el Bahri. Nearly a dozen of these had fallen victim to the enemy's archers, whose arrows were still found in situ, several of which had completely penetrated the torso.

Sacrifice victims

Bog bodies

Bodies with preserved soft tissue recovered from the peat bogs of northern Europe are well-known. Their preservation is secondary to the highly acid, anaerobic nature of peat as well as its content of sphagnan, a constituent of sphagnum (peat moss), having chelating, tanning and antimicrobial action (Painter, 1991). The most well-known are from Denmark's Roman Iron Age (about 400 B.C. to A.D. 400). In those with adequately preserved soft tissues, evidence of violence is abundant. Dieck (1965) reviewed literature reports of more than 700 bog bodies and found evidence of nonmilitary lethal violence in about 30% of the 263 retaining sufficient detail for evaluation. Lindow Man from England demonstrated a slashed throat and other traumatic lesions (West, 1986) as did those of Graubelle Man and a body from a Danish island. An adult female's arms were staked to the ground, and a rope around the neck of Tollund Man and Elling Woman suggests several others may have been strangulated or hanged (Glob, 1969; Fischer, 1980). They are

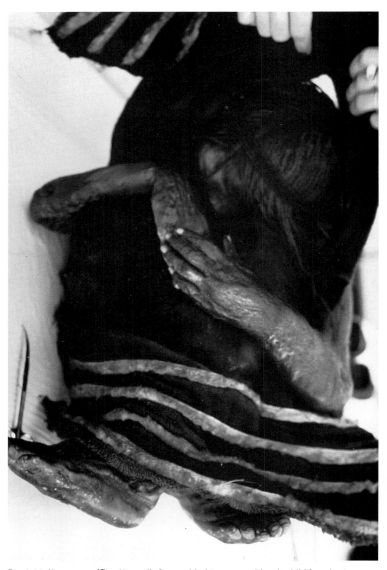

FIG. 3.25. **Human sacrifice.** Naturally freeze-dried 8–10 year old male child found at Inca stone altar at 5400 m altitude on El Plomo mountain near Santiago, Chile. Mountain sacrifice victim. Photograph by and courtesy of Patrick Horne.

commonly believed to represent human sacrifices as part of an agricultural fertility ritual (Glob, 1969:190).

Andean Mountain sacrifices

Ethnohistorical accounts suggest that the Incas probably viewed the Andean peaks as sites of their deity's incarnation (Schobinger, 1966:200). On several of the highest peaks stone altars have been identified. One of these included the spontaneously freeze-dried body of an 8–10 year old child ('El Plomo') who most likely was a human sacrifice (Mostny, 1957) (Fig. 3.25). No localized traumatic lesions were present on the body of this boy, though some associated artifacts implied elite status. Speculation regarding his manner of death has included strangulation, as well as the suggestion (based on ethnology) that he may have been buried alive

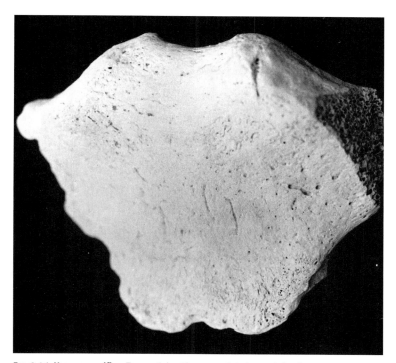

FIG. 3.26. **Human sacrifice.** Tangential cut has amputated manubrium's left upper corner. Spanish chroniclers describe extirpation of war captives' beating hearts through tangential incision beginning in suprasternal notch. Pacatnamu site, Peru, ca. A.D. 1150–1250. Courtesy Dr John Verano (1995).

after sedation with chicha (corn beer) (Mostny, 1957; Ramos Gavilan, 1621 cited in Vreeland & Cockburn, 1980), or possibly even freezing (Schobinger, 1966,p.198). However, Verano (1995) cites Duviols (1976) as noting the Inca practice of burying alive young children sacrificed at some of their recurring rituals (especially capa hucha). The El Plomo mummy, showing no wounds of violence, is consistent with that practice (Horne et al., 1982).

A young adult was found buried (with part of the skull exposed) in a flexed position atop El Toro, a 6300 m high peak in the Andean range about 29°10'S that separates Argentina and Chile. The body was surrounded by a rectangle of large stones. He was clothed only in a wool loin cloth, though several wool shirts, caps, a cape and sandals were beneath the body. Other artifacts included a variety of cords, feathers and other textile fragments. The absence of a wound implies a peaceful compliance on the part of the sacrificial victim, with death by freezing suggested to be the most probable (Schobinger, 1966).

Other Andean human sacrifice sites have also been found at Cierro del Chaña in the puna (a child) (Millán de Palavecino, 1966) and at Nevada Pichu-Pichu near Arequipa in southern Peru (Linares, 1966). Occasionally, however, young adults were offered for certain, infrequently recurring Inca rituals as was evident on El Toro (young adult male in his early twenties) and on Pichu-Pichu (a female of about 18 years of age).

In October, 1995 the well-preserved, frozen body of a teenage girl, wrapped in woollen clothes was found at the 6370 m (20 700 foot) summit of Mount Ampato in southern Peru, in association with a stone altar platform and abundant artifacts. The frozen body of an 11 year old girl and the skeleton of a 13 year old child were found nearby. At the time of this writing [April, 1996] no scientific report has appeared that details findings of their examination. A total of at least 13 'mountain sacrifices' have been recorded in the Andean area.

Andean coastal sacrifices

Allison et al. (1974b) report a young Tihuanaco child killed by strangulation, the body accompanying that of an adult. The sling was found still in situ around the neck. These authors also cite Latcham (1929) as stating that Andean area sacrificial victims were usually killed by strangulation, crushing the neck with a heavy stone, burying them alive or excising the beating heart. They add an additional case they view as a sacrifice – that of a spontaneously mummified young male from a Tihuanaco-type tomb at Nazca, Peru whose body had been transected at the waist and most organs (except the liver and one lung) removed. The lower half of the body was missing, though the severed end of the body was covered by a folded flap of skin. They express their belief that this is an example of the most common purpose of Andean sacrifice: removal of entrails for purposes of divination (Cobo [1653]1990:115). Vreeland (1978) found a pre-Inca Peruvian coastal mummy bundle containing only a pair of lower legs and feet, which he suggests represents a sacrifice.

One of the mummies from the Pachacamac site dating to about the late sixth century A.D. was that of a child. The bundle was radiographed at the University of Pennsylvania in 1981, revealing the body of a 1 year old infant. The skull demonstrated a blow to the head, but of greater interest was the presence of a stone knife that had been thrust through the base of the neck. After the child had been sacrificed the body was transected at the thoraco-lumbar junction, the thighs cut from the trunk and the legs crossed (Fleming, 1987).

Retainer sacrifices

Burials of elite Nubian (Bonnet, 1986:i–vii; O'Connor, 1993:41 and 54) and early Egyptian rulers sometimes contain many bodies believed to be those of servants, concubines, and others sacrificed to accompany the deceased ruler in the afterlife. Garland (1985) describes a tenth century B.C. Greek shaft grave at Lefkandi on Euboia as a 'hero shrine' in which three female skeletons lay adjacent to an amphora containing the hero's ashes. At the A.D. 250–500 site of Alto Vista, Zacatecas, Mexico a burial contained a young adult male's headless decapitated skeleton with remains of a broken flute and the detached bones of two legs. Adjacent to him were the stacked bones of eight other young adult males above which were eight skulls with detached mandibles. These and accompanying rich artifacts suggested this was the local (Chalchinhuites) equivalent of the Mexican Tezcatlipoca impersonator sacrifice ritual, part of the annual Tokcatl ceremony. In this rite a young male was prepared to impersonate the flute-playing God Tezcatlipoca and at the ritual he broke the flute, was killed (beheaded?) and eight other 'retainers' were also killed and buried in the same tomb after their bodies were partially dismembered and the muscle eaten ceremoniously. At Alta Vista the elite circumstances of the primary, intact skeleton buried with two extra legs and ritual artifacts, and the dismembered, nonelite, partial skeletons (retainers?) suggest a process analogous to the Tezcatlipoca ritual (Holien & Pickering, 1978).

It is, however, at the Peruvian site of Chan Chan that archaeological evidence of retainer burial on the grandest scale has been found. At least 24 burial platforms surround the central one believed to have housed the body of a Chimo culture ruler. Within the burial platforms are the skeletons of hundreds of mostly young adult females in an atypical burial position. The sacrifice mechanism of death, however, is not obvious in these bones (Conrad, 1982).

Historical accounts suggest that the practice of vast numbers of retainer human sacrifices (e.g. 1 000 for the Inca Huayna Capac) continued until contact times in South America (Rowe, 1946:286). Ethnographic accounts indicate that the Ashanti (Ghana) chief's female retainers were strangled (Fisher, 1984:620).

Unfortunately the manner of death of these victims is not often detailed. At the Pachacamac site near Lima, Peru the pioneering German archaeologist Max Uhle (1903) described the mummified bodies of a group of females buried in association with a temple there, who had been strangled with ligatures. This is a very useful observation, since the bulk of descriptions of retainer sacrifices involve no demonstrable lethal wounds, and are so interpreted on the basis of the indirect evidence of body location or position and the absence or paucity of artifacts reflecting elite status. Thus, while ethnohistorical accounts of retainer sacrifice are abundant (Cobo [1653] 1990:112) the paleopathological evidence of their implied violent deaths is sparse.

Sacrificed war captives

Egyptian iconography is replete with scenes demonstrating a broad range of lethal violence, such as decapitation, inflicted on war captives. In view of the known practice of historical distortion and exaggeration (designed to enhance the pharaonic image) indulged by the Egyptian royal artists, it may not be surprising to learn that only the most meager paleopathological evidence to support this is available. One example of such involves eleventh dynasty Pharaoh Nebhepetre's slain soldiers (Winlock, 1945) whose wounds were noted above. Not only were these buried very unceremoniously with little preparation, but their bodies had been left exposed after death to scavengers for some time. Evidence of stripping of muscles from tendons, a feature characteristic of vulture

feeding, is prominent, though it is possible such exposure was inadvertent, secondary to battle conditions.

More certain are the wounds described by Verano (1986) in the bodies of 14 adolescent and young adult males believed to be war captives found in three superimposed layers in a trench at the Pacatnamu site in Peru, adjacent to a ceremonial structure. Insect evidence suggests postmortem exposure, and two sacrificed vultures were included in the burial. The dismembered bodies showed abundant and unmistakable signs of violent deaths, including cut wounds, fractures, decapitation, slit throats and traumatically opened chests. The thoracic incision traversed the left part of the manubrium and perhaps the costochondral junctions of the left chest's upper ribs, a method consistent with pre-Columbian Mexico's Mixtec iconography (Nuttall, 1975:81) as well as Aztec and Peruvian chronicles (Garcilaso de la Vega, [1616] 1987:33) (Fig. 3.26). Stable isotope ratios of nitrogen reflected such marked differences between samples from these bodies and those of the area's residents that the victims were concluded to have been foreigners. These findings also support the iconography of Moche and Chimu art that depict the type of treatment of war captives (Alva & Donnan, 1993:132), even including exposure to vultures (Verano, 1986). Robicsek & Hales (1984) provide a detailed reconstruction of the Toltec-Maya ritual cardiectomy, including the knives employed and the procedure's surgical anatomy.

Dedicatory burials

Some Peruvian mortuary practices included human sacrifice at the initiation of construction of important buildings. Although some groups used llamas for that purpose, Andrews (1974) found the bodies of adolescent females, accompanied by elaborate grave goods, beneath certain architectural parts of Chimu buildings suggestive of dedicatory burials. Frazer (1976) identified the goal of human sacrifice as divine enhancement of agricultural fertility among the Druids (p. 762) and early Norwegians (p. 440) as well as appeasement of the deity by eastern Caucucus Albanians (p. 662) and Nigerian Onitscha (p. 659).

Accidental injuries

Massive body injuries

Typical of crushing injuries are those found in the 'frozen family of Utqiagvik' at Point Barrow, Alaska by Zimmerman & Aufderheide (1984). While the family was sleeping in a driftwood hut on the Arctic Ocean beach 650 years ago, a storm-driven mass of pack ice crushed the house. The dislodged ridgepole collapsed atop two fleeing occupants, pinning them to the soil floor where the permanently frozen soil (permafrost) maintained the integrity of the bodies' soft tissues until they were discovered while workmen were digging a trench for a municipal natural gas line in A.D. 1982. The ridgepole had collapsed the upper thoracic cage in each of them. The presence of hemoglobin-containing pleural effusion in each of the bodies suggested that death may not necessarily have been instantaneous.

Asphyxia

Approximately A.D. 400 an Inuit adult female was trapped by a massive landslide on one of St. Lawrence Island's (Bering Strait) steep slopes, apparently covering her body completely. When beach erosion uncovered her body nearly 1600 years later, Zimmerman & Smith (1975) found her trachea and upper airway completely obstructed by moss and earth, indicating she had asphyxiated.

Another example of aspiration was reported by Allison *et al.* (1974d) in which an aspirated deciduous tooth lodged in and obstructed a bronchus, inducing what probably was a fatal pneumonia distal to it. An aspirated deciduous tooth may have been the cause for the death of an infant whose spontaneously mummified body was found in the southwestern area of the U.S.A. A radiograph demonstrated its presence in the larynx or upper trachea (el-Najjar *et al.*, 1985).

Thermal injuries

Although we have been unable to identify any reports of antemortem accidental soft tissue burns in ancient bodies, Post & Donner (1978) reported a case of probable frostbite. Characteristic features were varying degrees of absorption of the digits on skin-covered feet and toes in a 2000 year old, spontaneously mummified, adult male body excavated from a site (Quitor 1) at 2500 m altitude near the Atacama desert community of San Pedro de Atacama in northern Chile. They effectively exclude leprosy, diabetes and congenital deformities as alternative explanations.

SOFT TISSUE INJURIES: MUTILATION

The compulsion to render one's appearance in a distinctive manner publicly is an ancient and universal human feature. Methods to achieve it have employed jewellry, clothing, unusual accouterments, hair styles and many others. Among the most unique, however, are various forms of mutilating the human body. Those involving skeletal deformations (e.g. artificial cranial deformation and foot-binding) are carried out during infancy or childhood. Deliberate tooth mutilation is an exception, usually limited to permanent teeth and performed after adolescence. Soft tissue deformities (ear, nose, lip perforations and distortions; tattoos) are induced commonly following cessation of body growth in early adulthood.

Labrets

Creation of lip perforations to accommodate ornamental or symbolic inserts is a well-documented practice among numerous tribes. Particularly well-known are Alaskan Inuit practices. In the Point Barrow region Spencer (1976:241–2) notes these are limited to males, initiated at a ceremony to mark the transition from boyhood to adulthood. They may also reflect status because various bone or wood inserts (three types) reflected 'expense' (i.e. high level of energy expenditure). In the Bering Strait region of Alaska north of the Kuskokwim, Nelson ([1899]1983:44-50) notes their location is most commonly the middle of the lower lip, and that the skin defect is increased in size with dilators to accommodate larger structures of ivory, beads or stone that are heavy enough to drag the lip downward to reveal the teeth. They were worn only after puberty and were removed on very cold days to avoid frostbite.

Surma women of Ethiopia's Omo valley insert wood discs as large as 10 cm in diameter into their lower lips, stretching and shaping these soft tissues to accommodate the disc's form (Virel, 1980:26). Sudanese Toposa women proclaim their married status via a brass wire traversing and dangling below the lower lip's midline (Fisher, 1984:604).

Nasal and earrings

Nasal perforations to accommodate beads (India) are common. Among the Bering Strait Inuit the practice was limited to prepubertal girls who removed them at puberty, suggesting they reflected a sexually immature status. In Colombia and Peru men wore elaborately carved nose ornaments, suspended from nasal septum perforations (Alva & Donnan, 1993). At least in Inca times these most probably reflected status since the wearing of jewellry was restricted to the nobility (Garcilaso de la Vega [1616]1987:394). New Guinea's Iwam people of the Sepik river perforated their nasal septum and inserted into the defect the wild boar's canine teeth to gain supernatural power in their hunt of the animal. Cassowary quills traversing their nasal alae served a similar purpose, while the women of Pakistan and Andhra Pradesh display jewels inserted into such nasal alae perforations for decorative purposes (Virel, 1980:28 and 46).

Ear lobe perforations to suspend ornaments is a very common, ancient custom. Among the Incas silver or gold earspools were a privilege of the nobility, commonly issued to the adolescent boys at the time of their graduation from the military academy during the Raymi festival (Garcilaso de la Vega, [1616]1987:394; Cobo, [1653]1990:74). The suspended item was of sufficient weight so as to stretch the perforations as much as several inches. Colonial Spaniards described these as *orejones* ('big ears') (Time-Life Books, 1992:59), and recognized them as a symbol of social elitism. Similar findings are described in a twenty-first dynasty

Egyptian mummy (Lady Teye) of clearly elite status. The earrings' weight had caused the perforation to sag to the point that it touched her shoulder so a later second perforation in the upper part of the same lobe was performed (Winlock, 1942:111). Heavy, ceramic rings worn by women of modern Sarawak's Kayan tribe produce an identical effect, and Kenya's Masai women support huge cloth pendants in large, lower ear lobe perforations while adorning smaller holes in the upper part of the same ear with jewels (Virel, 1980:48-9). Soto-Heim (1987) describes a variety of ear lobe perforations found among mummies in coastal areas of northern Chile, ranging from simple, 1 mm perforations to those greater than 2 cm. Allison et al. (1983) found 21 mummies among 650 examined from the same northern Chile geographic area, all of which demonstrated such perforations. They represented individuals from cultural groups ranging in time from A.D. 350 to 1350. All were males between 15 and 40 years of age. Some of these still retained the suspended ornament, which included such items as knotted cords, threads, corn tassels and many camelid hide/fur items. Accompanying grave goods in several of these denoted social stigmata, suggesting possible shamanic features.

In Burma ear lobe perforation was an important pubertal rite. The puncture was performed with gold or silver needles and enlarged subsequently by the use of string and cord, and later by the use of a screw device composed of a flexible, expansile, cylindrical metal tube. When large enough, a dumbbell-shaped, jewel-encrusted plug was inserted into the aperture by the wealthy, while the poor employed colored glass rods (Yoe, 1963).

Hair and nails

Among many tribes hair is believed to house part of an individual's spiritual essence (Karsten, 1968:46). It may be guarded jealously for fear that enemies' possession of it could permit them to employ it for malicious purposes. Braids may be detached, fashioned into some design and worn as amulets. Among the Chinchorros, a preceramic, coastal group from northern Chile, a wig of long, adult human hair was often fashioned and attached to the head of mummified infant bodies. Fingernails seem to have been regarded similarly. In one Chinchorro infant the hand was encased in sand-cement from which painted (red ochre), adult fingernails protruded (Aufderheide et al., 1993) while another wore a necklace of adult fingernails.

Circumcision

Development of the operation consisting of amputation of the male penile prepuce has been called 'the dawn of surgery' (Wright, 1923). While this is probably an exaggeration, the procedure does appear to enjoy a generous record of antiquity. If a lithic phallus from the European Neolithic period is correctly interpreted as representing a circumcised penis (Sandison & Wells, 1967:514), the procedure is probably at least 7000 years old. The strictum jus use of the term 'surgery,' however may prevent its application to circumcision because surgery is usually defined in a manner implying a technique involving mechanical manipulation designed to promote healing of a diseased tissue. Circumcision is most commonly a procedure carried out on a healthy tissue for a purpose more related to ritual than medicine. Consequently, only a portion of the prepuce may be removed (e.g. only the skin portion), and in some areas only a slit in the dorsal part of the prepuce may be performed (sometimes accompanied by pushing the glans penis through the created defect), though in most cases both the skin and mucous membrane are amputated by a circumferential incision at the base of the glans penis.

We have satisfactory evidence that the Egyptians carried out this procedure throughout most of their history. A bas relief from the tomb of Ankh ma Hor at Saqqara from about the time of Ramses II (1310–1243 B.C.) demonstrates a surgeon carrying out the procedure with a flint knife on pubescent boys; a partially preserved one in the temple of Khons near the great temple of Maut at Karnak suggests a similar theme. In addition the Ebers papyrus prescribes an application of honey and assorted ingredients to a bleeding circumcision wound. We also have the evidence from the mummies themselves. E. Smith (1906:29) comments that all males in the cemetery of Naga-ed-Der were circumcised and says mummified bodies prove it was general at all periods in Egypt. However, initially it appears to have been restricted to the royalty and elite members, involving the lower-ranking social levels later but it probably never became universal.

While there was a great deal of discussion about its spread 100 years ago, most historians now believe the Phoenicians acquired the practice from Egyptians, while the Hebrews may have learned about it either from the Phoenicians or the Egyptians (perhaps during their residence there?). Hebrew belief attributes origin of the practice to Abraham, though if the popular practice of estimating that event at about 1500 B.C. is correct, both the lithic phallus noted above and the Egyptian practice would have preceded it. The antiquity of the practice of circumcision by Islamics has not been dated reliably. The procedure may have an even greater antiquity elsewhere. The Australian aborigines had incorporated the custom when Europeans first encountered them, though modification (subincision – an incision into the urethra on the 'under' side of the penis, permitting escape of urine via that defect) was popular there (Morrison, 1967).

The practice of circumcision was and is widely spread throughout the world and includes not only the Near East, but also Africa's west coast, the pigmies of central Africa, the Abyssinian Christians, the Malay peninsula, all of Polynesia, Madagascar and parts of North (Chippewa Native Americans), Central and even foci in South America.

The stated purposes are enormously varied. The Jews cite a divine command. The modern impression attributes Arab use of the practice to religious dogma, though the Koran does not include it. Their practice precedes the Prophet and the interpretation of reference to Mohammed's writings remains controversial. Among many of the African tribes it is quite clearly a rite of passage, performed in elaborate ceremonies on prepubertal or adolescent boys. Arabs perform it at age 13 years while the Hebrew tradition is quite demanding about meeting the eighth postnatal day that their religious literature demands. Modern custom among western populations tends to justify it on the basis of health advantages (Morgan, 1965; Morrison, 1967) but Hackett (1984) and others note that these are minor and may be outweighed by its disadvantages. Other suggestions have included 'penis envy,' a tribal marker, phallic worship, fertility symbol, Victorian attempts to reduce sexual desire, increased fertility, and bonding within a tribal male group.

Recognition of the condition of the prepuce in a mummified body is not as simple as might be expected. Among spontaneously mummified bodies in a sitting position, the external genitalia are unidentifiable in about half of the bodies; even if a penis can be identified, the postmortem changes commonly prevent evaluation of the prepuce. In many the penis may be 2 cm wide but only 1 mm thick, and in others it can be indistinguishable among the folds of the scrotal skin. If resins were not applied, the external genitalia of Egyptian mummies were more regularly preserved.

In some areas females were also subjected to mutilating genital operations. The most conservative of these ('sunna') was the equivalent of the male counterpart; simple removal of the clitoral prepuce. A more extensive operation included total clitoridectomy, usually accompanied by at least partial removal of the labia minora. In its most destructive form (pharaonic circumcision – tahara farowntyya or infundibulation) the clitoris and both labia minora and majora were totally excised and the raw surfaces sutured to each other, effectively sealing the entire vaginal orifice except for a diminutive aperture just large enough to permit escape of urine and menstrual products. The alleged purpose of such mutilating alterations was to reduce sexual stimulation and frustrate premarital sexual intercourse, thus contributing to the maintenance of lineage purity. The infundibulation form required surgery to undo its effects at the time of marriage. Assaad (1980) cites Maspero (1899:523) that this was practiced in ancient Egypt but offers no supporting evidence. Gordon (1991) suggests that, while common among African Muslims today, the practice was probably not of Islamic origin and that it may have been absorbed from western and central African groups as well as from those in present day Mali, Somalia, Ethiopia and Nigeria following the sweep of Islam across northern Africa. Such operations are unknown among about 80% of modern Islamic groups. On the other hand, recent surveys reveal that this type of surgery was performed on about 98% of natives in western Sudan, 83% of which were of the infundibular form, though less than half of Nile valley Egyptians had suffered this form of mutilation, most of whom had had the much more conservative modification (Gordon, 1991).

The infundibular form of this surgery ought to be quite easily discerned in a mummified body with preserved external genitalia, though the more conservative operations may not be detectable at all.

Tattoos and scarification

The compulsion to decorate the human body reaches back into antiquity more than five millennia. Tattooing (insertion of insoluble pigment into or under the skin) is included within the many methods employed to achieve this, and probably evolved as an effort to perpetuate designs painted on the body. Scarification (production of raised skin scar patterns) is a closely related practice whose roots are more apt to lie in medical therapy.

Methods

Modern observations and ethnographic studies have identified three methods that were employed to insert pigment into the body tissues.

1. Needle prick. A small amount of pigment was picked up with a needle and inserted into the skin by a direct prick.
2. Pigment-soaked thread. Pigment was loosely attached to a thread by suspending it over a smoky flame or soaking it in a pigment solution, then drying it. After attaching the thread to a needle it was then drawn through the dermis; pigment became detached and deposited within the tissue.
3. Scarification. In India pigment was applied to a hot iron which, when pressed against the skin, produced a third degree burn. In Timor Laut the branding is preceded by an incision (Hambly, 1925:168) and some of the pigment becomes detached and lodges in the burned tissue. The resulting inflammation and organization entraps the pigment within the scar. The goal of this method is really production of a scar pattern (scarification); inclusion of the pigment is an inconstant feature. Heat, however, is not imperative and most scarification is performed without it. Incision length is variable but usually short (a few mm to 3 or 4 cm), probably to prevent major wound infections that would be common with widely gaping, elongated gashes. The Kaleri tribe of the Niger causes exuberant production of fibrous scar, generating a foreign body reaction by rubbing powdered leaves, ashes or plant juices into the wound, though it is conceivable that some of these also exert an antibacterial effect (Virel, 1980:134). Designs are created by rows of scarified dots or short lines. Abscess complications introduce more pattern irregularities with scarification than with tattooing methods. Knives were and are of obsidian, metal or bone.

The instrument employed for tattoo pigment insertion varied in place and time. The arctic Inuit's bone needle is simple, crude and ancient. Polynesians used a small, rake-like instrument whose cutting points often were constructed of multiple shark teeth; the instrument was struck with a mallet (Burchett, 1968:65). Burmese used a 61 cm (24 inch), pen-like structure with a brass head and whose needle points sometimes were slotted to suspend the pigment-containing fluid (Hambly, 1925:271).

Nature of the pigment

The most commonly used pigment was carbon. North American Inuit, for example, passed a thread, commonly made from dried, split caribou fascia, over the yellow flame of a seal oil lamp; soot collected on the thread (Spencer, 1976:243). Burmese suspended 'lampblack' in sassamum oil. North American Kwakiutl Indians also created a black pigment from a fungus (*Aspergillus niger?*) or coal (Hambly, 1925:250). Celtic Picts in Europe tattooed themselves with an indigo-like extract of the woad plant (Fairbanks, 1994). Ocher (a common form of naturally occurring, multicolored iron oxides in soil) has also been used for this purpose. The pigment particles were recognized by the body tissues as foreign materials and macrophages phagocytized (ingested) them. A few macrophages managed to escape the area with their contained pigment. However, the soot and other materials used for this purpose cannot be liquefied by the hydrolytic enzymes in macrophage lysosomes. Thus many macrophages died with the pigment unchanged, leaving it deposited near where the pigment was injected. The result was some degree of blurring of the deposited pigment aggregate when viewed from the skin surface, as well as a mild decrease in pigmentation intensity due to some pigment removal, local limited diffusion and occasionally some fibrosis. The bulk of the pigment, however, remained in the general area of deposit, sufficient to retain the desired pattern. The perceived, usually bluish, color is the result of the color of the pigment as well as that of the blood and tissue components that lay between the pigment and the skin surface.

Modern tattooing practices have expanded the list of materials injected into the skin to include over 50 different colors including metallic salts and synthetic dyes. These have introduced new hazards for the procedure (hypersensitivity reactions and allergic contact dermatitis; heavy metal toxicity by elements such as mercury, cadmium and lead), added to those problems that must also have plagued the ancients: bacterial infection and transfer of blood borne infections such as hepatitis when needles were reused without sterilization (Food and Drug Administration, 1994).

Antiquity and geography

Both tattooing and scarification practices are spread worldwide and from the most southern to the high arctic latitudes.

Within many broad regions, however, are areas such as northern China, that have never included these activities within their culture. Scarification has been more popular throughout Sub-Saharan Africa, where further pigment introduced into an already darkened skin is not easily perceived; this is also true of Australia's aboriginals. Elsewhere scarification was practiced in focal areas of the New World, and more widely in southeast Asia and the Torres Straits. In some of these latter locations it was combined with tattooing (Armelagos, 1969).

Tattoo practices are even more widely distributed, being found in North and South America including their arctic regions, Europe, North African coastal and Saharan region, India, Malay Peninsula, Japan and southern China (Hambly, 1925, see world map). While clay dolls with painted patterns resembling tattoos have been found in predynastic Egypt and Nubia, actual corporeal archaeological evidence begins with the 5300 year old 'Iceman' mummy recovered from a glacier of Austria's Tyrolean area. Egypt has contributed only a few tattooed bodies from the eleventh and eighteenth dynasties. New Kingdom art from the tomb of Seti I depicts Libyans with religious tattoos on their legs and arms from about 1330 B.C. (Hambly, 1925:105). The grasslands of central Asia have preserved the tattooed Pazyryk bodies of several

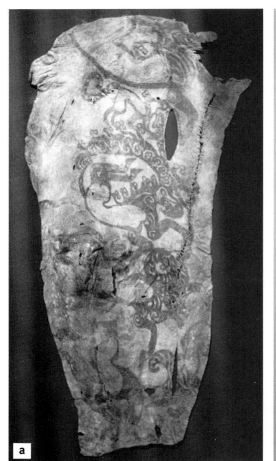

FIG. 3.27. **Tattoo.** (a) Tattoo over shoulder and arm as illustrated on (b) adjacent drawing. Scythian (Pazyryk, Russia) burial. Courtesy Dr Leonid Marsadolov, Hermitage Museum, Leningrad.

tattooed chiefs who were buried there between 1000–500 B.C., while various groups in southern China were probably indulging in this practice before 1100 B.C. but tattooed bodies of the Wu people there have been dated to about 500 B.C. The Japanese were already highly skilled in tattoo art by A.D. 500 but probably learned it from the earlier residents (Ainu) who may have been engaged with this technique as much as a millennium earlier (Hambly, 1925:313). Peruvian tattooed mummies have been reported from about A.D. 1000 (Vreeland & Cockburn, 1980:155), but most likely the practice is much older there. Marquesan and Maori mummification dates to the Polynesian dissemination, probably during the fifth century A.D. (Burchett, 1968:16).

Travelers' and ethnographic accounts document that these practices continued into the recent past and, indeed, continue today in a few focal areas. Widely expanding cultural contact has resulted in reduction or disappearance in tattoo practices due to evangelical efforts by those embracing the principles of Christianity, Judaism and Islam, all of which groups oppose it (Wrobelewski, 1987).

Purpose(s)

Ritual

The earliest (and most persistent) purpose of tattooing is linked inseparably to supernatural beliefs and magic. Hambly (1925:234ff) calls attention to some of its features: production of bleeding (associated with rejuvenation) and body perforation (providing ingress or egress for spirits). Designs are rich in animal and plant motifs most likely related to totemism. In some parts of Oceania (Samoa; Formosa) tattooing is controlled by clerics. Sexual orgies that marked the completion of tattooing in the Marquesas and that led to tattoo prohibitions by Christian missionaries probably reflected their association with divine fertility rites (Handy, 1965:154). For the Fiji and Ainu, tattoos were a passport into the postmortem spiritual world, and in most areas are associated with rites of passage (Hambly, 1925:164).

Proclamation

Not only the presence of the tattoo, but its location and design convey messages. Tribal and clan identification are self-evident. In Samoa and the Marquesas these also declare social rank and lineage (Virel, 1980:35) and sometimes even items of personal achievement. Intimidation of enemies may be a deliberate goal. They may also announce marital status of the tattooed person (Burma; Inuit), or identify participation in social subgroups. Nazi elite of World War II had their blood type tattooed in the axilla; modern criminals may be 'branded' as among some recent Cuban exiles, or boast of their illegal actions (Bronnikov, 1993).

Decorative

In addition to the ritual-related purpose, Marquesan women are as proud of the appearance enhancement of their elabo-

rate, skillfully-applied tattoo patterns (some of which resemble brilliantly-patterned, clinging slacks) (Stewart, 1831; Handy, 1965:64) as the Wodaabe of the Niger (Fisher, 1984:604) and Kenya's Poxot people (Meyerhoff, 1982:135) are of their facial and abdominal scarification designs.

Therapeutic

In many groups tattooing and (especially) scarification is related to therapeutic efforts to allay pain and illness (Rolle, 1992). In these circumstances the design is placed on the skin overlying the localized problem. The 'sincipital T' cauterization of the scalp still is used occasionally for headache or convulsions, and tattooing or scarification over the major joints is used to palliate the pain of arthritic disease. Both Capasso (1993) and Spindler (1994:167-73) believe this best explains the tattoo pattern over the 'Iceman' mummy's knee and spine, in view of the radiological demonstration of underlying osteoarthritis.

Paleopathology

The earliest tattooed body reported is that of the more than 5000 year old 'Iceman' (Spindler, 1994:167-73). The Bering strait Inuit carried out simple linear tattoo patterns primarily in the facial, forearm and back of the hand areas although upper trunk and breasts were included in some parts of the arctic; regional variations were substantial (Nelson, [1899]1983:51; Smith & Zimmerman, 1975). The tattooed Pazyryk burials of Scythian chiefs in the central Asian area of Altai were buried about 500–1000 B.C. Their elaborate patterns were similar or identical to those found on leather and wood goods in their graves (Rudenko, 1970). Such tattooing clearly reflected the social and political status of the deceased (Fig. 3.27). However, these graves had many other features strongly suggestive of spiritual or supernatural nature (Marsadolov, 1993), so that both the tattoos and the designs on their saddles and other items may be related to ritual as well. Zimmerman & Hart Hansen (1986) note that the tattoo patterns can be useful for dating purposes. Winlock (1942: figs. 15 and 20, pp. 22 and 28) excavated an eleventh dynasty ceramic figurine at Deir-el-Bahri, Egypt, that had a painted design suggestive of tattooing, and later identified the same pattern tattooed on the skin of a body in a nearby tomb. Amenophis and his queen of the eighteenth dynasty also had a tattoo pattern on the skin of the ventral thoracic surface (Hambly, 1925:321). Armelagos (1969) has described geometric tattoo patterns painted on a femur among X-group (A.D. 350–550) lower Nubians. Capasso (1993) cites the Hippocratic corpus as recognizing the practice among the residents of the Scythian area, while Vreeland & Cockburn (1980:151) reveal linear tattoos on the back of the hand of a Late Intermediate period Peruvian mummy. The elaborately tattooed ('Moko'), decapitated and desiccated heads of New Zealand's Maoris in today's museum collections may represent war trophies. It is the Japanese, however, who have carried decorative tattoo designs to their ultimate, both in imaginative composition as well as dramatic use of color, using mineral salt and organic pigments.

Paleopathologists must be alert to the fact that localized congestion in the skin secondary to postmortem effects can simulate a tattoo (Spindler, 1994:167-73). Furthermore, the dark brown color of the skin effected by postmortem changes in many mummies can obscure antemortem tattoos. Their delineation can be made more apparent by photography with infrared film (Zimmerman & Hart Hansen, 1986). The tattoo patterns often can be of valuable assistance for identification of cultural affiliation.

PART FOUR

Congenital anomalies

CONGENITAL SKELETAL ANOMOLIES

Congenital anomalies or malformations are produced by pathological changes in the normal development during intrauterine life. These anomalies can be observed at birth or years later, and may be hereditary or acquired between fertilization and birth. Many of these affect the skeleton: 40 % of the congenital malformations among live births in England and Wales between 1960 and 1980 were skeletal (Manchester, 1983a:28). The etiology of many of these defects is poorly understood, but in the industrial countries 90 % of congenital malformations are genetic disturbances. Therefore the differing rates must be evaluated from the perspective of population genetics, even though the genetic background is 'complex and obscure' (McKeown, 1988). From a genetic point of view, three categories of factors affect development (Barnes, 1994):

1. Single gene disorders (33.3 % of congenital defects).
2. Chromosomal disorders (8.3 %).
3. Multifactorial disorders (the remainder of congenital defects). These are the result of interaction among intrinsic factors (genetic) or between intrinsic and extrinsic factors (environment).

Any organ may be involved. Congenital malformations of some kind are observed in 4–5 % of the newborns, and 40 % of these individuals die in the perinatal period (Sandritter & Thomas, 1981). Other epidemiological studies show an incidence around 27 per 1000 (including those malformations that are not recognized at birth) (McKeown, 1988). However, several factors confound comparisons of the incidence of congenital malformations among different populations (Turkel, 1989):

1. The lower priority given to congenital malformations compared with other diseases (nutritional or infectious) in poor populations.

2. The number of births that occur outside of a health system.
3. Lack of any statistics in many underdeveloped countries.
4. Variations in the methods of observation, definition, and diagnosis.

Since most congenital malformations appear in low frequencies in a population, increased prevalence may have significant anthropological implications, such as inbreeding (Turkel, 1989). Thus, consanguineous parents have a higher probability of bearing malformed children than do unrelated parents. Major contributions to the understanding of hereditary transmission of disease were made in the early twentieth century (Devor, 1993).

A large number of congenital malformations and variants can occur in the skeleton. The degree of severity varies from minimal variants (that do not represent malformations *strictu sensu*) to very severe, and sometimes lethal deformities. Congenital malformations tend to decrease the life expectancy or the quality of life, whereas minor variants do so minimally or not at all. Examples of severe congenital malformations are uncommon in prehistoric times because most infants affected by them died at or shortly after birth. If the affected infant did not die due to the defect, its abnormal appearance may well have caused the infant to be destroyed and the fragile immature skeleton would not survive the taphonomic process (Barnes, 1994). As a result, major or lethal skeletal congenital anomalies are uncommon in archaeological skeletal populations of children.

Skull malformations

Craniosynostoses

Suture closure in the cranial vault occurs during adulthood between 30 and 40 years on the endosteal surface and 10 years later on the external surface. However, variation in age of suture obliteration is great. Normally, obliteration initiates in the bregma region, and then occurs successively in the sagittal, coronal, and lambdoid sutures. Therefore, craniosynostosis (premature fusion of the cranial sutures) can be considered as a normal process that occurs at an abnormally early age. Barnes (1994) notes that if the suture never forms, it is preferable to call this condition suture agenesis rather than craniosynostosis. The fused sagittal and sometimes coronal sutures may be seen as broad ridges of solid bony overgrowth or as completely obliterated sutures that are indistinguishable from the surrounding bone. Craniosynostoses or suture agenesis can occur as isolated conditions or forming part of polytropic syndromes.

The relationship between skull deformities and craniosynostoses was suspected as early as at the beginning of the nineteenth century and during the following decades it became evident that some of those craniosynostoses were associated with other congenital defects (David *et al.*, 1982). As these authors note, premature suture closure is a pathological process, but without etiological specificity. The nature and degree of the skull deformity depends on the number of sutures involved, the order of the synostosis, the age, and the underlying mechanisms that produce that deformity. The limited growth in the direction perpendicular to the involved suture is compensated for by increased growth in other directions.

Primary craniosynostosis (idiopathic developmental failure) can be the result of intrauterine growth aberration recognizable at birth and some of these result from genetic errors; in other instances premature fusion can be secondary to other processes. Less than one-third of the craniosynostoses cases can be assigned to a specific etiology. The relationship between craniosynostosis and mental or neurological problems is not always clear. Certainly, occasionally extensive craniosynostosis can produce increased intracranial pressure due to the reduced cranial capacity. The etiology could be under genetic control, although the manner of transmission is not yet known. The exact prevalence of craniosynostoses is not known, but it seems to be more common in males than in females. There is no racial predilection.

Although craniosynostoses are quite common today, not many cases have been described in the paleopathological literature. Guillen (1992), however, includes in her doctoral dissertation at least a dozen cases of her own observations and those of others in the Spanish literature of the Andean region. She also implies that excessively tight head bands employed to bring about intentional cranial deformation may somehow impair suture physiology and produce synostosis, occasionally with fatal results. White (1996) reports a similar experience in pre-Hispanic Maya skulls.

Scaphocephaly (heel-shaped skull)

Definition, Etiology, Epidemiology and Pathology

Scaphocephaly is the premature fusion of the sagittal suture. It is the most common of all the craniosynostoses (50–80 % of the total). Familial cases occur, but the role of genetic factors is not clear. This condition seems to have a male predilection and perhaps racial or geographic preponderance, but further epidemiological studies are necessary to evaluate these possibilities. This pattern of craniosynostosis limits the development of the skull in the transverse direction and thus generates an abnormally long and narrow skull in which the cephalic index is below 70 (hyperdolichocephaly) (Fig. 4.1). Widening and elevation of the forehead also occurs, with prominent frontal bosses. The skull base and the maxilla are narrowed. A bony ridge in the sagittal line between the bregma and lambdoid suture is commonly observed. An overgrowth on the endosteal surface of the sagittal suture is sometimes apparent. Scaphocephaly normally only involves the sagittal suture and has no complications. However, premature fusion of other sutures, especially the coronal, occa-

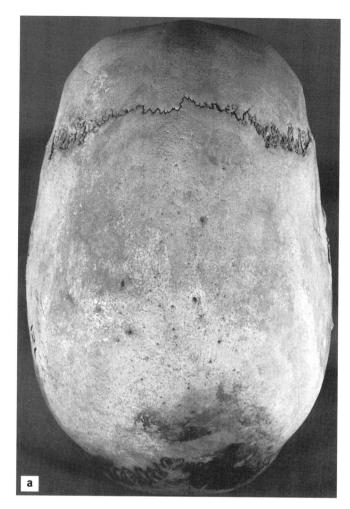

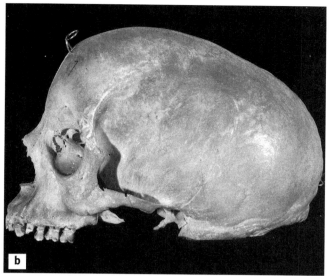

Fig. 4.1. **Scaphocephaly.** (a) Sagittal suture agenesis. (b) Dolichocephaly. (a) G26. Adult. Guanche ca. A.D. 1000. MAT, OAMC (b) T-97. CMNH.

sionally accompanies the sagittal synostosis. Less commonly, scaphocephaly forms part of a more major craniofacial malformation, such as Crouzon or Carpenter syndromes.

Paleopathology

One of the first scaphocephalic skulls was officially registered as early as the seventeenth century. It is that of a child of 8 years of age that was shown at the Natural History Museum of Paris (France). Since then other cases have been described in several parts of the world: Arizona, California, Kansas, and Maryland (U.S.A.); British Columbia (Canada); Marseilles (France); Karga (Egypt); Senegal and others. Comas (1966) described four cases from Mexico (Chihuahua, Tlatilco, Piedra Gorda at Baja California, and one other without provenance). Recently, Campillo (1993) described two cases of scaphocephaly: one of the Eneolithic period from Cova del Palanqués (Navarrés, Valence, Spain) as well as a medieval skull from Sant Miquel de Cardona (Bages, Catalonia, Spain). More scaphocephalic skulls have appeared in the Canarian archipelago (Spitery, 1983). Four scaphocephalic skulls belonging to the pre-Hispanic population of the Canaries are curated in the Verneau Collection of the Musée de l'Homme at Paris. Two of them come from the island of La Gomera (western Canary Islands) and two other skulls are from Gran Canaria

(eastern Canary Islands). A Guanche male skull from the island of Tenerife (western Canaries) is curated at the Museo Arqueológico of Tenerife (Rodríguez-Martín et al., 1985b).

Plagiocephaly

Definition and etiology

This is the result of asymmetrical suture closure producing a 'lopsided' skull. The skull appears laterally or anteroposteriorly asymmetrical (Morse, 1978). A multifactorial inheritance seems to play a role in the development of this malformation.

Pathology

David et al. (1982) describe three types of plagiocephaly:
1. Frontal plagiocephaly: this is the product of premature synostosis of the ipsilateral and sphenofrontal sutures. The skull base is also involved and the bony orbit is deformed. This is the most common form of plagiocephaly, and one of the most common of all forms of craniosynostoses. Sexual predilection is not well established.
2. Occipital plagiocephaly: this malformation is caused by abnormalities of the ipsilateral lambdoid suture with flattening on one side of the occipital region and prominence of the ipsilateral frontal region. Male preponderance has been observed.
3. Hemicranial plagiocephaly: is associated with multiple sutural fusions on one side of the skull, involving the coronal, squamous, and lambdoid sutures.

Paleopathology

A plagiocephalic skull from Saint Victor cemetery (Marseilles, France) with synostosis of the right coronal and marked asymmetry was reported by Spitery (1983). Campillo (1993) diagnosed plagiocephaly with marked digital impressions (a sign of increased intracranial pressure in the opinion of the author) in an individual from the 'Talaiot de Biniadrís', Talayotic Culture (Alaior, Minorca, Balearic Islands). A plagiocephalic skull with unilateral synostosis of the coronal suture coming from Tejeriguete (La Gomera) is curated in the Verneau Collection from the Canary Islands, now curated in the Musée de l'Homme at Paris. Two cases, curated at the Museo Canario of Las Palmas de Gran Canaria, come from Barranco de Orchilla (San Miguel, Tenerife) and Barranco de Guayadeque (Gran Canaria) (Spitery, 1983).

Turricephaly (acrocephaly; acrobrachycephaly)

This condition is produced by premature bilateral coronal synostosis associated with closure of the sphenofrontal, and, probably, sagittal sutures. Turricephaly may be part of a syndrome, such as Apert, Pfeiffer and the milder forms of Crouzon syndromes. As an isolated condition, turricephaly is not very common. This condition is more commonly seen in females. The typical picture is that of an abnormally broad skull with a high, tower-like, forehead, and discrete hypertelorism (wide-set-eyes). The cephalic index is over 85. This type of craniosynostosis is associated frequently with increased intracranial pressure and causes characteristic 'digital impressions' that are visible in the radiographs. The case of a child of 10–12 years of age coming from Barranco de Guayadeque (Gran Canaria, Canary Islands) has been recognized.

Trigonocephaly

The metopic suture usually fuses at about 2 or 3 years of age, remaining unfused to varying degrees in 10 % of individuals. Trigonocephaly is an uncommon cranial malformation that is the consequence of premature synostosis (commonly during intrauterine life) of this suture, resulting in a triangle-shaped skull. A familial incidence has been detected on rare occasions, although the exact etiology is not clear. This condition normally affects males. The forehead is narrowed and close-set-eyes (hypotelorism) are obvious. The cephalic index is within the normal range. A bony ridge is observed between the glabella as far as the bregma. Few cases have been reported in the paleopathological record. Spitery (1983) refers to two cases: one from the Réville cemetery (France) of the Mérovingian period (sixth–seventh centuries A.D.) and another curated at the Dupuytren Museum.

Oxycephaly

Several writers equate this term with turricephaly, although others identify oxycephaly with an abnormally high and conical head showing anterior–posterior shortening and increased height near the bregma region (David et al., 1982). Barnes (1994) uses the term oxycephaly when lambdoidal and coronal sutures are both involved. Several of the few cases of oxycephaly reported in the paleopathological literature come from the Canaries: one is the skull of a 12 year old

child from Acusa and another is that of an adult male from Barranco de Guayadeque (both on Gran Canaria).

Triphyllocephaly (cloverleaf skull deformity)

This condition refers to a trilobular skull that is caused by multiple sutural fusion. A constriction ring develops in the lambdoid–squamosal region and causes a marked bulging in the frontal and temporal bones (David et al., 1982). This condition is usually associated with hydrocephalus (Raspall, 1990) and mental retardation is frequent.

Early synostosis of the lambdoid suture

This very uncommon condition limits the anteroposterior development of the skull producing a flat aspect to the occipital region. One of the prehispanic Canarian skulls from Gran Canaria, curated with the Verneau Collection (Paris), shows complete synostosis of the lambdoid suture along with partial synostosis of the sagittal (Spitery, 1983).

Complex craniofacial deformities

Crouzon's syndrome (craniofacial dysostosis)

This is a hereditary (autosomal dominant with incomplete penetrance) and familial disease characterized by early synostosis of the coronal and sagittal sutures causing oxycephaly. Most often the disease is not recognizable until the end of the first year of age and is accentuated during the child's development. The skeletal changes of this syndrome are almost limited to the skull bones.

The morphological characteristics of Crouzon's syndrome are:

- Skull: oxycephaly due to the early closure of the coronal and sagittal sutures, although early lambdoid suture closure is also observed in 80 % of the cases (McAlister, 1989). These craniosynostoses usually begin during the first year of life and are complete between the second and third year). Bossing of the bregma region occurs due to the fact that this is the less ossified of the skull regions and offers a lesser resistance to the intracranial pressure. A long foramen magnum, decreased angle of the petrous temporal portion and a thin and prominent frontal bone are also found. Well marked digital impressions, increased radiological density at the level of the occipital bone and petrosphenoidal region as well as hypertelorism accompany the changes. Hydrocephaly is not uncommon. The skull is brachycephalic (Fig. 4.2).
- Face: hypoplasia of the maxilla and small paranasal sinuses; ogival palate; certain degrees of prognathism; decreased orbit volume; depressed nasal apertures; deviated nasal septum; and dental anomalies (malpositions, supernumerary teeth, dental crowding, etc.).

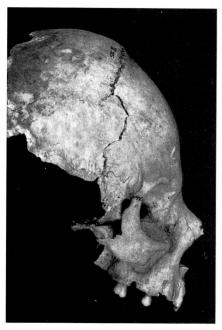
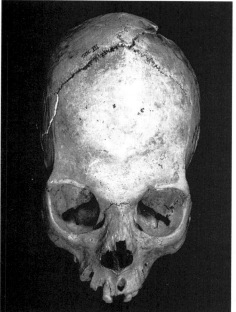
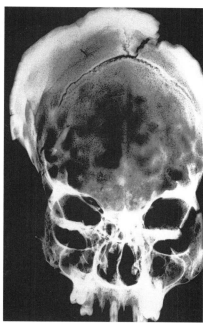

FIG. 4.2. **Crouzon syndrome.** Note frontopteric suture synostosis, elevated frontal bone, shallow orbits. X-ray: digital impressions. Medieval child 12 years, Catalonia, Spain. Courtesy Dr D. Campillo, MAC.

Paleopathology

A probable case of craniofacial dysostosis of Crouzon has been diagnosed by Campillo (1993) in a medieval child from Sant Miquel de Cardona (Bages, Catalonia, Spain).

Apert's syndrome (acrocephalosyndactyly)

Etiology and pathology

This is a hereditary disease (autosomal dominant), although sporadic cases are not uncommon; it is recognizable at birth. This condition affects three different levels:

- Skull: coronal synostosis at birth; flattening of the frontal bone and occiput; possible secondary sagittal suture closure; and oblique skull base. The skull is brachycephalic. Hydrocephaly may participate in the syndrome.
- Face: maxillary hypoplasia; flat nasal base; frequent hypertelorism; deep palatal vault; and possible palatal division. Delayed dental eruption and dental crowding are also observed.
- Extremities: syndactyly in the hand and foot (especially in the fingers and/or toes 2, 3 and 4); carpal and tarsal fusion; possible bone ankylosis; and shortening of the upper limbs.

Paleopathology

Brothwell (1967c:441) refers to a probable case of Apert's syndrome in a child from Nubia, and calls attention to inconsistencies about this condition:

There is still much confusion regarding the use of terms acrocephaly and oxycephaly, and whether acrocephaly is quite distinct from acrocephalosyn-dactyly or is purely a milder expression of the same syndrome.

Carpenter's syndrome

This condition, which is also known as acrocephalosyndactyly type II, is similar to Apert's syndrome. This is an autosomal recessive trait showing craniosynostosis involving the coronal, sagittal and lambdoid sutures, and syndactyly. Other features are: micrognathia, ogival palate, genu valgum, coxa valga, acetabular hypoplasia, coccygeal agenesis, spina bifida occulta, and scoliosis.

Anencephaly

Definition, etiology and epidemiology

This is a lethal congenital malformation of the posterior embryonic neural tube showing a small mass of amorphous brain tissue and absence of the skull vault (Figs 4.3 and 4.4). Only 25 % of anencephalics are born live but these die prior to the seventh day of life. Other congenital malformations (organic or skeletal), especially total or partial rachischisis are observed commonly in relation with anencephaly. The etiology of this lethal condition is not yet known. Genetics could play a role in its development, but it is probably a product of multifactorial influences. The present incidence of anencephaly is about 1 per 1000 births. Anencephaly constitutes an exception with regard to other congenital malformations because it appears with higher frequency in poor families than in families with higher social and economical status (McKeown, 1988). Anencephaly seems to be less common in Eastern and African people than in the Western countries. Failure of skull development in anencephalics

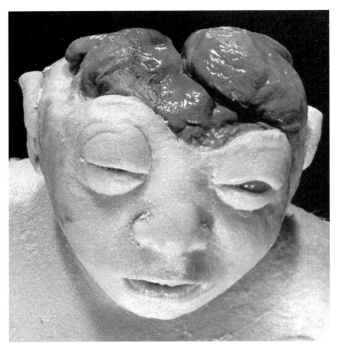

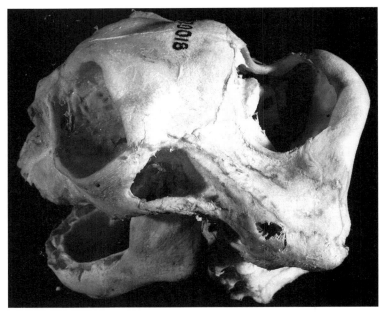

FIG. 4.4. **Anencephaly, skull.** Note absence of cranial vault bone development. Courtesy P. Sledzik. 1987.0018. NMHM.

FIG. 4.3. **Anencephaly.** Small malformed mass of cerebral tissue at skull base in modern newborn. Failure of cranial vault bone development dramatically exemplifies that neural tissue directs growth of those bones, not vice versa: no brain, no bone. BM.

is often cited as evidence that neural tissue governs related skeletal growth.

Paleopathology

One of the earliest (and according to Barnes, 1994 the only) case of anencephaly described in the paleopathological literature is that of an Egyptian mummy coming from the catacombs of Hermopolis (Palés, 1930; Brothwell & Powers, 1968).

Microcephaly

Definition and etiology

This condition refers to a statistically significant subnormal skull circumference, and usually is the result of failure of brain development (microencephaly), probably due to genetic factors. The term microencephaly is also known as true microcephaly, as it demonstrates underdevelopment of all parts of the brain with the exception of the cerebellum, resulting in a brain weight one-half to one-fourth that of normal. Microcephaly may be associated with congenital infections, Tay-Sachs disease, radiation, or phenylketonuria (Zimmerman & Kelley, 1982). Familial cases suggesting autosomal recessive inheritance occur. Consanguinity seems to play a role in the development of this condition because its frequency in isolated populations can reach 1 in 2000 births.

Pathology

Irregularities in the thickness of the cranial bones producing lacunae (lacunar or fenestrated skull) may also be present (el-Najjar & McWilliams, 1978). Mental retardation is common in this condition. The characteristics of microcephaly include:
1. Recession of the frontal and parietal bones.
2. Flattening of the occipital bone.
3. Prominent nose and receding mental protuberance.
4. Cranial capacity is always less than 1000 cc and head circumference is below 46 cm.
5. Smaller cranial measurements than normal.
6. Early synostosis of all or most of the cranial sutures and bregmatic fontanelle.
7. Large face in comparison to the head.
8. The skull has a conoidal shape.

Cases of extreme microcephaly (with cranial capacity below 600 cc) are very uncommon, and most individuals die before reaching adulthood (Dokládal & Horácková, 1994).

Paleopathology

The number of reported microcephalic cases in ancient populations is very small. Brothwell & Powers (1968) refer to those found in Donnybrook (Ireland) in the last third of the nineteenth century and dated to the tenth century A.D.; Hythe, Kent (England) dated to the twelfth century A.D.; and a case observed in a pre-Hispanic Peruvian skull. Campillo (1977) found a microcephalic skull from the Cova d'Es Morro at Manacor, Talayotic Culture of Minorca. He also cites a report of a French skull from Rochereil en la Dordogne apparently from the Magdalenian period and two reported by Wells (1964:43)

– one of 699 cc cranial volume from South Africa and one of 490 cc from Peru. Morse (1978) describes two microcephalics from a Late Woodland mound at the Riviera aux Vase Site, Macomb County, Michigan (U.S.A.). More recently, Dokládal & Horácková (1994) describe two cases with extreme microcephaly coming from the Czech Republic: one of an adult female with cranial capacity of 355 cc and horizontal circumference of 351 mm, and another, an old male, with cranial capacity of 405 cc and horizontal skull circumference of 365 mm. Comas (1968) tells the tale of two microcephalic 'Aztecs' (although they were born in El Salvador) that were exhibited as circus attractions during the last half of the nineteenth century and that were examined by Virchow and Warren, among other prestigious physicians and anthropologists.

Macrocephaly

Macrocephaly is a term used to define a brain with a weight ranging between 1600 and 2800 g, associated with enlargement of the cranial vault. Mental retardation is not uncommon in true macrocephaly. It is very difficult (usually impossible) to determine whether a specimen with such features is affected by macrocephaly or by one of the forms of hydrocephalus in archaeological human remains.

Hydrocephalus

Definition and etiology

Hydrocephalus results from abnormal accumulation of fluid in the lateral, third and fourth ventricles and/or subarachnoid space. Hydrocephalus occurs when the equilibrium between secretion of fluid and its resorption fails and the volume of the skull fluid content increases. Without proper surgical treatment 50 % of the children affected by hydrocephalus at birth die within the first 5 years of life. Of all the cases of this condition, 25 % are congenital; the rest can be due to trauma, infections, or tumors. Hydrocephalus has the most heterogeneous etiology of all the congenital malformations (McKeown, 1988).

Pathology

The appearance of the skull is large and globular, revealing a frontal bossing (Fig. 4.5). Several features in archaeological specimens are important to consider in order to diagnose the condition (el-Najjar & McWilliams, 1978):
1. Enlargement of the head.
2. Thinning of the skull bones.
3. Bulging fontanelles.
4. Widely separated sutures often showing wormian bones.
5. Atrophy of the supraorbital ridges.
6. Flattening of the cranial base.

Paleopathology

Brothwell (1967c:428) states that it is impossible to determine whether hydrocephalic dry skulls occurred prenatally, perinatally, or postnatally and if induced by trauma, anoxia, infection or tumor. Hydrocephalus developing in late childhood may not result in appreciable enlargement of the skull and, therefore, the specimens of paleopathological interest must be those of less than 6 months of life (Manchester, 1983a:33). In a review of cases of hydrocephalus in the paleopathological literature, Richards & Anton (1991) state that 30 possible cases have been reported ranging from 10 000 B.C. to A.D. 1670. However, they found that diagnostic criteria for this condition have not been established. One of the first cases of hydrocephalus diagnosed in ancient human remains was that of a Guanche (pre-Hispanic inhabitant of Tenerife, Canary Islands) in 1877 (Verneau, 1879). This skull was diagnosed by the French anthropologists Armand Quatrefages and René Verneau. It was excluded from their osteometric studies on the Guanche population because this malformation prevented their measurements.

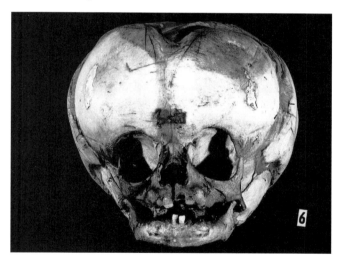

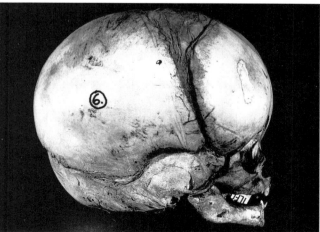

FIG. 4.5. **Hydrocephalus.** Note suture separation and rounded skull shape. Modern specimen. Pathology Museum of Barcelona University School of Medicine. Courtesy Dr D. Campillo.

One of the most ancient cases of hydrocephalus we could find in the literature is that of a child from Seeburg (Germany) and is dated to the Neolithic period (Brothwell, 1967c:428). However, Spitery (1983) described a probable case of hydrocephalus in a Neanderthal from Starocelje, Crimea. Other Romano-British cases come from Norton, Yorkshire (England); two Gallo-Roman cases from Boulogne-sur-Mer, Viel-Atre; one case from la Rochereil III (Dordogne) dated to the Magdalenian period; Col Sainte Anne (Simiane-Collongue, Bouches-du-Rhône) to the Iron Age; Roaix (Provence) from the Chalcholithic epoch (France); a Neolithic case from Zambujal (Portugal); another from Tell Duweir-Lachish, Palestine (Iron Age); two cases from Egypt's Roman period and first dynasty (Sakkara); and finally one from Sudanese Nubia.

An interesting case of hydrocephalus with other skeletal anomalies is described by Richards & Anton (1991) in a child of less than 1 year of age from the Middle period (2500 B.C. to A.D. 500) of Central California. This child shows a unique craniofacial configuration and malformed postcranial elements. The cranial capacity was 3300 cc. The upper limbs were longer than normal while the lower limbs were shorter, and the femoral morphology showed anterior–posterior compression of the shaft, neck and head, with a markedly prominent linea aspera and altered trochanters. Campillo (1993) observed a hydrocephalic child (7 years of age), from Sant Vicenç de Malla (Osona, Spain) and dated to the seventeenth or eighteenth century, showing a cranial capacity of 3900 cc. Recently, Kreutz & Schultz (1994) describe a case of hydrocephalus externus from the early medieval cemetery in Straubing (Germany), belonging to a 2–3 year old child showing enlargement of the skull with thin bones, dehiscence of the sutures, lambdoid wormian bones, and flattened orbital roofs with *absence* of digital impressions that are typical of internal hydrocephalus.

Congenital herniation of meninges and brain

Definition and etiology

This defect is similar to that of spina bifida, and consists of a cleft of the skull vault through which the meninges and cephalic mass protrude externally (meningoencephalocele). If only the meninges protrude, the condition is known as meningocele. The etiology is not yet known, but sporadic cases are most commonly observed (Raspall, 1990).

Pathology

These defects occur in three locations:

1. Occipital: this is the most common type (75 %). Hydrocephalus may exist with involvement of the ventricular system in severe cases.

2. Anterior defects: 15 % of cases. These are divided into two types: visible or basal, and non-visible or sincipital. This defect is localized in the nasal base and usually demonstrates hypertelorism. Hydrocephalus can be present.

3. Parietal: 10 %.

Paleopathology

One of the rare cases of this condition reported in archaeological material is that of a 6–8 year old child from Ancon, Peru (1000–1200 A.D.) showing the defect in the frontal bone (Stewart, 1975). Differentiation must be made between congenital herniation of meninges and brain and trepanation. Such a separation is based on the herniation's more gradual border.

Cleft palate (palatoschisis)

Definition, etiology, and epidemiology

It results from arrested development during embryogenesis. A certain degree of familial incidence has been detected, suggesting a genetic component (perhaps multifactorial) in the development of this condition. Cleft palate is a midline defect of the palate that permits open communication between the oral and the nasal cavities. Cleft palate can be part of multifeature syndromes such as Kniest's disease, progressive hereditary arthro-ophthalmopathy, diastrophic nanism, congenital spondyloepiphyseal dysplasia and others. The present incidence of cleft palate is 1 per 1000 living births.

Pathology

The range of cleft palate varies from a minor cleft or dorsal notch in the posterior edge of the palate to a large and U-shaped cleft resulting from aplasia of the palatal processes (Barnes, 1994). The palate is shorter and broader than normal. This is more commonly observed in females than in males. Nutritional and respiratory problems related to cleft palate are common and therefore in ancient times, without proper medical and surgical treatment, many of the affected infants died due to this defect.

Paleopathology

There are few cases of cleft palate in the paleopathological literature. The most ancient cases are from Nubia and from San Francisco (California), dated 2000 to 0 B.C. Other possible cases come from the Cambridgeshire Anglo-Saxon period in England, Hungary, Nubia, Sudan, Peru, South Pacific islands and Greenland. Ortner & Putschar (1985) report three cases of cleft palate: a young adult female from southwestern Colorado (U.S.A.), another case from Kentucky (U.S.A.) and an

8–10 year old child from Nazca (Peru), all of unknown chronology. More recently, Gladykowska-Rzeczycka (1989), described two cases of cleft palate in the Neolithic cemetery of Zlota (Tarnobrzeg District, Poland). Despite prevalence values among living Native Americans greater than the general U.S.A. population, few paleopathological reports of this lesion among ancient North Americans can be found (Gregg & Gregg, 1987:136).

Enlarged parietal foramina (foramina parietalia permagna; Catlin Mark)

Normal parietal foramina are located, uni- or bilaterally in both parietals by Santorini's emissary vessels in 60 % of the normal population. The normal diameter of these foramina is 1–2 mm. However, this diameter may be considerably larger. The problem such enlargements generate is its separation from trepanation or traumatic injuries. Enlarged parietal foramina are located near the sagittal suture and are usually bilateral. This anomaly probably results from autosomal dominant genes and a familial relationship has been observed (Barnes, 1994). It occurs more commonly in males than in females, and is found in 1 per 25 000 persons (Swoboda, 1972). One archaeological case has been found in a probably medieval skull from Eastry (Kent, England) and another in an Amerindian individual from Palo Alto (California, U.S.A.).

CONGENITAL MALFORMATIONS OF THE SPINE

Atlas occipitalization (atlanto-occipital fusion; atlanto-occipital assimilation)

Definition and epidemiology

This condition results from the complete or partial congenital fusion of the arch of the first cervical vertebra (atlas) with the occipital bone while the posterior element usually remains unfused. This is considered a transitional vertebra at the occipitocervical border (Fig. 4.6). Atlas occipitalization is the most common of all the anomalies at this level, and its frequency in the general population is around 1 %.

FIG. 4.6. **Atlas occipitalization, platybasia.** Note fusion of part of atlas to skull base. G25. Adult male Guanche, ca. A.D. 1000, ICPB.

Pathology and paleopathology

This malformation can result in shortening of the neck and neurological compression by the part of the odontoid process that is elevated in half of the patients, although platybasia and basilar impression are not as common. Half of the patients also have vertebral fusion at the C2–C3 level (Ozonoff, 1989). Other malformations can accompany atlas occipitalization including mandibular anomalies, cleft palate, cervical ribs, and urinary tract anomalies. One of the earliest descriptions of this lesion is that of a Peruvian skull diagnosed by the American investigator MacCurdy. Other cases come from Spain (Majorca, Valence and Catalonia), Taforalt (Morocco – that 9000 B.C. specimen is perhaps the oldest case known), Indian Mound Park (Late Woodland Culture , Illinois, U.S.A.) and from a Guanche site on the island of Tenerife (Canary Islands).

Basilar impression

Definition and etiology

This uncommon anomaly is characterized by an indentation of the occipital bone and may be found associated with atlas occipitalization (Barnes, 1994). A variety of conditions can produce basilar impression such as Paget's disease, osteogenesis imperfecta, rickets, osteomalacia, osteoporosis and cleidocranial dysostosis.

Pathology

In severe cases the proximal cervical spine has an appearance as if it were pushed into and imprinted on the skull. The foramen magnum is usually deformed and often smaller than normal. In the opinion of Barnes (1994), any indentation

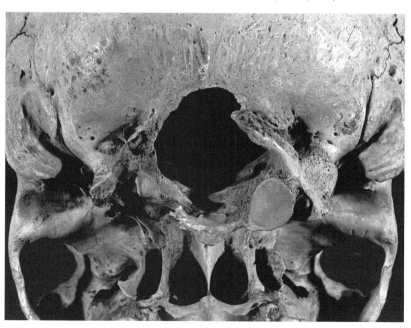

around the foramen magnum indicates basilar impression. Neurological or circulatory disturbances can be the result of compression by the odontoid. The clinical symptoms may not appear until adulthood. Although the terms platybasia and basilar impression are often used as synonyms, these are two different conditions. Platybasia has no clinical significance, being an anthropological term used to define flattening of the angle between the anterior fossa plane and the clivus plane (Hensinger & MacEwen 1986).

Paleopathology

Campillo (1993:64) describes three cases of basilar impression – two from the Iron Age of Valence, Spain (Cova del Palanqués, Navarrés, and Barranc de Llopis, Castelló de Rugat), and another belonging to the Talayotic Culture of Son Real (Majorca, Balearic Islands). This last case was associated with vertebral fusion between C2 and C3.

Klippel–Feil syndrome (congenital shortened neck)

Definition, etiology, and epidemiology

First described by Klippel & Feil in 1912, this condition demonstrates congenital fusion of two or more vertebral segments into a block with a single spinous process, neural arch, and vertebral body. Shortening of the neck is uniformly present. Scoliosis of the cervical vertebrae, malformation of the occiput and spina bifida commonly (but not invariably) accompany this vertebral lesion. The term Klippel–Feil syndrome is used by most to refer to those individuals with congenital fusion of cervical vertebrae, whether the fusion involves two segments, a block, or the whole cervical spine (Hensinger & MacEwen, 1986) (Fig. 4.7). The etiology of this condition is not absolutely clear. It is often hereditary, sometimes inherited as an autosomal recessive and sometimes as an autosomal dominant (López-Durán, 1995). Although familial cases have been observed on a few ossacions, sporadic cases are much more common (Raspall, 1990). Its prevalence is 1 in 30 000–40 000, with slight predilection for females.

Pathology

The involved vertebral bodies are flattened or widened and the intervertebral disc spaces narrow or absent. In some cases, even the upper thoracic vertebrae may be involved. This fusion is the result of segmentation failure of the spine that occurs

between the third and eighth weeks of embryogenesis. Up to one-third of the patients affected by Klippel–Feil syndrome show uni- or bilateral elevation of the scapula. Associated scoliosis or kyphosis appear in 60 % of these individuals. Posterior spina bifida is found in 45 % and cleft palate in 5–20 % of the cases (Hensinger & MacEwen, 1986). Hemivertebrae are also commonly present.

Paleopathology

Dastugue & Gervais (1992) recommend the term Klippel–Feil syndrome in paleopathology when the entire cervical and thoracic segments of the spine are involved. Examples of Klippel–Feil syndromes have been reported in specimens from Peru, Anasazi (Arizona, U.S.A.), proto-Arikara (Upper Missouri River Basin, U.S.A.), Sakkara (Egypt dated to Ptolemaic or earlier period) and S'Illot des Porros (Talayotic Culture, Majorca, Balearic Islands). Recently Urunuela & Alvarez (1994) reported a case involving most of the cervical vertebrae in pre-Hispanic remains from Mexico.

Jarcho–Levin syndrome of vertebral anomalies

Definition, etiology, and epidemiology

In 1938 Jarcho & Levin described an uncommon syndrome that is also called occipito-facial-cervico-thoracic-abdomino-digital dysplasia, and spondylo-costal dysplasia. Its etiology is genetic (autosomal recessive) and it is particularly common in Puerto Rico.

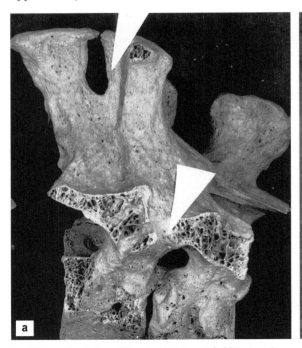

FIG. 4.7. **Fused vertebrae (Klippel–Feil deformity).** (a) Fusion of two cervical vertebrae. (b) Vertebral block C2-C7. (a) XXX1. Precontact North American aboriginal; (b) Talayotic culture, Balearic Islands, Spain, fifth century B.C. (a) Courtesy Dr John Gregg and USDAL; photograph by Glenn Malchow. (b) Courtesy Dr D. Campillo.

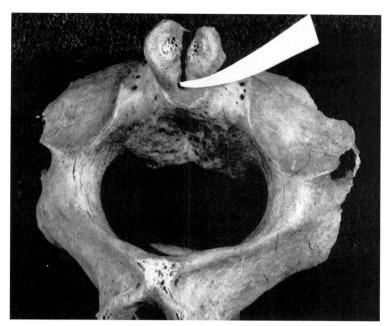

FIG. 4.8. **Bifid odontoid process.** XXV. Precontact upper midwestern North American aboriginal. Courtesy Dr John Gregg and USDAL. Photograph by Glenn Malchow.

Pathology

This syndrome is characterized by the Klippel–Feil syndrome combined with malformations of the thoracic spine (hemivertebrae, fusions and agenesis), shortening of the trunk, decreased thoracic capacity, thoracic lordosis, and approximation of the lower ribs to the iliac crests. Other skeletal signs that have been described since the initial study of Jarcho and Levin include dwarfism with relatively long limbs, prominent occiput, broad forehead, dolichocephaly, and wide nasal bridge. Afflicted individuals die early due to atelectasis and secondary pulmonary infections. No cases have yet been reported in the paleopathological literature.

Congenital absence of the odontoid process (odontoid aplasia)

Definition

This is an uncommon condition that results from the failure of the three centers of ossification of the odontoid process of the axis (second cervical vertebra). This process normally ossifies between the first and fourth years of age, reaching complete fusion by the age of 5 years.

Pathology

The defect may be partial or complete and can result in subluxation or dislocation of the atlanto-axial joint that may sometimes result in paraplegia. Less than 30 cases are reported in the medical literature (el-Najjar & McWilliams 1978), and none are reported in paleopathology. Other rare

types of congenital anomalies of the odontoid process include agenesis of the dens odontoideum (the apical segment has no base, or odontoideum) and agenesis of the apical segment with a hypoplastic base. A split (bifid) odontoid process is also known (Fig. 4.8).

Spina bifida (rachischisis)

Definition

This is the most common of all spinal congenital defects in which incomplete midline bony closure appears in one or more neural arches, most cases occurring in the lumbosacral region of the spine, especially in the sacrum. It was first described by Recklinghausen (in 1882) during the last part of the nineteenth century.

Pathology and epidemiology

There are two types of defects

Spina bifida occulta (SBO)

This consists of incomplete fusion of the posterior neural arch and can involve one or more sacral segments when it affects that bone. The meningeal or neural structures do not protrude through the defect, and commonly the defect is only diagnosed during a routine radiological examination in clinical practice. The lumbosacral area is the most commonly involved spinal region and usually only one or two vertebrae are involved. The prevalence of SBO of S1 is high (5–25 % of the population). The vertebral arch may not fuse dorsally until later than is usually accepted in the medical literature, and, therefore, the prevalence of SBO is probably lower than 25 % (Turkel, 1989). In general, spina bifida decreases with age, especially among females. The exact cause of this difference between sexes remains obscure.

Spina bifida aperta or cystica (SBA)

This is a more severe form than SBO and is often fatal. SBA includes three grades of severity:
- Meningocele: meninges and nerve roots extrude through the defective neural arch, but the spinal cord remains in the vertebral canal. This defect occurs most commonly in the lumbosacral region and represents 5 % of SBA.
- Myelomeningocele: the spinal cord, along with the meninges, are extruded through the defect. This is the most common type of SBA (60 % of all the cases) and most frequently occurs in the lumbosacral area. Hydrocephalus may be associated with myelomeningocele (Barnes, 1994).
- Myelocele: the skin and dura fail to close at the level of the defect and subsequent death from infection occurs shortly after birth if the infant is not treated. This is the most severe of all the cases of spina bifida.

Other features associated with SBA are vertebral hypoplasia, hemivertebra, laminar and pediculate fusion, diastematomyelia, and scoliosis (50 % of the afflicted) and kyphosis (20 %) (Ozonoff, 1989). Modern medical or surgical treatment offers an almost normal life to only a small number of children affected by SBA (McKeown, 1988).

Paleopathology

Spina bifida constitutes a problem for paleopathologists due to the difficulties in distinguishing both types. In the opinion of Barnes (1994):

the spinal canal is widened with neural tube defect, pushing the edges of the bony cleft outward. In contrast, the spinal canal remains normal and the edges of the bony cleft are not raised when no neural tube defect is present.

Morse (1978) affirms:

The presence of a meningocele or a myelomeningocele results in severe neurological symptoms and is incompatible with long life; so when an archaeologist finds such a defect in an adult skeleton, it can be safely assumed that the condition was a spina bifida occulta.

Many early cases of spina bifida occulta come from many different sites: North Africa, Near East, South America (Peru), Central America (Mexico), North America (U.S.A. and Canada), and Europe as well as from many different periods. In contrast, very few cases of spina bifida aperta or cystica are reported in the archaeological records. One of the most interesting population studies is that described by Ferembach (1963) in the human group of Taforalt (Morocco) (10 070 to 8500 B.C.) where she found a high frequency of this condition and other vertebral anomalies, suggesting that this was an endogamous group.

Of great interest is the example of the Guanche population of Tenerife (Canary Islands). Rodríguez-Martín (1995b) found that the most frequent spinal congenital malformation in this group was sacral spina bifida occulta. The mean prevalence of SBO among the Guanche population was almost 30 % (including all the degrees of this condition), and the traditionally isolated areas of the island showed a frequency around 50 %, suggestive of inbreeding and biocultural isolation.

Butterfly vertebra

Definition, epidemiology, and pathology

This uncommon anomaly rarely has symptomatic significance, although it can coexist with pes cavus and vertebral or rib defects. Commonly, only one vertebra is involved, usually in the lumbar or thoracic area. It is a sagittal defect or cleft in the central part of the vertebral body without neural arch involvement (Fig. 4.9). Males are more commonly affected

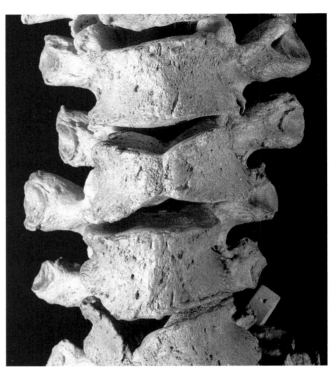

FIG. 4.9. **Vertebral sagittal cleft centrum, partial (butterfly vertebra).** Notochord regression failure in modern adult. T-899. CMNH.

than females. The disc may be absent or hypoplastic and calcified. Compensatory changes in the adjacent vertebral segments can result in scoliosis or kyphosis.

Paleopathology

Few cases have been reported in the paleopathological literature: one in an adult Tanoan burial at the Henderson site in the Pecos Valley (New Mexico, U.S.A.), five cases in Sadlermiut skeletons (Canada) and one case in a female from Pacatnamuu (Peru) (Barnes, 1994).

Anterior spina bifida

This defect consists of the lack of fusion in the anterior part of the vertebral body. It is much less common than spina bifida involving the posterior arch. It produces no symptomatic manifestations and the defect normally is found as an isolated feature during a routine radiological examination (Swoboda, 1972).

Incomplete segmentation of vertebral segments

Definition, etiology, and epidemiology

This anomaly usually occurs at the level of the cervical spine, below the axis, although sometimes the thoracic and lumbar spine may be involved. This abnormality usually involves two adjacent vertebrae and they appear in the radiograph as solid masses. The etiology of this condition remains obscure, although it seems that its origin is the congenital absence of the intervertebral disk that appears around the first month of embryogenesis. There is no proof of its hereditary origin, although familial cases do exist (sometimes dominant and others recessive). On the other hand, sporadic cases are not uncommon. The exact incidence of block vertebrae among the general population is not known, but it is estimated around 2–4 % (López-Durán, 1995).

Pathology and paleopathology

Congenital failure of spinal segmentation is often and erroneously referred to as congenital fusion (Murray et al., 1990). Fusion of the neural arches and partial or complete fusion of the spinous processes can be present. Unilateral failure of segmentation of the vertebral bodies, posterior vertebral elements, or both, produce scoliosis due to asymmetrical spinal growth. The oldest case of cervical block is that of the man of Combe-Capelle (Upper Paleolithic) that shows a double vertebral block: C3-C4 and C5-C6 (Spitery, 1983). Many other cases come from different archaeological sites: Columnata (Algerie-Epipaleolithic), Gayole, Var (France), Son Reial (Spain), Tenerife (Canary Islands), Peru and the U.S.A. In a recent study of historic skeletal samples from Lithuania, Jankauskas (1994) found a prevalence of 2.57 % for cervical, 1.59 % for thoracic and 0.54 % for lumbar regions.

Spondylolysis and spondylolisthesis

Definition

Spondylolysis is the ossification union failure of the pars interarticularis of the vertebra, resulting in separation of the vertebra into two parts: a ventral part formed by the vertebral body, the pedicles, and the transverse and superior articular processes; and a dorsal part formed by the laminae, spinous process and inferior articular processes.

Etiology

The etiology of spondylolysis is controversial. Earlier concepts viewed spondylolysis as a congenital malformation due to developmental ossification failure of the laminae. A strong genetic component seems to play a role in spondylolysis (Turkel, 1989). However, Stewart (1953) demonstrated that the frequency of spondylolysis increases with age and suggested that hyperflexion of the lumbar spine with simultaneous extension of the knees cause repeated microtrauma of the pars interarticularis resulting in stress fractures. Porter & Park (1982) feel that these two causes (congenital and traumatic) are not mutually incompatible and one individ-

ual may be congenitally predisposed to a stress fracture of the pars interarticularis. On the other hand, these authors note that the existence of unilateral spondylolysis must question the concept that spondylolysis is always the result of stress fractures.

Epidemiology

No clear gender differences are demonstrable although a small predilection for males has been observed. This condition is found in 4–8 % of the general population. Blacks are less frequently affected than Caucasians. No cases at birth are reported and spondylolysis among children is uncommon before 5 years of age (Hensinger, 1992). The frequency of the defect then increases with age until 20 years.

Radiology and pathology

An interesting prospective radiological study was performed by Fredrickson et al. (1984) in 500 unselected first-grade schoolchildren. The data support the hypothesis that spondylolysis is the result of a defect in the cartilaginous anlage of

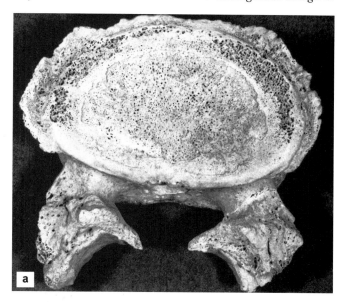

FIG. 4.10. **Spondylolysis.** (a) Neural arch separation. Osteophytic lipping – spondylolisthesis? (b) Separation through pars interauricularis. (a) LII, precontact North American aboriginal. (b) G31, Guanche ca. A.D. 1000, Canary Islands. (a) Courtesy Dr John Gregg and USDAL; photograph by Glenn Malchow. (b) MAT, OAMC.

the vertebra, that there is a hereditary predisposition to such a defect and that spina bifida occulta is strongly associated with it. The consequence of this condition is the separation of the vertebra into the body with the superior articular facet, and the neural arch with the inferior articular facet (Fig. 4.10). The health problem arises because the vertebral body can slide or slip forward due to loss of the anchoring effect of the inferior articular facet, resulting in so-called 'spondylolisthesis.' This usually occurs when the body of L5 slides onto the sacrum, although slippages of L3 on L4 or L4 on L5 have been observed. Spondylolysis is usually bilateral. Sclerosis is found in the margins of the lesion reflecting the nonunion of the fragments. It is important to note that the existence of spondylolysis or defective posterior vertebral elements are not necessary for the development of spondylolisthesis. This can exist as a consequence of severe spinal degenerative disease, pathological fractures by localized or generalized skeletal disease, or by vertebral fractures.

Paleopathology

Stewart in 1953 carried out one of the first archaeological populational studies of spondylolysis in Alaskan Eskimo populations and recorded frequencies between 15.3–40.3 % Gunnes-Hey (1981) found a frequency of 25.7 % of this condition in Koniag populations with a higher incidence in older males, although not a statistically significant difference. More than 90 % of cases showed bilateral separation, and over 75 % had only one involved vertebra (usually L5). In a more recent study on Canadian Eskimos skeletons from the area north and west of Hudson Bay and the coast of Labrador, Merbs (1990) found 30 vertebrae of 89 individuals affected by spondylolysis, showing incomplete defects. These defects most commonly involved the pars interauricularis, but other sites were affected too: pedicles, the area between the transverse process and the superior articular process, and the lamina. The most frequently affected vertebrae were L4 and L5, but examples of L3 and sacrum involvement were also present. The male/female ratio was nearly four to one. The great majority of cases occurred in adolescents or young adults.

Morse (1978) reported a frequency of 31 % spondyloses among the Morse Red Ocher Site (Illinois, U.S.A.). Jankauskas (1994) found considerably fewer (6.64 %) of lumbar spondylolysis, principally involving L5, in Lithuanian historic skeletal populations, but noted spondylolysis was much more common (15.8 %) in persons with total lumbarization of S1. Spondylolysis with clearly associated spondylolisthesis is scarcely reported in paleopathology. One unequivocal example is that described by Merbs (1980) in an adult historic Eskimo from St. Lawrence Island (Alaska) and belonging to the Hrdlicka Paleopathology Collection (San Diego Museum of Man). This specimen demonstrates complete spondylolysis of L3 with spondylolisthesis of L3 on L4.

Hemivertebrae

Definition and etiology

Vertebral bodies ossify from two independent ossification centers. If these centers do not develop appropriately, or if they do not fuse, a ventral defect ('fissured body') of the vertebral body results. This causes no spinal deformity (Duthie & Bentley, 1987). However, if one of the two centers does not appear at all, the consequence of such a failure is a hemivertebra. This asymmetry disturbs the weight-bearing equilibrium of the spine, with secondary production of lateral curvatures (scoliosis) as compensation for this alteration.

Pathology and paleopathology

A typical triangular-shaped vertebral body is located between adjacent normal vertebrae. Hemivertebra may vary in size, and the contralateral defect may be completely absent or only hypoplastic. On the other hand, it may replace a normal vertebra, or be a supernumerary structure. The adjacent vertebrae can compensate for this defect by deformation or fusion with the hemivertebra. Multiple hemivertebrae in the same spine is more common than a solitary hemivertebra. If the hemivertebra is located in the cervical spine or lumbosacral region, dysequilibrium effects are worse than at other sites of the spine (Malagón & Arango, 1987). Hemivertebrae are usually wedged in the coronal plane. Anterior wedging produces kyphosis. Few examples are described in the paleopathological literature. Two interesting cases come from Paucarcancha, Cuzco (Peru), and a Pueblo Indian site at Quarai, New Mexico (U.S.A.) (Barnes, 1994:62).

Sacrococcygeal agenesis

This is an uncommon condition (about 200 cases are recorded in the medical literature) affecting the normal development of sacrum and coccyx and appearing in stages of early embryogenesis. The etiology of this defect remains unknown and hereditary factors have been suggested. Other skeletal changes associated with this condition include prominence of the lumbar region, clubfoot, hemivertebrae, narrowing of the pelvis, dislocation of the hip, and congenital subluxation of the knees. No cases are reported in the paleopathological literature.

Sacral agenesis

Definition and etiology

One or more segments of the sacrum are absent in this malformation. This is a very uncommon anomaly. Less than 25 cases have been reported during this century (Hensinger &

MacEwen, 1986). Varying degrees of neurological disturbances and deficits affecting the legs, as well as urological incontinence and infections accompany the defect. The etiology is completely unknown, but some data suggest a genetic mutation as the cause of this severe condition.

Pathology

Most cases of sacral agenesis are accompanied by congenital absence of the coccyx, narrowing of the pelvis, spina bifida cystica, and spinal deformities, especially in the lower thoracic and upper lumbar vertebrae. Usually it is associated with arthrogryposis (López-Durán, 1995). Visceral anomalies of the anogenital area and urinary system have been detected in 35 % of the cases.

Two types of sacral agenesis have been defined:
- Complete: Both ilia are deformed, and these may articulate with each other. Standing and walking are impossible in this type (Barnes, 1994).
- Incomplete: the deformed sacrum is sickle-shaped through which a meningocele may protrude (Resnick, 1989a).

Sacral agenesis is not reported in the paleopathological literature.

Congenital absence of the pedicles

Absence of the pedicles is due to defects in the cartilaginous neural arch occurring during the first 8 weeks of fetal life. Several pedicles may be absent in the same arch and the associated changes can include absence of the laminae, absence of the articular processes in the transverse processes, enlarged intervertebral foramen, defective transverse processes, and dense neural arches (el-Najjar & McWilliams, 1978).

Transitional vertebrae

Definition and general pathology

Transitional vertebrae are those that incorporate the morphological characteristics of parts of adjacent vertebrae. The neural arches are primarily involved and the vertebral body shows minor or no changes (Barnes, 1994). Changes may be uni- or bilateral, complete or partial, and symmetrical or asymmetrical. The most frequently involved segment of the spine is the lumbosacral area. However, other regions of the spine (occipitocervical, cervicothoracic, thoracolumbar, and sacrococcygeal) can also be affected. Population differences have been reported. From a paleopathological point of view, sometimes it is difficult to assess the presence of transitional vertebrae if the spine is not completely preserved (Dastugue & Gervais, 1992).

Transitional vertebrae at the lumbosacral level

Definition and Epidemiology

It is difficult to be certain what kind of lumbosacral shift has occurred without an exact count of lumbar and sacral segments. These types of anomalies occur in 3–5 % of the population, and two-thirds are sacralizations of L5 (López-Durán, 1995) (Fig. 4.11c). Sacralization of L5 is the defect in which this vertebra is incorporated into the sacrum and the lumbar spine loses a segment. The morphological aspect of the sacrum is normal but shows an extra sacral foramen (five sacral foramina). On the contrary, when the first sacral segment is separated from the rest of the sacrum assuming the form of the last lumbar vertebra the defect is called lumbarization of S1 (Fig. 4.11). In both cases the defect may be complete or incomplete, unilateral or bilateral, symmetrical or asymmetrical.

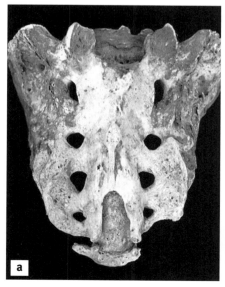 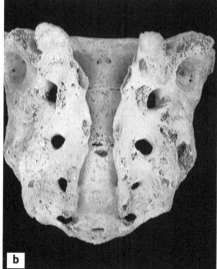 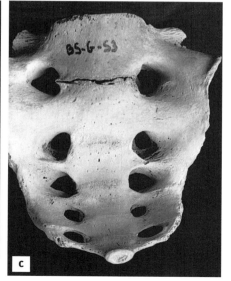

FIG. 4.11. **Sacral malformations.** (a) Coccyx sacralization. (b) Spinal bifida occulta. (c) L5 sacralization. G29, 35, 36. All adult Guanches ca. A.D. 1000. MAT, OAMC.

Pathology

In sacralization, the anomalies in development of one or both of the transverse processes of the fifth lumbar vertebra may produce fusion with the base of the sacrum, producing a 'butterfly wing' appearance (Duthie & Bentley, 1987). The pedicle and transverse processes can also articulate with the ilium if they have enough length and are directed laterally (Barnes, 1994). However, if the shift is mild, the transverse processes of L5 are wide, resembling sacral alae without articulation with the sacrum. In those cases with unilateral sacralization (most commonly seen on the right side), progressive scoliosis can develop, generating rotation and curvatures of several spinal segments. A lumbarized S1 segment is completely or incompletely separated from the rest of the sacrum and shows a short and widened body, assuming the characteristics of a lumbar vertebra. Females are more commonly affected.

Paleopathology

The most ancient case of sacralization is that of the man of La Ferrasie II, a Neanderthal showing partial sacralization of the fifth lumbar vertebra. The oldest example of lumbarization is one case from Téviec. Since then cases have been described among various ancient cultures. Campillo & Rodríguez-Martín (1994) observed 6.28 % of L5 sacralization and 5.44 % of S1 lumbarization among the aboriginal (Guanche) population of Tenerife, Canary Islands. Sacralization was almost equally distributed between males and females while lumbarization was much higher among females (9.3 %) than in males (1.7 %). All the cases of hemisacralization of L5 were associated with scoliosis. When considering the diagnosis of sacralization of L5 and lumbarization of S1 in archaeological bones it is important to determine whether the sacrococcygeal junction is normal, in order to avoid misdiagnosis because of confusion with transitional vertebrae at that level.

Transitional vertebrae at the sacrococcygeal level

Definition, pathology, and epidemiology

Sacralization of the coccyx is more commonly observed than is the separation of the last sacral segment. Reed (1967) found such a high frequency of sacrococcygeal fusion in skeletal material from southwestern U.S.A. that he usually did not consider it as an anomaly. Sacralization of the coccyx may be complete (in which case extra sacral foramina will be apparent) or incomplete (Fig 4.11a). Sometimes this malformation is difficult to differentiate from sacralization of L5. Males seem to be more frequently affected than females.

Paleopathology

The aboriginal Guanche population of Tenerife (Canary Islands) had a coccyx sacralization rate of 2.9 % (Campillo & Rodríguez-Martín, 1994). Rodríguez Maffiotte (1974b) also described an interesting case of sacralization of the first coccygeal segment associated with lumbarization of the first sacral segment in a Guanche from Roque de Tierra (Anaga, Tenerife, Canary Islands).

Scoliosis

Definition, epidemiology, and etiology

Scoliosis is the lateral curvature of the spine with rotation of the vertebrae and the spinous processes towards the concavity of the curvature. In the concavity the ribs are approximated among them, pedicles and laminae are thinner and shorter than normal, and the disc spaces are shortened. Vertebrae assume a cuneiform shape. Scoliosis usually has a double curve, permitting the head to be located in the midsagittal plane. The frequency of some types of scoliosis is about 2 % of the European population, but only in a fraction of the cases do skeletal changes develop (Brothwell & Powers, 1968). Scoliosis has multiple etiologies. It is often found to accompany congenital malformations of the spine, such as hemivertebrae (this form has the worst prognosis), block vertebra, congenital bar, or transitional vertebrae. This type of scoliosis is the so-called congenital scoliosis and is much less frequent than the idiopathic form. Other associations include: osteochondrodystrophy, neurofibromatosis, chondrodysplasia punctata, pseudoachondroplasia, parastremmatic nanism, osteodysplasia (Melnick–Needles' syndrome), Marfan's syndrome, osteogenesis imperfecta, untreated infantile hypothyroidism, paralysis, and trauma.

Idiopathic scoliosis

This is the most common type of scoliosis (80 %) and appears after birth or during childhood, most commonly between 10 and 12 years of age. Although the etiology remains obscure, population studies of idiopathic scoliosis have demonstrated that this is a familial disease in 30 % of the cases. It is probably inherited as a dominant character linked to the X chromosome with incomplete penetrance and variable expression. In school screenings idiopathic scoliosis has been observed in between 5 and 8 % of the children, although less than one-third are true scoliosis with deviation and rotation. The prognosis depends on the age of onset, and is worst if it appears early in life (Adams, 1986). It is believed that the problem arises in unilateral epiphyseal arrest of the vertebrae producing a wedge-like deformity of the vertebral body (Fig. 4.12). Idiopathic scoliosis is divided into three types depending on the age of onset:

- Infantile (from birth to 3 years): this is slightly more frequent in males and normally involves the thoracic region, and usually located on the left side. Spontaneous resolution of the deformation may occur in more than half of the cases while the remainder can reach curvatures up to 100 degrees. This type is almost unknown in North

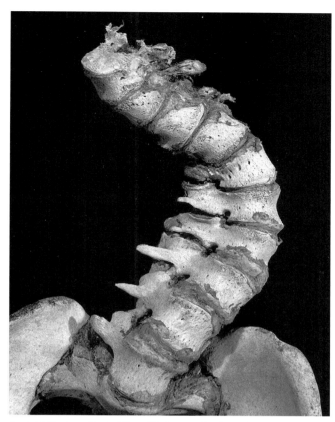

FIG. 4.12. **Kyphoscoliosis, idiopathic.** Note wedged vertebrae. Modern case. T-391. CMNH.

America. The U.K. and other European countries show the highest incidence of idiopathic scoliosis. Associated plagiocephaly is observed in more than 75 % of the patients, and hip dysplasia appears commonly.

- Juvenile (from 4–9 years). This type of idiopathic scoliosis shows a familial history and is equally distibuted between both sexes, although some statistics show a small predilection for females. It involves the lumbar and thoracic region, as does the adolescent type. The curvature is usually located in the right side. This is not a homogeneous group and some patients show features of the infantile type while others those of the adolescent type (Murray *et al.*, 1990). Spontaneous resolution occurs very uncommonly and almost 90 % of untreated individuals show severe scoliosis in adolescence with probable pulmonary dysfunction.
- Adolescent (more than 10 years). A familial history is present and the mode of inheritance seems to be multifactorial. As with the juvenile type, usually the curvature is located on the right side. Among severe cases of adolescent scoliosis, females are much more frequently affected than males (5–8:1).

Paralytic scoliosis

Paralytic scoliosis is less common than the idiopathic form and it is observed principally in the thoracolumbar region. This results from weakening of the spinal muscles by neuro-

logical disorders such as poliomyelitis, cerebral paralysis or muscular dystrophy. The consequences are structural and postural imbalance with pathological curvatures. Different types of vertebral rotation may be present in this type of scoliosis:

1. Unilateral vertebral rotation affecting one or two vertebrae.
2. Segmented vertebral rotation involving most vertebrae of the same spinal segment that are rotated in the same direction.
3. Alternating vertebral rotation that is similar to number 2 above, but the segments are rotated in alternate directions.

Paleopathology

Paleopathological diagnosis of scoliosis is not difficult if the spine is complete and well preserved. The problem arises when only a part or a segment of the spine is available for examination. Dastugue & Gervais (1992) describe three features that can help in the diagnosis:

- Lateral wedging of the vertebral body at the apex of the curve.
- Asymmetry of the neural arch and vertebral processes.
- Horizontal torsion of the vertebral body and spinous processes showing deviation from the median plane.

Ortner & Putschar (1985) add several other features for the diagnosis of scoliosis on dry bone:

- The transverse processes of the thoracic vertebrae are deflected backward in the convexity and forward in the concavity.
- The transverse processes of the lumbar spine are short and plump on the convexity, and long, slender, and pointed on the concavity.
- The spongiosa architecture in the wedged side of the vertebra shows sclerosis in the concavity and reduction in the size and number of trabeculae on the convexity.

Very few true examples of scoliosis have been described in the paleopathological literature because it is necessary to find complete and well preserved skeletons to diagnose scoliosis with certainty. The several reported cases have originated in the following sites: Crichel Down (Dorset, U.K.), Saint Philbert and the Medieval necropolis at Creuzier-Le-Vieux in Vichy (Allier) (France), an Indian Knoll site from Kentucky (U.S.A.) and Paucarcancha (Peru). One of the oldest examples of scoliosis is that of the Paleolithic man of Combe-Capelle. This specimen shows lateral inclination of the sacral promontory that, in the opinion of Dastugue & Gervais (1992), is an unequivocal sign of scoliosis. Ortner & Putschar (1985) describe an interesting case of scoliosis from the archaeological site of Hawikuh (New Mexico, U.S.A.). This is the skeleton of a Spanish priest massacred during the Pueblo Revolt of 1680 and shows a combination of scoliosis and slight deformity of the limbs that suggest it may indicate the possibility of rickets in early childhood as the cause of scoliosis.

Congenital kyphosis

Definition, etiology, and pathology

Kyphosis is the term used to define the angular deformity of the spine with convexity directed dorsally or dorsolaterally, having angulations in excess of 40 degrees. The etiology of congenital kyphosis remains obscure, although hereditary factors can play a role. The most commonly involved region is the thoracic spine. There are two main types of kyphosis:

1. Kyphosis associated with ossification disorders (cretinism, achondroplasia, osteochondrodystrophy, etc).
2. Kyphosis due to localized spinal malformation (posterior hemivertebra or failures of segmentation).

This anomaly appears as a consequence of the same segmentation defect as congenital scoliosis and the direction of the curvature will depend on the location of the spinal defect (congenital scoliosis and kyphosis commonly coexist). Spinal progressive angulation is unavoidable in congenital kyphosis and surgical treatment will be required (Apley, 1981).

Paleopathology

Paleopathological examples of congenital kyphosis are scarce probably because the presence of a complete, or almost complete and well preserved spine is required to make the diagnosis (Dastugue & Gervais, 1992). Recently, Nivaud & Gervais (1991) have described six cases of kyphosis from Saint-Philbert (France).

CONGENITAL MALFORMA-TIONS OF THE THORAX

Cervical ribs

Definition, etiology, and pathology

This common congenital condition was first described during the Roman imperial period by Galen and results from the elongation of the transverse process of one of the cervical vertebrae, normally the seventh cervical vertebra. The etiology of this condition is not yet known. The transverse process demonstrates the features of a true rib with head, neck, and body, although it very uncommonly reaches the sternum (Fig. 4.13). Even more rarely will the sixth cervical vertebra be involved. Cervi-

cal ribs are often bilateral and symmetrical; the cervical vertebra may articulate with the superior aspect of the first rib (Murray et al., 1990). In 10 % of the cases (especially after trauma, occupational stress, or progressive ossification) cervical ribs can compress the subclavian artery and vein and/or the brachial plexus producing obstruction of the blood supply ('scalenus anterior syndrome'). This usually appears at about 30 years of age.

Paleopathology

Few cases of cervical ribs have been reported in the paleopathological literature: an adult from Lewistown (Illinois, U.S.A.); an Anasazi Indian from Alkali Ridge (Utah, U.S.A.); two cases from Las Humanas, Gran Quivira (New Mexico, U.S.A.); and a few other specimens (Barnes, 1994). Campillo

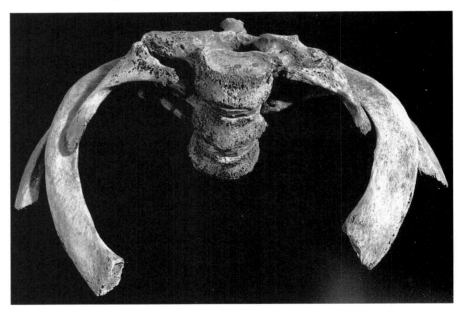

Fig. 4.13. **Cervical rib.** Additional, short rib just superior to first rib is a product of the ossification center of the seventh cervical vertebra's costal process. CMNH.

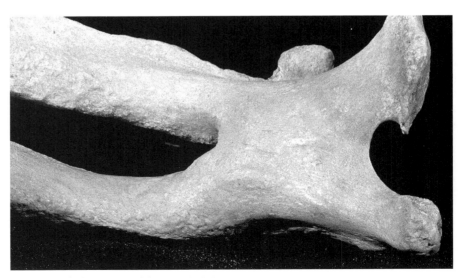

Fig. 4.14. **Rib fusion.** Modern adult. T-309. CMNH.

(1980) describes the case of an ectopic cervical rib in an individual from the Talayotic Culture of Minorca (Balearic Islands, Spain). If a cervical rib is missing in paleopathological studies, a facet on the superior surface of the first rib can serve as a marker for this anomaly, because it reflects the joint with the anterior end of the costal arch of the seventh cervical vertebra (Dastugue & Gervais, 1992).

Costal fusion

This congenital malformation represents the fusion of two ribs (normally, the first two ribs) (Fig. 4.14). Such an anomaly is very commonly associated with thoracic vertebral abnormalities. Radiographs are very helpful in the paleopathological diagnosis because they permit exclusion of fracture or callus formation. One of the few examples of costal fusion cited in the paleopathological record is that described by Cybulski (1978) in a skeleton from Hesquiat Harbour (British Columbia, Canada).

Other rib anomalies

Other rare anomalies of the ribs include intrathoracic ribs (usually on the right side) and pelvic or lumbar ribs. The latter arise adjacent to the lumbar spine, ilium, acetabulum, and sacrum-coccyx. They result from a complete shift of the costal portion of the transverse process of the first lumbar vertebra.

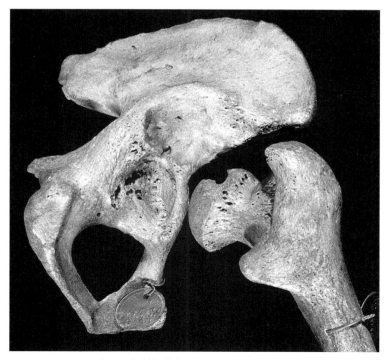

FIG. 4.15. **Congenital hip dislocation.** Acetabulum is incompletely formed and a rounded depression above it reflects site of dislocated femur head. E-1. CMNH.

CONGENITAL MALFORMATIONS OF THE PELVIS

Congenital dislocation of the hip

Definition, etiology, and epidemiology

Congenital dislocation of the hip is the loss of the normal relationship between the femoral head and the acetabulum. The femoral head is not appropriately positioned in the acetabulum and undergoes complete or partial displacement out of the acetabulum. Without proper treatment muscular action will exaggerate the proximal and lateral displacement of the femoral head along the iliac bone. As a result the acetabulum becomes dysplastic and the head will be deformed and flattened. These alterations bring about anteversion and valgus change of the femoral head and neck, and a neoacetabulum (false acetabulum) is formed in the pelvis (Fig. 4.15). Some do not consider this disorder strictly congenital because it comes to attention when the child begins to walk (Revell, 1986). Genetic factors seem to play an important role in the development of this entity. In affected families, normal parents can anticipate about a 6 % risk of congenital hip dislocation in their children, but this rises to about 36 % if one parent is also affected (Sartoris & Ogden, 1989). The prevalence of this condition reflects considerable population variation. Lapps have frequencies as high as 4–5 % of the skeletal series (Brothwell & Powers, 1968). In a more recent study, Holck (1991) found that the frequency of congenital hip dislocation among skeletal Lapp populations is more than 30 times the prevalence of this anomaly in other Scandinavian populations. In contrast, it is extremely rare in Blacks and uncommon among Chinese. Modern clinical statistics show a range of frequency fluctuating between 1 and 15–20 per 1000 live births. Females are affected five to eight times more frequently than males. Among affected individuals, breech deliveries are six times more frequent than those with vertex presentation.

Pathology

About 10 % of affected infants will show signs of dislocation (Murray et al., 1990). Morphological changes they describe appear at different levels:
- Acetabulum: aplasia of the lunate surface results in flattening and elongation. A false acetabulum develops at the pelvic level.
- Femoral head and neck: Ossification development of the femoral head is delayed. It becomes flattened and oval-shaped. The femoral neck is short with increased anteversion that can reach 90 degrees; this results in shortening of the limb. The cervical–diaphyseal angle is valgus.

■ Pelvis: In unilateral dislocation the pelvic development is impaired, causing lateral inclination. In cases of bilateral dislocation the pelvis may be atrophic and assume a vertical position.

The left hip is more commonly involved (3:1); 25–50 % of congenital dislocations are bilateral. If this condition remains untreated, the consequence of the dislocation is secondary degenerative joint disease at relatively early adulthood, dislocation of the femoral head, coxa vara, or coxa valga, along with shortening of the lower limb and tilted pelvis. Associated anomalies may appear in some cases: torticollis, spina bifida, sacral agenesis, femoral and/or fibular hypoplasia, and club foot (Revell, 1986). Alciati et al. (1987) call attention to the fact that congenital dislocation of the hip is a distinctly different condition from that of the much less common hip dysplasia. They note that congenital hip dislocation shows a true lack of a hip joint and the acetabular aplasia is the result of prior dislocation of the femoral head. Cases of hip dysplasia, however, reveal a complete joint but with malformed and defective elements that cause a superior–external subluxation of the femoral head, producing a new joint above (cranial to) the acetabulum. Displacement is always upwards but there can be additional anterior, posterior or lateral displacement. Presently, few authors accept the concept of primary acetabular dysplasia (Murray et al., 1990).

Paleopathology

Congenital dislocation of the hip may have been more common in ancient times than it is at present (Alciati et al., 1987). This could be an expression of defective adaptation to bipedalism or perhaps the result of inbreeding in those populations. It is not easy to assess whether a dislocation is traumatic or congenital in dry bones. Ortner & Putschar (1985) point out that the pathological features of congenital hip dislocation in dry bones are:

■ Neo-acetabulum on the lateral cortex of the ilium.
■ Degenerative joint disease in the neo-acetabulum even showing eburnation.
■ Flattening of the femoral head that contains a vertical groove corresponding to the round ligament.
■ A marginal exostosis pointing downward is common.
■ The true acetabulum is small, flat, and triangular.

Perhaps the earliest example of congenital dislocation of the hip is that of the australopithecine specimen Swartkrans SK 50, dated to 1.7 million years B.C. That specimen, according to Spitery (1983), demonstrates a false acetabulum above the true one. This feature, in her opinion, could correspond to a dislocation of the hip, though it is impossible to exclude its congenital origin. Others of the most ancient examples are described by Dastugue & Lumley (1976) in the skeleton of Baume-de-Montclus (France); Spitery (1983) in two Mesolithic skeletons from Téviec (Morbihan, Bretagne, France); and Palés (1930) in a specimen acquired from a Neolithic

site in France. Other cases were found in the United Kingdom, two cases dated to the Saxon period (Guildown, Surrey, and Lincolnshire), Denmark (Middle Ages), Greece (early Iron Age), Nubia (Christian Period), Egypt, Peru and Kwasteyerkiva – a Pueblo Indian site (New Mexico, U.S.A.). A case of bilateral congenital dislocation of the hip is described by Morse (1978) in a 10 year old child from Morse Site at Fulton (Illinois, U.S.A.) belonging to the Red Ocher Culture (Late Archaic).

An interesting case of combined skeletal malformations is that described by Wakely (1993) in a female skeleton (21–23 years of age) found in the medieval cemetery of Abingdon Vineyard, Abingdon, Berkshire (England). It revealed bilateral congenital dislocation of the hip joints (more pronounced on the right side), spina bifida occulta at the level of the first sacral segment and spondylolysis of L5.

Extrophy of bladder and cleft pelvis

Failure in the development of the lower abdominal wall may be accompanied by a defect of the anterior bladder wall, exposing the interior of the bladder ('extrophy of bladder': Ortner & Putschar, 1985). This malformation is compatible with life and, although the pubic and ischial rami are fused, the pubic symphysis is absent. Hence, a separation of several centimeters between the two halves of the pelvis results in the so-called 'cleft pelvis.'

APLASIA AND HYPOPLASIA OF THE EXTREMITIES

There are almost as many classifications of limb development aberrations as there are publications about them. In an effort to avoid contributing still another, we will avoid classification controversies by first discussing developmental failures of whole limbs followed by those involving individual bones.

Failures in the development of a limb

Amelia is the term used to define the absence of the whole limb or all the limbs of the body (Fig. 4.16). Hemimelia consists of a partial defect in which the upper segments of the limb are well developed but the distal segments are defective and appear as a stump. In contrast to the previous case, phocomelia is the failure in the upper segments with normal development of the distal portions, creating the shape of a 'seal winglet.' Micromelia is a defect characterized by the presence of abnormally small limbs.

Paleopathology

Congenital absence of limbs, as well as congenital absence of bones, is difficult to assess in paleopathology because of taphonomic changes that affect the skeletons (Ortner & Putschar, 1985).

Failures in the development of bones

Agenesis (congenital absence) or hypoplasia of the long bones reflects failure in formation of the entire bone or a portion of it. Agenesis is recognized at the end of the shafts that are normally in contact with the absent bone: articular surfaces are absent or malformed. The most frequently involved bones are the fibula, radius, femur, ulna, and humerus. A typical example of this type of failure in the upper extremities is the so-called 'club hand' that consists of radial aplasia with the result that only one bone (the ulna) is present in the forearm. The ulna is shorter than normal, bowed and thickened

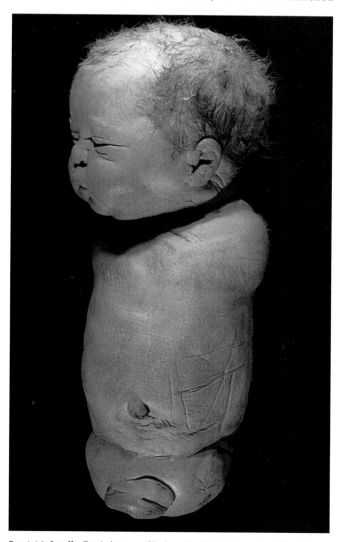

FIG. 4.16. **Amelia.** Total absence of limbs or limb buds in modern infant. X-rays revealed diminutive pelvic bones. BM.

and the thumb and carpal bones on the radial side are absent. The frequency of this anomaly is 1 in 50 000 births. Associated carpal anomalies may be present: absence of the scaphoid or lunate (this is an uncommon finding), or carpal blocks between the scaphoid and other carpal bones. Besides the complete absence of radius, there are two other types of club hand: absence of the distal half of the radius, and a complete, but abnormally short radius. Congenital absence of the ulna is much less frequent and less severe than the radial defect. In almost all cases there is unilateral involvement. Males are more often affected than females. Proximal femoral focal deficiency (congenital femoral shortening) consists of partial absence and marked shortening of the proximal portion of the femur. This occurs most commonly as an isolated entity, and is unilateral in 90 % of the cases. Four types of defects have been described:

1. Rudimentary development of the proximal third of the femur with prominent coxa vara. The most important features of this type of defect in the mature skeleton are subtrochanteric varus deformity or pseudoarthrosis and ossification of only the distal part of the femur, with pelvic and acetabular anomalies.
2. Coxa vara with normal femoral shaft. The trochanter never ossifies.
3. Femoral diaphyseal shortening accompanied by a normal upper third of the femur.
4. Dysplasia of the distal third of the femur with knee synostosis.

Congenital absence of the patella may exist as an isolated entity, but most cases are related to a hereditary syndrome: nail-patella syndrome (Murray et al., 1990).

Agenesis or hypoplasia of the fibula is the most common manifestation of all the congenital bone absences and can be classified into three different groups: unilateral and partial agenesis, without tibial angulation; partial or complete agenesis with tibial angulation; and partial or complete bilateral agenesis (Malagón & Arango, 1987). Fibular agenesis may be associated with tibial shortening and bowing, tarsal block, aplasia of the fourth and fifth metatarsals and related phalanges, equinovalgus foot, and shortening of the femur. Females show a slight preponderance.

Tibial aplasia or hypoplasia is less common than that of the fibula – 1 case in 1 000 000; about 200 cases have been reported in the medical literature. Tibial hypoplasia is the common feature of this failure but at least a portion of the proximal third is almost always present. It is usually associated with clubfoot and agenesis of the medial metatarsal and related phalanges in the foot along with malformations of the hip, knee and upper limbs.

In contrast to the previously mentioned defects, skeletal hyperplasia consists of the enlargement of a bone, portion of a limb, or the complete limb. These conditions are usually idiopathic. However they can be a feature of different diseases, such as neurofibromatosis, hemangiomatosis, lymphangiomatosis, endocrine disorders, arteriovenous abnormalities and others. No cases have been described in the paleopathological literature.

UPPER EXTREMITY MALFORMATIONS

Dysostosis cleidocranialis (cleidocranial dysostosis or dysosteogenesis; cleidocranial dysplasia; congenital cleidal dysostosis; congenital cleidal agenesis; or Marie-Sainton syndrome)

Definition and etiology

This relatively uncommon congenital malformation is characterized by aplasia, hypoplasia, or pseudoarthrosis of the clavicles, especially in the lateral portions. Anomalies of the skull bones commonly accompany the clavicular changes. It is inherited as an autosomal dominant with varying degrees of penetrance and both sexes are affected equally. Sporadic cases can occur.

Pathology

In addition to the clavicular deformations, accompanying anomalies include delayed or incomplete ossification of the skull, widening of the cranial sutures that have wormian bones (these can persist in adulthood) as well as the metopic suture, frontal bossing, absence or hypoplasia of the mastoidal antrum and other cranial sinuses and a widened and deformed foramen magnum. Basilar impression may be present. A clear disproportion of the facial skeleton is common, showing midfacial hypoplasia in comparison with the skull, which is brachycephalic. The unformed ossification centers of the skull give the appearance of a mosaic of small bones (Revell, 1986). Bilateral defects are seen in more than 75 % of the cases.

Other skeletal changes are also found commonly: delayed vertebral ossification with the vertebrae producing a biconvex vertebral shape over time, spina bifida occulta, scoliosis, short and deformed scapulae, delay and failures in the ossification of the pubis, narrowing of the iliac wings, shortening of the femoral neck, blunting of the femoral head, coxa vara or coxa valga (quite frequent), shortening of the phalanges, maxillary hypoplasia, arched palate and dental aberrations of development (delayed eruption of deciduous dentition with enamel hypoplasia, tooth impaction, retention of deciduous dentition, and supernumerary tooth buds). Adult stature is often slightly reduced, but dwarfism is very uncommon.

Differential diagnosis

Differential diagnosis must rule out pycnodysostosis (in which the pelvis is absolutely normal and the bones are abnormally dense) and with osteogenesis imperfecta (fragile bones and normal pelvis and clavicles:Wynne-Davies & Fairbank, 1982).

Paleopathology

Salvador & Carrera (1995) comment that this syndrome has been diagnosed in the skull of a Neanderthal, but they do not reference the chronology and site of origin of this specimen.

Sprengel's deformity

Definition, etiology, and pathology

This congenital disorder is characterized by supraelevation of the scapula, of either side, more commonly the left; 30 % are bilateral. The etiology is poorly understood. Females are more commonly affected than males. The scapula is widened and its superior-inner angle is hook-shaped. From one-quarter to one-third of these patients show the so-called 'omovertebral' bone or 'os omovertebrale' that is formed in the upper-internal portion of the scapula and is joined with the spinous process of a cervical vertebrae. This malformation is commonly associated with vertebral abnormalities (Klippel–Feil syndrome in 25 % of cases, spina bifida, or congenital scoliosis due to hemivertebrae), costal anomalies (ribs agenesis, synostosis of the ribs and cervical ribs) and other syndromes (cleidocranial dysplasia).

Paleopathology

Few cases of this deformity have appeared in the paleopathological literature. Perhaps the most ancient case is that of a Mesolithic skeleton from Rochereil (6000–3000 B.C.: Dastugue & Lumley, 1976).

Madelung's deformity (congenital subluxation of the wrist)

Definition, pathology, and etiology

Madelung's deformity consists of shortening and bowing of the distal third of the radius with oblique articulation with the carpus, and dorsal dislocation of the ulna, that is longer than the radius and shows enlargement and distortion of the head. This condition is usually bilateral (70 %) and is commonly diagnosed about 6–12 years of age. It may appear in association with other syndromes such as diaphyseal aclasis (multiple hereditary osteocartilaginous exostoses) and nail-patella syndrome (osteo-onychodysostosis or Fong's disease). The etiology is unknown although inheritance seems to play a role (autosomal dominant of variable expression). Females are more commonly affected than males (3–4:1).

Paleopathology

A unilateral deformity conforming to the definition of this entity was described recently in a medieval elderly male from Canterbury, U.K. (Anderson & Carter, 1995). The authors suggest that its unilateral presentation, gender and an associated shortening of the ulna may favor a traumatic rather than congenital etiology.

Congenital radio-ulnar synostosis

Definition, etiology, and epidemiology

This rare malformation occurs by fusion of the proximal portions of the radius and ulna, resulting in inability to pronate and supinate the forearm (Fig. 4.17). The etiology is not yet understood. A familial history has been observed in some cases. In these families it is inherited as an autosomal dominant with variable expression. Both sexes are affected equally.

Pathology

Duthie & Bentley (1987) describe three types of radio-ulnar synostosis:

- True congenital radio-ulnar synostosis: the upper end of the radius is underdeveloped and fused to the ulna (both medullary cavities are fused). The radial shaft shows anterior bowing and is longer and more robust than that of the ulna. Most (80 %) of these are bilateral.
- Congenital dislocation of the radial head which is underdeveloped, and the radio-ulnar synostosis involves a few centimeters of their upper extremities, normally at the level of the coronoid process.
- Malformed radial head joined to the upper end of the ulna. Of these 60 % are bilateral (Resnick, 1989a).

Paleopathology

As is also true about tibia–fibula synostosis, the non-traumatic origin of this kind of synostosis can only be established by radiological demonstration of normal skeletal structure at the level of the bony fusion. Several paleopathological examples of radio–ulnar synostosis exist. One of the first cases was found near Lake Como (Italy) and is dated to the Paleochristian period (Alciati et al., 1987). Two interesting examples of synostosis in the left upper limb come from the Crable Site, Fulton County, Illinois (Morse, 1978). Polidoro & Antón (1993) document the presence of two archaeological examples from California in the Hearst Museum of Anthropology.

Congenital dislocation of the radius

This very rare condition involves the radial head which is rounded and hypoplastic with thinning and elongation of its neck. The malformation is usually bilateral and the radius length is normal or slightly increased while the ulna is short. Other features include defective trochlea, prominent ulnar epicondyle, and hypoplasia or aplasia of the capitulum. A familial history is present in many cases. This condition is present at birth. It may appear as an isolated condition or forming part of other skeletal syndromes (60 % of the cases) such as hereditary osteo-onychodysostosis; multiple exostosis; or Hajdu–Cheney syndrome (familial idiopathic acro-osteolysis).

Congenital pseudoarthrosis of the clavicle

Congenital pseudoarthrosis of the clavicle is a rare condition that usually involves the middle third of the clavicle and is visible at birth. This condition occurs almost exclusively on the

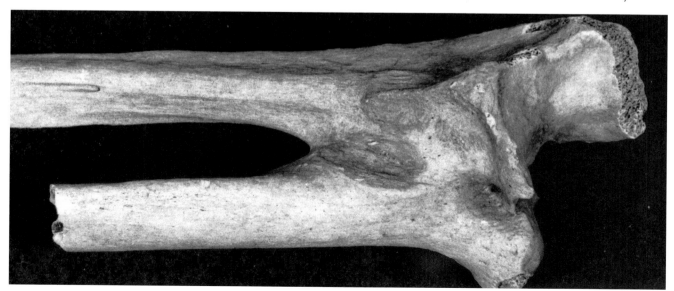

FIG. 4.17. **Radioulnar synostosis.** Precontact upper midwestern, North American aboriginal. LIV. Courtesy Dr John Gregg and USDAL. Photograph by Glenn Malchow.

right side, although 10 % of cases show bilateral lesions. In some cases a familial occurrence has been detected (Resnick, 1989a). Congenital ulnar psuedoarthrosis is a very uncommon condition that involves the union between the middle and distal ulnar shaft. It appears at or shortly after birth.

Carpal blocks (carpal coalition)

This relatively common condition is characterized by fusion of two or more carpal bones. It may be isolated or associated with other syndromes. Carpal blocks most often occur between the triquetral and the lunate bones, rarely in other bones (capitate-hamate, pisiform-hamate, and trapezium-trapezoid).

LOWER EXTREMITY MALFORMATIONS

Developmental coxa vara (infantile coxa vara; idiopathic coxa vara)

The etiology remains obscure, but it has been observed in association with osteogenesis imperfecta, rickets, fibrous dysplasia, and renal osteodystrophy. Both sexes are affected equally. The femoral neck is short; the neck-shaft angle of the femur is less than 120 degrees (this angle normally is about 150 degrees at birth and 120 to 130 degrees during adulthood), the femoral head is osteoporotic, the greater trochanter is elevated and the limb is shortened more than 5 cm. The length of the femoral shaft is normal, as is the shape of the acetabulum. Bilateral involvement occurs in one-third of the cases. If this condition remains untreated it will result in degenerative joint disease of the hip in early adulthood. Two possible examples of developmental coxa vara are described by Merbs (1980) in two pre-Hispanic skeletons from the Valley of Chicama (Peru).

Genu recurvatum congenitum (congenital dislocation of the knee)

This uncommon condition, described by Chatelaine during the first third of the nineteenth century, is characterized by anterior tibial dislocation on the femoral condyles, accompanied by aplasia or hypoplasia of the patella. The most common etiology is trauma caused by malposition in *utero*. Other causes may be primary embryonic defect, or excessive contracture of the quadriceps muscle. Genetic factors cannot be excluded. There is no sexual predilection. Bilateral dislocation is the rule although one side is always more severely affected than the contralateral one. Other skeletal anomalies related to this condition are congenital dislocation of the hip, patellar agenesis, and congenital dislocation of the elbow.

Bipartite patella

This fairly common condition (1 % of the normal population) represents a persistence of accessory ossification centers of the patella. Bilateral involvement of the patellae along with its high incidence in some populational groups are considered by Dastugue & Gervais (1992) proof of the genetic origin of bipartite patella. The alteration presents a notch with a rough surface in the superior-lateral portion of the patella in the dry bone. Bilateral involvement is common. Though often considered as a normal variation , the alteration may be related to chronic tensile failure of the bone in skeletally immature persons (Resnick, 1989a,c). Vastus-notch, a discrete skeletal trait showing smooth surfaces and of a lesser size, must be differentiated. Patellar fractures are less easily excluded, though radiological study can be useful.

Congenital angulation of the tibia (congenital tibial kyphosis)

Anterior angulation of the tibial shaft produces this malformation, very similar to that produced by rickets, Paget's disease, or tertiary syphilis. These can usually be excluded by the absence of their other commonly associated changes. It may be uni- or bilateral, and is usually accompanied by talipes equinovarus, fibular agenesis, and/or congenital dislocation of the hip.

Congenital pseudoarthrosis of the tibia

Definition, etiology, and epidemiology

True congenital pseudoarthrosis is rare in a newborn infant and presents as a defect resembling a fracture that never ossifies. Infantile pseudoarthrosis (more common) appears during the first or second year of age. The defect is at the union between the middle and distal third of the tibia. This may be an isolated feature, but 10 % of neurofibromatosis cases have this defect (Bullough, 1992). To date, the relationship between pseudoarthrosis and neurofibromatosis and fibrous dysplasia is not yet understood in detail (Resnick, 1989a). No gender predominance is evident.

Pathology

The affected tibia is characterized by sclerosis, narrowing of the medullary cavity, and tapering of the bone ends at the level of the pseudoarthrosis with a large gap separating them. The bone ends may be superimposed. The fibula is usually also involved and the leg shows anterior angulation and shortening. The reduction in length is exaggerated if the defect involves the shaft near the growth plate. This entity is normally unilateral. Spontaneous resolution does not occur and surgical correction is difficult.

Tibial-fibular synostosis

The paleopathological diagnosis of this condition in dry bone depends upon demonstration of the continuity of the skeletal structure and the absence of signs of fracture by radiography (Dastugue & Gervais, 1992). Some cases from La Cariguela (Granada, Spain) are described in the paleopathological literature (Spitery, 1983).

Tarsal blocks (tarsal coalition)

Tarsal blocks may be congenital (the etiology is unknown) or secondary to extrinsic factors (infection, trauma, etc), and may be isolated or form part of other syndromes (Apert's syndrome, arthrogryposis, symphalangism, etc). These blocks may occur between any of the tarsal bones, but the most common of the tarsal blocks are:

- talocalcaneal coalition: bilateral in 25 % of cases and occurs between the talus and the sustentaculum tali.
- calcaneonavicular coalition: may be bilateral and shows hypoplasia of the head of the talus.
- talonavicular coalition: this is much more uncommon than the blocks listed above.

Paleopathology

These are uncommon malformations and the few cases described in the paleopathological literature are from the following sites: Notre-Dame and Caen Saint Martin (France) Blain Mound (U.S.A.) and an additional one in a Merovingian skeleton (Spitery, 1983).

Talipes equinovarus (club foot)

Etiology, epidemiology, and pathology

This anomaly is the most common congenital malformation of the foot and may be uni- or bilateral (35–50 % of the cases). It can appear as an isolated deformation of the foot or take part in multiple malformative syndromes. The exact etiology of club foot is not clear. There is no model of inheritance that can be applied to this disorder, although some studies have shown the possibility that club foot may be transmitted as an autosomal dominant. A familial history is present in many cases. The actual incidence is 1 in every 800–1000 births, and is more common in males than in females (2–3:1), although severity is greater in females. The basic pathological features of club foot are varus of the heel, equinus deformity and varus deformity of the forefoot. All these changes appear as a result of prolonged contractures of the soft tissues; during the early stages they are limited to the talus and later extend to the calcaneus, cuboid and scaphoid bones (Duthie & Bentley, 1987: Fig. 4.18).

Paleopathology

This condition is more easily diagnosed in mummies and artistic representations (like those of Egypt and South America) than in dry bone (Morse, 1978). When club foot is suspected, it is useful for the paleopathologist to attempt to realign the foot and ankle bones, and compare them to the other foot or to other normal feet. Brothwell (1967c) describes the following changes as probable features of talipes equinovarus in dry bone:

1. Tibial distal articular area is altered, especially at the level of the medial malleolus which can show additional degenerative signs.
2. The talus and especially the calcaneus show important morphological changes.
3. The cuboid can form a pseudo-heel due to the extreme inversion of the foot.
4. Due to the inversion, metatarsals form the under surface of the foot and show additional flattened areas of bone that correspond to the superior aspects.

Morse (1978) suggests several additional criteria helpful for diagnosing club foot in dry bone:

1. The only bone that is always abnormal is the talus. This bone has a shortened neck that is sometimes completely absent, producing an appearance as though the head is fused to the talar body.
2. Minor changes of shape in the body of the talus.
3. Secondary adaptive changes develop in other bones such as shortening and widening of the calcaneus, decrease in the size of the tarsal scaphoid, curving medial deviation

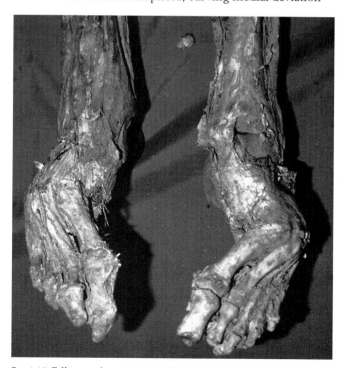

FIG. 4.18. **Talipes equinovarus.** Note characteristic equinovarus foot deformity, bilateral in Guanche mummy. G38. Adult mummified Guanche ca. A.D. 1000. MAT, OAMC.

of the metatarsals, flattening of the distal articular surface of the tibia and posterior displacement of the fibula.

Few paleopathological examples of true club foot have appeared in the paleopathological literature. Dzierzykray-Rogalsky & Prominska (1994), after examining the mummy of Pharaoh Siptah (1209–1200 B.C.), observed that the left foot compensated the shorter left leg by dislocation of the tarsal and metatarsal bones, tendons and muscles and they question the previous diagnosis of poliomyelitis suggested by Harris & Weeks in 1973. The Polish authors feel that probably Siptah was affected by club foot rather than by poliomyelitis. Morse (1978) records four cases of club foot among 1200 pre-European Polynesian skeletons, principally from Mokapu, Oahu, Hawaii (U.S.A.).

FIG. 4.19. **Polydactyly.** Supernumerary digit without metacarpal articulation in modern infant. BM.

Metatarsus varus congenitus

This is an entity that is usually bilateral and with unknown etiology (a familial history has been observed in many cases). It results in adduction of the forefoot. This may be evident at birth or during the first months of life.

Talus verticalis congenitus

A congenital vertical talus is much more uncommon than club foot and may occur as an isolated condition or associated with other neurological disorders (arthrogryposis or myelomeningocele), lumbosacral agenesis, syndactyly, or club foot. The etiology is not yet known. The talus is underdeveloped and heel valgus is present. This condition is essentially a congenital dislocation of the talonavicular joint, that can be uni- or bilateral. Sexual distribution is similar in both sexes (Murray *et al.*, 1990).

MALFORMATIONS OF FINGERS AND TOES

Adactyly

Agenesis of a finger or toe, including the metacarpal or metatarsal.

Syndactyly

This common inherited anomaly is characterized by a lack of differentiation (appearance of fusion) between two or more

digits. This condition may occur as an isolated one or in association with other syndromes.

Polydactyly

An increased number of digits can occur in the hand or in the foot, often in association with a number of syndromes called short rib-polydactyly syndromes that have a lethal course (Fig. 4.19). These include two major syndromes: chondro-ectodermal dysplasia or (Ellis-van Creveld syndrome) and asphyxiating thoracic dysplasia of Jeune. Another group, that is transmitted as an autosomal recessive and has a lethal course within the neonatal period due to lung hypoplasia, includes three types of disorders: (i) Saldino–Noonan; (ii) Majewski; and (iii) Verma–Naumoff (Murray *et al.*, 1990). Sometimes, polydactyly may be rendered occult by syndactyly due to partial fusion of the extra digits (Sandritter & Thomas, 1981).

Symphalangism

This inherited (dominant) entity is produced by the fusion of one phalanx to another in the same digit (usually in the proximal interphalangeal joints of the fingers and the distal interphalangeal joints of the toes). The first digit is very uncommonly affected.

Hyperphalangism

Hyperphalangism is the term used to define an increased number of phalanges and this is almost limited to the thumb. This may appear as an isolated condition or associated with other entities (polydactyly, trisomy 13, etc).

PART FIVE

Circulatory disorders

A broad array of lesions can affect arteries and veins other than the coronary vessels of the heart itself that are discussed in Chapter 8. Those beyond the heart are referred to by the term 'peripheral vascular system.' The etiologies of these range from infectious to autoimmune conditions. In most instances the arterial lesion is small enough to escape detection by the examiner and consequently these diseases will not be discussed in detail. The tissue effects resulting from such arterial obstructions, however, may be apparent to the unaided eye. Arterial obstruction results in decreased blood flow (ischemia). If the process develops slowly (e.g. atheromatous stenosis) the affected organ or tissue often undergoes atrophy with gradual reduction in volume. Sudden obstruction of an artery (e.g. clot formation) deprives the tissue it normally perfuses of blood so abruptly that the ischemic cells cannot survive. The result is cellular death (necrosis). An area of tissue necrosis resulting from such rapid ischemia is called infarction. The periphery of the infarcted soft tissue is usually sharply demarcated, delineated by the area normally perfused by the obstructed artery. If the individual survives the episode, such necrotic tissue usually is liquified, absorbed and replaced by fibrous tissue. The end result is a localized, depressed focus of scar. Skeletal tissue infarcts also undergo necrosis and the necrotic tissue is often absorbed. If the lesion is near the bone surface, the result is often a cortical defect.

This initial section dealing primarily with soft tissues will limit itself largely to conditions affecting the larger arteries, principally the aorta, whose abnormalities are of a magnitude large enough to be recognized readily by the examining paleopathologist. These are followed by those producing primary skeletal changes.

ANEURYSMS

Atherosclerotic peripheral vascular disease and aneurysm formation

This condition is characterized by arterial wall injury secondary to the development of a lesion called 'atheroma.' The atheroma begins as a localized deposit of fat in the blood vessel wall, accompanied by a prominent proliferative response of the artery's smooth muscle cells. A cellular infiltrate follows and necrotic areas develop that frequently become fibrotic and/or calcified. Multiple atheromas are common and occur most often in the larger arteries (aorta and its principal branches), although no artery is immune to the process. In some circumstances, especially in the presence of high blood pressure (hypertension) and diabetes mellitus, even microscopic-sized arteries are affected. The ultimate cause of this condition is unknown, but risk factors include male gender, age, hypertension, elevated blood lipid factors secondary to dietary fat or genetic aberrations of fat metabolism, smoking and others. Complications of this condition that could be encountered by a paleopathologist include:

1. Aneurysm formation – a localized dilatation of an artery whose wall has been weakened by atherosclerosis.
2. Stenosis – a gradual narrowing of the arterial lumen by an expanding atheroma.
3. Thrombosis – ulceration of the atheroma with sudden obstruction of the arterial lumen by thrombosis (clotting).

Atherosclerotic aortic aneurysm

This type of aneurysm may involve any of the larger arteries but most commonly affects the descending (abdominal portion) aorta between the renal arteries and the aortic bifurcation where the aorta divides, each artery descending into the leg. The aortic wall, weakened by atheromatous replacement of much of its elastic tissue, begins to yield to the stretching effect of the intra-arterial pressure. Expanding gradually over a period of years, the aorta may reach diameters four to five times greater than its normal width of less than 4 cm (Fig. 5.1). Untreated, it eventually ruptures, usually with sudden, rapid exsanguination (fatal hemorrhage).

The outer layer (adventitia) of the posterior part of the aorta blends intimately with the ligamentous and fascial fibers that lie anterior to the vertebral bodies and usually

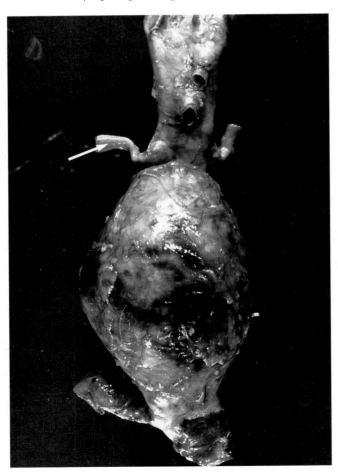

FIG. 5.1. **Aortic aneurysm.** The renal arteries are indicated by an arrow. The diameter of the aorta above it is normal, below the renal arteries the aorta is dilated (aneurysm). PBL.

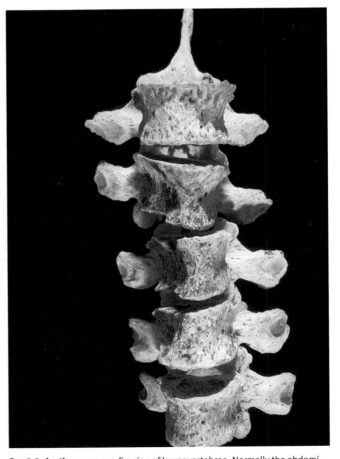

FIG. 5.2. **Aortic aneurysm.** Erosion of lower vertebrae. Normally the abdominal aorta is attached to the spine's anterior longitudinal ligament just to the left of the midline. Pulsations of an atherosclerotic aneurysm in this area have eroded the left lateral aspects of the vertebral bodies. T-532. CMNH.

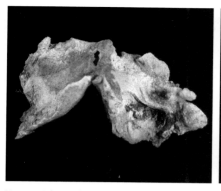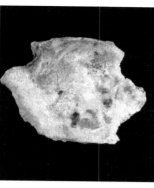

Fig. 5.3. **Atherosclerotic plaques.** Two calcified, atherosclerotic plaques found where the femoral artery must have been located in a skeleton from about 250 B.C. in Egypt's western desert. Soft tissue had all decayed but calcified plaques were recovered by meticulous excavation techniques. The larger one is about 2 cm long and of tubular form. Courtesy Dr J.E. Molto. PBL.

slightly to the left of the midline, binding this part of the aorta firmly to the spine at that site. Thus, the anterior end of the vertebral bodies, most commonly in the lumbar segment, are subjected to the constant compressive effect of the aneurysm's pulsations, resulting in shallow, concave erosions there. In mummified tissue aortic atherosclerosis is usually recognized easily; the fibrous nature of the aneurysm wall can be expected to weather the postmortem environment more easily than epithelial and other visceral structures. In skeletonized bodies, erosions of the anterior vertebral bodies may betray the aneurysm's antemortem presence (Fig. 5.2).

Arteries elsewhere may also develop aneurysms. These may thrombose (clot) and may stop expanding before they rupture. An exception is a cerebral artery whose wall undergoes aneurysmal dilatation because of either atherosclerosis or a congenital flaw in its muscular wall ('berry aneurysm'). These may rupture while still very small, and the resulting intracranial hemorrhage is often fatal. While the fragmented, ruptured cerebral artery aneurysm may not be recognizable in ancient human mummified remains, the hemorrhage can be expected to be readily apparent.

Atherosclerotic thrombosis, embolism, and infarction

The principal other hazard of atheromas is thrombosis. Endothelial cells lining arteries have an anticlotting effect. Any process that destroys an arterial lining and exposes blood within the artery to the structures composing the arterial wall usually results in clot formation. An expanding atheroma will frequently cause ulceration of the endothelium overlying it. In very large arteries the rapid blood flow will often limit the resulting thrombus to a flat clot 2 or 3 mm thick on the ulcerated surface. Fragments (emboli) may become detached from the surface of such clots and be swept 'downstream,' lodging in a distal smaller branch and occluding it (embolism). This is a common sequence of events in the instance of an ulcerated atheroma of a carotid artery of the neck, whose emboli can obstruct a large cerebral artery

with resulting death or necrosis (infarction) of the ischemic (blood-deprived) brain tissue. If the individual survives this for several weeks, liquefaction and collapse of the affected brain area conceivably might be discernible in ancient mummified bodies. A clot in the leg veins, on the other hand, will embolize to the lungs (pulmonary embolism), producing a hemorrhagic-appearing infarct there.

Complete obstruction of the artery by the clot may also occur in other areas with resulting tissue infarction. Larger branches within a visceral organ (especially the spleen or kidney) will produce changes similar to that described above in the brain. Such acute thromboses may also occur in the leg arteries where a more proximal point of obstruction may deprive the limb of virtually all of its blood supply. Such an infarcted extremity is said to suffer 'gangrene,' and the appearance of its shriveled, black tissues (stained by hemoglobin breakdown products) contrasts sharply with that of the other extremities. Careful excavation can detect the presence of calcified remains of an atheroma in a large artery, such as the femoral, even in skeletonized bodies. These are often simply irregular, flattened, thin, calcified flakes varying from a few millimeters up to 2 cm long (Fig. 5.3). Occasionally circumferential calcification will form a tubular structure whose diameter approximates that of the artery it occupied. Awareness of these lesions' appearance combined with careful excavation can be expected to identify these conditions much more regularly in the future. Diffuse narrowing (stenosis) of smaller arteries with resulting impairment, but not complete arrest, of blood flow may result in generalized atrophy of the affected organ. Renal arteriosclerosis in hypertensive or diabetic individuals may produce diminutive kidneys and death by chronic renal failure (uremia).

Infectious aneurysm

Syphilitic aortic aneurysm

As the aorta leaves the heart it reaches the top of the thoracic cavity, arches 90 degrees to the left and, after sending branches to the head and arms, descends to the pelvic level just anterior to the spine. In advanced (tertiary) syphilis the spirochetes infect the microscopic-sized arteries in the inner portion of the aortic wall involving its initial course immediately beyond the aortic valve. Its weakened, spirochete-damaged wall will then gradually expand to aneurysmal proportions, compressing or stretching the soft tissues surrounding the base and parts of the ascending aorta. Even the aortic arch (but rarely any more distal segment) may be involved. Eventually the aneurysm comes into contact with the inner face of the manubrium, sternum and/or attached parts of clavicles and ribs. The constant, pulsating aneurysmal impact often erodes these skeletal structures (Fig. 5.4). Now unrestrained by these bones, the aneurysm soon presents as a heaving, throbbing mass in the upper anterior chest covered only by a thin layer of

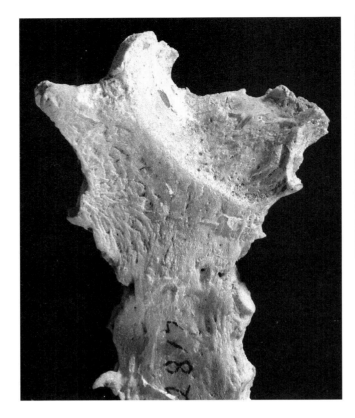

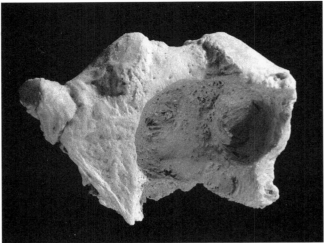

FIG. 5.4. **Aortic aneurysm.** Erosion of manubrium of two modern persons. Syphilitic aneurysms of the ascending aorta and arch often erode the upper sternum overlying the aneurysm. T-2817 and T-580, CMNH.

stretched skin. Eventual necrosis of the latter with inevitable infection is usually followed by aneurysmal perforation in a final, dramatically catastrophic and fatal exsanguination. In mummified bodies the dense fibroelastic aneurysmal wall should be evident, while in skeletons the pattern of bone erosion can be diagnostic (Kelley, 1979).

Traumatic ('false') aneurysms

In addition to these causes, aneurysms of the extremities can also be created by trauma, usually inflicted by a sharp-edged item that perforates the arterial wall without severing the artery. The blood leaking from the perforation may be constrained by a surrounding mass of muscle. The inflammatory response to the blood may result in the production of a fibrous wall that surrounds the hematoma. This may eventually become lined by endothelium, creating a spherical, hollow structure whose lumen communicates with the artery via the persisting perforation and thus becomes filled with circulating blood. Such an aneurysm of traumatic origin commonly is termed 'false aneurysm' because its wall is not composed of the arterial wall itself.

Aortic dissection (dissecting 'aneurysm')

Persons afflicted with this condition commonly suffer from an inherited defect in the integrity of collagen and/or elastic tissue structure, sometimes associated with other features composing Marfan's or Ehlers–Danlos syndrome. Focal foci of degeneration and liquefaction (cystic medial necrosis) develop in the aortic wall. When one of these eventually communicates with the aortic lumen, the blood within the aorta is directed into one of these necrotic areas within the aortic wall. Driven by the pulsating aortic pressure, the blood then dissects from one necrotic focus within the wall to the next along the length of the aorta, splitting the wall into an inner and a thin, fragile outer later. Ultimately this outer layer is perforated, with fatal results. The site of perforation most commonly is the base (origin) of the aorta, producing hemorrhage into the pericardial sac surrounding the heart (hemopericardium), but occasionally hemorrhage into the thoracic or abdominal cavities occurs from perforating dissections in those segments of the aorta's course.

CONGENITAL AORTIC DISEASE

Coarctation of the aorta

A large and often bewildering array of congenital cardiac abnormalities may occur whose effect can cause shunting of blood through abnormal defects or obstruct its flow by stenosing malformations. In mummified bodies the rapid postmortem alterations to which the heart is subject may impair their recognition, especially in the small hearts of infants. None are common, but a vascular anomaly paleopathologists may encounter is coarctation (compression) of the aorta. The effects of this malformation will often accommodate life into adulthood. This lesion is characterized by a usually sharply localized constriction of the aorta most commonly located near the origin of the left subclavian artery. The pressure just proximal to the constriction is high and just distal to it is abnormally low; this is reflected in such differing blood pressure readings measured respectively in the arm and leg. The blood is rerouted through a detour of collateral, connecting branches that enlarge to accommodate the increased flow. Thus, the increased amount of blood under high pressure causes the intercostal arteries coursing along the inferior edge of the ribs, and the internal mammary arteries under the sternum near the costochondral junctions to assume a serpentine shape. During the growth period these bones will conform to the pulsating loops of the engorged, sinuous arterial loops, generating a 'notched' appearance of the bone edges in these areas that has diagnostic value to either modern radiologists or paleopathologists even when the soft tissue lesion has undergone postmortem degeneration.

Paleopathology of aneurysms

Tangible evidence of easily recognizable atherosclerotic arterial disease is so abundant in Egyptian mummies (Shattock, 1909; Smith, 1912; Williams, 1927; Long, 1931; Sandison, 1962) that it led Ruffer (1911b) to speculate that Egyptians must have suffered from it as regularly as modern Europeans do. Moodie (1923b:394; 1931), Gray (1967b), Vhnanek & Strouhal (1975), Harris & Wente (1980) all were able to detect radiologically the calcification in larger arteries of Egyptian mummies. Rowling (1961) suggests an Egyptian inscription depicts cerebral hemorrhage (ruptured aneurysm ?). In spite of this as well as the quite clear description of an aneursym in the Ebers papyrus (Ebbell, 1937: 125, column 108), no aneurysm has been reported in an Egyptian mummy. The skull base lesion suggested by Smith & Wood Jones (1910) and illustrated in Moulin (1961) is less than diagnostic.

While the antiquity of the atherosclerotic process is quite ancient (Peng, 1995) (discussed in Chapter 8), recognition of an aneursym is more recent. Though the Ebers papyrus reference is quite convincing, it may well relate to traumatic aneurysm as do the comments of Galen and Rufus of Ephesus (Moulin, 1961). The Hippocratic corpus is silent on this topic. Antyllos (second or third century A.D.) not only is the first to separate true from false (traumatic) aneurysm but also details a method for their surgical removal when they occur in the extremities.

The points of aneurysmal impact on the bones are marked by relatively smooth, sharply-demarcated areas of erosion. The anterior and anterolateral (left of the midline) portions of the vertebral bodies will demonstrate such defects as demonstrated in modern cases (Kelley, 1979). Increased resistance by the vertebral body end-plates often produces a 'scalloping' effect (Ortner & Putschar, 1985:247). The sternum, left sternoclavicular junction and left costochondral junction skeletal structures are all common sites of aneurysmal erosion by syphilitic aneurysms and parts or all of these

osseous structures can completely disappear. The atherosclerotic aneurysm, usually located in the abdominal segment of the aorta, will produce such characteristic vertebral lesions on the lumbar vertebrae.

The nonsyphilitic bacterial type of aortic aneurysm is so rare that its encounter in paleopathological tissue would be remarkable, while the dissecting form does not produce dilatation until the dissection actually occurs, and the patient usually dies within hours or at least days, so these do not produce bone erosion. They are, however, often associated with Marfan's syndrome. This is characterized by skeletal deformities including excessively lengthy long bones and fingers, and the closely related Ehlers–Danlos syndrome also reveals a dislocated lens. Congenital and traumatic aneurysms similarly rarely erode bone because of their usual peripheral location. If they lie adjacent to a bone such as the femoral shaft or pelvis, shallow pressure erosion can occur (Murray et al., 1990).

Congenital vascular changes can, however, produce unique effects. Congenital arteriovenous aneurysm delivers a greatly increased flow of oxygenated, arterial blood to the regional affected limb, the result of which can be a powerful growth stimulus leading to an inappropriately elongated long bone with a slightly expanded diaphysis and irregular inner (marrow) radiological lucency (Murray et al., 1990).

Included in this section of the chapter are a variety of alterations impacting the skeleton whose vascular origin ranges from certainty to controversial or presumptive.

OSTEOCHONDRITIS DISSECANS

Synonymy and definition

Osteochondritis dissecans (König's disease; post-traumatic subarticular necrosis; transchondral fractures) is a benign, noninflammatory condition of young adults characterized by the production of small, focal epiphyseal areas of necrosis on the convex surfaces of diarthrodial joints resulting in partial or complete detachment of a segment of the subchondral bone and articular cartilage.

Etiology and epidemiology

A few familial cases have been reported (Jaffe, 1972; Adams, 1986) in which it appears to be transmitted in an autosomal dominant pattern (Bullough, 1992) often involving multiple joints. Most cases, however, are sporadic. Its common appearance in young athletes (Forrester & Brown, 1990; Kulund, 1990; Brower, 1994) has led to the suggestion that trauma, especially repeated, low-grade chronic or microtrauma, may play a role in the etiology of this process. The early necrotizing lesion has also been postulated to result from defective blood flow, perhaps septic or aseptic emboli, but support for ischemia as an etiological factor is less than it was several decades ago (Carnevale, 1971). Some authors believe that the evidence for any proposed factor is unconvincing and simply regard the condition as currently idiopathic (Helms, 1989).

Osteochondritis dissecans affects patients between the ages of 10–25 years most commonly. Children under 10 years are infrequently involved, but those that do suffer from it are often obese. It is uncommon after the fourth decade of life, though recently an increasing number of cases have been observed in middle-aged or elderly women (Forrester & Brown, 1990; Murray *et al.*, 1990). Males are affected two to three times as frequently as females although the number in women rises after menopause.

Pathogenesis

The initial lesion of this process is a focal area of bone necrosis 10–20 mm long and up to 5 mm deep on the convex surface of a joint beneath the articular cartilage. Indeed, Murray *et al.* (1990) have suggested this disorder may more properly be named descriptively as post-traumatic subarticular necrosis. It is found most commonly on the lateral and anterior aspects of the medial femoral condyle near the attachment of the posterior cruciate ligament. Only 15 % are on the lateral condyle. The talus is the next most frequent site followed by the elbow (capitulum), while the radius head and virtually any other joint can be involved.

Following necrosis the lesion may persist, and Bullough (1992) notes that clinically resected specimens may show viable overlying cartilage. Eventually the lesion's roof often becomes detached, surviving as a loose body in the joint

('joint mouse'). In some patients this may remain viable in the synovial fluid and even remodel into other sizes and shapes (Murray *et al.*, 1990), though more commonly it persists unchanged. To complete the analogy, the residual bone defect with its irregular lining is commonly termed the 'mouse bed' (Sandritter & Thomas, 1981). Osteochondritis dissecans is the most common cause of intra-articular loose bodies. In some cases the loose body may be resorbed, and in others a thin layer of bone may cover the defect although its surface remains depressed (Ortner & Putschar, 1985). Reactive bone sclerosis eventually surrounds the defect. Features of interest in the various locations include the following:

- Femoral condyle. This is the site involved in 85–90 % of the cases (Fig. 5.5). It is bilateral in only 20 % of cases (Muñoz Gómez, 1983). With the exception of Schinz *et al.* (1953), most authors feel it is uncommon in the third and fourth decades of life and rare after 40 years. In other features it also conforms to the model described above. A history of previous knee trauma is evident in half the cases (Resnick *et al.*, 1989a). The most probable cause is believed to be traction of the internal ligament of the knee on the osteochondral surface (Kulund, 1990), although others (Duthie & Bentley, 1987; Johnson & Brewer, 1987) have related prominent tibial spines to this condition. Prognosis is dependent upon age of onset and lesion size.

- Talus. This is the second-most common site of involvement by this condition, and appears between the second and fourth decade of life. The proximal surface is affected on its posterior-medial aspect as well as the lateral border, and 'joint mice' are not uncommon (Helms, 1989). Older patients often have a history of athletic stress (Murray *et al.*, 1990).

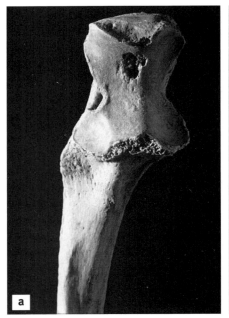 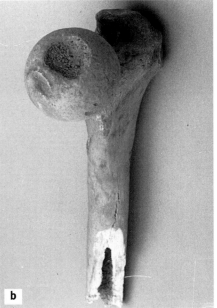 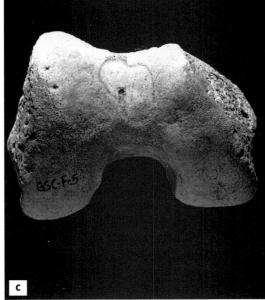

Fig. 5.5. **Osteochondritis dissecans.** Note healed lesion in femur's intercondylar area (c) while active lesions are present in the femur head (b) and in the ulnar trochlear notch (a). G11, 12, 13. Adult male Guanches ca. A.D. 1000. MAT, OAMC.

■ Elbow. The third most common site for this lesion of about 10 mm diameter appears in the humeral capitulum during adolescence or young adulthood, generating its crater on the humeral condyle, often with associated radial head hypertrophy. The much higher involvement of the right side may reflect its relationship to strong activity of the right arm. The appearance of secondary degenerative joint disease may follow many years after the onset of the dissecans lesion. The radius and ulna may also be involved showing the same characteristics.

Involvement of bones other than the three sites mentioned above is quite unusual. They include the following:

■ Shoulder. The first radiological sign at this location is alteration of the trabecular architecture near the humeral head's articular surface followed by subchondral radiolucency after which the articular bone collapses. The final product commonly consists of secondary degenerative joint disease (Brower, 1994).

■ Patella. The medial facet or the convex intercondylar ridge are the usual locations, though the lateral facet and the middle of the lower portion of the bone are occasional alternative sites. These may be due to tangential fractures or subluxations of the patella (Johnson & Brewer, 1987), and the lesion is usually unilateral.

■ First metatarsal head. A large, dissected fragment of the convex articular surface is seen only rarely.

■ Hip. Either the femoral head (see Fig. 5.5) or, less often, the acetabulum may be involved. While Schinz et al. (1953) found the frequency at this location second only to the knee, most other authors encounter it only occasionally.

Radiology

Concordant with its pathologic appearance, osteochondritis dissecans presents radiologically as a well-demarcated, radiolucent defect in the articular surface of the affected joint, surrounded by a sclerotic repair zone (Rothschild & Martin, 1993; Brower, 1994).

Complications

Degenerative joint disease may appear at an early age as a consequence of osteochondritis dissecans, and may be accelerated in athletes (Apley, 1981; Johnson & Brewer, 1987).

Paleopathology

The gross appearance of the lesion in dry bones conforms to the description detailed in the Pathogenesis section above. Dastugue & Gervais (1992) divide the progression of the lesion into three phases:

1. Necrotic phase: the sequestrum is not yet detached from the articular surface and is limited by a sharply defined border.
2. Exposition phase: the sequestrum is detached, exposing the crater in the underlying spongiosa.
3. Cicatrization phase: a layer of new bone lines the crater.

Zimmerman & Kelly (1982) describe a similar sequence. The 'joint mouse' surface may mirror the bone defect (Rothschild & Martin, 1993) though occasionally the resemblance may be distorted by remodeling of either the loose joint body or the crater. The latter is particularly apt to occur by revascularization and new bone formation if the surface fragment maintains some degree of attachment to the joint surface. Joint space narrowing with osteophyte formation is an indicator of secondary degenerative joint disease.

Although osteochondritis dissecans is not normally very common among ancient populations (Mann & Murphy, 1990), Martín Oval & Rodríguez-Martín (1994) found a high percentage among the Guanches (ancient inhabitants of Tenerife, Canary Islands). Wells (1974) also found osteochondritis lesions more frequently in Romano-British and Anglo Saxon than in earlier Bronze age populations. Loveland et al. (1984) also described femoral condylar lesions in prehistoric bones from the U.S.A. Plains area.

A cautionary note about the diagnosis of osteochrondritis dissecans in archaeological bones was sounded by Birkett (1982), noting that small, irregularities representing normal variations in bone joint surfaces are difficult to separate from osteochondirits dissecans. An interesting example of bilateral osteochondritis dissecans with peripheral sclerosis in the humeral trochleae was noted by During et al. (1994) in the skeleton of the helmsman of the seventeenth century Swedish warship *VASA*, considered to be occupational lesions. Seventeen individuals with osteochrondirits lesions with peripheral sclerosis were found in a Merovingian populations (A.D. 500–725) in southern Germany (Schulz, 1981).

OSTEOCHONDROSES

A variety of conditions may produce osteochondroses of almost any epiphysis. These include trauma, steroid therapy and other diseases where the cause appears to be of an idiopathic nature. Multiple, simultaneous joint involvement may occur. The common features characterizing this group of conditions is the absence of an inflammatory element and their onset under age 10 years (Duthie & Bentley, 1987; Resnick, 1989a). With the exception of Scheuermann's and Freiberg's diseases, the osteochondroses are most commonly seen in males. Radiologically these diseases are heralded by increased joint density followed by subchondral radiolucency that leads to articular surface collapse and joint fragmentation (Helms, 1989).

Legg–Calvé–Perthes disease (juvenile deformans; osteochondritis of the hip; coxa plana; superior femoral epiphysitis; Perthes disease; Legg–Perthes disease; Legg–Calvé–Perthes–Waldenström's disease)

Definition, etiology, and epidemiology

Legg–Calvé–Perthes disease is osteochondrosis of the femoral head in children. Almost all authors agree the condition represents obstruction to the blood supply of the growing femoral head with resulting avascular necrosis. No definitive familiar or hereditary features have been identified, though more than one child in the same family can be involved. Affected children display some growth retardation.

It affects children from 3–10 years of age (average about 6 years) with a few cases at children's age extremes. Cases over age 12 are considered adolescent avascular necrosis and have a worse prognosis (Thompson & Salter, 1992). A disproportionately larger fraction of children come from low socioeconomic families. Blacks, Polynesians, American Indians and Australians enjoy a lower frequency of this problem than do Caucasians, Inuit, Japanese and Mongoloids (Duthie & Bentley, 1987). As in most other osteochondroses, males outnumber females about 4:1.

Pathogenesis and pathology

The disease is usually unilateral; in the 10 % of bilateral cases the onset in the two sides is not simultaneous but occurs successively at an interval of 2–4 years between them (Piulachs, 1959; Resnick, 1989a). The superior and anterolateral aspects of the femoral head are the most affected, showing deformation, flattening and widening with the femoral neck demonstrating shortening and widening, producing coxa vara. The final product is often described as a 'mushroom-shaped' femoral head that is commonly lower than the position of the greater trochanter. The acetabulum, too, is deformed, demonstrating flattening, elongation and an irregular articular surface. Indeed, the volume of the femoral head may so exceed that of the acetabulum that secondary subluxation of the hip results, together with the then inevitable degenerative joint disease. In the untreated case restoration and remodeling of the bone fixes the 'mushroom' shape of the femoral head that lacks the fovea capitis for ligamentum teres attachment (Mann & Murphy, 1990). Later an ischium varum deformation often occurs with medial displacement of the ischium producing a decreased diameter of the obturator foramen (Piulachs, 1959). In treated cases regeneration requires 2–5 years.

Radiology

The first radiological sign is that of decalcification of the femoral head (without narrowing of the joint space or alterations of the acetabulum: Brower, 1994), followed by flattening and fragmentation, characterized by increased radiological density mixed with the bands of radiolucency and disorganization of the skeletal architecture. The next stage involves increased flattening. The epiphyseal bone tissue covers the neck, producing the typical image of coxa plana and mushroom-shaped femoral head. The femoral neck is short and wide (Resnick, 1989a), showing coxa vara, and the acetabulum is longer than normal. The 'sagging rope' sign (a curved line that crosses the base of the femoral neck) is caused by the superimposition of the anterior margin of the flattened femoral neck (Resnick, 1989a; Murray et al., 1990). Metaphyseal cysts, radiolucent lesions that may simulate an abscess or tumor, are characteristic features of Legg–Calvé–Perthes disease (Resnick, 1989a).

All these pathological and radiological changes are grouped by Thompson & Salter (1992) into four different phases:

1. Growth arrest: immediately after the ischemic episode (interval: 6–12 months).
2. Subchondral feature: beginning of true Legg–Calvé–Perthes features (interval: 3–8 months).
3. Resorption: fragmentation appears (interval: 6–12 months).
4. Resolution: complete epiphyseal ossification with or without deformity of the femoral head.

Complications

Legg–Calvé–Perthes disease is an autolimiting condition with a strong tendency to spontaneous resolution, although its global prognosis is not as good as many authors believed years ago (Duthie & Bentley, 1987). It depends on the degree of deformity of the femoral head, the degree of osteonecrosis, the location of the lesion, and the age of the onset of the disease (the prognosis for children under 5 years of age is better than that for older children). The most important and common complication of Perthes' disease is degenerative joint disease that will appear in 38 % of the patients affected by the disease at the age of 6–9 years and 100 % of those affected at ten or more years of age (Thompson & Salter, 1992).

Paleopathology

The morphological changes detailed in the Pathogenesis and Pathology section, above, are overt and easily recognized in dry bones. Much more difficult, however, is the differentiation of Legg–Calvé–Perthes disease from other conditions producing similar changes. These include principally slipped capital femoral epiphysis, trauma and congenital dislocation of the hip. Mann & Murphy (1990) suggest that the first of these can be separated by its shortened femoral neck, but as we point out above, this can also be a feature of Legg–Calvé–Perthes disease. It may not be possible to separate multiple epiphyseal dysplasia (or even tricorrinophalangic syndrome) from Legg–Calvé–Perthes disease. McKusick's metaphyseal chondrodysplasia produces similar pelvic changes. Other rare mimicking conditions are juvenile hemochromatosis, Gaucher's disease, infantile hypothyroidism and several hemoglobinopathies (Wynne-Davies & Fairbank, 1982). Finally, coxa vara with a flattened femoral head and shallow acetabulum can follow Legg–Calvé–Perthes disease and be mistaken for evidence of femur head osteonecrosis or slipped capital femoral epiphysis (Murray et al., 1990). An adult female at the National Museum of Natural History (Smithsonian Institution), from Peru's Chicama valley, had a porous, mushroom-shaped femoral head with thickened trabeculae under the porous lesion (Ortner & Putschar, 1985).

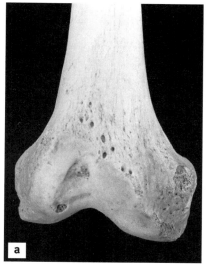
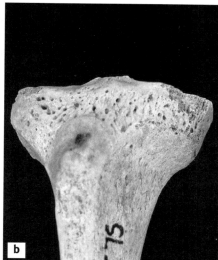

FIG. 5.6. **Osteochondritis dissecans; Osgood–Schlatter's disease.** (a) Note active dissecans lesion in the anterior portion of the femur's lateral condyle. (b) Demonstrates roughened tibial tubercle (Osgood–Schlatter's disease?). G14, G16. Adult male Guanches ca. 1000. MAT, OAMC.

Osgood–Schlatter's disease (anterior tibial apophysitis; surfer's knee; tibial traumatic epiphysitis)

Definition and epidemiology

This condition is simply osteochondritis of the tibial tuberosity. It is found most commonly in boys of 10–15 years of age (girls that do develop this lesion do so about 2 years earlier). More than one out of five is bilateral (Golding, 1984; Ortner & Putschar, 1985; Resnick, 1989b).

Etiology and pathogenesis

Speculations regarding its etiology revolve about two considerations: direct trauma to the tibial tuberosity or excessive traction of the patellar ligament that is rooted to the tuberosity. Earlier it had been suggested that such traction might interfere with blood flow to the tuberosity but it is now felt that the contractions (especially pliometric exercises) producing the injury actually results in an avulsion fracture of the tibial tuberosity (Piulachs, 1959; Kulund, 1990). The latter view is supported by the observation that is seen today particularly commonly among athletes especially in the fields of soccer or basketball. In a few cases the lesion has occurred in combination with late rickets (Sandritter & Thomas, 1981).

Paleopathology

Four features characterize the tibial tuberosity in this condition:
1. Thickening;
2. Irregular surface with calcification in adjacent areas (radiologic study often reveals a gap between the tuberosity and the tibia) (Fig. 5.6);

3. Fragmentation (some authors [Schinz et al., 1953] consider this the sine qua non for the diagnosis of this lesion);
4. Actual detachment of the tuberosity from the tibia.

This condition is an uncommon one in ancient populations (Mann & Murphy, 1990). A probable case of Osgood–Schlatter's disease was reported in the tibia of a late Saxon individual in England (Wells, 1968b).

Sinding–Johansson–Larsen's disease

Epidemiology and pathogenesis

This lesion is an avulsion fracture of the patella's lower pole (apex), induced by mechanisms similar to that noted above in Osgood–Schlatter's disease (trauma and/or excessive traction of the patellar ligament). Both unilateral and bilateral forms are seen. Its typical onset is in the early teens, but it may appear even earlier.

Paleopathology

The changes on the patellar apex are very similar to those listed for the tibial tuberosity in Osgood–Schlatter's disease.

Blount's disease (tibial osteochondrosis deformans; developmental tibia vara; nonrachitic tibia vara)

Definition and pathogenesis

Blount's disease is an osteochrondrosis of the tibial proximal epiphysis' postero-medial surface. Excessive weight applied to this area results in delay in growth of the medial tibial plate. Although all its features have not yet been explained, it is clear that genetic transmission as an autosomal dominant plays a major role. American Blacks are more commonly affected than Caucasians. It is an uncommon condition, presenting in two forms. The infantile form presents between ages 2 and 6 years and is usually bilateral, appearing when an often obese infant begins to walk. The epiphyseal plate is wider than normal and fragmented. The juvenile form appears at about 8–10 years, is usually unilateral, and is less common and less severe than the infantile form. The tibia and femur are rotated medially and the limb is shortened 1–2 cm.

Paleopathology

The medical concavity of the proximal tibial epiphysis is depressed with consequent widening of the epiphyseal plate. In the infantile form fragmentation of the affected area is common and in the very young there is even irregularity of the metaphysis. The juvenile form affects the same area, the posterior aspect of the medial concavity of the tibia's proximal epiphysis, but fragmentation is unusual, the epiphyseal bone dysplasia is lacking and metaphyseal irregularity is unusual. Internal rotation of the tibia and femur with limb shortening of 1–2 cm is common to both. A probable case of nonrachitic tibia vara (Blount's disease) was found in a medieval teenager from the ninth century in Switzerland (Lagier et al., 1991). The left tibia was 5.5 cm shorter than the right with a deformed epiphysis of the medial condyle sloping posterolaterally.

Osteochondrosis of the proximal tibia epiphysis

This extremely uncommon condition consists of osteochondrosis of the medial half of the proximal tibial epiphysis with features similar to those of Legg–Calvé–Perthes disease, and is a cause of bowing of the leg (Duthie & Bentley, 1987).

Necrosis of distal tibial epiphysis

Definition and pathogenesis

Reports of this condition are limited largely to radiological observations without clinical details. The distal tibial epiphysis is flattened (thus increasing its density) and fragmented. The appearance strongly resembles that of the process involved in Legg–Calvé–Perthes disease. Beyond this no data is available (Murray et al., 1990).

Haglund's disease (Sever's disease)

Osteochondrosis of the calcaneal tuberosity is the lesion constituting this entity. Its onset appears between 10 and 15 years

of age and spontaneous resolution over several weeks or months is the rule (Golding, 1984). Only radiological descriptions are available and they describe irregularity of the calcaneal tuberosity with fragmentation and increased density. No paleopathological reports of this condition have appeared.

Köhler's disease

Definition, pathogenesis, and pathology

Osteochondrosis of the tarsal navicular is known as Köhler's disease. Its onset usually occurs between 4 and 8 years of age, though both younger and older ages have been reported. Males predominate (5:1), and while a clinical history of trauma can be extracted in many cases, the exact etiology remains unknown. Generally flattened, sclerotic tarsal navicular bones in children have been assumed to represent osteochondritis in the past. However, recent reports indicate that some such lesions in asymptomatic children are congenital variations (Helms, 1989; Resnick, 1989b; Murray et al., 1990). Complications are rare and the lesion usually heals due to revascularization without therapy in 2 or 3 years. The navicular is deformed into the appearance of a biconcave lens of irregular contour, is often fragmented and smaller than normal. Radiologically it often appears as a thin, flat, dense plate.

Freiberg's disease (Köhlers II disease; Freiberg–Köhler's disease)

Definition and pathogenesis

Osteochondrosis of the metatarsal head usually involves the second metatarsal only, rarely the others simultaneously. It appears between 10 and 18 years of age and is one of the few osteochondroses that afflicts primarily females (3:1). The cause is usually attributed to trauma because of the frequency of a traumatic history and Freiberg (1914) himself cited a traumatic fissure on the articular surface in support of that etiological factor. More recently, however, Duthie & Bentley (1987) feel that the condition is a product of developmental anomalies in which the first metatarsal is shorter than the second, placing pressure on the latter. Most cases are unilateral.

Paleopathology

The involved metatarsal is shorter than normal, has a virtually absent neck and thickened distal portion. Its head is flattened, collapsed and shortened ('cup' shape) with an irregular articular surface. Radiologically the involved area is dense and sclerotic with diaphyseal cortical hypertrophy (Helms, 1989). In severe cases the head may separate from the shaft (Ortner & Putschar, 1985). Late complications include the development of degenerative joint disease and hyperostosis of the metatarsal diaphysis. An alleged first archaeological example of Freiberg's disease was found in a medieval adult British male (Anderson & Carter, 1993). The head of the second metatarsal showed destruction and collapse with dorsal bony overgrowth and the proximal phalanx had dorsal subluxation with osteophytes.

Epiphysitis of the first proximal phalanx of the foot

The principal signs of this condition are radiological, and not even very well documented (Duthie & Bentley, 1987). They include phalangeal radiodensity and irregular contour of the affected foot. These changes may predispose to *hallux rigidus*. No paleopathological cases of this condition have been recognized.

Scheuermann's disease (Scheuermann–Delahaye's disease; Scheuermann–Schmorl's disease; juvenile disco-genic disorder; juvenile thoracic kyphosis; adolescent kypho-sis; true adolescent kyphosis; vertebral epiphysitis)

Definition and epidemiology

Osteochondrosis of the apophyseal rings of the vertebral bodies is the lesion unique to this condition. Its onset usually occurs between 12 and 18 years of age although extension to an additional 5 years of this range has been reported. Some series report a male predominance while others show no gender predilection. While familial patterns suggestive of a genetic etiology have been described, traumatic influences are gradually gaining credibility. In some cases only one or two vertebrae may be involved while others have been seen in which the entire thoracic and upper lumbar spine is affected (Murray *et al.*, 1990), while frequently sparing the cervical and lower lumbar levels (Golding, 1984).

Pathogenesis and complications

The anterior–superior aspect of affected vertebral bodies undergo osteochondritic erosion and epiphyseal ring fragmentation with loss of height anteriorly, generating a vertebral body of cuneiform shape leading commonly to kyphosis and often scoliosis as well. The common presence of Schmorl's nodes may be related to disc degeneration. Spontaneous resolution has been observed, but untreated cases usually develop early spondylosis with kyphosis. Helms (1989) however, notes that if only a few vertebrae are involved the condition may not necessarily lead to kyphosis. In addition to the spondylosis with kyphosis that commonly characterize this condition, other complications include flattened intervertebral discs, disc hernias and rigid kyphotic deformity (Schinz *et al.*, 1953).

Paleopathology

The anatomic changes noted above are quite apparent in paleopathological specimens. Probable cases of Scheuermann's disease in antiquity have been identified from the Bronze age in Dorset, U.K.; the fifth century B.C. at Kamid-el Loz, Lebanon; the medieval period at Aebelholt Abbey in Denmark; and the Iron age from St. Richard's Road at Deal, Kent, U.K. (Anderson & Carter, 1994). The latter case is a juvenile male skeleton whose two lower thoracic vertebrae display irregular, linear defects in the central part of the superior surface of the vertebral body accompanied by slight kyphosis and Schmorl's nodes. These authors alert excavators to consider this disease, implying that the paucity of reported cases may represent an artifact related to its recognition.

Calvés disease (vertebra plana)

Definition and pathogenesis

This form of vertebral osteochondrosis is produced by aseptic necrosis of a vertebral body. It is rare, affects children between 2 and 6 years of age and involves only a single vertebra. In addition to interruption of blood supply, weight-bearing and occupational stress may play a role in its induction. The prognosis is benign since reactive changes often restore the original vertebral structure without permanent sequelae (Casagrande & Frost, 1955).

Paleopathology

The 'Calvé vertebra' is characterized by flattening and cuneiform deformation secondary to the aseptic necrosis of the vertebral body. Secondary kyphosis is not uncommon (Sandritter & Thomas, 1981). The diagnosis can be established if the following three features can be identified: (i) only one vertebra is involved; (ii) intervertebral discs are not involved; and (iii) the affected vertebra demonstrates increased radiological density. Although differential diagnosis must include skeletal cystic angiomatosis (the collapsed vertebrae look quite similar), this condition usually involves multiple vertebrae while disease described by Calvé is commonly limited to a single vertebra.

Panner's disease

In 1927, Panner described this rare condition as osteochondrosis of the distal humeral capitulum with pathological changes similar to Legg–Calvé–Perthes disease (Krebs, 1927). It involves the dominant arm of almost exclusively 4–10 year old boys (Resnick, 1989*a*) giving rise to a speculative hypothesis of a traumatic origin. Lack of supportive evidence led to considerations of genetic or endocrinological influences, but no universally accepted etiology has evolved. The condition is usually bilateral and spontaneous resolution over a 1 or 2 year period is the rule. Osteochondritis dissecans of the elbow can be differentiated on the basis of age at onset, because that disease occurs during adolescence or young adulthood.

Kienböck's disease (Lunate's malatia)

Definition and epidemiology

Osteochrondrosis of the lunate (or sometimes any other carpal bone: Duthie & Bentley, 1987) is an uncommon condition. Its relationship to trauma (and especially repeated microtrauma) is much more prominent than in osteochondroses at most other sites. Carpenters, air-drill or clinch machine operators are particularly susceptible. In addition, reduction in blood flow to the bone in patients with primary circulatory disorders, traumatic circulatory problems or degeneration and collapse due to ligament lesions can all result in osteochondrosis in the wrist. Some workers (Helms, 1989) still consider the etiology idiopathic. It appears in early adulthood or as late as 50 years of age, is usually (but not invariably) unilateral and commonly on the right side (Schinz et al., 1953; Piulachs, 1959).

Pathology

The usual osteochondrosis sequence of events occurs here as elsewhere: subchondral alteration, radiolucency and then usually (but not always: Helms, 1989) fragmentation, flattening, subchondral cysts and finally bone collapse with increased density. In addition the hamate often migrates proximally with associated shortening of the ulna (Piulachs, 1959; Kulund, 1990). Secondary degenerative joint disease occurs rapidly and is prominent in late lesions, especially those in which the affected carpal bone completely disappears and degenerative joint disease involves all the carpal bones (Schinz et al., 1953; Piulachs, 1959). Occasionally recovery from this lesion does occur, though continued hand use discourages this desirable result.

Preiser's disease (Preiser–Kohler–Mouchet disease; post-traumatic osteitis)

Osteochondrosis of the carpal navicular (scaphoid) bone usually provides a history of trauma or microtrauma, though the vascular factor cannot be excluded. It usually appears in adults and many authors consider it a form of occupational disease. The affected navicular is irregular and deformed. Pseudocystic lacunae limited by a dense, sclerotic line can be identified radiologically. The late stages reveal disintegration and complete absorption. No previous paleopathologic cases

have been reported, but Fig. 5.7 demonstrates an example from the Spanish Roman period, identified by Dr D. Campillo (personal communication) in a Barcelona collection.

Fig. 5.7. **Preiser's disease.** Note fracture and slight ischemic necrosis of carpal navicular (specimen length is 3.3 cm). C17. Adult, Roman period, Catalonia, Spain. Courtesy Dr D. Campillo. MAC.

Thiemann's disease

Osteochondrosis of the proximal interphalangeal joints of boys in the second decade also seems to be related primarily to trauma, though some with familial relationships have been described. Metacarpophalangeal, tarsometatarsal and interphalangeal toe joint involvement also can occur (Resnick, 1989a). The expected osteochondritic pathology of bone irregularity, fragmentation and sclerosis of the epiphysis is present.

Van Neck's disease

This is epiphysitis of the ischial tuberosity due to a traumatic lesion at the origin of the ischio-tibial tendons, generating a large hematoma with subsequent new bone formation (Duthie & Bentley, 1987).

Necrosis of the femoral head

Synonymy and epidemiology

Also called avascular or ischemic necrosis of the femoral head, its etiology is obscure. The blood supply of the femoral head makes possible aseptic necrosis on either a traumatic or non-traumatic basis. Intracapsular (transcervical and subcapital) fractures of the femoral head appear to be more common than extracapsular or intertrochanteric fractures (Resnick et al., 1989a). It has been seen also in a long list of other conditions including traumatic (especially posterior) hip dislocations which have a 50 % frequency of femur head necrosis (Ortner & Putschar, 1985); simple hip trauma without either fracture or dislocation; femur head epiphysiolysis; hemolytic anemia; corticosteroid therapy; Gaucher's disease; lupus erythematosus; fat or air embolism; limb immobilization; idiopathic (in adults, uncommon, 50% bilateral) and even degenerative joint disease (although Duthie & Bentley, 1987, question the latter). This is a disease of primarily male (4:1) adults between 30 and 60 years of age. In 30–50 % of cases both hips are involved. Such necrotizing events are much more common in the hip than in the remainder of the skeleton.

Pathogenesis and radiology

The femur head's blood supply comes from the anterior and posterior circumflex arteries and the artery of the round ligament. Circular anastomoses occur at the metaphysis where subsynovial vessels originate that pass into the epiphysis. Occlusion of these arteries produces bone necrosis. Avascular necrosis of the femur occurs in its head's central area that is the site of maximal stress and lesser blood supply (Golding,

1984). In late cases the femoral head morphology is profoundly deformed, assuming a flattened ('mushroom') shape with varus formation.

In living, modern patients Muñoz Gómez (1983) has described the radiological progression of this process through four stages:
1. Normal or osteoporotic bone status.
2. Irregularity, increased density and sclerosis of upper part of femoral head, but not subchondral fractures or joint space narrowing.
3. Spherical femoral head becomes deformed with a subchondral bone fragment separating from the head; sclerosis present.
4. Femoral head collapsed, articular destruction, osteoarthritis. If the articular surface is not altered, spontaneous resolution of this condition may occur in 25 % of the cases. In untreated cases secondary degenerative joint disease with joint space narrowing and hip osteophyte formation is the rule.

Paleopathology

Only a few of these cases have been reported in the paleopathology literature. Ortner & Putschar (1985) described a probable case in an Arkansas Native American Indian.

Primary necrosis of the medial femoral condyle

Epidemiology and etiology

About 8 % of persons affected by this recently-described condition are women over 50 years of age, and simultaneous bilateral cases are common. While numerous cases remain of idiopathic nature, in some it appears to have occurred as a compilation of corticosteroid therapy (Brower, 1994). Other diseases seen in these patients include cardiovascular disorders, diabetes mellitus, lupus erythematosus, diabetes and others (Muñoz Gómez, 1983). The lesion affects the weight-bearing portions of the medial femoral condyle, and only rarely the lateral condyle (Resnick et al., 1989b).

Pathology

The radiological progression has been defined as follows:
1. No changes or medial femoral condyle flattening with lucent areas mixed with reparative zones.
2. A condylar concavity of about 10–25 mm diameter surrounded by a band of osteosclerosis. Later an area of increased density with vaguely defined borders appears. These borders become more sharply defined

and radiolucency is seen over the lesion together with a line of calcified cartilage, but without fragment separation. It requires about 2 years to reach this point.

3. The calcified line and osteosclerotic halo disappear.
4. Large areas of osteosclerosis surround the lesion with flattening of the condyle, representing reconstruction and remodeling. An additional 2 years is usually required for the last two stages.

Very late phase cases demonstrate severe secondary degenerative joint disease. No such cases have been recognized in ancient human remains.

SLIPPED FEMORAL CAPITAL EPIPHYSIS (ADOLESCENT COXA VARA; EPIPHYSIOLYSIS OF THE FEMORAL HEAD; EPIPHYSIOLYSTESIS; EPIPHYSEAL COXA VARA)

Definition, epidemiology, and etiology

Slipped femoral capital epiphysis is an adolescent condition characterized by an inferior-posterior displacement of the femoral capital epiphysis, fusing with the neck in that position. Its etiology is not yet completely understood. About 7 % (or greater: Rennie, 1967) demonstrate a familial relationship, leading Rennie (1967) to suggest these are of genetic origin transmitted as a recessive with low penetrance. Some authors emphasize that the epiphyseal union with the neck in these cases is weak and that this point is a focus of shear stress (Duthie & Bentley, 1987). It occurs during the rapid growth of adolescence, coinciding with puberty (ages 10−15 years in boys, 2 years earlier in girls); thus it is rare under age 8 or over 17 years (Ortner & Putschar, 1985; Murray et al., 1990). Males predominate (2.5:1) and Blacks are affected twice as frequently as Caucasians (Ortner & Putschar, 1985; Resnick et al., 1989a). The condition is bilateral in only about 25 % of the cases (Duthie & Bentley, 1987) and among these, simultaneous involvement is seen in no more than about 10 % (Carnevale & Salvati, 1971). The unilateral cases are more common on the left side.

Pathology and complications

Movement of the femoral head during development of this condition is gradual, slipping slowly into its inferior-posterior position. The degree of such 'slippage' varies from mild to severe. In long-standing cases an osseous callus is formed at the union of the femoral head with its neck and the proximal aspect of the metaphysis can be absorbed during remodeling. The medial cortex of the femoral diaphysis may become thickened from the secondary stress applied to it by

this deformity (Resnick et al., 1989a; Murray et al., 1990). The growth plate demonstrates an upward convex contour and is little altered because it remains with the epiphysis. In severe cases the cartilage may suffer pathological changes similar to those of degenerative joint disease. Radiographically foci of osteopenia and areas of bone condensation are often present (Schinz et al., 1953).

MacEwen (1992) identifies three, classifiable degrees of severity based on the degree of epiphyseal slipping expressed as a fraction of the femoral neck width: (i) less than one-third; (ii) more than one-third but less than one-half; and (iii) more than one-half. Murray et al. (1990) describe an unusual form of this condition with backward and outward displacement of the capital epiphysis, calling it 'reverse slipped epiphysis.'

The most frequent complication of this condition is the development of secondary degenerative joint disease whose severity is usually related to the degree of head displacement. Bilateral cases are also susceptible to more severe complications. Others include varus deformity, shortening and widening of the femoral neck and osteonecrosis.

Paleopathology

The findings described in the preceding section can be clearly visualized in paleopathological specimens.

Differential diagnosis

- Rickets: This can be excluded by the normal thickness of the epiphyseal plates, normal bone density and the normal pattern in the remainder of the skeleton.
- Idiopathic coxa vara: Exclude this on the basis of the absence of femoral neck hypoplasia or epiphyseal plate alterations (Murray et al., 1990).
- Tuberculosis of the hip: Tuberculosis has prominent demineralization of the femoral head and acetabulum without epiphyseal slippage (Duthie & Bentley, 1987).
- Legg–Calvé–Perthes disease: This disease involves deformation of the femoral head but no slippage.
- Congenital dislocation of the hip: This condition creates a new joint for the femoral head that does not occur in slipped femoral capital epiphysis.

An advanced degree of secondary degenerative joint disease may not be seen as frequently in paleopathological specimens as in modern ones because the prognosis during the first 20 years after diagnosis is good or excellent (Murray et al., 1990).

Ortner & Putschar (1985) describe a male whose remains were excavated from a Chacama, Peru site and are now housed at the National Museum of National History (Smithsonian Institution). These bones demonstrate a slipped femoral capital epiphysis with a well-defined ligamentum teres, short and thickened femoral neck, an identifiable growth plate and well-organized trabecular structure − features they feel that differentiate this condition from Legg–Calvé–Perthes disease.

HYPERTROPHIC OSTEOARTHROPATHY

(TOXIC HYPERTROPHIC OSTEOPATHY; MARIE-BAMBERGER'S DISEASE; PNEUMONIC HYPER-TROPHIC OSTEOARTHROPATHY)

Definition and epidemiology

Hypertrophic osteoarthropathy demonstrates a symmetrical pattern of new bone formation on the diaphyses of the tubular bones of the appendicular skeleton with peripheral arthritis. Etiology is unknown, though some evidence suggests it represents a response to increased peripheral blood flow (Jaffe, 1972; Golding, 1984). The primary form of the disease is called 'idiopathic pachydermoperiostosis' or, simply, 'pachydermoperiostosis.' Only a small minority (3–5 % of all cases of hypertrophic osteoarthropathies) fall into this group (Howell, 1987; Resnick & Niwayama, 1989a). These are of genetic origin and follow two different inheritance patterns: a more common, dominant pattern affects primarily males in a severe form (Wynne-Davies & Fairbank, 1982) and a milder recessively-inherited pattern. Usually these are accompanied by skin lesions (Swoboda, 1972). The idiopathic form has a long evolution and usually does not shorten life expectancy.

The secondary form of the disease was formerly called 'pulmonary hypertrophic osteoarthropathy,' but when evidence accumulated that extrapulmonary conditions could cause this condition it was changed to 'secondary hypertrophic osteoarthropathy.' Diseases that have been related to this form include bronchogenic carcinoma, congenital cyanotic heart disease, pulmonary fibrosis, tuberculosis, bronchiectasis, empyema, pleural neoplasia, polycythemia vera, dysentery, pyelonephritis, extrathoracic carcinomas, alcoholism, bacterial endocarditis, auricular myxoma, aortic aneurysm, cirrhosis, Hodgkin's disease, ulcerative colitis, intestinal neoplasia, thyroid diseases and others. Of these, modern experience indicates that intrathoracic cancer is the most common cause (Lax et al., 1981). When the primary disease is treated the skeletal lesions resolve. Most cases appear in the older age group. When detected in children the lesions are usually related to congenital intrathoracic lesions (Wynne-Davies & Fairbank, 1982).

Pathology

Typical pathologic features (called Marie's signs) are widening of the digits, skeletal disturbances and joint alterations (Duthie & Bentley, 1987). These include:

1. Periosteal new bone formation of long and short tubular bones without endosteal bone deposition.
2. Clubbing of fingers and toes, especially the distal phalanges.
3. Lesions are symmetrical.
4. New bone can be separated from the cortex.
5. Mid-diaphysis is most common site.
6. If epiphyses are involved the lesion is indistinguishable from degenerative joint disease (Wynne-Davies & Fairbank, 1982; Zimmerman & Kelley, 1982). However, this condition does spare the bone ends and tendon insertions (Ortner & Putschar, 1985).

The most commonly involved sites are the wrist (radius-ulna), ankle (tibia-fibula) and the knee. The femur, humerus, metatarsals, metacarpals and the first and second phalanges are involved much less frequently while only in the most advanced cases does this condition affect the clavicle, ribs, scapula, pelvis, spine and malar bones (Revell, 1986; Howell, 1987). The idiopathic form, however, is more apt to show calvarial and skull base enlargement as well as paranasal and frontal sinuses, while the vertebrae in that form demonstrate a mixed radiographic pattern of rarefaction and sclerosis.

Radiological features

Characteristic features of hypertrophic osteoarthropathy are symmetrical diaphyseal periostitis of long and short tubular bones. Osteoporosis in periarticular areas is common (Murray et al., 1990), but the articular space is not narrowed nor are skeletal erosions apparent (Golding, 1984). Densities at ligament and tendon insertions have been observed (Bullough, 1992).

Differential diagnosis

The idiopathic form of hypertrophic osteoarthropathy should be differentiated from the secondary form on the basis of the former's appearance early in life because it is of genetic origin. Rarely hyperthyroidism will produce hypertrophic osteoarthropathy but that is limited to the upper limbs. Congenital finger and toe clubbing can also be excluded on the basis of age. Epiphyseal involvement produces a picture indistinguishable from degenerative joint disease. Absence of axial skeleton and skull involvement as well as absence of endosteal apposition in hypertrophic osteoarthropathy are features useful to exclude treponematosis, fluorosis and hypervitaminosis A. The symmetrical nature of the lesions can also be employed to exclude melorheostosis (Martínez-Lavín et al., 1994).

Paleopathology

Allison et al. (1976) reported a case from the area of Ica, Peru from the Huari culture about A.D. 1000. The looted tomb revealed only a few bones; the only tubular bone present was a femur with an enormously thickened diaphysis due to periostitis. Because it was a femur and in such an advanced state, the authors felt that the primary, idiopathic form of hypertrophic osteoarthropathy was the most probable diagnosis. The study by Pineda et al. (1987) suggests this criterion is not an absolute one. Gladykowska-Rzeczycka & Prejzner (1993) describe an adult male skeleton from a medieval cemetery in Poland in which extensive diaphyseal periostitis on the forearm and lower leg bone were clearly evident, and without epiphyseal or metaphyseal involvement. Radiologically the stratified layers of periosteal new bone were obvious together with focal osteopenic foci in the subperiosteal area. The authors felt these changes were most consistent with a secondary (pulmonary) form of the disease.

Two further examples were found by Martínez-Lavín et al. (1994) during an examination of 1000 skeletons in a Mesoamerican osteological collection at the National Museum of Anthropology in Mexico City. The first was a young adult female found in a tomb on the island of Jaina just off the western coast of Mexico's Yucatan peninsula, a Maya site from the Classic period (A.D. 300–900). Both tibiae and fibulae demonstrated a multilayered thickening due to new bone formation of their cortical surfaces without endosteal apposition. The axial skeleton was uninvolved. A single terminal digit was truncated and the authors could not be certain whether this was an antemortem or postmortem loss. The second case was that of a young adult male from the Ticoman site of Central Mexico dating to the Formative period (2000 B.C.–A.D.100). These bones revealed widespread, shaggy periostosis involving tibiae, fibulae, femora radii, ulnae and metatarsal bones. Two distal toe phalanges demonstrated prominent remodeling changes consistent with digital clubbing. No alterations of the axial skeleton or skull were noted. Radiographs showed widespread periosteal proliferation of the tubular bones without marrow involvement. Two examples of hypertrophic osteoarthropathy from pre-Hispanic Mexico were noted by Martínez-Lavín et al. (1994). A young adult male and female were found to demonstrate hypertrophic periostitis of both tibiae and femora with lesser involvement of other long bones but without axial involvement. The male had distinct digital clubbing. An example of secondary osteoarthropathy (Marie-Bamberger disease) with iliosacral synostosis was identified in a female skeleton from the Slav period (ca. A.D. 800) (Arendt & Ullrich, 1970).

PART SIX

Joint diseases

DEGENERATIVE JOINT DISEASE
(OSTEOARTHRITIS; HYPERTROPHIC ARTHRITIS; DEGENERATIVE ARTHROPATHY; DEFORMING ARTHROPATHY)

Definition, epidemiology, and etiology

Degenerative joint disease (DJD) is a noninflammatory, chronic, progressive pathological condition characterized by the loss of joint cartilage and subsequent lesions resulting from direct interosseous contact within diarthrodial joints. Preconditions necessary to produce this disease are a lesion affecting cartilage that exposes the bone surfaces, and joint mobility that permits bone-to-bone movement, causing the new bone formations that are a principal feature of DJD. The disease is the most common form of joint pathology and is usually detectable during the fourth decade of life. Thereafter it is age-progressive and without gender predilection. DJD is commonly subclassified as either primary or idiopathic (80 % of cases) in which no cause is evident, and secondary in which the joint has been altered by some other disease or event. The latter may be physical (trauma, congenital hip dislocation), infectious, metabolic (rickets, ochronosis), vascular (osteochondritis dissecans); neurotrophic (peripheral neuropathy) or other arthritis type (rheumatoid) in addition to extra-articular causes (obesity, occupational stress, congenital deformities, diaphyseal angulations or limb asymmetry).

Pathology and radiology

Principal features of DJD

These include (i) loss of the cartilage (perhaps due to loss of chondroitin sulfate in its matrix) normally covering the central areas of bone ends in diarthrodial joints with consequent exposure of the bone surface within the joint; (ii) bone remodeling producing focal nodules of new bone formation at the bone margins (osteophytes, 'lipping') and calcification of cartilage; (iii) small (up to 1 cm) cysts and surrounding sclerosis within the bone in areas devoid of a cartilaginous cover; (iv) eburnation (a smooth, shiny, polished surface produced by bone-to-bone contact in cartilage-free areas during joint movement and (v) fibrotic, thickened capsule (late). Radiological features include nar-rowing of joint space (a nonspecific change produced by many other forms of joint disease), as well as visualization of the subchondral cysts and their surrounding sclerosis in addition to the osteophytes. Epiphyseal osteoporosis may be due to immobility (Amillo et al., 1991). Many different joints can be involved by DJD but the large, weight-bearing joints (especially those of the lower extremities) are usually affected earliest and most commonly. The reader should understand that the features listed above are so regularly present in joints affected by DJD that no further comment about their presence is offered in the individual locations that follow below unless they differ in some unique way.

Locations of DJD

Knee

This is the most commonly involved joint, especially in women. The femur usually displays greater deformity than the tibial plateau, and joint mice (loose fragments of partly calcified cartilage) are common (Fig. 6.1 and 6.2). The medial or lateral femorotibial compartments are commonly affected, often accompanied by changes in the femoropatellar as well, the latter often showing the earliest changes. Knee subluxation may occur in later stages. Genus varum production is common.

Hip

This joint is also a common target of DJD (Thillaud, 1996), being seen in more than half of persons over 60 years of age, particularly also in women. Acetabular osteophytes are prominent, and the femoral head may reveal a 'mushroom' type of deformation, contributing further to limb shortening secondary to joint space loss.

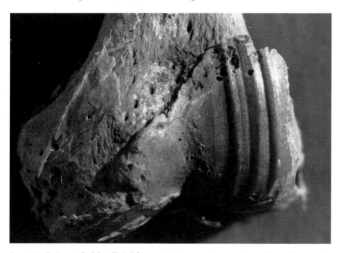

FIG. 6.1. **Osteoarthritis, distal femur.** Note massive new bone formation and eburnation with production of grooves separated by ridges. DK2, Aut. 12. Elderly Egyptian male spontaneously mummified. A.D. 300. PBL.

FIG. 6.2. **Osteoarthritis, patella.** Bone-to-bone movement has produced a pattern of ridges and grooves complementary to that of distal femur shown in Fig. 6.1. DK2, Aut. 12. Elderly Egyptian male spontaneously mummified. A.D. 300. PBL.

FIG. 6.3. **Osteoarthritis (degenerative joint disease), shoulder.** Note osteophytes at glenoid cavity border (a) and at margins of humerus head (b). G39, G40. Adult male Guanche ca. A.D. 1000. MAT, OAMC.

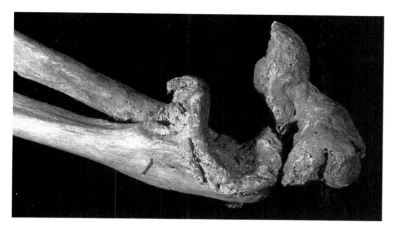

FIG. 6.4. **Osteoarthritis, elbow.** Extensive new bone formation over joint surface and margins, all areas, probably post-traumatic. E330. Modern case. CMNH.

Ankle and foot

With the exception of the first tarsometatarsal joint and subsequent production of hallux valgus or rigidus, DJD in these areas is usually secondary to trauma.

Sacroiliac

DJD is most commonly secondary to occupational stress with osteophyte formation in the superior and inferior margins with incomplete or complete joint ankylosis (Brower, 1994).

Shoulder

Trauma secondary to occupational stress is the usual etiology of DJD in the glenohumeral joint where both the fossa and the humeral head display the effects of DJD (Fig. 6.3). Involvement of the acromial end of the clavicle may cause its subluxation in the elderly.

Elbow and wrist

Rarely involved except secondary to trauma (Figs. 6.4 and 6.5) (including occupational) or rheumatoid arthritis (Golding, 1984). An exception, especially in females, is involvement of the trapeziometacarpal joint of the thumb with subluxation of the metacarpal head or the trapezioscaphoid joint.

Hand

Multiple digit involvement is common. Osteophytes of the distal interphalangeal joints (Heberden's nodes) or the proximal (Bouchard's nodes) are usually prominent.

Temporomandibular joint (TMJ)

This joint involvement by DJD is usually secondary to extreme lateral extension of the mandible in an effort to approximate several teeth during mastication in an individual who has suffered extensive tooth loss (see Fig. 14.6).

Variant form of DJD

While this condition is controversial, many consider it a unique form of DJD (Cobby et al., 1990). Its distinctive char-

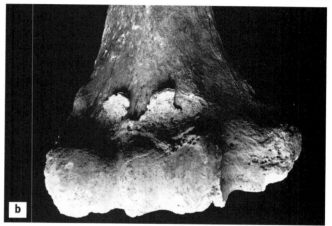

FIG. 6.5. **Osteoarthritis, elbow.** Note osteophytes on trochlear margin and coronoid fossa of distal humerus (b) and new bone formation in olecranon fossa (a). G41, G42. Guanche ca. A.D. 1000. MAT, OAMC.

acteristic is erosive osteoarthritis. Involvement of the distal and proximal interphalangeal joints of the hand and the first metacarpophalangeal joint is almost always seen but other joints (TMJ, acromioclavicular, elbow, sacroiliacs, symphysis pubis and even cervical spine) may accompany the hand lesions. A female predilection is clear.

Paleopathology

DJD is the most frequently identified disease in archaeological bones, though a lack of standardization of features required for qualitative and quantitative analysis limits comparison of results by different authors (Ortner & Putschar, 1985). The elbow, hip, knee and foot joint changes are most frequently seen in dry bones. Some employ principally eburnation as the diagnostic criterion (Cockburn et al., 1979) while others include osteophytes, subchondral cysts and/or sclerosis as well as joint surface pitting and alteration of joint surface contours (J. Rogers et al., 1987).

In Canadian Inuit archaeological samples Merbs (1983) found greater involvement of lower limbs and lumbar spine in males while lesions of the TMJ and thoracic spine predominated in females, consistent with stresses in these respective locations according to their occupational activities. Similarly lesions of a northern California hunting–gathering coastal population (A.D. 500) were predominantly in the lower spine, hands and feet, at a frequency intermediate between that of sedentary prehistoric agriculturists from the Pecos Pueblo site in New Mexico and that of the Arctic Inuit (Jurmain, 1990). In a study of aboriginals (Guanches) from Tenerife (Canary Islands), Rodríguez-Martín (1995c) also found a gender difference in DJD location patterns. Principal involvement in upper limb joints (elbow and shoulder) in females versus lower limb (hip) in males was consistent with stresses predicted from archaeologically determined subsistence activities.

Involvement of the TMJ by DJD was found in 20 % of skulls from Sayala (in ancient Nubia, Egypt) by Strouhal & Jungwirth (1980), who believed it to be the consequence of extensive tooth loss due to rapid abrasion, periodontal disease and caries. Extensive antemortem molar tooth loss was also blamed for a high frequency of DJD in a different set of Nubian skulls found by Sheridan et al. (1991). A similar explanation was offered for the high frequency of TMJ involvement in aboriginals of Gran Canaria (Canary Islands) by Pérez (1980–81). On the other hand, Pérez & Martinez (1995) found DJD of the TMJ in five of seven mid-Pleistocene skulls from central Spain, related it to their craniofacial architecture and felt this supported the hypothesis of phylogenetic proximity among the hominoids and Neanderthals.

An interesting example of the DJD variant known as an erosive osteoarthritis was identified in an approximately fifteenth century adult female near London with a characteristic pattern of hand lesions in the central joint areas, new bone proliferation and ankylosis (J. Rogers et al., 1991).

DEGENERATIVE DISEASE OF THE SPINE (VERTEBRAL OSTEOPHYTOSIS; SPONDYLOSIS; DEFORMING SPONDYLOSIS)

Definition and epidemiology

This designation includes the alterations produced by intervertebral disk degeneration, spinal osteophytosis, spinal ligament disturbances and degenerative joint disease of the articular facets that lead to nerve or blood vessel compression. These changes are uncommon under age 30 years and are age-progressive thereafter, reaching 80–90 % involvement after age 75 years.

Pathology

Osteophytosis (marginal spondylosis)

Degeneration of the intervertebral disk permits closer approximation of the vertebrae. Irritation from vertebral contact at the vertebral margins stimulates the periosteum to form nodules of new bone (osteophytes) (Fig. 6.6) in such areas and whose growth can reach a size great enough to fuse the adjoining vertebrae, resulting in osseous ankylosis. The involved locations are those most commonly flexed: lower cervical (C5-C6), lower thoracic (T8-T9) and lower lumbar (L4-L5) (Duthie & Bentley, 1987). Porosity and pitting of the vertebral bodies is also often seen.

Apophyseal joint degenerative disease

The articular facets are synovial-lined joints and when involved by DJD they demonstrate lesions characteristic of DJD as described in the preceding section: loss of cartilage, subchondral sclerosis, porosity eburnation, etc. Most commonly affected are the lower cervical (C6-T1), upper thoracic (T2-T5) and lower lumbar (L2-L4) areas. Osteophytes in the transverse foramina of C2-C6 can compress the vertebral artery to the point of arterial flow insufficiency. In some areas nerve compression can occur.

Intervertebral disk hernia

These hernias do not always induce degenerative spine alterations but they can do so. The mechanisms are the same for all forms of disk hernia: the hernia results in narrowing the

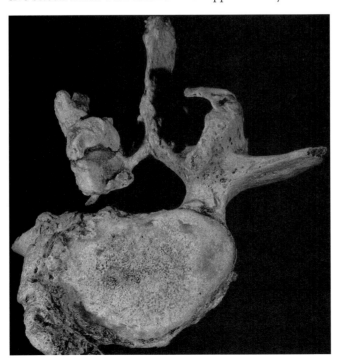

FIG. 6.6. **Degenerative joint disease, spine.** Extensive osteophytosis on vertebra with hemispondylosis. T899. Modern Case. CMNH.

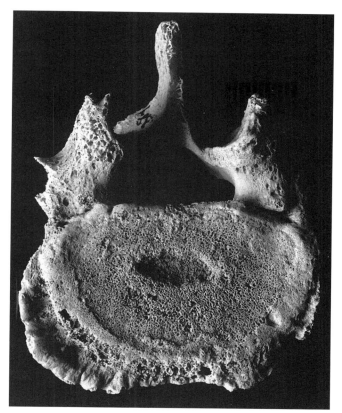

FIG. 6.7. **Osteoarthritis (osteophytosis) of vertebra and Schmorl's node.** Note osteophytes on vertebra and defect (Schmorl's node) in upper vertebral face. G51. Guanche ca. A.D. 1000. MAT, OAMC.

disk space, permitting contact between two adjacent vertebrae. The different forms of disk hernia include:

- Vertical disk hernia. In these cases the disk protrudes through the vertebral surface facing the disk and extends into the trabecular bone of the vertebral body (Fig. 6.7). The defect it creates is usually up to 5 mm in diameter and 1–1.5 cm in depth. The herniated defect is called Schmorl's node and these can be found in most individuals over 45 years.
- Lateral and anterior disk hernia. These cause osteophytosis, but produce no osteolysis.
- Posterior disk hernia. Causes osteolysis of the posterior margin of the vertebral surface and commonly induces radiculopathy.

Radiology

Disk space narrowing, subchondral cysts, Schmorl's nodes and osteophytosis are all radiographically detectable.

Paleopathology

Degenerative disease of the spine is among the most common lesions found in archaeological bones. Unfortunately the size of the disk space can not be assessed accurately in disarticu-

lated archaeological skeletons, but the horizontal growth of osteophytes is recognizable (J. Rogers et al., 1987). As yet no method of scoring severity has been standardized, but many workers follow that developed by Stewart (1958b):

1. Slight lipping at vertebra's inferior and superior margins;
2. Pronounced marginal lipping;
3. Extensive lipping with spurs;
4. Lipping that fuses two or more vertebrae.

A late Roman population from Sayala, ancient Nubia demonstrated a greater frequency of osteophytosis and apophyseal DJD among males than females involving principally the lower thoracic and lumbar areas (Strouhal & Jungwirth, 1980). A group of precontact North American aboriginals from Alabama showed severe DJD of the cervical area, interpreted by the investigators as stress from the common use of a tumpline to carry loads on the upper back (Bridges, 1994). Up to one-half of the aboriginal Guanches of Tenerife (Canary Islands) had degenerative disease of the spine in both males and females involving the lower cervical and lower lumbar spine, believed to reflect a vigorous lifestyle in the mountainous terrain of the island (Rodríguez-Martín, 1995c).

DIFFUSE IDIOPATHIC SKELETAL HYPEROSTOSIS (DISH) (FORESTIER'S DISEASE; FORESTIER–ROTÉS QUEROL DISEASE; SPONDYLOSIS HYPEROSTOTICA; SPONDYLITIS OSSIFICANS LIGAMENTOSA; DIFFUSE ENTHESOPATHIC HYPEROSTOSIS)

Definition, etiology, and epidemiology

Diffuse idiopathic skeletal hyperostosis (DISH) is an ossifying diathesis producing ankylosis of the spine due to ligament ossification without intervertebral disk disease. It is not a true arthropathy because neither cartilage nor synovium are involved. Its cause is unknown. It is rarely detected before age 40 years. Though more than half of adult autopsies show some degree of the changes seen in DISH, less than 15 % of these manifest symptoms during life (Bullough, 1992). About two-thirds of the cases are males.

Pathology and radiology

Diagnostic criteria are the following:

- Fusion of at least four vertebrae by bony bridges arising from the anterolateral aspects of vertebral bodies, involving the anterior and right aspects (Fig. 6.8). These bridges

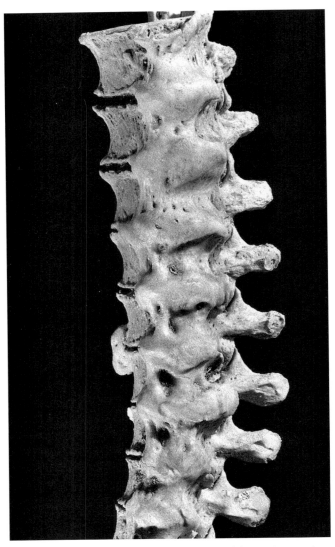

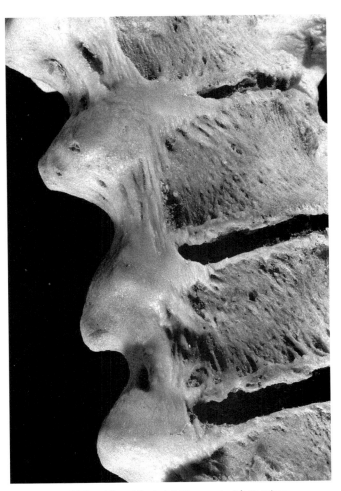

FIG. 6.9. **DISH (diffuse idiopathic skeletal hyperostosis).** Note how calcification is rooted to vertebral bodies. Also note absence of disk space involvement. T3350. Modern case. CMNH.

FIG. 6.8. **DISH (diffuse idiopathic skeletal hyperostosis).** Note the smooth-surfaced calcification ('dripping candle wax') on anterolateral surface of vertebral body. T3350. Modern case. CMNH.

Differential diagnosis between DISH and ankylosing spondylitis

In ankylosing spondylitis the individual is usually younger, syndesmophytes (bony bridges) are thinner and vertically oriented, apophysial and sacroiliac joints are fused and no extraspinal bone formation is seen (Roberts & Manchester, 1995:121).

Paleopathology

Prior to the 1981 study by J. Rogers *et al.* on British Saxon and medieval skeletons, ankylosing spondylitis and DISH were not separated. Crubézy (1990), however points out DISH was present in ancient populations and found it in a Shanidar 1 Neanderthal fossil (Crubézy & Trinkaus, 1992). That body had characteristic vertebral osteophytoses, most prominent on L3 and L5 as well as enthesopathies of several bones. The body of the prince of Stigliano, Italy (1511–1576) had diffuse calcification of the anterior longitudinal spinal ligament

have a flowing ('dripping candle wax') appearance that is rooted on the vertebral body in an oblique progression with dense and homogeneous structure (Fig. 6.9). They do not involve apophyseal joints (Crubézy, 1990). The process usually begins in the midthoracic spine.

- Intervertebral disk space is spared.
- Vertebral end plates are spared.
- Anterior longitudinal spinal ligament is ossified.
- Extraspinal ligamentous and muscular attachments are prominently calcified (enthesopathies). These include ischial tuberosities, ilial crests, pubic symphysis, trochanters, patella, femoral linea aspera, Achilles tendon attachment and the calcaneus. DJD, when present, is co-incidental but exaggerated.
- Sacroiliac joint may be fixed by several bony bridges but not by intra-articular bony ankylosis.

This set of features is also evident radiographically.

on the right side of the midthoracic spine with bony bridges between the vertebrae, calcification of the nucleus pulposus and diffuse exostoses at the elbows, shoulders, hips and knees including also a calcaneus spur (Fornaciari *et al.*, 1989*a*). A medieval case of DISH from Canterbury, England showed vertebral osteophytes of the lower thoracic and lumbar spine and enthesopathies of the radial tuberosity, ulnar olecranon, greater trochanter and calcaneal tuberosity. Though lacking the 'dripping candle wax' appearance Anderson *et al.* (1992) consider it an example of DISH. A 45 year old female skeleton from Herculaneum demonstrated not only characteristic spinal features but also had enthesopathies in the Achilles tendon attachment and bilateral calcaneus heel spurs. A twelfth–nineteenth century site from Sant Pere, Spain demonstrated a spine with classic DISH features in two vertebral blocks as well as many enthesopathies in characteristic areas (Puchalt *et al.*, 1996). Arriaza (1991) studied DISH in North and South America, finding a low frequency in hunter–gatherer populations, increasing in later sedentary societies.

Variant DISH

A condition characterized by calcification of the posterior spinal ligament of the midcervical spine has been described that can lead to spinal cord compression. The disks are not involved but most have hyperostosis of the anterior longitudinal spinal ligament and half show characteristic DISH extraspinal enthesopathies. Occasionally thoracic or even lumbar spine segments may also be involved (Murray *et al.*, 1990)

RHEUMATOID ARTHRITIS (PROGRESSIVE CHRONIC POLYARTHRITIS; PRIMARY CHRONIC POLYARTHRITIS; CHRONIC ARTICULAR RHEUMATISM; RHEUMATOID DISEASE)

Definition, etiology, and epidemiology

Rheumatoid arthritis (RA) is a chronic, nonsuppurative, systemic, inflammatory disease of synovial joints and connective tissue producing both articular and extra-articular signs and symptoms. Its cause is unknown but it demonstrates many features of an autoimmune nature. These include a high frequency of HLA-DR4 and/or DW4 histocompatibility antigens, the presence of an abnormal immunoglobulin (rheumatoid factor) in the blood and synovial fluid, the presence of many lymphocytes and plasma cells of the immune system in affected soft tissue some of which have been demonstrated to produce the rheumatoid factor locally, and a low level of complement in synovial fluid. In an anal-

ogy to acute rheumatic fever, it is tempting to speculate that an infectious agent sharing such tissue antigens may have initiated the immune response (Pitzen & Rössler, 1993). This may then have been perpetuated by continual release of tissue antigens from the necrotizing lesions. However, this concept has received no investigative confirmation, nor have a host of others that have suspected climate, diet, or alterations of vascular, endocrine, metabolic, or other systems. About 2 % of the adult population is affected by RA (and three-quarters of these are women), whose onset begins between 20 and 50 years of age.

Natural history

Clinical stages

While variations abound, RA commonly passes through a succession of three stages.
- Stage 1. Simple synovitis showing lymphocytic infiltrate and proliferation of the synovial membrane ushers in the disease. Fingers, wrists and later elbow, shoulder, knee, ankle, and foot joints are affected.
- Stage 2. The inflammatory lesion in this stage has resulted in necrosis of the synovium with an intense local inflammatory response ('pannus'). It advances as a frontal process, extending across the joint cartilage itself, including the cartilage in its necrotizing process. Cartilaginous destruction exposes the underlying bone where the process results in focal areas of cortical erosion, bone destruction and reactive sclerosis (subchondral radiological 'cysts' and pitting lesions) with more peripheral bone becoming osteoporotic. Articular movements are limited and tendon rupture may occur.
- Stage 3. Responses to the destructive processes of stage 2 produce joint deformity with capsular distention and tendon rupture. Ulnar finger deviation is common together with subluxation at the metacarpophalangeal level. Muscular atrophy and fibrous ankylosis occurs, the latter often ultimately progressing to bony ankylosis.

Joint involvement

The pattern of joint involvement tends to conform to the inclusion of several features. The condition is polyarticular (involves multiple joints) and is commonly bilaterally symmetrical. The early lesions usually involve the small joints, especially those of the hands (Figs. 6.10 and 6.11). Interphalangeal joint involvement (with the exception of the second) is especially common. These and the metacarpophalangeal joints are affected in 85 % of the cases. The foot is also frequently targeted by the disease. Later the knee (most commonly involved large joint), shoulder, elbow, wrist (Fig. 6.11) and TMJ become part of the disease as does the spine (particularly the cervical segment) where erosions, disk space narrowing and even ankylosis results (Fig. 6.12). In one-third of these the odontoid is involved by erosions creating the potential for disastrous complications that can threaten the underlying spinal cord's integrity. In about half of the cases other joints are affected.

Narrowing of the joint space is a common form of change and bone erosion at the joint margin induced by the cartilage-necrotizing inflammation are hallmarks of RA, but the joints show little evidence of any reparative (new bone formation) response to the intense inflammation. Indeed, weakening of soft tissue integrity may even result in subluxations or dislocations.

Systemic effects

In addition to fever, weight loss, anemia and fatigue, specific extra-articular manifestations are common, especially during the second stage of the disease. These include:

- Skin phenomena: rheumatoid nodules (foci of necrosis in subcutaneous tissue with reactive, inflammatory swelling), especially at bony prominences, tendons, joint capsule, etc.
- Vasculitis: small blood vessel inflammation with thrombosis (clotting).
- Enlarged lymph nodes.
- Eye involvement: inflammation of almost any ocular structure.
- Visceral involvement: inflammation of the lung, pericardium, spleen (Felty's syndrome), kidneys, brain, and gastrointestinal system.
- Nerve: inflammation (neuropathy) or compression by inflamed tissue (carpal tunnel syndrome).
- Liver: inflammation (hepatitis).
- Amyloidosis (deposit of unique protein in many body tissues causing tissue death, commonly by kidney failure).
- Blood: immunologically detectible ('seropositve') unique serum protein – 'rheumatoid factor'.

Radiology

In stage 1 radiology can detect only periarticular osteoporosis, cortical thinning and early diaphyseal periostitis. In stage 2 marginal erosions of affected joints appear as well as decreased joint space (cartilage destruction effect) and central subchondral cysts in large joints. In stage 3 the more severe and advanced effects become apparent: irregular surfaces, subluxation, osteoporosis, ankylosis, and joint deformity (described below).

Paleopathology

Differential diagnosis

DJD can be separated by the age group, location and symmetry of the lesions, marked osteoporosis and ankylosis of RA

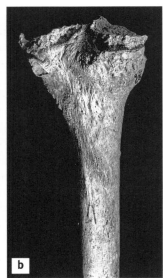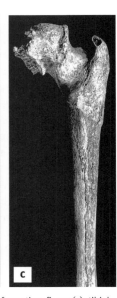

Fig. 6.10. **Rheumatoid arthritis.** Note ulnar deviation and paw formation, finger (a); tibial menisci calcification (b) and femur head deformation and erosion (c). Case 1. Late Roman. Catalonia, Spain. Courtesy Dr D. Campillo. MAC.

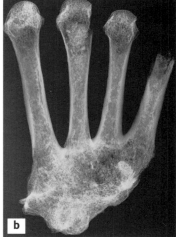

Fig. 6.11. **Rheumatoid arthritis.** (a) Bony ankylosis of carpal and metacarpals with erosions. (b) X-ray: ankylosis. Case 16. Menorca, Spain. Date? Courtesy Dr D. Campillo. MAC.

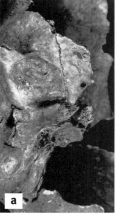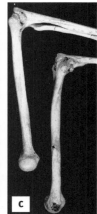

Fig. 6.12. **Rheumatoid arthritis.** Erosion and deformation in glenoid cavity of temporo-mandibular joint (a). (b) and (c) ankylosis of both elbows. Case 1. Late Roman, Catalonia, Spain. Courtesy Dr D. Campillo. MAC.

(the latter unusual in DJD). However DJD and RA can coexist. Ankylosing spondylitis commonly involves the sacroiliac joints and spine in a characteristic manner. Gout lesions are less symmetric than RA. Psoriatic arthritis presents both asymmetry and the typical 'pencil and cup' deformity.

As recently as 1974, Short noted that RA could be traced back to the seventeenth century by literary methods but paleopathology had no earlier convincing examples. While J. Rogers *et al.* (1987) indicate that RA is the least common arthropathy likely to be found in ancient bones, it is now clear that RA was present in archaeological populations. Its recognition, however, has probably been hampered by poor preservation of hand and foot bones as well as misdiagnosis of DJD, and its frequency most likely diminished because of the younger age at death in ancient societies. In addition, the disease may be in the process of evolution (Dieppe, 1989). Another factor that has been suggested by Rothschild & Woods (1991) is that trabecular loss under RA erosions contributes to poor preservation of the lesion in the postmortem environment. They also note that joint fusion in RA occurs primarily in individuals treated with adrenal cortical steroids.

Probably the earliest suggestion of the finding of RA in ancient remains was by Ruffer (1918) in a third dynasty mummy with a distal and middle phalangeal ankylosis, a questionable diagnosis unsupported by other RA features. Lipping with minimal erosion in many joints of a Native American from Illinois led Morse (1978) to suggest RA, but again the changes are of unsatisfactory degree and specificity. Characteristic lesions in both hands of a 40–50 year old male from a tenth or eleventh century site in England included subarticular erosions and cysts that led J. Rogers (1981) to suggest RA. A medieval adult specimen from the Natural History Museum of London had bilateral ankylosis of most tarsometatarsal joints and interphalangeal ankylosis of the right great toe as well as associated osteoporosis that Ortner & Putschar (1985) feel could be RA. They also believe RA could be responsible for the changes in an undated Alaskan skeleton. Those lesions included spine and rib fusion, apophysial joint involvement in thoracic and lumbar spine, distal femur erosion and porosity, pubic symphysis erosion and metacarpal changes.

A late Roman Iron Age adult Danish male had RA-like erosions of several metacarpals and a Danish early Bronze Age adolescent presented carpal and metacarpal erosions of possible RA nature (Bennike, 1985). Rothschild *et al.* (1988) described six individuals (3000–1000 years B.C.) for North America (Alabama) with very characteristic RA-like symmetric, lytic erosions in peripheral joints without vertebral syndesmophytes, sacroiliac changes or evidence of reactive inflammatory responses as well as characteristic hand and feet changes and including also odontoid erosions in two cases. In a 50+ year old female skeleton from modern Sudan dated c. A.D. 700–1450, Kilgore (1989) identified lytic, erosive lesions and subchondral cysts in wrist joints and metacarpophalangeal joints of the hands that are characteristic of RA.

In modern cases from the Todd collection at Cleveland's Natural History Museum, Rothschild *et al.* (1990) examined 59 individuals with known RA to establish parameters. The collection's prevalence was 4.2 % in females and 1.6 % in males. They identified the following features:
1. Erosive arthritis with smooth, rounded edges and smooth trabeculae.
2. Extensive symmetrical diarthrodial joint involvement, predominantly hands and feet.
3. Most severe were metacarpophalangeal, metatarsophalangeal and interphalangeal joints; least severe were distal interphalangeals.
4. Carpal involvement was common.
5. Radiography: marginal erosions with little or no sclerotic border; periarticular osteopenia uniformly present.
6. Most consistently involved: metacarpals, metatarsals, proximal and middle phalanges, carpals, humeri and ulnar styloids.

A study of modern surgical tibial plateaus and metacarpal head specimens by Leisen *et al.* (1991) both before and after maceration revealed partial or complete resorption of the articular surface, obliteration of the chondro-osseous junction and minimal periarticular osteophytosis. Surface perforations frequently exposed the epiphyseal trabecular bone and marrow space. Scanning electron microscopy demonstrated continuous resorption at the eroded surfaces and lining the lumen of many defects.

JUVENILE CHRONIC ARTHRITIS (STILL'S DISEASE; JUVENILE RHEUMATOID ARTHRITIS; JUVENILE CHRONIC POLYARTHRITIS)

Definition, etiology, and epidemiology

This condition is characterized by a noninfectious articular inflammation persisting for more than 3 months in an individual less than 16 years of age. Its cause is unknown. Onset occurs during the subadult period, peaking at 2–4 years and again about puberty. Like adult rheumatoid arthritis, a 3:1 predilection for females is seen. Its prevalence is more than one order of magnitude less than adult rheumatoid arthritis.

Pathology, radiology, and natural history

Features differing from adult rheumatoid arthritis include its monoarticular or at least pauciarticular (few joints) onset in over half the cases, not becoming polyarticular until later. In addition, large joints (especially the knee) and cervical spine commonly are affected early; in a minority both large and small joints are involved simultaneously. A distinctive feature is epiphyseal overgrowth, pronounced in the knee, though joint destruction is not inevitable. Nevertheless, unremitting progression in untreated cases can produce crippling, long-term results such as bony ankylosis, spinal apophysial fusion and even atlantoaxial subluxation. Like the adult form of rheumatoid arthritis, systemic effects suggestive of immunological disturbances occur, including lymphadenopathy, splenomegaly, pericarditis, rash, eye inflammation, erythema multiforme (focal skin inflammation) and amyloidosis, though the rheumatoid factor in the serum is not produced (seronegative).

Radiological features include periarticular osteopenia, periostitis of hand and foot tubular bones, early fusion of the growth cartilage, epiphyseal overgrowth and ankylosis. These features are often indistinguishable from those seen in hemophilic arthritis and may also closely resemble the epiphyseal overgrowth seen in joint disuse secondary to paralysis.

Paleopathology

Two features helpful in differentiating juvenile chronic arthritis from rheumatoid arthritis are the asymmetry commonly seen in the former and the fact that the spine often fuses in the juvenile form while erosion predominates in adult rheumatoid arthritis (Cockburn *et al.*, 1979). One paleopathological example comes from the precontact period on Kodiak Island, Alaska where the remains of a 30–35 year old female demonstrated destruction of joint surfaces, periarticular cystic erosion, porosity and hypertrophic bone formation in multiple joints, especially the knee, ankle and elbow as well as hands and feet (Ortner & Utermohle, 1981), believed to be late changes of juvenile chronic arthritis with onset during childhood.

ANKYLOSING SPONDYLITIS (AS)
(BECHTEREW'S DISEASE; HLA-27 SPONDYLO-ARTHROPATHY; MARIE-STRÜMPELL DISEASE; BAMBOO SPINE; POKER SPINE; ANKYLOPOIETIC SPONDYLITIS; RHEUMATOID SPONDYLITIS)

Definition, etiology, and epidemiology

Ankylosing spondylitis (AS) is a systemic, progressive, non-infectious, inflammatory disorder of connective tissue calcification involving the spine, sacroiliac and peripheral major joints. It is of unknown etiology, though the extraordinarily high (95 %) frequency of the histocompatibility complex antigen HLA-B27 suggests the operation of a genetic factor in this disease. Its prevalence is only about 1 in 2000 individu-

als. About 90 % of the cases are males. Usual age of onset lies between 15 and 35 years; it is rare before puberty (Murray *et al.*, 1990). Caucasians appear especially susceptible.

Pathology, radiology, and natural history

Development of the lesion

The initial change is inflammation of the joint, followed by granulation tissue formation that produces joint surface erosion. Fibrous tissue healing is followed by calcification, producing joint bony ankylosis. Spine ligaments pass through this same sequence.

Joint alterations, locations, and sequence

Sacroiliac joints
The disease is usually initiated by involvement of these joints, the earliest erosions occurring on the iliac side of the joint, followed by erosions on the sacral margins that are surrounded by a zone of reactive new bone formation (Brower, 1994). The end result of this progressive process is bony ankylosis of the joint and its associated ligaments. The presence of sacroiliac involvement is a *sine qua non* feature of ankylosing spondylitis. Other pelvic areas less regularly involved are the pubic symphysis (though usually not achieving complete ankylosis: Ortner & Putschar, 1985:411) and roughening of iliac crests and ischial tuberosities.

Spine
While sacroiliac involvement often initiates the disorder, it is the spine involvement that dominates both the clinical and

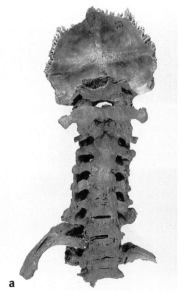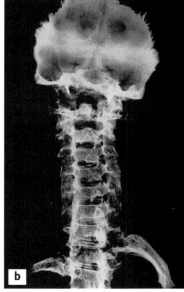

FIG. 6.13. **Ankylosing spondylitis.** (a) Note ligament calcification, ankylosis of upper spine to skull and rib ankylosis. (b) X-ray: ankylosis. Case 18. Late medieval, Catalonia, Spain. Courtesy Dr D. Campillo. MAC.

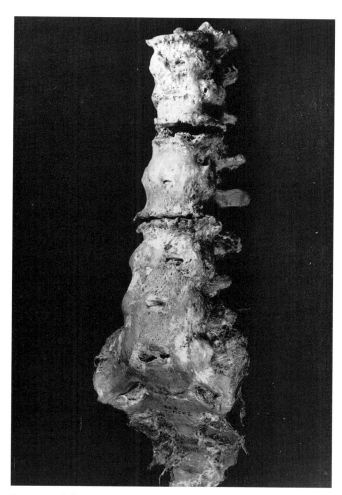

Fig. 6.14. **Ankylosing spondylitis.** Extensive calcification of anterior longitudinal and some adjacent spinal ligaments; disk edge elevations generate bamboo-like appearance. Courtesy Dr B. Arriaza. MAUT.

results in profound vertebral body osteopenia. Early erosion of the anterior vertebral body edge presents a radiological (lateral view) image of lost 'flairing' of the body, referred to by radiologists as a 'squaring' effect. The apophyseal involvement usually also terminates with fixation of the rib heads to the vertebrae.

Other joints

This disease often involves other joints where the sequence of events and final effects are indistinguishable from those of rheumatoid arthritis (RA). However the pattern of joints differs: AS tends to involve the major joints (the knee in 50 %, often with ankylosis (Golding, 1984), while RA regularly involves the small joints, especially the hands. AS also generates a more vigorous response of new bone formation and juxtacortical osteopenia is of lesser degree.

Paleopathology

Differential diagnosis

Features useful in the separation of AS from RA are listed in the preceding paragraph. AS is, however, a condition most frequently confused with DISH. Differentiating features between these two include the observation that in DISH the age of onset is usually later, the sacroiliac joints are not significantly involved, fewer vertebrae are involved, apophysial joints are not involved, syndesmophytes are horizontally oriented and enthesopathies are common (Zimmerman & Kelley, 1982). In less advanced cases the syndesmophytes of AS may be confused with osteophytes of degenerative disease of the spine. Features of syndesmophytes of AS that can help such separation include their vertical orientation, they arise 1–2 mm below the vertebral angle and they are more slender (Thillaud, 1996).

AS paleopathology reports

Reports of AS in the paleopathology literature are so abundant that we will comment primarily on some of those reported in the past several decades. A 1976 report by Steinbock identifies fusion of C1, 2 and 3 and apophysial joints to the skull of a New Mexico, U.S.A. adult male. A possible case of AS in Guanche (Canary Islands) aboriginal was noted by García Sánchez (1979) on the basis of ankylosis of two lumbar vertebrae with marked osteoporosis and a radiologic image suggestive of 'bamboo spine.' A similar radiological appearance was reported by Pérez (1980–81) in an aboriginal from Gran Canaria (Canary Islands) with thoracic and lumbar ankylosis and ligament ossification. A kyphotic, medieval 60 year old male from Geneva, Switzerland had fusion of all vertebrae, calcification of the anterior longitudinal spinal ligament, sacroiliac fusion, characteristic radiologic picture of AS and hyperostosis of iliac crests

the gross skeletal appearance. Following modern patients radiologically has helped establish the sequence of events. Erosion of the vertebral bodies' anterior angles in the T12-L1 region is usually the initial visible lesion that is followed by reactive sclerosis. Calcification of the periphery of the annulus fibrosus of the intervertebral disk follows promptly in the T11-12 and L1-2 disks, resulting in the formation of marginal, symmetric syndesmophytes (bony bridges) between the vertebrae. It is the anterior projection of these excrescences (in the region of the intervertebral disk area) at regular intervals as the disease spreads up and down the spine that has given rise to the simile 'bamboo spine' (Figs. 6.13 and 6.14). Simultaneously and subsequently calcification of the anterior longitudinal and other vertebral ligaments as well as involvement of the apophysial joints add to the fusion of these structures and assist in smoothing the bands of excrescences to produce the final effect of anterior and lateral calcification of the spine with regularly-spaced, smooth, elevated bands of calcification at the levels of the disk spaces. The resulting absence of vertebral movement and probably sharing of the weight-bearing by the surface calcification and other pelvic joints (Pérez, 1980–81). Ortner & Putschar (1985:413) suggest AS in the skeleton of an undated Alaskan aboriginal with fusion of several spine segments, sacroiliac joints and rib head fusion to vertebrae as well as a radiologic picture of vertebral squaring.

A dramatic example of advanced AS was presented by Gómez Bellard & Sánchez Sánchez (1989) in an eighteenth century 50 year old male from Granada, Spain in which the entire spine, sacrum and both iliac bones are fused into a single block. Apophysial fusion with costovertebral joints, bilateral syndesmophytes of the entire spine and appendicular joint involvement were also noted. Rodríguez-Martín (1989c) reported two examples in Tenerife (Canary Islands) aboriginals. In one of these both iliosacral joints, L4 and L5 with apophysial joints were fused, 'squared' and osteoporotic. The other adult male had incomplete but central fusion of one sacroiliac joint but many missing bones prevented further verification. An eighteenth century male from Granada, Spain examined by Yoldi et al. (1996) had extensive spinal and apophysial fusion with thoracic kyphosis.

PSORIATIC ARTHRITIS

Definition, etiology, and epidemiology

Psoriatic arthritis (PA) is a systemic disease with prominent cutaneous manifestations that can involve joints in a manner similar to that of RA and AS. Its etiology remains unknown but, like AS, the histocompatibility complex antigen HLA-B27 is present at increased frequency (60+ %) though lower than in AS (90+ %). This condition shows a strong familial tendency but the affected individuals are seronegative (do not have rheumatoid factor protein in their serum). Population prevalence of psoriasis is similar to that of AS. Of the individuals with PA 5–10 % have arthritis that affects women more often than men.

Pathology and radiology

Skin lesions usually precede arthritis by many years. Erosion of distal interphalangeal joints of hands and feet is the hallmark lesion of PA. In the severe form of the disease lytic destruction of fingers and toes occurs with later joint deformation ('arthritis mutilans'). In an interphalangeal joint a rounded, cup-like erosion on the end of one bone facing the other joint bone whose end has been tapered into the shape of a pencil point by the osteolytic erosive process is called a pencil-in-cup deformity by radiologists. Osteolysis of these small bones can be profound, and the shortened bones cause soft tissue overlap on the fingers. Subchondral cysts, ankylosis and subluxations are common. Lesions are asym-

metric and juxtacortical osteopenia is often absent (distinguishing features).

Sacroiliac and vertebral lesions occur in up to 25 % of the cases. However, both of these are often asymmetric, including syndesmophyte formation and ligament ossification. Enthesophytes may be seen at the Achilles tendon insertion and a calcaneus heel spur is also common.

Paleopathology

We could only find a single case report of PA in a complete skeleton from England (J. Rogers, 1981) of a 45 year old male with flexed, arthritic knees and ankylosed tarsal bones of both feet as well as some interphalangeal joints. Non-ankylosing changes were also present in the shoulders, elbows, wrists, hips, knees and ankles. Osteophytic lipping and roughness of one sacroiliac joint was present. The author made a diagnosis of seronegative arthropathy, possibly PA. Zias & Mitchell (1995), however, found changes of the arthritis mutilans form in two males and suggestive findings in a female among the commingled bones of a fifth century tomb at a Judean desert monastery.

REITER'S SYNDROME
(REACTIVE ARTHRITIS)

Definition, etiology, and epidemiology

Reiter's syndrome (RS) consists of the triad of nonspecific urethritis, conjunctivitis and polyarthritis. Most cases recently have been shown to be related to the bacterium *Chlamydia trachomatis*. The conjunctivitis and urethritis are clearly direct infections by this organism, the latter usually sexually transmitted. Whether the arthritis is a nonspecific, reactive form or whether it is a direct infection by the disseminated organism remains to be defined with certainty, since only about 1 % of chlamydial urethritis is accompanied or followed by arthritis. In Europe, Asia and North Africa there may be a relationship to infection by *Shigella dysenteriae*.

Ninety percent of affected persons are men. The histocompatibility complex antigen HLA-B27 is present in three-quarters of the cases, suggesting a genetic contribution to this condition, and a familial pattern occurs in some areas.

Pathology, radiology, and natural history

The similarity between RS, PA, AS and RA is so close that it seems most practical to call attention to differences. Joints involved in PA are primarily those of the lower limb. Involvement of knee, ankle and foot joints is seen in about one-half of RS cases but hand joints are affected in only the minority. Most cases of RS are pauciarticular (few joints affected). The arthritis of RS is usually less destructive than in the other seronegative types and indeed, the disease may be self-limiting, though chronic cases may result in joint deformities (Pitzen & Rössler, 1993). Calcaneal spurs and Achilles tendon insertion new bone formation are common. Asymmetric sacroiliitis can occur in up to half of the cases but only in 10 % is it seen early. Cervical spine instability can occur. Radiological findings reflect the above observations.

Paleopathology

A single paleopathological report of probable RS by Bruintjes & Panhuysen (1995) was that of a 40 year old male from Maastricht, Netherlands from the ninth century. They report spine ankylosis (T3-L5) with asymmetrical nonmarginal syndesmophytes, costovertebral and apophysial joint ankylosis and ossification of supraspinous ligaments. Bilateral, slightly asymmetric sacroiliac inflammatory changes were present as were enthesopathies of the iliac crest and right calcaneus. In the study of PA by Zias & Mitchell (1995) described in the preceding section, the female bones were suspected possibly to represent RS, not PA.

ENTEROPATHIC ARTHROPATHIES (ENTEROARTHROPATHIES)

This group of diseases is usually considered to represent reactive phenomena to extra-articular infections, and include chronic ulcerative colitis, Crohn's disease, Whipple's disease, primary biliary cirrhosis, salmonellosis, shigellosis and other gastrointestinal infections. Arthritic changes in these are usually transient but frequently recurrent. They are commonly oligoarticular and asymmetric forms of arthritis, may involve major or minor joints, and involve principally those of the lower limb. Arthritic changes are similar to those of RS but minor variations include the following:

- Ulcerative Colitis. Primarily involves distal interphalangeal joints of the feet in an asymmetric pattern. Only severe, chronic cases result in erosions and joint deformity.
- Crohn's Disease. Similar pattern as ulcerative colitis but more severe involvement.
- Yersinia Enteritis. Similar to the above but often includes sacroiliitis.
- Whipple's Disease. Permanent joint changes are not produced in this condition. This is somewhat surprising since the etiology of this disease has been established recently as the bacterium *Tropheryma whippelii* , and the organism has been identified within synovial membranes of affected joints and other soft tissues.

TRAUMATIC ARTHRITIS

Definition and pathology

Traumatic arthritis refers to permanent joint changes secondary to trauma (fractures, wounds, dislocations). The most commonly affected joints are those of the lower limb (hip, knee, ankle) followed by the elbow and shoulder. The lesions induced by such trauma are themselves indistinguishable from degenerative joint disease: narrowing of joint space, eburnation, erosion of joint cartilage with subchondral bone changes and marginal osteophyte formation (Fig. 6.15). Osteochondral microfractures are limited to the cartilage and subchondral bone surface. These changes are most apt to occur on the convex articular surfaces of the humeral head, femoral condyles, capitulum and medial aspect of the talus but not the femoral head. Features distinguishing traumatic arthritis from DJD include (i) any age group may be involved; (ii) traumatic arthritis is monoarticular, and (iii) severe injury commonly produces bony ankylosis (Steinbock, 1976; Zimmerman & Kelley, 1982).

Paleopathology

Many reports exist but we call attention to two. An adult Late Woodland culture female skeleton from Illinois, U.S.A. demonstrates a healed fracture of the radial neck that caused elbow dislocation with marked degenerative changes: eburnation of lateral condylar articular surface of the humerus

FIG. 6.15. **Fracture with traumatic arthritis.** Intra-articular fracture radial base with degenerative joint disease (DJD). G53. Adult male Guanche ca. A.D. 1000. MAT, OAMC.

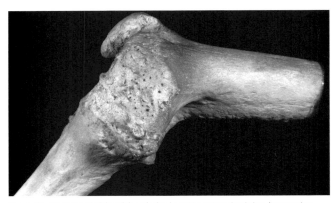

FIG. 6.16. **Septic arthritis with ankylosis.** Note extensive joint destruction and bony ankylosis. 1002834. Courtesy P. Sledzik. NMHM.

a

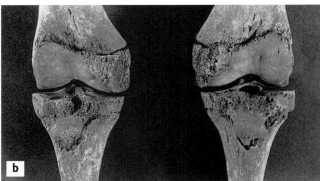

b

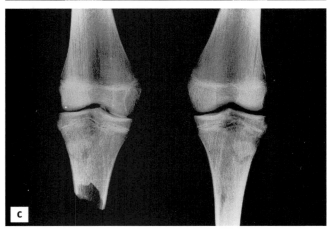

c

FIG. 6.17. **Septic (tuberculous) arthritis.** (a) Perforation of tibial plateau. (b) and (c) Tibia defects (fistulae?). Case 3. Age 15 years, medieval, Catalonia, Spain. Courtesy Dr D. Campillo. MAC.

with pronounced osteophyte formation; marked marginal proliferation of the ulnar articular surface as well as distortion and angulation of the radial head (Morse, 1978). In a 30 year old adult male from a prehistoric site near Valencia, Spain, Campillo (1978) reported a mandibular condylar fracture with defective healing and later bone resorption and apposition producing an abnormal articular surface of the temporomandibular joint.

NONSPECIFIC SEPTIC ARTHRITIS
(NONSPECIFIC PYOGENIC ARTHRITIS; INFECTIOUS ARTHRITIS; PURULENT ARTHRITIS)

Definition, etiology, and epidemiology

Septic arthritis can be defined as infection of the synovium and later all structures within a joint by a pathogenic infectious agent (bacterium, fungus, etc) that can lead to joint destruction. The section on osteomyelitis in Chapter 7 includes detailed discussion of the infecting organisms and methods of infection. Hence they will merely be summarized here. The most common infecting organisms are *Staphylococcus aureus* (more than half the cases); in very young children *Hemophilus influenzae* and hemolytic streptococci are often responsible. Other pathogens include the gonococcus (an aggressive joint invader), pneumococcus, pseudomonas, salmonella and others. Routes of infection can be direct inoculation (penetrating wounds, the most common method in modern adults), contiguous infected source (usually an extension from bone abscess) and hematogenous dissemination from a distant, infected source (most common method in children). The hip is especially vulnerable in children because blood-borne pathogens target the trabecular bone of the long bone metaphysis and the proximal femoral metaphysis lies within the hip joint. About 15 % of osteomyelitis cases are complicated by septic arthritis.

Pathology and radiology

Microorganisms reaching the joint create an exudate there. Enzymes of the bacteria and the white blood cells disrupt the synovium and cartilage, reaching the underlying bone, initiating osteomyelitis there and destroying joint architecture. Subluxation and dislocation with their effects may complicate chronic cases and ankylosis may be a product of healing (Figs. 6.16 and 6.17). Radiologic changes may not become visible for several weeks after initiation of the infection, when narrowing of the joint space is evidence followed by the subchondral bone changes and the eventual complications of subluxation or dislocation.

Paleopathology

Differential diagnosis

Septic arthritis can be differentiated from degenerative joint disease by monoarticular involvement of septic arthritis, demonstrable abscesses and fistulae as well as ankylosis. Joint tuberculosis is more difficult to separate but this usually produces far greater bone destruction and limb shortening than septic arthritis, and often is accompanied by evidence of a tuberculous infection elsewhere (especially the spine) from which it spread.

Case reports

Septic arthritis is an uncommon archaeological finding (Roberts & Manchester, 1995:115). The head of an otherwise normal humerus of an adult, early Saxon period female in England showed severe destruction with an eburnated surface (Wells, 1962). Septic arthritis of the hip was described by Morse (1978) in a 60 year old North American aboriginal from Illinois, U.S.A. Alterations included a shallow, enlarged acetabulum, femoral head deformation and an acetabular sequestrum. Rodríguez-Martín et al. (1985a) identified ankylosis of a tibiofibular joint together with substantial erosive lesions and destruction of the tibial plateau and with new bone formation at the joint margins. Radiographic osteoporosis was evident as was a healed tibial diaphysis fracture. Ortner & Putschar (1985) observed septic arthritis of the knee with fusion of the tibia and femur in an undated Peruvian body together with periosteal reactive bone and a cloaca in the posterior cortex.

NEUROTROPHIC ARTHROPATHY
(CHARCOT'S JOINT; NEUROPATHIC ARTHROPATHY; NEUROPATHIC ARTICULAR DISEASE)

Definition, etiology, pathology, and epidemiology

Neurotrophic arthropathy represents traumatic joint changes experienced as a result of a central lesion in the spinal cord or a lesion of the peripheral nerve that renders the individual insensitive to joint pain. Such joints are commonly and repetitively exposed to hyperextension, often with sufficient force to damage the internal joint cartilage and other structures. Erosion of the cartilaginous structures exposes subchondral bone with its traumatic degenerative effects, while capsule-stretching leads to subluxation and dislocation. Continued joint movements and the exuberant new bone formation in response to these ongoing changes generate greater

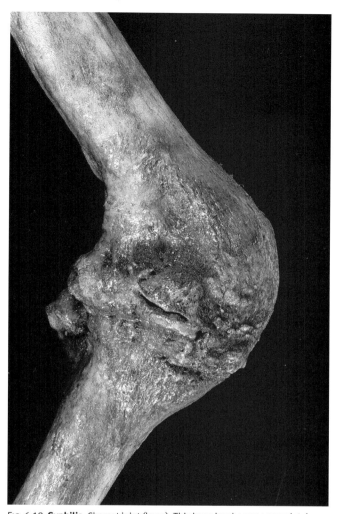

FIG. 6.18. **Syphilis.** Charcot joint (knee). This knee has become completely immobilized by osseous ankylosis secondary to repeated local trauma due to anesthesia caused by spinal cord myelopathy (tabes dorsalis). No. T-2799, Modern adult. CMNH.

joint destruction and more frequent ankylosis than most other forms of joint pathology. Pathologic fractures add further complexity to such pathologic changes. Periarticular soft tissue calcifications of such destroyed joints are common. Such joints can undergo profound destructive changes in just a few months.

In up to one-third of the cases the pathological lesion is one or more developmental cysts in the upper spinal cord (syringomyelia) whose expansion impinges on and destroys the cord's nerve columns. Loss of function may include sensations including those of position and/or pain. The joints involved in these cases are often those of the upper limb including the shoulder and elbow, sometimes even wrist and hands. Most are unilateral and monoarticular. In tertiary syphilis the posterior cord columns are destroyed by the treponemal spirochete (tabes dorsalis) affecting sensation awareness of the lower limbs. The knee is the most commonly affected (Fig. 6.18), though hip and ankle may be involved. It, too, is usually monoarticular and unilateral. The lower spine may participate in such a process with sclerosis, vertebral body fragmentation, osteophytosis and even vertebral collapse (Golding, 1984).

In addition to these central lesions are a variety of causes that result in loss of function of peripheral nerves. A congenital form is known but rare. In the developed countries, diabetes mellitus is certainly the most common cause. The mechanism of peripheral neuropathy induction is incompletely understood but is most probably metabolic and thus capable of affecting any peripheral nerve. Leprosy is a common cause of peripheral neuropathy in endemic areas. Chemical poisons including lead and a heterogenous variety of other causes are also known. All of these act by depressing or obliterating the affected person's perception of position and/or pain. These lesions commonly affect the feet (less often hands) where, in addition to the traumatic small joint changes, the breakdown of traumatized skin and soft tissues is followed by bacterial infection. When this reaches the joints it adds the destructive effects of septic arthritis to those of traumatic origin (see Leprosy in Chapter 7).

Radiological evidence of these processes are predictable. In advanced cases no other conditions generate such a dramatic mixture of destructive effects (Helms, 1989).

Paleopathology of Charcot's joint

Cassidy (1979) has cautioned that meticulous excavation methodology including sieving soil of appropriate regions should be carried out when such described joint changes are encountered, since isolated soft tissue calcification or separated fragments from pathologic fractures may otherwise be lost. A female adult skeleton from the first dynasty at Abydos, Egypt demonstrating gross degenerative disease with loss of both humeral heads and without pathology in the rest of the skeleton led Bourke (1967) to suggest neurotrophic arthropathy. A tenth century Hungarian skeleton of a 55 year old female with nasal and cranial features of leprosy revealed characteristic osteolysis and joint destruction in the feet (Palfi et al., 1992b).

GOUT (URIC ARTHRITIS)

Definition and etiology

Primary gout is a disease of metabolic aberration characterized by elevated serum levels (hyperuricemia) of urate ('uric acid') and a well-patterned tissue deposition of urate crystals into joints and periarticular soft tissues associated with intense local inflammation (Kelley & Palella, 1991). Its precise etiology remains unclear. Uric acid is the end-product of metabolized purine nucleotides, and is largely excreted by

the kidneys. Hence, its blood level represents a balance between production (purines ingested as meat as well as those synthesized and finally enzymatically catabolized to uric acid by the tissues), and its elimination (excretion into the urine by the kidneys). In a very small fraction of gouty individuals the cause of hyperuricemia is obvious: inherited enzyme deficiencies and overactivities, some of which are linked to X-chromosome mutations. In the bulk of cases, however, no such specific change is apparent though a positive family history (noted even by Galen: Schiller, 1994) in up to about 20 % of cases suggests the possibility of some heritable factor in many of these. Thus, genetic features presently only partly defined, but influenced by dietary and/or other environmental factors seem to be responsible for the hyperuricemia of primary gout. Secondary gout, however, is perhaps easier to understand. Anything that interferes with renal excretion of even normally produced quantities of uric acid will result in its retention and quantitative increase in the blood. The well-known causes of renal failure described in Chapter 8 can be responsible. Damaging effects of lead excreted by the kidney (lead nephropathy) deserve special comment because this form of kidney injury can impair renal excretion of uric acid long before other signs of kidney failure are apparent (Garrod, 1848:96; Wedeen, 1984:183ff). Uric acid overproduction due to great increases in cell death (e.g. some forms of leukemia) can overwhelm normal renal excretory mechanisms. The factors that induce the often sudden deposition of urates into the soft tissues are unknown.

Epidemiology

Gout is a worldwide condition with varying frequency among geographically separated populations and whose distribution seems to be changing coincident with western development. For example, ethnological and early contact records strongly imply its virtual absence among the thirteenth century Maoris colonizing Australia, while recent evaluation of the current Maori group documents one of the highest gout prevalence values in the world (10 % of the male population: Rose, 1975). A similar pattern has presented in the Pacific islanders generally as one large, gouty family (Kellgren, 1964; Benedek, 1993). Neel's (1962) 'thrifty gene hypothesis' (see also 'Diabetes' in Chapter 10) has also been invoked to explain these observations. The recent subsidence of gout in Europe suggests further that the condition is environmentally modifiable.

Natural history

Gout is normally divided into four chronological phases: (i) asymptomatic (hyperuricemia), (ii) acute gouty arthritis, (iii) intercritical, and (iv) chronic tophaceous gout. The initial period is usually of uncertain duration since it is asymptomatic, characterized only by an elevated level of sodium urate usually expressed as uric acid in the blood. It can be detected by chemical analysis of a blood sample. In antiquity, therefore, it would have been unidentifiable. Of those persons with gout, 95 % are males over 50 years.

The first event in phase two (acute gouty arthritis) is the abrupt appearance of pain in the affected joint. This is usually the first metatarsal-phalangeal joint and is commonly unilateral. Occasionally it is accompanied by fever. The swollen joint, covered by reddened soft tissues is so exquisitely tender that Thomas Sydenham (the seventeenth century physician who recognized the condition we call gout) noted that such patients cannot even tolerate the weight of a bed sheet on the afflicted area. The joint fluid contains inflammatory cells (leukocytes) containing sodium urate crystals, though it is not clear why the crystallization of urates in synovial fluid should evoke such a vigorous tissue response. Untreated this initial attack subsides spontaneously after several pain-filled days.

The interval between attacks is known as the intercritical phase. Recurrence of such acute attacks on the same or other joints can occur after an interval of unpredictable length ranging from weeks to years. While as many as 60 % of persons will have a second attack within a year after the first, about 7 % will never have another. Between acute gouty attacks the affected person usually has no symptoms.

The final, chronic phase of gout is initiated by massive tissue deposition of urate crystals. Metabolic or other changes acting as a trigger to initiate such crystallization in tissues have not been defined. The accumulation of these crystals in and around hand (Fig. 6.19) and foot joints (Fig. 6.20) can produce large, space-occupying masses within tissue called tophi (singular: tophus). These incite a prominent, foreign-body form of tissue reaction. In contrast to acute, gouty arthritis, this inflammatory response is accompanied by only a minimum of pain. The initial target for joint urate crystal deposit is the synovium, though deposition ultimately may involve periarticular soft tissues, the joint space, or joint cartilage or even the trabecular bone bordering the joint. The location of the tophi is similar to that involved in acute gouty arthritis and is detailed in the paleopathology section. Here we can point out that, while any joint in the body can be affected, most frequently involved are the joints of the lower extremities (Cotran *et al.*, 1989:1358). In addition, cartilage of the ear helix, forearm ulnar surface, olecranon bursa and Achilles tendon may participate as well. Skin breakdown over these lesions may result in external drainage of the crystals (Kelley & Palella, 1991). Cartilage destruction is followed by changes very similar to those of osteoarthritis (chronic degenerative joint dis-

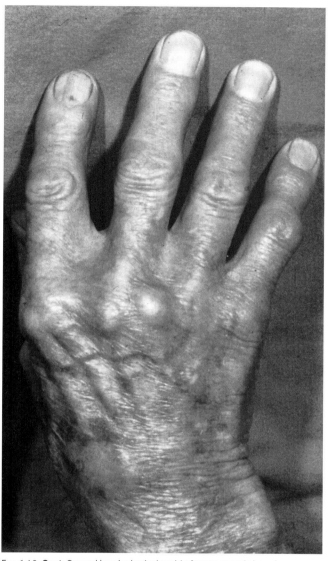

FIG. 6.19. **Gout.** Several hemispherical tophi of urate crystals have been deposited in tendon tissues near metacarpophalangeal joints. Modern elderly female. Courtesy R. Leff, Duluth, MN.

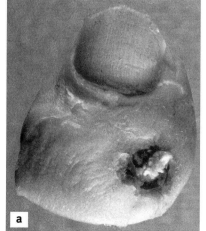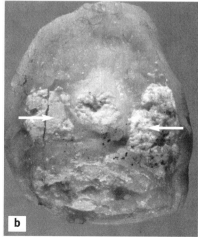

FIG. 6.20. **Gout.** (a) Amputated toe of elderly male. Note skin ulcer over surface of underlying tophus of urate crystals. (b) Plane of toe amputation. The lighter areas (arrows) are tophi of urate crystals. Courtesy of Dr R. Leff, Duluth, MN.

ease) that can limit ambulation seriously. The kidney, normally responsible for the bulk of uric acid secretion, may also be a site of crystal deposition in the form of microscopic obstruction of renal tubules by crystal aggregates (acute uric acid nephropathy), or by diffuse crystal deposition in kidney interstitial tissue (chronic urate nephropathy). Both of these are microscopically detectable phenomena. In addition, gradual aggregation of urate crystals in urine can produce macroscopic urate renal calculi. About 10 % of deaths in gout patients can be traced to such renal complications.

Radiologic changes appear 4–6 years after the first attack of acute gouty arthritis. They resemble the alterations seen in DJD including joint erosion, punched-out, cystic changes in subchondral bone that are surrounded by a zone of sclerosis and eventually gross deformity of the epiphysis, changes in position of fingers and toes and subluxation. Advanced cases may suffer ankylosis. Juxtacortical osteopenia, however, is unusual.

Antiquity and history

Gout was not really firmly separated from other arthritides until the sixteenth century. Greeks grouped all forms of arthritis, though they tended to specify its location by a descriptive term. Thus, when it involved the great toe (gout?) it was called podagra. The Hippocratic corpus comments on acute flares of arthritis that appeared related to eating, drinking and sexual excesses, at least some of which conceivably could have represented gout. Galen also described similar episodes among such ancient notables as Priam and Achilles of the Trojan war and Oedipus of Thebes (Copeman, 1970). In addition, this condition may have afflicted Alexander the Great. Biblical and Talmudic references to the foot disease of Judah's King Asa may also be gout (Rosner, 1969). Nriagu (1983) suggests that emperors and aristocrats during Rome's imperial period may have suffered gout secondary to renal effects of lead poisoning ('saturnine gout'), and skeletal lead measurements in Roman bones from that period support excessive lead exposure among Romans (Aufderheide et al., 1992). The Renaissance artist Michaelangelo has been suggested to have been a gout victim (Bluhm, 1979). While Thomas Sydenham (the ultimate champion of observational medicine) provided the description of gout in clear, graphic terms as a unique entity in the late seventeenth century (cited in Lyons & Petrucelli, 1987:440), we are indebted to Garrod (1859) (whom Ball, 1971 called the 'high priest of gout') for our awareness of the role of uric acid in all the varied manifestations of gout including renal effects and the contributions of lead poisoning. Eighteenth and nineteenth century historical figures plagued by gout include Benjamin Franklin, Charles Darwin and certainly Samuel Johnson (Bluhm, 1979). Colchicine was found to relieve acute gouty attacks when it was administered as early as the mid-seventeenth century as a purgative (Copeman,

1970), though it was not until 100 years after Garrod's identification of uric acid's role in gout (Copeman, 1970) that a drug (probenecid) became available whose urate-excreting effect enabled prevention of the disease.

Skeletal pathology

While the above descriptions emphasize the soft tissue deposits of urate crystals, bones are not completely spared. Intra-articular deposits usually occur early, not only in the synovium but also in the articular cartilage, accumulating there as a crystalline encrustation. This results in its eventual ulceration and destruction with exposure of the underlying bone (Jaffe, 1972:496). Loss of this protective cartilage not surprisingly can induce changes in the bone ends that may be indistinguishable from osteoarthritis. More distinctive, however, are periarticular bone lesions. They are often described as a consequence of pressure (from overlying soft tissue tophi, recognizable as such by bulging into the bone but separated from the marrow by a thin shell of cortical bone (Ortner & Putschar, 1985:416). In view of the fact that marrow deposition of urate crystals occurs in trabecular bone of persons with gout, another option for reconstruction of their origin could be made by assuming replacement of marrow elements by the crystals that may interfere with the vascular network sufficiently to produce trabecular resorption (Jaffe, 1972:498). Alternatively, after cartilaginous ulceration, some crystal masses may be extruded into subchondral bone. In any of these cases, subsequent changes include extremely dense reactive new bone formation, described by Rothschild & Heathcote (1995) as having ivory-like texture. Postmortem resorption of the crystals by groundwater and breakage of the overlying thin, skeletal shell in an archaeological bone produces a periarticular, scooped-out appearance of a discrete, circumscribed lytic lesion with overhanging, sharply defined edges rimming the surface defect (Ortner & Putschar, 1985:416; Rothschild & Heathcote, 1995). Usually only one joint is involved – most commonly the first metatarsal-phalangeal joint or interphalangeal joints or the equivalent hand joints. While ankles and wrists are commonly involved clinically, their less frequent involvement in archaeological bones suggests that crystal deposition in this area is probably mostly in soft tissues (Rothschild & Heathcote, 1995). Only an occasional individual will demonstrate polyarticular gouty deposits and these are rarely symmetrically distributed. The major joints, such as the knee, can be affected but infrequently. Urate deposits in the vertebrae can be found occasionally, usually relating to similar deposits in intervertebral cartilage (Jaffe, 1972:498).

Differential diagnosis

The lytic lesion of gout is so distinctive that, when present, its characteristic features detailed above are often sufficient for the diagnosis. The following, however, may be helpful in cases of doubt:

- Osteoarthritis: rarely limited to distal hand and foot joints; large joints commonly affected; polyarticular.
- Rheumatoid arthritis: undermining of joint cartilage, when demonstrable, is helpful; polyarticular and symmetrical joint involvement common.
- Pseudogout (calcium pyrophosphate crystal deposition): primarily a disease of the very aged (often 80+ years) (Rubin & Farber, 1994a:1339). Traumatic cartilage injury acts as a nidus for crystal deposition. Cartilage calcification is common. Occasional lytic lesions similar to gout, but no dense peripheral sclerosis. Larger joints affected. Tophi outside the joint.
- Osteomyelitis: gout lacks features of involucrum, sequestrum and cloacae and involves small joints.

Paleopathology

Few cases of gout lesions in archaeological bones have been reported, probably because the etiology of the lytic lesions was not recognized after groundwater had removed the urate crystals. Recognition of gout in ancient human remains is enabled by unique circumstances that permit retention of the urate deposits. This will occur primarily when the body is interred under circumstances preventing the access of groundwater. Thus Smith & Dawson (1924:157) describe the body of an elderly priest from the temple at Philae near the Nile's first cataract. Massive, chalky-white crystal deposits in and around distal hand and foot joints were identified chemically to be of urate composition. Though lower extremities were predominantly involved, some were present in the knee and elbow area. The shoulder was described as showing substantial effects of osteoarthritis which might have been of gouty origin. Though the skeletal lesions can be distinctive, remarkably few other ancient case reports can be found.

With the knowledge that modern Pacific islanders have a markedly high prevalence of gout, Rothschild & Heathcote (1995) examined 250 skeletons dated about A.D. 950–1450 from the Gognga-Gun Beach locale in Guam and found 5.6 % of the population demonstrated the lytic lesions characteristic of gout. Their report is accompanied by some superb examples of the periarticular, sharply defined lytic lesions showing a surface defect with overhanging edges and perilesional sclerosis. J. Rogers et al. (1981) add two additional cases from British skeletal collections. A probable case of gout is that reported by Wells (1973a) in a 55 year old male in England from about A.D. 150. Well-documented lytic lesions were found on the metatarsophalangeal joint of the first toe, other lower limb joints (metatarsals, tarsals and fibula), hands and both elbows. No doubt review of existing skeletal collections searching specifically for the lytic lesion of gout would uncover other cases.

Ochronosis (alkaptonuria)

Definition, epidemiology, etiology, and natural history

Ochronosis, also called alkaptonuria, is a condition characterized by precipitation of an organic pigment into the body's cartilaginous and fibrous tissue and the reactive changes which that deposited pigment initiates. It is a disease of inborn error of metabolism, inherited as an autosomal recessive. It has a world-wide distribution but, except in consanguineous marriages is found in only about 5 cases per 1 000 000 population. The biochemical defect is lack of homogentisic acid oxidase, an enzyme that normally enables a key step in tyrosine metabolism. Absence of the enzyme permits accumulation of homogentisic acid (HA), which binds to collagen and cartilage matrix where it oxidizes into a pigmented HA polymer that binds to the tissue irreversibly. HA is also excreted into the urine. If the urine is alkaline, HA polymerizes (molecules combine to form a chain) upon standing, exposed to air. This discolors the urine deep brown or black (Rosenberg, 1991:1876). Men and women are affected with equal frequency.

Diagnosis is sometimes made shortly after birth when the alkaline, urine-soaked diapers are found to be discolored. Symptoms usually appear in midlife as a chronic backache due to spine involvement. In later life larger joints, usually the knees, hips and shoulders (but not the small hand and foot nor the sacroiliac joints) demonstrate inflammation followed by features of osteoarthritis. Pubic symphysis sclerosis has been described. Pigmentation of ear or eyelid cartilage can become noticeable during the midlife years. Lifespan is usually not impaired (Jaffe, 1972:552).

Pathology of skeletal and soft tissue lesions

Deposition of the pigment is most obvious in the cartilage of diarthrodial joints, tracheal rings, intervertebral disks, ear and eyelid cartilage and to a lesser degree in the collagenous areas of tendons, ligaments, joint capsules, heart valves and fibrous scars. The effect of such deposited pigment is usually manifested first in the spine where sufficient pigment is laid down to turn the disk black. Much of the disk is resorbed as are parts of the cartilaginous vertebral plates facing the disks. The resulting narrowing of the disk space results in approximation of the vertebral faces, causing the backache. Advanced resorption can eventuate with fusion of the two vertebral faces, while lesser degrees of narrowing will induce an osteophytic response that is sometimes great enough to fuse the vertebrae by this method. Radiology at this stage demonstrates a striking picture of diffuse opacity of the disk space, but it is not known with certainty whether the radiodensity is due to the pigment *per se* or to the calcification involved in the process of osteophytosis or fusion.

In major joints, usually the knees, the pigment is deposited in the deeper layers of cartilage. Later pigment-laden cartilage fragments break off, becoming loose bodies (joint mice), that irritate the synovium sufficiently to generate a painful serious joint effusion. Pigmented cartilage fragments eventually become incorporated into the synovium which responds by chronic inflammation and hypertrophy, thickening the joint's synovial lining. In later stages the sloughing pigmented cartilage exposes the underlying bone, leading to secondary changes of osteoarthritis. In some cases the synovium may form cartilaginous bodies of affected tendon sheath linings and periarticular tissues (Aegerter & Kirkpatrick, 1975:633).

Antiquity, history, and paleopathology

We know little about the antiquity of this condition. It was first described as a disease by Rudolph Virchow in 1866 and was, together with several other diseases, recognized as a disease of 'inborn error of metabolism' (Garrod, 1908), a previously unknown concept. Subsequent increasing understanding of the condition paralleled the expansion of chemical methodology.

Since the skeletal changes of the joint lesions are indistinguishable from those of osteoarthritis, except for joint loose bodies and intervertebral disk calcification, and since ochronotic pigment is deposited only in tissues not normally preserved in skeletonized bodies, it is obvious that we can expect to encounter this disease only in human remains that are at least partly mummified. While several such bodies have been reported, it is not probable that these were true examples of ochronosis.

The possibility of ochronosis was raised when radiographs of Egyptian mummies demonstrated radiopacity of the intervertebral disk quite similar to the pattern seen in living ochronosis patients (Simon & Zorab, 1961). In a series of 64 British Museum Egyptian mummies as many as one in four demonstrated this finding (Gray, 1967). Radiological survey of the Egyptian mummies in the Manchester Museum by Isherwood *et al.* (1979) also revealed that 10 of 17 of those mummies had opacified intervertebral disks. These high frequencies led many to reject the possibility of ochronosis, a disease rare in modern times. Nevertheless, some argued that the practice of consanguineous marriages carried out by some pharaohs for political reasons may have made this possible. However, Stenn *et al.* (1977) obtained a needle biopsy of the hip from a wrapped, intact Egyptian mummy (Harwa) who had radiopaque disks and compared the infrared and ultraviolet absorption pattern of Harwa's black-pigmented hip cartilage with that of a synthetically-produced black polymer of oxidized homogentisic acid. Similarity of these patterns led them to suggest Harwa's cartilage had become

blackened by deposit of HA and therefore that the radiopaque disks did reflect the presence of ochronosis.

The question was ultimately resolved by application of more specific methodology. In 1962 Wells & Maxwell from England had unwrapped an Egyptian mummy that had demonstrated radiopacification of the intervertebral disks. Separation of the vertebrae demonstrated black deposits in the location of the intervertebral disks. They reported only their gross observations and were careful not to equate the black disks with ochronosis in the text (though the article's title implied it) but carried out no chemical studies. A three-vertebra section of this mummy was studied and reported 24 years later (Wallgren *et al.*, 1986). When the segment was again radiographed in an oblique plane, the radiopacity was obviously due to multiple localized clusters that proved to coincide with the presence of colorless crystalline masses surrounded by black, friable material. The black material was only of minimal radiodensity. This black material was then studied further by the technique of nuclear magnetic resonance spectroscopy, a method designed to help identify molecular structures. A sample of Egyptian embalming juniper resin ('cedars' of Lebanon resin) (Coughlin, 1977) was compared with the black material from the Wells & Maxwell (1962) mummy and these produced identical spectra, demonstrating that the two samples were of identical molecular structure. The crystalline substance that had been shown to be responsible for the radiopacity of the intervertebral disks was then subjected to energy-dispersive X-ray analysis, a method of identifying elemental composition of a substance. The crystals proved to be made entirely of the same elements that composed natron, the dehydrating compound used by Egyptian embalmers to desiccate the body.

The interpretation of these findings was that the natron was responsible for the disk space radiopacity and that the embalming resin in which the natron was embedded had imparted the black color to the disk space. As both Gray (1967) and Isherwood *et al.* (1979) had predicted on the basis of the disproportionate frequency of disk space radiopacity in Egyptian mummies and the modern prevalence of ochronosis, the radiopacity of Egyptian mummies' intervertebral disk spaces was proved to be an embalming artifact. The proposed mechanism by which this artifact probably had developed began with the initial act of evisceration followed by packing the abdominal and thoracic cavities with natron. The subsequent desiccation of soft tissues was accompanied by sufficient shrinkage to provide communication between these body cavities and the intervertebral disk spaces via the intervertebral foramina. After desiccation most of the natron was removed and hot, liquid resin was poured into the abdominal cavity, some of it flowing into the disk spaces *via* the intervertebral foramina, washing in some residual clusters of powdered natron. Cooling of the resin then fixed both the resin and its contained, discrete clusters of natron into the disk space. The resin has often been found to infiltrate even joints including the hip, so the finding of black hip joint lining via the needle biopsy of Harwa can be explained on such a basis as well. To date no chemically confirmed case of true ochronosis has been found in the paleopathology literature.

HEMOCHROMATOSIS

Definition

Hemochromatosis is a disorder in which the total body content of iron is substantially increased with visceral iron deposition and organ dysfunction. Hereditary and acquired forms exist.

Genetic (primary, hereditary, idiopathic) hemochromatosis

Genetic Aberration

A gene (HLA-H with C282Y mutation) located on chromosome 6 is responsible for the disorder (Feder *et al.*, 1996). It is transmitted as an autosomal recessive and only homozygotes develop clinical disease (although the mild iron metabolism dysfunction in heterozygotes is detectable and useful for diagnosis). Among Anglo-Saxons the gene frequency is 5 % and the homozygous state occurs in 0.3 % of the population (Powell & Isselbacher, 1991). The male/female ratio is about 7.5.

Mechanism

Adequate iron stores are so important to human survival and function that the body recycles much of its iron, limiting excretion to only about 1 mg/day. Since meat-including diets commonly contain much more than this, the adult human intestinal mucosa normally limits absorption of ingested iron to only such replacement quantities. In spite of intensive study, the details of the mechanism responsible for maintaining this homeostatic condition have not been defined. It is clear, however, that the effects of the genetic aberration result in interference with this discriminating mechanism, the consequence of which is iron absorption in excess of physiological needs. Absorption rates in hemochromatosis patients may be four-fold greater than normal (Powell & Isselbacher, 1991) in the absence of demonstrable need for additional iron.

Tissue injury

The surplus, absorbed iron is deposited as hemosiderin and ferritin especially in epithelial cells, particularly those of the viscera. When sufficient iron has accumulated within these cells' cytoplasm, its presence becomes toxic to the cell (lyso-

somal damage? cell wall injury?). Liver cells are especially susceptible; others include those of the pancreas and the myocardium. Dysfunction of these organs is detectable in early stages by laboratory testing. In later stages cellular necrosis with fibrotic scarring may be evident, the most obvious usually resulting in cirrhosis of the liver. Pancreatic dysfunction manifests as diabetes mellitus, while myocardial iron accumulation may induce heart failure or with electrical conductance interference which is responsible for the sudden death that commonly is the terminal event in this disease (Cotran *et al.*, 1989). Iron deposition, together with increased melanin production, darkens the skin ('bronzing'). Pituitary deposition leads to reduced gonadotropin production resulting in hypogonadism and decreasing libido. Arthritic symptoms are common (see below).

Natural history

Symptoms usually appear after age 40 years or more. The characteristic presentation is the triad of liver cirrhosis with 'bronzed diabetes' (dark-skinned diabetic). The enlarged liver is usually easily palpable. Diagnosis can be established by elevated values for serum iron, ferritin and iron-binding capacity as well as liver biopsy that reveals cirrhosis with heavy iron deposition. Today treatment involves iron removal by repetitive phlebotomy and by leeching the iron out via the urine using chelation agents. Such treatment is cumbersome but at least partly effective. After 5 years of such treatment a mortality of 11% has been reported in contrast to 66% without it. Death occurs most commonly from liver failure (sometimes with associated carcinoma) or from cardiac complications.

Arthritis

As many as one-third of individuals with hemochromatosis develop arthritic symptoms. Iron is deposited also in synovial cells and presumably the resulting cellular toxicity may initiate an inflammatory repsonse (synovitis). Deposition of calcium pyrophosphate crystals in the joint often exaggerates the destructive process. Nevertheless, the degree of hemosiderin deposition does not approach that seen in pigmented villonodular synovitis, nor does the synovial hypertrophy reach the profound degree seen in that latter condition. The hands are affected initially, especially the metacarpophalangeal and interphalangeal joints, but the problem subsequently quite commonly spreads to many of the other joints including the shoulder, elbow, hip and knee (Powell & Isselbacher, 1991). Recurrent acute exacerbations are also common and not easily explained.

Acquired hemochromatosis

Abnormalities of iron absorption may accompany several other illnesses. The mechanism is most obvious in long-standing conditions requiring frequent blood transfusions, such as aplastic anemia or sickle cell anemia. Each such blood transfusion injects about 0.25 g of iron. Without an effective method to excrete it, this iron is deposited in the various soft tissues – initially in the tissue macrophages but eventually in a cell distribution pattern similar to that of the genetic form. In a few reported cases the protective action of the intestinal mucosa has been overwhelmed by chronic, excessive iron ingestion either as a self-medication with therapeutic iron tablets or inadvertently ('Bantu siderosis').

Paleopathology

The dark brown color of skin and viscera, so striking in fresh tissues of hemochromatosis victims is not obvious in mummified human remains since this is the appearance of normal preserved ancient soft tissues. However, the liver cirrhosis can be expected to be quite easily identified without magnification and also be readily demonstrable microscopically. Similarly, the spleen is several-fold greater than normal. The heavy iron deposition will react readily with stains employing the Prussian Blue reaction (Lillie, 1965), confirming the diagnosis. The arthritic changes in the small hand joints are diagnostically helpful. To our knowledge this condition has not been reported in human mummies, though its modern prevalence (3 per 1000) suggests paleopathologists need to be alert to this possibility. The population to which an ancient individual with hemochromatosis belonged was probably little affected by the impact of the disease on those few of its members afflicted by this disease. Decreased gonadotropin excretion by the affected pituitary probably had no demographic impact because it occurs after the childbearing period has passed, and death usually occurs today in the late sixth or seventh decade – a lifespan longer than most ancient individuals reached.

CALCIUM PYROPHOSPHATE DEPOSITION DISEASE (PSEUDOGOUT)

Definition, etiology, and epidemiology

This disease is characterized by the deposition of dihydrate calcium pyrophosphate crystals in the articular tissues with calcification within the cartilage. It is a hereditary condition with a distinct familial tendency. Its cause is unknown, although associations with a variety of endocrine or metabolic states has been reported including diabetes, hyperparathyroidism, hypothyroidism, gout and hemochromatosis (Brower, 1994). Autopsies reveal a high prevalence, though a large fraction remains asymptomatic. No gender predilection exists.

Pathology and radiology

Of the cases, 95 % are monoarticular or oligoarticular. The knee is involved in three-quarters of the cases but the wrist, hand, shoulder, elbow, hip, ankle and symphysis pubis can all be affected, but not the great toe and only occasionally the spine. Clinical variant patterns include (Golding, 1984):
1. True pseudogout (recurrent acute attacks of major joint arthritis;
2. Polyarticular chondrocalcinosis (resembles rheumatoid arthritis);
3. Chronic chondrocalcinosis with DJD (cause joint destruction);
4. Destructive chondrocalcinosis (severe joint destruction mimicking neurotrophic arthropathy).

The principal intra-articular findings are calcified cartilage with destruction of joint structures. Radiologic study identifies calcification of knee menisci and articular cartilage that can closely resemble an exaggerated form of DJD. Linear calcifications in the fibrocartilage of the symphysis pubic is almost diagnostic of this disease.

Differential diagnosis

Gout is the most common condition resembling chrondrocalcinosis and can be separated by the latter's tendency to involve the knee quite regularly but only affect the first tarsometatarsal infrequently, to ossify knee menisci, involve women as often as men and only uncommonly generate the lytic defects around the joints like gout does.

JOINT SARCOIDOSIS

Joints may also be involved by small nodular granulomatous foci of inflammation in this systemic disease of unknown cause that also affects lymph nodes, spleen, lungs, skin and many other organs. Skeletal changes are seen particularly in small hand bones, less often the feet, causing small, cystic-appearing lytic lesions (called Junglin's cystic osteitis). Endosteal bone sclerosis, subperiosteal erosions or mild periosteal reaction are occasionally encountered as well as changes resembling DJD.

OSTEITIS CONDENSAS ILII

This idiopathic, peculiar phenomenon is an unusual, self-limited, uni- or bilateral, symmetric, periarticular, roughly triangular area in the inferior aspect of the ilium showing radiologically dense sclerosis near the sacroiliac joints but not involving them in a postpartum woman. It rarely produces permanent changes.

AMYLOIDOSIS

Unique amyloid protein is deposited in many scattered body sites in both the primary form (sometimes associated with multiple myeloma) or the type secondary to chronic inflammatory processes such as rheumatoid arthritis or tuberculosis. The amyloid may be deposited in soft tissue around the joint or within it as well as within bones, producing subchondral cysts, erosions and periarticular osteopenia, though joint destruction is unusual. The hand, wrist, shoulder and hip can be involved. Pathologic fractures occur but are uncommon. Because it occurs primarily in the elderly,

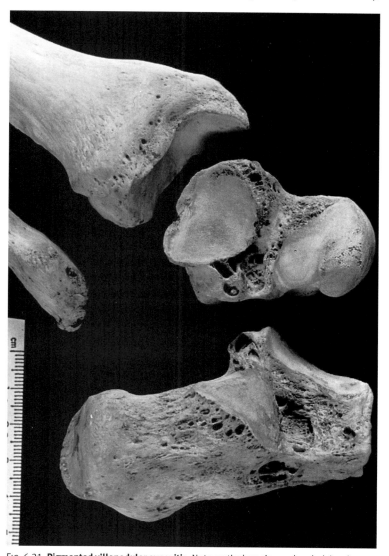

FIG. 6.21. **Pigmented villonodular synovitis.** Note cortical erosion and underlying, irregular lytic changes. 347. Courtesy Dr B. Ragsdale.

paleopathological encounters with this disease can be expected to be rare.

JOINT NEOPLASMS

Pigmented villonodular synovitis (benign synovioma; giant cell tumor of tendon sheath)

This is a benign neoplasm most commonly affecting the 20–40 year age group, arising from the synovial cells of tendon sheaths or major diarthrodial joints, most commonly the knee. It is a localized lesion affecting only one joint or tendon sheath. Histologically it is composed of benign-appearing cells arranged as a single mass or, more frequently, a papillary-surfaced tumor. These papillae are highly vascular and fragile. Given their location in major joints it is not surprising that they are often subjected to trauma sufficient to disrupt them with resulting bleeding. Consequently the hemoglobin breakdown pigments and the synovial inflammatory response to the trauma can be sufficient to dominate the picture, and originally led to the mistaken view that the entire lesion was a reactive process. Hence, the misnomer that labels this discussion. Though a benign neoplasm, the tumor can ulcerate the joint surface, leading to subchondral bone involvement (radiological 'cysts'), and decreased disk space (Gilliland, 1991) (Fig. 6.21). Rarely capsular penetration with periarticular nerve compression has been reported (Rubin & Farber, 1994a:1340).

Synovial osteochondromatosis (synovial chondromatosis; primary chondrometaplasia)

Benign metaplasia of the synovium causes cartilage deposition in these joints for unknown reasons. It affects adults of all ages and two-thirds are men. All major joints are affected but rarely hands and feet. Involvement is monoarticular. The calcified foci of cartilage are radiologically evident and frequently separate, moving about the joint as loose bodies ('joint mice'). Occasionally bone erosion is seen in the hip. Articular cartilage calcification or DJD changes secondary to this process may be found. Malignant degeneration is rare.

Synovial hemangioma

Benign hemangiomas (vascular tumors) may occur in many parts of the body, and joints are no exception. They most commonly affect the knee, are unilateral and monoarticular. Intralesional calcification is common, and they may demonstrate radiologically evident periosteal reaction or radiolucent areas in adjacent bone (Bullough, 1992). The increased blood flow these tumors induce may stimulate skeletal growth and maturation of epiphyseal end plates, causing limb length discrepancy. Joint destruction can occur.

Synovial sarcoma (malignant synovioma)

In spite of its name, this highly malignant tumor has not been established as originating from the synovium. It originates outside the joint in the periarticular tissues (joint capsule, tendon sheath, bursa, etc) and involves the joint interior in only about 10 % of the cases (Schiller, 1994:1345). It is seen primarily in adolescents and young adults. Two-thirds of the cases involve lower limb joints. Periosteal reaction may occur and there may be joint surface erosions with juxtacortical osteopenia. Partial calcification of the tumor may occur. Untreated this tumor metastasizes readily as it must have in antiquity, though it does spread to bones. The nonspecific nature of its local effects on bone makes it likely it will be identified only in mummified human remains.

PART SEVEN

Infectious diseases

Nowhere other than in the study of human infectious diseases is it so obvious that humans are only one of a vast array of life forms on this planet. Furthermore, the relationship between humans and these other life forms is so complex that the time interval necessary to evolve some of these adaptational relationships can be beyond our comprehension. The specificity of the multiple host adaptations by various malarial parasites, for example, seems almost incredible. So few malarial sporozoites are injected by an infected mosquito into a susceptible human, that these would surely yield to nonspecific immune action were the sporozoites unable to find an immune haven in which to multiply before challenging the human host. Thus, how many mosquito and how many human matings as well as how many mosquito bites were required to evolve a chemical and metabolic milieu that allowed the sporozoites to find their long-sought haven, the hepatic cells. There, sheltered from the host's immune surveillance, they can multiply exuberantly, be given time to evolve into merozoites and, when the hepatic cell dies, emerge in numbers large enough to reach their second haven − the red blood cells − *via* a different receptor before the immune system can recognize and destroy them all. Introduction to the other, often unique mechanisms that the many human pathogens have evolved to elude human biological defenses leads us to an understanding of the enormous complexity involved in human–pathogen confrontations.

The subject of human infectious diseases can fill several volumes the size of this one, so we have had to be selective in our discussions. Our choices have been based on several features, not all of which are associated with every discussed disease. These criteria include the disease's prevalence, its anthropological significance, recognizable tissue alterations it produces and its potential demographic effect. It is ironic that, in all probability, acute, often lethal infections were probably the most frequent in antiquity as suggested by findings in mummified human remains; yet these usually leave few recognizable skeletal changes. Those infections to which the body has developed at least sufficient immunity to prolong its coexistence as a chronic infection are the most apt to generate obvious skeletal lesions, though quantitatively these chronic infections probably had lesser demographic impact (unless, of course, they cause nonproductive, long-term incapacitation).

Our presentation of the more than 40 infectious diseases is divided into 4 agent-related groups (bacterial, viral, fungal, and parasitic). Space did not permit inclusion of those meeting our criteria less precisely – the rickettsia and the difficultly classifiable (mycoplasma, prions, etc).

BACTERIAL INFECTIONS

TUBERCULOSIS

Definition and taxonomy

Human tuberculosis is an acute or chronic infection of soft or skeletal tissues by Mycobacterium tuberculosis or M. bovis. Human infection by Mycobacteruim leprae is called leprosy. Human infections by all other species of Mycobacterium will be referred to in this text as atypical mycobacterioses. The many different features of this bacterial genus' species share one common characteristic: a staining affinity for fuchsin (red) of an intensity sufficient to resist destaining by acid solutions ('acid-fast'). The species are differentiated on the basis of cultural colony differences (e.g. colony form, rate of growth, pigment formation) and biochemical features (niacin secretion, catalase production, etc.). Recent advances in molecular biology provide promise for the application of this approach to bacterial taxonomy.

Most members of this genus are free-living environmental saprophytes (Table 7.1). The species that are regularly pathogenic to otherwise healthy humans are the first three listed. Each of the diseases caused by these three species usually presents clinical features distinctly different from those produced by either of the other two. Human infection by M. tuberculosis is usually acquired by inhaling bacilli-laden moisture droplets coughed into the air by a lung-infected human and thus this disease commonly begins as a respiratory infection. The reservoir of M. bovis, however, is in animals – especially cattle – though the specific animal type varies geographically and with cultural practices. In Kazakhstan, for example, 30 % of the camels shed this organism in their

secretions (Kovalyov, 1989). Consumption of food, especially milk, from these infected animals produces bacterial oropharyngeal penetration with infection of the cervical (neck) lymph nodes draining that area and, less frequently, gastrointestinal infection. In 1951, 20 % of bone and joint tuberculosis in children was caused by M. bovis (Griffith, 1937). This difference in pattern of organ involvement, however, is primarily a product of the route of infection. If M. bovis does reach the lung, it is fully capable of reproducing the pulmonary (and subsequently extrapulmonary) lesions normally expected in M. tuberculosis infections (Innes, 1940). In England in 1932 only 2.3 % of pulmonary tuberculosis was caused by M. bovis but 35 % of extrapulmonary sites were due to the same organism (Griffith, 1932). For this reason, as well as biochemical similarities, some workers classify M. bovis as a variant or strain of M. tuberculosis, though today most categorize it as a separate species. Several uncommon mycobacteria recovered more recently from apparently immunologically normal humans have been assigned species status. These include M. africanum and M. microti. These two, together with M. tuberculosis and M. bovis are now often referred

Table 7.1. Features of Mycobacterium Species

Species	Human disease[3]	Reservoir[4]	Pigment[5]	Geographic distribution[6]
M. tuberculosis[1]	L, N, D, B	Humans	N	W
M. bovis[1]	G, N (L)	A	N	W
M. leprae[1]	S, D	U	–	W
M. kansasii	L, N	W, M	P	NA
M. intracellulare	L, (N, D)	W, S, H, A	N	W
M. avium	L, (N, D)	W, S, H, A	N	W
M. simiae	L	U	P	NA, E
M. szulgai	L	U	S	
M. maimoense	L	W, S, H, A	N	E, AU, NA
M. xenopi	L	U	S	E, NA
M. asiaticum	L	U	P	E, AU, NA, AS
M. chelonei	(L, S)	U	N	
M. scrofulaceum	N (L)	W, S	S	
M. marinum	S	W	P	W
M. haemophilum	S	W, S, H, A	N	AU, NA
M. ulcerans	S	S	N	W
M. fortuitum	(E)	W, S, H, A	N	W
M. gordonae	0	W, S, H	S	
M. flavescens	0	W, S, H	S	
M. gastri	0	W, S	N	
M. terrae complex[2]	0	W, S	N	
M. phlei	0	W, S	S	
M. smegmatis	0	W, S	N	
M. vaccae	0	W, S	S	

[1] These organisms produce primary disease in apparently otherwise healthy humans. The remaining organisms usually produce disease in humans with at least partial immuno-suppression or in organs compromised by other disease states. In a minority, primary infections of apparently normal humans occur. These species are termed 'atypical mycobacteria' or 'MOTT' (mycobacteria other than tuberculosis), and newly identified species of this group continue to be reported.
[2] Includes M. terrae, M. triviale, M. novum and M. nonchromogenicum.
[3] B, bone; D, disseminated; E, eye; G, gastrointestinal; L, lung; M, meninges; N, lymph node; S, skin.
[4] A, animals; H, sputum of healthy persons; M, milk; S, soil; U, unknown; W, Water.
[5] P, photochromogen; S, scotochromogen; N, nonchromogen.
[6] AS, Asia; AU, Australia; E, Europe; NA, North America; SA, South America; W, Worldwide.

to as the 'M. tuberculosis complex.' In 1993, Cousins et al. described a tuberculosis infection shared by a human seal trainer, his colony of captive seals and several wild seals in Australia. Biochemically it was similar to, but not identical, with M. bovis. The authors suggest inclusion of this organism in the M. tuberculosis complex. Human infections by M. leprae, however, generate a unique pattern of skin and peripheral nerve involvement.

Collectively, based on their patterns of biochemical and culture characteristics, the species other than the first three listed in Table 7.1 are commonly called 'atypical' mycobacteria. A recent suggestion to refer to them by the acronym 'MOTT' (Mycobacteria Other Than Tuberculosis) is gaining popularity but this discussion will use the term 'atypical' for reference reasons. Their pathogenicity level is so low that they are encountered in human infections primarily in a subpopulation of at least partially immunosuppressed patients or in those with organs already compromised by other disease (e.g. an emphysematous lung). Occasionally some of these species are recovered from deep-seated infections (even bone) in immunologically normal persons (Williams & Riordan, 1973). Of these, M. kansasii has been the most commonly encountered species. Recently, however, patients suffering from infection by the virus of acquired immunodeficiency disease (AIDS) have experienced a high frequency of complications, including miliary spread, by M. avium-intracellulare complex infections as well as by an occasional member of the other species. It is even possible, though not yet demonstrated, that in such severely immunocompromised patients any of the 'atypical' species might be capable of infecting humans. In addition, it is important to note that while the demonstration of acid-fast bacilli in archaeological human tissues can be expected to reflect antemortem infection in most instances, the possibility of postmortem contamination by a saprophytic soil species of Mycobacteria must always be kept in mind. In at least one instance, such was the interpretation of the finding of stainable acid-fast bacilli in skin and muscle fragments adhering to a rib section of a century-old Native American burial (Bewtra et al., 1994).

Pathogenesis and natural history

Primary infection

Although exceptions abound, tuberculosis expresses itself as a biphasic disease – a primary infection phase and a reinfection (or reactivation) phase. The reservoir of M. tuberculosis is primarily infected humans. While Kovalyov (1989) points out that 7.5 % of tuberculous Kazakhstan cattle are infected with M. tuberculosis, human-to-human transmission is the most common way people acquire the disease in developed countries today. Human infection with M. tuberculosis usually begins as a lung infection, secondary to inhalation of the organism. The upward flow of mucus propelled by cells lin-

ing the bronchi (pulmonary mucociliary cleansing system) can eliminate occasional inhaled bacteria but if exposure is recurrent or the inhaled dose of bacilli is large, a lung infection is initiated. Most commonly this occurs at a peripheral, subpleural site in the mid-lung area.

Bacterial multiplication follows and some of these escape into the surrounding tissues where the lymphatic flow carries them into the lymph nodes of the lung 'root' (hilum), resulting in separate infections there. The organism's waxy coat resists the envelopment and digestion by enzymes of one of the lung's principal immune cells – the macrophage. Thus, the bacillus proliferates freely within the macrophage's cellular fluid (cytoplasm). During this early period, however, antigenic proteins from the infecting bacilli alert ('sensitize') a mobile subgroup of the host's immune system cells (T-lymphocytes) to the presence of these foreign bacilli. This can be demonstrated by injection of such antigens into the host's skin (tuberculin or Mantoux test); the lymphocytes in a sensitized host will react at the injection site causing accumulation of macrophages and lymphocytes at the site that secrete chemicals ('lymphokines') whose effects cause tissue injury. This becomes visibly apparent as a local firm, reddened, swollen area, a response termed 'delayed hypersensitivity.' A similar response occurs at the site of the lung infection where the reaction includes death of the macrophages (arresting proliferation of their enveloped tubercle bacilli) as well as necrosis (death) of the tissues in the affected lung area. In an otherwise healthy host, such a cottage cheese-like (caseous) area is walled off rapidly by an envelope of scar; an identical response also arrests the nodal lesions. Nonspecific healing changes may progress to replace the entire affected area with scar, often partly or even entirely calcified. In some cases the necrotic tissue may be large enough to persist in the central area of a partly calcified scar. In such cases the tubercle bacilli may survive (but usually do not proliferate), entrapped and contained by the shell of scar and calcium. Bacteria surviving under these conditions represent the potential for later reactivation of the infection in the event of changes in the lung environment (e.g. invasion of the lesion by a lung cancer) or immunological status (AIDS, lymphoma, etc).

This sequence of events occurring in a host who has never been exposed previously to tubercle bacilli (usually a child) is known as a 'primary' infection. In most cases the entire infective episode is without noticeable clinical effects (asymptomatic). The overwhelming majority of primary infections terminate with only a combination of a fibrocalcific scar in the lung accompanied by one or two others in the hilar lymph nodes. This pattern (lung and node calcification), known as 'Ghon complex,' (Ghon, 1912) may be evident radiologically. In a minority of cases variations in dosage of inhaled organisms, host immune response, nutrition or other factors occasionally impair the host defense sufficiently to permit progression of the primary infection. This usually takes the form of rapidly progressive pneumonia ('galloping consumption'), erosion into a bronchus with 'seeding' of new lung areas via the bronchi or erosion into a pulmonary vein. The latter will result in dissemination of the bacteria by the blood stream, with the potential for infection of any or all organs of the body ('miliary tuberculosis') and often terminating as tuberculous meningitis.

Secondary infection

Years later a person who has arrested and contained a primary tuberculous infection may become infected again by tubercle bacilli. This may occur because of a breakdown of such a primary lesion that then releases the long-dormant tubercle bacilli contained within it (reactivation) or because the individual again has been exposed to another large or repeated dose of inhaled tubercle bacilli (reinfection). This episode, called 'secondary infection,' commonly results in infections located in the upper lung near the level of the clavicle where the high oxygen tension encourages bacterial growth. This time, however, the host's immune system is already 'primed' and responds promptly with a powerful activation of the cell-mediated mechanism. The result is often a much larger area of tissue necrosis and its accompanying, vigorous, granulomatous inflammatory reaction. Structures bordering the infected area may become involved in the necrotizing process. Thus, infection of a lymph node adjacent to a bronchus may erode the bronchial wall. The liquified caseous content may then be discharged into the bronchial lumen, and be coughed out, together with its contained infective bacteria, rendering the patient infective to others. Alternatively, fragments of caseous material may be transported via the bronchi to other parts of the same or to the other lung, initiating new infective foci there. The evacuated caseous area, now permanently communicating with the bronchial opening (lumen), becomes an air-filled cavity that continually feeds bits of its fragmenting and infected lining into the bronchus. Erosion of the cavity lining into a branch of the pulmonary artery often produces hemorrhage with episodes of coughing up blood (hemoptysis), sometimes fatal. In this manner the secondary infection phase, usually in an adult, frequently results in progressive pulmonary infection inadequately controlled by host defenses. Clinical experience during a period prior to the availability of effective, specific therapy indicates that a 'seesawing' sequence of periods of disease progression alternating with episodes of partially effective host defense response accom-

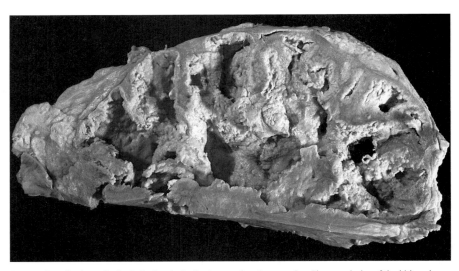

FIG. 7.1: **Renal tuberculosis.** Only the shell of outer renal cortex remains. The remainder of the kidney has been replaced by the caseous ('cheesy') necrosis of a tuberculous infection. Modern adult. BM.

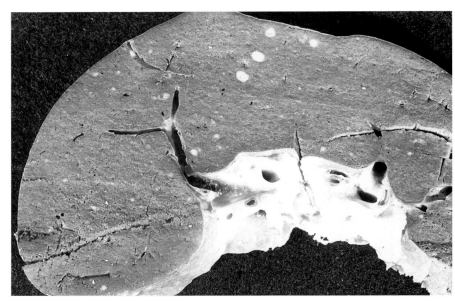

FIG. 7.2: **Miliary tuberculosis of the spleen.** The multiple white nodules visible on the sectioned surface of this spleen are foci of caseous ('cheesy') tuberculous necrosis. The tuberculous bacilli arrived at the spleen by hematogenous dissemination. Modern child. BM.

panied by clinical remission could continue for years, resulting eventually in death of one-third to one-half of those so affected.

Complications altering this course of events are legion, but of greatest interest to the paleopathologist is the involvement of organs other than the lung. Swallowing of infected sputum infrequently (probably because of the acid gastric environment) produces infection of the gastrointestinal tract. Transient episodes of dissemination by the blood stream may produce tuberculous kidney (Fig. 7.1) and/or adrenal destruction. Involvement of testes, ovaries and especially the mucosal lining of the uterus (endometrium) may cause infertility. While tuberculous meningitis is seen more commonly in children, adults are not immune to this lethal

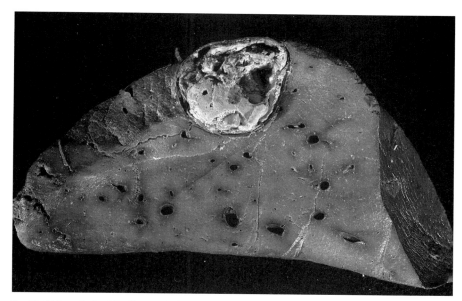

FIG. 7.3: **Tuberculosis of the liver.** A single large area of tuberculous caseous ('cheesy') necrosis is visible in this sectioned surface of the liver. Modern adult. BM.

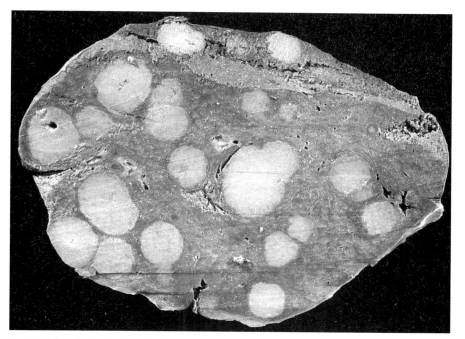

FIG. 7.4: **Tuberculosis, lymph node.** The multiple pale areas in this cervical lymph node represent foci of caseous ('cheesy') necrosis due to tuberculous infection (scrofula). Modern young adult. BM.

Table 7.2. Distribution of vertebral lesions.

Vertebral level	%
Cervical	6
Thoracic	45
Lumbar	48
Sacral	1

The vertebral distribution of 2504 spinal localizations of tuberculosis lesions is represented, pooling the findings of five authors (Sorrel and Sorrel-Dejervine, 1932; Cleveland, 1939; Sevastikoglou & Wernerheim, 1953, who also cite work by Sanchis-Olmos, 1948 and Garophalides, 1953).

Development (pathogenesis) of the skeletal lesions

Because the distribution and appearance of tuberculous lesions in dry bones are direct reflections of the anatomical features of vascularization and joint structure related to a bone, they are most easily recognized and interpreted if their antemortem genesis is understood. The following discussion details the mechanisms of their development.

Tuberculosis of the spine

More than 40 % of skeletal tuberculous lesions involve the spine (Table 7.2). This may be because it houses the skeleton's largest mass of trabecular bone. In addition, tubercle bacilli are known to thrive best under conditions of high oxygen tension, and the vertebrae are particularly well-endowed with arterial blood supply. The structure of the spine after birth reflects its embryological development from the body segments called somites. In each somite a segmental artery enters laterally from each side, branching to vascularize the lower half of the vertebral body developing above (cranial to) it and the upper half of that below (caudad to) it (Rothman & Simeone, 1975:39; Tuli, 1975:7) (Fig. 7.5). Called the intercostal and lumbar arteries after birth, their posterior spinal branches enter the vertebral bodies and branch into a web of small vessels just above the cartilaginous plate facing the intervertebral space, reaching to the midline from each side but with only minimal connections between the two sides. The bacilli in the arterial blood are deposited in this same distribution, disseminated along a plane of spongy, trabecular bone separated from the intervertebral disk space by only a thin cartilage layer. During the growth period this cartilage functions as a growth plate, enabling elongation of the vertebral body. Not surprisingly, the earliest detectable focus of the blood-disseminated tuberculous infection in the vertebral body occurs in just this area – adjacent to the cartilaginous plate. In about 80 %

complication. The spleen (Fig. 7.2), liver (Fig. 7.3) and abdominal lining (peritoneum) may be involved. Probably no organ, not even the eye, is totally free from the hazard of infection in a patient with M. tuberculosis in the bloodstream (bacteremia). Though neck (cervical) lymph nodes (Fig. 7.4) and, less frequently, the intestine are most commonly involved (usually without pulmonary infection) as a consequence of drinking milk infected by M. bovis, advanced pulmonary disease from M. tuberculosis infection can also discharge enough organisms into its lymphatic drainage system to reach and infect the cervical lymph nodes.

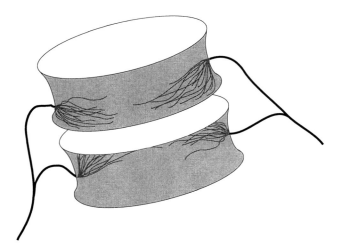

FIG. 7.5: **Schematic arrangement of lumbar and intercostal artery branches to vertebral body.** This simple diagram emphasizes the arrangement in which terminal ramifications of segmental lumbar and intercostal branches to vertebral bodies divide to nourish both halves of a vertebral body facing the disk space, providing an anatomical explanation for the frequent finding of such a pattern of tuberculous spine infections (based on Tuli, 1975). Drawing by Mark Summers, Duluth, MN. PBL.

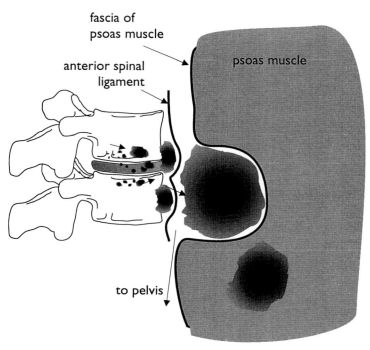

FIG. 7.6: **Frequent paths for spread of tuberculosis infection from vertebral body.** Commonly two vertebral bodies adjacent to a disk space are seeded hematogenously with tubercle bacilli. Subsequent possible paths, indicated by dark gray areas, include abscess growth within vertebral body, extension to disk space, migration to anterior longitudinal spinal ligament, enlargement of abscess there with anterior vertebral body erosion, extension to adjacent vertebrae, perforation of the ligament to produce peripsoas or psoas abscess, and ultimately extension distally and caudally, directed by psoas fascia to pelvic area. Drawing by Mark Summers, Duluth, MN. PBL.

of the cases this occurs in the anterior end of the vertebral body (Westermark & Forssman, 1938), though the anatomic feature responsible for this anterior localization has not been defined. Erosion through the cartilaginous 'end zone' not only permits extension of the abscess into the intervertebral space, but also permits the intervertebral disk to herniate through the cartilaginous defect into the vertebral body. This results in what is often the earliest observable radiological abnormality: narrowing of the affected intervertebral disk space.

The frequent finding of abscesses in adjacent vertebral bodies flanking an infected disk space is usually attributed to initiation of an abscess in a single vertebral body that eventually reaches its neighboring vertebra via perforation of the disk space (Aegerter & Kirkpatrick, 1975). Such findings, however, are more credibly explained by initial, simultaneous dissemination of tubercle bacilli to both vertebrae abutting an intervertebral disc, based on the unique vascular supply described above.

Because the vertebral body's periosteum does not extend into the intervertebral space, the abscess commonly dissects along the plane of the intervertebral disk until it reaches the anterior periphery of that space. Here the disk fibers blend with the densely woven fibers of the anterior longitudinal ligament. In many cases this structure resists, at least temporarily, the horizontal progression of the abscess' passage (fistula), directing it peripherally around the disk and often deflecting it vertically upward or downward.

The adherence of the anterior longitudinal ligament to the vertebral body is so dense that the fistula's retarded progression provides sufficient time to develop a roughly spherical abscess between this ligament and the vertebral body anteri-

orly. While the anterior longitudinal ligament may develop a focal, anterior or more lateral bulge to accommodate such an abscess, the pressure appears to be great enough to cause localized resorption of the vertebral body adjacent to the abscess, generating an appearance of the anterior vertebral surface that radiologists call a 'gouge defect' (Fig. 7.6).

Eventually such a fistula may reach the next vertebra, carrying the infection to a similar location at the adjacent vertebra or beyond. In this way the multiple, anterior vertebral body erosions produce a 'scalloped' appearance of the spine. Alternatively, the fistula eventually may perforate the anterior longitudinal ligament and extend into the paravertebral musculature. In the lower spinal area the most commonly affected soft tissue structure is the psoas muscle where an abscess of very impressive magnitude may develop. The psoas muscle fascia is also dense enough to redirect the fistula along its fascial plane or tendon. Following the downward course of the psoas fascia to its tendinous insertion at the femur's lesser trochanter, subsequent abscesses often develop in the pelvis, especially the groin or iliac fossae, and commonly reach the hip joint (discussed below).

The earliest lesion in the vertebral body is in the posterior part in only about 20 % of the cases. Even these usually dissect laterally or anteriorly after they reach the intervertebral space, but occasionally the subsequent dissection breaks through or dissects around the more narrow posterior longitudinal ligament and may even fistulize through the skin surface of the back. Only occasionally are the vertebral processes, neural arch or articular elements directly involved. Since the posterior longitudinal ligament is applied to the vertebral body within the neural canal, a posterior abscess often lies in the extradural space of the spine, and can compress the underlying spinal cord sufficiently to result in dysfunction and even paralysis.

The trabecular bone of the infected vertebral body may become destroyed by several mechanisms. These include expansion of the initial abscess within the vertebral body, initiation of multiple abscesses there or deprivation of blood supply to the trabecular bone (infarction) with bone necrosis. This latter complication may result from tubercular involvement of a segmental artery branch with consequent clotting (thrombosis), or the abscess underlying the anterior longitudinal ligament may dissect under the vertebral body's periosteum, lifting it off the bone, and thereby devascularizing it with subsequent bone infarction and necrosis. Such necrotic bone fragments ('sequestra') may be incorporated into a posterior abscess and become lodged against the spinal cord, compressing it. Progressive destruction of the vertebral body by any or all of these methods eventually often reaches a point at which insufficient vertebral trabecular bone remains to support the weight of the upper part of the trunk. Collapse of the vertebral body commonly causes not only shortening of the trunk but also anterior bending of the spine above the collapsed vertebrae (kyphosis), since the posterior vertebral structures are either usually intact or at least less destroyed (Fig. 7.7). If, as is most common, only, two or three vertebrae are involved, the angulation of the kyphotic deformity can be very acute, especially in the involved thoracic areas. In the minority of cases the collapsed area may involve six or more vertebrae; this tends to produce a more rounded, obtuse angulation. In spite of the spinal deformity, spinal cord compression sufficient to produce paraplegia only occurs in about 10 % of the cases. This deformity was described by Sir Percivall Pott in 1779, a full century before Koch (1882) established its cause.

This discussion has described a sequence of events based on arterial tuberculous bacteremia with osseous dissemination of the bacilli. The reader should be aware that alternative vascular routes have been proposed and are considered quite plausible. These are also vascular, involving veins and probably also lymphatics in the venous walls. The veins begin, of course, at the venous end of the capillaries in the vertebral marrow. When they emerge from the vertebral body they join (anastomose) with a paravertebral ('Batson's') venous plexus. This extends vertically along the spinal column, anastomosing (connecting) with intercostal veins of the chest wall and even branching into and joining with cerebral veins. Directional flow in this plexus is fluctuant, subject to body position and is particularly vulnerable to flow reversal during coughing. Anastomosing veins and their lymphatics from affected visceral areas such as the thorax can deliver tubercle bacilli into Batson's plexus, and pulses of reversed flow due to forceful coughing could force such contaminated blood back into the vertebral bodies. That such a mechanism occurs in situations of urinary organ pathology is well accepted. On the basis of experimental and clinical observations Hodgson (1975) has proposed this as a common method of vertebral infection and suggests that bacilli in cases of isolated involvement of the first lumbar vertebra may originate in infected kidneys. The skeletal paleopathologist, however, can expect the same pattern of osseous lesions in spines infected by either route.

Other items of interest relating to tuberculosis of the spine include the fact that children predominate in most of the reported series although many currently active specialists comment on the marked decline of skeletal tuberculosis, including the spine, in this age group. As many as one-half of persons with vertebral tuberculosis have demonstrable visceral lesions that could be the source of the bacilli; this figure varies widely in different series depending on the diligence of their search. Untreated cases carry about 50 % mortality rate after 5 years, about one-half of which is due to tuberculous infections of tissues other than the bone. Additional deaths occur secondary to the complications of paralysis of lower trunk and legs (paraplegia), respiratory dysfunction secondary to Pott's deformity, amyloidosis and others. Prior to available, effective treatment about one-third to one-half of patients with skeletal tuberculous vertebritis underwent

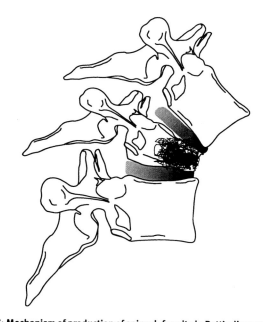

FIG. 7.7: **Mechanism of production of spine deformity in Pott's disease.** Growth of an abscess in the vertebral body may demineralize the bone sufficiently to render it unable to support the trunk's weight. Because the usually unaffected neural arch provides support, collapse involves primarily the anterior part of the vertebral body, creating a wedge-shape that tilts the upper trunk forward, generating the hunchback or gibbus of Pott's disease. Drawing by Mark Summers, Duluth, MN. PBL.

spontaneous healing, the rate being influenced by nutritional, socioeconomic and hygienic factors. Either fibrous or, more commonly, calcific replacement of the diseased area occurred, often with fixation of the affected structures. The remainder commonly lived sometimes for decades with their chronic but active disease, often deformed, and some with multiple, perpetually draining sinuses while others suffered on with paralyzed legs.

Tuberculosis of bones and joints other than the spine

About 90 % of tuberculous skeletal lesions involve a joint. There are also anatomically-related reasons for this. Since the same principles apply to most joints, we will use the hip as our model. Trueta (1957) has detailed the anatomy of the hip in relation to tuberculous infection. The results of his injection studies on specimens and his clinical observations can be summarized as follows. While fistulae from a psoas or other abscess may extend directly to skeletal structures, bones are most commonly infected by hematogenous dissemination of bacilli from an infected visceral source. The bacilli are deposited in the trabecular bone, not the compact bone of long bone diaphyses. In long bones, trabecular bone is in the metaphysis (including femur neck and its head). In the femur the head and neck derive their blood supply from three vascular sources: lateral epiphyseal, metaphyseal and ligamentum teres vessels. The active epiphyseal growth plate blocks the passage of vessels. Therefore the source of vascularization (and, accordingly, the location where bacilli would be deposited) varies with age according to the following sequence. Until birth all three sources function but at birth the ligamentum teres vessels cease their flow, and until age 3–4 years the metaphyseal vessel flow predominates over the lateral epiphyseal vessel source. Then the growth plate blocks that source; hence, between 4 and about 10 years the femur head is totally dependent on the epiphyseal vessels that are closely applied to the lateral aspect of the femoral head. As puberty approaches the ligamentum teres vessels reach the epiphysis, the epiphyseal plate begins to break down (permitting metaphyseal vessels to cross) leading to the adult pattern of anastomoses between all three circulations. There are also free anastomoses in the adult between synovial vessels and those of the epiphysis. A network of epiphyseal vessels exists under the joint's cartilaginous surface. Finally, the synovium lining the hip joint also extends over the femur neck. Vessels to the femur head traverse the neck and are covered only by synovium, making the femoral head's blood supply vulnerable in the event of injury to the neck.

The clinical consequences of these anatomical realities now become apparent. Primary infection of a long bone diaphysis is unusual – the trabecular bone is in the metaphysis. Because during active growth the epiphyseal plate blocks the traverse of metaphyseal vessels, hip infection at that time is most commonly initiated in the metaphysis. In the adult the generous anastomoses throughout the hip area, including the regional pelvic bones, often result in multiple infected sites in the area. A metaphyseal cancellous bone abscess that fistulizes to the surface will usually involve the joint because the hip joint capsule extends to the metaphyseal portion. Bacilli deposited in the vascular rete of epiphyseal vessels just under the joint cartilage will initiate focal areas of infection there that will ulcerate through the cartilage, exposing the underlying bone. At the same time, rich anastomoses with synovial vessels may produce a tuberculous pannus (plate of tuberculosis-infected granulation tissue) with cartilaginous erosion, also exposing bone. The resulting bone-to-bone contact can cause eburnation changes similar to that seen in degenerative joint disease. Crumbling of the femur neck secondary to tuberculous destruction of cancellous bone can injure neck vessels, adding bone necrosis to the destructive changes experienced by the femoral head. Penetration of the joint capsule by the tuberculous infection within the joint results in soft tissue, cold (tuberculous) abscesses, often with skin fistulae. This process is so destructive to joint structures that the end result is often complete, fibrous (sometimes osseous) obliteration of the joint. In untreated cases persistence of the infection, frequently with draining sinuses, leads to a chronic, disabling condition.

Among patients with tuberculous arthritis, hip involvement is second only to the spine, although the knee actually exceeds it in some series. Lower extremity joints are involved much more frequently than those in the arm.

Other sites

A primary diaphyseal infection without joint involvement is rare in the major long bones though it may involve the metacarpals, metatarsals and phalanges, probably because of their frequent trabecular bone structure in children. A unique response to tuberculous dactylitis (spina ventosa, finger and/or toe infection) is a sometimes vigorous, linear periosteal reaction. Involvement of ribs, flat pelvic bones, sternum (especially the sternoclavicular junction) and even occasionally the skull in adults (Scoggin et al., 1976; Brown et al., 1980) is again probably the consequence of their marrow-forming structure. Finally, attention needs to be called to the presence of tuberculous pleuritis, commonly with empyema (thoracic cavity abscess) formation. This is an extremely common part of active pulmonary tuberculosis. Of interest is the reactive periostitis occurring on the visceral aspect of ribs underlying such an empyema. Kelley & Micozzi (1984) feel that this reaction is distinctive enough to be predictive of its cause when found in a skeletonized body. While nontuberculous, pyogenic empyema secondary to extension of pneumonia to the pleural cavity could be expected to induce a similar periosteal rib response, it is probable that, without the availability of modern surgical drainage techniques, fewer ancient persons developing empyema from acute pneumonia rarely survived long enough to produce such a chronic periosteal reaction.

Epidemiology, antiquity, and history

Three potential sources of information about tuberculosis in antiquity are available to the historian: iconography, texts and bodies. They are, however, not of equal value. Most fallible are images, whether as rupestrian art, as monumental and textual illustrations or as sculptured figurines. In these the feature suggestive of tuberculosis is usually their pronounced kyphosis. Southwestern Native American rock art commonly includes a flute-playing hunchback once suspected of portraying Pott's disease but now generally accepted as related to a religious representation of a Hopi Katcina character Kokopolo (Morse, 1967a). The many Egyptian tomb inscriptions demonstrating what appear to be rounded spinal deformities (Ruffer, 1921a, plate ix, figures. 14 and 15; Vandier, 1964, figure 2; Baud, 1978, plate 16) are primarily the product of the unique and distorting Egyptian artistic tradition of presenting the upper trunk in frontal view while the remainder of the body is seen in profile. Wood, clay or ivory figurines (Ruffer, 1921a, plate x, figure 3; Jonckheere, 1948, figure 5; Ghalioungui & Dawakhly, 1965, figure 64) only rarely conform well to the anatomical characteristics of a tuberculous gibbus. This is also true of Peruvian ceramic herb containers. Morse (1967a) demonstrates the nonspecific nature of such profiles in his figure 2, by presenting pictures of four modern patients with distinct hunchback spinal deformities that are of nontuberculous and noninfectious nature.

Almost as treacherous are ancient literary sources. Since the relationship of a symptom cluster to a single, specific infective agent ('disease') is a relatively recent medical concept, these older descriptions must be approached with utmost caution and with the full knowledge that ancient views of the medical cosmos provided no stimulus to separate out various diseases producing similar symptoms or to recognize the common cause of a condition such as tuberculosis when it produces lung disease in one patient and ulcerating neck sores in another.

If images and texts, then, are only rarely sufficiently specific for useful diagnostic predictions, we are left primarily with the evidence provided by changes observed in the excavated corpses. When soft tissues are preserved the Ghon complex of primary infection (partly calcified, subpleural lung nodule with similar hilar lymph node involvement) is generally sufficiently distinctive (Salo et al., 1994) as are the larger caseous and cavitary lesions of active, progressive secondary pulmonary tuberculosis (Allison et al., 1981b) (though these, too, can be simulated by certain fungal infections: see below). The demonstration of acid-fast bacilli within such mummified lesions can raise the degree of diagnostic confidence to a much higher level. Recently the extraction from the lesion of a segment of DNA unique to the Mycobacterium complex (Salo et al., 1994) has provided the ultimate in diagnostic specificity. When only skeletal tissue is available for study, the nonspinal lesions can be of suggestive

morphology but are often not pathognomonic. It is possible, however, to reach a useful level of specificity if one restricts the diagnosis of skeletal tuberculosis to those bodies demonstrating the characteristic vertebral alterations seen in Pott's disease. While this approach is far too restrictive for routine applications, it is a practical compromise for efforts such as tracing the antiquity of this disease, where the presence of even a single case may alter substantially the reconstruction of this condition's evolution in a certain geographic area. However, even this lesion has been reproduced in modern patients by Blastomyces dermatididis and in an ancient skeleton by Coccidioides immitis (Harrison et al., 1991). In our subsequent discussion of tuberculosis' antiquity, therefore, we will use all of the information available from all sources, but place the greatest weight on the presence of Pott's vertebral deformity.

Epidemiological factors influencing the prevalence of tuberculosis include environmental features, differences in biology of the organism itself and host variations. Tuberculosis is a world-wide disease that can flourish in almost any climate. Reservoirs of the principal mycobacterial species are three: humans themselves, animals and, finally, soil and water. Lung-infected humans are the main source of infection by M. tuberculosis for other humans. It is true that many animals can also become infected by this organism (Kovalyov, 1989), most probably contracting the disease from a lung-infected human; while animal-to-man transmission of M. tuberculosis is believed to occur, though infrequently. The most common organism infecting animals is M. bovis. Kovalyov (1989) cites a Russian study (Kolokshanskaya & Kolokshanskaya, 1975) in which 60 % of tuberculous organisms recovered from cattle responding positively to tuberculin skin testing were M. bovis, 7.5 % were M. tuberculosis and the remainder were atypical mycobacterial species. Probably very few vertebrates are not susceptible to infection by M. bovis.

Both feral and domesticated animals are vulnerable. Animal-to-animal transmission of M. bovis was long thought to occur primarily by feeding in pasturage contaminated by animal droppings, and maternal–offspring transmission via infected udder ducts. Francis (1947), however, provides strong evidence that moisture aerolization not only can occur, but that among cattle it may be the most common form. Our experience with modern, free-roaming buffalo herds clearly demonstrates that tuberculosis can be perpetuated in such a herd without significant human intervention, implying the buffalo was at least capable of such a role in the New World prior to 1492 (Hawden, 1942). Animal-to-human transmission primarily occurs through human consumption of unpasteurized milk from animals with infected udders, though lung-infected cows can also transmit the disease to their handlers by aerosolization.

We are much less certain how humans contract infection by atypical mycobacteria. In some cases it is obvious: the reservoir of M. marinum is water (Williams & Riorden, 1973), and an ulcerated skin infection ('swimming pool granuloma') occurs when a human shares that environment (American Thoracic Society, 1990). However, while birds are particularly susceptible to infection by *M. avis*, the organism is normally found in soil and unique avian exposure is not found among humans infected by that species. Nor is the transmission method of infection by the other atypical species well established. Table 7.1 indicates their low virulence but widespread distribution. It is conceivable that frequent human exposure is unavoidable, but invasive infection is possible by these organisms primarily in those individuals rendered less resistant by chronic organ impairment or immunosuppression. Nevertheless, Iseman (1989) points out the reported but unemphasized observation that 24–46 % of infections by atypical mycobacteria occur in immunocompetent persons without other apparent disease. Hofer *et al.* (1993) document such an example. Iseman (1989) also suggests such apparently normal individuals with primary atypical mycobacterial infections may share a latent defect (possibly of collagen structure) that enhances their vulnerability to infections by these organisms.

The profound impact of host factors is detailed below. Poor nutrition, an immune system impaired by disease (AIDS, leukemias and lymphomas: Barnes *et al.*, 1991) or simply by age, and cultural or socioeconomic factors including densely crowded living conditions are of prime importance in human exposure to and invasion by mycobacteria.

The consequence of these variables is that both the form (e.g. pulmonary *versus* cervical adenitis) and the frequency of human tuberculosis will show great geographical and chronological variations. Abrupt, severe demographic and environmental upheavals that usually accompany major wars are almost predictably accompanied by an equally abrupt and marked rise in tuberculous infections within such a population. Application of these principles will lead to a better understanding of the history of tuberculosis outlined below.

Antiquity

No iconography or skeletal lesions consistent with tuberculosis from the Paleolithic period has ever been found. Morphologically, however, bone lesions with tuberculous fractures can be traced to the fourth century B.C. Evidence of this infection appears first in the New Stone Age. Formicola *et al.* (1987) report the skeleton of a 15 year old male member of an agropastoral group excavated from Arene Candide cave in Italy and radiocarbon dated at 3500–4000 B.C. A 90°, sharply angulated, thoracolumbar kyphosis secondary to complete destruction of the vertebral bodies of T11 and T12 (with partial destruction also of T9, T10, L1 and L2) with minimal new bone formation documents the features of Pott's disease. Recently Canci *et al.* (1996) described another example of Pott's disease from a cave very near the Arena Candide cave whose date (ca. 4000 B.C.) is contemporary with that reported by Formicola *et al.* (1987). A similar kyphotic change due to destruction of vertebral bodies T3 and T4 with multiple fistulae were found in the spine of a

22–30 year old woman excavated from the Karlstrup mound in Zealand, Denmark from the Danish Neolithic Age 2500–1500 B.C. (Sager *et al.*, 1972). Bartels (1907) also reported an adult male excavated from a Neolithic site near Heidelberg, Germany with a 45 degree angular, thoracic kyphotic spine lesion due to complete destruction of the bodies of vertebrae T4 and T5 with partial destruction of T3 and T6. Multiple fistulae involved this area and the four involved vertebra had stabilized by osseous ankylosis. While several other examples of possible tuberculous lesions have been reported, the three examples showing features characteristic of Pott's disease detailed here provide evidence as convincing as dry bone morphology can be that tuberculosis was a well-established condition in Europe during the Neolithic Age there. At the modern rate (1–3 %) of skeletal involvement in tuberculous patients (Resnick & Niwayama, 1981: 2165–84), these three cases imply the presence of 100–300 humans infected with tuberculous organisms.

In North Africa, Egyptian records say nothing about tuberculosis and the limitations of the tomb images have been discussed above. However, some corporeal alterations from this area are early enough to be considered Neolithic. Derry (1938) identified spine lesions in two Egyptian and five Nubian bodies several of which showed characteristic Pott's deformities and some of these he felt were from as early as 3300 B.C. In 1964, Morse *et al.* reviewed 31 cases of which about half seemed to satisfy the criteria for the Pott lesion. The 1895 excavation of an upper Egyptian site, Nagada, by Petrie and Quibell uncovered some mostly isolated spine sections a few of which appear to be of Pott's disease morphology (Petrie & Quibell, 1896). Dating of individual specimens was not always secure but some may have been predynastic (3700 B.C.). Elliot Smith described a Pott's type of kyphotic deformity in a child from the Old Kingdom (about 2700 B.C.), as well as a similar lesion from a much later period (New Kingdom, nineteenth dynasty: 1320–1200 B.C.) in a young male (Smith, 1927). However, the most convincing example from Egypt occurred in an adult male priest of Amen called Nesperehan from the twenty-first dynasty: 1085–945 B.C. (Smith & Ruffer, 1910; Ruffer, 1921b). In addition to a characteristic skeletal lesion of Pott's deformity, the adjacent soft tissues of a large paravertebral (psoas) abscess were preserved, although no acid fast bacilli were demonstrable in sections prepared from the abscess' lining. Strouhal (1991c) added two more cases with characteristic Pott's deformity, one in a Middle Kingdom mummy (without a psoas abscess) and the other in a Christian era skeleton. Zimmerman (1977) reported a 5 year old child with recent pulmonary hemorrhage and tuberculosis of the lung and vertebra in the New Kingdom upper Egypt tomb of the first high priest of Amun of Ramses II. Acid-fast bacilli were demonstrated in vertebral sections. Although the dating of the 'predynastic' cases is uncertain, the examples from the Middle and New Kingdom leave no doubt about skeletal evidence characteristic of tuberculosis in Egypt, supported in one instance by an adjacent abscess. To date, however, the cases are too few to calculate prevalence rates.

In addition to these findings there are some literary suggestions of tuberculosis in Asia during a period contemporary with the ancient Egyptian state. A Mesopotamian text from about 675 B.C. is cited by Castiglioni (1941) as describing tuberculosis-like symptoms of fever, cough, purulent and bloody sputum. Even less specific are descriptions in the religious hymns of Hindu Vedas (2000–1500 B.C.) (Sarma, 1939; Sigerist, 1961, 148–65). Chinese texts, probably from about 2700 B.C. during the reign of the first ruler Emperor Shen Nong of what can be called a nation suggest remedies for what is called 'consumption' (Johnston, 1993). A little (but only a little) greater certainty is provided by fibrous pulmonary scars found in the body of a woman of the Han Dynasty about 200 B.C. (Anonymous, 1980). Better, more tangible evidence must be awaited before we can be certain about the presence of tuberculosis in Asia during the Neolithic Period.

Although they are too recent to be considered Neolithic, the discourses of the Greek physicians constituting the Hippocratic corpus (about 400 B.C.) are an exception to the usually vague literary references to tuberculosis. While physicians of Hippocrates' era can not be expected to have understood clearly that the pulmonary, lymphatic and skeletal forms of tuberculous infection were but different manifestations of a single infectious agent, they appear to have been acquainted with them individually. Specifically, the Hippocratic authors describe the Pott's deformity with surprising specificity, not only the kyphosis-producing changes but even the increased vertebral body length of the lordotic spinal segment, the paravertebral (psoas) abscess, and comment further that 'they have, also, as a rule, hard and unripened tubercles in the lungs.' (Hippocrates, ca. 400 B.C. [1959]:279). In subsequent paragraphs the Pott's deformity is clearly separated from kyphosis secondary to trauma, congenital and other causes of spinal curvature.

The pre-Columbian presence of tuberculosis in the New World remained controversial for many years. An 1886 report by Whitney demonstrated a cervico-thoracic, kyphotic vertebral destruction with fusion from a Tennessee site. Morse et al. (1964) points out that the case from Pecos Pueblo (see Hooton, 1930: 319), though described by el-Najjar (1979) as a Pott's lesion, is probably from a post-Spanish period. Several others, such as that in a Peruvian mummy (Garcia-Frias, 1940) also could not be dated definitely to a pre-Columbian period. However, there seems to be no reason to reject three cases of Pott's disease from New York (Ritchie, 1952). The Lichtors (1957) described an osseous ankylosis of a Pott's deformity from Tennessee (A.D. 1200–1400), suggesting the disease may have been contracted from a buffalo. The modern, free-ranging buffalo is certainly known to be susceptible to tuberculous infection (Hawden, 1942). El-Najjar (1979) added an additional thoracic kyphotic lesion of the Pott's type from Arizona while

Widmer & Perzigian (1981) contributed three similar cases from Ohio, radiocarbon dated to A.D. 1275 ± 150. Morse et al.'s (1964) review of the New World cases reported up to that time resulted in a somewhat skeptical conclusion, based partly on dating and partly on morphological reservations. However, the subsequent addition of well-dated and anatomically well-defined cases (Buikstra & Cook, 1981; Hartney, 1981) gradually eroded that skepticism. Buikstra & Cook (1981) demonstrated little evidence for tuberculosis at an Illinois site before A.D. 1000, providing demographic and cultural features consistent with that observation. Probably the most convincing of those reports was that of Allison et al. (1973) in which they described a Nazca culture (radiocarbon dated A.D. 700) mummified child with characteristic Pott's deformity, psoas abscess and miliary lesions in the kidney, lung, liver and heart, acid-fast bacilli being demonstrable in abundance in the miliary lesions. In addition, sequencing a segment of DNA unique to the M. tuberculosis complex in the extract of a sample from a 1000 year old southern Peruvian mummy's hilar lymph node (part of a Ghon complex), Salo et al. (1994) seem to have settled the issue of the presence of pre-Columbian tuberculosis in the New World affirmatively beyond reasonable doubt. Subsequently Arriaza et al. (1995) used the same technique successfully on a bone sample from a diseased vertebra in the mummified remains of a 1000 year old female with Pott's disease from a northern Chile site, as did others (Dixon et al., 1995) on medieval British skeletons.

During this interval, epidemiological considerations fed the controversy. Several assumptions influenced these viewpoints. The acute infections, such as smallpox, introduced by contact with European immigrants frequently raced through a tribe with overwhelming ferocity and devastating mortality (Dobyns, 1992). These dramatic episodes spawned a concept that native North Americans were uniquely susceptible to European infectious agents because they had 'lost their immunity' during the millennia of separation following their New World colonization (the 'virgin soil' syndrome of a virulent infectious agent suddenly gaining access to a non-immune population). Later, when chronic illnesses such as tuberculosis reached epidemic proportions on reservations it was not unexpected that the etiological contribution made by the squalor, malnutrition, crowding and effects of social upheaval on the reservations would be obscured by a cultural concept that was content to explain the phenomenon on an immunological basis. Examples of such effects on Native Americans abound (Thornton et al., 1992). Because widespread European presence in North America's arctic areas was delayed, the Inuit experienced these effects later, but by the 1950s it had reached a point where it has been estimated that a very large fraction of Canada's arctic Native Americans had active tuberculous disease. Even in 1961 the 'virgin soil' viewpoint was strong enough to make Morse question the numerous examples of skeletal lesions (whose morphology actually conformed well to his own rigid, conservative criteria for the diagnosis of Pott's disease), suggesting that if they really were of tuberculous nature they should not be so infrequent in native skeletal collections.

Classical and Medieval Ages in Europe

We have only a few non-European data sources for this interval. Several Chinese medical texts dating to the Sui (A.D. 581–617) and Tang (A.D. 618–907) dynasties describe chronic, lingering illnesses with pulmonary symptoms that might be those of tuberculosis (Morse, 1967a). We also have available some writings by Chinese Taoist priests from the twelfth century suggesting that consumption may be due to the breathing of 'evil airs,' and that living agents ('animalcules') may play a significant role (Johnston, 1993). This was several centuries before western physicians considered an infectious origin seriously enough to record it though, as noted below, both Aristotle and Galen had earlier warned about its contagiousness. These limited observations compel us to search for our understanding of this period of tuberculosis' history in European history.

The information from Greece's classical period is largely literary. Homer (probably about 800 B.C.) is often cited as referring to tuberculosis, but his quotation only includes whatever it was that he meant by the word 'consumption,' though in another area he refers to a 'wasting away' sickness. Euryphon (fifth century B.C.) at least lists cough and hemoptysis as symptoms (Meinecke, 1927). We have already described the observations in the Hippocratic corpus. Therein is described a pulmonary condition characterized by fever, cough, foul-smelling sputum, hemoptysis, and emaciation as well as terminal hair loss and enteritis, calling it 'phthisis,' a term commonly borrowed and employed by later authors. This term for a symptom complex undoubtedly encompassed also many other lung entities, though tuberculosis was surely part of this syndrome. Furthermore those authors' independent description of tuberculous spondylitis (that would later be described in 1779 by Sir Percivall Pott as a unique vertebral deformity with paralysis) actually included identification of paravertebral (psoas) abscess formation. The Hippocratic corpus also makes reference to consumption of the hip, larynx and kidneys. Although these authors comment further that patients with the spine lesion also commonly had soft, pulmonary nodules, there is no clearly-defined or unequivocal statement that Hippocratic authors (Hippocrates, ca. 400 B.C. [1959]) recognized these very dissimilar clinical presentations as the product of a single etiological agent. By the late fourth century B.C. both Isocrates and Aristotle clearly understood the contagious nature of consumption. Galen, through intensely detailed observations, refined the symptom complex of phthisis and was sufficiently impressed by the etiological role of climate that he included a change of residence to the arid regions of North Africa as a therapeutic measure.

Among the Roman writers, Seneca (who probably suffered from the disease), Ovid and Celsus all described consumption during the first century A.D. as did many others. Columella (A.D. 50) and Vegetius (A.D. 420) both noted that consumption also affected animals (Meinecke, 1927).

It is clear that the term 'consumption' was originally used for a condition whose principal manifestation was a lingering, emaciating disease. By the age of Hippocrates pulmonary symptoms had been linked to it. Both he and especially Galen later refined these features into a more specific complex, often referred to as 'phthisis.' Although this most probably still remained a mixture of multiple etiologies, pulmonary tuberculosis in all probability constituted a significant fraction of these, varying with the perceptions of the different authors. Furthermore, the descriptions of some extrapulmonary forms of tuberculosis are of sufficient specificity to leave little doubt about their most probable cause. While no quantitative estimate is possible on the basis of such observations, it is evident that these conditions occurred during this interval at a frequency high enough to allow an active medical practitioner experience sufficient to recognize them as syndromes.

The feudal pattern during much of medieval Britain committed the majority of its population to a rural lifestyle. They lived in small, relatively self-sufficient family clusters and villages, usually walked to their work areas and had only limited opportunities for extensive social contact with large groups. Much of the European continent differed little from this pattern. Such are not the conditions expected to be conducive to spread of a disease like pulmonary tuberculosis, but available skeletal collections to search for the evidence are limited. Stirland & Waldron (1990) provide examples of several cases, including Pott's disease, from the fourth century Roman period in Britain, while Ulrich-Bochsler et al. (1982) found a case of Pott's disease in Switzerland dating to the seventh or eighth century. Such findings document the medieval presence of tuberculosis in Europe but they cannot establish its prevalence. Not until the sixteenth century did the writings of Girolamo Fracastorius initiate the concept of the germ theory of disease by suggesting that not only phthisis but many other conditions may be caused by living agents: 'animalculae' (Ackerknecht, 1972).

The later part of the Middle Ages and early Renaissance were characterized in part by two closely-linked events that acted to alter the frequency of tuberculosis in the European population and simultaneously to provide us with data from which some concept of tuberculosis prevalence can be derived. One of these can be traced to a philosophical concept of governance while the other related to dramatic demographic shifts. During this period both religious and secular movements stimulated development of alternative speculations regarding population governance. Among these was a view that an elite population subset with natural leadership qualities had an obligation and right to rule over the remaining bulk of the population. As early as about A.D. 1100 in France and Britain the royalty embraced this concept by claiming their talents were of divine origin and therefore they enjoyed a 'divine right' to rule. One of the methods employed to publicize this viewpoint (with its enhancement of centralization of power) was a claim of royal supernatural healing power of disease, specifically the ulcerating lesions of tuberculous cervical adenitis (lymph node infection: scrofula). It was performed in a ritual during which the king touched the sufferer, made a sign of the cross and then provided the afflicted commoner with a gold coin (Bloch, 1973:21). In England the practice endured until the early nineteenth century (Roberts, 1987a). We can gain some insight into the prevalence of tuberculosis in Europe from such British gold coin payment records. These indicate relatively constant but low level from their introduction in the eleventh through the sixteenth century. This was followed by a sharp rise in the early part of the seventeenth century from 300 to about 9000 persons annually in Britain and probably also in France (Ackerknecht, 1972:103).

The cause for this apparent rapid increase might, of course, lie in the social realm. It may, however, reflect a real increase in the disease's prevalence. The problem of supplying milk to the burgeoning population in British cities during the seventeenth century was solved by creation of 'town dairies.' These were wood buildings in city centers that housed cows under densely crowded, unhygienic conditions. These cows formerly had been pastured, but now were permanently contained in circumstances ideal for animal-to-animal (as well as human-to-cow and cow-to-human) transmission of tuberculosis. Such transmission is well-known (Stamp, 1961; Collins & Grange, 1983). Francis' observation (1947) that town dairies were major contributors to widespread expansion of tuberculosis in cattle offers an attractive explanation for an abrupt rise of scrofula in the seventeenth century (as measured by 'royal touch' payments) at the very time urban populations increased.

The other, major change at this time was a rural to urban demographic shift. This actually had begun much earlier when a resurgence of trade led to the crowded English walled towns of the eleventh century. Many other forces contributed to their gradual expansion. Much later, when the textile industry expanded following mechanization inventions, the focus of its activities shifted from a cottage industry to riverside sites where the necessary water power was available. The consequence of this shift included the development of cities there. The rate of this change, however, increased so rapidly that the cities could not accommodate such a massive demographic shift from rural to urban living. The many sixteenth century paintings of Peter Bruegel (ca. 1525–1569) and especially the etchings of W. Hogarth (1697–1764) have left us vivid images of how intensely crowded many European cities became as the former rural workers streamed into them, populating the limited available housing with ever increasing density. These circumstances provided the ideal conditions for aerial transmission of the tubercle bacillus causing lung infection. The fraction of tuberculous deaths in relation to deaths from all causes in

London rose to 15 % by the mid-seventeenth century and reached almost twice that figure 100 years later. Ackerknecht (1972:104) points out that the practice of taxing a building based partly on its number of windows tended to affect building design to minimize window construction, exaggerating the rebreathing of exhaled air by the people in such crowed, airless rooms.

Although the evidence is largely literary, we can tentatively use the above-noted observations to hypothesize the pattern of tuberculosis during medieval and early Renaissance times in England and a little later on the continent as follows. During the first part of this period the relative stability of rural life imposed by feudal governance minimized aerial, human-to-human transmission of the disease. Its reservoir at this time may have been in a small but constant fraction of pastured cattle. Transmission of tuberculosis to humans probably occurred, but the life style of both humans and cattle probably kept its prevalence low. Crowded living conditions are evident as early as the rise of Britain's trade-stimulated walled towns in the eleventh century. However, crumbling of Britain's feudal system in the latter part of the Middle Ages and early Renaissance resulted in an urban population explosion under circumstances ideal for respiratory bacillary transmission. A rapid increase in the pulmonary form, a fraction of which also had cervical node involvement, was predictable. Simultaneously, development of unhygienic town dairies to supply milk to the people in the city spread tuberculosis widely among cows. Consumption of their contaminated milk generated a seventeenth century scrofula epidemic. Together these events could account for both the documented increase in urban tuberculosis mortality from the pulmonary form as well as an explosion of scrofula patients seeking relief via the 'royal touch.'

Renaissance and industrial revolution

The increase in tuberculosis prevalence and incidence, noted so prominently in the seventeenth century, continued throughout the next hundred years. As it approached epidemic proportions physicians devoted increasing time and energy to it. These efforts gradually expanded both experience with and understanding of tuberculosis. Sylvius de Boe (Dutch) dissected the victims and called attention to the caseous nodules in the lung, declaring them to be the origin of 'phthisis.' Extrapulmonary forms were also described by Manget in 1700 (miliary tuberculosis), R. Whytt in 1768 (tuberculous meningitis) and that most meticulous of eighteenth century observers, Sir Percivall Pott (1779, spine tuberculosis). The latter actually rediscovered it, since Hippocrates had described it almost as well as did Pott; indeed, it was the Hippocratic report of the therapeutic value of paravertebral abscess aspiration that led Pott to use it successfully more than two millennia later. Still, the commonality of these different manifestations of tuberculosis continued to elude physicians, leading to etiological and therapeutic controversy. Failure to alter the course of the pulmonary form and its tendency to involve entire households led many physicians to view it as a 'constitutional' (i.e. hereditary) and therefore untreatable disorder. Hippocratic authors themselves had said 'consumptives beget consumptives' (Ancill, 1852:39; Flick, 1925:257). This bred a *laissez faire* attitude toward treatment among physicians.

By the early nineteenth century tuberculosis had become the most common cause of death by single diseases. In Britain the annual tuberculosis mortality rate peaked at about 400–500/100 000 population, while in Philadelphia it reached 618/100 000. These rates were highest in urban areas; female textile workers seemed particularly susceptible. Autopsies in major European centers were identifying the active disease or its healed stigmata in nearly 100 % of cases (Johnston, 1993). However, such autopsy studies continued to broaden the understanding of the disease. In 1821 Laennec, inventor of the modern stethoscope's progenitor, suggested that scrofula and other tubercle-forming, extra-pulmonary forms of the disease were merely involvement of other organs by the same agent as that causing the lung disease. Rudolph Virchow, the father of cellular pathology, still opposed this idea and described both an inflammatory and a neoplastic form of the disease based on cellular changes. However, by 1865, Villemin in France had injected rabbits with the contents of such tubercles and reproduced the disease, establishing the condition as an infectious one. Seventeen years later Robert Koch (1882) identified *Mycobacterium tuberculosis* as the etiology of tuberculosis, clarifying with certainty the unitarian and infectious nature of tuberculosis and initiating the era of its rational treatment and prevention.

The modern era (1882 to date)

Actually the tuberculosis epidemic had begun to subside in both Britain and the U.S.A. 30 years before Koch (1882) identified its cause (Fig. 7.8). Both its incidence and its mortality reached an apogee in these countries about 1850 (Johnston, 1993). Based on an assumption of the beneficial effects of fresh air (especially if laden with the scent of pine), sanatoria were built during the first quarter of the twentieth century for tubercular patients in rural, often mountainous areas. Whatever personal health value these had for such individual patients, it is debatable how much sanatoria influenced the incidence of new cases. Admission to most of these was voluntary, and for many years the available beds could only accommodate a fraction of existing infectious patients. Nor did their introduction produce any obvious alteration in the rate of decline of the disease. Except for a small and transient increase immediately following World Wars I and II (Dubos & Dubos, 1952: chart C), the decline in tuberculosis deaths between the middle of the nineteenth and twentieth centuries continued unabated and at a virtually constant rate (Fig.7.8). While the introduction of effective, specific drug therapy about 1950 did steepen the rate of decline, this effect is almost lost on a century-wide graphic scale. The drugs'

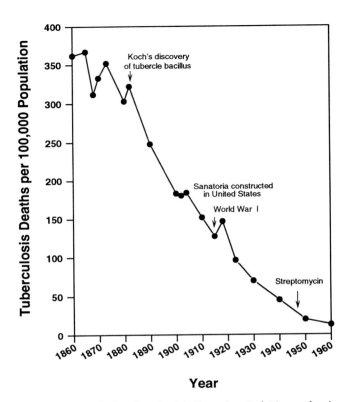

FIG. 7.8: **Frequency of tuberculous death in Massachusetts (1860–1900) and United States of America(1900–1960).** The progressive decline began before Koch established it as an infectious disease, continued at an unchanging rate through the period of sanatorium construction and had reached a low point even before specific antibiotic and chemotherapy was established. Figure composed from Massachusetts and United States of America census data.

effectiveness in rendering patients noninfectious by eliminating bacilli in the sputum was so dramatic by 1975 that most tuberculosis sanatoria closed or were converted to other uses. Coupled with an intensive case-finding program based on the tuberculin test (Pan American Health Organization, 1986), the disease had been reduced to one found primarily in the elderly or the disadvantaged. No longer a public health problem, officials began to speculate about and hope for complete eradication of the disease. Treatment returned to an individualized, outpatient basis, case finding programs lost funding support and research interest in the disease waned. By 1980 it was no longer viewed as a major public health problem among the developed countries.

The causes of this decline are not easily identified. As Bates (1992) points out, the decline began before the cause of the disease was identified; the sanatoria's contribution to the decline can not be demonstrated objectively and specific, effective therapy did not become available until more than 80 % of the decline had already occurred. It seems far more probable that socioeconomic factors are responsible for the majority of the effect. Better housing and working conditions decreased exposure to inhalation of tubercle bacilli, and better nutrition increased host resistance. Decreased bacterial virulence, suggested by some, is a theoretical but unconfirmed possibility. Operation of natural

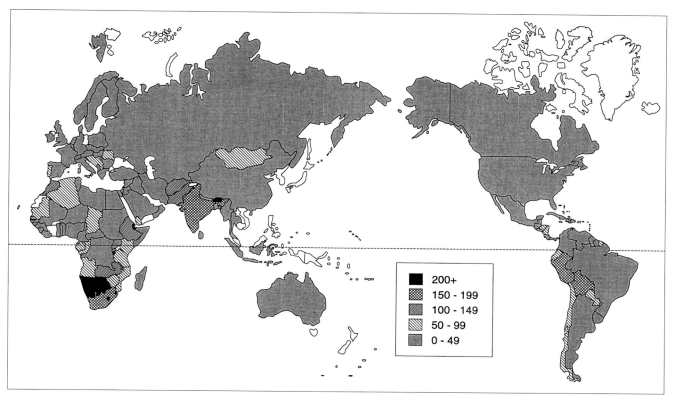

FIG. 7.9: **Cases of tuberculosis per 100 000 population reported to WHO in 1992.** Map created from statistical data published by the World Health Organization in Sudre *et al.* (1992), and used with their permission.

selection cannot be excluded (See Features of special bioanthropological interest, below).

Ironically, during the 1980s the tubercle bacillus once more demonstrated that the form, frequency and mortality of its disease is shaped by environmental and host factors (Bloom & Murray, 1992; Snider & Roper, 1992). A nidus of the disease persisted among the older members of the population (probably on the basis of age-related, spontaneously declining immunocompetence) and a heterogeneous subgroup including individuals with immunosuppression acquired by disease (leukemia, lymphoma) or of iatrogenic origin (cancer chemotherapy). Increased immigration from developing countries also imported new cases. In addition, for reasons still unclear, an increasing frequency of primary invasion by atypical mycobacteria in otherwise healthy persons was detected (Iseman, 1989). By 1990 it also became apparent that recurrences were evident in patients who had interrupted their treatment regimen, and in these the organisms frequently were resistant to available drugs. Such patients suffered a mortality similar to that of the preantibiotic era. Finally, a high fraction of AIDS patients were succumbing to miliary tuberculosis. In the absence of an effective vaccine or new drugs and in view of the difficulty in effecting behavior change among those engaging in high-risk activities, tuberculosis in the 1990s once again is presenting the potential of becoming a major threat to the public health of developed countries' populations.

It must be emphasized that the described decline also occurred but was of much lesser degree in developing countries (Daniel, 1978). Tuberculosis remains a world-wide disease of major concern in many countries (Fig. 7.9), continuing to infect about 9 million new individuals annually, one-third of whom die (Bloom & Murray, 1992).

Features of special bioanthropological interest

Transmission

Today, humans are infected primarily by inspiring air containing bacilli-laden moisture droplets coughed up by another human whose lung is infected, usually with *Mycobacterium tuberculosis*. In developing countries milk from animals infected primarily with *M. bovis* (though with *M. tuberculosis* in some cases) is still a significant source. It is important to remember that the route of entry is the principal single determinant of the form of the clinical disease caused by these two organisms because either of these two species may cause the same lesions if introduced in the same way to the same organ. When we find both cattle and their handler infected, we usually assume the organism was transferred to the human by consumption of milk from the infected cattle, but about half of infected cattle have pulmonary disease. If the human handler also does, the human-to-cattle aerial route is not excluded.

Conditions of aerial transmission in antiquity can be expected to have been more optimal in the sedentary ancient populations, because of their often poorly ventilated and densely crowded housing arrangements. In large populations familial foci probably were prominent. Marginal nutritional status in some of these also increased their susceptibility to infection. Finally, social turmoil including war or equivalent societal disruption even today in developed countries leads to a prompt increase in the number of tuberculosis-infected persons and undoubtedly did so in antiquity. Demonstration of an abrupt rise in tuberculous lesions among archaeological populations should include consideration of such social stress as an explanation.

Effect on the individual

The mortality of 35–40 % within 5 years after diagnosis seen in individuals with major pulmonary involvement was probably as common in antiquity as it was in the eighteenth to twentieth centuries before antibiotic and chemical therapy. Chronic but active illness of one or more decades duration can be expected to have characterized a significant fraction of infected persons. In all probability their course was marked by recurrent acute exacerbations and episodes of pulmonary hemorrhage as well as reduced work capacity. Specific mechanical disabilities secondary to bone and joint involvement would have limited physical effort. Emaciation and the general effects of major chronic illness undoubtedly arrested ovulation and menstruation; fertility was reduced further in those whose gonads and other portions of the genital system were directly infected.

Effect on the community

A population's birth/death equilibrium can be significantly disturbed by a tuberculosis epidemic. The younger age groups are more apt to become infected and, among these, infants have the highest probability of dying. Conditions of social disintegration provide an ideal soil for the rapid spread and increased mortality of tuberculosis. With every severely ill member a population loses not only the services of the person incapacitated by the disease but also those of the individuals burdened with the invalid's care. During an epidemic this can contribute substantially to breakdown of community infrastructure.

Role of the immune system in the human response to the tubercle bacillus

Following Koch's identification of the tubercle bacillus great interest was generated in the epidemiological aspects of the disease. Many observations were reported suggesting that various human populations (especially races) had differing 'resistance' to the disease. Few of these were carried out under conditions controlling for such obviously important variables as malnutrition, living conditions, etc. In spite of this the impression grew that 'natural resistance' (i.e. inherited) factors operated to render individuals variably susceptible to infection by the tubercle bacillus and variably capable of recovering from such an infection. These assumptions appeared to gain considerable support during the Native American Indian epidemics of the nineteenth century and those of the Inuit in the present century. Both the high rates of infection and the very substantial mortality suffered by these populations were explained on the basis of an absent 'natural resistance' factor secondary to their lack of exposure to tuberculosis for the many millennia during their residence in the New World, isolated from the tuberculosis-ridden Old World populations. In brief, natural selection had not operated during that interval to maintain an hypothesized previous resistance level.

However, increasing reports of New World pre-Columbian bones with characteristic tuberculous changes (Pott's deformity) are not compatible with such a view. Development of understanding of the human immune response as a hypersensitivity (type IV) reaction also led to a rational explanation of the differences in behavior of the disease in what is now called primary and secondary stages of tuberculosis. Re-examination of these Native American tuberculosis epidemics following European contact uncovered other factors that could have contributed significantly to the native populations' disastrous experience with the tubercle bacillus. Social upheaval, community function breakdown, malnutrition and densely crowded living conditions were such common experiences among the affected groups, that no nebulously hypothesized 'natural immunity' factor was felt needed to explain the course of the disease among these peoples.

Still more recently, however, attention has been called to relatively ignored observations made about 30 years ago. Several strains of mice had been developed by Lurie (1964) and others that demonstrated clear and unequivocal evidence of substantially different resistance responses to quantitatively standardized exposures to tubercle bacilli. Carried out during the years of the almost deliriously successful efforts at antibiotic and chemotherapeutic control of tuberculosis, these experimental study results may not have received the attention they deserved. With the availability of currently sophisticated laboratory methodology these findings are being re-examined, and have been successful in dramatically narrowing the chromosomal localization of 'host resistance factor' (bcg gene?) (Malo et al., 1991) as well as establishing a model to identify the intracellular reaction of the hypothesized gene's product within the macrophage (Radzioch et al., 1991). The difficulty in controlling variables in human clinical studies Stead et al. (1990) will make it unlikely that this approach can settle the issue satisfactorily until a specific, laboratory-identifiable alteration of the immune defense process becomes available.

It is now obvious that socioeconomic and other similar nonbiological factors have an enormous impact on the epidemiology of tuberculosis. However, some of the observations of the disease's behavior over the past several centuries would support acceptance that a 'natural resistance' factor may be contributing to modulate that behavior further. Recent experimental work suggests the issue may be resolved in the near future.

Paleopathological appearance of lesions

Appearance of soft tissue lesions of tuberculosis

Several examples of primary pulmonary tuberculosis have been reported from southern Peru and northern Chile (Allison *et al.*, 1973, 1981b; Salo *et al.*, 1994) (Fig. 8.8). These consist of at least partially calcified, solitary, subpleural nodules 1–2 cm in diameter with similar involvement of the hilar lymph nodes. Acid-fast bacilli found in one of the three cases reported by Allison *et al.* (1981b) provide diagnostic reassurance and Salo *et al.* (1994) generated evidence representing the greatest diagnostic specificity by recovering from the hilar node lesion a segment of DNA unique to the *Mycobacterium* tuberculosis complex. Allison *et al.* (1981b) also reported two adults with single pulmonary cavities (one filled with blood), each with abundant acid-fast bacilli in the cavity lining.

Other soft tissue evidence included a psoas abscess in association with the lesion of Pott's disease in an Egyptian mummy from the twenty-first dynasty published by Smith & Dawson (1924; figure 62). A similar abscess was present in a Peruvian child with Pott's disease (Allison *et al.*, 1973), adjacent renal involvement was evident also in this person and multiple focal fibrotic areas in the lung and other organs suggested the terminal episode was hematogenous dissemination (miliary tuberculosis). In an Egyptian child mummy from the New Kingdom, Zimmerman (1979) found acid-fast bacilli in the lytic lumbar vertebral lesions, but felt the lung was also involved because multiple pulmonary fibrotic areas contained blood pigment (hemosiderin) and blood was present in some of the bronchi.

This small number of reported soft tissue lesions can not be interpreted to reflect the frequency of tuberculosis. The paucity of tuberculosis soft tissue reports is most surely the result of preservation factors as well as the limited number of serious and detailed studies on mummies with well-preserved viscera, carried out by experienced operators. Furthermore, application of molecular biology methodology to suggestive lesions can be expected to result in more certain (and, therefore, reported) examples in the future. Arriaza *et al.*, 1994; Salo *et al.*, 1994).

Appearance of skeletal lesions of tuberculosis

Almost all physicians agree that the diagnosis of skeletal tuberculosis is not a simple matter, but the task is much more complicated when we are confronted solely with dry bones (Morse, 1978). Under such circumstances diagnostic error will certainly be multiplied many times, and the opportunity to achieve even a modicum of certainty will be enhanced in cases with involvement of the spine. The lesions of skeletal tuberculosis in nonspinal locations may be indistinguishable from those of other etiologies. For these reasons it becomes especially important to study not only the lesions themselves, but also their distribution within the skeleton and within the populations that are being examined (Pfeiffer, 1991). Buikstra (1976) includes the following parameters in the diagnosis of tuberculosis in skeletal populations:

1. Age of death of the individual.
2. Lesion morphology.
3. Lesion location.
4. Extra-vertebral location.

As explained above, tubercle bacilli, distributed by the blood, become arrested particularly in the areas of hematopoietic marrow (trabecular bone) rather than in the cortex or medullary cavity of the diaphysis and this explains the frequency of tuberculosis of the spine at all ages (Ortner & Putschar, 1985). According to these authors, joint tuberculosis is intimately linked to involvement of the adjacent bones, but the process may begin in the synovial membrane or in the bone or in both simultaneously.

Variation in host resistance, bacillary virulence and size of the inoculum influence the disease manifestations (Morse, 1978; Piulachs, 1957). The disease progresses most rapidly and often fatally in people who have little resistance. On the contrary, tuberculosis becomes chronic in those who have a good immune response. In this latter case it is possible to find the changes associated with bone regeneration and healing. It is important to note that only a small %age of individuals die from skeletal tuberculosis itself. Cases of skeletal tuberculosis exhibiting pulmonary or other soft tissue lesions of tuberculous origin are associated with high mortality rates, with peaks in the mid-20s and 30s (Palkovich, 1981).

Recent clinical reports indicate that skeletal tuberculosis is observed in about 1 % of all patients with tuberculosis (Davidson & Horowitz, 1970; Zimmerman & Kelley, 1982). However, in the preantibiotic era the incidence of skeletal involvement averaged 5–7 % (Cheyne, 1911; LaFond, 1958; Steinbock, 1976). In the past the bulk of such patients were children. Modern specialists, however, have commented on the decreasing frequency of bone tuberculosis in children ever since the 1930s, 20 years before effective treatment of tuberculosis was available. Similarly, the male predominance seen often several generations ago is gradually subsiding. In the opinion of Kelley & Micozzi (1984), the diagnosis of tuberculosis in human skeletal remains has been based upon the detection of secondary osseous lesions that result from hematogenous dissemination of the tubercle bacilli. Since those lesions develop in less than 7 % of cases, the paleodemography and paleoepidemiology of this disease have been difficult to assess from skeletal remains (Palkovich, 1981;

Kelley & Micozzi, 1984). Bennike (1985), therefore, warns that the absence of reported tuberculous findings in archaeological bones gives us no cause to conclude that the disease had not been present in a studied population.

Tuberculosis is characterized predominantly by destruction of the skeletal tissue, appearing as a pattern of resorptive lesions with little evidence of proliferative, reactive changes. Powell (1992) notes that this pattern has important implications for paleopathological criteria. However, an additional and often insufficiently emphasized factor must be considered. The bones predominantly affected by tuberculosis are fragile and susceptible to postmortem resorptive processes; frequently they may not be systematically collected in archaeological excavations. This is applicable especially to children's bones, because they are more apt to become eroded and to disintegrate (Brothwell, 1981).

Although the morphology of tuberculous lesions in dry bone is not specific, Ortner & Putschar (1985) suggest that the general pattern of bone and joint tuberculosis is characterized by:

1. Very little, if any, perifocal reactive bone formation is shown; the lesion is primarily or exclusively a lytic process.
2. In long bones, the process is localized in the metaphyses or in the epiphyses.
3. Sequestra are very uncommon. Except for spina ventosa, periosteal reactive bone formation is very limited.
4. Involvement of soft tissue adjacent to bone, often with skin fistulae, is commonly found.
5. Hematogenous dissemination to the synovium can preserve joint structure, but joints becoming infected by perforation from a metaphyseal abscess will commonly suffer severe anatomic disruption and even ankylosis.
6. Like osteomyelitis, peripheral involvement of the growth palate in a growing bone may stimulate growth, but destructive involvement can arrest growth.
7. Healed areas remodel.

Buikstra (1976) describes tuberculous skeletal lesions in a group of native arctic bones as 'concave, smooth-walled reaction areas that are oval, circular, or coalesced, ranging from 5 to 32 mm diameter in vertebral and long bone articular areas, but less than 3 mm in rib and nonarticular surfaces.'

Certain features of tuberculosis can be exploited for assistance in paleopathological diagnosis. These include the fact that osseous tuberculosis is a disease of young people and both sexes are equally affected (Bullough, 1992), but males predominate (Schinz et al., 1953). Direct progression of primary tuberculosis to a fatal outcome is more common in younger individuals than adults (Palkovich, 1981).

Multiple skeletal lesions are more common in children than in adults, but constitute the minority (5–15 %) of all patients with skeletal tuberculosis (Messner, 1987), although Kelley and El-Najjar (1980) suggest these low figures may be an artifact of radiological and autopsy dissection limitations, and that the actual figure may approach 40 %.

While most skeletal tuberculosis involves joints, it is not always possible in living patients (nor in archaeological bones) to be certain whether the infection began within the joint or in the cancellous tissue of the metaphysis (Aegerter & Kirkpatrick, 1975).

Tuberculosis of the spine

The organisms arrive at the spine from a primary extraspinal focus in the lungs, urinary system or others sites as described earlier. Table 7.2 and Fig. 7.10 indicate distribution of affected vertebrae. The spine is usually infected via hematogenous dissemination, but can be involved by direct extension from adjacent visceral lesions. The organisms spread from an involved area in the trabecular bone of the vertebral body to a site beneath the anterior longitudinal ligament. They may also

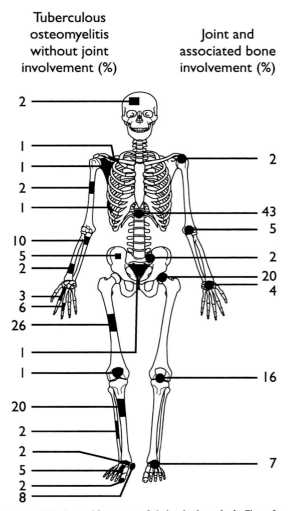

FIG. 7.10: **Distribution and frequency of skeletal tuberculosis.** These frequencies were calculated by pooling the published results of multiple major studies including Fraser (1914), Johansson (1926), Sorrel & Sorrel-Dejerine (1932), Sevastikoglou & Wernerheim (1953), LaFond (1958), Somerville & Wilkinson (1965), Tuli (1975), Martini et al. (1986) and Martini (1988). Numerical values were also included as cited in Sevastikoglou & Wernerheim (1953) for studies by Frosch, Whitman, Valtancoli, Brolin, Sanchis-Olmos and Garophalides.

FIG. 7.11: **Tuberculosis, spine.** Several vertebral bodies have been partially or completely destroyed by tuberculosis infection causing a sharp angulation in the spine (Pott's disease). No. MM4318. Modern adult. Courtesy P. Sledzik. NMHM.

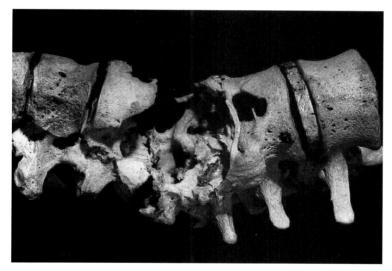

FIG. 7.12: **Tuberculosis, spine.** Note absence of new bone formation. Spine angulated (same specimen as shown in Fig. 7.11), but straightened for the photograph to reveal more structural detail. No. MM4318. Modern adult. Courtesy P. Sledzik. NMHM.

spread directly by necrosis of intervening tissue from one vertebral body to the next (Aegerter & Kirkpatrick, 1975), although such a pattern is probably more plausibly explained as simultaneous delivery of tubercle bacilli to vertebral bone located on adjacent aspects of an intervertebral disc, based on the aforementioned distribution pattern of the arterial blood supply. Distribution within the vertebral body may be (La Rocca, 1986; Bullough, 1992):

- *Anterior* (20 %) leading to cortical destruction under the longitudinal ligament and extension of the infection to adjacent vertebrae. The disk height is preserved. Anterior tuberculous disease is associated with spine deformation only infrequently.

- *Paradiskal* location (more than 50 %) eroding the cartilaginous end plate with narrowing of the disk space and causing kyphosis by bone destruction in the metaphyseal region of the vertebrae.

- *Central* (20–30 %) that starts in the middle of the vertebral body and spreads to involve the entire vertebral body, producing collapse and kyphosis Figs. 7.11 & 7.12).

This latter complication can appear at all ages, but the peak incidence is usually cited as 20–30 years. However, more recently Murray et al. (1990) found that almost half of those involved by spinal tuberculosis are under 10 years of age. Spinal tuberculosis or Pott's disease is the most common of the skeletal lesions in tuberculosis and it accounts for up to 50 % of all cases presenting skeletal involvement (Table 7.2), affecting especially the lower region from T8 to L4 vertebrae (Jaffe, 1972; Aegerter & Kirkpatrick, 1975; Manchester, 1983a; Resnick & Niwayama, 1989b). Some workers even believe that spinal lesions are more frequent than the sum of all other sites of skeletal tuberculosis (Murray et al., 1990). The extreme upper and lower (sacral) ends of the spine are less often involved. Steinbock (1976) notes that the initial site of spinal tuberculosis is usually the first lumbar vertebra and suggests organisms may reach it from the adjacent affected kidneys via Batson's paravertebral venous plexus or lymph nodes. Intervertebral disk involvement is often early (though complete destruction is rare). In some cases, the lesion appears to be restricted to the disk, sparing the vertebrae (Adams, 1986), though the absence of a blood supply to the disk area makes it more probable that in such cases a small vertebral abscess beginning adjacent to the cartilaginous plate may be beyond radiological resolution.

The most prominent features for a paleopathological diagnosis of spinal tuberculosis suggested by Morse (1961) are still cited frequently and remain of value:

- Spinal tuberculosis infrequently involves more than one to four vertebrae.

- Destruction of skeletal tissue is the most prominent feature. Bone regeneration is rare.

- In tuberculous vertebrae, destruction of the trabecular bone of the vertebral body results in its failure to support weight of the upper trunk, and its collapse produces the hump-backed condition or gibbus (angular kyphosis) that is typical in advanced Pott's disease (Fig. 7.13). The anterior portion of the vertebral body is usually most seriously involved. Kyphosis is most marked in the thoracic spine, while lumbar lesions may terminate with telescoping of the defect rather than severe angulation. In spite of the vertebral collapse and deformity, the diameter of the spinal canal is infrequently narrowed (Steinbock, 1976).

- Posterior vertebral element involvement (neural arches, transverse and spinous processes) can occur but is uncommon. However, an exception to this rule is suboccipital tuberculosis involving the atlas and axis; this can lead to subluxation (Ortner & Putschar, 1985; Resnick & Niwayama, 1989b). Posterior element findings include destruction of the laminae, erosion of the cortex of the vertebral bodies and adjacent ribs, paraspinal mass and relative sparing of the intervertebral discs (Resnick & Niwayama, 1989b).

■ Extravertebral cold (tuberculous) abscesses are frequent (50–90 % of the cases). This occurs posteriorly in the cervical and upper thoracic vertebrae and the sinus tracts may drain externally. The much more common anterior abscesses in the lower thoracic and lumbar areas have been described above. The 'scalloped' radiological appearance resulting from multiple abscesses lying between the anterior spinal ligament and the vertebral body is apparent also in archaeological bones as an excessively deep concavity of the anterior vertebral surfaces of several, adjacent vertebrae.

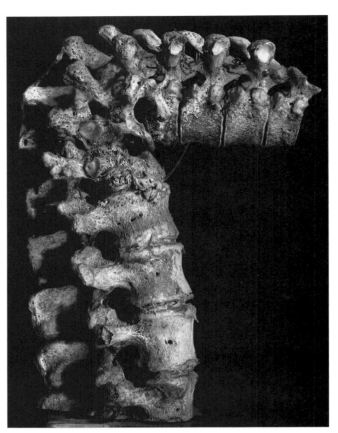

FIG. 7.14: **Tuberculosis, spine.** Pott's deformity with stabilization by new bone formation due to healing. No. 1194.55. Modern adult. Courtesy G. Worden. MM.

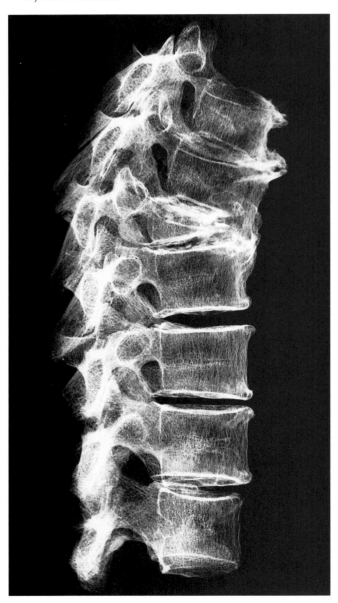

FIG. 7.13: **Tuberculous vertebritis (Pott's disease).** X-ray demonstrates wedge-shaped collapse of infected vertebra. Case 5, 17-18th century, Catalonia, Spain. Courtesy Dr D. Campillo. MAC.

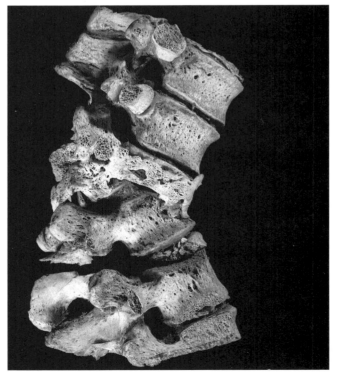

FIG. 7.15: **Tuberculosis, spine.** Several vertebrae show tuberculous destruction and collapse. Some new bone formation may represent fracture response or healing. Note spinal angulation (Pott's disease). No. 1194.16. Modern adult. Courtesy G. Worden. MM.

- Massive regeneration of bone is very uncommon. Spontaneous fusion occurs but is infrequent. However, in some cases the periosteum will respond to the vertebral fracture effects sufficiently to fuse the vertebrae, as it also does when complete healing occurs (Schinz *et al.*, 1953; Brothwell, 1981; Resnick & Niwayama, 1989*b*) (Figs. 7.14 & 7.15).

Buikstra (1976) believes that Morse's definition is unnecessarily narrow because bone involvement frequently includes extravertebral areas, commonly joints. Other useful diagnostic criteria of spinal tuberculosis include:

- Isolated lesions in widely separated vertebrae occur very uncommonly (about 5 % of the cases: Schinz *et al.*, 1953; Revell, 1986; Bullough, 1992).
- An early tuberculous focus is often located near either end plate of the vertebral body. This distribution is consistent with the vascular distribution described above. However, initial involvement of one of the vertebral processes is not uncommon (Murray *et al.*, 1990).
- If healing occurs, the osseous contour is smooth-walled and the earlier osteopenia is replaced by restoration of normal bone density (Adams, 1986).

Tuberculosis of the ribs

Involvement of ribs in tuberculosis is not rare. Kelley & Micozzi (1984) found the following features in the ribs of people killed by *Mycobacterium tuberculosis*, whose skeletons are curated in the Hamann–Todd Collection of the Cleveland Museum of Natural History:

- Nearly 9 % of the individuals with pulmonary tuberculosis have rib lesions that can be found in two forms: diffuse periostitis (more common) and localized abscess (much less frequent).
- Mild to moderate periostitis is restricted to the internal surface of the ribs usually involving several adjacent ribs, most commonly ribs four to eight. They suggest that the lesions develop from a subjacent infection of the pleura and lungs (tuberculous empyema).
- Much less commonly, the infection penetrates deeper into the cortex involving the central portion of the rib body. The costal head and neck are not affected.
- Rib lesions are twice as common in the left hemithorax.

As noted above, the tuberculous specificity of these lesions is controversial.

Pfeiffer (1991) describes three somewhat differing categories of rib lesions:

1. Plaque (84.5 %): these are distinct layers of dense periosteal bone deposited as a discrete plaque. These sometimes become detached, leaving traces too subtle to assess with confidence.
2. Expansion (13.6 %): a puffy, porous cortical expansion is differentiated from plaque primarily by its porosity and lack of distinct edges. As in the previous condition, expansion affects the interior aspect of the ribs and extends from the rib head or neck.
3. Resorption (1.9 %): erosive lesions of the rib head and neck appear, comparable to those of the vertebrae. Pfeiffer feels that these resorptive lesions are the only potentially diagnostic category of tuberculosis.

Comparison of these findings with those of Kelley & Micozzi (1984) suggests that Pfeiffer's no.3 lesion may be similar to the deeper one described by Kelley & Micozzi, and even her no.2 lesion might also be, but Pfeiffer's no.1 lesion is not described as having the broad area of distribution over multiple ribs as is Kelley & Micozzi's 'periostitis' lesion. Furthermore, the fragility and detachable character of Pfeiffer's 'plaque' lesion suggests it is not likely to represent a later, remodeled stage of that periostitis lesions. The issue remains unresolved.

Tuberculosis of the sternum

Sternal involvement in tuberculosis is uncommon in Caucasians (Murray *et al.*, 1990). When it does occur, the manubrium is most frequently involved by a lytic lesion, commonly resulting in complete destruction of the sternal body. Sclerosis and loss of the normal texture constitute the late deformity.

Tuberculosis of the diaphyses of the long bones

These lesions are rare in adults. Even in children they are not really common. The bones affected most frequently are tibia, ulna, radius, humerus, femur, and fibula (Konschegg, 1934 cited in Ortner & Putschar, 1985:161). Tuberculous infection of the diaphysis heals more readily and extensive bone destruction is unusual. The condition occurs by hematogenous dissemination; involvement by direct expansion from an adjacent focus is uncommon (Casagrande & Frost, 1955). The disease usually begins under the periosteum and may spread into the epiphysis. In children lesions near the bone ends may involve the growth plate, distorting bone development sufficiently to cause deformity (Turek, 1982; Revell, 1986). Osteopenia is the earliest sign of skeletal tuberculosis in these areas. Later eccentric cavitation, usually in the metaphysis, leads to bone destruction. The osteolytic areas are surrounded by diffuse osteopenia (Turek, 1982). Only the cortex overlying the lesion responds with marked reactive bone formation (Ortner & Putschar, 1985:159). Sequestra are rare and small, with little osteosclerosis, although sometimes with abscess and fistula formation. Paradoxically, occasionally the periosteum responds with a burst of activity resulting in a hypertrophic lesion with increased radiological density (Casagrande & Frost, 1955).

Tuberculous dactylitis (spina ventosa)

The short, tubular bones of the hands and feet in children represent an exception to the general rule that the diaphysis of a bone is usually not affected primarily by tuberculosis

(Schinz et al., 1953). This is probably because in children they contain trabecular bone with actively productive marrow; the lesion is rare in adults. The condition is produced by osteolysis followed by cortical erosion of the short tubular bones of the hands and feet. The apparent lack of agreement about the actual frequency of spina ventosa in the literature may be due to differences in patient population seen by the reporting investigators. When its frequency is assessed by age group it is apparent that spina ventosa is one of the most frequent manifestations of skeletal tuberculosis in the period of infancy and early childhood, and that the lesion is rare after the first decade of life. The condition generally spares the joints (Murray et al., 1990). Early lesions show thickening of the periosteum of the metacarpals and phalanges. Destructive lesions appear later, but new bone formation is found under the periosteum, generating the typical fusiform appearance (Adams, 1986). Destruction of the growth plate can lead to marked shortening.

Tuberculosis of the joints: general features

The fourth decade of life is the most frequent age of tuberculous joint involvement (Rotés Mas, 1983; Resnick & Niwayama, 1989b). Involvement of the joints in tuberculosis can occur via hematogenous dissemination or by direct extension of a bone lesion (Jaffe, 1972). Frequently, articular tuberculosis results from a combination of osteomyelitis and arthritis (Messner, 1987). Uribarri Murillo & Palacios y Carvajal (1990) believe synovial infection extending to the bone is the most frequent form of articular tuberculosis. A characteristic feature of tuberculous arthritis is that it tends to produce an identical lesion on the two opposing surfaces of the joint (Steinbock, 1976). The joints are destroyed by a replacement of the synovial lining with tuberculous granulation tissue (Aegerter & Kirkpatrick, 1975). Articular tuberculosis usually only affects one joint (85 % of the cases). Bilateral involvement of the same joint is very uncommon (Jaffe, 1972; Aegerter & Kirkpatrick, 1975; Resnick & Niwayama, 1989b). Aside from the spine, the joints of the

hip and knee are the most commonly affected (Table 7.3). Tarsus, elbow, wrist, and shoulder joints are also affected.

Several features in joint tuberculosis are almost always present:
- Osteopenia: deossification of the bones distal and proximal to the joints is usually dramatic (Edeiken, 1976), commonly not produced until the limb is at rest (Schinz et al., 1953).
- Marginal erosion of the bone.
- Destruction of the subchondral bone, that can be very deep on many occasions (Dastugue & Gervais, 1992).
- Frequently the periarticular destructive lesions are of oval shape, with well marked edges and without periosteal reaction (Messner, 1987).
- Sequestrum formation is rare.
- New bone formation is of much lesser degree in osteoarticular tuberculosis than in other infectious osteoarthropathies.
- The primary osseous focus is not located in the diaphysis of the long bones but in the metaphysis.

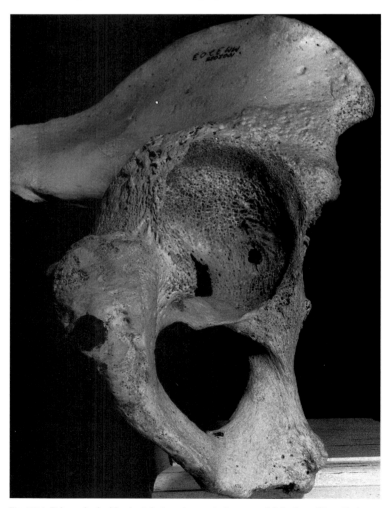

FIG. 7.16: **Tuberculosis, hip.** Acetabulum demonstrates several defects and its articular surface is granular. The periphery of the acetabulum is characterized by new bone formation probably representing healing phase of this tuberculous infection. No. 1000235. Modern adult. Courtesy P. Sledzik. NMHM.

Table 7.3. Distribution of joints involved in 7300 localizations of tuberculous joints

Joint involved	Number of localizations	% of all localizations
Spine	3101	43
Hip	1489	20
Knee	1151	16
Foot and ankle	514	7
Sacro-iliac	159	2
Shoulder	164	2
Elbow	367	5
Hand and wrist	323	4
Other	32	1
Total	7300	100

These are pooled figures from the findings of five authors (Sorrel & Sorrel-Dejerine, 1932; Cleveland, 1939; Sevastikoglou & Wernerheim, 1953; Somerville & Wilkinson, 1965; Martini, 1988).

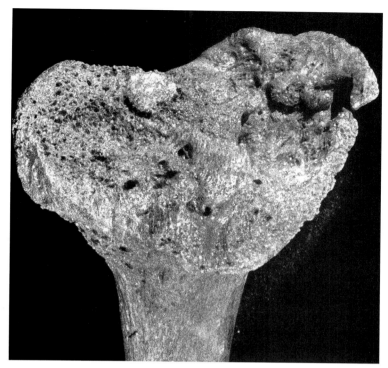

FIG. 7.17: **Tuberculosis, knee.** The tibial surface has undergone much destruction by the tuberculous process. No. E1. Modern case. CMNH.

The destructive changes of the joints can progress ultimately to ankylosis (Manchester, 1983a). The extensive articular destruction that is so typical of tuberculous arthritis is a late phenomenon, appearing years after the onset of joint involvement (Rotés Mas, 1983). In the most severe cases, secondary deformities and pathological fractures appear (Schinz et al., 1953). A well established infection rarely heals without considerable bone and joint destruction (Aegerter & Kirkpatrick, 1975).

Hip joint

The hip represents 20 % of the cases of skeletal involvement, making it the second most frequent skeletal lesion after vertebral involvement (Table 7.3). It is most common in children between 3 and 10 years of age, and 80 % of all modern patients are under 25 years (Schinz et al., 1953). In addition to a hematogenous origin, the hip can be involved by direct extension of the bacilli from an adjacent paravertebral or pelvic abscess. Tuberculous bacilli can escape from capillaries located in the synovial membrane, in the acetabulum or in the proximal femur (Messner, 1987). Bone destruction is seen most commonly in the acetabulum though head, femoral neck and trochanter are also frequently affected. In the late stages of the disease severe destruction of the femoral head and acetabulum is produced, and soft tissue cold abscesses and fistula formation are present (Fig. 7.16). The destruction may be so extensive that the hip can be partially or completely dislocated (Turek, 1982). Growth arrest secondary to fusion of the femoral growth plate

results in shortness of the affected limb (Schinz et al., 1953; Turek, 1982). If healing occurs, bony ankylosis is a common feature. Coxa valga and, most rarely, coxa vara are common deformities in persons with a tuberculous hip (Schinz et al., 1953).

Knee joint

Involvement of the knee is seen in about 16 % of cases of skeletal tuberculosis (Table 7.3). Some authors (Turek, 1982) state that tuberculosis of the knee is seen most frequently in adults while spinal and hip involvement affect children most commonly. During the first decade of life, however, children are affected as often as adults. Others (Ortner & Putschar, 1985) feel that the majority of cases start in infancy, childhood, and adolescence with an equal distribution between the sexes. These differing views probably reflect differences in observed patient populations. Most patients present with bone and synovial involvement at the same time.

The majority of cases begin as synovial tuberculosis and deforming lesions of the knee surface (femoral condyles, tibial plateau) are the product of a primary or simultaneous hematogenous osseous focus (Ortner & Putschar, 1985:154; Fig. 7.17). In archaeological bones, however, it is often not possible to be certain whether the lesion initiated in the synovium or the metaphysis. In the very advanced cases, posterior subluxation of the tibia may occur (Zimmerman & Kelley, 1982). Occasional valgus or varus deformity is seen (Turek, 1982). Isolated skeletal foci in the patella presenting small, rounded cavities with slight sclerosis are reported but uncommon (Schinz et al., 1953). If healing occurs, ankylosis may develop.

Sacroiliac joint

Sacroiliac joint involvement occurs in up to 2 % of cases of skeletal tuberculosis. The joint is one of the few in which tuberculous involvement commonly is bilateral. This is most likely because almost all of the cases are associated with spinal involvement, affecting the sacroiliac joint by direct extension, which is probably why the lesion is usually not encountered until very late childhood or even young adulthood. The majority of the lesions are destructive and abscess formation is common. Prolonged survival almost always leads to bony ankylosis, often with asymmetrical deformities (Ortner & Putschar, 1985:149).

Ankle and foot

These are involved simultaneously in most cases due to expansion from an adjacent soft tissue focus or by hematogenous dissemination. The tibiotalar joint is usually involved in children, while in adults the talus and other tarsal bones are commonly affected. Early abscess and fistula formation are common complications (Ortner & Putschar, 1985:155). Centrally destructive and isolated lesions are seen in the talus and calcaneus. Such an isolated lesion leads to extension to the metatarsal bones and toes (Turek, 1982). One-third of the patients show articular deformities: pes equinus, pes varus or pes valgus. Healing ankle lesions commonly progress to ankylosis.

Elbow

The elbow is very frequently involved (see Fig. 7.10). The initial lesion usually begins in the humerus. Bone destruction can be very severe in the elbow joint, extending into adjacent structures. The joint commonly becomes completely deformed and the head of the radius is often dislocated posteriorly. Healing usually begins by neoarthrosis formation and bony ankylosis may occur. Pseudoarthrosis is a rare finding.

Shoulder

Tuberculosis of the shoulder is uncommon and adults are more often affected than children. The process is commonly located in the anatomical neck of the humerus and in the glenoid cavity of the scapula, although extension of the process to the acromioclavicular joint may occur. The right side is affected three times more frequently than the left (Kremer & Wiese, 1930, cited by Ortner & Putschar, 1985:157). In the final stages of the disease in children, shortening of the upper limb follows involvement of the growth plate.

Wrist

Involvement of the wrist is not common. This occurs most commonly in children due to extension from a carpal infection. In adults the disease is the result of extension from an adjacent soft tissue focus in the tendons of the wrist (Turek, 1982). In children, the carpometacarpal joint is mainly involved and the radiocarpal joint is spared while, in adults, the process usually begins in the radiocarpal joint and spreads rapidly throughout the other joints of the wrist (Ortner & Putschar, 1985:159).

The pathological features most commonly seen are those of osteopenia and destruction of the wrist bones, usually the distal articular surface of the radius, navicular, lesser multangular, capitate and the proximal extremities of the second and third metacarpals. Sometimes cold abscess and fistula formation develop.

Tuberculosis of the skull

The skull is a rare site of skeletal tuberculosis and it affects young adults almost exclusively secondary to hematogenous dissemination. The cranial vault is the most common site of cranial tuberculosis. Murray et al. (1990) found that tuberculosis of the skull appears as numerous small areas of destruction of less than 2 cm in diameter, with poorly defined margins and some surrounding reactive sclerosis. Abscess and fistula formation occur. Not uncommonly, the lesion crosses the cranial sutures (Ortner & Putschar, 1985:163). The tuberculous focus is rarely solitary in children, although in adults it almost always is. Dastugue & Gervais (1992) allege that tuberculous lesions in the skull are purely destructive (with isolated sequestra) from the outside to the inside of the skull. Involvement of the cranial base (tuberculous otitis media and suboccipital tuberculosis), facial bones and mandible occurs but is less common.

Differential diagnosis of tuberculosis-like lesions

Many pathological conditions can be diagnosed mistakenly as tuberculosis in dry bone, especially when they affect the spine. The most important are listed below.

Chronic pyogenic osteomyelitis

It is important to note that tuberculous vertebral changes are brought about over a much longer period of time than the usual course of chronic pyogenic osteomyelitis. Therefore, tuberculosis can produce a much greater degree of vertebral destruction and deformities. On the other hand, in spinal tuberculosis new bone formation is not produced until the infection is in a much more advanced stage than in chronic pyogenic osteomyelitis (La Rocca, 1986). In contrast to pyogenic osteomyelitis, sequestra are either small or absent in tuberculosis. Finally, gibbus and paravertebral abscess formation are only uncommonly found in vertebral osteomyelitis.

Brucella osteomyelitis

In this disease, paravertebral abscess formation is uncommon and periosteal proliferation in long bones may be prominent.

Fungal infections (especially blastomycosis and coccidioidomycosis)

Involvement of posterior elements is common in fungal infections affecting the spine, a feature that is very infrequently found in tuberculosis.

Typhoid spine

Most of these lesions centralize in the lumbar region. They have a close resemblance to other pyogenic infections and are separated from tuberculosis by the same other criteria as for vertebral osteomyelitis as described above.

Healed vertebral fractures

In these, usually only one vertebra is involved and there is much less destruction of the vertebral body (Ortner & Putschar, 1985). Kyphosis is not angular. A large, localized, calcified callus may be distinctive (see Fig. 3.6).

Actinomycosis

Osseous involvement by actinomycosis is rare; the mandible is the most commonly affected area. In the spine neural arch lesions occur as frequently as those of the body, while the disk space is spared.

Echinococciasis

Skeletal involvement is not as common as in tuberculosis. In the spine the laminae and adjacent ribs are involved while the disk is usually spared.

Histoplasmosis

Skeletal lesions are rare in this disease and vertebral involvement is very uncommon.

Histiocytosis-X

In the age group affected by tuberculosis of the cranial vault the lesions must be differentiated from eosinophilic granuloma. In the latter disease the solitary lesions usually do not contain a central sequestrum and do not cross the cranial sutures (Ortner & Putschar, 1985:163).

Sarcoidosis

This disease can produce multifocal lesions of vertebrae and intervertebral disks with paraspinal masses (Resnick & Niwayama, 1989b) but is extremely rare (Buikstra, 1976).

Septic arthritis

In septic arthritis the process is much less destructive and much more rapid than in tuberculosis.

Traumatic arthritis

True osteoarthritic changes in synovial joints are frequently seen in association with compression fractures (Buikstra, 1976).

Malignant bone tumors

The angle of the gibbus is usually very acute when the vertebra is destroyed by spinal tuberculosis, while it is more obtuse when malignant bone tumors replace the vertebral body (Schinz et al., 1953). Cancers frequently involve more than two noncontiguous vertebrae and neural arch and ribs often display associated lesions (Buikstra, 1976).

Rheumatoid arthritis

All forms of infective arthritis, including tuberculosis, are more often unilateral than is rheumatoid arthritis. However, the differential diagnosis between both entities can be extremely difficult.

Paget's disease (osteitis deformans)

There are no resorptive foci and kyphosis is due to compression fractures. In general, vertebral lesions are rare (Buikstra, 1976).

Ankylosing spondylitis

Although involvement of the anterior aspect of vertebral bodies occurs in ankylosing spondylitis, rarefaction is much more common than cyst formation in vertebral bodies (Buikstra, 1976).

Scheuermann's disease

Kyphosis in this disease is not angular and the resorptive areas are not round but more rectangular.

LEPROSY

Definition and taxonomy

Leprosy (Hansen's disease) is a chronic infectious disease of humans, affecting skin, nasal tissues, peripheral nerves and bone caused by *Mycobacteruim leprae*. Its two clinical forms, tuberculoid (TT) or lepromatous (LL) leprosy are reflected by the degree of the host's immunological response. Hence intermediate or borderline forms occur.

The taxonomic position of *Mycobacterium leprae* is discussed in the section on 'Tuberculosis,' above. Like the other species in this genus, its waxy coat is intensely resistant to removal of the fuchsin (red) stain by acid solutions ('acid-fast'). In contrast to all other mycobacteria, however, the leprosy bacillus has never been cultured successfully in vitro. This has restricted the study of its biochemical and immunologically-related features profoundly. After considerable effort, several animals have been found to be vulnerable to infection by this organism. Injection of mouse foot pads with this organism has evolved as a standard laboratory model (Shepard, 1982). The nine-banded armadillo (*Dasypus novemcinctus*) develops widespread disease after *M. leprae* injection (Storrs, 1972), and the huge numbers of bacilli in its lesions are useful for studying the organism's biochemical features. However, its slow growth rate (often years) in this animal has made the mouse the preferred experimental animal for routine applications. Immunosuppression can increase the infectivity of injected animals. Temperatures closer to 30 °C than to the usual 37 °C of mammalian core temperatures enhance growth of M. *leprae*. Study of this organism is expected to be broadened by successful cloning of its DNA into *Escherichia coli* recently. To date no strain differences have been related consistently to the two major clinical forms of the disease described below.

Epidemiology

Leprosy has a worldwide distribution. Today its principal locations are characterized by tropical conditions (Fig.7.18). However, factors other than those of temperature and humidity appear to influence its distribution. Central China, Korea and even the southern U.S.A. are exceptions to the largely tropical predominance, and during the Middle Ages the disease was endemic throughout northern Europe at latitudes as high as Norway (Carmichael, 1993b). Indeed, Hunter & Thomas (1984) point out that 2 billion people (half of the world's population) live in countries where leprosy prevalence exceeds 100/100 000 population and thus puts them at risk for this disease. Recent data (WHO, 1992) has reduced the estimated number of persons who are infected with leprosy worldwide from the former 10–12 million to about 5 million. Prevalence figures are highest in Asia and Africa, then South America and then Oceania in that order.

Geographic, socioeconomic and other, often undefined, variables can produce striking epidemiological differences. Howe (1977) notes that only 10 % of tropical African cases are of the lepromatous (most infectious) type while in the Americas it represents about 60 % of the cases. In India about one-third of clinical cases experience their first symptom or sign during childhood and only 7 % become infected after age 35, while the numbers for the U.S.A. are 10.1 and 43 % respectively (Badger, 1964). Newborns of infected mothers, however, manifest no lesions. While the latent interval between infection and clinical manifestations is not known with certainty, most leprologists feel it is usually between 3 and 4 years. The disease is known to affect family members preferentially, although even prolonged exposure, e.g. between spouses, still results in a transmission rate of only about 5–10 %. Adult-to-child transmission rates are about five times greater, although three-fourths of children becoming infected within leprosaria experience only a single skin lesion after which they often heal spontaneously. Here, too, geographic differences are of major magnitude. The contact source is identifiable within the victim's extended family

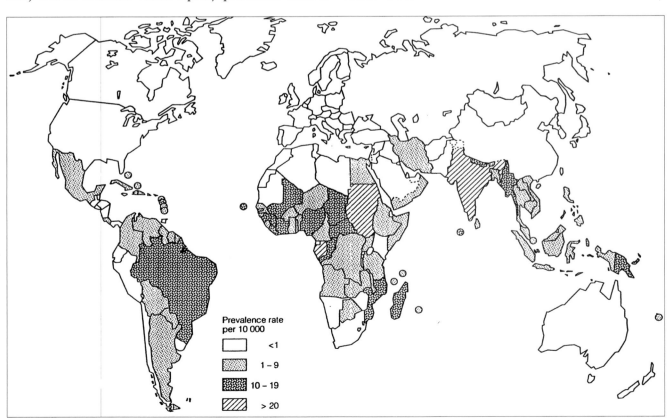

Prevalence rate per 10 000

☐ <1

▦ 1 – 9

▦ 10 – 19

▨ > 20

FIG. 7.18: **Prevalence of registered leprosy cases as at February 1992.** Update by the Leprosy Unit of the World Health Organization of a map origi- nally published in *World Health Statistics Quarterly* **44(1)**:3, 1991. By permis- sion of the World Health Organization.

62 % of the time but only in 34 % of U.S.A. cases (Badger, 1964). Reasons for male predilection are not clear. May (1958:151) laments that 'nothing...really explains satisfactorily the geographical pattern of occurrence.'

Leprosy appears to flourish best in rural environments as it did in northern Europe during the Middle Ages. Muir (1968) described leprosy as a disease of villages. Reasons for this remain obscure. Its prevalence as judged by leprosaria construction, increased initially with urbanization in England during the eleventh century, but declined rapidly after the thirteenth and also somewhat later in parts of Africa (Hunter & Thomas, 1984; Manchester, 1992). In addition to nonspecific health factors such as nutrition, leprosy prevalence is influenced greatly by apparent organism virulence as well as the cross-reaction effects of exposure to mycobacterial antigen by infection with M. tuberculosis or an atypical species as well as immunization by BCG vaccine (see Interactions between leprosy and tuberculosis, below). Today, of course, active drug treatment programs are also very influential.

Although 10 % of feral armadillos in parts of the southwestern U.S.A. are infected with a bacillus indistinguishable from M. leprae and it has been found also in a New World monkey (sooty mangabey Cerrocebus torquatus), transmission to humans is still considered to be person-to-person. Inability to culture the organism has hindered such studies and for years transmission methods were speculative. Injections of humans with leprosy-infected tissue suspensions have usually failed to transmit the disease although surgical implantation in one patient was successful (Arning, 1884, cited in Skinsnes, 1973). Experimentally the clinical form of the disease can be shown to be related to the method of transmission in mice, skin entry developing the immune response characteristic of the tuberculoid form and intraperitoneal or other routes resulting in the anergic state found in persons with lepromatous leprosy (Shepard et al., 1982). Because of the cited problems in determination of infection routes in naturally-occurring infections, we have no data whether this is also true in humans. While some uncertainty persists, demonstration that a single sneeze from a nasally-infected person with lepromatous leprosy can aerosolize millions of leprosy bacilli (Davey & Rees, 1974; Pedley & Greater, 1976) has led to general agreement that inhalation of moisture droplets laden with infective bacilli is the most probable route by which leprosy is commonly contracted. Direct skin-to-skin contact involving an ulcerated, infected lesion remains a realistic possibility in occasional patients as a primary inoculum. Nevertheless, Badger (1964:70) suggests that tuberculoid leprosy patients (who do not develop nasal mucosal lesions) are capable of infecting others, noting that on the South Pacific island of Nauru and in Nigeria a substantial fraction of the population developed leprosy, 70–90 % of which was of the tuberculoid form. Currently, however, most leprologists feel that only lepromatous patients are infectious.

Immunological modulations of leprosy infections

The clinical forms of leprosy are influenced profoundly by the immunological status of the patient. The immune status of patients known to be infected with M. leprae can be established by the lepromin test. Described by Hayashi ([1918] 1953) and Mitsuda ([1919] 1953) this is an intradermal injection of lepromin, an extract of leprosy bacilli harvested from diseased tissues. Fernandez's reaction occurs within 48 hours after injection and appears as a reddened, firm area at the injection site. Although the papular reaction described by Mitsuda ([1919] 1953) requires 4 weeks to develop, it correlates better with the patient's immune status. The Mitsuda reaction is regularly negative in lepromatous leprosy patients, but positive in the tuberculoid form. Positive reactions seen commonly in normal persons prevent its employment as a diagnostic test, making it useful only for immune status classification in a known leprosy sufferer.

Leprosy patients with a positive Mitsuda reaction to the lepromin test generally manifest a histological tissue reaction closely resembling that of tuberculosis and the clinical disease associated with this tissue response is appropriately called tuberculoid leprosy (TT). The lepromin reaction and tissue histology suggest these patients are manifesting a delayed hypersensitivity response of a cell-mediated immunity type similar to that seen in patients infected with M. tuberculosis. Few bacilli can be demonstrated in the lesions of tuberculoid leprosy, and for that reason it is sometimes referred to as a paucibacillary form. The infectivity of these patients is believed to be substantially less than that of the lepromatous form. In contrast, patients with a negative Mitsuda reaction demonstrate minimal resistance to actions by the leprosy bacillus. Its relatively uninhibited proliferation in these patients results in huge masses (globi) of accumulated organisms in the tissues, rendering the patient much more infectious to others. These patients are said to have lepromatous leprosy (LL). Laboratory studies suggest a deficient T-cell response to the antigens of M. leprae (Shepard, 1982).

The differences in the clinical appearance and disease course that characterizes these two disease forms is discussed in the natural history of leprosy; section below. It can be stated here, however, that the reason for the differences in immune response remains enigmatic. The fact that linkage to HLA antigens exists (TT-HLA DR3; LL-HLA MT1) suggests that host genetic factors may be responsible. Spitznagel (1989), however, voices an intuitive reservation probably shared by a significant number of other immunologists when he writes that '…suspicion lingers that the infecting organisms themselves play a role in this immunosuppression.' To compound the confusion, experimental data proposes a role for the route of infection (Shepard et al., 1982). Current preventive approaches are based on the assumption of host differences. Conversion from a negative to a positive lepromin reaction following tuberculosis infection or BCG vaccination is discussed in the section Interactions between leprosy and tuberculosis, below.

In addition to the two extremes or polar responses of the immune system described above as the TT or LL forms of the disease, a significant number of patients demonstrate a partial but incomplete response. The degree of this response varies, but encompasses the full spectrum between the two polar extremes. Such intermediate forms are called borderline (BB). Recent attempts to express such degrees of response semiquantitatively have led to the designations borderline toward tuberculoid (BT) or borderline toward lepromatous (BL) leprosy (WHO, 1980). While the position of a given patient along this spectrum is usually quite stable, the prominent immune response that characterizes tuberculoid leprosy may gradually deteriorate in prolonged, untreated cases especially in patients subjected to malnutrition or other infections (Manchester, 1991). In such circumstances the clinical picture begins to acquire some lepromatous features resembling BT, BB or, rarely, BL forms – a process referred to by leprologists as downgrading. The reverse (upgrading from a well-established LL form toward the tuberculoid type) very rarely occurs spontaneously, though treated patients may show some degree of a shift in this direction.

Natural history

The various clinical forms of this disease proved to be so confusing to earlier leprologists that as late as 1935 McCoy wrote '…if we are honest with ourselves we must admit there is no problem about which we know less than we know of this one.' Since that time advances in immunology have led to better recognition of the immune system's relationship to the leprous manifestations, though many questions still remain unanswered. The disease can be viewed as presenting in two different forms: lepromatous and tuberculoid. They are described separately below, followed by a discussion of intermediate or mixed forms.

Lepromatous leprosy (LL)

Facial Features

This form usually initiates as a chronic rhinitis. Symptoms are often so nonspecific as to elude suspicion of leprosy until skin lesions occur. The nasal mucosa becomes ulcerated and crusted, occasionally bleeding sufficiently to lead the patient to seek medical evaluation. Penetrating infection produces septal perforation. Extension to the superior surface of the hard palate may evoke sufficient periostitis to be observable radiologically. More obvious clinically is involvement of the nasal bone, nasal spine and even central maxilla, whose erosion or complete destruction becomes evident when its collapse is betrayed by a sinking and widening of its overlying skin and other soft tissues (saddle nose). This externally obvious soft tissue deformity constitutes one of the major features of a leprosy-sufferer's facial alterations. Nasal secretions literally teem with leprosy bacilli and their documented aerosolization by sneezing is believed to be the most probable method of leprosy transmission today. This rhinomaxillary syndrome (Andersen & Manchester, 1992) is unique to the lepromatous form of leprosy.

At some undetermined point during this interval the patient experiences the first of what often proves to be recurrent episodes of bacillemia that commonly progress to continuous bacteremia. Multiple organs are exposed to the bacilli during these episodes; the circulating bacteria are so plentiful, they may even be observed in peripheral blood smears. Those becoming resident within the internal organs, however, are effectively eliminated via macrophage phagocytic action. Consistent with the bacillus' well-known preference for temperatures lower than 37 °C, the pattern of subsequent invasive infection is that of body areas whose normal temperature is near 30 °C : skin, superficial subcutaneous structures (especially nerves), eyes and testis. The facial skin develops localized swollen areas, with deep lines between them; these nodules may ulcerate. The swollen upper eyelids impart a sleepy appearance and involvement of the supraorbital tissues commonly results in loss of eyebrow hair, particularly in the lateral areas. Later involvement of the sclera and/or iris may lead to blindness. This nodular dermal appearance, often referred to as leonine, is another face-deforming feature characteristic of leprosy.

Finally, the lepromatous rhinitis may extend to the maxilla, complicated further by secondary pyogenic infection. Beginning in the midline, the maxillary bone becomes eroded even to the point of palatal perforation, with consequent loosening of the upper central incisors anteriorly, leading to their loss. In very advanced cases the process may extend laterally as far as the canines. Such loss of maxillary osseous structure with its associated teeth is an additional feature of leprous facial alterations.

Thus facial changes represent a trio of deformities secondary to leprous destruction of the nasal area and the maxilla as well as swollen, infected, nodular lesions of facial skin. Two of these, the nasal spine and maxillary changes, are apparent in archaeological skulls. They are sufficiently unique to suggest strongly that they were caused by leprosy, and their combined presence in dry, archaeological bones has been termed facies leprosa by Møller-Christensen (1965) who found these features commonly in skeletons he excavated from medieval Danish leprosaria cemeteries. The morphological changes induced by these processes as seen in dry bones is detailed in the Skeletal pathology of leprosy section, below.

Nerve lesions

Peripheral nerves are commonly involved by the bacillus in lepromatous leprosy and eventually can produce a palpable, lumpy, hard and stiff nerve trunk in the more superficial (and cooler?) areas around the elbow (ulnar nerve) or the fibula head (peroneal nerve) (Jopling, 1982). The lack of a granulomatous form of inflammatory response, however, reduces the tissue destruction that is characteristically seen early in the tuberculoid form. Hence the leprosy bacilli can accumulate in huge masses (globi) within the nerve sheath, accompanied in some patients by hyperesthesia. More than one-third of a nerve's fibers need to be destroyed to manifest dysfunction. Thus nerve function in this form of leprosy persists much longer than in the tuberculoid form. Only at a later stage will the nonspecific fibrotic reaction to the bacillus' presence destroy enough nerve fibers to produce eventual anesthesia of the hands and feet. While the superficial portions of the nerves are the most severely involved, some lesions may be encountered in the deep areas proximally as far as the posterior root, but not the spinal cord or brain (Jopling, 1982). Traumatic soft tissue changes secondary to the neuropathy are discussed below.

Skin lesions

In addition to the facial lesions described above, multiple dermal lesions are commonly present in the cooler areas of the body (extremities, buttocks). They are hypopigmented in dark-skinned persons and erythematous in lighter-skinned. Their periphery is much more poorly-defined than in the tuberculoid form. The trunk is involved, but usually fewer lesions are located there.

Bone lesions

In only about 5 % of hospitalized patients are bones directly invaded by leprosy bacilli. This occurs commonly by direct extension from a more superficial, overlying soft tissue infected area and less frequently by a hematogenous route (Edeiken & Hodes, 1973; Resnick & Niwayama, 1981). The former generates considerable periostitis while in the latter this is not a prominent feature. Among bones involved by direct extension of leprous infection, the small bones of the hand and feet are involved most commonly. The vascular route can also infect the long bones of extremities. In that event lesions usually begin in the metaphysis but can spread to either the epiphysis or medullary canal.

In the remainder of the cases bone involvement is usually secondary to the peripheral neuropathy. Skin areas rendered anesthetic by nerve infection become vulnerable to tissue destruction because the affected patient is simply not aware of the injury. In addition to fractures, trauma producing loss of skin integrity leads to pyogenic infection, ulceration and extension into deeper tissues. There, nonleprous septic arthritis and/or osteomyelitis results in bone destruction with prominent periosteal reaction. Cessation of locomotion may occur due to muscle paralysis (secondary to nerve involvement) with resulting osteoporosis and bone atrophy. Involvement of the small bones of hands, wrist, foot and ankle is a common pattern. In the hand, phalangeal involvement is the rule, and eventual complete destruction or atrophy of distal phalanges is often accompanied by subsequent

loss of the infected soft tissue as well, producing finger shortening. This can extend progressively as far as the metacarpophalangeal joints. In the foot the process quite commonly involves the metatarsal bones as well, including the tarsus and calcaneus. The end result of these tissue losses can change these distal extremities into club-shaped stumps. The appearance of these changes in dry, archaeological bones is detailed in the Skeletal pathology of leprosy section, below.

Miscellaneous changes

Testicular involvement can cause extensive destruction. Ocular infection often results in complications leading to blindness.

Soft tissue pathology

The gross lesions have been described above. Histologically leprous lesions in LL patients induce a nonspecific inflammatory reaction within which leprosy bacilli abound. Healing occurs by nonspecific fibrosis.

Immunology

In the polar type of lepromatous leprosy described above the lepromin test is invariably nonreactive.

Tuberculoid leprosy (TT)

As its name implies, this clinical disease form shares certain of its features with tuberculosis. Among these are a similar response to the leprosy bacillus' antigens – so similar that most patients with a positive tuberculin test also react positively to intradermal injection of lepromin (see 'Interactions between leprosy and tuberculosis' below). This is also expressed histologically in the form of a prominent granulomatous type of inflammation, though with much less cellular necrosis than in tuberculosis. This immune response can be of clinical benefit in many patients. Children, for example, may develop only a single skin lesion (Bullock, 1985) that frequently progresses to complete healing without further evidence of disease. It also profoundly reduces the number of bacilli in the soft tissue lesions – so much so that tuberculoid leprosy patients are usually considered to be a much lesser infectious hazard to others. Their differences in the clinical disease manifestations are detailed below.

Facial features

The rhinomaxillary complex of features is absent in TT patients. While ocular lesions may be present, these are usually secondary to nonleprous corneal ulceration due to lagophthalmos (incomplete eyelid closure: Jopling, 1982).

Skin lesions

These are fewer than in the LL form; in the pure TT form they are usually single. The location may be anywhere on the body except the warmer areas of axilla, groin and perineum. They begin as macules, commonly in hypesthetic areas, with centrally depressed, sometimes erythematous but usually hypopigmented lesions demonstrating discretely circumscribed, peripheral elevations. The lumpy facial lesions separated by deep lines that make up the striking 'leonine' appearance in LL patients are not seen in those having the TT form. The lesions, though fewer, however, often extend to deeper areas, involving nerves and other tissues in the progressive form of the disease.

Nerve lesions

TT is essentially a peripheral neuropathic disease. While LL patients eventually produce enough scarring to generate anesthetic complications, nerve dysfunction dominates the clinical picture in TT patients. The granulomatous inflammatory tissue response (characteristic of the cell-mediated immunity seen in delayed hypersensitivity), while limiting the number of bacilli present, accomplishes this at the expense of extensive nerve fiber destruction, resulting in damage to enough nerve fibers so that anesthetic complications often are the complaints that bring TT patients to medical attention. They are most common in the distal parts of the extremities.

Bone lesions

The effects on the bones have been described under LL above, but occur earlier and more intensively in TT patients. Repeated, unsensed and therefore often neglected trauma to soft tissues of the hands and feet commonly result in pyogenic, nonleprous infections with all of its complications in the deeper tissues. Muscles innervated by affected nerves become atrophic and may undergo contracture (claw hand). Locomotion loss secondary to muscle paralysis is followed by bone atrophy. Distal phalanges of hands and feet become thinner (pencilling) and may resorb completely. The then unsupported soft tissues, abused and infected by neglected trauma, are lost. The process is then repeated in the next phalanx. It usually stops at the metacarpophalangeal joint in the hand but commonly involves also the metatarsals and even the larger foot bones, until the affected leg supports weight largely on the stump of soft tissue overlying the distal end of the tibia.

Immunology

Patients with the TT form of the disease react positively to the lepromin test.

In addition to the two polar extremities of the LL and TT forms characterized above, the intermediate forms (BT, BB and BL) demonstrate mixtures of features normally associated with either the LL or TT forms (Table 7.4). The degree of response to lepromin is also variable in these intermediate ('borderline') forms. It is also of interest that the ratio of lepromatous to tuberculoid forms demonstrates great geographic variability, being about 1/9 in Africa and as high as 4/1 in Europe (Hunter & Thomas, 1984).

Interactions between leprosy and tuberculosis

Antibodies generated by a given bacterial species may be capable of binding with cell membrane receptors of another species. Not only have such epitopes been demonstrated among the species of numerous genera, but there is increasing evidence that an entire disease entity, rheumatic fever, may be the result of such an event. The concept of such cross reactions, therefore, is not a unique one, although it is much better documented in examples of humoral than in cell-mediated immunity (CMI).

As early as 1924, Rogers suggested that differences in reactions to using an extract of attenuated tubercle bacillus (the bacillus of Calmette-Guérin or BCG) for vaccination were consistent with a protective effect relationship to tuberculoid leprosy. In 1939, J.M.M. Fernandez in Brazil called attention to the common experience in uninfected, normal persons of lepromin test conversion from negative to positive following BCG vaccination (Fernandez, 1957).

More recently massive BCG vaccination programs were carried out as tuberculosis control measures in various countries with high tuberculosis frequencies. Several of these countries

Table 7.4. *Clinical and immunological differences among the various clinical forms of leprosy.*

Feature	TT	BT	BB	BL	LL
Rhinitis	No	No	No	Occasional	Yes
Maxillary destruction	No	No	No	No	Yes
Ocular involvement	No	No	No	Rare	Yes
Testis involvement	No	No	No	Rare	Often
Skin lesions	Single	Multiple; satellite	Numerous; bilateral	Numerous; bilateral; homogeneous	Numerous and prominent (leonine facies)
Anesthesia	Prominent	Prominent	Less than TT	Much less than TT	Least
Lepromin reaction	Prominent	Mild	Variable	Negative	Negative
Granulomatous inflammation	Prominent	Moderately developed	Some features	No	No
Bacilli in lesions	Rare	Few	Moderate	Abundant	Teeming

Table constructed from data in Hansen & Looff (1895), Cochrane *et al.* (1964), Ridley (1972), Jopling (1982), WHO (1985) and Spitznagel (1989).
TT, tuberculoid leprosy; BT, borderline toward tuberculoid; BB, borderline; BL, borderline toward lepromalous; LL, lepromalous leprosy.

also were afflicted by a high leprosy prevalence. The protective effect of BCG vaccination against subsequent development of leprosy as compared with controls varied considerably but was usually a positive value, ranging from 20 % (Burma) to 42 % (New Guinea) to 80 % (Uganda) (Fine, 1988). Possible explanations to explain the variation include (i) prior exposure to atypical mycobacterial antigens, (ii) differences in preparation of the BCG vaccine, (iii) known geographical differences in lepromatous / tuberculoid leprosy form ratios (high in Europe, low in Africa); (iv) host genetic differences and (v) research design differences. More than one of these factors are probably operative. While the vaccination provided the greatest protective effect against the TT form, most studies showed at least some protective effect also for LL.

Fernandez (1957) suggested that a similar mechanism may be operating in other circumstances. He cites Neyra Ramirez' observation that tuberculosis was extremely common in Peru in 1952 but that leprosy was rare. Fernandez noted that, after the Conquest, the Spanish found leprosy in Peru so common that they built a leprosarium. He speculated that the spread of tuberculosis (92 % positive tuberculin reaction rate in Peru in 1953) after the Conquest provided so much protection against leprosy infection that it virtually extinguished leprosy there.

Manchester (1984, 1992) proposes a similar explanation for the change from the high leprosy / tuberculosis ratio in medieval Europe and especially England to the present reversed ratio. He cites some direct, skeletal evidence and considerably more indirect source data such as leprosarium construction rates and literary data. It is concluded that, with the advent of, and increase in, urbanization and the consequent increased population density in city and township (Pounds, 1974:267), both leprosy and tuberculosis incidence and prevalence increased since both are diseases spread by droplet inhalation and therefore are population density-dependent diseases. Consequently the growing population became increasingly tuberculin-positive, which conferred a degree of immunity to infection by *M. leprae*. In those individuals subsequently infected by *M. leprae* the tuberculin-positive status caused a population shift along the immune spectrum towards tuberculoid (i.e. low-infectious) leprosy. In so doing, the incidence of leprosy in the population declined to its ultimate extinction in England.

Still more recent field observations by Kaklamani *et al.* (1991) in Athens and Abel *et al.* (1990) in Vietnam, while less comprehensive, also demonstrate a negative correlation between tuberculosis and tuberculoid leprosy. Chaussinand (1948) regarded leprosy and tuberculosis as antagonistic infections. He felt tuberculosis could extinguish leprosy and urged universal BCG vaccination to enhance that effect. Hunter & Thomas (1984) also note a similar pattern with increase of urbanism in parts of Africa, but observe that a simple antagonism between the two diseases does not explain all the observations, suggesting that rainfall and other climatic factors probably also play a role. Leiker (1971)

also feels that the cross-reactive explanation must be supplemented by other operating factors.

It is evident, then, that the patient's immune status plays a major role in the types of clinical manifestations of leprosy infection, and that it influences the relationship between leprosy and tuberculosis. It is equally clear that much more needs to be learned about the mechanism by means of which these effects are carried out before we can feel content with our understanding of them.

Clinical course

We know that lepromatous leprosy sufferers are highly infective, although most immunologically normal, exposed patients do not get the disease. An average of at least one-third of the clinical infections manifest the disease during childhood. Its incubation period is long – up to 6 years. Once symptoms appear, the untreated disease usually progresses slowly. Its predilection for cooler temperatures results in a pattern of organ involvement that spares the vital viscera. Accordingly, leprosy is a lifelong disease during which the afflicted commonly suffer progressive, crippling losses of distal extremity parts as well as socially-isolating facial deformities. Local, pyogenic infections secondary to ulcerative skin involvement exaggerate such complications. In spite of these problems, the tendency for the disease to spare the viscera results in only a modest decrease in lifespan. Some complications, such as pyogenic infection with abscess formation and septicemia can cause an abrupt and fatal change in the course of the disease. In more modern times complicating tuberculosis was the most common cause of death in leprosaria patients. This, however, has been demonstrated to have been an artifact of leprosarial living conditions as well as the prevalence of tuberculosis at the time; leprosy patients have no greater immunological susceptibility to tuberculous infection than normal persons (Jopling, 1982). Amyloidosis, a common, nonspecific complication of many chronic infections is a not uncommon terminal event but usually only after decades-long infectious intervals. It is characterized by deposition of an abnormal protein in various soft tissues (most commonly liver, spleen, adrenals and kidney), gradually destroying these organs. Thus leprosy progressively impairs individual physical productivity but does not reduce the lifespan dramatically.

Antiquity and history

The scholar who attempts to establish the antiquity of leprosy must deal with the fact that the earliest available evidence is of literary and iconographic nature. While these are of great interest, their interpretation demands special caution because artistic license and the vagaries of linguistic practices commonly becloud the diagnostic certainty of the evidence.

Most historians believe the disease originated in Asia (China?) and spread westward, entering Europe centuries later. Since the documentation for this pattern is literary, it is subject to the possibility that it may represent a preservational artifact. Grmek (1983) suggests an African origin with subsequent radiation from there. The oldest reference to leprosy is from Leviticus in the Bible's Old Testament, probably written about 1500 B.C. (Gramberg, 1961). All agree that the term employed there, zara'ath or tsara'ath was used for a broad range of skin diseases (Cochrane, 1961), though it is not certain that leprosy was one of them (Yoeli, 1955). The New Testament Greek word lepra similarly can not refer to modern leprosy because the Greek term for that was elephantiasis graecorum (Browne, 1970). Validity for the claim that leprosy probably was included within what was called tsara'ath rests largely on the socially stigmatizing nature of that term, as described in Leviticus. Furthermore, the skin disease to which that word was applied was of temporary nature, precluding leprosy. Sushruta Samhita from India describes the condition quite well and even offers therapeutic suggestions as early as about 600 B.C (Skinsnes, 1973). The term kushta in the Vedas is believed to refer to leprosy, though its description is less detailed (Dharmendra, 1947). An early (500 B.C.) Chinese document attributes an illness suffered by Pai-Niu, a Confucian, to leprosy (li), but the specificity of that term has been questioned (Feeny, 1964). Skinsnes (1980), however, cites a reference from an excavated bamboo book written about 250 B.C. using the term li for a disease characterized by nasal destruction, eyebrow loss, crippled, broken legs, anesthetic mucosa and hoarseness. Skinsnes suggests this provides strong support for the accuracy of the diagnosis of Pai-Niu's disease. He also suggests that the 500 B.C. Chinese document by Nei Ching Su Wen provides a convincing description of leprosy. Thus, several of these references strongly suggest that leprosy as we know it today was present in India and China as early as five centuries before the Christian era, but they are unaccompanied by skeletal or even iconographic findings. Zias (1985) cites the absence of biblical Old Testament references to forbidden sexual practices as an etiology of leprosy as suggestive that leprosy appeared in the Holy Land some time after the first temple period and was well-established there by the first centuries of the common era. However, Dzierzykray-Rogalski (1980) describes four skulls from the Dakhleh Oasis in Egypt's western desert dating to the Ptolemaic period (second century B.C.) each of which reveals at least two features of Møller-Christensen's (1983: 130) 'facies leprosa'. Phalanges with leprous changes were also present but burial conditions did not permit associating them with the individual skulls. A sixth century A.D. Nubian cemetery has produced two cases: one mummy with characteristically deformed hands and feet described by Smith & Dawson (1924: figures 66 & 67, p. 160), and the other with facies leprosa (Møller-Christensen & Hughes, 1966; Møller-Christensen, 1967).

The second century of the Christian era provides us with two, nearly unmistakable descriptions of leprosy. One of these is by a Chinese surgeon, Hua T'o in about 150 A.D. and the other by a Greek physician in Cappadocia, Aretaios Kappadox, who documents the leonine facial features of the disease, but calling it elephantiasis, unfortunately a term Arab physicians used for filariasis (Andersen, 1969). Dols (1983) cites a third century reference to leprosy suffered by the Islamic king of al-Hirah near Syria.

The fourth century A.D. provides the earliest nonliterary evidence for the antiquity of leprosy, for during that period the first hospitals (called lazar houses) reserved for lepers were constructed in Cappadocia and in Europe (Ackerknecht, 1972). The emperor Constantine himself suffered from the disease. During the following century Sanskrit mythology documents the presence of leprosy in India. The Hippocratic corpus, however, provides no convincing evidence that Greek physicians knew leprosy. A fourth century A.D. skeleton from England shows features characteristic of leprosy in leg and foot bones (Reader, 1974), but the absence of a cranium prevents confirmation of the diagnosis. However, recent re-evaluation of that evidence suggests a more receptive viewpoint than in the past (Farwell & Molleson, 1993).

By the sixth and seventh centuries the presence of leprosy was being confirmed in many geographic areas and documented by a variety of methods. The skeletal evidence for leprosy from this period is documented in the Paleopathology of leprosy section, below. A Chinese book, Ch'ao's Pathology, describes leprosy well and a therapeutic manual written by Ch'ien Chin Yao Fang and compiled by Sun Szu-mo, titled One Thousand Golden Remedies reflects their awareness of this condition (Skinsnes, 1973). The first lazar house in England was built in 638 and Komyo, wife of emperor Sho'mu constructed the first leprosarium in Japan about the same time (Wells, 1964), while another was built in Constantinople. Dols (1983) also notes that the Islamic caliph U'mar's army encountered a Christian leper colony in the Palestinian desert during the seventh century.

In Europe the later medieval period is characterized by a continuous increase in leprosy prevalence until, by the thirteenth century the construction of 19 000 lazar houses can be documented (Roberts, 1986). While many authors have questioned how many of the patients in these houses really had been misdiagnosed, Møller-Christensen's (1961) excavations of the Danish lazar house cemeteries demonstrate that about 70 % of those skeletons reveal changes characteristic of leprosy. This is not only a testament to the diagnostic accuracy of the priests (who commonly evaluated the signs and symptoms), but that these leprosaria's occupants were primarily those with advanced disease (Andersen, 1969). By the sixteenth century, however, most of these had been closed or directed to some other use. These changes in frequency coincided with demographic changes believed to be related to the rise of tuberculosis that peaked in the seventeenth century in Europe (Dubos & Dubos, 1952). These relationships are discussed in the Interaction between leprosy and tuberculosis section, above. By 1300 Grön (1973) reports that leprosy was common enough to have become incorporated into an epic German poem about a leprous knight. Enough knights participating in the Crusades had contracted the disease to form a spiritual order (of Lazarus) for those afflicted. The return of many infected knights probably contributed to the spread of leprosy throughout Europe.

The disease was transported from Spain and Africa in the sixteenth and seventeenth centuries to the New World whose populations had not harbored leprosy in pre-Columbian times. During the nineteenth century importation of Chinese coolies into many Southern Ocean islands as common laborers by the colonizing Europeans distributed the disease throughout Oceania. The first reference to leprosy in Hawaii was in 1823, but two generations later 5 % of Hawaiians were infected with leprosy (Ackerknecht, 1972). The small South Pacific island of Nauru suffered a disastrous epidemic, 35 % of its population becoming infected during the 17 years after introduction of leprosy in 1912 (Bray, 1934; Wade & Ledowsky, 1952). By 1908 the disease had also reached Australia.

Nine years before Koch identified the bacterium causing tuberculosis, Gerhard Armauer Hansen (1874) discovered the leprosy bacillus. While inability to culture this organism retarded its study, Arning (cited in Skinsnes, 1973) transmitted the disease experimentally (surgically) in 1884. By 1918, Hayashi reported the lepromin reaction and the following year Mitsuda (1919) described his modified interpretation of the intradermal reaction that is employed commonly today. Seven years later a vaccine prepared from M. leprae was tested without satisfactory results. The use of BCG vaccine using an attenuated tubercle bacillus 50 years later is discussed in the Interactions between leprosy and tuberculosis section, above. Dapsone, the first form of drug therapy having a clinically demonstrable anti-leprosy effect began to be employed during the 1950s. Discovery of animals (mice and armadillo) vulnerable to experimental infection in the 1960s and 1970s had great laboratory value, enabling drug sensitivity testing and biological study of the organism. Some of the anti-tuberculous agents have been added to the therapeutic armamentarium since then. Not only can these drugs arrest the disease in many patients, but the fact that they render the patient noninfectious quite promptly has great epidemiological value for the population as a whole and enormous social benefit for the patient.

No historical review of leprosy is complete without a reference to the social stigma almost inseparably associated with this disease. Leviticus' comments indicate that even as early as 1.5 millenia before the Christian era, society was repulsed by at least some eruptive skin diseases that may or may not have included leprosy. They were expelled from the cities by the priest who made the diagnosis. Even at that time, their treatment suggests moral judgement.

This becomes very clear in the medieval period when we can be reasonably certain of the diagnosis. Ackerknecht (1972) points out that the European church viewed the lep-

rosy-afflicted with distinct ambivalance. While the establishment of sainthood for some who devoted their lives to lepers' needs reflects a supportive demeanor in some areas and times, leprosy was commonly viewed as a divine punishment, inflicted in retribution for the diseased victim's misbehavior (frequently implied to be of a sexual nature: Dols, 1983). Once the diagnosis had been established, commonly by a cleric, the afflicted person was often viewed as eclesiastically dead and sometimes even provided with a graveside ceremony including last rites while standing in the grave. Thereafter they were ostracized. Grön (1973) cites an interesting observation by Epstein that medieval nobility harbored a belief in the healing power of blood and that Emperor Constantine wanted to heal his own leprosy by bathing in the heart blood of a virgin. These attitudes further strengthen the moralistic viewpoint with which both state and church viewed leprosy. The taint of evil associated with leprous patients was manifested as late as 1896 in Paris when an opera dramatized a legendary tale of a leprous mother who deliberately infected her daughter's fiancée (Grön, 1973). The church at one time supported establishment of the Order of Lazarus, designed for lepers. The order was created in 1048 for crusading knights who became infected while attempting to return Jerusalem to the Christians. Pope Innocent VIII suppressed the order at the end of the fifteenth century, 100 years after the Crusades had ended (as had leprosy as a European epidemic). There were, of course, many individual acts of compassion. Of these, the most well-known is the founding (1873) and personal direction of the leprosarium on the Hawaiian island of Molokai by Father Damien, whose courage became a sacrifice when he also contracted and died of Hansen's disease in 1889.

The view of state government also was hardly compassionate. Laws were enacted to minimize contact between the infected and noninfected. These included denial of optional access to crowded, urban areas, and regulations requiring public announcement of their leprous status. On pain of death European lepers were required to announce their infected condition in loud voices upon approach by noninfected members of the population, to stay 'a spear's distance' from nonleprous persons and, later, to replace such shouts with the striking of wooden clappers. These latter are so distinctive that the skin sores in many seventeenth century paintings are recognizably meant to represent leprosy by the clappers their victims carry. Perhaps an extreme of this attitude was represented by Philip IV (Philip the Fair) about 1490 when he advocated that all lepers should be collected and burned until the epidemic ended (Skinsnes, 1973). Construction of the leprosaria may well be viewed more as isolation practices for protection of the public than actions motivated by compassion for the afflicted.

Dols (1983) points out that the Islamic world was an exception in that it did not view a leprous person as undergoing spiritual punishment for a moral violation, nor did public policy ostracize lepers, although examples of segragation may reflect contagion concerns. He traces this attitude to the fact that their religious texts viewed leprosy as neither a divine affliction nor as a condition for which the victim bore any responsibility. Oriental practices, however, commonly also involved leper disenfranchisement and persecution. The intensity of the leprosy stigma has little precedence among other diseases and its etiology remains enigmatic.

Skeletal pathology

The reported frequency of skeletal involvement in leprosy sufferers fluctuates between 15 and 50 %, although, as Zimmerman & Kelley (1982) point out, leprosarium skeletal populations have exhibited even higher percentages. Møller-Christensen (1978) found the typical skeletal changes of leprosy in nearly 70 % of the skeletons excavated from the medieval leprosarium at Naestved (Denmark). This high incidence is similar to that reported in modern leprosaria (Steinbock, 1976). In present populations about 25 % of all patients have some degree of disability (Paterson & Job, 1964). A large fraction of these people have bone changes in the fingers and toes.

Bone changes in leprosy can be viewed as the consequence of local tissue invasion by the bacilli, involvement of the nerves with motor and sensory loss (anesthesia), or circulatory disturbances producing local gangrene. The changes usually are confined to the small bones of the face, hands, and lower leg bones (Resnick & Niwayama, 1989b).

Paterson & Job (1964) group bone changes in leprosy into the following three types:

1. Specific. Those changes due to the action of M. leprae in bone. These changes are rare (5–6 %), and appear as lytic foci that may extend into the adjacent joint (Ortner & Putschar, 1985). Periosteal reaction and sclerosis are usually absent (Paterson & Job, 1964).
2. Non-specific inflammatory or degenerative. Those changes that occur in patients due to local trauma secondary to sensory loss (acute nonleprous osteitis and osteomyelitis, with identical bone changes to those seen in patients who have no sensory loss; non-specific periostitis; chronic periostitis and concentric absorption; and arthritis). These are the most frequent bone lesions found in Hansen's disease, and the bones of the hands and feet are almost exclusively affected.
3. Osteoporosis. Due to disuse, present only in severe cases. The almost total absence of periosteal reaction and callus formation in pathological fractures is characteristic of both lepromatous and tuberculoid leprosy (Schinz et al., 1953).

Rhinomaxillary syndrome

This is a new term introduced by Andersen & Manchester (1992) to substitute for that of 'facies leprosa' proposed by Møller-Christensen et al. in 1952, who applied it to the con-

dition characterized by the following skeletal signs (Møller-Christensen, 1983):

1. Atrophy and disappearance of the anterior nasal spine.
2. Atrophy and recession of the alveolar process of the maxilla confined to the incisor region, beginning centrally at the prosthion and resulting in loosening and eventually loss of the anterior teeth.
3. Endonasal inflammatory changes that constitute the pathological basis of this condition. It must always be present, together with one or both of the other signs. Rounding and widening of the nasal aperture occurs.

According to Andersen & Manchester (1992), in clinical contexts the facial disfigurement associated with the rhinomaxillary syndrome has been known as Bergen syndrome and its osteological significance, as noted above, was first recognized by Møller-Christensen who proposed the term facies leprosa for the cranial skeletal features. The problem for paleopathologists with this term 'rhinomaxillary syndrome' arises from its emphasis on the associated soft tissue changes since these are not evident in skeletal paleopathological studies.

This syndrome is present only in lepromatous and near-lepromatous leprosy. In that form of leprosy, bone involvement usually occurs by direct spread from overlying dermal or mucosal lesions, so that the skull is, along with the hands, the most often affected (Jaffe, 1972; Revell, 1986; Resnick & Niwayama, 1989b). In lepromatous periostitis normally little periosteal new bone formation is evident (Revell, 1986).

Bone Changes

The presence of all components of the rhinomaxillary syndrome is pathognomonic of lepromatous or near-lepromatous leprosy, but it must be taken into account that in any one individual the anatomic components of the syndrome may occur singly or in combination. The osseous lesions are found in the nasal cavity, the alveolar process and the oral surface of the palatine process of the maxilla (Andersen & Manchester, 1992) . The skeletal changes in this syndrome are infectious and erosive. The mandible is not affected.

Maxillary alveolar process

The first stage is a smooth resorption of the prosthion followed by a lateral and bilaterally symmetrical extension of the lesion involving the alveolae of the central and lateral maxillary incisors (first in the anterior walls and then in the posteriors). Finally, the incisors become loose and fall out due to lack of anchoring tissues and the maxilla becomes resorbed. As Andersen & Manchester (1992) point out, minor surface pitting, indicative of superficial inflammation, is noted.

Although the bone resorption is extreme, the cortical bone thickness is maintained, presumably through endosteal deposition. Møller-Christensen (1967) notes that the area of bone destruction is far too limited to be mistaken for periodontal disease and he suggested the term of 'paradentosis leprosa'.

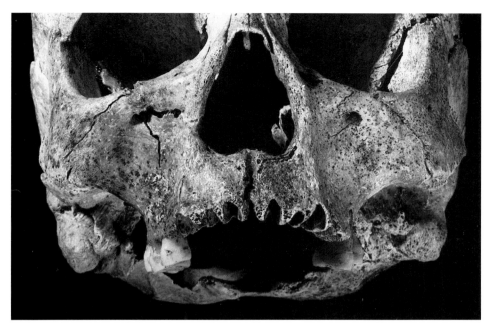

FIG. 7.19: **Rhinomaxillary leprosy.** Frontal view of this skull demonstrates one feature of Møller-Christensen's 'facies leprosa' triad: erosion of at least part of the nasal spine (osseous midline projection at inferior edge of nasal aperture). More subtle are the early erosive changes of the maxilla, and this view does not visualize the area of involved palate. No. 707457. Modern adult. Courtesy P. Sledzik. NMHM.

Anterior nasal spine

Atrophy of the anterior nasal spine is apparent both in archaeological skeletal material and in living people (Møller-Christensen, 1967). At the beginning of the process, surface pitting, progressive resorption of the anterior nasal spine and loss of cortical bone with exposure of cancellous bone are noted. At the end, there is a total loss of the nasal spine with its original base covered by cortical bone. These changes are compatible with local inflammation (Andersen & Manchester, 1992; Fig. 7.19, and see Fig. 7.24).

Margins of the nasal aperture

In this part of the face bilateral symmetrical resorption and smooth remodeling of the margins of the nasal aperture occur. At the inferior border some surface pitting develops and, at the beginning of the process, resorption causes exposure of cancellous bone (at the end of the process it will be covered by cortical bone; Andersen & Manchester, 1992).

Palatine process of the maxilla

Two patterns of lesions occur predominantly in the midzone area of the nasal surface on each side of the nasal septum (Andersen & Manchester, 1992):

1. Early fine pits develop which expand until they become confluent. Later, plaques of subperiosteal new bone are observed. Finally, the process becomes relatively smooth and inactive.
2. Discrete, roughly circular, shallow erosive lesions with irregular, aggressive-appearing single or multiple bases occur, rarely larger than 0.5 cm in diameter.

The earliest changes on the oral surface of the palatine process are small erosive pits near the palatine suture in the midportion of the palate. Later, confluence of the erosive lesions develops. In the very advanced cases perforation of the hard palate may occur. Proliferative new bone formation is not common. Zivanovic (1982:232) regards the facial features as the only lesion diagnostic of leprosy in a skeletonized body.

Intranasal structures

The above-described processes may progress to total absorption of the septum. Coarse pitting of the conchae with progressive absortion and loss is also observed. In paleopathological specimens the appearance resulting from destruction of the intranasal structures and remodeling of the margins of the nasal aperture is that of a wide, empty cavity.

Lesions of the cranial vault

Lepromatous scalp lesions may lead to erosions of the cranial vault (Ortner & Putschar, 1985), but there are no recognizable specific lepromatous changes on the skull (as occur in the treponematoses).

Lesions of the postcranial skeleton

Hands and feet

Diaphyseal remodeling is a pathological process of the proximal phalanges, metacarpals and metatarsals in all established types of clinical leprosy (Andersen et al., 1992). It is often bilateral but is rarely truly symmetrical (Steinbock, 1976). The changes are the result of sympathetic neuropathy and alteration of peripheral vascular bed dynamics selectively stimulating extracortical osteoclastic and endosteal osteoblastic activity, with extracortical absortion of bone and endosteal bone deposition at the same time (Murray et al., 1990; Andersen et al., 1992). In the opinion of Revell (1986), the bone changes associated with the sensory loss are much more severe than those caused by lepromatous osteomyelitis because the leprosy sufferer is more prone to injury of anesthetic limbs and to secondary infection with ulcerations, thrombosis and gangrene. Ultimately, pathological fractures in the diaphysis and subsequent resorption of the distal and proximal remnants can occur due to combined continued diaphyseal remodeling and achroosteolysis. As Revell (1986) observes, reactive periostitis, osteitis, bone necrosis and sequestration may all contribute to the final result.

In the hands, the terminal phalanges erode into points or resorb completely, leaving stumps in place of fingers

(Fig. 7.20). In the opinion of Møller-Christensen (1967) the metacarpals are rarely involved in this change). In the feet the pathological resorptive changes appear in the metatarsophalangeal joints. After that, deformation and misalignment can develop (Mann & Murphy, 1990). The resorption of the hand phalanges probably reflects neurotrophic changes associated with diminished blood supply due to the bacterial invasion of peripheral blood vessels (Murray *et al.*, 1990).

In the last stages of the disease there can be true neuropathic joints with complete disorganization of the weight-bearing surfaces and the subchondral bone. Destruction of the sensory nerves resulting in anesthesia, circulatory disturbances, and local pressure lead to concentric resorption of terminal phalanges of fingers, metatarsals, and toes (Fig. 7.21). These kinds of lesions are much more common than those of specific lepromatous arthritis and are evident in 20–70 % of patients. The result is a tapered appearance to the end of the bone ('licked candy stick': Figs. 7.22 & 7.23). In the opinion of Resnick & Niwayama (1989b) specific arthritis is rare, and joint involvement results from intra-articular extension of an osseus or periarticular infective focus or, much less commonly, from hematogenous invasion of the synovial membrane.

In 30 % of the cases, a typical enlargement of the nutrient foramen occurs in the hands (Campillo, 1983) and the joints may show all degrees of arthritis, subluxation and dislocation (Møller-Christensen, 1967). Paterson & Job (1964) define the enlargement of nutrient foramina as one with a diameter exceeding 1 mm. Ankylosis is not common but may occur in any of the phalangeal and tarsal joints (Steinbock, 1976). In the hands the process begins in the nails of the third phalanx and then it continues to the second phalanx that is also destroyed, the proximal phalanx and, rarely, the metacarpal. In the feet there is initial involvement of the metatarsal with the subsequent pencilling and the creation of a space between the phalanges and metacarpals (Schinz *et al.*, 1953). It is possible that the different localization of the lesions between hands and feet would be due to mechanical factors. It has been demonstrated that the areas of weight-bearing are more prone to atrophy and destruction (Forrester & Brown, 1990). Superimposed infection from trophic ulcers, more frequently seen on

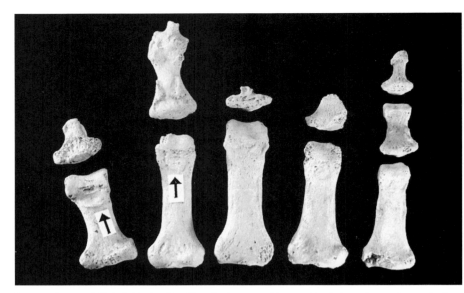

FIG. 7.20: **Leprosy.** This individual suffered from both yaws and leprosy. The deformed or totally resorbed terminal phalanges are probably the effects of leprosy. Skeletal collection on Guam, 26 year old female, ca. A.D. 830. Photograph courtesy of Diane Trembly and Paul Rosendahl, PhD, Inc.

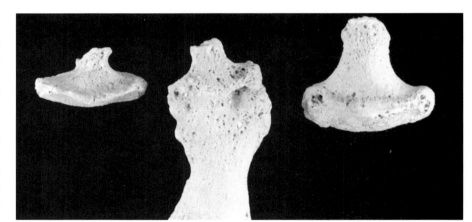

FIG. 7.21: **Leprosy.** Resorption and atrophy of the distal phalanges is dramatically portrayed in this leprous individual. Skeletal collection on Guam, 26 year old female, ca. A.D. 830. Photograph courtesy of Diane Trembly and Paul Rosendahl, PhD Inc.

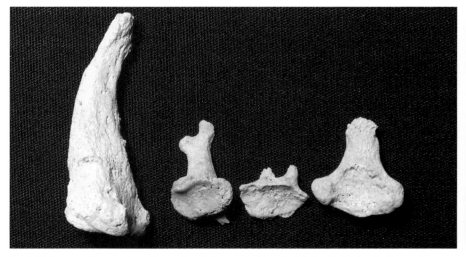

FIG. 7.22: **Leprosy.** Closeup view of several partially resorbed terminal digits. Skeletal collection on Guam, male, ca. 26 years, ca. A.D. 1150. Photograph courtesy Diane Trembly and Paul Rosendahl, PhD, Inc.

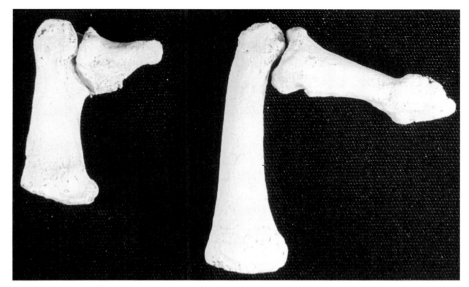

FIG. 7.23: **Leprosy.** Claw hand deformity and partial resorption of terminal digits. Skeletal collection on Guam, 26 year old female, ca. A.D. 830. Photograph courtesy of Diane Trembly and Paul Rosendahl, PhD, Inc.

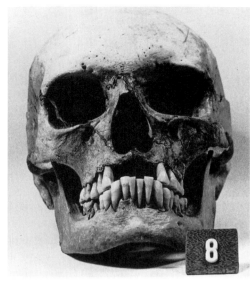

FIG. 7.24: **Leprosy.** Necrosis of the central maxillary region. Anterior tooth loss is evident. Courtesy Dr K. Manchester.

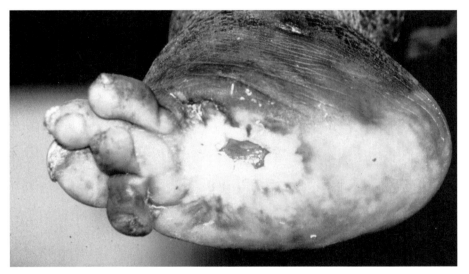

FIG. 7.25: **Leprosy.** Swollen, ulcerated and infected foot with digit deformity. Courtesy Dr K. Manchester.

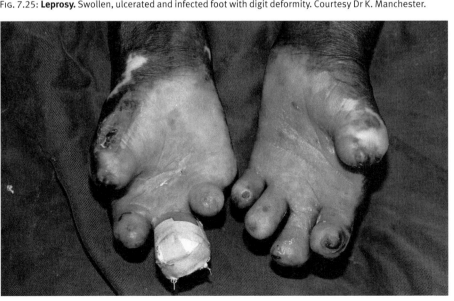

FIG. 7.26: **Leprosy.** Foot soft tissue edema with digit deformity. Courtesy Dr K. Manchester.

FIG. 7.27: **Leprosy.** Soft tissue infection with digit loss of fingers secondary to inadvertent trauma due to sensory motor impairment caused by the peripheral neuropathy of leprosy. Courtesy Dr K. Manchester.

the plantar aspect of the first metatarsophalangeal joint, hastens destruction (Murray et al., 1990) (Figs. 7.25, 7.26 & 7.27).

Long bones

Periostitis with subperiosteal new bone deposits is not uncommon in long bones (Ortner & Putschar, 1985). Møller-Christensen (1967) found such periostitis in 78 % of the cases observed, and has noted that leprosy often severely affects the tibia and fibula, producing pitting and irregularities in their surfaces due to infection of the periosteum with fine, longitudinally striated subperiosteal bone deposits (lepromatous periostitis). The tibia shows vascular grooves on the lateral surface. The fibula is rarely involved to the same degree. The involvement of the tibia and fibula is often bilateral and symmetrical, and it may occur anywhere, although usually located in the distal third (Mann & Murphy, 1990). Soft tissue lesions have been described in detail in the Natural history of leprosy section, above.

In the past decade methods of identification of *Mycobacterium leprae* by molecular biology techniques have been reported (Hackel et al., 1990; Nishimura et al., 1994) and will probably be applied commonly to ancient DNA samples to enhance the diagnosis in archaeological bones in the future (Spigelman & Lemma, 1993).

Paleopathology

The earliest skeletal evidence comes from the Dakhleh Oasis in Egypt's western desert where Dzierzykray-Rogalsky (1980) found two skulls from about 200 B.C. that demonstrated the lesions of facies leprosa. The Roman army may have carried the disease to England, where the next-oldest is the Romano-British partial adult skeleton in which Reader (1974) identified leprous changes in the distal tibia, fibula and feet. Møller-Christensen & Hughes (1966) and Møller-Christensen (1967) also noted facies leprosa in fourth to seventh century skulls excavated from sites near Aswan in upper Egypt. Further leprous skeletons have been reported from British sites from the sixth century (Andersen, 1969) and the seventh century (Møller-Christensen & Hughes, 1962), the latter revealing both the cranial and distal changes of leprosy. In 1953, and subsequently, Møller-Christensen published his findings from his excavations of medieval Danish leprosarium cemetaries and in which he defined the features of facies leprosa. The medieval period in England was a period of rapid increase in leprosarium construction (Roberts, 1986) and Møller-Christensen (1983) established on the basis of facies leprosa that the Scottish King Robert, who died in 1329, had leprosy. Eight cases of leprosy identified in a skeletal collection from the pre-Spanish period in the Mariana Islands suggests a greater antiquity there than had been previously supposed (Trembly, 1994).

TREPONEMATOSIS

Definition and taxonomy

Treponematosis is a chronic or subacute infection caused by microorganisms called spirochetes of the genus *Treponema*. On the basis of clinical and geographic variation, the infection is divided into four types: pinta, yaws, bejel (or endemic syphilis) and venereal syphilis. Controversy about the treponematoses centers on whether these are different disease entities caused by different bacterial species within the genus, or whether they are merely different clinical manifestations of infection by one species, *Treponema pallidum* (Manchester, 1983a). Recognizing the lack of common agreement, in this volume we discuss them as separate species. The worldwide distribution of the four syndromes is not isomorphic but is associated with distinctive geographic, climatic, and sociocultural features (Powell, 1988).

- Pinta is the most geographically restricted of the four syndromes. It is limited to the tropical regions of America, from Mexico to Ecuador. *Treponema carateum* (described in 1938) is responsible for the disease.
- Yaws or frambesia affects especially those populations with a low level of hygiene in tropical and subtropical humid areas. It is caused by *Treponema pertenue*, first described in 1905.
- Bejel (endemic syphilis or nonvenereal syphilis) is present in rural populations in temperate and subtropical nonhumid regions, and caused by *Treponema pallidum endemicum*.
- Venereal syphilis is the most ubiquitous of the four syndromes, occurring primarily in urbanized populations in all geographic regions (Powell, 1988). It is caused by *Treponema pallidum pallidum*, described in 1905.

All of these diseases are characterized by self-limited, primary and secondary lesions, a clinically disease-free latent period and late lesions that are frequently destructive, particularly of bone and skin (with the exception of pinta, which never involves internal organs or bones). Pinta, yaws and bejel (unlike syphilis), are commonly transmitted by fomites and nonvenereal contact. Furthermore, yaws can be transmitted by small flies, notably *Hippelates* species (Howe, 1981).

The order Spirochaetales (or spirochetes) includes spiral, flexible bacteria. As Howe (1981) points out, the spirochetes are structurally the most complex of bacteria. In general, spirochetes are not readily stained and are commonly examined in the living state in moist material by application of darkfield microscopy. All pathogenic spirochetes are quite fragile and readily killed by drying, heat, and disinfectants. However, they can survive for years at −76 °C (Howe, 1981). The pathogens are indistinguishable under the light or electron microscope. Furthermore, their DNA sequence homology suggests that all the treponemes are identical, and partial cross-immunity exists between the treponemal syndromes (Baker & Armelagos, 1988).

The pathological changes of three of the four syndromes (bejel, yaws, and venereal syphilis) are identical; differences between them are purely quantitative and of degree, not qualitative (Manchester, 1983a). Examples of transition of one syndrome to another due to alterations in the climate and/or living conditions are numerous: when people in hot and humid regions infected with yaws move to cooler regions they lose the generalized lesions of yaws and develop the restricted lesions of bejel (Steinbock, 1976). Therefore every human population has the kind of treponematosis that is adapted to its physical environment and sociocultural status. For these reasons Cockburn (1963) and others have suggested that many or all of these infections are merely forms or variants of one basic infection, the differences being due chiefly to modes of transmission, climate, geography or humidity.

Ortner & Putschar (1985) feel that in all treponematoses the infecting organisms enter the body through the skin or mucous membrane near the skin surface and, in the three forms that affect the skeletal system, the organisms are disseminated throughout the body and reach the bones by the bloodstream.

Pinta (mal del pinto [pinto disease]; carate; overia; lota; mal azul)

Definition, etiology, and geographic distribution

Pinta is a nonvenereal form of treponematosis with an evolution characterized by acute and chronic phases (Benenson, 1984). The lesions of pinta are commonly found in the face and extremities, affecting only the skin. Internal organs or bones are not involved, and it never causes serious morbidity or death. The infectious organism is the spirochete *Treponema carateum*. Pinta is found endemically in rural populations in the western world and in the tropical regions of Central and South America and Mexico under conditions of poor hygiene. The climate in which the disease occurs most commonly is semiarid and warm. Since pinta is probably not found outside of the New World it must have evolved in Latin America, possibly from a treponeme carried across the Bering Strait. Guerra (1990) asserts that the disease already existed in the New World before the discovery of the Americas, pointing out that the first chronicles of the conquest made by the Spaniards clearly identified the disease and describe such lesions in the skin of the Indians.

Pathogenesis

Humans are the reservoir for this organism. Transmission from person-to-person occurs through direct and long contact with the early cutaneous lesions. However, transmissibility is low (Arrizabalaga, 1993). The incubation period is 3–60 days and the transmission mechanism is not yet known, though Cockburn (1963:173) reminds us that the long-standing lesions of the blue-pigmented stage are teeming with organisms. It has not yet been demonstrated that certain hematophagus arthropods can be biological vectors of the disease (Benenson, 1984). Pinta behaves like a disease that has had time to evolve a less pathological but more infectious relationship with its host, and it may be a good example of a disease that is evolving an even more advantageous relationship with its host (Way, 1981). Resistance to pinta may be similar to that of other treponematoses. Pinta is rare in Caucasians and it is possible that some degree of natural racial resistance exists. Pinta is a disease of late childhood and young adults, with a peak incidence between 15 and 30 years.

Yaws (frambesia; pian; tropical frambesia; bubas; parangi)

Definition, etiology and geographic distribution

Yaws is a chronic and recurrent form of treponematosis of nonvenereal origin characterized by early and contagious, hyperkeratotic, eventually ulcerative skin changes and late, destructive, and non-contagious lesions. These heal spontaneously but relapses may occur both in the early and late stages. It never involves the brain, eyes, heart, aorta and abdominal organs as syphilis does (Benenson, 1984). The spirochete *Treponema pertenue* is the causative organism. Yaws is an endemic disease of rural areas in western and equatorial Africa, certain sites in Latin America, Caribbean islands, southeastern Asia, northern Australia, New Guinea, and the islands of the southern Pacific Ocean. In some endemic areas 10–25 % of the entire population may exhibit some form of yaws. The disease develops in a humid and warm climate. Garruto (1981) believes that yaws is the most important and widespread nonvenereal treponemal infection in man. Because of its long infectious stage it may persist in small isolated tropical populations where it remains endemic, affecting a few newly susceptible children each year.

Pathogenesis

Humans (by contacts in the house, village, school, etc) represent the principal reservoir, and possibly also the higher primates (Benenson, 1984). Transmissibility is high. It occurs mainly by direct contact with the exudates of the early skin lesions. Although it is possible indirect transmission can occur by lacerating and penetrating objects as well as by flies and insects contacting open wounds, the importance of such methods has not been elucidated. Transmission of the disease is rarely associated with sexual contact. Congenital transmission never occurs. Yaws is an infectious disease that is seen primarily in infancy (usually in the first decade of life: 2–10 years) by contact with open lesions containing the spirochetes, and it is more frequent in males than in females. The existence of natural or racial immunity has not been proved although it is possible that genetic factors do exist in the manifestation of the late lesions. It has been demonstrated that immunity against yaws provides partial immunity against syphilis. Unlike venereal syphilis, the other treponemal infections—yaws, pinta and bejel—elicit a natural immunity (Garruto, 1981).

Skeletal pathology

The initial lesion in the primary stage is a granulomatous, primary skin lesion at the point of infection. This is also called the 'mother yaw.' Between 1 and 5 % of the cases develop skeletal involvement some years after the primary stage without proper treatment. In the secondary stage there may be bone involvement with local rarefaction showing thinning by resorption of bony tissue and commonly periostitis (Powell, 1988). Periosteal reactions are often exuberant and result in considerable cortical thickening and bony expansion. Periostitis may be prominent on the plantar side of the calcaneus. Lytic defects can be seen within the cortex. There is predilection for involvement of bones distal to the knee and elbow. The lesions are commonly bilateral. Metaphyseal lesions may affect the joints producing bony ankylosis. Joint involvement may be extensive. Spontaneous resolution of secondary stage skeletal lesions over a few months is the rule (Steinbock, 1976; Ortner & Putschar, 1985; Powell, 1988; Murray et al., 1990).

The more destructive and extensive skeletal lesions of the tertiary stage appear 5–10 years after the primary stage. The tibia is the most common bone involved followed by the fibula, clavicle, femur, ulna, radius and bones of the hands and feet. Except for the osteochondritis and dental stigmata of congenital syphilis no bone lesion is found in yaws that may not be observed in syphilis. The differences are merely quantitative (Steinbock, 1976). The most typical feature of the tertiary stage is the saber shin, so-called because the tibia's curved anterior surface and posterior flattened surface conforms to the contour of a saber. This deformity is the result of extensive deposits of subperiosteal bone tissue in the tibial crests, and has also been called boomerang leg. This asymmetrical tibial new bone formation is the most consistent finding in yaws (40 %), and is rarely seen in the fibula (Mann & Murphy, 1990). Radius, fibula, and ulna may also present thickening of the cortex and pathological fractures may occur. There are, however, other important features in yaws.

Dactylitis

Bone changes in the hands of young individuals are found frequently. On the contrary, dactylitis is uncommon in syphilis. The changes are due to subperiosteal bone apposition parallel to the cortex with resorption of the original cortex. Involvement of multiple short bones is common in young individuals, but not in adults where only one is usually involved.

Gummatous osteomyelitis of the long bones

Localized cortical destruction produced by gummas (focal areas of necrosis) is a prominent feature in yaws (Steinbock, 1976). The lesions are oval and with their long axis parallel to the shaft. Periosteal reaction is not as prominent as in syphilis.

Joint involvement

Although joint involvement is rare, Ortner (1992) declares that in some cases of yaws many of the joints and para-articular areas exhibit major destruction of bone tissue accompanied by considerable reactive repair. This type of joint and para-articular involvement is not seen in syphilis. Ortner uses this feature to help him differentiate between archaeological cases of yaws and syphilis.

Skull involvement

This is uncommon in yaws and when it occurs the destruction is less severe than in syphilis. The usual result is a few irregular, crater-like depressions of the vault surface (Manchester, 1983a; Ortner & Putschar, 1985). However, in 7–8 % of the cases with skeletal involvement there is extensive destruction of the nasal area and maxilla and it may result in the condition known as gangosa or rhinopharyngitis mutilans. The word gangosa is derived from the Spanish (nasal voice) and describes the extensive destruction of the nasal region (Steinbock, 1976). Perforation of the hard palate occurs in 5 % of the cases of yaws with skeletal involvement while in syphilis the involvement of the nasal region is not so severe. The lesion begins in the soft tissue and from there it spreads to the skeletal structures. In the most severe cases the destruction spreads to the adjacent structures, uniting the nose, pharynx, and orbital cavities in a single space due to the destruction of the nasal bones, hard palate, and some parts of the maxilla. Bone regeneration is minimal.

Goundou

This is an African word meaning large nose and describes a tumor-like expansion of the maxilla, often bilaterally (Steinbock, 1976). Goundou appears almost exclusively in children and is less common than gangosa.

Differential diagnosis

It is very difficult to differentiate between syphilis and yaws. Epidemiological and geographic factors play a very important role in this task. In addition to syphilitic lesions, there are others that must be taken into account.

Neoplasms

Localized expansile lesions in the epiphyses of tubular bones may simulate bone tumors.

Leprosy and psoriatic arthritis

Destructive lesions in the fingers and toes may resemble abnormalities of leprosy and psoriatic arthritis. Leprosy may also produce similar lesions in the nasal palatal region although periosteal new bone formation on the long bones is not as common.

Uta or spundia (American leishmaniasis)

This disease may cause as extensive destruction of the nasopharynx as in gangosa. Unfortunately, the geographic distribution of uta in the New World is almost identical to that of yaws.

Bejel (nonvenereal syphilis; endemic syphilis; nonvenereal endemic syphilis; dichuchwa; njovera; treponarid – this term was introduced by Wells, 1973*b*)

Definition, etiology, and geographic distribution

Bejel or nonvenereal syphilis is an acute disease of children with restricted geographic distribution caused by *Treponema pallidum* subspecies *endemicum* (Arrizabalaga, 1993). It is characterized by a cutaneous and mucosal rash, commonly without a visible primary lesion. Inflammatory or destructive lesions in the skin, bones and nasopharyngeal region are late manifestations of the disease. In contrast to venereal syphilis, nervous and cardiovascular system involvement is extremely rare. Mortality is low. The clinical manifestations of bejel are intermediate between those of venereal syphilis and yaws (Steinbock, 1976).

Bejel is an endemic disease commonly found in limited regions with low socioeconomic levels and bad hygiene. It occurs in countries of the eastern Mediterranean Sea (mainly in Bosnia) and southwestern Asia. There are also a number of foci in Africa (dry subsaharan regions). It develops in arid and warm climates but, as Steinbock (1976) and Garruto (1981) point out, all of these foci have disappeared or are rapidly disappearing as living conditions improve and venereal syphilis is replacing the disease. Arrizabalaga (1993) sees bejel as the 'venereal leprosy' of the Middle Ages, the 'sibbens' of Scotland, the 'button-scurvy' of Ireland, the 'radesyge' of Norway, the 'skerljevo' of the Balkan countries, the 'saltflus' of Sweden, and the 'spirocolon' of Greece and Russia.

Pathogenesis and clinical features

Humans are the reservoir for this disease, contact occurring in the house, school or village. Transmission occurs by direct or indirect contact with the early infectious lesions of the skin and mucous membranes (favored by the shared use of eating and drinking implements) and, in general, under poor hygienic conditions. Congenital transmission does not occur. Where bejel predominates the great majority of conceptions occur in women whose disease was acquired at least 10 years prior to the menarche. Therefore the small number of spirochetes in their blood greatly reduces the likelihood of passage through the placenta to the fetus (Powell, 1988). Transmissi-

bility is high. The incubation period fluctuates between 2 weeks to 3 months, and the transmission period is highly variable depending on the duration of the wet skin and mucous membrane lesion stage. The host response is similar to that of venereal syphilis. Bejel occurs in childhood with peak incidence between 2–10 years. With improvement in living conditions the cycle of childhood infection is broken.

Skeletal pathology

Bejel shows stages of development and distribution of the skeletal lesions that are almost identical with those of yaws. Both of these conditions are characterized by spontaneous healing and periodic recurrence, depending on the immune response of the previously sensitized tissues (Powell, 1988; Arrizabalaga, 1993). In the tertiary stage gummatous granulomas and periostitis predominate, and destruction of bone and soft tissue in the nasal area may occur. Cardiovascular and central nervous system involvement are uncommon. The frequency of bone lesions is low in this disease fluctuating between 1 and 5 % of all cases in various, reported skeletal series.

In bejel the tibia is the most commonly affected bone, and its typical feature is the saber shin deformity. This is one of its first manifestations (although other bones may be affected in this way), and the layers of new bone are usually parallel to the shaft. The early lesions may heal spontaneously or progress to the stage where the medullary cavity is narrowed by endosteal bone (Steinbock, 1976). In addition, gummatous destruction of cortical tissue ensues, creating circumscribed areas of rarefaction. At a nasal-palatal level the destructive lesions closely resemble those of gangosa in the tertiary stage of yaws. The frequency of the nasal-palatal destruction is only a little less than that of saber shin.

As in yaws, bejel produces skeletal lesions that are morphologically indistinguishable from those of venereal or acquired syphilis. Notwithstanding, as also occurs in yaws, the location of the lesions in the skeleton is different depending on the syndromes. In yaws and bejel nasal-palatal destruction and tibial involvement are frequently found, but the other lesions that are seen in syphilis are unusual (less than 5 %). Other commonly involved bones are: fibula, ulna and radius, clavicle, phalanges and calcaneus. According to Zimmerman & Kelley (1982), Hutchinson's teeth, mulberry molars, and osteochondritis are never found in yaws and bejel because these occur when the treponemes invade the fetus 'in utero.'

Venereal syphilis (syphilis; acquired syphilis; lues)

Definition, etiology, and geographic distribution

Acquired or venereal syphilis is an acute, subacute, or chronic treponematosis clinically characterized by a primary lesion or chancre, a secondary rash affecting the skin and the mucous membranes with long latent periods and late lesions affecting skin, bones, viscera, cardiovascular and central nervous systems (tabes dorsalis) in 20–50 % of cases without treatment. The clinical features of syphilis are so variable that it has been called 'the great imitator.' The microorganism responsible for the disease is the spirochete *Treponema pallidum* subspecies *pallidum* (Arrizabalaga, 1993). As is true also of the other treponemes, it does not produce any kind of toxin. Venereal syphilis is a sporadic and urban worldwide disease. It is one of the most commonly diagnosed transmissible diseases. The differences in racial incidence are more related to sociocultural than biological factors (Benenson, 1984). Its prevalence is higher in urban than rural regions. Since 1957 early venereal syphilis has increased substantially all over the world. Before the antibiotic era the prevalence of syphilis in a civilized, urban adult population can be estimated to have been around 5 % (Steinbock, 1976). Climate has not influenced the development of this disease.

Pathogenesis and clinical features

Humans are the only reservoir. Transmission occurs by direct contact with infected exudates of the early moist lesions located on skin and mucous membranes and with organic liquids and secretions (semen, saliva, blood, vaginal secretions) of infected persons through sexual contact (vaginal or oral). Indirect transmission is possible, although uncommon, by contact with infected objects (needles, syringes, etc) or by nonsexual contact with fresh exudates from any open lesions at any stage (0.01 %). The incubation period varies from 10 days to 10 weeks but averages 3 weeks. The transmission period is quite variable and the disease is contagious through the primary and secondary stages as well as during the interval of mucocutaneous recurrence. In some cases it may be intermittently contagious over 2–4 years.

Host response

Susceptibility is universal, although only 10–25 % of exposures to microorganisms are followed by infection. There is no natural immunity to infection and the probability of an acquired immune response is influenced by sexual and hygienic practices, inoculum size, environmental and body temperature, and other factors (Arrizabalaga, 1993). Partial cross-immunity against the other treponemal infections exists. Demonstrable acquired immunity (related to inoculum size and length of infection) appears in 2–4 weeks after the debut of the primary lesion or chancre. Primary and secondary stages subside with developing resistance (Howe, 1981). Sometimes the latent period continues throughout life. In other cases spontaneous healing may occur. In still other cases, incapacitating lesions in the central nervous (6.5 %) and cardiovascular systems (20–30 %) appear suddenly 5–20 years after the infection (Benenson, 1984). Early

acquired syphilis is not lethal or incapacitating but the late manifestations of the disease affect health, restrict the individual productivity and shorten life mainly due to cardiovascular complications.

Age and sex groups

Acquired syphilis primarily affects young people between 15 and 30 years with a peak between 20 and 24 years of age – the most sexually active period of life. It is found two to threefold more commonly in males than in females. Recently a 50 % increase has been identified among homosexuals (Lozano Tonkin et al., 1984).

Skeletal pathology

Acquired syphilis manifests in three different clinical stages: a primary stage that corresponds with that of the initial ulcerative genital infection (chancre); a generalized secondary stage with a rash; and several tertiary manifestations that may occur years later, as long as 50 years after the chancre (Strong, 1981). The frequency of skeletal lesions in acquired syphilis has decreased dramatically due to improvement in diagnosis and treatment.

Of all the skeletal lesions in venereal syphilis, the most characteristic are those of the skull bones, most commonly affecting parietal and frontal bones. The bones of the facial skeleton are often affected showing severe and destructive lesions. Steinbock (1976) demonstrated that the frequency of bone lesions ranges between 10 and 20 %. The most commonly affected bones, in decreasing order of frequency, are the tibia, frontal and parietal, nasal-palatal region, sternum, clavicle, vertebrae, femur, fibula, humerus, ulna, and radius.

Both gummatous and nongummatous lesions are seen in somewhere between 10 and 20 % of the cases. The gumma is the most characteristic but not the most common lesion of tertiary syphilis and may occur in any tissue. The most frequently involved organs are the skin, the liver, the testes and the bones. Pathologically, the most striking and significant difference from the other syndromes is the severe, incapacitating, and frequently fatal circulatory and nervous system involvement. It is important to note that the most consistent feature shared by the tertiary lesions of syphilis is an exceedingly prominent osteosclerotic response to the infection (Ortner & Putschar, 1985).

Nongummatous lesions

Nongummatous lesions include periostitis, osteitis and osteoperiostitis, and are frequently seen in the tibia (saber shin), fibula, clavicle, femur, ulna, and radius. In the skull periostitis may be found in the nasal, palatal, frontal, and parietal bones (Zimmerman & Kelley, 1982). Bilateral involvement of this type, mainly in tibiae, is strong evidence of tertiary syphilis (Murray et al., 1990). In most cases the periosteum is involved first and the infection may spread into the cortex and even through the cortex to the medullary tissues. Sequestra are uncommon. In some cases there can be joint involvement.

- Periostitis. This begins in the metaphyses of the long bones and is characterized by formation of subperiosteal bone as a reaction to the periosteal inflammation (Steinbock, 1976; Powell, 1991). The medial third of the clavicle is thickened as well as the distal portion of the tibia. However, sometimes involvement of the entire periosteum with thickening and deformity of the whole bone appears (Fig. 7.28). When it is localized, periostitis can leave plaque-like exostoses on the cortex of the bone (Fig. 7.29). Almost all authors agree that the new bone located over the cortex is progressively remodeled into the cortex as the soft or fiber bone is replaced by lamellar bone. The outer surface is rough and markedly hypervas-

cular. Where the new bone layer is thick it may substitute for the original cortex. The latter may sometimes be resorbed gradually or rapidly destroyed by a syphilitic medullary gumma that later may invade the subperiosteal new bone and destroy it as well (Steinbock, 1976; Ortner & Putschar, 1985; Powell, 1991).

- Osteoperiostitis and osteitis. The medullary cavity commonly is greatly narrowed by the cortical thickening (Fig. 7.30). In late stages the medullary canal may be completely obliterated by sclerotic trabeculae. Sequestration in the long bones is uncommon. Osteoperiostitis and osteitis are seen in dry skeletal material as roughened external surfaces, thickened cortices, and scattered patches of increased radiodensity in the radiographs (Fig. 7.31).

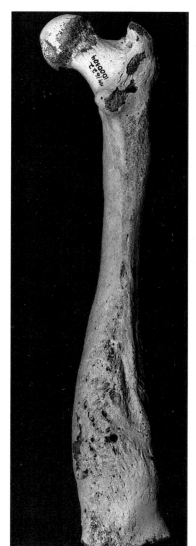
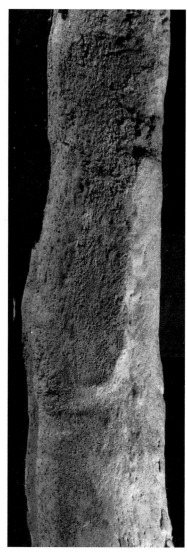
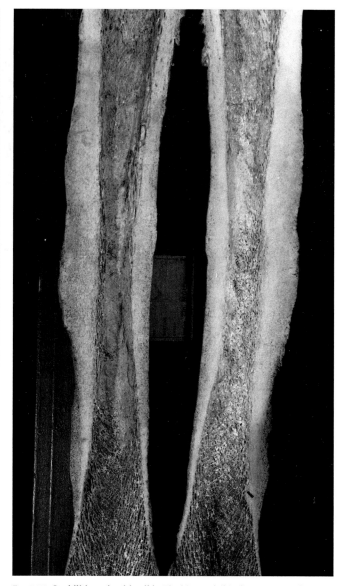

FIG. 7.28: **Syphilitic periostitis, femur.** The widened area of the femur's lower diaphysis is the product of periostitis. Some of the larger surface defects are undoubtedly the effects of gummas. No. 1000304. Modern adult. Courtesy P. Sledzik. NMHM.

FIG. 7.29: **Syphilitic periostitis.** A thick layer of localized periosteal new bone has been deposited on the diaphysis, most of which has not been remodeled into the cortex. No. 1449.10. Modern adult. Courtesy G. Worden. MM.

FIG. 7.30: **Syphilitic periostitis, tibia.** The bisected tibia demonstrates that, while the deposition of periosteal new bone encircles the entire diaphysis, that on the anterior surface is thicker than that on the posterior (saber shin). Note narrowed medulla. No. 1449.45. Modern adult. Courtesy G. Worden. MM.

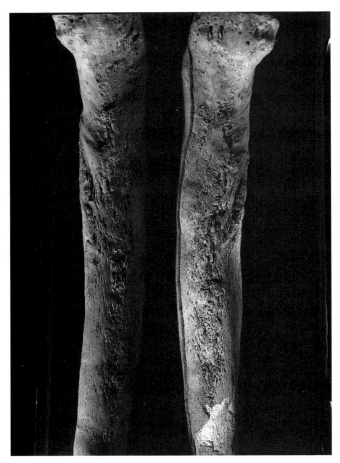

FIG. 7.31: **Syphilitic periostitis, tibia.** The entire diaphysis is coated with a thick layer of periosteum-formed new bone that has a very irregular, roughened surface and has not been remodeled into cortical bone. No. 1449.45. Modern adult. Courtesy G. Worden. MM.

Gummatous lesions

Alteration of the blood supply secondary to arteriolar inflammation induces both necrotizing and proliferative reactions in the tissues involved. The necrotizing reaction (tissue infarction) may be circumscribed and surrounded by a zone of collagenized connective tissue. The central portion of the lesion undergoes a characteristic process of coagulation of infarcted, necrotic tissue called gumma formation (Aegerter & Kirkpatrick, 1975). Gummas appear in the more advanced stages of syphilis (Casagrande & Frost, 1955). These lesions are found both in the skull and the long bones. Coalescence of the common, smaller lesions may form a large mass of dry, crumbly matter filling the entire medullary cavity (Jaffe, 1972). The macroscopic appearance in skeletal material is that of thickened cortices and rough external surfaces. Sequestra are uncommon.

It is important to note that periosteal gummas are usually much smaller and fewer in number than those occurring in the medullary cavity. All bone is destroyed in the space occupied by the gumma but the surrounding bone often becomes sclerotic. In dry bone the localized, surface depressions represent the foci of necrotic bone. These are usually quite sharply

defined, and encircled by an elevated rim of reactive, sclerotic bone that reflects the local reaction to the necrotic, gummatous bone. Mingling of such sunken, destructive areas with elevated foci of reactive new bone formation and partial coalescence of the lesions can generate a dramatically tumultuous irregular cranial vault surface known as caries sicca (dry rot). Occasional long bone lesions may present a similar, but rarely as well-developed process. In the skull the lesions appear in the frontal and parietal bones with the outer tables being affected first (Zimmerman & Kelley, 1982). Nasal palatal destruction is another important feature of cranial syphilis. In the long bones the underlying cortex is hyperostotic and endosteal bone formation may encroach upon the medullary cavity (Ortner & Putschar, 1985). Pathological fractures may be seen in the bones affected by the gummatous periostitis.

Joint involvement (gummatous arthritis)

Gummatous arthritis is uncommon and its origin is usually a gumma located in the synovial membrane or in the subchondral bone that produces destructive lesions in both tissues. The most frequently affected joint is the knee. Resnick & Niwayama (1989a, b) believe syphilitic joint disease can be caused by a variety of mechanisms:
1. Spread from a contiguous source of infection from the periarticular bone.
2. Direct involvement of the synovial membrane.
3. Sympathetic effusions that may relate to periosteal irritation from a neighboring intraosseous focus.
4. Neuroarthropathy (discussed separately below).

These joint changes are commonly unilateral and monoarticular. Only occasionally will the disease affect more than one joint. Granulation tissue production and pannus formation occur in this disease with destruction of the articular cartilage. Osteophytes, marginal lipping and eburnation, all features typical of degenerative joint disease, are seen in gummatous arthritis. Discrete areas of destruction may be present in the articular surfaces as a result of gummatous involvement (Steinbock, 1976; Ortner & Putschar, 1985). Progression of these processes may end in joint ankylosis.

Skeletal changes in neurosyphilis

Neurosyphilis appears in between 10 and 20 % of cases affecting large joints, especially those of the lower limbs (60–75 % of the neurosyphilitic cases). Spine involvement is seen much less frequently. The disease usually presents in the latter half of life, without gender bias; it is almost unknown in the immature skeleton (Murray et al., 1990). Monoarticular presentation predominates although polyarticular involvement is not uncommon. The knee, hip, ankle, shoulder, and elbow joints are altered in descending order of frequency.

The French physician Charcot was the first to describe the lesions of neurosyphilis in a lecture in in 1868. Subsequently, the arthropathy has been known as Charcot's joint. The condition evolves in the following manner. In the neurosyphilitic form known as tabes dorsalis, demyelinization of the posterior columns of the spinal cord results in a variety of dysfunctional changes. Of these, the most important, leading to joint involvement, is loss of deep pain sensation. In the absence of protective pain awareness, commonly used joints will be exposed to excessive and repeated trauma, the cumulative effect of which can be disastrous (see Fig. 6.18). Initially, the affected individual experiences instability of one or more joints with little or no pain. This is the result of subarticular fractures that become progressively more numerous and cause increasing disorganization of the affected joint, producing instability and hypermobility (Murray *et al.*, 1990). As there is no pain because of the neural involvement, trophic ulcers of soft tissues may appear, from which bacteria can gain entry into the joint complicating the skeletal degeneration with superimposed infection. Juxta-articular osteopenia is absent and <u>increased</u> radiological density often appears around an affected joint. In the early stages the lesions simulate degenerative joint disease (and fragmentation) but later subluxation and dislocation appears. After months or years gross disintegration of the joint may be evident with clearly defined margins of bony destruction or large multiple bone fragments detached from the articulator surfaces. Complete resorption of bone fragments may occur. Because the pathological condition underlying Charcot joint formation is anesthesia, other conditions producing loss of pain sensation may duplicate these effects. Among these are lesions of the spine including meningocele and syringomyelia, as well as peripheral neuropathy such as that often associated with diabetes mellitus.

Vertebral involvement (primarily in the lumbar region, less frequent in the thoracic spine, and very rarely in the cervical) initially is difficult to differentiate from the much more common appearance of degenerative spondylosis. Unusually severe degenerative changes accompanied by sclerosis and malalignment of vertebral bodies ('toppling brick' sign) should suggest the diagnosis. Fractures may appear.

Skull pathology

The pathognomonic lesion of syphilis is that of a tertiary gummatous osteoperiosteal lesion that was defined as 'caries sicca' by the German pathologist Rudolph Virchow in 1896. Virchow described the typical lesions of caries sicca as follows:

The only reliable and pathognomonic lesion of syphilis is…the scar which remains after superficial gummatous osteitis…always showing the same characteristics…I do not know other disease causing such changes. It is easy to recognize such foci,…, but it is difficult to say how they differ from other bone defects. Frequent and characteristic are the jagged, radiating, and stellate scars showing depressed centers and round borders. The diagnosis can be reached only by considering the appearance as a whole. The changes are grouped round a center and radiate and fuse to produce a uniform pattern. This is what is decisive.

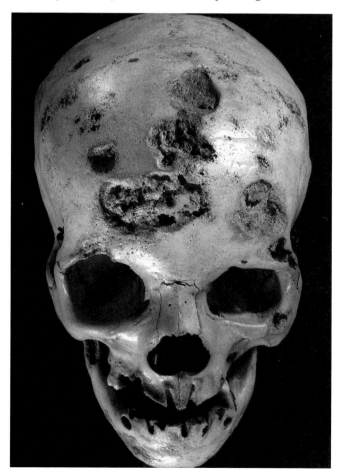

FIG. 7.32: **Syphilis, skull (caries sicca).** The frontal bone is extensively destroyed by bone gummas with only a modest periosteal response in the lesions' periphery. No. 1161.07. Modern adult. Courtesy G. Worden. MM.

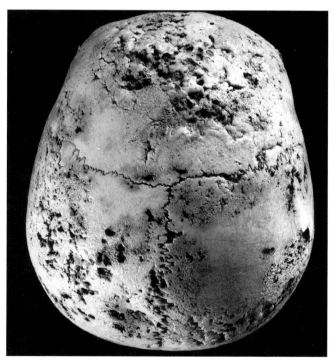

FIG. 7.33: **Syphilis, skull (caries sicca).** The depressed areas over the posterior half of the calvarium represent sites of necrotic bone tissue of gummas, while the frontal bone shows areas of irregular thickening adjacent to such bone defects that represent periosteal sclerotizing response. No. 1161.12. Modern adult. Courtesy G. Worden. MM.

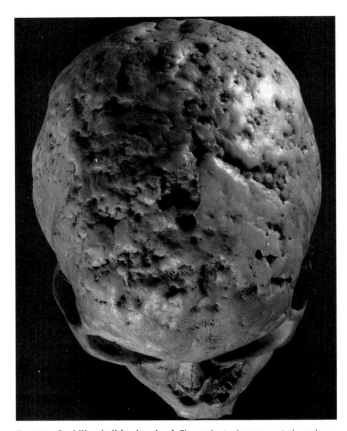

FIG. 7.34: **Syphilis, skull (caries sicca).** The periosteal response to bone loss secondary to skull bone gummas has almost bridged some of the depressed gummatous areas. No. 1161.10. Modern adult. Courtesy G. Worden. MM.

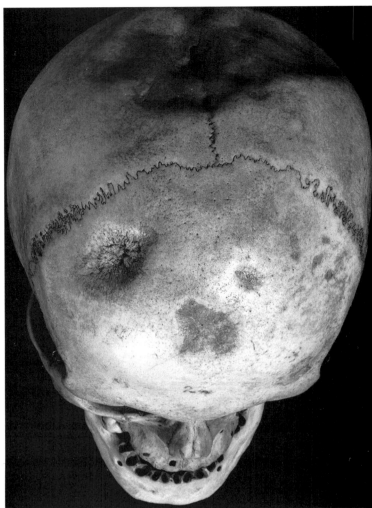

FIG. 7.35: **Syphilis, skull (caries sicca).** The broad, sunken areas are sites of bone gummas that involve principally the outer table and diploe. No. 1161. Modern adult. Courtesy G. Worden. MM.

FIG. 7.36: **Syphilis, skull (caries sicca).** A huge area of gummatous necrosis has destroyed much of the anterior half of the calvarium with only a few, irregular, scattered areas of new bone formation. No. 1161.04. Modern adult. Courtesy G. Worden. MM.

Steinbock (1976) describes two apparently opposed processes that are evident in each area of calvarial erosion. In the center the destruction produces a depression representing the partially resorbed, infarcted bone of a gumma (Fig. 7.32), but at the same time a regenerative process is seen around the circumference laying down new bone that gradually becomes sclerotic (Fig. 7.33). Further progression of the erosion increases the extent and depth of the depression and new bone is deposited around this depression, so the borders acquire a folded or wrinkled appearance. Individual foci will heal, but new foci will form in the vicinity. When numerous lesions of this type overlap, the distinctive features of the solitary lesion become more difficult to recognize. Blending of the collapsed foci of necrotic bone with the raised areas of reactive new bone formation may result in an elevated, smooth-surfaced 'plateau' of reactive bone, irregularly intersected by depressed grooves (valleys?) of scarred bone and broad lakes of depressed gummas, generating a surface of geographic appearance (Fig. 7.34). The erosive and reparative

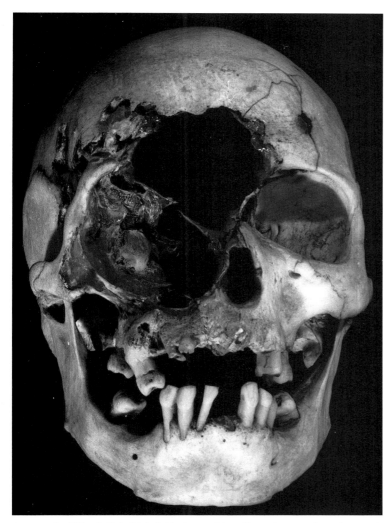

FIG. 7.37: **Syphilis, skull.** In this individual necrotizing effects of gummas have destroyed much of the right orbit and frontal bone and right nasal bone as well as the right and central maxillary area. No. 1177. Modern adult. Courtesy G. Worden. MM.

processes may completely obliterate the diploe. As Ortner & Putschar (1985) point out, the syphilitic lesion leads to a destruction of the outer table and part of the diploe but often spares the inner table almost completely (Fig. 7.35). Perforation of the three portions of the calvarium (inner table, diploe, and outer table) occurs largely in the final stage (Fig. 7.36).

Necrosis may occur secondary to ischemia resulting from syphilitic arteritis, but also by the rapid progress of gummatous granulation or the occurrence of secondary pyogenic infection. Sequestra are only rarely present but may present foci of radiologically irregular density. Although there can be changes in the nasal and palatal areas, these are not so characteristic as in yaws and bejel. These thin bones may be destroyed, enlarging the nasal cavity, which appears empty in dry skeletal specimens (Fig. 7.37). When the bone underlying the nasal soft tissues at the base of the nose becomes necrotic and is resorbed, the overlying and now unsupported soft tissues sag, producing a visibly sunken area often called saddle nose (Ortner & Putschar, 1985). The diagnostic criteria of syphilis in dry bones are based on three developmental sequences of skull changes. As described by Hackett (1983) they are:

I. Initial sequence:
　1. Clustered pits.
　2. Confluent pits.
II. Discrete sequence:
　3. Focal superficial cavitation.
　4. Circumvallate cavitation.
　5. Radial scars.
III. Contiguous sequence:
　6. Serpiginous cavitation.
　7. Nodular cavitation.
　8. Caries sicca.

It is important to point out that, as Hackett (1983) states, group I of the above cranial lesions can lead to either II or III. In all these caries sequences the changes on the surface of the outer table are more marked than those on the inner, and they do not involve the sutures themselves (Ortner & Putschar, 1985). Steinbock (1976) also notes that the gummatous destruction begins almost invariably on the outer table of the calvarium by extension of the infection from the soft tissues of the pericranium. The frontal bone is frequently the first bone involved from where the lesions may spread to the adjacent parietal and facial bones (Ortner & Putschar, 1985).

Differential diagnosis

Syphilis may resemble some other skeletal lesions from which it must be differentiated. Among others, Bogdan & Weaver (1992) compare the signs of treponematosis with trauma, hematogenous osteomyelitis, mycotic infection, tuberculosis, leprosy, myeloma, carcinoma, and osteosarcoma. The most important differential diagnoses are:
1. Tumors.
   - Primary osteogenic sarcoma. This malignant bone tumor almost exclusively involves only one bone while skeletal syphilis often appears bilaterally and in a much older age group.
   - Meningioma. Is exclusively a tumor of the skull and, although the age group falls within that of syphilis, it never affects the postcranial skeleton as syphilis does.
   - Metastatic carcinoma. This may be confused when it affects the skull vault. However, the cranial lesions of metastatic carcinoma are expansile lesions and not totally necrotic, are smaller than those of syphilis and are accompanied by little if any bone regeneration (Steinbock, 1976).
   - Multiple myeloma. The same criteria as those for metastatic carcinoma are applicable. The lesions are smaller and are purely lytic.
2. Infections.
   - Tuberculosis. Skeletal tuberculosis often proves difficult to distinguish from skeletal syphilis (Steinbock, 1976).

In tuberculosis, destruction of the bone tissue predominates with very little new bone formation. Therefore, hypertrophic expansion of the long bones is rarely found. Furthermore, cranial erosion in tuberculosis begins in the inner table.

■ Pyogenic osteomyelitis. Usually this disease does not involve as many bones as does syphilis. In addition, pyogenic osteomyelitis produces sequestrum and cloaca formation, lesions that are rarely observed i n syphilis.

3. Miscellaneous conditions.

■ Paget's disease. This may create postcranial lesions very similar to those of syphilis. However, the massive thickening of the skull vault is very different from cranial syphilis (Steinbock, 1976). Conveniently, the characteristic histologically demonstrable mosaic structure of Paget's disease is not found in syphilis.

Congenital syphilis

Congenital syphilis is a special form of the disease transmitted by hematogenous dissemination of the spirochetes through the placenta from the mother to the fetus, usually after the sixteenth to eighteenth weeks of life in utero, although it has been suspected that transmission may occur sometimes prior to the sixteenth week. The fetus, heavily infected with the spirochetes, is likely to abort or to die soon after birth. Mortality is particularly high without treatment and the prognosis is significantly worse if the affected infant is born prematurely (Murray et al., 1990). The attack rate of congenital syphilis is about 80 % in the offspring of infected mothers.

Congenital syphilis may adversely affect the development of vital systems, in addition to producing severe osteochondritis, periostitis, and diaphyseal osteomyelitis in young children (Powell, 1988). The typical 'Hutchinson's triad' of deformities includes:

■ Deafness, due to a lesion in the eighth cranial nerve.
■ Notched permanent incisors (Hutchinson's teeth).
■ Interstitial keratitis.

The toll levied upon population fertility by spontaneous abortions and stillbirth caused by congenital syphilis is substantial (Casagrande & Frost, 1955; Powell, 1988). In fact, as Mann & Murphy (1990) point out, the infection often kills the child before birth while milder cases or syphilis congenita tarda may remain dormant for many years. Surprisingly, late congenital syphilis does not produce cardiovascular lesions, even though occasionally neurosyphilis may develop (Strong, 1981).

Pathogenesis

The lesions of congenital syphilis originate from transplacental migration of the spirochetes and invasion of the perichondrium, periosteum, cartilage, bone marrow, and sites of active endochondral ossification. The spirochetes inhibit osteogenesis and lead to degeneration of osteoblasts (Resnick & Niwayama, 1989a, b). The skeletal lesions appear in the form of an osteochondritis at the sites where endochondral ossification takes place. The growth plates of the long tubular bones and costochondral junctions may be the only areas affected (Revell, 1986). However, in severe cases flat and short tubular bones and vertebrae can be involved. Epiphyseal separation may occur if the vascular granulation tissue invades the epiphyseal cartilage extensively. Periosteum is a site of active bone formation in the developing fetus and a periostitis is often seen (Revell, 1986). Subperiosteal new bone growth appears by osteoblastic activity in the elevated periosteum. This change is seen in surviving neonates rather than in fetuses and its combination with osteochondritis is exceptional (Jaffe, 1972).

Murray et al. (1990) describe three stages of congenital syphilis:

1. First stage. It appears at birth or shortly after, involving approximately 75 % of infected infants. Described as 'osteochondritis' or 'metaphysitis,' it occurs primarily around the knees, elbows, wrists, and shoulders. It produces irregular and multiple erosive lesions most characteristically affecting the proximal end of the tibia. Spontaneous regression takes place but slowly. Symmetrical erosions on the medial surfaces of the proximal ends of the tibiae and the distal end of the femora represent Wimberger's sign, detectable in 25 % of the affected individuals. Resnick & Niwayama (1989a, b) add that epiphyseal separation may result from the metaphyseal destruction.

2. Second stage. This appears by the age of 2 years. This stage shows periostitis due to periosteal infiltration by syphilitic granulation tissue. Periosteal reaction is diffuse, widespread and almost always symmetrical, affecting most long bones, but much more rarely the tubular bones of the hands and feet. If this new bone formation is accompanied by cortical thickening, it may produce an appearance of bone within a bone. Lesions are also seen in the skull, the mandible, and the scapula. Spontaneous slow resolution will occur.

3. Third stage (syphilitic osteitis). This stage develops in fewer than 10 % of the cases, in the later part of the first decade or in the second decade of life. It manifests as a spirochetal invasion of the cortex and medullary cavity of the shafts of major long bones. Elliptical or fusiform defects are seen, and organized periosteal reaction may persist.

Paleopathological diagnosis

The rarity of congenital syphilis in a paleopathological context is largely due to the fact that the disease causes about 50 % case fatality rate of affected fetuses. The skeleton of a new-born affected by congenital syphilis will only infrequently be diagnosed as syphilitic. Subsequently transverse pathological fractures through the metaphysis may occur (Parrot's pseudoparalysis: Ortner & Putschar, 1985). In such a case paleopathological diagnosis is dependent upon age at death, preservation, and recognition (Manchester, 1983a).

Skeletal pathology

Early or infantile form of congenital syphilis

This form is present at birth or during early infancy (always before 2 years of age, and most commonly between the third and the sixth months of life). The spirochetes characteristically attack the metaphyseal areas of the fetus, replacing the normal metaphyseal tissues with syphilitic granulation tissue (Aegerter & Kirkpatrick, 1975). Radiological features include rarefaction of the juxta-epiphyseal portion of the diaphysis, patchy diaphyseal rarefaction, and thickening of the short and long bones by subperiosteal deposition of bone (periostitis) which commonly begins at the sixth month of life (Piulachs, 1957; Zimmerman & Kelley, 1982). Jaffe (1972) points out that there is a nearly pathognomonic sign in the early form of congenital syphilis: Wimberger's sign, which consists of rarefaction of the medial tibial metaphysis.

Osteochondritis or metaphysitis is evident in the majority of syphilitic fetuses. Casagrande & Frost (1955) believes these lesions constitute the most positive sign of congenital syphilis and that they have a limited course. A diffuse form of periostitis, commonly located in the proximal third of the tibia and in the distal third of the femur is also present uniformly. Resnick & Niwayama (1989*a*, *b*) add a third sign: diaphyseal osteomyelitis or osteitis. Thus, this phase is characterized by these changes in archaeological bones:

1. Syphilitic osteochondritis. This often occurs during the first 6 months of life and affects the epiphyseal–metaphyseal junction of long bones' (tibia, ulna, radius, femur, humerus, and fibula) costochondral regions. In more severe cases the flat and short tubular bones and ossification centers of the sternum and vertebrae are also affected. The calcification zone widens, increasing from a thickness of 0.1–0.3 mm up to 3 mm. Unfortunately, these bands of increased calcification may not be preserved in archaeological specimens (Schinz *et al.*, 1953). Serrations ('saw-toothed' metaphysis) and adjacent osseus irregularity are seen in the metaphyses of the long bones. The epiphysis may be displaced or even crushed down into the defective ends of the shaft (Steinbock, 1976) .

2. Diaphyseal osteomyelitis (osteitis). Osteolytic lesions with surrounding bone eburnation and overlying periostitis appear in the long bones, mainly in the metaphyses (Resnick & Niwayama, 1989*a*, *b*). Sequestra are rare.

3. Periostitis. Periostitis is a less frequent manifestation of congenital syphilis than osteochondritis. It is seen well in the femur and tibia, extending through the entire diaphysis (Schinz *et al.*, 1953). New bone is laid down over the affected region and the cortex becomes thickened. The periosteum may cover the entire area with fiber bone that may be converted gradually into dense, lamellar bone ensheathing the cortex (periosteal cloaking: Steinbock, 1976). Skull involvement is relatively infrequent (5–10 % of cases with skeletal involvement). Two types of lesions may affect the skull: hypertrophic periostitis, or necrotizing osteitis that may involve both tables and form sequestra (Steinbock, 1976).

Differential diagnosis of the early form of congenital syphilis

1. Rickets. Syphilis appears before 6 months of life, while rickets is observed later. The deformation in rickets is a consequence of deformation due to static forces, while in syphilis the deformity is at sites of active bone formation (Turek, 1982).

2. Scurvy. The metaphyseal irregularity itself may be accompanied by fragmentation and fractures that sometimes resemble the lesions of scurvy (Turek, 1982; Murray *et al.*, 1990).

Late form of congenital syphilis

Skeletal involvement is not as common in the late as in the early form. Skeletal changes are seen after 2 years of life, between childhood and early adulthood and basically are similar to those of venereal or acquired syphilis: periostitis and gumma formation. The most frequently affected bones are the tibia, radius, and ulna (Jaffe, 1972). The tibia shows 'saber-shin' type of thickening and the skull exhibits changes similar to those of acquired syphilis. Other stigmata include dactylitis, Hutchinson's teeth (see Fig. 14.10), and mulberry molars (see Fig. 14.11: reduced, dome-shaped, first molars). Syphilitic arthritis is rare (Zimmerman & Kelley, 1982). Bone lesions in the late form of congenital syphilis are usually chronic and the deformities persist for many years. The skeletal manifestations of this disease rarely resemble those of the early form, but more probably will mimic those of acquired syphilis. Contrary to the early form, the late form is not a systemic pattern and only a few bones are involved (Schinz *et al.*, 1953). Gummatous or nongummatous osteomyelitis or periostitis result in diffuse hyperostosis of the involved bone (Resnick & Niwayama, 1989*a*, *b*).

1. Nongummatous periostitis. This primarily involves the diaphyses of the long bones. The tibia is the most commonly affected bone with the typical 'saber shin' deformity or 'saber tibia' of Fournier due to a marked subperiosteal apposition of new bone on the anterior surface. The normal, sharp anterior aspect of the tibia becomes rounded. In addition new bone is laid down endosteally, causing a narrowing of the medullary cavity. After years, the normal bone is replaced by very dense, sclerotic bone fused to the cortex (Steinbock, 1976).

2. Gummatous osteomyelitis. This is a diffuse osteomyelitis with patchy destruction of bone in the sites of the gummas. Sequestrum and sinus formation are uncommon. The tibia is the most commonly involved bone. The skull is less frequently affected than the long bones but its involvement is important for the diagnosis. The saddle nose (destruction of the bony and cartilaginous elements of the nose) appears in 15–30 % of the cases but it is nonspecific (Steinbock, 1976). Ortner & Putschar (1985) point out that skull lesions occur but usually appear as multiple, rounded, destructive foci without the characteristic features of caries sicca sequence. Occasionally, extensive involvement of the facial bones may occur.

3. Syphilitic dactylitis. An important feature in the late form of congenital syphilis is that of syphilitic dactylitis. This is more frequent in congenital than in acquired syphilis. Involvement of the fingers is more commonly seen than that of the toes. Phalanges and metacarpals increase in size and commonly demonstrate osteoblastic-induced deformation (Turek, 1982). Syphilitic dactylitis may be confused with the spina ventosa of children's skeletal tuberculosis. Bilateral involvement is not uncommon, although not symmetrical.

4. Joint pathology. Syphilitic arthritis in the late form of congenital syphilis is known as 'Clutton's joints,' which usually is the result of involvement of the synovial membrane. The lesion is commonly located in the knee and it is commonly bilateral. This inflammation is rarely seen in the dry bone because it is primarily a soft tissue process. It is only observed in dry bone in the very chronic cases and its appearance is that of an infectious arthritis.

5. Dental pathology. Dental stigmata are important for the diagnosis but almost all authors agree that they are not pathognomonic. The frequency varies from 30–50 % of the series. The permanent dentition and in some instances the deciduous molars are the only teeth affected (Steinbock, 1976). The most frequently involved teeth are the maxillary incisors and the first molars. Hutchinson's teeth are notched and narrowed incisors (primarily permanent maxillary central incisors, with a barrel shape). The mulberry molar (also known as Moon's molar, dome-shaped molar or Fournier's tooth) is a first molar considerably smaller than normal showing an irregular and rough occlusal surface with small protuberances that represent atrophic cusps.

Origins of the treponematoses

Stirland (1991) points out that there are two major problems to be addressed in any attempt to discuss the origins, history, spread, epidemiology, and evidence of treponematoses in ancient times:

1. What evidence is there for the origin and subsequent spread of treponemal disease, especially syphilis?
2. Do the treponemes represent four discrete diseases or only one?

At present two major approaches to these questions try to provide an explanation for the surprising similarities of the human treponematoses.

Unitarian theory

The most outstanding defender of this theory is Hudson (1965) who maintains that there is only one treponemal disease that assumes different clinical patterns under different epidemiological conditions. Hudson suggests that the first treponemal infection was yaws and that it probably appeared in central Africa. From there it spread, accompanying the human migrations to the rest of the world 100 000 years ago. Therefore, the defenders of this theory believe it is not appropriate to refer to transmission of syphilis from the New World to the Old World or vice versa. Cockburn (1963) suggests that since the organisms responsible for the four treponematoses must have descended from a common ancestor there must have been some connection between the infections. The difficulty, however, arises in finding some link between the populations on the two continents. Cockburn believes it is possible that some recent migrant groups brought the treponemes to the New World, or that the original settlers of the New World were already infected when they first crossed the Bering Strait. The problem is there is no evidence for either of these two speculations.

Nonunitarian theory

The most articulate and well-known defender of this viewpoint is Hackett (1963, 1967), who suggests that the different clinical patterns of human treponematoses are probably due to mutational changes in the treponemal strains. He suggests that at least four mutations have occurred in the last 10 000 years. In his opinion, the first form of treponematosis was pinta, which extended from Africa and Asia to America during the last part of the last glaciation (15 000 years ago). An initial mutation took place by about 10 000 B.C. The stimulus for the mutation probably was a warm and humid environment, resulting in yaws which extended through Africa, Southeast Asia, and probably the Pacific islands and Australia. It did not reach America. The second mutational change occurred around 7000 B.C. changing the clinical features from those of yaws to bejel or endemic syphilis, triggered by a warm, arid climatic change. The new disease appeared in northern and Saharan Africa, southwestern and central Asia, and central Australia. Yaws persisted in the areas of more humid environment. The third mutation appeared around 3000 B.C. with the development of urban areas and use of clothing in the regions of the eastern Mediterranean Sea and southwestern Asia. Here bejel (nonvenereal and typical of rural children) changed to acquired or venereal syphilis (urban adults). By the year 0 of our era, venereal syphilis had spread to the Mediterranean Sea but in a mild form. The fourth and last mutation took place in Europe in the late fifteenth century – probably favored by environmental and social conditions in the European cities at that time – and resulted in a much more serious disease. Livingstone (1991) sees no similar environmental or demographic circumstances in the situations postulated by this nonunitarian hypothesis. In his view the failure of this hypothesis to conform to epidemiological expectations strains the credibility of this theory. Until more tangible evidence becomes available, we can expect the issue to remain unresolved.

Geographic origins of the treponematoses

Sigerist (1951) points out that for centuries historians and physicians have debated whether syphilis was indigenous to America and was brought to Europe by Columbus' crew, and from which it spread to other parts of the world, or whether the disease existed in Europe before the end of the fifteenth century, possibly since remote antiquity. The question, for this medical historian, is obviously very important in the case of a disease that is contagious, renders people seriously ill for a long time, and has dire social consequences. With regard to the Columbian or pre-Columbian origin of treponematoses (and especially syphilis), Laín Entralgo (1963) observes:

1. The existence of syphilis in America prior to its discovery by Columbus is clear (a number of pathological samples confirm this).
2. Abundant medical and nonmedical literary documents and images (such as that by Jaime Huguet, 1461, representing the miracles of St. Cosme and St. Damian) prior to 1492 offer descriptions of lesions, bearing other contemporary diagnostic terms but that could be syphilitic, suggest the presence of European syphilis prior to the epidemic of 1495.
3. It is difficult to assess if the European epidemic of 1495 and its later terrible consequences was due to the new American importation or was the effect of an increase in the virulence of the European endemic organisms. Goff (1967) suggests that the epidemic probably was caused by the introduction of either a new strain or a mutant of high infectibility. In addition, in areas of the New World in particular, immunity had developed.

According to Stewart & Spoehr (1967), it appears that shortly after the discovery of America, what is interpreted as syphilis spread rapidly among the American Indians. As judged by the skeletal evidence for its presence in pre-Columbian Indian remains, the spread of this disease in America in post-Columbian times appears to have been of almost epidemic proportion. Stewart & Spoehr suggest that one possible explanation of these phenomena is that Europe and America each had its own variety of syphilis and therefore may have exchanged treponemes for which the recipient populations lacked immunity. An alternative explanation suggests that the treponemes of syphilis may have developed or differentiated locally in the West Indies from the treponeme causing yaws, and that the Spaniards carried the new disease first to Europe, then to the rest of the Americas, and eventually to other parts of the world. This last theory assumes that syphilis is of very recent origin and yaws was present in the Americas in the pre-Columbian period.

Thus, two principal concepts have evolved with regard to the geographic origin of syphilis: the Columbian theory and the pre-Columbian theory. However, recently a third theory has emerged (Livingstone, 1991).

Columbian theory

This hypothesis proposes that syphilis was introduced to Europe and the Old World after the return of the first trip of Columbus and his crew in 1493. This theory's defenders suggest that the introduction of a totally new disease would explain its rapid spread to every part of Europe. However, Steinbock (1976) finds it interesting that it was not until 40 years after Columbus' return that the New World is mentioned as the source of syphilis in the works of the Spanish authors Gonzalo Fernández de Oviedo (1537) and Rodrigo Ruiz Díaz de Isla (1539). By the 1560s almost all physicians accepted the American origin of syphilis. Steinbock (1976) also thinks the major impetus for regarding the New World as the cradle of syphilis was the discovery of guaiac, guayacán or palosanto (*Guaiacum officinale*), a type of wood, as a remedy for the disease. He notes that 'According to the reasoning of that period God always provides a remedy where He inflicts a disease.': therefore, it is not strange that the physicians of that time thought that since what was assumed to be an antisyphilitic agent (guaiac) came from the New World, then syphilis must have originated there as well.

Pre-Columbian theory

This theory maintains that the disease was present in the Old World a long time before the discovery of the Americas. The first supporters of this theory were the Italian physicians Niccoló Leoniceno and Niccoló Massa (1532). The defenders of this theory suggest that acquired or venereal syphilis was present in Europe before Columbus' return in 1493 but that it was indistinguishable from other diseases grouped as leprosy. Steinbock (1976) notes the many references to 'venereal leprosy' in the thirteenth and fourteenth centuries and later to 'hereditary leprosy.' Steinbock also points out that in the twelfth and thirteenth centuries the Crusaders returned from the Holy Land with 'Saracen Ointment' containing mercury to treat leprosy. However, leprosy is not transmitted by sexual contact or transplacentally but syphilis is, and while mercury is completely ineffective against leprosy it was used as the only remedy against syphilis for four centuries.

Livingstone's 'alternative hypothesis'

According to Livingstone (1991), there is no reason to assume that the treponemes have been undergoing similar adaptations throughout their evolution in the human species: some of the existing differences among them are adaptations to environmental temperature. He suggests that the post-Columbian increase in the number of cases in the Americas was due to the introduction of a virulent strain from the Old World at the time of Columbus' discovery. At the time of the discovery of America, there was increased contact with tropical Africa. The Portuguese had established a fort and trading post in what is now Ghana 15 years before Columbus' arrival in the New World, providing an opportunity for a nonvene-real treponeme from Africa to make the adaptation to the Americas. Ortner (1992a) finds that Livingstone's response to the question of the virulence associated with the disease during the epidemic in Europe in 1495 is equally important and intriguing. Rapid passage of microorganisms between hosts can result in increased virulence, and Livingstone thinks the sexual practices in Europe at that period would have increased the rate of transmission of the microorganisms from one human host to another, and thus its virulence. Resolution of these contrasting hypotheses also awaits the generation of new data relevant to the question.

History of the treponematoses

Palés (1930) believes that syphilis, as well as osteomyelitis, spondylitis and tumors, existed in prehistoric times, and the problem is not to demonstrate the antiquity of 'morbus galli-cus' but to determine its existence or nonexistence thousands of years ago. This means that it is absolutely necessary to establish the true history of the disease. Cockburn (1963) thinks human treponematoses in the very early days would have differed from those of the present time due to the small populations living in the earth at that period. In migrant groups (hunter–gatherers) only saprophytic infection or infections of a low grade of pathogenicity could survive. With population increase at the origin of agriculture, strains of pathogens producing more acute infections could exist. Under the conditions of life of those populations, only chronic infections like pinta or low-grade sores could survive. So, by the year A.D. 1000 treponemes would exist either as commensals or parasites on all continents but, because of the small size of the populations in most areas, any disease would be of a mild type and chronic in nature. Baker & Armelagos (1988) present several questions about the true history of treponematoses (especially of syphilis):

1. Did an epidemic of syphilis begin in the last years of the fifteenth century? It seems difficult to answer this question with complete security. Baker & Armelagos think that the numerous ordinances passed throughout Europe in those years in an effort to control the disease and the proliferation of publications regarding it indicate that a highly contagious disease that caused genital and cutaneous lesions was raging at this time.

2. Was this epidemic the result of differentiation of syphilis and its widespread recognition as a disease distinct from leprosy? In support of the pre-Columbian hypothesis Baker & Armelagos (1988) note that leprosy declined in those years and the ordinances about the 'new epidemic' were similar to those of leprosy.

3. Was the epidemic of venereal syphilis due to increasing urbanization and improved hygiene in late fifteenth century Europe? Leprosy declined in the fourteenth century with improved living conditions; almost all authors agree

that nonvenereal treponematoses would also have decreased with such improvement. It is possible that endemic syphilis was present in the Old World and during those years the treponeme was increasingly being transmitted sexually until syphilis was identified at the end of the next century.

According to these authors, the case of pre-Columbian syphilis in the Old World rests solely on vague and ambiguous disease descriptions, and in their opinion it must be rejected. However, there are several examples of probable pre-Columbian syphilis in Europe (see below) that have been described at the time of and more recently than the Baker & Armelagos paper.

As we have seen, the origins of syphilis, and in general of all treponematoses, is one of the most controversial problems in the history of infectious diseases. The disease was first recognized as a distinct pathological entity in Europe following epidemics that developed at the end of the fifteenth century, shortly after the return of Columbus from his first trip to the New World (Prioreschi, 1991). The concluding section of the history of the disease follows.

In 1495 (three years after the return of the first trip of Columbus) the Spanish Army of Gonzalo de Córdoba, the Great Captain, besieged the French troops of Charles VIII who, a short time before, had conquered Naples. During the siege a strange and severe epidemic appeared among the defenders. The disease began with loathsome sores and ulcers, terrible aches in the bones, and, shortly after, invalid status or death. With two such terrible enemies (the Spaniards outside and the treponemes inside Naples), the French troops surrendered and as they returned to their countries they spread the disease throughout Italy, France, and Germany. By 1500 all of Europe was afflicted by the terrible effects of the epidemic. 'It was a pestilence never seen before,' wrote López de Villalobos, a Spanish physician, in 1498. So, as Laín Entralgo (1963) affirms, remembering the origin of the disease, the French called it 'mal napolitanicus,' the Italians 'mal franzoso,' and the Spaniards 'mal francés.'

It is not strange that a huge amount of medical and non-medical literature about syphilis emerged during those years. The first reference was that of Niccoló Leoniceno with his 'Libellus de epidemia quam Itali morbum gallicum vocant' (Handbook of the epidemic that the Italians call the French disease) (1497). This was followed by others such as López de Villalobos with his 'Tratado sobre las pestíferas bubas' (Treatise concerning the bubic plaque) (1498), Gaspar Torrella (1497), Juan de Almenar (1502) or Giovanni da Vigo (1514), who introduced the mercurial ointment in the treatment of syphilis. But perhaps the most important text on syphilis was that of the Italian Girolamo Fracastoro – who, in the opinion of Laín Entralgo (1963), can be considered as the pioneer of modern epidemiology with his theory of 'contagium animatum' or the transmission of certain diseases by germs – who invented the technical name of the new disease with his famous poem, 'syphilis sive Morbus

Gallicus' (syphilis is a Gallic disease) written in 1521 and published in 1530. As Arrizabalaga (1993) points out, 'morbus gallicus' is the name that soon became dominant in designating a disease generally considered as new in Europe in that time. For the Europeans of the Renaissance 'morbus gallicus' was an incurable disease that manifested by severe pain in the bones and sores, beginning in the genitalia but could extend to the whole body.

The French rejected the name of 'morbus gallicus' and called it 'morbus neapolitanicus,' 'morbus italicus,' or 'morbus hispanicus' (Rodríguez Maffiotte, 1981). However as Arrizabalaga (1993) states, throughout the sixteenth century the phrase 'French pox' achieved an overwhelming dominance over any other names in Europe and overseas. In addition Leonardo Botallo, an Italian surgeon of the sixteenth century, proposed the term 'lues venerea,' and since then that name was adopted in the Old Continent together with that of 'French pox.'

The question at that time was: is morbus gallicus a new disease or is it an old one? Niccoló Massa, the author of an important 1532 text entitled 'De morbo gallico,' and Niccoló Leoniceno proposed that this was not a new disease, but only a new form of another one. On the contrary, two Spanish authors, Rodrigo Ruiz Díaz de Isla, from Seville in 1539 and Gonzalo Fernández de Oviedo (1537) suggested that syphilis was brought from Haiti by the sailors of Columbus and that the first cases appeared in Barcelona (Spain) in 1493, and that the Spanish soldiers of the Great Captain were the 'carriers' of this disease to Naples 2 years later. This last hypothesis was accepted promptly by most authors of the sixteenth century. Syphilis was considered a new disease coming from America not only in Europe but also in India where it appeared in 1498 with the arrival of the Portuguese sailors of Vasco da Gama, and in China and Japan where the disease emerged in 1505, 15 years before the arrival of the first Portuguese in Canton (McNeill, 1984). The first outbreak of a virulent venereal infection appeared in Japan in the decade following 1510 (the late Muromachi period) and expanded suddenly to epidemic proportions (Suzuki, 1991). The oldest documents describing the appearance of syphilis in that country were written in 1512 and 1513. Three of Suzuki's cases came from the Muromachi period and 50 from the subsequent Edo period.

Although it was horrible for the people affected, syphilis did not have a very important demographic impact. At the end of the sixteenth century the disease began to decrease in frequency and to soften its fulminating forms and disabling manifestations in the Old World (McNeill, 1984). Modern evaluation of the disease's description by Díaz de Isla suggests it is probable that the disease imported by the Spanish sailors was yaws and that until then only endemic and venereal syphilis resided in the Old World until 1493 (Guerra, 1982–85). Further refinement of the disease occurred after 1750 when the concept of lues venerea began to be challenged as a result of nosological efforts made by the pathologists of enlightenment who questioned whether lues venerea

was a single disease. The initial result was the progressive disappearance of the expression lues venerea, and its replacement by the plural expression of 'morbi venerei' (chancre, gonorrhea, bubo, and syphilis: Arrizabalaga, 1993). Syphilis was a term that became dominant after the third decade of the nineteenth century. A decade later, Philippe Ricord, a French physician working in the Hôpital du Midi at Paris and who specialized in venereal diseases, demonstrated the existence of the so-called 'virus syphilitique.' Thereafter syphilitic chancre and gonorrhea could be definitely separated. Ricord also proposed the division of syphilis into different stages (primary, successive, secondary, transitional, tertiary).

Albert Neisser discovered the gonococcus, the microorganism responsible for gonorrhea in 1879. Ten years later August Ducrey identified *Haemophilus ducreyi*, causing chancroid, ulcus molle or soft sore (a disease that emerged as an entity in 1852 due to the studies of the Frenchman Leon Bassereau). The discovery of the microorganism responsible for syphilis took place in 1905 when Fritz Schaudinn, a young German bacteriologist, isolated *Treponema pallidum* in serum from a lesion of secondary syphilis. One year later, A. Wassermann, A. Neisser, W. Bruck and other German scientists developed the first serological procedure for the diagnosis of syphilis: the Wassermann reaction. According to Laín Entralgo (1963), this reaction and the introduction of chemotherapy (salvarsan and neosalvarsan) by the German bacteriologist, Paul Ehrlich, were fundamental in the decisive change in venereology between 1848 and 1914. E. H. Hudson published the first description of nonvenereal syphilis or bejel after observing the disease among the Bedouin Arabs in 1928 (Kiple, 1993a). He emphasized the intermediate nature of this disease between yaws and syphilis and presented the unitarian concept of treponematosis.

Paleopathological evidence of syphilis

Paleopathologically there is an imbalance in the number of specimens with treponemal disease reported in the Old and the New World prior to 1492 with an abundance of cases in America and a dearth in Europe, Asia, and Africa (Stirland, 1991).

Old World

According to Baker & Armelagos (1988), the evidence of possible pre-Columbian treponematosis presented in Europe since 1930 is sparse and inconclusive. Most examples, in their opinion, consist of isolated long bones with inadequate archaeological provenance. Important negative evidence is provided by the absence of syphilitic stigmata in the large skeletal series coming from Egypt (Steinbock, 1976). In addition, excavations at several cemeteries of European medieval leprosaria have failed to demonstrate clear evidences of treponematosis before the sixteenth century. However several possible examples of pre-Columbian treponematosis have been diagnosed recently. Stirland (1991) found a well-preserved skeleton of a young adult coming from Magdalen Street site, Norwich (England), dated A.D. 1100–1468, that shows widespread, bilateral, florid periostitis. This involved mainly the tibiae and fibulae, and the radiographic changes support the diagnosis of treponemal disease. Stirland describes the coarsely striate and pitted expansions as 'diagnostic criteria of syphilis.' Her differential diagnosis includes pyogenic osteomyelitis, osteomyelitis of Garré, and Paget's disease. She concluded that the bilateral and widespread nature of the changes present in the skeleton do not occur in the other three diseases. The differential diagnosis and the geographical situation suggest that the skeleton displays evidence of syphilis. Other skeletons in the same cemetery show similar lesions although they are not as florid. Palfi *et al.* (1992c) described a probable case of congenital syphilis in the skeletal remains of an approximately 7 months old fetus coming from the cemetery of Costebelle (Hyéres, Var, France) dated from the third to the fifth centuries A.D. The authors state that the case constitutes an argument against the theories about the migration of *Treponema pallidum* from the New World back to the Old starting at the end of the fifteenth century.

Some examples come from Iraq (A.D. 500) and India (100–700 B.C.) (Baker & Armelagos, 1988). On the other hand, Australia and the Pacific islands have yielded many examples of treponematosis in skeletal remains. Ortner (1989) reports a possible case of yaws from an aboriginal burial near Coolab (Australia). This specimen, however, is an adult female dated as post-European. Ortner creates the following differential diagnosis: treponematosis complicated by a non-treponemal, hematogenous osteomyelitis; treponematosis triggering an inflammatory, erosive arthropathy; and treponematosis complicated by a secondary mycotic infection. However, the Australian origin of the specimen suggests to Ortner that yaws is the most likely treponemal syndrome. Borobia Melendo & Mora Postigo (1992) describe a possible case of treponematosis in an adult female skull coming from the Samar Cave (Philippine Islands) that shows typical lesions on the frontal, left parietal and both malar bones. They do not provide radiocarbon dates, so the exact chronology of this specimen remains unknown.

New World

The first diagnoses of treponematosis in pre-Columbian skeletal remains of the New World were made by J. Wyman in 1871 in specimens discovered and recovered in the caves of southeastern U.S.A. (Guerra, 1990). Five years later Jones (1876) made a diagnosis of treponematosis in skeletons removed from stone coffins and burial mounds at Nashville, Franklin, and Old Town (Tennessee, U.S.A.), and Hickman (Kentucky) (Steinbock, 1976; Hackett, 1983). However, the German pathologist Rudolph Virchow rejected these diagnoses in 1898 and they were also rejected by F.W. Putnam. In 1886 Mathews, Wortman and Billings carried out a careful study of nearly 3500 bone specimens, detecting treponemal lesions in some of them. In South America perhaps one of the most detailed studies is that of the Peruvian archaeologist and anthropologist Julio Tello (1909). However, its results are under serious challenge at present.

It is impossible here to list all the specimens showing treponemal changes that have been found in the New World representing a period prior to the European conquest. The following indicates the sites of origin in 80 % of the cases of Baker & Armelagos (1988). In the U.S.A. there is an abundance of cases. In the southeastern U.S.A. reported evidence of pre-Columbian treponematosis abounds: Lighthouse Mound (northeastern Florida); Tick Island archaic site and Palmer Mound (Weeden Island Period) in Florida; Irene Mound, near Savannah (Georgia); Moundville (Alabama); Late Woodland Hardin (North Carolina); Delaware; Virginia; Maryland. More recently, Reichs (1989) described a case of treponemal disease in an adult female from the Hardin Site (Gaston County, in the piedmont region of North Carolina), and the radiocarbon date suggests a fifteenth century occupation. Reichs suggests that the treponemal disease is possibly that of the endemic variety of syphilis (endemic syphilis or bejel). Ortner (1986) presents a case of congenital treponemal disease in a pre-Columbian child (3–4 years old) from the Fisher Site in Virginia. This case shows a combination of dental enamel hypoplasia and widespread periostitis. An adult male skull in close proximity to this child shows chronic granulomatous lesions in the cranial and postcranial skeleton. The only evidence of pre-Columbian treponematosis in northeastern U.S.A. is that from the Veddar site in the Mohawk Valley of New York.

A considerable number of purported cases of treponematosis have been discovered in Woodland and Mississippian remains in Illinois (Lower Illinois River Valley). According to Cook (1984) periostitis and osteitis are very common in skeletal collections from the American Midwest. Overall prevalence is slightly more than 50 %, with closer resemblances to endemic syphilis or bejel in the Middle Woodland and to yaws in the Late Woodland sample. Additional cases have been reported somewhat farther up the Illinois River in Schuyler and Fulton counties. In Arkansas, some probable cases of treponematosis have been discovered in St. Francis, White, and Black Rivers and in northeastern Arkansas (Crittenden and Mississippi counties). A site near Kansas City (Missouri), Morris Site (southeastern Oklahoma), and Crow Creek Site (South Dakota) are the sites of central U.S.A. at which some examples of treponematosis have been described. Evidence of pre-Columbian treponematosis is lacking in northwestern North America, while in the southwestern U.S.A. evidence of treponemal disease has accumulated: California, New Mexico, Colorado, and Arizona.

Human remains from pre-Columbian Mexico also provide evidence of the disease: Tula (Hidalgo), Cueva de la Candelaria (Coahuila), Santiago Tlatelolco and Ochicalco (Morelos), all of them coming from the Postclassic period, and Valle de Tehuacán, from the Preclassic period. In Central America there are several examples reported from Guatemala (Zaculen and Altar de Sacrificios), in Belize, in Antilles, and in Santo Domingo (Cucamana, Constanza, and Samaná). Most examples of pre-Columbian treponematosis in South America came from ancient Peru, and some of the first cases in the paleopathological literature were reported by the Peruvian Julio Tello and by the North American Herbert U. Williams, although many of their diagnoses are being questioned. The specimens came from different places: Paracas (early Nazca Culture); Cañete Valley; Machu Picchu; Urubamba Valley (near Cuzco); Paucarcancha; and Patallacta. Other South American examples of treponemal disease came from Colombia (Aguazuque) and Argentina (Río Negro, Valle del Río Chubut and Calchaqui). Three cases coming from Aguazuque (an archaeological site in the municipality of Soacha, Departamento de Cundinamarca, Colombia) have been described recently by Correal Urrego (1990). Several of those skulls also demonstrate very credible caries sicca lesions. The radiocarbon dating of these specimens is 5025–4030 years B.P. and Correal Urrego believes the most probable diagnosis in these cases is that of yaws. The soft tissue lesions of the primary and secondary changes can be expected to be preserved only rarely because the chancre and rash are transient and not lethal. Fornaciari et al. (1988a), however, has used immunohistochemical and ultrastructural methods to identify the presence of treponemes in an ulcerated skin lesion from a sixteenth century Italian mummy. The soft tissue and skeletal changes of syphilitic aneurysms are discussed in Chapter 5 (Circulatory disorders).

Paleopathological criteria

Baker & Armelagos (1988) allege that, since skeletal lesions resulting from yaws, endemic syphilis, and venereal syphilis are identical, speculation regarding the mode of transmission of the treponeme in a single individual is impossible. Reliable conclusions with regard to the prehistoric distribution of treponemal disease may, however, be drawn from skeletal evidence. The pattern of treponemal infection discerned in entire skeletal series, viewed in conjunction with social and climatological factors, may permit epidemiological inferences. Steinbock (1976) finds the paleopathological literature on syphilis and other form of treponematosis disappointing. The diagnosis, when based on a single bone exhibiting nonspecific periostitis or osteoperiostitis, is very difficult and vulnerable to error. He adds that until recently the epidemiology of treponematosis in early human populations has been ignored. Morse (1967b, 1978) emphasizes that syphilis and yaws produce similar pathological changes in the human skeletal remains. It is difficult to compare these because different degrees of destruction and sclerosis will occur in the various stages of both diseases. Morse feels that the outstanding characteristics of these diseases are

- Gummatous osteitis and periostitis that affect the shafts of the long bones, most frequently the tibia.
- New bone formation on the surface of the diseased areas. When this new bone formation occurs on the anterior portion of the tibia it may result in saber-shin deformity.
- Thickening of the cortex that sometimes causes localized swelling of the bone and/or a narrowing of the medullary cavity.
- Occasionally a gumma extends into the marrow space.
- Sequestra are rare.
- In the skull there can be periosteal osteitis sometimes only located in the outer table, although sometimes a gumma can produce a large area of destruction. The most frequently affected are the parietal and the frontal bones.
- A facial lesion can destroy the nose, palate, and the anterior alveolar area.

Morse (1967a) points out that the main differences between syphilis and yaws are:

- Presence of osteochondritis in the very young appears in congenital syphilis, but never occurs in yaws.
- Joint involvement is rare in syphilis and occurs even more rarely in yaws.

Ortner et al. (1992), however, call attention to the ability of yaws to produce a distinctive, subchondral, erosive form of joint involvement not duplicated by bejel or syphilis.

Recently a formal attempt to exploit the epidemiological differences between venereal syphilis, yaws and bejel when dealing with skeletal populations of adequate size has been suggested (Rothschild & Rothschild, 1995b). Features occurring within these three diseases at sufficiently different frequencies to permit distinction include saber shin without visible surface periostitis, prepubescence, involvement of tibia bilaterally, routinely affected hand or foot, average number of bone groups affected greater than three, and lacking periostitis of tibia but flattened (they note that the first letters of the first word in each of these features spells the acronym SPIRAL, that can serve as a memory aid). Differences of these features were documented by the study of three skeletal collections from the precontact period in Guam (yaws), nineteenth century Negev desert Bedouins in Israel (bejel), and the twentieth century anatomy cadavers (Todd collection) in Cleveland, Ohio (syphilis) (Rothschild & Rothschild, 1995b). Applying the developed criteria, they identified the distribution and time of transition of these treponemal forms among skeletal collections from 40 different New World sites (Rothschild et al., 1995). If subsequent studies support these initial findings, this approach has the potential to make an enormous contribution to the solution of persisting questions relating to the evolution of the treponematoses.

A serological approach identifying antitreponemal antibody in skeletal tissue was able to confirm treponemal infection in an archaeological (1240 year B.P.) tibia of a native North American (Ortner et al., 1992), but this method cannot distinguish between the various forms of treponemal disease.

OSTEOMYELITIS

Osteomyelitis is an inflammation of bone (osteitis) and bone marrow (myelitis) caused by pus-producing bacteria. Osteitis can occur independently of marrow infection or, more commonly, as a phenomenon related to it. The infection spreads to marrow space, Haversian canals, and subperiosteal space (Turek, 1982). Radiographic and pathologic differentiation of osteomyelitis and osteitis can be extremely difficult (Resnick & Niwayama, 1989a). Other authors affirm that osteitis and osteomyelitis are synonyms (Adams, 1986). Suppurative (pus-forming) osteomyelitis has a high incidence in debilitated individuals and in injured bones (Aegerter & Kirkpatrick, 1975). Clinically, osteomyelitis may show three different stages: acute, subacute, and chronic. The last two stages indicate a high resistance to treatment of the organisms, an inadequate immune response of the patient or an unsatisfactory treatment. Acute hematogenous osteomyelitis or indirect contamination by pyogenic bacteria in the blood stream from a focus elsewhere in the body is the most common form of the disease, followed by acute osteomyelitis resulting from direct contamination (traumatic injuries) (Adams, 1986; Powell, 1988). The site and type of osteomyelitis changes with the age and type of the subject (Revell, 1986).

Acute osteomyelitis

Taxonomy and epidemiology

Staphylococcus aureus is the bacterium most commonly observed in acute osteomyelitis, accounting for 90 % or more of the cases (Aegerter & Kirkpatrick, 1975; Morse, 1978; Blockey, 1984). *Streptococcus pyogenes, Haemophilus influenzae, Bacillus coli, Bacillus aerogenes capsulatus* and others such as pneumococcus, meningococcus, *Proteus vulgaris, Salmonella, Staphylococcus albus*, etc are less commonly isolated (about 10 %). Osteomyelitis has a worldwide geographical distribution. Although osteomyelitis can occur at any age, it is most often observed in children between 3 and 12 years when skeletal growth is most active (Jaffe, 1972; Robbins, 1975). Within this age range, incidence peaks occurs in infants under 2 years and children between 8 and 12 (Calandruccio, 1967). In adults, the clinical features of acute osteomyelitis are less marked than in children (Murray *et al.*, 1990). There is a male preponderance (two to four times more frequent in males than in females) that perhaps is due to the greater occurrence of trauma in the former (Piulachs, 1957). The mortality rate before modern medical and surgical treatment was more than 20 %, but, as always in infectious diseases, the prognosis depends on the virulence of the organisms and the resistance of the host. An episode of acute osteomyelitis can be fatal rapidly if the conditions are not favorable for the host. On the other hand, if the host survives, the infection can become chronic (Morse, 1978).

Pathogenesis

Hematogenous dissemination from an existing infectious focus is the most common route of infection. However, acute osteomyelitis can begin by bacterial penetration through a wound or compound fracture, or by direct extension from an adjacent infectious focus in the soft tissues surrounding the bone.

Acute hematogenous osteomyelitis

Long and large cylindrical bones of the extremities are most susceptible to osteomyelitis, especially at the ends where most rapid growth occurs, although any part may be involved. Perhaps this is due to the increased susceptibility of rapidly growing cells, the fact that these parts have the richest blood supply, and the slower blood flow in the metaphysis (Aegerter & Kirkpatrick, 1975; Apley, 1981). In adults diaphyseal involvement is as common as metaphyseal. The most commonly involved bones, in order of frequency, are femur, tibia, humerus, and radius (Robbins, 1975).

The organisms invade the metaphyseal area *via* a nutrient artery forming an infective focus in the sinusoidal veins. The growth cartilage may prevent spread of the infection into the epiphysis and joint, and then the infection spreads laterally and perforates the thin metaphyseal cortex by lifting the periosteum (the exception to this rule occurs in infants where the metaphysis is intracapsular and the protection of the joints is less common than in other age groups as Murray *et al.*, 1990, have noted). A subperiosteal abscess is formed and it raises the periosteum over a large area of the cortex (Steinbock, 1976). Thus, the infection produces an acute suppurative local inflammation with abscess formation. Septic thrombophlebitis and thromboangiitis (infection of blood vessels) develop producing local ischemia (reduced blood flow) and subsequent necrosis (cell death) of a bone segment (Calandruccio, 1967). Extension of the infection to the surrounding bone, particularly the medullary cavity, occurs through the Haversian and Volkmann canals (structures of low resistance) that have become enlarged by the process until finally, it arrives at the subperiosteal space (Robbins, 1975; Steinbock, 1976; Revell, 1986; Hughes, 1990). Large parts of the bone suffer ischemic necrosis forming a sequestrum (an area of necrotic bone surrounded by living bone) that may separate from the rest of the bone. In the meantime, the detached and elevated periosteum is stimulated to form new bone (involucrum) that tends to enclose the affected portion (Hughes, 1990). This new bone further impairs the blood supply of the involved bone region. The involucrum can be perforated by cloacae, channels through which the abscess can drain out of the bone into the soft tissues, and from there perforate the skin, forming a chronic drainage channel (fistula).

According to Steinbock (1976), if the infection subsides and if the sequestra are absorbed or extruded through the

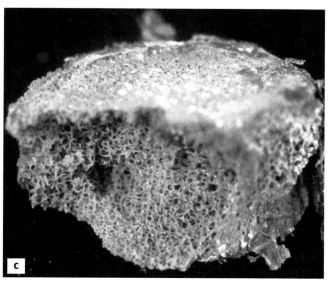

Fig. 7.38: **Osteomyelitis: metastatic abscesses.** Hematogenously disseminated bacteria established multiple bone abscesses in the cancellous bone of (a) rib, (b) scapula and (c) vertebra. Northern Chile, A.D. 1100. IQU-95, T-2. Courtesy Cora Moragas, Iquique, Chile. PBL.

draining sinuses, the thickness of the involucrum becomes reduced and is replaced by mature lamellar bone. If the process heals completely the bone is remodeled and trabeculae and Haversian systems align themselves along the lines of functional stress.

Acute hematogenous osteomyelitis in infants

This type of disease accounts for 7 % of all osteomyelitis cases. According to Revell (1986), important predisposing factors in infant osteomyelitis are pre-eclampsia, premature rupture of membranes and local infections. In this age group streptococci are responsible twice as often as staphylococci (Robbins, 1975). However, up to 40 % of *Staph. aureus* infections demonstrate polyostotic involvement (rare in other age groups), while streptococcus infections only involve a single bone (Bullough, 1992). Commonly, the infection involves the adjacent joint because some of the metaphyseal vessels penetrate the growth plate (Piulachs, 1957). Epiphyseal involvement can produce growth arrest (Resnick & Niwayama, 1989a). The process can break out through the periosteum and invade the adjacent soft tissue. Sequestra are formed uncommonly and, therefore, the chronicity of this kind of infection is exceptional. However, periosteal detachment can produce an involucrum (Calandruccio, 1967). Sinus tracts are not commonly found in infantile osteomyelitis (Resnick & Niwayama, 1989a).

Acute hematogenous osteomyelitis in children

Children account for 80 % of all cases of osteomyelitis. According to Calandruccio (1967) the growth cartilage very commonly prevents the spread of infection to the epiphysis. The exception is the hip and shoulder where the metaphysis is partially located within the articular space. Because the cortical

bone is thicker and the cancellous bone more dense than in infants, these present more resistance to metaphyseal subperiosteal abscess formation. The spread of the process tends, instead, to be directly toward the diaphysis, with periosteal detachment. The elevated periosteum produces new bone formation in the form of an involucrum (Resnick & Niwayama, 1989a) that can favor a later reinfection of the diaphysis through Haversian or Volkmann canals. In contrast with infants, the large periosteal detachment and the involvement of the endosteal blood vessels can produce a sequestrum. The internal bone pressure does not play an important role in the destructive process (Blockey, 1984). Any bone may be involved in children's osteomyelitis, although the most common are those of the lower limb, especially the distal femur and the proximal tibia that account for 75 % of the cases, followed by the proximal third of the humerus and the distal portion of the radius. Resnick & Niwayama (1989a) point out that hematogenous osteomyelitis of the child is not limited to tubular bones. Other bones may be involved: clavicle, pelvis, calcaneus, and others.

Acute hematogenous osteomyelitis in adults

With the exception of the spine, this is a rare process in adults: 13 % of all cases (Calandruccio, 1967; Murray et al., 1990). It occurs in people over 50 years or with debilitating concomitant conditions (Revell, 1986; Bullough, 1992). The infection can develop in any part of the bone, being more common in the subperiosteal space. Spread of the abscess is into the medullary cavity, although the cortical skeletal sinuses can produce extraperiosteal abscesses (Fig. 7.38) and chronic fistulae – one of this condition's most common complications. Large cortical sequestra are uncommon, though cortical bone resorption can cause pathological

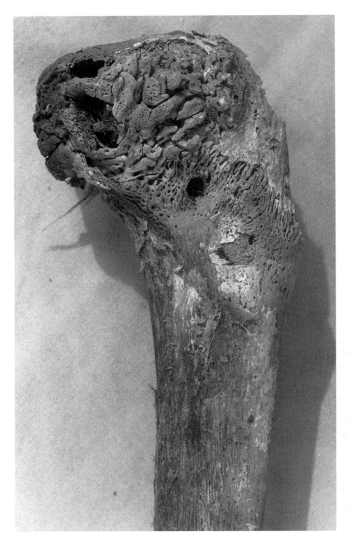

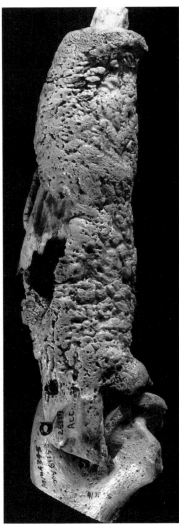

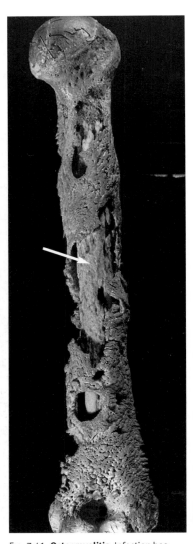

FIG. 7.39: **Osteomyelitis, tibia.** Involucrum covers much of the destroyed proximal tibia. Defects are cloacae through which pus drained. CHA Aut. 6. A 15 year old female, ca. A.D. 1100, Peru. PBL.

FIG. 7.40: **Osteomyelitis.** An enormous shell of reactive new bone formation (involucrum) surrounds a segment of nonvital diaphysis (sequestrum). Exudate drained out through the huge defect (cloacae) in the involucrum. No. 26119. Modern adult. Courtesy P. Sledzik. NMHM.

FIG. 7.41: **Osteomyelitis.** Infection has impaired blood supply to much of this modern humerus' diaphysis, resulting in its death (sequestrum formation shown by arrow). Dead bone is surrounded by an irregular shell of new bone formation (involucrum). No. MM 4346. Courtesy P. Sledzik. NMHM.

fractures. The rarity of subperiosteal abscess formation, involucrum formation, and periostitis is due to the fact that the firm attachment of the periosteum to the cortex in adults resists displacement much more effectively than in children (Resnick & Niwayama, 1989a).

Acute osteomyelitis caused by direct infection

This form of osteomyelitis, usually in the tibia and femur, is not as common as that caused by the hematogenous spread of the organisms. The infection spreads from an adjacent focus of infection resulting from compound fractures, injuries or surgery. Though possible at any age, it most often is observed in adults older than 40 years (Steinbock, 1976; Elena Ibáñez et al., 1984). In elderly patients (50–70 years) with diabetes mellitus or arteriosclerosis, osteomyelitis may be related to vascular insufficiency. The most common location of this ischemic form of osteomyelitis is the hands and feet (Elena Ibáñez et al., 1984). In accident cases the infection can be polybacterial, often including staphylococci, streptococci and gram-negative bacteria (Bullough, 1992). Its pathological findings are similar to those of acute hematogenous osteomyelitis, although the initial focus commonly affects the diaphysis. Presence of fractures, sequestrum and involucrum formation are common findings in acute osteomyelitis caused by direct infection.

Skeletal pathology

The knee region, followed by the distal third of the tibia and proximal third of the femur, account for 80 % of osteomyelitis locations (Calandruccio, 1967) and the humerus for 10 % (Ortner & Putschar, 1985). In children the most rapidly

FIG. 7.42: **Osteomyelitis.** Involucrum evident on proximal tibia. Diaphysis thickened. Septic arthritis has fused fibula to tibia. C27. Late medieval, Catalonia, Spain. Courtesy Dr D. Campillo. MAC.

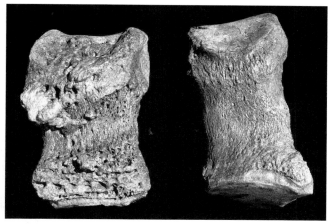

FIG. 7.43: **Osteomyelitis.** Normal metatarsal of the juvenile mammoth (*Mammuthus primigenius*) on the right measures 12 x 7 x 5 cm. That on the left is of similar size but deformed by a thick involucrum with multiple fistulous openings and cloacae from 3–10 mm in diameter. Secondary osteoarthritis changes are evident. Radiology showed medullary involvement. Infection had also spread to adjacent phalanges and interphalangeal joints. Butchering cut-marks and lithic knives found with specimen suggest injury may have enabled ancient hunters to subdue it. Southeast Wisconsin site (Hebior), U.S.A. ca. 11 000 B.P. Courtesy of John Kramer, Potomac Museum Group.

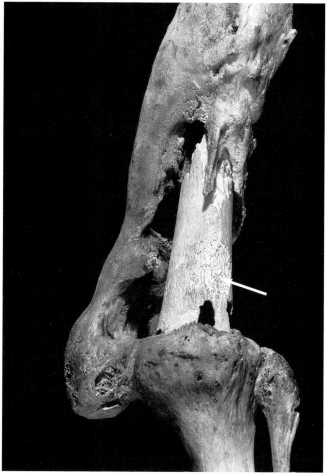

FIG. 7.44: **Osteomyelitis.** The devitalized diaphyseal segment (sequestrum, shown by arrow) is exposed and partly enveloped by reactive new bone formation (involucrum). Modern adult. No. E157. CMNH.

growing end of the bone is more susceptible to the infection (Fig. 7.39), while in adults the shafts are involved as often as the metaphyseal area. In hematogenous osteomyelitis, multiple skeletal lesions occur only in 5–25 % of all cases of acute osteomyelitis, while in the rest of cases only a single bone is involved (Steinbock, 1976). The pathological findings in osteomyelitis are those of bone destruction and reactive new bone formation (Fig. 7.40) along with the presence of necrotic bone or sequestrum (Fig. 7.41). Therefore, the involved bones are enlarged and deformed (Manchester, 1983*a*). The involved bone shows an irregular surface with pitting and cavities (that correspond with abscess formation (Figs. 7.42 & 7.43) in the living tissue). At the same time, and as a consequence of the reaction of the bone to the infection, plaques of new bone are seen on the skeletal surface. The new bone can surround the sequestrum that, according to Piulachs (1957), is pearly white (Fig. 7.44). Its location can be pandiaphyseal, hemidiaphyseal, or cortical, forming

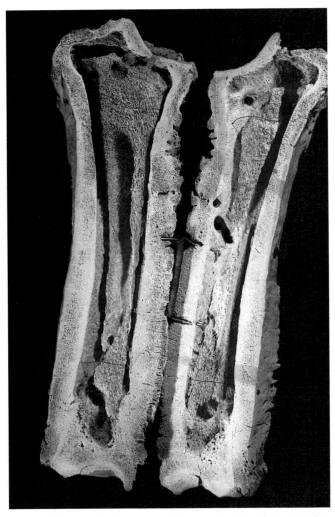

FIG. 7.45: **Osteomyelitis.** This bisected tibia has been reduced to an irregular, deformed porous mass of nonvital bone (sequestrum) surrounded by an enormous, thick involucrum that has become sclerotic. Modern adult. University of Pennsylvannia. Courtesy G. Worden. MM.

FIG. 7.46: **Osteomyelitis.** An enormous shell of reactive new bone formation (involucrum) surrounds a segment of nonvital diaphysis (sequestrum). Exudate drained out through the huge defect (cloaca) in the involucrum. No. 26119. Modern adult. Courtesy P. Sledzik. NMHM.

an involucrum that is irregular and bulky. This new bone is mechanically less efficient than normal bone because there is no alignment of the trabeculae to the lines of stress (Manchester, 1983*a*). Sometimes fistulae and cloacae are present. In very advanced cases, all the cortical bone can be surrounded by pus with subsequent blood flow restriction that can lead to sequestration of the whole shaft (Turek, 1982) (Figs. 7.45 & 7.46). Although healing occurs, irregularities of bone architecture with some sclerosis and cavities commonly remain (Steinbock, 1976). The involved bone is thicker and grows to about 1 cm more in length than the normal contralateral bone (Swoboda, 1972).

Radiology

The radiological findings of suppurative osteomyelitis are bone destruction, reactive new bone formation, bone necrosis, and the typical lytic areas in combination with other areas of increased bone density (Aegerter & Kirkpatrick, 1975; Revell, 1986). During the first 7–10 days of the disease no radiological findings are observable because no lytic changes are detectable until 30–50 % of bone mineral content has been removed (Revell, 1986). After that, a radiolucent area of bone destruction, surrounded by a large band of partially decalcified bone, is observed in the metaphyseal area with variable shape and size (Swoboda, 1972; Murray *et al.*, 1990). A periosteal detachment with later elevation at the same level appears several weeks later. Thin, visible layers of bone deposition parallel to the diaphysis follow, though sometimes this can occur simultaneously with the presence of lucency in the medulla. The necrotic bone is more dense than that of the surrounding decalcified bone. Extension of infection through the tissues of the medullary canal results in the expansion of osseous destruction and the presence of more and often large areas of radiolucency (Aegerter & Kirkpatrick, 1975).

Complications

Besides septic arthritis, other complications of acute osteomyelitis are:

1. Epiphyseal slipping of Klose. This is produced by pyogenic dissection of the growth cartilage (Piulachs, 1957).
2. Bipolar osteomyelitis. Involvement of the opposite thirds of the same bone occurs by extension through the medullary cavity.
3. Pathological fractures. An uncommon phenomenon, observed in adults more than in other age groups because the periosteal reaction restrains this kind of fracture.
4. Growth disturbances. Involvement of the cartilage produces bone longer or shorter than normal, with varus or valgus deviation (Piulachs, 1957).

Chronic pyogenic osteomyelitis

Acute pyogenic osteomyelitis can become chronic for different reasons. The most frequent cause of chronic osteomyelitis is the presence of a sequestrum that acts as a foreign body, perpetuating the infection. Other cases are due to the persistence of a low grade infection in the bone and adjacent soft tissues, or extension of the infection into a joint (Steinbock, 1976; Apley, 1981; Hughes, 1990). The process can recur as acute episodes of remissions and exacerbations over a period of many months or years. Hematogenous infection by a low virulence organism can produce chronic osteomyelitis from the infection's onset (Turek, 1982).

Taxonomy

Staphylococcus aureus is the most common organism responsible for chronic osteomyelitis. Sometimes the infection is produced by multiple organisms. *Haemophilus influenzae* is a common cause of bone and joint infection in patients under 2 years of age. Other organisms are *Proteus mirabilis, Streptococcus, Pneumococcus, Pseudomonas, Aerobacter aerogenes*, and others. Recently a variant of osteomyelitis has been described in children and young adults called 'chronic recurrent multifocal osteomyelitis' that is characterized by insidious onset and radiological findings of osteomyelitis (Bullough, 1992). This disease affects the metaphysis of tubular bones and clavicles and these show extensive periosteal new bone formation. Its etiology remains completely unknown. No bacteria, fungi or viruses have been isolated. To date there is no known genetic component in the origin of the disease, and no findings common to all the patients have been identified (Bullough, 1992).

Pathology, radiology, and complications

Chronic osteomyelitis is more common in the long bones. Very often it is limited to the extremity of the bone, although less commonly it can involve all of its length.

Chronic osteomyelitis is characterized by bone destruction and abscess formation, as well as draining sinuses and involucrum formation (Morse, 1978: Fig. 7.47). At the beginning of the process the bone has an osteoporotic, worm-eaten appearance; later areas of osteosclerosis develop. Periosteal detachment with subperiosteal new bone deposition follows. In the radiographs the dense

FIG. 7.47: **Osteomyelitis.** A segment of the sequestrum is evident. The irregular-surfaced involucrum with many cloacae and fistulous openings envelops the bone. No. E85. Modern adult. CMNH.

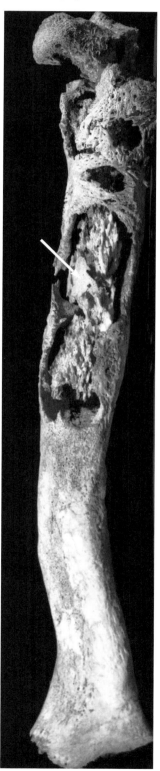

FIG. 7.48: **Osteomyelitis.** The nonvital, tubular segment of this modern adult femur's diaphysis (sequestrum, shown by arrow) is evident, surrounded by an enveloping shell of irregular new bone formation (involucrum) with multiple cloacae through which exudate drained from the infected area. The extensive diaphyseal destruction has bowed the femur. No. 1448.60. Courtesy G. Worden. MM.

necrotic area is surrounded by a white halo that represents the reactive new bone or involucrum that becomes riddled with cloacae. The diaphysial cortex can increase its thickness and show deformity with enlargement of the entire infected bone (Steinbock, 1976; Turek, 1982). Holes and cavities (honeycomb appearance) develop, inside of which a sequestrum can appear (Adams, 1986; Hughes, 1990: Fig. 7.48). Squamous cell carcinoma, developing in the skin surrounding a fistula opening, can be a late complication of chronic osteomyelitis, occurring in 1 % of the cases, often 30–40 years after the onset of the infection (Bullough, 1992). Another uncommon complication of chronic osteomyelitis, is systemic amyloidosis.

Brodie's abscess

In certain cases of suppurative osteomyelitis the host may be able to confine the process to cancellous bone without spread to the subperiosteal space. No acute episode precedes this lesion (Adams, 1986; Hughes, 1990). This condition accounts for 2.8 % of pyogenic osteomyelitis and it commonly affects adolescents and young adults (14–20 years of age: Aegerter & Kirkpatrick, 1975). The paucity of cases in children could be due to the long time required to develop osteosclerosis (Blockey, 1984). Some authors (Swoboda, 1972), however, have reported series in which Brodie's abscess is observed rather commonly in children. The area of infection and necrosis remains limited by a wall of granulation tissue forming a fibrous capsule that gradually becomes sclerotic and the abscess can become static (Aegerter & Kirkpatrick, 1975; Robbins, 1975). The immune system destroys the organisms so the pus becomes sterile, but because drainage is impossible the abscess may persist for a long time (Apley, 1981). This abscess is small (1–5 cm in diameter) and of circular or oval shape. It develops in the cancellous tissue of the metaphyseal area of a long bone, most commonly in the distal end of the tibia. The distal radius, proximal tibia and distal femur are also common areas of involvement. Very frequently, it is located in the epiphysis, very near the joint, although it rarely traverses the growth plate (Schinz et al., 1953; Resnick & Niwayama, 1989a). When Brodie's abscess occurs in children, it is not uncommon to find the abscess in the diaphysis of the adult long bone.

The diagnosis of Brodie's abscess in dry bone depends on the use of radiology or cross sectioning, because the external appearance of the overlying bone appears nearly normal (Steinbock, 1976; Morse, 1978). It appears radiographically as a translucent oval area in the central part of the metaphysis with its long axis parallel to the axis of the long bone, and the margins being sclerotic. Periosteal reaction is not present, although the cortex can be thickened (Schinz et al., 1953; Piulachs, 1957). If the abscess is located in the diaphysis, the cavity can be located in the cortex or in central or subcortical areas of the cancellous bone. Sometimes the accompanying hyperemia produces longitudinal growth of the bone if the growth cartilage is not destroyed (Ortner & Putschar, 1985).

Sclerosing osteomyelitis of Garré (chronic non-suppurative osteomyelitis; osteomyelitis of Garré; cortical idiopathic sclerosis)

The predominant feature in this rare chronic condition is the sclerotic and fusiform thickening of the cortex of the affected bone. The disease is confined normally to a single bone, limited commonly to one side of the diaphysis (Morse, 1978; Turek, 1982); however, multiple areas of bone can be involved. Infants and children are affected more commonly. The usual location is the tibia, followed by the femur. No pus is formed and no acute phase occurs. Instead of producing localized areas of necrosis as in Brodie's abscess, the infection spreads extensively throughout a segment of bone, inciting osteoblastic activity (Steinbock, 1976:77). The cortex thickens with consequent narrowing of the medullary cavity and fusiform expansion of the shaft (Piulachs, 1957). In dry bones bone sclerosis and thickening, with little or no evidence of abscesses or sinuses, are seen.

Septic arthritis

Bacterial infection can involve the joint in one of several ways. Direct spread from an osteomyelitic focus in the metaphysis adjacent to the joint is the most common manner of articular infection, occurring in about 15 % of all cases (Robbins, 1975; Steinbock, 1976). The route of the infection is the common vascular pathway of the epiphysis and synovial membrane or as a transchondral extension (Resnick & Niwayama, 1989a). Alternatives include hematogenous dissemination from a distant focus and direct infection of the joint through a penetrating wound in the skin, though the latter is very uncommon (Morse, 1978; Hughes, 1990; Bullough, 1992). Septic arthritis commonly involves the hip and knee, these two sites constituting 70 % of all cases (especially in infants and children), followed by the shoulder, ankle, elbow, and wrist. Besides infants and children, debilitated older adults are susceptible to septic arthritis. The process is usually monoarticular (Steinbock, 1976:79). The microorganism most commonly found in this condition is *Staphylococcus aureus*; gonococcus, streptococcus and pneumococcus are less commonly isolated. The pathological changes and the course of the disease in infectious arthritis depend on the type of microorganism involved, its virulence, and the resistance of the host (Morse, 1978). Although septic arthritis can be seen in all ages, it is a disease most commonly observed during the second, third and fourth decades of life (Robbins, 1975).

Osteomyelitis normally involves the metaphyseal region and there is no spread through the epiphyseal cartilage. However, if the joint capsule is attached under that cartilage, it is possible for the pus to invade the joint (Hughes, 1990). In infants under 1 year, the metaphyseal blood vessels penetrate the growth cartilage, providing access to the joint or the organisms (Schmid, 1987). In adults the epiphysis and the metaphysis are fused and vascular connections commonly are established between the two regions. This constitutes a route of infection of the joint through erosion of the articular cortex and cartilage (Steinbock, 1976:29). In children between 1 and 16 years the metaphyseal capillaries do not penetrate the growth cartilage and, therefore, joint infection is rarely found in this age group.

Inside the joint, pus destroys the articular cartilage by proteolytic enzyme action and this destruction is most rapid at sites of contact of the articular surfaces. Subsequent arthritic changes follow because joint cartilage does not regenerate. The osseous erosions at the margins of the joint lead to defects similar to those of rheumatoid arthritis and subchondral extension of pannus can destroy the bone plate, producing gaps in the subchondral bone (Resnick & Niwayama, 1989a). Sequestrum formation is rare. In infants under 1 year, the femoral head can be involved forming a whole sequestrum that can be expelled through an inguinal fistula. If the patients survive, the arthritis becomes chronic and fibrous ankylosis appears, followed by deposition of cartilage and bone (Morse, 1978). Calcification of the fibrous adhesions impairs the mobility of the joint and can produce permanent ankylosis (Robbins, 1975; Blockey, 1984). The healing stage is usually characterized by the formation of a tremendous amount of bony regeneration. Archaeological specimens frequently show evidence of sinus tracts (Morse, 1978).

Periostitis

Periostitis (inflammation of the periosteum) can occur in three different ways: (i) by extension of an adjacent soft tissue infection to the bone; (ii) as a manifestation of a generalized disease; (iii) by involvement of the surface of the bone from an osteitis or osteomyelitis (Morse, 1978). Capasso (1985) notes that in cases of prehistoric and protohistoric periostitis an additional route of periosteal infection could be the direct spread of the organisms from a compound fracture. It is important to note that periostitis is not always the consequence of infection. It can be the product of other causes, such as trauma, hemorrhage or chronic skin ulcers. The bone surface may appear irregular because of varying degrees of thickness, nodulation and pitting secondary to hypervascularity. The anterior tibial surface lies beneath the skin, and can be subjected to recurrent minor trauma (Manchester, 1983a). The periosteal new bone is unevenly distributed along the diaphysis. The differential diagnosis of periostitis is very difficult in ancient skeletal material because it can be caused by multiple factors independent of their nature (aseptic hemorrhage; trauma, ulcers, and infections) and these produce no specific pathological findings (Capasso, 1985).

Differential diagnosis of osteomyelitis

1. Rheumatoid arthritis. In this condition there is polyarticular involvement while osteomyelitis is monoarticular.
2. Ewing's tumor. Ewing's tumor shows layered ('onion skin') subperiosteal bone deposition and the skeletal destruction is limited to the diaphysis (Steinbock, 1976; Turek, 1982).
3. Osteosarcoma. Thick and short bony projections seen in spicular periostitis caused by acute or chronic osteomyelitis contrast with the long and thin radiating spicules associated with osteosarcoma (Zimmerman & Kelley, 1982).
4. Tertiary syphilis. In syphilis, multiple skeletal lesions and cranial involvement with the typical finding of 'caries sicca' occur. Sometimes, there can be confusion between tertiary syphilis and sclerosing osteomyelitis of Garré due to deposition of bone and narrowing of the medullary cavity.
5. Tuberculosis. Tuberculosis can produce abscesses similar to a Brodie's abscess, but without the typical sclerotic changes seen in Brodie's abscess. Sequestrum and diaphyseal involvement is uncommon. In the vertebrae, osteomyelitis involves not only the body but also the neural arch and the vertebral processes. On the other hand, in osteomyelitis only one vertebra is involved while in tuberculosis multivertebral involvement is common (Ortner & Putschar, 1985).
6. Benign bone cysts. May resemble Brodie's abscess but do not show osteosclerosis.
7. Benign giant cell tumor. This never has the prominent sclerosis of Brodie's abscess.
8. Osteoid osteoma. Can produce lesions identical to those of Brodie's abscess (Steinbock, 1976:81).
9. Fibrous cortical defect. This condition may resemble a Brodie's abscess due to its shape, especially when it is located in the distal femur.
10. Osteoblastoma. Sclerosing osteomyelitis of Garré with a central sequestrum may simulate osteoblastoma (Murray et al., 1990).

Paleopathological evidence

Sigerist (1951) thinks osteomyelitis was frequent not only in man but also in fossil animals. The oldest example is that of a Permian reptile, probably a Dimetrodon, that shows signs of fracture in the spine complicated by osteomyelitis. Other examples come from Pleistocene animals, bison, cave bear, various carnivores, etc (Janssens, 1970).

Osteomyelitis as a complication of compound fractures is said to be very common in prehistoric skeletal material, especially in the lower limbs (Capasso, 1985). However, other authors (Manchester, 1983a) feel that the more common route of infection in preantibiotic antiquity is the hematogenous route. It is difficult to decide how common this disease was. Ortner & Putschar (1985) have noted few references to it in the paleopathological bibliography, and suggest that the frequency of osteomyelitis in an archaeological population might not differ very much from that of a primitive modern population. If cloacae, sequestra or involucra are not present in dry skeletons, it can be very difficult to diagnose osteomyelitis. Most authors agree that osteomyelitis became more common (with a prevalence of about 1–4/1000: Birkett, 1983) since the Middle Ages as a result of more crowded living conditions and poor nutrition. This rate also held during the Industrial Revolution in England. Thus, it appears that increased morbidity of nonspecific bone inflammation in ancient history coincided with important socioeconomical changes (Capasso, 1985). Bacterial dissemination through the community was probably enhanced by an extension of trade networks and increased population density (Manchester, 1983a). Almost all the examples in which ages are given show osteomyelitis to have been a disease of adults (Birkett, 1983). Because traces of destructive bone changes may persist long after the infection has disappeared, the presence of healed osteomyelitis lesions in the adult skeleton can reflect subadult involvement with this disease (Powell, 1988).

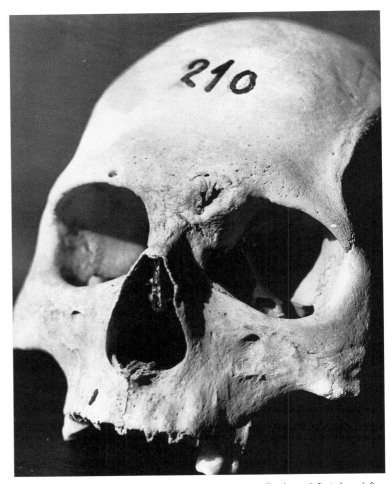

FIG. 7.49: **Frontal sinus fistula.** New bone formation surrounding bone defect above left orbit communicates with frontal sinus. R3. Adult Guanche ca. A.D. 1000. ICPB.

While some of them may be cases that began in childhood and became chronic in adult life, this does not explain the absence of children in the series.

Recently, Marcsik & Oláh (1991) describe a case of chronic pyogenic osteomyelitis resulting from an infection that spread into the femoral medullary cavity of a 30–40 year old male excavated from a tenth century site at the village of Sárrétudvari near the town of Debrecen on the Great Hungarian Plain. Marcsik & Oláh think that the probable cause of the lesion is trauma to the distal femora or soft tissue involvement of the lower thigh. Powell (1988) reports five cases of hematogenous osteomyelitis found at the archaeological site of the Moundville chiefdom in west central Alabama, U.S.A. (a half millennium immediately preced-

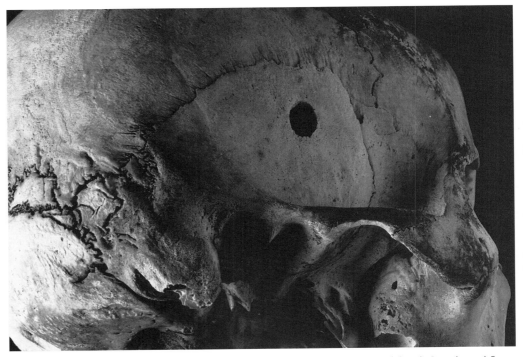

FIG. 7.50: **Cranial fistula.** Round defect, in the temporal bone, drained brain abscess. G20. Adult male Guanche ca. A.D. 1000. MAT, OAMC.

ing the European discovery of the New World). Four males and one female displayed extensive pathology characteristic of hematogenous osteomyelitis, combining both resorptive and proliferative lesions. Their age at death matched or exceeded both the modal age of the entire sample (30–35 years) and the mean age of adults who demonstrate osteoblastic reaction.

Canci et al. (1991) reported osteomyelitis of probable hematogenous origin in a child about 5 years old from the site of Toppo Daguzzo (southern Italy) belonging to the Bronze Age (fifteenth to fourteenth century B.C.). All the long bones and both scapulae show signs of infection in varying degrees of severity. The most severely affected bone is the left fibula; it shows involucrum formation, cloacae and a cortical sequestrum. Considered but excluded were tuberculosis, syphilis, leprosy and osteomyelitis due to direct infection.

Morse (1978) described a case of sclerosing osteomyelitis of Garré in a 20 year old male (burial number 293 at Dickson Mound, Illinois, U.S.A.) that showed thickening of the left femur and right tibia without abscesses or sinuses. He also felt that multiple or generalized periostitis is encountered rather commonly in prehistoric skeletal collections, examples of which were found at Dickson Mounds and Klunk Site (Illinois). Manchester (1983a) has noted that periostitis of the tibiae occurred in Anglo-Saxon skeletons more commonly than in many other groups. The diagnosis of primary periostitis in archaeological skeletons may mean only that it is impossible to deduce a more specific diagnosis (Ortner & Putschar, 1985). Cloaca, involucrum, or sequestrum formation are never seen in periostitis alone. However, it is not always easy to separate periostitis from osteomyelitis.

Rodríguez Martín et al. (1985a) reported a probable case of septic arthritis in the right knee of a 50–60 year old Guanche female skeleton from Tenerife (Canary Islands), dated A.D. 800–1000. This specimen shows destruction of the tibial plateau, with cavities in the subchondral bone, and ankylosis of the fibula and tibia. Cranial fistulae draining chronically infected cranial sinuses were also evident in Guanches (Figs. 7.49 & 7.50).

PNEUMONIA

Definition and epidemiology

For purposes of this discussion, pneumonia can be defined as an acute condition characterized by infection of the lower respiratory tract due to any infectious agent. As a primary condition pneumonia is not an epidemic disease, but it can be a complication of a primary epidemic condition such as viral influenza. Because many different organisms can infect pulmonary tissue, this discussion will deal initially with bacterial pneumonia, discussing lung infections by other agents in the latter section. When the frequency of pneumonia due to the pneumococcus (Streptococcus pneumoniae) is plotted on the vertical (y) axis against age on the horizontal (x) axis, a steep-walled, U-shaped curve is produced; the excessive vulnerability of the very young and very old becomes obvious. The newborn infant is partially protected by maternal antibodies for only a few months and can be viewed as partially immunocompromised until about age 2 years. Similarly the elderly are known to demonstrate a declining ability to respond to pneumococcal antigens. The spleen probably plays a specific but currently poorly understood role in such pneumococcal immunity, since splenectomy at any age (though more obviously in the young) distinctly increases the hazard of pneumococcic septicemia. Immunodeficient states, including the nutritionally-induced form often accompanying chronic alcoholism, render the affected individuals profoundly vulnerable. Fulminating pneumonia, often by organisms that rarely invade healthy human tissues, are the most common immediate cause of death in the acquired immunodeficiency syndrome (AIDS). Certain occupations, such as gold or diamond mining in South Africa, enormously increase the pneumonia risk.

A variety of pulmonary defense mechanisms operate to keep the lung microbiologically sterile in normal humans. Saliva normally contains antibacterial chemicals as well as antibodies secreted by tonsillar and adenoidal lymphocytes. Swallowed saliva carries bacteria from the oral cavity to the stomach where most do not survive that organ's acid environment. As the inspired air traverses the nasal and upper respiratory passages, turbulence causes bacteria-laden particulate matter in the air to come into contact with the sticky mucus lining those areas, effectively removing these particles before the air reaches the lower lung areas. Probably more important than any one of these, however, is the ciliary action of the mucosa lining the bronchi and upper respiratory passages. The microscopic-sized, whisker-like cilia attached to the surface of the bronchial mucosal cells have a unidirectional, whip-like, beating motion whose rapid component is directed upward toward the larynx. The mucus layer floats on their surface, perpetually propelled upward by ciliary action. This continually moving blanket of mucus bearing its burden of trapped inhaled dust, bacteria, fungal elements, pollen, soot, sloughed cells and other particulate matter is a highly effective cleansing system, delivering its content to the pharynx where it is swallowed.

Pulmonary protection from these mechanisms is heavily dependent upon the integrity of the ciliary system. Oral bacteria, even if pathogenic, rarely can reach the lung via the bronchi if the ciliary system is operating normally. Anything that impairs ciliary action imperils the lung. Examples include smoke, foreign bodies, certain anesthetics, reduced ventilation in the post-operative state, heart failure and others. More frequent than any of these, however, are upper respiratory infections. Many of these, such as the common cold, may in themselves be rather benign, but by impairing the ciliary action of the infected bronchi, may permit pathogenic oral bacteria to reach the lung unscathed and initiate a bacterial infection (pneumonia) there. This is not merely a theoretical possibility; examples are legion. The high mortality of the 1918 influenza pandemic was due not so much to the action of the influenza virus itself, but rather the bacterial pneumonia produced by the streptococci that invaded the lung by traversing the infected, cilia-impaired bronchi as a complicating event. Most cases of pneumococcic lobar pneumonia are preceded by an acute upper respiratory infection. The geographical distribution of pneumonia is worldwide and, except for a few areas such as South Africa where occupational activities impair pulmonary defense mechanisms, quite uniform. The most common cause of lobar pneumonia, *Streptococcus pneumoniae* (pneumococcus), is a gram-positive coccus surrounded by a capsule containing powerful polysaccharide antigens, more than 30 of which have been identified. Virulence correlates at least in part with the antigenic type (they have been assigned Roman numerals). Pathogenic pneumococci can be transiently found in the oral cavity of asymptomatic normal humans quite commonly.

Natural history

The enormous variety of organisms capable of causing pneumonia predictably produces a wide range of severity and pattern of lung infections. Their discussion here will be grouped under the type of infecting agent (bacterial, viral, fungal and other). Bacterial infections will be separated into acute and chronic forms. Because many of the common lung infections are discussed elsewhere as separate entities (e.g. tuberculosis), our approach to pneumonia in each of the categories will be to present one form of infection as a model, discussing the others related to the group only to the extent that they differ from the model.

Bacterial pneumonia

Pneumococcic lobar pneumonia

The clinical course of a typical, untreated acute pneumococcic pneumonia is quite characteristic. A few days after an upper respiratory infection of variable severity, the patient suffers a sharp rise in temperature often exceeding 40 °C, commonly associated with shaking chills (usually reflecting pneumococcic bacteremia), headaches and profound malaise. During this onset phase the bacteria are disseminated throughout one lobe of either lung; in about 10 % the condition is bilateral. The infection is commonly sharply limited to the lobe, for reasons not understood. Vascular penetration spills the bacteria into the blood stream, which circulates them; blood culture in this phase can help establish the diagnosis. In the affected lobe of lung the organism's

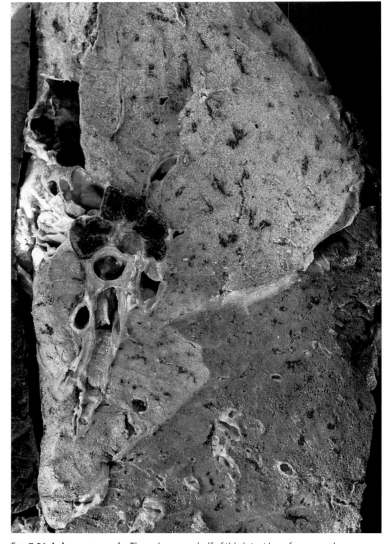

FIG. 7.51: **Lobar pneumonia.** The paler upper half of this intact lung from a modern autopsy is infected by the pneumococcus; its lighter color is imparted by neutrophiles (the white blood cells of pus). Note the sharply demarcated edge of the involved area, reflecting limitation of the process to a single lung lobe. Modern adult. BM.

presence induces the capillaries to leak protein-containing fluid that displaces air; if sufficient lung tissue is involved, shortness of breath (dyspnea) may ensue. Efforts by bronchial mucus flow to remove this fluid may produce an exaggeration of the cough that the upper respiratory infection often has already initiated.

Further capillary damage by the infecting organisms results in leakage of red blood cells (RBCs) which then fill the alveoli, displacing virtually all the air from the alveoli. As these RBCs find their way into the mucus flow, the coughed-up sputum may acquire a reddish color. By the third or fourth day white blood cells have usually leaked from the injured pulmonary capillaries to an extent that they have replaced most or all of the RBCs in the alveoli. When the red or white blood cells replace all the air normally present in lung tissue, such a lobe when palpated manually at autopsy resists compression and is said to be 'consolidated.' The absence of air in such an affected lung lobe produces a liver-like appearance to the surface of a lung transected with a knife known as red or white 'hepatization' (Cotran *et al.*, 1989:782: Fig. 7.51). Bacteremia may be maximal at this time. and between one-quarter and one-third of untreated patients die in this stage. The bacteria circulating in the blood may also produce infections in other tissues through which they pass. The most frequent of these secondarily-infected tissue complications is meningitis, particularly in children.

The pleura overlying the infected lobe is commonly involved by direct extension. Its capillaries will also leak, the fluid collecting in the pleural space between the lung and the chest wall. The protein in this pleural 'effusion' includes fibrinogen, which commonly coagulates as fibrin. This is a sticky material that frequently causes the surface of the visceral pleura (that covering the lung tissue) to adhere to the nearby parietal pleura (that covering the inside of the chest wall), resulting in adhesion of the lung lobe to the inside of the chest wall. The roughened surfaces of these pleural areas may rub over each other with each breath, causing breathing-related chest wall pain ('pleuritis').

Untreated this stage of the disease is characterized by continuing chills and high fever, profound weakness and malaise, cough and pleuritic pain for 5–7 days. At that point (commonly termed 'crisis') the disease follows one of two patterns: the fever rises still further, cardiovascular collapse with delirium and multiple organ failure ensue and the patient dies; or the fever declines abruptly to near-normal levels and all symptoms resolve during the subsequent week to 10 days. The rate and quality of the immune response is most probably responsible for the direction of the course following the crisis.

This entire pattern may be aborted at any point with modern therapy. Complications may also occur at almost any point. The most common of these is development of empyema. This complication occurs when bacteria extend through the thin layer of fibrous tissue (pleura) covering the infected lobe. Bacteria gaining access to the pleural fluid may convert the pleural space into a massive abscess. In most cases this becomes walled off in the most dependent part of the thoracic cavity and usually requires surgical drainage (obviously not available during antiquity and so this was probably often a lethal complication at that time). Another complication is extension of the infection to the pericardial sac surrounding the heart (acute suppurative pericarditis) when the affected lobe of lung, usually left lower lobe, overlies the pericardium. This is commonly a fatal complication even today. Though rare, hematogenous dissemination of the bacteria may produce osteomyelitis, as may many of the other bacterial pneumonias discussed below.

Diagnosis of pneumonia may be made simply by observation of the above-mentioned signs and symptoms, but is aided by listening (auscultation) to the breath sounds transmitted through the chest wall using a stethoscope and ascertaining the presence of chest fluid by tapping on the chest with one's fingers (percussion). Chest X-rays reveal increased density in the affected lobe. Blood and sputum cultures can confirm the diagnosis.

Case fatality rates in the U.S.A. before specific therapy was available were approximately 25–30 %, higher at the two age extremes (Heffron, 1939: 657). Similar rates have been identified in antiquity (see below). Aided by host antibodies, the white blood cells in lung alveoli can phagocytize the bacteria and their enzymes can liquefy the fibrin that leaked from the pulmonary capillaries. Unless complications occur, the disease resolves without permanent lung destruction. However, the fibrinous adhesion of the lung to the chest wall usually becomes scar tissue, permanently fixing that portion of the lung in that position (pleural adhesions). This has no effect on lung function and is asymptomatic, but in mummies can be recognized as a 'marker' for an episode of pneumonia with recovery.

While pneumococci are responsible for the overwhelming bulk of the form of lobar pneumonia described above, occasionally other organisms also assume a lobar form. Some of these (e.g. *Legionella pneumophila*) are described below.

Another, and today much more common, pneumonia form is bronchopneumonia in which the infection develops around multiple small bronchi that may involve more than one lobe. The pneumonia complicating pertussis (whooping cough) is of this type as are those of many other infectious agents. This is also the form of pneumonia seen when an individual aspirates food or similar foreign material, or when bronchial secretions are retained in postoperative patients, as well as those with heart failure or other causes of secretion retention. Pneumococci may be the responsible infecting bacteria in cases of bronchopneumonia but a wide variety of others may also be operative, depending on the cause and oral cavity flora.

Selected other bacterial lung infections include are listed below.

Anthrax

Bacillus anthracis is a gram-positive rod that forms an incredibly durable spore. Shed in horse or cattle feces, it may penetrate the skin upon contact but is usually inhaled with field dust. Recognized as an infectious disease of animals as early as 1836, the organism was cultured by R. Koch in 1872 and by L. Pasteur in 1873. By 1881 Koch had established the role of its spores while Pasteur demonstrated the human protection from the disease that was afforded by inoculation (Hutyra *et al.*, 1938:1). It is an occupational disease of animal handlers and produces a febrile illness with bronchopneumonia (if inhaled) and septicemia. Untreated cases are commonly fatal.

Legionellosis

The organism *Legionella pneumophila* is a gram-negative rod that thrives in moist environments. Its presence was first recognized when many attendees at an American Legion convention developed pneumonia. The organism was traced eventually to the hotel's cooling tower (though intensive epidemiological studies subsequently have usually linked the disease with ingestion and aspiration of contaminated potable water supplies: Yu, 1993). Both broncho- and lobar pneumonia forms occur (Cotran et al., 1989:348).

Klebsiella pneumoniae

This is a gram-negative rod and produces tissue necrosis. Consequently, lung infections often result in lung abscesses, a serious complication that must have been lethal quite regularly in antiquity (Schaberg & Turck, 1991: 601–2).

Staphylococcus aureus

This gram-positive coccus produces a powerful necrotoxin. It often enters the lung as a 'passenger' on aspirated foreign bodies (pills, beads, food). The excessively viscid (and therefore, retained) lung secretions of untreated children suffering from cystic fibrosis of the pancreas almost invariably become infected with this organism. Disastrous lung destruction secondary to multiple lung abscesses commonly occurs in any of these circumstances.

Streptococci

In addition to Strep. pneumoniae, a variety of other streptococcus species may infect the lung. The more virulent of these may produce multiple, confluent bronchopneumonia or occasionally lobar forms with a fulminant, fatal course, often even if treated. Such patterns are usually seen in individuals with lungs impaired by other conditions such as influenza, emphysema and others.

Pertussis

'Whooping cough,' so-named because of the inspiratory crescendo sound secondary to narrowing of bronchial and laryngeal air passages, is a disease of childhood caused by Bordetella pertussis. This organism has a special affinity for bronchial mucosal cells on whose surface colonies of the organisms thrive (Cotran et al., 1989:350), generating coughing paroxysms that may exhaust the child. In only a fraction of the patients does the infection extend distally, producing bronchopneumonia that occasionally is fatal even today. Before development of a vaccine that has controlled, but certainly not eliminated this disease in developed countries, pertussis killed more children in the U.S.A. than all other childhood contagious diseases combined (Smith, 1983:972), suggesting a similar prognosis in antiquity.

Diphtheria

This contagious disease in children (and rarely adults) is caused by the gram-positive bacillus Corynebacterium diphtheriae, and is transmitted by inhalation of bacteria-containing droplets. The bacterium invades the pharynx, larynx and bronchi. Its exotoxin produces necrosis of the mucosa and elicits such a vigorous white blood cell response that the exudate, mixed with the necrotic mucosa, creates a mem-

brane-like structure. Its detachment, sometimes in the form of an extensive, branching bronchial cast, can block the bronchial lumen sufficiently to produce fatal asphyxia (Cotran et al., 1989:351). The infection may extend to the lower respiratory tract, producing bronchopneumonia. Other organs targeted by its powerful, necrotizing exotoxin may cause toxic myocarditis, peripheral neuropathy and nephritis. Without antitoxin therapy the case fatality rate is about 35 % (Holmes, 1991: 570).

Botulism

The cause of this worldwide disease is Clostridium botulinum, a gram-positive rod that, under anaerobic conditions, produces a group of exotoxins that block neuromuscular transmission, resulting in muscular paralysis. While a form of wound infection exists, most humans acquire the disease by ingestion of toxin-containing food that has been kept under conditions permitting the bacterium to proliferate and permeate the food with its exotoxin. Consumption of such toxin-laden food results in respiratory (and other) muscle paralysis (Abrutyn, 1991:579). Reduced respiratory excursions produce retention of bronchial secretions and often fatal bronchopneumonia (Cotran et al., 1989:359). While this condition is seen most commonly today in persons consuming improperly home-canned foods, in antiquity it can be expected to have occurred as a result of storing meat (contaminated with the very durable clostridial spores) of mammals too large to be consumed entirely soon after they were killed, then eating the remainder of the meat later without heating it (the toxin is thermolabile). In arctic areas today the disease is a well-known hazard of eating the raw meat of stranded whales, and therefore it probably has been so for millennia.

Viral pneumonias

While bacterial pulmonary infections evoke a powerful white blood cell response with resulting cough (producing purulent sputum), pulmonary viral infections stimulate a lymphocyte and macrophage response. They affect the cells lining the alveoli and involve the alveolar wall itself ('interstitial pneumonia'), interfering with oxygenation of blood in pulmonary capillaries. Hence even when cough is present, it does not create sputum with pus, but instead the cough is 'dry.' Fever and general malaise are prominent. Many of these viruses commonly cause upper respiratory infections. Their involvement of the lower portion of the tract in some persons may be the result of an immunological dysfunction. Viruses that usually cause benign childhood illness may produce lethal pneumonia in adults. Only a few examples of specific agents are listed below.

Respiratory syncytial virus

This virus, innocuous in normal older children and adults, can cause serious and even fatal interstitial pneumonia in newborns and infants.

Cytomegalovirus (CMV)

Producing mild or asymptomatic infections in normal adults, CMV infections in newborns and infants as well as in immunocompromised adults can be lethal. Such infections are among the principal major complications in immunosuppressed patients who have undergone organ transplantation from nonidentical donors.

Measles and varicella (chickenpox)

The measles virus produces a febrile rash syndrome in normal children. In the age extremes it can involve other organs including the lung (and brain); this is particularly true in immunocompromised adults where the interstitial pneumonia it causes may be fatal. This is also true of chickenpox.

Fungal pneumonias

Fungi vary enormously in their human pathogenicity. Some, like *Blastomyces dermatididis*, quite commonly (though far from invariably) invade the lungs of healthy people unfortunate enough to inhale them. Others, like *Candida albicans*, lack such invasive potential unless the subject's immune system has been seriously impaired. The more common fungal pulmonary pneumonias with septicemia due to *Candida, Mucor* and *Aspergillus* spp. are often common terminal complications in AIDS patients. *Aspergillus fumigatus* or *A. niger* may colonize (without invasion) the bronchi of persons with impaired lungs (e.g. emphysema), causing allergic symptoms, but can be invasive in immunosuppressed patients. Fungal infections are discussed in detail in a separate section of this chapter.

Chronic pulmonary infections

Pulmonary tuberculosis, separately discussed in this Chapter, is the model for chronic lung infections. Histoplasmosis, blastomycosis and coccidioidomycosis closely resemble the pattern of tuberculosis. In persons with normal immune systems, chronic lung infections are most commonly complications of acute pneumonia or are perpetuated by other, coexisting lung conditions.

Antiquity and history

The presence of pneumonia has been documented in mummified human bodies more than 5000 years old (Allison, 1984a; Aufderheide & Allison, 1994). Authors of the Hippocratic corpus were well acquainted with the disease, but clinical diagnostic specificity was increased substantially in 1826 when René Laennec invented and popularized the stethoscope, a simple device to facilitate detection of breath sounds transmitted through the chest wall when the air of an affected part of the lung has been replaced by pus (Duffin, 1993). The latter part of the nineteenth century witnessed the birth of modern microbiology and pneumonia was one of the areas studied intensively because of its high prevalence. The 'father' of this specialty, Louis Pasteur, and G.M. Sternberg both independently isolated the pneumococcus in rabbits from the saliva of asymptomatic carriers in 1881. During the rest of that decade Osler (1881), Friedländer (1882) and many others found the pneumococcus in living, diseased patients or at autopsy in the lungs, blood, heart valves, meninges, middle ear, joints and other locations (Austrian, 1981). Thus the clinical features of pneumonia had been reasonably well defined by the early part of the twentieth century.

The prevalence and death rate of the disease in most of the world can probably be judged by that of the state of Massachusetts, where reporting of the disease by physicians was made compulsory early, and in the whole U.S.A., for which statistical data are readily available. The decade of the 1920s in the U.S.A. recorded 1 006 869 pneumonia deaths, accounting for 8.3 % of all deaths, of which 525 465 were of the lobar form. The pneumonia death rate in Boston in the early 1930s was about 135/100 000 population, compared to 780 in Bombay, 350–500 in Cairo, 200–350 in Panama City, and 100–200 in Buenos Aires and Copenhagen (Heffron, 1939:265, 280). Although socioeconomic factors and living conditions played a major role in transmission of pneumonia, the wealthy or well known were not immune to this disease. Pneumonia killed King George V, Sir William Osler, Kipling's daughter and one of Lincoln's sons (Dowling, 1973).

In 1891 Klemperer & Klemperer demonstrated in rabbits and later in humans the protective effectiveness of administration of serum from an individual who had recovered from pneumonia. Such serum contains antibodies against the 'type' (capsular antigen) of pneumococcus (antiserum) such an individual had suffered but survived. The results of efforts to employ this as a therapeutic method were clouded by the failure to recognize that many different pneumococcal types existed and that the antibodies that patients formed were specific to and therapeutically effective only for each type. By 1925, Avery & Heidelberger had identified the three most common polysaccharide antigens in the pneumococcus capsule that were responsible for specific types. Two years later Rufus Cole (1929) reported that antiserum administration had reduced the mortality rate of pneumonia in 371 patients treated with Type 1 antiserum from the expected 25–30 %, to 10.5 %.

In 1931, Massachusetts launched a major educational campaign and provided financial support for antiserum production and administration. Within the next few years several other states followed that example. While striking results were reported by some large, urban hospitals, the routine employment of this therapy in smaller communities was retarded by its somewhat cumbersome requirements. Neufeld had reported as early as 1904 that immersion of pneumococci in antiserum specific for the type caused its capsule to swell ('quellung reaction'), but this method was not employed clinically to type pneumococci until a generation later (Armstrong, 1931). Program leaders called for federal support to expand the educational program and the American national legislature did appropriate some funds in 1938. However, simple chemical chemotherapy with sulfapyridine became available in 1939 and soon demonstrated its superior effectiveness over antiserum therapy, so the antiserum therapy programs promptly faded away (Dowling, 1973). World War II experience revealed the effectiveness of penicillin, followed subsequently by many other antibiotics for pneumonia due to other organisms.

Within the general public is a cohort of individuals especially vulnerable to pneumonia. Among others, this subgroup includes the very aged, those whose spleens have been removed or destroyed by disease, and the immunocompromised. Since 1977 vaccines containing antigens of up to 23 pneumococcic types have been available to protect this subgroup from developing pneumonia. Protectiveness has been established by field tests, but the overall level of effectiveness (57 % in a study by Butler *et al.*, 1993) is less than anticipated for a number of reasons, of which the declining ability of older people to produce antibodies to these antigens with advancing age is the most prominent (Sims, 1992).

The frequency of the lobar form of pneumococcic pneumonia has decreased substantially in developed countries during the past few decades, perhaps because the widespread use of antibiotics has decreased the pneumococcus carrier state. However, increase in the geriatric population of those countries is probably responsible for the increase in bronchopneumonia, since that is commonly a terminal complication of other geriatric diseases such as cerebral hemorrhage and metastatic cancer.

Implications for ancient populations

Heffron (1939:316, 334–40) points out that factors contributing to the vulnerability to pneumonia development include crowding, malnutrition, dust inhalation, physically fatiguing occupations, coexistence of chronic disease, trauma and age extremes. One might expect, then, that the crowded conditions suffered by many sedentary agriculturalists in ancient times might be accompanied by an increased prevalence of pneumonia, particularly in those arid areas that are capable of producing dusty conditions. This might be exaggerated during periods of famine with associated malnutrition. A high frequency of trauma (with its accompanying incapacitation and resulting pulmonary secre-

tion retention) found among some groups living in a hazardous terrain would produce the same effect. Because age at death in excess of 55 years is usually found in only a small fraction of an ancient population, many of the above effects may be manifested principally by an increase in an ancient burial site's <u>infant</u> fraction due to the greater vulnerability of this age group to pneumonia.

Modern case fatality rates of lobar pneumonia from the years before specific, effective therapy became available ranged from 23.9–32.8 % (Heffron 1939:657, 659). The probability of death among the ancient people who developed pneumonia could be expected to be roughly similar to these rates among modern people untreated with specific therapy. In fact, this is precisely what was found in a study on a 4000 year old northern Chile coastal population of preceramic mariners (Aufderheide & Allison, 1994).

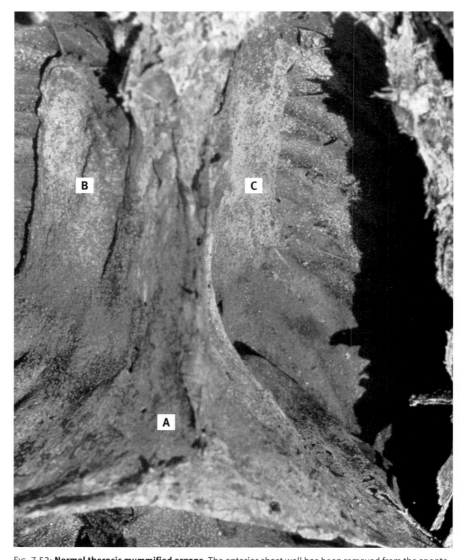

FIG. 7.52: **Normal thoracic mummified organs.** The anterior chest wall has been removed from the spontaneously mummified body of an Egyptian (Dakhleh oasis) 14 year old boy. The central, roughly triangular shaped structure (A) in the midline is the intact pericardium within which the desiccated heart was found. The elongated, roughly rectangular (B and C) flat structures on each side of the pericardium are the dried, normal, collapsed lungs, flattened and conforming to the curvature of the posterior chest. EG-2, T-1. PBL.

Soft tissue lesions in ancient human remains

In desiccated bodies the air in lungs at the time of death diffuses out of the lungs, and the blood in the pulmonary vascular bed dries. The lungs thus collapse. If the body is in a supine position, normal lungs will be found as relatively thin (often less than 1 cm thick) folds of tissue extending from the mediastinal tissues, draped across the lateral aspect of the thoracic vertebrae and flowing out onto the posterior rib cage, reaching about halfway to the lateral chest wall and commonly conforming to the curvature of the posterior chest wall (Fig. 7.52). The color is often dark brown or black, usually due to hemoglobin breakdown products. The section on Natural history of pneumonia (see above) describes how a lung lobe with pneumonia often becomes permanently adhesive to the chest wall adjacent to it. Such an adhesion

will prevent that portion of the lung from collapsing postmortem. This is easily identified by examination if it is located posteriorly, or by simple visualization if the adhesion is anterior or lateral. Such an adhesion produces no impairment of lung function, but its presence documents an episode of pneumonia suffered at some time in the person's life, and that the person had recovered from that episode of pneumonia. These adhesions may be localized (Fig. 7.53) or may involve the whole lobe or even the entire lung surface (Figs. 7.54 & 7.55).

If the studied individual died during an acute episode of pneumonia, the displacement of lung air by fluid or exudate (containing red and white blood cells) will prevent the affected part of the lung from collapsing. Furthermore the expanded portion of lung will not only be thicker than average, but will also be much firmer than normal (consolidated: Fig. 7.56). Transection will commonly demonstrate a dense, black parenchyma. In addition to its expansion and consolidation, evidence of pleural fluid is commonly present in the form of crystalline deposits on both visceral and parietal pleural surfaces. The more well-formed crystals are usually electrolytes (mineral salts such as ordinary salt or sodium chloride: Fig. 7.57), while the more powdery deposits are

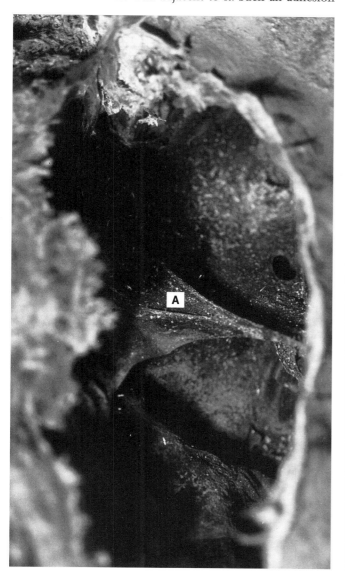

FIG. 7.53: **Pleural adhesion.** Interior of left thoracic cavity is exposed. Most of the left lung has collapsed except for a triangular, black segment (A) whose apex is attached to the parietal pleura of the lateral portion of the chest wall. A-142, T-5. Modern adult, colonial period, northern Chile. MAUT. PBL.

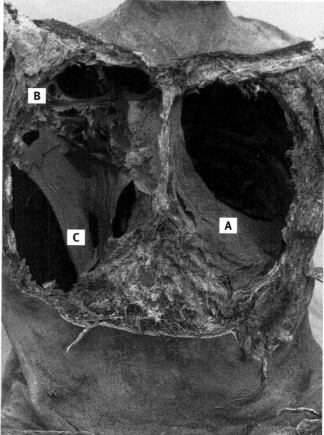

FIG. 7.54: **Pleural adhesions.** The normal left lung (A) of this spontaneously mummified body has collapsed and the lower lobe is draped over the left diaphragm. Right lung is adhesive to chest wall (B) and right diaphragm (C). Adult male ca. A.D. 600, northern Chile. PBL.

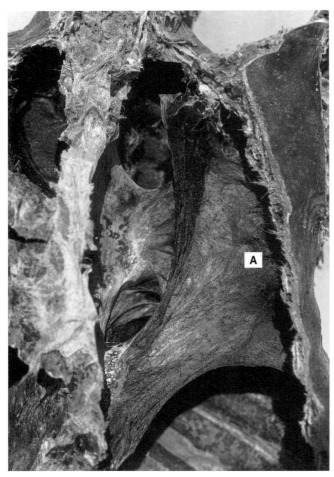

FIG. 7.55: **Pleural adhesion.** Left thoracic cavity is exposed. A broad area of adhesion (A) along the left chest wall has prevented the airless, desiccated and otherwise flattened normal lung from collapsing and retracting to the hilum at the mediastinum and posterior chest wall. AZ-141, T-26. MAUT. PBL.

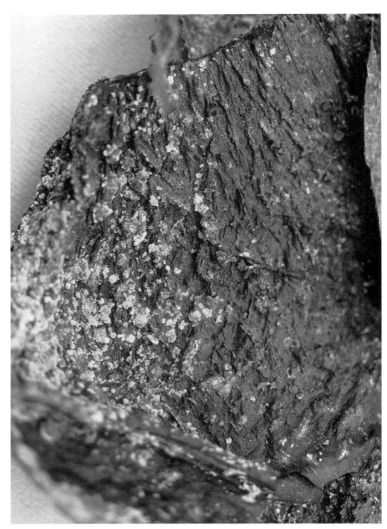

FIG. 7.56: **Acute pneumonia.** The lung of this adult female is thick (4.5 cm) and covered with crystals that were deposited on the lung after death when the pleural effusion secondary to the pneumonia dried, and the electrolytes and proteins in the fluid exudate crystallized. Northern Chile, 2000 B.C., Chinchorro culture. M01-6, T-14. MAUT. PBL.

commonly proteins, usually predominantly albumin (Fig. 7.58). Fragile pleural adhesions that did not have time to become scarred before death may also be seen. If the pneumonia was of the lobar form, it will demonstrate such a distribution; in about 10 % of the cases the condition is bilateral. Bronchopneumonia type of involvement will present a smaller and more localized involvement. However, the involvement is commonly multiple, with several focal areas being apparent, sometimes within only one lobe and sometimes involving more than one lobe or even all lobes of both lungs.

The examiner must be careful in interpreting the lower lobes. Normal lower lobes without disease are often draped partly over the surface of the diaphragm. When these become desiccated they may be so thin that segments of bronchi within them, being more rigid than the surrounding alveoli, may produce nodular, small elevations on the pleural surface of the collapsed lung. These can be mistaken for pathology, especially on the right side where the right lower lobe is draped over the diaphragmatic surface of the liver. In this area the lung may be so difficult to separate from the diaphragm and underlying liver that the lung thickness can

be difficult to evaluate. Within the lung, development of a lung abscess is normally characterized by an air-containing defect of any size, often communicating with a bronchus. The presence of an empyema can be recognized as a walled-off area of exudate (that may have the consistency of sand or fine gravel) between the lung and the chest wall (Fig. 7.59). It can be differentiated from a lung abscess by the fact that the chest wall forms the outer wall of the involved area.

Microscopic study is often not easy to interpret. All epithelium is usually degenerated. If alveoli are preserved (more often they are not) the content may appear as a uniform, structureless, hyaline material reflecting protein-containing (often fibrin) fluid. The large number of white blood cells present at death usually largely disappear after death. While stainable bacteria are often present, the problem of resolving whether they are of antemortem or postmortem origin may not be simple If they are all of the same type and if other organs do not show the same bacteria, or at least not at the same concen-

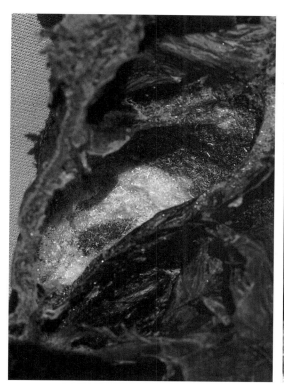

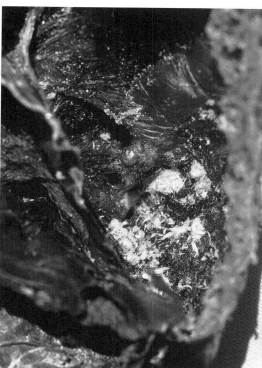

FIG. 7.57: **Pneumonia, acute with bilateral pleural effusion.** Lower half of each thoracic cavity of the spontaneously mummified body of a 1 ½ year old infant. The left lower lobe is thick (4.0 cm), indicating the presence of acute pneumonia. Crystalline deposits are due to bilateral pleural effusion. AZ-141, T-54. Cabuza culture ca. A.D. 800, northern Chile. MAUT. PBL.

FIG. 7.58: **Acute Pneumonia.** Thickened left lower lobe of lung. Electrolyte and protein content of pleural fluid crystallized during spontaneous postmortem desiccation. Cabuza culture, ca. A.D. 800, northern Chile. MAUT. PBL.

tration, then the bacteria visualized in the lung can usually be considered to have been there at the time of death.

Ruffer (1910) was the first to describe the gross and microscopic evidence of pneumonia in mummified tissue. He found pneumonia in an Egyptian mummy from the twentieth dynasty and in another from the Ptolemaic period. Allison (1984) described his experience with pneumonia in 51 spontaneously desiccated bodies. Both lobar and bronchial forms of pneumonia were encountered. He identified the nature of the infecting agent in some of these by several different methods including gram-staining, electron microscopy and antibody induction. In one of those mummies he found pneumonia in a segment of lung distal to a bronchus occluded by an aspirated tooth (Allison et al., 1974d).

In a group of 69 spontaneously mummified mummies, Aufderheide & Allison (1994) identified evidence of 26 former and terminal (at time of death) pneumonia episodes of which five were acute and the cause of death. This suggests a minimal pneumonia frequency (not every pneumonia episode produces pleural adhesions) of 38 % and a case fatality rate (5 fatal episodes out of 26 in total) of 19.2 %, similar to those respective values occurring in the U.S.A. in the 1920s prior to specific therapy availability.

There are usually no skeletal lesions secondary to a fatal episode of acute pneumonia, though rarely an individual, recovering from the pulmonary involvement, may develop osteomyelitis from the accompanying septicemia.

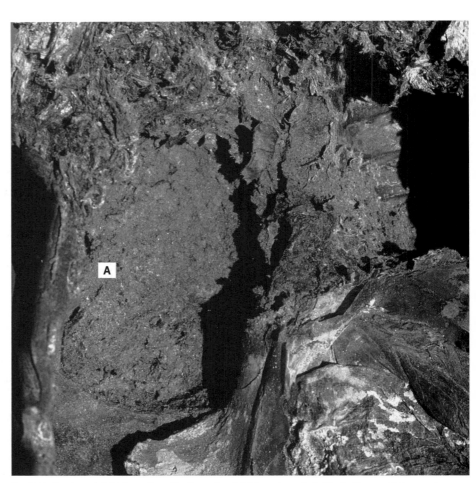

FIG. 7.59: **Empyema, right thoracic cavity.** The entire right thoracic cavity is filled with necrotic lung and exudate (A). A thick, consolidated right upper lung lobe was identified within the exudate. AZ-75, T-131, C1. Spontaneous mummification. San Lorenzo culture ca. A.D. 500, northern Chile. MAUT. PBL.

SALMONELLOSIS

Definition, epidemiology, taxonomy and geography

The species of the gram-negative rods, genus *Salmonella*, produce a variety of clinical syndromes in humans including diarrhea, septicemia and the asymptomatic carrier state. *Salmonella typhi* is the etiological agent for typhoid fever; *S. enteriditis* (including subgroups *S. paratyphi*, *S. typhimurium*, *S. heidelberg*) produce a condition in which the intestinal symptoms predominate, usually with a milder component of bacteremia. Only humans harbor *S. typhi* and only humans are infected naturally by this organism. Other *Salmonella* species are found in many animals as well as humans. Recovery from infection with *S. typhi* is followed by immunity that may tolerate the carrier state in a small number of patients (less than 5 %). The gallbladder is a common residence site for the bacillus in carriers. In both patients and carriers bacilli can be shed in the urine as well as in feces. Transmission is by the fecal–oral route. This is a disease of worldwide distribution but socioeconomic factors can influence prevalence and create endemic foci.

Natural history of typhoid fever

Typhoid fever will be our model for discussion of *Salmonella* sp. infections. A few days following ingestion the organism gains access to the blood stream and is widely disseminated, generating the symptoms of bacteremia: fever, chills, malaise and even vascular collapse in some patients. At this stage fever dominates the disease manifestations, though in children abdominal symptoms are common (colic, mild diarrhea) but not invariable. By the end of the first week a blotchy skin rash ('rose spots') may appear, and the liver and spleen enlarge. Abdominal symptoms are usually related to gallbladder infec-

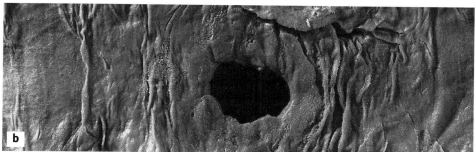

FIG. 7.60: **Typhoid fever.** (a) The circular, raised modern intestinal structures are hyperplastic lymphoid foci (Peyer's patches), a common source of tissue entry for the typhoid bacillus. (b) The demonstrated perforation of one of these is a common fatal complication. Modern autopsy. BM.

based on a disease description in early literature is the inconclusive effort made by Janssens (1083) to determine whether the epidemic reported by Gregory of Tours (sixth century A.D.) as *morbus desentericus* really was typhoid fever. However, on a purely clinical basis, by 1837 William W. Gerhard had separated the disease that we know now is caused by *S. typhi* from the other infectious enterides (especially those that had been gathered together under the appellation 'typhus') and called it typhus-like, or typhoid fever. Acceptance that it was transmitted by the fecal–oral route, however, was not embraced until nearer the end of the nineteenth century, reflected in the 1875 British Public Health Act. Rapid accumulation of knowledge thereafter was a benefit of the enormous breadth of bacteriological investigation initiated by Pasteur, Koch and their pioneering bacteriological colleagues. Many examples can be cited to demonstrate that, in appropriate circumstances, a single human carrier may be responsible for large typhoid epidemics. Of these, perhaps the tale of 'Typhoid Mary' is particularly poignant. This woman was a professional cook who ultimately was demonstrated bacteriologically to be a typhoid carrier. Over a decade she left, in her wake of families for whom she cooked, sufficient epidemic foci related to those family contacts, so that an investigating epidemiologist traced the problem to her presence. Her stool samples persistently revealed typhoid bacilli, so she was warned not to pursue her cooking career. When a subsequent epidemic was attributed to her continuing occupation she was forcibly isolated for the rest of her life.

Although sanitation engineering has dramatically reduced the frequency of typhoid fever in the developed western countries, recurring imported cases occur in focal areas of unsatisfactory sanitation. It remains a global problem in developing countries.

tion or intestinal hemorrhage. Bacilli invade the lymphoid foci (Peyer's patches) normally present in the small intestine causing them to enlarge and ulcerate (Fig. 7.60). Occasionally these perforate through the full thickness of the intestinal wall, leading to a fatal peritonitis if not closed surgically. In others the ulcerated areas may bleed, sometimes seriously. Within a month after onset sufficient immune response normally occurs to result in clinical improvement with recovery by at least 6 weeks in most untreated patients. Diagnosis is established by recovery of the organism from the blood, urine or feces, assisted by serologic response (Widal test).

Complications other than intestinal perforation or hemorrhage may include infection of other tissues, including meninges, kidneys, bones and joints (see below).

Probably 90 % recover from the disease spontaneously without treatment, an observation relevant to paleopathological implications. Modern specific antibiotic therapy decreases the frequency of complications (and, therefore, deaths) but does not eliminate them. Furthermore, it is not clear that such therapy diminishes the duration of the illness. Immunization with either an antigen preparation or with a live, attenuated organism results in some, but less than absolute, protection, which declines with time.

Antiquity and history of typhoid fever

Unfortunately the clinical features of typhoid fever are not sufficiently specific to separate it from the many other febrile or infectious diarrhea conditions. Typical of the problems encountered when trying to establish an etiological diagnosis

Skeletal pathology of typhoid fever

Osteomyelitis is a complication of the bacteremia and occurs in only 1 % of infected persons, regardless of age. The most commonly involved sites of the skeleton are ribs, tibia and spine (lumbar vertebrae). The lesion in the long bones, especially tibia, is a diaphyseal abscess near the periosteum (Putschar, 1976). In the spine, the typhoid lesions often involve two, and sometimes more, vertebral bodies with erosions of the adjacent vertebral plates, reactive perifocal sclerosis, marginal bony bridging, and narrowing of the intervertebral disc.

BRUCELLOSIS (MALTA FEVER; MEDITERRANEAN FEVER; UNDULANT FEVER; BANG'S DISEASE; GIBRALTAR FEVER)

Definition, taxonomy, and geography

An acute or recurrent infectious disease caused by any species of Brucella and characterized by invasion of the reticuloendothelial system. Brucellosis may be caused by any species of the gram-negative genus Brucella: B. melitensis, B. abortus and B. suis. Brucella species are distinguishable by agglutination tests with adsorbed, monovalent serum and by special biochemical tests. All of these organisms are highly endotoxic and are typically intracellular parasites (Howe, 1981). The species names refer to the origin or special affinities for respective animal hosts (Howe, 1981). B. abortus (cattle and horses); B. melitensis (from Malta where the principal vector is infected goat's milk that produces most cases of Brucella osteomyelitis: Jaffe, 1972:1048); and B. suis (swine transmitted through infected meat). Cross infections by any of these organisms can occur between various animal species. B. canis may be infectious for laboratory dog handlers.

Brucellosis is a worldwide disease. Although it has been eradicated in certain countries, brucellosis continues as an important disease in several farming areas such as the Mediterranean countries (both in Europe and Africa) as well as in other regions located in New Zealand, Asia, Central America and Mexico, and South America (Benenson, 1984; Murray et al., 1990). In the U.S.A. the most important pathogen is B. abortus. Undulant fever is most prevalent in rural areas.

History

Malta or Mediterranean fever was noted in the Hippocratic corpus as a type of fever with regular remissions or intermissions (hence the term undulant fever). In 1863, J. A. Marston separated undulant from other fevers and called it 'gastric remittent fever.' However, it was not until 24 years later that a British military surgeon, Sir David Bruce (1855–1931), isolated the organism responsible for the disease, which he called Micrococcus melitensis. In the decade of the 1920s the name was changed to Brucella melitensis in his honor (Laín Entralgo, 1963). In 1905, T. Zammit discovered the relationship between Malta fever and goat's milk. In 1897 the Danish physician Bernhard L. F. Bang isolated Brucella abortus as the agent responsible for infectious abortion in cattle (Laín Entralgo, 1963). Not until 1918, however, did Alice Evans note a close similarity between B. melitensis and B. abortus. The first case of undulant fever caused by B. suis was diagnosed in the U.S.A. in 1922, although even then the identity of the agent was not inmediately recognized.

Epidemiology and natural history

Goats, sheep, pigs, cows and horses are the most important reservoirs for human infection . The organism usually enters the body by ingestion of milk and dietary products from infected animals, especially in the types caused by B. melitensis and B. abortus. Also important are cuts and abrasions of the skin (that admit the organism upon contact with tissues from infected animals, especially those due to B. suis). Later, the pathogens spread via hematogenous dissemination to the organs of the reticuloendothelial system: liver, spleen, lymph nodes and the bone marrow. Person-to-person transmission is very uncommon. Brucellosis is considered as an occupational or professional disease in those people who work with cattle and other animals that compose the reservoir for this disease.

The incubation period is quite variable. While the average interval is about 5–30 days, it can be as much as several months. Adults are more prone to show clinical features. The great majority of cases reported are over 30 years, and males are more frequently affected than females; sexual ratio is about 2:1 (Aegerter & Kirkpatrick, 1975). There is no racial predilection. Although susceptibility and resistance to infection vary a good deal, brucellosis is rarely fatal. However, it can be a debilitating disease with a lengthy course. Duration of the acquired immunity is uncertain, although it seems prolonged. B. melitensis and B. suis are most virulent for humans.

Skeletal pathology

Skeletal involvement is present in only about 10 % of cases in most studies, although a few series report values as high as 70–75 %. Organisms reach the bone by hematogenous dissemination. Vertebrae are most commonly involved, especially in the lumbar vertebral bodies. Long bones are affected much less frequently than is the spine, while flat bones are least often infected. Vertebral lesions are often multiple and begin with an abscess causing a local lytic area in one or several vertebral bodies. Rapid progression without sequestrum formation follows (Ortner & Putschar, 1985). The intervertebral disc may be involved, and other adjacent vertebrae can be affected by direct extension (Putschar, 1976). In the final stage, osteosclerotic reaction and hypertrophic new bone formation without osteoporosis is characteristic (Murray et al., 1990). Eventual healing may produce localized vertebral fusion (Dastugue & Gervais, 1992). Osteophyte-like overgrowth of reactive new bone is not uncommon (Revell, 1986; Resnick & Niwayama, 1989a, b). In long bones, brucellosis is similar to suppurative osteomyelitis with a pattern of bone destruction, abscess formation and periosteal thickening. Joint involvement, usually monoarticular, is possible and it may occur independent of bone infection (Aegerter & Kirkpatrick, 1975). The hip is the most commonly affected joint, followed by the wrist and knee (Murray et al., 1990). Sacroiliac joint abnormalities also are common (Resnick &

FIG. 7.61: **Brucellosis?** The partially eroded archaeological vertebral body may represent brucellosis (Pedro Pons' sign). Chalcolithic period, northern Spain. Photograph courtesy Dr Francisco Exteberria, San Sebastian, Spain.

Niwayama, 1989*a*, b), half of which are bilateral (Uribarri Murillo & Palacios y Carvajal, 1990). Rapid destruction of the articular cartilage occurs with subchondral erosion, but complete destruction of the joint is unusual (Ortner & Putschar, 1985).

Vertebral brucellosis can be separated from tuberculosis because the former does not usually cause paravertebral abscesses, vertebral collapse or gibbus formation and tends to present destructive and reparative processes simultaneously, whereas tuberculosis is largely destructive (Zimmerman & Kelley, 1982:92).

Paleopathology

Several paleopathological cases have been thought to be brucellosis. The first possible case was reported by Brothwell (1965) in a specimen dated to the Middle Bronze Age from Jericho. The most clearly defined example comes from the National Museum of Natural History (Smithsonian Institution), in Washington, DC. It is a female Lapp skeleton (20–25 years) from Norway showing lytic lesions and erosions in several bones (left humerus, several thoracic and lumbar vertebrae, sacrum and pelvis, sacroiliac joints and left femur). After discussing the differential diagnosis with tuberculosis, mycotic infection and cancer, Ortner & Putschar (1985) suggest brucellosis as the most probable (principally based on the fact that the vertebral bodies have not collapsed).

One other possible case of skeletal brucellosis is reported by Soulié (1982) in a skeleton excavated at Raucourt (Meurthe-et-Moselle, France) belonging to an early medieval cemetery (last half of the seventh century). This specimen is a female aged 35 years showing ankylosis in the right elbow joint, spondylodiscitis from T4 to T10, osteomyelitis of the right tibia, and other infectious lesions in the left calcaneus and left fifth metatarsal. The skull shows a healed left frontal

trepanation hole that the author attributes to nervous complications associated with brucellosis, for functional impotence, or for local surgical treatment of a cranial osteomyelitis focus.

Three examples of epiphysitis with erosion of anterior vertebral rims and radiological sclerosis in adult males from medieval and Chalcolithic periods were found in Spain's Basque country and believed to represent early lesions of brucellosis (Etxeberria, 1994: Fig. 7.61).

ACTINOMYCOSIS

Definition, taxonomy, and epidemiology

Actinomycosis is a chronic granulomatous, suppurative disease of humans and cattle that may be systemic or localized, caused by the endogenous oral cavity bacterium *Actinomyces israelii*. *Actinomyces israelii* is an anaerobic, gram-positive and not acid-fast, filamentous and branched bacterium with a diameter of 0.5–1.0 μ. Oral cavity lesions are often precipitating conditions, providing the actinomycetes access to subcutaneous anaerobic conditions necessary for their reproduction (Molto, 1990). The actinomycetes then spread to adjacent tissues and are aspirated into the lungs. Systemic dissemination *via* the blood stream may occur, although this is not very common. *Actinomyces bovis* is the pathogen that affects animals and is isolated very infrequently from humans. It was more common in the preantibiotic populations than it is now. *Actinomyces israelii* was only classified correctly as a bacterium in 1981. Prior to that time it was believed to be a fungus (Shafer *et al.*, 1983; Molto, 1990).

Actinomycosis is a sporadic disease with worldwide distribution. The reservoir is the human oral cavity. The incubation period is not exactly known, although it can be several

FIG. 7.62: **Actinomycosis.** Much of this bovine mandible has been destroyed by osteomyelitis due to the anaerobe *Actinomyces bovis*. Human infections are usually due to *Actinomyces israeli*. No. MM3872. Modern case. Courtesy P. Sledzik. NMHM.

years. While it may occur at any age, there is a predilection for the ages between 15 and 35 years. The male–female ratio is 2:1 and any race can be affected. Natural susceptibility to the infection is low.

Natural history and skeletal pathology

Actinomycosis presents in three different forms depending on the location of the lesion: cervicofacial, abdominal and pulmonary, or thoracic (Robbins, 1975). The most common of these three forms is that of cervicofacial involvement (50–60 %) where it is an extension from a lesion in the oral cavity in either mandible or maxilla, presenting as multiple, small lytic lesions (Zimmerman & Kelley, 1982:88) sur-

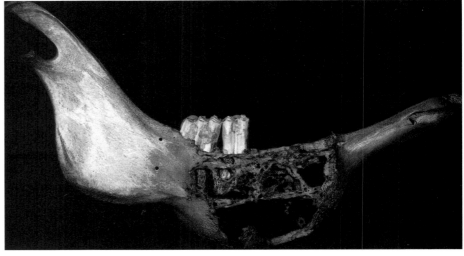

FIG. 7.63: **Actinomycosis.** This bovine mandible has been expanded and extensively destroyed by osteomyelitis with huge abscesses due to the anaerobe *Actinomyces bovis*. Human infections are usually due to *Actinomyces israeli*. No. 709. Modern case. Courtesy G. Worden. MM.

rounded by reactive bone sclerosis (Resnick & Niwayama, 1989a, b). Bone involvement is rather uncommon (Bullough, 1992), and is caused by direct extension from an adjacent focus rather than by the hematogenous route (Putschar, 1976; Resnick & Niwayama, 1989a, b: Figs. 7.62 & 7.63).

The thoracic and lumbar regions are the principal sites affected in the postcranial skeleton along with ribs, cervical vertebrae and sacrum, although any bone may be affected. In the spine, the posterior elements of the vertebrae are often more affected than the vertebral bodies, and the intervertebral discs are usually spared. Pulmonary infections can invade the chest wall. Rib lesions appear most often in the right hemithorax (Molto, 1990). The initial rib response (like skeletal lesions elsewhere: Murphy, 1992) is a diffuse, hypervascular, periosteal reaction that can be identified on dry bones by an increased number and size of the vascular channels and foramina (Ortner & Putschar, 1985). Later, reactive ossifiying periostitis and osteolytic foci appear with or without a small amount of endosteal osteosclerosis. The result is a thickening of the involved area (Murray *et al.*, 1990).

The lesion may remain limited to the periosteal surface while joint involvement may occur secondary to an adjacent focus in the bone whose healing can result in ankylosis (Ortner & Putschar, 1985). Actinomycotic spinal involvement can be separated from spinal tuberculosis by the former's tendency to involve the posterior elements, sparing the disk spaces, extending to adjacent ribs and only rarely producing vertebral body collapse (Zimmerman & Kelley, 1982:89).

Paleopathological evidence

The first probable case of actinomycosis in human paleopathology was recently described by Molto (1990) in an adult male (30–40 years old) excavated from the Le Vesconte Burial Mound in southern Ontario. The lesions were restricted to the pleural surface of the ribs of the right hemithorax, with thickening, diffuse hypervascular periostitis and osteolysis. Dental, periapical abscesses and periodontitis may have provided the nidus for the organism.

NOCARDIOSIS

Definition, taxonomy, epidemiology, and clinical features

Nocardiosis is an acute or chronic disease produced by *Nocardia asteroides* that often begins as a primary pulmonary infection and secondarily, but very uncommonly, can disseminate to other locations (principally to the brain and meninges where it produces abscesses). *Nocardia* species are acid-fast aerobic actinomycetes. The pathogen grows slowly, producing branching filaments. Biopsies of the deep tissues are cultured on Sabouraud's dextrose or blood agar without added antibiotics and incubated aerobically and anaerobically at 22 and 37 °C, respectively. *Nocardia* produces colonies that appear as dry, brittle, orange or yellow, brain-shaped growths often covered with a short mycelium. Nocardiosis is a sporadic disease with worldwide distribution. The soil is the reservoir for the disease. Infection occurs by inhalation of contaminated dust. No transmission from person-to-person or from animals-to-humans has been documented. The incubation period is unknown (probably several weeks). There is no sex or age predilection. All races may be affected. Susceptibility and resistance are unknown.

Soft tissue and skeletal pathology

When hematogenous dissemination occurs the central nervous system commonly develops abscesses in the meninges and brain, although any organ may be affected. Skeletal involvement is uncommon and the lesions occur primarily in cancellous bone. Morphologically, they are lytic with little, if any, reactive bone formation. Fistulae may be present. Joint involvement is uncommon but possible.

PLAGUE (PESTE; BLACK DEATH)

Definition and taxonomy

Plague is a specific zoonosis affecting rodents and their fleas (*Xenopsylla cheopis*). It is an acute and severe infectious disease caused by the bacterium *Yersinia* (formerly *Pasteurella*) *pestis* that can affect humans in three different forms: bubonic, septicemic, and pneumonic plague. *Yersinia. pestis* can liberate both endo- and exotoxins. This organism is a small, non-motile, pleomorphic, non-spore forming, and bipolar-staining gram-negative bacterium transmitted from rodent-to-rodent and then to man through the bites of fleas and arthropod parasites of ground squirrels and rodents of forest and prairie. The bacterium can develop in aerobic or anaerobic conditions. It belongs to the group of *Yersinias* species that are more frequently responsible for hemorrhagic sepsis in animals.

Epidemiology

The natural reservoir of plague is wild rodents, causing an acute, subacute, or chronic disease. Transmission to urban or domestic rodents can occur. The most important domestic hosts are the rats *Rattus rattus* and *Rattus norvegicus*. Transmission to humans occurs through bites of the flea *Xenopsylla cheopis*. The flea is the vector of the disease and when the rat dies due to the disease, the flea abandons the cooling corpse and attacks humans. It can inoculate 100 000 bacteria with each bite. *Xenopsylla cheopis* is an efficient vector of plague because the proventriculus of its feeding tube creates a location for the bacterium, whose growth blocks the flea's gut passage. Unable to swallow the meal, the flea attempts to dislodge the bolus, thus infecting the new host. Another flea, *Pulex irritans*, has an important role in the transmission of plague because it feeds upon both humans and the house rat (Carmichael, 1993a). Very probably, one of the causes of the rapid spread of the Black Death pandemic in the fourteenth century was due to the action of *P. irritans* in the transmission of the disease.

After the bite, *Y. pestis* becomes drained *via* lymph vessels into the lymph nodes, producing infection there (buboes). If the bacteria reach the blood stream, any organ can be affected, and if pneumonia and/or meningitis develop, the disease is almost always fatal. Average mortality associated with plague is about 25–50 % in untreated cases. According to McKeown (1988), the most important influence on plague mortality in the past was not the occasional epidemic outbreak, but the endemic causes of death whose level is determined by availability of food and by population size.

Transmission from person-to-person also occurs and is due to the inhalation of droplets aerosolized by persons affected by pneumonic plague. Pharyngeal asymptomatic carriers have been recognized in bubonic plague. Less frequently, transmission can occur by handling of contaminated objects. Another important form of transmission is the inhalation of dried feces of rats.

Susceptibility is universal. Immunity after recovering is only relative, though some authors (Ramenofsky, 1987) suggest a permanent immunity. Some evidence suggests that natural selection results in genetic resistance to *Yersinia pestis* (the Black Death could have effected this: Robins, 1981). Only when the disease attacks rodents or human populations not previously exposed, do epidemics with the severity of the 1347 pandemic appear (McNeill, 1984).

Because diffusion of the disease depends on rat migration, in many regions of the world plague is a possible hazard due to the persistence of infection in wild rodents and their contact with urban rodents (domestic rats: Benenson, 1984). There are several foci in the western U.S.A.; large areas of South America; central, northern, and southern Africa; the Near East; Kurdistan; the border between Yemen and Saudi Arabia; central and southeastern Asia; Indonesia; and some regions of the former USSR. Sporadic cases have been detected recently in South America and Asia.

Natural history

In all forms of plague, the incubation period fluctuates from 2–5 days. The onset of the disease is acute with signs and symptoms common to all forms: high fever (39.5–41 °C), tachycardia, headache, and chills.

Bubonic plague

This is the most common form (80 % of the reported cases of plague). Coinciding with the fever or a little later (4–5 days after infection), hemorrhagic inflammation, necrosis and edema develop within the lymph nodes. These painful lymph node abscesses, called buboes, appear in the axilla, groin and cervical region. They can reach the size of an egg, especially in the inguinal area. At this point of the disease 50 % of cases recover (Ramenofsky, 1987), but the disease may progress and spread to secondary lymph nodes and then to the blood stream. Occasionally, a primary skin lesion appears at the point of the flea bite. Delirium, mental confusion or incoordination may be present. At an organic level, there can be hepato- and splenomegaly. Mortality rate in untreated cases is about 60–70 %. Bubonic plague is transmitted from person-to-person only if a pneumonic complication is present (Benenson, 1984). Such complications appear in about 5–15 % of bubonic plague cases.

Septicemic plague

This form may be present with the bubonic form of plague, but is more commonly associated with the pneumonic form.

It is very acute and fulminating, killing the patient as a result of diffuse hemorrhage with marked terminal cyanosis, often without inflammation of the superficial lymph nodes.

Primary pneumonic plague

This is less common than the bubonic form, and it occurs when the bacteria reach the lungs. The incubation period is about 2–3 days, and its debut is very acute with high fever, headache, and tachycardia. Cough is not very prominent at the beginning of the clinical picture, but 20–24 hours later it increases with the appearance of highly infectious bloody sputum and respiratory symptoms (dyspnea and cyanosis). Radiography reveals pneumonia that very frequently is bilateral. Nearly all of the patients without proper antibiotic treatment die in a period of 48 hours to 5 days.

Cutaneous form of plague

This accounts for 5 % of all cases of plague, and is characterized by hemorrhagic spots on the skin that destroy the tissue, forming sores. Other symptoms are: fever, delirium, splenomegaly and nephritis. It can be fatal.

History and antiquity

When the history of plague is evaluated, a problem arises: most cases of biblical epidemics were attributed to plague by earlier translators (McNeill, 1984). However, some of the other organisms known to be responsible for certain modern epidemic diseases could have been responsible for the mortalities described in the Bible. The plague of the Philistines in 1320 B.C. has been suggested by many authorities to be the first epidemic of bubonic plague, but others attribute the episodes described in the Bible to bacillary dysentery or intestinal schistosomiasis (Davis *et al.*, 1975). It is believed that plague may have appeared initially as an inapparent infection of gerbils, and that the first pandemic occurred in the years A.D. 592–594 (McKeown, 1988). This pandemic killed thousands of people in a short time, and this important population decrease (along with the mortality caused by other terrible pandemics in the seventh century) had important demographic effects over a period of many centuries. However, based on the long description of Procopius, the earlier, so-called Justinian plague (A.D. 542–543) that killed millions of people (25 % of the population of the Roman Empire) and that has been suggested as being responsible for the fall of the Byzantine empire, can be identified with the bubonic form of plague (O'Neill, 1993). If so, then plague was present in Europe 50 years before the A.D. 592–594 pandemic (Davis *et al.*, 1975; McNeill, 1984). Other more recent, probable episodes of plague affected residents of Rome (1167 and 1230), Florence (1244), Spain and the south of France (1320 and 1333: O'Neill, 1993). The first description of bubonic plague in China is dated to A.D. 610 and the second one 32 years later. In A.D. 762 more than 50 % of the population of Shandong province died in a plague epidemic (McNeill, 1984).

The black rat (*Rattus rattus*) was responsible for the introduction of plague in Europe, accompanying marine commerce between the Mediterranean countries, Egypt and India. Over a period of several centuries the rats spread from the coast into central and northern Europe (McNeill, 1984). Both in Europe and Asia plague affected a region at regular intervals of 20–50 years, when a new generation was substituted for that previously exposed to the infection.

The greatest disaster that Europe ever experienced was known as the Black Death, Universal Plague, Great Mortality or Great Pestilence (A.D. 1346–1350). It was imported from Central Asia and began its spread during the siege of the small town of Kaffa (today Feodosiya) in the Crimea by the Tartars (the inhabitants of Kaffa reported that the Tartars shot the corpses of soldiers killed by the disease into the small town with catapults in hopes that the disease would attack the besieged people). From there the disease expanded to Messina and Genova, creating the first European foci, and in A.D. 1347 to Crete, Constantinople, Egypt, and southern France. By A.D. 1348 it had arrived at Italy, Cyprus, Rhodes, northern Africa, Spain, Portugal, the whole of France, Switzerland, Palestine and Syria. After that, England, Germany, Poland, the Scandinavian and Baltic countries, the Middle East, Arabia, and, in general, all the known world of that time became affected by this disastrous disease. There is good evidence that plague traveled via the international trade pathways (O'Neill, 1993). The average length of the disease in any given place was about 5–6 months. Due to the ecology of the disease the most unfortunate regions were those of Lower Egypt, Veneto (Italy), Provence (France), and Ireland, all of whom experienced recurrent waves of pneumonic and bubonic forms, or were reinfected in successive years. On the contrary, remote areas, like the Pyrenees (Spain-France), central Balkans, and the sub-Atlas region (Africa), escaped largely or entirely, due to their isolation from the ports and trade routes (Park, 1993).

The initial impact was tremendous, although the mortality rate varied geographically. Three forms of the disease were present: bubonic (77 %), septicemic (19 %) and pneumonic (4 %: Sendrail, 1983; O'Neill, 1993). This pandemic may have killed one-third of the European population (15–25 million). In England 30–50 % of the population died and in Norway and Iceland it was fatal for two-thirds of the population (McNeill, 1984; Crosby, 1986). Garrison (1966), has calculated that 25 % of the world population (more than 60 million people) died in this pandemic. Mortality was so great that the dead were abandoned in streets or stacked one on top of another and burned, because there were few survivors to prepare the burials. Paris, with 200 000 inhabitants lost 150 000. It was said that 500 people died every day within the Hotel-Dieu (Sendrail, 1983). Only 30 000 of Florence's

previous 100 000 residents survived; the disease killed 25 000 of the 40,000 inhabitants of Siena; Magdeburg lost 50 % of its population, Hamburg 60 %, and Venice 75 %.

The principal features of the Black Death were: rapid course of the disease; pain; swelling in the groin and armpits; the victim remained conscious until late in the disease; and, finally, characteristic black bruising. Guy de Chauliac, surgeon of Pope Clement VI at Avignon, described two forms of the disease:

Pestis, habuit duos modos. Primus fuit cum febre continua et sputo sanguinis. Et isti moriebantur infra tres dies. Secundus fuit cum febre etiam continua et apostematibus et anthracibus in exterioribus, potissime in subasellis et inguinibus. (Plague had two forms. The first one was with continuous fever and bloody sputum. And these died within three days. The second one was also with continuous fever and abscesses and anthraxes in the exterior of the body, especially in the axilla and groin).

de Chauliac (ca. 1350)

The European socioeconomic structure and almost that of the entire known world was highly disrupted. A great part of the nobility died; cities lost as many as half of their population; medicine could not prevent or treat the disease and the church failed to offer comfort (Ell, 1993). According to Park (1993), '…the Black Death seems to have been more universal and more virulent than many historians a generation ago believed…' Overall mortality associated with bubonic plague during the fourteenth century in Europe has been estimated at 25 % (Ramenofsky, 1987). Nothing was the same in the European continent after the Black Death pandemic.

Since the epidemic of Black Death, plague has been chronic in Europe and the Middle East until recently, especially in eastern Europe. During the second half of the sixteenth century several epidemics of plague attacked Europe, the first one in A.D. 1555, with the initial focus in Venice; the second one, between 1562 and 1565, affected much of central Europe; and the last one, in 1597, killed 600 000 in Spain alone. During the seventeenth century plague periodically attacked Europe causing thousands of victims. However, the new public hygienic measures and isolation of the infected reduced the mortality below the previous record levels (Garrison, 1966). However, in several later epidemics mortality was high again. In 1764 the famous epidemic of London killed thousands of people; in Moscow plague claimed more than 50 000 inhabitants (McNeill, 1984) in 1771. Other researchers (McKeown, 1988) attribute the decline of mortality during the eighteenth century to fortuitous changes in the behavior of the disease.

Thus for many centuries plague periodically attacked the Old World, killing thousands or millions of people. And the rats? Nothing was done with regard to the rats because no one knew that they were the carriers of the vector of the disease (the flea). It was only at the end of the nineteenth century that the form of transmission of the disease was elucidated. Without modern diagnosis, hygiene measures, and treatment the epidemics of the last years of the nineteenth century would have reached the same proportions as those of the medieval pandemics (Garrison, 1966). In 1894 the third great pandemic of plague affected Canton and Hong-Kong. Several bacteriologists belonging to the teams of Pasteur and Koch made the trip to Asia trying to discover the agent responsible of the disease. It was in Hong-Kong that a Swiss and a Japanese bacteriologist, Alexandre J. E. Yersin and Shibamiro Kitasato, discovered Yersinia (*Pasteurella*) *pestis*. Kitasato was the first to discover the bacillus but it was Yersin who gave the more accurate morphologic description (Davis *et al.*, 1975). However, the transmission of the disease remained unclear until 1896, when an epidemic exploded in Bombay and a European medical mission moved there to study the problem. Ogata, working in Formosa, discovered that *Yersinia pestis* was transmitted through the bite of the rat flea. It followed, then, that the most important prophylactic measure was rat control. A few years later, Simond (French) discovered that the disease was transmitted from the rat corpses to healthy rats through the fleas, and the 'theory of the fleas was confirmed.'

In 1895, Alexandre Yersin, Albert Calmette and Borrell prepared the first anti-plague serum therapy, and, in 1896 W.M.W. Haffkine prepared the first vaccine. Since 1900, plague has appeared sporadically in North America, South America and South Africa until the discovery of antibiotics in the decade of the 1940s. It was in 1907–1908 when the first focus of plague appeared in San Francisco and the rapid intervention of the experts of the Marine Hospital, diagnosing the disease and destroying the rats, avoided the spread of the disease to the rest of the city and the whole country (Garrison, 1966).

Paleopathology

The lung lesion of those who die of the pneumonic form can be apparent in mummified bodies, but the pneumonia is not recognizable as specific for plague. Occasionally the bubonic areas may be apparent, but, if so, they can be expected to present as hollow defects because the cellular content of pus will usually liquefy postmortem before spontaneous mummification occurs. The multiple hemorrhagic areas (disseminated intravascular coagulation), common in plague deaths, may be apparent as dark tissue stains. Unless the buboes can be clearly demonstrated, together with at least one of the other two features, it is unlikely that a firm diagnosis of plague could be made without unequivocal staining features of the organism in sections of affected tissues. The authors have not identified such cases reported in the literature. If a mummified body with features suggestive of plague does become available, identification of the organism by immunological methods or those of molecular biology would be a significant contribution to the field. The enormous demographic impact of plague in Europe was devastating and is mentioned in the History and antiquity section above. The labor shortage it created has been considered a significant contribution to the dissolution of feudalism in England.

CHOLERA

Vibrio cholerae is a gram-negative bacterium that produces an enterotoxin targeting gut mucosal cells, causing them to leak fluids into the gut lumen so abruptly and voluminously that the resulting diarrhea threatens life by producing profound dehydration. It is transmitted by the fecal–oral route, though a common mechanism involves eating raw fish or shellfish from waters that have become contaminated with the organism from human feces. Because the lost fluids contain salt and other plasma electrolytes, vigorous oral or parenteral replacement of the lost fluid and its solutes will usually produce spontaneous healing, since the organism does not invade the tissues. If such treatment is delayed or insufficiently aggressive, however, death ensues via vascular collapse secondary to the dehydration hypovolemia. This must have occurred in antiquity. The condition is commonly of epidemic nature. While the onset of epidemics sometimes can be traced to environmental causes or to human behavior, often no such specific factor is identifiable. Recently a bacteriophage (CTX) has been described that can be transferred to benign *V. cholerae* organisms. The phage's genes become incorporated into the bacterium's chromosome and cause the bacterium to pump out its dangerous toxin (Williams, 1996). Conceivably such a molecular event could usher in a new epidemic. In Burma (Myrmar) it is an annual event coinciding with the southwest monsoon in May in spite of religious exorcising rituals (Yoe, 1963:396–400). We do not know how ancient the disease is, but in some areas like India and Bangladesh, epidemics with high fatality rates are known to have been recurrent for at least centuries (Cotran *et al.*, 1989:356). Indeed, Cloudsley-Thompson (1976:131) believed that a monolith from about 350 B.C. in a western India temple describing the profoundly dehydrated appearance of local epidemic victims was relating a cholera epidemic. The most recent epidemic in the Americas was of marine nature occurring in western South America in 1992. It is highly probable that the disease occurred among ancient populations in an appropriate environment. It produces no anatomic lesion of either soft or skeletal tissues, and is included here only because of its potential massive mortality and contagiousness during epidemics.

GAS GANGRENE

Clostridium perfringes is a gram-positive rod that proliferates under anaerobic conditions. Small numbers of these spore-forming organisms can be found in the intestinal lumen of many animals as well as a significant fraction of asymptomatic humans in whom their growth appears to be inhibited by the overwhelming numbers of other, normal colon bacilli. Contamination of human wounds by the species in an anaerobic environment will foster its growth. Clinical circumstances under which this occurs include non-aseptic abortion and tissue devitalization with necrosis ('gangrene'), by accidental crushing of muscle, surgical amputation or ischemic necrosis. Once introduced into the necrotic tissue in one of these or similar manners, the organism quickly reaches the blood stream and is distributed widely to all tissues. This septicemia stage often prostrates the patient, with the clinical picture of fever, followed by shock, complicated further by two features: (i) profound anemia secondary to red blood cell (RBC) destruction by an enzyme (lecithinase) produced by the organism that destroys the RBC membrane, and (ii) the production of gas by the organism, (gas 'gangrene'). The latter is most obvious clinically as a crunchy sensation ('crepitus') upon palpation of the swollen, affected area due to the presence of bubbles of free gas formed by the bacteria in the subcutaneous tissue (Cotran et al., 1989:360). Even today the fatality rate is very high with the best of treatment and in antiquity can be expected to have been uniformly fatal.

While no skeletal lesions are produced, the gas formation by the bacteria continues postmortem until the body has cooled enough to arrest bacterial growth. Hence, within 4 hours after death the body tissues have a spongy consistency, most obvious grossly in the liver. Indeed, an older laboratory diagnostic method involved injection of a patient's sample of blood into a rabbit; after 5 minutes (to allow for body-wide dissemination of the organism in the blood sample) the animal was killed, the entire, intact rabbit placed into an incubator at body temperature for 4 hours, and then autopsied to observe the liver. A spongy appearance was obvious if the patient's blood sample contained *Clostridium perfringes* (see Fig. 8.14).

This condition has not been reported in ancient human remains. However, numerous *skeletal* examples of amputation have been published, and it is not inconceivable that abortion may have been practiced occasionally. Hence the circumstances under which gas gangrene might occur appear to have existed in ancient times. Those investigators examining mummified human remains need to remain alert to this possibility, because the gross lesions (organ parenchyma riddled with 'bubbles') are characteristic. Under postmortem circumstances that preserved soft tissues sufficiently well to permit recognition of the gross lesions, one would also expect to demonstrate the microscopic presence of the spore-forming clostridial bacteria.

LYME DISEASE

The tick *Ixodes dammini*, common in parts of the boreal forests of North America, is being recognized now also in many other areas including Europe and Australia (Cotran et al., 1989:366). It can transmit the infectious agent of this disease, the spirochete *Borrelia bergdorferi*. An erythematous trunk or thigh skin rash of characteristic pattern (erythema migrans) follows the tick bite in up to 80 % of people, accompanied by fever and malaise. Neurological, meningeal, cardiac and other organ involvement are features in some patients. In addition, arthritis occurs in major joints. Clinically this may be monoarticular initially but is frequently migratory, with fluctuating intensity. The knee is affected in 80 % of cases. The condition may be self-limiting and affect only the joint's soft tissues. However, in 10 % of the cases a chronic arthritis develops and juxtacortical osteoporosis, osteophyte formation and marginal bone erosion may appear (Resnick & Niwayama, 1989a). Calcification of the soft tissues, articular cartilage and menisci may also develop (Murray et al., 1990). Synovial histological lesions resemble those of rheumatoid arthritis (Cotran et al., 1989:367). Diagnosis is not always easy, and is aided by a history of exposure, tick bite and tick identification as well as serologically demonstrated antibody response. Selective antibiotic therapy in the earlier stages may abort progression of the disease. If untreated, permanent joint injury may occur. In paleopathological specimens the joint lesions may be indistinguishable from those expected in degenerating joint disease.

GLANDERS

Pseudomonas mallei, a gram-negative bacillus, is responsible for this condition. Horses and donkeys represent the principal reservoir, and humans become infected by contact with a lesion or by inhalation. The acute condition, often lethal in the untreated individual, may take the form of an overwhelming septicemia with multiple metastatic abscesses or vascular collapse and death. Inhalation can result in an equally serious, fulminating bronchial or lobar form of pneumonia, rapidly progressing to multiple lung abscess formation. The chronic form is characterized by subcutaneous, often ulcerating abscesses. Local complications become fatal in nearly 50 % of patients (Cotran et al., 1989:365).

Glanders (then called 'malleos') was recognized as an infectious disease of animals as early as the fifth century A.D., and the extensive loss of military horses prompted regulation in the eighteenth century, leading to its control in Europe 100 years later (Hutyra et al., 1938:722). It is rare in developed countries today.

Skeletal involvement in glanders is unusual. The skull (nasal bones and septum, ethmoid and sphenoid bones) is the most commonly involved skeletal site, due to the presence of infection of the nasal soft tissues and oral mucosa.

When this does occur periosteal reactive new bone formation may be prominent. Perforation of the hard palate and joint involvement may also occur. These dry bone lesions are not specific and must be differentiated from those seen in tertiary syphilis and leprosy (Ortner & Putschar, 1985). Joint infections are less common, resulting primarily from hematogenous bacillary dissemination from the nasal area to the synovium, rarely as an extension from an osteomyelitis. A literature review found the knee to be the most frequently involved joint, followed by the elbow and ankle (Beitzke, 1934: 589–93).

TROPICAL ULCER

Definition, epidemiology, and clinical features

Tropical ulcer is a chronic infection of skin, subcutaneous tissues and bones, produced by organisms of the Vincent type of fusiform bacilli (although other organisms such as spirochetes and staphylococci have also been isolated in the ulcers) mainly affecting the lower limbs. This disease is most commonly observed in Central and East Africa. There is no sex predilection and the peak age incidence is 20–30 years, although the disease can affect all ages.

Skeletal pathology and differential diagnosis

Skeletal lesions appear after the ulcer erodes muscle and tendon tissues. The most common location is the middle third of the tibial diaphysis (Resnick & Niwayama, 1989a); the fibula is involved less frequently. Deformities of the knee, ankle and foot may be encountered (Murray et al., 1990). Periostitis is often the first skeletal lesion and may result in fusiform excrescences or in bony growths with a 'sunburst' appearance, similar to that seen in certain malignant bone tumors. After this first stage, cortical destruction and sequestra appear, with abscess and fistula formation. Both cortical and cancellous bones are affected. If healing occurs, a thickened sclerotic cortex results, often described as 'ivory ulcers osteoma' (Murray et al., 1990). The final stage of chronic cases shows bowing deformities of the leg, and flexion deformities of the knee, ankle and foot appear. One of the most important complications of tropical ulcer is the development of epidermoid carcinoma in the skin margin of the lesion (2–25 % of cases), that can contribute to bone destruction. In paleopathological specimens the destructive changes of the invading skin cancer could lead to a mistaken diagnosis of primary osteogenic sarcoma. Differential diagnosis of tropical ulcer includes osteomas, malignant tumors of bone, pyogenic osteomyelitis, infarction of bone and hypertrophic osteoarthropathy.

AINHUM (DACTYLOLYSIS SPONTANEA)

Ainhum, a disease of unknown cause, is characterized by the development of constricting bands about the fifth toe, that finally can progress to autoamputation. Little or no pain accompanies the process. Risk factors include infection, chronic trauma, hyperkeratosis, poor vascular supply, or impaired sensation. It was first described in Brazilian Black slaves in 1867 by a Portuguese-Brazilian physician (José Francisco da Silva Lima) of the Hospital de Caridade in Rio de Janeiro (Guerra, 1982–1985; Cooper, 1993), and since then many cases have been reported. The disease is common in Nigeria and East Africa, where it may afflict as much as 2 % of the entire population (Cooper, 1993). It has been reported also in Asia (India and Burma) and in the Americas (U.S.A., Panama, Antilles and Brazil).

Ainhum is a disease of a subset of Black people who wear no shoes. It is very uncommon among other races (no cases are recorded in Caucasians). Both sexes are almost equally affected (though some studies report a slight difference in favor of males) in the middle ages of life (30–50 years).

The first radiological sign of ainhum is osteoporosis. Bone resorption is seen on the medial aspect of the distal portion of the proximal phalanx or the middle phalanx of the fifth toe (Resnick & Niwayama, 1989a, b). Other toes also may be involved, particularly the fourth toe (Murray et al., 1990). As more bone is resorbed, fractures and autoamputation are seen as long as 5 years after the onset of the disease. No example has yet been reported in archaeological bones.

VIRUS INFECTIONS

INTRODUCTION

Viruses are among the most diminutive of all the infectious agents. Most lie beyond the resolving power of the light microscope, requiring magnification that only an electron microscope can achieve in order to be visualized. Furthermore, their structure is also infinitely less complex than that of most bacteria, fungi or protozoan parasites. It is useful to conceive of a virus as composed of a central core consisting of an RNA or DNA segment surrounded by a protein envelope. Thus, lacking such vital features as energy production, and others, that all independent living agents require, most pathogenic viruses reproduce by devising ways of employing the intracellular reproductive machinery of the very cell that they parasitize. Some viruses, for example, use enzymes to splice their core segment into the parasitized cell's DNA;

subsequent cell division will also result in reproduction of the included virus. Consequently some viruses, such as smallpox, survive extracellular milieus so poorly that they can be maintained in a population only if they are continually transmitted from an infected to a nonimmune individual. In addition, some viruses are capable of altering the nature of their enveloping protein coat. Since the antigens presented by the virus commonly are present on the surface of the protein envelope, a change in such antigenic structure can render the virus unaffected by antibodies generated by the host against the antigens present initially. Recurrent influenza epidemics occur by this mechanism, and the AIDS virus alters its antigenic structure so rapidly that to date it has frustrated attempts to develop an effective vaccine. One consequence of some of these characteristics is that some viruses (smallpox is the classical model) have such specific requirements of population size or other features that their existence during the pre-urban period seems improbable.

While methods of transmission, principally contact, ingestion and inhalation, are similar to those of bacterial infections, the immune response to viral infections is commonly both humoral (antibody production) and cellular but does not usually employ the neutrophile. The responding cells are largely lymphocytes and macrophages, so viral infections rarely generate pus and abscesses. Most elicit no or only mild, nonspecific bone reactions, and few of them are chronic diseases. Because of their takeover of cellular mechanisms and intracellular growth, pathogenic virus infections are often characterized by cellular necrosis. Epithelial cells are common targets, including hepatic, bronchial and epidermal cells, though such specialized cells as neurons (poliomyelitis) and pulmonary alveolar cells are preferred by some viruses.

While virus infections unique to certain visceral organs are discussed in Chapter 8, those affecting the body more diffusely are included here. Although some of these may produce no diagnostic gross lesion in either skeletal or mummified soft tissue they are included in this text because their often devastating demographic impact on populations merit the attention of paleopathologists.

SMALLPOX (VARIOLA)

Definition and taxonomy

Smallpox (variola) is an acute, febrile illness of humans caused by the variola virus, and characterized by a vesicular skin eruption. Its severe form (variola major) carries a case fatality rate of 25–40 % while the separate strain causing variola minor (alastrim), found mostly in Africa and South America, is fatal in less than 1 % of the cases. Although the disease has now been eradicated from the entire world, it will be discussed here in the present tense. The variola virus is a member of the family Poxviridae, genus *Orthopoxvirus*. Some members of this genus infect only lower animals. It is a large, double-stranded, DNA-containing virus of 200–400 μ (Friedman, 1991) whose protein envelope shares antigenic structure with other pox viruses. Other features of these viruses include the skin as a target organ and production of focal lesions when inoculated on the chorioallantoic membrane of the chick embryo. Smallpox derives its name from the diminutive size of such chick embryo vesicular lesions.

Epidemiology

The disease, before eradication, had worldwide distribution. It is unique in that it has no known animal or extracorporeal reservoir. While laboratory monkeys suffer a mild disease if injected with the virus under appropriate conditions, only humans contract smallpox naturally, and all transmission, therefore, is human-to-human. Transmission may be by contact but is more probably by aerosolization and inhalation. Nasal secretions are infectious before eruption of the rash, and most transmission is probably acquired by their aerosolization. The lesions themselves remain infectious until the scabs are spontaneously desquamated, but transmission via inanimate sources is probably uncommon. Placental transmission also occurs. Experimentally it has been shown that the scabs may be infectious for long periods whose duration is affected by temperature and humidity (Meers, 1985). The virus has been demonstrated by electron microscopy in the lesions of an exhumed body after 100 years of interment, but did not grow on chick embryo membrane (el-Mallakh, 1985). While Meers (1985) found viable virus in variola scabs stored in envelopes for as long as 13 years, Zuckerman (1984) recovered the virus in only 4 of 45 scabs stored for 9 months. Concern about the contagiousness of possible smallpox-infected human tissue in a British excavation led to excavation precautions, but no such disease was identified (Anonymous, 1985; Dixon, 1985; Waldron, 1993). Nevertheless, it appears wise to respect the ability of this virus to survive some specialized postmortem conditions for a long (presently undefined) time, and the clothing of infected persons needs to be treated appropriately.

Understanding of smallpox's epidemic patterns rests on the recognition that humans are the only reservoir of the disease and that such human infections result in either the patient's (and the accompanying virus') death or lifelong immunity to the disease (also resulting in death of the virus within that individual). Accordingly, all members of an isolated group never previously exposed will be susceptible to infection and most will contract the disease. Several months later the survivors will be immune. Thus, unless nonimmune individuals are introduced into the group before the last victim's lesions heal, the infection will not be sustained within that group. Smallpox will not reappear in that group until nonimmune members are added to the group either by birth or from exogenous sources and are exposed to a newly infected person. Continuous endemic infection thus will only occur in groups large enough to provide the appropriate circumstances for the virus to escape perpetually from an infected individual into a susceptible one within the few weeks of the disease. In rural areas exposure can only occur through contact with a larger population that is serving as endemic host to the disease, and thus that probability becomes a function of human mobility and sociocultural intercourse.

All ages are susceptible. However, in large populations among whom smallpox is endemic (such as were common in the cities of seventeenth century Europe) ordinary social exposure to infected persons is often unavoidable during childhood. In such groups smallpox became largely a disease of children, described picturesquely by Crosby (1993b) as 'Trial by smallpox was a prerequisite for adulthood for all but a small minority.' On the other hand, European introduction of smallpox to Hispaniola in the West Indies in 1518 found the entire island's native population susceptible, and virtually everyone, regardless of age, contracted the disease.

Natural history

Pathogenesis

After the virus has been introduced into the body, commonly by inhalation, the organism enters a stage of amplification,

probably within bronchiolar and regional lymph node cells followed by viremia and further multiplication within tissue reticuloendothelial cells during an interval of about 10 days called the 'incubation period.' Large quantities of virus are then released into the blood stream (viremia) to the accompaniment of fever, chills, muscle pain and often headache. This prodromal period lasts only a few days after which the skin lesions appear. Their appearance evolves over several days, but most of the lesions within an area of eruption occur within a short time. Indeed, the fact that most of the lesions in local areas are in the same stage of development is an observation useful for excluding the diagnosis of chickenpox (varicella) with which smallpox can be confused.

Skin eruption

The lesions involve all parts of the body (Fig. 7.64). On mucosal surfaces they are usually simple ulcerations but on epidermal surfaces they initially present as dry, raised, nonulcerated papules. Their distribution excludes few areas but often initiates on the face and the distal portions of the arms and legs. Commonly most of the body surface becomes involved eventually to some degree. Necrosis of epidermal cells within the Malpighian layer and skin appendage cells results in central liquefaction within the lesion. The lesions' roof is thinned to the point where the liquid content within the lesion becomes visible, at which point the lesion is called a 'vesicle.' Many vesicles ulcerate. Sloughing of the necrotic

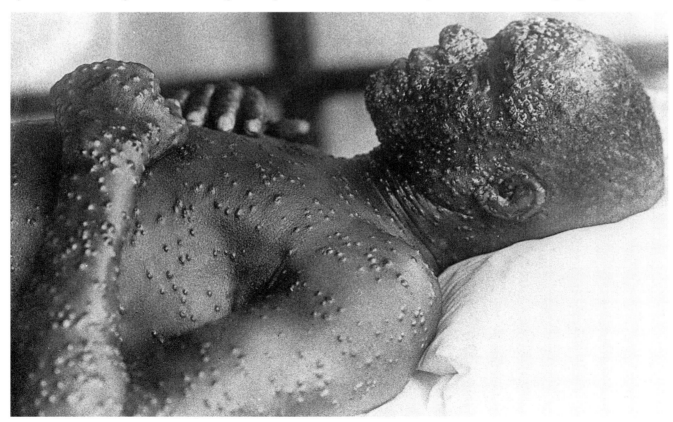

FIG. 7.64: **Smallpox.** The body of this modern adult male is covered with the characteristic vesiculations of smallpox. Courtesy P. Sledzik. NMHM.

epithelial cells into the lesion's fluid clouds the previously clear fluid of the vesicle, then termed a 'pustule' (even though the white, cloudy material is not pus). In the most severe form of the disease the lesion's blood vessels are injured sufficiently to leak red blood cells ('hemorrhagic smallpox'). In uncomplicated cases the vesicle's fluid is gradually resorbed. The vesicle collapses and the cells composing its roof dry, producing a crust or 'scab.' The deeper surface of the lesion extends into the lower dermis. Healing by fibrosis results in a pitted scar, sometimes darkened by inclusion of blood pigment. If the lesion becomes infected secondarily by bacteria, the involvement may be much deeper, resulting in an even more contracted scar.

During the vesicular stage the patient's fever, which usually subsides at the end of the prodromal stage, often recurs. In patients dying during the exanthematous (rash) stage autopsies commonly reveal foci of lymphocytic cells in many different organs, including the central nervous system (Councilman *et al.*, 1904; Bras, 1952). The degree of tissue destruction in such foci is often not great, but Chiari (1886) has described histologic evidence of frank necrosis in testicular lesions. They do suggest, however, that the variety of lesser, nondermal symptoms have an organic basis and probably reflect at least transiently dysfunctional focal areas of involvement of these organs.

Severity

The severity of the disease varies significantly from patient to patient, even in variola major. It will obviously be influenced by previous vaccination, but other, undefined factors also play a role. The virus that produces the mild form of the disease we call variola minor (alastrim) is believed to be a distinct strain because persons contracting smallpox from a patient with variola minor rarely have a severe form of the disease. At the other extreme is a disease so fulminant that all symptoms are exaggerated and the patient may die in a febrile state within a few days even before the rash appears. Such patients often die of diffuse hemorrhage or marrow aplasia (nonproductive state) complications. Shock, dehydration and secondary bacterial infections with pneumonia and/or septicemia as well as viral encephalitis are often lethal complications. Ocular and testicular involvement occurs but is less common.

Diagnosis

Diagnosis can often be made on a clinical basis during an epidemic. In sporadic cases the virus can be recovered from vesicle fluid by growing it on chick embryo allantoic membrane or demonstrating it morphologically in biopsy material. Conventional microscopy reveals an intracytoplasmic eosinophilic (red-staining) inclusion body surrounded by a clear halo ('Guarneri body') within affected, reactive squamous epidermal cells (Strano, 1976). Immunofluorescent antibody staining can often be employed to reveal the presence of the virus. Alternatively, electron microscopy can detect the typical envelope structure of the virus itself. Differential diagnosis includes chickenpox and meningococcemia (blood stream infection by the meningitis bacillus). In the former the lesions appear more abruptly (hours instead of several days as smallpox does), the lesions are in different stages of development, and the prodromal stage is shorter or even absent. The fulminant form of smallpox may develop a form of disseminated intravascular coagulation (a form of clotting within blood vessels that impairs further clotting) that results in diffuse hemorrhage similar to that seen in meningococcemia or other hemorrhagic febrile illnesses.

Prevention

Vaccination with the virus of a related species, vaccinia virus, provides complete immunity for several years with subsequent decline of resistance of the disease over about a decade. In susceptible, exposed individuals gamma globulin and methisazone may be employed in addition, but their value is controversial.

Eradication

Among infectious diseases smallpox is unique. Only humans are susceptible to infection, eliminating the concerns over animal reservoirs. Furthermore, there are no carriers; i.e. all infected persons have recognizable symptoms or signs. This led the World Health Organization (W.H.O.) to suggest in 1958 that it may be possible to eradicate this disease completely. By 1966 funds were specified for such an effort and the following year an eradication unit began its work. It was not an easy task. There were numerous skeptics within the W.H.O. itself. Much vaccine was donated by various countries but not all met quality standards. Insufficient supplies were common initially and there were priority conflicts on the part of some countries. In spite of all these problems, North and South America were variola-free by 1971, Indonesia by 1972, Asia, East and South Africa by 1975. The last person on earth to suffer a natural infection from smallpox was a 23 year old Somalian native (Ali Maow Maalin) in 1977 (Anonymous, 1980), dramatically fulfilling Edward Jenner's 1801 prediction (cited in Crosby, 1993b) concerning his recently reported discovery of vaccination: 'The annihilation of the smallpox – the most dreadful scourge of the human species – must be the final result of this practice.'

Globally, laboratories in six countries continued to maintain smallpox, but four of these have now been closed. The virus today is kept under heavy security in only two, specially designed laboratories in the U.S.A. and Russia. Laboratory accidents can occur, and one of these caused two deaths in England. A year after eradication had been accomplished the virus escaped through a laboratory ventilation duct from a Birmingham (England) laboratory, infecting and killing a young adult woman working in the floor above it; her mother also contracted the disease but survived. In both cases, however, strict quarantine contained further spread (Breman & Arita, 1980). Continued surveillance during the subsequent years has detected no subsequent case, though enough vaccine is stored to vaccinate 200 million people. Both countries have now agreed to destroy the last of these living smallpox viruses and it is expected this will take place before this volume goes to press.

Variola and vaccinia viruses are of such differing DNA structure that one would not expect vaccinia virus to evolve into variola. Other pox viruses include monkeypox, found in laboratory monkeys in 1958, but this has never been identified in feral monkeys. In 1970 a human case of monkeypox infection was identified and between 1970 and 1985 surveillance has detected 150 such cases, all in West and Central Africa. The human-to-susceptible-human infection rate is about 10 %, much less than smallpox. The disease is also milder with a case fatality rate of only 16 % (Nakano, 1985). The same vaccination for smallpox also protects against monkeypox. Cowpox is a disease of cows producing a mild pox disease in humans. Milker's nodule is also a cow disease producing a vesicle localized to the hand of a milker. Whitepox is a virus indistinguishable from variola reported in monkeys and rodents in Zaire but, because the laboratory was also handling the variola virus, contamination has not been excluded (Breman & Arita, 1980). Tanapox is a virus from the Tana River area in Zaire and has been found in two human cases (Nakano, 1985).

History and prehistory

Antiquity

For reasons given above, it is clear that smallpox can only be perpetuated in large, densely populated concentrations of humans such as are found in large cities. Hence, its antiquity cannot be older than the Neolithic period. However, there are few documents in the pre-Christian era containing descriptions sufficiently specific to be diagnostic of smallpox. A Chinese alchemist, Ko Hung, in about the third or fourth century A.D., described a skin eruptive disease suggestive but not diagnostic of variola that included a body-wide, pustular exanthema that 'looked like burns covered with white starch' (Lyons & Petrucelli, 1987:124) in which the majority died if not treated and the survivors bore deep scars. However, erysipelas and several other diseases could fit that description. Henschen (1966) cites Roman descriptions of smallpox in 'modern' Egypt from about the sixth century; if these really were smallpox, the 'sweep of Islam' through North Africa may have brought variola into Italy by the seventh century and into Spain by the eighth. Crosby (1993b), however, feels that the initial unequivocal documentation of smallpox was written by a ninth century Baghdad physician named Rhazes, *The Treatise on Smallpox and Measles*, in which the author differentiated these two conditions so clearly that there can be no doubt about the specificity of the diagnoses. Variola had reached Denmark by the thirteenth century, Iceland the fourteenth and Greenland the seventeenth. He also points out that prior to A.D. 1500 smallpox in Europe never achieved the prominence that plague did.

Smallpox during the historical period

The sixteenth century was a watershed for many cultural and biological features of western people and smallpox was no exception. Factors contributing to increased mobility are probably responsible for the rapid spread of this disease during the several centuries following A.D. 1500. Crosby (1993b) also noted that the immunity enjoyed by the previously exposed Russians and Dutch was an asset during their actions in Siberia and South Africa while the lack of it acted as an additional burden to isolated populations like the Mongols. It is in the New World, however, that we have enough data to appreciate the complex interactions between the biological features of the disease and the cultural characteristics of the populations. It is clear now that smallpox was absent from pre-Columbian New World populations. It had arrived in the West Indian island of Hispaniola by December, 1518 and virtually extinguished its aboriginal Taino population during the subsequent 25 years (Cook, 1992). An infected Negro on Panfilo de Narváez' ship may have transferred smallpox either to one of Hernan Cortés' soldiers during their clash or directly to local natives in 1520; alternatively, smallpox may have preceded Cortés into Mexico *via* Yucatan (Crosby, 1967). In the 1520s it was involving Veracruz natives and rapidly extended to the Aztecs in Tenochtitlan (modern Mexico City) where probably half of the Aztec population died (Diamond, 1990). Indeed, based on tax returns, Borah & Cook (1963:88) estimated the pre-Columbian population of Central Mexico at 25.2 million, declining to 16.8 million a decade after contact with Cortés and falling further to 2.5 million (a total of 90 % population reduction) by 1608, much of it the result of smallpox epidemics (Russell, 1983:222).

At this point readers need to be reminded of the imprecision of pre-Columbian Native American population estimates. Very few regions provide the kind of tribute records that Borah & Cook (1963) used so meticulously and skillfully to arrive at the Central Mexico estimates. Epidemic population mortality rates are calculated from pre- and post-epidemic population estimates. In many examples cited below, pre-epidemic estimates are pre-Conquest values. Because actual census data are available often only decades after Spanish contact, pre-Conquest estimates must be reconstructed for many areas from numerous different observations using multiple assumptions. Errors inherent within each assumption can generate a substantial, cumulative potential error for an estimate. Population epidemic mortality rates can be expected to be greatest during the initial infections of a nonimmune population. Yet it is precisely that exposure that is most apt to escape historical documentation, especially since a disease as highly infectious as smallpox may precede actual physical contact between the aboriginal and the Spaniard, the epidemic thus proceeding unwitnessed by the latter's chroniclers. Current estimates for North American pre-Columbian populations can differ by as much as tenfold (Cook, 1992; Crosby, 1992). Estimates of population decline listed below are those most commonly cited but, for the reasons given, they vary significantly in their reliability.

Extension to the South American continent probably followed several routes. Exploration voyages along the coast of Veragua by Alonso de Ojeda in 1509 and Vasco Núñez de Balboa's finding of the Pacific Ocean in 1513 led quickly to settlement of Panama's isthmus and the exploration of the coast to the south by Pascual de Andagoya in 1514. Ferdinand Magellan stopped at Rio de la Plata (now Argentina) in 1520 before circumnavigating South America's southern tip. Francis Drake's crew was infected with a lethal disease (smallpox?) when he occupied Cartagena in 1585 and he had previously engaged in piratical action on South America's western coast beginning in 1577 (Cook, 1992). These and other sources may all have created infectious foci from which smallpox may have spread. What we do know is that the disease preceded European presence in Ecuador where the Inca leader Huayna Capa and his family are believed to have contracted the illness and died in 1524 or 1525 (Wood, 1979), leading eventually to the Incan civil war encountered by Francisco Pizarro in 1531. Spread of the disease southward, perhaps enhanced by the return of Huayna Capa's remains to the Peruvian Cuzco capital, must have contributed to the success of Pizarro's conquest (Cook, 1992). Dobyns (1963) describes recurrent, massive epidemics between 1520 and 1600 in the Andean area, many of which were principally smallpox, with devastating effects. If his pre-Conquest population estimates are accurate, the Andean area suffered 90 % population depletion. Crosby (1992), however, cautions against universal extrapolation of such high mortalities, noting the very significant, documented variation of population responses to their encounter with new European pathogens.

Aldin & Miller (1987) also document the Portuguese contribution to the problem on South America's eastern coast. By 1560 a smallpox epidemic in the Rio de la Plata region killed 100 000 natives and in 1562 a ship from Lisbon imported the disease into Bahia (as others had before it), but which then spread southward via the Jesuit missions producing a smallpox pandemic. For several decades thereafter no major new outbreaks occurred, probably more due to the immunity that surviving natives had acquired than to absence of imported infected persons. During the seventeenth and eighteenth centuries, however, recurrent epidemics occurred leading to the pandemic of the late eighteenth century. After 1560 the disease was imported largely as a result of the African slave trade. Indeed, Aldin & Miller (1987) were able to correlate Brazilian outbreaks of smallpox with droughts in Angola (the principal source of the Portuguese slaves), because such droughts forced Angolan natives to concentrate

in the cities having water sources. The density of those urban populations led to their infection by smallpox and their presence there resulted in their capture by slavers.

Probably the best-documented North American smallpox epidemic occurred in the Missouri River valley in 1837–1838. As described by Trimble (1992), a crew member of the steamboat 'St. Peters' developed smallpox after the boat left to supply various forts upstream. The infection spread to passengers who disembarked at the various forts being resupplied, all the way to the northern part of the valley. Each of these became a focus for a new epidemic. At the two northern forts the case fatality rate was high: 50–66 % among the Assiniboine and Blackfeet near Ft. Union and 50 % for the Arikara and Hidatsi near Ft. Clark. The Mandan group suffered a case fatality rate of 88 %. The more southern groups experienced lesser rates, principally because an 1831 epidemic had been followed by a partially completed vaccination program. About 17 000 natives are estimated to have died in this disaster.

Less than 30 years later a smallpox epidemic was initiated on the northwest coast when a ship from San Francisco unloaded an infected passenger at Victoria. When the infection spread to Indians camped at the city's periphery, local authorities did not quarantine them but expelled them. The Indians returned to their homelands, spreading the disease as they scattered through the Queen Charlotte Islands and mainland coast, triggering an epidemic involving Haidas, Tlingits, Tsimshians and Kwakiutls that had a case fatality rate approaching 80 % (Boyd, 1992).

By 1789 English settlers had also carried the disease to Australia where its effects on the aborigines were equally catastrophic (Crosby, 1993b).

Severity

Case fatality rates of 25–50% characterize many of the described epidemics. While such rates are high enough to cause profound changes in any population's activities, it must be emphasized that they are no different from those suffered by contemporary European victims of the disease. Furthermore, smallpox was the cause of death in 13 % of deaths in the New England colonies (Robins, 1981). Differences in the impact on native and European populations were due not to differences in case fatality rates of those who became ill, but in the fraction of each population that was susceptible to infection (i.e. not immune).

In addition to these, however, there are credible estimates of Native American case fatality rates of 80–90 % during smallpox epidemics. This is often ascribed to a general immunologic resistance deficit secondary to the absence of exposure during pre-Columbian times (which presumably would have removed those theoretical persons who were genetically uniquely susceptible to smallpox). Such a postulated, nonspecific, general immunological susceptibility, different from the specific immune response to the variola virus in survivors or in vaccinated persons, has never been demonstrated scientifically (Crosby, 1976), although Black (1992) has suggested that a virus may enhance its virulence by multiple passages through a more genetically homogeneous population like that of the New World. Native Americans respond to vaccination in exactly the same manner as do Europeans. The additional mortality suffered by native Australian and New World aborigines can be satisfactorily accounted for by the following: (i) the absence of *specific* immunity results in simultaneous illness of virtually all population members of all ages; (ii) this commonly results in collapse of the group's infrastructure leading to deaths from otherwise nonlethal complications like simple dehydration of young children; (iii) post-epidemic census errors secondary to population dispersion; (iv) despair and lack of population leadership amidst such chaos, and (v) weakened body defenses resulting from preceding or concurrent other imported European disease. Trimble (1992) also points out that nomadic groups may be less affected because they normally live in small, mobile, fairly self-sufficient groups that often react to an epidemic threat by dispersion. Sedentary populations, however, may be more susceptible because their population density enhances transmission of the disease, the simultaneous illness of all members impairs crop attention causing famine, they are more affected by the loss of specialists, they cannot readily flee the area and community breakdown is more disastrous because of their greater degree of interdependence.

History of smallpox prevention efforts

Variolation

This method uses the fluid removed from a skin vesicle of a person with active smallpox infection. Such fluid contains the variola virus. It is introduced into the skin of a nonimmune, susceptible person by placing a drop on the skin and applying multiple pinpricks to the skin underlying the drop (identical with the method of vaccination but using the vesicle fluid containing live smallpox virus). This induces permanent immunity. The Chinese blew powdered smallpox scabs into the nose of the person to be rendered immune (Prioreschi, 1991:56). In most persons variolation does not produce smallpox disease, although the biomedical explanation for this failure is unknown. In some persons a mild form of the disease occurs, but in a few a full-blown episode of smallpox develops with all its complications. The commonly observed 4 % death rate of variolation is still much less than that of the natural disease, and skilled application may reduce this to 1 % or less. Nevertheless, a lethal reaction is an inseparable hazard of variolation.

This procedure is of undetermined antiquity but commonly is believed to have originated in China about the eleventh century (Aldin & Miller, 1987) although that documentation is poor. From there it seems to have passed to the Near East.

Interestingly, the technique appears to have been more a part of the folk-healing tradition than one used by medical professionals. From Turkey it is thought to have been carried to England in 1718 by Lady Mary Wortley Montagu, wife of the British ambassador (though this is challenged without explanation by Lyons & Petrucelli, 1987:493). It reached the North American colonies through the influence of the Boston clergyman Cotton Mather, who learned of it from one of his slaves (Crosby, 1993b). In Europe variolation services during the fifteenth to sixteenth century were offered for sale and the practice became known as 'buying pox' (Henderson, 1976). Initially it was used only during epidemics, probably because its hazards at that time were perceived as a more desirable risk than those of the naturally acquired disease. Crosby (1993b) notes that the death of Louis XV by variola and the fact that Louis XVI underwent variolation enhanced its acceptance in Europe. It never, however, enjoyed the enthusiastic and widespread use as did later vaccination.

Vaccination

In 1796 the British physician Edward Jenner observed that milkmaids frequently developed cowpox, a mild skin disease, but rarely contracted smallpox. Suspecting that the infectious agent causing cowpox might transfer immunity to the much more serious illness smallpox, he vaccinated his son (and several others) with fluid from a vesicle in a patient with cowpox. Subsequent efforts to vaccinate them by the variolation method were unsuccessful, confirming his expectations. He published his results in 1798.

The timing of his finding could not have been better. Major epidemics were raging in South America as well as North America, Europe and Australia. Its effectiveness without the risks of variolation led to rapid acceptance. Application in 1803 to the problems of smallpox importation by the slave trade dramatically 'broke the relationship between African drought and Brazilian smallpox' (Aldin & Miller, 1987) and vaccination was soon used widely in North America as well, where some areas even made it compulsory during an epidemic (Lyons & Petrucelli, 1987:551, figure 890). In 1870 a smallpox epidemic during the Franco–Prussian war killed more than 23 000 French soldiers while the largely vaccinated German army lost less than 300 (Arita, 1980:24–5). There have been few medical observations that have had greater positive impact on human health and society than that of Edward Jenner's.

Eradication

The dramatic control of smallpox by the simple process of vaccination led to the concept of total eradication of this disease. That successful process is described in moderate detail in the Natural history section, above. Here we will comment on the nature of the immunizing virus. The medical term for the virus producing the immunizing effect of vaccination is vaccinia virus. When Jenner carried out his initial vaccination he used fluid from a skin vesicle of a cowpox-infected person, and thus he assumed that the infectious agent producing the immune effect was the agent producing cowpox. Twentieth century studies, however, have revealed that this agent, termed vaccinia virus, is different from either cowpox or variola viruses. It is now not clear whether the fluid Jenner used was contaminated with what we now call the vaccinia virus (which has not been found in nature) or whether it is a mutant, altered by continuous and endless passage (Crosby, 1993b). With the disappearance of smallpox as a disease, we probably shall never know.

Tissue lesions of smallpox in ancient human remains

Soft tissues

The much-cited skin lesions on the mummified body of the Egyptian Pharaoh Ramses V are disappointing. Their gross appearance is consistent with smallpox but also with a variety of other vesicular skin conditions, or even postmortem artifact. Efforts to identify the virus by electron microscopy of skin scrapings from this body failed (Hopkins, 1980), as did a radioimmunoassay (Lewin, 1984). Since the specimen collection for those studies was far from ideal, our current knowledge about Ramses' lesions is such that it adds nothing to our search for variola's antiquity. The twentieth dynasty Egyptian mummy described by Ruffer & Ferguson (1911) had lesions grossly suggestive of smallpox, but his histological study demonstrated large numbers of bacilli in the lesions. Ruffer seems to have felt that this person suffered antemortem, terminal septicemia with postmortem bacterial proliferation (a not uncommon event in lethal smallpox cases), but that this did not exclude smallpox. Moodie (1923b:395-6), however, appears to suggest that the lesions themselves could be a postmortem product by gas formation of the proliferating bacteria. The issue remains unresolved. While smallpox in ancient Egypt remains unsubstantiated, Fornaciari & Marchetti (1986) have presented a convincing case of a sixteenth century mummified child in Italy in which not only was the virus visualized by electron microscopy, but it also demonstrated appropriate immunoreactivity. The rash pictured on the face of an eighteenth century priest whose preserved body was found entombed in the Mexico City church Iglesia del Carmen (Allison & Gertzen, 1989) certainly has the morphologic appearance of smallpox, but we could not find reports that the diagnosis has been pursued by laboratory methods.

Skeletal lesions of smallpox

We agree with Aegerter & Kirkpatrick (1975) that virus-induced bone infection is extremely rare. Other than rubella,

most of the few accounts of bone infection of viral origin are due to complicated smallpox. In smallpox epidemics, 2–5 % of children and adolescents develop osteomyelitis and arthritis variolosa 2–3 weeks after the skin lesions appear (Putschar, 1976; Zimmerman & Kelley, 1982:109). Skeletal involvement is not seen in adults (Ortner & Putschar, 1985). The lesions are restricted to the limb bones and they frequently are bilateral and multifocal. The proximal radius and ulna and distal humerus are the most common sites of skeletal lesions. Eighty % of the patients show articular infection in the elbow and this is an important datum in the differential diagnosis of osteomyelitis. The next most frequently involved skeletal elements are the bones of the ankle and foot. Shoulder, knee, hip and the small joints of the hand and wrist can be involved. Ribs, spine, pelvis and cranium are usually spared in smallpox osteomyelitis (Ortner & Putschar, 1985). Very commonly, osseous and articular changes coexist. The lesion usually starts in the metaphysis near the growth plate and often spreads to the adjacent joint (Ortner & Putschar, 1985). Smallpox infection in bone is characterized by juxtametaphyseal destruction of the skeletal tissue (resembling the pattern of pyogenic osteomyelitis), periostitis and articular involvement (Resnick & Niwayama, 1989a). Although involucrum formation can be quite marked, diaphyseal sequestra are uncommon (Putschar, 1976). A common characteristic of this disease is the complete detachment and displacement of the epiphysis. In severe cases, pathological fractures can occur. The bone changes in smallpox tend to disappear after several months to 1 year (Steere & Malawista, 1989), although growth retardation, bone or fibrous ankylosis, subluxation and secondary degenerative joint disease commonly develop (Resnick & Niwayama, 1989a, b).

Differential diagnosis

Resnick and Niwayama (1989a, b) point out that, although radiographic findings in smallpox simulate those of pyogenic infection, certain differences can be seen in smallpox: changes are symmetrical, their elbow predilection, extension into epiphyses with their destruction and the long bone extensive diaphyseal osteoperiostitis.

MEASLES (MORBILLI; NINE DAYS MEASLES; HARD MEASLES; RED MEASLES; SARAMPIÓN)

Definition, taxonomy, and epidemiology

Measles is an acute infectious disease of viral origin, highly contagious, and epidemic during the winter and the spring, that usually affects children under 5 years of age (50 % of the cases). The virus responsible for measles is a paramyxovirus of the genus *Morbillivirus* (family Paramyxoviridae) that spreads through microscopic respiratory droplets in the prodromic or early eruptive phases of the disease. It is a spherical RNA virus, with a size fluctuating between 125 and 250 nm, that can survive drying in droplets.

Humans are the only reservoir of the virus responsible for measles. The form of transmission is via respiratory droplets and, very uncommonly, by contact with contaminated objects. Except for varicella (chickenpox) measles is the most easily transmissible disease we know. The incubation period is about 10 days (8–13) following contact until the beginning of the clinical picture with the onset of fever, and 14 days until the rash appears. The transmission period begins a few days before the prodrome and lasts until 4 days after the rash.

Measles is universal and almost all people are susceptible, unless they have been vaccinated or have suffered the disease. The expected morbidity may be estimated as 100 % and the expected mortality between 10–25 % without proper treatment (Ramenofsky, 1987). The disease results in permanent immunity among the survivors. It had been suspected that American Indians lacked genetic resistance to measles because of the devastation brought about by the disease among those populations when the Europeans arrived in the Americas. However, it has been demonstrated that social disorganization contributed significantly to the high mortality caused by measles among Native Americans (Way, 1981). When the disease attacks isolated populations without previous contact with it, it affects all age groups and the attack rate and mortality increase substantially. Kim-Farley (1993) reports two clear examples: in 1848, 40 000 of a population of 150 000 people died in Hawaii; and, in 1874, Fiji lost 20–25 % of its people. Such kinds of epidemics produce complete collapse of community life functions with almost everyone acutely ill simultaneously (Garruto, 1981). Measles has a winter–spring seasonality in temperate climates and hot–dry seasonality in equatorial areas (Kim-Farley, 1993).

Measles is an endemic disease of children in the large urban populations, and epidemic at intervals of 2 to 4–5 years (Verger Garau, 1983; Benenson, 1984). Measles precipitates malnutrition, since it is a disease that in developing countries appears during the first 3 years of life, a period in which the children are at nutritional risk. In those countries, measles may show a mortality 300–400 times as great as in a well-nourished population (McKeown, 1988).

Natural history

Measles is a disease with a peak incidence between 5–9 years of age, being uncommon during adolescence and very rarely found in adulthood. In the less-developed countries the disease occurs earlier in life (children under 5 years of age) and almost all children are involved (Verger Garau, 1983). The prodromic period has a length of 2 days and is characterized by catarrhal symptoms in the eyes, nose and respiratory tract, fever (40 °C), and Koplik's spots on the buccal mucosa (area of first and second molars). These are small, bluish-white spots surrounded by a red areola that are pathognomonic of the disease. Two to four days after the emergence of the fever, Koplik's spots disappear and the rash appears behind the ears and/or on the forehead, spreading by the face, neck and thorax and then to the rest of the body in 2–3 days. Without complications, the disease has a short course of 7–10 days between the prodromic period until the resolution of the rash and fever.

Complications

The complications of measles appear as a result of viral replication or bacterial superinfection: otitis media, laryngitis, sinusitis, pneumonia (especially in infants) and encephalitis. Encephalitis is a complication uncommonly seen today (0.5–1 in 500 to 1000 cases), but it is very dangerous, usually appearing 2 days to 3 weeks after the rash. Mortality rate is very high in this complication and many survivors are handicapped by neurological sequelae. A defective form (devoid of the protein coat) of the measles virus is also associated with the delayed complication of subacute sclerosing panencephalitis of Dawson. This is seen in children and adolescents months or years after a measles attack. This kind of encephalitis produces intellectual damage, convulsions, and may be lethal. This is the only situation in which measles virus is latent and able to be reactivated (Garruto, 1981). In the developing and underdeveloped countries, diarrhea is one of the most important causes of measles-associated death.

History

Although the origin of measles remains unknown, measles virus is a new organism that probably is related to rinderpest and/or canine distemper (McKeown, 1988). Measles spreads among urban populations as a wave with the crests appearing at intervals of 2 years. This kind of spread requires a concentration of a minimum of 5000 to 45 000 susceptible people per year in order to maintain the disease. In an isolated population (whose demographic maintenance depends entirely on its own new births) a minimum of 30 000–50 000 people would be required. With a number less than this it is impossible for the virus to survive. Probably no other infectious disease requires so large a number of people for its perpetuation. Therefore, this kind of contagion was probably impossible before about 3000–2500 B.C. and its origin must be associated with the growth of human populations in large communities (McNeill, 1984; McKeown, 1988; Cohen, 1989; Kim-Farley, 1993). Several factors are important to the size of population required by the disease

(Garruto, 1981):

1. Measles virus has no reservoir other than humans.
2. Measles produces lifelong immunity and, therefore, the virus needs a continuous supply of new susceptibles persons.
3. It has an infectious acute stage of only several days.
4. Measles virus is not latent and able to be reactivated (with the exception of the cerebral complication known as sub-acute sclerosing panencephalitis).

All data suggest that measles was present among the Mediterranean populations during the second and third centuries A.D., with devastating epidemics (specially those of 165–180 and 251–266: McNeill, 1984; Kim-Farley, 1993). Measles arrived in China between the first and seventh centuries, and it was not until the sixteenth century when the disease appeared in the Americas (1530–1531) with its catastrophic effects on the native population there (Ramenofsky, 1987). One of the last points where measles arrived on this planet was New Zealand, in 1854, killing 4000 people (Crosby, 1986).

However, it was not until the sixteenth century that measles was clearly recognized as an independent disease. Prior to that century it was confused with smallpox, with the exception of the descriptions made by the Persian physician Rhazes in A.D. 910 and Avicenna, or Ibn-Sina, one century later. According to Kim-Farley (1993), the first demonstration that measles is an infectious disease was made by Francis Home in 1759. Kim-Farley notes that Peter Panum, in 1846, demonstrated that the disease is transmitted by the respiratory tract and that the disease produces permanent immunity. He also confirmed the length of the incubation period. Fifty years later, Henry Koplik described the pathognomonic mucosal lesions that presently are known as Koplik's spots.

Paleopathology

Because of its large population size and density requirement, measles is certainly no older than Jericho and probably much younger. Unfortunately, it produces no unique, grossly recognizable skeletal or soft tissue lesion that can serve as a paleopathological 'marker' for the disease. If the virus really is a product of a relatively recent mutation then all humans exposed to it would have been susceptible to infection, generating epidemics in the densely populated areas. However, its symptoms and signs are not sufficiently distinctive to permit great diagnostic precision from historical descriptions. While vaccination programs coupled with excellent supportive medical care in developed countries have lulled many into viewing measles as a relatively benign disease, it is important to remember that the absence of these preventive and therapeutic measures during antiquity as well as other, nonmedical effects of 'virgin soil' epidemics in ancient times must have exacted mortality rates similar to that experienced in the New World

aborigines during the post-Columbian period. The demographic effects of such epidemics must have been formidable.

RUBELLA (GERMAN MEASLES; 3-DAY MEASLES)

Definition, taxonomy, geography, epidemiology, and natural history

Rubella is a common, acute, contagious disease caused by a virus (rubella virus) that usually affects children and young adults and is characterized by a benign rash and lymphadenitis. However, if the mother is infected in the first trimester of pregnancy it can lead to serious fetal abnormalities, prominent among which are major anatomic cardiac structural alterations. Rubella virus is included in the genus *Rubivirus*, family Togaviridae. Its diameter is 50–60 nm and contains a single-stranded RNA genome. Rubella is worldwide. In areas with no vaccination coverage, rubella is primarily an endemic disease of children with periodic epidemics, although a number of adults are susceptible (Kim-Farley, 1993). In isolated populations, a very important proportion of the population can be susceptible when the virus is introduced in them. It is more prevalent in the winter and spring months.

Humans are the only reservoir. Infection is produced by droplet spread, by air-borne transmission, or by direct contact with infected articles, blood, feces or urine (Benenson, 1984). Major epidemics occur occasionally. For example, in the U.S.A. the epidemics of 1935, 1943 and 1964 were widespread. It is important to recognize that rubella affects 1:1000 pregnant women in the years without epidemics, but the frequency increases to 20:1000 during the epidemics. The incubation period is 14–21 days. There is no sexual or racial predominance. Rubella has predilection for children, although in those places where the children are immunized, infection of adults is becoming the most commonly affected age group. Susceptibility is universal. Immunity is lasting, so that second attacks are rare.

Rubella was first described in 1619 by the German physician Daniel Sennert (who, with others wrote 'de morbis puerorum' – 'on the disease of children'; Laín Entralgo, 1963). However, it was not separated as a distinct disease until the decade of 1750s. The early interest in the disease by German physicians apparently led to the use of the term 'German measles,' although the Germans termed it 'röteln' (Kim-Farley, 1993). Then 125 years later, the Scottish physician Henry Veale (1866) proposed the term 'rubella,' and 15 years after that, during the International Congress of Medicine (held in London in 1881), a general consensus was reached that rubella was an independent entity (Kim-Farley, 1993). In 1938, the Japanese workers Y. Hiro and S. Tasaka discovered that the disease is caused by a virus. Only three years later, the Australian N.M. Gregg demonstrated that congenital cataracts, along with other congenital abnormalities, appeared in the fetus following the infection of the mother with the rubella virus (Gregg, 1941). The rubella virus was finally isolated in 1962, independently, by T.H. Weller and F.A. Neva at Harvard University and Parkman et al. in the Walter Reed Army Institute (Washington, DC) (Kim-Farley, 1993). The first vaccine became available in 1969, and new vaccines have been introduced in medical practice since then.

Skeletal pathology

Intrauterine rubella infection

The importance of rubella lies in the fact that fetal abnormalities appear in 20–25 % of mothers infected with the rubella virus during the first 3 months of pregnancy (Papper, 1981). This may result in stillbirth (40 %), to delivery of a fetus with neurological defects or to congenital malformations (cataracts and other ocular abnormalities, deafness, congenital cardiovascular disease, microcephaly, neonatal jaundice, hepatosplenomegaly, retardation of growth that may lead to dwarfism, and osseous alterations). The probability of congenital malformations declines rapidly when maternal infection occurs after the third month of pregnancy (Robbins, 1975).

Skeletal changes occur in 35 % of cases and involve the metaphyses of the long bones, especially the distal femur and proximal tibia and the long bones of the upper limb. Ribs, vertebrae and skull may be also affected. The mechanism of production of the skeletal abnormalities is not completely understood and may be due to metabolic or nutritional disturbances, or a viral inflammatory process. The most characteristic radiological lesions in rubella are seen in the metaphyses of the distal femur and proximal tibia. These show poor mineralization and coarsening of the trabecular pattern, with longitudinal streaks of alternating sclerosis and lucency, or even a transverse broad band of lucency (Aegerter & Kirkpatrick, 1975; Ortner & Putschar, 1985). These lucent osteopenic regions are subject to pathological fractures (Murray et al., 1990). The diaphyses are not involved. Periostitis is absent. The skull may show enlargement of the anterior fontanel and poor mineralization. The bone changes disappear at about 2–3 months of age (if the infant survives) without leaving residual irregularities, with the exception of thickening of the zone of provisional calcification.

Postnatal rubella infection

This is of little interest for paleopathologists because skeletal manifestations are very uncommon. In general, there are arthritic changes in the small bones of the hand and wrist, knee, and ankle (Resnick & Niwayama, 1989a, b).

INFLUENZA (FLU; GRIP; GRIPPE; GRIPE)

Definition, taxonomy, and epidemiology

Influenza is an acute and very contagious infectious disease of the respiratory tract, produced by viruses, and characterized by fever, chills, headache, runny nose, myalgia and generalized pain in joints, prostration, weakness, coryza, and mild pharyngitis. This is the most common of human viral diseases. Today the mortality is usually low. Influenza is caused by several antigenically different strains of influenza virus: A, B, and C. The A and B types are associated with epidemics while the C type has been found only in sporadic cases. The three types may be identified by complement fixation and neutralization tests. The influenza viruses are spheroidal RNA viruses of medium size (80–120 nm). They can be included within the family of Orthomyxoviridae, in the genus Influenzavirus (Pumarola, 1983).

The type A influenza virus is described by geographical origin, number of the type and year of isolation, and the index that identifies the character of the associated hemagglutinin (HA) and neuraminidase (NA). At irregular intervals, averaging about 10 years, new subtypes appear that are completely different due to major changes in the genome (antigenic shift); these may cause pandemics. The most important pandemics of influenza in the last century have been those of 1889, 1900 and 1918. The latter was the most severe pandemic in the recent history of humankind; more than 20 000 000 died. Also severe was that of 1957 that began in northern China and spread rapidly throughout the world, and the 1968 pandemic that began in Hong-Kong. The interpandemic epidemics are due, at least in part, to minor antigenic changes (antigenic drift) in a very limited part of the genome (Pumarola, 1983; Benenson, 1984). Examples of these minor changes are the epidemics Hong-Kong (1971), England (1972), Port-Chalmers (1973), Scotland (1974), Victoria (1975), Texas (1977), and Bangkok (1979).

Garruto (1981) suggests that influenza represents an example of a disease of very important medical significance when introduced into isolated populations without prior exposure. It is associated with high morbidity and mortality in these populations, as well as a short contagious period, producing profound short-term effects (McKeown, 1988; Cohen, 1989). Humans are the reservoir of the type A human influenzal infections, although it is suspected that mammals, such as pigs or horses and several species of birds, may constitute sources of new human subtypes. Transmission occurs by inhalation of airborne virus containing the microscopic droplets exchanged between persons in limited spaces. The incubation period is 24–72 hours, and the transmission period is probably no more than 3 days after the debut of the clinical symptoms. Susceptibility is universal and the infection confers immunity specific to the type of virus causing the disease. Infection with related viruses increases the immunity base (Benenson, 1984). The mortality rate is usually low, (1 % or less) being a real threat to life for only the very young, the immunosuppressed and the elderly (Crosby, 1993a). However, this disease, when combined with pneumonia, was one of the ten leading causes of death in the U.S.A. in the 1980s (Crosby, 1986).

The attack rates during the epidemics fluctuate between 15 and 25 % in large populations and 40 % or more in small populations. In the U.S.A. influenza type A appears at intervals of 1–3 years, while influenza type B appears at greater intervals, 4–6 or more years. In temperate countries the epidemics are more commonly found in the winter, while in the tropics they have no seasonal relationship.

Natural history

Influenza shows a peak incidence in children and the incidence decreases with age (although there are other peaks in older people). Benenson (1984) affirms that during the epidemics of 1978 and 1978–1979 (influenza H1N1, Russian) the incidence was high in people under 25 years of age, while the people older than that group were immune. The clinical debut is very abrupt with general symptoms such as chills, fever, headache, myalgia, fatigue, and respiratory symptoms including cough, substernal and throat pain, and rhinitis. Healing occurs after 2–5 days, although fatigue may continue for several weeks. Influenza is characterized by acute inflammation of a catarrhal type affecting the air passages, sometimes with necrosis and desquamation of the lining cells (Strong, 1981). In some cases interstitial pneumonitis may be present, and bacterial pneumonia may be a complication. In neither human nor experimental influenza have inclusion bodies been demonstrated (Strong, 1981). Localized alveolar or interstitial emphysema may be present.

Complications

In severe cases, hemorrhagic bronchitis and pneumonia can occur within a few hours or days. Influenzal pneumonia is rare, but it runs a rapid course and is often fatal (Crosby, 1993a). Bacterial pneumonia (caused by pneumococci, streptococci, and *Haemophilus influenzae* in young people, and by pneumococci, staphylococci, and *Klebsiella pneumoniae* in older patients) is another important and common complication of influenza, especially in epidemics, and can be fatal. The most dangerous is that produced by staphylococci (Knight, 1981). With proper, modern treatment mortality is low. Other common complications of influenza are sinusitis, otitis, and bronchitis.

According to Crosby (1993a) and Ravenholt (1993), a serious complication of influenza is that of encephalitis lethargica. There is evidence that the global pandemic of encephalitis lethargica of the 1920s had its origin in the great influenza

pandemic of 1918–1919 (Crosby, 1993a). Epidemics of encephalitis lethargica have occurred in conjunction with many influenza epidemics (1580, 1658, 1673–1675, 1711–1712, 1729, 1767, 1780–1782, 1830–1833, 1847–1848, 1889–1892) but the global pandemic of encephalitis accompanying and following the 1918–1919 influenza pandemic was unique with respect to virulence and sequelae (Ravenholt, 1993). It is clear now that encephalitis cases previously thought to have occurred independently of influenza usually were actually sequelae.

History

Although the origins of influenza remain unknown, it is a disease well known since antiquity, appearing as explosive epidemics and major pandemics affecting great populations. It was cited and described in the Hippocratic corpus (Pumarola, 1983). Between 1570 and 1920 at least 30 pandemics and a number of epidemics have been registered, although Pumarola (1983) feels that as many as 120 epidemics can be identified between the fourth century A.D. and 1918. However, clear evidence of the disease before the European Middle Ages is lacking, and no undeniable evidence is apparent until the transition between the Middle Ages and the Renaissance period of the fifteenth and sixteenth centuries (Crosby, 1993a). The frequency and severity of influenza increased after 1889 until the terrible pandemic of 1918 that killed millions of people (Knight, 1981). In 1933, W. Smith *et al.* isolated the influenza virus and reproduced the disease in animals. Both Francis (1940) and Magill (1940), during an influenza epidemic, discovered an antigenically different virus from that discovered in 1933. They called this new virus 'B' and labeled the virus previously discovered by Smith and collaborators as 'A.' Taylor isolated a new type of virus ('C') in 1949.

Based on historical sources, Rodríguez Martín (1994) recently described an important epidemic of influenza that killed more than 20 % (3000–4500 people) of the aboriginal Guanche population of Tenerife (Canary Islands). The Spanish conquerors in 1494 introduced the influenza virus into this isolated population whose members had no prior exposure to the disease. The Spaniards called this epidemic 'modorra' (meaning drowsy) due to the lethal coma that complicated the disease in many cases. It was influenza, but complicated with pneumonia and encephalitis lethargica. In the opinion of C.R.M., its very high mortality rate was due to the fact that it was a virgin soil epidemic (a new disease for the Guanches but not for the Spaniards).

It is useful to review some of the most important influenza epidemics among isolated populations during the last 130 years. In 1860, influenza swept the Waikato (New Zealand) affecting 50 % of the population (Crosby, 1986). In 1949, an epidemic of influenza among the North American Indians of the Canadian Northwest suffered an attack rate of 100 % with a mortality rate of 11.1 % (Ramenofsky, 1987). The natives of the Caroline Islands were affected by the 1966 epidemic with a 100 % attack rate and mortality rate of near 30 %. During the 1970s, the Kren-Akores of the Amazon basin, contacted for the first time by Europeans during those years, lost 15 % of the population in a brush with influenza (Crosby, 1986).

Impact of influenzal infections on ancient populations

Compared with the degree of modern social interchange between populations, examples of isolated populations can be expected to have been more common in antiquity. Introduction of the virus into such a population may well have produced a 'virgin soil' type of epidemic, such as occurred in the Canary Islands. The principal effect then, on ancient populations was probably a demographic one, in which mortality is commonly exaggerated by the collapse of community function secondary to the paralysis of social activities when nearly all members become seriously ill simultaneously. Current methods do not allow detection of the disease in the bodies of those who recover and die later of other causes, but pneumonia should be identifiable (though not the infectious agent) in the mummified remains of those who suffered this fatal complication.

POLIOMYELITIS

The poliovirus, classified as an enterovirus, produces only a mild clinical affliction in most humans. In a small fraction of infected persons it invades the central nervous system where it targets the lower motor neurons in the spinal cord with resulting paralysis of related muscles. It may affect any age, though the fatality rate is higher in adults (up to 25 %) than in children (usually less than 5 %). Death is commonly the result of respiratory muscle failure (Ray, 1991:714). Survivors suffer varying degrees of permanent neurological deficit and consequent muscle paralysis and atrophy ranging from mere weakness of a single muscle to a quadriplegic state. Recent reports suggest the possibility of virus latency following recovery with acute recurrence several decades later. Findings in archaeologically recovered skeletons can expect to demonstrate diffuse osteoporosis involving both cortical and cancellous bone in affected limbs as a result of disuse atrophy of bone secondary to the muscle paralysis (Sissons, 1976). In children underdevelopment and deformities, such as coxa valga or pes cavus, of the affected extremity bones frequently occur (Resnick, 1989b). Osteopenia in the debilitated bones may be severe enough to cause pathological fractures (Preiss, 1953). In developed countries this disease has almost been eliminated by vaccination programs.

We do not know the antiquity of poliomyelitis. While the diagnosis has been suggested in the Egyptian Pharaoh Siptah whose radiologic study has revealed a shortening of the right leg with associated soft tissue atrophy (Harris & Weeks, 1973) and also in an example of Egyptian art with apparent similar changes (Wyatt, 1993:947), these could have alternative explanations as orthopedic diseases. Mitchell (1900) has suggested poliomyelitis as an explanation of unilateral shortening of a femur in a largely skeletonized Egyptian mummy from about 700 B.C. In the historic period it can not be recognized with certainty in epidemic form prior to about the early nineteenth century.

MISCELLANEOUS VIRUS INFECTIONS

In addition to the diseases caused by viruses discussed in this section, the pneumonias caused by the viruses of rubeola and varicella, as well as the cytomegalovirus (CMV) and respiratory syncytial virus (RSV), are included in the Pneumonia section of Bacterial diseases, above.

FUNGAL INFECTIONS

INTRODUCTION

The study of fungal infections (mycoses) has gained remarkable impetus in the past decades, because these diseases are far more common than was previously thought (Shafer *et al.*, 1983). Fungal diseases may be produced in humans and animals by several routes. One type of mycosis is that of the cutaneous mycoses or dermatophytoses. These are superficial and usually not lethal. Skin trauma is an important route. With the exception of mycetoma, this leads to a localized lesion (subcutaneous mycosis) which heals without dissemination.

The systemic fungi invade the deep tissues and viscera and are acquired by inhalation of the fungal spores, causing a primary infection of the lungs. Later dissemination through the blood stream or lymphatic system occurs, with subsequent bone involvement (systemic mycoses). Almost all these fungi were first found in the New World (Shadomy, 1981). Revell (1986) thinks that systemic mycoses should not be regarded as exotic diseases at present, since it is the mobility of people and the widespread use of corticosteroid and cytotoxic forms of therapy that has made these diseases well known by the microbiologists, pathologists and practitioners. When fungi normally present in the environment infect humans as a complication of therapy, their pathogenicity is regarded as 'opportunistic' or 'iatrogenic' (Ainsworth, 1993a). These disease patterns could have been different in ancient and pre-modern therapy times.

The systemic mycoses are caused by soil-inhabiting, dimorphic or diphasic fungi (Howe, 1981). The free-living or saprophytic form is a filamentous mold whereas the pathogenic, tissue-invading form is unicellular and yeast-like. The exceptions to this are: *Candida albicans*, which is indigenous in man and, when invasive, forms mycelia and pseudomycelia; *Coccidioides immitis*, which produces sporangiospores in mammalian tissues; and *Cryptococcus neoformans*, which is a monomorphic yeast.

Bone infection is secondary to dissemination by the blood stream. It actually constitutes a very small percentage of bone infections. The exception to this is coccidioidomycosis in which bone often is a feature of generalized infection (Aegerter & Kirkpatrick, 1975). The spine, postcranial bones and joints may be affected by fungal infections (Bullough, 1992). Morphologically, the skeletal lesions are mainly lytic with little if any perifocal bone reaction, similar to those of neoplastic disease and tuberculosis. However, features distinctive to each agent are lacking and the individual lesions are not distinguishable from each other on X-ray or dry bone specimens. Hence, the geographical distribution becomes a key factor in the diagnosis of these infections (Turek, 1982; Ortner & Putschar, 1985; Murray et al., 1990). Multiple bone involvement is not uncommon and soft tissue abscesses, fistula formation, and extension of the lesion into adjacent joints are observed (Putschar, 1976). Some of these mycotic infections show marked predilection for the male sex, often the result of occupational exposure (Putschar, 1976; Reichs, 1986a).

HISTORY OF THE FUNGAL INFECTIONS

Fungi were the first pathogenic microorganisms to be recognized. In the late eighteenth century and the early nineteenth century, it had been proved that some diseases in animals and plants were caused by these pathogens. For a short period of time, fungi were blamed for causing many diseases (Ainsworth, 1993a, b). However, with the discovery that bacteria, and later viruses, were the most important organisms in causing human and animal diseases, fungi were neglected and it was only during the decade of the 1930s that mycology acquired its own role in medicine due to increasing knowledge of fungal identity, epidemiology, ecology and geographical distribution.

Mycetoma was the mycosis first described in the Indian vedic medical treatises (2000–1000 B.C.) as 'padaavalmika' (foot ant-hill), while the initial modern report is from southern India by members of the Indian Medical Service in the nineteenth century (Ainsworth, 1993a, b). After 13 years

of studies the English–Indian physician Henry Vandyke Carter coined the name 'mycetoma' in 1874. He suspected that the disease was of mycotic nature (Vilaplana, 1992), and submitted material from an infected focus to the British mycologist M.J. Berkeley who provided the description of the fungus. Today, more than 25 different fungi have been identified as responsible for this condition.

In addition to mycetoma and candidiasis or moniliasis (whose pathogen, *Candida albicans*, was discovered by the Hungarian physician David Gruby, in 1842), another of the early mycotic diseases to be reported was that of coccidioidomycosis, caused by the fungus *Coccidioides immitis*. The first case was described by the Argentinian physician Alejandro Posadas in 1892 (Ainsworth, 1993a). About the same time a case was also studied in California by Rixford & Gilchrist (1896, cited in Ainsworth, 1993a). Laín Entralgo (1963) says this report was also the first to describe another important fungal infection: North American blastomycosis, caused by *Blastomyces dermatidis*, that was also studied by G. Busse. These last two authors attributed the cause to a protozoan that they called *C. immitis* in 1896, but 9 years later, another American scientist, W. Opuls identified its mycotic nature. In the decade of 1930s, two Americans (M.A. Grifford & E. Dickson) established that 'San Joaquin Valley fever' (southern California) was, in reality, a mild form of coccidioidomycosis. *Coccidiodes immitis* was isolated from the soil and very soon it became clear that both animals and humans were infected by this soil-inhabiting fungus. Rodents, especially, were found to be a target for this disease by C.W. Emmons, who created one of the initial botanical classifications of the mycoses in 1934 (García Pérez, 1975).

Another systemic mycosis, histoplasmosis (caused by *Histoplasma capsulatum*) was first considered to be produced by a protozoan, but in this century it was demonstrated that, in reality, this is a mycotic disease that affects millions of people in the midwestern regions of the U.S.A. The term histoplasmosis was first introduced by S.T. Darling in 1908 (Vilaplana, 1992)

Sporotrichosis, caused by the fungus *Sporothrix schenckii*, was first described by the American pathologist and dermatologist Benjamin R. Schenck in 1898 in the U.S.A. (Laín Entralgo, 1963; Vilaplana, 1992). Subsequently many cases were reported from Europe, especially in France after the studies of C.L. de Beurmann and H. Gougerot (Ainsworth, 1993a). The largest outbreak of sporotrichosis ever recorded was in the Witwatersrand gold mines of South Africa during 1941–1943, when approximately 3000 miners became infected. This epidemic was controlled by the use of potassium iodate therapy and fungicide treatment of the mine timbers from which the infection was contracted.

Cryptococcosis was initially described in Europe in the year 1895 by the German physician Otto Busse, and 1 year later by other German dermatologist, Abraham Buschke. In 1946, L.B. Cox and J.C. Tolhurst, studying several Australian cases, termed the disease 'torulosis' and felt that the disease was caused by the fungus *Torula histolytica*.

In 1850, J.B. Fresenius proposed the term *Aspergillus fumigatus* for the pathogen of aspergillosis, based on an isolate from a bustard (*Otis tarda*). The classical examples of potentially fatal human pulmonary aspergillosis were those of French pigeon (squab) feeders in the decade of 1890, who chewed in their own mouths the grain used for fattening the birds (Ainsworth, 1993a).

Thus, the history of these infections is relatively short. The recognition of fungi as agents of human disease belongs to the late eighteenth century. Many of the now well-known fungal infections were identified during the nineteenth century and the development of laboratory methodology during the twentieth century enabled the creation of an orderly taxonomy.

SYSTEMIC MYCOSES

BLASTOMYCOSIS (NORTH AMERICAN BLASTOMYCOSIS; GILCHRIST'S DISEASE; FONSECA'S DISEASE; EXOASCOSIS)

Definition, taxonomy, and geographical distribution

Blastomycosis, or North American blastomycosis, is an uncommon, chronic, exogenous mycotic infection endemic to northeastern North America. It affects primarily the lungs due to the inhalation of the fungus *Blastomyces dermatididis* causing pulmonary granulomatous or suppurative lesions and can affect other organs and bones via blood dissemination. It is a spherical, yeast-like, budding fungus. This fungus appears in the lesions as large, ovoid to spherical, thick-walled organisms. *Blastomyces dermatididis* is thermally dimorphic; the tissue phase may be obtained *in vitro* by inoculation onto most laboratory media and by incubation of the culture at 36 °C. At 22 °C in soil or artificial media, the organism is filamentous (Howe, 1981). Cross-reactions between blastomycosis and histoplasmosis antigens can make interpretation of serological study results difficult.

It is possible that blastomycosis originated in Africa and may have been brought to America via the slave trade, because there is no evidence of the disease prior to that time (Shadomy, 1981). However, Buikstra (1977) suggests that exposure to *Blastomyces dermatididis* probably increased with the adoption of agriculture by the American Indians, and Kelley & Eisenberg (1987) report several possible pre-Columbian cases. The disease is found in the cooler parts of North America, mainly in the Ohio and Mississippi valleys (where an endemic focus lies in the boreal forest of northern Min-

nesota) and in the Middle Atlantic states. In North and South Carolina its incidence is also quite high, as well as in southern Manitoba, southwestern Ontario, and the Saint Lawrence River area. It is also found in some parts of Africa (Tunisia, Morocco, Congo, South Africa, Uganda, Rhodesia, Tanzania, and Malagasy Republic).

Epidemiology and natural history

The soil is the most probable reservoir of this fungus, but the source of infection in humans is unknown. At present, blastomycosis is becoming an important medical problem, particularly in the central U.S.A. Experimental transmission to animals is difficult, negating its use as an aid in the diagnosis of the disease (Shafer et al., 1983).

Recent epidemiological evidence suggests an association with bird hunting, whereby exposure to the animal and/or its excreta may be the vector of transmission (Molto, 1990). Zimmerman & Kelley (1982) suggest a puncture wound as an alternative method of transmission. The environment of northern Minnesota beaver houses has also been implicated. The incubation period fluctuates between a few weeks and several months. Unlike tuberculosis, which often favors subadults, blastomycosis is age progressive (20–50 years: Kelley, 1989; Molto, 1990).

Blastomycosis is about 10 times more common in males than in females. This may be because males are more exposed to soilborne fungi in their roles as farmers, as may have occurred in some ancient cultures of the Americas (Widmer & Perzigian, 1981) though in many prehistoric populations females worked on the land as much as or more than males.

There is no distinct racial predilection (Benenson, 1984). Little data about immunity to blastomycosis is available, although in some cases infection is asymptomatic, suggesting that humans are relatively resistant to the disease.

Skeletal pathology

The fungus induces a granulomatous infection in the lung that may lead to dissemination of the pathogen to other locations through the blood stream. The systemic disease is fatal in approximately 90 % of cases (Zimmerman & Kelley, 1982). In contrast to paracoccidioidomycosis, the mucocutaneous tissues and viscera are usually spared (Howe, 1981). When disseminated, blastomycosis may involve almost any organ of the body, but skeletal involvement can be as high as 50 % (Resnick & Niwayama, 1989a, b; Molto, 1990) and even reaches 75 % in some studies (Murphy, 1992). Vertebrae (especially the thoracic and lumbar regions), ribs, tibia, tarsus, and carpus are the prime foci of infection, though no part of the skeleton is immune. The lesions are more lytic than sclerotic (Casagrande & Frost,

1955; Putschar, 1976). The skull can be also affected. Involvement of the ribs is almost invariably extensive in patients with advanced pulmonary blastomycosis and it occurs by direct extension from the pleural cavity (Molto, 1990). Skeletal involvement also may occur as a result of direct spread from a soft tissue focus (Revell, 1986).

Postcranial bones

Necrosis, abscess and fistula formation are commonly found in skeletal blastomycosis. The lesion is mostly lytic with sharp borders and a punched-out appearance, though sometimes with sclerotic margins (Jaffe, 1972; Revell, 1986; Resnick & Niwayama, 1989a, b; Bullough, 1992). One or several bones may be involved and there may be periosteal reactive bone formation, although this last feature is not very common. In the long bones it is common to observe both osteoporosis and periostitis and the lesions often involve the metaphyses and diametaphyses though lesions may also be subchondral (Murray et al., 1990).

Joints

Joint involvement is not uncommon, particularly in the knee and ankle, and often is monoarticular. This complication is related to hematogenous dissemination of the infection in 70 % of the cases, and to extension from an adjacent osteomyelitis in the remainder (Messner, 1987). In these cases the destruction of the joint is very severe and subluxation is common. Extension from the infected foci to soft tissues is not uncommon (Resnick & Niwayama, 1989a, b).

Spine

When the spine is affected, the vertebral body is eroded anteriorly and the posterior elements show destruction, an observation useful for the differential diagnosis with tuberculosis, although blastomycosis involves the spine less commonly than does tuberculosis. While paravertebral abscess may occur, vertebral collapse is infrequent, unless the destruction is very extensive (Ortner & Putschar, 1985). Intervertebral disk space involvement, however, is common, especially in the thoracolumbar area (Resnick & Niwayama, 1989a, b).

The individual soft tissue lesions are indistinguishable from those of tuberculosis.

Radiology

Jaffe (1972) notes that in long bones the shafts may show large areas of radiolucency with thinning of the cortex, and small foci of radiolucency occur in the subchondral or metaphyseal–epiphyseal areas. Other radiographic signs include osteoporosis and periostitis (Murray et al., 1990). The anterior portion of the vertebral bodies may show erosion.

Paleopathology

Kelley & Eisenberg (1987) describe several possible cases of North American blastomycosis in early American Indians of the Averbuch series (U.S.A.). Similarities of tuberculous and blastomycotic lesions led these authors to suggest that several of those cases show simultaneous infection by B. dermatididis and Mycobacterium tuberculosis.

COCCIDIOIDOMYCOSIS (VALLEY FEVER; SAN JOAQUIN VALLEY FEVER; DESERT FEVER; DESERT RHEUMATISM; COCCIDIOID GRANULOMA; POSADAS' DISEASE; POSADAS–WERNICKE'S DISEASE; OIDIOMYCOSIS)

Definition, taxonomy, and geographical distribution

Coccidioidomycosis is an inflammatory granulomatous disease endemic to arid and semiarid regions of the southwestern U.S.A., Mexico and South America, caused by Coccidioides immitis a pathogenic saprophyte (Long & Merbs, 1981). The disease can appear as a primary, benign, self-limited form affecting the lung, and a progressive, chronic, often fatal, disseminated form (less than 1 % of the cases). The fungus reproduces in tissues as a sporangium, liberating spores to repeat the process (Howe, 1981). The soil-inhabiting, saprophytic phase is truly mycelial, producing many infectious arthrospores on special hyphal branches from the vegetative mycelia, and, when disturbed, these arthrospores become airborne. Mixed with dust, they are inhaled by animals and human hosts. In the lung it reproduces as a sporangium, creating endospore-filled spherules up to 80 μ in diameter that eventually rupture, liberating spores to repeat the process (Howe, 1981). Coccidiodes immitis may be cultured in special media (Sabouraud).

This is a relatively common mycotic disease endemic to the southwestern regions of the U.S.A., especially in the San Joaquin Valley and Los Angeles area of California. Its range in the U.S.A. also includes Arizona, New Mexico, Texas, Nevada and Utah, as well as northern Mexico, Central America, South America (Argentina, Colombia, Bolivia and Venezuela) and even Europe.

Epidemiology and clinical features

The fungus' reservoir is the soil since coccidioidomycosis is acquired by inhalation of spores of Coccidioides immitis, human or animal contacts are of little or no importance (Long &

Merbs, 1981; Shadomy, 1981). Summer dust storms followed by an incubation period of 1–4 weeks make it a seasonal disease. Eighty percent of affected persons are adult males, suggesting an occupational exposure (Resnick & Niwayama, 1989a, b).

Some Native American populations of the southwestern U.S.A. have high rates of acute disease and suffer greater morbidity and mortality from the disseminated form than Whites in the same area (Sievers & Fisher, 1981). However, environmental and occupational activities leading to increased exposure as well as socioeconomic circumstances appear to be a more plausible explanation for this observation than an assumed heritable immunological vulnerability. Blacks are particularly prone to dissemination and skeletal lesions.

Recovery from the disease provides immunity. As in tuberculosis, most infections with this fungus are short, asymptomatic and pass unnoticed; however, they are both immunizing and sensitizing (Howe, 1981). Before antimycotic treatment became available, mortality in the disseminated form caused death within a year (Casagrande & Frost, 1955). This is of considerable importance in paleopathology.

FIG. 7.65: **Coccidioidomycosis.** This spherule of the pathogenic fungus was found in a microscopic section of a collapsed vertebral body of a skeleton with Pott's deformity. Pre-Spanish site, southwestern U.S.A. Photograph courtesy of William Harrison and the University of Chicago Press. (Reprinted from Harrison *et al.* (1991) *Journal of Infectious Diseases* **164**:436–7.)

Skeletal pathology

The disseminated form usually runs a rapid course and spreads from the lung to the other soft tissues (liver, spleen, kidneys, pericardium, peritoneum, skin and lymph nodes), bones and joints. In 30–50 % of the disseminated cases it reaches the central nervous system (Halde, 1983) where it causes meningitis and subsequent death (Shafer *et al.*, 1983). Bones are affected in the disseminated form in about 25 % of the cases. Some authors (Murphy, 1992) insist that the disease has the highest rate of skeletal involvement among all the fungal infections. The disease usually is monostotic (Casagrande & Frost, 1955; Putschar, 1976; Reichs, 1986b). The small bones of the hands and feet are especially susceptible, and then the spine and ribs. In reality, no part of the skeleton is immune to the disease (Murray *et al.*, 1990).

Postcranial bones

Long bone lesions are most often found in the distal portions (metaphyses and epiphyses) and within the prominences, in the areas of insertions of tendons and ligaments (especially in the ischial tuberosity), the outer margin of the iliac bone,

the patella, the olecranon, the calcaneus and the malleoli of the ankle (Shadomy, 1981; Murray *et al.*, 1990). In flat bones, the lesions are produced more centrally and tend to be discrete, but may be confluent and expanding. Morphologically, the lesions in this disease are lytic and well-demarcated, with massive destruction of the cancellous bone producing a punched-out appearance. They demonstrate minimal, if any, periosteal reaction, showing central cavitation, combined with osteoporosis. Eventually, the lesion can break through the cortex and at that stage periosteal proliferation ensues (Zimmerman & Kelley, 1982).

Joints

Joint involvement is not uncommon (Jaffe, 1972) and the ankle, knee and elbow are the most commonly affected joints. The articular changes result from an osteomyelitic focus that breaks through the epiphysis and extends into the joint (Casagrande & Frost, 1955). Degenerative lesions lead to osteophyte development (Long & Merbs, 1981). More than 40 % of the patients show often severe evidence of destructive changes.

Spine

A wide variety of polymorphic lesions commonly involve the various segments of the spine (Long & Merbs, 1981). Most lesions do not show bone regeneration, while a few show periosteal bone deposition around the lesion's borders. They are mainly resorptive with well-defined, punched-out areas

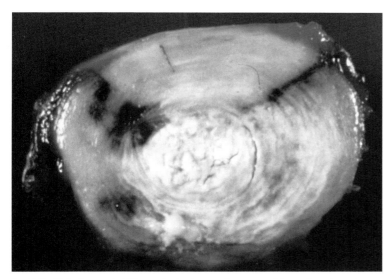

FIG. 7.66: **Histoplasmosis.** This 2 cm lesion has a soft, caseous ('cheesy') center and a peripheral envelope of fibrous tissue, grossly indistinguishable from a tuberculous lesion. PBL.

and diffuse erosive activity. Healing may produce sclerotic vertebral lesions (Murray et al., 1990). The posterior elements of the vertebrae are usually not spared, which is an important point in the differential diagnosis with tuberculosis. Collapse and subsequent kyphosis, however, are uncommon, and the intervertebral disks are usually spared (Putschar, 1976; Resnick & Niwayama, 1989a, b). Radiographically, cavitation combined with osteoporosis, perifocal reactive osteosclerosis, and fistula formation are commonly seen.

As indicated in Chapter 8, the individual soft tissue lesions are indistinguishable from those of tuberculosis.

Paleopathological evidence

Spherules and endospores of *Coccidioides immitis* have been identified histologically within the affected vertebrae of a pre-Columbian skeleton with a gross morphological lesion identical with Pott's disease from Nuvakwewtaqa, Arizona (Harrison et al., 1991) (Fig. 7.65).

HISTOPLASMOSIS (DARLING'S DISEASE; AMERICAN HISTOPLASMOSIS)

Definition, taxonomy, epidemiology, and natural history

Histoplasmosis is a generalized mycosis of variable severity caused by *Histoplasma capsulatum* or *duboisii*, and which primarily affects the lungs, but from which hematogenous dissemination may occur. The infection is common but clinical symptoms are uncommon, most cases presenting as an asymptomatic or mild and self-healing disease. The disease is unique among the systemic mycoses because it primarily involves the reticuloendothelial system (spleen, liver, lymph nodes and bone marrow), in which the fungus is found almost exclusively intracellularly within macrophages and histiocytes (Howe, 1981).

Histoplasma capsulatum and *duboisii* are culturally indistinguishable pathogenic, aerobic fungi 1–5 μ in diameter that grow in vitro under CO_2 at 36 °C in artificial media enriched with blood, glucose and cysteine (Howe, 1981). Histoplasmosis due to H. capsulatum is widespread in its geographical distribution (North, Central and South America; Africa and Southeast Asia) and endemic in the Ohio and Mississippi River Valleys and northeastern U.S.A. in soil of damp, fertile areas polluted by birds, dogs, bats and skunks. Skin tests indicate that up to 75 % of the more than 5 million people in those areas of the United States have had a primary but subclinical infection (Shadomy, 1981; Shafer et al., 1983; Messner, 1987), and that more than half of the reported cases have come from there (Murray et al., 1990). *Histoplasma duboisii* has a habitat restricted to Africa, between the deserts of Sahara in the north and Kalahari in the south. All people affected with this species presenting in Europe and America have lived at some time in Africa (Murray et al., 1990).

Poultry soils, bat caves and starling-inhabited locations are the fungus' reservoir. Inhalation of dust contaminated with the spore-containing excreta of pigeons, starlings and blackbirds (Shafer et al., 1983) is the common route of infection. Symptoms appear from about 10 days after the exposure. The prevalence of the disease increases from childhood to 30 years. There are no sexual differences in frequency, although males are more severely affected than females. *Histoplasma duboisii* causes severe systemic infections in young Negroes in tropical West Africa (Nigeria) where susceptibility is universal (Ortner & Putschar, 1985:225). Subclinical infections are extremely common in endemic areas, and they increase resistance to the infection.

Skeletal and soft tissue pathology

While H. capsulatum has a predilection for the reticuloendothelial system, on very rare occasions, the often fatal, disseminated form produces skeletal lesions, most commonly affecting the skull, the small bones of the hands and feet and the radius. The lesions are multiple, punched-out foci with cortical thickening and surrounding bony sclerosis of the long bone shafts (Zimmerman & Kelley, 1982). The African type of histoplasmosis due to H. duboisii involves the skeleton in 80 % of infected persons. The multiple, round, lytic foci affect short and long bones and cranial vault more commonly than flat bones, and often cause a considerable amount of periosteal reaction (Ortner & Putschar, 1985:225; Murray et al., 1990).

Individual soft tissue lesions are indistinguishable from those of tuberculosis (Fig. 7.66), except for the primary lesion in which the tuberculous pulmonary nodule is solitary; in histoplasmosis, 15 to 20 nodules may be present and whose healed, calcified residue produces a characteristic radiological pattern.

CRYPTOCOCCOSIS (TORULOSIS; EUROPEAN BLASTOMYCOSIS; BUSSE–BUSCHKE'S DISEASE)

Definition, taxonomy, and epidemiology

Cryptococcosis is a chronic fungal infection caused by *Cryptococcus neoformans* (*Torula histolytica*) and *Cryptococcus bacillispora* that may involve the skin, oral cavity, subcutaneous tissues, joints and meninges from a primary focus in the lungs. Meningitis is the most common form of presentation.

Cryptococcus neoformans is a monophormic, spherical, thin-walled, encapsulated yeast-like organism that shows predilection for the central nervous system but also affects the lungs (where the primary lesions appear), the skin and other organs. Following entry into a mammalian host the yeasts quickly acquire a demonstrable capsule, the chemical nature of which permits it to escape detection by immunosurveillance of the human host's immune system (Howe, 1981). This fungus may be isolated on any good bacteriologic media (Howe, 1981). The microorganisms are widespread and frequently found on the skin or in the bronchi of healthy persons. The mechanism of human infection is not known but is probably inhalation of airborne microorganisms (Shafer *et al.*, 1983; Benenson, 1984). Aerosolized pigeon excreta may be involved but this is uncertain (Shadomy, 1981).

Geographical distribution is worldwide. There is no transmission from person-to-person or from animal-to-person. The incubation period is unknown, and no racial predilection is demonstrable. Although it can appear at any age, this is largely a disease of the older adult period. Cryptococcosis is often an opportunistic infection, and in recent decades the incidence and mortality of the disease have increased, as corticosteroid and immunosuppressive therapy have become more prevalent (Shafer *et al.*, 1983) and as a complication of several underlying diseases (Hodgkin's Disease, AIDS, sarcoidosis, tuberculosis, and diabetes mellitus). Spontaneous resolution in some patients with cryptococcosis of the lungs has been reported (Halde, 1983).

Skeletal and soft tissue pathology

Skeletal cryptococcosis occurs in 5–10 % of infected persons with disseminated disease, often secondary to the common complication of chronic meningoencephalitis (Bullough, 1992). Other common sites are pelvis, femur, tibia and spine as well as skull. These multiple, disseminated, discrete, lytic lesions are distributed in the metaphyses and bony prominences. Sclerosis and local subperiosteal new bone formation are only seen occasionally (Shadomy, 1981; Resnick & Niwayama, 1989a, b; Murray *et al.*, 1990). Neither the lesions nor their pattern are specific. Joint involvement that may be very destructive is uncommon (10 % of the patients) and occurs by extension of the infection from an adjacent skeletal focus. The knee is the most commonly affected joint. In the vertebrae, involvement of two or more adjacent vertebrae with paraspinal masses is characteristic. Brain abscesses may be recognizable in human mummified remains, in which the organism's capsule could make it identifiable histologically. We were unable to find ancient examples of this infection in the paleopathology literature.

PARACOCCIDIOIDOMYCOSIS (SOUTH AMERICAN BLASTOMYCOSIS; BRAZILIAN BLASTOMYCOSIS; LUTZ'S DISEASE; LUTZ–SPLENDORE–ALMEIDA'S DISEASE; PARACOCCIDIOID GRANULOMA; ZIMENEMATOSIS; ESCOMEL'S DISEASE.)

Taxonomy, epidemiology, and skeletal pathology

Paracoccidioidomycosis or South American blastomycosis is a chronic pulmonary infection caused by the fungus *Blastomyces* or *Paracoccidioides brasiliensis*, commonly found in South America. This is a severe, often fatal mycotic disease that in disseminated cases can affect all the internal organs. The gram-positive organism appears in tissues and in vitro at 37 °C as a spherical, multiple-budding, yeastlike cell (5–20 μ in diameter) with a thick capsule, while in nature and on agar is a filamentous mold. The capsule reacts positively with the periodic acid Schiff (PAS) stain, and may be cultured on Sabouraud's glucose agar.

Paracoccidioidomycosis is almost exclusively seen in the tropical or subtropical areas of South America (Brazil, Colombia and Venezuela) although there may be occasional human infections in a large region from Mexico to Argentina, with the exception of Chile, El Salvador and Panama (Reichs, 1986b). Spores in dust or soil represent this fungus' probable reservoir, and transmission is suspected to be by inhalation of contaminated dust, though infection from person-to-person is unknown. It has a very variable incubation period ranging from 1 month to several years. Paracoccidioidomycosis is a disease of midlife (30–50 years) with a male–female ratio of 12:1. Whites are affected most frequently, while Blacks are the least affected group (Ortner & Putschar, 1985:224). Few data are available about the post-infectious immune response.

Skeletal pathology

Bone involvement is relatively common in the disseminated form of the disease, affecting the clavicle, ribs, vertebrae and extremities with round, lytic, often multiple lesions found in areas of the skeletal system with a good blood supply. However, information regarding osseus lesions varies from author to author (Shadomy, 1981).

Paleopathology

Allison *et al.* (1979) reported a case with histological demonstration of the organism in the mummy of a 56 year old woman of northern Chile who died about A.D. 290 and demonstrated pulmonary and renal lesions. This author argues that it is probable this was an imported disease in northern Chile acquired during a trading expedition to a tropical area, since among grave goods were examples of tropical bird feathers. The age of the individual and the nature of the lesions are similar to those seen in modern cases of this disease.

CANDIDIASIS (MONILIASIS; CANDIDOSIS; THRUSH; MUGUET)

Taxonomy and epidemiology

In 1890 the thrush fungus was assigned to the genus *Monilia* because moniliasis became the generally accepted name for what we now call candidiasis. The genus *Candida* was proposed in 1923 (Ainsworth, 1993*a*). Candidiasis is a mycosis that normally is limited to the cutaneous system and the mucous membranes. In addition to *Candida albicans*, other species may also be involved (*C. tropicalis, parapsilosis, stellatoidea, krusei*). *C. albicans* is an endogenous, yeast-like organism that is commonly found in the oral cavity, vagina and gastrointestinal tract of healthy persons. The fungus may become invasive only under certain circumstances (especially those diseases characterized by immunosuppression), attacking organs such as lungs and kidneys (Shadomy, 1981). *Candida albicans* is a nutritionally dependent dimorphic organism that grows as a yeast in its natural habitat or *in vitro* in the presence of glucose, and as mycelia or pseudomycelia when it invades tissues or *in vitro* in the presence of dextran, glycogen or starch (Howe, 1981). Its distribution is worldwide and its reservoir is humans.

Transmission occurs by contact with fluids of the mouth, skin, vagina and feces of infected individuals or carriers. It can also be transmitted from the mother to the fetus during parturition and by endogenous dissemination. Its incubation period is variable, and there is no sex and age predilection. This disease is the most common opportunistic infection in the world, and its incidence has increased remarkably since the use of antibiotics and immunosuppressive drugs (Shafer *et al.*, 1983). Dissemination in antiquity, however, must have been rare.

Skeletal pathology

Bone involvement in cases of disseminated candidiasis is relatively uncommon and occurs by hematogenous dissemination to a bone or a joint, or extension from an overlying soft tissue abscess (Resnick & Niwayama, 1989*a*, *b*). The osteomyelitic lesions may be single or multiple, and the preferred sites are the flat bones (scapula, sternum, vertebrae, ribs, and pelvis) and the long bones. Joint involvement is not uncommon and there is a predilection for the large weight-bearing joints, the knee being the most commonly affected joint in 75 % of patients with bone lesions. The hip and the shoulder account for most of the remainder (Messner, 1987).

ASPERGILLOSIS

Taxonomy, epidemiology, and skeletal pathology.

Aspergillosis is a systemic mycosis produced by several species of *Aspergillus*, especially *Aspergillus fumigatus*, that primarily affects the lungs and occasionally may produce hematogenous dissemination. *Aspergillus* may act as an opportunistic invader in debilitated individuals. In persons with chronic lung disease such as emphysema or chronic lung abscess, this organism may line the bronchial or abscess surfaces without invasion, and its allergenic structure may produce an asthma-like syndrome. The pathogenic species of aspergillosis are *A. fumigatus* (the most common pathogen) and *A. flavus*. Occasionally the disease may be produced by another species. Aspergillosis is a sporadic disease with worldwide distribution. Its reservoir is dung in the process of fermentation and decay, and it can also be found in stored wet hay as well as other stored food under hot conditions (Benenson, 1984). Inhalation of airborne spores is the manner of transmission. Its incubation period is from several days to several weeks. There is neither sex, age nor racial predilection. The tissues of healthy people are very resistant to infection by this organism. If the skull is involved, destruction and necrosis of bone between affected paranasal sinuses and orbit or anterior cranial fossa occur (Ortner & Putschar, 1985). When, very uncommonly, the spine is affected by contiguous spread from a pulmonary focus, vertebral collapse and gibbus may result. The ribs may also be affected by the same route.

MUCORMYCOSIS (PHYCOMYCOSIS; CIGOMYCOSIS)

Taxonomy, epidemiology, and skeletal pathology

Mucormycosis is a rare and serious systemic fungal infection caused by several genera of the environmental saprophytes of Mucoraceae that can occasionally become invasive opportunistic pathogens in immunosuppressed persons. This disease is very uncommon in healthy people. Corticosteroid and immunosuppression therapies predispose to the disease. As an opportunistic infection, mucormycosis affects debilitated patients, especially those affected by diabetes mellitus in the acidotic state. Dissemination in antiquity can be expected to have been most infrequent. *Mucor, Rhizomucor* and *Rhizopus* are the main causes of the pulmonary, gastrointestinal and fungicemic forms of mucormycosis. However the disease also may be caused by the genera *Absidia* and *Cunninghamella* (Benenson, 1984). Infection is produced by inhalation or ingestion of the fungi by susceptible individuals or the infection may follow minor trauma. There is no transmission from person-to-person or from animals-to-person. Its incubation period is unknown and there is no sex and age or race predilection. The most common mechanism of death is cerebral ischemia secondary to diffuse occlusion of small brain arteries by intravascular mycelial fungus masses in fungicemic individuals. The isolation of mucormycosis from specimens other than blood is of little value because the fungi of these genera are ubiquitous in the environment.

Extension of the infection into bone is seen in the cranial form of mucormycosis involving the nasal cavity and extending into the paranasal sinuses, producing sinusitis. One of the most important features of skeletal mucormycosis is unilateral perforation of the hard palate with sequestrum

formation (Ortner & Putschar, 1985:227). Putschar (1976) reports a case in an Iranian boy with progressive destruction of the cranial vault due to a mixed staphylococcal and mucor osteomyelitis.

SUBCUTANEOUS MYCOSES

SPOROTRICHOSIS (BEURMANN–GOUGEROT'S DISEASE; SCHENCK'S DISEASE)

Subcutaneous mycoses are chronic infections, localized in the skin, underlying dermis and occasionally the deep tissues (muscles and bones). Occasionally these diseases may involve any exposed body surface. Both dimorphic and monomorphic fungi are responsible for these mycoses (Howe, 1981).

Taxonomy and epidemiology

Sporotrichosis is a chronic mycotic disease usually localized in the skin and subcutaneous tissues, produced by *Sporothrix schenckii*. Because the infection seldom disseminates, arthritis, pneumonitis and other organ involvement are uncommon and only rarely is the disease fatal. *Sporothrix beurmanni* is the other species that can cause sporotrichosis (Vilaplana, 1992). *Sporothrix schenckii* is a small, dimorphic, ovoid, branching microorganism with septate hyphae, measuring 3–5 μ,

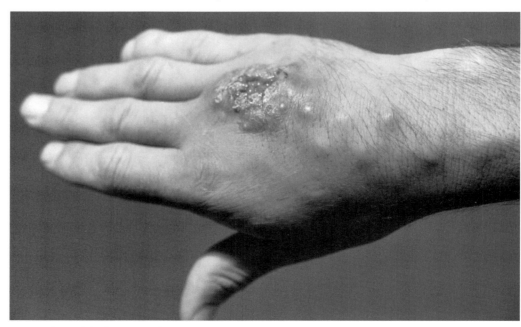

FIG. 7.67: **Sporotrichosis.** Primary infection is a puncture wound represented by a fungating ulcer on the back of the hand. Modern adult. Photograph courtesy Dr George Sarosi, Indianapolis.

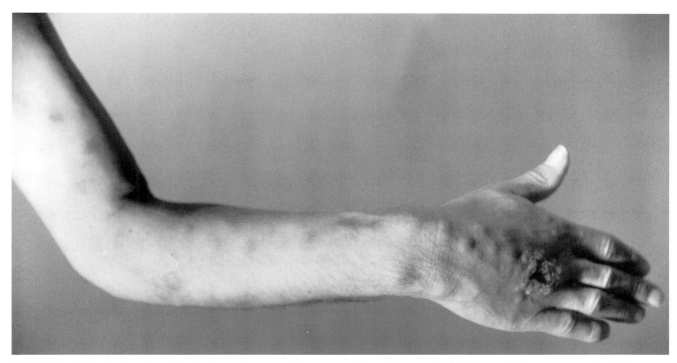

Fig. 7.68: **Sporotrichosis.** The primary infection is a puncture wound (now ulcerative) on the dorsum of the hand. Satellite abscesses along the course of a lymphatic are evident. Modern adult. Photograph courtesy Dr George Sarosi, Indianapolis

and it can be cultured on Sabouraud's medium. The fungus reproduces in tissues and in vitro at 36 °C on Sabouraud's medium as oval, round or elongated, yeast-like cells but as a hyphae-forming mold at 25 °C and in the environment (Howe, 1981). This fungus is very difficult to visualize in biopsy material (Turek, 1982).

Sporotrichosis is worldwide between 50° North and South latitudes (Ortner & Putschar, 1985:225). *Sporothrix schenckii* lives in the vegetation, especially in very humid places, such as the cranberry bogs of the upper midwestern U.S.A. It usually enters cutaneous and subcutaneous tissues *via* a penetrating skin wound (Fig. 7.67) from a thorn, often on the hand, and is an occupational disease of farmers, fruit gatherers, florists and other plant handlers. Lymphatic infection may spread up the arm (Fig. 7.68) to axillary nodes from 1 week to 3 months after the skin lesion. Three-fourths of infected persons are males. However, sometimes it may be inhaled and subsequently it can disseminate (Benenson, 1984). Alternatively, entry can occur by accidental laboratory or clinical inoculation (Shafer *et al.*, 1983). Transmission from person-to-person does not occur. Humans probably are more susceptible than animals. Infections are immunizing and sensitizing and elicit a cell-mediated immune response (Howe, 1981).

Skeletal Pathology

The most common locations of sporotrichosis are the skin and the soft tissues, following traumatic implantation. Skele-

tal involvement does occur in about 10 % of the general disseminated cases, producing multiple localized lytic lesions in the skull, long and short tubular bones (Putschar, 1976). Osteolysis predominates and periostitis is usually absent (Resnick & Niwayama, 1989a, b). However, localized but extensive periostitis is the most common feature in some authors' experience (Ortner & Putschar, 1985:226). Mandible, skull and vertebrae are uncommonly involved (Messner, 1987). Severe damage in the elbow, wrist, knee and sternoclavicular joints may occur. While spontaneous fractures may result, the lesions may be mild, healing without residual complications (Ortner & Putschar, 1985:226). No case of sporotrichosis in ancient human remains appears to have been reported to date.

MADUROMYCOSIS (MYCETOMA; MADURA FOOT; ACTINOMYCOTIC MYCETOMA; MYCOTIC MYCETOMA; EUMYCETOMA; ACTINOMYCETOMA; BALLINGALL'S DISEASE)

Taxonomy and geography

The term maduromycosis is used to describe those mycetomas that are produced by true fungi (Halde, 1983). Mycetoma is caused by a variety of bacterial and fungal agents that occur in soil, producing a rare and chronic disease principally involving the foot (Jaffe, 1972). Untreated, it may be fatal. These lesions can be caused by a wide variety of organisms: bacteria (*Nocardia* in 20 % of the cases, *Streptomyces* and *Actinomyces*) and fungi (*Madurella*, *Allescheria*, *Cephalosporium*, *Pyrenochaeta*, *Neotestudina*, *Phialophora* and *Leptosphaeria*). All these organisms are widely distributed in nature (Revell, 1986).

Maduromycosis is very common in southern India, where it is also known as Madura foot, although similar mycetomas may occur in other regions of the world, especially in tropical and subtropical regions: Africa (Senegal, East Africa, Tunisia, Madagascar, Algeria, Southwest Africa, and Zanzibar); America (Brazil, Argentina, Chile, Guyana, Central America, Cuba and the south-western U.S.A.); Europe (Greece, southern Italy and Sardinia); and Asia (Sri Lanka and the Philippine Islands). Maduromycosis is a disease of locations with a dry season and poor hygienic conditions occupied by bare-footed peoples, since the infective organisms are present in the soil and decaying vegetation (Revell, 1986).

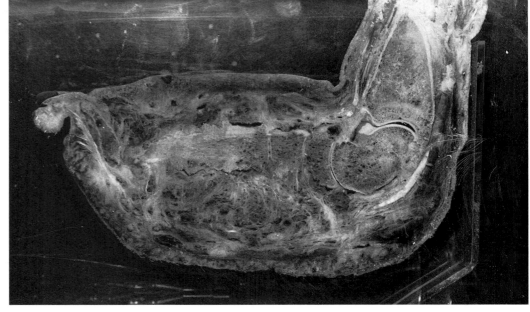

FIG. 7.69: **Maduromycosis.** Transected modern adult foot and ankle with associated soft tissues preserved in formaldehyde. Note erosion of the metatarsals and phalangeal destruction with soft tissue fibrosis. No. 224201. Courtesy P. Sledzik. NMHM.

Epidemiology and clinical features

Transmission occurs by subcutaneous implantation of spores due to wounds by splinters or thorns; thus the lesion is not contagious. Its incubation period is several months. No special age or sex distribution is apparent, although mycetoma is now considered by some as an occupational disease because the condition has a peak incidence between 20–40 years of age (Turek, 1982). Host response is unknown.

Skeletal pathology

A penetrating wound initiates soft tissue infection whose necrotizing effects eventually reach the underlying bones. Localized destruction and generalized osteoporosis occur in the tarsals and metatarsals (Reichs, 1986b) (Fig. 7.69). The tibia and fibula, along with the metatarsals, may show multiple areas of cortical destruction with little reactive bone formation (Figs. 7.70 & 7.71). Ankylosis is common in the interphalangeal and metatarsophalangeal joints due to destruction of articular cartilage. Sequestra are uncommonly found because of cortical perforation. Sometimes lesions may simulate osteosarcoma because of excessive proliferative periosteal and cortical reaction (Murray *et al.*, 1990). Distant bones may be affected, probably by hematogenous dissemination.

An example of Madura foot from the Byzantine period (A.D. 300–600) in Israel was reported by Hershkovitz *et al.* (1992). The distal segments of both tibiae and fibula as well as the tarsal and metatarsal bones showed periostitis, plaques and spicules but no medullary involvement was present. Ligament calcification was noted.

PARASITIC INFECTIONS

Roy Moodie (1923b:96), paleontologist-turned-paleopathologist, notes that parasitism provides us with the most ancient evidence for the presence of disease on Earth. He calls our attention to the tumor-like excrescence in a Paleozoic fossil crinoid's perianal area secondary to the attachment of a snail (that probably fed off the crinoid's discharge). He also cites (p.103) Van Tieghem's 1877 observation of bacterial cellular destruction of a pre-Cambrian plant structure. In addition to the obvious concern for the impact of parasitic infestation on the health of ancient populations or individuals, paleopathologists also have an interest in these conditions because human parasitism does not occur in isolation from other ecological factors. Many parasites have complex or unique life cycles. Human exposure to such parasites commonly results from human intrusion into that cycle with unexpected parasitic invasion of the human

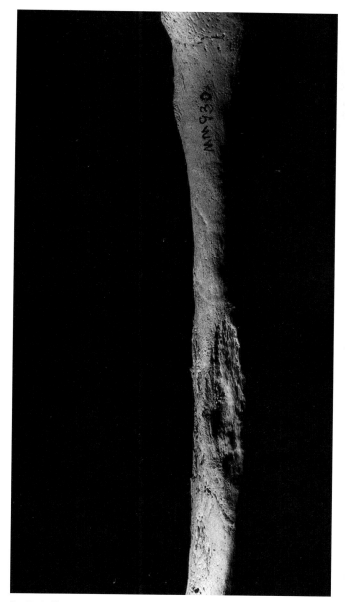

Fig. 7.70: **Mycetoma.** This tibia's midshaft area demonstrates a reasonably sharply demarcated, oval area of irregularly-surfaced new bone formation. Its shape suggests an overlying soft tissue ulcer, and this, plus its location, are characteristic of mycetoma. No. 1002626. Modern adult with a clinically confirmed diagnosis of mycetoma. Courtesy P. Sledzik. NMHM.

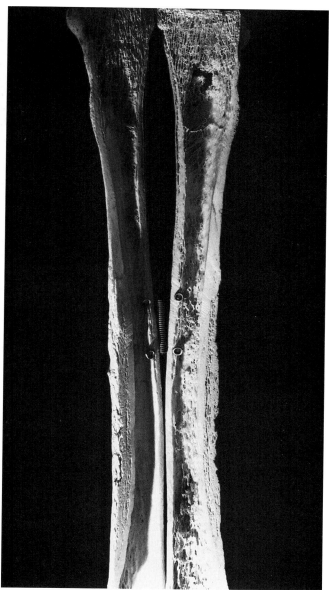

Fig. 7.71: **Mycetoma.** Bisection of the tibia shown in Fig. 7.70, revealing the multiple layers of periosteal new bone on the cortical surface not yet remodeled. No. 1002626. Modern case. Courtesy P. Sledzik. NMHM.

body ('accidental host'). Thus, if the features unique to a parasite's life cycle are known, then the finding of that parasite in an ancient human body often can be translated into prediction of an aspect of the human's behavior such as diet, occupational activity or domestication of certain animals.

Models for the negative effect of a parasite on the health of its human host are abundant. The lethal nature of falciparal malaria is an overt example. Perhaps more subtle would be the increased frequency of infections that commonly complicate the chronic anemias. Such anemia often is a feature of certain forms of parasitism: severe iron deficiency anemia in children with hookworm infestation; the anemia of chronic

malaria, as well as the folate and vitamin B12 deficiency anemia seen in some adults with fish tapeworm (*Diphyllobothrium latum*) infection. Other diseases caused by parasites include the cachexia of the malabsorption state that frequently characterizes chronic giardiasis, and also the cerebral cystic lesions of cysticercosis produced by the larvae of pork tapeworm, or the large, cystic lesions in the liver or lung resulting from dog tapeworm infestation. Identification of these and many other parasitic conditions supplies useful information to the paleopathologist interested in reconstruction of the health status of an ancient population.

Documentation of parasitism also provides an opportunity to expand cultural or ecological understanding of an archaeological population. Reinhard *et al.* (1986*b*) demonstrated status differences in two families at the same American colonial site based on the differences of frequency of *Ascaris* ova in their latrine content. In a different study the presence of *Diphyllobothrium pacificum* ova in coprolites of several members of a northern Chile Archaic period coastal population not only amplified our knowledge about the marine nature of their diet, but also reflected their maritime subsistence strategy. In addition, it provided an example of mechanisms that are operational in adaptive radiation of parasites (Reinhard & Aufderheide, 1990). Similarly, the dog–sheep cycle of the tapeworm, *Echinococcus granulosus*, can help establish the domestication of these animals when an ancient human body is found to have evidence of the hydatid disease that organism causes. Karl Reinhard (University of Nebraska) has also used differences in the frequency of *Pediculus humanus* var. *capitis* as a measure of social interaction between two contemporary pre-Columbian valley populations from southern Peru (personal communication). Clearly there are many different ways that establishment of the presence of a parasite in an ancient body can be employed to increase our knowledge about the nature of that population's cultural characteristics. Thus, the presence of certain parasites can be predictive not only of the health but also the behavior of the parasite's host.

Clues to the presence of the parasite vary among the many organisms infesting and infecting humans. Some, like lice, can be recognized by the unaided eye. Another is the guinea worm *Dracunculus medinensis*. Some of the intestinal roundworms, like *Ascaris lumbricoides*, are large enough to be seen easily; yet, in spite of their frequency as established by the presence of their ova, recognition of the adult in a mummified body has not been reported. Others are of microscopic size and can themselves be expected to be identified only rarely in archaeological bodies, but documentation of their presence may be possible by the morphology of the gross changes they induce in affected viscera. *Trypanosoma cruzi* has been visualized directly with electron microscopy and immunostaining only once (in a Peruvian Inca mummy: Fornaciari et al., 1992a) but the unique, massively dilated esophagus and colon it causes in the form of Chagas' disease enabled Allison (1993) to recognize it in numerous mummified bodies from an endemic area in South America. In the same way, Carrion's disease (bartonellosis) produces no 'marker' in its severe, acute stage of hemolytic anemia, but becomes recognizable easily in the chronic, skin eruptive stage because of these lesions' unique form and pattern. Although the methods of molecular biology have not yet been applied at the time of this writing to nonbacterial parasites in ancient bodies, successful identification of DNA unique to *Mycobacterium tuberculosis* in a pre-Columbian Peruvian mummy with pulmonary lesions characteristic of tuberculosis (Salo et al., 1994) suggests broad application of this approach to archaeoparasitology as well. Undoubtedly, however, parasite ova identification in specimens (most commonly coprolites) is the most extensively used technique, and its simplicity will keep it so for the enteric helminths that can be so characterized. Rectosigmoidoscopic biopsy of coprolites in human mummies may even avoid destructive dissection of such bodies (Filho et al., 1988). Interpretive caution must be employed in coprolite analysis, because consumption of parasitized animal tissue by ancient humans can result in the appearance in coprolites of parasite ova of species that do not invade humans. Fish trematode (*Cryptocotyle lingua*) ova found in the feces of a 1600 year old Alaskan female body is an example of this hazard (Zimmerman & Smith, 1975).

In the following discussion, we have been selective in our coverage of this field, including only those parasites that are large enough to be seen with the unaided eye or, at most, use of a simple hand lens, and those that produce a distinctive, grossly recognizable morphological change in the viscera they invade. We have chosen not to include most of that multitude of parasites identifiable in ancient bodies only histologically by the appearance of their ova, cysts or other unique product.

PROTOZOAN INFECTIONS

AMEBIASIS

Definition and epidemiology

Amebiasis is an intestinal infection by the protozoan *Entamoeba histolytica* that may present as an acute or chronic diarrhea or as an asymptomatic intestinal infection (carrier state). Extraintestinal complications are principally abscesses in the liver, lung or brain. While the condition is worldwide, it flourishes in areas that combine warm temperatures with poor sanitation, common in tropical and subtropical areas. Among the several species composing this genus, only *E. histolytica* can invade human tissue and humans are the only reservoir for this species. Different strains have varying virulence. Trophozoites live in the colon and their cysts are discharged in enormous numbers with the feces. Completion of the cycle occurs upon ingestion of cyst-contaminated food or water.

Natural history

Pathogenesis

The ingested cysts exist in the small intestine, and the trophozoites then pass to the colon where a lectin on the protozoan's surface causes it to bind to a receptor on a colon mucosal cell. This is followed by the epithelial cell's death, which opens the path to invasion of the colon wall by the parasite. Reproduction of the trophozoite by binary fission creates further cellular death, eventually resulting in a flask-shaped mucosal abscess (Connor et al., 1976). Subsequent enlargement of the involved area produces a grossly visible ulcer that may fuse with a neighboring mucosal abscess to generate an ulcer several centimeters in diameter. Erosion of an artery in the base of such an ulcer can produce an alarming degree of acute hemorrhage into the colon. Only occasionally will deeper erosion occur and penetrate the bowel wall, terminating in colon perforation and fatal peritonitis when feces escape through the colon wall defect.

Clinical Features

In the very acute form, the above-described sequence of events initiates as abdominal pain, often crampy with fever, toxicity and diarrhea. Much more commonly the systemic reaction is mild or absent, abdominal pain is mild and the clinical picture is dominated by diarrhea that comes on gradually over a period of days or a week. Blood loss sufficient to be obvious in the passed stool is common but only occasionally will massive lower intestinal hemorrhage occur.

In endemic areas the disease often progresses to the chronic stage, characterized by recurrent, acute flares of the condition, separated by long, nearly asymptomatic intervals. Because such individuals continue to pass cysts in the feces, they remain infectious. Eventually all symptoms may subside yet the continuous cyst excretion makes the individual a 'carrier' for amebiasis.

Complications

The healing process in the chronic stage may generate enough scar tissue to produce a stricture that obstructs the passage of stool. Rarely a mass of granulation tissue will become so exuberant that it resembles a tumor ('ameboma'). However, while the preservation of the colon in a mummy may rarely be of sufficient quality to reveal amebic ulcerations, it is the escape of the ameba from the intestine to produce abscesses in other viscera that is most apt to be recognized by the paleopathologist and that justifies its inclusion in this volume.

Amebae commonly escape the colon by entering an eroded vein in the wall of a mucosal ulcer. The venous blood carries the trophozoite down the mesenteric veins to the portal vein that enters the liver and branches to the capillary level. The parasite that lodges in such a liver capillary then penetrates its wall and establishes one or more liver abscesses (see Fig. 8.15). While these are often small, they can exceed 12−15 cm in diameter and produce abdominal pain, fever and a tender enlarged liver. Because the intestinal infection may have healed by the time the abscesses becomes symptomatic, diagnosis may be difficult and require needle aspira-

tion to establish its etiology. Medical therapy usually cures the smaller abscesses, only the larger requiring surgical evacuation (Reisberg, 1992). The marked male predominance in persons with liver involvement remains unexplained (Plorde, 1991a).

From the liver the abscess may penetrate the diaphragm to reach the lung and establish an abscess there. Occasionally such extension may also penetrate the pericardium. Transport of the trophozoite from lung abscess via the pulmonary vein blood to the systemic circulation occurs only very rarely, but can result in abscesses elsewhere (especially the brain).

Diagnosis is usually made by demonstration of the organism in stool or aspirated fluid. Recently developed serologic tests are producing results of gratifying specificity and sensitivity. Medical therapy includes medications effective for cysts only (diloxanide furoate) as well as others that act against both cysts and trophozoites (metronidazole).

Morbidity

It has been estimated that 10 % of the world's population is infected with E. histolytica, that prevalence rates may reach 50 % in endemic areas and that disabling infections may, at least transiently, incapacitate 40 million persons annually of which 40 000 die (Plorde, 1991a). Variations in the proportions of virulent strains rather than immunological causes are believed to be a better explanation for differences in disease severity. It is fortunate that only a minority of infected persons suffer a debilitating form of the disease. Nevertheless, the high prevalence found in endemic areas can be responsible for major effects on affected populations in terms of loss of productivity, susceptibility to bacterial infections, and population growth and stability.

Antiquity and history

Neither the acute nor the chronic stages of amebiasis can be separated from bacillary dysentery in earlier literature, although some of the outbreaks described among British troops in Africa most probably were related to E. histolytica infection. Patterson (1993a) described how Lösch (1875), a Russian physician, first identified the pathogen in 1875 and that two North American investigators (Councilman & Lafleur, 1891) described the clinical disease well. However, confusion between intestinal and extraintestinal lesions as well as nonpathogenic and invasive species of ameba prevented clear understanding of the clinical and epidemiological variables associated with amebiasis until the observations and human feeding experiments by E.L. Walker in the first quarter of the twentieth century (Walker, 1931; Patterson, 1993a).

Considering the durability of most parasitic cysts, it is surprising that so few have been found in coprolites. Pizzi & Shenone (1954) found ova of what they suggested might be *Entamoeba coli* in a pre-Columbian spontaneously (frozen) mummified Inca child's coprolites. Although this species is not pathogenic for humans, it does demonstrate that the cyst can survive in mummified bodies. Witenberg (1961), moreover, identified cysts from *E. histolytica* in two 1800 years old coprolites from a cave near the Dead Sea in Israel. It could be argued that it is unlikely amebiasis would have evolved as a disease entity until subsistence strategies were developed that led to large, sedentary populations. Confalonieri *et al.* (1989), however, found *E. histolytica* in 40 % of Brazil's Yanomamö Indians before they established permanent contacts in the Amazon forest with non-Indians. Certainly the size of amebic liver abscesses ought to make them detectable in mummified human remains, as should those in the lung. Microscopic examination of the lining or contents can confirm the diagnosis. Even though most of the organisms in such a cyst are trophozoites (which conceivably may not survive desiccation), the organism does form cysts under adverse circumstances (especially lowered temperatures and dehydration) and thus would be likely to form some cysts postmortem that could survive mummification.

Toxoplasmosis

Definition, taxonomy, and geographical distribution

Toxoplasmosis is a severe, generalized disease caused by the sporozoan protozoan *Toxoplasma gondii* (class Sporozoa, subclass Coccidia) that principally affects the central nervous system. *Toxoplasma gondii* is a small (2.5–5 µ), oval or rounded, intracellular protozoan belonging to the Sporozoa (Benenson, 1984). This protozoan may affect any warm-blooded vertebrate. It has a multiphasic life cycle. The sexual stage develops in the intestine of cats, and the asexual stage in the muscles and other tissues of feline and nonfeline mammals, including man. In the cat's intestine, the sexual stage results in production of infective oocysts and these may be ingested (with the feces of the cat) by other mammals. The oocysts then develop into trophozoites that multiply asexually by fission and invade the tissues (Howe, 1981). They may eventually form cysts and remain encysted in the tissues (chronic toxoplasmosis). In any form (cyst, oocyst or trophozoite) animals eating them may become infected. Only the feline mammals are able to produce feces with oocysts (Benenson, 1984).

Worldwide

This worldwide protozoan was observed originally in North African rodents called gundi, hence its name (*Toxoplasma*

gondii: Howe, 1981). In reality, it may affect mammals, birds and man. However, because domestic animals are the intermediate hosts, transmission to humans probably occurred only sporadically until humans domesticated animals.

Epidemiology and natural history

Cat is the reservoir. Rodents, pigs, cattle, sheep, other homeothermic mammals, chickens and birds are only intermediate hosts. Humans become infected by ingestion of undercooked meat containing cysts. Infected pregnant women can infect the fetus and this may cause serious fetal damage with hydrocephaly, ocular damage, brain involvement, microcephaly, etc (Howe, 1981; Benenson, 1984). The incubation period is not exactly known but it may be between 5 and 25 days. There is no age, sex or race predilection. Susceptibility is universal. The length of immunity is not yet well defined. There are four different clinical and pathological syndromes in toxoplasmosis: acquired toxoplasmosis in the normal host, acquired toxoplasmosis in hosts with immune system impairment, eye infection (retinochoroiditis), and congenital infection. The sites of predilection are central nervous system, skin, lymph nodes, tendon sheaths and skeleton (Murray *et al.*, 1990). In the congenital form, there is a tendency for stillbirth or prematurity. The disease is characterized by fever, rash, mental retardation, jaundice, hepatosplenomegaly, chorioretinitis, convulsions and death occurring in the 10–20 % of acute cases.

History

Our knowledge of the infectious agent of this condition began with its observation in the tissues of a Tunisian rodent, the gundi, described in 1909 (Patterson, 1993c). Fourteen more years passed before the first human case was described. Because this parasite's life cycle is so complex, it was not defined until 1970, and it was in that year that J.K. Frenkel and collaborators demonstrated the transmission of the organism to humans (Robbins, 1975).

Paleopathology

Osseous lesions are unusual, and when they do occur in the congenital form they are located in the metaphyses of the long bones as nonspecific metaphyseal abnormalities simulating those of rubella and syphilis (Resnick & Niwayama, 1989a). Calcifications of the brain, often paraventricular, could survive the postmortem environment. The most important manifestations of acquired toxoplasmosis in the musculoskeletal system are those of periarticular swelling and tenosynovitis, mainly around the wrist and ankle (Murray *et al.*, 1990), but these are not visible in pale-opathological specimens. Occasionally the soft tissue lesions of heart failure, secondary to myocardial involvement, might be apparent. Toxoplasmosis has not been reported in archaeological human remains.

CHAGAS' DISEASE (AMERICAN TRYPANO-SOMIASIS)

Taxonomy, epidemiology, and natural history

The protozoan, *Trypanosoma cruzi*, is hosted by many feral and domestic animals of Central and South America, to which regions this disease is largely restricted. Nevertheless, most human infections are passed on human-to-human, mediated by the reduviid ('assassin' or 'kissing') bug. This insect lives in the thatched roofs of humble dwellings, dropping from there to the house's occupants (often infants or children), usually while they are asleep. After a blood meal from

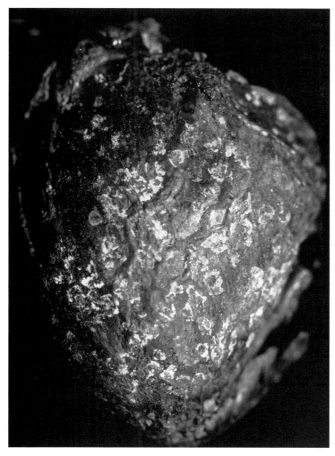

FIG. 7.72: **Exudative pericarditis.** White patches on this dilated heart represent acute exudative pericarditis. Similar exudate was present over liver. Probably acute myocarditis due to *Trypanosoma cruzi* infection (Chagas' disease). A 14 year old male of the Alto Ramirez culture ca. 250 B.C. from near Arica, northern Chile. MAUT. PBL.

their exposed skin (frequently the face) the insect commonly deposits its parasite-contaminated feces on the skin's bite defect. Because of variation in host resistance a local swelling (chagoma) may or may not occur, and the bitten individual may not even have significant symptoms from the subsequent blood dissemination of the organism. An acute, febrile response often accompanies the blood dissemination of the trypanosomes. The parasites enter such a person's cells and proliferate there. In about 10 % myocardial fiber involvement is extensive enough to generate the picture of acute, diffuse myocarditis of a fatal degree (Fig. 7.72). The great majority recover and have no further acute symptoms (Kirchhoff, 1991:791–3).

The disease then enters an asymptomatic phase during which the disseminated organisms will survive at their multiple sites, producing slow, localized tissue destruction with intermittent parasitemia. The tissue lesions may be the product of an autoimmune mechanism. After an apparent disease-free interval often of many years following the acute attack, about one-third of these individuals (now viewed as having <u>chronic</u> Chagas' disease) become symptomatic. Most persons with the chronic form of the disease will present with an enlarged heart (dilated cardiomyopathy) and with heart failure that may progress to a lethal outcome. In the minority (especially in Brazil) the parasites target the nerve cells of the myenteric plexus in the gut wall. These are destroyed (by parasites? autoimmune?), with resulting peristaltic paralysis. Food accumulates in these static, paralyzed bowel segments with consequent dilatation of the affected areas, producing megaesophagus or megacolon. Although this is a disease primary in Latin American countries, many immigrants from such areas to the U.S.A. and Canada have been found to be in the asymptomatic, chronic stage of Chagas' disease (with intermittent, low-grade parasitemia), and transmission of the disease via blood transfusion has now been reported in North America (Kirchhoff, 1993).

In summary many persons bitten by the infected insect have mild or no symptoms, a minority suffer an acute but self-limited illness and a substantial fraction of these develop a serious chronic condition usually dominated by heart failure. Varying immune responses as well as try-panosome strains probably form the basis of the differing outcomes of this infection. The disease flourishes under conditions of primitive housing facilities that accommodate insect infestation commonly found in poverty-stricken rural areas.

Chagas' disease is a condition about which paleopathologists working with New World human remains need to be knowledgeable. Gross lesions suggesting this possibility are primarily the segmentally dilated, food-filled areas of paralyzed esophagus or colon, although an enlarged heart with apical fibrosis (Acquatella, 1993) and with evidence of pleural effusion secondary to heart failure (abundant, crystalline, pleural surface deposits) may be more common, though less specific. In modern Chile 90 % of hospitalized patients with megacolon and all of those with both mega-esophagus and megacolon are serologically positive for Chagas' disease (cited by Fornaciari *et al.*, 1992a).

Chagas' disease in antiquity

Rothhammer *et al.* (1985) found the dilated gut lesions in 9 of 22 spontaneously mummified bodies in the lower valleys of northern Chile's Atacama desert; these ranged from about 470 B.C. to A.D. 600. Two bodies also showed cardiomegaly with fibrosis. No organism was identified in the tissues but the pattern of pathologic lesions strongly suggested that Chagas' disease was responsible. They speculate further that the reduviid bug (*Triatoma infestans*) adapted to the vegetal-roofed dwellings of the studied sedentary agropastoralist populations prior to about 500 B.C. Fornaciari *et al.* (1992a, b) studied the spontaneously mummified body of a young adult female from a member of the Inca culture from Cuzco, Peru, and now housed in a Florence, Italy museum. They demonstrated megacolon, megaesophagus and myocardial fibrosis, but in addition they also identified by both light and electron microscopy organisms in the heart and esophagus tissue sections that had a morphology consistent with *Trypanosoma cruzi* . Their identity was confirmed immunologically using immunoperoxidase staining methods. Thus, the pre-Columbian presence of Chagas' disease in the New World appears to have been established satisfactorily. If the

behavior of the disease then was similar to what it is now, we can expect a large fraction of the more sedentary populations to have become infected by this organism. In only a minority did the acute form of the condition cause death, but probably a larger number succumbed in the chronic stage.

MALARIA

Definition, taxonomy, epidemiology, and geography

Malaria is an acute or chronic, recurrent, febrile, human infection by the protozoan *Plasmodium sp.* transmitted by a mosquito of the genus *Anopheles*. The blood, liver and spleen are the most commonly involved organs. A very large number of species compose the genus *Plasmodium*. The four that commonly infect humans, in order of highest to lowest frequency, are *P. vivax*, *P. falciparum*, *P. malariae* and *P. ovale*. In addition, other members of the genus parasitize a large number of animals, such as *P. brasilianum* (New World monkey), *P. knowlesi* (simian), *P. berghei* (mouse) and numerous others including those hosted by birds (*P. lophurae*), reptiles (*P. mexicanum*) and many mammals. All plasmodial species are characterized by a biphasic growth cycle involving a phase in the vector (sporogony) and another (schizogony) in the host. Within the species, development of strains with unique, clinically relevant features is common.

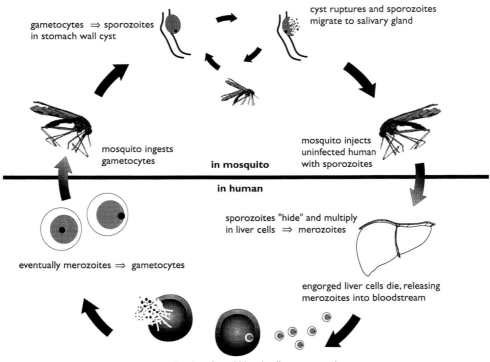

gametocytes ⇒ sporozoites in stomach wall cyst

cyst ruptures and sporozoites migrate to salivary gland

mosquito ingests gametocytes

in mosquito

mosquito injects uninfected human with sporozoites

in human

sporozoites "hide" and multiply in liver cells ⇒ merozoites

eventually merozoites ⇒ gametocytes

engorged liver cells die, releasing merozoites into bloodstream

merozoites invade red blood cells, mature and release new generations of merozoites which invade uninfected RBCs

FIG. 7.73: **Cycle of malaria organism in mosquitos and in humans.** Drawings by Mark Summers, Duluth, MN.

In spite of massive efforts to control this disease, worldwide 3000 people die of malaria every day, 90 % of which are African children (Taylor & Molyneux, 1995). The epidemiology of very few diseases is affected by a greater number of variables than is that of malaria. These variables can be grouped according to those dealing with the vector, the host and the environment. Only the anopheline mosquito can support the sporogony cycle that enables it to transmit the disease. However, the many species within the *Anopheles* genus vary substantially in their preferences for host blood, type of water conditions for breeding, luminosity, forest level (ground/canopy), shelter circumstances, activity temperature, geographical distribution and many other features. The epidemiological implications of each of these is self-evident. For example, most of the falciparal form of malaria in tropical Africa is transmitted by one of three species – *A. gambiae*, *A. arabiensis* and *A. funestus* – because these prefer human environments, human blood and adapt superbly to environmental changes (Collins & Besansky, 1994). Environmental factors involve rainfall, the presence of appropriate water conditions (a majority of the species prefer standing or slow, running water), temperature (the different species have varying optimal temperatures for the sporogony cycle) and altitude. Host factors include genetic features, behavioral (occupational exposure, selection of residence site with respect to mosquito breeding water locations), acquired immune resistance, and socioeconomic circumstances that permit construction of physical features that minimize exposure to mosquitoes and many others. Add to this the differences in virulence and other biological features of individual strains that often develop within any of the four species of *Plasmodium* affecting man, and the varying epidemiological and clinical presentations of malaria become understandable (Plorde, 1983). While malaria is characteristically seasonal, a combination of variables can obliterate even this feature.

The geographic pattern of malaria encircles the globe, but operation of the above-listed variables is responsible for its irregular distribution. Although other factors also contribute, the disease is only infrequently identified in areas where the average midsummer temperature is lower than 58 °F (13 °C), effectively restricting it to tropical and subtropical regions. Nevertheless, considerably more than half of today's world population lives in areas at risk for malaria infection. Residents of sub-Saharan Africa as well as much of eastern Asia and part of Oceania are at high risk as are those of portions of Venezuela, Brazil and Colombia. The U.S.A., Europe, Australia, Canada and most Caribbean islands have largely eliminated their endemic foci. Yet, while local sources in such countries have been minimized, some are experiencing a resurgence of the disease secondary to rising international tourism, refugee immigration, recreational intravenous drug use and even blood transfusion transmission.

In addition to the distribution irregularities of malaria's presence, the ratios of the four species affecting humans contribute further heterogeneity to malaria's global picture.

Plasmodium vivax is the most widely distributed and, in most areas where it occurs is also the most frequent. The outstanding exception to this is western Africa where the otherwise rare red blood cell genotype Fy(a-b-) (homozygous absence of the Duffy blood cell antigen) is nearly universal, probably reflecting an evolutionary response to the immunity to *P. vivax* parasitism that this genotype confers, because *P. vivax* uses a Duffy antigen (Fy6 which is absent in Fy(a-b-) persons) as a receptor for its red blood cell transmembrane passage (Gelpi & King, 1987; Mollison et al., 1993:253). In South Africa, however, *P. falciparum* is responsible for 99 % and *P. malariae* for 1 % of the malaria there (Hansford, 1977). At the other extreme is *P. ovale*, which is limited largely to Africa and certain parts of southeastern Asia such as Vietnam (Connor et al., 1976). The frequency of *P. malariae* has fluctuated significantly even in historic times; it was the most common form during the centuries of malarial endemicity in Europe, but is rare there now. *Plasmodium falciparum* remains the major threat to life in many parts of Africa, Brazil and other areas of malarial concentration.

Natural history

The acute phase: the malaria cycle

Figure 7.73 demonstrates the complex sequence of events occurring in the human-to-human transmission of malaria. If we initiate our discussion of this cycle with the mosquito ingesting blood from any infected human, the red blood cells of significance are those that contain the sexual forms (gametocytes). Within the mosquito's stomach these forms are released by gastric lysis of the red blood cells. Finding each other, the fertilization of the gametocytes leads to growth of the resulting mass of sporozoites within a cystic structure (ookinete) in the mosquito's stomach wall. When this eventually ruptures the sporozoites migrate to the mosquito's salivary glands and accompany the saliva that is injected into the victim's blood when the infected mosquito bites a susceptible human. This vector phase of growth is termed sporogony.

Within the now infected human, the sporozoites target liver cells, enter them and multiply asexually, each sporozoite producing many others that become transformed into merozoites. Few, if any, symptoms occur during this interval. The length of this clinical 'incubation period' varies from 2 weeks for the common species to 6 weeks for *P. malariae*. At the end of this time the newly produced merozoites escape from the hepatic cells and enter the blood stream. In the ovale and vivax forms of the disease some commonly re-enter an hepatic cell and repeat the hepatic phase, continuing to multiply and contribute new merozoites to the blood (providing the potential for relapse following treatment); in the other two species the hepatic phase constitutes only a single cycle and thus, unless reinfected, are self-limited diseases.

The freed merozoites emerging from the liver cells now attach to a red blood cell (RBC). The receptor site is probably unique to each species. That for *P. vivax* is known in detail: the previously-mentioned Duffy Fy6 RBC antigen. This antigen has been shown to be identical to the erythrocyte chemokine receptor (Horuk *et al.*, 1993), and an antibody directed against it has been demonstrated experimentally to be capable of blocking the penetration of the RBC membrane by *P. knowlesi*, the simian equivalent of *P. vivax*. Camus & Hadley (1985) suggest a falciparal protein product (subsequently named EBA-175) they isolated may serve as a bridge between the *P. falciparum* merozoite and the RBC. Wyler (1983a, b) suggests that glycophorin, an RBC membrane protein, appears to play a central role in falciparal transmembrane passage, though the effect is more probably achieved by this protein's stimulation of the RBC membrane to undergo the appropriate movement, rather than its functioning as a chemical receptor. More recently EBA-175 has been found to bind to glycophorin A on the RBC membrane (with the help of sialic acid) and, in contrast to *P. vivax*, can use alternative pathways (including glycophorin B), enabling it to bind to all human RBCs (L.H. Miller *et al.*, 1994; Sim *et al.*, 1994). Subsequent invagination of the RBC membrane interiorizes the merozoite where it assumes the ring form of a trophozoite. Its nucleus undergoes division (schizony), and accumulation of cytoplasm around each of these nuclear fragments generates new merozoites. The parasite consumes from 25–75 % of the RBC's hemoglobin content in the process of its intraerythrocytic multiplication (Wyler, 1983a, b) and the resulting hemin product is toxic to the RBC (Orjih *et al.*, 1981). Its rupture releases the newly formed merozoites, each of which promptly re-enters an intact RBC and repeats the intraerythrocytic cycle.

The interval required to complete an intraerythrocytic cycle is constant for the species (48 hours for *P. vivax* and *P. ovale*, 72 hours for *P. malariae*) and after about a week ('prodromal stage') the cycles become synchronized. Thereafter the massive, simultaneous RBC rupture and merozoite release produces the clinical picture of a malarial paroxysm, characterized by sudden onset of high fever, chills, headache, and muscle pains. It is not known if these symptoms are responsive to the presence of the newly released parasites in the blood, or to the potassium and fragmented cell products of the lysed RBC. As the merozoites re-enter RBCs the symptoms subside, leaving the patient exhausted as the fever falls, only to recur again after completion of the next intraerythrocytic cycle 2 or 3 days later. *Plasmodium falciparum* produces less well-defined paroxysms because it usually does not synchronize its RBC invasion and growth stages.

Continued repetition of these cycles eventually reduces their severity and regularity, though release of new crops of merozoites from the liver can renew them in infections by *P. vivax* and *P. ovale*. The cellular destruction occurs primarily in the spleen, which organ enlarges because of this additional workload, and becomes easily palpable. This occurs with such regularity that the 'splenomegaly rate' (% of examined population in whom the spleen is palpable) can serve as a reasonable assessment of chronic malarial infection frequency in endemic areas. After many intraerythrocytic cycles have been completed, sexual forms (gametocytes) instead of more merozoites are formed. These do not cause RBC rupture, with the result that the merozoite intraerythrocyte cycles cease. These sexual forms are included in the blood meal of a mosquito that bites a malarial person with circulating intraerythrocytic gametocytes, completing the overall malarial cycle (see Fig. 7.73).

Clinical features

Knowledge of the malarial cycle explains many of malaria's major features: (i) endemicity can only occur where one or more of the 67 (of the more than 400 total) species of anopheline mosquitoes are found that are capable of supporting the sporogony phase of the malaria cycle, in proximity to a sufficiently dense, infected human population susceptible to infection by the plasmodial species the mosquitoes can transmit; (ii) the acute symptoms of the paroxysm are associated with synchronized RBC destruction and release of their enclosed merozoites; (iii) the regular recurrence of the paroxysms at fixed intervals is related to the time interval needed for reproduction and maturation of new merozoites within the RBC (i.e. the intraerythrocytic cycle period) which is a feature of the plasmodial species.

Some other clinical features also have a demonstrably pathophysiological basis. The anemia that malarial victims commonly suffer is frequently greater than can be accounted for on the basis of the number of parasitized RBCs. This is because the RBC destruction (hemolysis) is not limited to the parasitized cells but also includes many normal-appearing, nonparasitized cells. The mechanism of destruction of these appears to have an immune basis, in which many circulating immune (antigen–antibody) complexes and/or complement become attached to nonparasitized RBCs that then are removed from circulation by the spleen. Removal and destruction of RBCs sensitized for any reason is a normal splenic function. Parasitized RBCs also modify the RBC surface proteins, resulting in a knob-like bulge that causes the infected RBC to adhere to endothelial cells and to normal RBCs (rosettes). Such a cluster of cells would also be removed by the spleen (L.H. Miller *et al.*, 1994).

As expected, severity of the symptoms is a function of the degree of parasitemia (the percentage of RBCs parasitized at any given moment). This is also plasmodial species-related. *Plasmodium ovale* and *P. vivax* produce milder disease in part because they primarily traverse the membranes of relatively young RBCs (the minority of a given RBC population). *Plasmodium falciparum*, however, can parasitize RBCs of any age, producing much higher parasitemia levels. Only falciparal malaria is commonly fatal, not only because of the higher parasitemia levels, but also because the expression of the parasite-induced protein 'EMP-1' (Nowak, 1995) on the cell membrane of RBCs parasitized by *P. falciparum*. This protein causes them to adhere to host cell surface proteins (CD36, ICAM-1, etc) on the endothelial lining of capillaries in many organs throughout the body but especially in brain venules, clogging these vessels and retarding or blocking blood flow through them (Chan-Ling *et al.*, 1992). It is this feature that is principally responsible for the lethality of untreated falciparal malaria. Damage to the affected organs produces clinical features of encephalopathy, cardiac arrhythmias and pulmonary insufficiency which, together with kidney glomerular damage from deposit of immune complexes and consequent renal failure, can cause death from failure of one or more of these organs (White & Plorde, 1991). While people infected with the species other than falciparal malaria are usually spared these lethal complications, an occasional death from fatal intra-abdominal hemorrhage may occur in patients with *P. vivax*-induced huge splenomegaly if the individual suffers sufficient local trauma to rupture the fragile, infected spleen.

The diagnosis of malaria can often be made on the basis of symptoms and signs. Regularly-spaced paroxysms with splenomegaly in a person with a history of exposure (residence in or visit to a known malarial area) can make possible a diagnosis on a purely clinical basis. However, experienced malariologists are well aware of the extreme variability of clinical features in this disease, and include malaria in the differential diagnosis of a diagnostic problem if the patient was at malaria risk. Diagnostic confirmation is achieved by morphologic identification of the parasite within the RBCs on a stained blood smear. If the degree of parasitization is low, concentrated smears are more apt to demonstrate the parasite, though a greater degree of skill is required to interpret them.

The chronic phase

In untreated patients the recurring paroxysms in the acute phase gradually subside in intensity and their sharply defined intervals become obscured. Blood smears demonstrate progressively decreasing parasitemia. After weeks the fever and general toxicity have subsided, and the infected person enters the chronic phase of the disease. It is characterized by a moderate anemia, with fatigue proportional to the anemia. Parasitization may be so low that only concentrated smears demonstrate the organisms. Such individuals, though not well, usually resume their daily activities. Persisting, low-level infection, however, maintains their enlarged spleen and often the liver also. This clinical picture, even in the absence of demonstrable parasitemia, is termed tropical splenomegaly syndrome. These persons commonly also have certain immunological changes reflecting previous malarial infection and malariologists diagnose patients with the syndrome as suffering from chronic malaria even though the organism cannot be identified. Antimalarial therapy usually produces a beneficial response in such persons (White & Plorde, 1991).

The progression from the acute to the chronic phase of malarial infection is accompanied by demonstrable immunological changes involving both humoral and cellular responses. Antibodies directed against the parasite are believed effective in the erythrocytic cycle phase, though the sporozoites within hepatic cells escape detection. The role of T lymphocytes is less well known, though it is clear they produce chemicals (cytokines) such as interferon-gamma and induce macrophages to release the inflammatory agent called tumor necrosis factor-alpha (L.H. Miller *et al.*, 1994). These lymphocytes' participation is clearly vital to eventual disappearance of the infection. For several years the chronic state may be interrupted by acute recurrences secondary to the discharge of additional merozoites into the blood stream from the hepatic cells where they continue to cycle, isolated from the immune responses in persons with *P. vivax* and *P. malariae* infections. Alternatively, residence in a malaria area may result in a new infection, perhaps by a different species. The immunity is not only species-specific, but often strain-specific.

As in other features, falciparal malaria also differs from the other three species infecting humans with respect to spontaneous immune responses. The absence, in falciparal malaria, of continuing intrahepatic merozoite production, as occurs in the vivax and ovale species, results in a greater effectiveness of the humoral (antibody) response, so that those who survive the complications of the acute phase of falciparal malaria enjoy a favorable prognosis for spontaneous cure, unless reinfected. Treatment and eradication attempts are discussed in the historical section below.

Interactions between malaria and red blood cell polymorphisms

The merozoites of all four malaria species infecting man must be able to complete a part of their total life cycle within the human host's RBCs. To accomplish this, two key conditions must be met: (i) the parasite must be able to bind to a specific protein on the outside of the RBC membrane; this bond will then stimulate the membrane invagination that carries the parasite into the RBC's cytoplasmic interior, and (ii) once inside the RBC the parasite must be able to utilize cytoplasmic proteins to meet the enormous nutritional demands of its growth and multiplication.

The first of these requirements (membrane receptor) has already been discussed. These membrane receptor proteins are species-specific. For *P. vivax* the receptor is the Duffy Fy6 RBC antigen. This Fy6 antigen is missing in people who manifest neither the a nor b Duffy antigen Fy(a-b-) on the RBC membrane surface. In such persons the parasite cannot enter the RBC to complete its cycle (Mollison *et al.*, 1993:253). Only in western Africa are huge populations found without either of the Duffy antigens, and such persons are immune to the vivax form of malaria (Gelpi & King,

1976). This circumstance is often cited as a model of how a random mutation (in this case absence of Fy6 RBC antigen) can confer such a great health advantage (freedom from vivax malaria) that the greater reproductive success postulated to occur in such healthier persons leads to its eventual replacement of other gene forms (in this case leading to the Duffy Fy(a-b-) phenotype) by natural selection. In modern studies, however, it has not been easy to demonstrate convincingly that increased reproductive success, postulated to be the mechanism of the evolutionary process, actually occurs with sufficient consistency to bring about the hypothesized consequence. While progress is being made, the nature of the receptor proteins for the other vivax and malariae forms has not yet been defined chemically with specificity, though we do know that P. falciparum can employ several alternative chemical routes (including glycophorin A and B), enabling it to enter all human RBCs.

The other requirement is more complex. The physiological function of the RBC is to transport oxygen from the inhaled air in the lung to all the metabolizing tissues of the entire body. This process is so vital that cessation of blood flow for even a few minutes results in irreversible brain damage. To maximize its efficiency the human RBC consists of little more than an anucleated, membrane-bound bag of hemoglobin. This hemoglobin is the only protein energy source present within the RBC in amounts sufficient to provide the energy demands of the reproducing and growing merozoites within it. Not surprisingly, these merozoites consume up to three-fourths of the hemoglobin within the RBC before it lyses and frees the newly-formed parasites (Wyler, 1983b:935). Anything that impairs the availability of such hemoglobin as an energy source for the parasite will function as a significant impediment to merozoite growth, and will tend to limit the ability to maintain malarial disease in such an individual.

A number of mutations are known that either alter hemoglobin directly so as to make it less suitable for the malaria parasite's consumption, or alter the parasitized cell in a manner that it is recognized and destroyed by the spleen. In either event, the survival of merozoites in such altered cells is threatened. Probably the best-studied of these is hemoglobin S (HbS). The altered gene coding for hemoglobin in such patients results in a 'point mutation' in which substitution of a single amino acid (of the 146 composing hemoglobin's beta globin chain) occurs: valine for glutamic acid at position 6 in the molecule. Trager & Jensen(1976) have developed a method for culturing falciparal parasites in vitro. Using this method, substitution of HbS in vitro for normal hemoglobin (HbA) has been shown to impair the rate of falciparal merozoite growth. In addition, the altered HbS is less soluble in an hypoxic environment, and in homozygous HbS persons the hemoglobin polymerizes into an insoluble, linear chain that deforms the RBC into an elongated, arc-like shape resembling a sickle blade, hence the name of the condition: sickle cell disease. The deformed RBCs are destroyed prema-

turely and tend to clog capillaries, reducing blood flow and injuring the ischemic organs.

In the past untreated homozygous HbS children usually died before puberty. Heterozygotes, however, produce both HbS and normal HbA. They have enough HbA to prevent the RBC deformation and thus have few or no clinical disease manifestations. However, they do have enough HbS in their RBCs to impair falciparal merozoite growth within such RBCs. Thus, heterozygotes (HbSA) escape the disease but gain the benefits of falciparal malarial suppression (Allison, 1954). Within a population, therefore, the loss of the occasional homozygote child is compensated, in part at least, by the hypothesized increased reproductive success of the much larger number of sickle cell heterozygotes, since the latter enjoy actually greater malarial resistance than those with normal hemoglobin. These two alterations, one (HbSS) threatening the population while the other (HbSA) benefiting it, are viewed as being in balance, maintaining not only the population but also the perpetuation of the S gene. Such a situation is called a balanced polymorphism. In this example malaria maintains the balance because it confers benefit to the heterozygote living in a malarial area. Without malaria only the prepubertal lethal action in the homozygote would operate, and thus eventually would be expected to extinguish the gene within the population.

Other gene alterations that have been postulated to have a similar effect are HbC, HbE, HbF, thalassemia and glucose-6-phosphate dehydrogenase (G6PD) deficiency (Roth, 1985; Kiple & King, 1981). The evidence for the mechanism of action in sickle cell disease as a balanced polymorphism is well-documented, but the quantitative effect (i.e. whether actual balance is achieved) has not yet won universal acceptance. The others listed above enjoy substantially less investigation and their current status must be viewed more speculatively.

Hunt & Stocker (1990) question whether the oxidative stress occurring in G6PD deficient RBCs actually is of an order of magnitude to inhibit malarial parasite growth within the RBC. Fava bean ingestion is followed by RBC lysis in people with G6PD deficient RBCs. The β-glycosides vicine and convicine, present in fava beans, are hydrolyzed in the bowel to divicine and isomural, whose oxidized forms can place sufficient oxidant stress on G6PD-deficient RBCs to cause their hemolysis. Clark et al. (1984) demonstrated that divicine killed intracellular malarial parasites (P. vinckei) in mouse RBCs in vivo. They suggested that fava beans (in subhemolytic dose) helped preserve G6PD genes by acting as an antimalarial agent. Using in vitro methods, Golenser et al. (1983, 1988) demonstrated that isomuracil enhanced the resistance of G6PD-deficient RBCs to parasitization by falciparal organisms. Roth et al. (1983) also demonstrated inhibition of in vitro growth of P. falciparum in G6PD deficient RBC. Greene (1993) concluded that well-designed population studies support the protective effects of G6PD deficiency against falciparal malaria parasitism predicted by the in vitro studies. Since the latter reveal enhancement of such effects by certain foods (fava beans), he suggests further that quinine taste sensitivity coevolved with G6PD polymorphic variants on the basis that ingestion of small amounts of such food items (kept small by the increased detection of their bitter taste) would prevent unfavorable major hemolysis but retain their antimalarial oxidant effect.

Nagel et al. (1981) note that the impairment of HbE on malarial parasite growth probably only is significantly effective in the homozygote. Roth (1985) cites Vogel & Motulsky's (1960) observation that thalassemia and malaria reveal geographical concordance but that in vitro studies reveal no suppression of malarial parasite growth, implying that thalassemia's protective effect must operate through some other mechanism. On the basis of α thalassemia's gene frequencies in Namibia's San (Bushmen) and South African Bantu populations and considering these tribes' origins, Ramsay & Jenkins (1984) suggest this may be the oldest of African malarial parasite traits.

In summary, the concept of malaria-driven balanced polymorphisms can be considered a very attractive explanation for the perpetuation of otherwise lethal or at least destructive genes in malarial geographic areas. The bulk of evidence supporting these suggestions has been derived from geographical correlations of malaria (principally falciparal) and the polymorphic gene of interest. Well-designed studies of living populations are consistent with these hypotheses. Only relatively recently have in vitro methods evolved to evaluate the degree of biochemical support for these associations. To date these suggest that, in addition to intraerythrocytic metabolic changes, alternative mechanisms such as premature cell death may also be operative. Hill et al. (1991) have also suggested that certain leukocyte HLA antigens common in West Africans provide antimalarial protection by affecting presentation of antigen to immune system cells. Continuing methodological progress can be expected to provide a future database that permits firmer conclusions than are possible currently.

Antiquity and history

Antiquity of the malarial parasite

Malarial organisms are among the most ancient of human parasites. While the fossil record provides only meager support for this point of view, the taxonomic distribution of these organisms among modern animals suggests a prolonged phylogenetic development. In addition to humans, malaria parasites infect many mammals, numerous avian hosts, some reptiles (mostly lizards) and perhaps even some amphibians (Russell et al., 1963). Furthermore, the high degree of specialization that characterizes the relationship between many of the plasmodial species, their insect vectors and their vertebrate hosts testifies to the length of the evolu-

tionary interval necessary to achieve this level of adaptation. Garnham (1963) postulates the presence of quartan-like parasites in lemurs during the Tertiary Age 60 million years ago (mya), benign tertian species during the Oligocene about 30 mya and malignant tertian probably during the Pleistocene. Their ancestors may have been members of the modern intestinal cell parasites of the order Coccidia.

Neither the place nor the time when the four species that currently infect humans evolved is known with certainty. While controversial, the origin of humans appears to be centered in Africa, and the similarity of some of the malarial species adapted to the African higher primates to those of humans suggests a possible common ancestor (Cockburn, 1963:2). This could have occurred during the Pleistocene because, in their relatively sheltered position within RBCs, the parasites may be spared some of the natural selective influences acting on their hosts, resulting in slower evolutionary adaptation of the malarial parasite than that of its vertebrate host. Indeed, Plasmodium cynomolgi bastianelli (a vivax-type malarial parasite isolated from a Malayan Macacus fascicularis monkey) was accidentally passed to humans in a laboratory accident, and then experimentally demonstrated to be able to be passed man-to-man by infected mosquitoes (Eyles et al., 1960; Contacos et al., 1962).

Thus, Cockburn (1963:2) feels malaria is older than humans, and that the two probably coevolved in tropical Africa, while Bruce-Chwatt (1965) suggests that human migration related to the Neolithic revolution carried it down the Nile to the Mediterranean shores, Mesopotamia, India and even to South China.

Human history of malaria.

General considerations

The nonspecificity of malaria's clinical features retarded the development of our understanding of this disease. Malaria has three significant clinical characteristics: febrile paroxysms, the periodicity of their recurrence, and splenomegaly. However, the first two of these are obvious only in their acute stage (falciparal forms frequently never become periodic), both the fever and its distinctive, recurrent interval subsiding with the development of partial immunity as it enters the chronic stage. Furthermore, splenomegaly may be most obvious in the chronic stage when fever is minimal or absent. The difficulty early physicians encountered in trying to separate malaria from the many other causes of fever is self-evident. This is particularly true during the period before medical concepts linked symptoms to specific etiological agents. In addition, the large number of variables involving the vector, host, parasite and environment contributed further to the inconstancy of clinical observations. These problems constrain our reconstruction of the disease's history.

The history of malaria is discussed below from a geographic perspective. Appreciation of these events, however, may well be enhanced by preliminary reference to Table 7.5.

Table 7.5. Chronology of discoveries leading to understanding of malaria cycle.

400 B.C.	Malaria separated clinically from other fevers: periodicity; splenomegaly (Hippocrates).
A.D.1640	Peruvian cinchona bark extract introduced to Europe (Countess of Chinchon?).
1650	Diagnostic value of therapeutic response to cinchona bark (T. Sydenham, T. Brady, R. Talbor).
1820	Quinine isolated from cinchona bark (French chemists Pelletier and Caventou).
1831	Association of swamps with malaria : 'malaria (bad air)' or 'paludism' (Boyle, 1931).
1837	Black granules in blood and spleen in malarial patients (Meckel).
1880	Exflagellation observed in malarial blood (Laveran, 1880).
1889	Exflagellation observed in avian malaria (Danilewsky, 1897 a, b).
1891	Giemsa stain developed (Romanowski, 1891).
1897	Gametogenesis described in avian and falciparal malaria (Ross, 1897 a, b).
1897	Exflagellation described in mosquito (Ross, 1897 a, b).
1897	Sporozoite cycle in mosquito described in avian malaria (Ross, 1897 a, b).
1900	Sporozoite cycle in vivax and falciparal malaria described (Grassi, 1900).
1922	Therapeutic value of malaria in neurosyphilis described (Wagner-Jauregg, 1922).
1947	Exoerythrocytic stage of *Hepatocystis* described in monkey liver (Garnham, 1947).
1948	Exoerythrocytic stage of human and simian malaria described (Shortt & Garnham, 1948).

This outline is distilled primarily from a detailed and authoritative narrative description in Garnham (1966:3–16).

This table provides a chronology of the discoveries over more than 300 years that eventually led to an understanding of all stages in the malaria cycle. It is presented in outline form, distilled primarily from an authoritative and detailed, 14 page narration presented by Garnham (1966:3–16).

Europe

Clearly malarial transmission would not have been possible during the Pleistocene's glaciation episodes that involved much of Europe, though the interstadial periods were warm enough to have supported the various stages of the diseases. Hints of the possible presence of malaria can be found in the Vedic literature, in the Ebers papyrus and in Homer, but nowhere in these earlier years are the disease descriptions diagnostic of malaria. Henschen (1966) observes no evidence of malaria in Egypt until the Hellenistic period. However, in an extraordinarily thorough review of paleoclimatological and geological evidence, Bruce-Chwatt & Zulueta (1980) concluded that Europe probably was not plagued with malaria epidemics until at least about 500 B.C. They base this prediction on the fact that population densities before that date were generally too low to support endemic malaria foci and that the efficient vectors *A. labranchiae* and *A. sacharovi* could not have survived the climatological circumstances. The principal European vector before 500 B.C. seems to have been *A. atroparvus*, an inefficient vector for *P. malariae* and *P. vivax*, and one which, at that time, was

immune to *P. falciparum* strains that may occasionally have been introduced from North Africa. In addition, falciparal malaria requires a midsummer temperature near 20 °C (not reached in Europe until later) while that for the other human malarial species is several degrees less. Thus, these authors argue that only *P. malariae* and *P. vivax* were found in Europe before 500 B.C. and then only in scattered foci of southern Europe, poorly transmitted and causing only a mild disease.

This reconstruction is in partial conflict with the now well-known Angel (1967) hypothesis that the malaria-driven spread of thalassemia in the eastern Mediterranean occurred during the Neolithic period. Using the thickened cranial diploe (porotic hyperostosis) in archaeological skulls as a marker for the congenital anemia of β thalassemia, he correlated its frequency with sea level fluctuations (which he postulated would provide new mosquito vector breeding areas) during Neolithic years. He attributed periods of decreased porotic hyperostosis frequency to the protection from malaria that he believed the relatively asymptomatic heterozygote state of thalassemia imparted. However, the reconstruction by Bruce-Chwatt & Zulueta (1980:14) does not predict the presence of these malarial species there until millennia later because of the lower temperatures, low population density and absent vector. In addition, the hypothesized protection of the heterozygous thalassemia state is supported primarily by correlations between the distribution of thalassemia and <u>falciparal</u> malaria presence, and they feel that such high correlations are found only in Italy and Sardinia.

Nevertheless, increasing Mediterranean commerce during the millennium before 500 B.C. disseminated both material and cognitive commodities. Among the latter was the concept of agricultural use of land. In Greece this developed at such a pace that by about 500 B.C. deforestation had created such major alluvial deposits at river mouths that large, newly-formed marshes emerged, which provided new mosquito breeding areas (Bruce-Chwatt & Zulueta, 1980). Increased trade activity also introduced both new falciparal strains as well as African mosquito species capable of transmitting it. Although malaria began to increase in frequency in Europe after 500 B.C., initially at least it appears to be limited largely to nonfalciparal forms. The Hippocratic corpus (400 B.C.) clearly recognized malaria as a unique fever form and also described the associated splenomegaly. This source, however, remains silent regarding the falciparal form of malaria. It has been suggested that Alexander the Great's returning soldiers may have brought malaria as well as booty back home with them. Malaria apparently expanded slowly and probably quite focally between the early and late classical Greek and Roman periods, though its presence there is confirmed by Celsus and Cicero. Detailed descriptions of military campaigns during this period identify bivouacs by huge armies in marshy areas that would surely have devastated them to a degree that would have entered the military record, had malaria then been as common in southern

Europe as it was later. Thus, it was not until the later Hellenistic and late Imperial Roman times that such episodes begin to appear in historical chronicles.

The Middle Ages following the collapse of Rome provide only meager data about malaria in Europe. While southern Italy probably does not reflect the status of malaria throughout all of Europe, we do have at least military histories of this area. During the several centuries following the fall of Rome, the many barbarian armies besieging that city repeatedly frequently paid a heavy price in malarial deaths or were totally driven out by the malarial mosquitoes of the Pontine marshes outside the city (Cloudsley-Thompson, 1976). In A.D. 587 St. Augustine probably died of malaria while traveling through this area. Between A.D. 900 and 1200 the armies of reigning European monarchs (Otto the Great, Frederick Barbarossa and others) attacking Rome suffered a fate similar to those of the earlier barbarians. Europe experienced its first malarial pandemic about the mid-sixteenth century (Cloudsley-Thompson, 1976). The term 'malária' (bad air) dates at least to the sixteenth century (Jarcho, 1993:189). The latter part of the seventeenth century was characterized by a high level of endemic malaria with periodic epidemics of 'the ague' sweeping Europe throughout the eighteenth and most of the nineteenth centuries. Spain, France, Germany, the Balkan areas and even much of Scandinavia suffered from malaria, though the falciparal form appears to have constituted a minor fraction of the cases and these especially in southern Europe or in port cities.

The U.K. participated in these patterns. Several of their monarchs contracted the disease and Oliver Cromwell may have died of it. The therapeutic value of extracts prepared from the bark of the Peruvian cinchona tree (Cortex cinchonae) was introduced in England during the mid-seventeenth century (legendarily by an aristocrat's wife, the Countess of Chinchon) and championed by Thomas Sydenham and Robert Brady. Robert Talbor's cure of Charles II's malaria with cinchona bark extract brought him fame and encouraged popular acceptance of such therapy, which had been resisted by some on a religious basis because of its dissemination by the Jesuits (Smith, 1976).

Kiple & King (1981) have graphically recorded the disastrous early European efforts to establish trade and colonization bases in West Africa, particularly those relating to the slave trade. The high mortality among European merchants and soldiers soon led to the view of the west African coast as the 'white man's grave,' and malaria (often then called the angel of death) was responsible for a large fraction of these deaths. In the late seventeenth century European visitors to West Africa suffered a 50 % annual mortality. Crews of French slavers, with a more transient exposure, still suffered a 20 % mortality per transatlantic voyage. Nineteenth century British Army records indicated a death rate of 15.3/1000/year for European soldier members stationed in England, contrasting with 483–688/1000/year among those stationed in West Africa. These rates are of special interest when compared to those for West

African and African West Indies members of the British Army extracted from military records by Curtin (1988) who found rates only about one-fourth to one-tenth as great for Africans as for their European fellow-soldiers. While many Europeans had been exposed to malaria (see above), this was primarily to P. malariae while the virulent form experienced commonly in West Africa was principally falciparal malaria. Furthermore, many West African natives enjoyed the increased resistance to malaria of both the acquired and the genetic types discussed above under the Interactions between malaria and red blood cell polymorphisms and Natural history sections, above. Disease, primarily malaria, remained a demanding price for permanent European presence in West Africa until the development of effective malaria prophylaxis at the beginning of the twentieth century. It remains a major public health problem for both natives and Europeans there even today.

The decline of malaria in Europe began about the mid-nineteenth century. It was an asynchronous movement, reflecting the complexity of malaria's epidemiology, and no single feature will explain the pattern's sequence. Factors involved include swamp drainage, increasing agricultural use of the land, increasing quality of building structures, separation of residence areas from swamps, mosquito control efforts, drug therapy (beginning with cinchona bark (1632) progressing to quinine (1820) and finally the synthetics such as mepacrine, etc (1940s)), increased understanding of the disease that resulted from experience with the therapeutic use of malaria for neurosyphilis in the 1920s (Wagner-Jaureagg, 1922), improved sanitation and socioeconomic conditions, insecticide use and others.

The New World

The question of the pre-Columbian presence of malaria in the western hemisphere has occupied many investigators, though controversy on this topic remains. Dunn (1965) points out that, in contrast to Africa, malaria is a natural infection of American feral mammals. Furthermore, the two malarial species identified in them (P. brasilianum and P. simium) are almost indistinguishable from the human species P. malariae and P. vivax, respectively. The falciparal form has no representation among New World primates. He notes that the numerous genetic polymorphisms that provide some degree of protection from malaria (hemoglobin S, C and E; thalassemia; glucose-6-phosphate dehydrogenase deficiency; absence of Duffy antigens) and which are common in malarial areas of Africa and Asia are almost absent in North and South America. The trans-Beringian passage by those populating the New World appears to have filtered out the disease. While occasional Pacific Islanders may have landed in South America over the past millennia, absence of appropriate vectors in Oceania at that time make it unlikely they brought malaria with them. Even the alleged South American indigenes' ancient recognition of cinchona bark's antimalarial properties proves to be anecdotal. Early American colonists did not suffer malaria until they introduced it from Europe.

Dunn concludes that malaria in the Americas is a post-Columbian disease. Wood (1975) also notes that hemolytic disease of the newborn based on the ABO blood group normally acts to reduce the A and B blood group antigens in a populations. Since malaria-bearing anopheline mosquitoes preferentially bite humans of blood group O, this would counterbalance the above-noted anemia's effect, maintaining the frequency of A and B antigens. Because most Native Americans are of phenotype O blood group, the absence of malaria's effect in pre-Columbian times is implied.

The findings of P. malariae and P. vivax without P. falciparum in a remote, forested Peruvian valley (Sulzer et al., 1975) could reflect the pre-Columbian status of malaria in the New World. However, Bruce-Chwatt (1965) examined all the evidence and arguments in exhaustive detail, particularly the literary references attributing indigenous familiarity with cinchona bark, and found evidence suggestive of both views but convincing of neither. He leaves the question unanswered, anticipating that application of new technology to South American mummified human remains may eventually supply the evidence required for an authoritative conclusion, a suggestion we endorse enthusiastically.

Although the conquistadors may well have been acquainted with the ague, they probably had just as much difficulty separating it from other febrile illnesses as we do today when reading their chronicles. Smallpox and measles were highly contagious and exacted a great toll among American indigenes shortly after contact. Though these two conditions were at least normally accompanied by skin rashes, a variety of dysenteries such as typhoid fever, and other febrile illnesses like yellow fever could simulate malarial symptoms so closely that unlettered sixteenth century explorers and adventurers could not be expected to differentiate them any better than could the European physicians of that time. Malaria may have joined smallpox and measles as agents responsible for the cascade of epidemics described by Dobyns (1963) flowing through the Andean area during the first few centuries after 1492, though the high fevers he cites can not be translated into a specific disease as easily as can the more familiar lesions of smallpox and measles. Several febrile illnesses of indeterminate nature decimated the early colonies on Hispaniola. In a search for pre-Columbian New World malaria, there is little value in detailing descriptions of the epidemics that raged throughout the New World during the early or midportion of the sixteenth century; unequivocal identification of malaria among them simply is not evident in these records.

However, within a few decades after contact, the importation of African slaves introduced an independent and obvious source of malaria. Disappointment with Native Americans as slaves by the New World colonizers led to the African slave trade whose role as mediators of transatlantic exportation of malaria has been well documented by both Kiple & King (1981) as well as Curtin (1988). Recruited from the western African equatorial coastal areas, many of these were malaria-infected (Merbs, 1992), often in the chronic phase and they therefore had partial immunity. The first of these began to trickle in about 1510. By 1576 an estimated 40 000 had arrived (Bruce-Chwatt, 1965) with rapid increases thereafter. Portuguese and German slavers delivered many to the Brazilian coasts. Certainly malaria soon became established even among the Spanish colonists, particularly in coastal areas and port cities. Thereafter it becomes a formidable problem to trace the ultimate origin of the malaria observed in the New World from historical sources.

Dunn (1993) describes how malaria had even spread up much of the Mississippi Valley by the nineteenth century and also involved both coasts. Malaria and dysentery combined to devastate populations along the southern periphery of America's southwestern region during the last half of the sixteenth century (Reff, 1992). The epidemics along the lower Columbia River, described as 'fever and ague' by Americans (and 'intermittent fever' by the British) during the early nineteenth century were new to that area's natives and almost certainly was malaria, probably a mixture of P. vivax and the falciparal form, causing an 87 % loss of the local population within a decade (Boyd, 1992). In 1914 the U.S.A. of America recorded 600 000 malarial infections, about half of which were of the falciparal form (Binford & Connor, 1976).

Control and eradication efforts

Diligent combinations of swamp drainage, chemical prophylaxis and especially liberal use of vector control by insecticides (DDT) following World War II led to the virtual extinction of endemic foci of malaria in the U.S.A. and several other countries. By 1955 the World Health Organization (W.H.O.) had become so encouraged that they launched a global effort to eradicate malaria. Although many different antimalarial approaches were employed, initially these eradication efforts were centered on residual insecticide spraying of homes, sometimes supplemented by nontechnical but labor-intensive techniques of wetlands drainage. By 1975 successful eradication had been achieved in Australia, the U.S.A. and most of Europe. An intensive campaign in Sardinia, for example, ended malarial transmission there for the first time since its probable introduction from Carthage during the Punic wars. It soon became apparent, however, that successful eradication required a basic health care infrastructure, national will and major capital expenditure. Subsequently the realities of conditions in many tropical developing countries led to a shift of emphasis from eradication to malaria control (Clyde, 1987). The success of chemical malarial suppressants, especially chloroquine during the Vietnam conflict, caused many of the developing countries to abandon all other more costly approaches. The subsequent development of falciparal malarial resistance to this compound has been followed by a resurgence in the disease frequency (Wyler, 1983a, b,1993) to which these countries, having abandoned nonchemical control methods, cannot now respond rapidly.

With these experiences, interest has shifted toward the development of an antimalarial vaccine (Miller, 1986). Production of such a vaccine against a protozoan with a life cycle as complex as that of *P. falciparum* presents unique problems. Immunity against malaria is not only specific for each plasmodial species, but also against each stage of the species. Furthermore, the intracellular parasites within the liver cells escape immunosurveillance. *In vitro* culture methods have enabled substantial progress at the molecular level of study (Barker *et al.*, 1986), including identification of genes coding for the major surface protein of the falciparal sporozoite (Dame *et al.*, 1984). Vaccination with isolated, attentuated merozoites has succeeded in simian malaria with *P. knowlesi* (Wyler, 1983a, b). Nevertheless the many complex biological interactions have, in spite of encouraging progress, retarded the availability of a vaccine demonstrated to be both safe and effective for human use to date (Miller, 1986). *Plasmodium falciparum* induces a wide variety of antigenic determinants on the RBC membrane, further complicating the vaccine problem. Recently Patarroyo (cited in Maurice, 1995) has claimed considerable success with a three-peptide vaccine. Experimental efforts using genetic engineering targeting the mosquito itself or the sporozoites developing within it are in their infancy (Aldhous, 1993; Zheng *et al.*, 1993).

Impact of malaria on ancient populations

The many millions of people suffering from malaria today provide us with a model, much of which can be extrapolated back to ancient populations. Adults with sufficient immunity to suppress many of malaria's symptoms still harbor the parasite in their blood. Mosquitoes can transfer the organism to nonimmune children who develop acute, severe disease. Thus, children under 5 probably bore much of the symptomatic burden evident in ancient populations as they do in modern ones (L.H. Miller *et al.*, 1994). In areas of low endemicity the cerebral form was especially common and its high mortality can be expected to have had a significant demographic impact on such populations. The relative state of partial immunodeficiency that characterizes the pregnant woman rendered her susceptible to malarial exacerbations that stunted fetal growth with resulting low birth weight hazards as well as intrauterine death. Additionally, neonatal infections contributed further losses.

In areas of high endemicity, severe anemia rendered infected children and even some adults susceptible to the well-established vulnerability of anemic patients to serious infections. Other complications including exsanguination from ruptured spleens contributed further to malarial deaths.

Children surviving the first 5 years of life gradually moved into the same status as adults – sufficient immunity to suppress at least the acute symptoms most of the time, though continuing to harbor the organism. Transient metabolic insults from other acute infections or episodes of malnutrition could produce transient partial immunosuppression, allowing exacerbation of malarial symptoms of sufficient severity to strain an already compromised immune status, converting a potentially reversible infection into a lethal one.

While undoubtedly falciparal malaria was responsible for most of the deaths, and while it was common for many adults to be free of the exhausting paroxysms of the acute disease, it must be understood that an adult with chronic malaria is not a healthy individual. Not only is such a person subject to the occasional acute exacerbations described above, but the constant parasitemia can reduce an adults' energy level and productivity. Thus, in addition to the actual deaths described above, reduced fertility commonly seen in many chronic infections most probably contributed further to such a population's demographic burden.

Finally, while ancient populations may not have understood the connection between malaria and the mosquito vector, they most surely did observe the differences in malaria frequency among various environmental circumstances and responded to them to the extent possible.

Soft tissue lesions of malaria in ancient human tissues

Chronic malarial soft tissue lesions can be expected to be characterized by moderate liver enlargement and varying degrees of enlarged spleens. Long-standing malaria commonly results in progressive occlusion of small splenic blood vessels with infarction and fibrosis. One could expect such a spleen to show only mild to moderate size increase but to be riddled with fibrous scar, a tissue type that resists decay better than the blood cells normally composing the bulk of living splenic mass. Traumatic rupture of the spleen in a person with acute malaria would be accompanied by massive intra-abdominal hemorrhage, probably detectable in well-preserved mummies. In fresh tissue the precipitated pigment of hemoglobin catabolism induced by malaria parasites is prominent (Yamada & Sherman, 1979), but in desiccated mummy tissues such pigment could be difficult to separate from many other (often postmortem) pigment forms.

Ruffer (1913) speculated that the presence of splenomegaly in several Egyptian mummies from the Coptic period might reflect malarial infection but demonstrated no organisms. Cockburn *et al.* (1980) found a small, dark piece of tissue in the Egyptian mummy Nakht (ROM-1, dissected by members of the Paleopathology Association) that he felt could be spleen. Attempts by Krotoski (1980) of the U.S. Public Health Hospital in New Orleans to demonstrate the organism by immunofluorescence with antibodies against *P. vivax*, *P. cynomolgi* and *P. falciparum* on sections of the rehydrated tissue all produced positive reactions, and Giemsa stains revealed no organisms. These reactions were interpreted by Krotoski (1980) as nonspecific reactions, not diagnostically interpretable. Cockburn (1980) commented that 'This report does increase the likelihood that ROM-1 died from a ruptured spleen resulting from malaria... .' Nevertheless, Guy, Krotoski & Cockburn (1981) coauthored a manuscript whose abstract concluded '... a diagnosis of malaria based on these results is not possible.' Unless subsequent more certain evidence is provided, it would appear that this mummy should not be cited as an established example of malaria in ancient mummies.

However, preliminary trials of an immunological approach on human mummy tissue extracts have produced titillating results. Howard *et al.* (1986) found a circulating anodic antigen secreted into the blood by P. *falciparum* and a monoclonal antibody targeting that antigen developed by Parra *et al.* (1991) led to the development of an enzyme-linked immunosorbent assay (ELISA) that proved to be 98 % sensitive and 96 % specific (Taylor & Voller, 1993). A commercial modification of this (ParaSight™-F test) designed for field use gave positive reactions in 7 of 18 Egyptian and Nubian mummies ranging from 1500 to more than 5000 years old (R.L. Miller *et al.*, 1994). To date malarial parasites have not been demonstrated convincingly by morphologic or nucleic acid methodology in any ancient human tissue.

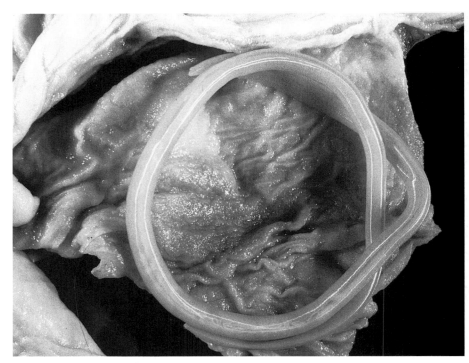

FIG. 7.74: *Ascaris lumbricoides.* This roundworm parasite was found upon opening the intestine during autopsy in North America. Modern adult female. BM.

HELMINTH INFECTIONS

ASCARIASIS

Taxonomy, epidemiology, and natural history

Ascaris lumbricoides is an intestinal roundworm that may exceed 30 cm in length. Although a porcine species exists, only humans act as hosts for this species. The adult worms normally reside in the jejunum. The female produces prodigious numbers of eggs – up to several hundred thousand daily – and often more than the males can fertilize. Several weeks after these have been discharged into the soil, the fertilized ova have developed into larvae. Human ingestion of these results in release of the larvae in the intestine. The larvae then initiate a rather circuitous route through the body, beginning by invasion of an intestinal mucosal capillary, being carried by the blood to the lung. Here they escape from the pulmonary capillary, penetrate the alveolar wall and reach the air-containing alveolus. Passing upward through the bronchi and larynx, larvae reach the pharynx, are swallowed with sputum and saliva, reaching the intestinal lumen from which their body tour originated. There they then grow to maturity (Fig. 7.74), completing the cycle. Their effect on the host during this extraintestinal part of their life cycle is largely limited to the pulmonary segment where they may produce cough, allergic responses or even bronchopneumonia.

Predictably, since human-to-human transmission is by the fecal–oral route, the condition is most common under circumstances devoid of latrine facilities or with poorly developed sewage disposal systems. Particularly vulnerable are populations indulging in night soil practices (use of human feces for garden fertilization), since the large number of ova excreted in the feces from an affected individual will contaminate the garden plants. Children playing in areas used casually for defecation are also very susceptible because the eggs survive desiccation quite well. Plorde & Ramsey (1991:818) suggest that perhaps one-fourth of the world's population harbors this parasite.

Adult worms within the intestine may reach surprising numbers (even hundreds) without producing significant symptoms. Most people hosting this parasite are asymptomatic. Occasionally migration into the bile duct orifices may block bile flow with resulting symptoms of pain, jaundice and fever. More commonly, migration to the cecum with blockage of the appendiceal orifice will result in acute appendicitis. Probably the most common complication occurs when adult worm numbers are so high as to produce a bolus large enough to block the intestinal lumen, causing intestinal obstruction. While this can be relieved surgically today, in antiquity it would have been a lethal complication in most cases.

Ascariasis in antiquity

Ascaris sp. may have great antiquity. Ferreira *et al.* (1993) found a nematode larva (genus and species indeterminate) in a fossilized hyena coprolite at an Italian site 1.5 million years old. *Ascaris lumbricoides* ova have been identified in a Middle Kingdom Egyptian mummy (Cockburn *et al.*, 1980). Patrucco *et al.* (1983) identified such ova in coprolites from bodies on the Peruvian coast dating to 2277 B.C. (Horne 1985). Dexiang *et al.* (1981) report evidence of the presence of this parasite in several bodies from the Ming dynasty in China (A.D. 1368–1644), and Aspöck *et al.* (1973) found *A. lumbricoides* ova in human coprolites of Austrian salt miners from about the same period. Several mummified bodies from 600 B.C.–A.D. 500 found in northern European bogs have harbored such ova (Szidat, 1944), as have late pre-Columbian sites in the southwestern U.S.A. and in cave sites from Kentucky. Reinhard *et al.* (1986*a*) used differing rates of *Ascaris* ova in latrine contents among early American colonial dwellings to identify status differences. A medieval English latrine has also yielded evidence of this parasite (Taylor, 1955). To date, however, no adult worms have been reported from ancient human remains. It may be that in the postmortem environment they do not survive the powerful enzymes found in their most commonly occupied site – the upper small bowel.

HOOKWORM

Taxonomy, epidemiology, and natural history

This condition is only marginally eligible for inclusion in this volume because the very slender, adult worm, usually not exceeding a length of 1 cm, is barely visible without magnification. The Old World species, *Ancylostoma duodenale*, is found in Europe, the Middle and Far East while its New World counterpart, *Necator americanus*, is now distributed through Africa, Asia and the Americas. The adult larvae from thousands of eggs discharged daily by each female hatch in the soil and penetrate the skin of barefoot humans. Distributed by the blood, they leave the lungs' capillaries, are carried up the bronchi via the cilia-propelled mucus blanket to the back of the throat (pharynx), are swallowed, mature and establish residence in their new human host's intestine.

Hookworm infestation is worldwide, probably involving 20–25 % of this planet's population. A warm, moist climate enhances the larvae's survival so that the disease's distribution is defined roughly by a tropical and subtropical belt 35° (±) 5 latitude North and South. Its epidemiological features are defined further by socioeconomic factors, because developed countries within such zones have minimized the condition by housing, nutritional and hygienic practices. The link between hookworm disease and poverty eventually frus-

trated early twentieth century efforts by the Rockefeller Foundation-funded Anemia Commission to eradicate the condition (Ettling, 1981).

Hookworm's impact on its host's health can be substantial. Except for minor effects on the lung and gut during larval transport, its single, significant clinical effect is iron deficiency anemia. This is because the adult worm derives its nutrition by sucking blood from a mucosal capillary. Daily blood loss averages only 0.2 ml/worm. Bone marrow red blood cell production rate can increase up to about sixfold. When the collective total blood loss from the intestinal worm burden exceeds the marrow's maximum output, anemia will result. This is commonly an iron-deficient form, the appearance of the anemia being accelerated in a population with reduced iron (meat) intake. Iron is an essential component of hemoglobin; body iron deficiency thus will limit the bone marrow hemoglobin production response to a submaximal level. In a growing child even a normal marrow is barely able to meet the rapidly increasing oxygen demands of the expanding body mass. Any impairment of its productivity will be manifested promptly as anemia. Thus the combination of intestinal blood loss with body iron deficiency will make the growing child especially susceptible to profound degrees of anemia. Barefoot children playing in areas of casual, uncontrolled defecation are particularly susceptible. Anemia *per se*, of course, is commonly coupled to increased infection rate, and in populations afflicted with hookworm infection, is often aggravated by general malnutrition. Adults usually manifest shortness of breath (dyspnea), fatigue and lethargy (Plorde & Ramsey, 1991: 820–1).

Hookworm in antiquity

The clinical nonspecificity of anemic symptoms makes it difficult to recognize in literary sources, nor are its morphological effects on either soft tissues or bone of diagnostic value. Nevertheless, Sandison (1967*b*) suggests it was described in ancient China. Interpretations of the Ebers papyrus descriptions vary but Hippocratic authors do describe geophagia (dirt-eating), though this nondiagnostic symptom can characterize a number of different, unrelated conditions. Documentation of this disease, therefore rests on identification of the worm. Its small size delayed this in modern autopsies until the nineteenth century (Dubini, 1843; cited in Ettling, 1993) and the large number of hookworm ova in the feces of Italian miners led Perroncito (1880; cited in Ettling, 1993) to conclude the infestation was the cause of epidemic anemia in these workers. When he infected himself accidentally, A. Looss established the parasite's cycle, while the U.S. Army surgeon B.K. Ashford identified the New World species *Necator americanus* in Puerto Rico (Ettling, 1993).

Such a small, delicate organism is understandably difficult to find in desiccated human tissue, yet Allison *et al.* (1974*c*) provide reasonably convincing photographs of these worms in a pre-Columbian Andean mummy from about A.D. 900. Unfortunately the tissue was too disintegrated to identify diagnostic ova, and Ayala (1978) questioned the identification. Ferreira *et al.* (1980) reported *Ancylostoma sp.* ova in what they felt was a human coprolite from a northeastern Brazil site dated about 5000 years B.C., but it was not within unequivocal human remains, so its human origin was disputed (Kliks, 1982). Subsequent finding of diagnostic quality ova in a coprolite removed from pre-Columbian mummified human remains from the same area by the same workers (Ferreira *et al.*, 1983 *a,b*; 1987) appears to vindicate their initial interpretation and establish the disease as a pre-Columbian one in South America. Since the arctic climate during the assumed early Holocene trans-Beringeal human migrations would be expected to be incompatible with larval persistence in the arctic soil, these investigators have suggested transpacific migrations as the vehicle for hookworm disease's transport to the New World, pointing to archaeological evidence (Meggers & Evans, 1966) that such routes were actually employed by early South American immigrants.

FILARIASIS

Taxonomy, epidemiology, and natural history

While seven different species of the filarial nematodes can infect humans, it is *Wuchereria bancrofti* (or, rarely, *Brugia malayi*) that is of interest to paleopathologists because of the enormous swelling of various body parts it can cause. The adult worm (up to 10 cm long) lives in a large lymphatic vessel, often in the groin area, discharging the microfilarial progeny (up to 300 μ long) into lymphatics and thence into the circulating blood (Greene, 1991). Only humans act as definitive hosts for this mosquito-transmitted nematode that is prevalent throughout the tropical areas of South America, Africa, Asia and the western South Pacific islands (Scholtens, 1975:572).

The acute febrile response to primary invasion is usually not severe, though allergic responses can be distressing. It is the chronic form of the disease that can be so debilitating. The presence of the adult worms stimulates a chronic inflammatory response that often evokes a powerful fibroblastic phase so extensive that the associated scarring process destroys local tissue architecture, including the lymphatics (Greene, 1991). Obliteration of the involved area's lymphatic drainage results in collection of fluid (edema) in the tissues normally drained by lymphatics in the now fibrotic region. This edema becomes chronic, progressively worse and can reach massive proportions (Meyers *et al.*, 1976). Swelling of the legs with its associated thickened skin can be incapacitating and is locally referred to as elephantiasis. Involvement of the groin areas can also produce grotesque enlargement of the external genitalia, especially the scrotum.

Axillary lymph node involvement produces similar distortions of the arm or breast. Dysfunction of these structures with skin erosion may eventually produce serious secondary bacterial infections. There is evidence to suggest that these late complications occur primarily as a consequence of repeated exposures over decades, resulting in the accumulation in the body of a very large number of adult nematodes (Cotran *et al.*, 1989).

Filariasis in antiquity

The antiquity of the disease may be great but the elephantiasis in Greek and Roman writings seems to refer to leprosy. Filariasis may have originated in Southeast Asia and accompanied migrants from there to Polynesia and Africa (Laurence, 1968). It appears to have been endemic in the Nile delta in Ptolemaic times (Savitt, 1993). Otto Wucherer from Brazil identified microfilaria in the urine of an affected patient with hematuria in 1868, and Joseph Bancroft in Australia found the adult worm in 1877 (Cobbold, 1887); their observations are memorialized in the organism's designation: *Wuchereria bancrofti* (Savitt, 1993). No skeletal lesion is produced. The swollen areas are so overt that one would expect them to be recognized easily in mummified bodies. However, filariasis is a tropical disease, prevalent in areas in which little spontaneous mummification occurs. We have been unable to find a published report of this condition in an archaeologically recovered body.

CESTODES (TAPEWORMS)

TAENIA SOLIUM

Taxonomy, epidemiology, and natural history

Tapeworms are flat, ribbon-shaped worms composed principally of a series of readily-detachable body segments (proglottids) that are shed and excreted with the feces. Some can reach the remarkable length of several meters, and attach themselves to the intestinal wall by means of a circular set of hooklets or suckers embedded in their head (scolex). Lacking a digestive system, they absorb nutrients directly from the intestinal lumen. The five common members of this group include *Hymenolapsis nana* ('dwarf tapeworm'), *Taenia solium* (pork tapeworm), *Taenia saginata* (beef tapeworm), *Echinococcus granulosus* (dog tapeworm) and *Diphyllobothrium latum* and *pacificum* (fish tapeworm). Our model for discussion will be the pork tapeworm.

Only humans function as the definitive host for *Taenia solium*. The adult worm, attached to the human intestinal wall, is hermaphroditic, shedding parts of its segmented body (proglottids) with their enclosed ova regularly in the feces. The pig is the common intermediate host. Ingesting food contaminated by the ova, the embryo is freed in the pig's intestine, invades the mucosa and is disseminated widely by the blood through the animal's various body tissues where it encysts, particularly in muscle. Human consumption of the pork muscle without heating it sufficiently to kill such encysted larvae will permit the larvae to emerge in the human intestine, attach to the wall and grow there into an adult worm. Thorough heating of pork prior to consumption effectively prevents transmission.

In spite of its size, the adult tapeworm can live for many years in the human intestine without producing symptoms. In some individuals mild intestinal irritability or distress may occur. Such a relatively benign relationship between the definitive human host and parasite contrasts with a (fortunately unusual) circumstance in which the human becomes the intermediate host. That will occur when the ovum-containing feces excreted by a human are ingested not by a pig but by another human. In that case the embryo will be liberated in the second human's intestine after ingestion and the larvae will be disseminated throughout the body tissues in the same manner as normally occurs when the pig ingests such contaminated feces. Similarly, just as in the pig, the larvae will encyst in the various human tissues. Such cysts usually range from 1–2 cm in diameter and are thus visible grossly. The term used to describe such a visceral dissemination of *T. solium* larvae in a human serving as an accidental intermediate host is cysticercosis (Cotran *et al.*, 1989:420). Cysticerci develop in any soft tissue (skin, subcutaneous tissue, muscle, heart, brain, liver, lung and eye) and are much less common in bones (Robbins, 1975). Calcification of encysted larvae occurs frequently, and sometimes, though not usually, the number of calcifications is huge (Zuppinger, 1954). This occurs in long-term survivors in whom the cysticerci eventually die. On radiographs, linear or oval, elongated calcifications appear in the soft tissues and muscles, and the long axis of the calcified cysts lie in the plane of the surrounding muscle bundles (Resnick & Niwayama, 1989a, b). It should be noted that a human definitive host (adult worm in the intestine) can also become an accidental intermediate host by ingestion of food or beverage contaminated with the person's own feces (fecal–oral route). Cysticercosis does not occur in beef tapeworm (*T. saginata*) infection because human tissue cells have no receptors for the larvae.

Taenia solium infection in antiquity

The presence of taeniid ova in antiquity has been documented in an Egyptian male buried in 1198 B.C. (Hart *et al.*, 1977) and similar ova were found in the body of an adult

Chinese male from the Western Han dynasty buried in 167 B.C. (Dexiang *et al.*, 1981), about the same time (180 B.C) that white, flat worms (Jao Ch'ung) in human intestines are described in Chinese literature (Chu & Ch'iang, 1931). Cahill *et al.* (1991) found taeniid ova in a latrine from an eighth century B.C. site near Jerusalem. While Fry (1977) has suggested such ova may be present in pre-Columbian bodies from Utah in the U.S.A., this appears questionable since neither pigs nor cattle, the specific intermediate hosts for *T. solium* and *T. saginata*, were present in the Americas before A.D. 1492. One would expect the cysticercosis cysts to be recognizable on gross examination of mummified soft tissues in the form of multiple small cysts which could be confirmed by histological demonstration of scolex hooklets; to date, however, this has not been reported.

ECHINOCOCCIASIS (HYDATID DISEASE)

Taxonomy and epidemiology

Two species of this tapeworm commonly infect humans. Echinococci are found worldwide, but *E. granulosus* is most common in North America, eastern Europe, Australia and New Zealand, while *E. multilocularis*, cycling normally between dogs and rodents, is found in humans especially in central and eastern Europe as well as in Arctic areas. Human infestation with *E. vogeli*, for whom pacas are the usual intermediate hosts, can be encountered in South America (Cotran *et al.*, 1989:421).

Life cycle and natural history

Echinococcus granulosus produces unilocular cysts and is the most common, while *E. multilocularis* produces multichambered cysts. *Echinococcus granulosus* normally cycles between the dog (acting as definitive host for the adult worm in its intestine) and sheep (the intermediate host). Humans ingesting the fertilized ova (fecal–oral route) become the accidental intermediate host, the larva behaving in the human as it does in sheep. After escaping from the digested eggs the larvae penetrate the human gut wall and are disseminated throughout the body by the blood. Any soft tissue structure may be involved as larvae lodge in capillaries. There they generate a cyst that has a hyaline, outer membrane and a cellular, germinating lining that produces many microcystic structures enveloping scolices (worm heads) suspended in a fluid medium. Growth of such hydatid (water-filled) cysts is slow but progressive, capable of expansion to a diameter of 15–20 cm in a decade.

Because the first set of capillaries that the larvae encounter after entering the blood stream is in the liver, this organ is

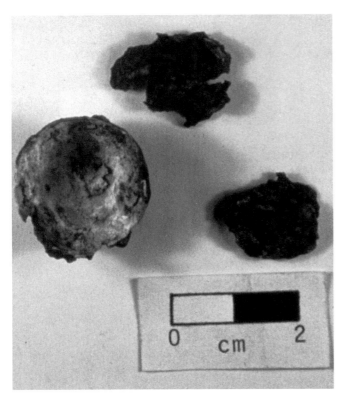

FIG. 7.75: **Hydatid cyst?** Calcified shell fragments from a burial in North Dakota, U.S.A. may represent a 2 cm cyst of the dog tapeworm *Echinococcus granulosus* (or possibly healed tuberculous node). A 45 year old female, Woodland period (ca. 1370 years B.P.). Photograph courtesy John Williams, Grand Forks, ND.

the most frequently involved by localized growth of the organism. Leakage of the hydatid cyst spills the scolices into the organ's parenchyma, which may then initiate the growth of one or more cysts. Those traversing the liver may produce pulmonary cysts and others, escaping the lung, reach the peripheral circulation where they may finally lodge in bone, brain or any other tissue.

Cyst expansion in these soft tissues compresses the surrounding parenchyma of the liver, lung or other affected organ with consequent atrophy of such tissue. Not surprisingly, the resulting symptoms vary, depending on the affected organ. Common bile duct compression or extensive parenchymal liver atrophy may cause jaundice and/or hepatic failure, while bronchial compression may generate pneumonia in the related pulmonary parenchyma. Bacterial access to a large hydatid cyst converts it into a spectacular, massive, suppurative abscess. Cyst rupture may result in multiple new cysts in the abdominal or pleural cavities.

Death of the developing progeny and the germinating layer within the cyst, commonly the consequence of bacterial infection, often produces calcification of the cyst wall (Fig. 7.75). Some of the sand-like scolices may persist, whose demonstration can establish unequivocally the nature of such a calcified shell. This may occur in any soft tissue organ (Cotran et al., 1989:422).

Pathology

Soft tissue lesions

Those that have been found in archaeological specimens are limited to the calcified hydatid cysts, usually of the liver or lungs. These, of course, can be found associated with skeletons as well as mummies, though their exact location would be more easily established in the latter. Few, however, have been reported in mummified human soft tissue remains (see Antiquity of Paleopathology section, below). The calcified wall, whose thickness varies from millimeters to centimeters, is often incomplete, in which case the central area is usually hollow and its noncalcified content has commonly become liquefied and disappeared. If the calcified wall is intact, the amorphous, often lipid-containing, central material may contain microscopically demonstrable scolex remnants, including the characteristic hooklets.

Skeletal lesions

Osseous involvement by hydatid disease is rare (only 1–2 % of cases) and is usually limited to a single bone or region. The most common site is the lower vertebrae (40–44 % of cases with skeletal involvement) where it may cause spinal cord compression and paraplegia (Zimmerman & Kelley, 1982:109). Other bones that may be affected are pelvis (16 %), femur (15–20 %), humerus (7–10 %) and tibia and fibula (6–9 %). Ribs, sternum, scapula, phalanges and skull may be also affected but less frequently. The lesion is seen initially at the epiphyseal-metaphyseal region of the long bones (Duró, 1983; Bullough, 1992). No part of the skeleton is immune.

Due to hematogenous dissemination, in skeletal echinococciasis the cancellous bone is filled with small, thin-walled cysts that expand and cause pressure atrophy of bone. A radiolucent area is seen in the radiographs, but a large cystic lesion such as occurs in soft tissues does not develop in bone (Revell, 1986; Bullough, 1992). It is usually a multiloculated, osteolytic lesion with an irregular outline, but normally the bone preserves its external contour. Internally disorganization and destruction are very prominent, and pathological fractures occur in the late stage of the disease (Duró, 1983; Resnick & Niwayama, 1989a, b). In general, skeletal hydatid lesions are slowly destructive without periosteal reaction. Draining sinuses and secondary infection are commonly seen. If the cyst breaks out through the cortex, the extraosseous component develops into the large cyst observed in the classical form of soft tissue hydatid disease (Schinz et al., 1953; Jaffe, 1972; Bullough, 1992). Calcification of the soft tissue mass may occur (Resnick & Niwayama, 1989a, b) . Osteolytic lesions may cross the joints (Murray et al., 1990). Bony destruction may be extremely extensive in later stages, leading to multiple large cystic areas separated by residual bony septa. In the vertebrae, progressive destruction of the vertebral bodies may lead to angular kyphosis, and the posterior elements are more often involved than in tuberculosis (Ortner & Putschar, 1985).

Antiquity and paleopathology

Echinococciasis is probably as old as animal domestication, or at least as dog-assisted sheep or cattle pastoralism, an activity Schwabe (1978:10) estimates was established in the Fertile Crescent by 9000 B.C.. Patterson (1993b:703) feels it accompanied the expansion of subsequent population distribution, particularly the European settlement of the New World and Australia. It is found today wherever dogs are incorporated into a sheep-herding economy. The highest modern prevalence is among the cattle-raising tribes of Kenya and east Africa. Literary descriptions include a comment in the fourth century B.C. Hippocratic corpus (Hippocrates [ca 400 B.C.] 1984: Aphorisms XVII, 55) that a burst water-laden liver fills the abdomen with fluid, usually a fatal complication. Wells & Dallas (1976) cite a sixteenth century observation of 'water-clear, egg-like' structures in slaughtered pigs in Copenhagen, reported by T. Bartholin. McClary (1972) found taeniid ova in a Late Middle Woodland coprolite from Michigan (U.S.A.) but could not be certain whether the specimen was of human or canid origin. Because neither pigs nor cattle (intermediate hosts for *T. solium* and *T. saginata*) were present in pre-Columbian America, this implies that the ova are those of *Echinococcus granulosus* and that this worm was present prior to A.D. 1492. Reports of calcified hydatid cysts found in archaeological human remains are not abundant. Zias (1991) found two such calcified shells in a 2000 year old tomb near Jerusalem. Ortner & Putschar (1985:232) identified three similar calcified shells from an adult Aleut female at a Kodiak, Alaska site probably dating to about A.D. 1700 Weiss and Møller-Christensen (1971) found 72 thin-walled, fragile, calcified cysts averaging 1 cm in diameter scattered throughout the abdomen and pelvis areas within a medieval skeleton of a 16 year old female leper at a Danish site. Although they comment that they contained no organic material, no histological search for hooklets is described. The cysts are viewed as abdominal implants secondary to a ruptured hepatic hydatid cyst.

Williams (1985) found a 25 mm cyst in the thoracic area of an adult female who had died in North Dakota, U.S.A. about A.D. 1370. Its calcified wall was intact, but unfortunately reburial was carried out before histological studies could be performed. A 3 cm, hollow calcified mass found in the abdominal area of a early medieval adult at a Winchester, England site reported by Price (1975) similarly was not examined histologically but was felt to be most probably a hydatid cyst. Wells & Dallas (1976), at a second century A.D. English site, found a small (less than 1 cm diameter), calcified shell in the thoracic cavity area of a female skeleton. Tapp (1986) comments on a hydatid cyst in an Egyptian mummy.

Thompson *et al.* (1986) describe a cerebral hydatid cyst in an Egyptian mummy curated in Manchester with scolices and hooklets that are, unfortunately, not recognizable in the accompanying photomicrograph of the cyst wall.

While surgical drainage, and more recently chemotherapy, can often cure this problem today, echinococciasis eventually must have claimed the lives of a large fraction of persons with this disease in antiquity, though its slow progress over one or even several decades probably permitted normal activities over most of that interval.

Differential diagnosis of hydatid cyst

On the basis of the above reports one might conclude that the finding of any spherical or oblate, hollow calcified structure most anywhere in or near human remains justifies the diagnosis of hydatid cyst. However, dystrophic calcification of necrotic tissue from almost any cause may result in calcification. This commonly begins at the lesion's periphery and the process may become arrested by its obliteration of blood vessels leading into the affected area. Separated from its source of calcium ions by such vascular obstruction, the central necrotic mass may remain uncalcified. In the postmortem state this organic material may liquefy and escape from the calcified shell.

Soft tissue tuberculous lesions commonly undergo such a transformation. While smaller lesions heal by calcifying the entire necrotic mass (that usually has the original consistency of cottage cheese, and is generally termed caseous), involved areas exceeding 2 cm frequently become calcified only around their periphery. If the infectious process becomes arrested, the central, caseous necrotic area may remain unchanged for the remainder of the individual's life. Indeed, its contained tubercle bacilli may remain alive and dormant within it, capable of reinitiating invasive infection many years later if liberated from its enveloping calcified prison by an invading cancer or decrease in the host's immune system. The size of such lesions may reach 6 cm or more. On a gross basis in archaeological human remains such a hollow, calcified shell of a tuberculous lesion would not usually be distinguishable from a calcified hydatid cyst. The case reported by Salo *et al.* (1994) is an excellent example of this phenomenon. The pulmonary nodule in the lung of that pre-Columbian adult was a hollow, spherical, calcified shell but a segment of DNA unique to *Mycobacteriun tuberculosis* was demonstrated in the extract of one of the involved hilar lymph nodes, thus establishing tuberculosis as the nature of the process. Similar structural changes can occur in lymph nodes, though the usual smaller size of these lesions more commonly results in complete calcification without a hollow center.

Furthermore, the sequence of described changes also can occur in pulmonary tissue infected by several fungal agents that commonly involve human lungs, including *Blastomyces dermatididis, Histoplasma capsulatum* and *Coccidioides immitis*. In fact, the spherules of *Coccidioides immitis* have been demonstrated to survive arid postmortem conditions sufficiently well to be recognizable in affected archaeological bone (Harrison *et al.*, 1991).

Thus tuberculosis, fungal or severe pulmonary infections other than echinococcal organisms can reproduce the gross appearance of hydatid cyst. The modern relative frequencies of these agents are such that the non-echinococcal etiologies would be seen far more frequently than those induced by the dog tapeworm, though geographic variables would influence the prevalence of the fungal infections. This would be even more probable if the location of the calcified structure could be recognized as intrathoracic. However, even this observation is not absolute in skeletonized bodies, because postmortem soft tissue changes can dislocate the liver into the chest cavity.

Even all abdominally located calcified cystic structures are not necessarily of echinococcal origin. Intestinal tuberculosis can involve mesenteric lymph nodes that may calcify, and we have observed at least one, currently unreported, such case. These, however, usually calcify completely if the infective process becomes arrested. Benign or low-grade renal, ovarian and even testicular tumors may calcify, especially when their original structure is cystic. Metabolically or traumatically induced areas of fat necrosis in or near the pancreas (and occasionally breast) can also terminate as calcified shells. Thus, an abdominal location of such a structure is not a firm basis for the diagnosis of hydatid cyst. None of these, however, would be expected to produce more than one or two such lesions, and these possible etiological origins of abdominal calcifications would become quite improbable in cases such as the one reported by Weiss & Møller-Christensen (1971) in which 72 calcified, hollow spheres were found, predominantly in the abdominal and pelvic region of a female skeleton.

If, then, the diagnosis of echinococciasis cannot be established with conviction on the basis of the gross morphology and location of a hollow, calcified shell, what can be done to increase the certainty of its origin? The simplest next step is the histological examination of a suspension or tissue section of a rehydrated sample of the calcified structure's central content or, if it is hollow, scrapings from its lining (Reinhard, 1990). Identification of the organism's characteristic hooklets, normally a part of its head (scolex) establishes the diagnosis with certainty. Since postmortem effects are variable, however, their absence does not exclude the diagnosis. In none of the above-reported cases from antiquity were hooklets identified (nor was any such study stated to have been made). Occasionally tissue sections of the calcified wall <u>might</u> reveal the triple-layered structure characteristic of echinococcal origin. If these histological methods do not produce positive results, further investigation by immunological methods or nucleic acid biotechnology can be employed (Salo *et al.*, 1994).

Differential diagnosis of intraskeletal lesions presents formidable problems. According to Zimmerman & Kelley (1982:109), it is doubtful whether one could diagnose this disease from skeletal remains alone. Skeletal hydatid disease may mimic a lot of pathologies, including:

- Tumors. Plasmacytoma, giant cell tumor, cartilaginous tumors (enchondromas, angiosarcoma, and especially skeletal metastases).
- Benign conditions. Fibrous dysplasia, hyperparathyroidism (brown tumor), hemophilic pseudotumor.

Because the morphology of the lesions is not specific, it becomes important to take into account archaeological, ethnohistorical and geographical factors as well as the need for canine domestication.

TREMATODES (FLUKES)

PARAGONIMIASIS

Taxonomy, epidemiology, and natural history

This condition is caused by more than 30 species of *Paragonimus*. Most cases have been reported from Far East countries where *P. westermani* predominates, though other species can be found in Africa and South America (*P. caliensis, P. mexicanus*). The World Health Organization estimates that a total of about three million people are infected, the majority of which are in Asia. Recent immigrants from southeastern Asia are bringing the disease to the attention of North American physicians (Plorde & Ramsey, 1991:829).

The definitive hosts for *Paragonimus* sp. are dogs, pigs, cats, wild carnivores and man. In these, the small (about 1 cm long) flatworm resides encysted, usually in the lung. Erosion of the cyst into a bronchus results in dissemination of the ova by sputum and feces. In water the embryo emerges, passes through several intermediate hosts, the last of which is a crustacean. Consumption of this (usually a crayfish) without heating results in release of the metacercariae in the intestine of the host (human or animal). These penetrate the intestinal wall and reach the lungs via the peritoneal cavity and diaphragm. In heavily infested persons they may reach the kidney, liver and other organs, the most disastrous of which is the brain (Barrett-Connor, 1982).

The cysts invoke an inflammatory response, resulting in an envelope of fibrous tissue around the cyst. The attempt at isolation of the lesion is, however, frequently incomplete, and eventual communication between a cyst and a nearby bronchiole is common. The cyst contents are coughed up, often mixed with blood. This completes the fluke's cycle, but not the patient's problems. Bacterial infection of the now-evacuated cyst may convert the larger ones into an abscess, while obliterating the smaller through fibrosis and even calcification. Migrating metacercariae that reach other organs may become encysted in such ectopic areas. In the brain major neurological deficit may result from such foci of cerebral necrosis; as many as half of those persons with involvement of the central nervous system will reveal radiological evidence of calcification (Plorde & Ramsey, 1991:829). The range of severity is related to the number of organisms ingested; hence, endemic areas will have a larger number of life-threatening infestations. In the majority the disease presents as a chronic bronchitis, sometimes with bronchiectasis that mimics tuberculosis (Cotran et al., 1989:424).

Antiquity and paleopathology

No skeletal lesions are produced by *Paragonimus* sp. The pulmonary cysts of 1 or 2 cm diameter ought to be recognizable in closely examined mummified human lungs, especially since the chronic form of the disease frequently involves at least partial calcification of some lesions. Rehydration of this tissue would permit histological identification of the enclosed ova. To date the fluke itself has not been reported in archaeological remains. However, the ova have been found in human coprolites from the Atacama desert in northern Chile (Gooch, 1976a, b; Hall, 1976, 1978; Hinz, 1990). Some uncertainty about the age of the studied specimens remains, since Hall's 1976 report lists them as 2500 B.C. and his 1978 report as 5900 B.C., together with a claim that this is the oldest established case of human paragonimiasis in antiquity.

FASCIOLIASIS

These small, worldwide, adult worms, *Fasciola hepatica* ('liver fluke') enter the human as metacercariae adherent to leaves of the freshwater plant watercress, commonly used as salad garnish. The larval forms penetrate the duodenum, are guided to the liver by venous and lymphatic channels where they burrow into the larger spaces where the adult worms, up to 4 cm long, establish residence in the major bile ducts and gall bladder. Their ova reach the gut, are excreted and, after passing through a snail phase, complete the cycle. Human symptoms are characterized principally by biliary obstruction and inflammation.

Though the adult worm is visible without magnification aids, its presence in ancient human remains has not been reported. The characteristic ova, however have been identified frequently in archaeological excavations. Fasciola ova, apparently from human sources, have been found in a 700 year old coprolite from the western U.S.A. (Moore et al.,

1974), and from latrine soils from medieval northern Europe (Herrmann, 1987), Germany (Reinhard et al., 1986a) and Viking Age Scandinavia (Nansen & Jørgensen, 1977).

FASCIOLOPSIASIS

The intestinal fluke, *Fasciolopsis buski*, has a similar life cycle, differing principally in that it remains within the intestine. It is found commonly in oriental countries. The mature worm is about twice the size of *Fasciola heptica*, and has not been identified in human remains. However, its ova were present in an ancient Chinese mummy from the Han Dynasty, about 167 B.C. (Dexiang et al., 1981).

CLONORCHIASIS

Clonorchis sinensis is a diminutive adult worm less than 2 cm long found principally in the Far East. It is acquired by eating raw, freshwater crayfish that harbor its metacercariae. The adult worms are small enough to occupy the smaller bile ducts in the liver, producing the clinical picture of biliary obstruction. They stimulate a proliferative epithelial response great enough to produce a malignant biliary tumor in many cases. No adult worms have been recognized in ancient human remains but their ova have been reported in several Chinese bodies from the Han Dynasty (167 B.C.), Sung Dynasty about (A.D. 100) and the Ming Dynasty (about A.D. 1500) (Dexiang et al., 1981).

ECTOPARASITES

PEDICULOSIS (LICE)

These varieties of lice infest humans: *Pediculus humanus* var. *capitis* (head louse), *Pediculus humanus* var. *corporis* (body louse) and *Phthirius pubis* (pubic or genital louse). The pubic louse is not known to transmit human disease (Plorde, 1991b). The body louse can also infest the scalp. The body louse is uniquely adapted to humans, and lives on the skin and especially in the clothing of a human. The body louse can transmit several different diseases including the spirochete-caused febrile illness called relapsing fever and a rickettsial febrile infection termed trench fever (Gillum, 1976). However, the reason for its inclusion in this text is primarily its ability to transmit the rickettsial agent, *Rickettsia prowazekii*, the agent of epidemic typhus. While this disease causes no gross skeletal or soft tissue lesions, its epidemic nature and significant mortality make it a disease of interest to paleopathologists who deal with population diseases. The only louse-transmitted disease that will be discussed here, therefore, is epidemic typhus.

Typhus

Rickettsiae are small (commonly 1 μ or less in diameter), bacteria-like, gram-negative organisms, most of which are obligate intracellular parasites. *Rickettsia prowazekii* lives in the louse's abdomen and is transmitted to the human by crushing the louse against the skin, creating a man-louse-man cycle (Pinkerton & Strano, 1976). It produces an acute, febrile disease affecting only humans, and is associated with a skin rash as well as enlarged liver and spleen. The severe degrees of this illness can be complicated by liver failure with jaundice and hemorrhage, myocarditis with heart failure or encephalitis. While overall mortality averages about 10 %, fatalities are more common at the two ends of age extremes, especially among the aged. Because lice are not restricted geographically, this can be a worldwide condition. Due to the louse's high prevalence under the unhygienic conditions common in extreme poverty or politico-socioeconomic turmoil, epidemics tend to appear under these circumstances and it is today particularly prominent in East Africa. Between 1918 and 1922 in eastern Europe, 30 million infections occurred with about 3 million deaths (Pinkerton & Strano, 1976).

Pediculosis in antiquity

The antiquity of pediculosis probably exceeds three millennia. Vreeland & Cockburn (1980) cite Villiar Córdoba (1935:227) as describing the presence of louse egg casings (nits) (Fig. 7.76) in Peruvian mummy hair from as early as A.D. 600–1000. Cloudsley-Thompson (1976:104) cites the Venetian writer of 1591, Prospero Alpini, as commenting on the frequency of lice in Egypt. Biblical references include lice in Egypt (Exodus 8:15–17). Herodotus, in the fourth century B.C. commented on the eating of lice by a central Asian population (Cloudsley-Thompson, 1976:105). Gardner (1924) identified nits of head lice on the hair shafts of a fourth century Egyptian mummy. W. Birkby (quoted in Cockburn & Cockburn, 1980:141; Reinhard & Hevly, 1991)

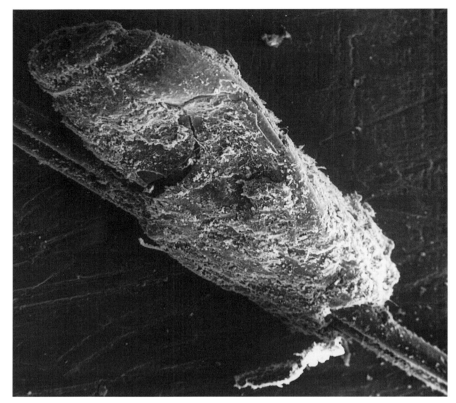

FIG. 7.76: **Pediculosis capitis.** This electron microscope image of a hair louse egg casing attached to a scalp hair shaft provides interesting detail but the 'nit' can be detected with the unaided eye. From an Aleutian mummy ca. A.D. 1700. Photograph courtesy Patrick Horne, Toronto.

found such egg casings in the hair of 8 of 18 pre-Columbian cave mummies from the southwestern U.S.A. K. Reinhard (cited in Aufderheide, 1990) found a much higher frequency of head lice infestation of Chiribaya mummies from the Chiribaya Alta site (about A.D. 1000–1200) in the lower Osmore Valley of southern Peru than he did from a similar site in the midportion of the same valley near Moquegua. He suggests such frequency differences could be a measure of social contact. Social implications of the presence of head lice abundance were also noted by Gill & Owsley (1985). They suggested it may reflect social isolation consistent with warrior outcast status. Hair combs from Dead Sea scroll caves in Israel from the Neolithic B period contained nits from mummies (Zias & Mumcuoglu, 1991). Cloudsley-Thompson (1976:106-110) documents well the close relationship between epidemic typhus and war. The Spanish army contesting the Moors for Grenada in 1489 suffered 17 000 typhus deaths and he suggests Napoleon's fate was partially shaped by this disease when he lost more men to typhus than to the enemy. Using the species of *Pediculus* as examples, Kellog (1913) has suggested that host genetic relationships are more determinative of ectoparasite distribution than environmental circumstances. Gardner (1924), however, cautions that prediction of biological distance between hosts based on *Pediculus* distribution may be limited by the ability of some species to 'cross over' phylogenetic barriers.

PART EIGHT

Diseases of the viscera

INTRODUCTION

This chapter deals with paleopathological changes in the body's soft tissues with special emphasis on the viscera. The diseases arising within these organs only rarely affect bone, and even when they do so, osseous changes are secondary to the effects on the primary soft tissue organ in which the condition arose.

Postmortem morphologic alterations are usually much more marked in soft tissues than in bone. While space does not permit a detailed discussion of postmortem taphonomic processes the reader's interpretive skills may be usefully enhanced by a review of a few basic principles operative to achieve preservation of soft tissues.

Factors influencing preservation

Postmortem decay is an enzymatic process. Enzymes require an aqueous medium. If tissue dries before it decays, it remains so until it is rehydrated. This simple truth is exploited by those who bring us beef jerky and dried fruit. Spontaneous ('natural') mummification occurs by this mechanism in hot, dry environments, such as deserts, that lead to rapid desiccation. However, the race between decay and dehydration is a highly competitive one and, like most races, small effects can determine the difference between a win or a loss. Thus, differences in delays in the interval between death and interment, presence of bacteremia at time of death, weather fluctuations and similar features are responsible for the broad range of variation in degree of soft tissue preservation usually observed in bodies from the same burial site. Other approaches to slowing or blocking enzymatic decay can make use of heavy metals to 'poison' the enzyme. For example, numerous reports document the localized conservation of skin and muscle of the wrist underlying a copper bracelet in an otherwise skeletonized body. Finally, an enzyme's action is usually highly specific, and if the chemical form of the tissue is altered (denaturation), the enzyme can not 'recognize' it and so does not act on it. Oxidation of fatty acids can so alter body fat (production of adipocere), rendering it immune to enzymatic decay. Anthropogenic ('artificial') forms of mummification have employed (sometimes even combined) all of these features.

Variable response of body tissues

Not all body tissues decay at the same rate. Epithelial cells deteriorate much more rapidly than do the supporting tissues such as collagen, elastic tissue and cartilage or skeletal muscle. Epithelial cells contain destructive enzymes normally carefully controlled to destroy undesired particles or organisms that gain access to the living cell's cytoplasm. After death this control is lost, and these same enzymes then destroy the cell itself. In general, the more metabolically active the living cell is, the more rapidly it will be destroyed after death. Thus the vital nature of the heart's muscle fibers, the kidney's tubular cells and the adrenal secretory cells predict their rapid postmortem dissolution while the body's large mass of skeletal muscle deteriorates so slowly that often much of it is still intact when tissue dehydration arrests decay. These selective decay rate differences will dictate the amount of information soft tissue paleopathologists can derive from the various organs.

Recognition of morphologic alterations by disease

From the above it will be clear that morphologic changes produced by taphonomic processes are much more profound in soft tissues than in bone. Loss of color and texture impair a soft tissue paleopathologist's ability to evaluate or even recognize an organ. Even anatomic location is not a sacrosanct feature, since an organ's attachment to a site may be lost with subsequent organ migration. We have found a stone-containing gall bladder lying free in the pelvis and the entire liver in the thorax. Thus in spontaneously mummified bodies adrenal pathology has only rarely been described, nor has the necrotic lesion of myocardium secondary to acute myocardial infarction been reported. Indeed, in some cases the heart is represented by only a black stain on the inner lining of the pericardial sac. The kidney may be identifiable in some only by a reniform space at the appropriate retroperitoneal location. Compared with hospital autopsies, paleopathological dissections of mummified human remains can be viewed as 'salvage pathology'. The above factors seriously constrain recoverable antemortem information and paleo-

pathologists need to keep their expectations realistic. Nevertheless, as in other fields, thorough knowledge of fresh tissue pathological changes combined with experience with advanced postmortem alterations can avoid the pitfalls of pseudopathology and enhance recovery of data. The experienced forensic pathologist brings highly applicable specialized skills to the field of soft tissue paleopathology.

Topics covered

As noted in the Preface, it is difficult to recognize a disease of whose existence one is not aware. Many modern diseases have not appeared in the paleopathological literature. This may be due to a difference in the frequency of a disease in antiquity versus the modern period. In many cases, however, it may be possible it is simply being overlooked. Hence we have chosen to discuss most common diseases affecting the visceral organs today, even if they have never been reported in archaeological bodies. Illustrations for such, of course, will need to employ modern examples, the paleopathological appearance of which the reader will need to extrapolate from the illustration. By employing all of one's knowledge, meticulous dissection and reasonably conservative reconstruction of findings, it is often surprising how much useful information about the individual's antemortem health status can be predicted from such careful dissections by properly prepared operators.

Soft tissue lesions of the head and neck

The brain and meninges

Brain preservation

Together with the adrenal and kidney, the brain is among the first organs to undergo postmortem autolysis. Every experienced medical examiner has seen repeated examples of near or actual brain liquefaction in corpses exposed to summer temperatures for even as little time as a week. Insects gaining access to the cranial cavity can accelerate the destructive process. Hope (1834) examined a series of mummified Egyptian heads in the British Museum and found residua of the genera *Necrobia, Dermestis* and even *Diptera* within the cranial cavity; the numbers and stages present led him to believe they entered the skull at the time of embalming. One of us (A.C.A.) examined the victim of a summer stabbing 18 days after the murder in which several wounds had penetrated the skull. The cranial cavity was devoid of brain or meningeal tissue but was filled with teeming blowfly larvae, indicating how rapidly the brain can be not only liquified but actually consumed after death.

Yet, in spite of the brain's tendency toward rapid post-mortem dissolution, examples of its unexpected preservation abound. In many of these adipocere formation from the brain's lipid content is responsible for the preservation. In others an excessively arid environment may prevent complete cerebral dissolution, while in still others the mechanism is not at all clear.

Probably the oldest preserved brain was reported from a site near Moscow (Walter, 1929) in which two cerebriform fossilized human brains (without skulls) were preserved together with parts of a wooly mammoth. In all probability, adipocere formation preserved the gross brain form initially and during the period that acid groundwater gradually dissolved the skull, eventually leading to mineral replacement of all the organic matter. Mineral springs have also preserved human brains by a means, probably chemical, not yet well understood but capable of retaining gross cerebral morphology for 7000–8000 years (Royal & Clark, 1960; Doran et al., 1986; Pääbo et al., 1988).

Adipocere formation was clearly the mechanism that preserved a clay-buried, 5000 year old Swiss brain (Oakley, 1960) as well as that of a Bronze Age bog body (Powers, 1960), although in other bog bodies in which some brain tissue remained, adipocere was not described (Brothwell, 1986:63). Klohn et al. (1988) described a cerebral concretion that appears to have originated by a combination of calcium with fatty acids hydrolyzed from the brain's neutral fat to form calcium soaps, and adipocere was also the effective agent in preserving brain tissue in 56 of 74 medieval skulls excavated at a Danish monastery (Tkocz et al., 1979). Finding retained brain tissue (some cerebriform) within the cranial cavities of persons who died 45 years prior to exhumation of cranial gunshot wounds, Radanov et al. (1992) suggested the microclimate within the cranial cavity (resulting from the crania's gunshot-induced perforations) permitted rapid evaporation of cerebral fluids and consequent brain preservation without adipocere formation.

The incredibly arid and rain-free climate of northern Chile's Atacama desert results in a high rate of soft tissue preservation of biological material interred in its nitrate-rich soil. Gerszten & Martínez (1995) examined the desiccated cerebral tissue from 15 of the many spontaneously mummified human remains excavated from sites in this area. Most preserved brains were shapeless, shrunken brown masses but at least one retained its gyriform surface morphology (see Intracranial hemorrhage, below). One of us (A.C.A.) has examined many mummies from this area and found the brown-stained dura mater present very frequently when abundant soft tissue of the rest of the body was also retained. In one 4000 year old population of 16 adults, all of whose heads were present, brain tissue was found in 8. This was usually present as an amorphous, brown mass of pasty consistency (Fig. 8.1). In several, however, about one-fourth of the cranial cavity was filled with granular, pebble-like, brown material, the individual granules averaging only a millimeter

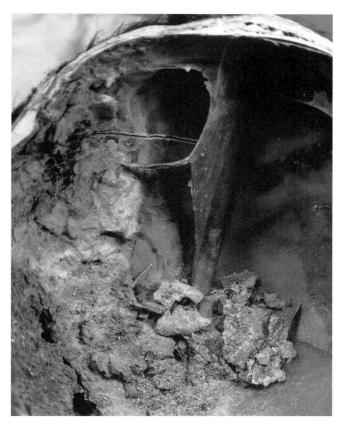

FIG. 8.1: **Brain and meninges preservation.** The calvarium (top of the skull vault) has been removed to demonstrate preservation of parts of the dura mater (falx cerebri). The brain has been reduced to several irregular, brown, amorphous masses of pasty material. Spontaneous mummification, adult male about A.D.100. PBL.

or two in diameter. The taphonomic process that generated this appearance was probably initiated by liquefaction of the brain with subsequent precipitation of the solutes as the body desiccated. In one body the particles were of sand-like quality.

Intracranial hemorrhage

In spite of all these observations of retained brain tissue, remarkably few paleoneuropathologic reports have appeared. Evidence of epidural hematoma was commonly found among 45 infants from 3 infant populations at a site in Germany (Teegen & Schultz, 1994), which the authors identified not on the basis of soft tissue changes, but of stained skull bones and attributed them to birth injuries or child abuse. Gerszten & Martínez (1995), examining 15 spontaneously mummified human remains at sites ranging from 100 B.C. to A.D. 800 in the Atacama desert identified several with retained brain tissue showing subdural hematomas related to head injuries. They also found one with subarachnoid hemorrhage over the cerebral convexity. In another, an example of intracerebral hemorrhage was obvious in a 45 year old male; severe renal atherosclerosis in that body suggested that hypertension, often related to this kidney condition, may have caused the cerebral hemorrhage (though the illustrated lesion is also consistent with a ruptured 'berry' aneurysm of a cerebral artery). Figure 8.2 is an example of this type of hemorrhage.

Infectious diseases

Dalton *et al.* (1976) describe a 2 year old child mummy from southern Peru with resolving pneumonia and a '…thick layer of dried pus on the spinal cord…' The brain had disintegrated. Histology revealed small bacilli consistent with *Haemophilus influenzae* (the most common cause of meningitis in infants today), but immunostaining efforts produced no reactive changes. Although osseous changes may sometimes reflect chronic meningitis, we have not been able to find other examples of pus-coated meninges in the paleopathological literature.

Neoplasms

Primary malignant tumors of cerebral tissue constitute about 10% of human primary cancers. Their frequency age distribution curve is bimodal with the first peak in children's age group and a second in that of older adults. Because of the generally poor postmortem preservation of cerebral soft tissue, we must keep our expectations of encountering these in ancient mummified bodies low. Clues to their presence could include focal areas of hemorrhage and necrosis, especially in the common high grade astrocytic tumors. Low grade astrocytic tumors of the cerebellum in children may be recognizable because of their cystic nature. Small foci of calcification may also betray the presence of an antemortem oligodendroglioma. Many of these tumors will block the flow of cerebrospinal fluid and produce obvious hydrocephalus. The possibility of a primary cerebral neoplasm should be suspected when finding hydrocephalus in the brain of an adult archaeological body. Most of these tumors in antiquity would have progressed to produce eventual increased intracranial pressure with convulsions, coma and death.

Meningiomas arise from the meninges in older adults and can be located anywhere within the cranial cavity. They have a dense, fibrous matrix that would be expected to survive the

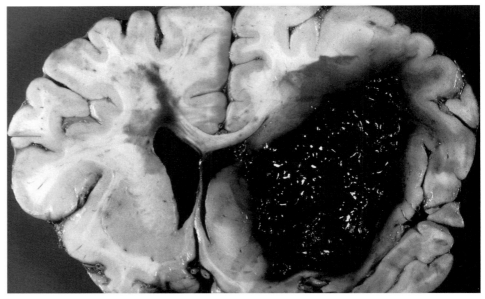

FIG. 8.2: **Intracerebral hemorrhage.** Section of gross brain demonstrates that a large area of brain tissue has been disrupted by hemorrhage from a ruptured cerebral artery. Modern adult male. PBL.

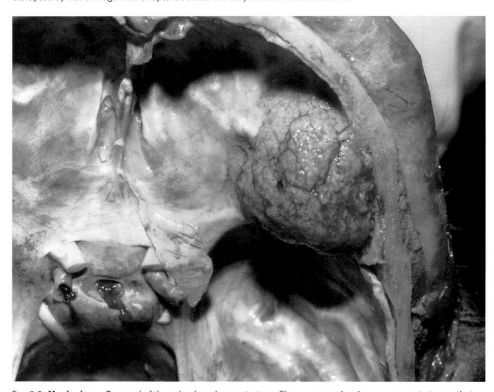

FIG. 8.3: **Meningioma.** Removal of the calvarium demonstrates a fibrous-appearing 6 x 5 x 4 cm ovate tumor that arose from the meninges in the lateral aspect of the right anterior fossa of the cranial cavity. Its benign histology is consistent with its discrete, sharply demarcated and noninvasive periphery. Modern adult male. PBL.

postmortem changes quite well. About one-fifth of intracranial tumors are meningiomas and, except for the occasional meningiosarcoma that is capable of brain invasion, meningiomas are generally benign. They present a mass of hard or rubbery, lobulated, sharply demarcated lump of tissue intimately attached to the meninges (Fig. 8.3). Although benign, their slow but progressive enlargement may compress the brain sufficiently to cause increased intracranial pressure and even death unless removed. In antiquity this tumor may well have produced symptoms of headache, personality change, focal motor loss and/or convulsions progressively over a period of many years eventually leading to death. The clinical symptoms and signs vary with location and size.

While we have no record of identification of the soft tissues of a meningioma, the tumor frequently has left an indication of its presence in the form of localized marked hyperostosis that meningiomas may induce in the bone overlying it. While the tumor may erode the skull's inner table, the most dramatic examples of induced hyperostosis we have are present on the outer table. Campillo (1994–95: 95) demonstrates what he suspects is a meningiosarcoma (or possibly even osteosarcoma) in a lesion presenting an enormous mass over the skull's frontal bone, similar to the well known Chavin culture skull from Peru (MacCurdy, 1923). He also cites five other cases his group has published demonstrating meningioma-induced hyperostosis, the oldest of which is of Neolithic age, and notes that the oldest example, published by de Lumley (1962), was found in a 200 000 year old skull of *Homo erectus* from a French cave. Rogers (1949) also found such characteristic cranial hyperostosis in a first dynasty Egyptian body and in another from the twentieth dynasty.

Soft tissue lesions of the eye

In spontaneously desiccated mummies the globe of the eye loses its fluid content, the muscles shrivel and the orbital soft tissues collapse into a small, irregular and inconspicuous mass at the rear of the orbit, often still anchored by the optic nerve. Among those Egyptian mummies in whom these dried tissues have not been replaced with artificial eyes, the appearance is not very different from that of naturally mummified bodies. The common conditions of conjunctivitis, trichiasis and others were well-known in antiquity as judged from the recommendations for their treatment in old medical texts such as the Ebers papyrus, the Vedic literature and others. However, without tissue rehydration most of these did not produce a lesion clearly visible to an examining paleopathologist. Consequently in this text we acknowledge the ancients' awareness of many ophthalmological conditions, but we will limit our discussion principally to those few that would be recognizable without further tissue manipulation by a paleopathologist.

Trachoma

The most common cause of blindness in the world today is trachoma. It is an infection most frequent in arid, sandy areas, caused by *Chlamydia trachomatis* and spread largely by person-to-person contact, though transmission by flies has also been suspected. It begins as an infection of the upper eyelid conjunctiva, penetrating to the cartilaginous tarsal plate where destructive abscesses may occur. Eventual spread to the lower lid is common, but more important is extension to the cornea. Here the inflammation stimulates extensive granulation tissue. Healing occurs by organization of the granulation tissue that involves fibrous tissue replacement, which impairs vision. Paleopathologists are most apt to encounter the end stages of this disease with eyelids often grotesquely deformed by the advanced destructive lesions. Defective closure of such deformed eyelids invites drying of the conjunctiva with secondary bacterial infection, especially by the bacterium *Hemophilus aegypticus*. The widespread scarring of the cornea usually renders it opaque and the eye becomes sightless (Strano & Font, 1976). The paleopathologist's attention will probably be attracted by the lid deformation, and subsequent rehydration of the eye will render the fibrotic cornea apparent.

Trachoma is, in all likelihood, an ancient disease. Egypt's Ebers papyrus, written ca. 1500 B.C. but containing portions written probably as early as 3000 B.C., includes specific remedies (application of antimony, ochre and natron) for trachoma ((Ebbell, 1937: p. 69, column 57). The Ayurvedic texts of India were probably organized about the sixth century B.C. but assumed their present form about the sixth century A.D. They describe an eye condition that most probably is trachoma (Chakravorty, 1993). Mi disease, described in the second century B.C. book *Shan Hai Ching*, is also most likely to be trachoma (Gwei-Djen & Needham, 1993). Trachoma ('aspritudo') was common in ancient Rome (Birely, 1992; Andersen, 1994: 17). While the Middle Ages and early Renaissance texts of Europe, the Middle and Far East commonly describe trachoma, Crosby (1986) doubts it was a pre-Columbian New World disease. In spite of this frequency, the condition has not been reported in mummified bodies. Webb (1990) feels that a localized, lytic lesion of the orbital roof is the osseous 'marker' for trachoma among prehistoric Australian aboriginal skulls. If so, the condition there can be traced back to the late Pleistocene period. The relationship of the osteological lesion to the soft tissue infection by *Chlamydia trachomatis*, however, is speculative and circumstantial. Karasch (1993) has prepared a superb history of trachoma under the title 'Ophthalmia'.

Blindness

In Egyptian art blindness is indicated by closed eyelids. Fuchs (1964) notes that, in addition, blind individuals are also characterized in tomb reliefs as having puffy eyelids and rolls of abdominal fat. These are features that he feels may have a metabolic and endocrine basis, resulting in focal fatty degeneration and water retention. Blind individuals are commonly pictured as harpists in ancient Egypt. Jantzen (1968) points out that one of these, from the eighteenth dynasty tomb of Paätenemheb, demonstrates a remarkably prominent, tortuous temporal artery, suggesting his blindness is the consequence of thrombosed ocular arteries secondary to their involvement by temporal (granulomatous; giant-cell) arteritis. He attributes this to the then current artistic fashion of literal rendition of models. The earliest evidence of recognition of this entity appears to be a report by an Arabian physician about A.D. 1000 (Andersen, 1994: 81). One of the well-known ceramics of Peru's Moche culture (A.D. 100–800) demonstrates the drooping corner of the mouth characteristic of left facial paralysis and a shrunken, empty right eye area (blindness) that might represent this same etiology.

In medieval Europe blinding was a common form of punishment as a substitute for capital punishment (hanging). It began with the support of the church. Crimes punished by blinding included rebellion and theft quite commonly, but the same penalty was also inflicted for arson, poaching, perjury, rape and counterfeiting. Blinding methods were violent and commonly carried out surgically. In some instances it may have been carried out with hot iron instruments (Bruce, 1941).

Symbol

The eye has an age-old history as a symbol. Ancient Egypt's principal Old Kingdom sun god was Horus, symbolized as a health-bringing, stylized 'wedjat' eye (related to his loss of an eye in a struggle for power with his uncle, the god Seth and which was restored by the god Thoth). Nordic mythology relates how their principal deity, Odin, traded one of his eyes for access to a well of knowledge (Guirand, 1978:257). Aztec iconography frequently depicts the gouging of an eye (which commonly dangles on the cheek, suspended by its optic nerve), but it is unclear if the depictions are literal or symbolic. Arrington (1959) comments that eye gouging was a common ritual element among many ancient groups. All of these examples appear to use the eye, or the loss of it, as being related to the acquisition of special knowledge. Donington (1974:122) cites the blindness of Samson and Oedipus as a 'turning of their sight inwards'; i.e. gaining unusual insight of the meaning of their actions dictated by their subconscious self.

Cataract

The eye's lens normally is transparent. Cataract is a term employed for the condition characterized by vision loss secondary to opacification of the lens. Such a process is the consequence of the precipitation of proteins within the lens. The most common form of lens opacification is due to aging. Lens proteins have virtually zero turnover (Berman, 1991:202) so that interactions with sugar (glycosylation) and changes in intermolecular linkages that produce protein precipitation will result in progressive accumulation of protein debris within the lens, leading to loss of its transparency and eventual blindness. While this process is age-related, certain conditions such as diabetes, ultraviolet radiation, drugs and many inherited enzyme deficiencies can accelerate it to a marked degree.

Cataract is surely an ancient disease (Andersen, 1994:49). The surgical approach called 'couching' (insertion of a needle into the eye and pushing the hardened, opaque lens downward, out of the path of vision) began in India certainly before the fifth century A.D. and was popularized by Arab physicians in the medieval period (Hirschberg, 1982). Reflection of light from the opacified lens in a living individual makes the presence of a cataract obvious to even a casual observer and its treatment today is simply surgical removal with replacement by a plastic lens. It is, however, not simply recognizable within the shriveled, desiccated remains of a mummy's eye, so that little has been written about it in the paleopathology literature. One would expect rehydration to make the lens identifiable, though whether the precipitated proteins of a cataract would become recognizable is not known. Now that chemical methods have become available to detect and quantify the insoluble lens' proteins we can expect the frequency and antiquity of cataract to be defined in the near future.

Artificial eyes

The use of artificial eyes in statuary has been known since ancient times. The 'wedjat' eye was one of the early symbols of dynastic Egypt's initial principal god – Horus (Sandison, 1957; Andersen, 1994:40). Highly stylized eyes composed of copper or brass outlines filled in with white plaster, shell, glass or porcelain and with obsidian for the iris were commonly attached to Egyptian coffins, statuary (Tonkelaar *et al.*, 1991) and (beginning with the New Kingdom) sometimes even in mummies (Wilson, 1972). Maegraith *et al.* (1991) feel the eye symbol of the Viking-type ship that appears on the Memoir II cover of the Liverpool School of Tropical Medicine, February 1990 issue (*Report of the Malaria Expedition to West Africa, August, 1889*) is the eye of Horus. The moai ('stone heads') of Rapa Nui (Easter Island), used by indigens as spiritual containers for both spirits of ancestors and those of deities, were fitted with artificial eyes of coral and red scoria (van Tilburg, 1994: plate 25). Thin silver and gold wafers were found beneath the eyelids of mummies representing the Chiribaya people of coastal southern Peru from about A.D. 1200 (Aufderheide, 1990). Rising (1866) found the crystalline lens of large, Pacific cuttlefish placed in the orbits of mummies from Arica, a northern Chile port city. However, in spite of extensive employment of the eye as a symbol, for decorative purpose, for statuary and even for mummies, there is no convincing evidence artificial eyes were ever used in antiquity for cosmetic purposes in living persons.

Neoplasms

The two principal eye neoplasms are malignant melanoma and retinoblastoma. Melanomas arise from pigment-forming cells in the eye and most (but not all) of these tumors retain their melaninogenic capacity, the gross tumor presenting a black appearance. Growth is slow but the neoplasm eventually destroys vision and both invades locally and metastasizes hematogenously. It affects primarily adults.

Retinoblastoma is a cancer of childhood arising in the eye's retina. More than 90 % are of sporadic origin; in the remainder a family history of these tumors is prominent. Such children inherit a mutation of the Rb gene (a tumor suppressor) on one of the two chromosomes for that site and thus are vulnerable for the development of this tumor if they suffer a mutation of the other also after birth since homozygous nonfunctional mutations of the Rb gene usually leads to growth of this neoplasm. It is a white or cream-colored tumor. It may spread into the brain by retrograde growth along the optic nerve, or it may metastasize hematogenously.

Thus an eye-destroying tumor may well remain recognizable in mummified human remains. The black pigmented appearance of a melanoma usually will be sufficient to separate it from neuroblastoma.

Soft tissue lesions of the ear

The only externally visible soft tissue lesions of the ear of interest to paleopathologists are the mutilations designed to support earrings. These are discussed in Chapter 3 (Traumatic conditions). Several examples of ear drum perforations have been reported. Both Egyptian mummies labelled PUM II and PUM III were found to have perforations of the tympanic membrane (Benítez, 1988) as was the 2100 year old body of the Marquis of Tai (Cockburn, 1974).

Otosclerosis

Sound is transferred from the vibrating tympanic membrane ('ear drum') to several articulated ossicles through the middle ear to the cochlea (hearing organ) in the inner ear. These ossicles must retain their normal articulation to transmit the sound vibrations. For reasons not yet well understood (though it behaves much like an autosomal dominant mutation), bony proliferation (otosclerosis) may occur at sites of articulation with subsequent fixation, resulting in decreased or absent sound transmission and consequent loss of hearing. Particularly common is fixation of the stapes footplate to the oval window. Using a surgical microscope, Birkby & Gregg (1975) were the first to report otosclerosis in the body of one of 11 Spaniards buried in a New Mexico (U.S.A.) cemetery about two centuries earlier. They found the stapes footplate fused to the round window by hard bone. Previously they had examined 4064 temporal bones harvested from 2600 Native American Indian skeletons without finding such a lesion. This was consistent with the virtual absence of this condition in modern U.S.A. Indian populations in contrast to the known clinical prevalence of 1 %

(and histologic evidence in about 9 %) among modern Caucasians (Dalby et al., 1993). In 1164 temporal bones from various British sites between the fourth and seventeenth centuries, Dalby et al. (1993) found a prevalence of about 0.9 %. This study used endoscopy to visualize the ear ossicles in the intact skull. The simplicity of this noninvasive procedure can be expected to encourage its application in the future.

Otitis media

Infection of the middle ear is primarily a disease of children; more than half acquire it under the age of 4 years (Rudberg, 1954: table 25). A wide range of bacteria can cause this disease, though the pneumococcus (Streptococcus pneumoniae) and Haemophilus influenzae are responsible for about half of the cases. Acute pharyngitis causes sufficient swelling to occlude the Eustachian tube, providing an opportunity for bacteria, trapped in the now undrained space, to proliferate. First fluid, then pus can fill the space, causing the tympanic membrane (ear drum) to become reddened and bulge into the external auditory canal. Eventually the exudate may digest a portion of the tympanic membrane, allowing the pus to drain by this route. Subsequent healing is the rule, though recurrences are common. The tympanic membrane defect may persist into adulthood, serving as an entry point for bacterial access with recurrent or chronic infections. In addition, the squamous epithelium lining the external auditory canal may extend through the defect into the middle ear where its desquamated cells (keratin) accumulate, blocking the lumen as an irregular expanding mass of material referred to clinically as a cholesteatoma. In spite of its name, this is not a neoplasm – merely a localized accumulation of exfoliated, dead, benign squamous epithelium.

Complications of otitis media include not only recurrent or chronic infection but also extension of the bacteria to the blood, resulting in a life-threatening septicemia. In addition, local destruction of the ear ossicles and/or cochlear branch of auditory nerve can lead to deafness, while extension to the cranial cavity can produce fatal meningitis or posterior extension can reach the air cells of the mastoid process. Since the air cells of the mastoid develop during the same period of infant growth that is coincident with a high prevalence of otitis media, extension of the infection to the mastoid may break down the thin walls between the cells and impair further air cell production. In some cases the mastoid abscess may perforate the cortical surface and drain exteriorly.

Paleopathology

The paleopathologist can expect to identify the perforated tympanic membrane by direct observation, though a simple, hand-held otoscope will provide a desirably illuminated view and, if required, a magnifying lens. Evaluation of middle ear ossicles for either destruction by otitis media or otosclerotic fixation is most simply and nondestructively achieved with an endoscope (Dalby *et al.*, 1993). Benítez (1985) extirpated the temporal bone and prepared histological sections, identifying an antemortem tympanic membrane perforation found in a young adult Egyptian mummy. Smith & Wood Jones (1910:284) found a draining sinus in the posterosuperior part of the mastoid in a Nubian mummy (subject no. 23:60:J) from the New Kingdom and Leek (1986:191) identified an even earlier example of such a sinus in the lower mastoid that exposed underlying air cells in an aged male excavated from Cheops' western necropolis of the Old Kingdom era. Gregg *et al.* (1965) and Gregg & Steele (1982) used radiological studies to evaluate the presence of mastoid air cell patterns demonstrating changes produced by otitis media in both living and ancient Native American skulls. They found that about half of the mastoids revealed evidence of alteration by otitis media with mastoiditis, and that pre-Columbian frequency of such changes was lower than that for those dating to the post-1492 period. In a large Swedish study of modern patients, Rudberg (1954) found clinical evidence of mastoiditis in 17.2 % of children with otitis media not treated with antibiotics while chemotherapy reduced this to less than 1.5 %. Comparison of the Gregg *et al.* study with that by Rudberg suggests that radiological evaluation may be the most sensitive method for detection of mastoiditis. Certainly persistence into adulthood of a draining sinus via the mastoid occurs so infrequently that it would serve as an insufficiently sensitive 'marker' for mastoiditis prevalence study.

Exostoses of the external auditory canal

Definition
This benign lesion is composed of a skin-covered, circumscribed mass of dense bone located at the meatus or within the external auditory canal (Fig. 8.4).

Nature of the lesion
Whether this lesion is a reactive change or a benign neoplasm is not at all clear. The very early literature refers to it as a benign neoplasm (osteoma) while the more recent articles favor the term 'exostosis.' Mingled within these are reports by several authors who feel that both occur and can be differentiated.

The floor, all of the anterior wall and about half of the posterior wall of the external auditory canal is formed by the tympanic portion of the temporal bone, while the roof and upper half of the posterior wall are created by the squamous portion (Sobotta & McMurrich, 1939:38–45). Collectively this tubular structure is termed the tympanic ring, while the posterior junction of the tympanic bone with the squamous roof (the latter forming part of the anterior mastoid structure) is named the tympanomastoid suture while the homologous junction on the anterior wall is termed the tympanosquamous suture. Graham (1979) defined what he felt were true benign, neoplastic (osteoma) lesions as roughly spherical but peduncu-

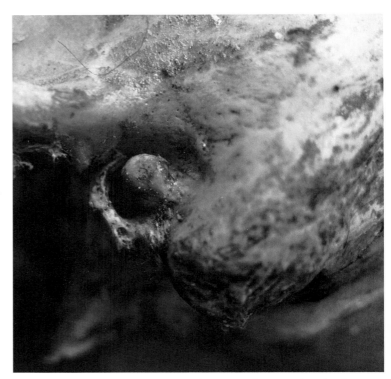

FIG. 8.4: **Exostosis at external auditory canal meatus.** A white, smooth-surfaced osseous nodule located on the anterior wall of the aural canal meatus was 4 mm in diameter. Spontaneously mummified adult male, coastal Peru, A.D. 1000. PBL.

lated nodules of dense osseous tissue arising from either of the two sutures (i.e. from either the anterior or posterior wall) that were solitary and tended to increase sufficiently so as to occlude the canal, with a histological structure of fibrovascular channels embedded in lamellar bone. He admitted that any given lesion might lack at least one of these features. He characterized reactive exostoses as being of sessile, broad-based forms, commonly bilateral and often multiple, invariably involving the tympanic bone and that its histological structure was composed of concentric layers of subperiosteal bone with abundant osteocytes and far fewer fibrovascular channels. Gregg & Bass (1970), however, described four different forms, later described simply as spongy, knob-like, linear and spicular (Gregg & Gregg, 1987:90). Of these only the linear type fits Graham's description of exostoses while a single, additional example of the nodular type was described that might conform to Graham's osteoma classification (but pedunculation is not noted though it was unilateral). These authors depict their single, nodular, fifth example as 'tumor type,' but seem to equate the terms exostosis and osteoma for all their other examples. While DiBartolomeo (1979) cites Graham's (1970) classification, he presents all of his own 50 cases as exostoses even though some are solitary and pedunculated. The custom of referring to these lesions as osteomas in the older literature appears to have evolved into terming them exostoses in more recent reports. There appears to be little sense of urgency to distinguish benign neoplasm from reactive exostosis today.

Antiquity

In Japan these lesions have been found in Neolithic bones from about 5000 B.C. Among early marine coastal populations of northern Chile, these structures were common as early as 7000 B.C. (Aufderheide et al., 1993), but were absent in nearby highlanders (Standen et al., 1995). A few Egyptian examples beginning with the twelfth dynasty (roughly 1800 B.C.) have been reported (Hrdlicka, 1935). Seligman (1870) found them in Inca skulls. Such lesions were also found in the fossil hominids of Shanidar 1 (Trinkaus, 1983) and LaChapelle Aux Saints (Trinkaus, 1985).

Location of the lesions

About 70 % of the lesions are found on the posterior wall, beginning near the tympanomastoid suture; most of the remainder are on the anterior wall (near that suture) with a minority on the floor near the tympanic membrane (Blake, 1880; Roche, 1964; Gregg & Bass, 1970; DiBartolomeo, 1979; Gregg & Gregg, 1987). Most report a high frequency of bilateral lesions (DiBartolomeo, 1979: 62 %), but Gregg & Gregg (1987:90, table 4.7) found that only 58 % of their upper Missouri river archaeological skulls of Native Ameri-

cans were bilateral. Of the unilateral lesions, 75 % were on the left side. All of DiBartolomeo's clinical cases revealed more than one lesion/meatus.

Age and gender

All series identify a high male/female ratio varying from 6/1 (Gregg & Gregg, 1987) to 14/1 (Roche, 1964). Both archaeological studies (Hrdlicka, 1935; DiBartolomeo, 1979; Gregg & Gregg, 1987; Manzi et al., 1991) and clinical studies (DiBartolomeo, 1979; Gregg & Gregg, 1987) identified either no or only an occasional such structure in individuals under age 20 years, strongly implying that this is an acquired condition. In 177 skulls from Peru, Capasso (1988) found 15 with ear canal exostoses; all but one were in males and all were adults. Similarly, none could be found in examination of about 10 000 schoolchildren (Bezold, 1885, cited in Hrdlicka, 1935).

Frequency

Archaeological population frequencies reveal some geographical differences. North American upper midwestern archaeological populations averaged about 4.9 % (Gregg & Gregg, 1987); Hrdlicka's (1935) multinational collection revealed about twice that many (10.8 %), while a large Australian collection demonstrated the highest recorded frequency of 27.9 %. Furthermore, Gregg & Gregg (1987:90) report that the frequency in their archaeological specimens (4.9 %) approximates that found in surveys of those groups' living descendants from the same region, suggesting that the soft tissue covering these lesions probably is not obscuring underlying lesions when examined in current populations. For that reason DiBartolomeo's (1979) finding of only 0.6 % in about 11 000 patients seen in a otolaryngologist's clinical practice is the product of patient selection, reflecting the asymptomatic nature of a large fraction of these lesions.

Etiology

The older literature contains a generous quantity of speculation about the cause of these lesions. DiBartolomeo (1979) and Kennedy (1986) have collected these and Table 8.1 has been constructed from their articles and some other sources. Some of these, such as gout or alcoholism, do not warrant serious consideration, while others (cranial deformation or mastication stress) appear conceivable but not probable. Racial affinity and 'constitutional predisposition' are general terms that assume the effect of some type of genetic population difference leading to this condition, but its virtual absence under age 20 years suggests an environmental mechanism instead.

Because chronic infections involving the periosteum are known to provide a powerful stimulus to new bone formation, the possibility of chronic external auditory canal infection has been postulated (Toynbee, 1849; Cassels, 1877). In spite of the plausibility of individual reports, however, DiBartolomeo (1979) found that while as many as 30 % of

Table 8.1. Proposed etiology of external auditory canal exostoses

Proposed etiology	References
Alcoholism	Toynbee, 1849
Genetic	*Seligman, 1864; *Turner, 1879; Blake, 1880; *Dalby, 1889; *Hartmann, 1893; Hrdlicka, 1935; *Adis-Castro & Neumann, 1947; *Berry & Berry, 1967
Gout and/or rheumatism	Toynbee, 1849; *Field, 1882; *Virchow, 1893; *Vail, 1928
Ear piercing	von Luschan, 1896 a, b
Cranial deformation	Jackson, 1909; *Oetteking, 1930; *Ostman, 1930
Bathing	*Tod, 1910
Chronic infection	*St. John Roosa, 1866; Cassells, 1877; *Field, 1878
Canal form	*Stewart, 1933
Mastication stress	*Burton, 1923
Chronic irritation	Hrdlicka, 1935; Sheehy, 1958; DiBartolomeo, 1979
Swimming	*Wyman, 1874; *Field, 1878; Kelson, 1900; *Moore, 1900; Jackson, 1909; *McKenzie, 1920; *Belgraver, 1938; *Harrison, 1951; Roche, 1964; *Starachowicz & Koterba, 1977
Cold water	van Gilse, 1938; Fowler & Osmon, 1942; *Adams, 1951; *Ascenzi & Balistreri, 1975; Kennedy, 1986.

This Table was created from the narrative portions of the above-mentioned references listed in Kennedy (1986) together with additions by us.
* For references not present in the bibliography of this volume, see Kennedy, (1986).

his patients admitted to a history of an acute ear infection in childhood, none had chronic infections.

The turn of the century produced a variety of reports dealing with individuals exposed to cold water immersion to a far greater extent than the general population (Kelson, 1900; Jackson, 1909). Thus, DiBartolomeo (1979) found many of his patients from California's southern coast were ocean surfers, swimmers or divers. Kennedy (1986) notes that populations in whom this lesion is common are those living between latitudes 30–45° N and S, and who exploit marine or freshwater resources. A study of British military recruits identified a frequency of about 5 % among swimmers (same among fresh- and seawater swimmers) compared with less than 1 % of nonswimmers (Harrison, 1962). Recently a high frequency of exostoses found among wealthy, male, imperial Romans (in contrast to none in nearby slaves and laborers) was attributed to their use of daily baths and the absence of lesions in their women was associated with the men's traditional use of cold water baths in the frigidarium (Manzi et al., 1991).

Only a few efforts have been made to reproduce these lesions experimentally. Van Gilse (1938), cited by DiBartolomeo (1979), observed that Italian swimmers in the warm Adriatic waters did not develop aural exostoses while the Dutch bathing in the cold milieu of the North Sea were vulnerable to these lesions. He attempted to test the role of the thermal element. Irrigating human external auditory canals with both warm and cold water he created no exostoses but found prolonged (45 minutes) hyperemia of the canal's epidermal lining following a 30 second cold water irrigation in contrast to only 1 minute of hyperemia after using warm water. A more aggressive attempt to reproduce these lesions employed cold water irrigation of the external auditory canal in guinea pigs (Fowler & Osmun, 1942). This produced no lesions in the external canal but did induce a diffuse proliferative skeletal response in the middle ear. Twenty years later Harrison (1962) also irrigated anesthetized guinea pig external aural canals at weekly intervals for a total of up to 11 hours. Histologic sections demonstrated vasodilatation in the underlying bone and in five animals diffuse histologic evidence of new bone formation was found deep in the meatus adjacent to the tympanic membrane and in one animal a 'seedling' osteoma was found at that site. Emphasizing the thin layer of soft tissue overlying the external auditory canal's bony structure, he postulated the increased blood flow stimulated by repeated cold water exposure may be sufficient to evoke a proliferative response in the underlying periosteum.

A critical summary of the evidence for the etiological role of cold water exposure in the development of external auditory canal exostoses and/or osteomas reveals that cold water exposure initiates a prolonged vasodilatation of the canal structures involving not only the soft tissues in humans, but also the superficial aspects of the underlying bone in guinea pigs. The implication that the demonstrated proliferative skeletal changes in the studied guinea pigs would have proceeded and eventually formed gross lesions characteristic of the exostoses under consideration in humans is provocative but speculative. While current authors frequently declare that these experimental studies have 'proved' the etiology of this condition, this body of evidence is fragile indeed. The simple fact remains that the gross lesions have not yet been reproduced experimentally. In addition, the cold water theory is not a plausible explanation for the presence of these bony nodules among inland populations that have a frequency rivalling that of coastal groups (Blake, 1880; Gregg & Gregg, 1987). We consider the etiology of external auditory canal exostoses and/or osteomas as an unresolved issue.

Recognition in archaeological remains

A defined, benign outgrowth of bony tissue of any form located anywhere from the meatus to the tympanic membrane is eligible for the assignation of 'exostosis'. Until the separation of benign neoplasm (osteoma) from exostosis is better defined, the term 'exostosis' is probably acceptable (though Kennedy's (1986) suggestion of the descriptive term 'auditory hyperostosis' could be a practical solution in the interim). More explicit description of the location, shape, base and size of the lesions as well as their histology in future reports could help resolve the reactive or neoplastic nature of these structures.

Soft tissue lesions of the nose

Nasal polyps

Nasal polyps have a considerable antiquity. An Egyptian remedy for 'fetid nose' (ozaena?) probably deals with an infected, ulcerated, foul-smelling nasal polyp (Ebbel, 1937: col. 20, p.105). The Hippocratic writers about 400 B.C. described five types of polyps, recommending removal with strings (Pahor, 1992c). Medieval Arabian physicians preferred to remove them with scissors while Fabricius (Renaissance) used copper forceps, tongs and scissors (Pahor & Kimura, 1990).

The nasal 'polyp' is not a neoplasm but an area of nasal mucosa in which a localized expression of allergy has resulted in so much fluid extrusion that its sheer weight causes the mucosa to descend to near (or actually protrude from) the nares in polypoid form. Drying with secondary infection results in ulceration and often bleeding. Their high moisture content would result in a dramatic size decrease in desiccated bodies, though fibrosis secondary to ulcerative infection can be expected to survive the desiccating process sufficiently for gross recognition. In spite of this, Allison (1992) found a nasal polyp large enough to fill the nasal space in a skull otherwise devoid of soft tissue from the Atacama Desert in northern Chile, dated to about A.D. 1000.

Syphilis

Nasal soft tissue destruction may be extensive. The earlier forms destroy the cartilaginous support of the nasal bridge and the resulting depression of the overlying skin is known as 'saddle nose'. Later destructive changes include the skin and bone, exposing the nasal chamber (see Treponematosis in Chapter 7 (Infectious diseases)).

Mucocutaneous leishmaniasis

This is a parasitic infection of the skin and mucous membranes. An isolated, often self-healing form of cutaneous leishmaniasis called 'Oriental sore' is found in the Old World caused by a variety of species. The mucocutaneous form of the New World is caused largely by *Leishmania braziliensis* and is present in Central and South America. The natural reservoir lies in many forest mammals and the organism is transmitted by blood-sucking sandflies such as those of the genus *Lutzomyia* (Connor & Neafie, 1976). Initial lesions appear on skin surfaces exposed to fly bites. Years later the nasal mucocutaneous areas and even associated bone may become involved and can be devastatingly destructive with extensive disfigurement. This form is called espundia, and ultimate death by bacterial infection is common (Locksley, 1991). A primary, localized facial lesion found in the Peruvian area is known as uta. Diagnosis is established by demonstrating the organism histologically. A skull of a 45–50 year old female of a population occupying a low valley (Azapa) site near the modern port of Arica, Chile about A.D. 1100 showed extensive skeletal destruction of the nasal areas as well as the right orbit and paranasal sinus walls, strongly suggestive of this disease (Allison, 1981a; Allison et al., 1982), though the absence of soft tissue prevented histologic search for the organism.

Sinusitis

Chronic infection of the paranasal sinuses with characteristic acute exacerbations provides recurring stimulation to the periosteum immediately underlying the mucosa lining. The eventual result is irregular first fibrotic and later calcific thickening of these structures. In an intact skull or head, these are usually visualized in skull radiographs. Frequently seen in modern individuals, examples have also been reported in the paleopathology literature. Lewis et al. (1994) report multiple cases from the collection at the University of Bradford characterized by maxillary antrum bone deposits and cite dental abscesses, poor ventilation, air pollution and allergies as etiological conditions leading to the infection.

Neoplasms

Nasopharyngeal carcinoma is the principal neoplasm of concern in this area. It arises from the soft tissues of the posterior nasopharynx, invades aggressively into the surrounding structures (including the bone) of the palate, sinuses, orbit and eventually even reaches the cranial cavities. Regional lymph node involvement is common and late stages include distant hematogenous metastases. Histologic type is most commonly squamous cell carcinoma of varying degrees of differentiation including one type exhibiting extensive lymphocytic infiltrate (lymphoepithelioma). Causes remain unknown. While it has a global distribution, the populations in southern China are particularly susceptible, where it constitutes almost 20 % of all cancers in contrast to its worldwide estimate of 0.25 % (Balogh, 1994). The tumor is also found in arctic natives, whose practice of chewing raw hides has been suggested as being an etiological contributor, but only on an anecdotal basis. The Epstein–Barr virus is frequently present in the cells of this tumor, but its causal status remains undefined.

Archaeological skulls demonstrating lytic lesions consistent with nasopharyngeal carcinoma have been reported frequently. In addition to an Egyptian case he reported himself (Strouhal, 1978), nasopharyngeal carcinoma was the diagnosis made by half of the authors of individual articles reporting primary soft tissue carcinomas collected and summarized by Strouhal (1994). Most were found in Egyptian mummies. A 1000 year old skull from a 45–50 year old female from northern Chile demonstrates a widely destructive process in the right facial bones consistent with either leishmaniasis (uta) or nasopharyngeal carcinoma (Allison & Gerszten, 1981). Brothwell (1967a) cites the description by Derry (1909) of the skull of a pre-Christian Nubian adult of the sixth century A.D. that had an extensive lytic process of the skull base including the nasopharyngeal area that Derry thought most probably began in the nasopharynx. Brothwell also cites a similar case reported by Wells (1963) in an early Old Kingdom mummy, as well as an example published by Krogman (1940) from an Iranian site more than 5000 years old. Unfortunately, in none of these was it possible to confirm the suspected nasopharyngeal carcinoma diagnosis by soft tissue histology. Compared to the relatively low frequency of this lesion today, the cases diagnosed as nasopharyngeal carcinoma in ancient bodies is proportionately very high, suggesting diagnostic imprecision (but see Fig. 13.18).

Transnasal craniotomy (TNC)

During the Egyptian mummification process a metal rod was inserted by the embalmers into one of the cadaver's nostrils (most often the left) and forced upward through the skull bones, penetrating the ethmoid sinuses and reaching the cranial cavity (Fig. 8.5). Allegedly this was done to enable subsequent brain extraction through the defect. This can be and was performed without visible external deformation. The modern paleopathologist can identify this defect easily by inserting a straight probe into the nostril. When the inner end has reached the cranial cavity, movement of the outer end in a circular manner can provide an impression of the

defect's size at the level of the cribriform plate. Visual inspection of the
nasal chamber permits a view of the
extent of nasal structure destruction
and whether resin or linen cloth are
visible. Radiology of the skull can detail
these changes. Sometimes the defect
will be large enough to accommodate
the passage of a pediatric endoscope,
permitting an internal view of the cranial cavity to determine the possible
presence of residual brain or meningeal
tissue as well as resin or linen.

The early Greek historian Herodotus
(ca. 450 B.C., II: paragraph 86)
described the creation of the defect by
embalmers using a hooked rod with
which they also removed the brain
through the channel they had produced. That this could have been performed was demonstrated by Karl
Sudhoff (1911) who collected instruments that were believed to have been
used by ancient Egyptians for that purpose, and used them to create the
transnasal craniotomy defect in human
cadavers, and also to remove some
brain tissue. The latter was achieved by plunging the metal
rod through the defect into the brain then withdrawing it
and wiping off the adherent brain tissue. Repeated efforts of
this nature resulted in the removal of a significant amount of
cerebral tissue. Subsequent brain maceration was achieved
by vigorous rotation of the metal rod, mixing the macerated
tissue with the cerebrospinal fluid from the brain ventricles.
Turning the body prone caused this semiliquid suspension to
drain out through the defect. These procedures were later
repeated on both sheep and human bodies with similar
results (Leek, 1969).

Earlier Smith (1902), Smith & Dawson (1924) and others
(Macalister, 1894) had noted that transnasal craniotomy
(TNC) first appeared in the eighteenth dynasty body of
Ahmose (Brier, 1994:62), leading to the conclusion that this
was a procedure limited to the latter half of Egyptian history.
However, Strouhal (1986) found TNC in four Middle Kingdom (twelfth dynasty) mummies and noted that one of Manchester Museum's 'Two Brothers' from the Middle Kingdom
also revealed such a defect as does the mummy from the same
period currently curated at the Boston Museum of Fine Arts.
He also cites the report of a body with TNC found in Imhotep's
tomb (third dynasty) though this would be more convincing
if it were radiocarbon-dated. Thus the initiation of this practice can be traced credibly to at least the Middle Kingdom.

Yet certain incongruities remain in our reconstruction of
this practice. Among these the most obvious is that, while all
tangible parts of an Egyptian ruler's body were considered

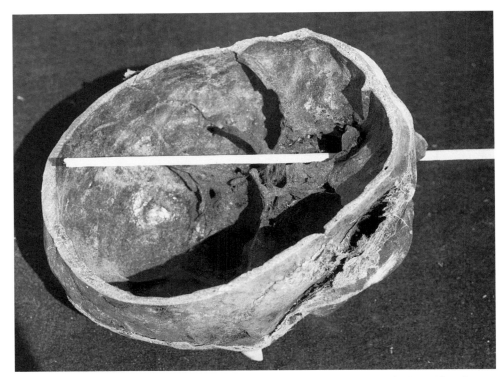

FIG. 8.5: **Transnasal craniotomy.** Egyptian mummification commonly involved the creation of a channel from the
nasal cavity to the cranial cavity via the ethmoid sinuses. The white rod in this illustration indicates the traverse of
this defect (titled transnasal craniotomy here) in the skull of an Egyptian mummy from Dakhleh Oasis from the Ptolemaic Period. PBL.

sacred and all his extirpated viscera were preserved, no one
has ever found brain included with those organs (Smith &
Dawson, 1924:68). This is most easily explained if the suggested method of excerebration (repeated insertion of a
metal rod into the brain followed by wiping off the soft,
cerebral tissue adhering to the withdrawn rod) is accurate,
since no cerebral structure would remain in recognizable
form. Such preserved brain-smeared bandages would not be
distinguishable from other masses of used natron-containing
packages often interred with or near the body. Strouhal
(1992:260) expresses doubt that the brain was removed
routinely in the manner described by Herodotus.

The most disturbing, however, is the presence of TNC in
bodies in which no other effort was made to preserve soft
tissues. For example, all ten of anthropogenically mummified Ptolemaic period bodies examined by one of us (A.C.A.)
at Egypt's Dakhleh oasis revealed not only the usual evisceration and other obvious soft tissue conservation procedures,
but also the expected TNC. The TNC defect, however, was also
present in 18 of 21 additional bodies removed from the
same tombs and that were clearly spontaneously mummified
without evisceration or other efforts to preserve soft tissue
(Aufderheide et al., unpublished results). If the purpose of
TNC was to remove brain in order to prevent its putrefaction,
then it would appear illogical to remove it without also evis-
cerating the abdomen, since the latter organs are obvious
sources of offensive putrefaction and are easily removed.
Furthermore, Egyptian belief system identified the heart, not

the brain, as the site of emotions and features of character. It is conceivable that the practice of TNC was initiated as part of the body soft tissue conservation effort and in later periods survived the curtailment of the other elements, such as evisceration, perpetuated only as a ritual feature. We have only the comment by Herodotus (not an eye witness) that the purpose of TNC was brain removal. Alternatively, therefore, creation of this defect could have been introduced initially solely for ritual purposes. That would be consistent with the religious nature of the entire mummification process. Many cultures have beliefs involving the postmortem exit or entry of souls (Frazer, 1976:208); for the Egyptians it was the *ka* and *ba* that would move out of and into the tomb and its contained body after death. The TNC defect thus could be conceived as an enabling device for such passage, similar to that of the door often painted upon the tomb wall. Such a viewpoint could accommodate the variations and inconsistencies in its application as well as the related variable cranial cavity content. Indeed, Smith & Dawson (1924:100) cite Maspero as explaining that a hole in the cranial vault of the skull of Meneptah (as well as Sety II and Ramses IV, V, and VI) was created by embalmers '…in order to allow evil spirits a free exit from the head…'

We are aware of no other cultural group that practiced TNC.

Soft tissue lesions of the neck

Cysts

These are usually embryonic remnants. Thyroglossal duct cysts, as their name implies, are products of that structure. During fetal life the thyroid migrates from a position equivalent to the base of the tongue, down to its final locale, resting on the trachea just below the larynx. Its 'wake' consists of the thyroglossal duct that normally atrophies and essentially disappears. Persistence of that duct's lumen in the central portion with obliteration at both ends results in entrapment of the fluid secreted by its epithelial lining, generating a cyst varying from a few millimeters to several centimeters in diameter. These are harmless and always in the midline.

Similarly, during the embryonic stage of 'gill clefts', the pharynx communicates with the skin surface of the side of the neck. Subsequent failure of obliteration of these structures may produce a cyst at any of the several branchial cleft levels. Fusion of the inner, pharyngeal level with lumen persistence of the central and outer portions may produce a skin surface defect. Complete persistence of the entire structure results in a skin–pharynx fistula. Other branchial cleft structures such as cartilaginous fragments are also often present. The cyst size range is similar to that of the thyroglossal duct origin, but one feature (location) easily differentiates the two: the thyroglossal duct cysts are in the midline while those of branchial cleft origin are lateral.

After desiccation such cysts lose their liquid content and often collapse to the point of difficult recognition. In others the globoid shape is retained in spite of its fluid loss often with a thin, peripheral rim of calcification. We know of only one paleopathology report of a young adult male from a Frankish thirteenth century cemetery in Greece that demonstrated a thyroglossal cyst (Barnes, 1995), though their frequency in most modern populations today suggests they are being overlooked in mummified, ancient bodies.

Torticollis

'Wry neck' is characterized by involuntary turning of the head secondary to dystonic muscle contraction. Initially it may be only transient, but it commonly progresses to a nearly fixed deformity. An Egyptian mummy of the Birmingham collection demonstrates this condition (Pahor, 1992c:864).

Thyroid lesions

These are discussed in Chapter 10 (Endocrine disorders).

HEART AND PERICARDIAL DISEASES

Examination of the heart in desiccated mummies is very difficult because of the brittle nature of the tissue. However, if the entire heart is immersed in rehydration fluid, the various structures of interest can be dissected in a useful manner. Parts of the heart intended for biochemical, immunological or other study methods can first be removed before rehydration from areas not expected to show anatomical changes and these samples can be retained for such other investigations.

The heart is a mass of muscle (myocardium) whose almost only purpose is to keep blood in motion so that oxygen and nutrients can be delivered to tissues while metabolic waste products are transported to excretory organs (lungs, kidney, gut) for elimination. The muscle mass is so thick that the heart has a set of its own vessels (coronary arteries) that nourish the heart muscle. The most common modern diseases of the heart involve conditions (especially atherosclerosis, discussed in Chapter 5 (Circulatory disorders)) that decrease or arrest blood flow through these arteries. The result of this is necrosis (infarction) of the myocardium. A weakened heart may not be able to pump blood at a normal rate ('heart failure'), resulting in accumulation of blood (congestion) in the lungs. Untreated this can displace air space for gas exchange to a degree sufficient to be lethal. Other diseases can affect the heart valves whose purpose is to regulate direction of blood flow. Diseased valves can either obstruct the flow of blood or permit reflux, either of which reduces its pumping efficiency and often leads to heart failure. Finally, these and many other heart conditions may interfere with the normal conductivity of the heart's electrical impulse that is necessary for muscle contraction, and this may result in sudden cardiac arrest. Those conditions that may result in a grossly recognizable lesion are discussed below.

Coronary thrombosis and infarction

Stenosing (narrowing) atheromas (fibrofatty plaques) in the coronary arteries are commonly accompanied by pain (angina) originating in the ischemic (oxygen-deprived) myocardium. Eventually ulceration of such an atheroma may be followed by acute coronary artery thrombosis ('heart attack') and the ischemic myocardium often becomes necrotic (infarcted). The heart muscle so weakened may not be able to carry out its pumping action efficiently, and death by cardiac arrest, heart failure, or rupture of the infarcted ventricular wall may occur. The latter will fill the pericardial sac (that envelops the heart) with blood, compressing the heart and producing cardiac arrest. If the affected individual survives, the infarcted myocardium eventually is replaced by fibrous scar. These complications

FIG. 8.6: **Heart: fibrinous pericarditis.** The light grey coating over the visceral pericardum of this heart represents fibrin that leaked from pericardial and epicardial vessels. Cause of death was end-stage renal failure with uremia. Spontaneously mummified young adult male from northern Chile, Cabuza culture, A.D. 350–1000. PBL.

can be expected to be recognizable in mummified remains, though postmortem autolysis often obliterates the evidence of antemortem myocardial infarction occurring shortly before death (Zimmerman, 1978). Arteriosclerotic disease of the peripheral vessels is discussed in Chapter 5 (Circulatory disorders).

Infections

Myocarditis

Various species of viruses, bacteria, fungi and protozoa can all infect the myocardium. Immunocompromised persons are particularly susceptible to myocarditis by organisms normally not virulent enough to produce human infection. Human hosts with a normal immune system, however, may suffer infection by many bacteria, especially if these have established an infective focus within the blood stream, such as a scarred heart valve deformed by a previous episode of rheumatic fever. In endemic areas of South America, *Trypanosoma cruzi* myocarditis (Chagas' disease) is a common and often lethal infection, and cardiomegaly in residents of such areas suggests the possibility of this condition. In mummified human remains all forms of myocarditis may be recognizable by the presence of an enlarged, dilated heart sometimes covered with fibrin (Fig. 8.6). Bacterial and fungal infective agents may be demonstrable with appropriate stains.

Valvular heart disease

The mitral and aortic heart valves (rarely those of the right heart) may be damaged by rheumatic fever, and the aortic may also be involved by atherosclerosis or by the dynamic stress to which a congenital bicuspid aortic valve deformity is subjected. The result of these conditions is commonly extensive fibrotic thickening and even calcification. The additional workload imposed on the heart by these deformities often causes heart failure that, untreated, may be fatal by early to middle adulthood (mitral) or 10–20 years later (aortic). Iron-containing macrophages in lung alveolae may testify to antemortem heart failure in human mummies. Such valves are also subject to local infection (endocarditis) with production of a clot upon the infected valve and whose untreated course is often fatal over a period of months. Calcification is frequently most extensive in the aortic valve, which can become so encrusted with calcium as to retain its diagnostic appearance even in skeletonized bodies. The larger mitral valve is often more irregularly and incompletely calcified. Their fibroelastic structure often permits the valves to survive postmortem changes far better than the muscle, permitting their evaluation for pathology even when much of the myocardium has decayed (Fig. 8.7).

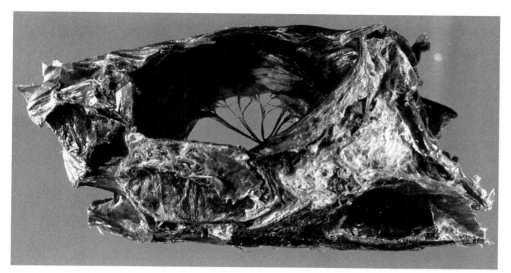

FIG. 8.7: **Heart: normal mitral valve.** The actively metabolizing myocardial fibers autolyze rapidly after death but the fibrotic and elastic tissues are more resistant. In this infant's heart most of the muscle was lost, but the delicate fibro-elastic structures of the normal mitral valve remain virtually unchanged. Spontaneously mummified 2 year old infant, A.D. 500–800, northern Chile. PBL.

Heart disease due to miscellaneous causes

Enormous heart enlargement due to indeterminate reasons has been termed idiopathic cardiomyopathy. It may present as a heart with markedly thickened walls (hypertrophic form) or one with increased musculature but whose striking change lies in enlargement of its chambers (dilated cardiomyopathy). Occasionally metabolic disturbances can result in inappropriate deposits of substances (glycogen, amyloid) into the heart muscle that weaken the myocardial fibers, causing heart failure. Nutritional deficiencies (thiamine: common in chronic alcoholics) can have a similar effect. While the enormously enlarged heart of dilated or hypertrophic cardiomyopathy can be expected to be recognizable in mummified tissue, only infrequently will its cause be demonstrable because of the myocardium's rapid postmortem autolysis.

Paleopathology of cardiac pathology

Column 37 of the Ebers papyrus from Egypt provides a graphic description of angina pectoris including the pain radiating to the arms (Ebbell, 1937:48): 'If thou examinest a man for illness in his cardia, and he has pains in his arms, in his breasts, and in one side of his cardia…it is death threatening him'. Mortuary inscriptions have been interpreted to describe acute, sudden death (Bruetsch, 1959). Peng (1995) reported a Chinese noblewoman buried about 200 B.C. who suffered coronary atherosclerosis with severe stenosis. That the process was not limited to highly structured civilizations is evident by observations of atheromas in aortic and coronary arteries of Alaskan spontaneously mummified bodies (Zimmerman *et al.*, 1971, 1981; Zimmerman & Aufderheide,

1984; Zimmerman, 1985). Experimental studies carried out by Zimmerman (1978) suggested that acute myocardial infarction could probably not be distinguished from postmortem autolysis of normal myocardium in spontaneously mummified bodies, but that the fibrotic scar of a healed infarct could be. These predictions are consistent with the observations by Long (1931) of fibrous foci in the myocardium of a twenty-first dynasty Egyptian mummy whose coronary arteries (as well as her aorta and renal arteries) were atherosclerotic.

Localized calcifications in otherwise undeformed mitral valves were interpreted by Long (1931) and by Zimmerman (1978) as healed endocarditis. No such reports have been described from the many spontaneously mummified bodies examined at the University of Tarapaca in Arica, Chile. *Trypanosoma cruzi* amastigote organisms have been demonstrated to be responsible for the enlarged heart of a Peruvian Inca mummy (Fornaciari *et al.*, 1992*a*, *b*). Another example of infectious myocarditis was the finding of multiple myocardial abscesses containing gram-negative bacilli in a late nineteenth or early twentieth century Aleutian mummy (Zimmerman, 1993*a*). The heart of an 8 year old child (from northern Chile, about A.D. 300) encased in pale exudate, was reported by Allison (1981*b*). The etiology probably was related to the pneumonia found in the lung. Extension of suppurative, bacillary lung infection to the pericardium, producing acute, purulent pericarditis is a well-known and often lethal complication of pneumonia. Blackman *et al.* (1991) found a similar-appearing fibrinous pericarditis enveloping the heart of an 18 year old male from the Cabuza culture (A.D. 350–1000) from northern Chile. In this case, however, it was not an infectious process but rather a metabolic complication of uremia due to renal failure with diffuse renal calcification, a product of secondary hyperparathyroidism.

The entire array of cardiac shunts, valvular deformities and malpositions that characterize congenital lesions may, of course, be encountered by the paleopathologist, but in most of these cases postmortem alterations can be expected to obscure and complicate their identification. In spite of myocardial preservation difficulties, Robertson (1988) reported an example of a congenital heart lesion (common atrioventricular canal) in a spontaneously mummified body of an infant member of the Anizazi culture from Canyon de Chelly, dating to about A.D. 600. Cardiomegaly was obvious and right heart failure was manifested by ascites. Lung fragments from tissue retrieved from an isolated canopic jar demonstrated microscopic presence of intra-alveolar fluid and protein that might have been the result of pulmonary edema secondary to left ventricular failure, though an inflammatory origin could not be excluded (Walker *et al.*, 1987).

PULMONARY DISEASES

Of all the viscera, the lungs (or at least part of them) are most frequently preserved in mummified remains. This is most probably due to the small fraction of their mass represented by epithelial cells, because epithelium is richly endowed with lysosomes filled with hydrolases that initiate the autolytic decay process. The rate of desiccation is also enhanced by the enormous collective surface area of the pulmonary capillary bed and the relative paucity of chest wall soft tissues.

Congenital conditions

Bronchogenic cyst

Derived from primitive foregut, these cysts are usually found near the tracheal bifurcation. The wall is composed of bronchial elements, though cartilage may not be prominent. Accumulated mucous secretion distends the lumen. This lesion has not been reported in archaeological remains.

Bronchopulmonary sequestration

This malformation is composed of pulmonary tissue located either within normal lung or adjacent to it, but whose bronchi and vasculature usually are separate from the normal lung. In such cases the bronchial secretions accumulate since they cannot drain via the normal bronchial system. The mucus-distended bronchi expand until they dominate the gross structure, compressing the softer intervening structure into a mass of scar. The anomaly has not been identified in mummified tissue.

Pulmonary infections

Pneumonia

The section dealing with pneumonia in Chapter 7 (Infectious diseases) includes the features of lung infections in both modern and ancient bodies. Here we will stress only a few additional items of special interest. We generate a working diagnosis of pneumonia upon finding a thickened or consolidated area in a desiccated, mummified lung. Validation of that approach was achieved by reviewing more than 250 autopsy records in a community hospital for the years 1925 through 1928, a period prior to the availability of effective pneumonia therapy. Only 5 % of pulmonary areas of consolidation or masses proved to be noninfectious lesions, most commonly pulmonary infarcts and metastatic carcinoma (A.C.A., unpublished results). Thus, a consoli-

FIG. 8.8: **Primary tuberculosis (Ghon complex).** The nodule at the bottom of the illustration is a 1.2 cm calcified shell located in the subpleural area of pulmonary parenchyma and represents the residuum of the initial (now arrested) pulmonary tuberculous infection. The two mounds present in the mediastinal tissues (upper half of the photograph) are partly calcified hilar lymph nodes, enlarged because tubercle bacilli had drained into them from the primary focus in the lung and infected these nodes. From an extract of one of these nodes DNA characteristic of the tuberculosis-causing bacterial complex was isolated and sequenced. Spontaneously mummified adult 30–35 year old female, Peru, A.D. 1000. PBL.

dated area of lung bears a 95 % probability of representing pneumonia. A diffuse area of pulmonary adhesions may prevent postmortem collapse of the lung, but will not result in consolidation.

Tuberculosis

Tuberculous changes may also be recognizable. The characteristic appearance of a primary tuberculous Ghon complex was obvious in the lung of an adult female Andean mummy from about A.D. 1000 (Salo et al., 1994). A pulmonary hollow, peripheral, calcified nodule was associated with two enlarged hilar lymph nodes (Fig. 8.8). Zimmerman (1979) identified pulmonary adhesions with recent pulmonary hemorrhage and found acid-fast bacilli in vertebral bone of an Egyptian mummy. Allison et al. (1973) were able to demonstrate acid-fast bacilli in soft tissues (including miliary tubercles) of several Andean mummies, as did Garcia-Frias (1940), though some question the pre-Columbian context of the latter. Thus it appears that ancient tuberculous lungs manifest the fibrotic and calcifying changes with which pathologists examining modern lungs are familiar, but without the inflammatory cellular infiltrate. More recently Salo et al. (1994) isolated a segment of DNA unique to the Mycobacterium tuberculosis complex from the partly calcified hilar lymph node of a 1000 year old Andean mummy. In future studies the methods of molecular biology can be expected to expand greatly the number of etiological agents responsible for deaths in antiquity. In the New World, soft tissue tuberculous infections date back to only about A.D. 300, but in the Old World it has been identified in Egyptian New Kingdom mummies. Excellent summaries of this disease's antiquity and history can be found in Morse (1961), Buikstra (1977, 1981), Manchester (1983a:39–41), Buikstra & Williams (1991), Strouhal (1991c) and Johnston (1993). Walker et al. (1987) identified foci of calcification in tissues removed from Egyptian canopic jars, and felt they probably represented earlier tuberculous infection.

Fungal infections

Since at least several common fungal agents such as Blastomyces dermatitidis and Coccidioides immitis would be expected to retain their diagnostic structure in tissues, one would anticipate reports of their presence in the lungs of occasional ancient bodies. Separation of the common saprophytes contaminating postmortem archaeological tissues is not usually difficult. However, few published cases of pulmonary infections by pathogenic fungi can be identified.

As mentioned in Chapter 7 (Infectious diseases), Aspergillus sp. can colonize lung cysts, abscesses or bronchial mucosa, particularly in previously diseased pulmonary parenchyma. Horne (1995) reported findings in an Egyptian mummy with Aspergillus sp. lining a lung cavity. A newspaper article (Vancouver Sun, December 20, 1995) stated that Aspergillus sp.

was recovered from the lung of the 'Iceman' (Tyrolean glacier mummy examined at Innsbruck, Austria) but at the time of this writing this information has not appeared in a scientific journal. Harrison et al. (1991) found Coccidioides sp. in the bone of an archaeological skeleton from the southwestern U.S.A. demonstrating the lesion of Pott's disease (see Chapter 7 (Infectious diseases)). In view of the current hazard of infection by this organism following exposure to dust inhalation in this geographical region, the lungs of mummies from this area should be examined with special focus on fungal infection. Allison et al. (1979) reported a case of pulmonary paracoccidioidomycosis in a northern Chile mummy and demonstrated the unique, 'spokewheel' structure of the organism in tissue sections.

Fornaciari & Marchetti (1986) and Fornaciari et al. (1989b) have identified smallpox virus in tissues of a medieval body in Italy, confirmed by immunostaining, and Dalton et al. (1976) have published an electron micrograph of a mummy kidney tissue section resembling a virus structure, but to date no convincing case of virus pneumonia in an ancient body has been reported.

Degenerative conditions

Emphysema

The lung is masterfully constructed to effect gas exchange with the blood efficiently. As the bronchi extend into the lung periphery they bifurcate into rami of ever-diminishing diameter, terminating as a series of blind-ended air sacs (alveoli). The walls of these alveoli are thin and fragile, occupied principally by thin-walled blood vessels and capillaries. It is here that gas exchange between inspired air and circulating blood occurs. Indeed, functionally a lung can be conceptualized as a mass of capillaries suspended in air, maximizing the surface area for such gaseous movement.

Emphysema is characterized by destruction of such alveolar walls, together with the capillary normally present in that wall. The two alveoli adjacent to the destroyed wall thus become a common chamber at the expense of reduced vascular surface area secondary to the loss of the capillary in the destroyed wall. Slow progression of this diffuse process eventually reduces the pulmonary vascular bed to the point of insufficient gaseous exchange to sustain life (pulmonary insufficiency) or places an intolerable strain on the heart's right ventricle, which is obligated to perfuse such a damaged lung (right heart failure).

While destruction of shared alveolar walls begins at the microscopic level, progression of the process eventually can produce easily recognizable, balloon-like cystic, air-filled structures called 'bullae' that may measure 10 or more centimeters in diameter (Fig. 8.9). The end result, however, varies in structure ranging from the bullous form to that composed principally of multiple diminutive cystic areas that are quite subtle visually and not easily defined without magnification.

The etiology and mechanism of the process is not understood satisfactorily. Lung structure integrity is viewed as the result of a balance between a certain tissue-destructive enzyme (elastase) released by inflammatory cells and the presence of a compound in the blood (alpha-1 antitrypsin) that normally inhibits this enzyme's action. Imbalance resulting from either an increase in elastase production or a decrease in the amount of inhibitor can result in destruction of the alveolar wall by the elastase.

The most common form of emphysema is related to chronic smoke inhalation. The irritative smoke effect on tissues attracts a surplus of inflammatory cells whose high content of elastase overwhelms the inhibitor. Another, less common mechanism involves the mutation of the gene responsible for the production of the inhibitor. Individuals homozygous for such defective alleles may produce little effective alpha-1 antitrypsin, permitting the unopposed elastase to carry out its destructive action.

The gross appearance of the bullous form of emphysema can be quite dramatic. For example, the entire right lower lobe in Fig. 8.10 has been converted into a single, large bulla without any internal structure. Differentiation of the two types of emphysema can be effected by determining the presence of soot particles in a microscopic section of lung tissue. This can not be evaluated with certainty grossly because hemoglobin breakdown products can impart a black color to the tissue that is just as intense as that due to extensive carbon deposition from chronic smoke inhalation. Emphysema in the absence of substantial carbon deposition suggests the possibility of alpha-1 antitrypsin deficiency. In such an instance, liver histology may be helpful. The inhibitor is formed in the liver but not released from the liver cell to the blood. Liver cells become engorged with the retained inhibitor where it may be demonstrable with immunostaining methods. In later stages, the injured liver cells may die and be replaced by scar, leading to cirrhosis of the liver.

In addition to these two principal forms of emphysema, any chronic, scarring lung disease can distort bronchial air flow sufficiently to result in multiple areas of hyperinflation of pulmonary tissue. Focal areas of localized emphysema are also common at the periphery of areas of pneumonia or calcification. These only rarely create health problems.

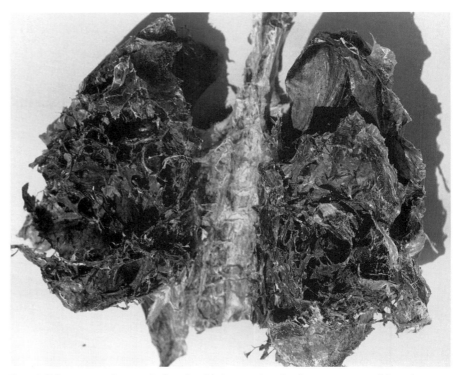

FIG. 8.9: **Pulmonary emphysema.** Bullous (cystic) changes of varying degree are scattered throughout both lungs. Spontaneously mummified adult male from northern Chile, A.D. 450-800. PBL.

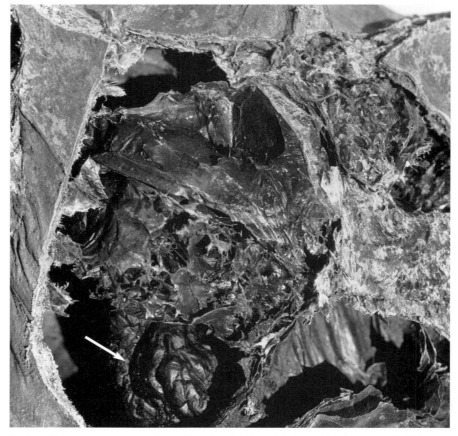

FIG. 8.10: **Pulmonary emphysema.** Almost the entire right lower lobe (arrow) has been converted into a huge, single, bloodless translucent bulla. The middle and upper lobes show similar but smaller cysts, exposed in this photograph by removing the overlying pleura that had made the lung adherent to the chest wall. Spontaneously mummified adult male from northern Chile, A.D. 500-800. PBL.

Primary emphysema has no lengthy historical record. It was not described until the publication of Rene Laennec's 1826 edition of *Treatise on Diseases of the Chest* (Knudson, 1993), and our understanding of the pathophysiological processes is still evolving. It is clear, however, that the disease is much older than its historical documentation. Allison (1984a:522, table 20.7) list emphysema as a common finding in the spontaneously mummified bodies from northern Chile, but it is not clear what fraction of these represent the focal, relatively benign form. Their illustration of the lungs of an 11 year old spontaneously mummified child from a northern Chile member of the Cabuza culture (A.D. 450–1000), however, is unmistakably an advanced, bullous form of emphysema, most probably (based on his age) a severe form of alpha-1 antitrypsin deficiency (Allison, 1984b). A moderate degree of emphysema was identified in an Egyptian early New Kingdom mummy (Shaw, 1938). Tissue from Egyptian canopic jars also demonstrated emphysema (Walker *et al.*, 1987).

Pneumoconioses: anthracosis

With every breath we inhale dust grains, germ-laden moisture droplets and other particles many of which may be potentially harmful. The lung has several defense mechanisms that are so

FIG. 8.11: **Anthracosis: pleural adhesion.** The left lung is adhesive to the chest wall over a broad area, preventing its postmortem collapse. The dark color proved to be anthracosis histologically. Spontaneously mummified 22 year old male from northern Chile, 2000 B.C. PBL.

effective they maintain a microbiologically sterile pulmonary environment. The most important of these is the mucosal lining of the bronchi. These cells not only secrete a mucous blanket but, using a surface-located, whip-like organelle (cilium), produce a constant upward, cleansing flow of mucus. Most inhaled particles adhere to this sticky mucus and are effectively removed. The process can, however, be overwhelmed. Frequent smoke inhalation introduces so many particles that some of them reach the walls of the lung alveoli. Smoke particles vary enormously in their composition and size, but most are carbon-containing compounds. While inflammatory cells can ingest, liquefy and remove many other foreign inhaled particles, the body has no effective method for disposal of most smoke particles. Many of those brown or black particles that manage to reach the alveolar walls are retained there; others are carried to lymph nodes in the hilum where they become trapped permanently. Continued smoke inhalation thus results in a cumulative lung burden of smoke particles that eventually discolor the lung. The quantity of accumulated smoke particles (and, therefore, the degree of dark discoloration), is a measure of past smoke exposure. This process is termed 'anthracosis' (Fig. 8.11) An alternative source of black discoloration of lung tissue is coal dust, usually inhaled by miners or as a result of other industrial coal exposure.

Although wood smoke includes an enormous range of chemically heterogenous particles, only a minority invoke locally toxic effects. Some coal miners, for example, may have completely blackened lungs that, however, function normally. The term 'anthracosis' is limited to deposition of carbon-containing pigment in the lung, and does not necessarily imply limitation of pulmonary function.

In other circumstances anthracotic pigment deposition is accompanied by reactive and destructive scar formation. Whether this is due to the deposited black pigment or whether another, different and toxic substance was inhaled and deposited simultaneously, is not always obvious. Some coal dust, for example, contains quartz, some forms of which are known lung toxins (see Pneumoconioses: Silicosis, below). Slatkin *et al.* (1978) found the stable carbon isotope ratio of pulmonary anthracotic pigment to be distinctly lower than that of endogenous tissues, indicating its exogenous origin (Fig. 8.10).

Simple anthracosis is a common finding in many mummies (Brothwell *et al.*, 1969; Zimmerman, 1977; Walker *et al.*, 1987). This is probably a reflection of poor ventilation in rooms with open hearths. Occasionally, however, additional smoke exposure may be related to rituals. Furthermore, scientists at the General Electric Environmental Science Laboratory found no dioxines or dibenzylforans in mummy lung 'soot', suggesting it was not derived from burning wood (*Wall Street Journal*, 24–25 October, 1989). The seal oil commonly used by arctic natives for both light and heat is also notorious for generating a smoky flame, and all such native lungs examined by us have been profoundly anthracotic (Zimmerman & Aufderheide, 1984), some of which have been accompanied by pulmonary fibrosis (Zimmerman, 1986). Shaw (1938) also found it in a New Kingdom mummy.

Pneumoconioses: Silicosis

Sandy soils contain abundant silicon, most of which is in the silicon salt form (silicate), but some commonly is combined with oxygen as silicon dioxide (silica). When inhaled and deposited in the lung, silica has a local toxic effect causing tissue necrosis that heals by fibrosis. Lesser exposure can riddle the lung with isolated, fibrotic nodules, but as these enlarge with further silica accumulation they coalesce to produce broad areas of fibrous replacement of lung tissue. Though the lung is more tolerant of silicate than of silica, even the silicate form can produce a diffusely fibrotic effect if the deposit is of major degree (Sherwin et al., 1979).

Given the inevitable dust exposure suffered by most agriculturalists, it is not surprising that varying degrees of pulmonary fibrosis secondary to silica or even silicate deposition have been reported in mummy tissues. Since such aboriginals commonly are also exposed to smoke, the combined effect may be a dark and fibrotic lung (anthracosilicosis). An example of such a seriously diseased lung is that of a pre-Columbian adult male from the southwestern U.S.A. in whom it was considered the cause of death by el-Najjar et al. (1985). Zimmerman (1977) has observed this condition in an Egyptian mummy and also in Peruvian (Zimmerman et al., 1981) and in arctic mummies (Zimmerman, 1995: and personal communication). Tapp et al. (1975) described it in an Egyptian mummy, calling it sand pneumoconiosis. Similar findings were noted in 26 mummified lungs from northern Chile (Abraham et al., 1990). The lesser degree of reactive fibrosis to the silicate inhaled from the Negev Desert dust has been attributed to changes in the crystal surface resulting from weathering, rendering it less tissue-toxic (Pollicard & Collet, 1952; Bar-Ziv & Goldberg, 1974) and leading these workers to suggest the term 'simple siliceous pneumoconiosis'. However, Sherwin et al. (1979) found a broad range of fibrosis, including severely destructive forms, in southern California farmers with pulmonary silicate deposition. Whether these different observations reflect differing soil composition (perhaps with varying silica content) or some other unidentified factor is not yet obvious. Munizaga et al. (1975) also described the condition in sixteenth century Chilean natives whom the Spanish compelled to work in dusty mines.

The diagnosis is not too difficult to establish in mummified lungs. The black color itself is suggestive of anthracosis, though it should be verified histologically because hemoglobin breakdown products can also blacken a lung. While silica itself (silicon dioxide) is not refractile when viewed by polarized light, silicate crystals are. Silicates are invariably inhaled and deposited with silica, and they are therefore of 'marker' value for the etiology of the fibrotic effects.

One important interpretive caveat is essential: bodies buried in sandy soils commonly accommodate the postmortem aspiration of sand into the bronchi. This can extend down into remarkably small bronchi. Such a postmortem artifact must be differentiated from dust silicates inhaled and deposited in lungs antemortem. This can usually be achieved by evaluating two criteria: silicates penetrating the lungs of a buried body postmortem will be characteristic of the burial soil (i.e. the range of crystal sizes will be great) in contrast, only the finer particles (usually 5 μ or less) of silicates will find their way into the tissues during life. The other criterion is location: postmortem sand contamination is found within bronchial lumens (though in histological sections the microtome blade may drag some of this into the adjacent tissues), while antemortem silicate deposits are primarily distributed within the pulmonary fibrotic areas. This source of contamination has also frustrated A.C.A.'s effort to quantitate the silica in fibrotic, mummified lungs. On the other hand, Abraham et al. (1990) describe a correlation between silica content and degree of pulmonary fibrosis in lungs of mummies from the Atacama Desert. These differing results may be related to selection of mummies for study and the anatomical portion of lung sampled.

Shaw (1981) cites Collis (1914–1915, 1915–1916) as suggesting that the modern curse of 'knapper's rot' (silicotic pneumoconiosis occurring in contemporary industrial knappers who shaped flint fragments into gunflints) also must have affected prehistoric populations who found, mined and knapped flint from these same mines making this the world's oldest occupational disease. However, Shaw (1981) pointed out that modern miners and knappers only created enough dust to be fibrogenic if they employed modern metal tools in unventilated enclosures, conditions not existing in ancient times.

Pneumoconioses: Asbestosis

The protein and iron-containing, coated, asbestos fibers called 'ferruginous bodies' could be expected to retain their appearance in mummified lungs, as would the often prominently thickened pleura found in asbestos-exposed tissues. No such findings have been reported, including one study in which the investigators specifically sought them in vain (Abraham et al., 1990). These observations emphasize the broad range of asbestos contamination of soils in different geographical areas.

Vascular conditions

Pulmonary embolism and infarction

The process of tissue necrosis following abrupt interruption of its blood supply (ischemia) is called infarction. If the individual survives the ischemic event, the infarcted tissue undergoes autolytic liquefaction, collapse, at least partial resorption and is replaced by a linear scar. Lung tissue, however, has two blood sources: the principal one is composed of pulmonary artery branches while the other consists of multiple branches from the aorta directed to the bronchi themselves. Thus, if a pulmonary artery branch is suddenly occluded, the lung tissue it normally supplies may become infarcted. However, the bronchial arteries supplying the bronchi of the infarcted lung area remain open and continue to pump blood into the area. Within 48 hours the necrotic vessels in the infarcted lung tissue will leak the blood from the bronchial artery supply, converting the dying lung tissue into a hemorrhagic mass. As stated above, up to 5 % of modern pulmonary consolidation areas are infarcts (and, except for neoplasms, almost all the others represent pneumonia). Such infarcts in mummies can expect to be discrete masses without demonstrable integrity of internal structure. The blood would make the affected area dark or even black. Red blood cells might or might not persist in recognizable form, but bacteria or fungi should be absent. In spite of its modern frequency and the favorable rate of lung preservation in mummies, to date no pulmonary infarct in mummified human lung has been reported. The most likely reason for this is that such lesions are being misinterpreted as pneumonia.

The usual cause of a lung infarct is an embolus. This is a clot, commonly formed in a leg vein, that becomes detached, is swept 'downstream' to the right atrium, then the right ventricle and finally enters the pulmonary artery where it is passed into successively smaller branches until it lodges in one slightly smaller than the clot itself. The clot is called a thrombus while still attached at its original site of formation in the leg vein, but called an embolus after it becomes detached and transported to the lung. The lung may survive occlusion of a diminutive arterial branch but become infarcted if a larger branch is blocked. On the other hand, if the embolus is huge (several centimeters or more in diameter) it may block the main pulmonary artery, causing sudden death. Given the brittle nature of the main, desiccated arterial trunks in mummified bodies, it would be difficult to demonstrate the presence of such a fatal embolus in the pulmonary artery, particularly since desiccation and at least partial autolysis would shrink it substantially. No such reports of paleopathological infarcts are identifiable.

Atherosclerosis

Atherosclerosis of the main pulmonary artery occurs only when the pulmonary systolic blood pressure (normally about 20 mm of mercury) rises above 60 for a prolonged period. If present the atheromas can be identified easily — they are identical with the much more common aortic atheromas. Their presence is proof of severe, chronic pulmonary hypertension, such as occurs either in chronic fibrotic pulmonary diseases or is of an idiopathic nature. Pulmonary artery atheromas rarely ulcerate or calcify, perhaps because the right ventricle cannot withstand pressures of this magnitude long enough. The accompanying thick-walled small pulmonary arteries and arterioles may be demonstrable histologically. Pulmonary artery atherosclerosis has not been reported in mummified bodies.

Neoplasms

Hamartoma

Few benign tumors occur in the lung. The most common of these is a hamartoma. By definition, a hamartoma is a benign tumor composed of cells normally present in the organ in which it is found but arranged in architectural disarray. Thus we could expect to find such a tumor made up of cells of bronchial mucosa, smooth muscle, cartilage and blood vessels. These are, indeed, found in lung hamartomas but cartilage is usually the dominant tissue and is easily recognizable. Since cartilage survives the postmortem environment better than epithelium, lung hamartomas could be encountered at mummy dissection. It usually presents in adults as spherical, solid masses up to 5–6 cm in diameter in any part of the lung. Its gross appearance depends on its structural elements but most commonly resembles a chondroma. It rarely impairs the lung function in any manner. It is, however, a quite uncommon tumor.

Brochogenic carcinoma

Most other lung tumors arise from bronchi (bronchogenic carcinoma). While these cancers are reaching epidemic proportions in modern developed countries, the bulk of them have been linked statistically to cigarette smoking. Hence their frequency in antiquity would be expected to differ little from that in modern communities where cigarette smoking is uncommon. Such populations rarely suffer from bronchogenic carcinoma. The occasional cancers of this type in such groups are probably the result of inhaling other carcinogens (radon gas, heavy metal mining dust, aerosolized asbestos and many unknown substances). Bronchogenic carcinoma tends to grow into the bronchial lumen, blocking it and causing pneumonia in the portion of the affected lung. Simultaneously and/or alternatively invasion through the bronchial wall into the pulmonary parenchyma is also common. In these, tumor cells enter lymphatics and spread to hilar lymph nodes and later to cervical nodes. They also penetrate bronchial veins where the detached cells are swept and transported by the blood to any organ of the body. The brain, adrenals and bones are particularly common metastatic sites, though no area or structure is immune to spread from bronchogenic carcinoma.

Mesothelioma

An extremely rare malignant tumor can arise from the lung pleura: mesothelioma. This usually quite fibrous tumor spreads diffusely and envelops the lung in a thick rind of white, usually quite fibrous, tumor as much as 6–8 cm thick. It is found almost exclusively in persons working with asbestos and is viewed as a malignant response to the inhalation of asbestos fibers. Hence encountering this tumor in ancient bodies would be expected to be exceptional.

Most of these tumors occur in the older age group after many years of exposure to the offending carcinogen. Since the malignant lung cancers today have a low rate of cure, the natural history we associate with them in modern times is probably quite similar to the occasional lung cancer that occurred in antiquity.

If a lung tumor is encountered in mummified human remains and it is not a hamartoma, it is more apt to be a metastatic carcinoma to the lung from an extrathoracic primary source. Osteosarcomas and other soft tissue sarcomas commonly metastasize to the lung, as do primary visceral cancers late in their course. If more than one tumor is found in the lung, the probability of its metastatic nature is high. In contrast to primary bronchogenic carcinomas, metastases are more apt to be spherical and multiple, with reasonably sharply defined periphery unless extremely large.

Foreign bodies

Probably the most common material aspirated in modern times is food. Precipitating factors include malfunction of the swallowing musculature secondary to cerebral disease (hemorrhage, infarction, neoplasm, demyelinating diseases, etc) or alcoholic intoxication. Local factors, such as dentures, may play a role. In antiquity some of these factors may have operated as well. The bronchi of a spontaneously mummified 22 year old male from northern Chile were found by one of us (A.C.A.) to be filled with masticated food items; the absence of pneumonia implied this was a terminal event. Fatal complications probably abbreviated the lifespan of individuals with chronic conditions. Nevertheless several reports document aspiration of nonfood items in prehistoric bodies. Zimmerman & Smith (1975) found the trachea and major bronchi obstructed by aspirated moss in a 1600 year old arctic female body. She had apparently been buried in a mud-slide, a fairly common arctic phenomenon in terrain of the type present on St. Lawrence Island where the body was found. Allison et al. (1974d) found that pneumonia in the mummified remains of an Andean adult male from A.D. 950 was due to bronchial obstruction by an aspirated tooth. Allison (personal communication) also found a lithic point embedded within the lung of a 40 year old northern Chile mummy from about A.D. 1350 without evidence of an entry wound, suggesting the injury had been incurred a long time previously. El-Najjar et al. (1985) also reported a probable tooth aspiration in a child mummy from the southwestern U.S.A..

LIVER AND BILIARY TRACT DISEASES

Preservation and appearance

The liver is essentially an epithelial organ. After death the prompt autolytic changes in hepatic cells often delete antemortem patterns of primarily hepatic epithelial cells, such as hepatitis. The liver at time of death weighs about 1500 g in an adult, but in desiccated cadavers weights of 100–200 g are common. While the liver normally is quite well anchored to the diaphragm and lower mediastinal tissues, degenerative postmortem changes abetted by gravity secondary to burial position can result in detachment of the liver from these structures. This can result in displacement of the liver into the pelvis, the left thoracic cavity or elsewhere.

While the hepatic cells usually degenerate rapidly, the fibrous portal skeleton of the liver commonly persists. Thus, antemortem conditions characterized by portal area alterations may remain recognizable. These include the various forms of cirrhosis. Evaluation of portal patterns in mummy livers, however, requires awareness of a possible common misinterpretation. In most mummies much of the degenerated hepatic cell debris remains (sometimes even the profile of the former living cells is still apparent), and in these circumstances the relationship of the portal areas to the hepatic cellular tissue can be judged reliably. In some bodies, however, the hepatic cell degeneration proceeded to liquefaction before desiccation occurred. Accordingly, the surviving fibrous portal areas collapse, closely approximate each other sufficiently to create the illusion of a pattern of interconnected, proliferative portal areas suggestive of cirrhosis. Simple awareness of this form of pseudopathology is usually sufficient to allow its recognition. Indeed, the gross appearance of a light brown, spongy structure (instead of the usual firm, black, often brittle appearance of a normal, desiccated liver) can anticipate the microscopic appearance of this phenomenon.

Hepatitis

For reasons given above it is not likely that a diagnosis of hepatitis can be made on the liver of a desiccated mummy. A possible exception could be an Egyptian mummy that was promptly eviscerated and the liver placed in a canopic jar with sufficient natron and/or resin to effect rapid desiccation. In chemical or thermal forms of mummification, suffi-

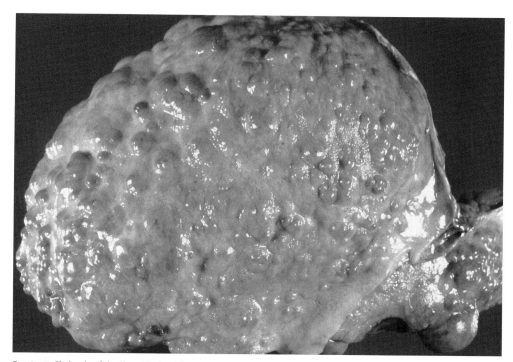

FIG. 8.12: **Cirrhosis of the liver.** The knobby surface of this liver is composed of regenerative nodules of liver tissue enveloped by dense scar. Modern adult male. PBL.

cient liver cell survival to allow diagnosis is also conceivable. However, we are not aware of any reports of hepatitis identification in the paleopathological literature.

Cirrhosis

Bile formed by liver cells is drained by a network of bile ducts at the periphery of the individual lobules of liver cells. Normally these are enveloped by a thin layer of fibrous tissue also containing blood vessels and collectively these are termed a 'portal area'. Chronic liver cell injury and destruction due to toxins (alcohol), microbiological agents (hepatitis viruses) or even autoimmune mechanisms is often followed by a proliferative, fibrous, scarring response in the portal structures surrounding the lobules of affected liver cells. Given enough time the portal areas enlarge substantially, intercommunicate freely and finally expand to an extent that virtually surrounds such liver lobules in a fibrous envelope (cirrhosis). The resulting antemortem gross appearance of such a cirrhotic liver is striking: a web of sunken, retracted fibrous bands with bulging masses of liver cellular tissue (representing compensatory hyperplasia) between the fibrous cords (Fig. 8.12). While every clinical pathologist is familiar with this picture, it must be emphasized that the bulging hepatic cell masses so prominent before death can be expected to have collapsed in the mummified body because of the postmortem epithelial cell degeneration. The gross cirrhotic changes may thus be too subtle for certain diagnosis. However, the persistence of fibrous tissue in desiccated cadavers usually permits ready recognition upon histological examination. Pathologists

examining the liver of an Egyptian mummy, Nakht, noted some surface irregularity but were not certain of the diagnosis of cirrhosis (in that case secondary to schistosomiasis) until it was studied in microscopic sections (Reyman, 1977).

The antiquity of cirrhosis is considerable. Chen & Chen (1993) note that Erasistratus (300 B.C.) associated abdominal fluid (ascites) with liver disease and that Aretaeus the Cappadocian in the third century A.D. recognized that cirrhosis could follow hepatitis and that carcinoma could arise in a cirrhotic liver. They also point out that the British physician Mathew Baille in 1793 recognized the role of alcohol in the production of this condition and that Rene Laennec assigned it the term 'cirrhosis'. In addition to the Egyptian mummy reported by Reyman (1977), cirrhosis has also been reported in two medieval mummies from Naples (Fornaciari et al., 1988b).

It is unlikely that tissue preservation in mummified livers will permit the separation of alcoholic or postviral cirrhosis from some of its less frequent forms (primary biliary cirrhosis or that following primary sclerosing cholangitis) since these differentiations are usually dependent on the demonstration of various patterns of inflammatory cells that only rarely survive the mummification processes. However, the cirrhosis representing a late complication of common bile duct obstruction (see below) should be recognizable in ancient bodies, but remains unreported to date.

Fatty degeneration of the liver

Accumulation of fat droplets within the cytoplasm of liver cells is frequently seen in alcoholics, certain types of toxin exposure and especially in circumstances of severe malnutrition. The fat *per se* is not injurious but the conditions producing it frequently are. It is a readily reversible phenomenon if the primary condition is treated appropriately. Its recognition in ancient bodies could serve usefully as a guide to the probability of a serious state of malnutrition before death. If present in a substantial fraction of a studied population, it might signal famine conditions. Since this condition is so frequent in malnutrition including the late circumstances accompanying a fatal chronic illness, the probability of its presence in at least a few of the mummies that have been autopsied is great. Yet this lesion has not appeared in the paleopathology literature. The most probable reason for this failure of recognition lies in the postmortem taphonomic processes. This fat accumulates as triglycerides, and these are normally split into fatty acids by the lysosomal enzymes during postmortem autolytic action. This would render the lipid invisible on histological examination. Thus this otherwise valuable clue is probably lost to us, at least in spontaneously desiccated bodies.

Congenital lesions

Both single cysts and a polycystic form have been reported in modern cases. These ought to be identifiable if occurring in mummified livers (Fig. 8.13). Their flattened epithelial lining, however, would probably not survive. The cysts could probably be separated from artifacts of gas bubbles produced by postmortem growth of bacteria by simply identifying the bacterial presence with appropriate histological stains. Cysts in the region of the extrahepatic bile ducts also occur.

Gas gangrene septicemia

Clostridium perfringens, a gas-producing gram-positive bacillus common in soil and even occasionally in normal human feces, flourishes in the anaerobic milieu of the necrotic muscle of a contaminated crushing injury and usually kills the affected individual swiftly by invading the blood stream. Before death the gas produced in the wound by the bacilli will accumulate locally there, but that produced by the organisms in the blood does not accumulate because during the blood's passage through the lungs the gas diffuses into the lung air and is exhaled. However, after death the blood no longer circulates. Bacterial growth for a few hours after death before the body temperature drops too low is common. At the moment of death when circulation ceases, hundred or thousands of bacilli in such an affected person will be present in the blood vessels of an organ as vascular as the liver. The continued production of gas postmortem by these bacteria in the liver will result in its accumulation in the form of trapped bubbles within the liver. Hence the transected liver of such an individual will produce the dramatic and easily recognizable spongy appearance seen in Fig. 8.14.

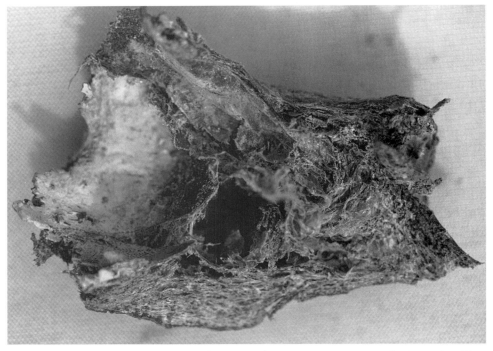

FIG. 8.13: **Congenital cystic disease of the liver (juvenile form).** The larger cyst demonstrated in this sectioned liver is 4 cm in diameter. Multiple others ranging from 1–2 cm were present in other areas. Histologically few normal portal areas were identified. Infant (2 years old) from northern Chile, A.D. 450-800. PBL.

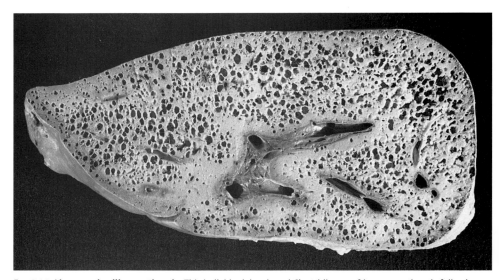

FIG. 8.14: **Liver: gas bacillus septicemia.** This individual developed *Clostridium perfringens* septicemia following surgical bone tumor removal from the femur. Gas bubbles formed by postmortem growth of bacteria present in the liver at the time of death produced this spongy texture. Modern adult female. PBL.

Abscesses

Single or multiple liver abscesses can occur as a consequence of septicemia by a virulent, pyogenic organism, but more common is the consequence of bowel organisms gaining access to the extrahepatic biliary tract. The most frequent mechanism for the latter is a gallstone impacted at the ampulla of Vater where the common bile duct drains into the intestine. Such an impaction disturbs the effectiveness of the sphincter

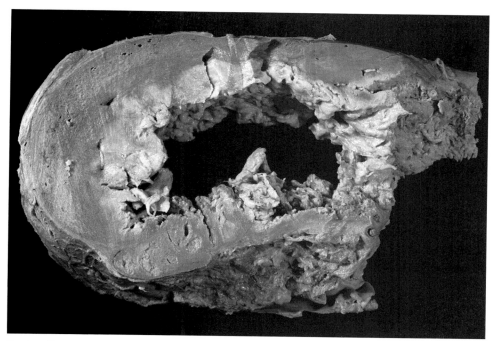

FIG. 8.15: **Liver: amebic abscess.** The central cavity represents an area of liquid pus that has drained from this liver. The pale area surrounding it is a mixture of amebae-containing pus infiltrating liver tissue. Amebae infected the colon, entered mesenteric veins and were transported by these and the portal veins into the liver where they flourished and produced this abscess. Modern adult female. PBL.

Neoplasms

Primary hepatoma

An occasional benign adenoma composed of liver cells can be found in the liver. The malignant tumor of importance is hepatocellular carcinoma arising from liver cells. This tumor today is of relatively low incidence in the developed world where most cases arise in a cirrhotic liver. In the Mediterranean countries, Africa and especially the Orient it is often the most common cancer in those populations, paralleling the frequency of hepatitis B virus (HBV). It has also been linked to the mycotoxin aflatoxin (see section on Poisoning in Chapter 9) in India. We do not know the frequency of these agencies in antiquity, but this tumor has not been described in mummified remains.

Metastatic carcinoma

Much more common than any of these today is carcinoma metastatic to the liver from a primary tumor elsewhere, usually the gastrointestinal tract, bronchus or breast. The cancers that are primary in the liver usually present as a large, irregular, knobby mass while the metastatic lesions commonly are multiple, smaller and often spherical nodules. While bone changes suggestive of metastases have been reported in ancient skeletons, no definite soft tissue liver metastases have been found, although Zimmerman's (1990) experimental work suggests such tumor cells would probably survive better than benign liver cells.

muscle there that usually effectively prevents bacterial entry. With this protective mechanism impaired by the gallstone, bacteria may enter the bile duct and ascend rapidly into the smaller biliary ducts within the liver (ascending cholangitis) giving rise to multiple abscesses there. These, in turn, may 'feed' their bacteria into the blood stream generating fatal septicemia. While this condition was not rare prior to effective antibiotic and surgical treatment, and while such abscesses should not present diagnostic difficulties at a mummy autopsy, we have not identified a published case of this kind in an archaeological body. We have had personal experience in the case of a spontaneously mummified body from a northern Chile coastal population of about A.D. 1300 in which a lobar pneumonia of the right lung was complicated by an empyema of the right lower thoracic cavity and a fistula from which had penetrated the diaphragm near the 'bare area' to produce a right subdiaphragmatic abscess penetrating into the liver. Like abscesses elsewhere, such an abscess may or may not retain grossly recognizable pus whose appearance can vary from a thin, light-colored membrane lining the abscess wall to a granular, sand-like material. Bacterial stains usually easily demonstrate the offending organism histologically.

Additional causes of abscesses include parasites. These include amebae (*Amoeba histolytica*) as seen in Fig. 8.15, dog tapeworm (*Echinococcus granulosus*) and the blood fluke, *Schistosoma* sp. The latter does not produce actual abscesses but its ova, deposited in the liver in large numbers initiate a destructive, scarring inflammatory response that results in a cirrhosis-like structure. All of these are discussed in more detail in Chapter 7 (Infectious diseases).

Biliary tract diseases

Bile serves as an excretory mechanism for cholesterol, bilirubin (a hemoglobin breakdown product derived from destroyed red blood cells) and bile salts (useful for fat digestion in the intestine). In addition, a stabilizing compound, lecithin, is also present. Since cholesterol is not water soluble, the proportions of these four substances in the bile becomes critical in order to keep them in solution. Circumstances substantially altering normal conditions may upset the equilibrium sufficiently to result in supersaturation of one of these substances with the consequence of its crystallization and ultimate formation of a precipitate in the form of a stone (Greek: lithos); gallstone or cholelith.

Bile is formed by liver cells, excreted into the smallest of the bile ducts ('canaliculi') that then join others to form ever larger ducts within the liver. These finally emerge from the liver as two hepatic ducts that unite into a single channel – the common bile duct. After traversing the head of the pancreas (where it is joined by the pancreatic duct) the common bile duct empties into the intestine through a sphincter-guarded nipple termed the ampulla of Vater. In about the middle of its course, the gallbladder joins the common bile duct *via* a smaller one called the cystic duct. Thus when the sphincter at the ampulla of Vater is closed, bile can 'back up' *via* the cystic duct into the gallbladder where it can be stored until the next meal is ingested.

Two problems of interest to paleopathology can arise within this system: the formation of calculi (bile precipitates: gallstones or choleliths) and infection of the biliary tract.

Gallstones (Cholelithiasis)

While mixtures are common, gallstones can be classified into two major groupings based on their predominant chemical element: cholesterol or pigment (bilirubin) stones. The frequency of gallstones is age-dependent. In the western, developed countries cholesterol stones are most common while in the remainder of the world pigment stones predominate. Their frequency at autopsy in aged U.S.A. Caucasians is about 25% (Fraire *et al.*, 1988), though some Native American groups are thrice that. Rural, developing countries often have much lower rates. Both environmental and hereditary ('thrifty gene?') factors probably are influential (Neel, 1982).

While gallstones can form within the common bile duct, most occur in the gallbladder, probably at least partly because bile stagnation favors precipitation of bile constituents. Initially these crystals formed are so diminutive that bile merely becomes more viscid ('sludge'). Larger agglutinations may form calculi 0.5–1.0 mm in diameter ('gravel') small enough to pass from the gallbladder through the cystic duct and out *via* the common bile duct. Physicochemical and mechanical factors determine the appearance of larger stones. Occasionally a single stone may be formed, assuming the egg-shape and size of the gallbladder lumen. More commonly multiple calculi averaging about 1 cm in diameter occur. Forced together by gallbladder contraction, such stones abrade each other, each gradually acquiring multiple flat (facetted) surfaces. Pure cholesterol stones are pale yellow and translucent while pigment (bilirubin) stones vary from brown to black. About 15 % of cholesterol stones and 50 % of pigment stones contain sufficient calcium salts to be detectable radiologically.

The majority of gallstones within the gallbladder are silent, producing no symptoms. A stone approximating the size of the cystic duct may be passed with painful difficulty. If a stone becomes impacted in the cystic duct and blocks it, bacteria may reach the gallbladder lumen and initiate a violent, acute infection, turning the gallbladder into a pus-filled bag (empyema) that may perforate, initiating a lethal acute peritonitis. Alternatively, erosion of the gallbladder mucosa by stones within its lumen may generate chronic inflammation (cholecystitis) that may be symptomatic intermittently. A cal-

FIG. 8.16: **Gallstones (cholelithiasis) and chronic cholecystitis.** Gallstones with flattened (faceted) surface are present within a gall bladder whose dense 1 cm wall has been thickened by fibrotic scar. Spontaneously mummified 60 year old male from northern Chile (Chinchorro culture), 2000 B.C. PBL.

culus that reaches the common bile duct but is not immediately expelled may continue to expand by further crystal deposition, then pass to the ampulla of Vater, blocking the main flow of bile at this constricted location. Unable to enter the intestine, the bile pressure rises and the smaller intrahepatic ducts rupture. The spilled bile is absorbed by the blood where the increase in reabsorbed bilirubin pigment imparts a yellowish-orange color to all body tissues including the skin (jaundice). Intestinal bacteria commonly also make their way into the biliary tract causing acute ascending cholangitis.

Aufderheide & Allison (1994) found a thick-walled (1 cm) gallbladder filled with brown and black, faceted gallstones lying loose in the pelvis of a spontaneously mummified body of a north Chile preceramic coastal population (Chinchorro) of about 2000 B.C (Fig. 8.16).

Angel (1973) describes two brown, facetted gallstones found between the ribs and iliac crest of an arthritic male skeleton from Grave Circle B at Mycenae, dating to about 1600 B.C. Several Egyptian mummies are known to harbor gallstones. Smith & Dawson (1924: p. 156 and figure 60) demonstrate a gallstone-filled gallbladder adherent to the liver of a priestess of Amen from the twenty-first dynasty, and Gray (1966) identified radiopaque gallstones in X-rays of an Egyptian mummy of unknown provenience curated at the University of Leiden. The body of a noblewoman from the Han dynasty (about 200 B.C.) in the Hunan province of China had multiple gallstones (Wei, 1973). Munizaga *et al.* (1978) found multiple gallstones present in 2 out of 75 spontaneously mummified bodies from coastal northern Chile who occupied that area about A.D. 100–200 while a north Colombian mummy (desiccated by exposure to heat from a fire) of the Muisca culture (about A.D. 1200) was X-rayed by Cardenas (1994) and demonstrated multiple gallstones. Studying a group of medieval mummies from a cathedral in Naples, Italy, Fornaciari et al. (1988b) found cholelithiasis and cholecystitis in a mummy that also demonstrated cirrhosis. In North America, Steinbock (1990) cites a personal communication from C.O. Lovejoy that 6 of more than 1000 burials at the Ohio Libben Woodland (A.D. 1000–1200) site were associated with gallstones.

Steinbock (1990) has also summarized the earlier literature in an excellent and well documented presentation in which he noted that Hippocrates and Aristotle discuss jaundice but do not mention gallstones. Nevertheless, animal gallstones from that general period were not only known but used as a source of yellow pigment. Interestingly Galen (A.D. 130–201, cited in Glenn, 1971), describing obstructive jaundice, may have mistaken a small gallstone for pomegranate or grain seeds. Not surprisingly, it was at those early universities at Padua and Bologna that the first accurate and detailed autopsy performed by a graduate (Gentile da Foligno) of the University of Bologna who carried out the postmortem dissection at Padua in 1341, includes a description of a gallstone imbedded in the gallbladder's cystic duct (Steinbock, 1993a). Later contributions by A. Beniveni, A. Vesalius and others finally led to G.P. Morgagni's (1682–1771) classical study of all clinical and pathological aspects of cholelithiasis (Glenn, 1971).

Miscellaneous conditions

Hypervitaminosis A

If enough is ingested, carnivore liver contains sufficient vitamin A to produce hepatotoxicity as well as periosteal stimulation. A pattern of coarsely-woven, periosteal new bone formation of the long bones and skull, with randomly placed lacunae found on fossil skeletal parts of a *Homo erectus* fossil from Kenya, East Africa, was felt to conform to the expected pattern for this condition (Walker et al., 1982; Zimmerman, 1990).

GASTROINTESTINAL TRACT DISEASES

The organ occupying the most space in the abdomen (gastrointestinal tract) is distinctly under-represented in the paleopathological literature. Examination of a mummy's gut provides the obvious reason. Most intestinal lesions are a product of the mucosal epithelium, but the mucosa rarely survives the postmortem process. The smooth muscle, collagenous and vascular elements of the wall fare much better, but the frequency of lesions arising primarily in these is low.

The mummified intestine is thin, translucent and friable. Tubular segments are common but perimortem compression and fracture from postexcavation handling often prevents detailed examination of much of it. Yet, in spite of all the factors, including its bacterial content, that act to generate postmortem loss of colon tissue for study, recovery of desiccated feces (coprolites) for laboratory study is common. Search for these can be facilitated by awareness that the lower rectum in both living and dead bodies is usually devoid of feces, but that gravitational forces commonly result in prolapse of the often coprolite-containing cecum into the lower pelvis where it frequently lies on the perineal floor overlying the anus or adjacent to it. Because the types of lesions affecting the various segments of the gastrointestinal tract are quite similar, we will review them by mechanism of pathological process rather than the more usual practice of dividing the tract into segmental levels.

Congenital lesions

Omphalocele

This is a rare lesion. During fetal development much of the bowel transiently enters the umbilical cord during a rotational process and subsequently re-enters the abdomen. Interference with this process may result in its arrest while the gut is enclosed within the cord's membranes. At birth the infant is born with not only most of the intestine but often also other abdominal organs, must commonly the liver, extruded from the abdominal cavity, covered by thin, translucent membranes from the center of which the umbilical cord emerges. This is not to be confused with a superficially similar-appearing lesion (*gastroschisis*) that consists of an anterior abdominal wall defect *adjacent* to the umbilicus through which much of the gut herniates, uncovered by a membrane. This can be differentiated by identifying a normal, intact umbilical cord arising from the skin of the defect's edge. While prompt modern surgical care can salvage some of these infants, the mortality is high.

Esophageal Atresia

This is also a rare lesion. It usually involves the proximal half. While variations are common, the most frequent form results in the upper portion of the esophagus ending in a blind pouch while the lower esophageal segment originates from the trachea and communicates with its lumen (*tracheoesophageal fistula*). Pneumonia due to aspiration of food is the principal cause of death in unoperated infants.

Imperforate anus

This is another segment of the gastrointestinal tract that can fail to develop a lumen – in this case that of the cloacal membrane. The complete anal closure causes prompt intestinal obstruction that can be relieved surgically today by anal incision. Atresia of any other level of the gastrointestinal tract may occur rarely, all of which cause intestinal obstruction.

Pyloric stenosis

This is a consequence of deficiency of an enzyme involving the production of nitric oxide. The absence of this endogenous smooth-muscle relaxant results in spasm of the pyloric muscle at the stomach's outlet, preventing the emptying of the stomach contents. It is characterized by the appearance of projectile vomiting, abdominal colic often with a palpable mass (the hypertrophic, spasmodic pyloric muscle) and sometimes visible reverse peristalsis all appearing during about the second week of life. The Ramstedt operation that incises and transects part of the pyloric muscle can cure the condition.

Meckel's diverticulum

A blind-ended outpouching of the gut is called a diverticulum. That described by Meckel is located near the end of the ileal part of the small intestine (Fig. 8.17). In most cases it produces no symptoms and is related to the intestinal movements described for the omphalocele lesion; therefore it may not be surprising that its wall often contains ectopic gastrointestinal tissues. The most common of these include pancreatic tissue and gastric mucosa. The former of these rarely may produce a lump large enough to generate the complication called intussusception (described under Intestinal obstruction, below) but much more common is ulceration of the diverticulum's mucosa from the hydrochloric acid produced by the ectopic gastric mucosa. Erosion of the ulcer into a submucosal artery can produce hemorrhage into the intestinal lumen serious enough to demand surgical excision.

Megacolon (Hirschsprung's disease)

Normal intestinal contractions need to be precisely coordinated in order to produce a progressive, peristaltic wave that effectively propels ingested food along the length of the gut. Such integration is achieved by nerves and their related ganglion cells located in the gut wall. In about 1 in 5000 births (Cotran et al., 1994:786) such ganglion cells fail to develop, most commonly in the rectosigmoid area. The aganglionic segment is therefore incapable of propelling food, and the ingested food accumulates in the colon just proximal to this defective segment, with progressive dilatation of the otherwise anatomically normal part of the colon. Eventually complete intestinal obstruction may occur; in some the dilated colon may become so thinned that it ruptures with resulting (usually lethal) peritonitis. Surgical excision of the aganglionic (not the dilated) segment is usually curative.

Diaphragmatic hernia

Normally the diaphragm effectively separates the abdominal from the thoracic cavities. Developmental failure of one side (usually the left) of the diaphragm permits the stomach, a variable amount of the intestine, sometimes the liver or other abdominal organs to move upward and occupy the thoracic cavity on the affected side (Fig. 8.18). The diaphragmatic defect is believed to be related to premature return of the intestine from the umbilical area during its development. The resulting lung compression may inhibit development of that organ to a degree that can not support life at

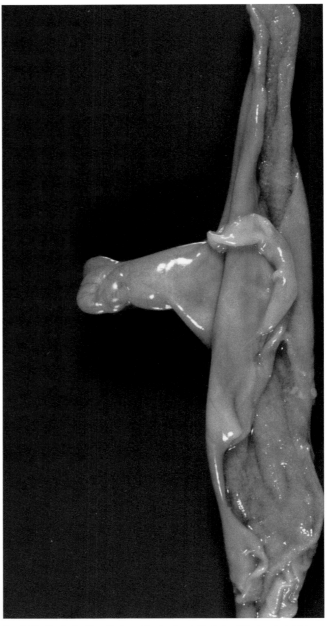

FIG. 8.17: **Meckel's diverticulum.** The horizontal tubular, blind-ended, 'side-arm' structure is a congenital anomaly related to the umbilicus. It is of clinical significance because some of these include ectopic gastric mucosa or ectopic pancreatic tissue. Modern adult female. PBL.

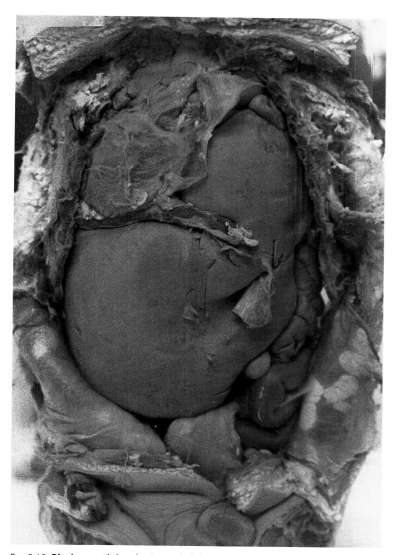

Fig. 8.18: **Diaphragmatic hernia.** Congenital absence of the diaphragm permits abdominal viscera to become displaced into the thoracic cavity, inhibiting growth of the lung. Modern infant. PBL.

adjacent to it permit a portion of the upper (cardiac) end of the stomach to squeeze upward into the thorax adjacent to the esophagus. Such a space is usually small, and this para-esophageal hernia can be more serious because the blood supply of the herniated portion may be so compressed that the herniated segment of stomach may become infarcted. In such circumstances only prompt, corrective surgery before it ruptures can avert a fatal outcome. Both sliding and parae-sophageal forms of hiatal hernia are acquired and occur commonly in adults. The mechanism is believed to be due to abdominal pressure generated while straining at stool to expel a relatively desiccated mass of feces. It is thought to be rare in undeveloped countries because of the large fecal content of dietary fiber in the latter (Burkitt, 1981:143).

Paleopathology reports

In antiquity both omphalocele and gastroschisis would have been fatal uniformly and promptly, the infants succumbing to infection. Furthermore, the cord membranes enveloping the omphalocele's content would rarely survive the mummifying process, increasing the difficulty of differentiating them in a mummified body. We have found no case reports of either of these in mummified human remains. Prompt recognition with immediate surgical repair of tracheo-esophageal fistula cases can save many of these infants, but in antiquity they all must have perished within the first 10 days as a consequence of aspiration pneumonia. The lesion, however, is unreported in the paleopathological literature, perhaps because mummification changes make it difficult to carry out the necessary delicate dissection, and attention may be diverted to the more obvious changes of pneumonia. Imperforate anus could probably have been relieved in some cases in antiquity by blind incision of the area if it were an entity known to them, but its low frequency would have prevented common knowledge of the condition. Atresia at other intestinal levels would all have ended with irreparable intestinal obstruction, as would congenital pyloric obstruction. Most cases of Meckel's diverticulum do not develop complications and one would expect them to be identifiable. The absence of any reports is probably simple testimony of postmortem preservation problems and the gut's fragility even if this lesion were present. Consequently we were unable to find reports of any of the above-mentioned conditions in archaeological bodies.

However, Munizaga et al. (1978) dissected an adult female mummy from coastal northern Chile who died about A.D. 250. They found two loops of jejunum that had herniated through a defect in the posterior part of the left diaphragm into the thoracic cavity. The blood supply of these jejunal loops had been sufficiently compressed to render the loops ischemic with subsequent infarction. The herniated bowel loops were thickened and black, reflecting the changes of hemorrhagic infarction. Gerszten et al. (1976b) reported a coastal Andean adult female from the colonial period that

birth. In some cases the diaphragmatic defect is not total. In these the smaller defect may produce a much lesser mass of herniated structures, producing no serious lung growth interference and these may be compatible with life, sometimes even if unrepaired.

This condition should not be confused with an acquired form called hiatal hernia. The esophagus, of course, must traverse the diaphragm to reach the stomach. As it does so, the diaphragmatic muscle fibers and ligaments are structured to support the esophagus in such a manner as to prevent reflux of the acid stomach secretions into the esophagus. In some individuals the esophagus-enveloping tissues are too loosely structured. In the simple 'sliding' form, this may permit an upward sliding movement of a portion of stomach into the thoracic cavity. The resulting reflux of acid gastric juice produces unpleasant but not life-threatening symptoms. In a small minority of cases the esophagogastric junction remains intact, but the tissues died of infarction of a part of the stomach that had formed a paraesophageal hernia.

The only case of congenital megacolon in an archaeological body that we could find was reported in a Roman Period Egyptian mummy by Ruffer (1911c).

Ulcerative gastrointestinal lesions

Gastric and duodenal ulcers

In modern western populations gastric or duodenal ulcers are found in about 10 % of males and about 4 % of females. Their direct cause is controversial but it is clear that gastric colonization with *Helicobacter pylori*, hyperacidity and ingestion of nonsteroidal anti-inflammatory agents play a major role. They begin as superficial mucosal erosions that extend to the submucosa where an intense chronic inflammatory response results in a thickened, fibrotic wall. Complications include gastric obstruction from the fibrosing base of a pyloric ulcer, a surgically remediable lesion today. Perforation of the gastric or duodenal wall by a penetrating ulcer occurs in about 5 % of the cases and may be a fatal complication. Gastric juices and food spill out of the bowel wall defect, commonly causing widespread peritonitis, though a slowly perforating ulcer may localize the infection in the form of an abscess. A more frequent complication is hemorrhage: about 20 % of ulcers bleed. Extension of the ulcer base may erode a capillary or venule that results in a constant trickle of blood. Such individuals may present with iron-deficiency anemia. Erosion of an artery in the ulcer base, however, results in a blood-spurting lesion that can produce a hemorrhage of massive proportions and prompt exsanguination.

Esophageal varices

Another cause of such massive upper gastrointestinal hemorrhage is ruptured esophageal varicose veins. Such persons usually have a liver so densely scarred by cirrhosis that the portal vein blood flow is impeded and the pressure within that vein rises substantially, forcing much of its blood into collateral vessels that bypass the liver. The esophageal submucosal veins form part of that collateral venous system and become engorged with blood under increased pressure. They are covered only by relatively thin and soft mucosa, erosion of which causes the underlying vein to bleed directly into the esophageal lumen, a complication with a 50 % mortality and almost inevitable recurrence in those surviving the first bleeding episode.

Mallory–Weiss syndrome

Yet another cause of upper gastrointestinal hemorrhage is the Mallory-Weiss syndrome, in which violent retching (usually in an inebriated person) can cause a laceration of the mucosa at the esophagogastric junction. Life-threatening hemorrhage can result when the laceration includes a large submucosal artery or vein, or when the laceration penetrates the entire wall, spilling stomach contents into the left thoracic cavity with resulting massive infection there.

Angiodysplasia

Lower gastrointestinal hemorrhage in the elderly can result from mucosal erosion of a focal, degenerative, tangled mass of blood vessels (angiodysplasia), most commonly found in the cecum. They, too, can bleed massively into the colon.

Paleopathological reports of ulcerations

In mummified bodies the mucosa is absent, making the mucosal part of the mucosal defect unrecognizable. However, the dense, fibrotic zone in the submucosa that extends even into the muscular wall underlying the ulcer can be expected

FIG. 8.19: **Megaesophagus.** The esophagus is dilated down to its junction with the stomach . In this case the dilatation resulted from destruction of esophageal ganglion cells due to infection with *Trypanosoma cruzi*. Adult female, northern Chile, A.D. 1100. PBL.

to survive the postmortem atmosphere quite well in an otherwise mummified body and should be easily detectable. In a perforated ulcer either the presence of a local abscess or exudate reflecting generalized peritonitis should stimulate a search for the origin – a search that should include not only appendicitis and other causes but also ulcer perforation. Similarly the blood-filled stomach, esophagus and upper small intestine from a bleeding ulcer, Mallory–Weiss syndrome laceration, or esophageal varix rupture (or even a colon distended with blood from a bleeding angiodysplasia lesion) ought to be obvious. While there is no reason to believe that many risk factors for gastric and duodenal ulcers and other bleeding lesions were not present in antiquity, the described lesions have not been reported in archaeological bodies. Sievers & Fisher (1981:212), however, report that today gastric ulcers are less common and duodenal ulcers rare among full-blooded Native Americans from the southwestern U.S.A., Rowling (1967) notes that, while no peptic ulcers have been found in Egyptian mummies, the Ebers papyrus (Ebbell, 1937; p.30, column 39) describes diagnostic findings strongly suggestive of upper gastrointestinal hemorrhage: '…if thou examinest his obstacle in his cardia, and thou findest that he has…turned deathly pale, his mind goes away, and his cardia becomes dry [thirst?], then thou shalt say of him: it is a blood-nest which has not yet attached itself…' Nevertheless, the characteristic, food-relieved, epigastric pain of ulcers is not mentioned in any Egyptian papyrus. However, while the Hippocratic authors did not mention ulcers, both Celsus and Pliny were familiar with peptic ulcers (Majno, 1975:360), testifying to an antiquity of at least two millennia for this condition.

Intestinal obstruction

Achalasia

This is a serious complication of a wide variety of bowel lesions and can occur at any level from the esophagus to the anus. Lower esophageal sphincter spasm results in retention of food in the esophagus with distention of that segment (achalasia). The distended esophagus (megaesophagus) can also be the result of destruction of its ganglion cells by infection with *Trypanosoma cruzi* (see Chagas' disease in Chapter 6; and Fig. 8.19). Obstruction of the gastric outlet by a scarring pyloric ulcer has already been mentioned above.

Adhesions

Abdominal adhesions, often from prior abdominal infections or surgery may provide a rigid, fixed structure that can impede an intestinal wave of peristalsis, permitting the intestine to twist around it and compress its own blood supply. A segment of bowel (most often the sigmoid colon) containing a heavy fecal load may even undergo such a twisting con-

tortion (volvulus) without prior adhesions. The resulting compression of the blood supply in its mesentery can lead to infarction of the twisted segment with hemorrhage into the infarcted portion, rendering it thickened and black.

Neoplasms

Neoplasms arising in the bowel mucosa (adenocarcinoma) or muscular layer (leiomyoma) of the wall can also obstruct the intestinal lumen, especially in the colon.

Intussusception

Intussusception is a process in which a usually upper small bowel segment 'telescopes' into the lumen of a lower segment causing bowel obstruction and (if untreated) also infarction. Imperforate anus has been discussed in the section on Congenital lesions, above.

Hernia

Perhaps the most common cause of intestinal obstruction is a hernia, which represents protrusion of a segment of intestine through a defect in the fascial layer of the abdominal wall, most commonly in the inguinal area or scrotum, producing a subcutaneous bulge in the affected area. If the fascial defect is large, pressure on the bulge can push ('reduce') the bowel back into the abdominal cavity. Sometimes inflammation will cause the bowel to become permanently adherent to the hernia sac, preventing reduction by manual pressure ('incarcerated' hernia). The herniated bowel, of course, also drags its mesentery into the hernia sac, and if the fascial defect is small, the mesentery (containing its blood supply) may become compressed and render the herniating bowel ischemic ('strangulated' hernia) – a surgical emergency.

In these various conditions the afflicted person suffers abdominal distention, pain and vomiting with loss of fluids that produces major metabolic changes. The distention of the bowel can impair its blood circulation, leading to gangrene and perforation with peritonitis. The inguinal fascial defects are responsible for the most common form of hernia and in the male occur there as the result of incomplete fusion of the canal along which the embryonic testis migrates from the intra-abdominal position to the extra-abdominal scrotal location. Another common hernia site is the umbilicus, though obstruction at this site is uncommon because of the usually wide mouth of the hernia sac.

Paleopathological reports of intestinal obstruction

Except for the paraesophageal and diaphragmatic hernias described under Congenital lesions in this chapter, we could find no examples of intestinal obstruction or any of the other discussed causes in mummies. Rowling (1967) suggests this may be the case in Egyptian mummies because embalmers would have removed the bowel from the hernia sac during evisceration. An enlarged scrotum found in the mummy of Ramses V has been suggested to have been caused by a hernia (Rowling, 1967), as was the large scrotum found by Dzierzykray-Rogalski (1988) in a baby. In neither case was bowel demonstrated in the scrotum. Pharaoh Merneptah's scrotum was removed by the embalmer though his penis remained intact (Smith & Dawson, 1924:100). Harris & Wente (1980) suggest its removal may have been performed by the embalmers because of a hernia. In view of the fact that scrotal enlargement could be due to a number of other causes such as hydrocele or, more commonly, postmortem putrefactive changes, assignation of hernia as the cause of an expanded scrotum rests on slender evidence indeed. Textual and other artistic evidence, however, more strongly suggests that the presence and mechanism of hernia production were known in antiquity at least as ancient as the Egyptian civilization. The Ebers papyrus (Ebbell, 1937: col. 106, p.123) describes a hernia quite convincingly in its instructions to a physician concerning'…a swelling of the covering on his belly's horns [i.e. inguinal areas]…above his pudenda, then thou shalt place thy finger on it…and knock on thy fingers; if…that has come out and has arisen by his cough…thou shalt heat it [i.e. the swelling] in order to shut (it) up in his belly…'

Umbilical hernias are clearly delineated in Egyptian funerary art, both paintings and reliefs, some of which (reliefs from mastabas of Ptah-Hetep and of Mehu, Old Kingdom, Saqqara) are of a degree of clarity that they leave no diagnostic doubt (Ghalioungui & Dawakhly, 1965: figures 43 and 44), but the diagnosis of inguinal hernias descending into the scrotum are of far more marginal diagnostic specificity and dependent on only modest degrees of scrotal enlargement (Ghalioungui & Dawakhly, 1965: figures 42 and 45 – reliefs from mastabas of Ankh-Ma-Hor and of Menu, Saqqara, Old Kingdom). However, a statuette, thought to be that of the imported god Bes commonly represented in lower Egypt, is more convincing. This stone figure was found in an ancient Phoenician cemetery at Sousa dated to about 900 B.C. by Gouvet but first reported by F. Poncet (1895) in a French journal Le Progres Medical (June 1, 1895). An English translation appeared in the Lancet (October 5, 1895). It demonstrates a seated male figure wearing a tough, fascial cloth skillfully bound to support what appear to be bilateral inguinal hernia masses – probably the earliest known truss. While perhaps not unequivocally diagnostic, the suggested diagnosis is certainly the most plausible.

No case report of intestinal obstruction by volvulus in ancient bodies could be identified by us, but again the Egyptian papyrus Ebers (Ebbell, 1937: p.39, col. 25) suggests its presence at that time: '…if thou examinest one who suffers…with colicky pains, and whose belly is stiff through it, and who has pain in his cardia…nor is there any way it can come out, then it shall rot in his belly…it grows into a twist in the bowel…'

Megaesophagus has been reported in ancient bodies with Chagas' disease (see Chapter 6), but we searched in vain for cases of intestinal obstruction in mummified bodies due to adhesions, intussusception or neoplasms.

Infectious conditions

Salmonellosis

The gastrointestinal tract is the target of viruses, bacteria and parasites so frequently that most modern people suffer at least one mild infection annually. Most of these, however, produce either no grossly recognizable lesion at all, or one that is limited to the mucosa and hence is lost in the process of postmortem mucosal autolysis. Among these are cholera, almost all the viral gastroenteritides, salmonellosis and others. Probably the only recognizable enteric lesion of typhoid fever in a mummy would be that of its complication: perforation with acute peritonitis. These lesions are discussed in Chapter 7. In view of the substantial fraction of infant mortality attributed to such infections in the developing countries of the modern world, the inability to recognize these anatomically in ancient mummies is a major impediment in the study of paleoepidemiology. More sophisticated laboratory methodology will need to be developed for their recognition. Sawicki et al. (1976) have identified one such possible path by inoculating a rabbit with solutions of powdered Peruvian mummies' coprolites and demonstrating a substantial rise in Salmonella antibody titer (method of antibody induction). Molecular biology methodology has also shown promise of its ability to demonstrate infectious agents' DNA in ancient tissue (Salo et al., 1994).

Appendicitis

There are, however, a few specific forms that can produce identifiable lesions. One of these is appendicitis. The usual cause of appendiceal infection is occlusion of its orifice, commonly by a fecalith (pebble of dried fecal material). The gas-forming, normal colon bacilli within the lumen continue to form gas, the escape of which the occluded orifice will now prevent. The pressure within the appendix rises, compresses the mucosal blood vessels and those in the wall. The bacteria then invade the ischemic, necrotic wall, which eventually perforates, producing either a localized abscess or, more commonly, generalized peritonitis.

Crohn's disease

An ulcerating enteritis that may be evident in a mummy is Crohn's disease. About two-thirds of the cases involve the small intestine and the remainder affect the colon. Its cause is unknown. It begins as a diffusely ulcerative mucosal process, but is accompanied by a very extensively granulomatous, scarring process that greatly thickens the wall. Extension to adjacent structures such as other bowel loops or the bladder results in fistulae between such structures. The disease is chronic and has no known cure.

Diverticulosis

While there are several forms of congenital diverticulum formation (jejunal; Meckel's) that bulge from the antimesenteric border of the bowel, acquired forms develop on the mesenteric border where blood vessels penetrate the wall. Bulging through such a wall defect, the soft mucosa is covered only by the thin serosal layer. Not surprisingly this fragile diverticular wall often ruptures when it becomes infected secondary to erosion of the mucosal lining by hard fecal fragments. Believed to be produced by years of straining at stool, their development becomes a function of age, found most commonly in the descending colon of elderly people. Perforation of diverticula below the peritoneal line of reflection commonly results in a localized abscess that may fistulize, frequently to the perineum. Perforation at higher levels usually spills the pus directly into the peritoneal cavity, causing generalized peritonitis.

Paleopathological reports

The description of right abdominal pain in Egypt's Ebers papyrus (Ebbel, 1937:p.52, col. 41) is too nonspecific to serve as evidence of appendicitis in that period, but a single case of healed appendicitis in a Byzantine Nubian, uneviscerated mummy was identified by Smith & Wood Jones (1910:268). The appendix was found in the pelvis of this young woman, attached to the opposite (left) pelvis wall by a thick adhesive band, suggesting she had survived appen-

diceal rupture with abscess formation. This finding is highly suggestive, but is not absolute proof of a primary appendiceal infection, because the appendiceal serosa can become adhesive to a nearby inflammatory process such as acute salpingitis. No other case was identified in the literature. It is conceivable that the highly fibrous, bulky diet of ancient people produced sufficiently rapid food transit to prevent fecal desiccation in the cecum, though the incidence of acute appendicitis has not been studied formally in human vegetarians versus those on a general diet. Modern epidemiological observations, however, note that acute appendicitis is rare in tribal societies (Burkitt, 1981:142).

Crohn's disease was first reported in 1932 in the U.S.A. It is believed to be of recent development. Its world prevalence pattern reveals a predominance in western developed countries (Hutt & Burkitt, 1986:22). One would expect that the thickly scarred wall would be recognized easily even in ancient bodies whose mucosa has dissolved and the muscle layer thinned, but it has not been seen in mummies.

Diverticulosis coli has not been reported in mummies. Being an acquired disease primarily afflicting the elderly, the small fraction of mummies reaching that age may explain the absence of this complication.

Neoplasms

Adenocarcinoma

The most common intestinal tumor today in western countries is colon adenocarcinoma. A similar tumor also affects the small intestine and even the stomach. It is believed to arise from a pre-existing adenomatous polyp. Most cases are sporadic but a small fraction occur within families demonstrating a heritable syndrome of one of several types. Multiple specific mutations involving both oncogene (*ras*) and suppressor genes have been shown to occur prior to the growth of invasive cancer. The cause of these mutations is unknown but epidemiological studies show significant correlations with increased dietary animal fat and decreased dietary fiber (and subsequent slow fecal transit time permitting longer exposure of colon mucosa to intestinal content: Hutt & Burkitt, 1986:27–30). The capacious lumen of the cecum and ascending colon can accommodate a very large tumor mass before the latter interferes with stool passage (Fig. 8.20). For this reason tumors of the proximal colon are usually

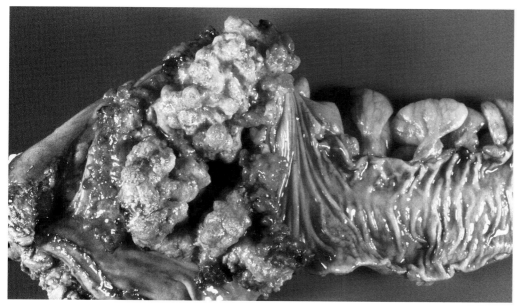

FIG. 8.20: **Colon carcinoma.** Because of the colon's large diameter, cancers can attain a substantial size before calling attention to themselves by obstructing the intestine. Modern adult female. PBL.

of considerable size before detection. The surface of these large cancers commonly erode, causing enough blood oozing from its ulcerated areas to result in anemia, a common initial symptom. In the smaller diameter of the more distal colon, similar tumors are more apt to call attention to themselves earlier by blocking the lumen and causing intestinal obstruction. The frequency of small intestine tumors is only about one-tenth that in the colon. The large volume of the stomach also permits the growth of very large tumors unless they arise at the relatively narrow opening of the esophageal junction with the stomach or at its pyloric outlet into the duodenum. All of these intestinal cancers tend to metastasize into the mesenteric lymph nodes and, later, invade veins that carry the metastatic cancer cells into the liver where they usually flourish.

Paleopathology

Because of their substantial size, one would normally expect to recognize gastrointestinal cancers readily in mummified human remains. Perhaps postmortem liquefaction and destruction by bacteria is responsible for the paucity of these paleopathological reports describing them, yet the colon is quite commonly recognizable in spontaneously mummified bodies. Fornaciari *et al.* (1993) have reported such a case in the mummified remains of a fifteenth century king from Naples, and recently Zimmerman (1995, and personal communication) found a similar one in a Ptolemaic period body from Dakhleh oasis in Egypt's western desert. Rowling (1961) suggests the possibility of carcinoma of the rectum in an Egyptian body, but the diagnosis is based entirely on pelvic bone changes, unfortunately without associated soft tissues. Leiomyoma, composed of smooth muscle cells, is a benign and common gastrointestinal tumor in modern times, and would be expected to survive postmortem effects even better than cancer, yet we can find no report of this lesion in archaeological bodies.

Miscellaneous lesions

Hemorrhoids

Hemorrhoids may be the lesion for which an ointment is described in the Eber papyrus (Ebbell, 1937: p.44, col. 33): '…to relieve the vessels of the hinder part…' In addition the same text (p.42, col. 31) may describe either *pruritus ani* or

fistula-in-ano: '…to expel burning in the anus…that is accompanied by many flatus without his perceiving it…to expel purlency in the anus…'

Rectal prolapse

Ruffer (1913) described a case of rectal prolapse in a Coptic mummy. The Ebers papyrus (Ebbel, 1937: p.43, col. 32) suggests this may have been a problem among living Egyptians when it recommends application of a mixture of compounds as a hot pack for '…dislocation in the hinder part…' In spontaneously mummified bodies, however, we have observed numerous examples of rectal prolapse with features that suggest these were postmortem processes of fermentation with gas formation and increased abdominal pressure (see Chapter 2 (Pseudopathology)).

Gastric contents and coprolites

Finally, gastric contents and colon feces (coprolites) (Fig. 8.21) contain an enormous mass of data about ancient diets and parasites, and these can be employed to predict season of death, method of subsistence and other features valuable for reconstruction of an ancient population's lifestyle. The details of these aspects are outside this book's remit, but interested readers can begin their search with references to Ruffer (1920), Halbaek (1959), Horne (1985), Scaife (1986), Aaronson (1989), Reinhard (1990), and Miller *et al.* (1993), in addition to the data provided in the Parasitic infections section of Chapter 7.

FIG. 8.21: **Coprolites (dehydrated feces).** After death the coprolite-filled cecum has become displaced by gravity from the right lower quadrant of the abdomen, sliding downward so that its medial aspect lies just above the anus. A 15 year old male, northern Chile, 2000 B.C. PBL.

URINARY DISEASES

Congenital lesions

Polycystic disease

While normal kidneys frequently have occasional, harmless cysts, the most common form of polycystic kidney disease (PKD) is the product of an autosomal dominant gene located on chromosome 16 (European Polycystic Kidney Disease Consortium, 1994) or another on chromosome 4 (Kimberling et al., 1993). PKD is characterized by the presence of a large number of cysts scattered throughout the renal parenchyma (Fig. 8.22). These cysts somehow induce self-destruction (apoptosis) of the intervening renal elements until insufficient functioning renal parenchyma remains to sustain life, and renal failure (uremia) ensues (Woo, 1995). The rate of progression, however, varies enormously (depending on the nature of the gene mutation?) and may lead to death in early childhood or as late as the ninth decade. The condition is bilateral and end-stage PKD commonly reveals kidneys of enormous size (10× increase) composed principally of fluid-filled cysts varying from microscopic size to some that are 4–8 cm in diameter. Treatment today consists of dialysis and transplantation. PKD patients constitute about 10 % of renal transplantations in most centers. In antiquity, of course, no effective therapy was available, and the common adult form onset was late enough to permit child-bearing and thus gene transmission. In addition to the renal pathology, nearly half of these individuals also have a few cysts in the liver (not enough to affect hepatic function) and a few demonstrate cerebral artery aneurysms whose rupture may be fatal. About one-third of PKD deaths are due to renal failure, another third due to a complication of the commonly accompanying hypertension and the remainder to unrelated causes (Cotran et al., 1994:935). Other, much less common forms of kidney cystic disease usually have small cysts, there are several in which the cysts are limited to the renal medulla, and that are inherited in a variety of patterns.

Horseshoe kidney

The other congenital renal lesion of a frequency about that of polycystic kidneys (about 1 in 750 in clinical, modern autopsy series) is fusion of the (usually) lower pole of both kidneys. This results in a horseshoe-shaped single structure, but commonly two ureters emerge. It normally does not interfere with function, although the renal arteries in some cases may compress one or both ureters sufficiently to cause ureteral obstruction.

Paleopathology of congenital renal lesions

We have been able to find the report of only one case of polycystic renal disease in an archaeological body. Allison (1981a) described this condition in a 17–19 year old spontaneously mummified body excavated from a site in northern Chile dating to about A.D. 300 and illustrated it in Case No. 7 in the Paleopathology Club series. The horseshoe malformation has not appeared in the paleopathology literature.

Infectious conditions

Pyelonephritis

Both the renal pelvis and the kidney parenchyma are so commonly involved in kidney infections as to justify use of the term pyelonephritis. While bacilli may reach the kidney via a septicemic episode, they usually arrive there as a result of infections in any part of the lower urinary tract (urethra, bladder, and ureters). The entrance of the ureters into the bladder is normally guarded by a valve-like structure that permits urine to enter the bladder, but prevents reflux of urine from the bladder back up into the ureter. In cases of bladder infection, dysfunction of these valves may permit reflux of bacteria-laden urine into the ureters that subsequently can reach the level of the kidney. Other obstructions may involve urethral constriction by an enlarging prostrate, tumors encroaching upon any part of the urine-conducting system or impaction of ureteral calculi. Because of the proximity of the external urethral orifice to the anus, particularly in females, it is not surprising that the most common organism involved

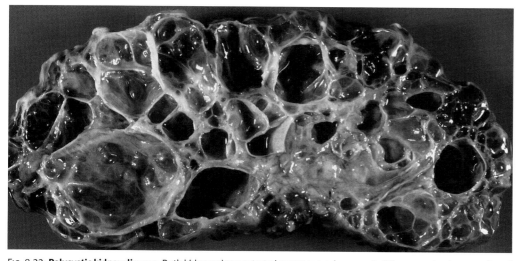

Fig. 8.22: **Polycystic kidney disease.** Both kidneys demonstrated enormous enlargement of the organ due to expansion of the many cysts with atrophy of the renal parenchyma between the cysts. Modern adult male age 50 years. PBL.

is the one most prevalent in the human colon: *Escherichia coli*. In diabetics staphylococcic infections are common, often reaching the kidney through the blood stream.

In acute pyelonephritis the onset may be quite abrupt, with chills, fever, malaise and burning urination. Subsequent course is dependent on the nature of the initiating factor, especially in those in whom obstruction played a role. Untreated multiple abscesses may develop in both kidneys (pyonephrosis); in some, (especially diabetics) bacilli may reach beyond the renal capsule, producing a perinephric abscess. Fatal septicemia by the infecting bacillus may terminate the process. Alternatively, a combination of the immune system's response plus at least temporary or partial relief of obstructive effects may allow recovery. Without correction of the obstructing effect (for example, passage of a ureteral stone), however, recurrences are common and lead to a continuing condition of chronic pyelonephritis with acute exacerbations. Since each episode results in some amount of renal parenchymal destruction, the end result often is bilateral renal fibrosis and atrophy manifested as chronic renal failure with uremia (Fig. 8.23). A chronic xanthogranulomatous form often extends beyond the kidney, involving retroperitoneal tissues with dense scar formation (Scully *et al.*, 1995).

FIG. 8.23: **Kidney: chronic pyelonephritis.** This kidney measured 7 x 4 x 2 cm and its mate was about two-thirds as large. In addition to the bilateral size reduction, they demonstrated both finely and coarsely granular surfaces reflecting profound, diffuse irregular parenchymal atrophy characteristic of chronic pyelonephritis or other causes of diffuse parenchymal damage (renal arteriolosclerosis, chronic glomerulonephritis). A small calculus found in the renal pelvis is pictured lying free beneath the right side of the kidney. An 18 year old male, northern Chile, A.D. 450–800. PBL.

Renal tuberculosis

Renal tuberculosis usually is the result of tuberculous septicemia (miliary tuberculosis). Subsequent lesion development follows the pattern already described in the lung (Chapter 7): i.e. caseous necrosis of a progressively expanding lesion until it coalesces with a neighboring lesion and /or erodes into a hollow viscus through which the necrotic caseous material is discharged. That hollow viscus in the lung is, of course, a bronchus while in the kidney it is commonly one of the urine-filled calyces of the renal pelvis. The bacilli-laden urine then passes down the ureters to the bladder and urethra. Secondary infection of these structures as well as others draining into them (prostate, seminal vesicles, epididymis and even testis) is a common complication. In a significant percentage of people suffering miliary spread of the tubercle bacillus, the body's immune system may eliminate organisms in all organs except one. Examples of such processes include those persons with active urinary tract tuberculosis but no evidence of active disease in the lung or elsewhere. Occasionally penetration of the renal capsule will result in a perinephric tuberculous abscess. The tuberculous process may reach the vertebrae via lymphatics and veins that drain into Batson's plexus of veins with the subsequent course described in Chapter 7. The progression of renal tuberculosis is slow, commonly involving many years before

renal failure or a complication of the disease leads to death in untreated persons.

Paleopathology of infectious renal lesions

Chronic pyelonephritis and perirenal abscess have both been reported in South American mummies by Gerszten *et al.* (1983). Ruffer (1921b) identified multiple, bilateral kidney abscesses with stainable gram-negative bacteria in an Egyptian mummy. He also found schistosome ova in two kidneys. We have been unable to identify tuberculous kidneys in the paleopathological literature, though psoas muscle abscesses in relation to tuberculous vertebritis are dramatically demonstrated in an Egyptian mummy reported by Ruffer & Ferguson (1911).

Hydronephrosis

This term applies to kidneys with greatly dilated calyces and renal pelvis due to urinary flow obstruction. However, the obstruction may occur at any point in the urinary tract with dilatation of structures proximal to the obstructed site. This would include the ureter (Fig. 8.24) (calculus; tumor; compression by gravid uterus of ureter at pelvic brim; defective

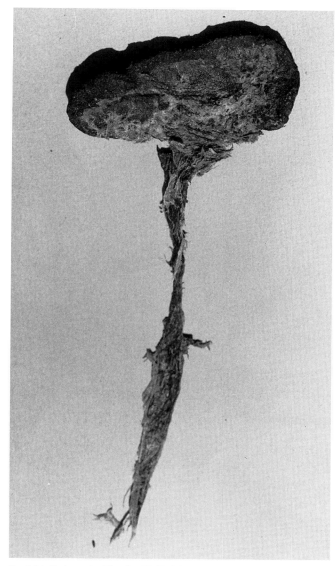

FIG. 8.24: **Hydroureter.** The distal half of this ureter is dilated to about three times its normal diameter. Two small calculi (renoliths) were present in the renal pelvis. Although no calculus was present within the ureter at the time of death, in all probability a small calculus had passed from the renal pelvis into the ureter, obstructing the ureter at about its midcourse long enough to dilate it, then was expelled into the bladder and excreted. An 18 year old male, northern Chile, A.D. 450–800. PBL.

valve at ureterovesical junction) or the urinary bladder (urethral stricture; tumor; prostatic hypertrophy − benign or malignant; calculus). Obstruction distal to the urinary bladder obviously would result in bilateral hydronephrosis. If the obstruction persists unrelieved, the elevated urinary pressure will result in atrophy of functional renal tissue and precipitate renal failure with uremia if bilateral. Such an affected kidney is enlarged due to the distended urine-filled calyces that eventually replace most of the renal parenchyma as the latter undergoes progressive atrophy (Fig. 8.25). Modern treatment involves endoscopic or open surgical relief of the obstruction. A serious complication of unrelieved obstruction occurs when bacteria gain access to the urine proximal to the obstruction, initiating an acute, violent pyelonephritis that can be lethal.

Paleopathology of hydronephrosis

We are aware of only one reported case of this lesion in antiquity. Allison & Gerszten (1983) demonstrated a hydronephrotic kidney in their Case No. 13 of the Paleopathology Club series. The right renal pelvis and upper quarter of associated ureter were clearly distended, though no calculi could be found. In modern clinical cases this circumstance is often due to ureteral compression by an aberrant renal artery or ureteral stricture.

Glomerulonephritis

The purpose of the kidney is to eliminate the body's metabolic waste products (MWP) and toxins. It achieves this in a two-step process.
1. The kidney first separates the plasma from the blood cells and proteins, returning the latter to the blood. This separation (filtration) is carried out within thousands of microscopic-sized, spherical masses of tangled capillaries called glomeruli. As blood flows through these capillaries the plasma leaks through the specialized capillary membrane into the space around it.
2. The microscopic, cell-lined tube (tubule) surrounding the glomerulus collects the plasma filtrate and eventually

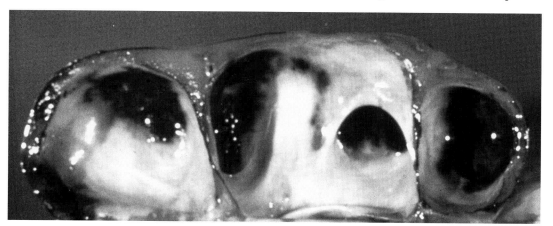

FIG. 8.25: **Kidney: hydronephrosis.** A bladder tumor obstructed the ureter, causing unilateral hydronephrosis. The increased pressure caused the renal pelvis and calyces to dilate enormously, resulting in atrophy of the renal parenchyma. Modern adult male. PBL.

empties into the renal pelvis to join that from other tubules; the filtrate is then called urine. However, during its traverse along the tubule, 95 % of the water and all of the sugar and other nutrients are reabsorbed into the blood, but the MWP remain within the tubule and form the principal solute of urine.

This process responds to many physiological stimuli to maintain a constant blood level of appropriate nutrients and other vital substances in spite of a wide range of continually changing food and beverage intake and varying metabolic expenditure. The integrity of the glomerular basement membrane is essential to this control. A vast array of conditions, however, can affect this membrane's structure negatively. The most common are the infectious or autoimmune diseases in which antigen–antibody protein complexes are deposited on or in the glomerular basement membrane and which tend to 'clog the filter'. Among the most frequent of these are infections by certain strains of beta hemolytic streptococci whose antibodies not only obstruct the filtering membrane, but also stimulate swelling of the cells lining the capillaries to a degree that obstructs their lumen. Without plasma flow through the capillaries or through a membrane partially obstructed by deposition of such protein complexes, no urine can be formed. Untreated, the MPW accumulate in the blood (uremia) and the individual may die within a few weeks. Modern dialysis therapy supports the patient through this often self-limited, acute phase. Still other antigen–antibody complex-producing conditions are often of autoimmune nature, the classic model of which is lupus erythematosus. A variety of other bacilli, viral or even protozoal infections occasionally produce a similar effect. Collectively these conditions are termed acute glomerulonephritis.

Other conditions may injure the membrane in such a way that it leaks proteins. Since renal tubules are not designed to reabsorb proteins, such proteins are lost to the body when excreted in the urine. Massive urinary protein loss lowers the serum albumin level dramatically so that it can not carry out its function of osmotic fluid balance (nephrosis). The result is accumulation of water in tissues, creating a bloated, edematous appearance.

If the acute forms of the nephritides are survived, the condition may progress into an often years-long chronic glomerulonephritis phase that may eventuate in the uremic state of end-stage chronic renal disease.

Death in the acute phase often presents a kidney of up to twice normal size. The progressive loss of glomeruli in the chronic phase is accompanied by the loss of their associated tubules. The result is usually diminutive, atrophic, granular-surfaced kidneys.

Paleopathology

Estes (1989:46) refers to reports of glomerulosclerosis in Egyptian mummies, but he does not cite them. End-stage renal disease due to chronic glomerulonephritis often demonstrates abundant fibrotic glomeruli, but this change also occurs with other chronic renal diseases. No other diagnoses of glomerulonephritis in archaeological kidneys could be found by us.

Metabolic conditions

Urinary calculi

The most common of these that confront the paleopathologist is the formation of urinary calculi (urolithiasis). Stones arise by precipitation of the urine's solutes. The precise circumstances leading to such a state of supersaturation are not well understood, but the chemical and physical state of the crystallized solute (urolith) varies in relation to location, secretion of hypernormal levels of the solute, age, gender, urine pH, crystal inhibitors, urinary infection and the presence of minute particles that serve as nucleating agents to initiate precipitation. The cause of the increased urinary solute secretion is clearly defined in some cases: hyperparathyroidism leaches calcium from bones and excretes it into urine in large amounts; metabolic derangements in gout patients cause elevated levels of uric acid in both blood and urine. In many persons, however, the cause is not obvious.

Calculi in the urinary tract create two types of problems: They may obstruct the flow of urine and they may erode the urinary tract's lining mucosa resulting in hemorrhage (hematuria) or rendering it susceptible to infection. Because the nature of the stones differ, it is customary to divide them into those that precipitate in the upper tract (renal or kidney stones) and those that form in the urinary bladder (vesical stones).

Renal calculi are most commonly formed by the precipitation of calcium in the form of calcium oxalate or calcium phosphate. If the mucosal areas abraded by the calculi become infected it is often by bacilli that split urea, producing ammonia. The resulting more alkaline urine will then often enlarge the calculus by precipitating magnesium ammonium phosphate ('struvite') onto it. Progressive crystal growth may produce a single calculus that fills the entire renal pelvis and its calyces ('staghorn calculus'). Alternatively, the renal pelvis may expel the stone into the ureter while it is still no more than 2 or 3 mm in diameter. The smaller stones may represent a greater hazard because they may enter the ureter, impact there and obstruct urine flow. The ureter's peristaltic contractions in its effort to propel the stone through the ureter into the bladder can produce notoriously agonizing pain. Permanent arrest of the stone in the ureter may cause total obstruction with subsequent hydronephrosis and loss of that kidney's function if the stone is not removed. Renal calculi occur largely in adults with little difference among the genders.

Urinary bladder calculi may occur in adults but are most common in children, and are 10-fold more frequent in boys. They may reach enormous size in the bladder; diameters of 8–10 cm and occasionally greater have been reported. While calcium oxalate composition is also common in these stones, uric acid calculi are frequent as well. Schistosome ova have been found in Egyptian uroliths, suggesting they acted as a nucleation particle for stone formation. In certain body positions, gravity-directed movement of the stone may obstruct the urethral opening, preventing micturition and causing painful bladder distention. Infection can also generate a struvite stone in the bladder.

The epidemiology of urolithiasis is unique. Bladder stones are common among the world's poor and largely vegetarian people (e.g. Thailand). During the past several centuries it has become clear that, as such populations develop modern economies and concordantly increase their dietary meat component, bladder stones disappear while the frequency of renal calculi increases. Certain obvious exceptions to this generalization, however, make it clear that factors other than meat protein are operating. Another major difference between renal and bladder stones is their response to surgical excision: renal calculi commonly recur while bladder stones do so only rarely.

Paleopathology

The interpretation of the history of this disease is challenging and the interested reader is referred to its superb documentation by Steinbock (1985, 1989, 1993c). Space restrictions compel us to extract from his account only a few of the essential features. Because uroliths are discrete, tangible structures, the diagnostic certainty of ancient literature is often reassuring. The Vedas of India include bladder stone as a proper prayer subject as early as 1500 B.C. Hippocratic writers recognized both renal and bladder stones. About 300 years later Ammonius of Alexandria created a stone-crushing instrument for use within the bladder. Rufus of Ephesus (first century A.D.) described a transverse perineal incision to remove bladder stones as did Celsus (Rome) about the

same time (cited in Steinbock, 1993c). In the eighteenth century, hospitals at Norwich, England and at Paris became centers for bladder stone removal, averaging about one case per month for more than a century.

The actual antiquity of urolithiasis, however, exceeds its literary record by a considerable margin. A calcium oxalate stone was found in the urinary bladder of a 1500 year old spontaneously mummified body of a native North American (Streitz et al., 1981: see Fig. 8.26). Paleopathologic findings of both renal and bladder stones have been documented carefully by Steinbock (1985) and his table is reproduced in Table 8.2 by permission. The Mesolithic bladder calculus from Sicily (Piperno, 1976) testifies to this condition's antiquity there of more than eight millennia. Though Smith & Wood-Jones (1910:56) were only able to identify a single Egyptian case among about 10 000 bodies (not all mummies), excavation methods and endemic geographic differences may be responsible for the larger number of finds subsequent to their studies. Both Europe and the Americas are well represented in Steinbock's table, to which we can add a renal calcium oxalate calculus from the skeleton of an adult Maori female in New Zealand from 150–200 years ago (Houghton, 1975). Steinbock's accompanying text annotates each of the reports.

Several further examples have appeared since that 1985 article. di Tota et al. (1992) reported at the ninth session of the Paleopathology Association in Barcelona, identifying a lamellated, concentric pattern of a 1.3 cm probable bladder stone found in the pelvic area of an adult female skeleton from Alfadena (Aquila, central Italy). Sánchez Sánchez & Góméz Bellard (1988) found renal and biliary calculi in a seventeenth century young adult female excavated in the Basque country in Spain and also found similar calculus forms in necropoles from two different archaeological sites from the seventh and sixteenth centuries. Morris & Rodgers (1989) also report two large calcareous bodies, composed of

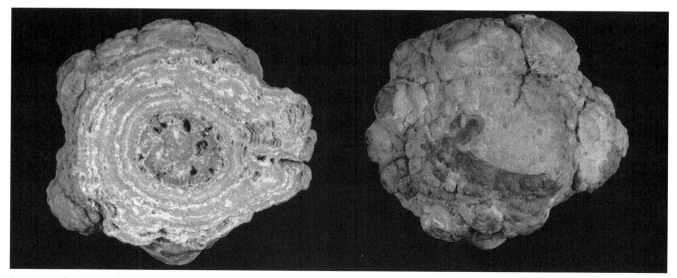

FIG. 8.26: **Vesical calculus (bladder stone).** This 3 x 2.7 x 2.5 cm calcium oxalate stone was found within an anatomically normal bladder. It has been bisected to reveal both its knobby surface and the concentric layers of urine solutes that precipitated around what was probably organic matter (protein?, pus?) now represented by the small central defects in the sectioned plane. Spontaneously mummified, 30–40 year old male, southwestern U.S.A., A.D. 500. PBL.

hydroxyapatite (calcium phosphate), each up to 4 cm in diameter, lying adjacent to the lumbar vertebrae of an adult woman's skeleton from a South African site. Fulcheri & Grilletto (1988) provided observations of a probable renal calculus in an Old Kingdom Egyptian body. Blackman et al. (1991) detected two small calcium oxalate stones in the left kidney of an 18 year old male spontaneously mummified body of a member of northern Chile's coastal Cabuza culture (A.D. 450–1000). Diffuse, punctate bilateral calcification of the renal parenchyma, bilateral hydroureter, osteopenia and fibrinous pericarditis suggested end-stage renal disease with uremia and secondary hyperparathyroidism leading to bilateral nephrocalcinosis. More recently Catalano & Passarello (1988) document the presence of 24 left renal calculi in an adult female from a fifth to sixth century B.C. site near Rome.

Individual case reports remain justifiable because the number of stones reported to date is not yet large enough to spell out specific patterns, though what we do have available supports the historical documents and the epidemiological concepts noted above.

Hypertension and diabetes mellitus

Atherosclerosis of the larger renal arteries is accelerated in individuals with supranormal blood pressure levels (hypertension). One of the effects of this process is stenosis (lumen size reduction) and complete lumen obstruction by thrombosis. The kidney parenchyma nourished by the now occluded artery commonly becomes necrotic (infarcted) and subsequently undergoes liquefaction, absorption and replacement by a localized and grossly visible scar. In addition, microscopic-sized arteries may suffer from stenosis due to smooth muscle proliferation of the wall at the expense of lumen size, or deposition of protein deposits in the wall of arterioles. These changes are exaggerated in diabetes in which further restriction of blood flow occurs by extension of this process to the glomerular capillaries. The consequence of this is atrophy of the individual, diminutive areas supplied by each of these arterioles, resulting in atrophy of the kidney as a whole, and a finely granular surface secondary to sunken atrophic microareas of renal parenchyma of pinhead size juxtaposed to surviving parenchymal portions. Thus these conditions may result in a collapsed, sharply defined fibrotic area in an otherwise grossly normal kidney produced by infarction secondary to occlusion of a large renal artery branch; or arteriolosclerosis and/or glomerulosclerosis can cause a granular-surfaced, small atrophic kidney. Most hypertensive individuals, however, do not have sufficient involvement to make these alterations recognizable in mummified tissue.

Paleopathology

Except for the occasional example of hand and/or foot joint destruction due to diabetic neuropathy, we have no reliable

Table 8.2. Paleopathology reports of renal and bladder calculi.

Date	Location	B/K*	Reference
8500 B.C.	Sicily	B	Piperno, 1976
3500 B.C.	Egypt	B	*Shattock, 1905
3500 B.C.	Egypt	B	Ruffer, 1910
3300 B.C.	Kentucky, U.S.A.	B, B, K	*Smith, 1948
3100 B.C.	Egypt	K	*Bitschai, 1952
2800 B.C.	Egypt	K	*Shattock, 1905
2100 B.C.	France	B	*Duday, 1980
2000–700 B.C.	England	B	*Mortimer, 1905
1500 B.C.	Illinois, U.S.A.	K	*Beck & Mulvaney, 1966
1000 B.C.	Egypt	B	Smith & Dawson, 1924
1000 B.C.	Egypt	K	Gray, 1966
1000 B.C.	Sudan	B	Brothwell, 1967 b
550 B.C.	Italy	K	Catalano & Passarello, 1988
100 B.C.	Italy	B	di Tota et al., 1992
100 B.C.–A.D. 500	Arizona, U.S.A.	B	*Williams, 1926
0-A.D. 200	Sinai	K	*Basset, 1982 (personal communication)
A.D. 450-1000	England	B	Brothwell, 1967 b
A.D. 500–750	Arizona, U.S.A.	B	Streitz et al., 1981
A.D. 1000	Chile	K	*Allison & Gerszten, 1982 (E. Gerszten, personal communication)
A.D. 1350–1500	Denmark	K	Møller-Christensen, 1958
A.D. 1500	Indiana, U.S.A.	K	*Beck & Mulvaney, 1966
A.D. 1650	W. Virginia, U.S.A.	K	*Metress, 1982 (personal communication)
A.D. 1650	Spain	K	*Sanchez Sanchez & Gómez Bellard, 1990
A.D. 1700	South Africa	K	Morris & Rogers, 1989
A.D. 1800	New Zealand	K	Houghton, 1975

*B, bladder; K, kidney. The content of this Table was abstracted from Steinbock (1985) with his permission and expanded with references post-1985.
* For references not listed in the bibliography of this volume see Steinbock (1989).

'marker' for the presence of diabetes in antiquity. Glomerulosclerosis and prominent arteriolosclerosis in renal arterioles could at least conceivably be suggestive of diabetes, but it has not been reported to date. Indeed, Long's (1931) histological observation of renal medium-sized arterial atherosclerosis in an Egyptian adult female (Teye), consistent with hypertension (though not necessarily diabetes) is an exception, and was accompanied by coronary atherosclerosis with myocardial fibrosis. Gerszten et al. (1983) identified both medium and small artery lesions in South American spontaneously mummified bodies.

Neoplasms

Hypernephroma

Hypernephroma (adenocarcinoma of the renal cortex) is the most common adult renal neoplasm. It often reaches an enormous size (Fig. 8.27), and invades the renal vein via which metastases commonly reach the lung. However, the paleopathological literature does not record any malignant kidney

tumor of any kind. Today this tumor represents about 2 % of all visceral cancers (Cotran *et al.*, 1994:986). If it had been this frequent 5000 years ago, one would surely have expected G. Elliot Smith or F. Wood Jones to have encountered it because Egyptian bodies commonly retained the kidneys, and renal cancers of this type are often so large they would be difficult to overlook. Even though most adult Egyptians died before age 60, a significant fraction reached an age in which this tumor commonly occurs. Papillary cancers of the renal pelvis are much less common and less obvious. In the bladder identical papillary carcinomas are more easily recognized, though other types, such as squamous cell carcinomas are more apt to be flat and obviously invasive into a thickened bladder wall.

FIG. 8.27: **Kidney: hypernephroma.** The uninvolved upper and lower ends of the kidney are visible at the left and right lower edges of the mass. The remainder of the kidney has been replaced by a huge, primary adenocarcinoma (hypernephroma) of the kidney that has extended considerably beyond the kidney itself and invaded surrounding tissue. Modern older female. PBL.

FIG. 8.28: **Male external genitalia.** Male genitalia are preserved in recognizable form more frequently than are those of females in spontaneously mummified bodies and both are preserved better with the anthropogenic mummification methods used in this example. A 23–27 year old male Egyptian (Ptolemaic), 140 B.C., Dakhleh Oasis. PBL.

GENITAL DISEASES

Preservation of external genitalia

In spontaneously mummified bodies the enzyme-laden fluids (especially those from the abdominal cavity) tend to gravitate to the most dependent portion of the body's burial position. In many cases this is a sitting position, and in such burials the perineum is the most dependent area. Post-burial desiccation in such mummies is frequently slow enough to permit the enzymatic decay process sufficient time to destroy the external genitalia beyond recognition in both males and females. Because of their prominence and contours, those of the male may remain identifiable more frequently than those of the female (Fig. 8.28). The supine position offers a higher frequency of identification. In anthropogenic forms of mummification, recognition of these structures is heavily dependent upon mummification practice traditions. Egyptian embalmers, for example, frequently made considerable effort to preserve external genitalia, at least among males of royal or noble classes. Unfortunately, during the later periods of extensive resin use, their common custom of wrapping the penis in hot, resin-soaked linen often destroyed the soft tissues; in some, such wrappings were used to model a penis whose soft tissues had not survived the desiccating action of natron. The presence or absence of circumcision can be judged quite frequently in Egyptian male bodies, even in many preserved by spontaneous mummification. Among Egyptian boys it was part of a puberty ritual even in predynastic times (Strouhal, 1992:28; Fig. 8.29). In those,

FIG. 8.29: **Male circumcision.** This appeared to be a puberty rite during Egypt's dynastic period, but was probably practiced even in pre-dynastic times. Young adult Egyptian male from Dakhleh Oasis, Ptolemaic period. PBL.

however, that were eviscerated via the perineum and the perineal defect closed with resin-soaked linen, dissection usually fails to identify the external genitalia. Evidence of the more mutilating types of female 'circumcision' has not been reported in Egyptian mummies and those of lesser degree probably would not be easy to detect. In spontaneously mummified bodies, genitalia are preserved less frequently. Aufderheide & Allison (1994) found 71 % of 21 males but only 29 % of 22 females had identifiable external genitalia in a preceramic group from northern Chile that had been buried in a supine position. Recognition of female breasts is discussed below in a separate section.

Sexually transmitted diseases (STD)

Three of these diseases common today are syphilis, gonorrhea and anogenital warts (condyloma acuminata). Acute gonorrheal urethritis produces a white discharge and intense burning on urination. Retrograde extension to the prostate and epididymis causes abscesses there that are exquisitely tender and can be serious by producing septicemia. In women the spread is from the cervix to the 'adnexae' (fallopian tubes and ovaries), producing serious abscesses there called pelvic inflammatory disease (Fig. 8.30) or leading to a chronic state of adnexal infection with extensive adhesion formation. Today chlamydial infections have replaced gonorrhea as the most common cause of such pathology in western countries. Syphilis has been described in Chapter 7 and will not be repeated here. Anogenital warts are virus-induced papillomas of the external genitalia and perianal areas of both genders, caused by certain subtypes of the human papilloma virus (HPV). They are not tissue-destructive, though some

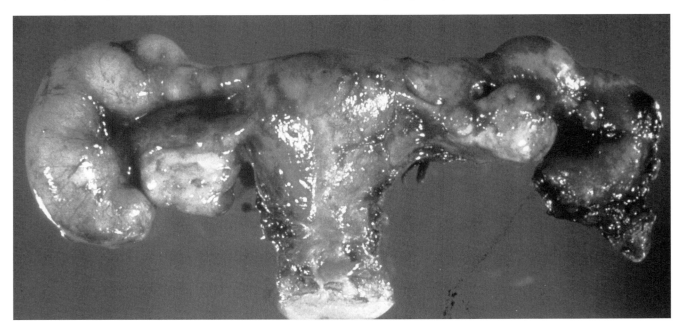

FIG. 8.30: **Acute pelvic inflammatory disease.** Both fallopian tubes are very distended with liquefied pus. Ovaries are enlarged due to diffuse infection without abscesses. Modern young adult female. PBL.

strains have been linked to cervix cancer in women and to anal cancer in immunosuppressed males.

Paleopathology

Whether or not the Hippocratic references to painful urination represent gonorrhea is controversial since they do not associate it with venereal transmission. Some (Rothenberg, 1993) regard Egyptian remedies for painful urination as supportive of the diagnosis of gonorrhea, and label this as the oldest of venereal diseases. Oriel (1973 a, b), however, feels that even the citations of Galen and Celsus (who describe urethral discharge) are not acceptable evidence of gonorrhea because they describe neither pain nor the association with sexual intercourse. While James Fernel (in France) challenged the prevailing opinion that gonorrhea and syphilis were manifestations of the same condition as early as the sixteenth century, it was not until the mid-nineteenth century that Phillippe Record clearly separated these two venereal diseases, and shortly thereafter (1879) Albert Neisser identified the gonorrheal organism that still bears his name (Rothenberg, 1993). The disease has, however, not been identified in mummified tissue, and is not likely ever to be except in testicular, joint or other complicating abscesses. The absence of reference to such a disease by Roman authors also led Oriel to doubt that gonorrhea existed in the western world at that time. However, the opposite is true about anogenital warts, which were called condyloma or thymion by the Greeks (slang: ficus or fig by the Romans). Celsus (first century A.D.) described penile warts and clearly associated this condition with intercourse. Lay writers viewed anogenital warts with amused contempt and commonly equated their presence on the male perineum with sodomy. We are, however, unable to find any reports of a paleopathological lesion of such papillomas. Thus, while the literary record of gonorrhea prior to the Middle Ages is not universally convincing, that of venereal warts certainly extends at least two millennia backward in time.

Testis

Though the scrotum is often identifiable, the testis rarely survives spontaneous mummification and does so only infrequently in anthropogenic forms of soft tissue preservation. Scrotal enlargements in mummies have been attributed to hernia (see Gastrointestinal tract diseases, above) but are most probably a postmortem artifact of bacterial fermentation with gas formation. One would expect that the fibrotic reactions of gonorrheal or tubercular testicular infections would remain detectable, but none have been reported, nor have testicular neoplasms, even though the most common of these (seminoma; embryonal carcinoma) today demonstrate frequencies that peak between 20 and 30 years – ages commonly represented in archaeological human remains.

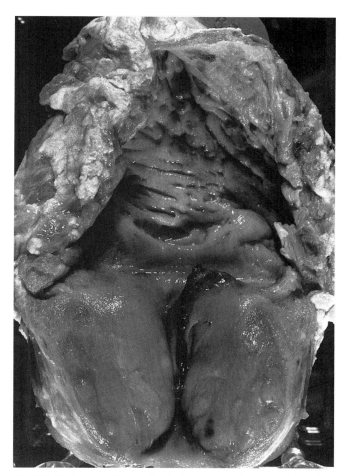

FIG. 8.31: **Benign prostatic hypertrophy.** The greatly enlarged prostate in the lower part of the picture surrounds and compresses the urethra, interfering with the outflow of urine from the bladder above it. The increased work required to force urine through the narrowed urethra has resulted in hypertrophy of the muscle in the bladder wall, reflected in the folds evident in its inner surface. Modern senile male. PBL.

Prostate

In males the urethra that drains the urinary bladder traverses the normal, walnut-sized prostate gland after which it enters the penis. It is, therefore, not surprising that enlargement of the prostate gland will constrict the urethra, impairing emptying of the urinary bladder (Fig. 8.31). The most common reason for such increase in size is benign prostatic hypertrophy (BPH), an age-related change probably secondary to a not-well-understood hormonal action. The expanding prostate, however, may be due to a malignant change in the organ, that invades surrounding tissue, metastasizes to pelvic lymph nodes and to the spine where the vertebral response is frequently both lytic and proliferative ('osteoblastic').

Paleopathology

Since remedies for a distended bladder mentioned in the Ebers papyrus (Ebbell, 1937:p.60, col. 48) are not always linked to the presence of bladder stones, it is probable that at least some cases of vesical distention may have been due to prostatic enlargement. The failure to identify even normal-sized prostate tissue at autopsy in spontaneously as well as in many anthropogenically mummified bodies is probably the result of the same processes as those related to the testis (see above). Consequently, neither benign nor malignant forms of prostatic enlargement have appeared in the paleopathology literature.

Abnormalities of female internal genitalia

Normal ovaries respond at roughly monthly intervals to pituitary hormones by 'developing' one of the many ova pre-

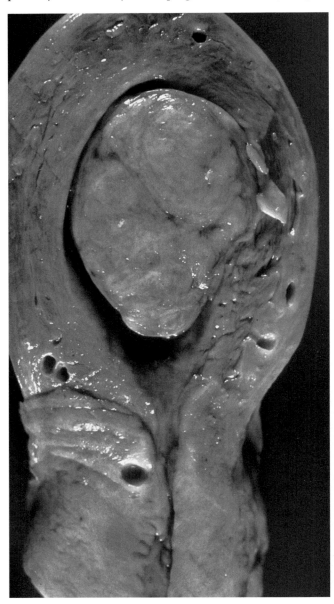

sent in adult ovaries. The uterine lining (endometrium) responds (by a rapid increase in thickness) to estrogen formed by the follicle of the developing ovum. About mid-cycle the ovarian-developed follicle ruptures, releasing the ovum which is drawn into the fallopian tube (salpinx) and transported to the uterine cavity on a layer of mucus propelled by the whip-like action of cilia on the surface of the tube's lining cells. Following follicular rupture the endometrium responds to progesterone now formed by the ovary and develops substantial and specialized mucous secretion, in anticipation of the needs of a fertilized ovum. If the ovum is not fertilized, ovarian secretions cease, the arterial supply of the now thickened, secreting endometrium undergoes clotting, the ischemic endometrium becomes necrotic and drains out of the uterus via the vagina as a trickle of bloody, necrotic debris (menstruation) after which the cycle is repeated.

Endometriosis

Endometriosis represents ectopic endometrium implanted outside the uterus, most commonly on the adnexal structures. Many of these respond to normal hormones and bleed. In their ectopic position, such recurrent hemorrhage into tissues of the tube and ovary commonly produces focal accumulation of old blood surrounded by a fibrous wall ('chocolate cyst').

Neoplasms

Abnormalities of menstrual chronology are commonly secondary to hormone production while changes in the amount of menstruation frequently are due to local organ pathology.

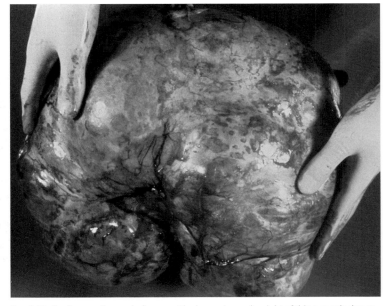

FIG. 8.33: **Benign ovarian cystadenoma.** The huge size and weight of this tumor is due to the fluid secreted by its lining cells and which collects in the smaller cysts within the main tumor. Modern middle-aged adult female. PBL.

FIG. 8.32: **Leiomyoma.** A 3.0 x 2.0 cm benign tumor of smooth muscle cells, arising in the smooth muscle of the uterine wall, is growing into the uterine lumen. In other examples it may be found entirely within the wall or projecting from the surface. Infarction with calcification is common in these benign tumors. Modern 43 year old female. PBL.

Those of interest to the paleopathologist are tumors affecting the endometrium. The endometrial mucosa covering the thumb-sized endometrial polyps often demonstrate surface mucosal erosion with subsequent bleeding unrelated to menstruation. The thick mass of smooth muscle constituting the uterus often produces benign smooth muscle tumors (leiomyomas: Fig. 8.32). Their twisted bundles of muscle frequently compress the tumor's blood vessels and occasional arteries undergo thrombosis, causing a local area of infarction in the tumor. Such necrotic tissue may liquefy and be absorbed, healing by scar formation, or it may be replaced by calcification. If the tumor is located under the endometrium, the mucosa may be stretched, become ischemic and bleed,

also resulting in vaginal bleeding not related to menstruation. Endometrial carcinoma usually ulcerates and causes bloody discharge. Untreated it invades the uterine wall and adjacent tissues including the bladder, adnexae (tubes and ovaries) and bowel, metastasizing to pelvic lymph nodes. These painful masses may destroy the tissues they occupy and produce dense adhesions. Carcinoma may also begin in the cervix, causing ulceration and a bloody discharge. Cervical carcinoma is probably related to strains of the human papilloma virus (which also causes anogenital warts), and spreads in a manner similar to that of endometrial carcinoma.

While pathology texts commonly present a bewildering complex of ovarian neoplasms, the postmortem loss of epithelium prevents the paleopathologist from identifying most of the specific histological types. A pragmatic paleopathological compromise, therefore, is to view ovarian tumors as either solid or cystic, each of which can display benign or malignant features. The lining cells of cystic tumors secrete a watery (serous) or a slimy (mucinous) fluid. Their size ranges from a few centimeters to some that have been reported to weigh more than 25 kg, almost all of it due to the contained fluid (Figs. 8.33 and 8.34). About one-third of serous cystadenomas are malignant while cancerous forms constitute only about one-tenth of the mucinous forms. A general, though not invariable rule is that the greater the mass of solid tissue within a cystic ovarian tumor, the more likely is its malignant nature (Fig. 8.35). The malignant forms tend to implant tumor cells at many sites on the peritoneal surface, each of which may grow into an independent tumor mass, interfering with bowel and other abdominal organ function, leading to death. A special form of cystic tumor unrelated to the above is a dermoid cyst, a cystic form of teratoma. Teratomas are tumors containing structures composed of all three germ layers (endoderm, mesoderm and ectoderm). When found in extraovarian locations most of these are solid, malignant tumors. Such may also occur in the ovary, but peculiarly, most ovarian teratomas are cystic and benign. Their cystic fluid is usually an oily secretion produced by glands of the skin tissue lining the cyst wall. The

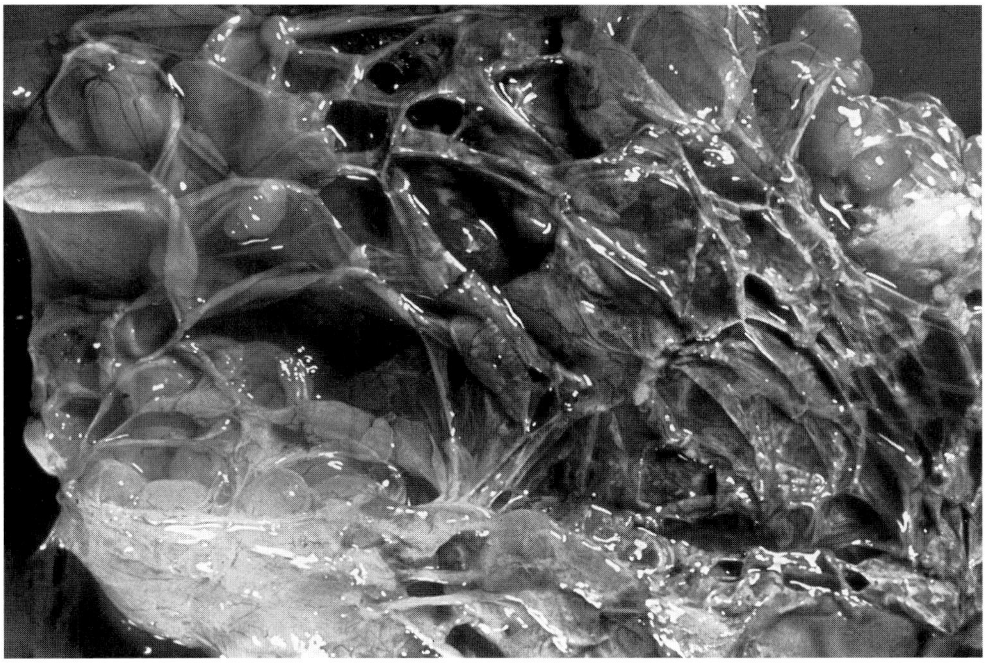

FIG. 8.34: **Benign ovarian cystadenoma.** Sectioned surface of tumor shown in Fig. 8.33. Note the multilocular internal structure (numerous smaller cysts) virtually devoid of solid tissue. Modern middle-aged adult female. PBL.

FIG. 8.35: **Ovary: cystadenocarcinoma.** Note the partly cystic and partly solid nature of this malignant cystic tumor. Modern adult female. PBL.

dermal elements in the tumor can also produce abundant hair. Especially striking is the production of calcified masses (in about 25–30 % of dermoid cysts) the majority of which prove to be malformed teeth, most prominently misshapen crowns that are radiologically and visually obvious (Figs. 8.36 & 13.16: Thornton, 1988).

Uterine prolapse

Prolapse of the vaginal mucosa or uterus occurs most commonly as a consequence of weakened pelvic ligaments and especially musculature, frequently following childbirth. Pressure of a urine-filled bladder or feces-laden rectum can push the vaginal mucosa toward and even through the vaginal orifice. The suspensory ligaments may permit the uterus to descend or actually protrude out beyond the labia.

Paleopathology of gynecological lesions

Apparent prolapse of the vagina, uterus or rectum are common forms of pseudopathology in mummified human remains. These are usually the consequence of postmortem fermentative processes with gas formation that result in intra-abdominal pressure increases, forcing viscera out of the available orifices (vagina, rectum or possibly even the para-esophageal area). We have seen one case in a spontaneously mummified body of the Chinchorro culture of northern Chile in which not only the uterus but both fallopian tubes and ovaries had prolapsed externally – undoubtedly a postmortem artifact. Smith & Wood-Jones (1910:268) feel, however, that a fibrous vaginal polyp may have been responsible for an antemortem vaginal mucosal prolapse in an adult Nubian female body from the Byzantine period, and in another from the same excavation area, a vaginal cyst had dragged the vaginal mucosa to the introitus. That uterine prolapse in living persons was familiar to Egyptian physicians is evidenced by the Ebers papyrus (Ebbell, 1937:p.109, col. 43): '…remedy to cause a woman's womb (uterus) to go to its place…' Janssens (1970:118) describes a vesicovaginal fistula in the mummified body of the Egyptian princess Hehenit of the eleventh dynasty, speculating it may have been the product of a protracted delivery.

At least two benign neoplasms of the uterine wall have been reported in archaeological bodies. These are believed to be smooth muscle tumors (leiomyomas, often called fibroids), but usually their survival of the postmortem decay process is enhanced by calcification of infarcted areas. Strouhal & Jungwirth (1977) found a 123 mm long nodular

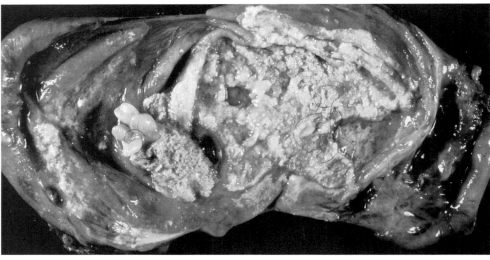

FIG. 8.36: **Benign ovarian teratoma ('dermoid cyst').** While structures of all three germ layers are usually present, in benign ovarian teratomas the ectodermal elements predominate. Epidermis lines the cyst, filling it with oily sebum from the sebaceous glands and hair from the skin's hair follicles. In addition malformed tooth crowns are commonly prominent in the cyst wall. The latter can be recognized by their malformed morphology when these are the only surviving tissues in skeletons. Modern adult female. PBL.

structure in the pelvis of an adult Nubian (Sayala) female skeleton dating to the third to fourth century A.D. It was extensively calcified but also demonstrated an organic matrix. Similarly, Kramar et al. (1983) also employed radiological, chemical, histological and ultrastructural techniques on a 50 mm calcified (hydroxyapatite) mass that was also found to contain collagen; this mass was associated with a group of human skeletons from a 5000 year old Neolithic burial ground in Switzerland. In both cases uterine leiomyoma seems the most probable diagnosis.

One would expect that the malformed teeth found in about one-third of ovarian benign teratomas (dermoid cysts) would have been identified even in skeletonized bodies but we have not been able to find such a report. Their small size and atypical appearance may escape attention at excavation and dissection of mummies, but in skeletons only awareness of the significance of finding isolated, misshapen teeth would lead to the diagnosis (Thornton, 1988). While no malignant tumors of female internal genitalia have been identified in mummified bodies, the Ebers papyrus suggests that Egyptian physicians may have been aware of them (Ebbell, 1937: p.111, col. 45): 'Remedy against "eating" [cancer?] in the womb which produces phagadena in her vagina.'

In addition to the above we have a description of an adult Egyptian mummy dissected by Granville (1825: 298) in which he states that '…the disease which appears to have destroyed her was ovarian dropsy attended with structural derangement of the uterine system general…' He also notes that the uterus was larger than that expected in a 50–55 year old woman, that there must have been '…a large sac connected with the left ovarium…' and that '…the ovarium and broad ligament of the right side are enveloped in a mass of diseased structure…' and that the right fallopian tube is normal. Figure 1 of Plate XXII (Granville, 1825: p.316) contains a drawing purporting to give evidence of these changes. The drawing reveals a normal-appearing right tube with the right ovary and parametrial tissues in a tangle of structures continuous with and overlying much of the uterine body. The upper part of what appears to be a bulbous uterus emerges from behind these tangled structures. The left tube area is shredded into three linear, strap-like structures terminating in two, rounded folds. Granville's interpretation of what today would probably be called bilateral ovarian cystadenomas or cystadenocarcinomas is consistent with this drawing. The uterus would not be expected to show a substantial enlargement without distortion of its form if it were invaded. The cystic nature of the lesions is not obvious in the drawing. If the lesions were not cystic, other causes need to be considered. Alternatively, malignancy of the uterus (either endometrial or cervical) with parametrial invasion is also possible. Even a simple cystadenoma of the left ovary and late stage pelvic inflammatory disease of the right ovary and parametrium cannot be excluded (though the uninvolved right tube would make that unlikely: see Fig. 1.3).

Pregnancy-related conditions

Ectopic pregnancy and abortion

We can expect women in antiquity to have been vulnerable to all of the pathophysiological, metabolic and hemorrhagic hazards of pregnancy as well as those relating to the placenta, to parturition and to postpartum complications.

Normally the ovum meets the sperm and is fertilized during its traverse through the fallopian tube, though sometimes this encounter occurs prior to entry into the salpinx. If the fertilized ovum never enters the tube, it may implant on the ovary (rarely the peritoneal surface). If its passage through the fallopian tube is delayed or arrested (often by mucosal scarring from previous infection with associated lack of mucus propulsion due to loss of ciliated mucosal cells), implantation in the tube (ectopic pregnancy) may occur. The latter is by far the most frequent ectopic site. The hazard at an ectopic site is one of hemorrhage, since the placenta invading the structure supporting the ectopic implantation commonly penetrates the full thickness of the supporting tissue. In the tube this occurs about a month after implantation (6 weeks after the last menstrual period). The external surface, with its exposed, highly vascular placental base, may result in serious and even lethal, sudden intra-abdominal hemorrhage (Fig. 8.37). Ovarian implantations may survive a few weeks longer but suffer the same hemorrhagic hazard. The muscle underlying peritoneal implantation sites, however, may support fetal growth into the third trimester.

A substantial fraction of pregnancies today terminate in spontaneous abortion – most in the first trimester. Death of the developing embryo is usually followed by placental necrosis as well. The entire necrotic mass may be sloughed with little greater bleeding than that anticipated in a normal menstrual period. Incomplete placental necrosis with continuing circulation of blood into the non-necrotic portion may result in more abundant bleeding and occasionally this can be life-threatening without some form of surgical intervention. The more advanced the pregnancy, the more probable is serious hemorrhage when spontaneous abortion occurs.

Paleopathology of ectopic pregnancy and abortion

Since almost 1 % of pregnancies implant at ectopic sites today, and since 90 % of these are in the tube, the soft tissue paleopathologist has a reasonable expectation of encountering this complication. In spite of these statistics, the condition has not been reported. If it has not been overlooked, the most likely reason for its absence is that the principal risk factor (pelvic inflammatory disease complicating gonorrheal or chlamydial venereal infections) was rare or did not exist in antiquity. While the lesion in the tube might not be identified with ease, the exsanguinating abdominal hemorrhage would be obvious.

A large number of abortions today are secondary to nonviable chromosomal damage or gross DNA alterations, so it is probable that this problem also plagued the women of ancient populations. Lethal hemorrhage from this source may not be obvious in a

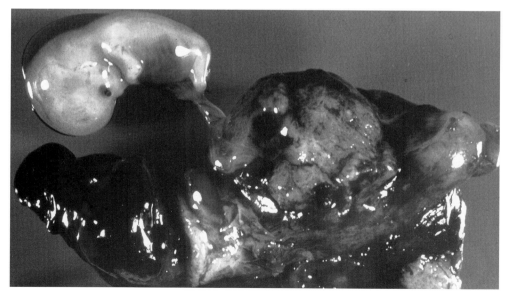

FIG. 8.37: **Fallopian tube: ruptured ectopic tubal pregnancy.** The placental growth has expanded the diameter of the tube. Complete placental penetration of the tube wall resulted in hemorrhage, rupture of the tube and expulsion of the fetus. Modern young adult female. PBL.

mummified body. Residual blood may still be found in the uterus or even the vagina, though the latter area may be cleaned by those preparing the body for burial. Furthermore, abortion may occur so early that the uterine enlargement may not be overt either. Control of family size may have included induced abortion by amniotic sac perforation in some ancient groups. This would surely have involved a greater hazard of hemorrhage because it most probably would have been performed at a somewhat later stage of pregnancy and the lack of aseptic technique can be expected to have been followed by a substantial increase in uterine infections. Whether or not abortion was induced (usually by a probe or chemicals as some were: Sandison & Wells, 1967:499) would not be readily detectable but the exudate in the uterus and its thickened wall together with parametrial tissue involvement might well betray the infectious complication.

Lithopedion

In exceptional circumstances (about 0.0005 % of all pregnancies) the dead fetus and pregnancy products become necrotic but are not expelled by the uterus. A few rare examples of this have been reported in cases of normal, intrauterine implantation, but the overwhelming majority are the product of ectopic, intra-abdominal, extrauterine implantation of the fertilized ovum. Christianson (1992) describes the earlier postmortem stages in swine. Autolysis of the fetus is initiated promptly after death with resulting edema and swelling of the body. This swelling may be equivalent to the human form of hydrops fetalis: an immediately premortem event in the human fetus. Uterine absorption of the fluid converts the body into a desiccated, shriveled 'mummy'. Such necrotic tissue will occasionally undergo dystrophic calcification. The form of the fetus is retained and often remains easily recognizable. More than 100 years ago Küchenmeister (1881) described the three forms such calcification may take, involving (i) only the membranes: lithokelyphos; (ii) both membranes and fetus: lithokelyphopedion (Fig. 8.38); and (iii) only the fetus: lithopedion. This useful classification is still employed today. The three forms of lithopedion may remain in situ for years and such women may be otherwise asymptomatic, although erosion of the bones into the colon may result in their eventual expulsion. More than 300 cases of such retained, calcified feti and/or pregnancy products have been reported (Spirtos et al., 1987).

Rothschild et al. (1994) found vertebrae and calcified membranes of a lithokelyphopedion in the level corresponding to 3100 years B.C. of a Texas sinkhole used as a burial site in Texas' archaic period. Their diagnosis rests entirely on the assumption that the concave calcified mass represents calcified placental membranes. This is a reasonable assumption, but weakened by its burial context. Had it been found in an isolated, adult burial, certainty would have been enhanced. The next-oldest case was reported by Caspar Bauhin (1586) followed by several other sixteenth century physicians cited by King (1954) and D'Aunoy & King (1922).

Eclampsia

During the later stages of pregnancy certain poorly understood physiological changes may occur that are grouped under the term eclampsia. This condition is characterized by a constellation of findings, the principal ones of which include hypertension, acute renal failure, convulsions and multifocal areas of hemorrhage. The kidney and brain lesions may be fatal. The glomerular changes are too subtle to expect them to be identifiable in a mummified body, but the uremic pericarditis with precipitated exudate on the visceral pericardium can be recognized grossly. The focal hemorrhages in the brain, liver or other organs are usually large enough to be apparent. Thus the finding of a fetus consistent with the third trimester in a mummified body showing either pericardial exudate and/or brain or other hemorrhages can suggest this diagnosis. To date it has not been reported in the paleopathology literature.

FIG. 8.38: **Lithokelyphopedion.** Both the calcified placental membranes (lithokelyphos) and calcified parts of the infant's lower extremities (lithopedion) are evident. Provenance data unavailable but specimen is from modern adult female. NMHM.

FIG. 8.39: **Obstructed birth canal.** Maternal female skeleton with near term fetal bones in pelvic area arranged in transverse (undeliverable) position. Note the right humerus present in the birth canal. All fetal bones were present except right forearm and hand. Young adult female, A.D. 1100. Personal communication, Joseph Bohlen, M.D., Springfield, IL.

secondary to nutritional deficiency (rickets), fracture deformations, infections (Micozzi, 1982) or skeletal neoplasms. While such problems today are dealt with surgically (cesarean section), in antiquity they could represent a survival threat to both mother and child. In marginal situations a good deal of soft tissue molding can permit eventual passage, but cranial dimensions dictate the ultimate parameters. On the other hand, certain fetal positions are incompatible with delivery, but conceivably in antiquity efforts (sometimes successful?) might be made by those attending the mother to alter the position.

Paleopathology of birth obstructions

The paleopathology literature provides examples of both types of problems. A pelvis deformed by the presence of multiple exostoses provided so much obstruction to fetal passage that it completely blocked delivery of a mature fetus in a medieval woman. The mother's skeleton with its restrictive pelvis was found with that of a full term child in the birth position (Sjovold *et al.*, 1974). In another case (Joseph G. Bohlen, pers. comm.) the mother's skeletonized body was found with that of the fetus in a transverse position but lacking an arm. The missing arm may represent an unsuccessful effort to extract the fetus, though it could of course have been amputated postmortem (Fig. 8.39). Williams (1929) also cites a description by Derry of a negress (in a Coptic cemetery) whose congenitally absent right sacroiliac joint and small right innominate bone narrowed the birth canal sufficiently to result in impaction of the fetal head at the constricted site. More recently van Gerven (1981) identified the skeleton of a Nubian woman from the Christian period who died with a term fetus in a breech position in the birth canal. A similar case has been reported by Regöly-Mérei (1961), cited in Sandison & Wells (1967).

Placenta previa

During labor two major maternal problems may occur: hemorrhage and obstruction to fetal passage; lesser but still major concerns include perineal lacerations. The lacerations themselves may result in vesicovaginal or rectovaginal fistulae. The past Arabian custom of packing the vagina with salt may initiate enough inflammation to generate such fistulae even without lacerations (Naim & Fahmy, 1965). Hemorrhage can be life-threatening in cases of placenta previa. In this circumstance the ovum implants in the lower portion of the uterus and part of its placenta may lie across the internal cervical os. Thus during labor that opening expands to allow the fetus exitus from the uterus. As it opens (usually to about 10 cm) the portion of the placenta covering it is torn. Resulting hemorrhage may be minor, especially if the amniotic sac ruptures and permits the fetal head to descend to the cervix and compress the placenta there. If the placenta completely covers the cervical exit area, however, the bleeding may be so major as to be fatal. Since, in antiquity, the infant might well be allowed to remain in situ at burial, this condition could be recognizable in a mummy. There is, however, no such report as yet.

Obstruction to fetal passage

This commonly is due to abnormal pelvic skeletal structure or an atypical fetal position. Skeletal alterations can be

Postpartum complications

These include infection (puerperal sepsis), placental hemorrhage and uterine prolapse. Infection of a recently pregnant uterus often produces septicemia quite abruptly. Occasionally maternal feces contain *Clostridium perfringens* and if the uterus becomes contaminated by such feces postpartum, gas gangrene septicemia may occur with fatal results. Such contamination may occur via manipulation by midwives (e.g. efforts to assist in expulsion of the placenta). Indeed, recognition of the cause of puerperal sepsis through contamination by attending physicians did not occur until 1795 when Gordon called attention to it and Semmelweis popularized the value of aseptic obstetrical techniques about 40 years later (Lowis, 1993).

In mummies puerperal fever may be so fulminant that only the indications of pregnancy may be apparent. If the process was less fulminant, intrauterine exudate and involvement of parametrial tissues may suggest the diagnosis. A 'foamy liver' (Fig. 8.14) in a mummy with signs of recent birth can reflect puerperal fever due to *Clostrium perfringes*.

Hemorrhage secondary to abruptio placenta may occur at this stage of pregnancy. In this condition the placenta is only partially separated from the uterine lining by uterine contractions. The opened veins may then suck in sufficient amniotic fluid to cause intravascular coagulation that depletes the blood's coagulation proteins, producing major or lethal hemorrhage. In a mummified body evidence of the multiple areas of hemorrhage in various organs and tissues of a body also showing signs of term pregnancy or recent delivery could imply this diagnosis. However, we could find no report of such a case in antiquity. In placenta accreta, the placenta can not be separated from the uterus after delivery due to fibrotic changes. This can also result in serious hemorrhage, and in mummies at least part of the placenta would be found still attached within the uterus.

At least one case of perineal laceration with resulting fistula between the bladder and vagina has been reported (Williams, 1929). Rabino-Massa (1982) has also demonstrated that a prolapsed uterus in an Egyptian naturally mummified body buried with a newborn child' was an antemortem finding by presenting histological evidence that the uterus showed complete inversion.

Maternal mortality in antiquity is difficult to evaluate. The expression of mortality rates in many ancient populations often demonstrates a distinct increase in female deaths in the 20–25 year age group (see Manchester, 1983a:9, figure 5). This is commonly interpreted as pregnancy-related deaths, though little supportive, specific physical evidence of such a cause is available. Mafart (1994), however, suggests that the maternal mortality in two French skeletal series from the fifth/sixth and the eleventh/twelfth centuries A.D. did identify childbearing risks, but that these were quantitatively insufficient to contribute significantly to the general female mortality. Interpretation of this demographic feature requires further analysis involving demonstrated causes of death. Increasing mummy studies may render this possible in the future.

A highly informative study of maternal mortality was carried out by Arriaza et al. (1988) on 18 examples of childbirth-complicated deaths extracted from 128 female, spontaneously-mummified bodies of childbearing age (12–45 years) who lived in a single northern Chile valley over an interval of 2700 years. This would suggest a maternal mortal-

ity rate of about 14 %. This is in sharp contrast to the approximately 1 % value in rural parts of undeveloped countries today (Harker, 1993). The large difference in these two figures probably lies in the small sample of the study involving ancient populations. These workers found that 3 of their 18 bodies had failed to complete delivery (one was breech presentation, one had failed to deliver the second twin and the third died of unknown causes with a 7–8 month fetus in the uterus – eclampsia?). The cause of death in the remainder was not obvious, but occurred in the puerperium, though in several the placenta was still present. Of diagnostic value for the recognition of death during or a short period before or after parturition are the intrauterine presence of a fetus, presence of placenta or umbilical cord, enlarged uterus, many redundant abdominal skin folds, lactating breasts as well as separation of the pubic symphysis and/or sacroiliac joint.

BREAST DISEASES

Normal

The normal human breast consists of 5–12 clusters of potentially milk-forming, glandular tissue separated by loose fibrous tissue interwoven with a variable amount of fat. Each cluster is drained by a duct leading to the nipple. Substantial differences in fat and fibrous content lead to a significant normal variation in size, texture and morphology not necessarily dependent on somatic size or total body fat. In addition the cells composing the ductular and glandular tissue contain estrogen and progesterone receptors, and thus respond to these blood hormone level fluctuations, both those involved in the normal menstrual cycle as well as in pregnancy. Thus the newborn breast of either gender will demonstrate a transient increase in the neonatal period in response to the maternal estrogen stimulus at term, and again at puberty (regularly in the female and transiently in some males). The prolonged estrogen elevations of pregnancy provide time for substantial increase in glandular tissue at the expense of the fat, with a further response to other hormones during the later pregnancy stages leading to production of milk. The retardation of ovarian function after menopause drops the blood estrogen level to the low quantities contributed primarily by the adrenal cortex, and the breast glandular tissue undergoes substantial atrophy, though only in the advanced elderly state does the glandular tissue virtually disappear, merely the ducts remaining embedded in fibrous stroma.

Prior to the domestication of cattle, the importance of the human breast was obvious: it was essential for the survival of the infant and, therefore, for that of the population. Human milk supplies all of the infant's essential nutrients except vitamin D and iron. The maternal antibodies of the IgG class present in the milk cross the placenta and provide at least a useful degree of protection until the infant's immune system can supply its own. Even the transient decline in body iron content in the purely milk-fed infant may have had some beneficial inhibitory effect against infection because most pathological bacteria require an abundant, readily available iron supply from their environment (Stuart-Macadam & Kent, 1992:5). Bottle-feeding with baby food 'formulas' has been associated with a striking increase in infant mortality in developing countries, due principally to lack of aseptic techniques with resulting infectious infant diarrhea (Lithell, 1981). Weaning time also influences infant mortality. Prema-

ture withdrawal of breast feeding may introduce pathogenic bacteria into the infant's intestine before its immune system is prepared to deal effectively with them resulting in similar infections (Rothschild & Chapman, 1981:586). Furthermore, lactation prolongs the postnatal period of amenorrhea with its associated lowered fertility level (Ellison, 1987).

Infectious lesions

In spite of every precautionary effort, even modern breast-feeding practices place the breast at increased risk for infection. Staphylococci, streptococci or other organisms may gain access to the dermal areas through small skin fissures. The resulting infection may spread widely and rapidly in the form of a cellulitis (commonly caused by streptococci) or, more frequently, produce a localized abscess (usually staphylococci). Untreated either of these, but especially the former, may spread to the blood stream and represent a threat to the mother. The localized lesions often drain spontaneously. The nursing infant is at risk in either form of infection. The localized abscess may reach substantial proportions, and usually heals by scar formation that may distort the breast.

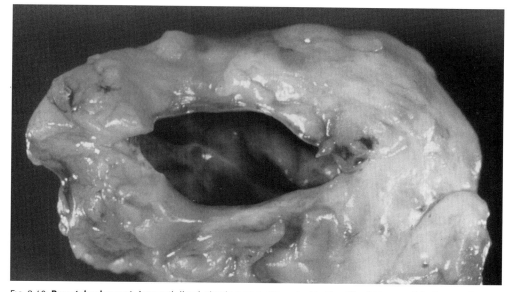

FIG. 8.40: **Breast: benign cyst.** A smooth-lined, simple 2 cm cyst is embedded in a fibrofatty area of the breast. These are very common in western countries today, and their size varies from microscopic to several centimeters in diameter. If they were present in antiquity, they would be expected to be recognizable in mummified human remains. Modern young adult female. PBL.

Fibrocystic disease of the breast

The cause of the condition in unknown but manifests as either the formation of one or more cysts within the breast, as foci of dense fibrosis or, most commonly, as both. The cysts may be diminutive but can reach 5 or 6 cm in diameter (Fig. 8.40). They are lined by epithelium similar to that lining normal breast ducts. Hence they frequently contain estrogen receptors and enlarge and become tender at certain stages of the menstrual cycle. This disease is very common in western countries today and usually appears during the late second or third decade of life. Except for a small subgroup that also demonstrates marked epithelial hyperplasia with dysplasia microscopically, the condition is benign.

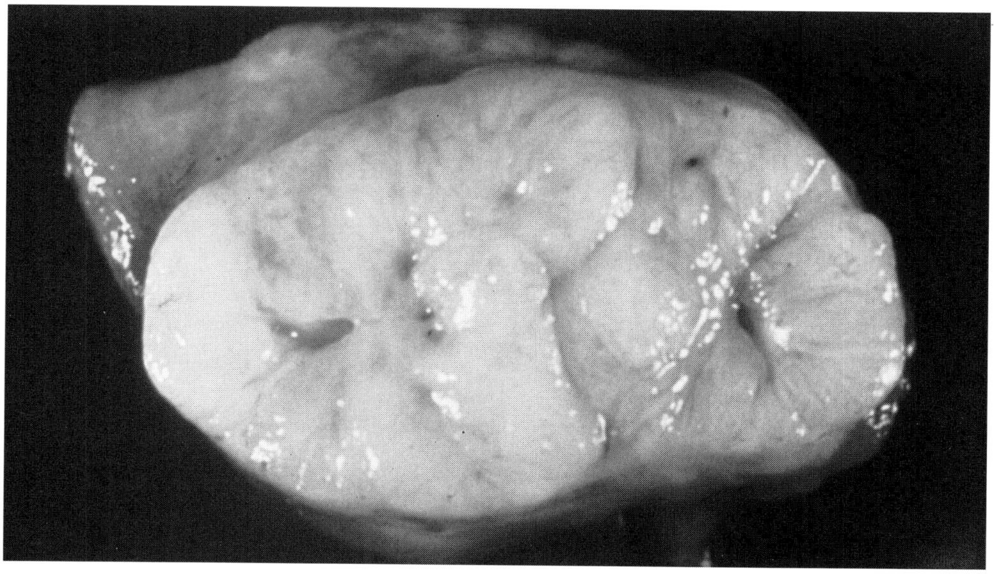

FIG. 8.41: **Breast: benign fibroadenoma.** A 3.5 x 2 x 2 cm white, predominantly fibrous breast nodule has been excised surgically. Its sharply demarcated periphery suggests benignity. Because of its almost exclusively fibrous tissue component this lesion has a high probability of remaining intact in a mummified body. Modern young adult female. PBL.

Neoplasms of the breast

Fibroadenoma

The most common breast tumor is a benign, sharply circumscribed lesion called fibroadenoma (Fig. 8.41). Its size varies from a nearly microscopic dimension to 4 or 5 cm. It is usually discovered and removed surgically when it is about 2 or 3 cm in diameter. It afflicts the same age group as fibrocystic disease, with which it occasionally coexists. Its histology is a simple mixture of breast ducts entwined within and compressed by lobules of fibrous tissue.

Papilloma

A far less common tumor of the breast is an intraductal papilloma. This is a benign, branching tumor with a tree-like structure. It arises as a solitary lesion in one of the main ducts along its course to the nipple. It seldom exceeds 2 cm in diameter and is so fragile that normal pressures on the breast may break off an 'arm' or 'branch', resulting in expulsion of a few drops of bleed from the nipple (which is the usual initial symptom). With few exceptions this, too, is a benign lesion.

Carcinoma

Carcinoma arising in the breast is the most feared neoplasm. It occurs infrequently in women less than 30 years of age, its frequency then rising subsequently with progressive age. Most cases occur after menopause. Variations in gross and microscopic features as well as location are enormous. Nevertheless, the most common forms are characterized by tissue hardness due to an abundant fibrous stroma that often shows focally calcified areas ('scirrhous' carcinoma). The tumor causes necrosis of normal structures, replacing them with tumor growth until a mass of about 1 cm or more is reached. Quite commonly tumor cells then infiltrate along local structures, resulting in a central tumor 'body' with numerous, linear extensions radiating from it

into surrounding tissues in every plane (Fig. 8.42). This gross appearance of a central mass with peripheral extensions suggested the structure of a crab to the early pathologists, leading to the term 'cancer' (Latin term for crab) for this and any other malignant tumor.

Untreated the tumor commonly extends to the breast's skin surface (Fig. 8.43) where it ulcerates and usually becomes infected (a stage one would expect in archaeological bodies if breast cancer occured in antiquity). It also may

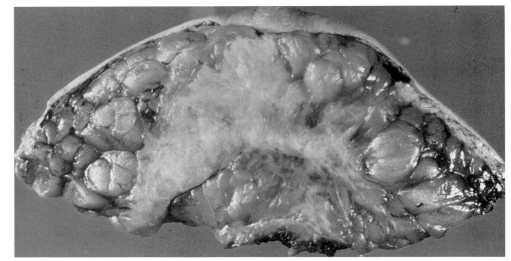

FIG. 8.42: **Breast: scirrhous carcinoma.** The breast has been bisected through the tumor. The nipple-containing skin is at the top of the photograph. The underlying breast tissue demonstrates the lobulated, fatty appearance of a non-lactating breast, much of which has been replaced centrally by an irregularly-shaped mass of white cancer tissue. This was hard (scirrhous) to palpation and at its periphery poorly-defined, finger-like extensions blend with the fatty tissue where the cancer is invading it. Modern adult female. PBL.

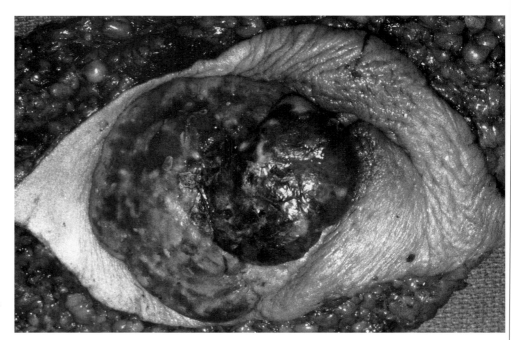

FIG. 8.43: **Breast: late stage carcinoma.** The cancer has extended through the skin. Its continuing expansion has caused it to project as an irregular mass above the level of the surrounding skin. If breast cancer occurred in antiquity one would anticipate that its untreated course would bring it to this easily recognized stage at the time of death frequently. Modern aged adult female. PBL.

grow into the chest wall, penetrate it and induce pleural effusion or even invade the lung. In later stages it spreads to the nodes draining lymph from the area. The most evident involved nodes are usually those in the axilla on the same side, though those above the clavicle or in the retrosternal regions are often involved as well. Finally, spread (metastasis) may occur through the blood stream, which can carry tumor cells to any organ in the body. Though no patterns of metastatic areas are unique to breast carcinoma, soft tissue sites that are particularly common include the lung and liver. In end-stage disease bones are often involved by metastases that are usually of lytic nature, though a minority induce distinct and even obvious osteoblastic features (see Chapter 13 (Neoplastic conditions)).

Gynecomastia

Enlargement of the male breast is called gynecomastia (literally: female breast). At birth and during childhood the histology of both male and female breasts is identical: simple ducts surrounded by fibrous tissue. Throughout life, in fact, male breast lining cells remain sensitive to estrogen as manifested by their identical response at birth and initially at puberty as outlined above. In females the rising and sustained estrogen and progesterone production from the ovary stimulates continued cellular proliferation with the final development of the glandular breast elements. In the male, normally testicular androgen production causes the stimulated cellular proliferation to cease and finally to subside, returning it to the prepubertal state. In addition, as in the female, small amounts of estrogen are also made by the male adrenal cortex (the testis also generates small quantities of estrogen precursors that can be converted into estrogen by enzymes in fat and muscle). Thus maintenance of the appropriate ratio of (large amounts of testicular-formed) testosterone to (the adrenal and extra-testicular sources of) estrogen will maintain a male breast in its usual atrophic, adult form. When the male ages and develops testicular atrophy, the testosterone level drops, and his breast elements may once again respond to the proliferative stimulus of endogenous estrogen that continues to be secreted from the extragonadal sources.

This discussion makes it clear that the male breast is free to respond to an estrogenic stimulus if the testosterone: estrogen ratio (about 300:1) is altered by either an increase in estrogen or decrease in testosterone. The latter is characteristic of the elderly male with testicular atrophy or the genetic XXY abnormality known as Klinefelter's syndrome in which no functioning testicular tissue is formed. Increased estrogen in males has several potential mechanisms that include estrogen-secreting testicular tumors or a variety of genetic mutations that affect the function of extragonadal enzymes that convert testicular precursors into estrogen, or that can block the action of testosterone on the breast cells. Some drugs (digitoxin, marijuana) can also duplicate these effects (Wilson, 1991c; Braunstein, 1993). Cirrhosis or other chronic liver injury (drugs) can reduce the liver's ability to metabolize and destroy estrogen, raising the effective estrogen level.

With this admittedly unpretentious background, the ongoing controversy of the presentation of apparent gynecomastia in certain royal Egyptian families presented below can be understood.

Paleopathological aspects of the breast

Appearance of the mummified breast

In addition to the variations in the size of the normal, resting (i. e. non-lactating) breast in living women, further variations are added by differing ratios of glandular:fat tissue (Fig. 8.44). Postmortem hydrolysis of neutral fat by endogenous and bacterial enzymes generates fatty acids which, in an alkaline environment become ionized and removable by groundwater (or seep diffusely into surrounding tissues). In women with a low glandular:fat breast tissue ration, removal of breast fat by the processes mentioned above can collapse the breast of a spontaneously mummified

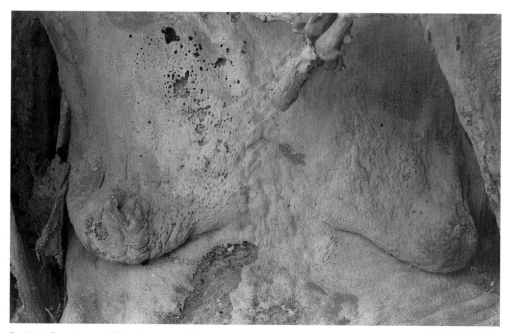

FIG. 8.44: **Breast: normal.** Varying rates and degrees of postmortem breast fat hydrolysis results in a wide range of breast prominence in spontaneously mummified bodies. Some, like this example, are obvious, but we have found sufficiently well-preserved breast tissue to permit gender identification in only about half of spontaneously mummified female human remains. Spontaneously mummified female, 55–60 years old, southern Peru, A.D. 1100. PBL.

body to a degree that minimizes the breast morphology beyond recognition. In an unpublished study by one of us (A.C.A.) the gender of only about half of spontaneously mummified adult, nonpregnant female bodies were identifiable with certainty on the basis of a grossly recognizable breast. Transection of nonpregnant and nonlactating breasts reveals what one would expect, since epithelium does not normally survive the postmortem environment: the 'fibrous skeleton' of the breast remains in the form of interconnecting, fibrous 'leaves' separated by empty space. In such a breast, scars from previous abscesses would not be easy to detect, but most invasive carcinomas would be overt, demonstrating a hard, fibrous mass of at least several centimeters in size, often ulcerating, with irregular peripheral 'fingers' reaching the skin surface and/or chest wall, and with secondary axillary masses. To date, no such lesion has been described in a mummy.

Lactating breasts, or those in later stages of pregnancy, however, are commonly obvious grossly. Histologically the glandular pattern can even be recognized after the epithelium has degenerated (Zimmerman & Aufderheide, 1984).

The breast as symbol

One would expect to find diseases affecting an external organ so visible, accessible and vital to the ancients as was the breast, to be well-represented in ancient lore, literature and art. The fact that they are not, suggests that the conditions of principal concern affecting the breast in modern populations (benign fibrocystic disease and carcinoma) may not have been common problems in antiquity. It is true that the female breast is a central feature in many items of ancient art, but it is employed there primarily in a symbolic manner, usually to represent fertility. The so-called 'Venus figures' (Lyons & Petrucelli; 1987: figure 16, p. 24) of paleolithic and mesolithic times demonstrate grotesque exaggeration of breast size, almost surely intended as symbolism (though at least one author has viewed them as literally representations of the pathological condition called 'massive' or 'virginal' breast hypertrophy: Harding, 1976). During the Hellinistic period we have no better example than the statue of Artemis in her temple at Ephesus where her nurturing character is portrayed as a human female body with 16 breasts. The importance of the breast in antiquity can be appreciated by noting that this organ was elevated to the level of divinity in Egypt (Hathor, the cow goddess) and reliefs demonstrate pharaohs and even commoners sucking at the teats of Hathor's exaggerated udder (Strouhal, 1992:25). The later Romans repeated the icon, substituting a wolf suckling Romulus and Remus, Rome's legendary founders. The breast is also occasionally used to symbolize close emotional attachment, as in the Chinese statuette demonstrating a woman breast-feeding her aged grandfather (Lyons & Petrucelli, 1987: figure 192, p. 122). A similar principle undoubtedly led to the former occasional Inuit practice of a mother greet-

ing an adult child (returning from a prolonged absence) by exposing her breast to which her child responded by kissing it. The nutritive image of the breast is also evident in an antipodal mode among the Amazons — a legendary tribe composed entirely of bellicose females whose armies beheaded or subjugated males. Whether or not the tale is based upon a historical group, as Schechter (1962) seems to feel, is less important for our consideration than that they were believed to have amputated their right breast in order to enhance the use of their weaponry.

Paleopathological aspects of breast feeding

Most of these relate to symbolism and have been dealt with in the first part of this section. In addition, we may note that weaning times were probably much later than at present. Aufderheide & Allison (1994) have used bone strontium levels to predict weaning in pre-Columbian, pre-ceramic natives of northern Chile, estimating the weaning time to have occurred between 2 and 3 years. Nitrogen stable isotope ratios may achieve similar predictions (Fogel et al., 1989). Sandison & Wells (1967) identify the weaning time in Mesopotamia and ancient Egypt at about 3 years, presumably based on literary sources. The vulnerability of the recently-weaned infant to enteric infections was also pointed out by Strouhal (1992:23) who found that childhood mortality peaked in that age group. The Egyptian papyri contain only a few references to breast problems including recommendation for application of a lotion to 'a breast that is ill' (Ebbel, 1937, p. 110, col. 95), though Sandison & Wells (1967) cite the Edwin Smith papyrus with inflammatory (probably lactation-related) breast conditions including abscess. They also cite Soranus (Alexandrian physician practicing in Rome about A.D. 100) with the observation that sudden regression of the breast was predictive of impending spontaneous abortion. Strouhal (1992:22) describes an exotic lotion believed to have properties that would increase the flow in a mother's breast, and notes that most aristocratic Egyptian mothers contracted with wet-nurses who often came to play an important family role. Seventh century Mesopotamian texts include symptoms of and treatment for breast diseases (Saggs, 1962:462). Because of breast-feeding's importance, the adequacy of milk flow appears always to have been an item of concern to mothers. Even as late as the Aztec period, Ortiz de Montellano (1990: 178) cites Hernández (1577) as stating that Aztec mothers employed sympathetic magic in order to stimulate their flow of milk by rubbing their breast with plants that exude milky latex. Lactation may have been employed deliberately as a method of family planning in antiquity. Although viewed as a notoriously unreliable contraceptive regimen today, Ellison (1987) notes that breast-feeding an infant 'on demand' (i.e. about every 15 minutes as is done today in many remote groups and was probably so performed in antiquity) enormously enhances its anti-ovulatory effect. Such an effect has been documented by the annual pregnancies of upper-class Elizabethan women and the much lower fertility of the poorer women to whom breast-feeding of the wealthy women's children was commonly delegated (McLaren, 1979).

Thus, while there is clear literary and graphic evidence that mothers have concerned themselves with the adequacy of their breast milk productivity for many millennia, and that they at least occasionally suffered inflammatory complications of lactation including abscess formation, such lesions have not been reported in ancient human bodies.

Fibrocystic disease

With its densely fibrous areas and gross cysts it would be expected that fibrocystic disease would be recognized in ancient mummified bodies, yet to date we could find only one reported case. The explanation may lie in its modern, worldwide epidemiological features. Although its etiology remains undefined, today it is a condition found with significant frequency primarily in western developed countries (Hutt & Burkitt, 1986:115). Similarly, the fibroadenoma, composed primarily of fibrous tissue, would be easily identifiable, but only one of these (in an adult, Egyptian female) appears in the paleopathological literature (Reyman & Peck:1980:93). The intraductal papilloma, however, is almost entirely epithelial and is rare, so the absence of this tumor among paleopathological reports is not surprising.

Neoplasms

Historical sources and artistic representations, however, can help us trace the antiquity of breast cancer back several millennia. A reference in the Edmund Smith papyrus has been interpreted to refer to breast cancer (Breasted, 1930:403–6; Baum, 1993), but is now believed to be too insubstantial for such a diagnosis. The Syrian surgeon Archigenes wrote profusely about cancer of both breast and uterus about A.D. 125. Benedek & Kiple (1993) provide a valuable compilation of ancient sources relevant to breast cancer. The following items are abbreviated from their listing. The Alexandrian surgeon Leonides not only recognized but incised and cauterized malignant breast lesions, and Galen (ca. A.D. 129–201) suggested the cancer lesion represented a coagulum of black bile. The ninth century Arabic physician Rhazes (A.D. 850–932) warned that operating breast cancer only made it worse unless excision was complete and accompanied by cautery. By the seventeenth century operations for breast cancer included the axillary nodes. Sandison & Wells (1967) also feel that Celsus (25 B.C.–A.D. 50) was familiar with breast cancer.

Reading breast cancer into artistic displays, however, is less convincing. Few examples of graphic art better exemplify the hazards of making medical diagnoses of artistic representations than that of Michaelangelo's La Notte (Night). On opposite walls of the Florentine Medici chapel lie the bodies of two, politically important Medici dukes, encased within sarcophagi. Above each the artist has created an exquisitely carved likeness of the entombed individuals. Two additional nude figures (one male and one female) are placed on the lid of each sarcophagus. The males are labeled Day and Dusk while the females are Dawn and Night. Michaelangelo considered this a major work and devoted a significant fraction of his working years to it.

Interest is directed at the breasts of Night (La Notte). These are deformed by multiple surface depressions up to about 5 cm in diameter, without evidence of ulceration. These 'lesions' have led to varying interpretations by several different professionals. Medically-trained persons are apt to agree with Rosenzweig (1983) that they represent the characteristic appearance of skin retraction produced by incorporation of the breast's Cooper's ligaments into a deep-lying scirrhous carcinoma. After viewing the statue, one of us (A.C.A.) felt that was certainly a serious consideration, but that other scarring processes such as healed fat necrosis or breast abscesses could duplicate such an appearance. Some poetic-minded viewers note that the physical features of the entire bodies of all four figures would be consistent with an interpretation that they represent the four stages of life: birth (Dawn), maturity (Day), decline (Dusk), and death (Night), and that the breast deformation of the latter simply indicates organ disintegration leading to death. On the other hand, viewers knowledgable about all other aspects of an artist's life and works (such as art historians) may incorporate this additional information into their judgments. Levy (1965:70) feels that 'the breast deformities reflect the deliberate expression of Michaelangelo's hostility toward women'. We feel that the sculptor intended La Notte's deformations to symbolize the physical and – by extension – probably also mental and emotional deterioration and exhaustion of the pre-death state and may even have deliberately selected a model possessing these features. Whether or not he was aware of the specific nature and appearance of breast malignancy is an interesting intellectual diversion but makes no contribution to the history and antiquity of breast cancer since abundant evidence of greater certainty (some of which is listed above) testifies to its recognition many centuries prior to the Renaissance. Probably viewers from other backgrounds have generated still other interpretations, but those listed above are sufficient to remind us of the uncertainties inherent in many medical interpretations of iconography. An ancient Greek statuette illustrated by Long (1965: 6, plate 1) stated to be of votive nature demonstrates a similar deformity in the left breast, which Long also interprets as carcinoma, though this judgment is subject to the same constraints as those of Michaelangelo's sculpture. Thus, literary sources suggest recognition of breast carcinoma about 2000 years ago, though iconography contributes little unequivocally supportive evidence.

Carcinoma of the breast has been suggested as causing metastatic bone lesions in a skeletonized body of a female from about A.D. 750 in northern Chile, representing a

Tiwanaku-related culture. Both lytic and sclerotic lesions were identified in the skull, pelvis, spine and femur (Allison et al., 1980). As those authors point out, it is not possible to indict the breast unequivocally as the primary source of the metastases since the metastatic pattern can be duplicated by other tumors. The presence of both a lytic as well as an osteoblastic feature in the metastases increases the probability of the breast as the primary tumor but, like other suggested cases of such a primary source, it requires demonstration of the soft tissue lesion to be certain of that specific diagnosis. Furthermore, Zimmerman & Kelley (1982:207) remind us that '…there is not one single instance of a tissue diagnosis in mummies of cancer of the…breast…' Nevertheless, if breast cancer had been as frequent during antiquity as it is in the U.S.A. today, it would still require examination of a huge number of mummified bodies to establish a statistically valid assessment of its prevalence — so many, in fact, that the absence of any reported malignant tumor in breast soft tissues to date can not be used to imply its absence in antiquity.

Gynecomastia

As explained above, enlargement of the male breast can occur under certain normal, physiological as well as pathological circumstances. The abundance of Egyptian graphic art and statuary includes some apparent examples of the finding. Undoubtedly, the most well-known example is the breast prominence of Tutankhamun, his two brothers (Smenkhare and Amenophis IV, also known as Akhenaten) and his father, Amenophis III. While the exact relationships between these four is not known with certainty, the above listing seems to be a most popular one currently (Harrison et al., 1969). Their mothers, however, have not been established. The appropriate interpretation of these enlarged breasts in paintings, relief and statuary has been the object of intense controversy. Arguments have been made to support a long list of possibilities that include artistic license (Drioton, 1950:84–9; Harrison, 1973; Hawkes, 1973:438; Swales, 1973; Taitz, 1973), mytho-theological significance (Fazzini, 1975:65); political significance (Fairman, 1972), acquired medical condition (Aldred, 1963; Ghalioungui, 1965:18, figure 37, schistosomal liver cirrhosis; Weller, 1972, adrenal feminizing tumor) and pathological medical genetic anomalies (Walshe, 1973, Klinefelter's syndrome (KS) or Wilson's disease (WD); Paulshock, 1980, familial gynecomastia). Many of the arguments supportive of or conflicting with these diagnoses are reviewed in Paulshock (1980). There are, however, other examples of enlarged breasts in Egyptian iconography: two Nile gods with obvious breasts are depicted on a ostracon from the Ramesside period (Peck & Ross, 1978:48, figure 48); in a Ramesside period erotic drawing the alleged male is pictured with a breast of a size equal to that of his apparent female partner (Peck & Ross, 1978:85, figure 84). Probably one of the best examples is that of the superbly crafted painted limestone statue of 'The Louvre

Scribe' originally in an Egyptian tomb chapel at Saqqara from the late fourth or early fifth dynasty and now in Paris (Strouhal, 1992:214). Unfortunately, no corporeal support for any of the medical suggestions has appeared for the Tutankhamun controversy (Harrison & Abdalla, 1972; Harrison, 1973) nor have we been able to identify a report of gynecomastia in any other mummy. We consider the question unresolved and await future reports of gynecomastia in mummified male human remains.

DERMATOLOGICAL DISEASES

The skin competes with muscle and bone for the distinction of being the largest body organ. It forms the interface between the body and its environment. Its protective function makes it vulnerable to the effects of its interaction with infectious and toxic agents as well as thermal and mechanical assaults. The openings of its sweat and sebaceous glands may become obstructed and the skin areas exposed to sunlight are subject to the effects of ultraviolet irradiation.

It is not surprising that skin should be one of the first mummified tissues studied. Some of these early efforts at rehydration and microscopic examination include those by Czermack (1852), Fouquet (1886), and especially by Wilder in 1904 as cited by Simandl (1928). Wilder examined skin from various areas including the head, thumb and limbs of several spontaneously mummified bodies from the southwestern U.S.A. (Basketmakers; Utah cliff dwellers) as well as several Peruvian bodies housed in New York museums.

The many references to dermatological conditions in the Bible, the Babylonian literature and others are almost irresistible to these who enjoy reconstructing diagnoses from ancient narrative clues. Sandison (1967c) lists some of the many diseases that have been suggested from such sources. However, except for a few obvious ones such as pediculosis, most descriptions are not sufficiently detailed to establish specific, etiological entities with any great level of certitude. Listed below are a few examples of conditions most of which were made possible by their identification in mummified human remains.

Preservation

The epidermis is often absent over much of a mummy's skin surface. During the early days of mummy studies in Egypt, Herodotus' (ca. 450 B.C.) description of Egyptian embalming was interpreted as involving immersion of the body in liquid natron ('…the body is then immersed in natron for the proscribed number of days…'). Perhaps suggested by their experience with modern examples of drownings, early Egyptologists attributed absence of much of the epidermis in

Egyptian mummies to such postulated immersion (Simandl, 1928). In fact, by somewhat circular reasoning, epidermal absence was considered supportive evidence of such an interpretation, and a good deal of nonsense was postulated on the basis of the use of absent epidermis as an immersion marker.

The current concept of Egyptian embalming methods does not include immersion. Natron is believed to have been employed as a pulverized, finely granular, dry salt applied directly to the skin and the surfaces of eviscerated body cavities. Efforts to reproduce this procedure demonstrated that the epidermis becomes so adherent to the encrusted natron that much of the outer skin layers are removed as the natron is peeled from the body (Notman & Aufderheide, 1995). Perhaps even more important, it must be remembered that all the moisture of the internal tissues (except for the eviscerated body cavities) must traverse the skin during the process of dehydrating the body, and that such moisture is laden with the endogenous proteases of destroyed cells by the time it reaches the skin surface. Thus it is not surprising that the skin (having been exposed to destructive enzyme action) is the last of the tissues to dry, and that it would disintegrate and peel off readily upon removal of the natron. For these reasons, areas containing minimal quantities of underlying soft tissues (ear, finger, scalp) commonly retain epidermis (Post & Daniels, 1969, 1973) even when it is lost over the abdomen or thigh of the same body (A.C.A., personal observation; Daniels & Post, 1970). This can be true even in spontaneously mummified bodies in whom soil is often adherent to skin surfaces, though Giacometti & Chiarelli (1968) found more frequent epidermal preservation in predynastic mummies. Thus, absent epidermis in a skin section from a mummy is more apt to reflect the quantity of soft tissue beneath the point of biopsy, than to be predictive of immersion in a liquid.

Traumatic dermatological lesions

Lacerations, mutilations such as scarifications, tattoos and perforations are discussed in Chapter 3. (Traumatic conditions).

Infectious dermatological lesions

An unmistakable example of smallpox in a seventeenth century priest found in a Mexico city church has been reported by Allison & Gerszten (1989). The face was literally replaced by hundreds if not thousands of pustules. In a medieval child mummy from Naples, Fornaciari & Marchetti (1986) demonstrated that the virus may retain its morphological appearance in tissues and even its antigenic structure, though unsuccessful culture efforts indicated it was no longer viable (Marennikova et al., 1990). The initial impression of smallpox in an Egyptian mummy by Ruffer & Ferguson (1911) proved to be a bacterial lesion histologically, and the facial lesions of

Ramses V have not been verified histologically. Smallpox in antiquity is discussed in greater detail in Chapter 7.

Other infectious conditions described in the paleopathological literature include infectious dermatosis (Wilder, 1904), subcorneal pustular dermatosis in an Egyptian mummy (Zimmerman & Clark, 1976), and the angiomatous eruptive lesions of the second stage (verruga peruana) of bartonellosis (Carrion's disease) reported by Allison et al. (1974b). Lice infestation (Aufderheide, 1990) is common in mummies from South America's Pacific coastal areas (see Chapter 7 (Infectious diseases)). An ulcerating, destructive facial lesion ('noma') has been seen by Pahl & Undeutsch (1988) in an Egyptian mummy, and Saskin (1984) reported acute vasculitis of unknown cause in a spontaneously mummified adult female body from about A.D. 350 in extreme northern Chile. Ruffer (1921d) identified a decubitus ulcer on the heel of Amenhotep II. The lesion known as histiocytoma found in an Egyptian mummy (Zimmerman, 1981) might also represent the residual scar of a local infection instead of a benign tumor. Rashes of unknown cause are displayed on clay Peruvian figurines in the Weisman (1965) collection.

Metabolic dermatological lesions

Obesity is not a commonly reported condition in mummified human remains. The exaggerated folds of abdominal skin seen in the royal mummies of Ramses III, Merenptah and Thutmose II by Ruffer (1921b) indicate it can be obvious when present, so the paucity of paleopathological reports imply that it was infrequent in ancient times. Baldness was not only recognized in Egyptian mummies by Ruffer (1921b), but Ebbell (1937: p.79, col. 66) found a suggested remedy for it in the Ebers papyrus; Ruffer also describes comedones in royal mummies. Since melanin is quite resistant to enzymatic decay, Frost (1988) suggests its use to predict skin color. Wilder (1904) has also described the dermatological changes of infantile eczema.

Dermatological neoplasms

Considering the amount of ultraviolet radiation that the exposed skin of many ancient groups probably endured, it is surprising that to date we have not been able to find reports of a verified, primary skin cancer in the paleopathological literature. In fact, only a few benign skin tumors have been reported. They include angiokeratoma circumscripta from the leg of an Inca child that had been left as a sacrificial offering at a ritual site on a high Andean peak (Horne, 1986a, b) and a common wart (verruca vulgaris' Fulcheri, 1987) in an Egyptian mummy. A simple lipoma on an adolescent male's chest was reported by Allison & Gerszten (1983), though observers must be careful not to confuse skin folds resulting from clothing compression for the true neoplasm these authors describe.

Miscellaneous conditions

Examination of the hairs enabled the identification of human skin that had been nailed to medieval church doors in England; these are believed to represent punishment for sacrilege (Quekett, 1848). Chest and leg papules found on a 2100 year old Chinese noblewoman's body proved to be an example of pseudopathology when Kuo-liang *et al.* (1982) showed them to be foci of adipocere formation.

Frost (1988) has also found that male skin has a darker color than that of females and that lighter skin color is generally perceived as a feminine feature. Hino *et al.* (1982) even identified a bacterial spore with intact morphological structure using electron microscopy of the skin of an Egyptian mummy from the Roman period. In past centuries dermatological problems were common enough in Ethiopia to develop a therapeutic industry in thermal baths (Pankhurst, 1990).

PART NINE

Metabolic diseases

VITAMIN D-RELATED SYNDROMES: RICKETS AND OSTEOMALACIA

Definition and epidemiology

The various syndromes caused by lack of effective vitamin D (hereafter written simply as D) availability are skeletal deformations characterized by a metabolic defect in mineralization of bone at sites of endochondrial bone formation. In children these effects are called rickets and in adults osteomalacia. The origin of the term rickets is uncertain. Suggestions have included English rucket (short of breath), rucken (to rock or reel), Middle English wricken (twist), Saxon rick (head, hump), Norman riquets (hunchback) or Greek rachitis (spine) (Steinbock, 1993b). While rickets has a distinguished antiquity, historically it came to medical attention particularly in the seventeenth and eighteenth centuries in Europe, not appearing in the U.S.A. until the latter part of the nineteenth century. Because the body's needs normally can be supplied almost entirely by the action of ultraviolet light on the skin, regions north or south of tropical areas are particularly vulnerable. Indeed, a popular, but controversial, theory postulates that the ultraviolet-absorbing melanin pigment in the skin of Negroid populations 'trapped' them in the sunlight-rich tropical zone (Neer, 1974). Consequently it is possible that the increased prevalence of rickets during these centuries was the consequence of the population demographic shifts, initiated by the industrial revolution, into the crowded, densely populated and sunlight-restricted cities. Support for such a suggestion is provided by observations that at its peak over 90 % of urban American children were affected while it was found only infrequently in the rural population. Our discussion in this section will focus on the changes known as rickets and will deal with osteomalacia separately and briefly.

Vitamin D metabolism

Knowledge of how the body acquires D is necessary for understanding of the circumstances under which rickets develops. Its principal function, together with parathyroid hormone (PTH), is to help maintain blood calcium and phosphorus levels necessary for bone mineralization. Precursor dietary substances include ergosterol (found in plants and grains). Following absorption it is hydroxylated in the liver, then undergoes a second hydroxylation in the kidney to form the most biologically active compound labelled 1,25 dihydroxyvitamin D_3. It is this compound we mean by the name vitamin D (D). Alternatively the action of ultraviolet light induces the skin's dermal cells to form a single hydroxylated compound from 7-dehydrocholesterol (D_2) which is somewhat biologically active itself, but is further hydroxylated to D_3 in the kidney. Thus we can anticipate that diseases affecting these various tissues would have an impact on D synthesis (Norman & Henry, 1993).

Vitamin D action

Though a host of body cells have a surface membrane receptor for D, we currently are aware of only three principal sites of its action: intestine, bone and kidney. In the gut D is very influential in stimulating the absorption of calcium (Ca) and phosphorus (P), though its molecular mechanism to achieve it there remains unknown. In bone it helps PTH to liberate calcium by increasing the number of osteoclasts indirectly, perhaps *via* its stimulatory effect on cell differentiation (Norman & Henry, 1993). In the kidney it salvages calcium by stimulating its reabsorption in kidney distal tubules.

Effects of deficiency

Calcification of the cartilage at sites of endochondrial bone ossification is dependent on D, though again its molecular mechanism has not been defined satisfactorily. It is obvious, then, that D deficiency will have its maximal manifestations in growing infants and children. Membranous bone formation remains unimpaired. Histologically proliferation of cartilage cells at affected sites is restricted, and their premature death is obvious (perhaps reflecting the cell differentiating feature of D action).

The cartilage's normal, columnar structure is poorly developed, producing a markedly irregular epiphyseal junction and leading to subsequent deformation of these structures. Since orderly cartilage formation followed by subsequent calcification must precede its replacement by mineralized osteoid, the cartilage aberrations retard this process, stunting linear growth (Jaffe, 1972:392).

Vascular alterations make a substantial contribution to such growth arrest. On the metaphyseal side a vertically-oriented vessel normally sends a branch to each individual cartilaginous column, and apparently plays a role in cartilage cell removal. In rickets these branches are not formed, probably because the noncalcified matrix does not support them. The absence of vessels prevents cartilage removal, and subsequent ossification can only occur in the vicinity of vessels. In severe cases the poorly calcified bones transmit increased pressure to this area resulting in compression and collapse of existing blood vessels (Trueta, 1968:58–64). Osteoid, the matrix for ossification is produced in abundance, though deficient deposition of bone mineral (hydroxyapatite) crystals cause an appearance of excess production (Teitelbaum, 1980). These changes underlie all of the subsequent skeletal growth alterations, modified by biophysical forces. Gross skeletal changes resulting from such impairment of bone

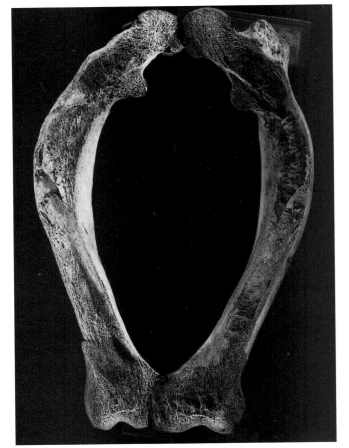

FIG. 9.1. **Rickets.** Space occupied by unresorbed, uncalcified cartilage and osteoid is apparent in the metaphyseal areas. Note thinned cortex. 1405.50. Modern case. Courtesy G. Worden. MM.

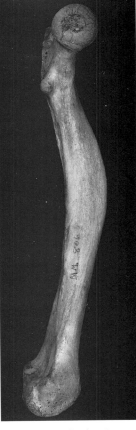

FIG. 9.2. **Rickets: bowing.** Femur demonstrates remarkable degree of bowing. 100, 2554. Modern adult. Courtesy of P. Sledzik. NMHM.

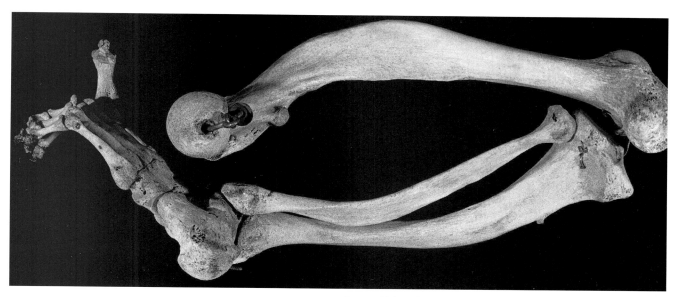

FIG. 9.3. **Rickets: bowing.** Femur, tibia and fibula have all become markedly deformed and bowed by the rachitic process. Modern adult. CMNH.

growth will now be itemized. These can be summarized as deformed, shortened and bowed long bones, kyphoscoliosis and craniotabes. Many of the drastic changes described only occur in the most severe cases. Others become modified as the child matures. Paleopathologists, therefore, can expect an enormously variable expression of these manifestations.

Long Bones

The cartilaginous architectural disarray results in irregular, nodular masses that produce a widening ('flaring') of long bone metaphyses. Wrists and ankles frequently are obviously wider than normal. The irregularity is often sufficient to tilt the epiphysis and produce a dysfunctional bone end as well as an appearance somewhat resembling the 'saber shin' deformity of treponematosis when the tilt is in the distal ends of the fibula and tibia posteriorly (Jaffe, 1972:391). The cortex, initially thin and porous (Fig. 9.1), later becomes thicker as a consequence of unimpaired membranous bone formation. This can be quite prominent in the fingers. The poorly mineralized bone is susceptible to fractures, but more frequently yields to the body's weight in the form of bowing − either inward ('knock-knees') or outward ('bow-legs') (Fig. 9.2). Extreme cases can produce functionally useless, grotesquely twisted femurs and tibias (Fig. 9.3) Horizontal, radiolucent lines (usually metaphyseal) were described by Looser (1920) as microfractures, but the subsequent demonstration that they are composed entirely of nonossified osteoid resulted in them being renamed as pseudofractures (Milkman, 1930). Though subjected to the biophysical forces of weight support, the leg bones are more frequently and severely bowed (Fig. 9.4), severe cases may also involve the upper extremity bones. Retardation of linear growth (enhanced by kyphosis and lordosis described below) produces a reduced stature that can reach dwarf proportions in advanced cases (Jaffe, 1972:386).

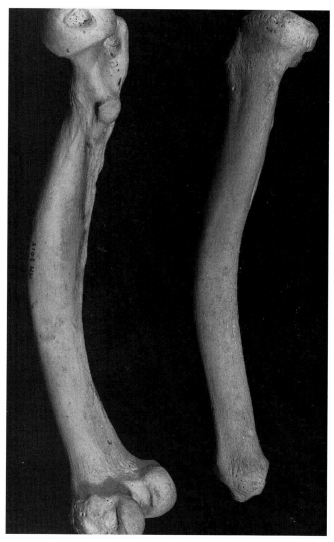

FIG. 9.4. **Rickets: bowing.** Both femur and tibia are bowed. 3019. Modern adult. Courtesy G. Worden. MM.

Skull

The anterior fontanel may persist for several years and most major cranial sutures are widened due to extensive endochondrial resorption, poor mineralization and fibrosis. Irregular, nodular masses in the outer table can produce nodular thickening, but generally the vault bones are thinner and softer than normal. Even the simple weight of the head can produce flattening of the parietal and occipital bones (craniotabes). Frontal bossing is so frequent that the 'square head' has become the clinical hallmark of a rachitic infant. Dentition abnormalities include late eruption as well as prominent enamel hypoplasia principally in the deciduous teeth.

Thorax

Rib ends, subjected to the same underlying changes as occur in the leg bones, react with metaphyseal flaring at their costochondral junctions. If the primary thrust of these is external they become obvious early in the disease. A linear array of these at such junctions produce the beaded appearance known commonly as 'rachitic rosary' and push the sternum outward, producing a 'pigeon breast' deformity. In others the arched costochondral junction pushes the sternum dorsally, generating a 'funnel breast' (Jaffe, 1972:390; Aegerter & Kirkpatrick, 1975:343). The softened, poorly mineralized bone also yields to the traction of the diaphragm at its points of attachment, the inward pull of which causes a circular depression in the lower rib cage (Harrison's groove).

Spine and pelvis

Thoracic kyphosis, in severe cases coupled to scoliosis affects the spine of the more severely affected children (Fig. 9.5). More commonly a prominent lordosis pushes the abdominal content forward, producing a pot-bellied child. At the spine's lowest end the lordosis pushes the sacral promontory forward (ventrally) folding the acetabulum upward and inward (protrusio acetabuli). These pelvic deformities threaten the possibility of later vaginal birth.

Causes of vitamin D deficiency

From the above description it is clear that alterations in several phases of D metabolism could lead to rickets. The changes can be grouped into four areas: (i) acquisition and stimulation of precursors, (ii) hydroxylation, (iii) respon-

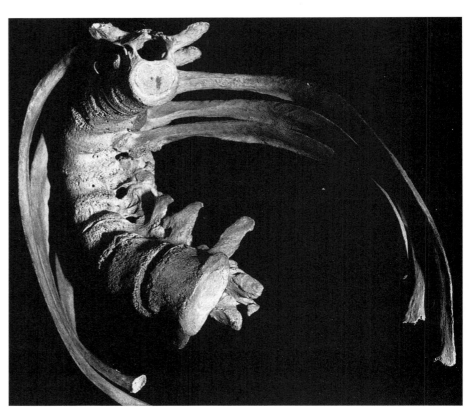

Fig. 9.5. **Rickets, kyphoscoliosis.** Spine has yielded and become deformed by body's weight on the hypomineralized vertebral bodies. E-325. Modern case. CMNH.

siveness of target organs, and (iv) interactions with PTH (Norman & Henry, 1993). Each of these is associated with distinct circumstances that are discussed below.

Acquisition and precursor stimulation

Reduction of sunshine exposure is the principal pathological agent, and probably responsible for the paucity of paleopathology specimens in contrast to its prevalence in industrializing Europe. Since many agricultural products have abundant ergosterol, simple dietary deficiencies are usually related to malnutrition. However, absorption from the intestine may be severely restricted by a constellation of diseases that are characterized by one common feature: malabsorption. These include celiac sprue (intestinal mucosa toxicity of gluten, a cereal grain protein), Crohn's disease (an idiopathic ulcerative intestinal condition), Wilson's disease (a chronic intestinal bacterial infection) and others.

Precursor conversion to bioactive form

While some of these conditions are acquired, many are hereditary. One of the best-understood involves a mutation of the gene that codes for production of the enzyme renal 1-hydroxylase that is responsible for converting D_2 to the much more active D_3 form (D) in the kidney. In modern cases certain drugs can block that enzyme's activity (Schiller, 1994:1305).

Responsiveness to target organs

An inherited mutation results in production of an altered D receptor on the surface membrane of cells normally influenced by D. Since the vitamin cannot recognize the target cells with these altered D receptors nor penetrate the membrane to exert its effects, these organs (including the epiphyseal plate's cartilage cells) cannot respond to the abundant D in the blood. In another disease (X-linked hypophosphatemia) a mutation prevents phosphate transport into the cell, limiting mineralization and producing rickets in male children only (Schiller, 1994:1305).

Interactions with parathyroid hormone

Since D plays a partial regulatory function in renal hydroxylation, hypoparathyroid persons may suffer the effects of D insufficiency. In addition D also plays a previously-mentioned role in bone resorption that is impaired in such individuals.

In addition, chemical changes involving phosphorus or alkaline phosphatase (both essential elements in bone mineralization) can result in a rickets-like effect. In Fanconi's syndrome an inherited defect in renal tubule action results in an extraordinary loss of phosphorus into the urine, while in hypophosphatasia production of the enzyme alkaline phosphatase is impaired because of a gene mutation.

Osteomalacia

This is the product of D deficiency in adults. It various enormously in degree and is the result of the mechanisms just described. It may be a rachitic condition perpetuated into adulthood but in most cases it is acquired. Because interference with bone growth in an adult is primarily effected during bone remodelling, manifestations are less dramatic since the period of bone growth has passed. Certainly in most cases the skeletal tissues grossly only manifest osteopenia (Jaffe, 1972:399). If, however, prolonged severe malnutrition accompanies the inciting condition, bone softening, even occasionally with bowing and vertebral body compression accompanied by kyphosis can occur. The more fragile bones also commonly lead to fractures. The most common cause is one of the malabsorption syndromes, especially if augmented by incapacitation that results in markedly reduced sunshine exposure (Schiller 1994:1306). Other causes include a protein produced by tumors. All of these can be exaggerated in the aged in whom osteoporosis may already have resulted in considerable bone demineralization. In the bulk of cases of osteomalacia in whom only osteopenia has occurred, the diagnostic separation from osteoporosis by gross analysis is usually impossible. Stout (1974) and Teitelbaum (1980) have indicated that microscopic identification of abundant unmineralized osteoid in the periphery of the trabeculae can enable the diagnosis.

Antiquity and history of rickets

While skeletal tissues testify to the antiquity of rickets as early as the Neolithic (see Paleopathology section, below), written descriptions are more recent. References to what might have been rickets can be identified in Chinese writings as early as 300 B.C., but the lack of particulars constrains their value (Steinbock, 1993b). Except for two cases reported by Ruffer in 1911 (cited by Pahor, 1992c), sun-drenched ancient Egypt appears to have escaped the plague of rickets. Most authors offer the second century physician Soranus of Ephesus as the best candidate for the distinction of being the first to provide a valid characterization of rickets as a discrete entity. About a century later Galen expanded the features mentioned by Soranus, adding pigeon breast and knock-knees to the list. Foote (1927) observed rachitic features portrayed in the infants in religious paintings of the fifteenth and sixteenth centuries (primarily bowed legs and square heads), and Cone (1980) added one more from the seventeenth century. Few additional reports appeared during the Dark Ages until the mid-seventeenth century when Daniel Whistler (1645) and Frances Glisson (1650) vied for recognition of rickets as the cause of 'The English Disease' becoming so prevalent at that time (cited in Clarke, 1962). Glisson also called attention to the frequency of scurvy concomitant with rickets (Fildes, 1986) In addition Arnold Boate (also spelled Boot) reported an example from Ireland in 1649 (cited in Fildes, 1986). Many subsequent articles about rickets appeared as its prevalence in England and the continent soared during the next two centuries. Fildes (1986) also notes that women of the poorer classes in the nineteenth and early twentieth centuries had to work in employers' buildings, reducing sunshine exposure. Losing the infertility effect of lactation, many had children almost annually, creating a strain on body calcium stores as well as reducing sunshine exposure. The resulting osteomalacia increased the hazard of rickets in their children. This period was characterized by a prevalence of rickets stigmata in urban children varying from 80 % in Boston (Morse, 1900) to 90 % in Dresden (Schmorl, 1909) and Vienna (Escherich, 1899: cited in Steinbock, 1993b). Subsequent fortification of food with D in the U.S.A. in the 1950s and in England in the late 1970s has had a profound effect, reducing the frequency of rickets to its present low level in these countries. Grimm (1985) collected 35 reports of definite or probable rickets cases from the Baltic and North Sea areas dating back to the early Iron and Bronze Age.

Paleopathology of rickets

Probably because of the sunshine to which hunters and gatherers were exposed, few ancient human remains have been found to harbor rachitic changes. Sigerist (1951:47) notes several from Scandinavia's Neolithic period and cites Poncet's report of rickets in a mummified, captive baboon in

Egypt. Zivanovic (1982:112) reports the skeleton of a child excavated in Yugoslavia with rachitic features including craniotabes, thick bones of the legs and characteristic rib cage lesions. Archaeological and radiocarbon methods dated the find to about 7000 B.C. In view of the sunshine in which ancient Egyptians carried out their agricultural subsistence, it is not surprising that the vast number of mummies and skeletons have revealed only the two cases reported by Ruffer (1911a) cited by Pahor (1992c). Ortner & Putschar (1985:284) comment on an isolated Egyptian sacrum from the twelfth dynasty demonstrating a profound angular change attributed to sitting, that appears to be a complication of osteomalacia.

Several medieval period skeletons have been reported. Møller–Christensen (1958, cited in Roberts & Manchester, 1995) found rickets in the Danish Aebelholt cloister graveyard and Wells (1964) cites the Hungarian study that demonstrated a threefold greater prevalence of rickets in a twelfth century cemetery than was found in one from the ninth century. Stuart–Macadam (1989a:212) reports a personal communication from K. Manchester in 1983 of a rachitic child and an adult with bowed legs from a medieval burial area at York. In a graveyard of an eighteenth to nineteenth century hospital (Spitalsfield) representing the peak of the European 'epidemic', Molleson & Cox (1993:153) identified rachitic changes in 20 children and 15 adults. From the same period Wells (1975) found that 25 % of a Norwich cemetery had rickets. Similarly, an Irish example from the nineteenth century at Waterford was reported by Power & O'Sullivan (1992).

Scurvy

Definition and chemical mechanism

Scurvy (adjective: scorbutic) is a condition caused by lack of vitamin C (C) resulting in defective collagen (and osteoid) synthesis with consequent skeletal growth retardation and hemorrhagic phenomena. While the tissues of most animals can produce C (now known to be L-ascorbic acid), from glu-

cose, a mutation of a gene coding for a specific enzyme (L-glucuronolactone oxidase) in its production has resulted in a blockage of a key step in its synthesis in monkeys, guinea pigs and humans. Hence, these must ingest and absorb the preformed vitamin. Ascorbic acid (AA) is found in a wide range of foods, being present in marine fish and in varying amount in numerous vegetals but demonstrating exceptionally high concentrations in citrus fruits.

While AA is a ready hydrogen donor and thus is involved in a broad array of body chemical reactions, in many of these, other substances can substitute effectively for AA. Consequently, deficient quantities of AA produce serious impairment primarily in collagen synthesis, whose complex triple helical structure can not be maintained because of defective interfibrillar bonding. This defect is responsible for the most prominent features of scurvy: defective osteoid formation with its attendant effect on skeletal growth in subadults and lack of small blood vessel wall integrity that result in accompanying hemorrhages. In addition failure of the normal role of AA in stabilization of folate and iron metabolism produces anemia in severely affected individuals.

Epidemiology and natural history

Any climatic, geographic, social or occupational circumstance that restricts access to C can be expected to generate examples of scorbutic individuals. Thus the condition is rare in the fruit-abundant tropical areas, but common at high latitudes. It may accompany the economic-based malnutrition of some urban center subpopulations as well as that of isolated elderly persons. Selective dietary restrictions in eccentric diets or certain bottle-feeding infant foods can also be responsible for scurvy. The historical section below notes various occupations characterized by the accompanying hazard of scurvy, of which the most common has been long sea voyages during the fifteenth to eighteenth centuries. Boiling destroys about 50 % of C effect and an additional 75 % of the remainder is lost under usual conditions of ship storage (Wyatt, 1976).

The adult body pool of C normally measures about 1500–3000 mg. The recommended preventive adult dosage is 60 mg daily. Symptoms do not appear until the body pool

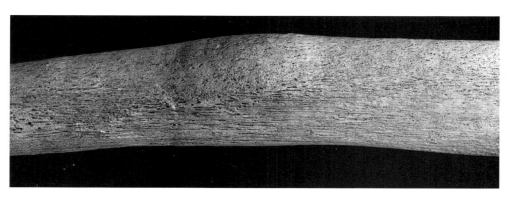

Fig. 9.6. **Hematoma, subperiosteal, organized.** Traumatic? In normal adults the periosteum is so tightly adherent to the bone that the periphery of an area of subperiosteal hemorrhage is usually quite sharply demarcated as in this lesion. Scurvy cannot be excluded. LXX. North American aboriginal, precontact, upper midwestern U.S.A. Courtesy Dr John Gregg and USDAL. Photograph by Glenn Malchow.

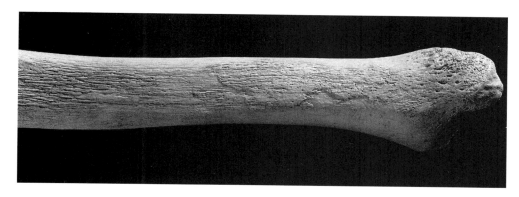

FIG. 9.7. **Hematoma, superiosteal, calcified.** Subperiosteal hemorrhage in scorbutics may not be sharply limited in the periphery because the connective tissue of scorbutics is defective and weak. The calcified layer has not yet been remodeled into the cortex. HTE-113. Modern case. CMNH.

is reduced to about 300 mg, though children are more susceptible than adults. Since about 4 % of C is destroyed or lost daily by normal catabolism, symptoms usually appear about 1–3 months following complete cessation of C intake. Ingestion of some but suboptimal amounts will delay onset of the deficiency symptoms. It should also be noted that , while scurvy is commonly encountered under circumstances that frequently also produce deficiencies of other substances, our discussion in this section is limited to those features unique to vitamin C deficiency.

The initial symptom of scurvy is usually the appearance of hemorrhages. An important characteristic of these is that they commonly are symmetrical. Skin involvement begins as those of pinpoint size (petechiae) that often expand into larger hemorrhagic blotches (ecchymoses) and whose color will vary from the initial bluish-black appearance to the kaleidoscopic pigments of late 'black and blue' bruises. While some are spontaneous, many are initiated by minor trauma and thus are more common in the lower extremities. A peculiar effect of bleeding into the region around hair follicles and sweat glands with resulting tissue reaction produces a characteristic hyperkeratotic (scaly) skin lesion that distorts growth of the hair shaft, causing it to grow in a corkscrew pattern (Meisel, 1995). Bleeding into the subperiosteal area of the orbital plate of the frontal bone may force the eyeball forward (exophthalmos). Many deeper hemorrhages involve muscle and subcutaneous tissues. Bleeding around nerves can compress and paralyze them, while hemorrhages around the major leg veins can compress and partially obstruct them leading to thrombosis and the serious consequences of pulmonary embolism.

Of special interest to paleopathologists is hemorrhage about and into bones and joints. These differ in subadults and adults. In adults the periosteum's normally tenacious adhesiveness to the bone is impaired to a moderate extent by the defective collagen in scorbutic individuals, rendering it susceptible to subperiosteal hemorrhage from minor trauma. These are usually diaphysial, restricted to a moderate size, the outer layers of which eventually heal by lamellar bone formation while the inner portion, if the hemorrhage is of substantial size, often has a more porous structure (Fig. 9.6). The periosteum of infants, however, normally is much more easily separated from the cortex. In scorbutic infants periosteal

attachment becomes so fragile that a subperiosteal hemorrhage often involves a proportionately much greater area and volume (Fig. 9.7). In contrast to the predominantly diaphyseal areas in adults, initial subperiosteal hemorrhages in infants occur far more regularly near the long bone joint in the metaphysis. In extreme cases these can dissect further, eventually reaching and involving a significant part of the diaphysis as well. Rarely, however, will the infant's joint interior suffer hemorrhage while intra-arthrodial hemorrhagic effusion is common in adults. Another consequence of these differences is the widening of metaphyses by such hemorrhages and their subsequent organization at wrists, ankles and knees in infants but not usually in adults. Adults usually also suffer hemorrhage into the marrow of long bones that heal by fibrous organization, speckled with the golden pigment of hemoglobin breakdown products (hemosiderin). In infants, however, the hemorrhage into the bone interior is usually targeted at the metaphysis – between the osseous end of the bone shaft and the zone of calcified cartilage. If substantial, such an area of bleeding is capable of shifting or completely separating the epiphysis. These dramatic changes in infancy are rapidly attenuated after age 2 years.

These same phenomena also distort costochondral junctions of ribs. Because the perichondrium does not separate easily as does the periosteum in infants, subperiosteal hemorrhage in this area usually begins abruptly at the osseous edge of the junction, spreading a variable but usually short distance along the rib. This produces a discrete, clearly demarcated knobby appearance of the ribs' costochondral junctions that bears some similarity to the 'rosary beads' expression of vitamin D deficiency (Hess & Unger, 1920). While other bones and joints can be involved by similar changes, they are much more frequent in the lower extremities in the adult, though arms (especially elbows and wrists) can be affected in infants.

The other region commonly involved both in infants and adults is the mouth region. Collagenous attachment of the gingiva to the periosteum is weakened, the resulting fissures leading to the red, swollen, often ulcerated, infected gums. Teeth are normally anchored firmly in the densely collagenous periodontal ligament. When this structure loses its integrity the teeth become loosened, the gingival infection extends to the teeth roots causing caries, and hemorrhage into the loose, infected tissues around the roots results in exfoliation of the teeth.

In addition to these subperiosteal changes complicated by the described hemorrhages, the growth plate itself is seriously affected. Cartilage is deposited and calcified in a normal manner. The defect of collagen synthesis, however, is here manifested by an inability to produce effective osteoid. Thus, the vascular extension into the cartilage zone to resorb the cartilage cells and replace the area with osteoid does not occur. The persistence of the calcified cartilage results in an expansion of this zone of calcification, creating the radiologically recognizable radiodense structure known as the 'white line of Fraenkel'. Absence of osteoid deposition prevents the subsequent ossification phase of remodeling but the osteoclastic phase is not impaired. Thinning and even complete removal of the preformed trabeculae at the junction with the zone of calcified cartilage, joined by foci of necrosis all of which are embedded in a gel of imperfect collagenous secretion generates a weakly-structured zone of detritus termed the Trümmelfeldzone (zone of ruins: Wimberger, 1923a, b). Not surprisingly, mechanical stresses (including weight-bearing) on such a fragile area produce infractions (partial fractures) that often extend into complete fractures. As noted, hemorrhage into such zones may completely separate the epiphysis. Similar foci of osteopenia surround and impair ossification centers at other sites of endochondral ossification. The continuing osteoclastic activity with osteoblastic activity impaired by defective osteoid formation during bone remodeling is also responsible for the thin diaphyseal cortex seen in scurvy as well as vertebral collapse with kyphosis in adults.

Other soft tissue effects produce areas of edema, and the often grotesque effect of reopening of long-healed wounds as the integrity of their collagenous scars becomes impaired. Internal hemorrhages may affect intestinal mucosa, brain and even heart muscle, and lung function is affected by the presence of pulmonary edema. The terminal, lethal effect of unrelieved scurvy usually is a severe infection, commonly pneumonia.

Treatment with ascorbic acid-containing foods (or the modern synthesized compound) can arrest the process within a few days and produce such prompt healing effects that caused early ship captains to recognize the antiscorbutic value of frequent port visits.

Antiquity and history

The essential milestones in the history of scurvy are listed in Table 9.1 The following observations may supply some perspective with which to view these events. Uncertainty about knowledge of scurvy by physicians of the classical period most probably is related to the fact that their temperate climate provided a diet of vitamin C-rich foods. Differences in the clinical pattern of affected areas in growing subadults

and adults no doubt delayed recognition that these had the same etiology until Barlow's description in 1883. Less obvious is why Lind's epic study published in 1753 (reprinted 1953) was not immediately implemented to prevent this disease. Lind was a ship's surgeon who separated 12 scorbutic crew members in the late 1740s into six pairs. One pair continued the standard shipboard diet, another pair added the consumption of an orange and lemon juice concentrate ('rob') and still another was supplemented with cider. Additions to the diets of the remainder included items we now know to contain little or no ascorbic acid. The citrus-supplemented diet induced a prompt cure (Fig. 9.8), the cider had a sluggish but positive effect while no change occurred in the remainder.

In spite of these clearly defined effects, Lind's 1753 report went unheralded by most. It is true that others (e.g. Hawkins, 1593 cited in Hess, 1920; Smith 1986 and Tilghman, 1980) had promoted citrus fruit as an antiscorbutic 150 years earlier, but dozens of others were recommending other products – all unsupported by controlled studies such as those by Lind. Even though Lind was a British naval surgeon, the admiralty did not make daily administration of lemon juice routine naval policy until 40 years after Lind's study. Certainly Captain James Cook's denigration of citrus in favor of malt (wort) as a seagoing antiscorbutic contributed to the delay. As late as 1854 the French army in the Crimea

Table 9.1 Events leading to the recognition and cure of scurvy.

400 B.C.	Hippocrates: may have known scurvy (gum lesion and leg pains)
ca. 200 A.D.	Romano–British: *Rumex* sp. antiscorbutic (Janssens *et al.*, 1993)
1498	Vasco de Gama to S.E. Africa = sea scurvy (French, 1993)
1519	Magellan: sea scurvy. Recovery at ports (French, 1993)
1541	Echthius: good description but thought it was contagious (cited in Smith, 1986)
1564	Ronsseus: identified scurvy in Germanicus' army (Pliny) (cited in Smith, 1986: 104)
1565	Word 'scurvy' in Oxford dictionary
1593	Hawkins: citrus fruits beneficial to scurvy (Lloyd, 1979; Smith, 1986)
1618	Birkenkamp: stomacace = gum and tooth lesions (Birkenkamp, 1618)
1650	Glisson: bleeding in rachitic = scurvy too (Glisson, 1650, cited in Clarke, 1962)
1713	Bergen & Feller: called gum lesions scurvy (Bergen & Feller, 1713)
1740	Anson: circumnavigated globe, 50% crew died – scurvy (Lloyd, 1979)
1753	Lind: treatise on citrus fruits preventing scurvy
1768	Cook: fresh meat, sauerkraut = no scurvy (Tilghman, 1980)
1776	Cook: prefers malt (wort) to lemons (Lloyd, 1979)
1793	British navy: lemon juice daily (Lloyd, 1979)
1825	Scurvy in prisoners cured by potato diet (Carpenter, 1987)
1847	Potato famine caused scurvy (Hess, [1920] 1983)
1848	Garrod: studied potatoes. Scurvy = diet deficiency (Lee, 1983)
1854	French lose 23 000 to scurvy in Crimea (Carpenter, 1987)
1883	Barlow: pathology of infantile scurvy (Barlow, 1883)
1907	Holst & Fröhlich produced scurvy in guinea pigs (Holst & Frölich, 1907)
1914	Funk suggests concept of vitamins (Funk, 1914)
1928	Szent–Gyorgyi: ascorbic acid = antiscorbutic (Szent-Gyorgyi, 1928)
1933	Scorbutic infant cured by synthetic ascorbic acid (Hirst & Zilva, 1933)
1982	Maat: first paleopathology description (Arctic bodies)

This table was created from narrative reports by Hess (1920), Hirst & Zilva (1933), Lloyd (1979), Tilghman (1980), Maat (1982), Lee (1983), Smith (1986), Carpenter (1987), Stuart–Macadam (1989), Adelfang (1991), Wilson (1991), French (1993) and Janssens *et al.* (1993).

lost 23 000 men to scurvy. It is true that Lind and others were not concerned with scurvy as a disease, but rather as an impediment to the marine-related function of the voyage and so it was to be prevented. It is also true that reduction of complete destruction of ascorbic acid by various food processing methods produced puzzling, varying effects in antiscorbutic tests. More fundamental, however, are the observations of French (1993) who points out that physician resistance may be reflective of their general concept of disease. The latter was rooted in Galen's' view of the body as an independent, self-sufficient whole (a 'microcosm' whose multiple parts were in a state of equilibrium) suspended in a macrocosm (the environment). As such, disease represented an influence of the external (macrocosm) that upset the body equilibrium. The nineteenth century popularization of the germ theory was consistent with such a concept, in which the intrusion of an external influence (bacterium) altered body system function. Thus, Lind's suggestion that scurvy was a condition arising de novo within the body (a deficiency) did not fit neatly into the basis of contemporary medical theory. It was not until the first quarter of the twentieth century that the full concept of scurvy and its treatment was completely accepted.

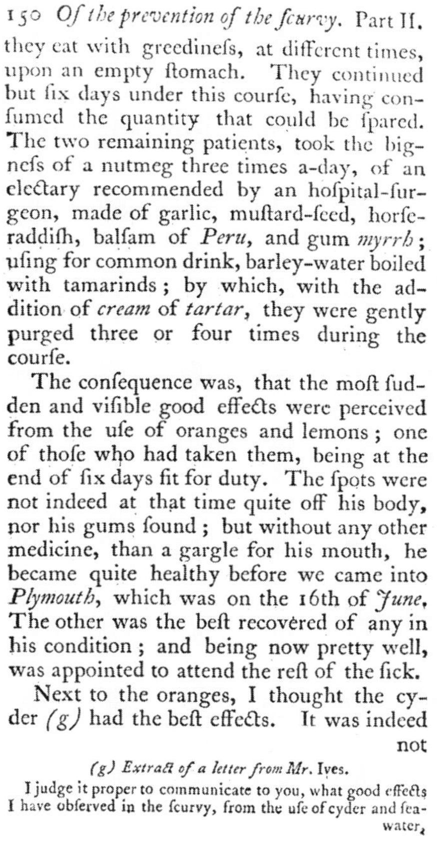

150 *Of the prevention of the scurvy.* Part II.

they eat with greedinefs, at different times, upon an empty ftomach. They continued but fix days under this courfe, having confumed the quantity that could be fpared. The two remaining patients, took the bignefs of a nutmeg three times a-day, of an electary recommended by an hofpital-furgeon, made of garlic, muftard-feed, horfe-raddifh, balfam of *Peru*, and gum *myrrh*; ufing for common drink, barley-water boiled with tamarinds; by which, with the addition of *cream* of *tartar*, they were gently purged three or four times during the courfe.

The confequence was, that the moft fudden and vifible good effects were perceived from the ufe of oranges and lemons; one of thofe who had taken them, being at the end of fix days fit for duty. The fpots were not indeed at that time quite off his body, nor his gums found; but without any other medicine, than a gargle for his mouth, he became quite healthy before we came into *Plymouth*, which was on the 16th of *June*. The other was the beft recovered of any in his condition; and being now pretty well, was appointed to attend the reft of the fick.

Next to the oranges, I thought the cyder *(g)* had the beft effects. It was indeed not

(g) *Extract of a letter from Mr.* Ives.

I judge it proper to communicate to you, what good effects I have obferved in the fcurvy, from the ufe of cyder and fea-water.

FIG. 9.8. **Scurvy.** Page 150 from James Lind's (1772) *A Treatise on the scurvy*, describing his 'controlled' shipboard study of 12 scorbutic patients, the results of which clearly established fruits as the most effective remedy. PBL.

Paleopathology and differential diagnosis

For reasons noted above it should come as no surprise that skeletons from temperate and tropical areas have only rarely demonstrated scorbutic changes. Even in arctic areas the social adaptations of native food practices (eating raw meat and many other body parts normally shunned by southerners) have prevented scurvy as a common problem. Holck (1984), however, notes that medieval Scandinavian skeletons suggest that scurvy may have been that region's most common health problem at that time.

Maat's (1982) study of the remains of Dutch sailors who had died on Spitzbergen during an arctic expedition provided a superb contribution to understanding the lesions of adult scurvy. Joint hematomas were common, as were infractions and overt long bone fractures. Ossification of diaphyseal localized areas of subperiosteal hemorrhage are the hallmark of adult scurvy. While gingival soft tissues are absent in ancient skeletons, blackened tooth roots, as described by Maat testify to the oral hemorrhagic areas in scorbutic persons. Janssens et al. (1993) examined bodies from the 1584–85 siege of Antwerp buried in a local cathedral and found similar changes. Their illustration of long bone cross-sections demonstrated dramatically how a shell of lamellar new bone on the surface is attached to the original cortex by a web of more porous bone. They also emphasize that the finding of symmetrical lesions can be very valuable in the differential diagnosis of scurvy. Mogle & Zias (1995) also suggest that their finding of a midline, anterior trephination in the skull of an 8–9 year old child whose skull revealed porous bones without proliferative features and mandibular edentulism represents an attempt to cure scurvy by trepanation.

It will be noted that scurvy and rickets superficially share several features: widened metaphyses of long bones, (especially those of the lower limbs), and prominent, 'knobby' costochondral rib junctions. These, however, are produced by completely different mechanisms, traces of which often persist sufficiently to permit their separation. Metaphyseal widening in rickets is the result of profound irregularity of the metaphyseal–epiphyseal junction due to multiple instead of single ossification centers and irregular cartilage proliferation. In scurvy it is usually the consequence of ossification of subperiosteal hemorrhages whose form is often discernible. The 'knob' at costochondral junctions in rickets is often produced by a proliferative, arching cartilaginous mass above which the edges of the osseous portion of the rib projects discretely. In scurvy the enlargement at that site is the consequence of subperiosteal hemorrhage whose ossification thickens the bony rib; since the perichondrial attachment remains firm, the involved, expanded bony part of the rib ends abruptly at its junction with the cartilaginous section. Alternatively, a fracture at that junction may also depress the cartilage attached to the sternum sufficiently to accentuate the sternal end of the osseous rib portion in the absence of hemorrhage there. Furthermore the feature of the thin meta-physeal and diaphyseal cortex of scurvy is not shared by rickets. Ortner & Putschar (1985: 270–3), though, note how antemortem healing and postmortem changes can obscure such features. Kato (1932) states flatly that the only scorbutic radiologic feature never shared by rickets is subperiosteal hemorrhage, in spite of the fact that Wimberger (1923a, b) earlier had felt that the more narrow radiologic seam at the epiphyseal ossification center of long bones in scurvy permitted its separation from coexisting rickets.

Osteoporosis

Definition, etiology, and epidemiology

Osteoporosis represents a condition of reduction of total bone mass per unit volume while retaining a normal ratio of bone mineral to bone matrix (Krane & Holick, 1991:1921). This definition will fit a substantial number of circumstances of known cause, such as bone changes in sudden immobilization of previously active persons, several endocrinopathies including Cushing's syndrome and others. Recent literature demonstrates an increasing clinical tendency to use the term osteoporosis, when expressed without modifying adjectives or phrases, as one that implies reference to that form of age-related bone loss without obvious etiology. Thus, idiopathic osteoporosis has been divided into two groups: Type 1 afflicting primarily postmenopausal women 51–75 years old, characterized by predominantly trabecular bone loss with fractures of the distal radius and vertebrae, and Type 2 that affects both genders above age 60, and features loss of both trabecular and cortical bone with hip and vertebral fractures.

Used in this way, by definition its etiology is unknown. In most populations bone mass peaks in the midportion of the fourth decade. Thereafter bone remodeling continues but the bone formation/resorption phase ratio is gradually altered from its previous equilibrium by continued resorption but

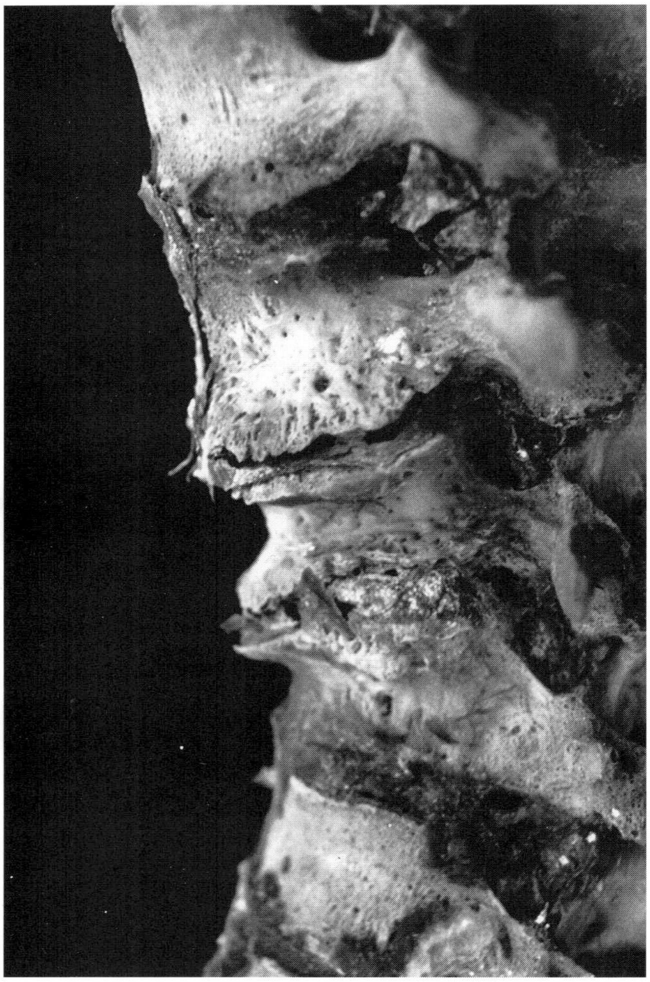

Fig. 9.9. **Osteoporotic crush vertebral fracture.** Lumbar vertebral body in center of photograph has collapsed as a result of loss of bone mineral and trabeculae. Elderly female of Tiwanaku culture about A.D. 700 in northern Chile. Photograph courtesy of Michael Zlonis, Duluth, MN. MAUT.

Fig. 9.10. **Osteoporosis with multiple crush fractures.** Spine with depleted mineral content and trabeculae. Vertebral bodies collapsed under strain of bearing normal body weight. Those near the center have collapsed so completely that they most probably compressed the spinal nerve with production of severe pain. Elderly adult of San Lorenzo culture about A.D. 800 in northern Chile. MAUT. PBL.

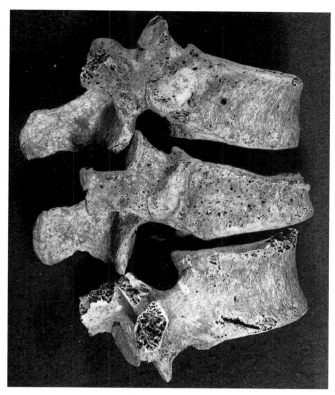

FIG. 9.11. **Osteoporosis, vertebral body.** The vertebral body's bone mineral content was depleted resulting in compression. Note that neural arch contributes some support to the posterior part of the vertebral body, producing a wedge-shaped compression fracture. CCVIII. Precontact North American aboriginal, upper midwestern U.S.A. Courtesy Dr John Gregg and USDAL. Photograph by Glenn Malchow.

lagging formation. Women normally suffer a substantial acceleration of this phenomenon during the post-menopausal state, while in men the change is more gradual, paralleling similar alterations in gonadal hormone production in the two genders, suggesting a possible causal effect.

Age-related bone mass loss is a global phenomenon and has been demonstrated in geographic areas spanning the climatic regions from the Arctic to the tropics. Ethnic and racial differences in degree of bone loss have been demonstrated. Afro-Americans suffer less from the complications of osteoporosis than do North American Caucasians, but this has been attributed to the larger bone mass at midlife. Over a lifetime women lose about 35% of their peak cortical bone mass and about half of their trabecular bone while men lose about two-thirds of those values.

Skeletal pathology

Spine

The most obvious gross change is a reduction of bone mass per unit volume. Transected vertebrae or metaphyses reveal an overtly porous pattern of cancellous bone. Closer inspec-

tion will allow recognition that horizontal trabeculae have suffered a disproportionately greater loss, providing greater prominence of the vertical trabeculae (Jaffe, 1972:371). In severe cases even gross observation can detect the more delicate trabecular structure, seen more easily with a hand lens and confirmed histologically. The supporting vertebral cortical plate adjacent to an intact intervertebral disk may be so thin that it yields to the mechanical pressure of weight-bearing, resulting in a concave bulging of the plate into the body of the vertebra ('codfish vertebra'). Eventually the thinned, remaining vertical trabeculae fail completely in their support of the weight in erect posture, and the vertebral body collapses. This collapse may be uniform; i.e. the upper vertebral plate may move downward uniformly, crushing all trabeculae and almost approximating the lower plate of the vertebral body (Figs. 9.9 and 9.10). More often the partial support of the neural arch attachments and the greater integrity of trabeculae in the posterior portion of the vertebral body will cause that area to maintain itself while the more anterior portion collapses (Fig. 9.11). This produces a wedge-shaped compression of the vertebral body, high in the posterior area and profoundly crushed at the anterior end, disturbing weight support and resulting in a forward bending of the spine (kyphosis) above the compressed vertebra. The most commonly affected area is the segment between the mid thoracic and upper lumbar spine portions. When several vertebrae suffer such effects the spine angulation is quite marked, producing what is often called the dowager's hump.

Long bones

The same process of trabecular thinning and loss described in vertebral bodies above is also experienced by the trabecular bone in metaphyseal areas of long tubular bones. Because body weight is transmitted through the femur neck in a manner tangential to the vertical plane, the loss of physical support of the more complex trabecular patterns in this area often leads to fractures of the femur neck and intertrochanteric fractures. The compact bone of these long bones is also eroded, though its gross recognition may appear as much as a decade later after the vertebral changes have become obvious. These initially present as endosteal erosion with resulting porosity gradually extending toward the periosteum, the resorption slowly but progressively widening the medullary cavity and reducing cortical thickness (Fig. 9.12). These processes eventually can also lead to fractures resulting from minor stress.

While the femur and distal radius are by far the most commonly fractured long bones in osteoporotic persons, the humerus may also yield to minor stresses and very much less commonly the tibia and fibula. Skull changes are very much less evident, though some authors include biparietal thinning as an osteoporotic rather than developmental effect (Epstein, 1953: Fig. 9.13). Histologically the principal change is simply loss of bone structures in both trabecular

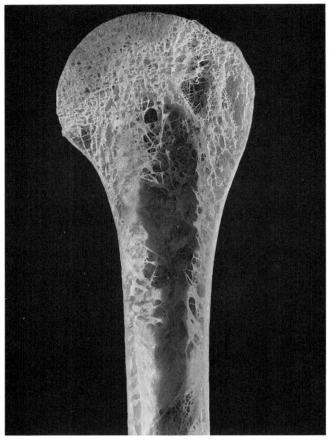

FIG. 9.12. **Osteoporosis, humerus.** Cortex of this modern, sagitally sectioned humerus is remarkably thin and cancellous bone demonstrates profound loss of trabeculae. T-22. CMNH.

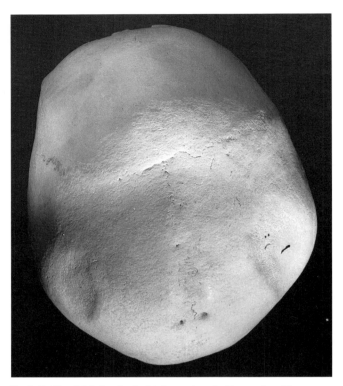

FIG. 9.13. **Biparietal atrophy.** Parietal areas have lost bone mineral from diploe and outer table, resulting in marked thinning of these areas, probably due to osteoporosis. 196. 439. Modern adult. Courtesy G. Worden. MM.

and compact bone sites, with thinner but otherwise normal-appearing trabeculae. Surfaces are smooth, demonstrating no evidence of increased resorption such as those found in hyperparathyroidism: tunnelling resorption and numerous osteoclastic lacunae.

The gross diagnosis of osteopenia is obvious in extreme examples. Efforts to identify less severe examples and provide at least semiquantitative evaluations have led to measures of bone density on an X-ray film (Allison, 1988), by computer tonnography (CT) evaluation, by absorption of an energy beam traversing vertebral bodies, distal radius or femur neck, trabecular micromorphology or weight of bone mineral in a sample of known volume. The Singh index represents an estimate of severity based on trabecular pattern of a sagittal section through the femur head and neck (Singh *et al.*, 1970). Lack of standardization has constrained application of these procedures.

Antiquity, history, and paleopathology

Numerous studies have documented the presence of osteoporosis in ancient human remains. Ericksen's (1976) study of three Native American archaeological populations found osteoporosis predominantly among females, and osteoporosis was found to afflict ancient Nubian women even earlier than in the modern population studied by Dewey *et al.*, (1969). Aufderheide & Allison (1994) found severe osteoporosis with multiple vertebral crush fractures, kyphosis and even scoliosis in 5 out of 59 (8 %) spontaneously mummified human remains of the Chinchorro culture that lived on Chile's northern coast more than 4000 years ago. Four were women (ages 35, 60 and 60 ± 5 years) and one was a man aged 40 ± 5 years. Zimmerman (1994) also demonstrated it in a 45 year old Alaskan mummy from 500 years ago.

INTOXICATIONS

FLUOROSIS

Definition, etiology, and epidemiology

Fluorosis is a condition caused by chemical intoxication by the fluoride ion. Though this may be inhaled by employees of industrial ore processing plants, it is most commonly acquired by unintentional ingestion of water in areas where the fluoride-bearing soil contaminates the water sources. Such areas have been identified in North Dakota, Texas and other states in the U.S.A., but can be found in many geographic areas throughout the world. Endemic fluorosis sites in southern India and Pakistan have been known for many years. More than 20 million Chinese have the dental changes of fluorosis, about 5 % of which also have skeletal lesions (Hall & Sidel, 1993). On the other hand, remarkably localized areas have been identified, some limited to a specific part of a city. Involved areas often come to attention because of the cosmetic dental effects that excess fluorine produces.

Pathophysiology of dental fluorosis

The fluorine ion can replace the hydroxyl ion in the bone (and tooth) hydroxyapatite crystal. This results in a greater degree of bone crystallinity with its attendant brittleness, leading to vulnerability of the involved structure to traumatic fracture. In teeth, such areas of affected enamel impart a chalky, dull white finish that contrasts with the highly reflective luster of the tooth crown's uninvolved portions. Such an enamel also chips more readily. Fluorine's cellular toxic effect also produces foci of enamel agenesis or dysgenesis. These pits absorb organic material and produce yellow to brown foci of discoloration. Fluoride-containing dentine may not function properly. Thus, teeth may be not only cosmetically marred, but abnormal in size and shape as well. In addition, the roots are often the target of hypercementosis, probably reflecting the type of periosteal stimulation seen so dramatically in skeletal fluorosis (Singh *et al.*, 1962). Affected teeth usually contain 3–10 mg F/g of tooth ash (Roholm 1937:258). In animals these dental changes can be induced by administration of about 1 mg/kg body weight/day. But in humans it has occurred at doses as low as 0.07 mg/kg. The caries-resistant quality of such teeth has been widely exploited by public programs of drinking water fluoridation at doses designed to capture the desirable caries-resistant feature, but too low to produce the cosmetic effects.

Skeletal pathology in fluorosis

Sodium fluoride directly stimulates osteoblasts to bone formation and is the only substance known to do so (Krane & Holick, 1991:1926). Furthermore, its effects are highly variable and sometimes bizarre. It may produce broad, flat sheets of periosteal new bone formation in some areas, discrete, localized, nodular excrescences in others and both in still others. Endosteal surfaces are also affected with resulting narrowing of the medullary cavity. The skeletal axis can be not only the first affected but also the most severe. These foci of new bone formation are so extensive that the pain

they cause upon movement impairs spinal mobility, especially in the cervical area. In addition, the spinal canal in this segment can be so diminished in its anteroposterior diameter that, in addition to the radicular pain, the features of spinal compression may be superimposed (Singh & Jolly, 1961; Singh et al., 1961). Interosseous ligaments, especially radioulnar and tibiofibular, are special targets of ossification as are muscular tendinous bone insertions. Joint capsules may calcify, though their interior surfaces usually remain uninvolved. The brittleness of long bone mineral results in increased fracture frequency. In the skull the tables may expand to the point of marrow space obliteration. Histological features indicate abnormalities including irregular structure, wide zones of unmineralized osteoid bridging trabeculae and marrow fibrosis (Weatherell & Weidmann, 1959; Faccini & Teotia, 1974). Some authors also emphasize evidence of resorption that may be noted grossly on the endosteal surface, radiologically as resorption of phalangeal cortices, and microscopically as tunneling resorption. These features, together with negative calcium balance and elevated parathyroid hormone blood levels, identified in some modern cases, suggest the possibility of additional effects of secondary hyperparathyroidism in cases of skeletal fluorosis (Faccini & Teotia, 1974).

Natural history of fluorosis

In addition to the mottled teeth, the earliest sign of skeletal fluorosis may be restriction of motion of the cervical spine. Eventually this may involve the entire spine and kyphosis is a common acquired deformity. Radicular pain can be intense, to which the individual commonly responds by progressive decrease in motion of all parts of the body until completely bedridden. Anemia with complicating infection may be lethal in advanced cases.

Paleopathology of fluorosis

The diagnosis of skeletal fluorosis should not be difficult in advanced cases. It is the very irregularity of the often bizarre structure and widespread distribution of new bone formation that suggests the etiology of fluorosis, especially if the characteristic advanced vertebral changes, as well as exaggeration of cristae and calcification of interosseous ligaments, are present. So much new bone has formed that the bone weight may be threefold greater than normal. The sheet-like new bone plates studded with up to thumb-sized exostoses on flat bones are characteristic as are the thick skull vault bones. Mottled teeth can support the diagnosis which can also be confirmed by chemical analysis demonstrating elevated fluoride content. However, because fluoride diagenesis is a potential problem, control bone samples of the same age from the same site are necessary to validate such measurements. Normal values are about 0.1–1.5 parts per 1000 (Roholm, 1937:258).

Lukacs (1984) and Lukacs et al. (1985) report what they identify as the first example of dental fluorosis in ancient human remains. In a Mehrgarh population from a prehistoric site in Pakistan (a known region of modern endemic fluorosis), they noted the chalky-white and yellow-brown discoloration of dental fluorosis in nine individuals. The population also had a low (1.3 %) frequency of dental caries and more than half also had enamel hypoplasia and dental calculus formation.

LEAD POISONING

Only a few areas on our planet today are relatively free from the effects of almost worldwide lead processing and use (Piomelli et al., 1980). If these modern, remote areas reflect the ancient environment, then studies suggest that human lead exposure was probably minimal during antiquity except at local ore outcroppings. However, because of its physical qualities lead was one of the first metals employed by humans for utilitarian purposes. Such use resulted in human exposure, leading to a long history of lead poisoning.

Metabolic and physiological features of lead

About half of modern populations' lead body burden is derived from inhaling lead-polluted air, but in antiquity human exposure probably occurred principally by ingestion of contaminated foods and beverages or by local application to the skin (cosmetics; therapeutics). Lead absorbed through the skin, intestine or lung is distributed throughout the body to all tissues. Modern degrees of exposure easily overwhelm the body's very limited ability to excrete this metal. Turnover rates create an average half-life ($T_{1/2}$ = the time interval necessary to remove one-half of the amount present at the beginning of the period) of lead in soft tissues of only a few weeks. However, the unexcreted portion accumulates in bone's hydroxyapatite crystal, and the $T_{1/2}$ of lead in bone is decades-long (Wittmers et al., 1981). Thus, continued or at least frequent lead exposure results in a progressive rise in bone lead content that, because of its long half-life can be interpretatively employed to reflect lifetime lead exposure. Since lead exposure from natural sources is minimal, skeletal lead content indicates the extent of exposure to anthropogenic lead manipulations. In brief, bone lead content, when integrated into other archaeological or anthropogenic data, can be predictive of certain aspects of individual or population human behavior (Aufderheide et al., 1985).

Lead is an enzyme poison capable of affecting an enormous range of chemical processes in the human body. Interference with several steps of the complex reaction sequence in hemoglobin synthesis can cause anemia. In the growing child low blood lead levels can retard intellectual development. Overt symptoms of lead poisoning include intestinal cramps (colic or 'dry gripes'), nerve paralysis producing muscle weakness (especially 'foot-drop' or 'wrist drop') and the potentially fatal toxic effect on the brain manifested as convulsions. Less obvious toxic effects include kidney failure and gout.

Grossly evident lesions of lead toxicity are few. Lead can combine with oral bacteria-produced sulfur, precipitating as a clearly visible black line in gingival tissue (gums), that may be preserved in mummies. Its interference with osteoblast function in long bone epiphyses results in accumulation of an excessively wide zone of calcified but unossified cartilage in the epiphyses. This becomes apparent as a transverse band of increased density radiologically (lead line). Bilateral renal atrophy is the only other occasionally recognizable tissue lesion of lead toxicity. Relatively simple methods of chemical analysis, however, can identify the amount of lead accumulated in bone. Clinical symptoms correlate at least roughly with blood levels. Recent in vivo studies offer some guides to translate bone lead into blood levels and hence into symptoms. Such an approach has enabled bone lead analysis to predict an eighteenth century lead poisoning epidemic in the Caribbean (Handler et al., 1986).

History of lead poisoning

Lead artifacts appear in the archaeological record at least as early as 5000 B.C. (Aufderheide, 1993). However, lead's effects on skeletal tissue becomes evident only radiologically or by chemical analysis. Hence, it is not surprising that evidence of its toxicity does not become available until the historical record of the Greco–Roman period. Their pursuit of the silver contaminating lead ore led these populations into exposure sufficient to become symptomatic (Aufderheide et al., 1992). In the first century A.D. Pliny warned the populace about the dangerous fumes in 'silver mines', but general population exposure resulted from employment of metallic lead – a silver mining and processing byproduct – as a utilitarian product for drinking-water pipes as well as foodware. Lead leaching from the containers into their contents of food and beverages resulted in inadvertent lacing of these items with lead. Roman wine production was especially susceptible to this, and Nriagu (1983) has suggested the toxic effects of such hidden sources of lead ingestion were responsible for some of the unrestrained behavior of certain Roman emperors. Gilfillan (1990) has even suggested that gonadal dysfunction and decreased fertility (demonstrated in animals but much less well in humans) induced by lead toxicity may have been responsible for the rapid decline of the wine-drinking Roman aristocracy during the imperial age, leading to the fall of the empire.

During Europe's Industrial Revolution, a series of population-wide exposures to lead *via* contamination of food and beverages were manifested by epidemics of colic, convulsions and paralysis – the classic triad of lead toxicity. They were known by different names, such as the colic of Pictou (French), colica pictonum (Holland), colic of Devonshire (England) and others. The American colonial period experienced similar problems through the use of pewter kitchenware (Aufderheide *et al.*, 1988).

Even though the toxicity of lead had been repeatedly defined by such experiences, the utility of this metal was so attractive that its employment penetrated almost every aspect of life. Today gasoline engine emissions, food can solders, painted children's toys or cribs, batteries and a thousand other sources continue to threaten health status in developed countries (Aufderheide, 1993).

Paleopathology of lead poisoning

No cases of lead toxicity in antiquity have been recognized on the basis of oral pigmentation, small kidneys or radiological lesions. Chemical analysis, however, has generated useful information in several areas.

Social correlates

Arguing that high bone lead levels in colonial Americans correlated with wealth (because only the wealthy could afford the British pewter that was the lead source), Aufderheide *et al.* (1981) demonstrated that skeletal lead content could separate plantation slaves from their owners and even white indentured servants from their white employers.

Health effects

Aufderheide *et al.* (1992), in a study of 20 Italian peninsula populations between the time of the Etruscans to the Middle Ages, found that the populations' bone lead content paralleled their intensity of lead ore mining, rising from a minimal level initially to a peak at the time of the Roman imperial age and decreasing again after the mines had been depleted. In a separate chemical study, Handler *et al.* (1986) identified lead intoxication as the cause of a Caribbean-wide, eighteenth century epidemic of colic and muscle weakness, eventually tracing its origin to the practice of distilling fermented molasses (a plantation product) into rum through a lead-lined distillation unit.

Another unique application of skeletal lead analysis involved an attempt to reconstruct the fate of nineteenth century Arctic expedition members. In 1845 Sir John Franklin used two ships of Britain's royal navy and 129 crewmen to open the last, unexplored section of what western nations had hoped could be made into a commercial waterway through the northern section of the New World (Northwest Passage). Not one of the expedition's members was ever heard from again. The graves of several crewmen who had died early in the expedition were found on Beechey Island off the coast of Devon Island in the Canadian arctic archipelago. A note in a rock cache on King William Island, describing how their ships became hopelessly ice-bound, was found eventually years later during a search that also revealed a trail of skeletons along the coast of that island. Owen Beattie, anthropologist from the University of Alberta (Edmonton, Canada), and colleagues exhumed the well-preserved, frozen Beechey Island bodies and carried out autopsies on them in the field (Beattie & Geiger, 1987). They also harvested skeletal tissue samples from some of the King William Island skeletons. Analyses revealed lead concentrations of several hundred parts per million (ppm or micrograms of lead per gram of sample tissue), about ten times the value found in bones of Inuit from that area and high enough to have been capable of causing serious degrees of lead poisoning. A thorough examination of expedition supplies and soil samples suggested the origin of the lead probably was the lead solder used to seal the group's food tins. This was established by demonstrating that the lead in the expedition members' bones had the same pattern of lead isotope ratios as that of the tins' lead solder (Kowal *et al.*, 1990).

Yet another example is that where similar methodology was employed by Reinhard & Ghazi (1992) at the University of Nebraska at Lincoln. Having found high skeletal lead content in bones of the Omaha tribe of North American Indians (some of which dated to the post-contact period), their initial suspicion was directed at musketballs and other lead product sources, to the manufacture of which the Native Americans were exposed during life, and also perhaps postmortem in some cases from grave artifacts. Nevertheless, some unphysiologically high values stimulated them to pursue alternative sources and eventually led them to awareness of the use of body paint acquired from eastern U.S.A. sources. Like Kowal *et al.* (1990), the Nebraska investigators used lead isotope ratios to demonstrate that most of the bone lead isotope ratio patterns, especially the very high values, matched that of the body paint from the eastern sources and only a small fraction of the total was similar to a local lead source from which the lead artifacts had been fashioned.

Clearly the devastating effects of excessive exposure to lead had become apparent by Greco–Roman times, yet the utilitarian value of lead has been so seductive that this lesson has had to be relearned during every subsequent century. The history of the human encounter with lead suggests that willingness to undergo long-term risk for short-term gain is a feature characteristic of the human personality. It is equally clear that the anatomic features of lead poisoning (gingival and metaphyseal 'lead lines') are so subtle that they will be overlooked in most cases. Fortunately, relatively simple chemical analyses of skeletal tissue can determine its presence in cases with possible exposure conditions.

MERCURY POISONING

While ancient humans may well have been exposed to mercury, modern anthropogenic processing of mercury has caused this toxic metal to be almost as ubiquitous in the current human environment as is lead.

Exposure

Humans are exposed to both organic and inorganic forms of mercury, but it is primarily the latter that exerts its toxicity. Elemental mercury has found a host of applications such as dental amalgam, thermometers, light switch components and many others. It vaporizes readily and thus is inhaled. Mercury salts are also highly toxic. One of them, mercurous chloride, has been used for years as a laxative. Although this form was believed to have little toxicity, if absorbed it is commonly oxidized to the highly toxic, mercuric form which is excreted by the kidney and which poisons the renal tubules during its renal transit. Mercuric salts' antiseptic qualities have resulted in its inclusion in many compounds directed at wound infections. Majno (1975:255) cites such an application by a second century Chinese commentator. Wood (1979:215) cites the sixteenth century physician Fracastoro as deliberately exposing his syphilitic patients to fumes of burning mercury ore. Later organic mercurials were used for antiluetic therapy.

Toxicity of mercury

Mercury produces its toxic effects by combining with sulfhydryl bonds, denaturing proteins and inactivating enzymes. Acute poisoning involves gastrointestinal symptoms and renal failure. Chronic poisoning affects the peripheral nerves producing tremors. In addition, the central nervous system is also involved with a resulting symptom complex called erethism that includes memory loss, excitability, insomnia, delirium and even coma (Graef & Lovejoy, 1991). These symptoms are so apparent to even the medical nonprofessional that they have generated the pejorative phrase 'mad as a hatter' because these industrial workers in the felt industry became exposed when employing mercury in daily use as a hide depilatory agent. Mercury mouthwashes and antisyphilitic therapy resulted in mercury absorption by the teeth, rendering them brittle and subject to accelerated attrition. The gingiva also suffered, becoming infected, darkly discolored (mercury combining with bacterial sulfur to precipitate as mercuric sulphide) and even ulcerated. Toxic effects on mandibular and maxillary periosteum and bone resulted in periostitis, necrosis and tooth loss (Thoma, 1944;478,1169).

Probably the most extensive episode of modern mercury poisoning occurred in Japan where mercury wastes discharged into Minamata Bay, became methylated and entered the marine food chain, poisoning the local populations exploiting that bay's resources (Graef & Lovejoy,1991).

Paleopathology of mercury poisoning

Objective evidence of mercury poisoning can be very subtle. The chronic form can terminate in renal failure and is associated with bilateral renal atrophy. One of us (A.C.A.) has observed a calculus in the renal pelvis composed almost entirely of mercury salt in a modern individual dying of uremia due to chronic mercury poisoning secondary to decades of use of a mercurous chloride compound as a laxative. Proof of the nature of the process, however, rests on the chemical analysis of tissue or calculi.

In 1988, d'Errico et al. examined the dentition from the remains of a Renaissance (1470–1524) Italian noblewoman, Isabella d'Aragona. The enamel of the facial surfaces had been completely and deliberately abraded to the level of the dentine while the lingual surfaces revealed intact enamel with a black patina. Electron microscopy demonstrated a wear pattern that reflected deliberate use of a metal abrading device to remove the enamel, presumably because of the black color. X-ray fluorescence analysis of the black patina indicated a high mercury content. The most probable explanation appears to be that the observed eroded enamel represents efforts by the individual to remove the black dental patina which was a deposit of mercury salt resulting from oral mercury therapy for syphilis, a popular therapeutic (but unsuccessful) effort to obtain a cure for syphilis contracted during the virulent European epidemic in the first decade of the sixteenth century. Since her bones revealed no evidence of tertiary lues the authors postulate she may have died (at age 54) from toxic renal effects.

Smith et al. (1978) have measured the mercury content of soft tissues from ancient (1600 years old) and modern humans – Alaskan Inuit – as well as ancient (A.D. 1015) and modern whale meat. While the modern human species revealed about twice the mercury content (3.962 ppm in hair, 0.334 ppm in muscle) of the ancient specimen (1.840 ppm in hair, 0.019 ppm in muscle), this still emphasizes that mercury contamination of food sources was significant in antiquity (ancient whale muscle = 0.006 ppm, modern = 0.010 ppm).

Long-Xiang Peng (1995) has attributed part of the excellent soft tissue preservation in a 2000 year old Chinese mummy to the effect of a weak mercuric chloride solution found within the coffin.

Because the tissue changes in mercury poisoning are not usually unique, a chemical study of mummified human tissue samples of worldwide distribution and depth in time would be very informative.

Though not an example of systemic mercury intoxication, Fornaciari (1985) reports an example of the external application of mercury paste as an effort at soft tissue preservation for the body of a medieval child, identifying yet another method of mercury exposure (to the 'mummifier') in the past.

ARSENIC POISONING

Although arsenic poisoning produces no characteristic skeletal lesion, toxic quantities do accumulate in bone, and grossly recognizable soft tissue lesions also occur. The condition has been recognized in mummified human remains (Figueroa et al., 1988). For these reasons a brief overview of poisoning with this heavy metal is provided in this volume.

Exposure

Today industrial exposure is the most common. The mining of certain ores, such as copper, may result in concurrent exposure to arsenic. Processing (smelting) of such ores generates the highly toxic arsine gas. The manufacture of many arsenic products may expose workers. Users of these products are especially vulnerable. Arsenic is used in fungicides, wood preservatives, pesticides and in glass manufacturing (Graef & Lovejoy, 1991). It was commonly used as a sheep dip (Savory & Sedor, 1977). It was also the active ingredient in intra-arterial embalming fluids during the nineteenth century. The nineteenth and early twentieth century physicians used organic arsenicals to treat a variety of illnesses including syphilis (arsphenamine), and inorganic arsenic is a common ingredient in many folk healing compounds in China and southeast Asia (Garry, 1987). In recent times the most frequent nonindustrial exposure has been arsenical pesticides, especially lead arsenate.

Exposure can be either intentional or accidental. Because the highly toxic inorganic arsenicals are tasteless but commonly available as pesticides, they became the time-honored vehicle for homicide. The forensic literature of the past two centuries abounds with examples. For the same reason arsenicals have been the preferred agents in suicides. Accidental arsenic poisoning has also occurred by ingestion of contaminated water supplies, often involving sizable cities (Zaldívar, 1974).

Metabolic aspects of arsenic

Absorption from either the gut, skin or lung is quite efficient (>80 %). The metal is widely distributed in the body by blood, bound to globin in hemoglobin. Almost all of it is excreted in the urine, with minor fractions in bile, skin and feces. In the liver the most toxic, trivalent ion is changed to the pentavalent form, then detoxified by methylation in which form it is excreted. Arsenic exerts its toxic effects by binding with sulfhydryl groups on proteins (e.g. those in renal tubular cells), and by binding to enzymes (inhibiting their action), especially those involved with energy reactions in carbohydrate metabolism (Moyer, 1993).

Toxic effects of arsenic

In the acute form of intoxication myocardial toxicity and even brain stem failure may occur, while the more common lesser doses generate symptoms involving the gastrointestinal tract, kidney and liver (jaundice: Savory & Sedor, 1977). The symptoms and signs in chronic forms of poisoning are more apt to include peripheral neuropathy (nerve cells are sensitive to reductions in available energy), skin changes (hyperpigmentation, hyperkeratotic lesions of the palms and soles) and respiratory inflammation (trachea and bronchi: Graef & Lovejoy, 1991). In addition the skin lesions may progress to malignancy (squamous cell carcinoma) and increased frequency of lung cancer has also been reported. Vascular wall injury with clot formation is common as well (Zaldívar, 1974).

Perhaps the most well-documented episode of chronic arsenic poisoning of an entire population is the one that occurred in the mid-twentieth century in Antofagasta, Chile (population 10 000). Incidence rates of arsenic intoxication were as high as 156 per 100 000 (Zaldívar et al., 1978). The exposure was traced to the city's drinking water (arsenic concentration of 0.58 ppm), drawn from the local river (Toconce). In this area the streams arise as melted snow in the nearby Andean peaks but flow through an arsenic-containing lava bed before descending to the city. River water had an arsenic concentration of 0.94 ppm (20 times the upper level of safety standard). Arsenical skin lesions were common and had progressed to malignancy in several adults. Several children had fatal vascular complications. Symptoms were related to total dose of arsenic (Zaldívar, 1974; Zaldívar & Ghai, 1980). Other episodes have been reported in Taiwan (Tseng et al., 1968), Canada (Hindmarsh & McLetchie, 1977) and Poland (Geyer, 1898).

Gerin & de Zorzi (1961) as well as Hansen & Moller (1949) found that the liver contained the highest concentration of arsenic in cases of acute poisoning, but that bone also had diagnostically elevated values. While both hair and nails have very high quantities of arsenic in such cases, these sources of specimens can be dangerously misleading. Hair and nails have a very high sulfur content (about 4 % by weight). Exogenous arsenic exposure (e.g. when washing hands or hair in arsenic-containing water) results in irreversible binding of arsenic to the hair and nail sulfur, resulting in insoluble arsenic sulfide. Such contaminating arsenic cannot be distinguished from endogenous arsenic in these samples, and thus the arsenic content of these sample sources does not reflect total body arsenic absorption.

Postmortem lesions of arsenic poisoning have been described by Thienes & Haley (1972) and include fatty degeneration of the liver, acute tubular necrosis of the kidney, edematous gut mucosa with abundant mucous and fluid content, heart petechiae, cerebral edema, peripheral nerve degeneration (with histological evidence of myelin degeneration) and leukonychia (a transverse, white band of arsenic deposit on the fingernails or toenails). Several of these, as well as skin lesions, could be recognized in mummified bodies. Tseng *et al.* (1968) noted that the vascular thromboses leading to leg gangrene (locally called 'blackfoot') revealed the histological structure of atherosclerosis or thromboangiitis obliterans.

History and paleopathology of arsenic poisoning

Borgoño & Greiber (1971) described results of arsenic analysis carried out on 51 samples of 35 mummies excavated from the Antofagasta region. Hair values ranged from 0.8–3.8 mg of arsenic per 100 g of specimen (8–38 ppm). Muscle samples ranged between 0.5 to 0.9 ppm, while bones had values as high as 9.0 ppm (compact bone) to 24.8 ppm (vertebral body) and teeth showed levels of 1.2 ppm.

The most detailed report of mummy studies for arsenic poisoning is that of Figueroa *et al.* (1988) who examined a group of Inca-period mummies (CAM-9 site) from the Camarones valley on the north coast of Chile, a short distance north of Antofagasta. The Camarones river is also contaminated with arsenic. The Camarones mummies (from about A.D. 1400) demonstrated numerous skin lesions, especially in the children, though the distribution pattern did not conform to that which is characteristic of chronic arsenicism. Elevated values of arsenic were found in all specimens examined. Mean values (ppm) were 3.9 for bone, 12.7 for hair, 18.8 for nail, 26.8 for kidney, 14.9 for liver, 8.2 for skin, 0.7–1.2 for Camarones river water and 17.0 for burial site soil. A progressively increasing concentration was noted with age.

The possibility of arsenic poisoning has been suggested as a possible cause of Napoleon's death. The emperor, himself, believed he was being poisoned during his exile. The autopsy report, however, identified perforated stomach cancer as the cause of death. More recently the validity of this diagnosis has been questioned. Increasing quality of analytical instrumentation following World War II led to the popular practice of quantitative trace metal measurements in human hair samples under the assumption that the body burden of metals important for nutrition could be predicted from the amounts in hair that could be sampled noninvasively. Inevitably the practice was extended eventually to the measurement of toxic metals, including arsenic. Retention of a lock of hair from the deceased as a personal memento was a popular funerary custom in past generations. Several surviv-

ing locks of Napoleon's hair have been subjected to chemical analysis. In 1961 neutron activation analysis found 10.4 ppm of arsenic in one such hair sample (Karlen, 1984). Smith *et al.* (1962) found fluctuating arsenic levels in segments of Napoleon's hair representing a whole year's growth. Twenty years later Lewin *et al.* (1982) used modern neutron activation analysis on yet another of Napolon's hair locks and found only traces of arsenic. However, we are now aware that hair can become contaminated entirely from exogenous sources by binding irreversibly with its high (4 % by weight) sulfur content. In view of the frequent opportunity for exogenous as well as medicinal arsenic exposure in the Napoleonic era, the variable introduced by potential contamination can be employed to support interpretation of the measured arsenic values as representative of either endogenous or exogenous origin. Thus the application of quantitative arsenic analysis has failed to bring about final closure to the continuing speculation about the role of arsenic in Napoleon's illness and/or death.

Also interesting was the case of the American arctic explorer Charles Francis Hall. While over-wintering on the west coast of Greenland with his ship frozen in ice, some expedition members developed an animosity against Hall, questioning his leadership ability. In November, 1871, Hall had returned to the ship, vigorous and apparently healthy at the end of a 14 day reconnaissance trip, but fell ill within a half-hour after drinking a cup of coffee prepared for him by the ship's steward. He suffered acute abdominal pain and other gastrointestinal symptoms as well as delirium. His diary entries during this period indicate his suspicion that he was being poisoned by the ship's surgeon (with whom he was not on good terms). Two weeks after onset of his complaints Hall died on November 8, 1871, during an exacerbation of his symptoms, and was buried on shore in a wooden coffin. In August, 1968, F. Paddock, a physician from Pittsfield, Massachusetts, and Chauncy C. Loomis, an English professor from Dartmouth College, exhumed the coffin. It had not been buried deep enough to keep the body permanently frozen, so considerable soft tissue decomposition was observed. However, hair, fingernail, bone and soil samples were acquired.

Tests at the Toronto Centre of Forensic Sciences indicated the presence of considerable arsenic (all values in ppm or μg of arsenic/g of tissue): bone, 11.0; hair, 10.6–29.4; fingernail, 20.7–76.7; soil, 21.9. Both hair and fingernail were sampled in segments, and highest values were found in the proximal segments, lowest in the distal. This pattern suggested chronic arsenic administration with larger, 'pulsed' doses during the last several weeks of Hall's life (Paddock *et al.*, 1970).

Certainly the nature and chronology of the social conditions and Hall's symptoms are consistent with arsenic poisoning, but several factors restrict the certainty of such a diagnosis. First, one might question whether a surgeon, the only crew member with convenient access to arsenic, would incriminate himself by using this compound. Secondly, the soil had a substantial arsenic content and the sampled tissues were bathed in this groundwater every summer. As noted above, the high sulfur content of hair (and also nail) will bind arsenic. The fact that some hair specimens have an arsenic content higher than that of soil does not necessarily indicate a substantial premortem content, since prolonged exposure of hair to arsenic-containing soil water can result in a cumulative concentration in hair greater than in soil water ('arsenic sink' effect). The same is true of fingernail matrix. Thus, while the presence of postmortem tissue values of arsenic are consistent with elevated antemortem values, it is equally true that all the analytical values are also explainable as postmortem contamination from the soil.

For the paleopathologist, the arsenical skin lesions can be expected to be the only gross anatomic finding of arsenic poisoning, though the distinctive line in fingernails could be identified if specifically sought. The keratotic lesions can involve almost any area, but are often most prominent on the palms and soles (fortunately because epidermis is often preserved on hands and feet in contrast to other sites in mummified human remains). Squamous cell carcinomas that evolve from the keratoses should be recognizable in mummies also.

MYCOTOXICOSIS

Mycotoxicoses are conditions characterized by various symptoms elicited by toxins produced by fungi, especially those of the genera *Aspergillus, Penicillium, Fusarium* and *Phoma* (Bennington, 1984). The genus *Penicillium*, for example, secretes a product, penicillin, that is highly toxic to many bacteria. Because penicillin is not toxic to humans, it may be employed as an antibacterial agent in human infections. In other cases the toxins are also toxic to humans. The mushrooms *Amanita muscaria* or *A. phalloides* forms of fungus, generate a mycotoxin so powerful that the cellular necrotizing effects in the liver and brain may be lethal only hours after ingestion. Ainsworth (1993a, b) traces recognition of poisonous fungi to a play by Euripides (450 B.C.) and to multiple Roman authors. The fungus *Aspergillus flavus* frequently contaminates cereal grains, especially wheat and peanut products (Ainsworth, 1993a, b), in India and other countries even today. Stored under damp conditions this fungus produces a mycotoxin called aflatoxin B_1. Especially in the presence of the hepatitis B virus, the liver insult by aflatoxin B_1 may progress to cirrhosis and even hepatocellular carcinoma (Patten, 1981).

The fungus *Claviceps purpurea* often attacks rye (*Secale cereale*) and other grains under moist field conditions, producing a hyphal mass (sclerotium) that includes several compounds collectively termed ergot. Ergotamine and ergonovine are alkaloid components of ergot whose effects are characterized primarily by smooth muscle contraction. These compounds remain intact during food preparation methods and are consumed with bread or other goods prepared from the rye contaminated by this fungus. Among the many symptoms resulting from the spastic contraction of smooth muscles are the ischemic effects of spastic arteries. In the legs profound and prolonged arterial spasm can actually restrict blood flow sufficiently to produce tissue death (gangrene), while in the brain and spinal cord foci of ischemic necrosis also occur. Symptoms of the latter effect generate involuntary and purposeless muscle contractions of varying degree that have been termed 'creepings' or even 'convulsions' in laic descriptions (though true seizures are rare). Lesser doses often cause bizarre behavior, and ergot's lysergic acid components may even cause frank hallucinations (Haller, 1993). The powerful smooth muscle constrictive action of ergot has led to its use as a uterine contraction agent in obstetrical practice today.

Sandison (1967d) states that ergotism has been recognizably described as early as the ninth century. By carefully detailing past weather records that would have favored the growth of ergot-producing *Aspergillus flavus* in the field, Matossian (1989:67–8) feels it is possible to predict episodes of ergotism during the past centuries. For example, a cold winter and wet spring in England in 1659 was followed by a fall (autumn) epidemic whose symptoms parallel those of ergotism. She also suggests that the unusual behavior that characterized the witchcraft period in Salem, Massachusetts could well have been the effects of chronic ergotism.

Paleopathology

Recognition of the cause of ergotism has led to practices in western countries that have virtually eliminated this condition there. There is little doubt that some clinical phenomena and even epidemics of the past were manifestations of ergotism. Unfortunately, the pattern of symptoms is not sufficiently unique to permit diagnostic certainty. Gangrenous changes can also be the effects of diabetes mellitus, atherosclerosis and other causes. Arterial histology, if soft tissues are preserved, reveals thickening of the muscular wall with fibrosis, changes consistent with hypertension, Raynaud's syndrome and other conditions. If these findings occur in certain contexts, such as some of Matossian's observations, ergotism becomes a more probable explanation. The hepatic fibrosis and even malignant hepatic tumor expressions of aflatoxin B_1's hepatotoxic effects can be expected to be recognizable in mummified bodies, but these too can occur in the absence of mycotoxins. Thus, the anatomic clues to mycotoxin effects in ancient human soft tissue remains may not be obvious, but could be discernible in some cases. Under such circumstances the diagnosis of ergotism would become more probable with demonstration of contextual support, especially if similar pathology is found in several contemporary individuals. The anatomic findings in association with circumstances supportive of ergotism have not been reported in mummified human remains.

PART TEN

Endocrine disorders

Some organs secrete biologically active substances into ducts that transport the secretions to the area where these compounds carry out their biological action. For example the liver secretes bile into the common bile duct that drains into the intestine where the bile's emulsifying effect aids the food digestive process. Similarly the digestive enzymes made by the pancreas reach the intestine *via* the pancreatic duct, saliva from salivary glands reach the oral cavity through the salivary ducts, etc. These ducts are large enough to be visible to the unaided eye and so were recognized by early anatomists whose observations soon led to experiments that identified the organ's function. Some organs, however, secrete their biologically active substance (hormones) directly into the blood circulating through those organs. Hormones thus reach their point of action *via* delivery through the blood, recognizing their target tissues and binding to them by specialized proteins (receptors) on those cells. Such organs earlier were called 'ductless' glands and later were grouped under the term 'endocrine' glands.

A feature common to many endocrine organs is a 'feedback system' in which the intensity of their hormone production is regulated by yet another endocrine gland that usually produces a stimulant and which, in turn, is directly or more often indirectly responsive to the original hormone's blood level. For example the amount of thyroid hormone released by the thyroid gland is dependent on how much thyroid-stimulating hormone is released by the pituitary gland which, in turn, gets its signal from cells in the hypothalamus that are responsive to the blood's thyroid hormone level.

This section deals with both the skeletal and soft tissue lesions some of which involve the glands themselves, while in others the anatomic changes are brought about in tissues directly affected by too much or too little secreted hormone. The principal endocrine organs with which we will concern ourselves are the pituitary, thyroid, parathyroid and adrenal glands as well as the endocrine portion of the pancreas (its islets of Langerhans), since these can produce grossly recognizable effects detectable by a paleopathologist.

THE PITUITARY GLAND

This remarkably small gland (usually less than 500 mm³) lies cradled in an enveloping, thin-boned cavity (sella turcica) centered in the cranial cavity's middle fossa. It is connected to the inferior aspect of the brain *via* a slender (1–2 mm wide) stalk only about 1 cm long that emerges from the hypothalamus. It is sometimes called the 'master gland' because it generates hormones that regulate the function of the thyroid, gonads, adrenal cortex, kidney tubules and breast tissue as well as a general growth hormone.

Disorders affecting this gland are primarily expressed as loss of function or as hyperfunction of the organs it normally controls. Pituitary insufficiency can be induced by trauma, infection, radiation therapy, hemorrhage, ischemia or congenital aplasia. However, the shell of protective bone around the gland limits expansion of the pituitary and acts to render the gland especially vulnerable to destructive effects of compression by a tumor arising within the pituitary itself, even if such a lesion is benign. Pituitary hypofunction generates a constellation of organ deficiencies, only some of which produce changes that can be detected grossly by an examining paleopathologist. For example, the reduction or absence of growth hormone in a developing child may result in a diminutive, but normally-proportioned skeleton with delayed epiphyseal closure (pituitary dwarfism) (Rubin & Farber, 1994d). Effects on the other endocrine organs are discussed in those specific sections. The skeletal effects are defined below.

Primary tumors may arise from cells within the pituitary gland. Hormone production by these tumors is often autonomous and not subject to normal regulating influences, resulting in overproduction and causing hyperfunction of their target organs or tissues. For example, a hyperfunctioning pituitary tumor generating supranormal quantities of growth hormone during childhood can cause a gigantic skeleton, while development of this same tumor in an adult stimulates excessive bone growth, most obvious in the facial and cranial structures (acromegaly). These tumors are usually small, some producing symptoms when they are less than 1 cm in diameter (microadenomas), but even the larger ones (macroadenomas) often only reach a diameter of 3 or 4 cm. Postmortem and desiccation shrinkage may reduce these tumors to a degree that their recognition may elude the paleopathologist unless the abnormalities resulting from insufficient or excessive hormone production alerts the examiner to the possibility of a pituitary abnormality. Macroadenomas commonly erode the skeletal shell of the sella turcica (Fig.

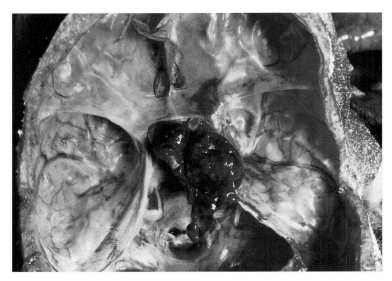

FIG. 10.1: **Pituitary adenoma.** A prolactin-secreting pituitary adenoma compressed and destroyed the normal portion of the pituitary, producing panhypopituitarism in this modern adult male, leading to death. Modern case. PBL.

10.1). This can be assessed by simple anteroposterior and lateral radiographs of the skull and the volume of the sella turcica can be calculated (Hawkins, 1992). The overwhelming bulk of pituitary tumors are benign adenomas, though rarely a malignant tumor primary in the pituitary or its stalk tissues can destroy not only the gland itself, but produce destructive invasion of surrounding cranial and cerebral tissues. These usually are not hormonally active.

Gigantism (Giantism)

Growth hormone
(GH or somatotropin)

Growth hormone (GH) is essential for normal growth of endochondral bone. It is stored in the pituitary's acidophilic cells that compose about half of the anterior lobe. Its secretion is regulated by two hormones from the hypothalamus: a releasing hormone (somatotropin-releasing hormone: GRH) that results in release of the stored GH into the blood, and an inhibitory hormone (somatostatin) that inhibits its secretion (Daniels &

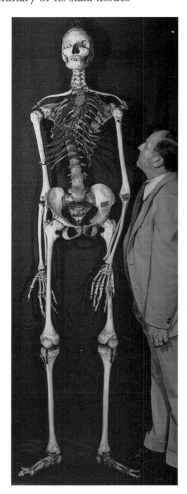

FIG. 10.2: **Gigantism.** The skeleton is 7 feet 6 inches (228.6 cm) tall while the living man's height is 5 feet 10 inches (177.8 cm). Modern case. Courtesy G. Worden. MM.

Martin, 1991:1661). While GH is essential for linear growth, it does not act on bone directly, but instead, stimulates the formation of other hormones (somatomedins) that mediate the action. Of these, somatomedin-C (insulin growth factor-1: IGF-1) is the most important; its blood concentration parallels linear growth (Wilson, 1991b:1651).

Most pituitary lesions causing excess growth hormone production are benign adenomas composed of acidophilic cells of the pituitary's anterior lobe. These are usually macroadenomas (2 cm or greater); a few are microadenomas and only occasionally is diffuse hyperplasia responsible. The end result of excess growth hormone in childhood is profound stimulation of all cells in the cartilaginous growth plate at all sites of endochondral bone formation. For this reason linear growth is accelerated when it occurs in childhood. Furthermore, GH suppresses gonadotropin production, thereby delaying epiphyseal fusion and prolonging the period of growth (Aegerter & Kirkpatrick, 1975:377). These effects lead to gigantism: stature three or more standard deviations greater than the population's mean value (Fig. 10.2). In western countries today gigantism could be defined roughly as total body height greater than 213 cm (7 feet). Fetal growth is independent of GH (Daniels & Martin, 1991:1661); hence the ultimate victims of gigantism are of normal birth weight.

When the pituitary lesion develops before about age 10 years, the epiphyses respond vigorously to the increased GH effect generating accelerated linear growth of normal body proportions with gross bone morphology differing from normal primarily only in magnitude. Gonadotropin suppression results in sexual immaturity. However, soft tissues also respond to the growth stimulus. When excessive size is reached the strains imposed by the great body weight may exceed the ability of even the larger bones to respond properly. Furthermore, prolonged GH exposure induces a neuropathy (nerve dysfunction) expressed as muscle weakness. The paradox of increased size and weight coupled with muscular weakness may lead to skeletal distortions. Kyphosis with or without scoliosis is a common response, later often of a degree that impairs respiration sufficiently to initiate pulmonary infections. Tarsal deformities frequently lead to loss of locomotion in early young adulthood. Most untreated giants die of cerebral or cardiac complications before age 30 years.

Eventually epiphyses often close sufficiently to impair further linear growth. Nonuniformity of closure leads to deforming growth asymmetry. Continued growth after this period initiates the same features as are seen in individuals whose tumors first appear in adulthood – a condition termed acromegaly.

Acromegaly

Giants whose untreated tumors continue to function after their epiphyses eventually close, as well as normal adults whose tumors develop after growth has ceased, undergo a

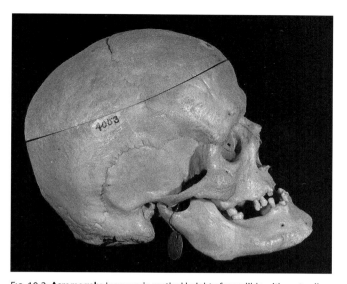

FIG. 10.3: **Acromegaly.** Increase in vertical height of mandible with protruding chin is a characteristic effect of excess growth hormone from a pituitary adenoma in an adult modern male. The greater growth of the mandible with respect to the maxilla commonly causes malocclusion and its destructive effect on the teeth. T-4053. CMNH.

dramatically different appearance. The GH reawakens endochondral bone growth, but the fused epiphyses no longer permit linear growth, and show only slight thickening. Joint cartilage proliferates and subsequent pressure may cause them to ulcerate and simulate osteoarthritis (Nabarro, 1987). Short tubular hand bones may demonstrate some terminal digit tufting but hand thickening is primarily the product of soft tissue proliferation. The costochondral junctions and even clavicles may respond dramatically, producing rounded masses ('beading') that may undergo cystic fibrous changes internally (Jaffe, 1972). Vertebrae develop subperichondrial thickening as well as new bone deposits on the vertebral body surface not facing the disk spaces that has the appearance of an envelope of new bone (Erdheim, 1931: figure 84; Ortner & Putschar, 1985:300, figure 464). Perhaps the most obvious changes occur in the facial bones. Mandibular lengthening generates prominent prognathism, exaggerated by further subperiosteal deposition of new bone at the chin (Fig. 10.3). Malar and other bones become prominent because of their thickening. Cartilage proliferation even enlarges the nose. Small benign adenomas may not alter the sella turcica, but larger ones compress and erode the posterior clinoids, while malignant lesions can destroy all sella structures as well as surrounding bone. A review of 30 clinical cases of acromegaly showed radiological evidence of sella abnormalities in only 25 (Hamwi et al., 1960). Sinus cavities are narrowed by their thickened walls (Hosovski, 1991). In adults the cranial cavity is not usually enlarged because the ossification centers are completely ossified before the condition develops. The frontal bone, however, often shows a prominent supraciliary ridge and the occipital prominence may become a torus (Aegerter & Fitzpatrick, 1975:377). The offending pituitary tumors sometimes undergo hemorrhage into their parenchyma that may destroy not only the tumor but the remaining pituitary tissue, arresting the process and inducing hypopituitarism. While most modern, treated acromegalics' age of death is only modestly shortened by their disease (Nabarro, 1987), earlier reports of substantially shortened life span (Wright et al., 1970) probably more closely reflect the acromegalic's fate in antiquity.

Paleopathology of gigantism and acromegaly

Review of the published record suggests that the giants of myth really are mythical (Todd, 1914). Nineteenth century literature reflects a common belief that modern humans descended from a race of giants. Documentation of excessive stature, however, is rare. All too often literature supplies no more satisfying evidence than Herodotus' comment (ca. 450 B.C.: IX, 83) that a dead Persian soldier at the battle of Plateae in 479 B.C. was 5 cubits tall (Bartsocas, 1985); at the accepted cubit measure of Greek antiquity (18.22 inches) this translates into 91.1 inches or about 7.6 feet. The literature, however, reveals that human height exaggeration was not limited to circus owners − numerous physician reports have been refuted by later measurements. Lewis Wilkins was measured in a Chicago hospital shortly before he died there at age 28 years of an ulcerative colitis. He was 8 feet 2 inches tall, and autopsy demonstrated a pituitary tumor that had invaded and destroyed much of the cranial base (Bassoe, 1903). Schereschewsky (1926) lists 24 reported giants between 230 and 283 cm stature (including three in excess of 272 cm or about 9 feet), but does not supply circumstances under which the measurements were made. Hayles' (1980) review declares that the tallest, documented human was Robert Pershing Wadlow, the Alton giant once displayed by Ringling Brothers Barnum and Bailey Circus, whose measured height at time of death was 8 feet 11.1 inches (272 cm) and who weighed 465 pounds (211 kg). Today skeletons of giants are curated at the Philadelphia Mütter Museum (229 cm), London's Hunter Museum (230 cm) and the Leyden Museum (221 cm). None of these died more than 250 years ago. Claims for gigantism in older specimens lack satisfactory documentation.

In contrast to gigantism, acromegaly has a respectable antiquity. An Egyptian skeleton in the British Museum displays skull features characteristic of acromegaly, particularly evident in the mandible (Brothwell, 1981:124, plate 5.1C). Perkins' (1931) review of the Nordic sagas reveals some vivid portrayals that led him to produce a familial pattern of acromegaly which, of course, lends itself to skeptical criticism of the descriptions' specificity. Keith (1931) felt that an adult skull from Gardar in southern Greenland (*Homo gardarensis*) had acromegalic features. A medieval acromegalic skeleton from Yugoslavia appears to be well-documented by Hosovski (1991). Medieval skull fragments from Oxfordshire demonstrate a largely destroyed sella turcica but no facial or postcranial bones were available for evidence of hormonal effect (Hacking, 1995). A North American aboriginal skull and long bones dating to about A.D. 900 with typical skull characteristics was excavated in Illinois (Morse, 1969) and Brauer (1991) found a complete skeleton with an eroded sella, characteristic facial and postcranial features in San Cristobal Ruins of New Mexico from the late prehistoric period. A pre-Columbian adult male skeleton from the Pottery Mound Pueblo site in New Mexico demonstrated both cranial and acral (extremity) changes characteristic of acromegaly, though the sellar region was too poorly preserved to evaluate adequately (Rhine, 1985). A historic period Native American skeleton in the Smithsonian Institution collections demonstrates changes suggestive but not diagnostic of acromegaly (Ortner & Putschar, 1985:301). Nehrlich et al. (1991) describe a dramatic degree of polyostotic fibrous dysplasia in the facial and many postcranial bones of the obviously acromegalic Tegernsee giant who died in 1876 and is displayed at the Munich Museum. They do not view this as a variant of Albright's syndrome but, instead, feel the fibrocystic changes are an effect of prolonged exposure to growth hormone excess.

Differential diagnosis of gigantism includes eunuchoid gigantism that can occur in circumstances of gonadal failure before puberty. Moderate increase in stature may be a product of this condition but it never reaches the extent seen in pituitary gigantism and the lower half of the body exhibits more growth than the upper (Aegerter & Kirkpatrick, 1975:378).

Summary of skeletal lesions in gigantism and acromegaly

1. Gigantism: Normally-proportioned and structured bones of excessive length with late superimposed degenerative changes secondary to increased weight and muscular weakness; especially kyphoscoliosis.
2. Acromegaly: Thickening of all bones; elongated, prognathic mandible; prominence of nose and facial bones; beaded costochondral junctions; wide ribs; enlarged vertebrae; subperiosteal bone envelope; thick hand bones; tufted digits; degenerative joint changes; thick long bones; enlarged or eroded sella turcica.

Pituitary dwarfism

Loss of pituitary function during childhood leads to a form of dwarfism characterized by short stature with normally proportioned body segments (above and below the symphysis pubis) as well as normally proportioned extremity lengths in relation to the trunk. Intellect is also usually within normal limits. The cause of pituitary insufficiency is usually compression by a pituitary tumor − either adenoma or craniopharyngioma. The adenomas in pituitary dwarfism are usually nonfunctional, generating their somatic effects by compressive destruction of residual pituitary tissue. Not surprisingly, not only is growth hormone synthesis suppressed but also that of thyroid hormone, gonadotropins and adrenocorticotrophic hormone. In some even the posterior pituitary lobe is crushed by the expanding tumor, adding loss of antidiuretic hormone synthesis to the spectrum of symptoms. In addition to adenomas that arise within the pituitary lying within the sella turcica, craniopharyngiomas arising from remnants of the pituitary stalk outside the sella and even primary tumors of the midbrain (Sandison, 1958) may invade or compress the pituitary. In such a case symptoms and signs of brain tissue destruction, especially the optic chiasm very near the sella turcica with its unique impairment of vision, may complicate the clinical picture further. Individuals with findings limited to evidence of only pituitary involvement are said to have the Paltauf or Lorain syndrome, while those with evidence of additional midbrain destruction are termed Fröhlich syndrome (Jaffe, 1972:342). Causes of pituitary dysfunction in childhood other than neoplasms are far less common but include trauma, congenital deformity, cystic degeneration and deposition of mucopolysaccharides in certain congenital enzyme deficiencies.

Nonskeletal effects of hypopituitarism

Lack of gonadotropin production usually results in lack of sexual development as well as the effect on epiphyseal closure discussed below. Mentation is usually normal. Effects of decreased thyroid hormone function and adrenal function are commonly identifiable but often not as profound as might be expected. Increased thirst and urine output, when present, reflect loss of antidiuretic hormone production by the compressed or destroyed posterior pituitary lobe. Thin skin and fine hair are common.

Skeletal effects of hypopituitarism

The fundamental skeletal lesion of hypopituitarism results from the loss of growth hormone effect. This is expressed as delay in development of ossification centers with consequent retardation of growth at the cartilage growth plate. Trueta (1968:47) has demonstrated that hypophysectomized rats show decreased epiphyseal vascularity on both sides of the growth plate, inhibiting cartilage cell reproduction and proliferation. Eventually a thin layer of bone covers the plate, terminating further growth. Thus the epiphyseal plate persists (though nonfunctional) far beyond the age of usual fusion; similarly sutures and synchondroses persist as well. The end result is gracile tubular bones of the extremity that are shorter than normal but, except for persistence of identifiable epiphyseal lines, are not otherwise deformed (Jaffe, 1972:344). The extremities are in appropriate proportion to the trunk, and body segments are also in appropriate proportion.

Dentition, however, is commonly distinctly abnormal. Since growth hormone affects primarily mesodermal structures, dental enamel (of ectodermal origin) is unaffected and tooth crowns are of normal size. However, tooth eruption is normally affected by changes in pulp, root and supporting tissues (all of mesodermal origin). Absence of growth hormone impairs these tissues, resulting in delayed eruption and shedding of the deciduous dentition. Delayed bone growth of the jaws also affects the mandible more than the maxilla, the disproportionate growth of upper and lower incisors producing a distinct overbite (Cohen & Wagner, 1948), as well as delay in eruption of the second mandibular molar teeth.

Paleopathology of pituitary dwarfism

In living individuals pituitary dwarfism can be separated easily from cretinism on the basis of intellect, the cretin usually demonstrating marked mentation impairment. In archaeological skeletons, however, the problem can be more complex. Key evidence, when present, is the finding of erosion or destruction of the sella turcica commonly found in pituitary dwarfs. Unfortunately, some tumors or other types of pathology destroy the pituitary soft tissues without altering the sella's skeletal structure. In such cases it may be helpful to note that cretinism affects the lower extremities more than the uppers. In addition, because cretins are affected since birth while pituitary lesions in childhood commonly appear only after several years of normal growth, the degree of stunted growth in pituitary dwarfs is usually not as extreme as it often is in cretins (Jaffe, 1972:342). Nevertheless, in the absence of sella turcica distortion, differentiation of cretinism from pituitary dwarfism may be impossible in some skeletons because of overlapping variations in the degree of the noted differences. Separation of either of these two from achondroplastic dwarfs on the basis of the gross disproportion of the trunk and the extremities rarely presents a problem.

Few skeletons of either pituitary or cretinous dwarfs from antiquity have been reported. One possible case of a young Romano-British adult female excavated from a Roman cemetery in Gloucester was suspected to be a pituitary form of dwarfism because of short stature (131.2 cm), gracile but normally shaped long bones, dentition showing unerupted third molars and just erupting mandibular canines and many unfused or delayed epiphyseal closures. New bone formation on both inner and outer cranial bone surfaces suggested a possible infectious etiology (Roberts, 1987b).

Another example comes from the collections at the Smithsonian Institution from a New Mexico site including both late prehistoric and early historic burials. Open or recently fused epiphyses of gracile bones and small stature in what appeared to be a grown male suggested pituitary dwarfism. Unfortunately the base of the skull that contained the sella turcica was missing.

Using a standardized radiological method to assess the volume of the sella turcica in intact ancient skulls, Hawkins (1992) found a mean value of 561.4 ±(157.7) mm³ in a series of ancient Egyptian skulls. In addition, a predynastic skull excavated from a Badari site had a volume of 1350 mm³. He states that modern imaging techniques have established that most pituitary tumors in excess of 1 cm diameter are associated with sellar volumes of less than 1200 mm³ only rarely. The Badari skull revealed evidence for neither dwarfism or acromegaly so he concluded it probably represented a nongrowth-hormone producing chromophobe adenoma of the pituitary first appearing in an adult.

Summary of skeletal changes in pituitary dwarfism

Short stature with extremities appropriately proportioned to trunk, upper and lower body segments appropriately proportionate, delayed ossification centers, delayed epiphyseal fusion, gracile bones of normal structure, and frequent sella turcica erosion or destruction.

THE PARATHYROID GLANDS

Four parathyroid glands are normally present, lying just posterior to the cranial and caudal poles of the lateral thyroid lobes. They are diminutive structures each normally weighing less than 50 mg. Their hormonal product, parathyroid hormone (PTH) maintains the blood calcium level within the normal range by stimulating release of calcium and phosphorus from bone, increasing phosphorus excretion and calcium reabsorption in the kidney, and stimulating the kidney to synthesize vitamin D which, in turn, increases calcium and phosphate absorption from the intestine (Kronenberg, 1993). The PTH synthesis and release is not regulated by the pituitary gland, but by the blood calcium level. Reduced calcium levels stimulate PTH synthesis and release.

Primary hyperparathyroidism

Though one of us (A.C.A.) has found normal parathyroid glands in ancient frozen Arctic bodies, they have not been described in desiccated archaeological bodies. Furthermore, while hyperfunction may be due to either a benign adenoma of a single gland or hyperplasia of all four glands, their combined weight is usually less than 5 g or a maximum diameter of about 2 cm. Thus, it is quite probable that a paleopathologist would overlook such alterations, unless attention would be directed by the skeletal changes resulting from PTH overproduction.

The features of primary hyperparathyroidism relate to the normal functions of PTH that is being secreted in abnor-

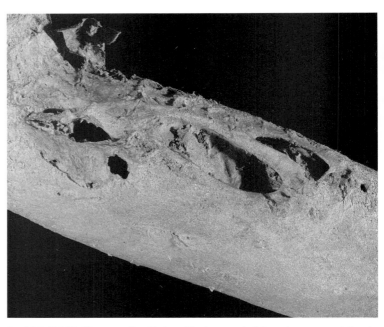

FIG. 10.4: **Osteitis fibrosa cystica.** Cortex of the humerus in this modern young adult male has become profoundly resorbed by prolonged hyperparathyroidism and a local area of osteitis fibrosa cystica, eventually exposing the underlying fibrocystic defect. T-391. Modern young adult male. CMNH.

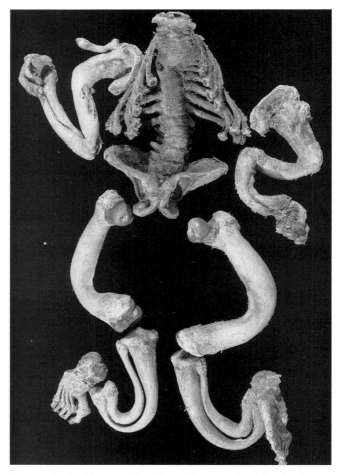

FIG. 10.5: **Osteitis fibrosa cystica.** Advanced hyperparathyroidism has demineralized bones to a degree rendering them unable to bear normal body weight without becoming deformed. T-391. Modern, young adult male. CMNH.

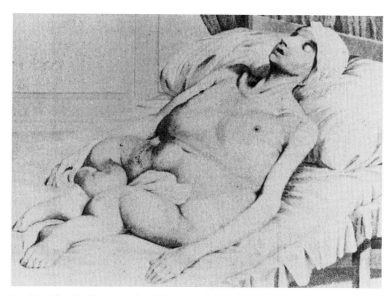

FIG. 10.6: **Osteitis fibrosa cystica.** This young adult male was the first recorded case (Buchanan *et al.*, 1981) of the complication of prolonged hyperparathyroidism with extreme deformation caused by profound bone demineralization and fibrotic osteoclastic lesions. Compare with Fig. 10.5. Illustration is courtesy Dr A. McNicol, Department of Pathology, Glasgow Royal Infirmary. Reprinted with permission from Buchanan *et al.* (1981) *Canadian Medical Association Journal* **124**:812–15.

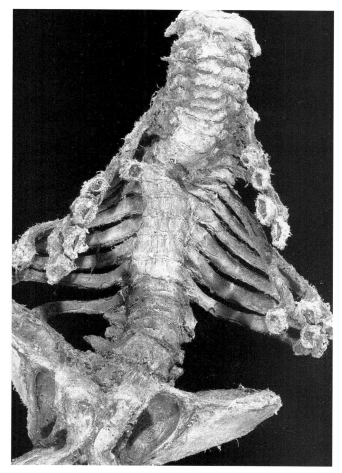

FIG. 10.7: **Osteitis fibrosa cystica.** Prolonged hyperparathyroidism with demineralization of vertebra. Subsequent weight-bearing produced kyphoscoliosis deformation. T-391. Modern young adult male. CMNH.

mally high quantities by a parathyroid adenoma that is no longer under the control of normal physiological regulatory mechanisms. Thus some of the characteristics of this condition result from the hormone's effect on bone and the remainder from the consequence of the hypercalcemia (elevated level of calcium in the blood).

Skeletal Changes

Parathyroid hormone, with the assistance of vitamin D, acts on bone osteoblasts in a mechanism not yet completely defined but which appears to incite exuberant osteoclastic activity, probably by osteoblastic secretion of an osteoclastic stimulant (Holick *et al.*, 1991:1897). As osteoclasts burrow into bone trabeculae ('tunneling resorption') the resorbed calcium enters the blood. The osteoclastic activity is so intense that the trabeculae are eventually completely destroyed and replaced by fibrous tissue. The osteoclast-resorbed, cookie-bite defects on the trabecular surface are easily recognized with modest, hand-lens magnification. The process is particularly active in the subperiosteal areas that acquire a porous radiological appearance, and may even obscure the lamina dura that surrounds the teeth. Thus the initial skeletal effect is diffuse osteopenia, rendering the bones weaker, fragile and more fibrotic (Aegerter & Kirkpatrick, 1975:392). In many areas this process becomes so advanced that routine, day-to-day stresses are sufficient to generate microfractures with small foci of hemorrhage. These are probably responsible for the bone pain so commonly present in this disease. Organization of this hemorrhage results in more extensive fibrosis and architectural disruption not very conducive to bone remodeling. Repetitive episodes of this type eventually produce grossly recognizable areas involved by the changes, measuring 5 cm or more in diameter. The tissue liquefaction phase of organization may eventuate as fluid- or fibrous-filled cystic areas. Some of these areas can become large enough to expand the bone diameter, covered only by a thin shell of cortex, rendering them susceptible to major fractures through these areas of weight-bearing long bones. The exposed mass of benign fibrous tissue stained by the brown-appearing hemoglobin breakdown products of blood (hemosiderin) have given rise to the misnomer 'brown tumors' for these non-neoplastic, benign, reactive changes. The process is known more formally as osteitis fibrosa cystica (Jaffe, 1972:310; Fig. 10.4). It may involve almost any bone in the skeleton but is especially obvious in the extremity bones. After years of such uncontrolled hyperparathyroidism, gross bone deformation can occur as a product of weight stresses on profoundly weakened and hypomineralized bones combined with fracture deformities (Fig. 10.5). These changes are demonstrated clearly and dramatically in a 33 year old male from the late eighteenth century, re-reported and illustrated again 200 years later (Buchanan *et al.*, 1981; Fig. 10.6). These effects of advanced, untreated hyperparathyroidism, are seldom seen today for uncertain reasons, perhaps because the condition is now usually recognized and treated at an earlier stage. If this condition existed in antiquity, however, its development in the absence of effective therapy can be expected to have complicated hyperparathyroidism quite regularly. Weakened, osteopenic vertebrae may also suffer collapse with resulting kyphosis (Fig. 10.7). Identification of the trabecular 'tunneling resorption' lesions can help separate hyperparathyroidism from conventional osteoporosis as the etiology of this complication.

Soft tissue changes

Even though the changes accompanying hyperparathyroidism are principally skeletal, the kidneys may also manifest changes. The excessive calcium leached from the bones and absorbed from the intestine raises the blood calcium level. The parathyroid cells of the adenoma or hyperplastic glands do not respond to this normal signal, and maintain the high calcium level. Thus the increased calcium and phosphate excretion into the urine can reach supersaturation levels, resulting in precipitation of calcium phosphate within the kidney. This precipitate eventually accretes into the form of a kidney 'stone' (renolith). Small calculi of this kind may be passed (painfully) through the ureter and excreted *via* the bladder urine, or they may block the ureter (Potts, 1991:1903). In the latter instance the rise in pressure proximal to the obstructing stone may dilate the proximal ureter and kidney calices (hydronephrosis). If the stone does not pass and relieve the obstruction, the kidney undergoes atrophy, and becomes functionless. Alternatively, continued deposition of calcium onto a stone in the renal pelvis may increase its size to a degree that can not pass through the ureter. Such stones tend gradually to conform to the shape of the renal pelvis and even its calices, eventually occupying most of the space within these structures and weighing up to 100 g. These often erode the cells lining the renal pelvis and subsequent severe infections (pyelonephritis) are common. In antiquity many such infections would have been fatal. Renal calculi and their complications are discussed in more detail in the Urinary Tract section of Chapter 8.

Summary of skeletal and soft tissue changes in hyperparathyroidism

Skeletal lesions include diffuse osteopenia, trabecular tunneling resorption, microfractures, macrofractures and osteitis fibrosis cystica. Soft tissue changes may produce diffuse nephrocalcinosis, renal calculi, hydronephrosis, pyelonephritis and parathyroid adenoma or diffuse hyperplasia.

Secondary hyperparathyroidism

In the secondary form of this disease, the inciting event is the gradual onset of kidney failure from any cause. Progressive loss of kidney function eventually results in inability to excrete sufficient phosphorus. The subsequent rise in blood phospho-

rus level has a reciprocal relationship to blood calcium levels, so the corresponding decrease in blood calcium seen in uremic states stimulates PTH synthesis and release. The consequent increased excretion of calcium into the urine (calciuria) with precipitation of calcium salts of microscopic size in the relatively stagnated urine results in diffuse deposition of these salts throughout both kidneys (diffuse nephrocalcinosis). Radiologic study demonstrates diffuse opacification of such kidneys in contrast to the discrete, gross calculi formed in cases of primary hyperparathyroidism.

Paleopathology of hyperparathyroidism

In most archaeological cases of hyperparathyroidism the skeleton will probably only reveal diffuse osteopenia. Subperiosteal porosity may be recognizable with the unaided eye but the ragged surface of bone trabeculae characteristic of the accelerated osteoclastic activity that is part of this condition usually requires at least moderate magnification for satisfactory evaluation. Radiological study of undeformed bones can identify localized foci of osteitis fibrosa cystica. Bone transection at such sites will reveal cortical thinning with irregular calcified plates and spicules reflecting dystrophic calcification of organized hemorrhagic areas. Brownish discoloration at such sites reflect hemosiderin deposits. In the most advanced examples long bone curvature with

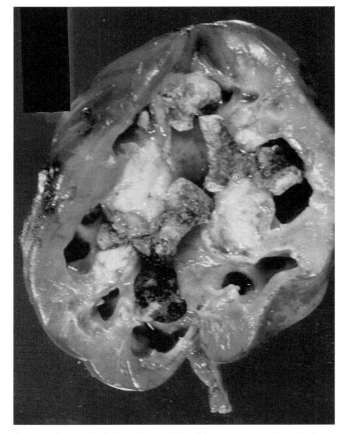

FIG. 10.8: **Renal calculi.** Multiple calculi lie within the renal pelvis and calices in this modern adult male with primary hyperparathyroidism. PBL.

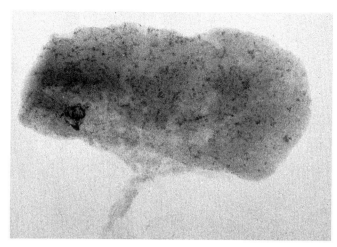

FIG. 10.9: **Diffuse nephrocalcinosis and renal calculus.** Contact print of an X-ray of an atrophic kidney in a spontaneously mummified body of a young adult male. Note diffuse calcification of renal tubules (punctate, dark spots) and small, oxalate calculus in renal pelvis (denser structure in left lower region of kidney). Death was due to renal failure and uremia from chronic renal disease with secondary hyperparathyroidism (Blackman *et al.*, 1991). Cabuza culture, AZ141, T-36, A.D. 350–1000, northern Chile. MAUT. PBL.

cortical thinning and even frankly expanded areas covered by thin cortical shells may be obvious, often with evidence of past or terminal fractures. Osteitis fibrosa cystica lesions are not limited to the long bones, but can also occur in the flat bones of the pelvis and skull.

Only the rare, unusually large parathyroid adenomas can be expected to be detected by paleopathologists. The publications by Steinbock (1989, 1993c) dealing with urolithiasis are particularly rewarding. A case of (primary?) hyperparathyroidism was diagnosed on the basis of focal osteoclastic 'tunneling resorption' seen in histologic sections of an osteopenic femoral trabecular bone in an adult Egyptian female from the Dakhleh Oasis (Cook *et al.*, 1988). Probable secondary hyperparathyroidism in a spontaneously mummified South American body has been reported in which both diffuse nephrocalcinosis and several discrete renal calculi were identified (Blackman *et al.*, 1991; Figs. 10.8 & 10.9). We are not aware of other published archaeological examples of hyperparathyroidism.

Hypoparathyroidism

Definition, etiology, and natural history

Hypoparathyroidism is a condition characterized by a low blood calcium level, elevated phosphorous levels, low blood parathyroid hormone (PTH) level and nonfunctioning parathyroid glands. When it develops later in childhood or adulthood its cause is usually accidental surgical resection of the parathyroid glands during thyroidectomy; in an occasional case the acquired condition is of idiopathic etiology. Clinical features are dominated by uncontrolled muscle

spasms (including those of the larynx) secondary to the hypocalcemia. No specific anatomic soft tissue or skeletal lesions are produced, so no further discussion of this entity will be presented here.

Pseudohypoparathyroidism

Definition

Under this designation are included several different syndromes all of which appear to be the product of genetic mutations and are characterized by resistance of the target organ to the action of parathyroid hormone (PTH). As a consequence the parathyroid glands produce an appropriately structured PTH molecule, but the cells responsible for mediating the effects of PTH do not respond to the hormone. Hence the blood chemistry pattern is similar to that of hypoparathyroidism: low calcium and high phosphorus (as well as the similar clinical features of muscle spasms and convulsions) but differ in that normal or even supranormal quantities of PTH are present in the blood and the parathyroid glands are hyperplastic. In its simplest form, this type (termed Ib) is probably caused by a chemical change in the target cell's receptor which is not being recognized by the normal PTH molecule.

In another form (type Ia) the target cells are resistant not only to PTH but also to thyroid-stimulating hormone (TSH), to gonadotropins and to glucagon. The defect in this group lies within the intracellular chemical machinery that normally responds to the binding of PTH to its cell surface receptor. In addition, these persons have a constellation of anatomical deformities including a short, stocky body build, round facies, obesity, mental retardation and skeletal defects characterized by abnormally shortened metacarpals 4, 5 and sometimes 1. This combination of physical features has been termed Albright's hereditary osteodystrophy (AHO), and the skeletal features can be expected to be recognizable easily in ancient human remains. The chemical findings are usually identical to those of Ib with respect to calcium, phosphorus and PTH levels (Levine, 1993:196).

Still another variant presents the physical features of AHO but the target cells are not resistant to PTH and thus such persons have normal blood levels of calcium, phosphorus and PTH. As one might expect, this syndrome of AHO without biochemical abnormalities has been called pseudopseudohypoparathyroidism (no, that is not a misspelling!) (Rubin & Farber, 1994d:1126). Biochemists are rapidly detailing other abnormalities of the target cell's complex chemical mediators of PTH's effects and we can anticipate other future subdivisions of this family of intracellular changes. Anatomic skeletal changes to date, however, have been limited to the shortened metacarpals identified above as well as occasional examples of irregular, small calcified, and even ossified nodules in the subcutaneous and especially periarticular soft tissues of the upper extremity (Aegerter & Kirkpatrick, 1975:405). To date we have been unable to identify a paleopathological report of this condition.

DISORDERS AFFECTING GENDER EXPRESSION

The great variety of these conditions lies beyond the scope of this volume. The abbreviated comments below are designed only to provide a perspective for the paleopathologist, serve as a guideline to search for certain key features at the time of body dissection and suggest an approach to resolve these problems with the assistance of specialized texts.

Metabolic causes of aberrant genital structures

The sex chromosome pattern in these persons is that of a normal female (XX) or normal male (XY). In these individuals the primary problems lie in extragonadal organs, usually the pituitary or adrenal glands. Congenital pituitary aplasia results in panhypopituitarism. In addition to evidence of nongonadotropic hormone deficiency (dwarfism reflecting growth hormone, hypothyroidism, etc), lack of the gonadotropins' luteinizing hormone (LH) and follicle-stimulating hormone (FSH) and decreased steroidogenesis by the adrenal cortex can lead to failure of secondary sex characteristics at puberty in both males and females. Mutations affecting the enzyme systems involved in steroidogenesis and androgen production by the adrenal cortex often are responsible for variations in external genitalia expression in congenital adrenal hyperplasia. A variety of chemical effects can lead to absent, decreased or overproduction of androgens. The most common form of the latter (21 hydroxylase deficiency) may result in virilization in females (labial fusion simulating a scrotum and clitoral enlargement resembling a penis). In the male it may produce hypospadias and sufficient distortion of other external genitalia features to cause uncertainty in gender identification. The term pseudohermaphroditism is applied when these alterations are sufficient to render a greater resemblance to the gender opposite that of the individual's chromosomal karyotype or internal genitalia (Peterson, 1994).

Genetic cause of aberrant genital structures

The sex chromosome pattern in these individuals is usually abnormal, commonly resulting from the addition or deletion of one or more X or Y chromosomes. The presence of a Y chromosome (which carries the gene for testis structure) generates a male phenotype. In Klinefelter's syndrome (XXY), the additional X chromosome renders the testicular structures resistant to pituitary gonadotropins, resulting in infantile male external genitalia, gynecomastia (enlarged male breast) and female pubic hair distribution. The loss of an X chromosome in Turner's Syndrome (45X,O) results in a female phenotype with infantile external genitalia (Rubin & Farber, 1994c:221–3). The term hermaphrodite is reserved for an individual with internal gonads containing both testicular and ovarian tissue structures and a bewildering array of mixed gender external genitalia.

THE THYROID

Thyroid structure and function

In the living individual, the thyroid gland consists of two lobes, each about $4 \times 1.5 \times 1.0$ cm lying on each side of the trachea, joined across the midline by a horizontal bridge ('isthmus') of thyroid tissue crossing the trachea distal to the lower end of the larynx. It normally weighs about 15–20 g, much of which represents stored thyroid hormone. The gland is composed of microscopic-sized sacs called follicles. The epithelium lining these follicles produces thyroglobulin, which is stored in the follicles. Tyrosine residues on thyroglobulin are iodinated and, when these residues are cleaved by stimulated follicular epithelial cells, a three (T-3) — as well as a four — iodine-containing fragment (T4 or thyroxine) is secreted into the blood. These metabolically active thyroid hormones are delivered to the tissues and bind to specific receptors. An additional iodine atom is then removed from T4. The remaining T3 compound exerts its hormonal effect on the cell. This thyroid hormone has a regulatory effect on the intensity of cellular function (metabolic rate) including the cells of muscle, bone, liver, and other organs. Thus, not only does thyroid hormone affect the quantitative features of tissue cells' specific products, but the heat generated by their collective metabolism helps maintain the overall body temperature.

The rate of thyroid hormone synthesis, in turn, is controlled by the hypothalamus and pituitary gland using a feedback system to maintain a stable, autoregulatory system. The brain's hypothalamus contains cells that monitor the blood level of thyroid hormone. If that drops to subnormal levels, the hypothalamus signals the pituitary by secreting thyroid-releasing hormone (TRH). The pituitary cells then secrete thyroid-stimulating hormone (TSH) that binds to thyroid follicular epithelial cells, stimulating them to accelerate thyroid hormone synthesis and release. If the blood level of thyroid hormone reaches supranormal levels, the monitoring hypothalamus cells sense this and secrete less TRH which, in turn, decreases the pituitary's output of TSH, resulting in a deceleration of hormone synthesis by the thyroid gland.

Clearly, all elements of this mechanism must be intact if the regulatory system is to function normally. Aberrations occur if disease affects the hypothalamus or either gland. Anything that interferes with the ability of the thyroid follicular epithelium to manufacture thyroid hormone results in a subnormal hormone blood level, causing the pituitary to release TSH. Failure of the impaired thyroid to respond by synthesizing and releasing thyroid hormone results in a continuing low blood hormone level and continuing high TSH production. Eventually the thyroid enlarges (hyperplasia) in response to the continuing, high TSH level, causing a goiter (enlarged thyroid).

The most common cause of this sequence of events is dietary iodine deficiency. Because iodine is a major element in thyroxine, an insufficient iodine supply will limit the thyroid's ability to produce adequate levels of hormone in response to TSH stimulation. The resulting growth of thyroid tissue can reach enormous, disfiguring proportions. In spite of this size, the amount of hormone production may still be subnormal, producing a hypofunctioning state (hypothyroidism). In most cases, however, the gland is so large that, while the concentration of hormone produced within the gland is low, collectively it makes sufficient hormone to maintain a normal state (euthyroidism).

Initially the gland enlarges proportionately, producing a simple, diffuse goiter (Fig. 10.10). Eventually, however, growth occurs irregularly, producing focal areas of enlargement that convert the gland into a continually enlarging, multinodular structure. Foci of necrosis, hemorrhage, scarring and even calcification are common in these huge goiters. Such glands can attain monstrous proportions, weighing several kilograms and causing disfiguring external deformations. Huge goiters may compress the trachea and esophagus, producing symptoms (dyspnea, dysphagia) of obstruction. Occasionally, after decades of such growth, one or more of the nodules may undergo sufficient hyperplasia to generate a surplus of thyroid hormone (hyperthyroidism), particularly if a high dose of therapeutic iodine is ingested. Thus, the individual with a multinodular goiter due to iodine deficiency may be in a hypothyroid, euthyroid or hyperthyroid functional state. Similar effects can be brought about by dietary substances that interfere with thyroid hormone synthesis. These are called goitrogens, and include members of the *Brassica* genus (cruciferous plants) such as cabbage, turnips, cassava and others. Thyroid injury by therapeutic radiation or infection are other conditions that can lead to goiter formation by a similar mechanism.

Pituitary dysfunction can also affect the thyroid status. Occasional pituitary tumors are composed of TSH-secreting cells that are not responsive to hypothalamic signals or high blood thyroid hormone levels, resulting in a perpetual stimulation of an otherwise normal thyroid gland. The result is a goiter with hyperthyroidism. Alternatively, pituitary destruction by tumor, trauma, infection or ischemia can eliminate all TSH production. The now unstimulated thyroid will atrophy and its reduced hormone production induces a state of hypothyroidism.

Grave's disease

This is an autoimmune disease in which antibodies are directed at the TSH receptor of the thyroid follicular epithelial cells. Some of these antibodies stimulate growth while others stimulate hormone production. As a consequence, a diffuse goiter develops that doubles or triples the size of the thyroid but does not reach the enormous magnitude sometimes seen with multinodular goiter. The effects of the increased hormone production are those of hyperthyroidism – thyrotoxicosis. However, the associated edematous pretibial skin lesions of the legs and feet as well as exophthalmos (protruding eyes) are probably also of autoimmune origin. Grossly the thyroid weighs up to 50–60 g and histologically shows prominent proliferative changes. Usually no nodular structures are found in the thyroid. The disease appears in mid-adult life and the female/male ratio is about 6/1.

Thyroiditis

The lymphocytic (Hashimoto) form of thyroid inflammation is also of autoimmune nature. Antimicrosomal antibodies are present, stimulating follicular epithelial growth without increased function. A familial pattern suggests a genetic influence, perhaps expressed through T-lymphocyte malfunction. The immune response system destroys much of the thyroid tissue over time. In the active phase the thyroid may enlarge to about triple its normal size. Several other forms of thyroiditis cause subacute or chronic inflammations (DeQuervain's & Riedel's thyroiditis respectively). DeQuervain's thyroiditis is thought to be of viral origin. Riedel's thyroiditis, of unknown etiology, is characterized by replacement of thyroid tissue by dense fibrosis that may

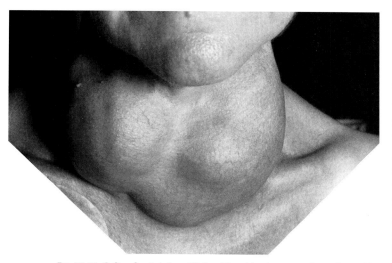

FIG. 10.10: **Goiter, frontal view.** Bilateral thyroid enlargement in modern middle-aged adult male. PBL.

incorporate adjacent structures, and in the final stage the thyroid may be of normal or smaller size.

Neoplasms

Adenoma

These are discrete, often encapsulated benign tumors composed of follicular epithelium embedded in an otherwise normal thyroid gland. They rarely exceed 4–5 in diameter. Most do not function but a few form enough thyroid hormone to produce symptoms of hyperthyroidism. The functional adenomas are indistinguishable anatomically from the nonfunctional either grossly or microscopically. Foci of degeneration similar to that described for multinodular goiter above may occur.

Carcinoma

Thyroid cancers assume a variety of forms. Follicular carcinoma has a gross appearance similar to that of the adenoma described above, although in its terminal, untreated state one would expect some gross evidence of invasiveness. Papillary carcinomas remain quite sharply demarcated and may contain cystic foci. They metastasize to the neck lymph nodes frequently but rarely reach distant organs or structures. They represent the most common form of thyroid cancer today and may appear as early as the third decade of life. Medullary carcinomas arise from the parafollicular cells that secrete bioactive peptides and sometimes are part of a genetic syndrome characterized by multiple endocrine neoplasms (MEN). All of these cancers, however, produce discrete masses in an otherwise normal-size thyroid, and their malignant nature may not be recognizable on gross examination alone.

Goiter

Epidemiology

Goiter is a worldwide condition affecting an estimated 200 million people (WHO, 1960a, b; Fig. 10.11). Its distribution takes two forms: endemic and sporadic. Endemic areas (more than 10 % of population afflicted) are quite sharply defined. Goiters are more common in inhabitants of mountainous areas. Areas of endemic frequency coincide with areas of low soil iodide content, consistent with the assumption that iodide has been leached from the scant mountain soil. Most goiters in these areas appear to be due to dietary iodine deficiency and dietary iodide supplementation is usually effective prophylaxis. Sporadic goiter appears as an isolated phenomenon almost anywhere in the world, including within the endemic areas. Such sporadic goiters are frequently due to conditions other than iodine deficiency, such as ingestion of goitrogens (cruciferous vegetables).

In the Americas endemic areas involve the Great Lakes region, upper Missouri River (Hrdlicka, 1916), Appalachia, Brazil and Andeana. In Europe the alpine region is a common location for endemic goiters, while in Czechoslovakia goiter

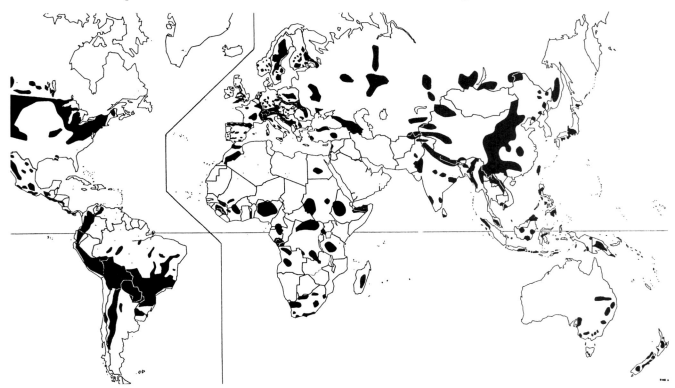

FIG. 10.11: **Geographic distribution of endemic goiter.** Reproduced with permission from p. 338 of WHO (1960b) Endemic goitre. *WHO Chronicle* **14(9)**:337–65.

has been attributed to a diet rich in goitrogenic cruciferous vegetables (cabbage). Asian endemic areas also cluster around the mountains. The incidence of goiters is extremely high in Russia's Pamir plateau. Other endemic areas include the Himalayas and China, but Japan and Iceland are probably spared because their marine diet of fish and seaweed is rich in iodine. The Atlas mountains of the North African coast and both the southern part of the Nile valley (Ghalioungui, 1965) and Congo river area of west central Africa are also endemic areas. Only the southeastern area of Australia is involved, though Tasmania has a high frequency due not to iodine deficiency, but to a derivative of thiocyanate in the milk of cows fed marrowstem kale feed (WHO, 1960*a*, *b*).

Clinical features of hyper- and hypothyroidism

Hyperthyroidism is characterized by hyperactivity, prominent eyes (ophthalmopathy), tremor, increased pulse and hypertension as well as heat intolerance. Its causes have been noted above. Hypothyroidism produces lethargy, cold intolerance, slow pulse with normal or low blood pressure, focal areas of brawny skin texture (myxedema) and impaired mentation. Congenital hypothyroidism is called cretinism. These unfortunate children have diminutive stature due to delay in development of ossification centers and frequently distorted spine curvature. The head may appear disproportionately large for the body, extremities (especially the lower) are short and mental retardation is common. An enlarged tongue may produce a ferocious expression (Giampalmo & Fulcheri, 1988). These persons may be the offspring of goitrous, iodine-deficient parents, but in many cretins the thyroid is absent or defective, such as in congenital thyroid aplasia. In others a familial form has been linked to defective thyroxine metabolism (WHO, 1960*a*).

History and antiquity of goiter

Huge multinodular goiters were treated in China with burnt or alcohol-extracted seaweed (Lee, 1941) as early as 1600 B.C. (Iason, 1946) (though Lee only claims third century B.C.). Bartsocas (1985) thinks Aristotle recognized Grave's disease. The Roman historian Juvenal describes the endemic presence of goiter 'in alpibus' (Switzerland's Valais valley) and Vitruvius mentions it in the Cottian alps (Merke, 1984). It was, however, not until about the time of Discorides (first century A.D.) who called it 'bronchocele' (Marketos *et al.*, 1990), and Galen (A.D. 130–200), that the existence of the normal thyroid was noted (Rolleston, 1936). Galen, however, thought its function was to lubricate the larynx (McCosh, 1977). The sixteenth century anatomist Vesalius provided a more comprehensive description (Rolleston, 1934) and Caserio of Padua noted the absence of a secretory duct. Although travelers had earlier (thirteenth century) observed cretinism in Europe's alpine goitrous area, it was the sixteenth century physicians Paracelsus and Felix Platter who associated cretinism with goiter (Sawin,

Table 10.1 Historical events leading to recognition of iodine's role in goiters.

1600 B.C.	China used burnt seaweed as goiter therapy.
A.D. before 1800	Observations of endemic goiter in alpine areas.
1811	J.B. Courtois identified the element iodine.
1818	J. Coindet: iodine in seaweed; Dumas found it there.
1825	J.B. Boussingault: iodine may cause goiter.
1850	A. Chatin: little iodine in water in endemic areas.
1860+	Several iodine prophylaxis trials. Inconclusive.
1885	Bacteriology born. Goiter infectious?
1895	E. Baumann isolated 'thyroiodine' from thyroid.
1899	C. Oswald identified thyroglobulin.
1915	E.C. Kendall crystallized thyroxine.
1920	D. Marine's large-scale iodine prophylaxis trials.
1924	Michigan, U.S.A. introduces iodized salt: success.
1926	C.R. Harington synthesized thyroxine.

This table was created by us from information supplied in narrative form in WHO (1960*a*, *b*), Iason (1946) and in Sawin (1993).

1993). Goiters are obvious in some Italian paintings and sculptures from the fourteenth to the nineteenth centuries (Giampalmo & Fulcheri, 1988), where individuals appear to have been specifically inserted into the paintings to help establish a pitiful milieu and reflect social attitudes. However, when such a diagnosis is made on the basis of a general rounding or prominence of the neck of a coin-imprinted figure such as those of Ptolemy (Hart, 1967) and Cleopatra (Iason, 1946) or on wood statuettes (Wells, 1968*a*), separation of goiter from features of artistic design may not be convincing (Harris & Wente, 1980). Borhegyi & Scrimshaw (1957) extend the antiquity of goiter in Guatemala (an endemic area today) to 2000 B.C. on the basis of two stone figurines with neck structures of questionable specificity. Byzantine physicians were interested in 'atheromatous' (partly calcified multinodular goiter) and 'steatomatous' (colloid) goiter (Marketos *et al.*, 1990). The century-long trail from early suspicion to identification of the role of iodine in goitre is outlined in Table 10.1. Confusion resulted in part because only some individuals in endemic areas were affected, response to iodide therapy helped many but in some it initiated thyrotoxicosis, sporadic cases occurred outside of endemic areas, and the evolving science of bacteriology suggested a possible infectious explanation. Though some questions have not even yet been answered, Kendall's (1915) identification of thyroxine, C.R. Harington's synthesis of it in 1926 (WHO, 1960*b*) and the effectiveness of D. Marine's 1920 large-scale iodine prophylaxis studies (Sawin, 1993) have established the importance of iodine deficiency in the development of goiter.

Paleopathology of goiter

The bulk of normal thyroid tissue is made up of a gelatinous liquid (thyroglobulin) called colloid, enclosed in thin-walled follicles. In most goiters colloid represents an even larger fraction of the total volume. One needs to expect a dramatic size reduction from that in the living individual as the liquid content of the follicles dehydrates. It is, then, perhaps not surprising that it is virtually impossible to identify normal thyroid tissue in a body that has been desiccated by either spontaneous or anthropogenic means. An identifiable thyroid in such bodies is usually a pathological thyroid. Thus, the huge multinodular goiters are most likely to be detected. It is also true that it is precisely in such large, multinodular goiters that compression of small vessels leads to sufficient ischemia to produce focal infarction with its subsequent events characterized by necrosis, hemorrhage and finally fibrosis and calcification. These latter features are apt to survive postmortem alterations and remain recognizable.

We were able to identify only a few paleopathological examples of soft tissue thyroid disease in ancient human remains:

CASE 1: The spontaneously mummified body of a young adult female of the Nazca culture in the Inca valley of southern Peru was radiocarbon-dated at about 100 B.C. Radiological examination revealed two areas of calcification about 1 cm in diameter in the neck. Dissection revealed these were lying within 'thick tissues'. Histological study identified occasional colloid-filled follicles. Additional findings included extensive, calcified atherosclerosis of the aorta, lumbar osteoarthritis, osteomyelitis of the left femur and many missing teeth. The degree of aortic atherosclerosis was considerably more advanced than would be expected in a 30 ($\pm$ 5) year old female. This finding, together with the thyroid findings and radiologically-demonstrated thickened cranial cortex suggest a diagnosis of goiter with hypothyroidism (Gerszten *et al.*, 1976*a*), but are also consistent with thyroiditis – particularly that described by Riedel, which is of idiopathic origin, destroying the thyroid and replacing it with an infiltrating fibrous mass with occasional foci of calcification. Hypothyroidism is a known complication of such thyroid destruction.

CASE 2: The spontaneously desiccated, mummified body of a young (about 25 years) adult male was found in the mortuary chapel of the church of Santa Maria della Grazia in Comiso, Sicily. The mummy was dated to A.D. 1748–1838. A 6 cm × 4 cm × 1 cm mass was found in the thyroid area. Histological study revealed numerous circular follicles embedded in fibrous tissue and containing amorphous periodic acid Schiff (PAS) positive-staining material. Immunohistochemical stains showed strong reactivity with anti-thyroglobulin antibody. The authors (Fornaciari *et al.*, 1994) made a diagnosis of thyroid goiter. Goiter is endemic to southern Italy and Sicily today.

ologically (Avioli & Krane, 1978). They consist of bone demineralization, increased growth rate and a peculiar complex of findings termed acropachy.

- Demineralization is due to excessive urinary excretion of calcium and phosphorus and is usually mild enough to escape detection, though after many years untreated persons may have bones whose reduced number of trabeculae may be recognizable in sectioned femurs and whose outer cortex porosity may include enlarged vascular channels. Vertebral osteopenia may lead to occasional kyphosis deformity (Jaffe, 1972:351).

- Skeletal growth rate. In subadults the rate of growth increase may lead to increased stature, though premature epiphyseal closure will almost always prevent gigantism.

- Acropachy (from the Greek words for extremity and thickening) is a unique phenomenon characterized by digital clubbing, new bone formation in hands and feet and prominent swelling of hand and foot soft tissues. The new bone formation is of variable degree, involves principally hand and foot digits, though metacarpal and metatarsal bones may participate. The new bone formation commonly takes the form of multiple subperiosteal layers, parallel to the periosteum, though in others it will be less uniform (radiologically described as of 'fluffy' appearance) and sometime spiculated with spicules oriented transverse to the long axis of the distal extremities' short tubular bones. Bony 'tufting' of the distal phalanx is occasionally evident (Thomas, 1933). In living individuals the soft tissue swelling involving hands and feet is out of proportion to the degree of bone thickening. Most of the reported cases have been seen in hyperthyroid persons, usually several years after effective thyroid therapy. However, no treatment had been given to some (King *et al.*, 1959), while others had no evidence of thyroid abnormality. Hypertrophic pulmonary osteoarthropathy may resemble this condition, though thickening in that process is usually due less to soft tissue swelling than to the prominent hypertrophic skeletal changes, and involvement of the forearm and lower leg long bones is more prominent and far more commonly present than in acropachy (Avioli & Krane, 1978: 455). Yet, in a single example these two diagnoses may not be separable. Evidence of prominent facial lesions in pachydermoperiostitis, however, can be employed to identify this rare condition (Nixon & Samols, 1970) whose hand and foot changes are similar to those of acropachy. Blood levels of long-acting thyroid stimulator protein are elevated in modern patients with thyroid acropachy (Gilliland, 1991:1487). The etiological mechanisms involved in all three of these conditions requires better definition.

Skeletal lesions in states of thyroid dysfunction

Hyperthyroidism

Bone lesions in hyperthyroid individuals are usually asymptomatic, mild, nonspecific and not easily demonstrated radi-

Hypothyroidism

Deficient hormone action at the epiphyseal cartilage plate retards long bone growth sufficiently to produce a form of dwarfism (cretinism) characterized by extremities of normal length in proportion to the trunk (Jaffe, 1972:196), but whose vertical body proportions (divided at the level of the pubic symphysis) remains infantile (Wilkins & Fleishman, 1941; Avioli & Krane, 1978:448). The fundamental skeletal lesion of hypothryoidism is failure to calcify the cartilage formed at the long bone epiphyseal plates and other sites of endochondral bone formation. Since such calcification must precede the deposition of osteoid and subsequent mineralization, long bone lengthening is retarded (Lichtenstein, 1970:76). Epiphyseal growth plates persist often until midlife and closure of sutures and fontanelles is delayed. Eventually skeletal maturation does occur at which time a thin layer of bone seals off the epiphyseal plate from the metaphysis and further lengthening ceases usually at a final total body stature of between 1–1.5 m. Normally epiphyses usually ossify from a single ossification center whose periphery gradually spreads to involve the entire epiphysis. In cretins multiple ossification centers appear and their enlargement is retarded, fusing eventually in an irregular and unpredictable pattern (radiologically, 'epiphyseal dysgenesis': Wilkins, 1941). The resulting distorted bone ends are often dysfunctional under the stresses of weight-bearing, precipitating premature changes of osteoarthritis.

Intramembranous bone formation, however, is not impaired. Consequently diaphyseal bone growth progresses, resulting in shortened but widened bones (Aegerter & Fitzpatrick, 1975:382). In the skull, too, formation of the vault bones proceeds in a normal fashion, while the growth at the synchondroses of the sphenoid and occipital bones is retarded, causing a brachycephalic head with a wide, deep sella and prognathism (Wilkins & Fleischman, 1941; Jaffe, 1972:346–51). The result is a body retaining infantile skeletal proportions, remaining closer to the upper (above pubic symphysis) *versus* lower segment value of infancy (1.7) than to that of normal adults (1.0) (Wilkins & Fleischman, 1941). Vertebral growth may be impaired sufficiently to produce smaller vertebrae with compression of the anterior portion of the body ('beaking') of the first lumbar kyphosis (Aegerter & Kirkpatrick, 1975:382). Other effects of thyroid deficiency are manifested as decreased mentation, brawny skin ('myxedema') and sluggish locomotion.

The skeletal changes are usually most obvious in the femur head, which can be quite deformed by the described processes. In an isolated femur head the differentiation between cretinism and osteochondritis (Legg–Calvé–Perthes disease: see Chapter 5) may be irresolvable, though the latter is bilateral in only about 10 % of the cases, and the pattern of involvement at other sites simplifies correct diagnosis when the entire skeleton is available (Jaffe, 1972:352). The possibility of rickets may also be excluded in a similar manner.

The alterations described above are characteristic of a child born with a virtual absence of thyroid hormone action secondary to thyroid aplasia, a genetic defect. This is the most common form of cretinism today. Thyroid deficiency acquired after birth commonly results in impairment of lesser degree than is seen in congenital aplasia. If it occurs late in childhood the deficiency may have little effect on mentation and body stature may approach the lower limits of normal, accounting for the existence of such modern clinical classifications as cretins, semi-cretins and cretinous persons (WHO, 1960*a*, *b*).

Paleopathology of cretinism

Given the evidence of low soil iodine content in modern endemic goiter and cretinism areas, one would expect bone collections from such locations to reveal skeletons with cretinous changes frequently. Yet we have not been able to identify a single, convincing report of ancient human remains with changes characteristic of cretinism. An isolated Egyptian skull from the eighteenth dynasty has been interpreted as cretinous (Seligman, 1912), but a subsequent evaluation declared the changes to be due to achondroplasia (Keith, 1931). Merke (1984) denies that Neolithic Swiss skeletons are unambiguously related to cretinism including that of a 14 year old female that Virchow thought was the result of iodine deficiency. Merke also declares a slipped femoral epiphysis housed at the Hallstatt museum is nondiagnostic of cretinism. DeVasto (1974) has noted the low soil iodine content of Andean highlands (1/35 of that on the Peruvian coast) and that the prehistoric diet included known dietary goitrogens. Regional pre-Columbian figurines suggest the presence of cretinism. Evidence of active trade of iodine-rich marine products with the highlands suggests ancient Andean people were aware of goiter, cretinism and their prevention. DeVasto also notes that earlier reports of underdeveloped nasal bones and late suture closure in Andean collections by G.E. Eaton, A. Hrdlicka and C.G. MacCurdy suggest such effects, but he offers no diagnostic skeletal morphology. Ortner & Putschar (1985:305) illustrate a recent cretinous pelvis whose femur head dramatically demonstrates the lobulated surface resulting from the irregular fusion of multiple ossification centers (figure 473), as well as another modern example whose mushroom-shaped deformity is an unfortunate product of years of weight-bearing on a femur head with inadequate skeletal support (figure 474). Conceivably cretins' usual mental retardation may have contributed to an early death in antiquity with subsequent dissolution of the fragile, infant bones. Yet the fact that none at all have been reported remains an enigma.

Summary of skeletal lesions in thyroid diseases

- Hyperthyroidism. Usually mild osteopenia, mildly increased stature and, rarely, acropachy (periostitis and soft tissue edema of hand and foot phalanges).
- Hypothyroidism. Cretinism-dwarfism with short extremities, infantile skeletal proportions, epiphyseal dysgenesis, prominent brachycephalic head and prognathism.

THE ADRENALS

Normal adrenal function

The adrenal glands are located immediately above and sometimes partially overlap the superior pole of the kidney on each side. The adrenal cortex secretes several hormones including aldosterone (enhancing sodium reabsorption and potassium excretion in the kidney) and cortisol (an essential hormone involved in electrolyte balance, immune function and other actions). The adrenal medulla secretes catecholamines that have a central role in vascular tone and blood pressure regulation. Adrenal pathology affects these functions. The adrenal gland, together with the pituitary gland and the hypothalamus, is part of a self-regulating system similar to that of the thyroid. The hypothalamus monitors the blood cortisol level (i.e. cortisol has an inhibiting effect on the hypothalamus), and a decline stimulates secretion of corticotropin-releasing hormone (CRH), delivered directly to the pituitary via the portal venous system. CRH stimulates the pituitary to release adrenocorticotropic hormone (ACTH) into the blood which, in turn, causes the adrenal cortical cells to release cortisol into the blood.

The normal adrenal gland undergoes rapid postmortem autolysis and thus is seldom identified in mummified human remains. No adrenal lesions have been reported in the paleopathology literature. Hence our discussion will be limited to those few pathological entities that might survive the postmortem changes sufficiently to be recognized grossly by the paleopathologist.

Acute adrenal insufficiency: Waterhouse–Friderichsen syndrome

This condition is characterized by bilateral, acute, massive hemorrhage into both adrenal glands of sufficient size to fragment and destroy these organs. This is often a consequence of septicemia from a virulent bacterium, usually *Neisseria meningitidis*. This organism normally produces acute infection of the meninges covering the brain and spinal cord. In occasional cases the degree of septicemia that normally precedes the meningitis is so severe that it initiates systemic activation of the coagulation system within blood vessels (disseminated intravascular coagulation' DIC). Rapid consumption of blood clotting factors results in a hemorrhagic state that is associated with massive bleeding into many body tissues including the skin. The extensive and fragile capillary and sinusoidal network of the adrenal gland is especially vulnerable and explosive hemorrhage frequently shatters both adrenals (Fig.

10.12). The loss of adrenal cortisol production and catecholamine secretion by the adrenal medulla is followed by profound and often lethal vascular collapse. Paleopathological clues would include not only extensive bilateral adrenal hematomas, but also evidence of bleeding into other tissues such as the skin, gastrointestinal tract and elsewhere.

Chronic adrenal cortical insufficiency (Addison's disease)

Destruction of both adrenal glands by any gradual process results in progressive atrophy of many body tissues and a cachectic state. In developed countries today, autoimmune adrenalitis is postulated as the most common cause of such adrenal loss. In earlier days tuberculosis was the most frequent disease responsible for such destructive adrenal effects and still is in developing countries (probably also in antiquity). In such cases the paleopathologist would find caseous masses mixed with fibrous tissue replacing the adrenal organs. Features characteristic of tuberculosis should be present in the lung and/or elsewhere.

The size of the adrenal glands and the level of their secretory function can also be affected by changes in the hypothalamus and /or pituitary gland. Trauma, infections, invasive tumors or ischemia of the hypothalamus and/or the pituitary will result in a loss of their secretory products and thus their interaction with the adrenal glands. Lacking stimulation by ACTH from the pituitary, the adrenals will undergo progressive atrophy causing adrenal insufficiency as described in the preceding section. Primary, nonfunctional pituitary adenomas are a common cause of such events.

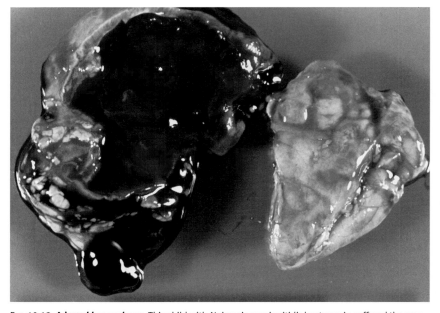

FIG. 10.12: **Adrenal hemorrhage.** This child with *Neisseria meningitidis* bacteremia suffered the complication of disseminated intravascular coagulation and resulting hemorrhage into skin and viscera. Acute adrenal destruction by hemorrhage frequently results in shock and death; in this case it was unilateral (uninvolved adrenal is on right). PBL.

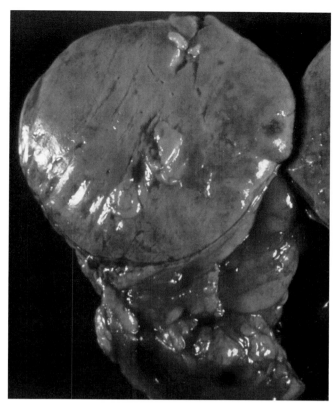

FIG. 10.13: **Adrenal cortical adenoma.** This benign, 4 cm tumor in a modern female of sixth decade was functional, secreting sufficient aldosterone to produce symptoms and signs of Conn's syndrome. PBL.

Adrenal hyperfunction (Cushing's disease)

Autonomously functioning tumors (usually in the pituitary gland) composed of cells that are derived from CRH- or ACTH synthesizing cells can result in the presence of a surplus of such hormones independent of need. The most common of these is an ACTH-producing pituitary adenoma. Continued adrenal cortical stimulation by ACTH results in progressive enlargement of both adrenals due to cortical hyperplasia. Such enlargement may reach a size up to tenfold greater than normal. It is conceivable that enlargement of this degree might result in a detectable mass in a mummified body in spite of some postmortem autolysis. Useful confirming evidence that could also be recognized in mummified human remains are some of the somatic effects of the high blood cortisol levels in such individuals. These include obesity and deposition of fat over the dorsal aspect of the spine producing a distinct bulge there ('buffalo hump'), as well as in the facial area causing it to assume a more round contour ('moon face'). The spinal curvature may be further distorted by vertebral osteoporosis with compression fractures of vertebral bodies. Except for muscle wasting and osteopenia, the extremities are not deformed. Hyperpigmentation of the skin is common and may be detectable. Cardiac and vascular complications of hypertension are common, as are those complications present in the minority that develop diabetes. Prominent facial hair and acne in adult females are manifestations of the virilizing effects in females (Rubin & Farber, 1994d:1135). This constellation of abnormalities can alert the paleopathologist to the possible presence of adrenal hyperfunction. Since the primary tumors in the pituitary and hypothalamus are not usually large enough to be detectable in human mummies, the resorption of the sella turcica's skeletal structure due to compressive effects of a pituitary tumor may help confirm such a suspected diagnosis. A similar degree of hyperfunction can be achieved by a functioning adrenal cortical adenoma or carcinoma. While adenomas are usually small (up to 4 cm), adrenal cortical carcinomas may be sufficiently large and infiltrating to be identifiable at a paleopathological autopsy.

An aldosterone-secreting adenoma of similar gross and microscopic structure will cause sodium retention with blood volume increase and hypertension (Conn's syndrome: Fig. 10.13). Uncommon tumors grossly and microscopically similar to those causing Cushing's syndrome occasionally secrete androgens and have virilizing effects in females. Finally, genetic mutations may interfere with normal steroid synthesis, causing continuous secretion of high levels of ACTH by the pituitary. The result of this is an infant with enormously (10–20x) enlarged adrenals (congenital adrenal hyperplasia). Anatomic effects vary with the affected enzyme, but may include virilized external genitalia in females. The principal skeletal change in Cushing's syndrome is simple osteoporosis with its potential for development of long bone fractures as well as vertebral body collapse and kyphosis.

DIABETES MELLITUS

Pathophysiology

Normally carbohydrates are metabolized in the body to provide the energy needed for the many chemical reactions that occur within cells to enable them to carry out their functions. The blood level of glucose ('sugar') necessary to make the amount required by the tissues is regulated by the hormone insulin. This is made by specialized (beta) cells within the pancreas. Dietary ingestion and absorption of glucose raises the blood glucose level (hyperglycemia), stimulating release of insulin from the pancreas' beta cells. Insulin binds to specific chemical receptors on tissue cells such as those in the liver, enabling them to store the surplus glucose as glycogen, until needed between meals. Diabetes mellitus is characterized by reduced production of, or peripheral impaired response to, insulin.

Two types of diabetic abnormalities are encountered. In Type 1 (insulin-dependent diabetes mellitus, IDDM) the onset

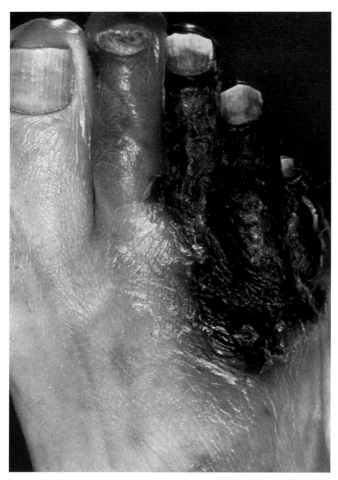

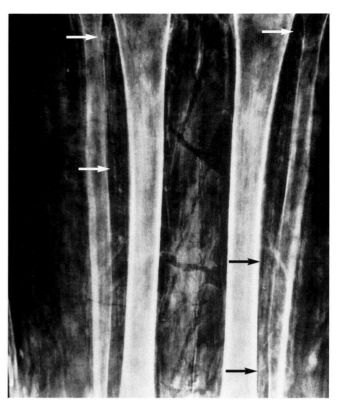

FIG. 10.15: **Diabetic arterial calcification.** Radiological study of extremities. Arrows indicate diffuse, heavy calcification in all three major calf arteries, a pattern often seen in diabetes mellitus, due to atherosclerosis or Mönckeberg's medial calcification. Twenty-second dynasty (930–880 B.C.) Egyptian mummy Nes-Ptah, barber of Amun, age 65 ± 5 years. Courtesy Dr Myron Marx, San Francisco, CA.

FIG. 10.14: **Gangrene of the toes.** Atherosclerotic narrowing of small arteries is a common complication of diabetes mellitus, the process producing ischemia with ultimate gangrene of several toes. Elderly modern male. PBL.

usually occurs during childhood or adolescence. Pancreatic beta cells are destroyed by an autoimmune mechanism with a resulting decrease or absence of insulin production. Without the ability to burn sugar appropriately, the body burns fat as an alternative. This generates so much organic acid that the resulting electrolyte abnormality (metabolic acidosis), if untreated, progresses to coma and death. In Type 2 (noninsulin-dependent diabetes mellitus, NIDDM) the onset is in adulthood, commonly in the elderly. The beta cells' insulin response is subnormal and the peripheral tissues are partially resistant to the insulin's action (Craighead, 1994).

In both types, the blood sugar level is elevated and the surplus sugar appears in the urine. This sugar causes an osmotic diuresis and the loss of plasma water may produce a dramatically increased urinary output (polyuria) and its associated thirst (polydipsia), two of the prominent clinical features of the disease. In addition, elevated blood sugar levels increase binding to (glycosylation of) certain proteins, eventually leading to the deposit of insoluble substances (advanced glycosylation products) on vascular basement membranes of small blood vessels throughout the body. In the retina, such deposits (diabetic retinopathy) weaken the arterial walls and

these often rupture; the resulting intraocular hemorrhage ends in blindness. Vision loss may also be the result of protein deposits in the lens (cataract), rendering it opaque. Further deposits in the kidneys (diabetic nephropathy) produces first atrophy of the entire organ and finally complete loss of function with death by renal failure (uremia). Destruction of peripheral nerves, with consequent anesthesia (peripheral neuropathy), commonly involves the feet and legs. Unable to feel pain, diabetics can injure their feet inadvertently . The consequent soft tissue ulcerations, usually on the ball of the foot, become infected and such processes may involve the bones of the arch (metatarsals). Simultaneous deposits in the small vessels of the foot may also cause ischemic osteolysis of the distal metatarsals and proximal phalanges. Remodeling often causes the metatarsals or phalanges to reform in a distinct, distally tapered shape (diabetic osteopathy). The ischemia may result in localized digital gangrene of one or more toes.

Aberrant fat metabolism commonly also accelerates the development of atherosclerosis. In fact, coronary artery atherosclerosis with its complications is a common method of death in diabetics. The large arteries of the legs may be so narrowed by such a process that the entire leg may become gangrenous (Fig. 10.14). Finally, though it has no effect on blood flow, calcification within the medial layer of small arteries (Mönckeberg's calcification) is often extensive and prominent in a radiograph (Marx & D'Auria, 1986) (Fig. 10.15). Obesity is common in type 2 diabetics (Craighead, 1994).

Epidemiology and history

This is a worldwide disease with enormous prevalence differences. Samoa and Fiji lead the list with 11.8 and 10.1 % of the population affected, followed closely by Native North Americans (10.0 %). The disease is rare in China, Japan (0.4 %), England, Wales (0.6 %) and Australia (0.9 %). Mortality figures are also widely disparate, ranging from 5.1/100 000 in Hong Kong to 45/100 000 in Mexico and the Caribbean (Lieberman, 1993). The rapid and extensive rise in the prevalence of diabetes during the past two generations among Native North Americans (Knowler et al., 1978; Weiss et al., 1989; Wendorf, 1989) and the South Pacific islanders on Nauru (Diamond, 1992) suggests this may be due to persistence of a genetic mechanism biologically useful in the past but detrimental now. In 1962, Neel suggested that the episodic nature of food availability to early hunter–gatherers would act as a selective factor for those individuals bearing a gene whose product would permit more efficient storage of food as fat that could be used for energy during the intervals of deprivation ('thrifty gene'). The modern high dietary burden of carbohydrate was postulated to exhaust the pancreas' beta cells, creating the diabetic state. In 1982, Neel presented a modification of this postulate, incorporating more recent data. Cahill (1979) offered a similar suggestion that emphasized the glucose-sparing effect of noninsulin-dependent diabetes mellitus, reducing the need to make glucose from fat; 10 years later, Szathmary (1990) made a similar suggestion. These hypotheses are not easy to test and the issue remains controversial, though accumulating data from genetic studies strongly imply some genetic influence in both Type 1 and Type 2 diabetes.

The antiquity of the disease is controversial. The suggestions of diabetes in ancient Egypt are based entirely on the recommended treatment for polyuria in the Ebers papyrus, an association of rather slender certainty. The East Indian Vedas (probably 2000–500 B.C.) use the terms *asrava* (flux or polyuria) and *prameha* (sweet like honey) for patients with polyuria. Most convincing of these, however, are descriptions by Susrata Sambita who described the sweet taste of such patients' urine (Lee, 1941 claims the Chinese made a similar observation in the third century B.C.) and divided them into genetic and acquired types (Raghunathan, 1976), made up of both lean and obese persons. The Arabian physician Rhazes of Baghdad recognized diabetic gangrene in the ninth century. Sixteenth century physicians Amatus Lusitanus (Portuguese) and (Belgian) Johann van Helmont wrote about diabetic diet and lipemia. Recognition that the widely varying symptoms, physiological changes and complications

of diabetes were due to a single disease were largely nineteenth and twentieth century accomplishments by such investigators as William Prout (diabetic coma), Rudolph Kulz (beta-hydroxybutyric acid), Adolph Kussmaul (air hunger of coma) and Paul Langerhans (pancreatic islets). The early twentieth century isolation of insulin by Frederick Banning, Charles Best and J. Macleod crowned the roster of achievements that led to our present understanding of this disease. A considerably more detailed discussion of this disease's history can be found in a 1976 article by Raghunathan, from which some of the above items have been abstracted.

Paleopathology

Since diabetes mellitus is a condition expressed as non-anatomic pathophysiological changes in carbohydrate metabolism we must look among its complications for gross anatomical changes that will serve as markers for its presence. Though not unique to diabetes, cataract (opaque lens) is a common diabetic complication, and the eye often survives the postmortem events in spontaneous (natural) mummification. Because the globe collapses during the desiccation process and surrounding tissues also become opaque, evaluation of lens opacity would require rehydration of the globe before inspection of the eye. Even then it is not likely that the other ocular tissues would acquire sufficient transparency to contrast with a cataract-bearing lens, though biochemical analysis could possibly establish the diagnosis. While epithelial cells disappear rapidly after death, tissues of mesenchymal origin often are preserved; this is especially true of arteries. Thus, retinal aneurysms in a person with advanced diabetic retinopathy could be expected to be recognizable in desiccated human bodies. This, however, would require special processing of the eye with subsequent microscopic study.

The kidneys in a person with diabetic nephropathy will often be recognizably smaller than normal. The hyaline change in renal arterioles of such diabetic individuals would usually be identifiable and the replacement of many glomeruli by large hyaline deposits could also be observed, but require a microscope. Their presence would be very strong evidence of the existence of diabetes before death. Pursuit of such evidence is encouraged by a report of recognizable hypertensive arteriolar disease in an Egyptian mummy (Long, 1931).

More easily recognized grossly would be evidence of atherosclerosis. Coronary artery stenosis, often with accompanying arterial calcification, is often a serious diabetic complication. Similar atherosclerotic changes in other major arteries, especially the abdominal aorta is often also seen. Atherosclerotic stenosis of the ilial, femoral and other proximal leg arteries is also often grossly observable. These may cause sufficient stenosis to produce grossly evident leg gangrene. All of these atherosclerotic changes can occur in nondiabetic individuals, but the more advanced degree of this process is found at a younger age in diabetes. Thus, a conflict between the stage of atherosclerosis and the estimated age of a mummified body should suggest the possibility of diabetes.

Changes in the feet and lower legs will probably be the most obvious changes suggestive of diabetes. Mönckeberg's medial calcification of small arteries (as described by Sandison (1962) histologically in a thyroid artery in an Egyptian mummy) will be most easily recognized on radiological examination, as will be the skeletal changes of diabetic osteopathy described above (Gondos, 1968; Plessis, 1970; Friedman & Rakow, 1971). The accompanying soft tissue ulcerations, infections and gangrenous toes (often bilateral) reflecting ischemic changes as well as traumatic effects secondary to peripheral neuropathy are overt. These arterial changes were recognized in radiological studies on an Egyptian mummy curated at the Boston Fine Arts Museum (Marx & D'Auria, 1986; D'Auria et al., 1988:221).

Alveolar bone loss, detectable by dental X-rays, has been reported in diabetes (Cheraskin & Ringsdorf, 1970). While one would expect this to be manifest in postmortem remains, it has not been evaluated in archaeological skeletons. Haversian bone formation rates have also been reported to be retarded in diabetics (Wu et al., 1970), though only a single report of this finding could be found by us.

PART ELEVEN

Hematological disorders

Since blood is made within bones, one could expect disturbances of blood production or destruction to generate structural changes in skeletal tissue. While they do, it is unfortunate that the induced anatomic lesions are mostly both subtle and nonspecific. However, several recent reports have appeared on the laboratory horizon that hint at the potential emergence of techniques for identification of some specific hematological disorders in human remains. For that reason we have chosen to review at least the principal aberrations of blood diseases in this Chapter, grouping them into the red blood cell, white blood cell and coagulation disorders.

DISORDERS OF RED BLOOD CELLS (ANEMIAS)

Biology of red blood cell production, function, and destruction

Red blood cells (RBCs) have only one function – to transport oxygen, essential to all living cells, from the lung to all cellular tissue throughout the body. In general, the more metabolically active the cell, the greater its oxygen need. For example, irreversible cerebral damage begins after as little as 3 minutes of anoxia. Oxygen is transported by its attachment to the iron molecule of hemoglobin. The RBC can be viewed simply as a bag of hemoglobin whose reactive nature causes it to bind oxygen as the RBC passes through the lung and releases the oxygen when it reaches the chemical milieu of the tissue cells. The survival and function of most metabolizing body cells is dependent upon a continuous adequate supply of oxygen.

In the adult, RBCs are produced in trabecular bone, found most abundantly in the spine, flat bones and long bone metaphyses. The adult bone marrow has about a sixfold reserve – i.e. it can increase its RBC production rate about six times greater than that necessary to maintain hemeostasis. The dramatically different status of the infant, however, must be appreciated. During pregnancy's third trimester and the postnatal infancy period, body mass is increasing at an exponential rate. The need to produce enough RBCs to nourish the enormous number of new cells exceeds the entire body's marrow capacity. Hence some blood is produced outside of bone marrow (extramedullary hematopoiesis), principally in the spleen, liver and adrenal as well as the long bone diaphyseal marrow space. The rapidly growing infant, therefore, is uniquely susceptible to any interference with RBC production.

Hemoglobin is manufactured in the bone marrow. Its three main constituents relevant to our interests are its basic protein structure (two pairs of globin chains – normally alpha and beta), and a structure called heme that contains the critical iron atoms. When the RBC is mature, its nucleus is expelled and it is delivered to the circulation to function as an oxygen carrier. Without a nucleus it cannot repair its protein content and thus eventually dies after a circulating life of about 120 days. Thus, roughly 1 % of RBCs need to be replaced daily. The dying RBCs are removed from the circulation by the spleen, which catabolizes the hemoglobin into major fragments, converting the heme into a yellow-green compound (bilirubin) that is excreted into the bile, but retaining the iron and sending it back to the marrow for recycling into new hemoglobin. This normal conservation of iron is so effective that, in adult males, iron deficiency is essentially evidence of chronic blood loss (adult females can lose blood by menstruation).

Anemia is the state of subnormal circulating hemoglobin (<13.5 g hemoglobin/dl in males, 12.0 g/dl in females). Clinical signs and symptoms of severe, prolonged anemia include skin pallor, fatigue, weakness, dyspnea (shortness of breath), vertigo and tachycardia (increased heart rate). Skeletal effects reflect the marrow's effort to increase RBC production by hyperplasia: widened medullary cavity with cortical thinning and trabecular pattern distortion with widened metaphyses in long bones (Aegerter & Kirkpatrick, 1975), while flat bones (especially the skull's frontal and parietal bones) show thickening due to widened diploe that demonstrate fewer but thicker, spike-like trabeculae lying perpendicular to the inner and outer tables, generating a 'hair-on-end' radiological appearance, and a resorbed overlying outer table.

Trueta (1968:229–30) suggests a mechanism by means of which these changes may be shaped. The peripheral blood's anemic status provides a powerful stimulus (erythropoietin) to the marrow's RBC production machinery. The marrow's RBC production response results in such an intense crowding of the intertrabecular space by the proliferating marrow cells that their sheer pressure produces resorption of trabeculae and outer table of the skull. This same pressure impairs blood flow through the osteogenetic periosteal vessels, hindering new bone formation. The consequence is accelerated resorption and decreased production of bone, the end product of which is a radiographic 'hair-on-end' skull appearance and diffuse osteopenia elsewhere. Trueta does not explicitly define how marrow crowding causes bone resorption, and we still have not defined that mechanism completely. However, the reader must understand clearly that our present concept emphasizes that the anemia does not directly cause trabecular resorption. Instead, subnormal hemoglobin levels in the peripheral blood provide a perpetual and potent activation of the kidney-produced hormone erythropoietin which, in turn, powerfully stimulates the marrow's RBC production machinery. It is this latter effect (marrow hyperplasia) that somehow induces bone resorption and the resulting gross skeletal manifestations described above. Thus we should not expect such skeletal changes in anemias whose marrow cannot respond: aplastic anemia due to marrow destruction by chemicals or by myelofibrosis. These, however, are rare in infancy.

Anemia can come about by any of three mechanisms: blood loss, decreased production rate or increased destruction rate. Below we present an example of each of these as a model, discussing others only to the extent that they differ from the model.

Anemias due to blood loss

Acute blood loss is usually temporary and produces no significant bone changes. Chronic blood loss usually depletes body iron stores and presents as iron deficiency anemia. This is, therefore, included in the following section.

Anemia due to decreased hemoglobin synthesis

Iron deficiency anemia

In a preceding section we pointed out that the marrow of infants normally is strained to the maximum to supply adequate oxygenation for the explosive increase in body mass that characterizes the first several years after birth. Breast milk contains a minimum of iron. Exclusive or predominantly breast-fed infants begin postnatal life with normal body iron content, extracted from the mother (even an iron-deficient one) during fetal life. Without dietary iron supplementation the hemoglobin demands of an expanding body mass cannot be met by the iron-insufficient state of the blood-forming marrow. In iron-deficient persons the marrow produces RBCs with subnormal hemoglobin content (anemia). The low level of hemoglobin in the blood, however, provides a powerful stimulus to increase RBC production. Thus, iron-deficient persons have subnormal blood hemoglobin levels but a marrow perpetually expanding in response to the RBC production stimulus. Such infants often come to maternal and then medical attention when the infant's anemia-induced weakness prevents it from walking. In antiquity, the infant's lowered serum iron level may have imparted some benefit – resistance to infection by bacteria that commonly require a milieu of enough iron to accommodate their reproductive needs (Stuart-Macadam & Kent, 1992:5–8). Armed with modern antibiotics, contemporary pediatricians do not view iron deficiency anemia as beneficial, and prevent its development with dietary iron supplementation. In antiquity the diets of some populations may have contained too little iron to restore normal body iron content of such affected infants as they progressed into childhood. The maize-dominated diet of late prehistoric southwestern Native American groups probably was such an example. In these the anemia persisted long enough to induce the skeletal changes of anemia noted earlier, though it is unusual to find more than the alterations of the frontal and parietal bones. Only in severe cases is pneumatization of facial sinuses affected.

In adults chronic blood loss leading to iron deficiency anemia is usually due to an ulcerating gastrointestinal condition, most commonly a peptic ulcer or colon cancer. An exception is the adult female whose body iron content is reduced to marginal levels by abnormal menstrual bleeding and who then experiences a succession of pregnancies. In adults the skeletal changes are commonly even less marked than in infants and cranial changes, if present in adults, are usually acquired in infancy.

Thalassemia (Cooley's anemia; Mediterranean anemia)

This is a group of anemias caused by a variety of genetic mutations at different sites of the gene coding for the structure of the globin chains of hemoglobin. They result in absolute failure or depression of synthesis of those globin chains, causing formation of RBCs with reduced hemoglobin content. They are named according to the globin chain affected (alpha or beta) each of which has variants. The consequence is a spectrum of severity, ranging from anemic fetal deaths to only modest anemia in adulthood. Populations bordering the Mediterranean sea and even those of Southeast Asia are most vulnerable, as are those of countries occupied by their migrants. Beta thalassemia is most common and the homozygote (thalassemia major) is far more seriously affected than is the heterozygote (thalassemia minor).

The most severe of anemic skeletal changes are those found in thalassemia major. The general changes of marrow hyperplasia may be extreme with metaphyseal flask-shaped deformity causing premature epiphyseal closure in long bones (especially proximal humerus and distal femur) with dwarfism. Osteoporosis with fish-like vertebrae may affect long bones to the degree of pathological fracture. Loss of trabeculae with thickening of the remainder can cause a 'honeycomb' pattern of hand and foot short tubular bones, while this same change in the skull generates the most obvious 'hair-on-end' appearance of the thickened cranial bones (Fig. 11.1). Survival to adulthood ameliorates these changes, especially those in the extremities (Murray et al., 1990). Long bones also show increased Harris (growth arrest) lines while ribs show expansion and cortical destruction with diagonal trabecular arrangement and right angle crossings (Ortner & Putschar, 1985).

While thalassemia is often thought of as an example of RBC production deficiency, it is the globin portion of hemoglobin whose synthesis is decreased. Responding to the low blood hemoglobin level, RBC production is increased enormously. However, before most RBCs have reached maturity in the marrow, their abnormally structured hemoglobin often precipitates. These abnormal RBCs are destroyed within the marrow and their components recycled for new RBC production ('ineffective erythropoiesis'). Abnormally-structured cells escaping such a fate in the marrow are removed prematurely from the peripheral circulation by the spleen. This enormous increase in RBC turnover rate is responsible for the highly cellular marrow of the thalassemic patients.

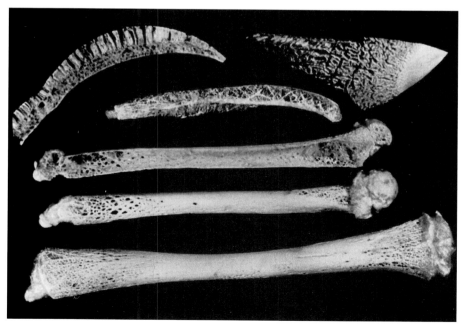

FIG. 11.1. **Thalassemia.** Note spiculations from outer table (left upper corner), coarse diploic trabeculation (upper center) and surface of outer table showing 'porotic hyperostosis' pattern of the spicules. Transected long bones demonstrate similar interior coarse trabecular and surface lacy pattern. All are the product of profound, life-long, anemia. Modern case. Photograph courtesy Dr Bruce Ragsdale, Birmingham, AL.

Anemias due to increased red blood cell destruction (hemolysis)

Sickle cell anemia (S hemoglobinopathy; drepanocytosis; Herrick's disease)

A genetic mutation at a single locus (position 6) of the gene coding for the hemoglobin beta chain in this condition results in the substitution of a single amino acid (valine for glutamate). Minor as this molecular change is, the altered beta chain causes the hemoglobin to polymerize into a long, insoluble molecule that distorts the RBC into an elongated, sickle-like arc when the RBC is exposed to a hypoxic environment. These deformed RBCs are recognized and removed from the circulation long before the end of the 120 day life of a normal RBC, placing an enormous replacement burden on the marrow. More important, the sickle-shaped RBCs are not easily passed through the capillaries. In these narrow blood vessels the deformed RBCs become entangled with each other, forming aggregates large enough to occlude the lumen, blocking blood flow. The ischemic tissue area then undergoes necrosis (infarction). This can occur in any organ but is especially common in the spleen and threatening in the brain.

The condition occurs predominantly in Blacks of African origin and is expressed only in homozygotes. Symptoms, triggered by hypoxia, are episodic but by age 5 or 6 years may becoming life-threatening. In addition to the usual skeletal signs of marrow hyperplasia, these children also suffer bone infarcts secondary to the described vascular occlusions (Steinbock, 1976:226), though these are more easily recognized in those who survive to the late teens or to young adulthood. Diffuse osteoporosis with vertebral 'cupping' may be obvious (Moseley, 1966; Murray et al., 1990). Necrosis of the femoral head with subsequent deformity is common and may mimic Legg–Calvé–Perthes disease. Infarction can also produce hand and foot bone changes (sickle cell dactylitis or hand-foot syndrome). Long bone infarcts can resemble osteomyelitis and may undergo pathological fractures.

Hereditary spherocytosis (Minkowsky–Chauffard's disease; familial hemolytic anemia)

In addition to the above-discussed, another group of mostly milder (with a few exceptions) hereditary hemolytic diseases occur, many of which involve mutations affecting the function of enzymes employed in the burning of glucose within the RBC. We will note here the more common one involving a mutation that alters the RBC membrane protein (spectrin), resulting in changing its shape from a normal pliable, biconcave disc to that of a rigid sphere. One of the spleen's functions is the recognition and removal of deformed (normally aging) RBCs. Thus, the normal spleen recognizes the shape of the spherocytes of hereditary spherocytosis (HS) as abnormal, even though they may be no more than a few days old. This premature RBC destruction

(hemolysis) requires RBC replacement at a much higher rate than normal, resulting in a generalized expansion of marrow with its attendant skeletal changes of modest degree. The transmission of HS is that of an autosomal dominant and its locale of highest frequency is northern Europe. The increased production of bilirubin resulting from the increased RBC destruction rate may raise the bilirubin concentration in bile high enough to make it precipitate as gallstones. A similar RBC shape alteration by a different mutation produces an RBC of oval shape (hereditary elliptocytosis).

Paleopathology of the anemias

The general response to anemia involves skeletal changes detailed above and merely summarized here as metaphyseal widening, cortical thinning, cranial bone thickening and coarsening of trabecular bone. Except for the bone infarcts of sickle cell disease, these changes are common to all the anemias discussed, making the diagnosis of a specific type of anemia on a skeletal morphological basis difficult or impossible. Nonmorphological data such as geography or ethnicity may make some anemia forms more probable than others (Ortner & Putschar, 1985:258). Their degree of expression varies with the severity and duration of the anemia, which may also be of some use in differential diagnosis.

Assignment of these changes, however, to a specific anemia with greater certainty will probably need to await other measurement methods. One recent study was able to make a specific diagnosis by recognizing the sickled RBCs in ancient remains by means of scanning electron microscopy (Maat, 1991). Immunological methods are also being explored in the hope that altered beta chains may have antigens not shared by normal beta chains. The first step in that direction is a report that an immunological method was able to detect a reactive result using an antiserum directed against normal human hemoglobin alpha and beta chains in extracts of lumbar vertebrae up to 2000 years old (Ascenzi et al., 1991).

Porotic hyperostosis (symmetrical hyperostosis; hyperostosis cranii; spongy hyperostosis) and cribra orbitalia (usura orbitae; hyperostosis spongiosa orbitae)

Definition

Porotic hyperostosis (PH) is characterized by usually symmetrically distributed cranial lesions involving the outer table only of the frontal and parietal bones and much less frequently of the occipital. In the fully developed lesion the involved areas of the skull are thickened by the expanded diploic layer and the outer table overlying the lesions has been resorbed completely. This permits direct visualization of the trabeculae of the expanded cancellous bone, and coarsening of these trabeculae is usually apparent (Fig. 11.2). In earlier cases or those of lesser degree the outer table is often

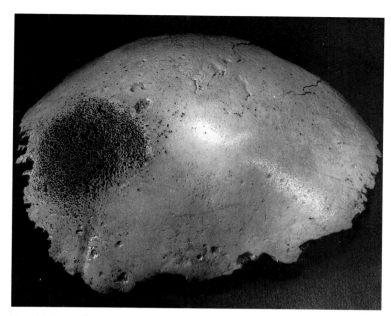

FIG. 11.2. **Porotic hyperostosis.** Parietal bone has thickened area with resorption of overlying outer table exposing diploe. Case 12. Infant of eneolithic period from Alacant, Spain. Courtesy Dr D. Campillo. Specimen curated at Museu Arqueologic d'Alcoi, Spain.

incompletely resorbed, the most minimal examples presenting only as multiple, discrete pinhead-sized perforations. In older individuals such an appearance may represent a healing stage of a previously more overt lesion. The lesion is commonly most fully developed in infancy (but not at birth).

Etiology

While K. Rokitansky and R. Virchow noted the orbital lesions of cribra orbitalia, the detection and detailed description of PH is usually attributed to Welcker (1888) even though he called it cribra orbitalia. Hrdlicka (1914) found PH in Peruvian skulls and Hooton (1930) described these lesions as 'osteoporosis symmetrica' in his widely publicized study of pre-Columbian Native American remains at Pecos Pueblo site. During these periods, causes of these changes were attributed to a wide variety of underlying conditions with little or no supporting evidence It was the report of the anemia we now call sickle cell disease by Cooley & Lee (1925) that suggested that skeletal reactions were associated with anemia. Probably the most well-known application of this observation is the hypothesis presented by Angel (1978) in which he used the presence of PH as a marker for thalassemia (see the section on Interactions of Malaria in Chapter 7).

A veritable cascade of articles, roundtable discussions and symposia since that time and dating to the present reflect the paucity of extant evidence that can lead to a clear and unequivocal understanding of these lesions. This evidence has been collected and well-presented by Stuart-Macadam & Kent (1992:151–6). She has emphasized that iron deficiency anemia is probably the most common cause of PH worldwide and notes that it should be considered an adaptive response because it may impart a beneficial effect in infancy since iron is essential for the growth of most bacteria. However, Martin et al. (1985) noted that individuals with iron deficiency are more susceptible to severe infections. Because iron is also required for the incorporation of hydroxylysine and hydroxyproline into collagen, Endt & Ortner (1982) examined the content of these amino acids in normal bone and in collagen from individuals with PH, finding from 5–25 % less of these amino acids in the PH bone. Roberts & Manchester (1995) also regard PH as a maladaptation and epidemiological studies have demonstrated an increased mortality in individuals with the closely-related lesions of cribra orbitalia (see below).

Several workers, however, have called attention to the presence of similar lesions that appear to be associated with intentional cranial deformation (Allison et al., 1981a; Guillen, 1992: 162–3). Individually the lesions appear indistinguishable from PH. The cranial deformation is produced by cloth bands that encircle the infant's head, applied shortly after birth and tightened by the mother to force cranial growth in the desired direction. The degree of tightening in some cases has been demonstrated to result in sufficient effect on the affected sutures to induce premature synostosis and even bone necrosis under pressure pads. In the third case reported by Allison et al. (1981a) the cloth deformer band had been tightened to the point that the parietal bones overlapped the temporals. It is, therefore, quite conceivable (though undemonstrated) that such tight deformer bands could apply sufficient stress to the suture vasculature to induce a periostitis type of response. This has also been the impression of one of us (A.C.A.), who has dissected mummies from this same area (southern Peru and northern Chile). In one such study only 72 (64 %) of 113 skulls showed intentional cranial deformation, yet all 24 examples of the PH-like lesions were found among those 72 cranially-deformed skulls (chi squared p<0.0001: Aufderheide, 1990). In some (but not all) cases the distribution of the lesions was quite strikingly related to the suture, appearing as a linear band 1 or 2 cm wide paralleling the suture but separated from it by at least 1 cm. In one of the examples transection of the vault documented the absence of the outer table. Unfortunately, there is a natural reluctance to incise a skull lesion, so the presence or absence of the outer table is seldom established. Guillen (1992:162–3) pleads for more precise recording of the lesions' locations to help determine whether or not this may be of differential diagnostic value.

Cribra orbitalia (CO) is a similar but smaller lesion located in the orbital roof (Fig. 11.3), usually predominantly in the anterolateral portion; 90 % are bilateral. Both PH and cribra orbitalia are found predominantly in infants and younger children. Cribra orbitalia has virtually identical morphological as well as demographic features and associations as PH. For example, in the study by Aufderheide (1990) noted above, all of the skulls with PH-like lesions also had bilateral CO, and only three additional examples of CO were found in

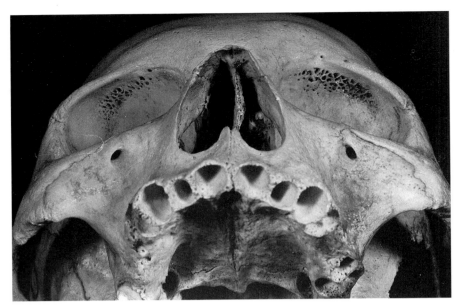

FIG. 11.3. **Cribra orbitalia.** Cribiform defects in orbital roof. Case 11. Late medieval adult. Valladolid, Spain. Courtesy Dr Gonzalo Trancho and Dr D. Campillo. Specimen curated at School of Biology, Universidad Complutense de Madrid.

Note that there are many things we do not know about PH and CO, including the answer to questions such as: How severe an anemia for how long is necessary to produce PH? Must coexisting conditions (protein malnutrition) exist? Can a cranial deformer really produce this lesion? If so, what is the mechanism? If a mechanism other than marrow proliferation is operative, is the radiological picture identifiable in such modern cases? Can severe anemia in individuals whose marrow response is impaired induce the PH lesion? And many more. In view of the fact that such questions can be expected to be resolved readily by relatively simple animal studies, it is surprising that we still need to debate them.

undeformed skulls. Cribra orbitalia is usually more common in a population than is PH and is therefore regarded as a more sensitive marker for whatever the underlying stimulating influence (anemia ?) is.

It may be useful to summarize now what we do know about PH and CO.

1. If the radiological 'hair-on-end' or 'hairbrush' appearance in modern living patients with severe congenital anemia is in actuality the lesion that paleopathologists call PH, the severe, prolonged anemia of any cause that will not hinder a compensatory proliferation marrow response can produce this lesion *in infancy*. If such degrees of anemia appear first in adulthood, marrow expansion takes other forms (reoccupation of long bone medullary space and extramedullary hematopoiesis including liver, spleen, and even paraspinal, extramedullary, soft tissue, marrow-producing masses).

2. Specific anemias in modern patients in whom such a radiological appearance has been demonstrated include thalassemia, sickle cell anemia, hereditary spherocytosis, iron deficiency anemia and congenital nonspherocytic anemias, most of the latter representing deficiencies of enzymes involved in glucose metabolism.

3. Both primary polycythemia vera and red blood cell polycythemia secondary to hypoxia (as in congenital heart disease) can also be associated with such a radiological picture. If Trueta's concept (see above) of the mechanism that brings about the PH lesion is correct, then this is not surprising because the primary stimulus for the lesion is excessive marrow cellular proliferation. Trueta (1968) even cites PH lesion production in the cases of acute leukemia described by Baty & Vogt (1935) as well as Cooley et al. (1927).

Paleopathology of porotic hyperostosis

Angel's (1978) hypothesis about malaria-driven thalassemia in the peri-Mediterranean area (using PH as a thalassemia marker) has been discussed in the section on malaria in Chapter 7. While some have predicted that Europe was too cold to permit the overwintering of anopheline mosquitoes before 500 B.C., Angel (1977) cites Garnham (1966) that falciparal malaria appears to have continued transmission at temperatures down to +14 °C. On the basis of PH, Angel had predicted an elevated frequency of thalassemia in the Middle East Neolithic period, so it is of interest that Hershkovitz et al. (1991) found a Neolithic skeleton in coastal Israel with an arm deformed by premature closure in a manner characteristic of thalassemia (absent humeral neck with laterally rotated head; sharp-edged, porotic-based furrow with small, adjacent fossa; premature fusion with shortening). Several other skeletons revealed suggestive but less diagnostic features.

There is no unequivocal evidence of sickle cell disease or thalassemia in the pre-Columbian New World, so iron deficiency anemia is usually invoked to explain the presence of PH and CO there. Two infants less than 2 years old from Grasshopper Ruins in Arizona had both PH and CO (Zimmerman & Kelley, 1982:77). Among 115 skeletons from an Alabama site of about A.D. 1050–1550, Powell (1988) found no PH, but CO was identified in only 2.5 % of the elite while those considered to be of two lower status groups had values of 6.5 and 9.9. %. Her conclusion was that fewer of the elite group had iron deficiency anemia. Stuart-Macadam (1989a, b), however, argues that archaeological evidence to support dietary deficiency of iron as a cause of iron deficiency is weak. At Arizona (Canyon del Muerto and Houck) and Colorado (Mesa Verde) sites Zaino (1967) found PH in about one-fourth of the infants and young children between the periods of Basketmaker II to Pueblo III. Many other reports document the presence of PH and CO in all parts of the world, but the validity of the interpretations is constrained by the limitations discussed above.

DISORDERS OF WHITE BLOOD CELLS

Plasma cell dyscrasias (multiple myeloma; plasma cell myeloma; myelomatosis; Kahler's disease)

This term specifies a group of conditions which all share one central feature: a malignant, monoclonal proliferation of plasma cells. A plasma cell is simply a B lymphocyte that is actively secreting an antibody. Antibodies are immunoglobulins (Igs) and the various plasma cell dyscrasias are classified on the basis of the type of Ig secreted. The proliferating cell mass is monoclonal; i.e. all cells are derived from a single, mutated plasma cell. Accordingly, all such plasma cells in a given patient secrete the same Ig (antibody) molecule.

An Ig molecule is Y-shaped in which the vertical segment is long, and of quite constant structure (heavy or H chain) that defines the Ig molecule class (gamma, beta, or mu) while the shorter, angulated segment (light or L chain) is of variable molecular structure, representing the portion designed to attach to a specific (often bacterial) antigen. Depending on the nature of its mutation, the malignant plasma cell clone may secrete an Ig of any of the three classes and may secrete the entire Ig molecule or any segment of it; usually L chains, occasionally H chains, are produced. L chains can be of two types: kappa or lambda but in the malignant, monoclonal cells only one of these is produced.

The various dyscrasias include the following:

■ Waldenström's macroglobulinemia. This is characterized by secretion of the large IgM molecule in amounts great enough to render the blood viscous, producing blood flow problems. While bone marrow as well as liver and spleen are infiltrated, no discrete bone lesions are produced.

■ Heavy chain disease. Only the heavy chain of the Ig molecule is secreted with soft tissue infiltration (especially lymph nodes) but no bone lesions are produced.

■ Primary amyloidosis. Excessive light chain production results in their deposition as an insoluble product (amyloid) in various soft tissue organs with tissue destruction, but no bone lesions.

■ Solitary plasmacytoma. This is a discrete soft tissue or bone tumor composed of plasma cells (Apley & Solomon, 1992). It eventually disseminates (multiple myeloma) after a

number of years in most cases (Ferrández Portal, 1996), though in a few cases surgical removal has effected an apparent cure.

■ Multiple myeloma. This disseminated form is the most common and is discussed in detail because of its paleopathological significance.

Multiple myeloma

Modern examples of this condition in ages 30 to 40 years are so few that paleopathologists should be reluctant to make this diagnosis in remains of individuals under age 40 at time of death. About two-thirds of the affected persons are male. Its etiology is unknown but most demonstrate an abnormality in chromosome 14. Since lymphocytes are central to the body's immune defense system, it may not be surprising that a malignant transformation of plasma cells would impair immune function. Indeed, bacterial infections are common and in some modern series bacterial pneumonia is the presenting complaint in 25–30 %. Infections are also common causes of death in multiple myeloma.

In about two-thirds of the cases the L chains, small enough to pass through the glomerulus, become detectable in the urine as 'Bence–Jones' protein, precipitate in and clog the renal tubules. In about 10 % the L chains are deposited in soft tissues as amyloid. These three (infections, renal failure and amyloidosis) account for most of the myeloma deaths.

The lesion that permits paleopathological recognition is the lytic bone lesion. Early in its course the proliferating plasma cells are distributed widely as focal nodules throughout the marrow (Roberts & Manchester, 1995). These plasma cells of multiple myeloma (but only rarely those of the other plasma cell dyscrasias) secrete a lymphokine that stimulates osteoclasts in the immediate vicinity of such a tumor mass to

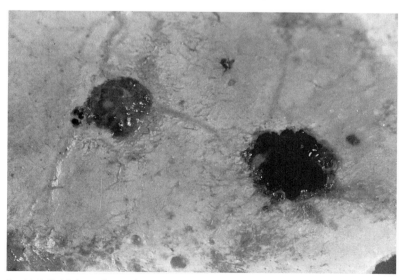

FIG. 11.4. **Multiple myeloma: skull defects.** A closeup view of several lytic myeloma lesions about 1.5 cm in diameter on the endocranial surface of the skull vault bones emphasizes the sharply demarcated periphery and the complete destruction of all osseous tissue within the lesion. Modern, elderly female. PBL.

resorb bone locally. The consequence is a sharply localized, completely lytic dissolution of bone without reactive new bone formation (Fig. 11.4). Such nodules vary from a few millimeters to a few centimeters in diameter. Most are between 0.5 and 2 cm in size, though adjacent lesions may coalesce to produce occasional larger ones. Initially they are scattered throughout trabecular bone and become most easily visualized radiologically in the flat bones, especially the skull, where eventually either or both tables may be penetrated (Fig. 11.5). At autopsy the lesions are discrete, completely devoid of any trabecular bone spicules which have been replaced by a translucent gel composed of a sea of plasma cells suspended in their immunoglobulin secretion. The radiographic appearance is that of a punched-out area. In later stages the lesions may be so abundant as to have a moth-eaten appearance on a skull radiograph, and then long bone metaphyses may be involved. Eventually sufficient bone destruction will result in vertebral body collapse (Fig. 11.6) with attendant neurological compression, scoliosis or kyphosis deformity. Later pathological long bone fractures occur. Endosteal diaphyseal involvement may produce a scalloped radiographic appearance. Compilation of several series suggests the following skeletal element involvement in descending order: spine, ribs (Fig. 11.7), skull, pelvis, femur, clavicle and scapula (Cotran et al., 1994). The paleopathologist, however, must remember that X-rays of modern patients are generally carried out at time of diagnosis and usually only repeated in the event of some local complication such as pathological fracture. Hence, an even more widespread involvement may well be encountered by paleopathologists (Figs. 11.8, 11.9 and 11.10).

Paleopathology of multiple myeloma

The principal condition from which myeloma must be separated is metastatic carcinoma. In contrast to metastatic carcinoma, Strouhal (1991b) noted that lesions of myeloma (i) very commonly involve the mandible, acromion, glenoid and olecranon, scapula, clavicle, radius and ulna, (ii) are more widely distributed, (iii) have sharply localized, discrete edges, (iv) are smaller; surrounded by smooth, unpitted bone, (v) affect males more commonly. Any evidence of sclerotic bone reaction (except in areas of healing pathological fracture) probably excludes multiple myeloma. The young ages affected by Ewing's tumor serve to exclude myeloma in such cases.

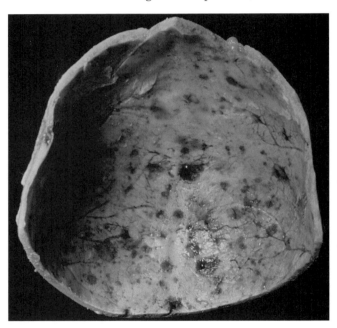

FIG. 11.5. **Multiple myeloma: skull defects.** The endocranial surface of the calvarium is studded with sharply-demarcated, 'punched-out,' lytic lesions in areas involved by this tumor in a modern, elderly adult. PBL.

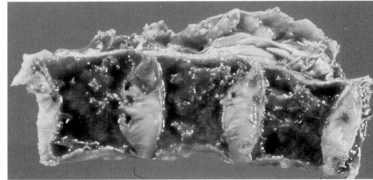

FIG. 11.6. **Multiple myeloma.** Osteoclastic activity, stimulated by a tumor-secreted factor, has destroyed virtually all trabeculae in these vertebrae of a modern, elderly female and replaced the destroyed area with a gel-like mass of tumor and secreted protein. PBL.

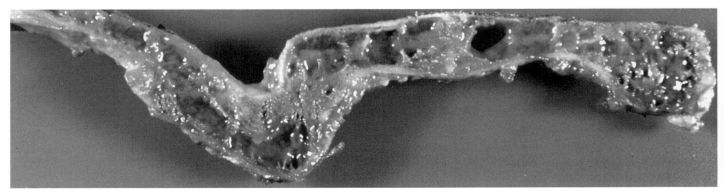

FIG. 11.7. **Multiple myeloma.** The multiple lytic areas, devoid of trabeculae, have produced gross deformation of the transected sternum in this modern, elderly female. PBL.

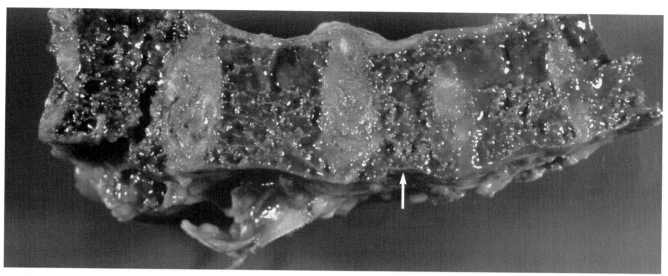

FIG. 11.8. **Multiple myeloma.** Destruction of trabeculae by tumor has weakened and collapsed central vertebra pictured here. Modern, elderly female. PBL.

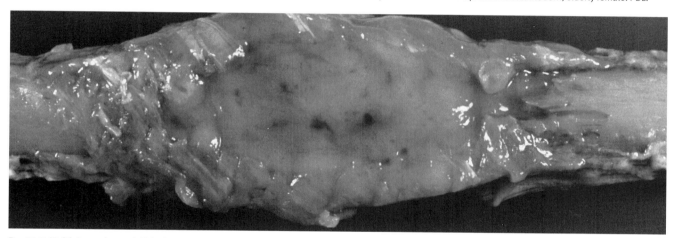

FIG. 11.9. **Multiple myeloma.** A rib lesion seen in this modern elderly female has not only destroyed all trabecular tissue, but eroded the cortex as well, expanding the area of involvement. PBL.

While many myeloma reports in ancient bones of young adults are probably examples of misdiagnosis, the following are examples whose descriptions are consistent with multiple myeloma. The oldest case is probably a Neolithic 40–50 year old female from Austria with many purely lytic lesions throughout the skeleton (Strouhal, 1991b). A medieval example estimated to be a 60–80 year old female from Germany had lesions (Alt & Adler, 1992). While two of four cases from North America reported by Morse *et al.* (1974) are young adults, a third is only 35 years and the fourth is a 45 year old male from Florida dated A.D. 500–1250. Morse later (1978) described another from California: a 45 year old female with appropriate lesions. Brooks &

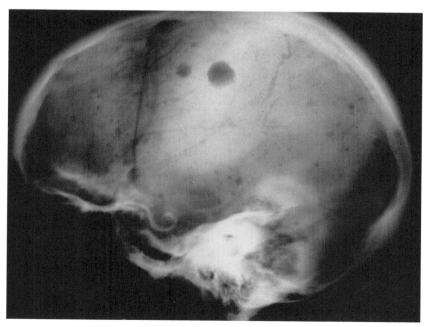

FIG. 11.10. **Multiple myeloma: skull defects.** Several larger lesions up to 1.8 cm in diameter are seen in this skull X-ray of a modern, elderly female. Note, however, the many smaller lesions scattered through the skull, many of less than 10 mm diameter. PBL.

Melbye (1967) identified a 40+ year old female from about A.D. 1200 in Missouri with characteristic myeloma lesions while Steinbock (1976:381) noted such lesions in an isolated, pre-Hispanic Peruvian skull and another was an approximately 50 year old female from Kentucky about 3300 B.C. with body-wide, typical myeloma skeletal changes. Both of these later examples are curated at the Smithsonian Institution.

Histiocytosis-X (Langerhans cell granulomatosis)

This group term includes several, age-specific, different clinical presentations affecting children, all of which are characterized by proliferation of histiocytes (more recently called Langerhans cells). These individual syndromes are called eosinophilic granuloma, Hand–Schüller–Christian disease and Letterer–Siwe disease. Although all have the common pathological feature of histiocytic proliferation, their differing clinical features justify our discussion of them as separate conditions. Recent studies, however, have demonstrated that the histiocytes in all forms of this condition are of clonal nature, suggesting this is a neoplastic and not reactive disorder (Willman et al., 1994).

Eosinophilic granuloma

This is commonly seen in predominantly male children 5–10 years old but can be found less often in adolescents and even young adults. It usually comes to attention as a serendipitous radiological observation. In the minority it may produce localized pain, usually associated with a pathological fracture. The lesion is quite sharply localized, small and essentially lytic (Fig. 11.11). In some locations it may erode the cortex and stimulate overlying reactive periostitis. However the range of the lesion's form is substantial (Helms, 1989) and in some the periphery is only vaguely defined. Its center may even contain a sequestrum (Ortner & Putschar, 1985). In living patients the radiologically lytic area is occupied by a granulomatous inflammatory area demonstrating histiocytic proliferation and commonly infiltrated by eosinophils. Involved bones in descending order of frequency include skull (especially frontal bone), mandible, humerus, ribs, thoracic and lumbar spine and femur, and less frequently in the clavicle, sternum, tibia and fibula. In long bones, involvement is primarily diaphyseal and metaphyseal. They are rare in hands and feet. The spine lesions may collapse the vertebral body (vertebra plana). In most cases the lesion is solitary and may resolve spontaneously (Bullough, 1992) but multifocal lesions are present in the minority.

In archeological bones they can be differentiated from multiple myeloma by the fact that myeloma lesions are smaller and both more abundant as well as more widely scattered. An example of eosinophilic granuloma in antiquity is a case reported by Morse (1978). Lytic lesions in the T12 and L1 vertebral bodies and a multilocular lesion in the ilium (the latter

showing some new bone formation) were present in a 2.5 year old child from an Illinois site dated to A.D. 1000–1600.

Hand–Schüller–Christian disease

This form involves principally boys aged 2–5 years old. The lesions in this form are multiple, widely disseminated and resemble those described above but frequently also contain lipid (mostly cholesterol) deposits. The clinical triad of (i) exophthalmos (bulging eyes), (ii) diabetes insipidus (excessive urine excretion due to antidiuretic hormone deficiency) secondary to posterior hypophyseal area involvement and (iii) indolent, scattered calvarial lesions characterizes the clinical presentation as well as fever, infections and visceral involvement in some cases. Untreated, some of these die while modern chemotherapy makes such an outcome unusual.

Letterer–Siwe disease

While the histological lesions are similar (though usually far more proliferative) this form is so aggressive that death in untreated cases is the rule. The affected age group ranges

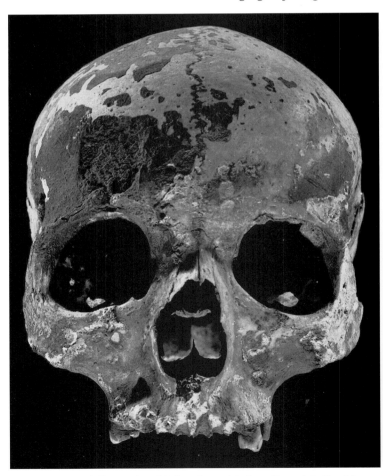

FIG. 11.11. **Eosinophilic granuloma?** Solitary, large, right frontal bone defect involving outer half of diploe without new bone formation. Case 24. Young adult eneolithic female, Valencia, Spain. Courtesy Dr D. Campillo. Specimen curated at Museu de Prehistoria de Valencia, Spain.

from birth to 2 years. The clinical features of visceral involvement (especially liver, spleen and lymph nodes) are prominent. Later histiocytes are abundant in the blood. Many regard this form as a leukemia-like form of histiocytic malignancy and even chemotherapy today salvages only about half of affected infants. Death is usually from pulmonary involvement. Skeletal lesions are multiple, their distribution similar to the other forms.

We could find no paleopathological reports of Hand–Schüller–Christian disease and Letterer–Siwe disease.

Leukemia

Leukemia consists of a malignant transformation of white blood cells with such malignant cells circulating in the peripheral blood and infiltrating soft tissues (especially liver, spleen and lymph nodes). They are grouped into those with an acute course (6 months or less) and those with a chronic course. Leukemias affecting children usually involve the lymphocytes and run an acute course (acute lymphoblastic leukemia) while adults may suffer either acute or chronic forms that may involve either the lymphocytes or the granulocytes (myeloid form). Etiology is unknown for all leukemias, but radiation, certain viruses and some chemicals are strongly suspected of playing some etiological role.

Though white blood cells (WBCs) are essential elements of the body's immune system, leukemic WBCs are usually dysfunctional. Thus major infections are common and often lethal, especially in the acute forms. In addition, the leukemic cells dominate the marrow, suppressing the formation of other, normal cells. Platelet production often virtually ceases and the infiltrated liver may not be able to form coagulation proteins at a normal rate. Hence major hemorrhage into the intestine, brain and other tissue is also a feature of acute leukemia.

Skeletal lesions include diffuse osteopenia, the product of extensive marrow involvement by leukemic cells. In addition, pressure of local marrow infiltrates commonly resorbs most if not all trabeculae in focal areas, generating lytic lesions that appear as radiolucent foci. About half of the children and lesser fractions of adults with acute leukemia demonstrate such widely scattered focal lesions in both trabecular and cortical bone sites. Some of the latter may also represent frank intramedullary hemorrhage. Trueta (1968:230) suggests that some of these radiolucent foci represent focal hemorrhage secondary to sinusoidal vascular injury by infiltrated leukemia cells, and provides photographs of vascular injections to support this interpretation. He also uses a photomicrograph from a paper by Kalayjian et al. (1946) to confirm his own observations that cellular leukemic infiltrates occur in subperiosteal locations in long bones, stimulating a layer of new bone formation. However, this layer is prevented from fusing to the outer cortical surface by a thick layer of leukemic cell infiltrate. The result is a radiographic appearance of an onion-like layer

of new diaphyseal bone separated from the underlying cortex by a thin radiolucent line. If sufficient vascular integrity remains to nourish the cortex, the cortex itself may respond by increasing density. Enlargement of vascular foramina as well as distinct grooving and porosity of metaphyses is common, secondary to cellular infiltration (Ortner & Putschar, 1985:264). The long bone ends commonly demonstrate transverse radiolucent lines in the metaphyses that could represent leukemic infiltrate. Vertebral bodies may become sufficiently demineralized to collapse. Rarely long bones will yield similarly to pathologic fractures.

The chronic leukemias in adults produce less striking changes. Usually only diffuse osteoporosis is apparent, while in some the marrow becomes more dense diffusely due to marrow fibrosis (see below).

Myelofibrosis

In this condition the marrow undergoes fibrosis. Extramedullary hematopoiesis (blood production at sites other than the marrow) is common in the liver, spleen and adrenal. An occasional case will even form a tumor-like swelling adjacent to a vertebra that proves to be a mass of blood-forming cells. Many of the white cells are atypical and dysfunctional. Some of the cases terminate after a prolonged course as forms of chronic myeloid leukemia. The term myelodysplasia is often used as a collective term for these variations. Skeletal findings include marrow fibrosis and osteosclerosis of the axial skeleton. Cortical thickening by endosteal apposition may be present in the proximal portions of the femur and humerus. In advanced cases radiographs may be unable to distinguish between cortical bone and the medullary cavity.

Lymphomas

We have noted above that malignant transformation of lymphocytes can produce the picture of leukemia. In another form (lymphoma) malignant lymphocytes infiltrate soft tissues, especially lymph nodes, commonly without involving the peripheral blood. Eventually they may extend to the bone marrow but only occasionally (and then terminally) 'spill' into the peripheral blood. Lymphomas are classified according to cell types and demonstrate a wide range of aggression. They usually present as tumors within lymph nodes in peripheral areas (groin, axilla or neck) or within the thoracic and abdominal cavities. Eventually they tend to spread to other lymph node-bearing areas. In the bone marrow they may present as a diffuse infiltrate that gradually erodes the trabeculae producing diffuse osteopenia much like some chronic leukemias do. More commonly they may form a tissue-destroying tumor that produces multiple radiolucent areas, often with cortical erosion, but they only uncommonly induce a periosteal response. In addition, in rare cases, the skeletal lesion may be the initial, identifiable area of involvement. The diffuse skeletal lesions are scattered through the common sites of bone marrow activity. Localized lesions often target vertebral body involvement with collapse and, in some cases, paraplegia. Long bone involvement is primarily metaphyseal and can cause enough destruction to produce a pathological fracture.

In addition to these various lymphoma forms (collectively called nonHodgkin's lymphomas) a less frequent form was described by Hodgkin and bears his name. Four histologic subtypes have been described with varying tumor behavior. Collectively, however, these four subtypes cover the same range of behavior that has been described above for non-Hodgkin's lymphomas. The skeletal lesions may be primarily lytic, sclerotic or mixed. Affected bones are similar to those involved by nonHodgkin's lymphoma.

Systemic mastocytosis

Mast cells are tissue cells containing histamine granules in their cytoplasm. Systemic mastocytosis is characterized by widespread proliferation of these cells in many visceral organs. It affects late adolescents and all adult ages. Widespread proliferation of mast cells can produce hematologic disturbances, infiltrate the liver with subsequent hepatic dysfunction and eventually lead to death in a few years. In about 10 % of cases skeletal changes are identifiable as diffuse osteopenia with multiple, small osteoblastic foci often not sharply defined. These are scattered through the usual marrow-forming bones. Occasional long bone metaphyseal involvement can lead to a pathological fracture.

BLEEDING DISORDERS

Hemophilia

While deficiencies of many different coagulation factors can occur, hemophilia is the most common and will be used here as a model.

Definition and features

The various coagulation factors have been given Roman numeral designation. The condition known as hemophilia was later found to be made up of two different coagulation deficiency types: VIII and IX. Hence VIII is now designated as hemophilia A and IX as hemophilia B. Hemophilia A (deficiency of factor VIII) is the common and classical deficiency. We will limit our discussion to VIII deficiency and hereafter refer to it simply as hemophilia.

Hemophilia (VIII deficiency) is transmitted as an X-linked recessive trait and thus is expressed in the male or homozygous female (a single normal X produces enough VIII to prevent bleeding). The degree of deficiency varies enormously from person to person. Frequency is about 3–4/100 000 male births. Clinical bleeding occurs when blood levels of factor VIII fall to about 1 % of normal. It usually becomes evident at about 3–5 years of age. Minor trauma commonly produces hemorrhage into muscle areas and, more seriously, into joints. Most commonly involved are the knee (above all), ankle and elbow since these are most commonly bumped in normal play or work. The hip, wrist, hand (metacarpophalangeal joints) and shoulder are less often involved. Recurrent joint hemorrhages over a period of several decades results in chronic synovitis with connective tissue proliferation as well as cartilage and skeletal disturbances, which upsets synovial fluid–blood balance, interfering with cartilage plate nutrition (Aegerter & Kirkpatrick, 1975). Subsequent degenerative joint disease with cartilage destruction, erosion and eburnation of subchondral bone and osteophytosis results, often with sufficient severity to cause complete destruction of the joint. Subluxation, deformation and growth retardation is often complicated eventually by joint ankylosis. Premature growth plate closure is common and epiphyseal hyperplasia may be associated with cortical thinning.

Special note must be made of the occasional example of bleeding into cancellous bone producing pseudotumors (Aegerter & Kirkpatrick, 1975). These are of variable shape or size and can cause massive bone destruction with new bone formation that can mimic true tumors. The femur, tibia and pelvis are the common sites of such events. Similar pseudotumors can result from hemorrhage into some of the soft tissues and superficial bone sites such as muscular musculoperiosteal and subperiosteal locations (Duthie & Bentley, 1987). Radiologically they appear as sharply demarcated radiolucent areas with or without an osteosclerotic halo (Brower, 1994). Harris (growth arrest) lines are common. The radiological appearance of a hemophilic joint may be indistinguishable from that of rheumatoid arthritis (Helms, 1989), though the young age can serve as a differential feature.

PART TWELVE

Skeletal dysplasias

INTRODUCTION

In this chapter we present a wide range of skeletal growth disorders. Even though the causes of only a few have been identified at the molecular level, undoubtedly the ultimate etiology most of them lies in the genetic realm. Some are the product of a 'point' mutation at a single base DNA locus, while others involve the loss, gain or translocation of a major chromosomal segment that may carry hundreds or thousands of genes. The latter can be expected to manifest itself in a cascade of aberrations. These alterations may affect morphology (e.g. amelia: absence of limbs) or function (e.g. a dysfunctional form of alkaline phosphatase leading to hypophosphaturia).

Such genetic changes may be isolated, acquired mutations that can result in death prior to childbearing age, but many are heritable — i.e. transmitted to progeny. If a heterozygote expresses the abnormality and the altered gene is not on a sex chromosome, it will be transmitted in an autosomal dominant (AD) pattern. When expressed only in homozygous individuals, the transmission pattern is autosomal recessive (AR). When the altered gene is on a sex chromosome the transmission pattern is sex-linked (SL). Isolated mutations without a family history are called sporadic (S). Our present knowledge of the specific molecular change responsible for the abnormal skeletal growth is slender indeed, though completion of the human genome project in the coming decade can be expected to clarify many of them.

Here we have found it necessary to compromise our general pattern of topic selections. In most of this volume we have attempted to include most conditions characterized by anatomic changes discernible with the unaided eye, even if they have not yet been reported in the paleopathology literature. The number of dysplastic skeletal syndromes, however, is infinite. For that reason we have selected primarily those that are common or produce unique alterations. These we have collected and divided into several groups, the syndromes of each group sharing some common feature. Because these syndromes often have been assigned different names by different authors, we have been guided by the recommendations of the Second International Nomenclature of Constitutional Diseases of Bone, listing the older terms in parentheses. With some modifications we have also grouped them according to their classification. In addition their transmission form is indicated when known (AD, AR, SL, S) or listed as I, if indeterminate. We generally present one (sometimes more) example from each group in some detail as a model, and comment much more briefly on other similar syndromes principally with relation to how they differ from our model. Unfortunately most of these syndromes have not been studied anatomically to a degree sufficient to lead us to an understanding of the morphologic histological mechanism leading to the abnormal skeletal structure. For these we can offer the reader only an itemization of the deformities. Most of the dysplastic skeletons encountered by paleopathol-

ogists will be examples of the syndromes we present here as models. For those that are not, our listings can be employed to narrow the range of possibilities. Final confirmation can be achieved by reference to more exhaustive presentations such as that by Sillence et al. (1979).

GROWTH DEFECTS OF LONG BONES AND SPINE

Most of these are characterized by defects of endochondral bone growth resulting in slowing or arrest of growth. Since membranous bone is not affected, the principal, obvious alteration is a body with shortened extremities relative to the trunk. Our model for this group is achondroplasia.

Achondroplasia (chondrodysplasia fetalis; fetal chondrodystrophy; heterozygous achondroplasia; micromelia; chondrodystrophic dwarfism) (AD)

Epidemiology, etiology, and prognosis

This congenital, hereditary and familial disease usually leads to a respiratory death at birth when two achondroplastic heterozygote parents produce a homozygote fetus. Thus, our discussion will concern itself with heterozygote-afflicted persons, since their life expectancy is near normal. It is the most common form of skeletal dysplasias (1 per 10 000 live births). Eighty percent of these individuals represent new ('sporadic') mutations. Intelligence is normal.

Pathology

Achondroplasia is the classic model for short-limbed dwarfism. The fundamental defect lies in depressed cartilage proliferation at the long bone growth plate. The usual cartilage columns are replaced by irregular chondrocyte masses without architectural structure. A thin, horizontal plate of fibrous tissue and bone soon separates the cartilage from the epiphysis and its blood vessels, halting further extremity growth (Cotran et al., 1994:1218). Membranous bone formation, however, is unaffected. The result is a dwarfed body with a normal-sized trunk but shortened extremities (Fig. 12.1). The head often appears disproportionately large, which is only partly an illusion due to its brachycephalic shape with frontal bossing and a shortened cranial base that leads to a depressed nasal bridge and a consistently prominent 'saddle nose'. Spinal lordosis is especially common and the shortened, thickened ribs contribute to a flat-appearing chest.

The limbs are all shortened – femur the most, then the humerus, then the bones of the lower legs and forearms (Figs. 12.2, 12.3, 12.4 & 12.5). Shortened fingers have been

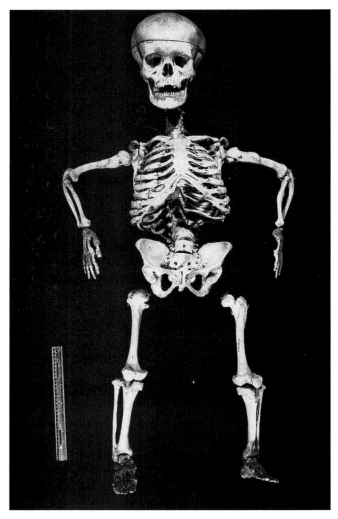

FIG. 12.1. **Achondroplasia.** A short-limbed dwarf skeleton. Modern case. 1002894. Courtesy P. Sledzik. NMHM.

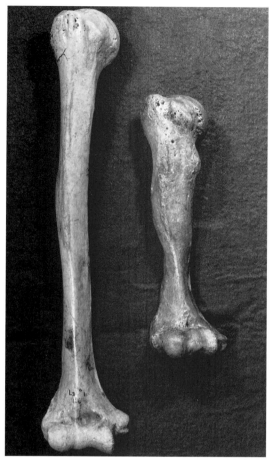

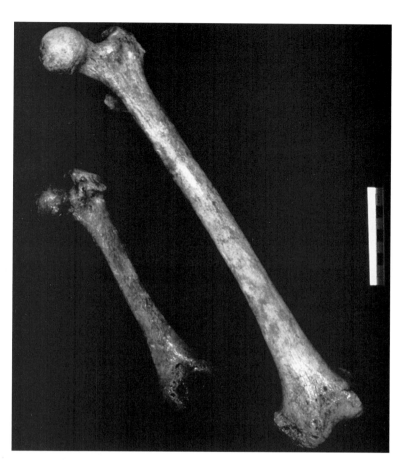

FIG. 12.2. **Achondroplasia.** A humerus of normal modern case is contrasted with the shortened and irregularly thickened humerus of an archaeological achondroplastic humerus. Turkey, about A.D. 1100. Courtesy Dr R. Pickering. DMNH.

FIG. 12.3. **Achondroplasia, femur.** The irregular, shortened femur of an adult achondroplastic dwarf contrasts with a normal femur of same age. Courtesy Dr R. Pickering. DMNH.

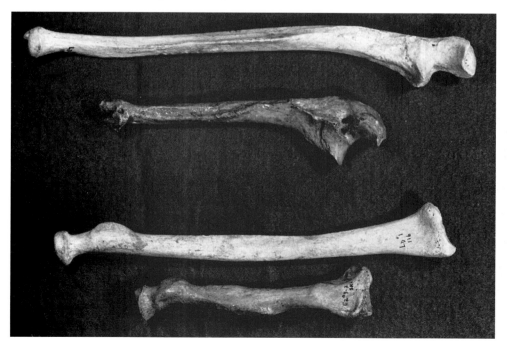

FIG. 12.4. **Achondroplasia, radius and ulna.** Abnormal bones are contrasted with normal bones of same age group. Courtesy Dr R. Pickering. DMNH.

FIG. 12.5. **Achondroplasia, tibia.** The prominent widening of the metaphysis is well illustrated in this infant. Modern case. PBL.

termed a 'trident' pattern. Long bone diaphyseal growth is unimpaired, causing them to thicken and the delayed but ultimately calcified metaphysis is commonly widened. Adult stature rarely exceeds 140 cm.

History

These unfortunate individuals were often viewed as unique in antiquity and commonly subjected to a variety of roles in royal European courts, where they provided amusement or were used as gifts to other monarchs. Egyptian pharaohs also employed them as craftsmen (Strouhal, 1992:154) and may even have attributed some ritual value to them.

Paleopathology

Its frequency and ready skeletal recognition have led to numerous case reports of achondroplasia in the paleopathology literature. K.R. Weeks (cited in Strouhal 1992:249) found nine Egyptian examples supplementing their common appearance in that country's iconography. North American examples include two from a prehistoric site in Alabama (Snow, 1943), one from California curated at the Lowie museum at Berkeley, dating to A.D. 1500–1800 (Hoffman, 1976), and an isolated skull from the Late Woodland period in Maryland (Ortner & Putschar, 1985:334). These all had the principal characteristic skeletal features of achondroplasia. Similar finds have been reported from Belgium (Susanne, 1970) and medieval Poland (Gladykowska-Rzeczycka, 1989). More recently Bortuzzo (1995) found an example in a middle Neolithic cairn at Ernes, France showing characteristic achondroplastic features except for the poorly-preserved skull.

Syndromes sharing some of achondroplasia's features include those listed below. In these the thoracic deformities are so severe that neonatal death or in infancy is the rule.

Pseudoachondroplasia (AD, AR)

Limb shortening in the condition is rhizomelic (Greek *rhiza*, root; *emos*, limb); i.e. most prominent at the hips (femora) and shoulders (humeri) with irregular epiphyses and widened metaphyses, resulting in premature degenerative joint disease.

Achondrogenesis (AR)

Stillborn or die at birth (respiratory). Disproportionate dwarfism, short extremities, poor ossification of whole skeleton.

Thanatomorphic dysplasia (thanatophoric dwarfism; death-bearing dysplasia) (S, AR)

Stillborn or die at birth (respiratory). Very short limbs with narrow thorax and short ribs, flattened lumbar vertebrae, otherwise similar to achondroplasia.

Short rib polydactyly syndromes (AR)

The three types composing this subgroup all demonstrate a thorax so abnormal that the more severe forms impair respiration sufficiently to cause death. The short, horizontal ribs impart a narrow, flat appearance to the thorax. They also share varying degrees of polydactyly and limb shortening, but differ in deformities of other bones.

Saldino–Noonan's syndrome (Type I)
Very short limbs that terminate in bony spurs; postaxial polydactyly.

Majewski's syndrome (Type II)
Moderately short limbs with rounded ends with preaxial and/or postaxial polydactyly. Occasional cleft palate and flat nose.

Verma–Naumoff's syndrome (Type III)
Like Type I but with skull and saddle nose like achondroplasia.

Asphyxiating thoracic dysplasia (Jeune's disease) (AR)

Short limbs like achondroplasia but extremely short, horizontal ribs reaching only to anterior axillary line. Postaxial polydactyly with shortened phalanges in 20 %. Spur-shaped os pubic (Wynne-Davies & Fairbank, 1982). Skull and spine uninvolved. Early respiratory and renal death common but not inevitable.

Chondrodysplasia punctata (Conradi's disease; stippled epiphyses)

This is a short-limbed dwarfism with radiographically granular epiphyses presenting in infancy in three forms:
- Severe rhizomelic form (AR). Short limbs with cup-shaped metaphyses and radiologically stippled epiphyseal calcification in hips, shoulders and spine. Saddle nose, flat face and bowed legs. Nonskeletal changes include cataracts (75 %), mental, cardiac and visceral abnormalities. Few survive the first year.
- Conradi–Hünerman Disease (S, AD). Usually only one limb shortened. Punctate calcifications in epiphyses of many bones. Craniosynostosis. Less severe.
- X-linked form (SL-D). Lethal for males so only affects females.

Camptomelic dysplasia (AR)

(Greek *kamptos*, bent). The shortened extremities are bowed anterolaterally (especially leg long bones). Thorax is bell-shaped, sufficient to impair respiration leading to death at birth or within the first year. Other skeletal changes include macrocephaly with a small face, depressed nasal bridge, multiple limb joint dislocations due to articular element hypoplasia, platyspondylia and sometimes cleft palate and micrognathia.

Multiple epiphyseal dysplasia (AR, AD) (dysplasia epiphysialis multiplex; Ribbing-Müller's disease; Fairbanks' disease; multiple epiphyseal dysostosis; hereditary epiphysiopathy or ribbing)

This probably heterogeneous group shows disproportionate, short-limbed dwarfism with enlarged epiphyses (radiologically stippled) showing delayed and irregular ossification involving the large joints. Premature advanced degenerative joint disease is a common complication. Life expectancy and intelligence normal. The spine is usually not involved.

SHORT-LIMBED DWARFISM WITH PROMINENT SPINE ALTERATIONS

Congenital spondyloepiphyseal dysplasia (spondyloepiphyseal dysplasia [congenita]) (AD, SL-R)

Epiphyseal ossification failure appears to be responsible for the severe degree of short-limbed dwarfism (100–120 cm) seen in this condition. Both vertebrae and limbs participate fully in the shortening process. Vertebrae are thick, irregular and flattened, encroaching on the intervertebral disk space. These changes generate an extreme lumbar lordosis and a moderate kyphoscoliosis. Odontoid aplasia often leads to atlantoaxial instability. Less common are cleft palate and hip dislocation. Additional radiological observations include poor ossification throughout the skeleton, especially in the pubic bone and the knee epiphyses.

A late form (Spondyloepiphyseal Dysplasia Tarda) is much less severe, manifests in the 5–10 year age group and is transmitted principally as an X-linked recessive, but occasionally an AD pattern. The marked spinal changes in both the usual and tarda forms make a major contribution to the dramatically subnormal stature.

Other conditions with prominent spinal involvement include those listed below.

Kniest dysplasia (Kniest disease) (?D)

Appearing at birth or soon thereafter, this condition shares the short limbs, short trunk, diminutive stature, lumbar lordosis and kyphoscoliosis of the syndrome preceding this one. In addition the femoral neck is wide and short, the facial skeleton flattened with hypertelorism, saddle nose and cleft palate. Radiography also reveals diffuse osteopenia. Histologically degenerative chrondrocyte changes and abnormalities of growth plate vasculature play a role in the epiphyseal dysplasia (Sillence *et al.*, 1979).

Larsen's syndrome (S, AD, AR)

Scoliosis and kyphosis reduce stature in this syndrome but in addition dislocations of many joints occur including elbow, hip, knee (with severe genu recurvatum) and less often the ankle and wrist. A round, flattened face with saddle nose, hypertelorism, micrognathia, cleft palate and frontal bossing is often striking. Hypoplasia of cervical and thoracic vertebrae contribute further to decreased stature and short, thick phalanges and metacarpals are common. Radiological demonstration of two ossification centers in the calcaneus is almost pathognomonic of this disorder.

METAPHYSEAL AND DIAPHYSEAL DISORDERS

Diaphyseal aclasis (hereditary multiple exostoses; osteochondromatosis; multiple osteochondromatosis; multiple exostosis; exostosing disease; deforming chondrodysplasia; multiple hereditary osteocartilaginous exostoses) (AD)

The outstanding feature of this relatively common disorder is the formation of many exostoses (osteochondromas) in areas of endochondral but not intramembranous bone. Thus variable numbers and sizes of these lesions occur at the ends of long bones, especially the distal femur, proximal tibia and fibula as well as the distal radius. Their presence in the knee region is a consistent feature. The extent of involvement may range from a single site to many areas throughout the skeleton. They are not present at birth but begin to grow symmetrically at 6–8 years, initially at the metaphyseal end of the long bones, deforming the metaphysis into a 'trumpet' shape. This often interferes with metaphyseal remodeling this area. Cortical thinning is often followed by pathological fracture. In some cases the lesions interfere with bone growth sufficiently to reduce stature. Of those afflicted, 2–10 % suffer malignant degeneration of one of the osteochondromas. A variety of other skeletal effects of the exostoses includes bowing of the radius, ulna shortening and radioulnar synostosis, shortened fibula and valgum of the knee and ankle. With continued growth of the skeleton, many of these exostoses migrate to the diaphysis. Other conditions with growth abnormalities prominent in the metaphyseal and diaphyseal region include those listed below.

Metaphyseal chondrodysplasia (McKusick's disease; cartilage–hair hypoplasia) (AR)

This short-limbed dwarfism (under 150 cm) is primarily the consequence of the metaphyseal accumulation of masses of cartilage without architectural structure as well as metaphyseal sclerosis in the knee region with uninvolved epiphyses. In addition, vertebrae that are smaller than normal contribute also to reduced stature. Accompanying coxa vera can be severe. Cranial brachycephaly with delayed ossification is also often a feature. Abnormalities of hair color and texture are consistently a part of the McKusick form of this syndrome. Two other (Jansen & Schmid) less common types of this syndrome have an AD transmission form. The Jansen form is accompanied by elevated blood calcium and hypercalciuria but, paradoxically low or normal parathyroid hormone (PTH) levels. This paradox may be explained by the recent identification of a gene mutation coding for the PTH receptor; this produces spontaneous activation of this receptor without PTH binding, explaining the atypical mineral pattern (Schipani et al., 1996). The syndrome is common in the American Amish community (1–2/1000 live births: Wynne-Davis & Fairbank, 1982). Intelligence is unimpaired.

Metatrophic dysplasia (metatrophic dwarfism) (AD, AR)

The responsible histologic changes in this condition are unknown but the gross alterations are focused on the long bone metaphyses that are irregularly widened into a 'trumpet' shape. The deformed and widened epiphyses appear to interfere with long bone growth. Other associated deformities include vertebral changes (platyspondylia with kyphoscoliosis), short ribs with production of a narrow thorax, small ilia and short bone deformities of hands and feet. The AR inheritance pattern is lethal. While the AD pattern is less severe, respiratory impairment shortens adult life.

Dystrophic dysplasia (dystrophic dwarfism) (AR)

This short-limb dwarfism shows prominent, widened metaphyses with deformed epiphyses. Severe scoliosis exaggerates the reduced stature. A prominent differentiating feature is a deformed femoral head on a short, wide femoral neck and irregular acetabulum.

Dyschondrosteosis (AD)

This short-limb form of dwarfism (under 150 cm) involves the forearms and legs, commonly including Madelung's deformity (dislocation of distal ulna), coxa valga and ankle deformities. A sixth century A.D. 60 year old female skeleton from Switzerland demonstrated the forearm changes and may be an example of this disorder (Kaufman et al., 1979).

Chondroectodermal dysplasia (Ellis–van Creveld syndrome) (AR)

This last of this section's syndromes bears features of many of those presented above. Consanguinity is common in parents of these cases as noted in a study of the Amish community. The most obvious feature is acromesomelic dwarfism (decreased stature due to shortening of the distal and middle segments of the limb). Thus the tibia, fibula, radius and ulna are shortened but only occasionally the femur and humerus. Polydactyly, sandal gap (increased space between first and second toes), carpal blocks and club foot deformity are common. Joining the extremity deformities are the thoracic alterations of short ribs and long, narrow thorax that impair respiration and even cardial function, commonly leading to a childhood death. The skull and spine, however, remain uninvolved, though dentition is often hypoplastic. Frayer et al. (1987) made this diagnosis in a 17 year old Paleolithic male (though hands and feet missing). Rogers (1986) also described a mesomelic Romano-British young adult female dwarf with small but not pathological hands or feet, which she felt represented the Langer type of mesomelic dwarfism.

DEVELOPMENTAL ANOMALIES OF CARTILAGINOUS AND FIBROUS COMPONENTS OF THE SKELETON

Dyschondroplasia (Ollier's disease; endochondromatosis; multiple endochondromatosis; multiple chondromata; internal chondromatosis) (I)

The fundamental abnormality in this disorder is the production of benign chondromas in the long bones' metaphyseal areas. Occasionally only a single bone is involved but far more commonly many bones are affected. Distribution is often bilateral but asymmetrical. The bone ends at the knees are most commonly involved but the small hand and foot bones may be so extensively replaced that pathological fractures and malfunction of these are often noted. While the metaphyseal involvement is most evident, radiological studies quite regularly demonstrate extension into the epiphyses, manifesting as irregular, mottled densities there. Metaphyseal areas reveal extensive structural replacement by cystic-appearing areas that represent the chondromas. Enchondromal growth ceases during the second decade but malignant change in a chondroma occurs in about 15 % of afflicted persons, usually in adulthood.

Such a distinctive pattern ought to be recognizable in dry bones, so it is not surprising that at least one case of this condition has been reported in a medieval adult male from a Swiss site in whom the left tibia and humerus, knee and fibula showed these changes as well as bilateral Madelung's deformity (Kramar *et al.*, 1995).

Maffucci's syndrome (enchondromatosis with hemangiomas) (I)

This rare syndrome consists essentially of the skeletal lesions of Ollier's disease accompanied by soft tissue subcutaneous and visceral hemangiomas, and thus cannot be differentiated from Ollier's disease in dry bones.

Dysplasia epiphysealis hemimelica (tarsoepiphyseal aclasis; epiphyseal hyperplasia; Trevor's disease) (S)

Hyperplasia of a single long bone epiphysis in a usually male infant characterizes this syndrome. Calcified masses may be periarticular or attached to the bone. The distal femur, talus or occasionally proximal tibia are the most common sites. Genu valgum and/or varum may be present, and metaphyses are usually spared.

DISORDERS OF DIAPHYSEAL DENSITY OR METAPHYSEAL REMODELING

Osteopetrosis (Albers–Schönberg's disease; marble bone disease; osteosclerosis fragilis generalisata) (AD, AR)

Failure of proper osteoclastic function underlies the several disorders grouped into this syndrome. The skeletal lesions are the product of the absence of bone remodeling. While the chemical mechanisms have not been defined with certainty in all forms of this disorder, in at least one it has been traced to a genetic mutation resulting in the absence of the enzyme carbonic anhydrase II. This enzyme allows osteoclasts to secrete hydrogen ions, creating the chemical milieu that allows the osteoclasts to resorb the bone matrix and mineral, an essential step in bone remodeling. In its absence new bone production is not matched with resorption, resulting in a continuing accumulation of membranous, unorganized bone. Animal models have created a similar disease through other mutations and even a retrovirus (Cotran *et al.*, 1994:1222). A severe form of this disease (AR) is present at birth and lethal in childhood, usually as a result of infection secondary to bone marrow failure as a consequence of marrow replacement by bone. The milder, later (tarda) form is transmitted by AD pattern and permits survival to adulthood, though life expectancy is subnormal.

The unopposed, life-long new bone formation obliterates the medullary cavity, creating the medical problems of ane-

mia and pancytopenia (low white and red blood cell counts). Enlarged liver and spleen reflect conpensatory hematopoiesis. Long bones become thickened, the metaphyses widened ('mace-shaped') and all trabecular bone replaced by unorganized membranous bone. This unorganized bone, while dense, has much weaker architectural integrity is and thus more vulnerable to trauma. Indeed, repeated fractures usually bring these individuals to medical attention. Radiologically the epiphyses reveal alternating layers of dense and lighter bone. The process is universal throughout the skeleton and may obliterate the skull diploe and replace cranial sinuses. Constriction of vascular and neural foramina impair the anatomic structures traversing them, generating facial paralysis, etc. An example of this disease was identified in an isolated child's mandible in ancient Nubia (Nielsen & Alexandersen, 1971), and children of several families were identified in human remains excavated from an eighteenth and nineteenth century British site (Waldron *et al.*, 1989).

Dysosteosclerosis (AR)

The hyperostosis in this disorder mimics that of osteopetrosis, involving not only the skull and long bones, but also showing platyspondylia and dental anomalies (enamel hypoplasia, delayed eruption).

Pyknodysostosis (AR)

A distinct but similar condition that differs from osteopetrosis in that the sclerosis does not replace bone marrow. The commonly reduced stature is due to the multiple fractures plaguing those afflicted with this disorder. In addition, a host of other isolated deformities affect various bones (vertebral blocks, clavicular and mandibular hypoplasia, tapered terminal phalanges and others). The generalized skeletal osteosclerosis is easily recognized radiographically. Probably the most well-known example of pyknodysostosis is the French impressionist painter Henri de Toulouse-Lautrec.

The remaining members of this group demonstrate various types of much more localized forms of hyperostosis. For these, we will discuss infantile cortical hyperostosis as our model.

Infantile cortical hyperostosis (Caffey's disease; Caffey's syndrome; tubular stenosis with periodic hypocalcemia) (I)

Usually a self-limited condition over a period of several months, the condition described by Caffey & Silverman (1945) and earlier by Roske (1930) commonly appears in infancy in the form of a localized, tender lump on a rib or mandible, much less frequently a long bone diaphysis. The rather abrupt onset of subperiosteal new bone formation produces local cortical thickening with eventual widening of the medullary cavity. While some metaphyseal widening may occur in an affected long bone, the epiphysis is never involved. Though usually an isolated lesion, distribution is asymmetrical when multiple. Skull lesions may thicken the cortex at the expense of the diploe and fontanelle closure may be delayed. Spontaneous resolution with ultimate remodeling is the rule.

Paleopathology

A Romano-British infant from England revealed multiple, asymmetrical localized hyperostoses throughout the skeleton. A second infant from the Saxon or medieval period showed similar lesions on the mandible, clavicle, skull and long bone diaphyses (Rogers & Waldron, 1988).

Diaphyseal dysplasia (Camurati–Engelmann disease; Engelmann's disease; diaphyseal sclerosis; hereditary and progressive diaphyseal dysplasia; infantile multiple hyperostotic osteopathy; progressive diaphyseal hyperostosis) (AD)

This variant demonstrates diffuse hyperostosis limited to the long bone diaphyses, converting them into fusiform-shaped thickened shafts of the tibia and femur (less frequently the humerus, ulna radius and hand and foot bones). The skull may be involved in some cases. The marrow may be obliterated in late stages.

Frontometaphyseal dysplasia (I)

An early childhood disease in which the hyperostotic process affects principally the skull. The postcranial skeleton has a short trunk with bowed limbs.

Craniometaphyseal dysplasia (AD, AR)

Craniofacial and long bone diaphyses are the targets of hyperostosis in this disorder of infants. Cranial sinus obliteration, frontal bulging, hypertelorism and facial deformity are obvious, while the diaphyseal lesions affect the lower limbs more than the upper.

Metaphyseal dysplasia (Pyle's disease; familiar metaphyseal dysplasia) (AR, AD)

Hyperostosis affects the skull, while the distinguishing feature is involvement of the metaphyses. These are enlarged, convex and shaped like an Erlenmeyer flask, rendering them susceptible to fracture. An example of this condition was identified in both tibiae, a humerus and pelvis of a pre-Hispanic skeleton from the Mochica culture (A.D. 200–800) in Peru (Urteaga & Moseley, 1967).

Craniodiaphyseal dysplasia (AR)

In addition to cranial and long bone diaphyseal osteosclerosis, this childhood disorder also demonstrates osteosclerosis of vertebral, rib, clavicle and short hand and foot bones.

Melorheostosis (Leri's disease; Leri's hyperostotic osteopathy; osteosis eburnisans monomelica; monomelic hyperostosis; dripping candle wax disease) (I)

The hyperostosis in this syndrome affects only one limb (usually the lower) and commonly only one bone. The cortical new bone is laid down as though in successive layers, generating an appearance resembling dripping candle wax that expands distally, sometimes from one bone to the next. Other deformities in the involved bone may include genu varum and valvum and patellar dislocation. Other bones are only rarely involved (Swoboda, 1972).

The lesion is so distinctive in dry bone that it becomes readily recognizable. An example has been identified in the fibula of an Alaskan Eskimo from A.D. 500 (Lester, 1969), and also in the humerus of a north-Chilean (Chinchorro culture) adult female from about 2500 B.C. (Kelley & Lytle, 1995). Both reveal the characteristic dripping candle wax structure.

In addition to the above, mutations affecting the synthesis or regulation of alkaline phosphatase (an enzyme central to bone production) produce unique skeletal dysplasias.

Hyperphosphatasia (AR)

This severe childhood disorder is characterized biochemically by blood levels of alkaline phosphatase 20 to 40 times greater than normal and anatomically by thick, bowed long bones with many pathological fractures that may impair growth, normal epiphyses, thick short bones of hands and feet, acetabular protrusion, coxa vara and kyphoscoliosis. Cranial bones are commonly thickened. A rare, milder form also occurs. The histology is identical with that of adult Paget's disease (Aegerter & Kirkpatrick, 1975:369; Avioli & Krane, 1978:678).

Hypophosphatasia (AD, AR)

The AR form produces a severe disease lethal at birth or in infancy and is characterized by severe, generalized osteopenia as would be expected in the absence of alkaline phosphatase, an enzyme vital to the deposition of new bone. Some of the resulting changes may mimic rickets, producing decreased stature, globular head, bowed limbs, osteopenia, widened metaphyses, dental anomalies and pathological fractures. The AD form is less severe.

COLLAGEN DISORDERS LEADING TO INAPPROPRIATE MINERALIZATION

Because collagen forms the matrix for deposition of the hydroxyapatite crystal of bone mineral, mutations affecting collagen structure have major impact on skeletal structure. However, collagen also forms the 'fibrous skeleton' of many vital soft tissue structures, so the skeletal dysplasias in this group are commonly accompanied by many visceral abnormalities. Our model for this group is osteogenesis imperfecta.

Osteogenesis imperfecta (brittle bone disease; osteitis fragilitas; fragilitas ossium congenita; osteopsathyrosis) (AD, AR)

Definition, etiology, and disease mechanism

Osteogenesis imperfecta (OI) is an inherited disease caused by defective collagen formation and clinically characterized by profoundly osteopenic bones that fracture readily in response to minor stress. Variations in clinical manifestations are correlated at least in part with a variety of differing mutations in at least one of the two genes coding for the synthesis of pro-alpha 1 or 2 chains of type I collagen heterotrimer. Since the stability of the collagen fiber is dependent upon the bonding between the fibrils at regular intervals, the impaired synthesis of these chains produces a lax, stretchable connective tissue texture with a low level of integrity. This is reflected at a number of different body sites, but in OI bone formation defects manifest themselves most obviously as recurrent fractures. Both autosomal dominant and recessive forms have been described. Birth frequencies range from 1/30 000 to 1/60 000 (Prockop, 1991:1864).

Natural history

Formerly classified as either severe (infantile) or mild (adult) forms, better understanding of inheritance patterns and clinical variations related to them resulted in the four-type classification (Sillence, 1981) used today, though recent genetic refinements promise further taxonomic changes in the near future (Hollister, 1987). In the most severe form (type II) the bones are so osteopenic that they yield to the normal stresses of intrauterine life. The number of fractures these feti suffer as well as the morphologic changes are detailed below, but type I collagen is present at many body sites and collagen abnormalities may be manifested as sclerae of bluish color (choroidal pigment effect becoming visible because of the thin, translucent collagen in the overlying sclerae). Skin is thin and joint capsules may become as stretchable as often seen in Marfan's or Ehlers–Danlos syndrome. Stretching of the collagen in cardiac valves (aortic, mitral) may cause regurgitation at those sites. While tooth enamel is formed appropriately from the uninvolved ectodermal structures, it chips easily because of the weak support it receives from the underlying dentine that is poorly formed and often pigmented. Individuals with the milder types are commonly edentulous by age 30 years. Affected teeth are also usually deformed in both the deciduous and permanent dentition (dentinogenesis imperfecta).

At the other variation extreme, type I OI persons may be unaware of their disease until they suffer a fracture in late adolescence or adulthood. Indeed, if the first fracture occurs in a postmenopausal woman, the osteopenia may be misdiagnosed as the usual form of postmenopausal osteoporosis. Intermediate types exist, some of which improve after puberty. In types other than II, hearing loss, due usually to temporal bone osteosclerosis, becomes apparent in young adults (50 % under age 30 years) and becomes almost universal in later life (Whyte, 1993:347).

In addition to the direct effect of the gene mutations on collagen synthesis cited above, observations in affected individuals suggest other metabolic effects not yet completely understood. These include increased urinary excretion of hydroxyproline and glycosaminoglycans (Trueta, 1968) and skeletal accumulation of glycosaminoglycans (Cruess & Rennie, 1984:438). It is also important to note that the callus formation response to the fractures, including its calcification, is normal in all types (actually progressive with startling rapidity in some cases) but the resulting transformation into bone undergoes the same impairment as does primary bone formation in OI.

Bone Pathology

Because of the stresses that weight-bearing and use place on them, bones most commonly and severely affected are those of the legs, clavicles, ribs and spine, though virtually any bone can be involved.

Long, tubular extremity bones

In many cases the endochondral bone formation at the epiphyseal plate functions well enough to permit these to approach their normal length. The poor quality of the bone at this site does yield to fracture stress (Figs. 12.6 & 12.7) whose corresponding callus formation can produce multiple foci of calcification there (popcorn calcification: Whyte, 1993:348) that in exceptional cases may destroy the plate, arresting growth and producing short stature. The bone in this area suggests that osteoid may have been formed directly by

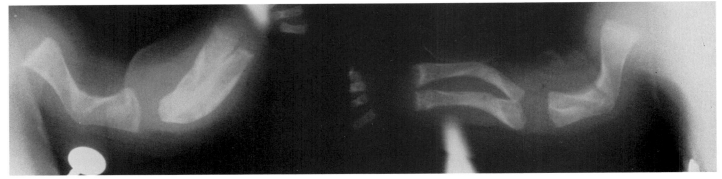

FIG. 12.6. **Osteogenesis imperfecta.** X-rays of this modern stillborn infant demonstrate multiple long bone fractures incurred during fetal life, affecting both arms. PBL.

metaplasia of cartilage cells (Aegerter & Kirkpatrick, 1975: 142). In many cases, however, the distinctive alteration of these bones is their advanced osteopenia with remarkably thin cortices. Periosteal osteogenesis is substantially limited with only primitive osteoid deposition poorly lamellated and usually not effectively remodeled into the original cortex (Ortner & Putschar, 1985:337). The trabecular bone of their metaphyses is also poorly formed with fewer and thinner trabeculae. Superimposed on these changes may be two further effects: bending from muscle strains and prominence of multiple calluses secondary to multiple fractures. In the lower extremities a linear array of these on long bones may generate a pleated (Jaffe, 1972:163) or accordion (Prockop, 1991:1864) simile. Combinations of these changes can result in grotesquely deformed bones without weight-bearing function.

Ribs

These are so frail that in severe cases nodular arrays of calluses produce obvious 'beading' effects. They are also often inwardly displaced by such fractures, and their expansive respiratory movements may be sufficiently restricted that pneumonia proves to be the most common cause of death in the neonatal period.

Vertebrae

Fractures of the neural arch are common. Compression fractures resulting from the sparse trabeculae of the vertebral bodies often produces kyphoscoliosis in those surviving long enough to assume independent erect posture.

Dentition

Dentine has a collagenous base and thus suffers the same deleterious effects as does the skeletal matrix. The result is delayed deciduous dentition and deformation of both deciduous and permanent teeth, the results of which have been noted above. Changes are often best seen in the lower incisors (Lichtenstein, 1977:23).

Skull

Skull bones in the severe forms are so thin that they have a parchment-like quality upon palpation. Sutures are wide. Particularly striking are the transformation of the usual broad vault bones into many diminutive wormian bones

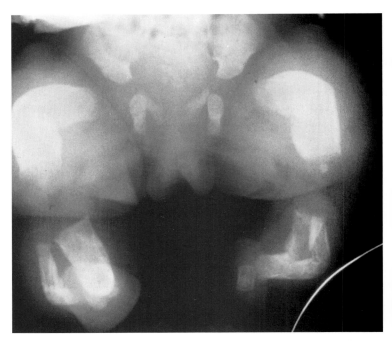

FIG. 12.7. **Osteogenesis imperfecta.** X-rays of legs of this modern stillborn infant demonstrating lower limb long bone fractures incurred during fetal life. PBL.

(see Jaffe, 1972:169, figure 35D for a dramatic example), while the skull base is normally less severely affected).

Paleopathology

An isolated adult femur from a burial (A.D. 650–850) in England revealed several deforming proximal diaphysis fractures with 90 degree angulation, cortical thinning and trabecular bone rarefaction (Wells, 1965b). A British Museum mummified Egyptian child from dynasty 21 revealed characteristic OI features in long bones, skull and dentition (Gray, 1969).

Fibrogenesis imperfecta ossium (I)

This disturbance of collagen synthesis permits modeling of normal skeletal contours but with profound osteopenia.

Fibrodysplasia ossificans progressiva (myositis ossificans progressiva; fibrogenesis ossificans progressiva) (S, AD)

This childhood syndrome is characterized by ossification of tendons, muscles, ligaments and aponeuroses and sometimes skin and joint capsules, incurred by trivial trauma or even spontaneously (Fig. 12.8). Initially the calcified masses are in soft tissues but with time they become attached to bone. It usually begins in the cervical areas, spreads to the limbs and eventually may involve most soft tissues except the heart, diaphragm and larynx. The entire spine and many ribs may fuse. Microdactyly with phalangeal synostosis is common, as are spina bifida and carpal blocks. Death commonly occurs at the end of the second decade. Recently at least seven

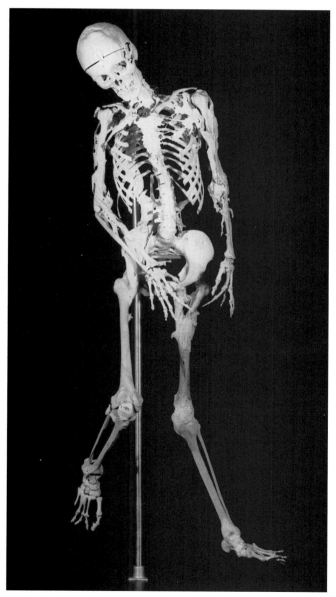

FIG. 12.8. **Fibrodysplasia ossificans progressiva.** The extensive soft tissue calcification of arms and, to a lesser degree, of legs is well demonstrated. Modern case. Courtesy G. Worden. MM.

different proteins have been identified that are major determinants of gross body morphology. Of these, protein 4 and its mRNA were found to be overexpressed in fibrodysplasia ossificans progressiva (Connor, 1996; Shafritz et al., 1996). The gene for bone morphogenetic protein 4 has been mapped to chromosome 14q22-q23.

Osteopoikilosis (osteopoikilia; generalized condensing osteopathy; spotted bones) (AD)

Bones in this condition have a normal contour and thus cannot be recognized as abnormal by external inspection only. However, radiology demonstrates disseminated, dense, small oval or rounded radiopacities around metaphyses and epiphyses with normal surrounding bone. Diaphyses are uninvolved, nor are the skull, spine and ribs. Etiology of these osteosclerotic foci remains unexplained.

Osteopathia striata (AD)

This syndrome, too, is limited to radiological detection. It involves most any trabecular bone except skull and clavicles. It is characterized by multiple lines of bone condensation in the epiphyseal line, parallel to the bone's long axis and extending into the metaphysis.

Nail–Patella syndrome (onyco–patellar syndrome; Fong's syndrome; Turner–Kieser's syndrome; hereditary osteoonychodysostosis) (AD)

Seen in late childhood or early young adulthood, this syndrome is characterized principally by patellar hypoplasia with recurrent dislocations as well as nail (ungual) hypoplasia. Other structural changes include hypoplasia of lateral femoral condyle, upper radial extremity (with Madelung deformity and elbow dislocation), small scapulae and mushroom-shaped metaphyses. Concurrent renal changes are common.

In addition to these, several dysplasias demonstrate both major skeletal and soft tissue alterations secondary to dysfunctional collagen. Our model for these is Marfan's syndrome.

Marfan's syndrome (arachnodactyly) (AD)

Defects in cross-linking of the collagen fibrils results in loss of their triple-helical structure with resulting loss of physical integrity. Eighty-five percent of cases are familial (Salvador & Carrera, 1995). The weakened fibers of the aortic wall often yield with consequent fatal aortic rupture in midadulthood. Joint capsules are weak and allow dislocations, while the ocular fibers suspending the lens also permit dislocation. Skeletal features are dominated by excessively elongated extremities, especially the uppers. The horizontal distance between fingertip of outstretched arms may exceed vertical stature (even though the latter usually exceeds 180 cm), and the elongated fingers have been dubbed arachnodactyly (spider-fingers). The former American president Abraham Lincoln may well have had this disorder. Specific skeletal features of this disorder include:

- Skull: dolichocephaly, frontal bossing, dental anomalies and malocclusion.
- Trunk: kyphosis, scoliosis (50 %), pectus excavation or carinatum.
- Limbs: dislocations of hip, clavicle, patella and genu recurvatum, club foot and hallux valgus.

Homocystinuria (AR)

The enzyme transforming serine and homocysteine into cystathionine is dysfunctional in this syndrome, producing a defective collagen as well as mental retardation. The changes in both skeletal and soft tissues resemble those of Marfan's syndrome. In addition, increasing tissue levels of homocysteine increase platelet adherence and the resulting thromboses may contribute to the mental retardation (Prockop, 1991:1873). However, epiphyses are flattened, metaphyses widened and punctate ossification of distal radius and ulna ends is radiologically evident, as well as increased numbers of Harris lines of growth arrest.

SKELETAL DYSPLASIAS DUE TO CHROMOSOMAL ABERRATIONS

In contrast to the probably localized mutations responsible for most of the syndromes described above, those listed below are examples produced by chromosomal changes. These are incurred during the mitotic phase of cell division *via* such mechanisms as translocation (of major portions of a chromosome within its own structure or added to another chromosome) or complete loss of part or all of a chromosome. Since loss or translocation of such large quantities of DNA often contain hundreds or thousands of genes, such alterations can be expected to result in a constellation of gross morphologic deformities. Below we identify five such examples.

Trisomy 21 (mongolism; Down's syndrome)

These individuals are usually born to cytogenetically normal parents. As a result of nondysjunction during meiosis, an additional chromosome 21 (trisomy 21) characterizes these individuals. Nonskeletal consequences of this chromosomal abnormality include mental retardation (one of its most common effects), impaired immune response leading to infections, congenital heart malformations and a 15-fold increase in acute leukemia. Skeletal features include short stature, short neck, brachydactyly, shortened femora and humeri, congenital hip dysplasia, ischiopubic ramus hypoplasia, 'sandal gap' and large iliac bones. Skull changes are flattened occiput, brachycephaly, nasal bone hypoplasia, delayed suture closure, small orbits, hypertelorism, often metopism with frequent other suture abnormalities, round face, dental alterations and ogival palate. Soft tissue changes include oblique orbital fissures, flat nasal bridge, often protruding tongue, broad hands with deformed fifth fingers, abnormal dentition, frequent cardiac malformations and increased frequency of childhood leukemia (German, 1991).

Paleopathology

Trisomy 21 may have been rare in antiquity (currently the rate is 1/800 live births) because its modern frequency is related to maternal age (as high as 1/25 births over maternal age 40) and the increased susceptibility to infection this defect imposes on those afflicted (Manchester, 1983a:28). However, an isolated child's skull from Britain's Saxon period showed small maxilla with a normal mandible, thin cranial bones, microcephaly, globular skull vault, hyperbrachycephaly, small sphenoid body and high basi-occipital angle, collectively believed to represent this syndrome (Brothwell, 1960). A second example from the late Hallstatt period (350 B.C.) in Austria was found in a necropolis by Czarnetzki (1980).

Trisomy 8 (Warkany's syndrome)

Mental retardation is only slight in this rare (1/25 000 births) trisomy form, but skeletal changes are abundant and include such otherwise unrelated alterations as patellar hypoplasia, butterfly vertebrae, hemivertebrae, spina bifida occulta, scoliosis, shortened metacarpals and metatarsals, hypertelorism, micrognathia, scaphocephaly, frontal bossing and long facial skeleton.

Deletion 5p (cat cry syndrome; cri du chat syndrome)

Features of this condition include profound mental retardation and delayed development. Skeletal features consist of microcephaly, hypertelorism, round face, cranial asymmetry and micrognathia with malocclusion. Noncranial features are scoliosis with hemivertebrae, short metacarpals, hip dislocation, hypoplastic ilia, syndactyly and foot deformities.

Deletion of the chromosomal 5p 14-15 region is responsible for these dramatic changes (Salvador & Carrera, 1995). The syndrome acquired its name because the sound of these infants' cries resemble the high-pitched cry of a cat.

Turner's syndrome (Ullrich–Turner syndrome)

The presence of only a single sex chromosome produces this 45X pattern, thus seen only in females. Most of these are aborted spontaneously in the first trimester (Salvador & Carrera, 1995). The alteration impairs growth and development, terminating at a stature below 150 cm. Skull changes include micrognathia, thick cranial bones and oval palate. Other features are diffuse osteoporosis, vertebral anomalies, Madelung's deformity, hand and foot bone changes, femoral condyle asymmetry, reduced upper tibia epiphysis and hip dislocation.

Klinefelter's syndrome

Such individuals have only one Y chromosome but more than one X chromosome; 47 XXY is the most common form. Clearly all these individuals have a male habitus. There are no characteristic skeletal features but stature is commonly more than 180 cm and a disproportion between length of the trunk and the limb long bones is common. Long bone synostoses and vertebral anomalies are more prevalent than usual. The diagnosis cannot be established in dry bones, but it is included here because the unique portrayals of Pharaoh Akhenaton (twenty-eighth dynasty) in Egyptian iconography have been interpreted as possible Klinefelter's syndrome because of the suggestion of gynecomastia, pelvic enlargement and descent scapulae (Spitery, 1983). Others, however, have interpreted these features as consistent with acromegaly, Fröhlich's syndrome and progressive lipodystrophy.

SKELETAL DYSPLASIAS DUE TO CONGENITAL METABOLIC DISORDERS

Mucopolysaccharidoses

Mutations affecting the production of several enzymes involved in mucopolysaccharide (MPS) metabolism are included in this subgroup. Because MPS composes the matrix of cartilage, faulty cartilage structure impairs long bone growth. Hence these come to attention primarily during the growth period after birth. The result is a form of dwarfism with osteoarticular deformities. Most have coarse facial features, cloudy corneas, mental retardation and joint stiffness (Cotran et al., 1994:144). They are classified as MPS I to VII.

Below we discuss the five principal members of this group. Our model is Hurler's syndrome.

Hurler's syndrome (gargoylism; Pfaundler–Hurler's disease; MPS I-H) (AR)

Absence of the enzyme alpha-L-iduronidase results in accumulation and excretion of dermatan sulfate and heparin sulfate. Neurological, cardiac, pulmonary and hepatic MPS accumulations usually lead to death in childhood. Mental retardation and corneal opacities are routinely present. This is the most severe form of the MPS syndromes.

Dwarfism is partly the result of thoracolumbar kyphosis or kyphoscoliosis. Lower limb bones are of normal length but display wide metaphyseal areas, coxa valga with acetabular flattening, resulting hip subluxation and genu valgum. The arm long bones are distinctly shortened, but especially distinctive are thick, short metacarpal metaphyses with hypoplasia of the distal phalanges. The skull shows macrocephaly, scaphocephaly, frontal bossing, bulging temporal areas, a small face with a large mandible and dental anomalies.

Scheie's syndrome (MPS I-S)

This is a variant of Hurler's syndrome involving the same enzyme deficit but of milder severity, appears later, is of near normal stature and of normal intelligence.

Hunter's syndrome (MPS III) (SL-R)

This is the product of iduronate sulfatase deficiency, yet effects are similar to Hurler's syndrome but of milder degree: dwarfism, large head and facial anomalies. Separation of MPS I and III can not be achieved in dry archaeological bones.

Morquio–Brailsford's syndrome (chondrosteodystrophy; deforming osteochondrodystrophy; Ullrich's disease; Brailsford's syndrome; epimetaphyseal dysostosis) (AR)

Multiple enzymatic defects result in keratan and chondroitin sulfate accumulation. Intelligence is usually normal. Severe disproportionate dwarfism is secondary to excessive trunk shortening. This is partly the result of platyspondylia with marked kyphoscoliosis and extreme lumbar lordosis. Odontoid agenesis or hypoplasia contributes to upper cervical instability. In addition epiphyses and metaphyses are wide and irregular with normal diaphyses, resulting in articular problems. Other bone alterations are similar to Hurler's syndrome.

Paleopathology

Two isolated humeri from early dynastic Egypt in London's Natural History Museum are abnormally short with severe malformation of the humeral heads' articular surfaces, believed to represent this syndrome (Ortner & Putschar, 1985:336).

Maroteaux–Lamy syndrome (MPS VI) (AR)

Dwarfism is severe in this form, usually a stature of 90–120 cm. This is the combined effect of platyspondylia and lumbar kyphosis as well as lower limb bowing. Separation from Hurler's syndrome in dry bones is impossible.

Mucolipidoses

These uncommon metabolic derangements produce effects that mimic those of MPS. Transmission pattern for all is AR. While they have been separated into three types, the skeletal changes they share include early cranial suture synostosis, widening of ribs, iliac hypoplasia, metacarpals that are short, wide and pointed and bullet-shaped phalanges.

Type I has minimal skeletal changes and is lethal in infancy. Type II is also lethal early, and its skeletal changes are those of Hurler's syndrome. Type III has normal life expectancy, but also demonstrates kyphosis, spondylolisthesis, claw hand and joint stiffness.

Lipid storage diseases

Sphingolipidoses

This group of diseases includes Fabry's disease, Niemann–Pick disease, Tay–Sachs disease and Gaucher's disease. The latter is the only one with major skeletal anomalies and will be our disease model.

Gaucher's disease (AR)

This is characterized by cerebroside-laden bone marrow and lymphoreticular cells. The infantile and juvenile forms are lethal and without skeletal deformities but the adult form has a normal life expectancy. Skeletal lesions in these include early onset (second decade) of degenerative joint diseases, pathological fractures, osteomyelitis, scalloping of the medullary lining, osteoporosis and subarticular sclerotic foci secondary to areas of bone necrosis. Vertebral collapse is common. The disease is especially common among Ashkenazy Jews.

PART THIRTEEN

Neoplastic conditions

GENERAL PRINCIPLES OF NEOPLASIA

Definition

A neoplasm ('new growth') can be defined as a mass of local-ized tissue growth whose cellular proliferation is no longer subject to the effects of normal growth- regulating mecha-nisms. The degree of growth autonomy enjoyed by any one neoplasm can vary widely. In some, such as the common wart, the neoplasm remains subject to most of the growth-regulat-ing compounds in the body, and forms only a small mass of tissue that is incapable of destroying surrounding cells or migrating to other parts of the body; such behavior is termed benign. Other neoplasms escape all physiological restrictions, are capable of destroying surrounding normal tissues, and cells from them can reach other body locations *via* blood or lym-phatic vessels, establishing new growths (metastases) at their new sites; such behavior is described as malignant and the genre of such neoplasms is called cancer. While the terms benign and malignant are products of our modern therapeutic limitations, and while the many neoplasms to which humans are subject include numerous examples of differing degrees of growth autonomy intermediate between that implied by these two terms, *most* neoplasms reflect behavior closely resembling one or the other of these extremes. Accordingly this volume will employ these two adjectives as characterizing the respec-tive neoplasms' predicted behavior, indicating exceptions by the addition of further descriptive adjectives.

Characteristics of benign and malignant tumors

Features of benign tumors, then, include those reflecting their limited growth potential. They impact their surrounding, unaffected tissue only by compression and often stimulate them to produce a fibrous wall (capsule) enveloping the neoplasm, which the latter rarely violates. Their peripheral borders are sharply demarcated. Benign tumors commonly are composed of cells normally present in the tissue from which they arose and closely resemble them histologically (are well differentiated). They are also usually named by adding the suffix -oma to the root of their cell of origin: osteoma, chondroma, fibroma, leiomyoma, neuroma are all benign neoplasms composed respectively of osteocytes, chondrocytes, fibrocytes, smooth muscle and nerve cells. The prefix adeno- is employed when the neoplastic cells are arranged in the form of glands. Thus an adenoma is a benign gland-forming neoplasm. Alternatively, if the cell of origin is uncertain a benign neoplasm may be assigned an eponym (usually the name of the investigator who originally reported the lesion), such as Wilms' tumor of the kidney. Distinctive features of a tumor may be emphasized by modifying adjectives or prefixes such as papillary, polypoid, mucinous and others. Teratomas have all germ layer cells (see Fig. 13.16).

Malignant neoplasms manifest their much greater degree of growth autonomy. Their rate of growth is commonly much greater. A capsule is often absent. They respect few surrounding natural borders, penetrating into regional tissues with tentacular projections that frequently obscure their peripheral border. They create space for their own expansion by inducing death of surrounding normal cells, often by obstructing their blood supply. These effects may be detectable grossly in the form of foci of necrosis and hemorrhage. Extension of a malignant tumor into surrounding tissue is termed invasion. The organ or tissue in which the malignant neoplasm originates is called the primary site. Eventually cells of a malignant tumor may penetrate into a lymphatic or blood vessel. Such cells can then become detached from the parent clone, be swept downstream and lodge in a distant tissue. There they may die or flourish to produce a new growth (metastasis) with similar features at such a separate, secondary (metastatic) site. If lymphatic, the metastasis usually is found in one of the regional lymph nodes; if hematogenous the metastasis usually is present in the first organ whose capillary bed is encountered by the metastasizing cells: commonly the liver for abdominal primary sources (stomach, bowel) or the lung for most other primary sites. Malignant neoplasms composed of epithelial cells are named by adding 'carcinoma' to the cell of origin and 'sarcoma' to malignant neoplasms of mesenchymal cells. Examples include squamous cell carcinoma of the epidermis or osteosarcoma of the femur. Descriptive adjectives and eponyms are also common, as with benign tumors. As a group, carcinomas are more apt to metastasize to regional lymph nodes initially, while sarcomas commonly metastasize hematogenously. Exceptions to this general rule are particularly common among carcinomas.

Function of neoplastic cells

Neoplasms, either benign or malignant, may be composed of cells containing genes from their cell of origin that code for the production of protein products. Thus adenocarcinomas of colon mucosa may produce sufficient mucus to generate a grossly slimy quality and liposarcomas can make fat. Some of the benign adenomas arising in endocrine glands may produce bioactive peptides that can produce grossly recognizable effects. A parathyroid adenoma may secrete sufficient parathyroid hormone to induce the well known osseous changes of fibrous dysplasia and 'brown' (giant cell) tumors of von Recklinghausen's disease. Metastatic osteosarcoma can produce an ossifying lung metastasis, while a pituitary adenoma can secrete sufficient growth hormone to cause gigantism in a subadult or the deforming osseous overgrowth in the adult facial bones that are characteristic of acromegaly.

Epidemiology

Today cancer deaths are exceeded only by those due to cardiovascular diseases in developed countries. In the U.S.A. about one-half of the men and one-third of the women develop cancer at some site during their life, and about one-fifth of all deaths are due to cancer. Cancer is an age-progressive disease, ranging from about 1.8 % prevalence rate below age 39 years to approximately 27 % in ages 60–79 years (Parker et al., 1996). In addition to age, geography is a risk factor. Among 48 countries for which statistics were available, the U.S.A. ranked about in the middle (27) for males and 8 for female, while Hungary had the highest rate (1 and 2, respectively) and Mexico the lowest (48, 41: Parker et al., 1996). Affected organ is also a substantial variable. In 1996 the U.K. recorded a breast cancer death rate of 27.7/100 000 population while that for rural Tajikstan was only 4.4. Extrapolation beyond such a database, however, is hazardous; the effect of time can be substantial. The U.S.A. male death rate for lung cancer rose from about 5 to 75/100 000 population during the past 65 years, while that for stomach cancer in males fell from about 38 to 7. Ethnic or regional effects are demonstrable for certain types of cancer and include positive correlations between the incidence of liver cancer and the prevalence of hepatitis B. Particularly interesting are migrant effects that demonstrate a progressive increase in breast cancer among Japanese in Japan, Hawaii and the U.S.A., though to date complete equilibration with that of the U.S.A. population has not yet been achieved.

Causes of neoplasia

The absolute etiology of most cancers is not known. We can, however, speak about exposures that increase the probability of acquiring the disease (risk factors). These include exposure to physical, chemical and viral agents.

Physical agents

Ultraviolet light is probably the best example. Excessive skin exposure to ultraviolet radiation at wavelengths between 290 and 320 nm can induce the development of basal cell carcinoma, squamous cell carcinoma and the pigment-producing malignant melanoma, all arising from normal cells present in the skin. Skin pigmentation and the atmospheric ozone layer have protective effects by filtering such radiation. At shorter wavelengths it can be noted that the 1945 atomic bomb explosions over Japan resulted in a dose-related increase in myelogenous leukemia. X-radiation of the thymus in infants (which included the thyroid in the radiated field) was followed by the development of thyroid cancer several decades later. Contamination by ingestion of the radioactive isotope thorotrast among Japanese watch dial painters produced osteosarcomas (the long-lived isotope was deposited in the bone marrow). While the latter-cited agents are of anthropogenic origin, ancient humans were exposed to ultraviolet light and the naturally-radioactive gas radon.

Chemical agents

A large number of chemicals are known carcinogens. Most of them are synthetic compounds or naturally-occurring but processed in a manner resulting in substantial exposure. They include vinyl nitrate (liver cancer), aniline dyes (bladder cancer), and even metals such as nickel and cobalt (probably lung cancer). Grouped among 'environmental pollutants' they are only a few for which the evidence is particularly strong. The mechanisms of action in some are directly mutagenic (gene-altering) while in others mutagenicity is the product of one of their metabolites. It has been estimated that the majority of modern human cancers are caused by environmental agents of which chemicals constitute a substantial fraction. The evidence, however, for most of these is less conclusive than for those discussed above.

Viruses

While numerous viruses can cause cancer in animals and the association with several of these with certain human cancers is strong, the latter fall short of absolute certainty. Our recently developed laboratory methodology for the study of genetics has increased our understanding of the chemistry of growth enormously, but substantial gaps in our knowledge base remain. For our purposes in recognition of paleopathologic lesions, it will suffice to view development of a neoplasm as a disturbance of the equilibrium normally operative between the product of a growth-stimulating proto-oncogene in the host DNA and those of growth-suppressing genes whose protein products counteract ('regulate') the cellular proliferation initiated by the activated oncogene. Certain DNA viruses have genes whose protein products bind to the proteins generated by suppressor genes, impairing their action and thus permitting a less regulated growth of the initiated area of cellular proliferation. Since several suppressor genes may contribute to the regulatory effect of cellular growth, the degree of regulatory liberation of autonomous cellular growth may vary from minimal regulatory loss to essentially unopposed, autonomous neoplastic growth. Examples include the human papilloma virus (cervix cancer), hepatitis-B virus (liver cancer) and Epstein–Barr virus (lymphoma and cancer of the nasopharynx: see Fig. 13.18). In addition, some RNA viruses may incorporate their own RNA into the host genome by employing an enzyme called reverse transcriptase. Subsequent division of the affected cell will, of course, duplicate its entire genome including that of the now included virus segment which can 'transform' the cell into a line of cells characterized by neoplastic growth. This mechanism is operative in the production of human T cell leukemia/lymphoma by the HTLV-1 virus.

Thus whether stimulated by physical, chemical, viral or other initiators, the ultimate expression of neoplastic tissue growth clearly is mediated by genetic mutations. It is also of anthropological interest that in many cases neoplastic growth only occurs in a homozygote. Hence an autosomal heterozygote at birth may not manifest the neoplasm but is more vulnerable to subsequent development of a neoplasm because only one additional mutation at the specified chromosomal locus is required to result in the homozygosity leading to neoplastic growth. The hereditary form of the ocular tumor retinoblastoma is such an example. The Rb gene has tumor suppressive action. A child of an affected family is born with one defective, nonfunctional Rb gene and one normal one. The single normal Rb gene is sufficient to suppress tumor growth, but if the child is subjected to a mutation of that single normal gene also, the total loss of suppressive action by gene products at that gene locus results in development of a tumor, usually involving the retina. A different form of that Rb gene mutation may result in a different neoplasm, the most common of which is osteosarcoma (Rubin & Farber, 1994b:181). Rapid progress in the field is expected to increase our understanding of neoplastic mechanisms enormously in the near future.

Cancer in antiquity

Most cancers occurring in antiquity were incurable. We can, therefore, anticipate that their paleopathological presentation would be similar to modern, neglected neoplasms that were allowed to progress without therapeutic efforts. In cases of primary cancers occurring external to the body cavities (such as breast cancers) we would anticipate much larger neoplasms than we normally encounter today in clinical practice – often with fungating, ulcerative lesions. Metastatic lesions may also be more extensive. On the other hand the growth of visceral cancers may terminate life earlier than in modern times because of interference with vital functions. For example, a cancer of the intestine often blocks the bowel, a complication which can be fatal within a few days in an untreated patient. Modern surgical relief of this complication may prolong life sufficiently to allow a more extensive pattern of metastases than would be found in an individual whose life was truncated by an untreated, earlier obstructive complication such as would be expected in antiquity. Such modifying variations must be kept in mind by the paleopathologist who must also be familiar with the natural history of the many neoplasms involving the body's various organs.

Because exposure to carcinogens leads to cancer in many circumstances, the expectation of fewer carcinogens in antiquity might generate expectations of fewer cancers in ancient populations. While it is certainly true that the ancients were spared exposure to many of our modern, synthetic carcinogens, natural environmental oncogenic substances must have plagued them. Local ore outcroppings of asbestos or other carcinogenic minerals surely were a hazard to residents of those sites; domiciliary occupation of caves may well have included some that trapped naturally-occurring radon gas, uranium or heavy metal ores; the social custom of chewing betel nuts with its attendant carcinogenic action on the oral mucosa (Hutt & Burkitt, 1986) must have caused local squamous cell carcinoma in some individuals; surely the mean sun exposure times of early hunters, gatherers and even agriculturalists must have equalled if not exceeded the average ultraviolet exposure of many modern populations. While the range and probably amount of carcinogen exposure in antiquity was most likely less than in modern populations, it was not absent. In fact, at least some influences may have enhanced the development of neoplasia. The groups from which marriage partners were drawn were surely smaller than in most parts of the world today, favoring transmission of heritable neoplastic conditions. Another obvious factor tending to modify the expression of neoplasia in antiquity is lifespan. In modern populations neoplasia is an age-related phenomenon. In 1996 about 87 % of U.S.A. cancer deaths occurred in individuals 55 years of age or older. Since probably about 90 % of ancient humans died prior to age 55, age alone could be expected to reduce the frequency of cancer in antiquity by about 90 % of the modern rate (assuming other modern causes to be of equal intensity in antiquity).

However, certain cancers, such as osteosarcoma, are most common in teenagers and young adults. Unfortunately for comparison purposes, osteosarcoma is not a common tumor even today. If we try to ascertain whether or not its frequency in antiquity was similar to that of the present, we face formidable obstacles, even if we hypothesize that a cemetery population reflects death rates of the total ancient population accurately. This tumor can be recognized with a desirable degree of certainty at the knee location, but often with less precision elsewhere. Thus, if we limit our study to the knee and, based on modern frequencies, reduce the expected number by corrections for only those occurring between ages 10 and 30 years, that are osteoblastic, and were fatal, one would expect only 1 in about 5000 (pairs of) knees (0.02 %) examined in skeletal populations. Thus, even if the frequency then was similar to that now, the number of individuals that would need to be examined to reach a statistical certainty would be prohibitive. Similarly, if we choose a currently much more common tumor – breast carcinoma – our efforts would be frustrated by an insufficient number of mummified human remains to carry out the comparison. Quantitative approaches to this type of question will need to await a currently unavailable method that can reflect the presence of a malignant neoplasm independent of its anatomic preservation.

Paleopathological study of neoplasms

Diagnostic methods

Our available resources for establishing a diagnosis of neoplasms in antiquity include historical records, iconography and preserved human remains. Historical records often offer tantalizing comments that suggest the possibility early writers may have had familiarity with cancer. Rarely, however, are these of a specificity sufficient for serious diagnostic consideration. Translations of Egyptological and Veda texts, infrequently carried out by persons with medical expertise, lead to such misrepresentations as characterizing as a neoplasm a lesion referenced in a Latin text as tumor. This term actually referred to any localized tissue swelling, regardless of its nature and was employed to identify abscesses, aneurysms, lymph nodes draining an infected area, malformations and others as well as neoplasms (Boulos, 1986). Similarly Galen and Greek physicians used the terms *onkos* and *karkinos* (from which the Romans derived the word *cancer* and the English *carcinoma*) in much the same sense as Latin's *tumor* (Micozzi, 1991). The healing of a 'breast cancer' present in Darius' (Persian) wife by Democedes of Crotona (Herodotus, III:33) was more likely inflammatory mastitis (Micozzi, 1991). Certainly some references appear to refer quite plausibly to our modern concept of cancer; a lethal oral lesion recorded by Sushruta in his Samhita, most likely written about 600 B.C., was quite probably a malignant lesion in view of the popularity of betel nut chewing in early societies of India (Suraiya, 1973). Retsas (1986), however, presents citations from the Hippocratic corpus that will satisfy the skepticism of even the most critical analysts in which ancient physician authors describe malignant lesions of the breast and uterus. In summary only a few of the alleged ancient references to what we view as malignant neoplasia today are considered satisfactory evidence of cancer, and these carry us back little further than the fourth century B.C. Interpretive constraints on most literary depictions of malignant neoplasm in antiquity apply equally well to iconographic representations. The alleged breast cancer in Michaelangelo's sculpture, La Notte (night), discussed in Chapter 8 is a good example. Micozzi (1991) identifies several commonly cited cases and expresses inconclusive evaluations of these. Neoplasms of the individual soft tissues are discussed in conjunction with other diseases of the various viscera in Chapter 8 and require no further elaboration here. Those involving the skeleton are described in this Chapter. Their presentation is grouped on the basis of their cell of origin.

TUMORS OF OSSEOUS ORIGIN OR DIFFERENTIATION

Osteoma (eburneous exostosis; spongy exostosis; ivory exostosis)

Epidemiology, etiology, pathology, and radiology

This benign tumor affects more adult men than women. Its frequency peaks in the fourth and fifth decades. Though it is not always easy to do so, this tumor should be separated from ossification foci that are a reactive change to some other pathological process and osteomas are, instead, considered true, primary neoplasms.

These benign, bone-forming, and slow-growing lesions are normally located on the outer surface, and more rarely inner table, of the skull and also on facial bones, near to or within the frontal and ethmoidal sinuses. The histology of cranial and facial osteomas is different. Osteomas of the outer table of the skull ('button' osteomata) are composed of mature lamellar bone, and have the appearance of a circumscribed, ivory-like tumor (Fig. 13.1), while those on the facial bones are composed of immature bone and are commonly related to the sinuses, especially the frontal sinus. Occasionally they represent only a minor manifestation of a constellation of malformations that constitute the autosomal dominant Gardner's syndrome, the most prominent feature of which is colon polyposis. These osteomas are smooth-surfaced, small lesions (most less than 1 cm), sharply demarcated, usually solitary, circular and rounded. Other bones (clavicle, humerus, femur and tibia) are only occasionally affected. Those presenting in the external auditory canal are discussed in detail in Chapter 8.

Paleopathology of osteomas

The oldest example of osteoma is that involving the dorsal vertebra of a Mosasaurus from the later Cretaceous period of the Mesozoic era (Abel, 1924). Many cases of cranial and facial osteomas have been described. Some of the most spectacular cases of 'button' osteoma of the skull are those reported by Moodie (1923a, b, 1926) in the left side of the skull of an ancient Peruvian from Ancón, now curated at the Peabody Museum of Harvard University; by Brothwell (1967a) in the right side of the skull of an Egyptian of Roman date; and by Steinbock (1976) on the left parietal of an adult pre-Hispanic Peruvian skull from Ancón. Another, with huge dimensions, in the left maxilla, is curated in the Musée Dupuytren at Paris (Thillaud, 1996). A survey of osteomas in earlier British populations found 17 cases on the skull: 7 in the frontal bone, 6 in the parietals and 4 in other regions (Brothwell, 1967a).

Solitary enostosis (bone island)

Epidemiology, etiology, pathology, and radiology

This is probably a developmental and usually single, oval island of compact, mature lamellar bone only occasionally exceeding 10 mm and seen in all age groups. It is commonly discovered radiologically in the intramedullary cancellous bone most frequently in the pelvis, ribs or proximal femur whose surface contours are not altered by the lesion's presence. Bony trabeculae extend into the surrounding bone in a spiculated pattern. The exceptional, larger examples could be mistaken for osteoblastic metastases.

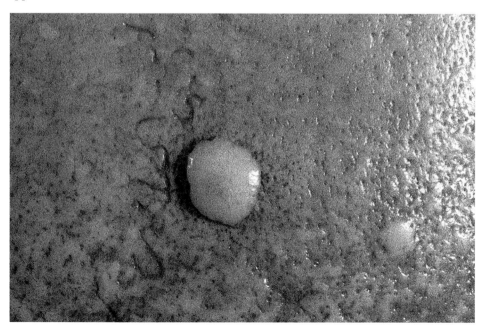

Fig. 13.1. **Osteoma, 'button'.** Tumor is an 8 mm nodule of ivory-like bone. It is adjacent to a partly obliterated cranial suture in an elderly modern male. Note satellite lesions in right lower region. 102-14. CMNH.

Osteoid osteoma

Epidemiology and etiology

This relatively common, usually solitary, small (< 2 cm), primary bone tumor accounts for about 10 % of all benign skeletal tumors. It affects more males than females (2.5:1). Seventy percent of the cases occur between 10 and 25 years. The principal symptom is salicylate-responsive local pain. Its etiology remains obscure, but some authors hesitate to label it a true tumor (Helms, 1989) while its discoverer considers it a hamartoma: a benign tumor composed of tissues normally present in the organ but assembled in architectural disarray (Jaffe, 1935, 1958:92–106).

Pathology and radiology of osteoid osteoma

About half of osteoid osteomas are in the diaphyses and may expand into the metaphyses of the long bones of the lower limb. The lumbar spine's vertebral neural arches are more commonly involved than their bodies. Metacarpals, proximal phalanges, humerus and fibula may all also be affected, while 20 % of the cases appear close to or within a joint (Bullough, 1992). Its center (nidus) is composed of osteoid and bone trabeculae and this is surrounded by new bone when it is located subcortically. This peripheral zone of sclerotic bone is absent when the tumor is located within the bone marrow. In cases of long duration in children, overgrowth of the involved bone may appear (Murray et al., 1990), while spinal involvement may produce scoliosis.

The most typical radiological image of osteoid osteoma is that of a central, rounded or oval, small (the lesion never exceeds 2 cm in diameter), radiolucent area corresponding to the nidus. As expected, the nidus is radiolucent, though some are obscured by calcification and the well-organized, newly-formed trabeculae produce a surrounding osteosclerotic margin that can be so dense it obscures the nidus (Spjut et al., 1971). The characteristic location is within the oft-thickened diaphysial cortex, but the tumor can be located in the subperiosteal region in cancellous bone (the endosteal type has a little larger nidus) or, more rarely, in a joint. Sclerosis is much less common in these last three locations.

Differential diagnosis of osteoid osteoma

The diminutive size (< 1 cm) of osteoid osteoma can separate it from osteoblastoma (see below). Calcification of the nidus can create a radiologically indistinguishable resemblance to an osteomyelitic sequestrum, especially when the shaft is thickened (Helms, 1989). Histological study can help separate Brodie abscess and nonossifying fibroma. Malignant tumors, such as osteosarcoma or Ewing's sarcoma may generate a superficial similarity when the osteoid osteoma is located in the periosteum where it stimulates substantial periostitis, but these have other features (described below) that distinguish them.

Paleopathology of osteoid osteoma

Steinbock (1976) suggests that three possible cases from antiquity have been reported. However, a Saxon tibia with a 10 cm diaphyseal swelling was not radiographed and is self-admittedly diagnostically uncertain (Brothwell, 1961; Brothwell & Sandison, 1967:325). A medieval Czechoslovakian example of the right tibia of an adult male (Vyhnánek, 1971), and an Anglo-Saxon femur (Wells, 1965a) demonstrate radiographic features quite characteristic of osteoid osteoma.

Osteoblastoma (giant osteoid osteoma; benign osteoblastoma)

Epidemiology, etiology, and pathology

This rare tumor is most common in the first two decades of life, peaking at an age slightly older than that of osteoid osteoma, though its degree of osteosclerosis surrounding the radiolucent center is also usually less dense (Revell, 1986; Bullough, 1992). However, this latter feature is often related to the duration of the lesion. Like osteoid osteoma, local pain is usually the presenting symptom, though that is not usually uniquely nocturnal nor distinctly salicylate-responsive. At least one-third of the lesions are found in the thoracic and lumbar spine (more often in the neural arches and processes than in the vertebral body) where the weakened structures may result in scoliosis (Murray et al., 1990). In this location the osteoblastic feature is often more prominent than the lytic. About one-third are in the extremity long bones (especially the femur), commonly involving the diaphyses (usually widening the cortex), sometimes the metaphyses but rarely epiphyses. The remainder are scattered through the pelvis, ribs, hands or feet and the skull and jaws. In the extremities they are usually predominantly osteolytic, though mixed patterns are not uncommon. In about one-third of the examples X-rays reveal some nidus calcification (López-Durán, 1995).

Differential diagnosis of osteoblastoma

Both osteogenic sarcoma and chondrosarcoma have some aspects that can simulate osteoblastoma but their invasive and other features (see below) usually permit their exclusion. A recently identified form of osteoblastoma has been described that is of larger size and sufficiently locally aggressive to penetrate the cortex. These may have some features overlapping those of low-grade osteosarcoma (Revell, 1986), though it very rarely metastasizes. Aneurysmal bone cyst, however, can have both gross and even histological similarities to those of osteoblastoma and some authors (e.g. Dahlin, 1967:75) have speculated about their identity. Ortner & Putschar (1985:369) question whether the diagnosis of osteoblastoma in archaeological skeletons is possible.

Ossifying fibroma

The term 'ossifying fibroma' is used variously in the literature. Some (Dahlin, 1967:70) employ it as a synonym for osteoblastoma, others regard it as a variant of fibrous dysplasia and still others as a tumor with aggressive local behavior (Bullough, 1992). It affects principally the long bones in the first two decades of life and the jaws in the third and fourth decades.

In the jaws it produces large (up to 5 cm) masses of osteolytic bone that expand and thin the cortex, especially in the mandible. The diaphysis and metaphysis of long bones (usually tibia) are common locations in growing children, and here the lesions may be extensive in the younger age group. The lesion may involve and distort the cortex but seldom penetrates it. The tibia may be sufficiently weakened to become bowed or suffer a pathological fracture (Bullough, 1992).

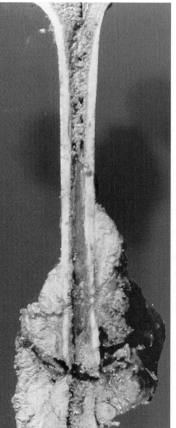

Fig. 13.2. **Osteogenic sarcoma, femur.** Cortical disruption, presence of medullary involvement and pathological fracture through the bone demonstrated in the sagitally sectioned bone establishes this as an osteogenic sarcoma (not a parosteal sarcoma) of conventional aggressive behavior. Modern young adult. PBL.

Osteogenic sarcoma (osteosarcoma)

Definition, epidemiology, and pathology

Osteosarcoma is a malignant tumor arising from the connective tissue elements in bone. It represents the most common malignant primary tumor of bone both in modern times as well as in antiquity. Nevertheless it remains a rare tumor with incidence rates estimated variously at 0.5–1.3 / 100 000 / year (Duthie & Bentley, 1987). Prevalence rates similar to these testify to its accelerated course. Its male:female ratio is about 2:1 (Vital Statistics of U.S.A., 1989). Current statistical data suggest a bimodal curve with one peak during the second and third decades and a second peak after age 40 years. The bulk of the later ones are osteosarcomas arising in areas exposed to irradiation (e.g. occupationally-ingested radioactive thorotrast) and in the lesions of Paget's disease, a condition commonly affecting the elderly of today's populations. Thus, in antiquity the bulk of osteosarcomas can be expected to be found in remains of adolescents and young adults under age 30 years. This age difference is also reflected by differences in location of this primary bone tumor. More than 80 % of the younger group are found in extremity long bones (primarily the knee region followed by the proximal femur and the humeral head), while about half of those in elderly people arise in the same areas that feature the lesions of Paget's disease: the flat bones and skull (especially the mandible).

To be classified as an osteogenic sarcoma a tumor must demonstrate a capacity for the production of osteoid. However, this need not be its dominant feature since many reveal extensive areas characterized by a chondroid or fibroid matrix. Its effect on pre-existing bone also varies from an osteolytic to an osteoblastic predominance as well as a generous fraction with mixed patterns.

The point of origin in most cases is in the region of long bone metaphyses (Fig. 13.2), only occasionally the diaphysis. In growing individuals the growth plate prevents epiphyseal extension as well as joint involvement until late in the disease's course. Hand and foot bones are almost never a primary site. Within the bone the lesion usually begins in the deeper, more central areas. Their expansion directs the growth both into the central area of the diaphysis as well as into the compact bone of the cortex. The resulting lytic action there gradually generates a 'cloudy' radiological appearance caused by irregularly alternating areas of osteopenia separated by regions of the normal density of uninvolved bone or increased density secondary to the tumor's osteoblastic character. Eventually its expanding front reaches the cortical surface where evidence of its cortical penetration serves as a valuable clue to its malignant nature (Fig. 13.3). Here the tumor often lifts the periosteum before penetrating it, producing a characteristic feature known as Codman's triangle at the tumor's edge on the cortical surface: an elongated, subperiosteal triangular area of radiolucency whose long axis is parallel to the cortical surface situated beneath the elevated periosteum and whose apex represents the tumor's periphery where the periosteum is still attached to the cortical surface. Though the frequency of Codman's triangle probably has been exaggerated in the past, its presence does remain a useful diagnostic feature.

The periosteum may respond to the tumor in a variety of patterns. Successive lamellae of new bone formation only occasionally produces an 'onion-skin' radiological effect that is most commonly seen in Ewing's tumor (see below). Irregular foci of new bone may occur. Many osteosarcomas assume a chondroblastic structure as they emerge from the bone and invade the surrounding soft tissues. In some of these the periosteum responds by the production of a radially-distributed series of bone spicules 1 or 2 mm wide and several centimeters long arranged in a plane perpendicular to the bone surface (Fig. 13.4). The soft tissue tumor between such spicules may enhance their size further by deposition of later mineralized osteoid on their surface. This results in a dramatic radiological appearance often termed a 'sunburst effect' (Fig. 13.5). More than half of osteosarcomas retain their ability to produce sclerotic areas of calcification inside and outside the bone, but the ratio of sclerotic to radiolucent areas varies greatly and mixed patterns are common (Resnick *et al.*, 1989c).

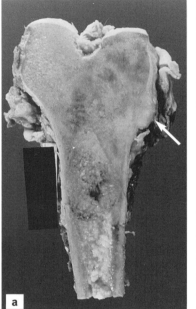

FIG. 13.3. **Osteogenic sarcoma, distal femur.** (a) Osteoblastic tumor has extended downward into diaphysis and upward into epiphysis producing dense sclerosis. (b) Area in upper right photograph of (a) shown by arrow, is shown here in greater detail, demonstrating the site where the tumor penetrated the cortex. Modern young adult. PBL.

FIG. 13.4. **Osteogenic sarcoma, distal humerus.** Periosteal response of spicules arranged perpendicular to bone surface ('sunburst' pattern) was ignited by lytic malignancy arising within bone and penetrating cortex. The space between spicules was occupied by tumor. CHA-47, spontaneously mummified body of a 30–35 year old female from a south Peruvian Chiribaya culture, ca. A.D. 1150. PBL.

FIG. 13.5. **Osteogenic sarcoma of the mandible.** Striking appearance of bone spiculation at right angles to plane of the bone cortex as discussed in the legend to Fig. 13.4 is again demonstrated by this tumor, here arising in mandible. 384642. Modern, 21 year old female. Courtesy P. Sledzik. NMHM.

Osteosarcoma metastasizes readily and almost invariably *via* the hematogenous route. Thus, 90 % of metastases are to the lungs. In the remainder, the afflicted person may live long enough to have some of the malignant cells traverse lung capillaries, reach the systemic circulation and metastasize to the various systemic organs including other bones.

Variants of osteogenic sarcoma.

- Periosteal osteosarcoma is limited to the cortical surface without demonstrable central involvement. A pronounced periosteal reaction in patterns described above is common with these. They usually begin in the mid-diaphyseal region of the femur or tibia, on any surface other than the posterior (Resnick *et al.*, 1989c). This is a rare form accounting for only about 1 % of osteosarcomas.
- Parosteal osteosarcoma (also called juxtacortical osteosarcoma) is two to four times more common than the periosteal variant, and occurs in slightly older adults. It begins quite regularly in the metaphysis and tends to envelop the bone, penetrating the cortex only very late in its course, remaining attached to the bone primarily only at its site of origin (sometimes simulating myositis ossificans).
- Telangiectatic osteosarcoma is distinguished by its extensive lytic features and little periosteal reaction, and whose destructive effects can be employed to differentiate it from aneurysmal bone cyst.
- Paget's sarcoma is an osteosarcoma arising within the lesion of Paget's disease in about 1 % of persons with Paget's disease. Most such individuals are in their sixth or seventh decades. Persons with multiple lesions may develop such tumors at multiple sites. These sarcomas are notoriously aggressive, invade soft tissues early and metastasize readily. Pelvis, femur, skull, tibia and humerus are the common primary sites.

Differential diagnosis of osteogenic sarcoma.

- Callus: an exuberant callus can usually be separated by its absence of aggressive invasion.
- Aneurysmal bone cyst and giant cell tumor are both benign lesions lacking the structural features of osteosarcoma.
- Chondrosarcoma affects older persons and its location is usually different (three-fourths are in the trunk and proximal femur and humerus; 10 % are secondary: Dahlin, 1967:139).
- Ewing's tumor is usually diaphyseal with a commonly layered or onion-skin periosteal reaction.
- Metastatic carcinoma is commonly multiple and in older individuals.
- Osteomyelitis can be separated from osteosarcoma when a sequestrum is present.

Paleopathology of osteogenic sarcoma

Many reports of osteosarcoma in archaeological bones are frustratingly difficult to evaluate because information crucial to the diagnosis is often not available. Esper (1774: plate XIV, figure 2) demonstrates a cave bear's long bone that more closely resembles a post-fracture callus than osteosarcoma. Even the familiar ancient Peruvian skull lesion thought by MacCurdy (1923) to be an osteosarcoma is now believed to be more probably an angioma or meningioma (Brothwell 1967a:337). What may be the oldest osteosarcoma has been reported in the jaw of a heavily fossilized bone from the Lower or Middle Pleistocene period in East Africa (Lawrence, 1935), though this example also remains controversial. Several Egyptian examples suggested by Smith & Wood Jones (1910) and Ruffer & Willmore (1914) do not offer morphological features or details, but a huge tumor about 25 cm in diameter involving the lower femur of an early Saxon in England can hardly represent any other diagnosis (Brothwell, 1967b:331), as is true also of a proximal humerus tumor in a Swiss Iron Age skeleton (Hug, 1956). Campillo (1984) also described a convincing example in a fifth century A.D. femur diaphysis of a Visigoth in Spain.

Strouhal (1994) made a major effort to identify all paleopathology reports of malignant tumors found in ancient remains in the Old World. He identified only 10 osteosarcomas in which he felt the diagnosis did not meet with serious objections; several of these were included in the preceding paragraph. Three were found in Egypt, two in Nubia and five in Europe (England, Switzerland, Italy and France). The oldest was of Neolithic age in Italy, one from Egypt's New Kingdom (1550–1070 B.C.), four from about 700–300 B.C. and one from upper Nubia's Islamic period (after the fourteenth century A.D.).

TUMORS OF CARTILAGE ORIGIN OR DIFFERENTIATION

Chondroma

Ten to twenty-five percent of benign bone tumors are isolated cartilaginous masses (chondromas) called enchondromas when located within the bone and periosteal or juxtacortical chondromas when they arise on the bone surface. They occur in either gender at any age, peaking at 25 years.

Pathology and radiology

About one-half of enchondromas are found in the medulla of short, tubular bones of the hand (though there they may extend also into the diaphysis), less often in the feet. About

25 % are in the metaphyses of the long bones of the extremities (humerus, femur, ulna, fibula and tibia in decreasing order (Jaffe, 1958:169) and the remainder scattered through ribs and other bones. They do not occur in bones formed by intramembranous ossification (Ortner & Putschar, 1985:370). Joint spaces are not involved. The periosteal chondromas are on the metaphyses of the long bones, principally the femur and humerus. Their size varies from 1–7 cm and they are solitary, well-demarcated, round or oval masses. Some may cause cortical thinning and mild expansion (Helms, 1989) but do not destroy the cortex, and the bone's external contours are usually intact. Radiology also demonstrates multiple foci of calcification within many of these lesions, as well as a sclerotic halo around the tumor's periphery (Helms, 1989).

Complications

The larger lesions may weaken the bone sufficiently to result in a pathological fracture. Malignant degeneration virtually never occurs in an isolated enchondroma but in the form of multiple enchondromatosis (Ollier's disease) the development of chondrosarcoma in one of the lesions occurs in 10–15 % of cases (see Chapter 12 (Skeletal dysplasias)).

Differential diagnosis

Bone infarction may simulate an enchondroma but can usually be recognized by its well-delineated periphery with scalloped or serpiginous borders, and is often densely sclerotic. Bone cysts and giant cell tumors may sometimes simulate enchondroma (see their description below). A low-grade chondrosarcoma could be confused with an enchondroma before it exerted its destructive effects.

Paleopathology

We are aware of only one enchondroma reported to have been found in ancient remains. It was present in a metacarpal bone from a Neolithic skeleton from the Zlöta cemetery in Poland (Capasso, 1985). We suspect that routine radiography of all bones in ancient skeletons would demonstrate the presence of many more.

Chondroblastoma (epiphyseal chondroblastoma, giant cell chondromatous tumor of Codman)

Epidemiology, pathology, and radiology

In spite of its ominous-sounding name, this is a benign tumor, and rare enough to represent only about 1 % of all benign tumors. It is found in adolescent males about twice as frequently as in females. These tumors are located only at sites of endochondral ossifications, and their diagnostically

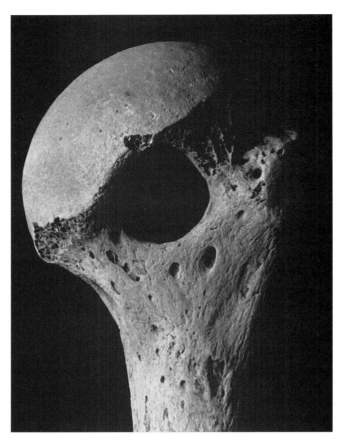

FIG. 13.6. **Chondroblastoma? Cyst? Giant cell tumor?** Note large, smooth-lined defect is in epiphysis. G19. Adult male Guanche ca. A.D. 1000. MAT, OAMC.

most useful feature is their location within epiphyses or apophyses (Fig. 13.6). Predictably, therefore, they occur most often in these sites of the upper and lower femur and tibia as well as the upper humerus. They are found only rarely in the hands, feet, flat bones or spine and virtually never in the skull. Thirty to fifty % of aneurysmal bone cysts have an accompanying chondroblastoma or osteoblastoma (Murray et al, 1990).

The lesions are small, only 1–5 cm, and are distinctly localized, destructive with lytic foci. Radiologically-demonstrable foci of calcification are present in about half of them as well as a band of 'soft' sclerosis. The cortex is commonly preserved but may be involved by expansion of the lesion, which also often induces a reactive periostitis.

Differential diagnosis

Its epiphyseal location is the most obvious diagnostic criterion, though that may be obscured in some cases by its expansion into the metaphysis or knee joint. Helms (1989) notes that 98 % of epiphyseal lesions are either osteomyelitis (the most common), chondroblastoma or giant cell tumor (it was not until 50 years ago that H.L. Jaffe and L. Lichtenstein differentiated the latter two conditions). Osteosarcoma and tuberculosis only rarely resemble these changes.

Paleopathology

Brothwell (1967a:324) pictures a large lesion in the humeral head of an early Nubian humerus, covered by a thin layer of bone that he feels is most likely a chondroblastoma or giant cell tumor. We are not aware of other ancient reported examples.

Chondromyxoid fibroma

Definition, epidemiology, and pathology

As its name implies, this is a benign tumor composed of cartilage cells in a matrix of myxomatous fibrous tissue. It is a rare tumor afflicting any age group, but more than half are found before age 30 years. The principal locations include the metaphyses of the knee and upper femur, though in about one-third other bones are affected including long bones, spine, scapulas, ribs, hands and feet. In the fibula and foot bones its position is central.

The lesion is localized, lytic, oval, less than 8 cm in greatest diameter, the larger of which can erode the cortex creating a characteristic surface defect (Resnick et al., 1989b). Periosteal new bone formation is minimal. Radiology may reveal a peripheral, narrow, sclerotic margin. The lesion has not been reported in ancient skeletons.

Osteochondroma (exostosis, osteocartilaginous exostosis)

Definition, epidemiology, and pathology

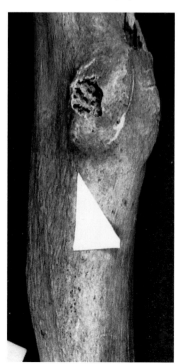

This lesion accounts for nearly half of all benign bone tumors. Most of them develop before age 30 years. Some regard the solitary osteochondroma as a *forme frusté* of hereditary multiple exostosis (see below and Chapter 12 (Skeletal dysplasias)) (Lichtenstein, 1977:17). About half of the tumors are found on metaphyseal surfaces of the lower femur and upper tibia, and the remainder at similar locations on other long bones, but not on diaphyses or epiphyses, and spine involvement is

Fig. 13.7. **Osteochondroma.** Femur diaphysis. Lobulated, expanded region of diaphyseal cortex contains many irregular defects scattered through it that reflect foci occupied by cartilage premortem. LXXXIX. North American aboriginal, precontact, upper midwestern U.S.A. Courtesy Dr John Gregg and USDAL. Photograph by Glenn Malchow.

uncommon. These represent little more than projections from the bone surface with a core of trabecular bone continuous with that of the metaphysis and covered by a layer of cortex that is also in continuity with the cortex of the adjacent, uninvolved bone area (Fig. 13.7; see also Fig. 1.7 in Chapter 1). In living persons a cartilaginous cap that may partially calcify crowns the osseous projection. The size range is broad, extending to more than 15 cm in some. Their shape can be sessile or pedunculated. Some have a lobulated surface (Spjut et al., 1971). Trauma applied to the tumor may result in its fracture. Radiographic demonstration of cortical and trabecular bone continuity with that of the bone from which it arises is key to the diagnosis. A very small fraction (1–3 %) of these tumors undergo malignant degeneration; they are usually those of larger size (Murray et al., 1990).

Differential diagnosis of osteochondroma

Myositis ossificans could be confused with osteochondroma but the former does not demonstrate the continuity of trabecular and cortical bone with that of the surrounding bone. In addition, the isolated osteochondroma must not be confused with the autosomal dominant, hereditary condition called hereditary multiple exostosis syndrome (diaphyseal aclasis), since the latter involves multiple bones in which an occasional one may undergo malignant degeneration.

Paleopathology of osteochondroma

Brothwell (1967a:323) confirms that a fifth dynasty Egyptian femur originally diagnosed as osteosarcoma is much more likely to be an example of isolated osteochondroma. Ortner & Putschar (1985:380) describe an example from a twelfth dynasty rock tomb at Lisht that arose from the junction of the fused pubic and iliac bones. Birkett (1986) found six osteochondromas in 1500 ancient skeletons from various British sites, all of which were located at the knee and four out of the five were in males. The diagnosis of osteochondroma in a 5 x 6 cm lesion of the distal femur of an adult female from the early Roman Iron age in Juellinge, Denmark seems sound (Bennike, 1985), and Ortner & Roberts (1985) also report an osteochondroma in the lateral aspect of the upper humerus in an approximately 30 year old male from the Romano-British period, while Chamberlain et al. (1992) describe an osteochondroma in a British Neolithic skeleton.

Chondrosarcoma

Definition, epidemiology, and pathology

This is the second most common malignant primary bone tumor after osteosarcoma. It may arise as an independent, primary bone malignancy, or be a product of malignant degeneration of a previously benign cartilaginous structure such as an enchondroma or osteochondroma. Current opinion is drifting toward the latter as the most common form of origin. Two-thirds of the cases occur in men, the age curve peaking at 45 years. Children under 10 years do not develop this tumor (López-Durán, 1995). Over half of the lesions develop in the pelvis and femur; the remainder occur in the tibia, ribs, sternum, scapula, spine and humerus medulla. Predictably its origin within a long bone most commonly is the metaphysis, with later expansion in both directions (Fig. 13.8). Subsequent growth produces a lytic effect that penetrates the cortex (often with a substantial periosteal response), and causes endosteal cortical scalloping in the medulla. Intralesional calcification is the rule. In hereditary multiple exostosis syndrome an occasional chondrosarcoma will develop from the surface lesion; such peripheral chondrosarcomas have a better prognosis than those arising centrally.

Differential diagnosis of chondrosarcoma

Intratumor calcification enables separation of central chondrosarcomas from many other lytic bone lesions (Spjut et al., 1971; Helms, 1989). Osteosarcoma occurs in a much younger age group and metastasizes much earlier to the lungs, thus running a much shorter course. Enchodromas and chondromyxoid fibromas do not have the aggressive and soft tissue invasive features of chondrosarcoma.

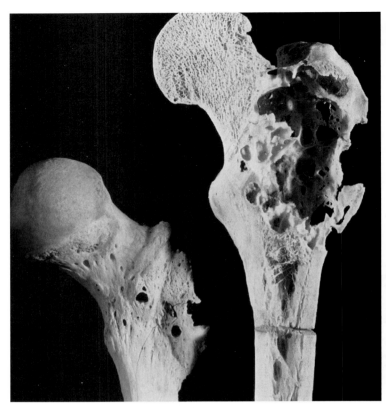

FIG. 13.8. **Chondrosarcoma, low grade.** Lobulated, metaphyseal lesion involves diaphysis and extends into soft tissues through eroded cortex. S94-9495. Modern adult. Courtesy Dr Bruce Ragsdale, Birmingham, AL.

TUMORS OF FIBROUS CONNECTIVE TISSUE ORIGIN OR DIFFERENTIATION

Connective tissue is a component of all principal parts of bone structure: the medulla, cortex and periosteum. It is, therefore, not surprising that connective tissue-derived tumors can be found at all such sites. In addition endothelial and other mature, differentiated cells can be derived from connective tissue elements. Understandably, then, some workers ('lumpers') simply lump all such lesions under a common, broadly interpreted term 'fibro-osseous bone defect' or similar inclusive denomination. Because the specific histology of the soft tissue component may range from simple fibrocytes to lipid, cartilage, vascular or other cellular types, some have proposed the term 'polymorphic' fibro-osseous lesions of bone (Ragsdale, 1993). Others ('splitters') feel that diagnostic terms should reflect the differences in clinical presentation, symptoms, gross structure, radiological appearance, behavior and histological composition that these lesions present in their different locations, genders and age groups. Having provided the reader with the above perspective, we have chosen an intermediate course in our following presentation, leaning in the direction of the 'splitters' in an effort to ease the reader's comprehension of the literature's confusing taxonomy for this group of lesions.

Desmoplastic fibroma (desmoid; aggressive fibromatosis)

Epidemiology, pathology, and radiology

It is a slow-growing, benign tumor arising primarily in the metaphyseal areas of long bones, mandible and pelvis. It appears under age 30 years without gender predilection. This lesion presents radiologically as a central, lucent, lytic lesion generating a 'soap-bubble' pattern that may expand the cortex, inducing reactive periostitis, but only occasionally penetrating into neighboring soft tissue and virtually never metastasizing. Its slow growth is commonly reflected by a surrounding sclerotic halo. The larger lesions make the bone vulnerable to pathological fracture which is the circumstance that brings modern cases to clinical attention.

A variation of this lesion arises in the periosteum (periosteal or juxtacortical desmoid). This variant affects mostly males under age 20 years. Most of these are small and compress the underlying cortex with resulting bone destruction, initiating reactive periostitis at its periphery and inducing a sclerotic margin at the depth of the eroded bone. Radiographs of Amenhotep III suggest the presence of such a lesion in the distal femur and several similar changes were found in collections at San Diego's Museum of Man (Braunstein et al., 1991).

Nonossifying fibroma (fibrous cortical defect; benign fibrous histiocytoma; metaphyseal fibrous defect; nonosteogenic fibroma of bone; polymorphic fibro-osseous lesion of bone)

Epidemiology, pathology, and radiology

Of the intraosseous fibrous bone lesions grouped under the above appellations, this is undoubtedly the most common. Indeed, radiological monitoring suggests that such lesions are demonstrable in up to one-third of otherwise normal children, especially in infants. Two-thirds are in males. In about half of the apparent solitary lesions, radiologic survey of the remainder of the skeletons will reveal additional involvement of other bones. They are characteristically localized, eccentric lesions usually in or near the metaphysis with scalloped margins and little reactive change in the periphery in the younger, but a sclerotic margin in the older. The radiological features frequently are of diagnostic quality (Spjut et al., 1971). The knee area is the most commonly involved region, though the polymorphic lesions (whose histology ranges from fibrous to fatty to vascular elements) are almost always in the proximal femur. The upper extremities are less frequently involved. The smaller lesions frequently fill in with bone and disappear by age 30 years, but the larger may persist, migrate into the diaphysis with bone growth, and produce pathological fractures in adulthood. The size range is enormous, extending from 1 cm to the full length of the diaphysis in adults (Murray et al., 1990). A small fraction of those with the liposclerotic myxofibromatous polymorphic histology patterns (see Fig. 13.17) undergo malignant change (Ragsdale, 1993) but this is rare in the others.

Fibrosarcoma

Definition, epidemiology, radiology, and pathology

Representing the minor fraction (< 10 %) of malignant bone tumors, fibrosarcoma is a malignant transformation of bone fibroblasts. It is a tumor affecting both genders equally and occurs predominantly in adults 30 to 60 years of age. It selects primarily the metaphyseal areas of long bones. More than half of these tumors affect the metaphyses in the knee region followed by those of the humerus. About one-fourth are associated with a pre-existing lesion (fibrous dysplasia, Paget's Disease or bone infarction).

The tumor begins as an eccentric, radiologically lytic lesion deep within the bone with irregular, geographic borders revealing cortical destruction and later expansion into both the epiphyseal and diaphyseal directions. Initially the periosteum tends to limit the tumor expansion (Revell, 1986) in that direction (often producing a Codman's triangle effect), and does not react to the tumor with new bone formation, but eventually the periosteum may yield, permitting the tumor to penetrate it and extend into the surrounding soft tissues (Lichtenstein, 1977). The tumor's histological structure is that of pleomorphic, spindle-shaped fibrocytes with moderate or poor differentiation. Fibrosarcomas metastasize hematogenously to the lungs but not as early as do osteosarcomas, resulting in a better prognosis (Duthie & Bentley, 1987).

Differential diagnosis of fibrosarcoma

Osteosarcoma is the tumor that shares the features of fibrosarcoma most intimately, as does malignant fibrous histiocytoma. Indeed, both these diagnoses are often considered simply as osteosarcoma variants by many orthopedic pathologists, and can be differentiated securely only by histological examination of the soft tissue tumor elements.

Fibrous histiocytoma and malignant fibrous histiocytoma (MFH)

The benign lesions are separable from nonossifying fibroma only by soft tissue histological study. This term for the malignant form was introduced by Spanier et al. in 1975, and most modern pathologists are now using it as a preferable synonym for fibrosarcoma (Revell, 1986). Eighty percent of fibrous histiocytomas are malignant (Murray et al., 1990). Features that are more common in MFH include the fact that three-fourths of these appear to arise in soft tissues, it affects more males than females and histologically has a cell structure suggesting a relationship to histiocytic cells. In archaeological bones the tumor is indistinguishable from fibrosarcoma and can, indeed, be treated as such, including its behavior.

Lipoma, liposarcoma, and leiomyosarcoma

The benign (lipoma) form of this tumor occurs as a sharply demarcated, lytic lesion with a sclerotic border found in the medulla most commonly, but less frequently in an intracortical or subperiosteal position. It is derived from the adipose cells of the bone marrow, and histologically can be composed entirely of fat (least common) or a mixture of fat and fibrous tissue with scattered foci of calcification - a description not inconsistent with that of some of the above-discussed fibro-osseous bone lesions. It also shares their gross features, bone involvement pattern and radiological structure as well as behavior.

Malignant variants exist and the few that have been described have arisen largely in long bones. Their diagnosis is possible only by histological identification of the lipid cell nature, and its course and appearance do not differ significantly from those of fibrosarcoma or malignant fibrous histiocytoma. For these reasons it has not been identified in ancient human remains.

Malignant tumors of muscle arising in bone are so rare as to be considered medical curiosities. Those of smooth muscle (leiomyosarcoma) have been reported several times but those of striated muscle (rhabdomyosarcoma) rarely (Lichtenstein, 1977). The gross appearance, radiological features and behavior are indistinguishable from other connective tissue-derived tumors. All of these can involve enough bone to result in pathological fractures.

TUMORS OF VASCULAR DIFFERENTIATION

Hemangioma of bone (capillary hemangioma; cavernous hemangioma)

Epidemiology, pathology, and radiology

This virtually always benign, solitary, small (< 2 cm) tumor of proliferating blood vessels and vascular sinusoids is found predominantly in older females. Most of them involve soft tissues (skin, liver, spleen) but in the skeleton they are found in the lower spine, skull (mandible, frontal and parietal bones) and ribs, and about one-fourth are present in long bones. The trabeculae are lysed and replaced by the tumor, only a few coarse ones spanning the full diameter of the lesion, generating a 'honeycomb' gross and radiological appearance. In ribs and skull it can cause thinning and expansion of the cortex. In the skull it may induce a 'sunburst' type of periosteal reaction by the formation of long, narrow bony spicules arrayed perpendicular to the outer table, though in almost all other areas no obvious periosteal reaction is apparent. In the vertebrae it may replace enough cancellous bone to collapse the body though it does not cross the intervertebral disc space (Steinbock, 1976:351). Thus the differential diagnosis in the spine includes Pott's disease, metastatic carcinoma or even perhaps Paget's disease, while the spicular periosteal reaction in the skull can simulate osteosarcoma or Ewing's tumor.

Multiple skeletal angiomas are present in a unique syndrome (skeletal hemangiomatosis) characterized by both hemangiomas and lymphangiomas that are scattered throughout many soft tissues including spleen, pleura and skin and in which the skeleton also participates. The syndrome is known under a variety of descriptive synonyms: cystic angiomatosis of bone; skeletal hemangiomatosis; lymphangiectasis of bone and cystic lymphangiectasis. It is found in more males than females under 30 years of age, affecting the flat bones more prominently than long bones. Individually each lesion does not differ from the solitary form described above.

Paleopathology of bone hemangioma

Moodie (1923a:frontispiece) has suggested that a lesion of a dinosaur tail's vertebra (found in the Como beds in Wyoming that are from the Mesozoic era 70–195 million years B.C.) represents a hemangioma, though this diagnosis is not considered as secure by many. A Peruvian skull in Harvard's Peabody Museum demonstrates a spiculated form of hyperostosis of the left frontal bone and is considered a probable hemangioma by Zimmerman & Kelley (1982:120). An approximately 40 year old female found in the necropolis of Fonte d'Amore near Sulmona, central Italy revealed a 6 cm defect in the left parietal bone without periosteal response that was felt to be a good candidate for the diagnosis of hemangioma (Capasso et al., 1991). Reverte (1986) also described a hemangioma in the vertebra of an ancient Spanish skeleton. A 20 mm lesion of the skull from the Middle Neolithic period in France resembles that of an angioma (Billard, 1994).

Glomus tumor, hemangiopericytoma, and hemangioendothelioma

A glomus tumor is a malformation of a normal arteriovenous shunting structure in the terminal phalangal soft tissues, more commonly fingers, consisting of vascular sinusoids around which specialized cells cluster. The entire normal system, designed to shunt blood directly from arterioles to venules and bypassing skin capillaries is known as a glomus body. Tumors derived from this structure are benign and represent a hamartoma (benign tumor composed of tissues normally present in that area but arranged in a pattern of architectural disarray). Their entangled nerve elements make them exquisitely sensitive. They can also appear within the bone of the terminal digit as a discrete, radiologically lytic area with sclerotic borders − a nonspecific pattern defeating specific identification in archaeological bone (Murray et al., 1990).

Hemangiopericytoma has a similar histology but is not limited to the glomus tumor's unique location. It may occur anywhere. While most are found at soft tissue sites, they can be present in many skeletal sites as well. Many of these behave as a low-grade malignancy and in most large series about 10 % metastasize to lungs, lymph nodes, liver and bone. Their gross and radiological appearances are nonspecific.

Hemangioendothelioma is an angioma composed of vessels of predominantly capillary size. Except for its more pale gross appearance, it resembles hemangioma in its distribution, radiological appearance and behavior, except that a very occasional one of these is capable of metastasis.

Angiosarcoma

This is a malignant variety of vascular tumor, most of which arise in soft tissues at many different sites. A small number of these arise in bone, where they are characterized by rapid growth, extensive bone destruction, erosion and perforation of the cortex and sometimes new bone formation (Bullough, 1992). A mild sclerotic reaction may surround the tumor. Direct extension into soft tissue is not common but distant metastasis is the usual final event.

Tumors of neural tissue

Neurilemmoma (Schwannoma), neurofibroma, and neurofibrosarcoma

Epidemiology, pathology, and radiology

While these tumors are derived from the Schwann cells of the nerve sheath (neurilemma), their histology, location and behavior differ. Neurilemmomas are solitary, nodular hamartomas most of which are located on retroperitoneal spinal nerves. Neurofibromas may be located on any peripheral nerve; many of them are subcutaneous. They appear as fusiform swellings of the nerve. Most of them are solitary and these are usually benign. When present as multiple lesions they are part of a neurofibromatosis syndrome. Late in the disease the affected individual may present with literally hundreds of such nodules, the subcutaneously-located ones often producing a lumpy, leonine facial appearance.

The solitary lesions of both have been found in long bones, jaws and sacrum as localized, ovoid lytic lesions with cortical erosion and overlying periostitis. The solitary neurofibroma arises in similar areas but also often intradurally in the spinal canal. Thus its radiological features there include thinning or erosion of both pedicles at a single vertebral site, erosion of the posterior aspect of vertebral bodies and enlargement of the exit foramen. These two lesions are found in adults of 30 to 50 years of age.

Neurofibrosarcoma (malignant schwannoma) usually represents malignant degeneration of one of the many lesions found in the neurofibromatosis syndrome. When this occurs in an intra-osseous lesion the bone demonstrates an irregular, destructive process with cortical erosion and prominent reactive periostitis, sometimes with pathological fractures. The affected age range is 20–40 years.

Paleopathology of neural tumors

Smooth, rounded cavities within the trabecular bone of several lumbar vertebral bodies of an adult Saxon (U.K.) led Brothwell (1967a:329) to a tentative diagnosis of neurofibromatosis. An early nineteenth century British male skeleton had skull, pelvis and spine changes characteristic of neurofibromatosis (Knüsel & Bowman, 1996). We were unable to identify other reports of either neurofibromas or neurofibrosarcomas.

Notochord tumors

Chordoma

Arising from residual notochordal tissue, a chordoma is almost always related to the spine. Specifically about half occur at the lower end in the region of the coccyx and sacrum while the remainder are at the upper end (most in the skull base and the bulk of the remainder related to cervical vertebrae). It is a solitary, lytic and expansile tumor that is not only locally destructive but frequently (about a fourth) metastasizes. In addition to demonstrating these features, radiology often identifies focal calcification within the tumor.

Miscellaneous tumors of unknown origin

Giant cell reparative granuloma (solid aneurysmal bone cyst)

Etiology, pathology, and radiology

This lesion is basically a localized, osteoclastic response to a local injurious event – often an infection. It affects either gender, commonly adolescents and young adults. Most of these lesions are in the maxilla and mandible, followed by the hand and foot bones. These are also the very locations subject to penetrating trauma by foreign objects as a result of mastication, weight-bearing or forceful movements. In living individuals the overlying soft tissues may be involved solely or in connection with the skeletal lesion. The bone lesion itself is discrete, radiolucent and sometimes with bone expansion and a thinned cortex but the latter is rarely destroyed. The body response is adequate to contain the process and reactive new bone formation is not uncommon. These findings are similar to those of giant cell tumor, aneurysmal bone cyst and the 'brown tumors' of hyperparathyroidism, but each of these has different preferential locations.

Meningioma

Etiology, epidemiology, pathology, and radiology

Meningioma is a soft tissue tumor arising from mesothelial cells of the meninges (dura mater). It is a soft tissue tumor, not a primary bone tumor. A few arise from the meninges of the spinal canal but the bulk of them are found intracranially. The average age of affected persons is 45 years and the genders are equally represented. Campillo (1991b) found about half of them underlying the skull vault convexity, 9 % over the lesser sphenoid wing (Fig. 13.9) and 5 % were parasellar. The feature of interest to paleopathologists is not the tumor itself, but rather the often remarkable degree of hyperostosis of the overlying bone that appears to be the effect of the increased vascularity stimulated by the soft tissue tumor.

The tumor itself may affect the skull's inner table overlying the tumor by evidence of its erosion by pressure atrophy or by direct invasion (Thillaud, 1996). It is, however, the outer table's periosteal response that is frequently so dramatic. Though all degrees of proliferation can be observed, the hyperostosis on the outer table's convex surface can thicken the skull, sometimes as much as 5–6 cm or more, the surface of which may assume a spiculated appearance (Fig. 13.10). Hyperostosis is not invariable; in fact only about 20 % of cases demonstrate any recognizable thickening, and only a minor fraction of these are of extreme degree. Ortner & Putschar (1985:378) note that differentiation of meningioma response from that of osteosarcoma can be enabled not only by the difference in age of the patient but also by the presence of bone spiculation only on the outer table.

Paleopathology

Probably the oldest case of meningioma is that found in a Neolithic adult skull from the Catalonia region of Spain, demonstrating an inner osteolytic lesion with exocranial bulging and a prominently imprinted middle meningeal artery; the diploe showed evidence of increased vascularization (Campillo, 1991b). The same author also reported an Enolithic period example from Catalonia as well as two medieval cases. Two Egyptian skulls from the first and the twentieth dynasties demonstrate characteristic responses (Rogers, 1949). Bennike (1985) also reported an example from the Middle/Late Neolithic in Denmark. Brothwell (1967a:327) identified a meningioma-type response in a Roman skull from the U.K. (originally believed to have represented an osteosarcoma). Another such altered opinion is cited by Steinbock (1976:355) in an adult pre-Hispanic Peruvian whose outer table demonstrated prominent spiculation but in whom the inner table was eroded. He also cites another Peruvian example from the Chimu culture (Moodie, 1926) and an adult male from southern California (Abbott & Courville, 1939). The other New World example is from Alaska (Ortner & Putschar, 1985); it was prominently lytic.

Giant cell tumor (osteoclastoma; myelogenic giant cell tumor; myeloplaxoma)

Epidemiology, pathology, and radiology

Giant cell tumor is derived from connective tissue but the stroma is infiltrated by huge numbers of multinucleated giant cells (osteoclasts). It is found almost entirely in individuals whose epiphyses have fused and so are rare before puberty (and also in the very elderly). It is responsible for about 5–15 % of benign bone tumors, but constitutes a much larger fraction in China. It is found in an eccentric position within the epiphyses, expanding there greatly and destructively, increasing the bone diameter until the thinned, expanded

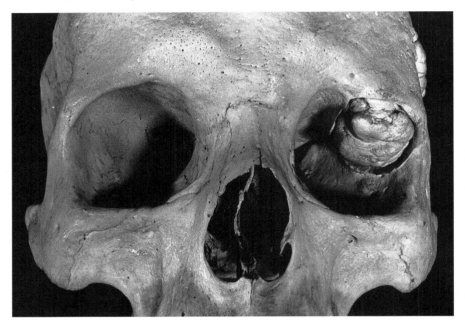

FIG. 13.9. **Meningioma.** Lobulated mass of dense bone in pteric region that penetrates orbit. Case 32. Colonial period. Iglesia Santa Cruz y Soledad de Nuesra Senora, Mexico. Courtesy Dr Maria-Elena Salas Cuestas and Dr D. Campillo. Instituto Nacional de Arqueologia y Historia, Mexico.

FIG. 13.10. **Meningioma with cranial hyperostosis.** The meningioma on the inner table has involved the cranial bone and stimulated a dramatic hyperostosis on the outer table equal to or greater than the thickness of the cranial vault bones. 1886740. Modern adult. Courtesy Dr Bruce Ragsdale, Birmingham, AL.

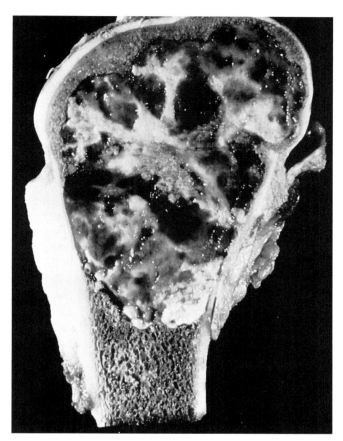

FIG. 13.11. **Giant cell tumor, humerus.** This tumor of osteoclasts has clearly arisen in the epiphysis, extended into the extreme upper end of the diaphysis, and fractured through the thinned cortex on the right side. The tumor's sharply-defined lower margin reflects its basically benign character. 73-2148. Modern case. Courtesy Dr Bruce Ragsdale, Birmingham, AL.

bone cortex merely forms an irregular shell in its periphery without peripheral sclerosis or periostitis (Fig. 13.11). Yet, in spite of such locally destructive and sometimes massive growth, it maintains some benign characteristics such as a nonsclerotic but sharply demarcated periphery and a reluctance to perforate the cortex (though the latter is so thin that its integrity is not easy to discern radiologically), but pathologic fractures are common. Any bone in the body may spawn a giant cell tumor, but about half of them arise in the epiphyses around the knee region, followed by the other extremity long bones (Fig. 13.12) followed in turn by the flat bones. Most of these tumors are benign; a small fraction are malignant and may metastasize. Untreated, as they must have been in antiquity, they reach a very large size and commonly suffer a pathological fracture (Steinbock, 1976:350).

Helms (1989) feels that the presence of the following radiological features will correctly identify 95 % of giant cell tumors: eccentric location within closed epiphyses abutting the articular space; central in the medulla; periphery is sharply demarcated but sclerotic.

Differential diagnosis of giant cell tumor

Chrondroblastoma is also an epiphyseal lesion but it affects a much younger age group than does giant cell tumor. Solitary bone cysts and aneurysmal bone cysts may resemble giant cell tumor but are smaller and not so destructive. The 'brown tumors' of hyperparathyroidism can usually be separated because these are multiple and bones show other effects of excessive parathyroid hormone action. Fibrosarcoma has peripheral sclerosis and induces periostitis.

Paleopathology of giant cell tumor

A Saxon age adult male skeleton reported by Brothwell (1967a:325) demonstrates a bulbous swelling of the distal femur just above the condyles covered by a thin shell of cortex that may be a giant cell tumor. It is surprising that more of these tumors have not been identified in archaeological bones.

Ewing's sarcoma

Epidemiology, pathology, and radiology

Less than 10 % of primary malignant bone tumors are Ewing's sarcoma. A tumor of strange histology, its growth pattern suggests an origin from marrow cells, while it shares a common chromosomal aberration (reciprocal translocation between chromosomes 11 and 22) with primitive neuroectodermal tumors (Schiller, 1994:1322). Most afflicted persons

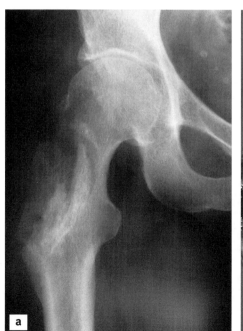
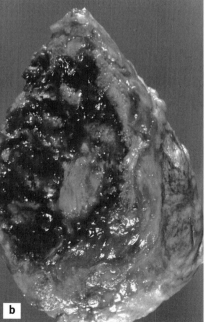

FIG. 13.12, **Giant cell tumor.** (a) X-ray reveals destruction of much of femur's epiphyseal area by the tumor. (b) The surgically enucleated mass is lobulated, without infiltrating edges and demonstrates foci of hemorrhage, both recent and old. Modern young adult. PBL.

are between ages 8 and 15 with only a minority over 20 years, and two-thirds are males.

The tumor presents in the medulla of the mid-diaphysis or in the metaphysis, completely lytic foci alternating with areas of infiltration of cancellous bone without destroying the trabeculae. This generates a striking radiologic picture of mottled involvement of the cortex and medulla including focal endosteal resorption areas (López-Durán, 1995). Although evidence of sclerosis is also identifiable, more eye-arresting is the periosteal response that classically consists of an onion-skin simulation resulting from multiple, circumferential layers of new bone formation. A spiculated surfaced periostitis pattern (simulating osteosarcoma) is known but exceptional. Advanced examples show cortical penetration with extension into soft tissues.

Long bones, especially humerus, tibia and femur are preferentially involved but many other skeletal sites have been reported and Helms (1989) notes that in persons older than about 25, flat bones are the most common primary locations. A small number progress to pathological fractures. This tumor metastasizes early by the hematogenous route to lungs and very consistently to other bones.

Differential diagnosis of Ewing's sarcoma

The occasional case showing a spiculated periosteal response may simulate osteosarcoma and it may be impossible to differentiate them, though Ewing's is usually a significantly more elongated tumor. Osteomyelitis may be a serious consideration, though in archaeological bones the presence of a sequestrum is often available to establish the infectious nature of such a lesion (Bullough, 1992). Lichtenstein (1977) suggests that metastatic neuroblastoma can simulate Ewing's sarcoma in children under 5 years, metastatic carcinoma in older adults and multiple myeloma in the aged.

Paleopathology of Ewing's sarcoma

A young male from the Late Neolithic in Catalona, Spain, demonstrating 16 different tumor foci in bones showing a honeycomb structure with irregular margins, was thought most probably to represent Ewing's sarcoma (Campillo & Marí-Barcells, 1984). A medieval Westphalia (German) site skeleton had a spindle-shaped expansion of the distal ulna that demonstrated a spongy, honeycomb internal structure suggestive of Ewing's sarcoma (Löwen, 1994).

Primary malignant lymphoma of bone (reticulum cell sarcoma)

Epidemiology, pathology, and radiology

Before the elaborate current taxonomy of malignant lymphomas was established based on lymphocyte phylogeny, these conditions were all lumped together under the term 'reticulum cell sarcoma'. Today it is clear that some of the lymphomas can originate in bone marrow (estimated to be about 40 %) and in others a primary soft tissue site can spread secondarily to the marrow. From this perspective it will be clear that lymphomas can produce a broad range of features in skeletal tissues and follow widely variable courses. The description provided here emphasizes the most common characteristics, but the reader must keep in mind that a substantial number of different entities are represented.

Predictably, the age range of affected individuals is wide, ranging from childhood (the minority) to the elderly. Similarly many different bones may be involved, though the cancellous portions of long bones of the legs are particularly common (especially the knee area) as well as vertebral bodies, pelvis and mandible. The infiltrate destroys both trabecular and cortical bone, and rarely incites any periosteal response. Osteosclerosis may occur as well as pathological fractures. Radiology demonstrates a spongy cortical involvement with endosteal focal areas of resorption. The nonspecificity of such changes is probably responsible for the absence of paleopathology reports of this tumor.

Metastatic skeletal lesions

Epidemiology and pathology

Most malignant skeletal lesions are metastases. López-Durán (1995) aptly noted that in persons over 40 years of age any malignant tumor identified in an organ could be a metastasis from a primary cancer in some distant organ. However, some primary cancers are more apt to metastasize to bone than others. The more common of these are prostatic carcinoma (70 % of which metastasize to the spine) and breast carcinoma (30–50 %). Lung, kidney and thyroid do so but less frequently. Since these primary sites occur principally in older persons, it follows that metastatic carcinoma of bone is largely a disease of the elderly.

The most commonly affected bones are vertebrae, pelvis, ribs, major long bones, sternum and skull. Since bone metastases are a target of hematogenous dissemination, it is not surprising that this list of metastatic bone sites reflects trabecular bone distribution. Metastases to bones distal to elbows and knees are uncommon (Thillaud, 1996). Within bone, metastases from lung, thyroid, kidney and gastrointestinal primary sites are all usually osteolytic (Figs. 13.13 & 13.14), those from the prostate (Fig. 13.15) are commonly osteoblastic and those from the breast are usually mixed. Osteoblastic metastatic lesions have been shown to produce fine spicules adherent to pre-existing bone (Bullough, 1992). Pathologic fractures and vertebral collapse are common effects of metastases. Neuroblastoma, a malignant adrenal tumor of children is unique in that it commonly metastasizes to bone (lytic lesions) prior to lung metastases.

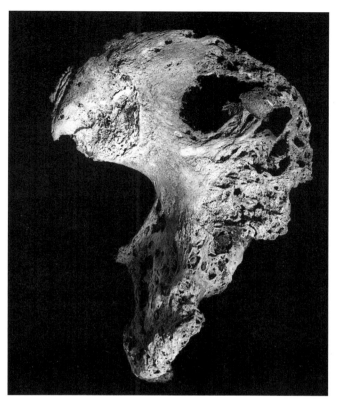

Fig. 13.13. **Metastatic carcinoma to the pelvis.** Much of the pelvic bone has been destroyed in an irregular and infiltrative manner by a largely lytic metastatic carcinoma. UK-105. Modern adult. NMHM.

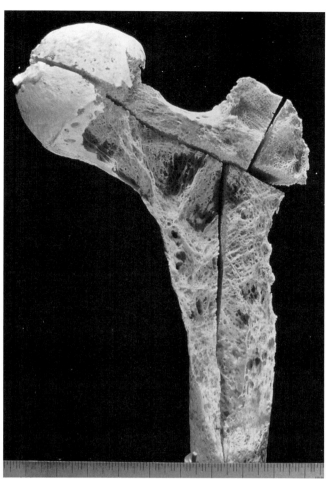

Fig. 13.14. **Metastatic carcinoma from the kidney to the femur.** Many various-sized, trabecular, lytic lesions have destroyed the cortex. S94-16581. Modern adult. Courtesy Dr Bruce Ragsdale, Birmingham, AL.

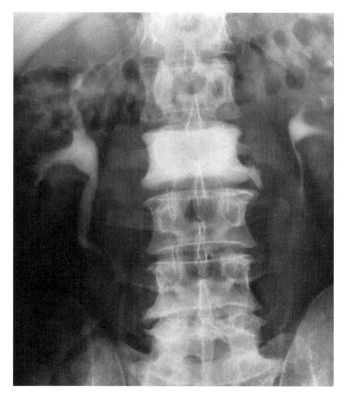

Fig. 13.15. **Osteoblastic metastatic carcinoma.** X-ray. Primary tumor in the prostate metastasized to the lumbar vertebra. This tumor often secretes an osteoblast-stimulating protein (as in this case) resulting in marked osteosclerosis. Modern elderly male. PBL.

Radiology and differential diagnosis

The range of bone changes induced by metastases is noted above. While most are rapidly progressive, a few may be deceptively indolent (Murray *et al.*, 1990). Furthermore, if a peripheral skeletal metastasis is evident, the spine should be examined because it will frequently house another. The age of the affected individual can be useful to separate a solitary metastasis from a primary malignant bone tumor. Given the wide range of possible appearances, it is nevertheless true that most metastases are discrete, often multiple, round, lytic, radiolucent lesions (Thillaud, 1996).

The primary site is not often predictable by the appearance of the metastatic lesion, though markedly osteoblastic metastases may incite suspicion of the prostate in a male and the breast in a female. An especially frustrating differential diagnosis can involve the separation of multiple myeloma from metastatic carcinoma since both can have multiple bone lesions in an older individual (Anton, 1988). Helpful features can be the discrete, totally lytic nature of the myeloma lesions, the larger size achieved by many metastases and the fact that any evidence of osteoblastic features excludes multiple myeloma. Radiological examination of dry bones in 128 cancer-diagnosed individuals of the Todd Collection demonstrated metastases in three times as many individuals as could be identified by simple gross visual examination (Rothschild & Rothschild, 1995a).

Paleopathology of metastatic carcinoma

Innumerable examples of metastatic carcinoma in ancient skeletons have been reported. They include those of Hooton, (1930), two females from Pecos Pueblo involving spine and forearms; Urteaga & Pack, (1966). melanoma? from Peru; Brothwell, (1967a), Saxon, U.K., scattered bone lesions; Steinbock, (1976), two skull lesions from Peru and two more from Alaska; Manchester (1983b) elderly female from England, skull and femur (breast?); Waldron (1987a), eighteenth century adult male, England, skull (from lung?); Ortner et al., (1991), medieval England, multiple bones (lung?); Strouhal (1991a), Nubian adult male, Christian period, jaws and facial bones (direct primary invasion?); Tkocz & Bierring (1984), medieval adult male, Denmark – spine, hip, scapulae – osteoblastic (prostate?); Anderson et al., (1992), fourteenth century U.K., osteoblastic pelvis, ribs skull (prostate?); Baraybar & Shimada (1993), pre-Inca Peru male, osteoblastic vertebra (prostate?); Allison et al., (1980), adult female, Peru-skull, pelvis, spine, mixed lytic and blastic (breast?).

Bone cysts (solitary bone cyst, juvenile bone cyst)

Unicameral bone cyst

Children are most commonly affected though the lesion may persist into adulthood. Two-thirds are found in males. The etiology is unknown, though G. Dupuytren and R. Virchow described it more than a century ago. The cyst is unichambered, located within the cancellous portion of a long bone metaphysis (in adults it may have migrated into the diaphysis), most commonly the proximal humerus and the femur. The lesion is radiologically lucent, sometimes fluid-filled, and has a sclerotic, sharply-defined periphery. Many resolve spontaneously (Murray et al., 1990) but some may respond to fluid pressure by expanding, thinning the cortex and even lead to pathologic fracture. Other lesions that may mimic such bone cysts include eosinophilic granuloma, Brodie's abscess, enchondroma and aneurysmal bone cyst (see below). Location and morphology may exclude some of these. A unicameral cyst was found in a medieval child (Lagier et al., 1987).

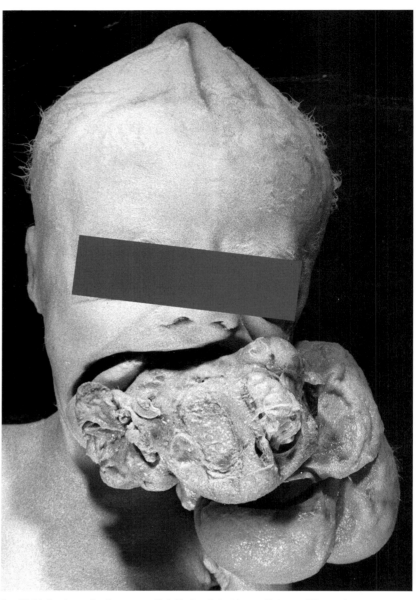

FIG. 13.16. **Teratoma, benign, congenital.** Modern infant born with tumor filling and protruding from oral cavity. It arose in Rathke's pouch. Biopsy demonstrated variety of benign tissues derived from all these germ layers. BM.

Aneurysmal bone cyst

Eighty percent of these lesions are found during the second and third decades of life. It constitutes only about 6 % of benign bone lesions. Perhaps as many as half of these have an underlying disorder (osteoblastoma, chondroblastoma, giant cell tumor) or trauma (Murray et al., 1990). Other reported associations include nonossifying fibroma, fibrous dysplasia and telangiectatic osteosarcoma. Jaffe (1950) and Lichtenstein (1950) independently described this condition, and each thought it was a vascular lesion.

Half of the lesions are found in long bone metaphyses, especially the femur and tibia, but also in the spine where they may involve several vertebrae. Hand and foot bones as

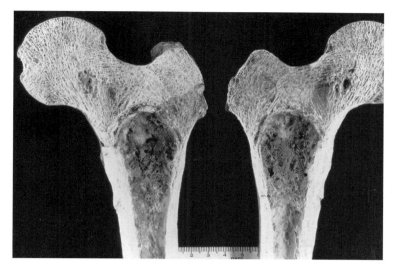

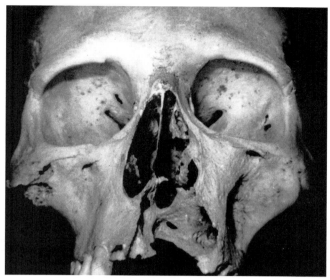

FIG. 13.17. **Liposclerosing myxofibrous tumor.** Metaphysis and upper diaphysis are occupied by lytic process that is not infiltrative but has sharply-defined upper border. Cortex is intact. Benign fibrous lesions of bone have a wide variety of principally descriptive names. A91-13. Modern adult autopsy specimen. Courtesy of Dr Bruce Ragsdale, Birmingham, AL.

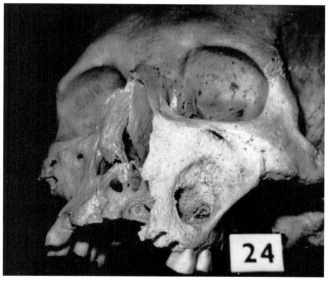

well as the pubic ramus are also common sites. In all these areas the lesion presents as a rapidly expanding, multiloculated lesion up to 25 cm in diameter, the individual, septum-separated spaces filled with blood. As expected, the radiological appearance is that of a 'soap-bubble' pattern. The cortex is thinned but only occasionally perforated. A thin layer of bone thus covers the specimen. It is noteworthy that the septa are fibrous and thus absent in archaeological dry bone. The cyst is usually limited by the growth plate, but can expand into both the epiphysis and diaphysis after growth ceases (López-Durán, 1995). Differential diagnosis includes unicameral bone cyst, osteoblastoma, osteogenic sarcoma and spinal hemangioma. Most significantly it should be separated from giant cell tumor (often by age).

We found one report of this lesion in antiquity. An adult Italian male skeleton (A.D. 1040–1270) had a large, discrete, sclerotic-edged, lytic defect of the iliac fossa with rounded margins, a hemispheric bottom of cortical bone and many thin spicules on the external iliac fossa that the authors felt probably was an aneurysmal bone cyst (Capasso et al., 1992a). Moodie's (1923a) diagnosis of this lesion in a dinosaur tail vertebra (illustrated in the frontispiece of his text) is controversial today.

Epidermoid bone cyst

Most of these occur in persons under 30 with a history of trauma. The bulk of these lesions are located in the distal hand phalanges and in the skull. The lesion is lined by squamous epithelium. They are sharply-demarcated and reflect this radiographically as a sclerotic zone at the periphery of a lytic, lucent area. The larger ones show cortical erosion and may

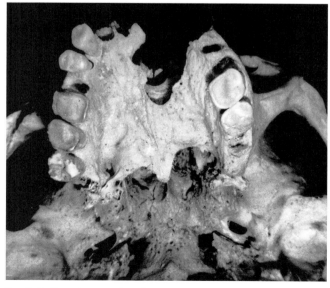

FIG. 13.18. **Nasopharyngeal carcinoma.** Nasal and palatal irregular bone destruction by a soft tissue malignant tumor. Case 20. Young adult, Talayotic culture, Balearic Islands, Spain. Courtesy Dr D. Campillo. MAC.

even cause pathologic fractures. Enchondroma, giant cell reparative granuloma and glomus tumor of bone can all have an identical appearance. An ancient example of this lesion was in the form of a crater-like lesion of 7 x 8 cm located just anterior to the skull vertex perforating the inner table also in a Late Dynastic Egyptian (Brothwell, 1967a:328).

PART FOURTEEN

Diseases of the dentition

by Odin Langsjoen

ORAL BIOLOGY

Introduction

The importance of the orofacial structures to the health, propagation and survival of the human race cannot be over-estimated. The basic needs of human life, food, water and oxygen all enter the body through this specialized area, in addition to being the location of the sense of smell and the ability to taste. Of major significance to health and survival is the masticatory component, a physical system for processing food into a digestible form from which nourishment may be extracted. The prominent features in this system are the temporomandibular joint and dental articulations.

Teeth are well preserved in archaeological remains, often surviving long after their supporting tissues have deteriorated. The physical condition of the dentition, as observed in archaeological material by paleopathologists can provide valuable information on individual health status as well as cultural influences and intercultural differences. Compared to other organs, the vulnerability of teeth to disease is enhanced because they act and react with the environment both physically and chemically. Although enamel cannot remodel itself as can bone, this fact does have a positive aspect for paleopathologists as the degree of wear observed at examination can provide a significant contribution to age estimation techniques.

Teeth possess features that have a high genetic component in their expression of form which has proved to be useful in establishing biological relationships between various human groups. Teeth provide evidence of cultural behavior patterns as well as the biocultural interrelationships between diet and dental decay. In enamel hypoplasia, a feature of growth arrest, teeth record evidence of stressful events such as malnutrition and childhood diseases.

Tooth surface anatomy may be altered irreversibly by wear (attrition) that often eliminates discrete traits. When severe, attrition can expose investing and supporting soft tissues to trauma and destructive microbial activity. Synergistic relationships between several pathologic events can complicate determination of initial cause, sequence of destructive processes and the assessment of responsibility. Despite the complex interactions between multiple destructive disease entities, gross examination is still the best, single method for determining the presence of dental pathology in archaeological remains and the dentition may often be used as a central feature in comparative population evaluation studies. Although much has been published on dental pathology, this aspect of paleopathology has not received the same attention as skeletal pathology (Ortner & Putschar, 1985:438).

Development of dentition

Vertebrate teeth always develop as a result of the interaction between two tissues. One of these is the epithelium lining the mouth; the other is the underlying mesenchyme. In mammals and reptiles these tissues give rise to enamel and dentin respectively. Dentin is one of the oldest of vertebrate tissues, recognized 400 million years ago in the Ordovician period in the form of skeletal plates of armor in the skin covering certain areas of anterior body parts of the members of the superclass Agnatha (armored fishes). Modern chondrichthyes also have tooth-like structures in the skin known as placoid scales, the precursor of dental enamel. These fishes have the capacity to form teeth, not only over the body surface but in the mouth as well. Teeth, then, are primarily structures that develop from the epithelium of the mouth lining and underlying mesenchyme; and only secondarily do they become attached to underlying bone. Mammals, perhaps because of their high metabolic requirements, have developed complex dentitions characterized by teeth confined to the anterior and lateral periphery of the oral cavity. Mammalian teeth have one or more roots that are covered with cementum and connected to alveolar bone by a specialized (periodontal) membrane. Mammals also develop two sets of teeth: a primary, or deciduous set that is shed during skeletal growth changes, and a secondary, permanent set. The two sets comprise a diphyodont dentition.

The human diphyodont dentition consists of a primary set of 20 teeth: 8 incisors, 4 canines and 8 molars, which provide rudimentary chewing functions during the early growing years from 6 months to 6 years of age. As dental arches extend in length, 4 first molars of the secondary dentition appear distal to the 4 primary second molars beginning at approximately 6–7 years of age. A concurrent expansion of the dental arches accommodates the emergence of the permanent incisors causing their primary predecessors to be shed. The appearance of permanent incisors and first molars heralds the beginning of a 6 year, mixed dentition period during which the remaining primary teeth are replaced. With the appearance of the second permanent molars distal to the first permanent molars at age 12 years, the primary–secondary exchange is normally completed. With maturity, approximately age 18, the third permanent molars can be expected to appear distal to the second molars and complete the adult dentition.

Mammalian dentitions are required to perform a variety of functions in order to reduce food particle size that include grasping, cutting, tearing and grinding. In response to these needs a variety of crown forms has evolved that are able to accomplish the specialized functional requirements. Such dentitions, composed of multiple forms for multiple functions, are called heterodont dentitions.

The human dentition is heterodont. Four distinct functions are needed to process food for digestion, requiring four classes of teeth: incisors to cut, canines to pierce and tear; premolars to grasp, hold, and reduce particle size; and molars to mill and grind. The human primary dentition has only three classes: incisors, canines and molars.

Descriptive terminology

Each tooth within a class has distinct 'type' traits that distinguish it from all other teeth in the class. These traits are unique to the arch and quadrant in which the tooth is located, its positional sequence within its class, and its set: primary or permanent. Identification by tooth type requires recognition of the special anatomic features of 52 teeth: 20 primary and 32 permanent. Five descriptors are necessary: set, arch, quadrant, sequence in class and class. Example: a permanent, maxillary, right first molar.

In order to promote concise and unambiguous communication among dental investigators, a common descriptive terminology must be applied uniformly from the initial data-gathering to final assessment of findings. To accomplish this the planes of reference and directional terminology of the Standard Anatomic Position (White & Folkens, 1991:28–31) must be applied consistently in which the subject's right is the observer's left and maxillae and mandibles are examined separately. However, because interarch relationships strongly influence the synergy of dental pathology, it is important to portray the maxilla and mandible, whether in open or closed relationships, in the standard anatomical position when describing and illustrating dental conditions.

Directional terminology and standard reference planes have assumed some modifications in nomenclature in order to be more dentally specific. The horizontal plane becomes the occlusal plane where the upper and lower teeth meet, separating upper and lower arches. The midsagittal plane divides the arches into right and left halves forming four quadrants. The anterior border of the midsagittal plane is the median line of the face. Tooth surfaces directed toward the median line of the face are termed mesial surfaces, those facing away are distal surfaces. Tooth surfaces facing the midsagittal plane are lingual or palatal surfaces, those facing away are labial, buccal or (collectively) facial surfaces. The functional tooth aspects facing the occlusal plane are occlusal or incisal surfaces.

Dental annotation

By connecting the anterior borders of the mid-sagittal and occlusal planes, quadrant brackets are formed that provide a condensed base for systems of tooth annotation. One such

		Median	Line	
Right				Left
Maxilla		55 54 53 52 51	61 62 63 64 65	
Occlusal	18 17 16 15 14 13 12 11		21 22 23 24 25 26 27 28	
Plane	48 47 46 45 44 43 42 41		31 32 33 34 35 36 37 38	
Mandible		85 84 83 82 81	71 72 73 74 75	

FIG. 14.1. **International coding system.** See the text for further details.

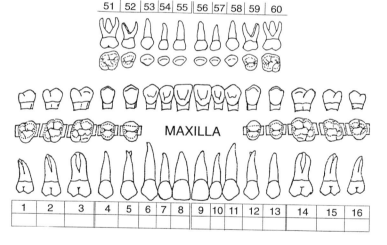

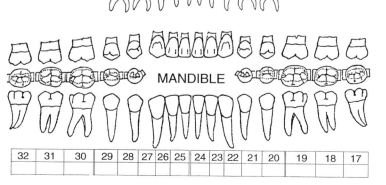

FIG. 14.2. **Dental field record.** Maxilla and mandible, with added data lines, are separate sheets in data-gathering note book. Courtesy Dr Odin Langsjoen. PBL.

system, the international system endorsed by the Federation Dentaire Internationale (FDI), is computer friendly because it is based on numbers alone. Each tooth, primary or permanent, is assigned a two-digit number (Fig. 14.1). The first digit designates the quadrant in which the tooth is anchored. Permanent tooth quadrants are numbered one through four, beginning with number one as the maxillary right quadrant proceeding clockwise around the arches to the mandibular right quadrant (number four). Following the same pattern primary tooth quadrants are numbered five through eight.

The second digit identifies individual teeth by type, based on their numerical relationship to the median line of the face. For example, all central incisors are numbered (1), all lateral incisors (2), and all canines (3). Since permanent dentitions have five posterior teeth per quadrant, and the primary dentitions only two, the permanent teeth conclude the arches with the third molars, second digit (8), and the primary arches end at their second molars, second digit (5). A tooth numbered 55 is the primary maxillary right second molar and a tooth numbered 33 is the permanent mandibular left canine.

A second coding system, that uses numbers only and is augmented with a visual format, is presented in Fig. 14.2. It is referred to here as the *Standards System* after its recommended source: '*Standards for Data Collection from Human Remains*' (Buikstra & Ubelaker, 1994:47–48). In this system the permanent dentition is assigned the numbers 1–32 beginning at the maxillary right third molar (1), moving clockwise to the maxillary left third molar (16), dropping to the mandibular left third molar (17) and concluding with the mandibular right third molar (32).

The primary dentition is assigned numbers 51–70 beginning at the maxillary right second molar, moving clockwise to the maxillary left second molar (60), dropping to the mandibular left second molar (61) and concluding at the mandibular right second molar (70).

Embryology of tooth development

In the sixth week of embryonic development the enamel-forming dental lamina invaginates into its supporting mesenchyme at sites of future primary teeth. These cap-shaped ingrowths sit atop a ball of ectomesenchymal cells called a papilla that forms the dentin and pulp. Ectomesenchyme also encapsulates the enamel-forming dental organ producing a follicle that gives rise to the tooth-supporting tissues: cementum, periodontal membrane and alveolar bone (Tencate, 1989:57–9).

Tooth development and eruption patterns appear to be programmed events influenced primarily by genetic factors. Ectodermal and mesenchymal tissues interact in a genetically-controlled reciprocal induction that precedes the differentiation of mesenchymal cells into dentin-forming odontoblasts and ectodermal cells into enamel-secreting ameloblasts. Embryonic ectoderm apparently stimulates the ectomesenchyme of the dental organ to differentiate into odontoblasts that arrange themselves at the site of future cusp tips and commence dentinogenesis. Not until after the first dentin-forming cells have been laid down do the cells of the internal enamel epithelium differentiate into ameloblasts and produce organic matrix against the newly formed dentin surfaces. This matrix is partially mineralized almost immediately. In brief, no dentin will develop in the absence of the epithelium and, reciprocally, enamel formation by the epithelium cannot begin until some dentin has been formed. The entire primary dentition is initiated between the sixth and eighth week of embryonic development. At birth the calcification of primary teeth is well advanced and calcification of the permanent first molars has begun.

Tooth eruption

The force for erupting tooth movement is believed to reside in the periodontal ligament (Tencate, 1989:280). Teeth and their supporting tissues, including alveolar bone, develop as a unit as root formation progresses. From the onset of root formation, teeth begin to move in an axial direction, continuing until they reach functional position with teeth of the opposing arch. At the time of crown emergence into the oral environment, its root is about two-thirds formed. Formation of the remaining apical third proceeds at a slower pace. After the emergence of tooth crowns into the oral cavity, permanent teeth require 2 or 3 years and primary teeth about 1 year before root formation is completed. A substantial amount of time is usually required before the crown reaches its final, functional position.

The clinical eruption charts, commonly used for age estimation of skeletal material, describe age ranges within which developing teeth may be expected to emerge through fixed gingiva into functional position in the oral cavity. Fully formed, though not fully mineralized, tooth crowns may be visible in skeletal material from 2–5 years earlier than clinical emergence. Failure to recognize these differences can result in higher than actual age estimates (Orban, 1986:372). Moore et al. (1986:325–30) studied a sample of medieval skeletons 12–23 years of age, they found the values were younger in 70 % of individuals whose ages were estimated by nondental skeletal criteria than in those for whom dental criteria were employed.

Description of tooth tissues

Enamel

Enamel is an ectodermally-derived tissue that covers the anatomic crown of a tooth. It consists of mineral (96 %) as well as organic material and water (4 %). Because of its high mineral content and crystalline arrangement, enamel is the hardest calcified tissue in the human body. The crystalline arrangement of the mineral salts also make it extremely brittle and subject to fracture when it loses its supporting foundation of dentin. It is semitranslucent, its color reflecting shades of its supporting and underlying dentin. It varies in thickness from 2–2.5 mm at cusp tips and incisal edges, tapering to a thin edge at its cervical margin. Ameloblasts that form enamel are highly vulnerable to local, systemic and hereditary disturbances during amelogenesis. Enamel, once formed, is a nonvital tissue and cannot be replaced.

Dentin

Dentin, a hard tissue of mesenchymal origin, is less hard than enamel but harder than bone. It forms the root of a tooth and is the supporting base of crown enamel providing the tooth with form and elastic strength. Its chemical composition is 70 % inorganic and 30 % organic material and water by weight. Dentin is a vital tissue. The dentin-forming odontoblasts, which remain vital within the pulp chamber, have cytoplasmic extensions within the dentinal tubules that traverse the thickness of the dentin to its exterior surface. Once the root (dentin) surface is exposed to the oral environment, the cytoplasmic extensions may transmit sensation to the pulp and the tubuli in which they are housed may provide a pathway for invading cariogenic microorganisms.

Periodontium

The periodontium is a collective term for the tissues that anchor, support and protect a tooth in the oral cavity. Beginning at the tooth root they include the following.

Cementum

A specialized, calcified connective tissue that covers the anatomical root to a depth of 0.02–0.2 mm, attaching itself to the principal fibers of the periodontal ligament. Cementum closely resembles bone in chemical composition, but differs from bone in that it has no blood supply and cannot remodel itself. It is considerably less hard than dentin. Regular cementum is acellular, since the cementocytes that form it retreat into the periodontal membrane after mineralization. Apposition of regular cementum continues for life with an ongoing mineralization of the principal fibers. A 'cellular' type of cementum, called osteocementum because the cementocytes are trapped in lacunae within the cementum similar to osteocytes in the lacunae of bone, is denser than acellular cementum (Fig. 14.3). Osteocementum forms in response to negative pressure in the periodontal ligament rather than to the positive stresses of function. A variety of circumstances favor the deposition of osteocementum: accelerated elongation of a tooth in its socket from lack of

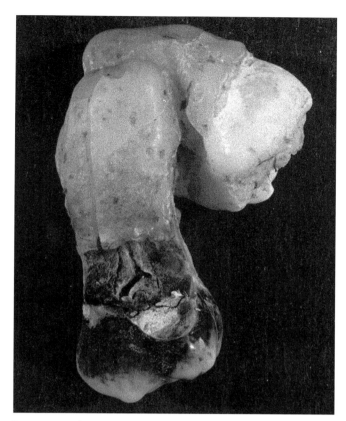

FIG. 14.3. **Dental concrescence.** Gradual second molar extrusion due to lack of functional stress resulted in osteocementum hyperplasia, fusing it to third molar. Courtesy Dr Odin Langsjoen. PBL.

functional stresses; tooth repair; negative intrasocket pressure associated with periapical inflammation at sites cervical to the inflammation; and loss of periodontal fiber attachment due to the loss of socket lamina dura in cases of Paget's disease (Shafer *et al.*, 1983:334).

Periodontal membrane

The periodontal membrane (ligament) is a sheet of connective tissue (0.15–0.38 mm thick) that decreases in thickness with age. It suspends a tooth in its socket in a relatively rigid articulation (gomphosis) prompting the use of the term ligament. The membrane's principal collagenous fibers attach the tooth cementum to alveolar bone. Other cellular components within the periodontal membrane include osteoblasts and osteoclasts that are functionally associated with alveolar bone remodeling as well as cementoblasts associated with cementogenesis. These cells are critical to the ongoing vitality of this specialized articulation.

Alveolar bone

Alveolar bone provides the rigid support of the periodontium. This bone has a specialized function: to support and maintain teeth in functional position. It is highly adaptable to forces of asymmetrical stress, but when deprived of its principal function of supporting teeth, it gradually resorbs. The alveolar process, which contains the individual tooth sockets, is made up of three distinct units: the cortical layers, the cribriform layer lining the sockets, and the trabecular bone between cortical plates. Radiologically the cribriform bone parallel to the plane of radiation appears dense and is radiographically described as lamina dura even though the lining layer is cribriform. The cribriform layer, in addition to providing attachment for bundles of periodontal ligament fibers, provides sensory and vascular elements an access to the periodontal membrane.

Enamel, dentin, cementum, periodontal ligament and alveolar bone together make a functional unit which is sealed and protected from the oral environment by the investing gingiva. The investing gingiva is part of the periodontium.

Gingiva

The investing gingiva has three components: an attached form and two unattached forms. The attached (fixed) gingiva is a firm, resilient band of keratinized oral epithelium extending from its junction with the oral mucosa to the cementoenamel junction on the teeth. Coronal to this junction the gingiva is unattached, forming a thin collar of keratinized epithelium separated from cervical enamel by a shallow sulcus. As this keratinized collar rises to fill the interdental space, it forms facial and lingual papillae that are connected by a 'col' or valley of delicate, nonkeratinized epithelium conforming to the shape of the contacting areas of adjacent teeth (Caranza, 1984:3–6).

Dental articulation

The cuspal design and position of upper and lower posterior teeth are essentially counterparts of each other. When jaws are closed in centric occlusion mandibular buccal cusps occlude with centrally placed fossae of the maxillary dentition and the maxillary lingual cusps occlude with centrally placed fossae of the mandibular teeth. All molars have central fossae; premolars have none. However, all posterior teeth, molars and premolars, have triangular hemifossae at their mesial and distal margins. These hemifossae, under conditions of proximal tooth

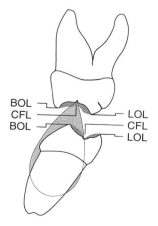

FIG. 14.4. **Chewing cycle diagram.** Frontal view of first molars' chewing cycle. BOL, buccal occlusal line; CFL, fossa line; LOL, lingual occlusal line; Shaded area, chewing cycle boundaries. Courtesy Dr Odin Langsjoen. PBL.

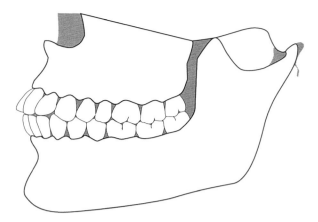

FIG. 14.5. **Jaws closed in centric relationship.** This figure demonstrates occlusal relationships, proximal contact and triangular interdental space. Courtesy Dr Odin Langsjoen. PBL.

contact, create diamond-shaped fossae in line with the central fossae of the molar teeth. This combined row of centrally placed, 'grinding pits' constitute a bimaxillary chewing table with mandibular buccal cusps working the central fossa line of the maxillary posterior teeth as the maxillary lingual cusps reciprocate within the cental fossa line of mandibular chewing teeth (Fig. 14.4). Centric cusps, also referred to as supporting and working cusps, experience wear patterns that differ from the wear patterns of noncentric, guiding or shearing cusps that fulfill a different masticatory role (see Physiological attrition, below).

In the centric relationship every posterior tooth has direct contact with two teeth of the opposing arch, with the exception of maxillary third molars and the mandibular first incisors. Incisors and canines normally do not make contact with their antagonists in centric position, but make contact only during protrusive and lateroprotrusive movements associated with biting and incising (Fig. 14.5).

ATTRITION

Dental attrition ('wear') is one of several regressive changes in dental hard tissues that are generally associated with the ageing process. It is a well-known phenomenon in archaeological skeletons and, because of its correlation with aging, is used as a method of estimating age. Other regressive changes that alter tooth forms are abrasion and erosion. None of these changes can be regarded as developmental anomalies or inflammatory lesions, nor are they necessarily related etiologically or pathologically. Yet, because they are all manifestations of hard tissue loss and often appear in combination, they are commonly treated as a group.

Attrition, by definition, is a physiological process, the wearing away of tooth hard tissue as a result of tooth-to-tooth contact during mastication and swallowing. Dental abrasion, however, is a wearing away of dental hard tissue by some abnormal mechanical process or abrasive material, and is considered pathologic. Dental erosion is a loss of tooth tissue by a chemical process that does not involve bacterial action. Although attrition, abrasion and erosion are three distinct processes, they are not mutually exclusive in action as evidenced by the role of abrasive materials in the severe loss of tooth occlusal surface experienced by ancient man.

Dental attrition occurs on occlusal, incisal and proximal surfaces (the latter are the surfaces with which a tooth is in contact with its two immediate neighbors) of all teeth as they rub together during mastication and swallowing. Proximal surface wear, though not as severe as occlusal wear, is not an insignificant phenomenon. The cushioning effect of the periodontal ligament allows sufficient tooth mobility within the socket to cause a perceivable flattening of proximal surface over time. It has been estimated that, by age 40 years, modern man has lost 1 cm of total arch length due to proximal attrition (Kraus et al., 1969:198).

The loss of proximal contact integrity, as well as the loss of crown height from occlusal/incisal wear, is normally accommodated by an ongoing physiologic remodeling of alveolar bone. In order to maintain the volume of interdental space needed for a healthy interdental gingival papilla, a modest lowering of interproximal alveolar bone becomes part of the bone remodeling effect. This adjustment is physiological, not pathological, as the term 'senile atrophy' implies.

All human dentitions show some loss of tooth enamel and dentin from functional wear. However, the degree of attrition experienced by our contemporary societies is much less severe than that of ancient populations in whom it appears to have been dental pathology's most destructive form.

Physiological attrition

The biomechanics of mastication are often reflected in the attrition patterns of ancient populations. Unfortunately, they are not routinely recognized in skeletal material due to the high percentage of dental arches that have been fragmented by tooth loss, both antemortem and postmortem. During mastication the mandible, with its bipolar, gliding hinge (temporomandibular articulation), rotates about and translates along a linear anteroposterior axis. If the chewing cycles are observed in frontal aspect along this axis the opening and closing movements describe a unilateral, pear shaped figure (Posselt, 1957:375). These tear drop-shaped cycles, when combined with opposite side chewing cycles and anteroposterior movements create a three dimensional dynamic that may be described as 'helicoidal'. The attrition pattern resulting from this physiological chewing pattern has frequently been reported for maxillary posterior teeth as 'ad palatum' wear of the lingual cusps. Seldom, however, is it recognized when it appears as a reciprocal pattern on the buccal cusps of the mandibular posterior teeth (Leek, 1980:41–2).

In a frontal section of first molar cusps closed in a centric relationship the mandibular buccal cusps fit into the central fossa line of the opposing maxillary teeth and the maxillary lingual cusps occlude in the central fossa line of the mandibular teeth, (Fig. 14.4). Cusps that function within the central fossa line of opposing teeth are 'working' cusps (pestle in mortar), and in a physiological occlusion they bear the brunt of crushing and grinding actions and can be expected to show higher attrition rates than the adjacent guiding or shearing cusps.

Physiological attrition patterns can provide a reliable estimate of age at death in homogeneous population groups if seriation procedures are employed (Lovejoy, 1985). Unfortunately such conditions are seldom observed in ancient populations due to the high percentage of damaged and missing teeth, both antemortem and postmortem. Nevertheless, reasonably intact helicoidal wear patterns can be expected among early and mid-adults and need to be recognized.

Deviations from normal chewing cycles necessitated by early posterior tooth loss typically result in an abnormal flattening of cuspids and incisors as extreme anterior excursions of the mandible are employed in search of new crushing and grinding surface. Similar anterior end-to-end wear patterns can also occur as a consequence of occupational use of anterior teeth as a third hand or as a result of parafunctional activities such as the action of bruxism (clenching of teeth, often while asleep) (Ramfjord & Ash, 1983:327).

Pathogenesis

It is clear that dental attrition, narrowly defined as tooth-to-tooth wear, can present as a solitary process only on proximal contact surfaces since all other surfaces may be influenced to a considerable degree by abrasive elements present in food or incorporated into it during its preparation. Abrasives are the foreign body elements that advance physiological attrition to pathological status. Considering the abundance of abrasive elements that are present in or added to the diets of prehistoric man, the pathological effects of tooth wear are not surprising. An exact point at which physiological attrition becomes pathological is difficult to assess, but may be described in terms of pathological consequences; i.e. attrition becomes pathological when tooth wear is so rapid and of such severity that associated alveolar bone is adversely affected (White & Folkens, 1991:352).

Attrition-related destruction of alveolar bone may take place along two pathways: internally *via* the pulp canal, or externally, *via* the periodontium. Access to the internal route is effected when attrition advances faster than odontoblasts of the dental pulp can deposit secondary dentin to protect tooth vitality, and attrition reaches and exposes the pulp canal. Pulp death is soon followed by infectious inflammatory destruction of periapical alveolar bone. Similarly when attrition erodes below the proximal contact level reducing

tooth contact more rapidly than alveolar bone can adjust by remodeling (Fig. 14.5), delicate interproximal periodontal soft tissues become exposed to the trauma of food impaction and stagnation. This is then followed by inflammation, localized periodontal abscess formation and destruction of alveolar bone as described in more detail in the periodontal disease section, below.

Paleopathology of attrition

Abrasive elements that augmented the wearing power of attrition were ubiquitous in antiquity, Lovell (1991) noted that foliage covered with abrasive volcanic ash accelerated enamel wear in howler monkeys. Mulholland (1989) and others have identified microscopic phytoliths with distinctive abrasive qualities in all parts of a plant leaf, stem, and root . In a study of Peruvian mummies, Leigh (1937:286) thought that the moderate attrition he observed was due less to the food than to the lack of abrasives incorporated into it during its preparation. Leek (1984:126–7), reporting on dental problems among desert dwellers of ancient Egypt, observed that the one abnormality from childhood onwards, common in every dentition, was tooth wear. His list of potential contaminants that were a part of early agriculture included contamination of grain from soil and air, flint particles from harvesting tools, wind-blown sand during the winnowing of grain, mineral fragments derived from milling stones and querns as well as inorganic materials that were purposely added to grain to hasten the grinding process.

Attrition among prehistoric populations was not only the most prevalent pathology, and most destructive of dental hard tissue, but also appears to have played a major initiating role in periapical and periodontal abscess formation, root caries, antemortem tooth loss and temporomandibular joint disease . A positive correlation also exists between degenerative temporomandibular joint disorders and the dental wear that accompanies aging.

Temporomandibular joint disease

The temporomandibular joint (TMJ) is a synovial joint cavity formed by the cartilage-covered condyle head and the cartilage-covered mandibular fossa of the skull. However, an additional flat, bonnet-shaped cartilaginous meniscus is interposed between these two surfaces, essentially dividing the joint into two compartments. One end of the meniscus is attached firmly to the mediolateral aspect of the condyle.

Each condyle is suspended by a loosely-fitting joint capsule that attaches the condylar neck to the cranial base. A loose fit permits the condyle and meniscus to slide as a unit between the mandibular fossa and the articular eminence of the temporal bone during multiple masticatory movements. Thus the flexible meniscus prevents direct articulation between the condyle and the fossa surfaces even during the many asymmetrical movements required for mastication. The force of clenched teeth (centric occlusion) is not transmitted to the TMJ, but instead is absorbed by the teeth.

Articular menisci of the TMJ are seldom recovered in archaeological materials and without guidance from all of the articular components of the TMJ, assessment of dental articulation is difficult. If such an assessment is based on attrition-flattened tooth surfaces alone, the mandible commonly will be erroneously positioned in an anterior, tooth-to-tooth, end-to-end, occlusal relationship thus perpetuating the myth that the one-tooth to two-teeth interarch occlusal relationship of modern populations is at odds with the observed apparent end-to-end occlusal relationship of ancient humans (Begg, 1965:5). 'Fitting' a mandible to a skull correctly must allow for the space occupied by the cartilage covering the TMJ surfaces plus that of the interposed meniscus.

FIG. 14.6. **Osteoarthritis of temporomandibular joint (TMJ).** Mandibular condyle (arrow) is nonanatomically positioned near TMJ for photographic reasons. Subchondral bone destruction on both and extending beyond mandibular fossa suggests subluxation due to extreme lateral mandibular shift in effort to bring few remaining teeth into occlusion during mastication. CHA-97. A 55 year old female, Chiribaya culture, A.D. 1150, coastal southern Peru. MAUT. PBL.

Diseases of the temporomandibular joint take on many forms from a variety of causes including developmental and endocrine disturbances, birth injuries, infections that spread by hematogenous routes such as middle ear infections, primary inflammation of the joint as in rheumatoid arthritis, and metastatic malignancies. One of the most incapacitating results of TMJ disease is ankylosis of the joint usually caused by traumatic injury to, or infections in or about, the joint (Shafer *et al.*, 1983:703–5). Alexandersen (1967:553–4), reporting the effects of unilateral traumatic injury to the TMJ that occurred during childhood, noted growth arrest and ankylosis of the injured joint that resulted in unilateral micrognathia with mandibular asymmetry and severe malocclusion. Most of these conditions occur at an early age and are quite rare. In older individuals the most common type of TMJ arthropathy, affecting contemporary as well as ancient populations, is degenerative osteoarthritis associated with the age-related breakdown of the masticatory system.

Antemortem tooth loss not only materially reduces masticatory function, but also creates further malfunction. Beginning with the initial breakdown of dental arch integrity the remaining teeth begin to tip, drift, rotate or extrude into malfunctional positions that interfere with the 'centric' occlusal position of the mandible where all chewing and swallowing movements begin and end.

In order to compensate for the lack of a stable centric position and to find new chewing surface the mandible must move into extreme lateral and protrusive positions that stress the temporomandibular joints. The deleterious effects of such parafunctional movements are reflected not only in the wear patterns of teeth that perform functions foreign to their morphology, but also in the temporomandibular joints that are stressed by the repeated subluxation movements required to position condylar heads into nonphysiological relationships with temporal articular surfaces.

The temporomandibular joint arthropathy that results from this chronic stress is a noninfectious, degenerative alteration of joint tissue surfaces resulting from repeated, intrinsic, microtrauma to joint tissues (Shore, 1959).

The earliest manifestation of the joint trauma is the destruction of the cartilaginous disc followed by changes in the cartilaginous surfaces of the condyle and temporal bone, reducing the joint to a 'bone against bone' articulation with subsequent deformation of the joints. The deformation presents varying degrees of surface roughness, a flattening of condylar heads, an enlarged mandibular fossa and a general disharmony in size and shape of the condyle and fossa (Fig. 14.6). Osteophytic lipping of bone at the joint capsule attachment area is also a common feature. The positional relationships between condyle and fossa are abnormal and usually dissimilar from those on the opposite sides.

PERIODONTAL DISORDERS

Classification and description

Periodontal diseases may be classified according to the stage of the inflammation present, as acute or chronic. However what is usually meant by the term periodontitis is a chronic

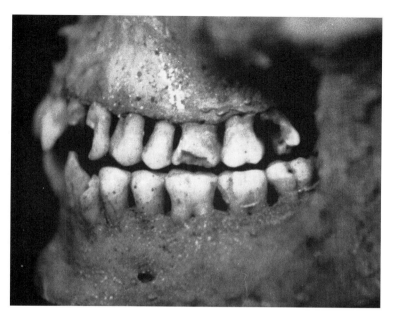

FIG. 14.7. **Periodontitis, generalized horizontal.** Alveolar bone recession has exposed tooth roots. Courtesy Dr Odin Langsjoen. PBL.

slowly progressive and destructive inflammatory process affecting one or more of the four components of the periodontium (Burnett & Schuster, 1978:213). With the exception of the early, acute and reversible inflammation of the investing gingiva, chronic periodontitis is essentially a connective tissue disease involving periodontal ligament, cementum and alveolar bone. Since only hard tissues are normally present in skeletal material, it is convenient to classify and describe chronic periodontitis in terms of the location and pattern of bone destruction as either generalized or localized.

Generalized periodontitis usually affects all teeth and is characterized by a horizontal reduction in alveolar bone height, the crestal margins being roughly perpendicular to the long axis of the affected teeth (Fig. 14.7). The reduction in alveolar bone and soft tissue height exposes significant root surface to the oral fluids. Though horizontal bone loss is quite common among contemporary adults its frequency in antiquity was less common (Clark *et al.*, 1986).

Localized periodontitis, the more prevalent form in antiquity, is tooth-specific, commonly occurring interdentally, creating vertical defects between tooth root and alveolar bone. In its early stages interdental defects appear as craters in the crestal bone confined within the facial and lingual cortical walls. As inflammation advances deep angular defects are formed in the cancellous bone. The facio-lingually broad posterior teeth are especially vulnerable to this inflammatory progression.

While the periodontium is subject to traumatic, neoplastic and other forms of pathology, such as the acute necrotizing gingivitis of Vincent's spirochete and fusiform bacteria, acute infection changes are rarely preserved for pathological examination. Hence in the remainder of this section we will discuss periodontitis only as chronic infection and its long-term effects on the periodontium, limiting our efforts to localized, tooth specific, chronic periodontitis.

Epidemiology and anatomic features relevant to periodontitis

Periodontitis is a global problem, estimated by the World Health Organization to affect 75 % of adults to some degree. It is responsible for more antemortem tooth loss than is dental caries (Shafer *et al.*, 1983:760). In contemporary populations it increases in frequency with every decade up to age 60. It is not gender-specific. In a normal, fully-erupted permanent dentition the mesio-distal diameters of all tooth crowns are wider through the occlusal and incisal thirds than they are at their cervical thirds. (see Fig. 14.5). As explained below, the loss of interproximal contact is the principal initiating event leading to periodontitis.

Pathogenesis of periodontitis

While the gingivitis that usually precedes periodontitis can begin with events such as a penetrating foreign body or major local trauma, by far the most frequent predisposing cause is loss of interproximal contact. Such contact loss may occur by a traumatic chip fracture of the enamel involving the contact area or even spontaneous lateral tooth drift following exfoliation of its neighbor. However, the cause most common in antiquity, was severe attrition. When wear on the occlusal surface has eroded beyond the contact areas of the crown, neighboring teeth are no longer in contact with each other. The enamel bridge at the former interproximal contact now no longer protects the tender gingival tissues occupying the interdental space. Lacking its protective enamel cover, food is now forced into this sulcus during mastication. With each subsequent meal the sulcus is traumatically expanded by retained organic matter, since the area has no self-cleansing method.

Chronic food retention in a protected niche provides opportunity for bacterial multiplication. A layer of such bacteria mixed with mucoid material (dental plaque) becomes attached to the tooth root at its cervical area. As food and microorganisms stagnate in the distended sulcus the transeptal fibers of the periodontal ligament are the first connective tissue elements to be victimized. Bacteria now invade, extending deeply into the periodontal ligament space and bacterial plaque begins to calcify, forming calculus.

Dental plaque, formed by bacterial colonization of the tooth pellicle (cuticle), is the single most important extrinsic factor in the development of periodontitis. Mineralized plaque is calculus. Supragingival calculus is mineralized by ions from the saliva, subgingival calculus by ions from gingival sulcular exudate. Besides differing in location and source of mineral ions, subgingival calculus differs from supragingival calculus in another basic feature: i.e. rather than being a direct etiologic agent of an inflammatory reaction it is a product of that reaction, forming at the bottom of an existing periodontal pocket (Shapiro & Stallard,

1977:77–8). It is so dense and firmly attached that it is often mistaken for osteocementum. Supragingival calculus, on the other hand, forms in large quantities, especially near the orifices of major salivary glands, is fragile and easily dislodged in dry skeletal specimens. In both types of calculus, however, the calcium is deposited as calcium phosphate in the form of hydroxyapatite.

The site of periodontal disruption gradually increases in this manner, creating vertical or angular defects in the bone alongside the root. The stripping of the periodontium from the tooth root exposes the root to the oral fluids, providing dental plaque with a site to initiate the necrotizing process of dental caries with its destructive effects (discussed in the next section). Purulent exudate collects in the lower recesses of the created periodontal defect, and the inflammatory process extends both more deeply and widely, eventually destroying the periodontal ligament and alveolar bone.

The body's defense mechanisms usually are inadequate to control the process, and in fact may at times even contribute to local tissue destruction (Williams, 1990) that has already been initiated by products of bacterial metabolism (Burnett & Schuster, 1978:227). Paleopathologists may observe evidence of such efforts at containment of the process in the form of peripheral buttressing bone or lipping on facial surfaces adjacent to osseous defects in alveolar bone (Caranza, 1984:243) (Fig. 14.8). Nevertheless, once firmly initiated the process is usually progressive and the ultimate effect is predominantly bone destruction. Eventually the process of periodontal tissue destruction extends around the tooth circumferentially, destroying its periodontal attachments sufficiently to result in tooth exfoliation. Following tooth loss the alveolar bone becomes resorbed since its only purpose was support and nourishment of the tooth (Moss-Salentijn & Klyvert, 1985:267). Such an effect is particularly obvious in *generalized* periodontitis in which diffuse periodontal recession results in such extensive exfoliation that the alveolar portion of the jaws may virtually disappear.

Antiquity, history, and paleopathology of periodontitis

Evidence of chronic periodontal disease has been described in a three million year old hominid (Lavigne & Molto, 1995) as well as in an example of the Pleistocene *Australopithecus africanus*, while acute periodontitis (probably Vincent's infection) was reported in soldiers of Xenophon's Greek army about 4000 B.C. (Shafer *et al.*, 1983:760). It is a commonly recognized condition in modern studies of ancient skeletal populations. These reports have a tendency to focus on *generalized* periodontitis with its diffuse, horizontal form of bone loss. Clark *et al.* (1986), however, noted that this form is not a common finding in ancient dry skulls. The tendency to lump the many forms and causes of periodontitis into a single category to the exclusion of multiple forms of *localized* periodon-

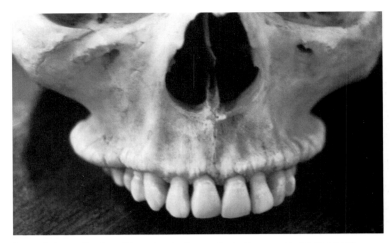

FIG. 14.8. **Generalized maxillary alveolar hyperostosis.** Enormous hyperostosis of maxillary alveolar bone is probably a process ('peripheral buttressing effect': Caranza, 1984:243) reactive to bone resorption and weakening by periodontitis. 14.10. Thailand. Courtesy Dr R. Pickering. DMNH.

titis risks omission of important diagnostic information. Such localized forms are abundant and correlate strongly with attrition and caries. Cultural practices can modify the prevalence of periodontitis. Langsjoen (1996) has demonstrated that the Andean practice of coca-leaf-chewing is a powerful predictor of periodontitis leading to a high rate of antemortem tooth loss, and betel nut-chewing is similarly suspected. More commonly, food collection and preparation practices that add grit to the ingested items, can accelerate attrition enormously, leading to premature interproximal contact loss.

Clearly, the consequences of the chronic periodontal disease syndrome in antiquity were very destructive. By middle age and beyond, periodontal disease was the major contributor to edentulism, and it affected principally the posterior chewing teeth.

DENTAL CARIES

Definition

Dental caries (from the Latin, rottenness) is a multifactorial, multibacterial disease of the calcified teeth tissues, characterized by demineralization of the inorganic portion and destruction of the organic component. It is both infectious and transmissible. Caries is a progressive disease in that a continuation of the same environmental conditions that induced the lesion will inevitably complete the destruction. Though the odontoblasts lining the pulp chamber wall can produce secondary dentin in response to the effects of attrition (see above) as well as caries, the absence of formative cells or vessels within enamel and dentin preclude the healing or replacement of tissue destroyed by a carious lesion.

Epidemiology

Dental caries is one of the most prevalent chronic diseases affecting the human body. In contemporary society it encompasses all races from all geographic areas of the world. It affects both sexes, every age group and all socioeconomic strata.

Pathogenesis

Patterns of dental caries

Fundamental to the reconstruction of dental carious disease is the clear understanding that dental caries presents as two, separate and distinctive patterns induced by different circumstances. These patterns can be recognized and separated on the basis of their differing locations: the tooth crowns and the tooth roots. Because the carious processes are induced by the bacteria and solutes of the oral fluids, subadults and young adults develop caries primarily of dental enamel, as only crowns are exposed to oral fluids in that age group. Several decades later the processes of chronic periodontitis discussed in the previous section may have damaged the tissues of the periodontium, exposing the roots to cariogenic activity. With these elementary principles in mind, the relevant details of these two patterns are discussed below.

Crown caries

Bacterial metabolic products contribute organic acids and proteases to the oral fluids. In sufficient concentration the first of these can dissolve the hydroxyapatite composing the mineral portion of dental enamel while the protease, especially the collagenase enzymes, are capable of digesting the organic matrix of the crown within which the apatite crystals are embedded. Normally the concentrations of these substances are too low to bring about such effects. Food-filled enamel pits and crevices, however, provide a haven within which bacteria can flourish, form a plaque-like mass attached to the enamel (Newbrun, 1977:44) and create a microenvironment within which the now more concentrated fluids can dissolve the enamel and initiate the carious process.

All tooth surfaces are not equally vulnerable to this process. The occlusal (chewing) surfaces of posterior teeth are formed by fusion of several developmental lobes. Fusion irregularities often generate depressed grooves and pits between the developing units, in which food can become trapped. While maxillary incisors often contain developmental pits, their anterior position and tooth form provide less opportunity for food particle entrapment. Most of the other tooth surfaces are sufficiently smooth to be self-cleansing.

Acidogenic, demineralizing bacteria predominate during the early, more superficial stages of the caries lesion. The demineralization process of pit and fissure caries follows the enamel rods, creating a cone-shaped area of decay whose apex is at the enamel surface and its base at the dentinoenamel junction (DEJ). At the DEJ it spreads rapidly affecting innumerable dentinal tubules en route, each of which provides a tract leading directly to the pulp. As decay penetrates the dentinal tubules, proteolytic bacteria predominate, destroying the collagenous dentin matrix (Shafer et al., 1983:440–2). The isolated dentin yields readily to the proteolysis of the decay process creating a large cavity communicating with the oral cavity through a smaller surface enamel defect. Thus the enamel surrounding the defect will be unsupported by the underlying decayed dentin, and the compressive forces of subsequent mastication soon fracture the unsupported enamel crystals away, generating a now obvious hemispherical surface defect (Fig. 14.9). Subsequent carious progression along the dental tubules soon leads to the pulp canal. Bacterial invasion produces rapid necrosis of the canal vasculature and soft tissues, extending the necrotizing process to the root apex and the surrounding trabecular bone producing a periapical abscess.

Some of the bacteria are gas-producing, and when accumulation of necrotic debris obstructs the canal the pressure within the periapical abscess creates the well-known throbbing pain of a toothache. More importantly it may force bacteria into some of the abscess wall's blood vessels, allowing them to circulate in the blood (bacteremia and septicemia). In this way bacteria may reach distant areas such as the vertebrae, heart valves or even brain, initiating abscesses in these new locations. Such complications may be fatal. Alternatively the abscess may fistulize through the alveolar cortical bone. Periapical abscesses frequently penetrate the thin layer of the facial alveolar cortex, to drain into the oral cavity. In addition to facial draining, maxillary periapical abscesses

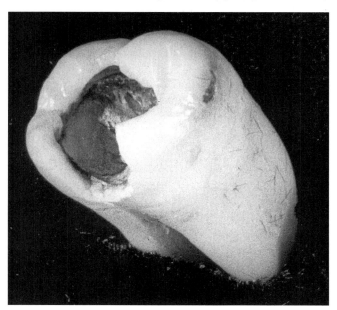

FIG. 14.9. **Dental caries.** Occlusal surface defect lined by dark-stained dentin. Note fracture of unsupported area of enamel. Modern case. Courtesy Dr Odin Langsjoen. PBL.

may also perforate into the maxillary sinus. As long as the drainage tract remains unobstructed the individual suffers little local distress, and the nonvital tooth may continue to carry out its masticatory functions because the periodontal ligament remains intact. Only in exceptional circumstances will the abscess fistulize from the periapical area along the outside of the root to emerge through the gingiva attached to the tooth's cervical area. Such a path traverses the periodontal tissues whose destruction can result in exfoliation of the tooth.

This discussion has emphasized developmental pits and fissures as the principal predisposing factors in the initiation of crown caries in crevices of congenitally malformed teeth as well as malpositioned and malfunctioning teeth. It is also axiomatic that tooth loss will result in drifting of adjacent teeth that often creates new opportunities for dental plaque development.

Root caries

Roots are normally covered by both soft and hard tissues. Hence, these must be diseased before roots are exposed to oral bacteria and fluids. As explained above, an occasional periapical abscess will fistulize along the root surface, permitting bacterial access to the root itself. This, however, is the exception. In the overwhelming majority of the cases, it is retraction or destruction of the gingiva and other periodontal elements that expose the root to the oral environment as defined in detail in the preceding section. The junction of the gingiva with the tooth is at its neck (the cemento-enamel junction: CEJ). This, then, is the site of initial root exposure and, logically, it is here that root caries is usually initiated (Banting & Courtwright, 1975; Hix & O'Leary, 1976). Expansion of the infected periodontium gradually creates a saucer-shaped defect at the CEJ that enlarges slowly (Hazen et al., 1973:132). The bacteria form a plaque on the cementum of that area, demineralize it and extend into the dentin. Crownward extension of the carious process undermines the enamel that often then fractures. The remainder of the process is similar to that described above for crown caries with one outstanding exception. Untreated, the periodontal infection often expands circumferentially until it has destroyed the tooth's attachment so extensively that spontaneous exfoliation results.

Because periodontal disease usually begins after age 30 years, root caries affects a substantially older population subgroup than does crown caries. Furthermore, root caries should be viewed not as a cofactor of the cause of periodontal disease, but rather as a product of the latter. Since root caries develops secondary to chronic periodontal disease, involves the same gram-negative anaerobic organisms as does the subgingival calculus of periodontal disease, occurs most commonly at the protein-rich CEJ and is predominately a proteolytic process, root caries should be looked upon as a process independent of a dietary carbohydrate factor.

Antiquity, history, and paleopathology

Dental caries can be traced far back in geological time and is present in all parts of the world. It appears to have affected hominids at all times during their evolution and has accompanied *Homo sapiens* from his advent in Paleolithic times (Clement, 1958). He also cites Rothpletz (1923) and Moodie (1948) as making similar observations involving parasite borings found in the calcareous cuticular teeth of lower Silurian creatures, two examples in a mosasaur mandible and caries in an herbivorous dinosaur (respectively). The Pleistocene also provides examples of caries. These include decay in a mastodon tusk in which the dentinal tubules of the tusk were filled with bacteria and carious spots were present on the outer edges of the dentin. Caries also has been reported in the teeth of a 75 000 year old camel. Caries appears to have affected hominids throughout evolution. Anthropologic studies by Lenhossek (1919) revealed that pre-Neolithic skulls did not exhibit dental caries, but that those of the Neolithic period did contain carious teeth. In most instances the lesions were noted in older persons in teeth that showed severe attrition and food impaction affecting the cervical areas.

Early humans appear to have been less affected than modern populations. If we limit ourselves to reports that differentiated clearly between crown and root caries we find that contemporary populations are characterized by a high caries susceptibility on all tooth surfaces, but in ancient populations caries was more prevalent on the roots. Indeed, a study of modern Britons and sixth century Saxons reported that not only was the caries rate of the contemporary English six times that of the Saxons, but that the majority of cavities in the modern group was located in pits and fissures of tooth crowns in sharp contrast to ancient Saxons' dentitions in which most of the cavities were at the cementoenamel junction. Moore & Corbet (1983) cited a number of investigators who had made similar observations in populations widely separated geographically: Turner (1913) reporting on ancient Egyptians, Leigh (1925) reporting on aboriginal Americans, Swärdstedt (1931) in his study of medieval Swedes, and Cook & Rothbotham (1968) in their examination of the Roman Britons. More recently Langsjoen (1995) described the same phenomenon in the Canary Island Guanches. All reported the majority of carious lesions to be at the cementoenamel junction area of tooth root and crown. The higher frequency of caries among agriculturalists *versus* hunter–gatherers commonly is attributed to the increased role of carbohydrate in farmers' diets. The importance of differentiating crown and root caries has particular relevance to this question. The addition of abrasives to the food by grinding grains with stone mills or manos and metates (grinding stones) can accelerate attrition enormously, leading to loss of proximal contact, periodontitis and root caries. In the absence of refined sugar, increased caries rates may be the product of this mechanism, recognizable by clearly defining the cervical location of the carious lesions.

Differential Diagnosis

Most carious lesions are self-evident, but the following precautions are useful.

■ Developmental enamel pits large enough to admit an examiner's probe may not be carious if they have a solid, enamel or dentin base. The absence of a halo of discolored decaying dentin visible through the semitranslucent enamel can confirm this.

■ Deep-pitted enamel hypoplasia may acquire an exogenous stain that is not caries, confirmable by the absence of cavitation or undermined enamel.

■ Secondary, physiologic dentin appearing on the biting surface of well-worn teeth is less mineralized than primary dentin and therefore absorbs stain more readily. Such brown spots are properly credited to attrition, not caries.

■ Brown-stained dentin surrounding an open pulp canal exposed by traumatic fracture or pathological attrition is not caries. The color is endogenous, not exogenous.

■ Saucer-shaped, shallow erosion of root caries can be differentiated from osteoclastic root resorption by the latter's sharply defined, irregular outline and scalloped resorption front (Caranza, 1984:46–8).

■ The chalky, white areas of early, smooth-surface enamel caries can acquire postmortem diagenetic stain resembling fluorosis; differentiation may be possible because fluorosis is usually more generalized throughout the skeleton (see Chapter 9).

ENAMEL HYPOPLASIA

Definition

Enamel hypoplasia is the term applied to a defect in the structure of tooth enamel resulting from a body-wide, metabolic insult sufficient to disrupt ameloblastic physiology. The enamel lesion has been called a biological window through which one can observe the long-term consequences of metabolic stress, providing a record from which investigators may infer the time at which the hypoplasia formed and therefore the time of the stressful event that caused it (Goodman & Armelagos, 1988). Hypoplastic enamel represents nonfatal stresses that can be induced by a variety of metabolic insults. To be eligible as a cause, the stressful condition is perceived as one of life-threatening magnitude of severity (starvation? major acute bacterial infection?),

sufficient to require the body to divert energy away from nonvital processes and redirect all its resources into processes essential for survival. Thus, arrest of growth in bone, teeth and other structures is viewed as the price of recovery from such an event. However, there is no one-to-one relationship between stressors and the resulting defect. Many stressors produce no obvious dental markers while disturbances of as few as 4 days can produce markings in long bones in the form of Harris growth arrest lines (Buikstra & Cook, 1980:444–9). The relationship of enamel hypoplasia to past general health makes it an important investigatory tool that may be used to identify visible manifestations of damage and provide clues to nutritional status, presence of infectious diseases, trauma or cultural activities. Thus, though the lesion is not a marker for a specific disease, it can be used to infer the general health status of a population.

Heritable forms of abnormal enamel formation are well-known though rare. The most studied of these is the autosomal dominant form of amelogenesis imperfecta. Gross enamel deformation is common among its different types. The following discussion will be limited to the far more frequent environmental form of enamel hypoplasia.

Description of the enamel hypoplasia lesion

In its classic form, lesions of environmental enamel hypoplasia consist of sharply-defined, linear, horizontal grooves of reduced enamel thickness extending circumferentially around the tooth crown. For reasons that remain unclear, linear horizontal defects are commonly limited to facial surfaces, and may appear as only a linear array of diminutive pits

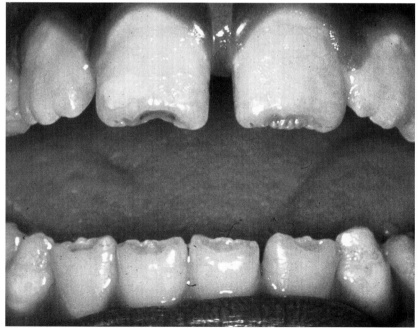

FIG. 14.10. Congenital syphilis ('Hutchinson's incisors'). Notched incisors due to diminutive or absent central lobe. An 80 year old modern female. Courtesy Dr R. Elzay. SDUM.

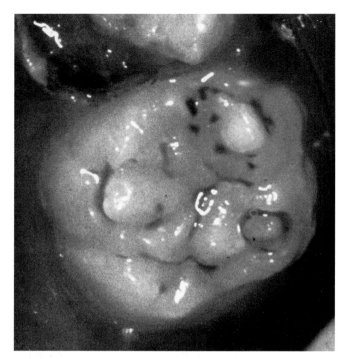

FIG. 14.11. **Congenital syphilis ('mulberry molar').** Irregular, lobulated molar occlusal surface. An 8 year old modern child. Courtesy Dr R. Elzay. SDUM.

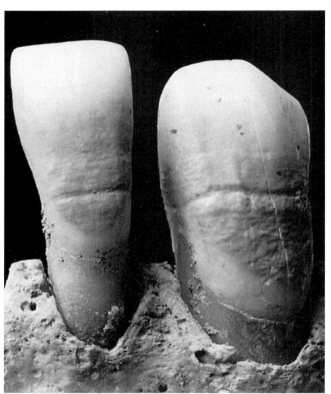

FIG. 14.12. **Chronological linear enamel hypoplasia.** Note the prominent, horizontal groove on the facial aspect of the lower right central incisor and the lower left canine. Teeth relocated for photographic purposes. Medieval young adult from England. Courtesy Simon Mays and the *Journal of Archaeological Science*.

or a focal cluster of pits. More major variations are broad, poorly-defined, chalky white areas of hypomineralization or honeycombed beds of cup-shaped enamel voids. Multiple lines suggest multiple stressful episodes. A few known stressors produce unique hypoplastic patterns. Among these are the lesions related to congenital syphilis: notched (Hutchinson's) maxillary incisors (Fig. 14.10) and cusp abnormalities (mulberry molars) (Fig. 14.11). These, however, are the exception. In most cases it has not been possible to associate hypoplasia patterns to specific metabolic or etiological circumstances consistently.

Not all teeth are affected. Most lines of enamel hypoplasia form during the first year after birth, a period of active amelogenesis for principally the maxillary central incisors and mandibular canines. Hence these are the teeth most frequently manifesting the lesions of environmental hypoplasia. At times they may be found on other teeth, even on second molars, but less than 2 % form between the ages of 3 and 7 years (Sarnat & Schour, 1941).

Pathogenesis

Several aspects of amelogenesis included in the opening section of this chapter are worthy of examination in detail here. The older concept of amelogenesis was that of a process in which all, or at least a major fraction, of the future crown was secreted as a matrix that later became mineralized as a whole. We know now that amelogenesis is an incremental phenomenon (Goodman, 1989; Tencate, 1989:197–210). Beginning at the dentin surface of the future cusp tip, matrix

is secreted by ameloblasts and then becomes mineralized. Thereafter another layer of matrix is secreted, followed again by its mineralization. The time lapse between matrix formation and its mineralization is an important variable that permits the development of the hypoplasia lesion (Suga, 1982). Suckling *et al.* (1983, 1986) have reproduced foci of enamel hypoplasia experimentally in sheep, based on this concept. Each such increment of amelogenesis betrays its origin as a line of junction on the enamel surface; the individual junction line is called perikyma (plural: perikymata). Growth is much slower when the final one-third of the crown is formed at the cervical end, causing the perikymata there to be closer together than at the tip. Near the incising edge a spacing interval of 10 perikymata per millimeter is common but near the tooth neck it may reach 30.

Formation of the linear groove of enamel hypoplasia is viewed as an arrest of amelogenic growth during a period of stress, halting the completion of that particular increment. Subsequent growth resumption following termination of the stressful episode will involve the formation of a new increment, leaving the previous one as an incomplete layer, viewed from the surface as a zone of thinner enamel representing the 'hypoplastic groove'. (Fig. 14.12). The other feature to be emphasized is that the acellular, avascular, secreted enamel can not repair, restore or remodel itself. Hence the groove remains as a permanent feature, a physical record of a stressful physiologic event.

Counting surface perikymata has limited usefulness because they wear off with age, restricting the practice to younger teeth. When visible, however, they do reflect a specific time interval (Hilson, 1993), useful for dating the stressing episode. Viewed in tissue sections they are termed striae of Retzius. If these striae are accentuated by a systemic metabolic disturbance they are referred to as Wilson's bands. Microscopic evaluation of these features is being carried out to supplement perikymata counting in an effort to increase the sensitivity of detection of the stress effects (Buikstra & Cook, 1980:444–9).

Conditions leading to enamel hypoplasia

A large number of environmental factors have been postulated as etiologic events resulting in this lesion. They include hemolytic disease of the newborn, premature birth, major febrile infections, dietary deficiencies of vitamins A, C and D, newborn hypoxia and others. The cause most frequently cited is malnutrition. Wells (1964:121) suggests that it was not starvation itself but the acute infections to which malnourished individuals are uniquely susceptible that are responsible for the dental hypoplasia. Berry (1985) also points out that prolonged malnutrition may produce no such lines since the hypoplasia lesion appears to be related to an acute, episodic insult.

Antiquity and paleopathology

Paleoepidemiological references to enamel hypoplasia go as far back as Neanderthal man. Although macroscopic enamel defects have been demonstrated in *Australopithecus crasidens* of the lower Pleistocene (Robinson, 1952), by and large this condition was not a major concern in the study of earlier hominids. Evidence of its antiquity is found in a general dental survey of British material of Bronze Age dates in which 58 % of the individuals examined were found to show hypoplastic defects on more than one tooth. In a comparison study of Hungarians and a Cro-Magnon group, Marksic & Baglias (1987) observed a higher frequency of enamel defects in the Cro-Magnon cohort, and suggested malnutrition as the cause and, less directly, infectious diseases.

The recognition of the classical linear enamel hypoplasia lesion in archeological teeth is not especially difficult. Problems may arise with atypical lesions. These can be particularly enigmatic when only pits are present. Certainly the occasional, common, minute developmental pit should not incite a search for a major stressful event, but the extent of pitting that is regularly correlated with such an event has not been standardized. Enamel lesions on only a single tooth may reflect a purely local phenomenon. Several other lesions that can cause confusion with the environmental enamel hypoplasia lesion include one of unknown (perhaps genetic?) etiology and is characterized by broad, undulating, circumferential, transverse grooves in the cervical third of permanent teeth in a pattern asynchronous with age. Appropriate interpretation of the identification of the linear enamel hypoplasia lesion in archaeological teeth currently is confounded by the many uncertainties in our knowledge. The presence of the lesion correlates statistically with at least some of the other biological markers for past stressful events such as porotic hyperostosis and cribra orbitalia. Its commonly bilateral presence is also consistent with a synchronous event. However, it correlates poorly or not at all with lines of growth arrest in long bones. The abundant current studies of this lesion can be expected to contribute significantly to the resolution of some of these questions in the near future. In the meantime, the suggestions of Goodman & Armelagos (1988) appear advisable. They note that, in view of the enormous range of metabolic and biological variables involved in both the host and the perceived nature of the stressful events, expectations of one-to-one correlations with other stress markers are probably unrealistic. Their extensive studies on living populations have shown correlations with more broadly-expressed differences in health status of different subpopulations. It appears that a pragmatic paleopathological approach that embraces conservative diagnostic criteria and the general concept that the lesion reflects a period of impaired health can be expected to provide workable results.

Unfortunately the teeth most useful for evaluation of enamel hypoplasia (the single-rooted anterior teeth) are the very ones that often become detached and separated from their sockets during interment, excavation and postexcavation handling activities. Fastidious excavation and curatorial practices can prevent such losses that may otherwise impair adequate evaluation for the presence and extent of enamel hypoplasia in archaeological skeletal populations.

MISCELLANEOUS DENTITION-RELATED CONDITIONS

Neoplasms

Ameloblastoma (adamintonoma; adamantine epithelioma)

This is a locally destructive but nonmetastasizing tumor arising from the enamel organ of the jaw. A histologically similar tumor is occasionally found in the tibia or the region of the sella turcica.

Epidemiology, pathology, and radiology
This peculiar tumor is commonly called adamantinoma when it appears in the tibia or base of the skull near the pituitary, while an identical-appearing tumor in the jaws has

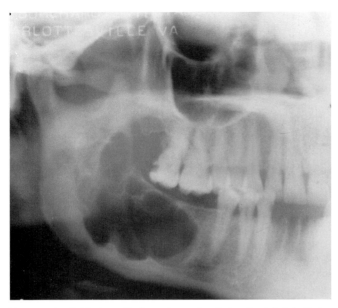

FIG. 14.13. **Ameloblastoma.** Radiograph reveals a destructive, lobulated but peripherally sharply demarcated neoplasm characteristic of ameloblastoma. 78-1014. Modern case. Courtesy Dr R. Elzay. SDUM.

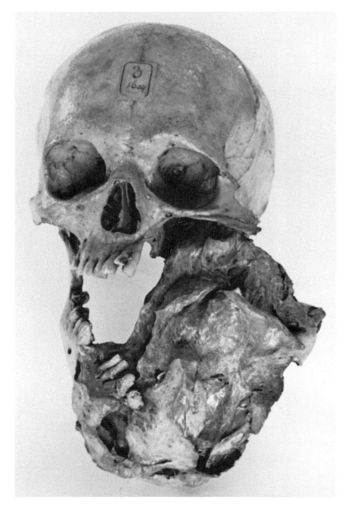

FIG. 14.14. **Ameloblastoma of mandible.** Mandible grossly distorted and destroyed by huge ameloblastoma. Early nineteenth century. Courtesy Dr P. Slootveg, Pathological Institute, State University, Utrecht.

been given the term ameloblastoma. Histologically these are composed of large masses of stellate cells arranged in a pattern suggestive of a dental enamel organ; thus it seems appropriate to label such a jaw tumor with a name suggesting its origin from an enamel-forming cell (though no enamel has ever been found in one) (Spjut et al., 1971). Why such a tumor should appear in the tibial diaphysis (where 90 % of those few outside the skull are found: Murray et al., 1990), remote from the dental apparatus, or the skull base is not obvious. These tumors are very destructive locally, replacing both bone and soft tissue at their site of origin, but they rarely metastasize. They affect persons between 15 and 40 years of age. Most (80 %) begin in the molar area of the mandible, but a minority is found in the maxilla. Radiologically the tumor presents a well-demarcated, trabeculated radiolucency showing multicystic osteolysis ('soap-bubble' pattern) (Fig. 14.3) and measuring from 3–16 cm in maximal diameter. While this appearance is not unlike that of fibrous dysplasia, an ameoloblastoma is generally much larger. A paleopathological example of a huge tumor of this type was found in the jaw of early nineteenth century human remains (Haneveld, 1977) (Fig. 14.14).

Tumors arising from the gingival epithelium are squamous cell carcinoma, identical to other oral cavity tumors discussed in Chapter 8.

Cysts of the jaws

Inflammatory cysts

The abscess forming at the tooth root is an extension of the bacterial infection of acute pulpitis. If the tooth is not extracted the body's immune and inflammatory response often contains the abscess, forming a wall around it composed of granulation tissue infiltrated by chronic inflammatory cells. The size of the abscess is usually between about 5–15 mm, and its cavity is often partially lined by benign squamous epithelium probably derived from some squamous cell rests of Malassez. Projection of the root apex into such a demonstrated cyst easily identifies its nature and origin. In such a chronic state of inflammation it is commonly termed a radicular cyst.

Dentigerous cysts

Unrelated to inflammation, these are related to maldevelopment of the enamel organ. Those that form early before calcified tissue develops are called primordial cysts and may be recognized by paleopathologists as simple unilocular cysts with a smooth lining and without other recognizable calcific tissue structures. Those that develop after the crown has at least partially formed are termed dentigerous follicular cysts. They are associated with unerupted teeth, are most common in the third molar position and betray their nature by a mass

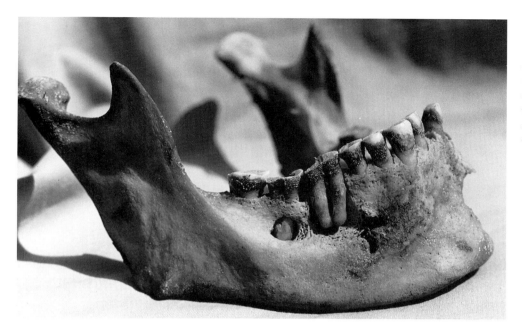

FIG. 14.15. **Osteomyelitis of the mandible.** The several dental-related abscesses have extended considerably beyond the tooth regions and destroyed the entire cortical area covering the roots of the first molar. CHA-40. Coastal southern Peru site, A.D. 1150, Chiribaya culture. Adult male. PBL.

of calcified tissue in the cyst wall that sometimes is even recognizable as a tooth crown. They are benign.

Osteomyelitis

If the infective process creating a root abscess is inadequately contained by the inflammatory and immune response a fistula frequently forms. Occasionally this will follow along a tooth root, emerging at the gingival epithelium attachment at the tooth's cervical area to drain into the oral cavity. More commonly, however, it will traverse the usually thin mandibular cortex over the root abscess, burrow through the overlying mucosa and drain into the oral cavity facially; the minority drain lingually. In the maxilla, perforation into one of the sinuses (usually the maxillary) is common where its suppurative drainage may initiate chronic sinusitis. Rarely it will not perforate the cortex early in either direction but instead will extend into the trabecular bone more distant from the tooth. Such an event will follow the sequence described for osteomyelitis in other bones in Chapter 7, except that sequestra in the mandible or maxilla are uncommon. Eventually a broad area of mandibular or maxillary cortex overlying such a huge abscess will become unroofed and drain (Fig. 14.15). Osteomyelitis of the jaws is a serious and potentially lethal lesion because of its frequently-associated bacteremia and surely must have been responsible for many deaths in antiquity.

Paget's disease

This condition of unknown cause is discussed in detail in Chapter 15. Here we will limit our comments to its effect on dentition. Jaw involvement is common, primarily in the maxilla. The earlier, lytic stage frequently destroys the lamina dura, the structure responsible for anchoring the tooth to the alveolar bone. Once destroyed, the lamina dura can not be reconstructed (Stafne, 1963:309–10). This event stimulates cementoblasts to generate excessive, cellular cementum as a reparative effort. Such a response, in the face of continuing active Paget's disease, is almost invariably unsuccessful and eventually the affected teeth are shed, together with their grossly evident, irregular masses of osteocementum clinging to their roots. Exfoliated teeth so deformed should arouse the suspicion of Paget's disease in the examining paleopathologist.

Acromegaly

Chapter 10 discusses this condition in considerable detail. It will suffice here to comment briefly on its dental effects. The mandible is often a special target for the action of excess growth hormone with the result that it increases in size more than does the maxilla. The increase involves both vertical height as well as length. A consequence of the latter is a more obtuse mandibular angle and a protrusion of the chin. The resulting malocclusion can be of major proportions. The enlarged tongue also impinges on the teeth, tending to separate them and creating a crenated lateral tongue margin. Hypercementosis of the unopposed teeth can be a prominent feature (Burkett, 1946:302–3), while the soft tissues around the separated teeth are vulnerable to development of periodontitis that can lead to tooth loss.

Osteogenesis imperfecta

The hereditary disease resulting in dysfunctional mesodermal products is discussed in Chapter 12 as a condition

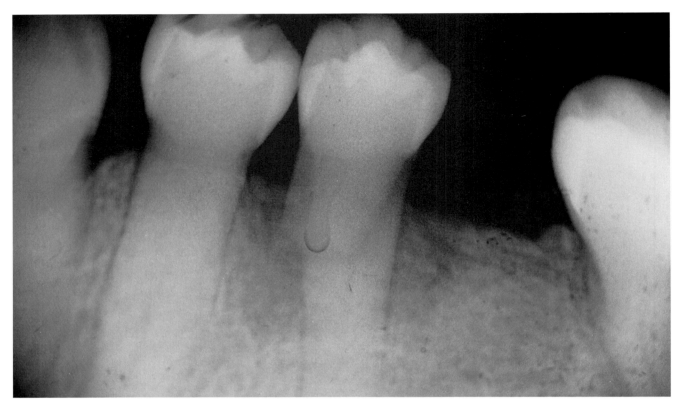

FIG. 14.16. **Odontogenesis imperfecta.** Crown deformities and tooth fracture are secondary to defective underlying dentin. D.K. Modern case.

Courtesy Dr R. Elzay. SDUM.

characterized by formation of abnormal organic, collagenous matrix of bone, rendering it susceptible to fractures. The dental effects, known as odontogenesis imperfecta, are equivalent. Dentin, being of mesodermal origin, is abnormal in structure and is often deposited in irregular, lobulated masses. Its support of overlying enamel is subnormal, resulting in both occlusal and incisal enamel loss through fracture (Fig. 14.16). Crowns already smaller than normal because of deficient dentin deposit,will be reduced further by such enamel fractures. The prematurely exposed dentin is then subject to attrition more rapid than normal. The shortened roots are usually well anchored by normal cementum and periodontium but the pulp canal commonly is diminutive or even absent (Shafer *et al.*, 1983:674).

Tooth mutilation

Unintentional (occupational) mutilation

Unintentional dental mutilation is the modification of tooth form that results from severe abrasion, excessive biting force or a combination of both. It is commonly present on anterior teeth that have been used as a third hand in domestic activities such as stripping plant fiber and softening leather. Stripping procedures create oblique grooves in the biting surface that describes the direction of the pulling force. After

incisal enamel is worn away, the rods of the remaining circumferential enamel, lying perpendicular to the biting force, are vulnerable to traumatic fracture under any number of third hand activities such as opening mollusc shells or cracking nuts. Circumferential enamel subjected to pressures of traumatic proportions may flake off in sizable pieces leaving characteristic vertical voids oriented in the direction of the excessive force. This type of unintentional tooth mutilation is often referred to as pressure chipping (Turner & Cadien, 1969).

Unlike the smooth enamel edges caused by abrasion, fractured enamel presents clear, unburnished margins similar to those of postmortem fracture. If the fractured edge has taken on a dark stain (patina), it is likely that the fracture occurred during life.

Intentional mutilation

Deliberate mutilation of teeth, for no apparent constructive purpose, unrelated to human needs or domestic activity and without therapeutic value, is intentional mutilation. Its purpose is speculative, possibly including personal expression, tribal identification, social stratification or ritual (Linne, 1940). Dental mutilation appears in a variety of loosely related forms ranging from total ablation of incisor teeth or the filing of teeth to the encrustation of teeth with jewelry of stone or metal.

Ablation of healthy teeth

Ablation of healthy teeth is known to have been practiced by young aboriginal Australian males as well as some African tribes (Thoma, 1944:473–55).

Tooth filing

Tooth filing was a common practice in Africa, South America, Mesoamerica and as far north as western Illinois, U.S.A. It persists in some remote South American tribes. It was practiced principally on the young adult as early as age 15 or at puberty. The imagination and creativity of the filers is expressed in a great variety of patterns ranging from shallow surface striations and holes to incisal notches or severe shaping of tooth crowns to a sharp point. Romero's classification of modified teeth in the Americas lists five basic types, each with a number of variants which total 59 individual forms of dental mutilation (Gill, 1985).

Young pulp chambers are large and pulp is very vulnerable to the traumatic insult of rapid removal of protective enamel and dentin. The finding of pulp degeneration and subsequent periapical abscess formation that commonly followed severe filing procedures verifies the antemortem nature of the mutilation. So filing not only severely reduced incisal function, but caused considerable pain and infection (Fastlicht, 1948:319).

The presence and pattern of mutilated teeth can have anthropological predictive value. Handler *et al.* (1986) identified western Africa as the site of tooth filing in several eighteenth century Barbados plantation slaves by demonstrating reduced or absent lead in their bones (implying African birth) in contrast to the high bone lead content of their fellow slaves born in Barbados.

Decorative inlays

The earliest New World cultures for which we have evidence of the preparation of cavities in living teeth for no preventive or therapeutic purposes, and inlay insertions to fit the cavities were the pre-Columbian Mayas and the inhabitants of Esmeraldas in Ecuador (van Rippen, 1917:861). Development of this art reached its peak during the zenith of Mayan culture (A.D. 460–600). Decorative inlaying of teeth, a later and less common practice than tooth filing, may represent a natural refinement of the more primitive filing techniques. Maxillary incisors and canines were the preferred sites for facial surface inlays, although mandibular anterior teeth were occasionally so decorated (Fig. 14.17).

In most instances the cavity preparation was of circular form, although rectangular forms were used in gold encrustation procedures (i.e. strips pounded or cold welded into undercuts in dentin). Unlike the straight-edged defects made by filing, creation of a circular cavity required drilling: the rotation of a stone with chipped edges about a central point in facial enamels. The procedure must have been a slow and meticulous one requiring many sittings in order to provide enough pulpal recovery time for reactive, secondary dentin deposition to preserve tooth vitality. Consequently the majority of cases of circular decorative inlays did not adversely affect pulp vitality (Fastlicht, 1948:320). Some of the numerous reported examples from antiquity could only have been achieved postmortem, but in others antemortem preparation cannot be excluded. The Esmeraldas of Ecuador filed horizontal grooves into facial enamel into which gold strips were fitted (van Rippen, 1917:872).

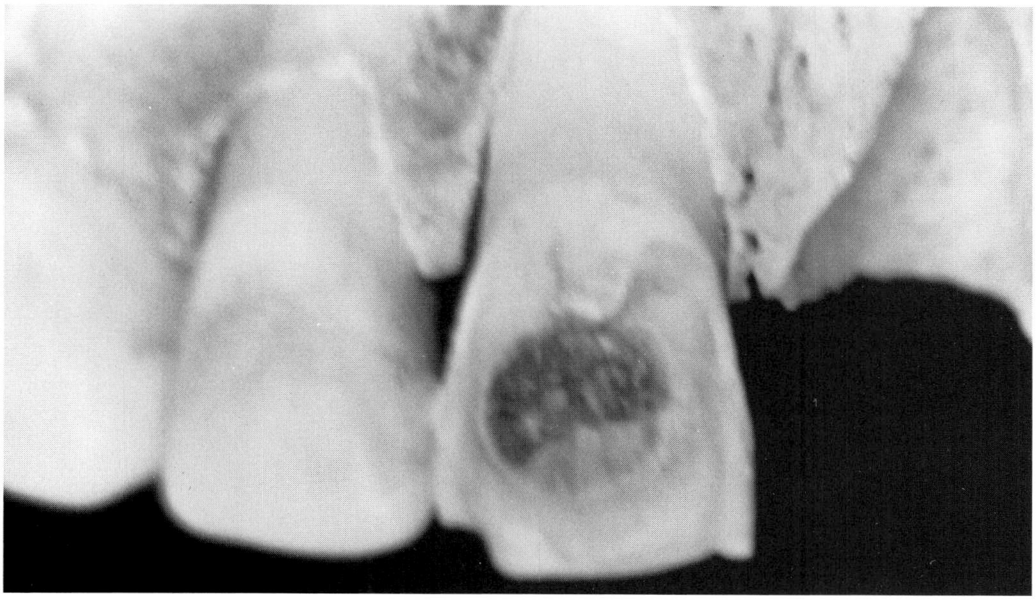

Therapeutics and prostheses

Abundant evidence suggests that botanicals were employed to counter toothache, but unequivocal examples of surgical intervention for pain relief, tooth repair or functional prostheses are rare (Leigh, 1937:294). One of the better-documented cases is that of the precontact skeleton of a New World Inuit (A.D. 1300–1700) in which a hole had been drilled into the root canal of a mandibular incisor, presumably to relieve pain from the pressure of an abscess (Schwartz *et al.*, 1995). However, the interpretation that carious teeth were filled with lead to prevent crown fracture during extraction is controversial. Most alleged examples of tooth stabilization devices or prostheses are either clearly, or most probably,

FIG. 14.17. **Dental inlay defect.** Maxillary central incisor has circular defect created by enamel milling. Inlay material is missing but dark stain in its base may represent adhesive material. To date this appears to be the only example of pre-Columbian inlay effort from Peru, ca. A.D. 250. Courtesy Dr Ellen FitzSimmons, University of Illinois, Chicago (see FitzSimmons *et al.*, 1994).

postmortem alterations. This includes the well-known 'Junker's bridge' from ancient Egypt (Ghalioungui, 1980:63–5) in which two molars abutting an empty socket were joined by fine wire. The one, highly credible Etruscan example (Becker, 1994:76–80) from Valsiarosa was fabricated with a gold band to fit over the lingual and facial surfaces of the four maxillary incisors, one of which was missing. A rivet in the band at the locus of the missing tooth undoubtedly supported a now-missing prosthetic tooth. It was probably designed for cosmetic, not functional purposes.

PART FIFTEEN

Miscellaneous conditions

PAGET'S DISEASE OF BONE

Definition, epidemiology, and etiology

First reported thoroughly as a discrete entity by Sir James Paget in 1876, this is a bone lesion of unknown etiology characterized by a profound increase in both bone resorption and new bone formation resulting in simultaneous mixtures of lytic and sclerotic processes, initiating as a localized condition but often terminating as a widespread state.

The clinical, symptomatic form of the disease is certainly one of older people, most commonly over age 60 years and the prevalence increases with age. However this is often preceded by a decades-long asymptomatic period during which it is found serendipitously, usually by a radiologic study carried out for some other reason. Overall it is found in 2–3 % of adults over 40 years (Krane, 1991:1937). Nevertheless, geographic prevalence rates vary greatly with higher frequencies present in parts of England, Europe, Australia and New Zealand, but rates less than 1 % have been reported from Scandinavia, African Blacks and India (Altman, 1993). Its cause is unknown, though a pattern suggestive of autosomal dominance has been found in about 15 % of the cases. A viral origin (measles? respiratory syncytial virus?) has been suspected on the basis of some morphologic and serologic findings but no unequivocal evidence for such a conclusion has emerged.

Natural history

Clinical features

About 80 % of individuals with Paget's disease of bone in a radiographically surveyed adult population are without symptoms. In the remainder, bone pain is the usual feature leading them to seek medical aid. Predominantly lytic lesions are more apt to be painful than the densely sclerotic ones. During the period of greatest activity the affected area is often palpably warm, probably because of the up to 20-fold increase in blood flow. Eventually compressive changes resulting from thickening of the cranium by new bone formation can produce dysfunction of cranial nerves especially near the skull base where even the brain stem can be compressed, and cord compression can occur due to vertebral involvement (Krane, 1991:1938). The vault bones can thicken sufficiently to compress the cerebral hemispheres, producing a melange of motor or behavioral symptoms. While high serum alkaline phosphatase levels reflect the new bone formation, most afflicted persons have a normal serum calcium level. Eventually widespread disease may become incapacitating.

External morphological changes

The alterations in the individual bones described below can produce certain characteristic effects. These include a moderate kyphosis that is due principally to vertebral body collapse in the lower spine, though in some individuals long bone leg fractures and bowing can also contribute to the shorter stature. Increased cranial blood flow includes the external carotid branches, producing bulging subcutaneous scalp arteries and veins. Frontal area bossing can be prominent. Altman (1993) has characterized the constellation of such effects in advanced stages of this condition as resembling a simian posture.

Skeletal lesions

The frequency of individual bone involvement in decreasing order is pelvis, femur, skull, tibia, lumbar spine, dorsal spine, clavicles and ribs (Krane, 1993: 1938).

Skull

The initial, predominantly lytic phase causes a localized region of radiolucency known as 'osteoporosis circumscripta'. Such an area grossly reveals a loss of trabeculae, though even at that stage the individual, surviving trabeculae already commonly are thickened by new bone formation. In addition both the inner and outer tables can be thinned to the point of difficult radiological recognition. Progression into a mixed and then predominantly sclerotic phase produces new bone at the inner and outer tables and eventually within the diploe as well (Figs. 15.1, 15.2, 15.3 & 15.4). During this phase of many years, new bone production and resorption occur simultaneously, though the degree of each varies from one area to the other. Jaffe (1972:250) emphasizes the enormous irregularity in radiodensity this pro-

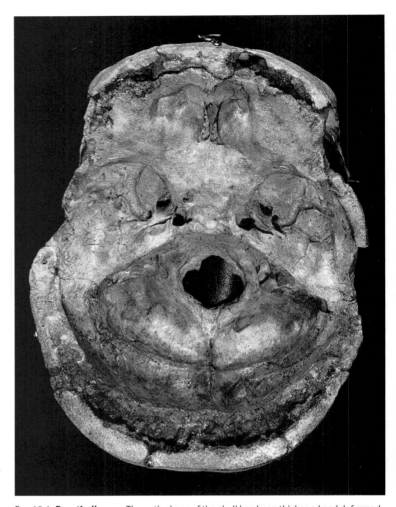

FIG. 15.1. **Paget's disease.** The entire base of the skull has been thickened and deformed by the diffuse action of Paget's disease. Modern elderly male. T-1625. CMNH.

FIG. 15.2. **Paget's disease.** The enormous thickening of the cranial vault bones is demonstrated clearly as are the sclerotic and lytic effects of diffuse Paget's disease. Modern elderly male. T-1625. CMNH.

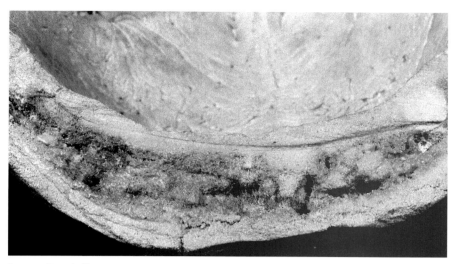

FIG. 15.3. **Paget's disease.** Cranial bone diploe. Combined and simultaneous effects of accelerated osteo-clastic and osteoblastic processes have not only resulted in thickening of the cranial bones, but both scle-rotic bone and bone defects are obvious in the thickened diploe. Modern elderly male. T-1625. CMNH.

FIG. 15.4. **Paget's disease.** Cranial bone diploe. Thickened skull vault tables are separated by diploe show-ing new bone formation ('pumice' appearance) alternating with lytic areas. T-1625. CMNH.

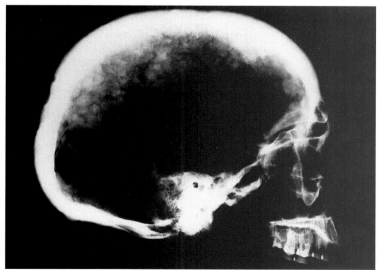

FIG. 15.5. **Paget's disease.** Skull radiograph shows bone thickening and irregular islands of dense, new bone producing characteristic mottled effect. Case 14. Modern old adult from Jaen cemetery, Spain. Courtesy Dr Miguel Botella and Dr D. Campillo. Specimen curated at Universidad de Granada, Spain.

duces and defines the radiologic picture of the lesions during this mixed phase as a 'cotton wool' appearance (Fig. 15.5). He likens the new bone to the granular structure reminiscent of pumice, and also notes that the eventual skull thickness usually does not exceed 2–3 cm (though extreme cases of twice that value have been reported). In addition, while facial bones are usually spared, when they do become enlarged in the late, predominantly sclerotic phase a distortion not unlike leontiasis ossea will result (Jaffe, 1972:250; Ortner & Putschar, 1985:312).

Spine

The lower end of the spine is most frequently involved and in a characteristic manner. All por-tions of the vertebra are affected, though the changes in the vertebral body are most appar-ent. There the periphery of the vertebral body's cancellous bone becomes most dense, often finely granular, while its central area is occupied by much fewer but thicker trabeculae. These localized differences become quite apparent radiologically. Weight-bearing may cause the central portion of the body to yield and become compressed. New bone formation on the hori-zontal surface may widen the vertebra and cause vertebral fusion if the disc degenerates.

Pelvis

The pelvic changes parallel those in the skull but usually do not achieve a similar degree of thickening.

Long bones

The spongiosa at either end of a long bone is usually the ini-tial area of involvement by the lytic process (Fig. 15.6) which then progresses toward the other end with a V-shaped leading edge, trailed by denser bone in the sclerotic phase (Krane, 1991:1939). The cortex becomes thickened, though the medullary cavity is retained (Fig. 15.7). New bone is deposited preferentially on the concave surfaces, causing anterolateral bowing of the femur and lateral tibia bowing. Fissure-like stress fractures (infractions) are com-mon. In addition, the newly-formed bone is lamellar, does not remodel in response to stress-produced effects and therefore does not have the strength of normal bone. The result is a vulnerability to complete, usually transverse, frac-tures that heal well but slowly (Fig. 15.8). In antiquity malalignment must have been common, contributing fur-ther to short stature.

Complications

Development of osteogenic sarcoma in an active lesion is the complication of greatest concern. It occurs in about 2–3 % of the cases, and is believed to arise from the fibrocytes that commonly occupy the space between trabeculae in involved areas. It is a devastating development and usually causes death from lung metastases within 2 years. Jaffe (1972:267) writes that he has never seen a person with Paget's disease survive 5 years after the diagnosis of osteogenic sarcoma.

Paleopathology

The paucity of archaeological case reports is usually explained by the late age at which the disease becomes manifest clinically. However, as noted above, a large fraction of the cases have asymptomatic but radiologically evident single lesions that may begin as early as 40 years of age. This certainly overlaps with the ages examined by paleopathologists. If the current prevalence of at least 1 % of the population was similar in antiquity, then the dearth of case reports more probably reflects the fact that X-raying normal-appearing ancient bones is not yet a universal practice.

No doubt the earliest suggestion of Paget's disease in an archaeological bone is that by Palés (1929:263–7) involving a French Neolithic femur. Ortner & Putschar (1985:315) regard this as a possible candidate for such a diagnosis but no histopathological studies have been performed on it. The exceedingly rapid bone resorption and production in Paget's disease results in a cement line pattern of architectural disarray producing an irregular, mosaic structure. It requires no more than the viewing of a histologic bone section to identify this highly distinctive appearance if the specimen has maintained sufficient postmortem integrity. Today a reader can expect reports of Paget's disease of bone in an archaeological specimen to be accompanied by a description and photomicrograph of such a section's appearance. To date this has not been carried out on this Neolithic specimen.

Saul et al. (1981) describe a partial Maya skeleton from Belize (A.D. 800–1000) including a skull, two humeri and a clavicle whose changes suggest Paget's disease. Unfortunately we have available only an abstract for the paper presented at a conference but he reports that 'preliminary histologic studies...support the strong possibility...' of Paget's disease. An

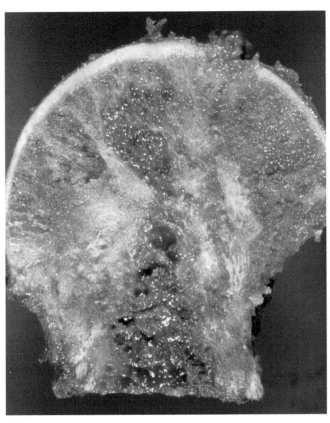

FIG. 15.6. **Paget's disease, humerus.** Irregular pattern of sclerotic and lytic bone reflect features of Paget's disease in this humeral head. Modern elderly male. PBL.

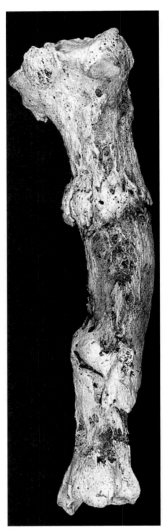

FIG. 15.8. **Paget's disease.** Tibia has become grossly deformed, not only in its diaphyseal silhouette but also its proximal and distal articular surfaces. Two healed transverse fractures testify to the weakness of new bone formed in Paget's disease. Malalignment is responsible for the apparent bowing. Modern elderly male. T-1625. CMNH.

FIG. 15.7. **Paget's disease.** The transected femur cortex of an elderly modern male demonstrates a mixture of bone destruction and production. PBL.

FIG. 15.9. **Leontiasis ossea.** Skull, facial view. Diffuse deposition by unknown causes has distorted the facial features to a grotesque degree. Eighteenth century site (Ohms) from the French Pyrenees. Case 3. Courtesy of Dr D. Campillo, Barcelona. UB.

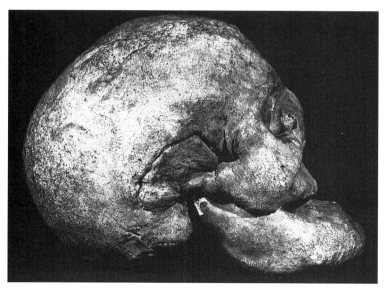

FIG. 15.10. **Leontiasis ossea.** Skull, side view. The deformation of the mandible as well as all facial features by diffuse deposition of new bone by unknown causes is evident. Eighteenth century site (Ohms) from the French Pyrenees. Case 3. Courtesy of Dr D. Campillo, Barcelona. UB.

Anglo-Saxon burial from about A.D. 950 was found to have abnormalities compatible with Paget's disease in most of the skeleton of an elderly male from an English site (Wells & Woodhouse, 1975). Morphologically and radiologically the changes appear consistent with Paget's disease but unfortunately bone architectural preservation was insufficient to permit histological confirmation. Five cases from the central U.S.A. region reported by Denninger (1933) and two by Fisher (1935) as examples of Paget's disease have been re-evaluated (Cook, 1980) and felt to be representative of treponematosis. An adult male skeleton from Norwich prior to A.D. 1468 may be an example of Paget's disease (Stirland, 1990). In addition two medieval skeletons (one an isolated sacrum) demonstrated both gross and histologic changes characteristic of Paget's disease, and the authors (Aaron et al., 1992) add that theirs may be the first example documented histologically.

LEONTIASIS OSSEA

This is a diffuse, chronic and progressive hyperostotic thickening of the cranial vault, facial and jaw bones, eventually distorting them in a cosmetically grotesque manner and frequently interfering with mechanical functions. Since variations are common, it is assumed that the abnormalities collected under this appellation are perhaps several different diseases. Nevertheless, no etiology has been identified for any of them. Until that becomes possible, this term will probably continue to include a potpourri of disorders. It is, however, common practice now to exclude cases in which involvement of bones other than the skull can be identified (Lichtenstein, 1970:132).

Leontiasis ossea was so named not because of its leonine features but because R. Virchow thought this entity was the osseous equivalent of a condition characterized by connective tissue overgrowth (fibroma molluscum) that did have leonine features (Knaggs, 1923). This disease can be subdivided into two main groups based on the nature of the skeletal response: the 'creeping periostitis' type and the 'fibro-osseous' type (Jaffe, 1972:276). The former is characterized by a profound periosteal stimulation that lays down multiple layers of woven bone which, after a long period, eventually become inseparably remodeled into the original bone underlying the new bone formation. Characteristically it begins in the nasal area, spreads to the sinuses, zygomas and orbits as well as the maxilla (Figs. 15.9 & 15.10). Eventually it extends upward to the cranial bones whose sutures retard the process only temporarily. Complications result from interference with sinus drainage, ocular pressure, nasal obstruction and dental function as well as nerve compression. The surface of the deposits is often lumpy and irregular. While an infectious origin has been postulated, none has been established.

The alternative form of skeletal response is one of fibro-osseous reconstruction. The bones may be thickened to the same degree as those with the 'creeping periostitis' form, but the alteration involves the full-thickness of the skull bones. The pre-existing bone structure is resorbed and replaced by areas of new bone of grossly irregular structure and pattern, twisted and separated from each other by fibrous tissue. In contrast to the 'creeping periostitis' type, this 'fibrous osteitis' type has a smoother surface without the lumpiness and excrescences found in the other form (Figs. 15.11 & 15.12). The only condition that could be confused with leontiasis ossea is cranial Paget's disease, but cranial involvement of this degree by Paget's disease could be expected to have accompanying lesions in noncranial sites as well (Jaffe, 1972:281).

Only a few cases of leontiasis ossea have been found in ancient human remains. The Peruvian case in Ortner & Putschar (1985:295, figures 455–7), as well as that in Zimmerman & Kelley (1982:134, figure 110), are dramatic examples and a similar one in Campillo's collections from Catalonia, Spain (Fig. 15.9) is equally characteristic.

Capasso (1989) found a plaster cast of a skull in the National Museum of Anthropology at Florence, Italy. The original skull was from an individual living between the eighteenth and nineteenth century in Italy's Tuscany region. The skull's cast revealed asymmetric enlargement, greater in the mandible, maxilla and zygoma than in the cranial vault. The hyperostosis diminished orbital volume and that of the cranial fossa, reduced cranial foramina and caused edentulism. The author ruled out fibrous dysplasia, Paget's disease, acromegaly, osteopetrosis, Caffey's disease, internal frontal hyperostosis and Brissaud's hemicraniosis, concluding it represented leontiasis ossea.

In addition the skull of an adolescent from the necropolis of La Olmeda (Pedrosa de la Vega, Palencia, Spain and of paleochristian date) showed bone thickening limited to the vault without facial bone involvement. The ectocranial sutures were open and the foramen magnum was so stenotic that the authors felt brain stem compression was the cause of death and the cause was leontiasis ossea (Prim et al., 1995).

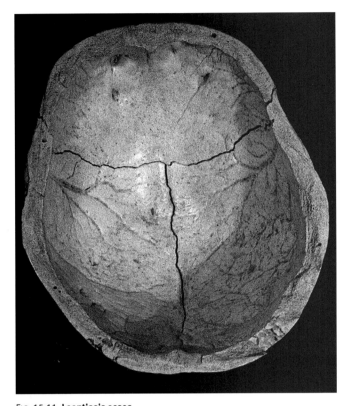

FIG. 15.11. **Leontiasis ossea.** Endocranial view of calvarium. Sclerosis of diploe with enormous thickening of cranial bone is evident. Note lytic effects of Paget's disease are absent. Modern elderly male. E159. CMNH.

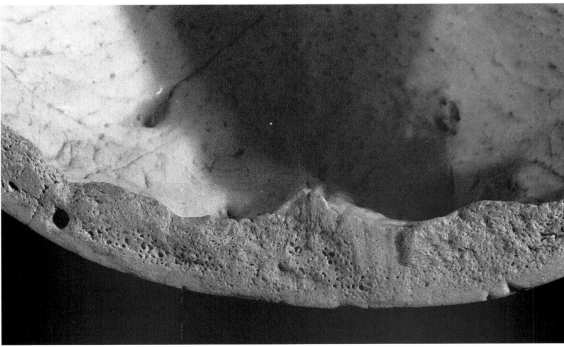

FIG. 15.12. **Leontiasis ossea.** The sclerotic process has almost completely obliterated the cranial bone diploe. Modern elderly male. E159. CMNH.

Hyperostosis frontalis interna

A peculiar thickening of the frontal bone composed of an expansion of the diploic trabecular mass but bulging only inwardly into the cranial cavity has been given this designation. Covered internally by a thin cortical layer it presents an irregular, nodular, cerebriform surface, encroaching as much as several centimeters into the anterior fossa of the cranial cavity but largely restricted to the dural surface of the squamous portion (Fig. 15.13). It is found almost exclusively in women, only about 10 % of which are under 30 years of age (Eldridge & Holm, 1940). In the late eighteenth century the anatomist Morgagni (1719, 1761) reported this finding in an elderly, obese woman with virilism and was rewarded for so doing by the subsequent labeling of this condition as 'Morgagni syndrome' – later also called Stewart–Morel syndrome or metabolic craniopathy (Moore, 1955:182; Jaffe, 1972:272). It has also been seen in acromegaly and pregnancy. For that reason it is assumed that some type of pituitary disorder is at the root of this alteration, but if so its nature has never been defined. The broad area of irregular thickening of the inner aspect of the squamous portion of the frontal bone is so distinctive that differential diagnosis is not a problem. While found in about 5 % of all adult women, the lesion has been identified radiologically in more than half of a studied group of women in the postmenopausal age period (Gerschon-Cohen et al., 1955).

Several paleopathology reports testify to its antiquity including cases from Nubia (Armelagos & Chrisman, 1988), Egypt (Watrous et al., 1993), Anglo-Saxon period in Britain (Anderson, 1994), Italy in the Roman imperial era (Sperduti & Manzi, 1990), Viking ship burial (Moore, 1955) and Poland (Gladykowsky-Rzeczcka, 1988).

Generalized hyperostosis with pachydermia (pachydermo-hyperostosis)

Jaffe (1972:291–8) describes the active phase of this strange, disabling disorder as usually beginning during adolescence, characterized by fibrous tissue thickening of subcutaneous fat in the hands and feet with production of clubbed fingers and spoon nails. The underlying bones demonstrate sufficient subperiosteal new lamellar bone formation to convert the phalanges into featureless tubular cylinders. This process of skin thickening with underlying new bone formation subsequently spreads to involve most of the skeletal elements, though the skull is relatively spared except for facial involvement. Late complications include joint ankylosis and ossification of the costovertebral, spinal and long bone interosseous ligaments, causing movement limitations and kyphosis. Radiculopathology and even cord myelomalacia can occur by involvement of the intervertebral foramina and spinal canal. The chronic phase persists long enough to allow the periosteal newly formed bone to be remodeled imperceptibly into the original long bone cortices. Histologically this remodeling encroaches upon and may seriously compromise the marrow space.

Differential diagnosis must exclude pulmonary hypertrophic osteoarthropathy and acromegaly. In the former, death usually occurs before the newly formed bone has had time to become incorporated into the original cortex (Jaffe, 1972:298) and the facial bones normally are not involved. Acromegalics commonly demonstrate an enlarged and often irregular sella turcica, an exceptionally prominent mandible and tufting of distal phalanges.

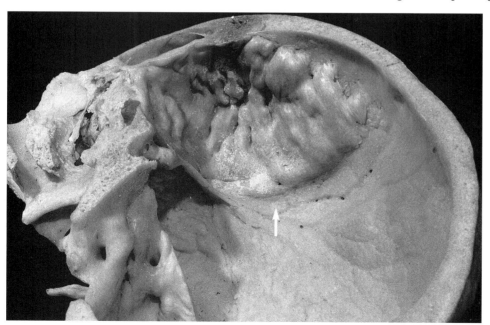

FIG. 15.13. **Hyperostosis frontalis interna.** Irregular, smooth-surfaced bone masses heaped up on endocranial aspect of the frontal bone. Modern, elderly female. T-967. CMNH.

Paleopathology

We could find only one report of this rare condition in the paleopathology literature. Allison et al. (1976) identified the condition in the partial, adult Peruvian skeleton from the Huari culture (about A.D. 1000) near Ica, Peru. A left femur, right hip and two ribs were recovered from a looted tomb. They were unusually heavy (the femur weighed 750 g) due to enormous cortical thickening that had also extended endosteally to virtually replace the marrow cavity. Unfortunately no soft tissue was available for study.

FIBROUS DYSPLASIA OF BONE
(FIBRO-OSSEOUS DYSPLASIA)

Definition, etiology, epidemiology, and pathology

Fibrous dysplasia is a common, idiopathic arrest of bone maturation resulting in localized foci of fibrous tissue with or without calcification within bone, sometimes accompanied by apparent endocrine disturbances. Its onset is commonly in childhood or adolescence, and almost always under age 30 years. Three-fourths of the affected persons are female; no familial pattern is known (Bullough, 1992).

The typically affected long bone demonstrates expansion of most any portion other than epiphyses (Fig. 15.14). Though the periosteum may often lay down a thin shell of new bone, the outer surface remains smooth while the endosteal surface of the thinned cortex is often ridged (Fig.15.15). Craniofacial lesions may produce asymmetry

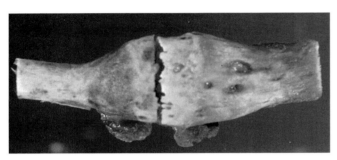

FIG. 15.14. **Fibrous dysplasia, rib.** Rib is expanded to twice normal diameter. Transection line is the result of a saw cut by the examining pathologist. Modern young adult male. PBL.

FIG. 15.15. **Fibrous dysplasia, rib.** Closeup view of transected surface of interior of the lesion shown in Fig. 15.14. It is about 2.5 cm in diameter, has a partly cystic and partly fibrous, benign structure. Modern young adult male. PBL.

sinus obliteration, hypertelorism, sphenoid wing and temporal distortion (Feldman, 1989) as well as mandibular involvement. Histologically the lesion's structure may be nearly entirely fibrous, though more commonly at least some calcification is scattered irregularly through the connective tissue. Quite frequently the calcification is the dominant feature of the lesion. The lesion's periphery is quite sharply demarcated. The condition may involve only one bone (monostotic form) or many (polyostotic form), but the pathologic nature of the lesion is identical in both forms. Malignant transformation (fibrosarcoma, malignant fibrous histiocytoma, chondrosarcoma, osteosarcoma) with metastasizing potential only occurs in less than 1 % of the cases (Spjut *et al.*, 1971; Aegerter & Kirkparick, 1975, Lichtenstein, 1977:17). Radiographically the sharply defined lesions may appear cystic and lytic or sclerotic ('ground glass': Helms, 1989) with a thin zone of reactive sclerosis, a thin cortex and cystic trabeculated medullary appearance.

Bone distribution in fibrous dysplasia

Monostotic form

Most (80 %) of the cases are monostotic (Feldman, 1989), usually coming to attention by an incidental X-ray or by pathological fracture. While no bone is immune to this condition, those of the lower limb are most commonly affected, followed by the pelvis, ribs, jaws, humerus and skull vault. Craniofacial bones are involved in 20 % of monostotic cases.

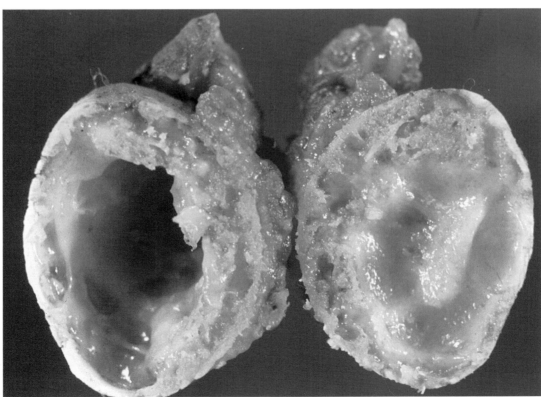

Polyostotic form

Though in most of these cases the distribution is uniquely unilateral, an occasional, florid expression of early childhood presents as a bilateral, extensively distributed, asymmetric process (Lichtenstein, 1977:11; Feldman, 1989). About half of these persons have skull and facial bone involvement; the pelvis, shoulder and proximal limb bones are affected preferentially and earlier (Ortner & Putschar, 1985). Spine lesions are uncommon, though ribs involved by this condition are the most common rib lesion of persons less than 30 years old.

Complications

Except for the rare, malignant degeneration, the most serious complication in either monostotic or polyostotic forms is pathological fracture. These heal promptly and well but recurring fractures can be quite deforming. A particularly common event is a succession of fractures in the subtrochanteric area of the femur that can distort the proximal femur into a 'shepherd's crook' shape whose appearance is considered almost diagnostic of fibrous dysplasia.

Extraskeletal features

The combination of polyostotic fibrous dysplasia and a variety of endocrine-like disturbances is known as Albright's syndrome or McCune–Albright's syndrome. These additional features may take the form of premature sexual development and blotchy skin pigmentation in girls. Other alterations include hyperthyroidism, disturbances of the ovary, pituitary and parathyroid glands as well as cardiovascular problems.

Paleopathology

If the fibrous lesion is not calcified or partially ossified, the degeneration of the fibrous tissue postmortem will present the lesion as an often smooth-lined, unicameral, empty cystic structure indistinguisable from unicameral bone cyst, non-ossifying fibroma, enchondroma, eosinophilic granuloma or even giant cell tumor. Preservation of fine or coarsely woven, irregular bone trabeculae will be more suggestive of fibrous dysplasia (Ortner & Putschar, 1985:317).

Case reports include an adult male from about A.D. 650 in England with a bowed, expanded humeral diaphysis with radiological and pathologically demonstrable cortical thinning and multiple cystic medullary lesions containing fibro-osseous tissue (Wells, 1963b). A dramatic example from Illinois, U.S.A. about A.D. 1000 was a 35 year old male whose bones of his entire left side and a few from the right were involved by expansion, bending, erosions, cortical thinning, cysts and areas of abnormal, sponge-like bone (Denninger, 1931). A twelfth dynasty young adult female skull from Lisht, Egypt is described by Ortner & Putschar (1985:231) as showing involvement of the frontal bone near the frontal sinus.

SKELETAL NEUROFIBROMATOSIS (VON RECKLINGHAUSEN'S DISEASE)

Definition, etiology, and epidemiology

Neurofibromatosis is a hereditary, sometimes congenital condition of the central and peripheral nervous system also involving the skeleton, skin (focal, brown pigmented areas called 'cafe-au-lait' spots) and other organs. The inheritance pattern is that of an autosomal dominant with variable penetrance and without gender or racial preference. Its frequency is about 1/3000 live births and the condition usually becomes detectible between 4 and 8 years of age. A mutated tumor suppressor called NF1 permits peripheral nerve tumor growth while that of a different gene (NF2) stimulates tumor growth of the eighth cranial (acoustic) nerve.

Natural history and pathology

The neurofibromatosis type 1 (NF1) condition is characterized by the production of often dozens or even hundreds of small tumor masses scattered throughout the cutaneous and subcutaneous tissues of the entire body. Derived from neuroectodermal and mesenchymal tissue, they are composed principally of nerve sheath (Schwann) cells, fibrous tissue and nerve elements. Their average size is about 1 cm but occasional huge tumors are encountered. Involvement of interspinal nerves is common. In about 4 % of the cases malignant degeneration (neurofibrosarcoma) develops that is capable of lethal, blood-borne metastases (Rubin & Farber, 1992c:229). Bones are involved in about 10–40 % of neurofibromatosis cases. Surface cortical erosion by a soft tissue neurofibroma adjacent to the bone may occur. Kyphosclerosis is seen in about half of the cases with vertebral wedging and scalloping as well as pedicle erosions. Interspinal nerve involvement may widen the interspinal foramina with smooth edges (Ortner & Putshcar, 1985). Lower limb involvement may cause bowing with unequal long bone lengths. Defective callus formation after pathological fractures leads to pseudoarthrosis, especially in the tibia and ulna. Enlargement of hand and foot bones is common. Cranial bone involvement can produce facial deformity, maxillary and ethmoid sinus hypoplasia and sphenoid distortion with orbital defects. Radiological features are variable

(Wynne-Davies & Fairbank, 1982), showing osteoporosis, hyperostosis and subperiosteal bone cysts (Duthie & Bentley, 1987) as well as cortical erosions: 'subperiosteal blisters' (Spjut et al., 1971). Associated anomalies include spina bifida, vertebral blocks and congenital hip dislocation. Accompanying intracranial meningiomas occur (Aegerter & Kirkpatrick, 1975). The condition has a tendency to slow its progression after epiphyses fuse but may be reactivated later. Pituitary compression from cranial involvement may superimpose the picture of panhypopituitarism.

Neurofibromatosis type 2 (NF2). These individuals lack peripheral nerve involvement, but they develop bilateral neurofibromas (Schwannomas) on the acoustic nerve. It is much more rare: 1/50 000 live births. Skeletal involvement is largely limited to enlargement of the acoustic meatus and canal secondary to the tumors (schwannomas) on the nerve. Despite the similarity of tumors, these two types are not merely variants but rather are distinct entities, each being brought about by mutations of different genes: NF1 on chromosome 17 and NF2 on chromosome 22 (Rubin & Farber, 1994c:230).

Paleopathology

Although soft tissue lesions ought to be obvious in well-preserved mummified remains, none have been reported. We could only find one case report in skeletal tissue, reported by Thillaud (1996) in the skull of a pre-Hispanic aboriginal from northern Chile. Predominantly osteoblastic lesions with deformity were noted in the left side of the skull.

HARRIS LINES (GROWTH ARREST LINES; GROWTH RECOVERY LINES; TRANSVERSE LINES; TRANSVERSE TRABECULAE)

Definition, etiology, and epidemiology

Harris lines are transverse lines of radiodensity at the ends of long bones (Fig. 15.16). They are of paleopathologic interest because of their alleged relationship to major physiological insults of sufficient magnitude to conserve the body's energy by transient retardation or arrest of long bone growth. Experimental reproduction of such lines in animals has demonstrated a slowing of the rate of cartilage cell division in the growth plate during such insults but with continuing mineralization, producing a segment of increased mineralization visualized radiographically as a transverse band of radiopacity (Goodman & Clark, 1981). In more detailed studies it was noted that the epiphyseal cartilage plate became thinner (decreased chondrogenesis) with increasing resistance of the immature cartilage cells to capillary and osteoblast penetration. A primary stratum of a thin osteoblastic layer is then laid down, replacing the mature cartilage cells below the epiphyseal plate. Upon cessation of the stressful episode osteoblasts of the primary stratum produce horizontally-oriented trabeculae (Fig. 15.17). This defines the production of the line as occurring during an interval following the stress,

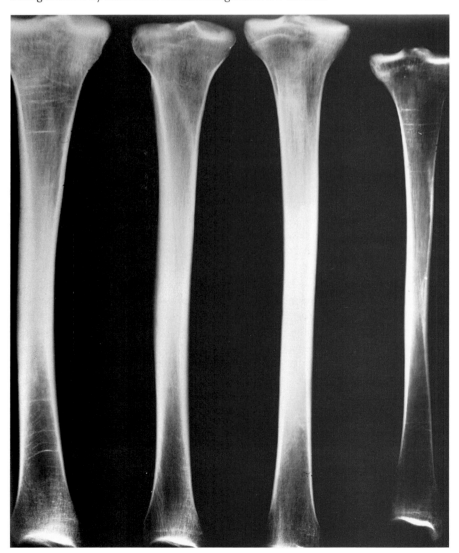

FIG. 15.16. **'Harris' lines.** Note multiple transverse radiologically-evident lines in distal ends of tibiae. G55. Guanches ca. A.D. 1000. MAT. OAMC.

leading Armelagos (1990) to note that such lines are evidence of the individual's ability to recover from a major, stressful episode.

Once formed, such lines are subject to the loss of bone mineral commonly beginning about age 20 years as well as bone remodeling effects. The result is that sufficient loss of bone mineral can occur so that the lines are no longer radiographically demonstrable (Larsen, 1987). Only about one-fourth of lines in subadults persist into adulthood (Steinbock, 1976). In many studies the number of lines in subadults are as much as four times greater than in adults. Furthermore the lines tend to cluster into a postnatal interval and again shortly before growth ceases in the mid-teens. Females tend to generate such lines substantially more often than males in most, but not all, studies, though some question that observation (Huss-Ashmore *et al.*, 1982). Lines are usually bilateral symmetrical (Vyhnánek & Stloukal, 1991).

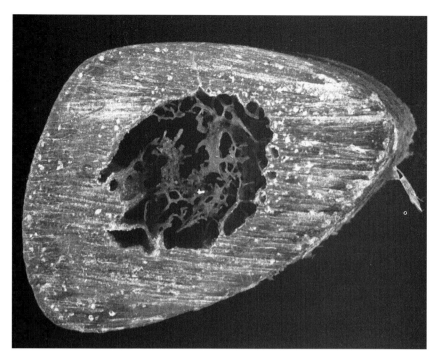

Fig. 15.17. **Harris line.** The line was located radiographically. The tibia was sectioned in that area to display it. Visualized transversely on the X-ray plate, this ragged web of delicate bone spicules appears as a distinct, narrow line. Adult male Guanche. PBL.

Interpretation of Harris lines

Variables involved in Harris line production and interpretation

- Radiological interpretation. Bone dissection following radiography demonstrates that a transverse radiographic line may be of incomplete or cribriform structure. Hence investigators vary in their definition of what is scored as a Harris line; some accepting a line that traverses only one-fourth of the medullary width while others demand the full diameter. Oblique lines are counted by some workers but not by others (Garn *et al.*, 1968; Martin *et al.*, 1985).
- Age. Since Harris lines gradually disappear with age, inclusion of subadults will result in larger numbers of lines than if only adults are measured (Martin *et al.*, 1985).
- Prediction of age of Harris line occurrence. Frequency of line formation correlates positively with the periods of greatest rate of growth in childhood (Symes, 1983). This suggests sensitivity of line formation to given physiological stresses may vary at different childhood ages. An assumption of growth linearity during childhood can also confound prediction of age at which the line was formed.
- Correlation of Harris line production with other alleged stress indicators (enamel hypoplasia etc) is poor. Whether this reflects differences in sensitivity, specificity or both is unclear (Wells, 1967*b*; Buikstra & Cook, 1980; Roberts & Manchester, 1995).

- A huge variety of conditions have been believed to be the cause of Harris line production including influenza, measles, surgery, starvation, vitamin deficiencies, emotional stress and others. However it is clear that it is not possible to predict the cause of a given line nor the duration of the condition.
- Bones and bone sites affected. Most common locations in order of frequency are proximal tibia, distal tibia, distal femur, distal radius, metacarpals and anterior rib ends (Garn *et al.*, 1968; Larsen, 1987). The number of lines varies among these sites in the same individual.
- Interobserver variations are substantial. Because these listed variables have not been standardized, present methods of Harris line assessment does not allow comparisons of interobserver results. Most workers, however, feel that a given observer can standardize a technique that incorporates the above variables and then employ such a method to compare two or more populations. Even then Huss-Ashmore *et al.* (1982) suggest conservative interpretations of results unless some other measurement of nonspecific stress indicator is also included in the study.

Paleopathology of Harris line studies

Wells (1967*b*) initiated the application of Harris line evaluation in archaeological population comparisons of health status. Allison *et al.* (1974*a*) compared highland with coastal populations on the basis of Harris lines, concluding that the higher values of coastal people may have been due to malaria. A study of aboriginal Americans (A.D. 959–1300) of the Dickson Mounds in Illinois found the distal tibia had more lines than the proximal; Harris lines resorbed in adulthood; distal bone lines peaked in infancy and again about puberty; males developed lines earlier than females and that no significant differences between Dickson cultural horizons were demonstrable (Goodman & Clark, 1981). Canary Island Tenerife's aboriginals (Guanches) showed no difference in Harris line patterns between the north and south sides of the island in spite of dramatic dietary differences, though females had almost twice as many lines as males. Using stable isotope ratios of nitrogen and carbon to assess the nature of the diet, no correlations with Harris lines could be demonstrated (Kelley & Boom, 1995). A further study of the same group by Rodríguez Martín (1995c) revealed that half of the males but only one-fourth of the females were free of lines, and that females not only had more lines per individual but that they developed them earlier, leading him to conclude that, compared with males, females played a secondary role in the Guanche society.

References

Aaron, J.E., Rogers, J. & Kanis, J.E. (1992) Paleo-histology of Paget's disease in two medieval skeletons. *American Journal of Physical Anthropology* **89**(3):325–31.

Aaronson, S. (1989) Fungal parasites of grasses and cereals: Their role as food or medicine, now and in the past. *Antiquity* **63**:247–57.

Abbott, K.H. & Courville, C.B. (1939) Historical notes on the meningiomas. *Bulletin of the Los Angeles Neurological Society* **4**:101–13.

Abel, L., Cua, V.V., Oberti, J., Lap, V.D., Due, L.K., Grosset, J. & Lagrange, P.H. (1990) Leprosy and BCG in southern Vietnam. *Lancet* **335**:1536. (Letter).

Abel, O. (1924) Neure Studien über Krankheiten fossiler Wirbeltiere (New studies of fossilized vertebrate diseases). *Verhandlung der zoologische botanische Gesellschaft Wien (Vienna)* **73**:104.

Abraham, J.L., Hunt, A., Burnett, B., Allison, M. & Gerstzen, E. (1990) Light microscopic and microanalytic study of lungs from pre-Colombian Chilean mummies: Correlations with cultural data and comparison with contemporary pneumoconiosis. (Department of Pathology, Medical College of Virginia, Richmond, VA) *Paleopathology Club Newsletter* **41**:3–5.

Abrutyn, E. (1991) Botulism. In *Harrison's Principles of Internal Medicine,* ed. J. D. Wilson, E. Braunwald, K. J. Isselbacher, *et al.*, 12th edn, pp. 579–80. New York: McGraw-Hill.

Ackerknecht, E.H. (1971) *Medicine and Ethnology. Selected Essays*. Baltimore: Johns Hopkins Press.

Ackerknecht, E.H. (1972) *History and Geography of the Most Important Diseases*. New York: Hafner Publishing Co.

Acquatella, H. (1993) Case records of the Massachusetts General Hospital. *New England Journal of Medicine* **329**:488–96.

Adams, J.C. (1986) *Manual de Ortopedia (Manual of Orthopedics)*, 4th edn. Barcelona: Toray.

Adelfang, K. (1991) Scurvy in medical dissertations of the seventeenth and eighteenth centuries. *Bulletin of the History of Dentistry* **39**:73–6.

Adelson, L. (1974) *The Pathology of Homicide*. Springfield, IL: C.C. Thomas.

Aegerter, E. & Kirkpatrick, J.A. (1975) *Orthopedic Diseases. Physiology, Pathology, Radiology*, 4th edn. Philadelphia: W.B. Saunders.

Ainsworth, G.C. (1993a) Fungus infection (mycoses). In *The Cambridge World History of Human Disease*, ed. K.F. Kiple, pp. 730–6. New York: Cambridge University Press.

Ainsworth, G.C. (1993b) Fungus poisoning. In *The Cambridge World History of Human Disease*, ed. K.F. Kiple, pp. 736–7. New York: Cambridge University Press.

Alciati, G., Fedeli, M. & Delfino, V.P. (1987) *La Malattia dalla Preistoria all'Età Antica (Disease: From Prehistory to Ancient Ages)*. Bari: Laterza.

Aldhous, P. (1993) Malaria: Focus on mosquito genes. *Science* **261**:546–8.

Aldin, D. & Miller, J. (1987) Unwanted cargoes: The origins and dissemination of smallpox via the slave trade from Africa to Brazil. In *The African Exchange*, ed. K. F. Kiple, pp. 35–109. Durham, NC: Duke University Press.

Aldred, C. (1963) *Akhenaten and Nefertiti*. New York: Viking Press.

Alexandersen, E.V. (1967) The pathology of the jaws and temporomandibular joint. In *Diseases in Antiquity*, ed. D. Brothwell &

A.T. Sandison, pp. 551–95. Springfield, IL: C.C. Thomas.

Allen, W.H., Merbs, C.F. & Birkby, W.H. (1985) Evidence for prehistoric scalping at Nuvakwewtaqa (Chavez Pass) and Grasshopper Ruin, Arizona. In *Health and Disease in the Prehistoric Southwest*, ed. C.F. Merbs & R.J. Miller. Anthropological Research Papers no. 34, pp. 23–42. Tempe, AZ: Department of Anthropology, Arizona State University.

Allison, A.C. (1954) Protection afforded by sickle cell trait against subtertian malarial infection. *British Medical Journal* **1**:290–4.

Allison, M.J. (1981a) Case No. 7: Polycystic kidney disease. (Department of Pathology, Medical College of Virginia, Richmond, VA) *Paleopathology Club Newsletter* **9**:1.

Allison, M.J. (1981b) Case No. 8: Fibrinous pericarditis. (Department of Pathology, Medical College of Virginia, Richmond, VA) *Paleopathology Club Newsletter* **10**:1.

Allison, M.J. (1984a) Paleopathology in Peruvian and Chilean populations. In *Paleopathology at the Origins of Agriculture*, ed. M.N. Cohen & G.J. Armelagos, pp. 515–29. New York: Academic Press.

Allison, M.J. (1984b) Case No. 16: Emphysema. (Department of Pathology, Medical College of Virginia, Richmond, VA) *Paleopathology Club Newsletter* **19**:1.

Allison, M.J. (1988) Simple techniques for the evaluation of osteoporosis in paleopathology. (Department of Pathology, Medical College of Virginia, Richmond, VA) *Paleopathology Club Newsletter* **33**:14–15.

Allison, M.J. (1992) Case No. 47: Nasal polyp. (Department of Pathology, Medical College of Virginia, Richmond, VA) *Paleopathology Club Newsletter* **51**:1.

Allison, M.J. (1993) Chagas' disease. In *The Cambridge World History of Human Disease*, ed. K.F. Kiple, pp. 636–8. New York: Cambridge University Press.

Allison, M.J. & Gerszten, E. (1978) Case No. 1: Primary, generalized hyperostosis. (Department of Pathology, Medical College of Virginia, Richmond, VA) *Paleopathology Club Newsletter* **1**:1.

Allison, M.J. & Gerszten, E (1981) Case No. 9: Uta, granuloma or carcinoma (Department of Pathology, Medical College of Virginia, Richmond, VA) *Paleopathology Club Newsletter* **12**:1.

Allison, M.J. & Gerszten, E. (1983) Case No. 13: Hydronephrosis of the kidney, trauma, homicide, decapitation, abdominal laceration. (Department of Pathology, Medical College of Virginia, Richmond, VA) *Paleopathology Club Newsletter* **16**:1.

Allison, M.J. & Gerszten, E. (1989) Case No. 35: Smallpox. (Department of Pathology, Medical College of Virginia, Richmond, VA) *Paleopathology Club Newsletter* **39**:2.

Allison, M.J. & Pezzia, A. (1976) Treatment of head wounds in pre-Columbian and colonial Peru. (Medical College of Virginia, Richmond, VA) *MCV Quarterly* **12**(**2**):74–9.

Allison, M.J., Mendoza, J. & Pezzia, A. (1973) Documentation of a case of tuberculosis in pre-Columbian America. *American Review of Respiratory Disease* **107**:985–91.

Allison, M.J., Mendoza, D. & Pezzia, A. (1974a) A radiographic approach to childhood illness in pre-Columbian inhabitants of southern Peru. *American Journal of Physical Anthropology* **40**:409–15.

Allison, M.J, Pezzia, A., Gerszten, E. & Mendoza, D. (1974b) A case of Carrion's disease associated with human sacrifice from the Huari culture of southern Peru. *American Journal of Physical Anthropology* **41**:295–300.

Allison, M. J., Pezzia, A., Hasegawa, I. & Gerszten, E. (1974c) A case of hookworm infestation in a pre-Columbian American. *American Journal of Physical Anthropology* **41**:103–6.

Allison, M.J., Pezzia, A., Gerszten, E., Giffler, R.F. & Mendoza, D. (1974d) Aspiration pneumonia due to teeth: A report of two cases, 950 A.D. and 1973 A.D. *Southern Medical Journal* **67**:479–83.

Allison, M.J., Gerszten, E., Sotil, R. & Pezzia, A. (1976) Primary generalized hyperostosis in ancient Peru. (Medical College of Virginia, Richmond, VA) *MCV Quarterly* **12**(**2**):49–51.

Allison, M.J., Gerszten, E., Shadomy, J.H., Munizaga, J. & Gonzalez, M. (1979) Paracoccidioidomycosis in a northern Chilean mummy. *Bulletin of the New York Academy of Medicine* **55**:670–83.

Allison, M.J., Gerszten, E., Munizaga, J. & Santoro, C. (1980) Metastatic tumor of bone in a Tihuanako female. *Bulletin of the New York Academy of Medicine, Second Series* **56**(**6**):581–7.

Allison, M.J., Gerszten, E., Munizaga, J., Santoro, C. & Focacci, G. (1981a) La práctica de la deformacion craneana entre los pueblos andinos precolombinos (The practice of cranial deformation among pre-Columbian Andean populations). *Chungará* (*Arica*, *Chile*) **8**:238–60.

Allison, M.J., Gerszten, E., Munizaga, J., Santoro, C. & Mendoza, D. (1981b) Tuberculosis in pre-Columbian Andean populations. In *Prehistoric Tuberculosis in the Americas*, ed. J. E. Buikstra, pp. 49–62. Evanston, IL: Northwestern University Archaeological Program.

Allison, M.J., Gerszten, E. & Fouant, M. (1982) Paleopathology: Today's laboratory investigates yesterday's diseases. *Diagnostic Medicine* (**Sept/Oct**) **1982**:28–44.

Allison, M.J., Arriaza, B.T., Focacci, G. & Muñoz, I. (1983) Los orejones de Arica (The orejones of Arica). *Chungará* (*Arica*, *Chile*) **11**:167–72.

Alt, K.W. & Adler, C.P. (1992) Multiple myeloma in an early medieval skeleton. *International Journal of Osteoarchaeology* **2**:205–9.

Altman, R.D. (1993) Paget's disease in bone. In *The Cambridge World History of Human Disease*, ed. K. F. Kiple, pp. 911–13. New York: Cambridge University Press.

Alva, W. & Donnan, C. (1993) *Royal Tombs of Sipán*. Los Angeles: Fowler Museum of Cultural History.

American Thoracic Society (1990) Diagnosis and treatment of disease caused by nontuberculous mycobacteria. *American Review of Respiratory Diseases* **142**:940–53.

Amillo, S., Villas, C. & Cañadell, J. (1991) *Manual de Ortopedia y Traumatología* (*Manual of Orthopedics and Traumatology*). Pamplona: EUNATE.

Ancill, H. (1852) *A Treatise on Tuberculosis. The Constitutional Origin of Consumption and Scrofula*. London: Longman, Brown, Green and Longman.

Andersen, J.G. (1969) Studies in the medieval diagnosis of leprosy in Denmark. An osteoarchaeological, historical and clinical study. *Danish Medical Bulletin* **16**:1–142.

Andersen, J.G. & Manchester, K. (1992) The rhinomaxillary syndrome in leprosy: A clinical, radiological and paleopathological study. *International Journal of Osteoarchaeology* **2**(**2**):121–9.

Andersen, J.G., Manchester, K. & Shahzady Ali, R. (1992) Diaphyseal remodelling in leprosy: Radiological and paleopathological study. *International Journal of Osteoarchaeology* **2**(**3**):211–19.

Andersen, S.R. (1994) *The Eye and Its Diseases in Antiquity*. Copenhagen: Rhodos.

Anderson, T. (1994) An Anglo-Saxon case of hyperostosis frontalis interna from Sarre, Kent. *Journal of Paleopathology* **6**(**1**):29–34.

Anderson, T. & Carter, A.R. (1993) The first archaeological example of Freiberg's infraction. *International Journal of Osteoarchaeology* **3**:219–21.

Anderson, T. & Carter, A.R. (1994) A possible example of Scheuermann's disease from Iron Age, Deal, Kent. *Journal of Paleopathology* **6**(**2**):57–62.

Anderson, T. & Carter, A.R. (1995) The first achaeological case of Madelung's deformity? *International Journal of Osteoarchaeology* **5**:168–73.

Anderson, T., Wakely, J. & Carter, A.R. (1992) Medieval example of metastatic carcinoma: A dry bone, radiological and SEM study. *American Journal of Physical Anthropology* **89**:309–23.

Andrews, A.P. (1974) The u-shaped structures at Chan-Chan, Peru. *Journal of Field Archaeology* **1**:241–64.

Angel, J.L. (1967) Porotic hyperostosis or osteoporosis symmetrica. In *Diseases in Antiquity*, ed. D. Brothwell & A.T. Sandison , pp. 378–89. Springfield, IL: C.C. Thomas.

Angel, J. L. (1973) Human skeletons from grave circles at Mycenae. In *The Grave Circle B of Mycenae*, ed. G.E. Mylonas, Appendix, pp. 379–97. Athens: Archaeological Society of Athens.

Angel, J.L. (1977) Anemias of antiquity: Eastern Mediterranean. In *Porotic Hyperstosis: An Enquiry, Monograph 32*, ed. E. Cockburn & A. Cockburn, pp. 1–5. Detroit: Paleopathology Association.

Angel, J.L. (1978) Porotic hyperstosis in the eastern Mediterranean. (Medical College of Virginia, Richmond, VA) *MCV Quarterly* **14(1)**:10–16.

Angel, J.L. (1981) History and development of paleopathology. *American Journal of Physical Anthropology* **56**:509–15.

Angel, J.L. & Caldwell, P.C. (1984) Death by strangulation. A forensic anthropological case from Wilmington, Delaware. In *Human Identification*, ed. T.A. Rathbun & J.E. Buikstra, pp. 168–75. Springfield, IL: C.C. Thomas.

Anonymous (1980) Decline and fall of the smallpox empire. *World Health* **May 1980**:24–5.

Anonymous (1985) The virus in the crypt. *New Scientist* **18**:19.

Anton, S.C. (1988) Bony criteria for differentiation of metastatic carcinoma, multiple myeloma, major infectious diseases and hyperparathyroidism: A case study approach. In *Human Skeletal Biology: Contributions To The Understanding of California's Prehistoric Populations*, ed. G.D. Richards, pp. 43–8. Archives of California's Prehistory no. 24. Salinas, CA: Coyote Press.

Apley, A.G. (1981) *Ortopedia y Tratamiento de Fracturas* (*Orthopedics and Treatment of Fractures*). Barcelona: Salvat.

Apley, A.G. & Solomon, L. (1992) *Manual de Ortopedia y Fracturas* (*Manual of Orthopedics and Fractures*). Barcelona: Masson-Salvat Medicina.

Arendt, W. & Ullrich, H. (1970) Vorkommen einer sekundären Osteoarthropathie (Marie-Bamberger) bei einem Slavenzeitliche Skelett (Presentation of a secondary osteopathy from a Slav period skeleton). *Beitrage zur Ortopaedie und Traumatologie* **17(7)**:458–64.

Arita, I. (1980) Can we stop smallpox vaccination? *World Health*, **May 1980**:27–9.

Armelagos, G. J. (1969) Disease in ancient Nubia. *Science* **163**:255–9.

Armelagos, G.J. (1990) Health and disease in prehistoric populations in transition. In *Disease in Populations in Transition*, ed. A.C. Swedlund & G.J. Armelagos, pp. 127–44. New York: Bergin and Garvey.

Armelagos, G.J. & Chrisman, O.D. (1988) Hyperostosis frontalis interna: A Nubian case. *American Journal of Physical Anthropology* **76**:25–8.

Armendariz, J., Irigarai, S. & Etxeberria, F. (1994) New evidence of prehistoric arrow wounds in the Iberian peninsula. *International Journal of Osteoarchaeology* **4(3)**:215–22.

Armstrong, R.R. (1931) A swift and simple method for deciding pneumococcal "type." *British Medical Journal* **1**:214–15.

Arriaza, B. (1991) *The Search For Seronegative Spondyloarthropathies and Diffuse Idiopathic Skeletal Hyperostosis in Ancient South America*. Unpublished Ph.D. Dissertation, Arizona State University.

Arriaza, B., Allison, M. & Gerszten, E. (1988) Maternal mortality in pre-Columbian Indians. *American Journal of Physical Anthropology* **77**:35–41.

Arriaza, B., Salo, W. & Aufderheide, A.C. (1995) Pre-Columbian tuberculosis in northern Chile: Molecular and skeletal evidence. *American Journal of Physical Anthropology* **98**:37–45.

Arrington, G.E. (1959) *A History of Ophthalmology*. New York: MD Publication, Inc.

Arrizabalaga, J. (1993) Syphilis. In *The Cambridge World History of Human Disease*, ed. K.F. Kiple, pp. 1025–33. New York: Cambridge University Press.

Ascenzi, A., Bellelli, A., Brunori, M., Citro, G., Lendaro, E. & Zito, R. (1991) Diagnosis of thalassemia in ancient bones: Problems and prospects in pathology. In *Human Paleopathology. Current Syntheses and Future Options*, ed. D.J. Ortner & A.C. Aufderheide, pp. 73–5. Washington and London: Smithsonian Institution Press.

Aspöck, H., Flamm, H. & Picher, O. (1973) Darmparasiten in menschlichen Exkrementen aus Prähistorischen Salzbergwerken der Halstatt-Kultur (800–350 v.Chr.) (Intestinal parasites in human excrements from prehistoric salt mines of the Halstatt period (800–350 B.C.)). *Zeitblatt Bakteriologie und Hygiene, I Abteilung Original A*, **223**:549–58.

Assaad, M.B. (1980) Female circumcision in Egypt. *Studies in Family Planning* **11(2)**:3–16.

Aufderheide, A.C. (1985) The enigma of ancient cranial trepanation. *Minnesota Medicine* **68**:119–22.

Aufderheide, A.C. (1990) Field Report of Results from Examination of 140 Chiribaya Mummies Excavated from Chiribaya Alta Site in Lower Osmore Valley near Ilo, Peru. Manuscript on file at the Department of Physical Anthropology, University of Chicago, Chicago, IL.

Aufderheide, A.C. (1993) Lead poisoning. In *The Cambridge World History of Human Disease*, ed. K.F. Kiple, pp.820–7. New York: Cambridge University Press.

Aufderheide, A.C. (1995) Preface. In *Proceedings of the First World Congress on Mummy Studies*, 1992, vol. 1, pp.21–4. Tenerife, Canary Islands: Museo Arqueológico y Etnográfico de Tenerife, Organismo Autónomo de Museos y Centros, Cabildo de Tenerife.

Aufderheide, A.C. & Allison, M.J. (1994) Bioanthropology of spontaneously mummified bodies of a Late Phase Chinchorro site (Morro 1–6) in northern Chile. Paper presented at the 59th Annual Meeting of the Society for American Archaeology, Anaheim, CA, April 20–24, 1994.

Aufderheide, A.C., Neiman, F.D., Wittmers, L.E., Jr & Rapp, G. Jr (1981) Lead in bone II: Skeletal lead content as an indicator of lifetime lead ingestion and the social correlates in an archaeological population. *American Journal of Physical Anthropology* **55**:285–91.

Aufderheide, A.C., Angel, J.L., Kelley, J.O., Outlaw, A.C., Outlaw, M.A., Rapp, G. Jr & Wittmers, L.E., Jr (1985) Lead in bone III. Prediction of social correlates from skeletal lead content in four colonial American populations (Catoctin Furnace, College Landing, Governor's Land, and Irene Mound). *American Journal of Physical Anthropology* **66**:353–61.

Aufderheide, A.C., Buikstra, J., Cartmell, L., Weems, C. & Springfield, A. (1991) The prehistory of Andean coca leaf chewing practices as reflected in radioimmunoassay measurement of cocaine in Chiribaya mummy hair. Paper presented at the 1991 Annual Meeting of the Society for American Archaeology, Chicago, IL, April 2–6.

Aufderheide, A.C., Rapp, G., Jr, Wittmers, L.E., Jr, Wallgren, J.E., Macchiarelli, R., Fornaciari, G., Mallegni, F. & Corruccini, R.S. (1992) Lead exposure in Italy: 800 BC–700 AD. *International Journal of Anthropology* **7(2)**:9–15.

Aufderheide, A.C., Muñoz, I. & Arriaza, B. (1993) Seven Chinchorro mummies and the prehistory of northern Chile. *American Journal of Physical Anthropology* **91**:189–201.

Aufderheide, A.C., Zlonis, M. & Cartmell, L. (1995) Unique mummification practices during the Ptolemaic period at Dakhleh Oasis, Egypt. Paper presented at the Second World Congress on Mummy Studies, Cartagena, Columbia, February 6–10, 1995.

Austrian, R. (1981) The pneumococcus: The first one hundred years. *Reviews of Infectious Diseases* **3**:183–9.

Avery, O.T. & Heidelberger, M. (1925) Immunological relationships of cell constituents of pneumococcus. Paper II. *Journal of Experimental Medicine* **42**:367–76.

Avioli, L.V. & Krane, S.M. (1978) *Metabolic Bone Disease*. Vol. 2. New York: Academic Press.

Ayala, S. (1978) Letter to the editor. *Paleopathology Newsletter* **21**:3.

Badger, L.F. (1964) Epidemiology. In *Leprosy in Theory and Practice*, ed. R.G.Cochrane, T.F. Davey & Sir G. McRobert, pp. 69–92. Baltimore: Williams & Wilkins.

Baker, B.J. & Armelagos, G.J. (1988) The origin and antiquity of syphilis. Paleopathological diagnosis and interpretation. *Current Anthropology* **29**(**5**):703–37.

Ball, G.V. (1971) Two epidemics of gout. *Bulletin of the History of Medicine* **45**(**5**):401–8.

Balogh, K. (1994) The head and neck. In *Pathology*, ed. E. Rubin & J. Farber, 2nd edn, pp. 1239–71. Philadelphia: Lippincott.

Bandelier, A.F. (1904) Aboriginal trephining in Bolivia. *American Anthropologist* 6:440–6.

Banting, D.W. & Courtwright, P.N. (1975) Distribution and natural history of carious lesions on the roots of teeth. *Journal of the Canadian Dental Association* **41**:45–9.

Bar-Ziv, J. & Goldberg, G.M. (1974) Simple siliceous pneumoconiosis in Negev Bedouins. *Archives of Environmental Health* **29**:121–6.

Baraybar, J.P. & Shimada, I. (1993) A possible case of metastatic carcinoma in a Middle Sican burial from Batán Grande, Peru. *International Journal of Osteoarchaeology* 3:129–35.

Barbet, P. (1953) *A Doctor at Calvary.* New York: P.J. Kennedy.

Barker, R.H., Jr, Suebsaeng, L., Rooney, W., Alecrim, G. C., Dourado, H. V. & Wirth, D.F. (1986) Specific DNA probe for the diagnosis of *Plasmodium falciparum* malaria. *Science* **231**:1434–6.

Barlow, T. (1883) On cases described as acute rickets. *British Medical Journal* **1**:619. (Abstract).

Barnes, E. (1994) *Developmental Defects of the Axial Skeleton in Paleopathology.* Niwot, CO: University Press of Colorado.

Barnes, E. (1995) Case No. 59: Thyroglossal duct cyst. (Department of Pathology, Medical College of Virginia, Richmond, VA) *Paleopathology Club Newsletter* **63**:1.

Barnes, P.F., Bloch, A.B., Davidson, P.T. & Snider, D.E., Jr (1991) Tuberculosis in patients with human immunodeficiency virus infection. *New England Journal of Medicine* **324**:1644–50.

Barrett-Connor, E. (1982) Parasitic pulmonary disease. *American Review of Respiratory Disease* **126**:558–63.

Bartels, P. (1907) Tuberkulose (Wirbelkaries) in der Jüngerer Steinzeit (Vertebral tuberculosis in the Neolithic). *Archiv für Anthropolgie* **6**:243–55.

Bartsocas, C.S. (1985) Goiters, dwarfs, giants and hermaphrodites. In *Endocrine Genetics and Genetics of Growth,* ed. C. S. Bartsocas, pp. 1–18. New York: Alan Liss.

Bassoe, P. (1903) Gigantism and leontiasis ossea, with report of the case of giant Wilkins. *Journal of Nervous and Mental Disease* **30**:513–32; 595–621.

Bates, B. (1992) *Bargaining for Life: A Social History of Tuberculosis, 1876–1938.* Philadelphia: University of Pennsylvania Press.

Baty, J.M. & Vogt, E.C. (1935) Bone changes in leukemia in children. *American Journal of Roentgenology* **34**:910–14.

Baud, M. (1978) *Le Caractère Du Dessin en Égypte Ancienne* (*The character of drawings in Ancient Egypt*). Paris: Libraire Adrien Masisonneuve.

Baudouin, M. (1923) Emploi de la Radiographie en Pathologie Préhistorique (The use of radiography in ancient pathology). *Nouvelle Journal des Mèdecins* **18**:250–1.

Baum, M. (1993) Breast cancer 2000 B.C. to 2000 A.D.– time for a paradigm shift? *Acta Oncologica* **32**(**1**):3–8.

Beattie, O. & Geiger, J. (1987) *Frozen In Time.* London: Bloomsbury.

Becker, M.J. (1994) Estruscan gold dental appliances: Origins and functions as indicated by an example from Valsiarosa, Italy. *Journal of Paleopathology* **6**(**2**):69–92.

Begg, P.R. (1965) *Begg Orthodontic Theory and Technique.* Philadelphia: Saunders.

Behr, D. von (1908) *Metrische Studien an 152 Guanchenschädeln* (*Metric Studies on 152 Guanche Skulls*). Stuttgart: Strecker & Schröder.

Beitzke, H. (1934) Rotz der Knochen und Gelenke (Bone and joint involvement in glanders). *In Gelenke und Knochen* (*Joints and Bones*), ed. H. Beitzke, H. Chiari, F. Klinge, T. Konschegg & F.J. Lang, vol. 9, part II, pp. 589–93 of *Handbuch der Speziellen Pathologischen Anatomie und Histologie* (*Handbook of Special Anatomic Pathology and Histology*). Berlin: J. Springer.

Benedek, T.G. (1993) Gout. In *The Cambridge World History of Human Disease*, ed. K.F. Kiple, pp. 763–72. New York: Cambridge University Press.

Benedek, T.G. & Kiple, K.F. (1993) Concepts of cancer. In *The Cambridge World History of Human Disease*, ed. K.F. Kiple, pp. 102–10. New York: Cambridge University Press.

Benenson, A.S. (1984) *El control de las Enfermedades transmisibles en el Hombre* (*Control of Transmissible Disease in Man),* 13th edn, 2nd impression. Washington, DC: Organización Panamericana de la Salud.

Benítez, J.T. (1985) Temporal bone paleopathological studies from two members of the Barrow frozen family. (Paper presented at the 12th annual meeting of the Paleopathology Association held in Knoxville, TE, 9–10 April 1985) *Paleopathology Newsletter* **50** (**June**) (**Supplement**): 5–6. (Abstract).

Benítez, J.T. (1988) Otopathology of Egyptian mummy PUM II: Final report. *Journal of Laryngology and Otology* **102**:485–90.

Bennike, P. (1985) *Paleopathology of Danish Skeletons.* Copenhagen: Akademisk Forlag.

Bennington, J.L. (1984) Mycotoxin. In *Saunders Dictionary and Encyclopedia of Laboratory Medicine and Technology*, ed. J.L. Bennington, pp.1028–9.

Bergen, J.G. & Feller, J.E. (1713) *De Scorbuto (On Scurvy).* Frankfurt am Oder. Thesis 11.

Berman, E.R. (1991) *Biochemistry of the Eye.* New York: Plenum Press.

Berman, S. (1995) Otitis media in children. *New England Journal of Medicine* **332**:1560–5.

Berry, D.R. (1985) Dental pathology of Grasshopper Pueblo Arizona. In *Health and Disease in the Prehistoric Southwest*, ed. C. Merbs & R.J. Miller. Anthropological Research Papers no. 34, pp. 266–8. Tempe, AZ: Department of Anthropology, Arizona State University.

Bewtra, C., Aufderheide, A.C. & Salo, W.L. (1994) Presence of acid-fast organisms in archaeological tissues. *Journal of Paleopathology* **6**(**1**):15–17.

Bietak, M. & Strouhal, E. (1974) Die Totessumstände des Pharaohs Seqenenre (17 Dynastie) (The Circumstances of Pharoah Seqenenre's death). *Annalen des Naturhistorischen Museums Wien* **78**:29–52.

Billard, M. (1994) Haemangioma of the cranial vault in a skull from the Middle Neolithic Period (France, 4312–3912 B.C.). In *Papers on Paleopathology Presented at the Xth European Members Meeting of the Paleopathology Association in Göttingen, Germany on 29 August–3 September, 1994. Paleopathology Newsletter* **88** (**Supplement**):4. (Abstract).

Binford, C.H. & Connor, D.H. (eds) (1976) *Pathology of Tropical and Extraordinary Diseases.* Washington, DC: Armed Forces Institute of Pathology.

Birely, A.R. (1992) A case of eye disease (Lippitudo) on the Roman frontier in Britain. *Ophthalmologica* **81**:111–19.

Birkby, W. H. & Gregg, J.B. (1975) Otosclerotic stapedial footplate fixation in an eighteenth century burial. *American Journal of Physical Anthropology* **42**(**1**):81–4.

Birkenkamp, U. (1618) *De Scorbuto (On Scurvy).* Helmstedt: Conrad Buscher & Johann Wolff (Publishers).

Birkett, D.A. (1982) Osteochondritis dissecans in ancient populations. *Paleopathology Newsletter (Supplement)* **39**:3. (Abstract).

Birkett, D.A. (1983) Non-specific infections. In *Disease in Ancient Man*, ed. G.D. Hart, pp. 99–105. Toronto: Clarke Irwin.

Birkett, D.A. (1986) Osteochondroma (Cartilaginous Exostosis). In *Papers on Paleopathology Presented at the VIth European Members Meeting of the Paleopathology Association in Madrid, Spain on September 9–11, 1986. Paleopathology Newsletter* **58** (**Supplement**): 3 (Abstract).

Björk, A. & Björk, L. (1964) Artificial deformation and cranio-facial asymmetry in ancient Peruvians. *Journal of Dental Research* **43**(**3**):353–62.

Black, F. L. (1992) Why did they die? *Science* **258**:1739–40.

Blackman, J., Allison, M., Aufderheide, A.C., Oldroyd, N. & Steinbock, R.T. (1991) Secondary hyperparathyroidism in an Andean mummy. In *Human Paleopathology*, ed. D.J. Ortner & A.C. Aufderheide, pp. 291–6. Washington, DC: Smithsonian Institution Press.

Blake, C. (1880) On the occurrence of exostoses within the external auditory canal in prehistoric man. *American Journal of Otology* **2**:81–91.

Bloch, M. (1973) *The Royal Touch*. London: Routledge and Kegan Paul. (Translated by J.E. Anderson).

Blockey, N.J. (1984) Conducta Adecuada en las Infecciones Óseas y Articulares (Appropriate treatment of bone and joint infections). In *Fundamentos Científicos de Ortopedia y Traumatología* (*Scientific Fundamentals of Orthopedics and Traumatology*), ed. R. Owen, J. Goodfellow & P. Bullough, pp. 530–42. Barcelona: Salvat.

Blondiaux, J. & Millot, F. (1991) Dislocation of the hip: Discussion of eleven cases from mediaeval France. *International Journal of Osteoarchaeology* **1**(**3&4**):203–7.

Bloom, A.I., Bloom, R.A., Kahila, G., Eisenberg, E. & Smith, P. (1995) Amputation of the hand in the 3600 year old skeletal remains of an adult male: The first case reported from Israel. *International Journal of Osteoarchaeology* **5**:188–91.

Bloom, B.R. & Murray, C.J.L. (1992) Tuberculosis: Commentary on a reemergent killer. *Science* **257**:1055–64.

Bloom, R.A. & Smith, P. (1991) A healed depressed frontal bone fracture in an early Samaritan (the Goliath injury). *Journal of Paleopathology* **3**(**3**):167–70.

Bluhm, G.B. (1979) Gout and pseudogout. *Henry Ford Hospital Medical Journal* **27**(**1**):14–17.

Bogdan, G. & Weaver, D.S. (1992) Pre-Columbian treponematosis in coastal North Carolina. In *Disease and Demography in the Americas*, ed. J.W. Verano & D.H. Ubelaker, pp. 155–63. Washington and London: Smithsonian Institution Press.

Bonnet, C. (1986) Archaeological excavations at Kerma (Sudan). In *Kerma (Soudan) 1984–1985–1986*. Tirage á part de Genava, n.s. tome **xxxiv**, 1986, pp. 5–19 (in French), pp.i–vii (in English). Excavation Reports. (Translated by Kitch Carter Young).

Borah, W. & Cook. S.F. (1963) *The Aboriginal Population of Central Mexico on the Eve of the Spanish Conquest*. Ibero-Americana no.45. Berkeley: University of California Press.

Borgoño, J.M. & Greiber, R. (1971) Estudio epidemiológico del arsenicismo en la ciudad de Antofagasta (An epidemiological study of arsenicism in the city of Antofagasta). *Revista Médico de Chile* **99**:702–7.

Borhegyi, S.P. & Scrimschaw, N.S. (1957) Evidence for pre-Columbian goiter in Guatemala. *American Antiquity* **22**(**2, part 1**):174–6.

Borobia Melendo, E.L. & Mora Postigo, C. (1995) Un Caso de Treponematosis Ósea en un Cráneo Femenino de la Cueva de Samar en Las Filipinas (A case of skeletal treponamatosis in a female skull from Samar Cave in the Philippines). In *Proceedings of the IXth European Meeting of the Paleopathology Association (Barcelona)*, pp. 47–54. Barcelona: Museu d'Arqueologia de Catalunya.

Bortuzzo, L. (1995) Un Achondroplase Bas Normand du VIe Millénaire B.P. Le Nain d'Ernes (A Bas Norman achondroplastic dwarf from the sixth millennium B.P. from le Nain d'Ernes). In *Proceedings of the IXth European Meeting of the Paleopathology Association (Barcelona)*, pp. 55–63. Barcelona: Museu d'Arqueologia de Catalunya.

Bosch Millares, J. (1975) *Paleopatología Ósea de los Primitivos Pobladores de Canarias (Skeletal Paleopathology of the Ancient Inhabitants of the Canaries)*. Las Palmas: Cabildo Insular de Gran Canaria.

Boulos, F.S. (1986) Oncology in Egyptian papyri. In *Paleo-oncology: The Antiquity of Cancer*, ed. S. Retsas, pp. 35–40. London: Farrand Press.

Bourke, J.B. (1967) A review of the palaeopathology of the arthritic diseases. In *Diseases in Antiquity*, ed. D. Brothwell & A.T. Sandison, pp. 352–70. Springfield, IL: C.C. Thomas.

Boyd, R. (1992) Population decline from two epidemics on the Northwest Coast. In *Disease and Demography in the Americas*, ed. J.W. Verano & D.H. Ubelaker, pp. 249–55. Washington, DC: Smithsonian Institution Press.

Boyle, J. (1831) *A Practical Medico-Historical Account of the Western Coast of Africa*. London: S. Highly, Edinburgh: Oliver and Boyd.

Bras, G. (1952) The morbid anatomy of smallpox. *Documenta de Medicina Geographica et Tropica* **4**:303–51.

Brauer, J.L. (1991) A case of acromegaly in a prehistoric skeleton from the San Cristobal Ruins, New Mexico. (Paper presented at the 18th meeting of the Paleopathology Association held in Milwaukee, Wisconsin, April 2–3, 1991). *Paleopathology Newsletter* **74** (**June: Supplement**):2 (Abstract).

Braunstein, E.M., Tyson, R.A. & Harris, J.E. (1991) Paleopathology and differential diagnosis of cortical desmoids. *American Journal of Physical Anthropology* **86**(**52**):54. (Abstract).

Braunstein, G. D. (1993) Gynecomastia. *New England Journal of Medicine* **328**:490–5.

Bray, G.W. (1934) The story of leprosy at Nauru. *International Journal of Leprosy* **2**:319–23.

Breasted, J.H. (1930) *The Edwin Smith Papyrus*. Chicago: University of Chicago Press.

Breman, J.G. & Arita, I. (1980) The confirmation and maintenance of smallpox eradication. *New England Journal of Medicine* **303**:1263–73.

Bridges, P.S. (1994) Vertebral arthritis and physical activities in the prehistoric United States. *American Journal of Physical Anthropology* **93**:83–93.

Brier, B. (1994) *Egyptian Mummies*. New York: William Morrow and Co.

Broca, P.P. (1867) Cas singulier de trépanation chez le Incas (A unique case of trepanation among the Incas). *Bulletin Mémoire Société Anthropologie de Paris* **2**(**2**):403–8.

Broca, P.P. (1875) Sur les trous pariétaux et sur la perforation congénitale, double et symétrique des pariétaux (On bilateral, symmetrical, congenital parietal defects). *Bulletin Mémoire Société Anthropologie de Paris*. Séries **2**(**10**):326–36.

Bronnikov, A.G. (1993) *Body language. New York Times*. **November 6**:17.

Brooks, S. T. & Melbye, J. (1967) Skeletal lesions suggestive of pre-Columbian multiple myeloma in a burial from the Kane Mounds, near St. Louis, Missouri. In *Technical Series Number 7. Miscellaneous Papers in Paleopathology: 1. Museum of Northern Arizona*, ed. W.D. Wade, pp. 23–9. Flagstaff, AZ: Northern Arizona Society of Science and Art.

Brothwell, D. (1960) A possible case of mongolism in a Saxon population. *Annals of Human Genetics* **24**:141–50.

Brothwell, D. (1961) The paleopathology of early British man: An essay on the problems of diagnosis and analysis. *Journal of the Royal Anthropological Institute* **91**:318–44.

Brothwell, D. (1965) The palaeopathology of the E.B.-M.B. and Middle Bronze Age remains from Jericho (1957–1958 excavations). In *Excavations at Jericho, 2*, ed. K.M. Kenyon, pp. 685–93. London: British School of Archaeology in Jerusalem.

Brothwell, D. (1967a) The evidence for neoplasms. In *Diseases in Antiquity*, ed. D. Brothwell & A.T. Sandison, pp. 320–45. Springfield, IL: C.C. Thomas.

Brothwell, D. (1967b) Evidence of endemic calculi in an early community. In *Diseases in Antiquity*, ed. D. Brothwell & A.T. Sandison, pp. 349–51. Springfield, IL: C.C. Thomas.

Brothwell, D. (1967c) Major congenital anomalies of the skeleton: Evidence from earlier populations. In *Diseases in Antiquity*, ed. D. Brothwell & A.T. Sandison, pp. 423–43. Springfield, IL: C.C. Thomas.

Brothwell, D. (1981) *Digging Up Bones*. Ithaca: Cornell University.

Brothwell, D. (1986) *The Bog Man and the Archaeology of People*. London: The British Museum Press.

Brothwell, D. (1994) Ancient trephining: Multifocal evolution or trans-world diffusion? *Journal of Paleopathology* **6**(**3**):129–38.

Brothwell, D. & Powers, R. (1968) Congenital malformations of the skeleton in earlier man.

In *The Skeletal Biology of Earlier Human Populations*, ed. D. Brothwell, pp. 173–203. Oxford: Pergamon Press.

Brothwell, D.R. & Sandison, A.T. (eds) (1967) *Diseases in Antiquity*. Springfield, IL: C.C. Thomas.

Brothwell, D., Sandison, A.T. & Gray, P.H.K. (1969) Human biological observations on a Guanche mummy with anthracosis. *American Journal of Physical Anthropology* **30**:333–47.

Brower, A.C. (1994) *Radiología Articular. Artritis en Blanco y Negro* (Joint Radiology. Arthritis in Black and White). Madrid: Marban.

Brown, T.S., Franklyn, P.P. & Marikkar, M.S.K. (1980) Tuberculosis of the skull vault. *Clinical Radiology* **31**:313–15.

Browne, S.G. (1970) How old is leprosy? *British Medical Journal* **3**:640–1.

Bruce, G. (1941) A note on penal blinding in the Middle Ages. *Annals of Medical History* **3**:369–71.

Bruce-Chwatt, L. (1965) Paleogenesis and paleo-epidemiology of primate malaria. *Bulletin of the World Health Organization* **32**(3):363–87.

Bruce-Chwatt, L. & Zulueta, J. de (1980) *The Rise and Fall of Malaria in Europe: A Historico-Epidemiological Study*. London: Oxford University Press.

Bruetsch, W.L. (1959) The earliest record of sudden death possibly due to atherosclerotic coronary occlusion. *Circulation* **20**(3):438–41.

Bruintjes, Tj.D. & Panhuysen, R.G.A.M. (1995) The paleopathological diagnosis of seronegative spondyloarthropathies. In *Proceedings of the IXth European Meeting of the Paleopathology Association (Barcelona)*, pp.73–7. Barcelona: Museu d'Arqueologia de Catalunya.

Buchanan, W.W., Kraag, G.R., Palmar, D.G. & Cockshott, W.P. (1981) The first recorded case of osteitis fibrosa cystica. *Canadian Medical Association Journal* **124**:812–15.

Buikstra, J.E. (1976) The Caribou Eskimo: General and specific disease. *American Journal of Physical Anthropology* **45**:351–68.

Buikstra, J.E. (1977) Differential diagnosis: An epidemiological model. *Yearbook of Physical Anthropology* **20**:316–28.

Buikstra, J.E. (ed.) (1981) *Prehistoric Tuberculosis in the Americas*. Evanston, IL: Northwestern University Archaeological Program.

Buikstra, J.E. & Cook, D.C. (1980) Palaeopathology: An American account. *Annual Review of Anthropology* **9**:433–70.

Buikstra, J.E. & Cook, D.C. (1981) Pre-Columbian tuberculosis in west-central Illinois: Prehistoric disease in biocultural perspective. In *Prehistoric Tuberculosis in the Americas*, ed. J.E. Buikstra, pp. 115–39. Evanston, IL: Northwestern University Archaeological Program.

Buikstra, J.E. & Ubelaker, D.H. (eds) (1994) *Standards for Data Collection from Human Skeletal Remains*. Arkansas Archeological Survey Research Series no. 44. Fayetteville, AS: Arkansas Archeological Survey.

Buikstra, J.E. & Williams, S. (1991) Tuberculosis in the Americas: Current perspectives. In *Human Paleopathology*, ed. D.J. Ortner & A.C. Aufderheide, pp.161–72. Washington, DC: Smithsonian Institution Press.

Bullock, W.E. (1985) Leprosy (Hansen's disease). In *Cecil Textbook of Medicine*, ed. J.B. Wyngaarden & L.H. Smith, Jr, 17th edn, pp. 1634–9. Philadelphia: Saunders.

Bullough, P.G. (1992) *Atlas of Orthopedic Pathology with Clinical and Radiologic Correlations*, 2nd edn. New York: Gower Medical Publishers.

Burchett, G. (1968) *Memoirs of a Tattooist*. London: Oldbourne.

Burkett, L.W. (1946) *Oral Medicine*. Philadelphia: J.B. Lippincott.

Burkitt, D.P. (1981) Geography of disease: Purpose and possibilities from geographic medicine. In *Biocultural Aspects of Disease*, ed. H. Rothschild, pp. 133–52. New York: Academic Press.

Burnett, G.W. & Schuster, G.S. (1978) *Oral Microbiology and Infectious Disease*. Baltimore: Williams and Wilkins.

Bush, H. & Stirland, A. (1987) Osteological evidence for decapitations in two British Roman cemeteries. Paper presented at the XIVth annual meeting of the Paleopathology Association held in New York City, 1–3 April, 1987. *Paleopathology Newsletter* **59** (**Supplement**):12. (Abstract).

Butler, J.C., Breiman, R.F., Campbell, J.F., Lipman, H.B., Broom, C.V. & Facklam, R.R. (1993) Pneumococcal polysaccharide vaccine efficacy. *Journal of the American Medical Association* **270**:1826–31.

Caffey, J. & Silverman W.A. (1945) Infantile cortical hyperostosis: Preliminary report on a new syndrome. *American Journal of Roentgenology* **54**:1–16.

Cahill, G.F., Jr (1979) Human evolution and insulin-dependent (IDD) and non-insulin dependent (NIDD) diabetes. *Metabolism* **28**(4):389–93.

Cahill, J., Reinhard, K., Tarler, D. & Warnock, P. (1991) It had to happen–scientists examine remains of ancient bathroom. *Biblical Archaeology Review* **17**(3):64–9.

Calandruccio, R.A. (1967) Diversas Afecciones Óseas (Diverse bone diseases). In *Cirugía Ortopédica* (Orthopaedic Surgery), ed. W.C. Campbell & A.H. Crenshaw, vol. **2**, pp. 1345–86. Buenos Aires: Inter-Médica.

Campillo, D. (1977) *Paleopatología del Cráneo en Cataluña, Valencia y Baleares* (Cranial Paleopathology in Catalonia, Valencia and Baleares). Barcelona: Montblanc-Martín.

Campillo, D. (1978) Dos Notas de Paleopatología (Two notes on paleopathology). *Archivo de Prehistoria Levantina* **XV**:311–23.

Campillo, D. (1980) Malformación Vertebral en un Indivíduo Perteneciente a la Cultura Talayótica Menorquina (Vertebral malformation in an individual of the Talayótica Menorca culture). *Asclepio* **XXXII**:65–76.

Campillo, D. (1983) *La Enfermedad en la Prehistoria (Disease in Prehistory)*. Barcelona: Salvat.

Campillo, D. (1984) Neurosurgical pathology in prehistory. *Acta Neurochirurgica* **70**:275–90.

Campillo, D. (1991a) Healing of the skull bone after injury. *Journal of Paleopathology* **3**(3):137–49.

Campillo, D. (1991b) The possibility of diagnosing meningiomas in paleopathology. *International Journal of Osteoarchaeology* **1**:225–30.

Campillo, D. (1993) *Paleopatología. Los Primeros Vestigios de la Enfermedad (Paleopathology. The First Evidence of Disease)*. Primera Parte (Part 1). Barcelona: Fundación Uriach 1838.

Campillo, D. (1994–95) *Paleopatología. Los Primeros Vestigios de la Enfermedad (Paleopathology. The First Evidence of Disease)*. Segunda Parte (Part 2). Barcelona: Fundación Uriach 1838.

Campillo, D. (1995) Agressivitat i Violença a les Societats Prehistóriques i Primitives (Aggression and violence in prehistoric and primitive societies). *Liines* **4**(5):4–17.

Campillo, D. & Marí-Balcells, V.J. (1984) Microscopy of osteal tumours in paleopathology. In *Proceedings of the Vth European meeting of the Paleopathology Association (Siena)*, pp. 35–43.

Campillo, D. & Rodríguez-Martín, C. (1994) Spinal congenital malformations in Spanish prehistoric populations. A comparative study between the Iberian Peninsula and Tenerife (Canary Islands, Spain). In *Papers on Paleopathology Presented at the Xth European Members Meeting of the Paleopathology Association in Göttingen, Germany on 29 August–3 September. Paleopathology Newsletter* **88**(**Supplement**):6. (Also published in: *Homo* (**Supplement**)**45**:29. (Abstract).

Camus, D. & Hadley, T. (1985) A *Plasmodium falciparum* antigen that binds to host erythrocytes and merozoites. *Science* **230**(4725):553–6.

Canci, A., Borgognini Tarli, S.M. & Repetto, E. (1991) Osteomyelitis of probable haematogenous origin in a Bronze Age child from Toppo Daguzzo (Bassilicata, Southern Italy). *International Journal of Osteoarchaeology* **1**(2):135–9.

Canci, A., Minozzi, S. & Borgognini, S. (1996) New evidence of tuberculous spondylitis from

Neolithic Liguria (Italy). *International Journal of Osteoarchaeology* **6**:497–51.

Capasso, L. (1985) *L'Origine delle Malattie (The Origins of Disease)*. Chieti: Solfanelli.

Capasso, L. (1988) Exostoses of the auditory bony meatus in pre-Columbian Peruvians. *Journal of Paleopathology* **1**(3):113–16.

Capasso, L. (1989) A paleopathological case of leontiasis ossea. *Journal of Paleopathology* **2**(2):85–8.

Capasso, L. (1993) A preliminary report on the tattoos of the Val Senales mummy (Tyrol, Neolithic). *Journal of Paleopathology* **5**:173–82.

Capasso, L., Di Muzio, M., Di Tota, G. & Spoletini, L. (1991) A case of probable cranial hemangioma (Iron Age, Central Italy). *Journal of Paleopathology* **4**(1):55–62.

Capasso, L., Capelli, A., Frati, L. & Pierfelice, V. (1992) Absence of the foramen nutricium with a probable aneurismatic cyst of the right ilium in a medieval subject from southwest Italy. *Journal of Paleopathology* **4**(3):185–92.

Caranza, F.A. (1984) *Glickman's Clinical Periodontology*, 6th edn. Philadelphia: W.B. Saunders.

Cárdenas, F. (1994) Form and function of aboriginal mummification in Colombia: A view from ethnohistory and modern technology. Paper presented at the 21st Annual Meeting of the Paleopathology Association Symposium, Modern Medical Research and Ancient Mummies, Denver, Colorado, March 29, 1994.

Carmichael, A.G. (1993*a*) Bubonic plague. In *The Cambridge World History of Human Disease*, ed. K.F. Kiple, pp. 628–31. New York: Cambridge University Press.

Carmichael, A.G. (1993*b*) Leprosy. In *The Cambridge World History of Human Disease*, ed. K.F. Kiple, pp. 834–9. New York: Cambridge University Press.

Carnevale, V. (1971) Patología articular (Joint pathology). In *Patología Quirúrgica (Surgical Pathology)*, ed. J.R. Michans, 2nd edn, vol. 2, pp. 347–86. Buenos Aires: El Ateneo.

Carnevale, V. & Salvati, A.A. (1971) Articulación de la Cadera (I) (The hip joint (I)). In *Patología Quirúrgica (Surgical Pathology)*, ed. J.R. Michans, 2nd edn, vol. 2, pp. 808–38. Buenos Aires: El Ateneo.

Carpenter, K. (1987) The problem of land scurvy, 1820–1910. *Bulletin of the Society for the Study of the Social History of Medicine* **40**:20–2.

Cartmell, L.W., Aufderheide, A. C., Springfield, A., Weems, C. & Arriaza, B. (1991) The frequency and antiquity of prehistoric coca leaf chewing practices in northern Chile: A radioimmunoassay study of a cocaine metabolite in human mummy hair. *Latin American Antiquity* **2**(3):260–8.

Casagrande, P.A. & Frost, H.M. (1955) *Fundamentos de Ortopedia Clínica (Fundamentals of Clinical Orthopedics)*. Barcelona: Salvat.

Cassels, J.P. (1877) On the etiology of aural exostoses. *British Medical Journal* **2**:845ff.

Cassidy, C.M. (1979) Arthritis in dry bones: Diagnostic problems. *Henry Ford Hospital Medical Journal* **27**(1):68–9.

Castaret, N. (1951) *Dix ans sous terre (Twenty Years Underground)*. Paris: Librarie Académique Perrin.

Castellano Arroyo, M. (1994) Consecuencias de los Traumatismos Según las Regiones (Trauma consequences by region). In *Medicina Legal y Toxicología (Forensic Medicine and Toxicology)*, ed. J.A. Gisbert Calabuig, 4th edn, pp. 361–75. Barcelona: Masson-Salvat.

Castigilioni, A. (1941) *A History of Medicine*. New York:Knopf.

Catalano, P. & Passarello, P. (1988) Renal calculi from a skeleton of Gabii Iron Age necropolis (Rome). *Rivista di Antropologia (Roman) Supplemento del Vol.* **66**:221–30.

Celsus ([c. A.D. 25] 1994) *De Medicina* VIII, 3–8. Loeb Classical Library. Translated by W.G.Spencer. Cambridge, MA: Harvard University Press. [First published in Loeb Library in 1938. Latest reprint 1994.]

Chakravorty, R.C. (1993) Diseases of antiquity in South Asia. In *The Cambridge World History of Human Disease*, ed. K.F. Kiple, pp.408–13. New York: Cambridge University Press.

Chamberlain, A.T.S., Rogers, S. & Romanowski, A.J. (1992) Osteochondroma in a British Neolithic skeleton. *British Journal of Hospital Medicine* **47**(1):51–3.

Chan-Ling, T., Neill, A.L. & Hunt, N.H. (1992) Early microvascular changes in murine cerebral malaria detected in retinal wholemounts. *American Journal of Pathology* **140**(5):1121–30.

Charcot, J.-M. ([1868] 1993) On arthropathies of cerebral or spinal origin. Reprinted in *Clinical Orthopaedics and Related Research* **296**:4–7. [First published in 1868].

Chaussinand, R. (1948) Tuberculose et lépre, maladies antagoniques (Tuberculosis and leprosy, antagonistic diseases). *International Journal of Leprosy* **16**:431–8.

Chen, T.S.N. & Chen, P.S.Y. (1993) Cirrhosis. In *The Cambridge World History of Human Disease*, ed. K.F. Kiple, pp. 649–53. New York: Cambridge University Press.

Cheraskin, E. & Ringsdorf, W.M. (1970) Alveolar bone loss as a prognostic sign of diabetes in patients of the 60-plus age group. *Journal of American Geriatrics Society* **18**(5):416–20.

Cheyne, W.M. (1911) *Tuberculous Diseases of Bones and Joints, Their Pathology, Symptoms and Treatment*. London: Henry Frowde.

Chiari, H. (1886) Über orchitis variolosa (Concerning orchitis variolosa). *Zeitschrift für Heilkunde (Wien)* **7**:385–406.

Chil y Naranjo (1878) Mémoire sur l'origine des Guanches ou habitants primitifs des îles Canaries (Report on the Origins of Guanches or Primitive Inhabitants of the Canary Islands). Congrés international des sciences anthropologiques tenu á Paris du 16 au 21 août, p.167.

Christianson, W.T. (1992) Stillbirths, mummies, abortions and early embryonic death. *Veterinary Clinics of North America: Food Animal Practice* **8**(3):623–39.

Chu, H.J. & Ch'iang, I.H. (1931) Extracts from some old Chinese medical books on worm infections. *National Medical Journal of China* **xvii**:655–66.

Clark, I.A., Cowden, W.B., Hunt, N.H., Maxwell, L.E. & Mackie, E.J. (1984) Activity of divicine in *Plasmodium vinckei*-infected mice has implications for treatment of favism and epidemiology of G-6-PD deficiency. *British Journal of Haematology* **57**:479–87.

Clark, N., Carey, S.E., Srikandi, W., Hirsch, R.S. & Leppard, P. (1986) Periodontal disease in ancient populations. *American Journal of Physical Anthropology* **71**:171–83.

Clarke, E. (1962) Whistler and Glisson on rickets. *Bulletin of the History of Medicine* **36**(1):45–61.

Clement, A.J. (1958) The antiquity of caries. *British Dental Journal* **4**:115–23.

Cleveland, M. (1939) Surgical treament of joint tuberculosis. *Journal of Bone and Joint Surgery* **21**:607–18.

Cloudsley-Thompson, J.L. (1976) *Insects and History*. New York: St. Martins Press.

Clyde, D.F. (1987) Recent trends in the epidemiology and control of malaria. *Epidemiologic Reviews* **9**:219–43.

Cobbold, T.S (1877) Discovery of the adult representative of microscopic filariae. *Lancet* **ii**:70–1. (Includes a letter from Joseph Bancroft reporting the discovery of the adult filarial worms in man).

Cobby, M., Cushnaghan, J., Creamer, P., Dieppe, P. & Watt, I. (1990) Erosive osteoarthritis: Is it a separate disease entity? *Clinical Radiology* **42**:258–63.

Cobo, Father B. ([1653] 1990) *Inca Religions and Customs*. Austin, TX: University of Texas Press. [First published in 1653].

Cochrane, R.G. (1961) Biblical leprosy. *Christian Medical Fellowship Quarterly (I.V.F.)* **24**:24ff.

Cochrane, R.G., Davey, T.F. & McRobert, Sir G. (eds) (1964) *Leprosy in Theory and Practice*. Baltimore: Williams and Wilkins Company.

Cockburn, A. (1963) *The Evolution and Eradication of Infectious Diseases*. Baltimore: Johns Hopkins Press.

Cockburn, A. (1980) News from the field: Egypt. *Paleopathology Newsletter* **31**:6–8.

Cockburn, A. & Cockburn, E. (eds) (1980) *Mummies, Disease and Ancient Cultures*. New York: Cambridge University Press.

Cockburn, A., Duncan, H. & Riddle, J.M. (1979)

Arthritis, ancient and modern: Guidelines for field workers. *Henry Ford Hospital Medical Journal* **27**(**1**):74–9.

Cockburn, A., Peck, W.H., Barraco, R.A. & Reyman, T.A. (1980) A classic mummy: PUM II. In *Mummies, Disease and Ancient Cultures*, ed. A. Cockburn & E. Cockburn, pp.52–84. New York: Cambridge University Press.

Cockburn, E. (1974) China. *Paleopathology Newsletter* 6:3–4.

Cockburn, E. (1994) The Paleopathology Association, "Mortui Viventes Docent." *ERES-Serie de Arqueologia* **5**(**1**):135–247.

Cohen, M.N. (1989) *Health and the Rise of Civilization*. New Haven and London: Yale University Press.

Cohen, M.N. & Armelagos, G.J. (eds) (1984*a*) *Paleopathology at the Origins of Agriculture*. Orlando, FL: Academic Press.

Cohen, M.N. & Armelagos, G.J. (1984*b*) Paleopathology at the origins of agriculture: Editor's summation. In *Paleopathology at the Origins of Agriculture*, ed. M.N. Cohen & G.J. Armelagos, pp. 585–601. Orlando, FL: Academic Press.

Cohen, M.N. & Wagner, R. (1948) Dental development in pituitary dwarfism. *Journal of Dental Research* **27**:445–58.

Cole, R. (1929) Serum treatment in Type I lobar pneumonia. *Journal of the American Medical Association* **93**:741–7.

Collins, C.H. & Grange, J.M. (1983) The bovine tubercle bacillus. *Journal of Applied Bacteriology* **55**:13–29.

Collins, F.H. & Besansky, N.J. (1994) Vector biology and the control of malaria in Africa. *Science* **264**:1874–5.

Collis, E.L. (1914-1915) Milroy lectures 1915. Industrial pneumoconiosis with special reference to dust-phthisis. *Public Health, London* **28**:252–64, 292–305.

Collis, E.L. (1915-1916) Milroy lectures 1915. Industrial pneumoconiosis with special reference to dust-phthisis. *Public Health, London* **29**:37–44.

Comas, J. (1966) La Escafocefalia en Cráneos Mexicanos (Scaphocephaly in Mexican skulls). Anales de Antropología III:99–118.

Comas, J. (1968) *Dos Microcéfalos Aztecas. Leyenda, Historia y Antropología (Two cases of Microcephaly in Aztecs. Mythology, History and Anthropology)*. México, D.F.: Universidad Nacional Autónoma de México.

Comas, J. (1972) La Supuesta Difusión Transatlántica de la Trepanación Prehistórica (The so-called transatlantic diffusion of prehistoric trepanation). *Anales de Antropología* **9**:157–73.

Concheiro Carro, L. (1994) Asfixias Mecánicas (Mechanical asphyxia). In *Medicina Legal y Toxicología (Forensic Medicine and Toxicology)*, ed. J.A. Gisbert Calabuig, 4th edn, pp.

376–96. Barcelona: Masson-Salvat.

Cone, T.E. (1980) A rachitic infant painted by Burgkmair 136 years before Dr. Whistler described rickets. *Clinical Pediatrics* **19**(**3**):194.

Confalonieri, U.E., Araujo, A.J. & Ferreira, L.F. (1989) Enteroparasitos em Indios Yanomámi (enteric parasites in Yanomami Indians). *Memoria de Instituto Oswaldo Cruz* (Rio de Janeiro) **84**:**Supplement IV**, 111–13.

Connor, D.H. & Neafie, R.C. (1976) Cutaneous leishmaniasis. In *Pathology of Tropical and Extraordinary Diseases*, ed. C.H. Binford & D.H. Connor, vol. 1, pp. 259–64. Washington, DC: Armed Forces Institute of Pathology.

Connor, D.H., Neafie, R.C. & Meyers, W.M. (1976) Amebiasis. In *Pathology of Tropical and Extraordinary Diseases*, ed. C.H. Binford & D.H. Connor, vol. 1, pp. 308–16. Washington, DC: Armed Forces Institute of Pathology.

Conner, J.M. (1996) Fibrodysplasia ossificans progressiva – lessons from rare maladies. *New England Journal of Medicine* **335**(**8**):591–3. (Editorial).

Conrad, G.W. (1982) The burial platforms of Chan Chan: Some social and political implications. In *Chan Chan: Andean Desert City*, ed. M. Moseley & K.C. Day, pp. 87–113. Albuquerque, NM: University of New Mexico Press.

Contacos, P.G., Elder, H.A. & Coatney, G.R. (1962) Man to man transfer of two strains of *Plasmodium cynomulgi* by mosquito bite. *American Journal of Tropical Medicine and Hygiene* **11**:186–93.

Cook, D.C. (1980) Paget's disease and treponematosis in prehistoric Midwestern Indians: The case for misdiagnosis. *Ossa* **7**:41–63.

Cook, D.C. (1984) Subsistence and health in the lower Illinois valley: Osteological evidence. In *Paleopathology at the Origins of Agriculture*, ed. M.N. Cohen & G.J. Armelagos, pp. 235–69. Orlando, FL: Academic Press.

Cook, M., Molto, E. & Anderson, C. (1988) Possible case of hyperparathyroidism in a Roman period skeleton from Dakhleh oasis, Egypt, diagnosed using bone histomorphometry. *American Journal of Physical Anthropology* **75**:23–30.

Cook, N.D. (1992) Impact of disease in the sixteenth-century Andean world. In *Disease and Demography in the Americas*, ed. J.W. Verano & D. H. Ubelaker, pp. 207–13. Washington, DC: Smithsonian Institution Press.

Cooley, T.B. & Lee, P. (1925) A series of cases of splenomegaly in children with anemia and peculiar bone changes. *Transactions of the American Pediatric Society* **37**:29–31.

Cooley, T.B., Witwer, E.R. & Lee, P. (1927) Anaemia in children with splenomegaly and peculiar changes in bones. *American Journal of Diseases of Children* **34**:347–63.

Cooper, D.B. (1993) Ainhum. In *The Cambridge*

World History of Human Disease, ed. K.F. Kiple, p. 561. New York: Cambridge University Press.

Copeman, W.S. (1970) Historical aspects of gout. *Clinical Orthopedics and Related Research* **74**:14–22.

Correal Urrego, G. (1990) *Aguazuque. Evidencias de Cazadores, Recolectores y Plantadores en la Altiplanicie de la Cordillera Oriental (Aguazuque. Evidence of Hunters, Gatherers and Planters on the Eastern Cordillera High Plateau)*. Bogotá: Fundación de Investigaciones Arqueológicas Nacionales. Banco de la República.

Cotran, R.S., Kumar, V. & Robbins, S. (1989) *Robbins Pathologic Basis of Disease*, 4th edn. Philadelphia: Saunders.

Cotran, R.S., Kumar, V. & Robbins, S.L. (1994) *Robbins Pathologic Basis of Disease*, 5th edn. Philadelphia: Saunders.

Coughlin, E.A. (1977) Analysis of PUM II mummy fluid. *Paleopathology Newsletter* **17**:7–8.

Councilman, W.T. & Lafleur, H. (1891) Amoebic dysentery. *Johns Hopkins Hospital Reports* **2**:395–548.

Councilman, W.T., Magrath, G.B. & Brinckerhoff, W.R. (1904) The pathological anatomy and histology of variola. *Journal of Medical Research* **11**:12–135.

Courville, C.B. (1967) Cranial injuries in prehistoric man. In *Diseases in Antiquity*, ed. D. Brothwell & A.T. Sandison, pp. 606–22. Springfield, IL: C.C. Thomas.

Cousins, D.V., Williams, S.N., Reuter, R., Forshaw, D., Chadwick, B., Coughran, D., Collins, P. & Gales, N. (1993) Tuberculosis in wild seals and characterization of the seal bacillus. *Australian Veterinary Journal* **70**:92–7.

Craighead, J.E. (1994) Diabetes. In *Pathology*, ed. E. Rubin & J.L. Farber, 2nd edn, pp. 1148–60. Philadelphia: Lippincott.

Crosby, A.W. (1967) Conquistador y pestilencia: The first New World pandemic and the fall of the great Indian empires. *Hispanic American Historical Review* **47**:321–37.

Crosby, A.W. (1976) Virgin soil epidemics as a factor in the aboriginal depopulation in America. *The William and Mary Quarterly, 3d Series* **33**:286–99.

Crosby, A.W. (1986) *Ecological Imperialism. The Biological Expansion of Europe, 900–1900*. New York: Cambridge University Press.

Crosby, A.W. (1992) Summary on population size before and after contact. In *Disease and Demography in the Americas*, ed. J.W. Verano & D.H. Ubelaker, pp. 277–8. Washington, DC: Smithsonian Institution Press.

Crosby, A.W. (1993*a*) Influenza. In *The Cambridge World History of Human Disease*, ed. K.F. Kiple, pp. 807–11. New York: Cambridge University Press.

Crosby, A.W. (1993*b*) Smallpox. In *The Cam-*

bridge *World History of Human Disease*, ed. K.F. Kiple, pp. 1008–13. New York: Cambridge University Press.

Crubézy, E. (1990) Diffuse idiopathic skeletal hyperostosis: Diagnosis and importance in paleopathology. *Journal of Paleopathology* **3**(**2**):107–17.

Crubézy, E. & Trinkaus, E. (1992) Shanidar 1: A case of hyperostotic disease (DISH) in the Middle Paleolithic. *American Journal of Physical Anthropology* **89**:411–20.

Cruess, R. & Rennie, W.R.J. (1984) *Adult Orthopedics*. London: Churchill and Livingstone.

Crump, J.A. (1901) Trephining in the South Seas. *Journal of the Royal Anthropological Institute* **31**:167–72.

Curtin, P.D. (1988) African health at home and abroad. In *The African Exchange*, ed. K.F. Kiple, pp. 110–30. Durham, NC: Duke University Press.

Cybulski, J.S. (1978) *An Earlier Population of Hesquiat Harbour, British Columbia. A Contribution to Nootkon Osteology and Physical Anthropology*. British Columbia Provincial Museum Cultural Recovery Papers, no. 1. Victoria, B.C.: British Columbia Provincial Museum.

Czarnetzki, A. (1980) A Possible Trisomy 21 from the Late Hallstatt Period. In *Papers on Paleopathology Presented at the IIIrd European Members Meeting of the Paleopathology Association in Caen, France. Paleopathology Newsletter* **32** (**Supplement**):107. (Abstract).

Czermak, J. (1852) Beschreibung und mikroskopische Untersuchung zweier ägyptischer Mumien. (Description and microscopic studies of two Egyptian mummies). *Sonder-Berichte Akademie Wissenschaft Wien* **9**:427–69.

Czermak, J.N. (1879) *Beschreibung und mikroskopische Untersuchung von Mumien. Gesammelte Schriften (Description and microscopic investigation of mummies. Collected papers)*. Leipzig.

D'Aunoy, R. & King, E.L. (1922) Lithopedion formation in extrauterine fetal masses. *American Journal of Obstetrics and Gynecology* **3**:377–84.

D'Auria, S., Lacovara, P. & Roehrig, C. (1988) *Mummies and Magic. The Funerary Arts of Ancient Egypt*. Boston: Boston Museum of Fine Arts.

d'Errico, F., Villa, G. & Fornaciari, G. (1988) Dental esthetics of an Italian Renaissance noblewoman, Isabella d'Aragona. A case of chronic mercury intoxication. *Ossa* **13**:233–54.

Dahlin, D.C. (1967) *Bone Tumors*, 2nd edn. Springfield, IL: C.C. Thomas.

Dalby, G., Manchester, K. & Roberts, C. (1993) Otosclerosis and stapedial footplate fixation in archaeological material. *International Jour-* nal *of Osteoarchaeology* **3**:207–12.

Dalton, H.P., Allison, M.J. & Pezzia, A. (1976) The documentation of communicable disease in Peruvian mummies. (Medical College of Virginia, Richmond, VA) *MCV Quarterly* **12**(**2**):43–8.

Dame, J.B., Williams, J. L., McCutchan, T.F., Weber, J. L., Wirtz, R.A., Hockmeyer, W.T., Maloy, W.L., Haynes, J.D., Schneider, I., Roberts, D., Sanders, G.S., Reddy, E. P., Diggs, C.L. & Miller, L.H. (1984) Structure of the gene encoding the immunodominant surface antigen of the sporozoite of the human malaria parasite *Plasmodium falciparum*. *Science* **225**:593–9.

Daniel, T. (1978) An immunochemist's view of the epidemiology of tuberculosis. Paper presented at the 47th meeting of the American Association of Physical Anthropologists held on April 13, 1978. Recorded and distributed on audio tape by Audio Archives of Canada. Abstract appeared in *American Journal of Physical Anthropology* **48**:388–9.

Daniels, F. & Post, P. (1970) The histology and histochemistry of prehistoric mummy skin. In *Advances in the Biology of Skin. Volume X. The Dermis*, ed. W. Montagna, J. P. Bentley & R.L. Dobson, pp. 279–92. Publication no. 396 from the Oregon Regional Primate Research Center. New York: Appleton-Century-Crofts.

Daniels, G.H. & Martin, J.B. (1991) Neuroendocrine regulation and diseases of the anterior pituitary and hypothalamus. In *Harrison's Principles of Internal Medicine*, ed. J.D. Wilson, E. Braunwald, K.J. Isselbacher, *et al.*, 12th edn, pp. 1655–82. New York: McGraw-Hill.

Danilewsky, B. (1889–1891) *La Parasitologie Comparée du Sanguine (Comparative Parasitology of the Blood)*, vol. 1 (Oiseaux), vol. 2 (Tortues) and vol. 3 (Reptiles). Paris: Kharkov.

Dastugue, J. (1973) Trephined skulls from the valley of Petit-Morin (France). *Paleopathology Newsletter* **5**:17.

Dastugue, J. & Gervais, V. (1992) *Paléopathologie du Squelette Humaine (The Paleopathology of the Skeleton)*. Paris: Boubée.

Dastugue, J. & Lumley, M.A. de (1976) Les Maladies des Hommes Préhistoriques du Páleolithique et du Mésolithique (Diseases of prehistoric man from the Paleolithic and Neolithic). *La Préhistoire Française* **1**(**1**):612–22.

Davey, T.F. & Rees, R.J.W. (1974) The nasal discharge in leprosy: Clinical and bacteriological aspects. *Leprosy Review* **45**:121–34.

David, A.R. (ed.) (1979) *The Manchester Museum Mummy Project*. Manchester: Manchester University Press.

David, J.D., Poswillo, D. & Simpson, D. (1982) *The Craniosynostoses. Causes, Natural History, and Management*. New York, Heidelberg, Berlin: Springer-Verlag.

Davidson, P.T. & Horowitz, I. (1970) Skeletal tuberculosis. *American Journal of Medicine* **48**:77–84.

Davis, D.H.S., Hallett, A.F. & Isaacson, M. (1975) Plague. In *Diseases Transmitted from Animals to Man,* ed. W.T. Hubbert, W.F. McCulloch & P.R. Schnurrenberger, 6th edn, pp. 147–73. Springfield, IL: C.C. Thomas.

de Chauliac, G. (1890) La Grande Chirurgie (Great Surgery), ed. E. Nicaise. Paris. (First written ca. 1350).

de Lumley, M.A. (1962) Lesions osseuses de l'homme de Castellar (Osseous lesions of the man from Castellar). *Bulletin du Musée d'Anthropologie PréChristorique de Monaco* **9**:191–205.

de Pina, L. (1965) Lights and shadows in the ancient art of dentistry. *Revista Portuguesa de Estomatologia e Chirurgie Maxilofaciale* **6**:17–44.

Denninger, H.S. (1931) Osteitis fibrosa in a skeleton of a prehistoric American Indian. *Archives of Pathology* **11**:939–44.

Denninger, H.S. (1933) Paleopathological evidence of Paget's disease. *Annals of Medical History* **5**:73–81.

Derry, D.E. (1909) Anatomical report. *Archives of the Survey of Nubia Bulletin* **3**:29–52.

Derry, D.E. (1938) Pott's disease in ancient Egypt. *Medical Press* **197**:196–9.

deVasto, M.A. (1974) The existence of pre-Columbian cretinism. Paper presented at the 2nd Annual Meeting of the Paleopathology Association held in Amherst, MA, April 11, 1974. *Paleopathology Newsletter* **6**(**June:Supplement**):6–7. (Abstract).

Devor, E. (1993) Genetic disease. In *The Cambridge World History of Human Disease*, ed. K.F. Kiple, pp. 118–19. New York: Cambridge University Press.

Dewey, J., Armelagos, G. & Bartley, M. (1969) Femoral cortical involution in three Nubian archaeological populations. *Human Biology* **41**:13–28.

Dexiang, W., Wenyuan, Y., Shenqi, H., Yunfang, L., Tiancheng, S., Jiahua, M., Wenxiu, H. & Nianfeng, X. (1981) Parasitological investigation on the ancient corpse of the Western Han Dynasty unearthed from tomb No. 168 on Phoenix Hill in Jiangling county. *Acta Academiae Medicinae Wuhan* **1**:16–23.

Dharmendra (1947) Leprosy in ancient Indian medicine. *International Journal of Leprosy* **15**:424–30.

Diamond, J. (1990) A pox upon our genes. *Natural History* (**February**) **1990**:26–30.

Diamond, J. (1992) Sweet death. *Natural History* (**February**) **1992**:2–6.

Díaz de Isla, R. (1542) Tratado Llamado Fructo de los Sanchos: Contra el Mal Serpentino Venido de la Ysla Española (Treatment Called the Fruit of the Saints for the Serpentine

Disease that came from the Island Hispaniola). Seville.

DiBartolomeo, J.R. (1979) Exostoses of the external auditory canal. *Annals of Otology, Rhinology and Laryngology* **88**(6) (**Supplement 61**):2–20.

Dieck, A. (1965) *Die Europäischen Moorleichenfunde (The European Bog Bodies)*. Neumünster: Karl Wachholtz Verlag.

Diego Cuscoy, L. (1986) El "Banot" como Arma de Guerra entre los Aborígenes Canarios (Un Testimonio Anatómico) (The 'Banot' as a war weapon among the Canarian aboriginals (anatomic evidence)). *Anuario de Estudios Atlánticos* **32**:733–81.

Dieppe, P. (1989) The history of rheumatoid arthritis. In *The Antiquity of the Erosive Arthropathies*, ed. P.J. Maddison, pp. 35–8. The Arthritis and Rheumatism Council for Research (ARC) Conference Proceedings no. 5. Bath, England: ARC.

DiMaio, D.J. & DiMaio, V.J.M. (1989) *Forensic Pathology*. New York: Elsevier.

di Tota, G., Capasso, L. & DiMuzio, M. (1992) A probable bladder stone from an Iron Age burial in central Italy. In *Papers on Paleopathology Presented at the IXth European Members Meeting of the Paleopathology Association in Barcelona, Spain. Paleopathology Newsletter* **79** (**Supplement**):10. (Abstract).

Dixon, B. (1985) Doubts that reach out from the grave. *New Scientist* **25**:58–9.

Dixon, R.A., Ensor, S., Lewis, M.E. & Roberts, C. (1995) The detection of *Mycobacterium tuberculosis* by PCR from human bone? Paper Presented at the 21st Annual Meeting of the Paleopathology Association, held in Denver, CO, 29–30 March. *Paleopathology Newsletter* **84** (**Supplement**):14. (Abstract).

Dobyns, H.F. (1963) An outline of Andean epidemic history to 1720. *Bulletin of the History of Medicine* **37**(6):493–515.

Dobyns, H.F. (1992) Native American trade centers as contagious disease foci. In *Disease and Demography in the Americas*, ed. J.W.Verano & D.H. Ubelaker, pp. 215–22. Washington, DC: Smithsonian Institition Press.

Dokládal, M. & Horácková, L. (1994) Two rare skulls with extreme microcephaly. *HOMO* **45** (**Supplement**):S40.

Dols, M.W. (1983) The leper in medieval society. *Speculum* **58**(2)(**July–Oct**):891–916.

Donington, R. (1974) *Wagner's Ring and Its Symbols*. Boston: Faber and Faber.

Doran, G.H., Dickel, D.N., Ballinger, W.E., Jr, Agee, F.O., Laipis, P.J. & Hauswirth, W.W. (1986) Anatomic, cellular and molecular analysis of 8000 year old human brain tissue from the Windover archaeological site. *Nature* **323**:803–6.

Dowling, H.F. (1973) The rise and fall of pneumonia-control programs. *Journal of Infectious Diseases* **127**:201–6.

Dreier, F.G. (1992) The paleopathology of a finger dislocation. *International Journal of Osteoarchaeology* **2**(1):31–5.

Drioton, E. (1950) *Egyptian Art*. New York: Golden Griffin Books.

Dubos, R. & Dubos, J. (1952) *The White Plague*. New Brunswick: Rutgers University Press.

Duffin, J. (1993) Pneumonia. In *The Cambridge World History of Human Disease*, ed. K.F. Kiple, pp. 938–42. New York: Cambridge University Press.

Dunn, F.L. (1965) On the antiquity of malaria in the Western Hemisphere. *Human Biology* **37**:385–93.

Dunn, F.L. (1993) Malaria. In *The Cambridge World History of Human Disease*, ed. K. F. Kiple, pp. 855–62. New York: Cambridge University Press.

During, E., Zimmerman, M.R., Krikun, M.E. & Rydberg, J. (1994) Helmsman's elbow: An occupational disease of the seventeenth century. *Journal of Paleopathology* **6**(1):19–27.

Duró, J.C. (1983) Osteomielitis. In *Reumatología Clínica (Clinical Rheumatology)*, vol. 2, ed. J. Rotés Querol, pp. 326–35. Barcelona: Expaxs.

Duthie, R.B. & Bentley, G. (1987) *Cirugía Ortopédica, de Mercer (Mercer's Orthopedic Surgery)*. Barcelona: Medici.

Duviols, P. (1976) La Capacocha. *Revista Allpanchis (Cuzco)* **9**:11–57.

Dzierzykray-Rogalski, T. (1980) Paleopathology of the Ptolemaic inhabitants of Dakhleh Oasis (Egypt). *Journal of Human Evolution* **9**:71–4.

Dzierzykray-Rogalski, T. (1988) Paleopathologic changes of the scrotum of a baby from the sixteenth century. In *Papers on Paleopathology Presented at the VIIth European Members Meeting of the Paleopathology Association in Lyon, France on 1–4 September. Paleopathology Newsletter* **62** (**Dec**) (**Supplement**):4–5. (Abstract).

Dzierzykray-Rogalski, T. & Prominska, E. (1994) A further report on Pharaoh Siptah's handicap (XIXth Egyptian Dynasty). *HOMO* **45** (**Supplement**):S45.

Ebbell, B. (Translator) (1937) *The Papyrus Ebers*. Copenhagen: Levin and Munksgaard.

Edeiken, J. (1976) Radiologic diagnosis of joint disease. In *Bones and Joints*, ed. L.V. Ackerman, H.J. Spjut & M.R. Abell, pp. 98–109. Baltimore: Williams and Wilkins.

Edeiken, J. & Hodes, P.J. (1973) *Roentgen Diagnosis of Bone*, vol. 1. Baltimore: Williams and Wilkins.

el-Mallakh, R.S. (1985) Night of the living dead: Could the mummy strike again? *Journal of the American Medical Association* **254**:3038. [Letter to the Editor].

el-Najjar, M.Y. (1979) Human treponematosis and tuberculosis: Evidence from the New World. *American Journal of Physical Anthropology* **51**:599–618.

el-Najjar, M.Y. & McWilliams, K.R. (1978) *Forensic Anthropology*. Springfield, IL: C.C. Thomas.

el-Najjar, M.Y., Aufderheide, A.C. & Ortner, D.J. (1985) Preserved human remains from the southern region of the North American continent: Report of autopsy findings. *Human Pathology* **16**(3):273–6.

Eldridge, W.M. & Holm, G.A. (1940) The incidence of hyperostosis frontalis interna in female patients admitted to a mental hospital. *American Journal of Roentgenology* **43**:356–9.

Elena Ibáñez, A., González Lanza, M. & García Vadillo, J.A. (1984) Infecciones Bacterianas del Aparato Locomotor (Bacterial infections of the locomotive system). *Medicine* **24**:984–94.

Ell, S.R. (1993) Disease ecologies of Europe. In *The Cambridge World History of Human Disease*, ed. K.F. Kiple, pp. 504–19. New York: Cambridge University Press.

Ellison, P. (1987) American scientist interviews. *American Scientist* **75**:622–7.

Endt, D.W. von & Ortner, D.J. (1982) Amino acid analysis of bone from a suspected case of prehistoric iron deficiency anemia from the American southwest. *American Journal of Physical Anthropology* **59**:377–85.

England, I.A. (1962) Trephining through the ages. *Radiography* **28**:301–14.

Epstein, B.S. (1953) The concurrence of parietal thinness with postmenopausal, senile or idiopathic osteoporosis. *Radiology* **60**:29–35.

Erdheim, J. (1931) Über Wirbelsäulenveränderungen bei Akromegalie (Concerning vertebral column changes in acromegaly). *Virchow's Archiv für Pathologische Anatomie und Klinische Medizin* **281**:197–296.

Ericksen, M.F. (1976) Cortical bone loss with age in three native American populations. *American Journal of Physical Anthropology* **45**:443–5.

Esper, J.F. (1774) *Ausführliche Nachrichten von Neuentdeckten Zoolithen unbekannter vierfüssiger Thiere (Report of newly-discovered, fossilized previously unknown four-footed animals)*. Nüremberg: Erben. (Facsimile copy printed 1978, in Wiesbaden, Germany by Guido Pressler Verlag).

Estes, J.W. (1989) *The Medical Skills of Ancient Egypt*. Canton, MA: Science History Publications.

Ettling, J. (1981) *The Germ of Laziness: Rockefeller Philanthopy and Public Health in the New South*. Cambridge, MA: Harvard University Press.

Ettling, J. (1993) Hookworm disease. In *The Cambridge World History of Human Disease*, ed. K.F. Kiple, pp.784–8. New York: Cambridge University Press.

Etxeberria, F. (1994) Vertebral epiphysitis: Early signs of brucellar disease. *Journal of Paleopathology* **6**(1):41–9.

Etxeberria, F. & Vegas, J. I. (1987) Violent injury in a Bronze Age individual in the Basque Country (Spain). *Journal of Paleopathology* **1**(**1**):19–23.

European Polycystic Kidney Disease Consortium (1994) The polycystic kidney disease 1 gene encodes a 14 kb transcript and lies within a duplicated region on chromosome 16. *Cell* **77**:881–94.

Eyles, D.E., Coatney, R.G. & Getz, M.E. (1960) Vivax-type malaria parasite of macaques transmissible to man. *Science* **131**:1812–13.

Faccini, J.M. & Teotia, S.P.S. (1974) Histopathological assessment of endemic skeletal fluorosis. *Calcified Tissue Research* **16**:45–57.

Fairbanks, V.F. (1994) Blue gods, blue oil and blue people. *Mayo Clinic Proceedings* **69**:889–92.

Fairman, H.W. (1972) Tutankhamun and the end of the 18th dynasty. *Antiquity* **46**:15–18.

Farwell, D.E. & Molleson, T.L. (1993) *Excavations at Poundbury 1966–80*. Vol. II: *The Cemeteries*. Dorset Natural History and Archaeological Society, Monograph Series, no. 11. Dorchester, England: Dorset Natural History and Archaeological Society.

Fastlicht, S. (1948) Tooth mutilations in pre-Columbian Mexico. *Journal of the American Dental Association* **36**:315–23.

Fazzini, R. (1975) *Images for Eternity*. New York: Brooklyn Museum.

Feder, J.N., Gnirke, A., Thomas, W., *et al.* (1996) A novel MHC class-I-like gene is mutated in patients with hereditary haemochromatosis. *Nature Genetics* **13** (**4**):399–408.

Feeny, P. (1964) *The Fight Against Leprosy*. London: Elek Books.

Feldman, F. (1989) Tuberous sclerosis, neurofibromatosis and fibrous dysplasia. In *Bone and Joint Imaging*, ed. D. Resnick, pp.1218–32. Philadelphia: W.B. Saunders.

Ferembach, D. (1963) Frequency of spina bifida occulta in prehistoric human skeletons. *Nature* **199**:100–1.

Fernandez, J.M.M. (1957) Leprosy and tuberculosis: Antagonistic diseases. *Archives of Dermatology and Syphilology* **75**:101–6.

Ferrández Portal, L. (1996) Tumores Óseos (Bone tumours). In *Cirugía. Tratado de Patología y Clínica Quirúrgicas (Surgery: Treatise on Surgical and Clinical Pathology)*, ed. H. Durán, I. Arceluz, L. García-Sancho, F. González Hermoso, J. Álvarez, L. Ferrández & J. Méndez, 2nd edn, vol. 3, pp. 3760–831. Madrid: Interamericana-McGraw Hill.

Ferreira, L.F., de Araújo, A.J.G. & Confalonieri, U.E.C. (1980) The finding of eggs and larvae of parasitic helminths in archaeological material from Unai, Minas Gerais, Brasil. *Transactions of the Royal Society of Tropical Medicine and Hygiene* **74**:798–800.

Ferreira, L.F., de Araújo, A.J.G. & Confalonieri, U.E.C. (1983a) The finding of helminth eggs in a Brazilian mummy. *Transactions of the Royal Society of Tropical Medicine and Hygiene* **77**(**1**):65–7.

Ferreira, L.F., de Araújo, A.J.G. & Confalonieri, U.E.C. (1983b) Parasites in archaeological material from Brazil: A reply to M.M. Kliks. *Transactions of the Royal Society for Tropical Medicine and Hygiene* **77**:565–6.

Ferreira, L.F., de Araújo, A.J.G. & Duarte, A.N. (1993) Nematode larvae in fossilized animal coprolites from Lower and Middle Pleistocene sites, central Italy. *Journal of Parasitology* **79**(**3**):440–2.

Ferreira, L.F., de Araújo, A.J.G., Confalonieri, U., Chamee, M.& Ribeiro, B.M. (1987) Encontro de ovos de ancilostomideos em coprolitos humano datados de 7230 ± 80 años, Piauí, Brasil (The finding of hookworm eggs in human coprolites dating to 7230 ± 80 years ago from Piauí, Brazil). *Ánales Académia Brasileira de Ciéncials* **59**(**3**):280–1.

Figueroa, L., Razmiliz, B.B., Allison, M.J. & Gonzalez, U.M. (1988) Evidencia de arsenicismo crónico en momias del Valle Camarones, región Tarapacá, Chile (Evidence of chronic arsenicism in mummies of the Camarones Valley in the Tarapaca region, Chile). *Chungará (Arica, Chile)* **21**:33–42.

Fildes, V.A. (1986) "The English disease": Infantile rickets and scurvy in preindustrial England. In *Child Care Through The Centuries*, ed. J. Cole & T. Turner, pp. 121–34. Cardiff: SST Publishing for the British Society for the History of Medicine.

Filho, L.F., de Araújo, A.J.G. & Confalonieri, U. (1988) The finding of helminth eggs in a Brazilian mummy. In *Paleoparasitologia No Brasil (Paleoparasitology in Brazil)*, ed. L.F. Ferreira, A.J.G. de Araújo & U. Confalonieri, pp. 41–3. Rio de Janeiro: PEC/ENSP, 1988.

Fine, P.E.M. (1988) BCG vaccination against tuberculosis and leprosy. *British Medical Bulletin* **44**:691–703.

Fischer, C. (1980) Bog bodies of Denmark. In *Mummies, Disease and Ancient Cultures*, ed. A. Cockburn & E. Cockburn, pp. 178–93. Cambridge: Cambridge University Press.

Fisher, A. (1984) Africa adorned. *National Geographic* **166**(**5**):600–33.

Fisher, A.K. (1935) Additional paleopathological evidence of Paget's disease. *Annals of Medical History* **7**:197–8.

FitzSimmons, E., Jones, G.K. & Steinberg, C. (1994) Report on Peruvian incisor inlay from the Late Intermediate period at Ancon. Paper presented at the 13th Annual Northeast Conference on Andean Archaeology and Ethnohistory, Ithaca, New York, 15–16 October, 1994.

Fleming, S. (1987) Infant sacrifice at Pachacamac, Peru: Dignity in death. *Archaeology* **40**(**2**):64–5,74,77.

Flick, L.F. (1925) *Development of our Knowledge of Tuberculosis*. Philadelphia, PA: Press of Wickersham Printing Company, Lancaster, PA. (Privately published).

Flinn, R.M., Corbett, M.E. & Smith, A.J. (1987) An unusual dental deposit – a taphonomic process? *Journal of Archaeological Science* **141**:291–5.

Fogel, M.L., Tuross, N. & Owsley, D.W. (1989) Nitrogen isotope tracers of human lactation in modern and archaeological populations. In *Annual Report of the Director of Geophysical Laboratory 1988–1989*, pp. 111–17. Washington, DC: Carnegie Institution of Washington.

Food and Drug Administration (1994) Tattooing. *FDA Medical Bulletin* **24**:8.

Foote, J.A. (1927) Evidence of rickets prior to 1650. *American Journal for Diseases of Children* **34**:443–52.

Formicola, V., Milanesi, Q. & Scarsini, C. (1987) Evidence of spinal tuberculosis at the beginning of the fourth millennium B.C. from Arene Candide cave (Liguria, Italy). *American Journal of Physical Anthropology* **72**:1–6.

Fornaciari, G. (1985) The mummies of the Abbey of Saint Domenico Maggiore in Naples: A preliminary report. *dall'Archivio per l'Antropologia e la Etnologia* **115**:215–26.

Fornaciari, G. & Marchetti, A. (1986) Intact smallpox virus particles in an Italian mummy of the sixteenth century: An immunoelectron microscopy study. *Paleopathology Newsletter* **56**:7–12.

Fornaciari, G., Castagna, U., Tognetti, A. & Tornaboni, D. (1988a) Syphilis teriarie dan une Momie du XVI Siécle: Étude Immunohistochimique et Ultrastructurelle (Tertiary syphilis in a sixteenth century mummy: Immunohistochemical and ultrastructural study). In *Papers on Paleopathology Presented at the VIIth European Members Meeting of the Paleopathology Association in Lyon, France on 1–4 September. Paleopathology Newsletter* **62** (**Dec**) (**Supplement**):7. (Abstract).

Fornaciari, G., Tornaboni, D., Pollina, L. & Tognetti, A. (1988b) Pathologie Pulmonaire et Hépatique (Pulmonary and hepatic pathology). In *Papers on Paleopathology Presented at the VIIth European Members Meeting of the Paleopathology Asocation in Lyon, France on 1–4 September. Paleopathology Newsletter* **62** (**Dec**) (**Supplement**):9. (Abstract).

Fornaciari, G., Bruno, J., Amadei, A., Tornaboni, D. & Tognetti, A. (1989a) Pathologie Rachidienne sur un Échantillon d'une Classe Socialement Élevée de la Renaissance Italienne (Spinal pathology in a specimen from an elite social class of the Italian Renaissance). La Sèrie de Momies de la Basilique de S. Domenico Maggiore à Naples (XVe–XVIe Siècles) (Mummy series from the Basilica of

St. Domenico Maggiore in Naples (XV–XVIth Centuries)). In *Advances in Paleopathology*, ed. L. Capasso, pp. 59–64. (Proceedings of the VIIth European Members Meeting of the Paleopathology Association in Lyon, France, September 1988.) Journal of Paleopathology Monograph Publications no. 1. Chieti: Marino Solfanelli Editore.

Fornaciari, G., Tornaboni, D., Castagna, M., Bevilacqua, G. & Tognetti, A. (1989*b*) Variole dans une momie du XIVe, siélle de la basilique de S. Domenico Maggiore a Naples: Etude immunohistochimique, ultrastructure et biologie moléculare (Variola in a fourteenth century mummy from the Basilica of St. Domenico Maggiore at Naples: Immunological, ultrastructural and molecular biochemical study). In *Advances in Paleopathology*, ed. L. Capasso, pp. 97–100. Chieti: Marino Solfanelli Editore.

Fornaciari, G., Castagna, M., Viacava, P., Tognetti, A., Bevilacqua, G. & Segura, E.L. (1992*a*) Chagas' disease in Peruvian Inca mummy. *Lancet* **339**:128–9.

Fornaciari, G., Castagna, M., Viacava, P., Tognetti, A., Segura, E.L. & Bevilacqua, G. (1992*b*) Malattia di Chagas in una mummia Peruviana Inca del Museo Nazionale di Antropologia ed Etnologia di Firenze (Chagas' disease in a Peruvian Inca mummy from the National Museum of Anthropology and Ethnology in Florence) *Archivio per L'Antropologia e la Etnologia (Firenze)* **122**:369–76.

Fornaciari, G., Castagna, M., Naccarato, G., Collecchi, P., Tognetti, A. & Bevilacqua, G. (1993) Adenocarcinoma in the mummy of Ferrante I of Aragon, King of Naples (1431–1494 A.D.). *Paleopathology Newsletter* **83**:5–8.

Fornaciari, G., Castagna, M., Tornaboni, D. & Lenziardi, M. (1994) Thyroid goiter in a XVIII century Sicilian mummy. *HOMO* **45**(**Supplement**):50.

Forrester, D.M. & Brown, J.C. (1990) *Radiología de las Enfermedades Articulares (Radiology of Joint Diseases)*. Barcelona: Salvat.

Forshufvud, S., Smith, H. & Wassén, A. (1961) Arsenic content of Napoleon I's hair probably taken immediately after his death. *Nature* **192**(**4798**):103–5.

Fouquet, D. (1886) Observations relevées sur quelques mommies Royale d'Egypte. (Relevant observations on several royal mummies of Egypt) *Bulletin de la Société d'Anthropologie de Paris* **3**:578–86.

Fowler, E., Jr & Osmun, P. (1942) New bone growth due to cold water in the ears. *Archives of Otolaryngology* **36**:455–66.

Fracastoro, G. ([1530] 1935) Fracastor, syphilis or the French disease. A poem in Latin hexameters. Translated by Heneage Wynne-Finch. London: William Heinemann Medical Books, Ltd.

Fraire, A.E., Johnson, E.H., Kim, H.S. & Titus, J.L. (1988) The relationship of obesity to gall-

stones – an autopsy study. Poster session at meeting of the United States and Canadian Academy of Pathology held at Washington, DC, February 28– March 4, 1988.

Francis, J. (1947) *Bovine Tuberculosis*. London: Staples Press, Ltd.

Francis, T. (1940) New type of virus from epidemic influenza. *Science* **92**:405–8.

Fraser, J. (1914) *Tuberculosis of the Bones and Joints in Children*. London: Adam and Charles Black.

Frayer, D.W., Horton, W.A., Macchiarelli, R. & Mussi, M. (1987) Dwarfism in an adolescent from the Italian Late Upper Paleolithic. *Nature* **330**:60–2.

Frazer, J.G. (1976) *The Golden Bough*. New York: Macmillan. (First published in 1922).

Fredrickson, B.E., Baker, D., McHolick, W.J., Yuan, H.A. & Lubicky, J.P. (1984) The natural history of spondylolysis and spondylolisthesis. *Journal of Bone and Joint Surgery* **66A**:699–707.

Freiberg, A.H. (1914) Infraction of the second metatarsal bone. A typical injury. *Surgery, Gynecology and Obstetrics* **19**:191–200.

French, R.K. (1993) Scurvy. In *The Cambridge World History of Human Disease*, ed. K.F. Kiple, pp.1000–5. New York: Cambridge University Press.

Friedländer, C. (1882) Über die Schizomyceten bei der acuten fibrösen pneumonie (Concerning acute, fibrotic pneumonia by schizomycetes). *Virchow's Archiv für Patologische Anatomie und Physiologie und für Klinische Medizin (Berlin)* **87**:319–24.

Friedman, H. (1991) Smallpox, vaccinia and other pox viruses. In *Harrison's Principles of Internal Medicine*, ed. E. Braunwald, K.J. Isselbacher, J.D. Wilson, *et al.*, 12th edn, pp. 709–12. New York: McGraw-Hill.

Friedman, S.A. & Rakow, R.B. (1971) Osseous lesions of the foot in diabetic neuropathy. *Diabetes* **20**(**5**):302–7.

Frost, P. (1988) Human skin color: A possible relationship between its sexual dimorphism and its social perception. *Perspectives in Biology and Medicine* **32**(**1**):38–58.

Fry, G.F. (1977) *Analysis of Prehistoric Coprolites from Utah*. Anthropological Papers no. 97. Salt Lake City, UT: University of Utah.

Fuchs, J. (1964) Physical alterations which occur in the blind and are illustrated on ancient Egyptian works of art. *New York Academy of Sciences* **117**(**1**):618–23.

Fulcheri, E. (1987) Case No. 27: Verruca vulgaris.(Department of Pathology, Medical College of Virginia, Richmond, VA) *Paleopathology Club Newsletter* **31**:2.

Fulcheri, E. & Grilletto, R. (1988) Sur un probable calcul rénal daté ancien empire Egyptien (Concerning a probable renal calculus dating to the ancient Egyptian empire). In *Papers on Paleopathology Presented at the VIIth Euro-

pean Members Meeting of the Paleopathology Association in Lyon, France, 1–4 September 1988. Paleopathology Newsletter* **62** (**Dec**) (**Supplement**):10. (Abstract).

Fulcheri, E., Rabino-Massa, E. & Doro Garetto, T. (1986) Differential diagnosis between palaeopathological and non-pathological postmortem environmental factors in ancient human remains. *Journal of Human Evolution* **15**:71–5.

Funk, C. (1914) *Die Vitamine (The Vitamins)*. Wiesbaden: J.F. Bergman.

García Pérez, A. (1975) Dermatología y Venereología (Dermatology and venerology). In *Historia Universal de la Medicina (Universal History of Medicine*, ed. P. Laín Entralgo, vol. 7, pp. 272–8. Barcelona: Salvat.

García Sánchez, M. (1979) Paleopatología de la Población Aborigen de la Cueva Sepulcral de Pino Leris (La Orotava, Tenerife) (Paleopathology of the aboriginal population of the burial cave at Pino Leris (La Orotava, Tenerife)). *Anuario de Estudios Atlánticos* **25**: 567–84.

García-Friás, J.E. (1940) La Tuberculosis en los Antiguous Peruanos (Tuberculosis in ancient Peruvians). *Actualidad Medica Peruana* **5**:274–91.

Garcilaso de la Vega ([1609] 1966) *Royal Commentaries of the Incas and General History of Peru*. Part 1. Translated by Harold V. Livermore. Austin, TX: University of Texas Press. [First published in Lisbon in 1609].

Garcilaso de la Vega ([1616] 1987) *Royal Commentaries of the Incas and General History of Peru*. Part 2. Translated by Harold V. Livermore. Austin, TX: University of Texas Press. [First published in Córdova in 1616].

Gardner, W.A. (1924) Lice from human mummies. *Science* **60**:389–90.

Garland, R. (1985) *The Greek Way of Death*. Ithaca, NY: Cornell University Press.

Garn, S.M., Silverman, F.N., Hertzog, K.P. & Rohman, C.G. (1968) Lines and bands of increased density: Their implication to growth and development. *Medical Radiography and Photography* **44**:58–89.

Garnham, P.C.C. (1947) Exo-erythrocytic schizogony in *Plasmodium Kochi* Laveran. A preliminary note. *Transactions of the Royal Society of Tropical Medicine and Hygiene* **40**:719–22.

Garnham, P.C.C. (1963) Distribution of simian malaria parasites in various hosts. *Journal of Parasitology* **49**(**6**):905–11.

Garnham, P.C.C. (1966) *Malaria Parasites and Other Haemosporidia*. Oxford: Blackwell Scientific.

Garrison, F.H. (1917) Memorial notice Sir Marc Armand Ruffer k.t., C.M.G. (1859–1917). *Annals of Medical History* **1**:218–20.

Garrison, F.H. (1966) *Historia de la Medicina (The History of Medicine)*, 4th edn. México, DF: Interamericana.

Garrod, A.B. (1848) On the nature, cause and prevention of scurvy. *Monthly Journal of Medical Science* **8**:457–71.

Garrod, A.B. (1859) *The Nature and Treatment of Gout and Rheumatic Gout.* London: Walton and Maberly.

Garrod, A.E. (1908) Inborn Errors of Metabolism. Alkaptonuria. *Lancet* **2**:73–9.

Garruto, R.M. (1981) Disease patterns of isolated groups. In *Biocultural Aspects of Disease*, ed. H.R. Rothschild, pp. 557–97. New York: Academic Press.

Garry, V. (1987) Arsenic intoxication. *Occupational/Environmental Pathology Review (Environmental Pathology Laboratories, Minneapolis)* **4**(**3**):1–3.

Gelpi, A.P. & King, M.C. (1976) Duffy blood group and malaria. *Science* **191**:1284.

Gerhard, W.W. (1837) On the typhus fever which occured at Philadelphia in the spring and summer of 1836. *American Journal of Medical Science* **19**:289–92, 298–9, 302–3.

Gerin, C. & de Zorzi, C. (1961) The arsenic content in the organs of the human body. *Zacchia. Rivista di Medicina Legale e delle Assicurazioni (Rome)* **14**:1–19.

German, J. (1991) Cytogenetic aspects of human disease. In *Harrison's Principles of Internal Medicine*, ed. J.D. Wilson, E. Braunwald, K.J. Isselbacher, *et al.*, 12th edn, pp. 40–55. New York: McGraw-Hill.

Germana, F. & Fornaciari, G. (1992) *Trapanazioni, Craniotomie e Traumi Cranici in Italia (Trepanation, Craniotomy and Cranial Trauma in Italy).* Pisa, Italy: Giardini Editori e Stampatori.

Gerschon-Cohen, J., Schraer, H. & Blumberg, N. (1955) Hyperostosis frontalis interna among the aged. *American Journal of Roentgenology* **73**:396–7.

Gerszten, E., Allison, M., Pezzia, A. & Klurfeld, D. (1976a) Thyroid disease in a Peruvian mummy. (Medical College of Virginia, Richmond, VA) *MCV Quarterly* **12**(**2**):52–3.

Gerszten, E., Munizaga, J., Allison, M.J. & Klurfeld, D.M. (1976b) Diaphragmatic hernia of the stomach in a Peruvian mummy. *Bulletin of the New York Academy of Medicine* **52**:601–4.

Gerszten, E., Allison, M.J. & Fouant, M.M. (1983) Renal diseases in South American mummies. *Laboratory Investigation* **48**(**1**):29A. (Abstract).

Gerszten, P.C. (1993) An investigation into the practice of cranial deformation among the pre-Columbian peoples of northern Chile. *International Journal of Osteoarchaeology* **3**:87–98.

Gerszten, P.C. & Martínez, J. (1995) The neuropathology of South American mummies. *Neurosurgery* **36**(**4**):756–61.

Geyer, L. (1898) Über die chronischen Hautveränderungen beim Arsenicismus und Betrachtungen über die Massenerkrankungen in Reichenstein in Schlesien (Concerning the chronic skin changes in arsenicism and considerations about the epidemic in Reichenstein in Silesia). *Archives of Dermatology and Syphilology (Berlin)* **43**:221–80.

Ghalioungui, P. (1965) *Thyroid Enlargement in Africa with Special Reference to the Nile Basin.* Cairo: S.O.P. Press.

Ghalioungui, P. (1980) Medicine in Egypt. In *An X-Ray Atlas of the Royal Mummies*, ed. J. Harris & E. Wente, pp. 52–79. Chicago: University of Chicago Press.

Ghalioungui, P. & el Dawakhly, Z. (1965) *Health and Healing in Ancient Egypt.* Cairo: The Egyptian Organization for Authorship and Translation.

Ghon, A. (1912) *Der primäre Lungenherd bei der Tuberkulose der Kinder (The Primary Lung Lesion in Childhood Tuberculosis).* Berlin: Urban and Schweizenberg.

Giacometti, L. & Chiarelli, B. (1968) The skin of Egyptian mummies. *Archives of Dermatology* **97**:712–16.

Giampalmo, A. & Fulcheri, E. (1988) An investigation of endemic goitre during the centuries in sacral figurative arts. *Zentralblatt für Allgemeine Pathologie und Pathologisches Anatomie* **134**:297–307.

Gilfillan, S.C. (1990) *Rome's Ruin by Lead Poison.* Long Beach, CA: Wenzel Press.

Gill, G.W. (1985) Cultural implications of artificially modified human remains from northwestern Mexico. In *The West and Northwest MesoAmerica*, ed. M.S. Foster & P.C. Weigand, pp.196–9. Boulder, CO and London: Westview Press.

Gill, G.W. & Owlsey, D. (1985) Electron microscopy of parasite remains on the Pitchfork mummy and possible social implications. *Plains Anthropologist* **30**(**107**):45–50.

Gilliland, B.C. (1991) Relapsing polychondritis and miscellaneous arthritides. In *Harrison's Principles of Internal Medicine*, ed. J.D. Wilson, E. Braunwald, K.J. Isselbacher, *et al.*, 12th edn, pp. 1484–90. New York: McGraw-Hill.

Gillum, R.L. (1976) Relapsing fever. In *Pathology of Tropical and Extraordinary Diseases*, ed. C.H. Binford & D.H. Connor, vol. 1, pp.106–10. Washington, DC: Armed Forces Institute of Pathology.

Gladykowska-Rzeczycka, J. (1988) Is this a case of Morgagni syndrome? *Journal of Paleopathology* **1**:109–12.

Gladykowska-Rzeczycka, J. (1989) Congenital anomalies of early Polish man. In *Advances in Paleopathology*, ed. L. Capasso, pp. 111–16. (Proceedings of the VIIth European Members Meeting of the Paleopathology Association in Lyon, France, September 1988). Journal of Paleopathology Monograph Publications no. 1. Chieti: Marino Solfanelli Editore.

Gladykowska-Rzeczycka, J. & Prejzner, R. W. (1993) A case of probable pulmonary osteo-arthropathy from the Polish medieval cemetery of Czarna Wielka, District of Grodzisk. *Journal of Paleopathology* **5**(**3**):159–65.

Glenn, F. (1971) Biliary tract disease since antiquity. *Bulletin of the New York Academy of Medicine* **47**:329–50.

Glisson, F. (1650) De rachitide sive morbo puereli, qui vulo The Rickets dicitur (Rickets, a disease of children, that is called The Rickets). Translated into English by Philip Arnim in 1651. (Cited in Clarke, 1962).

Glob, P.V. (1969) *The Bog People.* Ithaca, NY: Cornell University Press.

Goff, C.W. (1967) Syphilis. In *Diseases in Antiquity*, ed. D. Brothwell & A.T. Sandison, pp. 279–94. Springfield, IL: C.C. Thomas.

Goldfuss, A. (1810) *Die Umgebringen von Muggendorf (The Destruction of Muggendorf).* Erlangen.

Golding, D.N. (1984) *Enfermedades Reumáticas (Rheumatic Diseases)*, 2nd edn. Barcelona: Salvat.

Golenser, J., Miller, J., Spira, D.T. & Chevion, M. (1983) Inhibitory effect of a fava bean component in the in vitro development of *Plasmodium falciparum* in normal and glucose-6-phosphate deficient erythrocytes. *Blood* **61**:507–10.

Golenser, J., Miller, J., Spira, D.T., Kosower, N.S., Vande waa J.A. & Jensen, J.B. (1988) Inhibition of the intraerythrocytic development of *Plasmodium falciparum* in glucose-6-phosphate deficient erythrocytes is enhanced by oxidants and by crisis form factor. *Tropical Medical Parasitology* **39**:272–6.

Gómez Bellard, F. & Sánchez Sánchez, J.A. (1989) Spondylarthrite Ankylosante: Un Cas Complet (Ankylosing spondylitis: A complete case). In *Advances in Paleopathology*, ed. L. Capasso, pp. 117–18. (Proceedings of the VIIth European Members Meeting of the Paleopathology Association in Lyon, France, September 1988). Journal of Paleopathology Monograph Publications no. 1. Chieti: Marino Solfanelli Editore.

Gondos, B. (1968) Roentgen observations in diabetic osteopathy. *Radiology* **91**:6–13.

González Antón, R. (1995) Guanches. Las momias Patrimonio de la Humanidad (Guanches. Mummies as Mankind's Heritage). In *Proceedings of the First World Congress on Mummy Studies*, 1992, vol. 1, pp. 27–32. Tenerife, Canary Islands: Museo Arqueológico y Etnográfico de Tenerife, Organismo Autónomo de Museos y Centros, Cabildo de Tenerife.

González Antón, R., Rodríguez Martín, C. & Estévez González, F. (1990) Proyecto CRONOS. Bioantropología de las Momias Guanches (The CRONOS project. The bioanthropology of the Guanche mummies). *ERES (Arqueología)* **1**(**1**):137–40.

Gooch, P.S. (1976a) Bibliographic Annotation re Helminths in Archaeological and Prehistoric Deposits. Annotated Bibliography no. 9. St. Albans, Herts: Commonwealth Institute of Helminthology.

Gooch, P.S. (1976b) Identification of a parasite (Paragonimus) in coprolite from Chile. Paleopathology Newsletter **15**:2–3. (Letter Report in News from the Field).

Goodman, A.H. (1989) A report from the New Zealand conference on dental developmental defects. Dental Anthropology Newsletter **4(1)**:4–6.

Goodman, A.H. & Armelagos, G.J. (1988) Childhood stress and decreased longevity in a prehistoric population. American Anthropologist **90**:936–44.

Goodman, A.H. & Clark, G.A. (1981) Harris lines as indicators of stress in prehistoric Illinois populations. In Biocultural Adaptation, ed. D.M. Martin & M.P. Bumsted, pp. 35–46. Amherst, MA: University of Massachusetts.

Gordon, D. (1991) Female circumcision and genital operations. Medical Anthropology Quarterly **5(1)**:3–14.

Gordon, I., Shapiro, H.A. & Berson, S.D. (1988) Forensic Medicine. A Guide to Principles, 3rd edn. New York: Churchill Livingstone.

Gosse, L.A. (1861) Présentation d'un Crane défermé de Nahoa. Trouvé dans la Vallée de Ghovel, Mexique (Presentation of a deformed cranium from Nahoa. Found in the Ghovel valley, Mexico). Bulletins de la Société d'Anthropologie de Paris **2**:567–77.

Graef, J.W. & Lovejoy, F.H. (1991) Heavy metal poisoning: arsenic. In Harrison's Principles of Internal Medicine, ed. J.D. Wilson, E. Braunwald, K.J. Isselbacher, et al., 12th edn, pp. 2181–3. New York: McGraw-Hill.

Graham, M.D. (1979) Osteomas and exostoses of the external auditory canal. Annals of Otology, Rhinology and Laryngology **88(4)**:566–72.

Gramberg, K.P.C.A. (1961) 'Leprosy' and the Bible. The Bible Translator (London) **11**:10–23.

Graña, Y.R., Rocca, E.D. & Graña, R.L. (1954) Las trepanaciones craneanas en el Perú en l a época pre-Hispánica (Cranial trepanation in pre-Hispanic Peru). Lima: Imprenta Santa Maria.

Granville, A. B. (1825) An essay on Egyptian mummy. Philosophical Transactions of the Royal Society of London **1**:269–316.

Grassi, B. (1900) Studio di Uno Zoologo Sulla Malaria (Zoological Study of Malaria). Rome: Accademia dei Lincei.

Gray, P.H.K. (1966) A radiographic skeletal survey of ancient Egyptian mummies. Excerpta Medica. International Congress Series **120**:35–8.

Gray, P.H.K. (1967) Radiography of ancient Egyptian mummies. Medical Radiography and Photography **43**:34–44.

Gray, P.H.K. (1969) A case of osteogenesis imperfecta associated with dentinogenesis imperfecta, dating from antiquity. Clinical Radiology **20**:106–8.

Greene, B.M. (1991) Filariasis. In Harrison's Principles of Internal Medicine, ed. J.D. Wilson, E. Braunwald, K.J. Isselbacher, et al., 12th edn, pp. 809–10. New York: McGraw-Hill.

Greene, L.S. (1993) G6PD deficiency as protection against falciparum malaria: An epidemiological critique of population and experimental studies. Yearbook of Physical Anthropology **36**:153–78.

Gregg, J.B. & Bass, W.H. (1970) Exostoses in the external auditory canals. Annals of Otology, Rhinology and Laryngology **79**:834–9.

Gregg, J.B. & Gregg, P.S. (1987) Dry Bones: Dakota Territory Reflected. Sioux Falls, SD: Sioux Printing, Inc.

Gregg, J.B. & Steele, J.P. (1982) Mastoid development in ancient and modern populations. Journal of American Medical Association **248**:459–64.

Gregg, J.B., Steele, J. P. & Sylvester, C. (1965) Ear disease in skulls from the Scully burial site. Plains Anthropologist **10(30)**:233–9.

Gregg, N. McA. (1941) Congenital cataract following German measles in the mother. Transactions of the Ophthalmological Society of Australia **3**:35–46.

Griffith, A.S. (1932) Observations on the bovine tubercle bacillus in human tuberculosis. British Medical Journal **10**:501–3.

Griffith, A.S. (1937) Bovine tuberculosis in man. Tubercle **18**:528–43.

Grimm, von H. (1985) Zür Rachitis-Hypothese der Entstehung von Bevölkerungsgruppen mit heller Komplexion (Concerning the rickets hypotheses regarding the development of population groups of light complexion). Biologische Rundschau **23**:181–2.

Grmek, M. D. (1983) Les Maladies à l'Aube de la Civilisation Occidentale: Recerches sur la Réalité Pathologique dans le Monde Grec Préhistorique, Arcaïque et Classique (Diseases at the Dawn of Western Civilization: Research on the Pathological Reality of the Prehistoric Greek World). Paris: Payot.

Grön, K. (1973) Leprosy in literature and art. International Journal of Leprosy **41(2)**:249–83.

Guerra, F. (1982–1985) Historia de la Medicina (History of Medicine), 2 vols. Madrid. Norma.

Guerra, F. (1990) La Medicina Precolombina (Pre-Columbian Medicine). Madrid: Instituto de Cooperación Iberoamericana. Quinto Centenario.

Guiard, E (1930) La Trépanation Craniénne chez les Néolithiques et chez les Primitifs Modernes (Cranial Trepanation Among the Neolithic and Modern Primitive Populations). Paris: Masson.

Guillen, S. (1992) The Chinchorro Culture: Mummies and Crania in the Reconstruction of Preceramic Coastal Adaptation in the South Central Andes. Ph.D. dissertation, Department of Anthropology, University of Michigan, USA.

Guirand, F. (ed.) (1978) The New Larousse Encyclopedia of Mythology. New York: Hamlyn. (Translated by Richard Aldington and Delano Ames.)

Gunnes-Hey, M. (1981) Spondylolysis in the Koniag Eskimo vertebral column. In Biocultural Adaptation, ed. D.L. Martin & M.P. Bumsted, pp. 16–23. Amherst, MA: University of Massachusetts.

Gurdjan, E.S., Webster, J.E. & Lissner, H.R. (1950) The mechanism of skull fracture. Radiology **54**:313–39.

Guy, M.W., Krotosky, W.A. & Cockburn, A. (1981) Malaria and an Egyptian mummy. Royal Society of Tropical Medicine and Hygiene **75**:601.

Gwei-Djen, L. & Needham, J. (1993) Diseases of antiquity in China. In The Cambridge World History of Human Disease, ed. K.F. Kiple, pp. 345–54. New York: Cambridge University Press.

Haas, N. (1970) Anthropological observations on the skeletal remains from Giv'at ha Mitvar. Israel Exploration Journal **20:(1–2)**:38–59.

Hackel, C., Houard, S., Portaels, F., van Else, A., Herzog, A. & Bollen, A. (1990) Specific identification of Mycobacterium leprae by the polymerase chain reaction. Molecular and Cellular Probes **4**:205–10.

Hackett, C.J. (1963) On the origin of the human treponematoses (pinta, yaws, endemic syphilis and venereal syphilis). Bulletin of the World Health Organization **29**:7–41.

Hackett, C.J. (1967) The human treponematoses. In Diseases in Antiquity, ed. D. Brothwell & A.T. Sandison, pp. 152–69. Springfield, IL: C.C. Thomas.

Hackett, C.J. (1983) Problems in the paleopathology of the human treponematoses. In Disease in Ancient Man, ed. G.D. Hart , pp. 106–28. Toronto: Clarke Irwin.

Hackett, E. (1984) The foreskin saga. The Medical Journal of Australia **141**:187–9.

Hacking, P. (1995) A pituitary tumor in a medieval skull. International Journal of Osteoarchaeology **5**:390–3.

Halbaek, H. (1958) Grauballemandens sidste mültid (The Grauballe man's last meal: An analysis of food remains in the stomach). KUML **1958**:83–116.

Halde, C. (1983) Enfermedades Infecciosas: Micosis (Infectious diseases: Mycoses). In Diagnóstico Clínico y Tratamiento (Clinical Diagnosis and Treatment), ed. M.A. Krupp & M.J. Chatton, pp. 932–9. México, DF: El Manual Moderno.

Hall, H.J. (1976) Chicago. *Paleopathology Newsletter* **13**:9. (News from the Field).

Hall, H.J. (1978) Paragonimus. *Paleopathology Newsletter* **21**:4–6. (News from the Field).

Hall, T. & Sidel, V.W. (1993) Diseases in the modern period in China. In *The Cambridge World History of Human Disease*, ed. K.F. Kiple, pp. 362–73. New York: Cambridge University Press.

Haller, J.S. (1993) Ergotism. In *The Cambridge World History of Human Disease*, ed. K.F. Kiple, pp. 718–19. New York: Cambridge University Press.

Hambly, W.D. (1925) *The History of Tattooing and its Significance*. London: H.F. & G. Witherby. (Republished in 1974 by Gale Research Co., Book Tower, Detroit).

Hamperl, H. & Laughlin, W.S. (1959) Osteological consequences of scalping. *Human Biology* **31**:80–9.

Hamwi, G.J., Skillman, T.G. & Tufts, K.C., Jr (1960) Acromegaly. *American Journal of Medicine* **29**(**4**):690–9.

Handler, J.S., Aufderheide, A.C., Corruccini, R.S., Brandon, E.M. & Wittmers, L.E., Jr (1986) Lead contact and poisoning in Barbados slaves: Historical, chemical and biological evidence. *Social Science History* **10**(**4**):399–425.

Handy, W.C. (1965) *Forever The Land Of Men*. New York: Dodd, Mead and Company.

Haneveld, G.T. (1977) An early nineteenth century case of ameloblastoma of the jaw. *Archivum Chirurgicum Neerlandicum* **29**(**1**):9–17.

Hansen, F. & Moller, K. (1949) Arsenic content of human organs after fatal poisoning with arsenic trioxide and other arsenical compounds, with some remarks on the manifestations of arsenic poisoning. *Acta Pharmacologica et Toxicologica* **5**:132–52.

Hansen, G.A. ([1874] 1955) Causes of leprosy. *International Journal of Leprosy* **23**:307–9. (Translated from the original Norwegian, first published in Norwegian in 1874).

Hansen, S. (1894) *Primitiv Trepanation (Primitive Trepanation)*. Copenhagen: *Bibliothek for Laeger* **5**(**7.R**).

Hansford, C. F. (1977) Malaria in South Africa. In *Medicine in a Tropical Environment*, ed. J.H.S. Gear, pp. 536–41. Capetown: A.A. Balkema.

Harding, J.R. (1976) Certain upper paleolithic 'venus' statuettes considered in relation to the pathological condition known as massive hypertrophy of the breasts. *Man* (*London*) **11**:271–2.

Harker, W.B. (1993) Health in Pharaonic Egypt. In *Bioanthropology and the Study of Ancient Egypt*, ed. W.V. Davies & R. Walker, pp.19–23. London: British Museum Press.

Harris, J.E. & Weeks, K.R. (1973) *X-raying the Pharaohs*. New York: Charles Scribner's Sons.

Harris, J.E. & Wente, E. F. (eds) (1980) *An X-ray Atlas of the Royal Mummies*. Chicago: University of Chicago Press.

Harrison, D.F.N. (1962) The relationship of osteomata of the external auditory meatus to swimming. *Annals of the Royal College of Surgeons in England* **31**:187–201.

Harrison, R.G. (1973) Tutankhamun postmortem. *Lancet* **1**:259.

Harrison, R.G. & Abdalla, A. (1972) The remains of Tutankhamun. *Antiquity* **46**:8–14.

Harrison, R.G., Connolly, R.C. & Abdalla, A. (1969) Kinship of Smenkhare and Tutankhamen affirmed by serological micromethod. *Nature* **224**:325–6.

Harrison, W.R., Merbs, C.F. & Leathers, C.R. (1991) Evidence of coccidioidomycosis in the skeleton of an ancient Arizona Indian. *Journal of Infectious Diseases* **164**:436–7.

Hart Hanson, J. P., Meldgaard, J. & Nordquist, J. (1991) *The Greenland Mummies*. Washington, DC: Smithsonian Institution Press.

Hart, G.D. (1967) Even the gods had goitre. *Canadian Medical Association Journal* **96**(**21**):1426–32.

Hart, G.D. (ed.) (1983) *Disease in Ancient Man: An International Symposium*. Toronto: Clarke Irwin.

Hart, G.D., Cockburn, A., Millet, N.B. & Scott, J.W. (1977) Autopsy of an Egyptian mummy (Nakht-Rom I). *Canadian Medical Association Journal* **117**:461–73.

Hartney, P. (1981) Tuberculous lesions in a prehistoric population sample from southern Ontario. In *Prehistoric Tuberculosis in the Americas*, ed. J.E. Buikstra, pp. 141–60. Evanston, IL: Northwestern University Archaeological Program.

Hawden, S. (1942) Tuberculosis in the buffalo. *Journal of the American Veterinary Association* **100**:19–22.

Hawkes, J. (1973) *The First Great Civilizations; Life in Mesopotamia, The Indus Valley and Egypt*. New York: Knopf.

Hawkins, D. (1992) The diagnosis of pituitary disease from human skeletal remains. *International Journal of Osteoarchaeology* **2**:51–64.

Hayashi, Y. ([1918] 1953) Skin testing with leprosy bacillus suspensions. *International Journal of Leprosy* **21**:370–2.

Hayles, A.B. (1980) Gigantism. *Pediatric Annals* **9**(**4**):163–9.

Hazen, S.F., Chilton, M.W. & Mumma, R.O. (1973) The problem of root caries. *Journal of the American Dental Association* **86**:137–44.

Heffron, R. (1939) *Pneumonia*. Cambridge, MA: Harvard University Press.

Helms, C.A. (1989) *Fundamentals of Skeletal Radiology*. Philadelphia: W.B. Saunders.

Henderson, D.A. (1976) The eradication of smallpox. *Scientific American* **235**:25–33.

Henderson, J. (1987) Factors determining the state of preservation of human remains. In *Death, Decay and Reconstruction: Approaches to Archaeology and Forensic Science*, ed. A. Boddington, A.N. Garland & R.C. Janaway, pp.43–54. Manchester: Manchester University Press.

Henschen, F. (1966) *History and Geography of Diseases*. New York: Delacorte Press.

Hensinger, R.N. (1992) Espondilolisis y Espondilolistesis (Spondylolysis and spondylolisthesis). In *Sistema Musculoesquelético. Parte 2. Trastornos del Desarrollo, Tumores, Enfermedades Reumáticas y Reemplazamiento Articular, de FH Netter (Colección Ciba de Ilustraciones Médicas) (Musculoskeletal System. Part 2. Developmental Disorders, Tumors, Rheumatic Diseases and Joint Replacement of F.H. Netter (Ciba Collection of Medical Ilustrations))*, ed. R.H. Freyberg & R.N Hensinger, p. 39. Barcelona: Salvat.

Hensinger, R.N. & MacEwen, G.D. (1986) Anomalías Congénitas de la Columna Vertebral (Congenital anomalies of the vertebral column). In *La Columna Vertebral (The Spine)*, ed. R.H. Rothman & F.A. Simeone, pp. 212–344. Madrid: Panamericana.

Hernández, F. ([1577] 1959) *Historia Natural de la Nueva España (Natural History of New Spain)*, 2 vols. Mexico City: Universidad Nacional Autónoma de Mexico.

Herodotus ([c. 450 B.C.] 1981) *Herodotus.* Book II: paragraph 86. Loeb Classical Library. Translated by A.D. Godley. Cambridge, MA: Harvard University Press.

Herrmann, B. (1987) Parasitologische Untersuchung mittelalterlicher Kloaken (Parasitological investigation of medieval cesspools). In *Mensch und Umwelt im Mittelalter (Man and Environment in the Middle Ages)*, ed. B. Herrmann, pp. 131–61. Stuttgart: Deutsche Verlags-Anstalt.

Hershkovitz, I., Ring, B., Speirs, M., Galili, E., Kisley, M., Edelson, G. & Hershkovitz, A. (1991) Possible congenital hemolytic anemia in prehistoric coastal inhabitants of Israel. *American Journal of Physical Anthropology* **85**:7–13.

Hershkovitz, I., Speirs, M., Katznelson, A. & Arenburg, B. (1992) Unusual pathological condition in the lower extremities of a skeleton from ancient Israel. *American Journal of Physical Anthropology* **88**:23–6.

Hess, A.F. ([1920] 1982) *Scurvy: Past and Present*. New York: Academic Press. (First published in 1920).

Hess, A.F. & Unger, L.J. (1920) Scorbutic beading of the ribs. *American Journal of Diseases of Children* **19**:331–6.

Hill, A.V.S., Allsop, C.E.M., Kwiatkowski, D., Amstey, N. M., Twumasi, P., Rowe, P.A., Bennett, S., Brewster, D., McMichael, A.J. & Greenwood, B. M. (1991) Common West

African HLA antigens are associated with protection from malaria. *Nature* **352**:595–600.

Hilson, S.W. (1993) Histologic studies of ancient tooth crown surfaces. In *Biological Anthropology and the Study of Ancient Egypt*, ed. R. Walker, pp. 75–85. London: British Museum Press.

Hindmarsh, J.T. & McLetchie, O.R. (1977) Biochemical evaluation of chronic arsenic poisoning. In *Clinical Chemistry and Chemical Toxicology of Metals*, ed. S. S. Brown, pp. 287–8. New York: Elsevier/North Holland.

Hino, H., Ammitzbøll, T., Møller, R. & Asboe-Hansen, G. (1982) Ultrastructure of skin and hair of an Egyptian mummy. *Journal of Cutaneous Pathology* **9**:25–32.

Hinz, E. (1990) Zur Herkunft der Helminthen des Mensche in Amerika (On the origin of Helminths in America). In *Geomedizinische und biogeographische Aspekte der Krankheitsverbreitung und Gesundheitsversorgung in Industrie - und Entwicklungsländern (Geomedicine and Biogeographic Aspects of Disease Dissemination and Health Impairment in Industry and in Developing Countries)*, ed. E. Hinz, pp.359–406. Frankfurt am Main: Peter Lang.

Hippocrates ([c. 400 B.C.] 1959) *Hippocrates*. Vol. III, On Joints: paragraph XLI, p. 281. Loeb Classical Library. Translated by E.T. Withington. Cambridge, MA: Harvard University Press.

Hippocrates ([c. 400 B.C.] 1984) *Hippocrates*. Vol. I, Epidemics I: paragraph XXIV. Loeb Classical Library. Translated by W.H.S. Jones. Cambridge, MA: Harvard University Press.

Hippocrates ([c. 400 B.C.] 1992) *Hippocrates*. Vol. IV, Aphorisms II: paragraph XV. Loeb Classical Library. Translated by W.H.S. Jones. Cambridge, MA: Harvard University Press.

Hiro, Y. & Tasaka, S. (1938) Die Röteln sind eine Viruskrankheit (Rubella is a virus infection). *Monatschrift für Kinderheilkunde* **76**:328–32.

Hirschberg, J. (1982) *The History of Ophthalmology*, 11 vols. Translated by Frederick Blodi, M.D. (University of Iowa). Bonn: J.P. Wayenborgh. (First published in German in 1899).

Hirst, E.L. & Zilva, S.S. (1933) Ascorbic acid as antiscorbutic factor. *Biochemistry Journal* **27**:1271–8.

Hix, J.O. & O'Leary, T.J. (1976) The relationship between cemenal caries, oral hygiene status and fermentable carbohydrate intake. *Journal of Periodontology* **47**:398–404.

Hodgson, A.R. (1975) Infectious disease of the spine. In *The Spine*, ed. R.H. Rothman & F.A. Simeone, vol. 2, pp. 567–98. Philadelphia: W. B. Saunders.

Hofer, M., Hirschel, B., Kirschner, P., Beghetti, M., Kaelin, A., Siergrist, C.A., Suter, S., Teske, A. & Bottger, E.C. (1993) Brief report: Disseminated osteomyelitis from *Mycobacterium ulcerans* after snakebite. *New England Journal of Medicine* **328**(14):1007–9.

Hoffman, M. (1976) An achondroplastic dwarf from the Augustine site (Ca-Sac-127). *Contributions of the University of California Archaeological Research Facility* **30**:65–119.

Holck, P. (1984) Scurvy as a paleopathological problem. *Paleopathology Newsletter* **47** (**Sept**) (**Supplement**):5. (Abstract).

Holck, P. (1991) The occurrence of hip joint dislocation in early Lappic populations of Norway. *International Journal of Osteoarchaeology* **1**(**3 & 4**):199–202.

Holick, M.F., Krane, S.M. & Potts, J.T., Jr (1991) Calcium, phosphorus and bone metabolism: Calcium-regulating hormones. In *Harrison's Principles of Internal Medicine*, ed. J.D. Wilson, E. Braunwald, K.J. Isselbacher, *et al.*, 12th edn, pp. 1888–1901. New York: McGraw-Hill.

Holien, T. & Pickering, R.B. (1978) Analogues in Classic period Chalchihuites culture to Late Mesoamerican ceremonialism. In *Middle Classic Mesoamerica: A.D. 400–700*, ed. E. Rasztory, pp. 143–57. New York: Columbia University Press.

Hollister, D.W. (1987) Molecular basis of osteogenesis imperfecta. *Current Problems in Dermatology* **17**:76–94.

Holmes, R.K. (1991) Diphtheria. In *Harrison's Principles of Internal Medicine*, ed. J.D. Wilson, E. Braunwald, K.J. Isselbacher, *et al.*, 12th edn, pp. 569–72. New York: McGraw-Hill.

Holst, A. & Fröhlich, T. (1907) Experimental studies relating to ship beri-beri and scurvy. II. On the etiology of scurvy. *Journal of Hygiene* **7**:634–71.

Home, F. (1759) *Medical Facts and Experiments*. London.

Hooton, E. A. (1925) *The Ancient Inhabitants of the Canary Islands*. Cambridge, MA: Harvard University Press.

Hooton, E.A. (1930) *The Indians of Pecos Pueblo: A Study of Their Skeletal Remains*. New Haven, CT: Yale University Press.

Hope, F.W. (1834) Notice of several species of insects found in the heads of Egyptian mummies. *Journal of the Royal Entomological Society of London* **1**:11–13.

Hopkins, D. (1980) Ramses V: Earliest known victim? *World Health* **May**:220.

Horne, P. (1985) A review of the evidence of human endoparasitism in the pre-Columbian New World through the study of coprolites. *Journal of Archaeological Science* **12**:299–310.

Horne, P. (1986a) Case No. 23: Angiokeratoma circumscriptum. (Department of Pathology, Medical College of Virginia, Richmond, VA) *Paleopathology Club Newsletter* **27**:1.

Horne, P. (1986b) Angiokeratoma in Inca mummy. Poster presented at the 13th Annual Meeting of the Paleopathology Association held in Albuquerque, NM, April 12–13, 1986. *Paleopathology Newsletter* **54** (**June**) (**Supplement**):16. (Abstract).

Horne, P. (1993) Spores or red blood cells? A case from Leptiminus. *Paleopathology Newsletter* **84** (**Dec**):13–14.

Horne, P. (1995) Aspergillosis and dracunculiasis in mummies from the tomb of Parennefer. *Paleopathology Newsletter* **92** (**Dec**):10–12.

Horne, P.D., Quevedo Kawasaki, S. & Gryfe, A. (1982) The prince of el Plomo. *Paleopathology Newsletter* **40**:7–10.

Horuk, R., Chitnis, C.E., Darbonne, W. C., Colby, T.J., Rybicki, A., Hadley, T.J. & Miller, L.H. (1993) A receptor for the malarial parasite *Plasmodium vivax* : The erythrocyte chemokine receptor. *Science* **261**:1182–4.

Hosovski, E. (1991) A case of acromegaly in the Middle Ages. *Anthropologischer Anzeiger* **49**(**3**):273–9.

Houghton, P. (1975) A renal calculus from protohistoric New Zealand. *Ossa* **2**:11–14.

Howard, R.J., Uni, S., Aikawa, M., Aley, S.B., Leech, J.H., Lew, A.M., Wellems, T.E., Rener, J. & Taylor, D.W. (1986) Secretion of a malarial histidine-rich protein (PfHRPII) from *Plasmodium falciparum*-infected erythrocytes. *Journal of Cell Biology* **103**:1269–77.

Howe, C. (1981) General microbiology and immunology. In *Rypin's Medical Licensure Examinations*, ed. E.D. Frohlich, 13th edn, pp. 336–448. Philadelphia: Lippincott.

Howe, G.M. (1977) *A World Geography of Human Diseases*. New York: Academic Press.

Howell, D.S. (1987) Osteoartropatía Hipertrófica (Hypertrophic osteoarthropathy). In *Artritis y Otras Patologías Relacionadas (Arthritis and Allied Pathological Conditions)*, ed. D.J. McCarty, 10th edn, vol. 3, pp. 1206–12. Madrid: Panamericana.

Hrdlicka, A. (1912) Artificial deformations of the human skull with special reference to America. In *Actas del XVII Congreso Internacionale de Americanistas*, ed. R. Lehmann-Nitsche, pp. 147–9. Buenos Aires: International Society of Americanists.

Hrdlicka, A. (1914) Anthropological work in Peru in 1913, with notes on the pathology of the ancient Peruvians. *Smithsonian Miscellaneous Collections* **61**(**18**):1–69.

Hrdlicka, A. (1916) Goiter among the Indians along the Missouri. *Science* **44**(**1128**):203–4.

Hrdlicka, A. (1935) Ear exostosis. *Smithsonian Miscellaneous Collections* **93**:1–100.

Hrdlicka, A. (1939) *Practical Anthropometry*. Philadelphia: Wistar Institute.

Hudson, E.H. (1965) Treponematosis and man's social evolution. *American Anthropologist* **67**:885–901.

Hug, E. (1956) *Die Anthropologische Sammlung im Naturhistorischen Museum Bern (The Anthropological Collection in the Natural History Museum of Bern)*. Bern: Natural History Museum.

Hughes, S. (1990) *Ortopedia y Traumatología (Orthopedics and Traumatology)*, 4th edn. Barcelona: Salvat.

Hunt, N.H. & Stocker, R. (1990) Oxidative stress and the redox status of malaria-infected erythrocytes. *Blood Cell*s **16**:499–526.

Hunter, J.M. & Thomas, M.O. (1984) Hypothesis of leprosy, tuberculosis and urbanization of Africa. *Social Science and Medicine* **19**(**1**):27–57.

Huss-Ashmore, R., Goodman, A.H. & Armelagos, G.J. (1982) Nutritional inference from paleopathology. In *Advances in Archaeological Method and Theory*, ed. M.B. Schiffer, vol. 1, pp. 395–474. New York: Academic Press.

Hutt, M.S.R. & Burkitt, D.P. (1986) *The Geography of Non-Infectious Disease*. Oxford: Oxford University Press.

Hutyra, F., Marek, J. & Manninger, R. (1938) *Special Pathology and Therapeutics of the Diseases of Domestic Animals*, 4th English edn, ed. J. Russell Greig. Vol. 1. London: Baillière, Tindall and Cox.

Iason, A.H. (1946) *The Thyroid Gland In Medical History*. New York: Froben Press.

Innes, J.R.M. (1940) The pathology and pathogenesis of tuberculosis in domesticated animals compared with man. *Veterinary Journal (London)* **96**:391–407.

Irish, J.D., da Silva, M.A.P. & Cussenot, O. (1993) Hard tissue regeneration of a gunshot wound in a historic North African skull: A paleopathological perspective. *Journal of Paleopathology* **5**(**3**):135–41.

Iseman, M.D. (1989) *Mycobacterial avium* complex and the normal host. *New England Journal of Medicine* **321**:896–8. (Editorial).

Isherwood, O., Jarvis, H. & Fawcitt, A. (1979) Radiology of the Manchester mummies. In *Manchester Museum Mummy Report*, ed. A. Rosalie David, pp. 25–64. Manchester: Manchester University Press.

Jackson, G. (1909) Etiology of exostoses of the external auditory meatus. *British Medical Journal* **2**:1137–8.

Jaén, M.T. (1977) Notas Sobre Paleopatología. Osteopatología (Notes on paleopathology. Osteopathology). *Anales de Antropología* **14**:345–71.

Jaffe, H. L. (1935) 'Osteoid osteoma': A benign osteoblastic tumor composed of osteoid and atypical bone. *Archives of Surgery* **31**:709–28.

Jaffe, H. L. (1950) Aneurysmal bone cyst. *Bulletin of Hospital for Joint Diseases* **11**:3–13.

Jaffe, H. L. (1958) *Tumors and Tumorous Conditions of the Bones and Joints*. Philadelphia: Lea and Febiger.

Jaffe, H.L. (1972) *Metabolic, Degenerative and Inflammatory Disease of Bones and Joints*. Philadelphia: Lea and Febiger.

Jankauskas, R. (1994) Variations and anomalies of the vertebral column in Lithuanian paleoosteological samples. *HOMO* **45** (**Supplement**):S63.

Janssens, P.A. (1957) Medical views on prehistoric representations of human hands. *Medical History* **1**:318–22.

Janssens, P.A. (1970) *Palaeopathology. Diseases and Injuries of Prehistoric Man*. London: John Baker.

Janssens, P.A. (1983) The *morbus dysentericus* in the Historia Francorum of Gregory of Tours (sixth century). In *Disease in Ancient Man: An International Symposium*, ed. G.D. Hart, pp.263–6. Toronto: Clarke Irwin.

Janssens, P.A., Marcsik, A., Meyere, C. de & Roy, G. de (1993) Qualitative and quantitative aspects of scurvy in ancient bones. *Journal of Paleopathology* **5** (**1**):25–36.

Jantzen, G. (1968) Der blinde Harfner auf dem Grabrelief Paätenemheb (The blind harpist on the tomb relief of Paätenemheb). *Materia Medica Nordmark* **20**:689–94.

Jarcho, S. (1966a) The development and present condition of human paleopathology in the United States. In *Human Paleopathology*, ed. S. Jarcho, pp. 3–30. New Haven and London: Yale University Press.

Jarcho, S. (ed.) (1966b) *Human Paleopathology*. New Haven and London: Yale University Press.

Jarcho, S. (1993) *Quinine's Predecessor*. Baltimore: Johns Hopkins University Press.

Jarcho, S. & Levin, P.M. (1938) Hereditary malformation of the vertebral bodies. *Bulletin of the Johns Hopkins Hospital* **62**:216–26.

Jenner, E. ([1798] 1966) *An Inquiry Into the Causes and Effects of the Variolae Vaccina*e. London: Dawsons of Pall Mall. (First published in London in 1798, reprinted in 1966).

Johansson, S. (1926) *Über die Knochen-und Gelenk-Tuberkulose in Kindesalter (Concerning Bone and Joint Tuberculosis of Childhood)*. Jena: G. Fischer.

Johnson, R.P. & Brewer, B.J. (1987) Desórdenes Mecanicos de la Rodilla (Mechanical disorders of the knee). In *Artritis y Otras Patologías Relacionadas (Arthritis and Allied Pathological Conditions)*, ed. D.J. McCarty, 10th edn, vol. 3, pp. 1233–44. Madrid: Panamericana.

Johnston, W.D. (1993) Tuberculosis. In *The Cambridge World History of Human Disease*, ed. K. Kiple, pp. 1059–68. New York: Cambridge University Press.

Jonckheere, F. (1948) Egyptian Chronicle. *Chronique et Egypte* **45–46**:24–53.

Jones, J. (1876) Explorations of the aboriginal remains of Tennessee. *Smithsonian Contributions to Knowledge* **259**:1–171.

Jopling, W.H. (1982) Clinical aspects of leprosy. *Tubercle* **63**:295–305.

Jurmain, R. (1990) Paleoepidemiology of a central California prehistoric population from CA-ALA-329: II. Degenerative disease. *American Journal of Physical Anthropology* **83**:83–94.

Kaklamani, E., Koumandaki, Y., Katsouyanni, K. & Trichopoulos, D. (1991) BCG, tuberculosis and leprosy. *Lancet* **337**:304. (Letter).

Kalayjian, B.S., Herbut, P.A. & Erf, L.A. (1946) Bone changes in leucaemia in children. *Radiology* **47**:223–33.

Karasch, M.C. (1993) Ophthalmia (conjunctivitis and trachoma). In *The Cambridge World History of Human Disease*, ed. K. Kiple, pp. 897–906. New York: Cambridge University Press.

Karlen, A. (1984) *Napoleon's Glands*, 3rd edn. Boston, MA: Little, Brown and Co.

Karsten, R. (1968) *The Civilization of the South American Indians*. London: Dawsons of Pall Mall.

Kato, K. (1932) A critique of the roentgen signs of infantile scurvy. *Radiology* **18**(**6**):1096–110.

Kauffman, H., Lagier, R. & Baud, C. (1979) Un Cas de Nanisme par Dyschondrostéose au VIe Siècle á Genève (A case of dyschondrosteotic dwarfism from the VIth century in Geneva). Association Internationale des Anthropologues de Langue Française. XIIIe Colloque-Anthropologie et Médecine (Caen), pp. 204–11.

Keith, A. (1931) *New Discoveries Relating to the Antiquity of Man*. New York: Norton.

Kelley, M.A. (1979) Skeletal changes produced by aneurysms. *American Journal of Physical Anthropology* **51**:35–8.

Kelley, M.A. (1989) Infectious disease. In *Reconstruction of Life from the Skeleton*, ed. M.Y. Iscan & K.A.R. Kennedy, pp. 191–9. New York: A.R. Liss.

Kelley, M.A. & Boom, K. (1995) Harris lines and environment: The early inhabitants of Tenerife. In *Proceedings of the First World Congress on Mummy Studies*, 1992, vol. 1, pp. 93–8. Tenerife, Canary Islands: Museo Arqueológico y Etnográfico de Tenerife, Organismo Autónomo de Museos y Centros, Cabildo de Tenerife.

Kelley, M.A. & Eisenberg, L.E. (1987) Blastomycosis and tuberculosis in early American Indians: A biocultural view. *Midcontinental Journal of Archaeology* **12**(**1**):89–116.

Kelley, M.A. & el-Najjar, M.Y. (1980) Natural variation and differential diagnosis of skeletal changes in tuberculosis. *American Journal of Physical Anthropology* **52**:153–67.

Kelley, M.A. & Lytle, K. (1995) Brief communication: A possible case of melorheostosis from antiquity. *American Journal of Physical Anthropology* **98**:369–74.

Kelley, M.A. & Micozzi, M.S. (1984) Rib lesions and chronic pulmonary tuberculosis. *American Journal of Physical Anthropology* **65**:381–6.

Kelley, W.N. & Palella, T.D. (1991) Gout and other disorders of purine metabolism. In *Harrison's Principles of Internal Medicine*, ed. J.D. Wilson, E. Braunwald, K.J. Isselbacher, *et al.*, 12th edn, pp. 1834–41. New York: McGraw-Hill.

Kellgren, J.H. (1964) The epidemiology of rheumatic diseases. *Annals of Rheumatic Diseases* **23**:109–22.

Kellog, V.L. (1913) Ectoparasites of the monkeys, apes and man. *Science* **38(982)**:601–2.

Kelson, W. (1900) Cause of aural exostoses. *Journal of Laryngology, Rhinology and Otology* **15**:667–76.

Kendall, E.C. (1915) The isolation in crystalline form of the compound which occurs in the thyroid: Its chemical nature and physiologic activity. *Journal of the American Medical Association* **64**:2042–3.

Kennedy, G.E. (1986) The relationship between exostoses and cold water: A latitudinal analysis. *American Journal of Physical Anthropology* **71(4)**:401–15.

Kerley, E.R. (1976) *The Teaching of Paleopathology in North America*. Monograph no. 1. Detroit, MI: Paleopathology Association.

Kilgore, L. (1989) Possible case of rheumatoid arthritis from Sudanese Nubia. *American Journal of Physical Anthropology* **79**:177–83.

Kim-Farley, R.J. (1993) Measles. In *The Cambridge World History of Human Disease*, ed. K.F. Kiple, pp. 871–5. New York: Cambridge University Press.

Kimberling, W.J., Kumar, S., Gabow, P.A., Kenyon, J.B., Connolly, C.J. & Somlo, S. (1993) Autosomal dominant polycystic kidney disease: Localization of the second gene to chromosome 4 q13-q23. *Genomics* **18**:467–72.

King, G. (1954) Advanced extrauterine pregnancy. *American Journal of Obstetrics and Gynecology* **67**:712–40.

King, L.R., Braunstein, H., Chambers, D. & Goldsmith, R. (1959) A case study of peculiar soft-tissue and bony changes in association with thyroid disease. *Journal of Clinical Endocrinology* **19 (10)**:1323–30.

Kiple, K.F. (ed.) (1993a) *The Cambridge World History of Human Disease*. New York: Cambridge University Press.

Kiple, K.F. (1993b) Syphilis, nonvenereal. In *The Cambridge World History of Human Disease*, ed. K.F. Kiple, pp. 1033–5. New York: Cambridge University Press.

Kiple, K.F. & King, V.H. (1981) *Another Dimension to the Black Diaspora*. Cambridge: Cambridge University Press.

Kirchhoff, L.V. (1991) Trypanosomiasis. In *Harrison's Principles of Internal Medicine*, ed. J.D. Wilson, E. Braunwald, K.J. Isselbacher, *et al.*, 12th edn, pp. 791–3. New York: McGraw-Hill.

Kirchhoff, L.V. (1993) American trypanosomiasis (Chagas' disease) – a tropical disease now in the United States. *New England Journal of Medicine* **329**:639–44.

Klemperer, G. & Klemperer, F. (1891) Versuche über Immunisirung und Heilung bei der Pneumokokkinfection (Investigation of development of immunity and healing of pneumococcal infections). *Berliner Klinische Wochenschrift* **28**:833–55, 869–75.

Kliks, M.M. (1982) Parasites in archeological material from Brazil. *Transactions of the Royal Society of Tropical Medicine and Hygiene* **76**:701. (Letter).

Klippel, M. & Feil, A. (1912) Anomalie de la colonne vertébrale par absence des vértébres cervicales; Cage thoracique remontant jusqu'a la base du crane (Spinal column anomalies of absent cervical vertebrae; thoracic cage extends to near the cranial base). *Bulletin et Mémoris Société Anatomie. Paris.* **87**:185–8.

Klohn, M., Susini, A., Baud, C.A., Sahni, M. & Simon, C. (1988) Taphonomy of an ancient Kerma (Sudan) burial: A biophysical and biochemical study. *Rivista di Antropologia* **66 (Supplement)**:21–34.

Knaggs, R.L. (1923) Leontiasis ossea. *British Journal of Surgery* **11(42)**:347–79.

Knight, B. (1991) *Forensic Pathology.* New York: Oxford University Press.

Knight, V. (1981) Influenza. In *Medicina Interna, de Harrison (Harrison's Internal Medicine)*, ed. G.W. Thorn, R.D. Adams, E. Braunwald, K.J. Isselbacher & R.G. Petersdorf, vol. 1, pp. 1171–5. México, DC: La Prensa Médica Mexicana.

Knowler, W.C., Bennett, P.H., Hamman, R.F. & Miller, M. (1978) Diabetes incidence and prevalence in Pima Indians: A 19-fold greater incidence than in Rochester, Minnesota. *American Journal of Epidemiology* **108(6)**:497–505.

Knudson, R.J. (1993) Emphysema. In *The Cambridge World History of Human Disease,* ed. K.F. Kiple, pp. 706–8. New York: Cambridge University Press.

Knüsel, C.J. & Bowman, J.E. (1996) A possible case of neurofibromatosis in an archaeological skeleton. *International Journal of Osteoarchaeology* **6**:202–10.

Koch, R. (1882) Die Aetiologie der Tuberculose (The etiology of tuberculosis). *Berlin Klinische Wochenschrift* **19**:221–30.

Kolokshanskaya, L.D. & Kolokshanskaya, Y.A. (1975) Bacteriological diagnosis of tuberculosis using biological material from tuberculin-positive cattle. In *Animal Husbandry – An Industrial Basis,* pp. 106ff. Kishinev:Shtinitsa. (In Russian).

Kovalyov, G.K. (1989) On human tuberculosis due to *M. bovis*. A review. *Journal of Hygiene, Epidemiology, Microbiology and Immunology* **33(2)**:199–206.

Kowal, W., Beattie, O.B. & Baadsgaard, H. (1990) Did solder kill Franklin's men? *Nature* **343**:319–20.

Kramar, C. (1983) A case of ankylosing spondylitis in medieval Geneva. *Ossa* **8**:115–29.

Kramar, C., Lagier, R. & Baud, C. (1995) Un Cas de Chondrodysplasie (A case of chondrodysplasia). In *Proceedings of the IXth European Meeting of the Paleopathology Association (Barcelona)*, pp. 199–200. Barcelona: Museu d'Arqueologia de Catalunya.

Kramar, C., Baud, C.A. & Lagier, R. (1983) Presumed calcified leiomyoma of uterus: morphological and clinical studies of a calcified mass dating from the Neolithic period. *Archives of Pathology and Laboratory Medicine* **107**:91–103.

Krane, S.M. (1991) Paget's disease of bone. In *Harrison's Principles of Internal Medicine*, ed. J.D. Wilson, E. Braunwald, K.J. Isselbacher, *et al.*, 12th edn, pp. 1938–41. New York: McGraw-Hill.

Krane, S.M. & Holick, M.F. (1991) Metabolic bone disease. In *Harrison's Principles of Internal Medicine*, ed. J.D. Wilson, E. Braunwald, K.J. Isselbacher, *et al.*, 12th edn, pp. 1921–33. New York: McGraw-Hill.

Kraus, B.S., Jordan, R.E. & Abrams, L. (1969) *Dental Anatomy and Occlusion*. Baltimore, London, Los Angeles: Williams and Wilkins.

Krebs, C. (1927) Maladie de Panner. Une affection du condyle de l'humerus ressemblant à la maladie de Calvé-Perthes (de l'articulation coxo-femorale). (Panner's disease, a condition of the elbow joint resembling Calvé-Perthes' disease of the hip joint). *Archives Franco-Belges de Chirurgie* **30**:608–9.

Kremer, W. & Wiese, O. (1930) *Die Tuberkulose der Knochen und Gelenke: Ihr Pathologie, Diagnostik, Therapie und Soziale Bedeutung. (Tuberculosis of Bones and Joints: Its Pathology, Diagnosis, Therapy and Social Significance).* Vol. 9 of the series: *Die Tuberkulose und Ihre Grenzgebiete in Einzeldarstellungen (Tuberculosis and its Limitations in Individual Presentations)*, ed. L. Brauer & H. Ulrici. Berlin: J. Springer.

Kreutz, K. & Schultz, M. (1994) A case of hydrocephalus externus from the early medieval cemetery of Straubling (Germany). *HOMO* **45 (Supplement)**:S71.

Krogman, W.M. (1940) The skeletal and dental pathology of an early Iranian site. *Bulletin of the History of Medicine* **8**:28–35.

Kronenberg, H.M. (1993) Parathyroid hormone: Mechanism of action. In *Primer on the Metabolic Bone Disease Disorders of Mineral Metabolism*, ed. M.J. Favus, pp. 58–9. New York: Raven Press.

Krotoski, W.A. (1980) Untitled. *Paleopathology Newsletter* **31**:7–8.

Küchenmeister, von (1881) Über Lithopädien (On lithopedion). *Archiv für Gynaekologie (Berlin)* **17**:153–252.

Kulund, D.N. (1990) *Lesiones del Deportista (The Injured Athlete),* 2nd edn. Barcelona: Salvat.

Kuo-liang, Y., Bing-Sen, Q., You-E, Z., Zhen-yuan, H., Ming-Yan, C., Gen-Sheng, W., Zu-yi, L., Zeng-shou, C., Guo-fang, L. & Wen-ying, C. (1982) Skin changes of 2100 year old Changsha female corpse. *Chinese Medical Journal* **93**(10):765–76.

La Rocca, H. (1986) Infecciones de la Columna Vertebral (Infections of the spine). In *La Columna Vertebral (The Spine)*, ed. R.H. Rothman & F.A. Simeone, 2nd edn, pp. 796–813. Madrid: Panamericana.

Lacroix, M. (1972) *Étude Medico-Legale des Partes de Substance de la Voute du Crâne (Medicologal Study of Cranial Vault Defects)*. Paris: Masson.

Laennec, R.T. (1826) *De L'Auscultation Médiate ou Traité ou Diagnostic des Maladies des Poumons et du Coeur (An Auscultation Method for Diagnosis or Treatment of Heart and Lung Diseases)*, 2nd edn. Paris: J.S. Chaudet.

LaFond, E.M. (1958) An analysis of adult skeletal tuberculosis. *Journal of Bone and Joint Surgery* **40**:346–64.

Lagercrantz, S. (1935) Fingerstümmelungen und ihre Ausbreitung in Afrika (Finger amputation and its dissemination in Africa). *Zeitschrift für Ethnologie* (**July**):129–57.

Lagier, R., Kramer, C. & Baud, C.A. (1987) Femoral unicameral bone cyst in a medieval child: Radiological and pathological study. *Pediatric Radiology* **17**(6):498–500.

Lagier, R., Baud, C.A. & Kramar, C. (1991) A case of tibia vara (Blount's disease) from the early Middle Ages. *Journal of Paleopathology* **4**(1):25–8.

Laín Entralgo, P. (1963) *Historia de la Medicina Moderna y Contemporánea (A History of Modern and Contemporary Medicine)*, 2nd edn. Barcelona: Científico-Médica.

Langsjoen, O.M. (1995) Dental pathology among the prehistoric Guanches of the island of Tenerife. In *Proceedings of the First World Congress on Mummy Studies*, 1992, vol. 1, pp. 79–92. Tenerife, Canary Islands: Museo Arqueológico y Etnográfico de Tenerife, Organismo Autoónomo de Museos y Centros, Cabildo de Tenerife.

Langsjoen, O.M. (1996) Dental effects of coca chewing in antiquity. *American Journal of Physical Anthropology* **101**:475–89.

Larsen, C.S. (1987) Bioarchaeological interpretations of subsistence economy and behavior from human skeletal remains. In *Advances in Archaeological Method and Theory*, ed. M.B. Schiffer, vol. 10, pp. 339–445. San Diego: Academic Press.

Lastres, J.B. & Cabieses, F. (1960) *La Trepanación del Cráneo en el Antiguo Perú (Cranial Trepanation in Ancient Peru)*. Lima: Universidad Mayor de San Marcos.

Latcham, R.E. (1929) *Las Creencias Religiosas de los Antiguos Peruanos (Religious Beliefs of Ancient Peruvians)*. Santiago de Chile: Balcells.

Laurence, B.R. (1968) Elephantiasis and Polynesian origins. *Nature* **219**:561–3.

Laveran, A. (1880) Note sur un noveau parasite trouvé dans le sang de plusieurs malades atteints de fièvre palustre (Note about a new parasite found in the blood of several diseases attributed to malarial fevers). *Bulletin Academie Médicine Paris* **9**:1235–6.

Lavigne, S.E. & Molto, J.E. (1995) System of measurement of the severity of periodontal disease in past populations. *International Journal of Osteoarchaeology* **5**:265–73.

Lawrence, J.E.P. (1935) Appendix A. In *Stone Age Races of Kenya*, L.S.B. Leakey, p.139. London: Oxford University Press.

Lax, E., Verstandig, A. & Sulkes, A. (1981) Hypertrophic pulmonary osteoarthropathy preceding metastases from transitional cell carcinoma. *Ossa* **8**:157–63.

Le Baron, J. (1881) Lésions osseuses de l'homme préhistorique en France et en Algerie (Bone lesions of prehistoric humans in France and Algeria). Thèse pour le Doctorate en Médicine, Paris.

Lee, R.V. (1983) Scurvy: A contemporary historical perspective. Part 1. *Connecticut Medicine* **47**(10):629–32.

Lee, T. (1941) A brief history of the endocrine disorders in China. *Chinese Medical Journal* **59**:379–86.

Leek, F.F. (1969) The problem of brain removal during embalming by the ancient Egyptians. *Journal of Egyptian Archaeology* **55**:112–16.

Leek, F.F. (1980) Observations on a collection of crania from the mastabas of the reign of Cheops at Giza. *Journal of Egyptian Archaeology* **66**:36–45.

Leek, F.F. (1984) Dental problems during the Old Kingdom – facts and legend. In *Evidence Embalmed. Modern Medicine and the Mummies of Ancient Egypt*, ed. R. David & E. Tapp, pp. 126–7. Manchester: Manchester University Press.

Leek, F.F. (1986) Cheops' courtiers: Their skeletal remains. In *Science and Egyptology*, ed. R.A. David, pp. 183–99. Manchester: Manchester University Press.

Lehmann-Nitsche, R. (1904) Lesions des Cranes des Îles Canaries (Cranial lesions from the Canary Islands). *Revista del Museo de la Plata* **11**:211.

Leigh, R.W. (1937) Dental morphology and pathology of pre-Spanish Peru. *American Journal of Physical Anthropology* **22**:267–96.

Leiker, D.L. (1971) Some aspects of the epidemiology of leprosy. On the relationship of leprosy and other mycobacterium diseases. *International Journal of Leprosy* **39**:610–15.

Leisen, J.C.C., Duncan, H. & Riddle, J.M. (1991) Rheumatoid erosive arthropathy as seen in macerated (dry) bone specimens. In *Human Paleopathology. Current Syntheses and Future Options*, ed. D.J. Ortner & A.C. Aufderheide, pp. 211–15. Washington and London: Smithsonian Institution Press.

Lenhossek, M. von (1919) Die Zahn Caries einst und Jetz (Dental caries: Then and now). *Archiv für Anthropologie* **17**:44–66.

Lester, C.W. (1969) Melorheostosis in a prehistoric Alaskan Eskimo. *Journal of Bone and Joint Surgery* **49**:142–3.

Levine, M.A. (1993) Parathyroid hormone resistance syndromes. In *Primer on the Metabolic Bone Diseases and Disorders of Mineral Metabolism*, ed. M.J. Favus, 2nd edn, pp. 194–200. New York: Raven Press.

Levy, M. (1965) *The Moons of Paradise*. New York: The Citadel Press.

Lewin, P.K. (1984) "Mummy" riddles unravelled. *Bulletin of the Electron Microscopy Society of Canada* (**May**):3–8.

Lewin, P.K., Hancock, R.G. & Voynovich, P. (1982) Napoleon Bonaparte – no evidence of chronic arsenic poisoning. *Nature* **299**:627–8.

Lewis, M., Roberts, C.A. & Manchester, K. (1994) Maxillary sinusitis in paleopathology: Its character and prevalence in urban and rural British medieval populations. In *Papers on Paleopathology Presented at the Xth European Members Meeting of the Paleopathology Association in Göttingen, Germany on 29 August – 3 September, 1994. Paleopathology Newsletter* **88** (**Supplement**):15. (Abstract).

Lewis, S. (1995) Some notes on crucifixion. *Organ: The Newsletter of the Osteoarchaeological Research Group* **8**:10–11.

Lichtenstein, L. (1950) Aneurysmal bone cyst: Pathological entity commonly mistaken for giant cell tumor and occasionally for hemangioma and osteogenic sarcoma. *Cancer* **3**:279–89.

Lichtenstein, L. (1970) *Diseases of Bone and Joints*. St. Louis: Mosby.

Lichtenstein, L. (1977) *Bone Tumors*, 5th edn. St. Louis: Mosby.

Lichtor, Major J. & Lichtor, A. (1957) Paleopathologic evidence suggesting pre-Columbian tuberculosis of the spine. *Journal of Bone and Joint Surgery* **39a**:1398–9.

Lieberman, L.S. (1993) Diabetes. In *The Cambridge World History of Human Disease*, ed. K. F. Kiple, pp. 665–76. New York: Cambridge University Press.

Lillie, R.D. (1965) *Histopathologic Technic and Practical Histochemistry*, 3rd edn. New York: McGraw-Hill.

Linares, M. (1966) *Restos Arqueológicos en el Nevado Pichu-Pichu, Arequipa, Perú (Archaeological Remains at Nevado Pichu-Pichu,*

Arequipa, Peru). Argentina: Mendoza. (Published as a supplement to *Anales de Arqueólogia y Etnologia*).

Lind, J. ([1753] 1953) *A Treatise on the Scurvy*. Edinburgh: Edinburgh University Press. (First published in Edinburgh in 1753).

Linne, S. (1940) Dental decoration in aboriginal America. *Ethnos* **5**:2–28.

Lisowski, F.P. (1967) Prehistoric and early historic trepanation. In *Diseases in Antiquity*, ed. D. Brothwell & A.T. Sandison, pp. 651–72. Springfield, IL: C.C. Thomas.

Lithell, U. (1981) Breast-feeding habits and their relation to infant mortality and marital fertility. *Journal of Family History* **6**:182–94.

Livingstone, F.B. (1991) On the origin of syphilis: An alternative hypothesis. *Current Anthropology* **32(5)**:587–90.

Lloyd, C. (1979) Cook and scurvy. *Mariner's Mirror* **65(1)**:23–8.

Locksley, R.M. (1991) Leishmaniasis. In *Harrison's Principles of Internal Medicine*, ed. J.D. Wilson, E. Braunwald, K.J. Isselbacher, *et al.*, 12th edn, pp. 789–91. New York: McGraw-Hill.

Long, A.R. (1931) Cardiovascular renal disease: Report of a case 3000 years ago. *Archives of Pathology* **12**:92–6.

Long, E.R. (1965) *A History of Pathology*. New York: Dover.

Long, J.C. & Merbs, C.F. (1981) Coccidioidomycosis: A primate model. In *Prehistoric Tuberculosis in the Americas*, ed. J.E. Buikstra, pp. 69–83. Evanston, IL: Northwestern University Archeological Program.

Looser, E. (1920) Über pathologische Formen von Infraktionen und Callusbildungen bei Rachitis und Osteomalakie und anderen Knochenerkrankungen (Concerning the pathological forms of infractions and callus formation in rickets and other bone diseases). *Zentralblatt Chirurgie* **47**:1470–4.

López de Villalobos, F. (1498) El Sumario de la Medicina, con un Tratado Sobre las Pestíferas Búyas (A Summary of Medicine, with a Discussion about Pustular Buboes). Salamanca.

López Piñero, J.M. (1975) Prologue. In *Paleopatología Ósea de los Primitivos Pobladores de Canarias (Bone Paleopathology of the Ancient Inhabitants of the Canaries)*, pp. 9–11. Book written by J. Bosch Millares. Las Palmas de Gran Canaria: Cabildo Insular de Gran Canaria.

López-Durán, L. (1995) *Traumatología y Ortopedia (Traumatology and Orthopedics)*. Madrid: Luzán 5.

Lorena, A. (1890) *La Medicina y la Trepanación Incásica (Medicine and Inca Trepanation)*. Lima: La Crónica Médica.

Lösch, F. (1875) Massenhafte Entwickelung von Amoeben im Dickdarm. (Massive development of amoeba in the colon). *Archiv für Patologische Anatomie und für Klinische Medizin (Virchow), Berlin* **65**:196–211.

Lovejoy, C.O. (1985) Dental wear in a Libben population – its functional pattern and role in the determination of adult skeletal age at death. *American Journal of Physical Anthropology* **68**:47–56.

Loveland, C. J., Gregg, J.B. & Bass, W.M. (1984) Osteochondritis dissecans from the Great Plains in North America. *Plains Anthropologist* **29(105)**:239–46.

Lovell, N. (1991) An evolutionary framework for assessing illness and injury in non-human primates. *Yearbook of Physical Anthropology* **34**:117–55.

Löwen, H. (1994) A Ewing's sarcoma from an early medieval hillside in Westphalia. In *Papers on Paleopathology Presented at the Xth European Members Meeting of the Paleopathology Association in Göttingen, Germany on 29 August – 3 September, 1994*. *Paleopathology Newsletter* **88 (Supplement)**:15. (Abstract).

Lowis, G.W. (1993) Epidemiology of puerperal fever: The contributions of Alexander Gordon. *Medical History* **37**:399–410.

Lozano Tonkin, C., Cigüenza Gabriel, R., García Tenorio, T. & Montero Ruíz, E. (1984) *Enfermedades Infecciosas e Intoxicaciones (Infectious and Toxicological Diseases)*, 2nd edn. Madrid: Luzán 5.

Lucas, A. (1926) *Ancient Egyptian Materials and Industries*. London: Edward Arnold and Co.

Lucas-Championniére, J.M.M. (1878) *La Trépanation (Trepanation)*. Paris: Delahaye.

Lukacs, J.R. (1984) Dental fluorosis in early Neolithic Pakistan. *American Journal of Physical Anthropology* **63**:188. (Abstract).

Lukacs, J.R., Retief, D.H. & Jarrige, J.F. (1985) Dental disease in prehistoric Baluchistan. *National Geographic Research* **1(2)**:184–97.

Lurie, M.B. (1964) *Resistance to Tuberculosis: Experimental Studies in Native and Acquired Defense Mechanisms*. Cambridge, MA: Harvard University Press.

Lyons, A.S. & Petrucelli II, R.J. (1987) *Medicine: An Illustrated History*. New York: Abradale Press.

Maat, G.J.R. (1982) Scurvy in Dutch whalers buried at Spitzbergen. In *Proceedings of the IVth European Members Meeting of the Paleopathology Association at Middleberg/Antwerp on 16–19 September 1982*, pp. 82–93. Utrecht.

Maat, G.J.R. (1991) Ultrastructure of normal and pathological fossilized red blood cells compared with pseudopathological biological structures. *International Journal of Osteoarchaeology* **1**:209–14.

Macalister, A. (1894) Notes on Egyptian mummies. *Journal of the Anthropological Institute* **33**:115–26.

MacCurdy, G.G. (1923) Human skeletal remains from the highlands of Peru. *American Journal of Physical Anthropology* **6**:217–330.

MacEwen, G.D. (1992) Epifisiolisis de la cabeza femoral (Epiphysiolysis of the femoral head). In *Sistema Musculoesquelético. Parte 2. Trastornos del Desarrollo, Tumores, Enfermedades Reumáticas y Reemplazamiento Articular, de FH Netter (Colección Ciba de Ilustraciones Médicas) (Musculoskeletal System. Part 2. Developmental Disorders, Tumors, Rheumatic Diseases and Joint Replacement, of F.H. Netter (Ciba Collection of Medical Illustrations))*, ed. R.H. Freyberg & R.N. Hensinger, pp. 70–1. Barcelona: Salvat.

Maegraith, B.G., Crewe, W. & Jones, K. (1991) The ship and the eye. *Annals of Tropical Medicine and Parasitology* **85(1)**:1–3.

Mafart, B.-Y. (1994) Approche de la Mortalité maternelle au Moyen Age en Provence (An approach to maternal mortality during the Middle Ages in Provence). Actes des 6e Journales Anthropologiques, Dussier de Documentation Archeologique 17. CNRS Editions, Paris. Cited and annotated in *Paleopathology Newsletter* **89 (Jan)**:17, 1995.

Magill, T.P., Jr (1940) A virus from cases of influenza-like upper respiratory infection. *Proceedings of the Society for Experimental Biology and Medicine* **45**:162–4.

Majno, G. (1975) *The Healing Hand. Man and Wound in the Ancient World*. Cambridge, MA: Harvard University Press.

Malagón, V. & Arango, S. (1987) *Ortopedia Infantil (Pediatric Orthopedics)*, 2nd edn. Barcelona: Jims.

Mallegni, F., Ragghianti, V. & Usai, L. (1994) Traumatic events, of which one was perhaps lethal in a skeleton of an individual of Etruscan culture of the 8th century B.C. from the Civita of Tarquinia. *Journal of Paleopathology* **6(2)**:93–101.

Malo, D., Schurr, E., Epstein, D. J., Vekemans, M., Skamene, E. & Gros, P. (1991) The host resistance locus Bcg is tightly linked to a group of cytoskeleton-associated protein genes that include villin and desmin. *Genomics* **10**:356–64.

Manchester, K. (1983a) *The Archaeology of Disease*. Bradford: University of Bradford.

Manchester, K. (1983b) Secondary cancer in an Anglo-Saxon female. *Journal of Archaeological Science* **10**:475–82.

Manchester, K. (1984) Tuberculosis and leprosy in antiquity: An interpretation. *Medical History* **28**:162–73.

Manchester, K. (1991) Tuberculosis and leprosy: Evidence for interaction of disease. In *Human Paleopathology. Current Syntheses and Future Options*, ed. D. Ortner & A.C. Aufderheide, pp. 23–35. Washington, DC: Smithsonian Institution Press.

Manchester, K. (1992) Leprosy: The origin and development of the disease in antiquity. In *Maladie et Maladies. Histoire et Conceptualisation (Disease and Diseases. History and Conceptualization)*, ed. D. Gourevitch, pp. 31–49. Geneve: Librairie Droz S.A.

Mann, R.W. & Murphy, S.P. (1990) *Regional Atlas of Bone Disease*. Springfield, IL: C.C. Thomas.

Manouvrier, L. (1895) Le T Sincipital: Curieuse Mutilation Crânienne Néolithique (Syncipital T: Curious neolithic cranial mutilation). *Bulletin et Memoires de Société d'Anthropologie, Paris* **6**:357–60.

Manouvrier, L. (1904) Incisions, cautérisations et trepanations crâniennes de l'epoque néolithique (Cranial incisions, cauterizations and trepanations in Neolithic times). *Bulletin et Memoires de Société d'Anthropologie, Paris. Série* **5**(**5**):67.

Manzi, G., Sperduti, A. & Passarello, P. (1991) Behavior-induced auditory exostoses in imperial Roman society: Evidence from Coeval urban and rural communities near Rome. *American Journal of Physical Anthropology* **85**:253–60.

Maples, W.R. (1986) Trauma analysis by the forensic anthropologist. In *Forensic Osteology*, ed. K.J. Reichs, pp. 218–28. Springfield, IL: C.C. Thomas.

Marcsik, A. & Olah, S. (1991) Case report of osteomyelitis. *International Journal of Osteoarchaeology* **1**(**2**):147–50.

Marennikova, S.S., Shellukhina, E.M., Zhukova, O.A., Yanova, N.N. & Loparev, V.N. (1990) Smallpox diagnosed 400 years later: Results of skin lesions examination of 16th century Italian mummy. *Journal of Hygiene, Epidemiology, Microbiology and Immunology* **34**(**2**):227–31.

Margetts, E.L. (1967) Trepanation of the skull by the medicine-men of primitive cultures with particular reference to present-day native East African practice. In *Diseases in Antiquity*, ed. D. Brothwell & A.T. Sandison, pp. 673–701. Springfield, IL: C.C. Thomas.

Marketos, S., Eftychiadis, A. & Koutras, D.A. (1990) Thyroid diseases in the Byzantine era. *Journal of the Royal Society of Medicine* **83**:111–13.

Marksic, A. & Baglias, B. (1987) The frequency of enamel hypoplasia from the 8th century, Hungary. *International Journal of Paleopathology* **1**:25–32.

Marsadolov, L.S. (1993) *Program of Saiano-Altai Archaeological Expedition of the State Hermitage Museum*. St. Petersburg, Russia: State Hermitage Museum.

Martin, D.L., Goodman, A.H. & Armelagos, G.J. (1985) Skeletal pathologies as indicators of quality and quantity of diet. In *The Analysis of Prehistoric Diets*, ed. R.I. Gilbert, Jr & J.H. Mielke, pp. 227–79. Orlando, FL: Academic Press.

Martín-Oval, M. & Rodríguez-Martín, C. (1994) Osteochondritis dissecans among the Guanche population of Tenerife (Canary Islands). *HOMO* **45** (**Supplement**):S83. (Abstract).

Martínez-Lavín, M., Mansilla, J., Pineda, C.J., Pijoán, C. & Ochoa, P. (1994) Evidence of hypertrophic osteoarthropathy in human skeletal remains from pre-Hispanic Mesoamerica. *Annals of Internal Medicine* **120**(**3**):238–41.

Martini, M. (ed.) (1988) *Tuberculosis of the Bones and Joints*. Berlin: Springer-Verlag.

Martini, M., Adjrad, A. & Boudjemaa, A. (1986) Tuberculous osteomyelitis: A review of 125 cases. *International Orthopaedics (SICOT)* **10**:201–7.

Marx, M. & D'Auria, S.H. (1986) CT examination of eleven Egyptian mummies. *RadioGraphics* **6**(**2**):321–30.

Mason, O.T. (1885) The Chaclacayo trephined skull. *Proceedings of the United States National Museum* **8**:410–12.

Maspero, G. (1899) *Les Momies Royales de Deir-el-Bahari (The Royal Mummies from Deir-el-Bahari)*. Vol. 1. Paris: Memories Mission Archaeologic Françaises.

Matossian, M.K. (1989) *Poisons of the Past: Molds, Epidemics and History*. New Haven, CT: Yale University Press.

Matto, D. (1886) *La Trepanación en la Época de los Incas (Trepanation in Inca Times)*. Lima: La Crónica Médica.

Maurice, J. (1995) Malaria vaccine raises a dilemma. *Science* **267**:320–3.

May, J.M. (1958) *The Ecology of Human Disease*. New York: MD Publications.

McAlister, W.H. (1989) Osteochondrodysplasias, dysostoses, chromosomal aberrations, mucopolysaccharidoses, and mucolipidoses. In *Bone and Joint Imaging*, ed. D. Resnick, pp. 1035–62. Philadelphia: W.B. Saunders.

McClary, A. (1972) Notes on some Middle Woodland coprolites. In *The Schultz Site at Green Point*, ed. J. Fitting, Memoir no. 4, pp.131–6. Ann Arbor, MI: Museum of Anthropology, University of Michigan.

McCosh, F. (1977) Malaria and goitre in South America one hundred and fifty years ago. *Central African Journal of Medicine* **23**:254–8.

McCoy, G. (1935) Leprosy. In *A Geography of Disease*, ed. E.B. McKinley, pp. 412–14. Washington, DC: George Washington University Press.

McGee, W.J. (1894) Primitive trephining, illustrated by the Muñiz Peruvian Collection. *Bulletin of Johns Hopkins Hospital* **5**(**37**):1–3.

McGee, P. (1897) On some uses of trepanning in early American skulls. *British Association for the Advancement of Science* **6**:146–78.

McKeown, T. (1988) *The Origins of Human Disease*. New York: Basil Blackwell.

McKinley, J. I. (1993) A decapitation from the Romano-British cemetery at Baldock, Hert-

fordshire. *International Journal of Osteoarchaeology* **3**(**1**):41–4.

McLaren, D. (1979) Nature's contraceptive. Wet-nursing and prolonged lactation: The case of Chesham, Buckinghamshire. *Medical History* **23**:426–41.

McNeill, W.H. (1984) *Plagas y Pueblos (Plagues and Peoples)*. Madrid: Siglo XXI de España.

McWhirr, A., Viner, L. & Wells, C. (1982) *Romano-British Cemeteries of Cirencester*. Cirencester, UK: Corinium Museum.

Meers, P.D. (1985) Smallpox still entombed? *Lancet* **i**(**8437**):1103.

Meggers, B.J. & Evans, C. (1966) A transpacific contact in 300 B.C. *Scientific American* **214**:28–35.

Meiklejohn, C., Schentag, C., Venema, A. & Key, P (1984) Socioeconomic change and patterns of pathology and variation in the Mesolithic and Neolithic of Western Europe: Some suggestions. In *Paleopathology at the Origins of Agriculture*, ed. M.N. Cohen & G.J. Armelagos, pp. 75–100. Orlando, FL: Academic Press.

Meinecke, B. (1927) Consumption (tuberculosis) in Classical antiquity. *Annals of Medicine History* **9**:379–402.

Meisel, J.L. (1995) Scurvy (Case Records of the Massachusetts General Hospital). *New England Journal of Medicine* **333**(**25**):1695–707.

Merbs, C.F. (1980) *The Hrdlicka Paleopathology Collection*. San Diego: San Diego Museum of Man.

Merbs, C.F. (1983) *Patterns of Activity-Induced Pathology in a Canadian Inuit Population*. Ottawa: National Museum of Man Mercury Series.

Merbs, C.F. (1989) Trauma. In *Reconstruction of Life from the Skeleton*, ed. M.Y. Iscan & K.A.R. Kennedy, pp. 161–89. New York: A.R. Liss.

Merbs, C.F. (1990) Spondylolysis and age at death in Canadian Eskimos. In *Papers on Paleopathology Presented at the XIIIth European Members Meeting of the Paleopathology Association in Cambridge, England on 19–22 September, 1990. Paleopathology Newsletter* **72** (**Supplement**):16. (Abstract).

Merbs, C. F. (1992) A New World of infectious disease. *Yearbook of Physical Anthropology* **35**:3–42.

Merke, F. (1984) *History and Iconography of Endemic Goitre and Cretinism*. Boston, MA: MTP Press Limited.

Messner, R.P. (1987) Artritis por micobacterias y hongos (Arthritis due to mycobacteria and fungi). In *Artritis y Otras Patologías Relacionadas (Arthritis and Allied Pathological Conditions)*, ed. D.J. McCarty, 10th edn, vol. 4, pp. 1698–1708. Madrid: Panamericana.

Meyerhoff, E.L. (1982) The threatened ways of Kenya's Pokot people. *National Geographic* **161**:120–40.

Meyers, W. M., Neafie, R.C. & Connor, D.H. (1976) Bancroftian and Malayan filariasis. In *Pathology of Tropical and Extraordinary Diseases*, ed. C.H. Binford & D.H. Connor, vol. 2, pp. 340–55. Washington, DC: Armed Forces Institute of Pathology.

Michaelis, L. (1930) Vergleichende mikroskopische Untersuchungen an rezenten, historischen und fossilen menschlichen Knochen, zugleich ein Beitrag zur Geschichte der Syphilis (Comparative microscopic studies of recent historical and fossilized human bones with a discussion of the history of syphilis). *Veröffentlichungen aus dem Gebiet der Kriegs- und Konstitutionpathologie* **6**:1–92.

Micozzi, M.S. (1982) Skeletal tuberculosis, pelvic contraction and parturition. *American Journal of Physical Anthropology* **58**:441–5.

Micozzi, M.S. (1991) Disease in antiquity. *Archives of Pathology and Laboratory Medicine* **115**:838–44.

Milkman, L.A. (1930) Pseudofractures (hunger osteopathy, late rickets, osteomalacia): Report of case. *American Journal of Roentgenology* **24**:29–37.

Millán de Palavecino, M.D. (1966) Material de yacimientos de altura del área de la Puna (Material from the high sites from the area of the highlands). *Anales de Arqueología y Etnología (Argentina: Mendoza)* **21**:81–100.

Miller, L. (1986) Research in malaria vaccines. *New England Journal of Medicine* **315**(10):640–1.

Miller, L.H., Good, M.F. & Milon, G. (1994) Malaria pathogenesis. *Science* **264**:1878–83.

Miller, R.L., de Jonge, N., Krijger, F.W. & Deelder, A.M. (1993) Predynastic schistosomiasis. In *Biological Anthropology and the Study of Ancient Egypt*, ed. W.V. Davies & R. Walker, pp. 54–60. London: British Museum Press.

Miller, R.L., Ikram, S., Armelagos, G.J., Walker, R., Harer, W.B., Shiff, C.J., Baggett, D., Carrigan, M. & Maret, S.M. (1994) Diagnosis of *Plasmodium falciparum* infections in mummies using the rapid manual *Para*Sight™-F test . *Transactions of the Royal Society of Tropical Medicine and Hygiene* **88**:31–2.

Mitchell, J.K. (1900) Study of a mummy with anterior poliomyelitis. *Transactions of the Association of American Physicians* **15**:134–6.

Mitsuda, K. ([1919] 1953). On the value of a skin reaction to a suspension of leprous nodules. *International Journal of Leprosy* **21**:347–58.

Mogle, P. & Zias, J. (1995) Trephination as a possible treatment for scurvy in a Middle Bronze Age (ca. 2000 B.C.) skeleton. *International Journal of Osteoarchaeology* **5**:77–81.

Møller-Christensen, V. (1953) *Ten Lepers from Naestved in Denmark*. Copenhagen: Danish Science Press.

Møller-Christensen, V. (1958) *Bogen om Abelholt Kloster (Rickets in Abelholt Cloister)*. Copenhagen: Munksgaard.

Møller-Christensen, V. (1961) *Bone Changes in Leprosy*. Copenhagen: Munksgaard.

Møller-Christensen, V. (1965) New knowledge of leprosy through paleopathology. *International Journal of Leprosy* **33**:603–10.

Møller-Christensen, V. (1967) Evidence of leprosy in earlier peoples. In *Diseases in Antiquity*, ed. D. Brothwell & A.T. Sandison, pp. 295–306. Springfield, IL: C.C. Thomas.

Møller-Christensen, V. (1978) *Leprosy Changes of the Skull*. Odense: Odense University Press.

Møller-Christensen, V. (1983) Leprosy and tuberculosis. In *Disease in Ancient Man*, ed. G.D. Hart, pp. 129–38. Toronto: Clarke Irwin.

Møller-Christensen, V. & Hughes, D.R. (1962) Two early cases of leprosy in Great Britain. *Man (London)* **62**:177–9.

Møller-Christensen, V. & Hughes, D.R. (1966) An early case of leprosy from Nubia. *Man (London)* **1**:242–3.

Møller-Christensen, V., Baake, S.N., Melsom, R.S. & Waaler, E. (1952) Changes in the anterior nasal spine and the alveolar process of the maxillary bone in leprosy. *International Journal of Leprosy* **20**:335–40.

Molleson, T. & Cox, M. (1993) *The Spitalsfield Project. Volume 2, The Anthropology. The Middling Sort*. Council for British Archaeology Research Report no. 86. York: Council for British Archaeology.

Mollison, P.L., Engelfriet, C.P. & Contreras, M. (1993) *Blood Transfusion in Clinical Medicine*. Oxford: Blackwell Scientific Publications.

Molto, J.E. (1990) Differential diagnosis of rib lesions: A case study from Middle Woodland southern Ontario. Circa 230 AD. *American Journal of Physical Anthropology* **83**:439–47.

Moodie, R.L. (ed.) (1921) *Studies in the Paleopathology of Egypt*. Chicago: University of Chicago Press.

Moodie, R.L. (1923a) *The Antiquity of Disease*. Chicago: University of Chicago Press.

Moodie, R.L. (1923b) *Palaeopathology. An Introduction to the Study of Ancient Evidences of Disease*. Urbana, IL: University of Illinois Press.

Moodie, R.L. (1926) Tumors of the head among the pre-Columbian Peruvians. *Annals of Medical History* **8**:394–412.

Moodie, R.L. (1931) *Roentgenologic Studies of Egyptian and Peruvian Mummies*. Anthropological Series 3. Chicago: Field Museum of Natural History.

Moore, J.G., Grundmann, A.W., Hall, H.J. & Fry, G.F. (1974) Human fluke infection in Glen Canyon at A.D.1250. *American Journal of Physical Anthropology* **41**:115–18.

Moore, K.P., Thorp, S. & van Gerven, D.P. (1986) Pattern of dental eruption, skeletal maturation and stress in a medieval population from Sudanese Nubia. *Human Evolution* **1**(4):325–40.

Moore, S. (1955) *Hyperostosis Cranii (Cranial Hyperostosis)*. Springfield, IL: C.C. Thomas.

Moore, W.J. & Corbett, M.E. (1983) Dental and alveolar infection. In *Disease in Ancient Man*, ed. G.D. Hart, pp. 139–55. Toronto: Clarke Irwin.

Morgagni, G.B. (1719) *Animadversaria Anatomica (Anatomic Observations)*. Padova. (Cited verbatim on pp.1–3 in Henschen, F. (1949) *Morgagni's Syndrome*. Edinburgh: Oliver and Boyd).

Morgagni, G.B. (1761) *Lib. II, Epistle XXVII. De Sedibus et Causis Morborum (Regarding the Body and the Causes of Death)*. Padova. (Cited verbatim in Henschen, F. (1949) *Morgagni's Syndrome*. Edinburgh: Oliver and Boyd).

Morgan, W. (1965) The rape of the phallus. *Journal of the American Medical Association* **193**(8):223–4.

Morris, A.G. & Rogers, A.L. (1989) A probable case of prehistoric stone disease from the Northern Cape Province, South Africa. *American Journal of Physical Anthropology* **79**:521–7.

Morrison, J. (1967) Origins of the practices of circumcision and subincision among the Australian aborigines. *Medical Journal of Australia* **1**:125–7.

Morse, D. (1961) Prehistoric tuberculosis in America. *American Review of Infectious Diseases* **83**:489–504.

Morse, D. (1967a) Tuberculosis. In *Diseases in Antiquity*, ed. D.R. Brothwell & A.T. Sandison, pp. 249–71. Springfield, IL: C.C. Thomas.

Morse, D. (1967b) Two cases of possible treponema infection in prehistoric America. In *Miscellaneous Papers in Paleopathology*, ed. W.D. Wade, pp. 48–60. Flagstaff, AZ: Museum of Northern Arizona.

Morse, D. (1969) *Ancient Disease in the Midwest*. Springfield, IL: Illinois State Museum Reports of Investigations, no. 15.

Morse, D. (1978) *Ancient Disease in the Midwest,* 2nd edn. Springfield, IL: Illinois State Museum Reports of Investigations, no. 15.

Morse, D., Brothwell, D.R. & Ucko, P. (1964) Tuberculosis in ancient Europe. *American Review of Respiratory Diseases* **90**:524–41.

Morse, D., Dailey, R.C. & Bunn, J. (1974) Prehistoric multiple myeloma. *Bulletin of the New York Academy of Medicine* **54**:447–58.

Morse, J.L. (1900) The frequency of rickets in Boston and vicinity. *Journal of the American Medical Association* **34**:724–6.

Morton, S.G.(1839) *Crania Americana (American Crania)*. Philadelphia: J. Dobson.

Moseley, J.E. (1966) Radiographic studies in hematologic bone disease: Implications for paleopathology. In *Human Palaeopathology*, ed. S. Jarcho, pp. 121–30. New Haven and London: Yale University Press.

Moser, C.J. (1973) *Human Decapitation in Ancient Mesoamerica*. Washington, DC: Dumbarton Oaks Research Library and Collection.

Moss, M.L. (1958) The pathogenesis of artificial cranial deformation. *American Journal of Physical Anthropology* **16**(**3**):269–86.

Moss-Salentijn, L. & Klyvert, M. (1985) *Dental and Oral Tissues,* 2nd edn. Philadelphia: Lea and Febiger.

Mostny, G. (ed.) (1957) La Momia del Cerro El Plomo (The Mummy of Cerro El Plomo). *Boletin del Museo Nacional de Historia Natural* **27**(**1**):1–120.

Moulin, D. de (1961) Aneurysms in antiquity. *Archivum Chirurgicum Nederlandicum* **13**:49–63.

Moyer, T.P. (1993) Testing for arsenic. *Mayo Clinic Proceedings* **68**:1210–11.

Muir, E. (1968) Relationship of leprosy to tuberculosis. *Leprosy Review* **28**:11–19.

Mullholland, S.C. (1989) Phytolith shape frequencies in North Dakota grasses: A comparison to general patterns. *Journal of Archaeological Science* **16**:489–551.

Munizaga, A., Allison, M.J. & Parades, C. (1978) Cholelithiasis and cholecystitis in pre-Colombian Chileans. *American Journal of Physical Anthropology* **48**:209–12.

Munizaga, J., Allison, M.J., Gerszten, E. & Klurfeld, D.M. (1975) Pneumoconiosis in Chilean miners of the sixteenth century. *Bulletin of the New York Academy of Medicine* **51**:1281–93.

Muñoz Gómez, J. (1983) Osteonecrosis y Fracturas de Marcha (Osteonecrosis and fatigue fractures). In *Reumatología Clínica (Clinical Rheumatology)*, ed. J. Rotés Querol, vol. 2, pp. 408–17. Barcelona: Expaxs.

Murphy, S.P. (1992) *Glossary of Paleopathological Terms. Paleopathology Course. National Museum of Health and Medicine.* Washington, DC: Armed Forces Institute of Pathology.

Murray, R.O., Jacobson, H.G. & Stocker, D.J. (1990) *The Radiology of Skeletal Disorders. Volume 1. Fundamentals of Skeletal Radiology,* 3rd edn. London: Churchill Livingstone.

Nabarro, J.D.N. (1987) Acromegaly. *Clinical Endocrinology* **26**:481–512.

Nadeau, G. (1944) Indian scalping technique in different tribes. *Bulletin of the History of Medicine* **10**:178–94.

Nagel, R.L., Raventos-Suarez, C., Fabry, M.E., Tanowitz, H., Sicard, D. and Labie, D. (1981) Impairment of the growth of *Plasmodium falciparum* in Hb EE erythrocytosis. *Journal of Clinical Investigation* **68**:303–5.

Naim, A.& Fahmy, K. (1965) Vaginal fistulae complicating salt atresia in Arabia. *Alexandria Medical Journal* **11**(**3**):218–26.

Nakano, J.H. (1985) Poxviruses. In *Manual of Clinical Microbiology*, ed. E.H. Lennette,

A. Ballows, W.J. Hausler & H.J. Shadomy, pp. 733–41. Washington, DC: American Society for Microbiology.

Nanson, P. & Jørgensen, R.J. (1977) Fun af parasitaeg i arkaeologisk materiale fra det vikingetidige Ribe (Parasite eggs identified in material archaeological excavations in Viking Age Ribe). *Nordisk Veterinaer Medicin* **29**:263–6.

Neel, J.V. (1962) Diabetes mellitus: A "thrifty" genotype rendered detrimental by "Progress?" *American Journal of Human Genetics* **14**:353–62.

Neel, J.V. (1982) The thrifty gene revisited. In *The Genetics of Diabetes*, ed. J. Kobberling & R. Tattersall, pp. 283–93. New York: Academic Press.

Neer, R.M. (1974) Evolutionary significance of vitamin D, skin pigment and ultraviolet light. *American Journal of Physical Anthropology* **41**(**3**):496. (Abstract).

Nelson, E.W. ([1899] 1983) *The Eskimo About Bering Strait*. Washington, DC: Smithsonian Institution Press. (First published in 1899).

Nerhlich, A., Peschel, O., Löhrs, U., Parsche, F. & Betz, P. (1991) Juvenile gigantism plus polyostotic fibrous dysplasia in the Tegernsee giant. *Lancet* **338**(**8771**):886–7 (Letter).

Neufeld, F. (1904) Über die Antikörper des Streptkokken-und Pneumokokken-Immunoserums (Concerning antibodies of streptococci and pneumococci immunosera). *Deutsche Medezinische Wochenschrift* **30**:1458–60.

Newbrun, E. (1977) Etiology of dental caries. In *A Textbook of Preventive Dentistry*, ed. R.C. Caldwell & R.E. Stallard, pp. 30–54. Philadelphia: W.B. Saunders.

Nielsen, O.V. & Alexandersen, V. (1971) Malignant osteopetrosis in ancient Nubia. *Danish Medical Bulletin* **18**:125–8.

Nishimura, M., Sool Kown, K., Shibuta, K., Yoshikawa, Y., Oh, C.-K., Suzuki, T., Chung, T.-A. & Hori, Y. (1994) An improved method for DNA diagnosis of leprosy using formaldehyde-fixed, paraffin-embedded skin biopsies. *Modern Pathology* **7**(**2**):253–6.

Nivaud, M. & Gervais, V. (1991) Étude Paléopathologique des Squelettes du Prieuré de Saint Philbert sur Risle (Eure) (Paleopathological study of skeletons from the priory of Saint Philbert on the Risle (Eure)). *Bulletin d'Anthropologie de Basse-Normandie* **16**:92–9.

Nixon, D. & Samols, E. (1970) Acral changes associated with thyroid diseases. *Journal of the American Medical Association* **212**(**7**):1175–81.

Norman, A.W. & Henry, H. L. (1993) Vitamin D: Metabolism and mechanics of action. In *Primer on the Metabolic Bone Diseases and Disorders of Mineral Metabolism*, ed. M.J. Favus, 2nd edn, pp. 63–70. New York: Raven Press.

Notman, D. (1986) Ancient scanning: The computed tomography of Egyptian mummies. In

Science in Egyptology, ed. R.A. David, pp. 251–320. Manchester, England: Manchester University Press.

Notman, D. & Aufderheide, A.C. (1995) Experimental mummification and computed imaging. In *Proceedings of the First World Congress on Mummy Studies*, 1992, vol. 2, pp. 821–8. Tenerife, Canary Islands: Museo Arqueológico y Etnográfico de Tenerife, Organismo Autónomo de Museos y Centros, Cabildo de Tenerife.

Nowak, R. (1995) How the parasite disguises itself. *Science* **269**:755.

Nriagu, J.O. (1983) Saturnine gout among Roman aristocrats. Did lead poisoning contribute to the fall of the empire? *New England Journal of Medicine* **308**:660–3.

Nuttall, Z. (1975) *The Codex Nuttall*. New York: Dover.

O'Connor, D. (1993) *Ancient Nubia: Egypt's Rival in Africa*. Philadelphia: The University Museum of Archaeology and Anthropology, University of Pennsylvania.

O'Neill, Y.V. (1993) Diseases of the Middle Ages. In *The Cambridge World History of Human Disease*, ed. K.F. Kiple, pp. 270–9. New York: Cambridge University Press.

Oakley, K.P. (1960) Ancient preserved brains. *Man (London)* **60**(**122**):90–1.

Orban, B. (1986) *Orban's Oral History and Embryology*, 10th edn. St. Louis: C.V. Mosby Co.

Oriel, J.D. (1973a) Anal and genital warts in the ancient world. *Paleopathology Newsletter* **3**:5–7.

Oriel, J.D. (1973b) Gonorrhea in the ancient world. *Paleopathology Newsletter* **4**:7.

Orjhi, A.U., Banyal, H.S., Chevli, R. & Fitch, C. D. (1981) Hemin lyses malarial parasites. *Science* **214**:667–9.

Ortiz de Montellano, B.R. (1990) *Aztec Medicine, Health and Nutrition*. New Brunswick: Rutgers University Press.

Ortner, D.J. (1976) The paleopathology program at the Smithsonian Institution: Purposes and present status. *Bulletin of the New York Academy of Medicine* **52**(**10**):1197–206.

Ortner, D.J. (1986) Skeletal evidence of pre-Columbian treponemal disease in North America. In *Papers on Paleopathology Presented at the XIth European Members Meeting of the Paleopathology Association in Madrid, Spain. Paleopathology Newsletter* **56** (**Supplement**):10–11. (Abstract).

Ortner, D.J. (1989) Case Report No. 11: Trepanematosis (yaws?). *Paleopathology Newsletter* **66**:9–11.

Ortner, D.J. (1991) Theoretical and methodological issues in paleopathology. In *Human Paleopathology. Current Syntheses and Future Options*, ed. D.J. Ortner & A.C. Aufderheide, pp. 5–11. Washington and London: Smithsonian Institution Press.

Ortner, D.J. (1992a) Livingstone's "alternative hypothesis." *Paleopathology Newsletter* **79**:5–6.

Ortner, D.J. (1992b) Skeletal paleopathology. Probabilities, possibilities and impossibilities. In *Disease and Demography in the Americas*, ed. J.W. Verano & D.H. Ubelaker, pp. 5–13. Washington and London: Smithsonian Institution Press.

Ortner, D.J. (1992c) *Pathology and Pseudopathology*. Paleopathology Course. National Museum of Health and Medicine. Washington, DC: Armed Forces Institute of Pathology.

Ortner, D.J. & Aufderheide, A.C. (eds) (1991a) *Human Paleopathology. Current Syntheses and Future Options*. Washington and London: Smithsonian Institution Press.

Ortner, D.J. & Aufderheide, A.C. (1991b) Introduction. In *Human Paleopathology. Current Syntheses and Future Options*, ed. D.J. Ortner & A.C. Aufderheide, pp. 1–2. Washington and London: Smithsonian Institution Press.

Ortner, D.J. & Putschar, W. (1985) *Identification of Paleopathological Conditions in Human Skeletal Remains*. Washington, DC: Smithsonian Institution Press.

Ortner, D.J. & Roberts, C.A. (1985) Case Report No. 5: Osteochondroma. Case Reports on Paleopathology. *Paleopathology Newsletter* **50**:7–8.

Ortner, D.J. & Utermohle, C.J. (1981) Polyarticular inflammatory arthritis in a pre-Columbian skeleton from Kodiak Island, Alaska, USA. *American Journal of Physical Anthropology* **56**:23–31.

Ortner, D.J., Manchester, K. & Lee, F. (1991) Metastatic carcinoma in a leper skeleton from a medieval cemetery in Chichester, England. *International Journal of Osteoarchaeology* **1**:91–8.

Ortner, D.J., Tuross, N. & Stix, A. I. (1992) New approaches to the study of disease in archaeological New World populations. *Human Biology* **64**:337–60.

Osler, W. (1881) Infections (so-called ulcerative) endocarditis. *Archives of Medicine* **5**:44–68.

Owen, R. (1842) *Description of the Skeleton of an Extinct Sloth*, Mylodon Robustus *Owen, with Observations on the Osteology, Natural Affinities, and Probable Habits of the Megatheroid Quadrupeds in General*. London 4to.

Oviedo y Valdés, G.F. (1851) *Historia de las Indias*. Madrid: Imprenta de la Real Academia de la Historia. (Translated in 1959 as *Natural History of the West Indies* by S.A. Stoudemire). Chapel Hill, NC: University of North Carolina Press.

Ozonoff, M.B. (1989) Spinal anomalies and curvatures. In *Bone and Joint Imaging*, ed. D. Resnick, pp. 1063–70. Philadelphia: W.B. Saunders.

Pääbo, S., Gifford, J.A. & Wilson, A.C. (1988) Mitochondrial DNA sequences from a 7000 year old brain. *Nucleic Acid Research* **16**(**20**):9775–87.

Paddock, F.K., Loomis, C.C. & Perkons, A.K. (1970) An inquest on the death of Charles Francis Hall. *New England Journal of Medicine* **282**:784–6.

Pahl, M. (1987) Operationen am Schädel im alten Ägypten (Operations on the skull of ancient Egyptians). *Mitteilungen der DFG* (Newsletter of the German Research Society) **February**:24–8.

Pahl, W.M. & Undeutsch, W. (1988) Differential diagnosis of facial skin ulcerations in an Egyptian mummy. *Medezinhistorisches Journal* **33**(**1/2**):152–65.

Pahor, A.L. (1992a) Ear, nose and throat in ancient Egypt. Part I. *Journal of Laryngology and Otology* **106**(**8**):677–82.

Pahor, A.L. (1992b) Ear, nose and throat in ancient Egypt. Part II. *Journal of Laryngology and Otology* **106**(**9**):773–9.

Pahor, A.L. (1992c) Ear, nose and throat in ancient Egypt. Part III. *Journal of Laryngology and Otology* **106**(**10**):863–73.

Pahor, A.L. & Kimura, A. (1990) History of removal of nasal polyps. *Folia Medica* **102**:183–6.

Painter, T.J. (1991) Lindow Man, Tollund Man and other peat-bog bodies: The preservation and antimicrobial action of sphagnan, a reactive glycuronalglycan with tanning and sequestering properties. *Carbohydrate Polymers* **15**:123–42.

Palés, L. (1929) Maladie de Paget préhistorique (Prehistoric Paget's disease). *L'Anthropologie Paris* **39**:263–70.

Palés, L. (1930) *Paléopathologie et Pathologie Comparative (Paleopathology and Comparative Pathology)*. Paris: Masson.

Palfi, G., Dutour, O. & Berato, J. (1992a) A Propos d'une Spondylodiscite Médiévale du Xe Siècle (La Roquebrussanne, Var) (On a medieval spondylodiscitis from the Xth century (La Roquebrussanne, Var)). Munibe, Supl. 8. *Actas del I Congreso Nacional de Paleopatología (San Sebastián-Donostia)*, pp. 107–10.

Palfi, G., Farkas, G. & Olah, S. (1992b) Maladies Articulaires d'une Sèrie Anthropologique de la Période de la Conquête Hongroise (Joint diseases in an anthropological sample from the Hungarian Conquest Period). Munibe, Supl. 8. *Actas del I Congreso Nacional de Paleopatología (San Sebastián-Donostia)*, pp. 111–14.

Palfi, G., Dutour, O., Borreani, M., Brun, J.-P. & Berato, J. (1992c) Pre-Columbian congenital syphilis from the Late Antiquity in France. *International Journal of Osteoarchaeology* **2**(**3**):245–61.

Palkovich, A.M. (1981) Tuberculosis epidemiology in two Arikara skeletal samples: A study of disease impact. In *Prehistoric Tuberculosis in the Americas*, ed. J.E. Buikstra, pp. 161–75. Evanston, IL: Northwestern University Archaeological Program.

Pan American Health Organization (1986) *Tuberculosis Control. A Manual on Methods and Procedures for Integrated Programs*. Scientific Publication no. 498. Washington, DC: WHO.

Pankhurst, R. (1990) The use of thermal baths in the treatment of skin disease in old-time Ethiopia. *International Journal of Dermatology* **29**(**6**):451–6.

Papper, S. (1981) Internal medicine. In *Rypin's Medical Licensure Examinations*, ed. E.D. Frohlich, 13th edn, pp. 693–746. Philadelphia: Lippincott.

Park, K. (1993) Black death. In *The Cambridge World History of Human Disease*, ed. K.F. Kiple, pp. 612–16. New York: Cambridge University Press.

Parker, S. L., Tong, T., Bolden, S. & Wingo, P. A. (1996) Cancer Statistics 1996. *CA (American Cancer Society)* **46**(**1**):5–27.

Parkman, P.D., Buescher, A. & Artenstein, D. (1962) Recovery of rubella virus from Army recruits. *Proceedings of the Society for Experimental Biology and Medicine* **111**:225–30.

Parra, M.E., Evans, C.B. & Taylor, D.W. (1991) Identification of *Plasmodium falciparum* histidine-rich protein 2 in the plasma of humans with malaria. *Journal of Clinical Microbiology* **29**(**8**):1629–34.

Pasteur, L. (1881) Note sur la maladie nouvelle provoquée par la salive d'un enfant mort de la rage (Note about a new disease caused by the saliva from an infant who died of rabies). *Bulletin de la Académie de Médecine (Paris)* [Series 2] **10**:94–103.

Paterson, D.E. & Job, C.K. (1964) Bone changes and resorption in leprosy. A radiological, pathological, and clinical study. In *Leprosy in Theory and Practice*, ed. R.G. Cochrane, T.F. Davey & G. McRobert, pp. 425–47. Baltimore: Williams and Wilkins.

Patrucco, R., Tello, R. & Bonavia, D. (1983) Parasitological studies of coprolites of pre-Hispanic Peruvian populations. *Current Anthropology* **24**:393–4.

Patten, R.C. (1981) Aflatoxins and disease. *American Journal of Tropical Medicine and Hygiene* **30**:422–5.

Patterson, K.D. (1993a) Amebic Dysentery. In *The Cambridge World History of Human Disease*, ed. K.F. Kiple, pp. 568–71. New York: Cambridge University Press.

Patterson, K. D. (1993b) Echinococcosis (Hydatidosis). In *The Cambridge World History of Human Disease*, ed. K.F. Kiple, p. 703. New York: Cambridge University Press.

Patterson, K.D. (1993c) Toxoplasmosis. In *The Cambridge World History of Human Disease*, ed. K.F. Kiple, pp. 1051–2. New York: Cambridge University Press.

Paulshock, B.Z. (1980) Tutankhamun and his brothers. *Journal of the American Medical Society* **244**(**2**):160–4.

Peck, W. & Ross, J.G. (1978) *Egyptian Drawings*. New York: Dutton.

Pedley, J.C. & Greater, J.G. (1976) Does droplet infection play a role in the transmission of leprosy? *Leprosy Review* **47**:97–102.

Peng, L.-X. (1995) Study of an ancient cadaver excavated from a Han Dynasty (207 B.C.–A.D. 200) tomb in Hunan Province. In *Proceedings of the First World Congress on Mummy Studies*, 1992, vol. 2, pp. 853–6. Tenerife, Canary Islands: Museo Arquelógico y Etnográfico de Tenerife, Organismo Autónomo de Museos y Centros, Cabildo de Tenerife.

Pérez, P.-J. (1980–1981) Nueva Aportación Paleopatológica Acerca de la Población Prehispánica Canaria (New paleopathological contribution about the prehispanic Canarian population). *El Museo Canario* **XLI**:29–45.

Pérez, P.-J. & Martinez, I. (1995) New evidence of temporomandibular arthrosis in human fossils from the Middle Pleistocene site of Atapuerca/Ibeas, Burgos, Spain. In *Proceedings of the IXth European Meeting of the Paleopathology Association (Barcelona)*, pp. 267–72. Barcelona: Museu d'Arqueologia de Catalunya.

Perkins, M. (1931) Acromegaly in the far north. *Nature* **128**:491–2.

Persson, O. (1976–77) A trepanned skull from the Gillhög Passage-grave at Barsebak in West Scania (Southern Sweden). *Ossa* **3**(**4**):53–61.

Peterson, R.O. (1994) Disorders of genetic and phenotypic sex. In *Pathology*, ed. E. Rubin & J.L. Farber, pp. 885–6. Philadelphia: Lippincott.

Petrie, W.M.F. & Quibell, J.E. (1896) *Naqada and Ballas*. London: Quaritch.

Pfeiffer, S. (1991) Rib lesions and New World tuberculosis. *International Journal of Osteoarchaeology* **1**(**3&4**):191–8.

Piggott, S. (1940) A trephanned skull of the Beaker period from Dorset and the practice of trepanning in prehistoric Europe. *Proceedings of the Prehistoric Society* **6**:112–32.

Pineda, C.J., Martínez Lavín, M., Goobar, J.E., Sartoris, D.J., Clopton, P. & Resnick, D. (1987) Periostitis in hypertrophic arthropathy: Relationship to disease duration. American Journal of Roentgenology **148**:773–8.

Pinkerton, H. & Strano, A. (1976) Rickettsial diseases. In *Pathology of Tropical and Extraordinary Diseases*, ed. C.H. Binford & D.H. Connor, vol. 1, pp. 87–100. Washington, DC: Armed Forces Institute of Pathology.

Piomelli, S., Corash, M.B., Seaman, C., Mushak, P., Glover, B. & Padgett, R. (1980) Blood lead concentrations in a remote Himalayan population. *Science* **210**:1135–6.

Piperno, M. (1976) Scoperta di una sepoltura doppia epigravettiana nella Grotta dell'Uzzo (Trapani) (Discovery of a double burial in the Uzzo (Trapani) Cave). *Kokalos* **22–23**:720–51.

Pitzen, P. & Rössler, H. (1993) *Manual de Ortopedia (Manual of Orthopedics)*, 2nd edn. Barcelona: Doyma.

Piulachs, P. (1957) *Lecciones de Patología Quirúrgica. I. 3ª parte. Afecciones Quirúrgicas de los Huesos y de las Articulaciones (Lessons in Surgical Pathology. I: Part 3: Surgical Conditions of Bones and Joints)*, 2nd edn. Barcelona: Vergara.

Piulachs, P. (1959) *Lecciones de Patología Quirúrgica. II. Afecciones de las Extremidades. 2ª parte. Afecciones Congénitas y Adquiridas (Lessons in Surgical Pathology. II. Conditions Affecting the Extremities. Part 2. Congenital and Acquired Conditions)*. Barcelona: Vergara.

Pizzi, T. & Schenone, H. (1954) Hallazgo de huevos de *Trichuris trichiura* en contenido intestinal de un cuerpo arqueológico incaico. (The finding of *Trichuris trichiura* ova in the intestinal contents of an Inca body). *Boletin Chileno de Parasitologia* **9**:73–5.

Plessis, D.J. du (1970) Lesions of the feet in patients with diabetes mellitus. *South African Journal of Surgery* **8**:29–46.

Plorde, J. (1983) Malaria. In *Harrison's Principles of Internal Medicine*, ed. R.G. Petersdorf, R.D. Adams, E. Braunwald, K.J. Isselbacher, J. Martin & J.D. Wilson, 10th edn, pp. 1187–93. New York: McGraw-Hill.

Plorde, J. (1991a) Amebiasis. In *Harrison's Principles of Internal Medicine*, ed. J.D. Wilson, E. Braunwald, K.J. Isselbacher, *et al.*, 12th edn, pp. 778–82. New York: McGraw-Hill.

Plorde, J. (1991b) Scabies, chiggers and other ectoparasites. In *Harrison's Principles of Internal Medicine*, ed. J.D. Wilson, E. Braunwald, K.J. Isselbacher, *et al.*, 12th edn, pp. 831–4. New York: McGraw-Hill.

Plorde, J. & Ramsey, P.G. (1991) Nematodes, cestodes and hermaphroditic trematodes. In *Harrison's Principles of Internal Medicine*, ed. J.D. Wilson, E. Braunwald, K.J. Isselbacher, *et al.*, 12th edn, pp. 817–30. New York: McGraw-Hill.

Polidoro, G. & Antón, S.C. (1993) Radio-ulnar synostoses and allied conditions: Archaeological cases and their implications for function. In *Papers on Paleopathology Presented at the 20th Annual Meeting of the Paleopathology Association, Toronto, Ontario, April 13–14, 1993. Paleopathology Newsletter* **82**(**Supplement**):16. (Abstract).

Pollicard, A. & Collet, A. (1952) Deposition of siliceous dust in the lungs of the inhabitants of the Saharan regions. *Archives of Industrial Hygiene and Occupational Medicine* **5**:527–34.

Poncet, F. (1895) A prehistoric truss. *Lancet* **2**:869. (Originally published in 1895 in French).

Porter, R.W. & Park, W. (1982) Unilateral spondylolysis. *Journal of Bone and Joint Surgery* **64B**:344–8.

Posselt, U. (1957) Movement areas of the mandible. *Journal of Prosthetic Dentistry* **7**:375–85.

Post, P. & Daniels, F., Jr (1969) Histological and histochemical examination of American Indian scalps, mummies and a shrunken head. *American Journal of Physical Anthropology* **30**:269–94.

Post, P. & Daniels, F., Jr (1973) Ancient and mummified skin. *Cutis* **11**:779–81.

Post, P.W. & Donner, D.D. (1978) Frostbite in a pre-Columbian mummy. *American Journal of Physical Anthropology* **37**:187–92.

Pott, P. (1779) *Remarks on That Kind of Palsy of the Lower Limbs Which is Frequently Found to Accompany a Curvature of the Spine*. London: J. Johnson, No. 72, St. Paul's Church Yard.

Potts, J.T., Jr (1991) Diseases of the parathyroid gland and other hyper- and hypocalcemic disorders. In *Harrison's Principles of Internal Medicine*, ed. J.D. Wilson, E. Braunwald, K.J. Isselbacher, *et al.*, 12th edn, pp. 1902–21. New York: McGraw-Hill.

Pounds, N.J.G. (1974) *An Economic History of Medieval Europe*. London: Longman Group Ltd.

Powell, L.W. & Isselbacher, K.J. (1991) Hemochromatosis. In *Harrison's Principles of Internal Medicine*, ed. J.D. Wilson, E. Braunwald, K.J. Isselbacher, *et al.*, 12th edn, pp. 1825–9. New York: McGraw-Hill.

Powell, M.L. (1988) *Status and Health in Prehistory. A Case Study of the Moundville Chiefdom*. Washington, DC: Smithsonian Institution Press.

Powell, M.L. (1991) Endemic treponematosis and tuberculosis in the prehistoric southeastern United States: Biological costs of chronic endemic disease. In *Human Paleopathology. Current Syntheses and Future Options*, ed. D.J. Ortner & A.C. Aufderheide, pp. 173–80. Washington and London: Smithsonian Institution Press.

Powell, M.L. (1992) Health and disease in the Late Prehistoric southeast. In *Disease and Demography in the Americas*, ed. J.W. Verano & D.H. Ubelaker, pp. 41–53. Washington and London: Smithsonian Institution Press.

Power, C. & O'Sullivan, V.R. (1992) Rickets in 19th century Waterford. *Archeology (Ireland)* **6**(**1**):27–8.

Powers, R. (1960) Ancient preserved brains: An additional note. *Man (London)* **60**(**122**):91.

Preiss, G.A. (1953) Fracturas Óseas y su Curación (Fractured bones and their healing). In *Röntgen-Diagnóstico (Diagnostic*

Roentgenology), ed. H.R. Schinz, W.E. Baensch, E. Friedl & E. Uehlinger, vol. 1, pp. 248–412. Barcelona: Salvat.

Price, J.L. (1975) The radiology of excavated Saxon and medieval human remains from Winchester. *Clinical Radiology* **26**:363–70.

Prim, J., Campillo, D., Ribas, E. & Turbón, D. (1995) Bone leontiasis in individiual No. 24 of the Paleochristian necropolis at "La Olmeda," in Pedrosa de la Vega (Palencia, Spain). In *Proceedings of the IXth European Meeting of the Paleopathology Association (Barcelona)*, pp. 287–9. Barcelona: Museu d'Arqueologia de Catalunya.

Prioreschi, P. (1991) *A History of Medicine.* Vol. 1. Lewiston, NY: Edwin Mellen Press.

Prockop, D.J. (1991) Heritable disorders of connective tissue. In *Harrison's Principles of Internal Medicine*, ed. J.D. Wilson, E. Braunwald, K.J. Isselbacher, *et al.*, 12th edn, pp. 1860–8. New York: McGraw-Hill.

Pruniéres, L. (1874) Sur les Crânes Artificielle-ment Perforés à l'Époque des Dolmens (Concerning artificial cranial perforation during the Dolmen period). *Bulletin et Memoires de Société d'Anthropologie, Paris (Série 2)* **IX**:185–205.

Puchalt, F.J., Castellá, M., Negre, M.C., Feucht, M. & Villalaín, J.D. (1996) Enfermedad de Forestier al Completo con Asociación de Alteración Sacra del Desarrollo (Forestier's Disease complete with a developmentally altered sacrum). In *Salud, Enfermedad y Muerte en el Pasado (Health, Disease and Death in the Past). Actas del III Congreso Nacional de Palaeopatología (Proceedings of the 3rd National Paleopathology Congress)*, ed. A. Pérez-Pérez, pp. 225–8. Barcelona: Fundación Uriach 1838.

Pumarola, A. (1983) Gripe (Influenza). In *Patología Infecciosa Básica. Enfermedades Víricas (Basic Infectious Pathology. Viral Diseases)*, ed. F. Gudiol Munté, pp. 91–102. Madrid: IDEPSA-Antibióticos.

Putnam, F.W. (1878) Archeological explorations in Tennessee. *Report of the Peabody Museum, Harvard University* **2**:305–60.

Putschar, W.G.J. (1976) Osteomyelitis including fungal. In *Bones and Joints*, ed. L.V. Ackerman, H.J. Spjut & M.R. Abell, pp. 39–60. Baltimore: Williams and Wilkins.

Quekett, J. (1848) On the value of the microscope in the determination of minute structures of a doubtful nature, as exemplified in the identification of human skin attached many centuries ago to the doors of churches. *Transactions of the Microscopical Society of London* **2**(**o.s.**):151–8.

Rabino-Massa, E. (1982) Postpartum inversion of the uterus in an Egyptian dynastic mummy. In *Papers on Paleopathology Presented at the IVth European Members Meeting of the Paleopathology Association in Antwerp, Netherlands on September 16–19, 1982. Paleopathology Newsletter* **39** (**Sept**) (**Supplement**):10. (Abstract).

Radanov, S., Stoev, S., Davidov, M., Nachev, S., Stanchev, M. & Kirova, E. (1992) A unique case of naturally occurring mummification of human brain tissue. *International Journal of Legal Medicine* **105**(**3**):173–5.

Radzioch, D., Hudson, T., Boule, M., Barrera, L., Urbance, J.W., Varesio, L. & Skamene, E. (1991) Genetic resistance/susceptibility to mycobacteria. *Journal of Leukocyte Biology* **50**:263–72.

Raghunathan, K. (1976) History of diabetes from remote to recent times. *Bulletin of the Indian Institute of the History of Medicine* **6**:167–82.

Ragsdale, B.D. (1993) Polymorphic fibro-osseous lesions of bone. *Human Pathology* **24**:505–12.

Ramenofsky, A.F. (1987) *Vectors of Death. The Archaeology of European Contact.* Albuquerque, NM: University of New Mexico Press.

Ramfjord, S. & Ash, M.M. (1983) *Occlusion.* Philadelphia: W.B. Saunders.

Ramsay, M. & Jenkins, T. (1984) Alpha-thalassemia in Africa: The oldest malaria protective trait? *Lancet* **2**(**8399**):410. (Letter).

Raspall, G. (1990) *Enfermedades Maxilares y Craneofaciales (Maxillary and Craniofacial Diseases).* Barcelona: Salvat.

Ravenholt, R.T. (1993) Encephalitis lethargica. In *The Cambridge World History of Human Disease*, ed. K.F. Kiple, pp. 708–12. New York: Cambridge University Press.

Ray, C.G. (1991) Poliovirus infections. In *Harrison's Principles of Internal Medicine*, ed. J.D. Wilson, E. Braunwald, K.J. Isselbacher, *et al.*, 12th edn, pp. 713–14. New York: McGraw-Hill.

Reader, R. (1974) New evidence for the antiquity of leprosy in early Britain. *Journal of Archaeological Science* **1**:205–7.

Redford, D.B. & Lang, C. (1996) Crucified! *The Akhenaten Temple Project Newsletter (University of Toronto, Canada)* **1**:1–2.

Reed, E.K. (1967) Variation of the spine in human skeletal material from southwestern archaeological collections. In *Miscellaneous Papers in Paleopathology*, ed. W.D. Wade, pp. 30–9. Flagstaff, AZ: Museum of Northern Arizona.

Reff, D. (1992) Contact shock in northwestern New Spain 1518–1764. In *Disease and Demography in the Americas*, ed. J.W. Verano & D.H. Ubelaker, pp. 265–76. Washington, DC: Smithsonian Institution Press.

Regöly-Mérei, R. (1961) Beiträge zur Geschichte der Krankheiten (Über einege interressante pälaopathologische Fälle) (Contributions to the history of diseases: Concerning several interesting paleopathological cases). *Therapia Hungarica* **9**:33–6.

Reichs, K.J. (1986a) Forensic implications of skeletal pathology: Sex. In *Forensic Osteol-ogy*, ed. K.J. Reichs, pp. 112–42. Springfield, IL: C.C. Thomas.

Reichs, K.J. (1986b) Forensic implications of skeletal pathology: Ancestry. In *Forensic Osteology*, ed. K.J. Reichs, pp. 196–217. Springfield, IL: C.C. Thomas.

Reichs, K.J. (1989) Treponematosis: A possible case from the Late Prehistoric of North Carolina. *American Journal of Physical Anthropology* **79**:289–303.

Reinhard, K. (1990) Archaeoparasitology in North America. *American Journal of Physical Anthropology* **82**:145–63.

Reinhard, K. & Aufderheide, A. (1990) Diphyllo-bothriasis in pre-Columbian Chile and Peru: Adaptive radiation of a helminth species to Native American populations. In *Papers on Paleopathology Presented at the VIIIth European Members Meeting of the Paleopathology Association in Cambridge, England on September 19–22. 1990. Paleopathology Newsletter* **72** (**Supplement**):18–19. (Abstract).

Reinhard, K.J. & Ghazi, A.M. (1992) Evaluation of lead concentrations in Nebraska skeletons using ICP-MS. *American Journal of Physical Anthropology* **89**:183–95.

Reinhard, K.J. & Hevly, R.H. (1991) Dietary and parasitological analysis of coprolites recovered from mummy 5, Ventana Cave, Arizona. *Kiva* **56**:319–25.

Reinhard, K.J., Confalonieri, U.E., Herrmann, B., Ferreira, L.F. & Araujo, A.J.G. (1986a) Recovery of parasite remains from coprolites and latrines: Aspects of paleoparasitological technique. *HOMO* **37**:217–38.

Reinhard, K.J., Mrozowski, S.A. & Orloski, K.A. (1986b) Privies, pollen, parasites and seeds: A biological nexus in historic archaeology. *Masca Journal* **4**:31–6.

Reisberg, B. (1992) Common intestinal parasitic infections. In *The Biological and Clinical Basis of Infectious Diseases*, ed. S.T. Shulman, J.P. Phair & H.M. Sommers, 4th edn, pp. 294–301. Philadelphia: Saunders.

Rennie, A.M. (1967) Familial slipped upper femoral epiphysis. *Journal of Bone and Joint Surgery* **49**(**3**):535–9.

Resnick, D. (ed.) (1989a) *Bone and Joint Imaging.* Philadelphia: W.B. Saunders.

Resnick, D. (1989b) Neuromuscular disorders. In *Bone and Joint Imaging*, ed. D. Resnick, pp. 932–45. Philadelphia: W.B. Saunders.

Resnick, D. (1989c) Additional congenital or heritable anomalies and syndromes. In *Bone and Joint Imaging*, ed. D. Resnick, pp. 1071–91. Philadelphia: W.B. Saunders.

Resnick, D. & Niwayama, G. (eds) (1981) *Diagnosis of Bone and Joint Disorders*, vol. 3. Philadelphia: W.B. Saunders.

Resnick, D. & Niwayama, G. (1989a) Osteomyelitis, septic arthritis and soft tissue infection: Mechanisms and situations. In *Bone and Joint*

Imaging, ed. D. Resnick, pp. 728–55. Philadelphia: W.B. Saunders.

Resnick, D. & Niwayama, G. (1989*b*) Osteomyelitis, septic arthritis and soft tissue infection: Organisms. In *Bone and Joint Imaging*, ed. D. Resnick, pp. 765–98. Philadelphia: W.B. Saunders.

Resnick, D., Goergen, T.G. & Niwayama, G. (1989*a*) Physical trauma. In *Bone and Joint Imaging*, ed. D. Resnick, pp. 801–98. Philadelphia: W.B. Saunders.

Resnick, D., Niwayama, G., Sweet, D.E. & Madewell, J.E. (1989*b*) Osteonecrosis. In *Bone and Joint Imaging*, ed. D. Resnick, pp. 959–78. Philadelphia: W.B. Saunders.

Resnick, D., Kyriakos, M. & Greenway, G.D. (1989*c*) Tumors and tumor-like lesions of bone: Imaging and pathology of specific lesions. In *Bone and Joint Imaging*, ed. D. Resnick, pp. 1107–81. Philadelphia: W.B. Saunders.

Retsas, S. (1986) On the antiquity of cancer: From Hippocrates to Galen. In *Paleo-oncology: The Antiquity of Cancer*, ed. S. Retsas, pp. 41–53. London: Farrand Press.

Revell, P.A. (1986) *Pathology of Bone*. Berlin and Heidelberg: Springer-Verlag.

Reverte, J.M. (1986) Hemangioma of corpus vertebrae. *HOMO* **37**:96–9.

Reyman, T.A. (1977) Schistosomal cirrhosis in an Egyptian mummy (circa 1200 B.C.). *Yearbook of Physical Anthropology (1976)* **20**:356–8.

Reyman, T.A. & Peck, W.H. (1980) Egyptian mummification with evisceration per ano. In *Mummies, Disease and Ancient Cultures*, ed. A. Cockburn & E. Cockburn, pp. 85–100. New York: Cambridge University Press.

Rhine, S. (1985) A possible case of acromegaly from New Mexico. In *Health and Disease in the Prehistoric Southwest*, ed. C.F. Merbs & R.J. Miller, pp. 210–19. Anthropological Research Papers no. 34. Tempe, AZ: Arizona State University.

Richards, G.D. & Anton, S.C. (1991) Craniofacial configuration and postcranial development of a hydrocephalic child (ca. 2500 B.C.–A.D. 500): With a review of cases and comment of diagnostic criteria. *American Journal of Physical Anthropology* **85**:185–200.

Riding, I.J. (1992) Six Pawnee crania: Historical and contemporary issues associated with the massacre and decapitation of Pawnee Indians in 1869. *Indian Cultural Research Journal* **16**(**2**):101–19.

Ridley, D.S. (1972) Review of the five-group system for the classification of leprosy according to immunity. *International Journal of Leprosy* **40**:102–3. (Abstract).

Rising, Lieut. R.N. (1866) On the artificial eyes of certain Peruvian mummies. *Transactions of the Ethnological Society of London* **4** (**New Series**):59–60.

Ritchie, W.A. (1952) Pathological evidence suggesting pre-Columbian tuberculosis in New York state. *American Journal of Physical Anthropology* **10**:305–11.

Robbins, S.L. (1975) *Patología Estructural y Funcional (Structural and Functional Pathology)*, 1 a Edicion. esp. Madrid: Interamericana.

Roberts, C. (1986) Leprosy and leprosaria in medieval Britain. *MASCA Journal* **4**:15–21.

Roberts, C. (1987*a*) Leprosy and tuberculosis in Britain: Diagnosis and treatment in antiquity. *MASCA Journal* **4**(**4**):166–71.

Roberts, C. (1987*b*) Possible pituitary dwarfism from the Roman period. *British Medical Journal* **295**:1659–60.

Roberts, C. & Manchester, K. (1995) *The Archaeology of Disease*, 2nd edn. Ithaca, NY: Cornell University Press.

Robertson, A.L. (1988) Autopsy findings in pre-Columbian Americans. (Department of Pathology, Medical College of Virginia, Richmond, VA) *Paleopathology Club Newsletter* **33**:4–5.

Robicsek, F. & Hales, D. (1984) Maya heart sacrifice: Cultural perspective and surgical technique. In *Ritual Sacrifice in Mesoamerica*, ed. E.P. Benson & E.H. Boone, pp. 49–90. Washington, DC: Dumbarton Oaks Research Library and Collection.

Robins, R.S. (1981) Disease, political events and populations. In *Biocultural Aspects of Disease*, ed. H.R. Rothschild, pp.153–75. New York: Academic Press.

Robinson, J.T. (1952) Some hominid features of the Apeman dentition. *Journal of the Dental Association of South Africa* **7**:102–13.

Roche, A. (1964) Aural exostoses in Australian aboriginal skulls. *Annals of Otology, Rhinology and Laryngology* **73**:82–91.

Rodríguez Maffiote, C. (1974*a*) Algunas consideraciones Acerca de la Trepanación en las Poblaciones Prehispánicas de las Islas Canarias (Some considerations about trepanation in the prehispanic Canary Island populations). *Medicina and Historia* **37**:3–4.

Rodríguez Maffiotte, C. (1974*b*) Anomalías Congénitas de un Sacro-Coxis de la Época Prehispánica de Tenerife (Islas Canarias) (Congenital anomalies of the sacrococcygeal area during the prehispanic period in Tenerife (Canary Islands)). *Acta Médica de Tenerife* **35**(**4**):229–34.

Rodríguez Maffiotte, C. (1981) *Historia de la Medicina (History of Medicine)*. Santa Cruz de Tenerife: Gráficas Tenerife.

Rodríguez-Martín, C. (1989*a*) La Paleopatología en Canarias. Visión Histórica (Paleopathology in the Canaries: An historical view). *Revista de Archaeología* **97**:29–37.

Rodríguez-Martín, C. (1989*b*) Earnest Albert Hooton y la Paleopatología Canaria (Earnest Albert Hooton and Canarian paleopathology).

Boletín de Historia de la Antropología **2**:16–21.

Rodríguez-Martín, C. (1989*c*) Reumatismo Articular en las Poblaciones Prehispánicas de Canarias. A Propósito de Dos Probables Nuevos Casos de Espondilitis Anquilosante en Aborígenes de Tenerife (Joint rheumatism in the prehispanic populations of the Canaries. Report on two new probable cases of ankylosing spondylitis in Tenerife aboriginals). *Anuario de Estudios Atlánticos* **35**:545–79.

Rodríguez-Martín, C. (1990) Una Perspectiva Histórica de la Paleopatología en Canarias (Historical perspective of paleopathology in the Canaries). *ERES (Arqueología)* **1**(**1**):21–50.

Rodríguez-Martín, C. (1991) Los Traumatismos en la Prehistoria de Tenerife (Islas Canarias) (Trauma in Tenerife's prehistory (Canary Islands)). In *Nuevas Perspectivas en Antropología (New Perspectives in Anthropology)*, ed. M.C. Botella, S.A. Jiménez, L. Ruiz & P. du Souich, vol. 2, pp. 829–37. Granada: Universidad de Granada and Diputacíon Provincial de Granada.

Rodríguez-Martín, C. (1992) Un Caso de Luxación Subastragalina Izquierda en un Guanche del Sur de Tenerife (Islas Canarias) (A case of subtalar dislocation in a Guanche from southern Tenerife (Canary Islands)). Munibe, Supl. 8. *Actas del I Congreso Nacional de Paleopatologia (San Sebastian-Donostia)*, pp. 125–8.

Rodríguez-Martín, C. (1994) The epidemic of Modorra (1494–1495) among the Guanches of Tenerife. *Journal of Paleopathology* **6**(**1**):5–14.

Rodríguez-Martín, C. (1995*a*) Biologia Esquelética de la Población Prehispánica de la Comarca Isora-Daute (Skeletal biology of the prehispanic population of the Isora-Daute District). In *La Piedra Zanata (The Zanata Stone)*, ed. R. González Antón, R. de Balbin Behrmann, P. Bueno Ramírez & C. del. Arco Aguilar, pp. 227–65. Santa Cruz de Tenerife: O.A.M.C.-Cabildo de Tenerife.

Rodríguez-Martín, C. (1995*b*) Patología de la Columna Vertebral en Poblaciones del Pasado. Revisión en la Población Prehispánica de Tenerife (Spinal pathology in past populations. A review in the prehispanic population of Tenerife). *ERES-Serie de Arqueología* **6**(**1**):157–70.

Rodríguez-Martín, C. (1995*c*) Osteopatología del Habitante Prehispánico de Tenerife, Islas Canarias (Osteopathology of the prehispanic inhabitant of Tenerife, Canary Islands). In *Proceedings of the First World Congress on Mummy Studies*, 1992, vol. 1, pp. 65–78. Tenerife, Canary Islands: Museo Arqueológico y Etnográfico de Tenerife, Organismo Autónomo de Museos y Centros, Cabildo de Tenerife.

Rodríguez-Martín, C. & Casariego Ramírez, C. (1991) Historical note on Canarian paleopathology. *Journal of Paleopathology* **4**(1):7–14.

Rodríguez-Martín, C., Rodríguez Maffiotte, C. & Rodríguez-Martín, B. (1985a) *A Propósito de un Caso de Gonartritis Grave con Fusión Tibio-Peronea en un Aborígen Canario (Report on a Case of Severe Knee Arthritis with Tibial-Fibular Fusion in a Canarian Aboriginal)*. Santa Cruz de Tenerife: CCPC, Parlamento de Canarias.

Rodríguez-Martín, C., Rodríguez Maffiotte, C. & Rodríguez-Martín, B. (1985b) *Notas Históricas de las Investigaciones de la Obliteración Precoz de las Suturas Craneales. A Propósito de un Caso de Escafocefalia Encontrado en la Isla de Tenerife (Historical Notes on the Research on Earlier Cranial Suture Closure. Report of a Case of Scaphocephaly Found in the Island of Tenerife)*. Santa Cruz de Tenerife: CCPC, Parlamento de Canarias.

Rodríguez-Martín, C., González Antón, R. & Estévez González, F. (1993) Cranial injuries in the Guanche population of Tenerife (Canary Islands). In *Biological Anthropology and the Study of Ancient Egypt*, ed. W.V. Davies & R. Walker, pp. 130–5. London: British Museum Press.

Rogan, P.K. & Lentz, S.E. (1995) Molecular genetics evidence suggesting treponematosis in pre-Columbian Chilean mummies. In *Proceedings of the Second World Congress on Mummy Studies*, ed. F. Cardenas-Arroyo, p.2.8. (Abstract). Bogota, Colombia: Universidad de los Andes.

Rogers, J. (1981) Two examples of erosive arthropathy in skeletal material. *Paleopathology Newsletter* **35**:7–10.

Rogers, J. (1986) Mesomelic dwarfism in a Romano-British skeleton. *Paleopathology Newsletter* **55**:6–10.

Rogers, J. & Waldron, T. (1988) Two possible cases of infantile cortical hyperostosis. *Paleopathology Newsletter* **63**:9–12.

Rogers, J., Watt, I. & Dieppe, P. (1981) Arthritis in Saxon and medieval skeletons. *British Medical Journal* **283**:1668–70.

Rogers, J., Waldron, T., Dieppe, P. & Watt, I. (1987) Arthropathies in palaeopathology: The basis of classification according to most probable cause. *Journal of Archaeological Science* **14**:179–93.

Rogers, J., Waldron, T. & Watt, I. (1991) Erosive osteoarthritis in a medieval skeleton. *International Journal of Osteoarchaeology* **1**:151–3.

Rogers, L. (1924) The epidemiology of leprosy. *Annals of Tropical Medicine and Parasitology* **18**:267–332.

Rogers, L. (1949) Meningiomas in Pharaoh's people: Hyperostosis in ancient Egyptian skulls. *British Journal of Surgery* **36**:423–4.

Rogers, S.L. (1985) *Primitive Surgery. Skills Before Science*. Springfield, IL: C.C. Thomas.

Roholm, K. (1937) *Fluorine Intoxication*. London: Lewis.

Rolle R. (1992) Die Skythenzeitlichen Mumienfunde von Pazyryk Frostkonservierte Graben aus dem Altaigebirge (The frozen tombs of Scythian mummies found at Pazyryk in the Altai mountains). *Veroffentlichungen der Universität Innsbruck* **187**:334–58.

Rolleston, H. (1934) The endocrine disorders. In *A Short History of Some Common Diseases*, ed. W.R. Bett, pp. 87–101. London: Oxford University Press.

Rolleston, H.D. (1936) *The Endocrine Organs in Health and Disease with an Historical Review*. London: Oxford University Press.

Romanowski, D.L. (1891) Zur Frage der Parasitologie und Therapie del Malaria (Concerning the question of the parasitology and therapy of malaria). *St. Petersburg Medizinische Wochenschrift* **16**:297–307.

Rose, B.S. (1975) Gout in the Maoris. *Seminars in Arthritis and Rheumatism* **5**:121–45.

Rosenberg, L.E. (1991) Storage diseases of amino acid metabolism. In *Harrison's Principles of Internal Medicine*, ed. J.D. Wilson, E. Braunwald, K.J. Isselbacher, *et al.*, 12th edn, pp. 1875–7. New York: McGraw-Hill.

Rosenzweig, W. (1983) Disease in art: A case for carcinoma of the breast in Michaelangelo's *La Notte*. *Paleopathology Newsletter* **41**:8–11.

Roske, G. (1930) Eine eineartige Knochenerkrankung im Säuglingsalter (A unique bone disease of infancy). *Monatsschrift Kinderheilkunde* **25**:385–400.

Rosner, F. (1969) Gout in the Bible and Talmud. *Journal of the American Medical Association* **207**(1):151–2. (Letter).

Ross, R. (1897a) On some peculiar pigmented cells found in two mosquitoes fed on malarial blood. *British Medical Journal* **2**:1786–8.

Ross, R. (1897b) Report on the Cultivation of *Proteosoma*, Labbe in Grey Mosquitoes. Calcutta: Government Press, May 21.

Rotés Más, M.I. (1983) Artritis Infecciosas (Infectious arthritis). In *Reumatología Clínica (Clinical Rheumatology)*, ed. J. Rotés Querol, vol. 1, pp. 189–96. Barcelona: Expaxs.

Roth, E.F., Jr (1985) Red cell polymorphisms and the malarial hypothesis. *Diagnostic Medicine* **May**:29–35.

Roth, E.F., Jr, Raventos-Suarez, C., Rinaldi, A. & Nagel, R. (1983) Glucose-6-phosphate dehydrogenase deficiency inhibits *in vitro* growth of *Plasmodium falciparum*. *Proceedings of the National Academy of Sciences of the USA* **80**:298–9.

Rothenberg, R.B. (1993) Gonorrhea. In *The Cambridge World History of Human Disease*, ed. K.F. Kiple, pp. 756–63. New York: Cambridge University Press.

Rothhammer, F., Allison, M., Nuñez, L., Standen, V. & Arriaza, B. (1985) Chagas' disease in pre-

Columbian South America. *American Journal of Physical Anthropology* **68**:495–8.

Rothman, R.H. & Simeone, F. A. (1975) *The Spine*. Philadelphia: W.B. Saunders.

Rothschild, B.M. & Heathcote, G.M. (1995) Characterization of gout in a skeletal population sample: Presumptive diagnosis in a Micronesian population. *American Journal of Physical Anthropology* **98**:519–25.

Rothschild, B.M. & Martin, L.D. (1993) *Paleopathology. Disease in the Fossil Record*. Boca Raton, FL: CRC Press.

Rothschild, B. M. & Rothschild, C. (1995a) Comparison of radiologic and gross examination for detection of cancer in defleshed skeletons. *American Journal of Physical Anthropology* **96**:357–63.

Rothschild, B. M. & Rothschild, C. (1995b) Treponemal disease revisited: Skeletal discriminators for yaws, bejel and venereal syphilis. *Clinical Infectious Diseases* **20**(5):1402–8.

Rothschild, B.M. & Woods, R.J. (1991) Spondyloarthropathy: Erosive arthritis in representative defleshed bones. *American Journal of Physical Anthropology* **85**:125–34.

Rothschild, B.M., Turner, K.R. & Deluca, M.A. (1988) Symmetrical erosive peripheral polyarthritis in the Late Archaic period of Alabama. *Science* **241**:1498–501.

Rothschild, B.M., Woods, R.J. & Ortel, W. (1990) Rheumatoid arthritis "in the buff": Erosive arthritis in defleshed bones. *American Journal of Physical Anthropology* **82**:441–9.

Rothschild, B.M., Rothschild, C. & Bement, L.C.(1994) Lithopedion as an archaic occurrence. *International Journal of Osteoarchaeology* **4**:247–50.

Rothschild, B.M., Rothschild, C. & Hills, M.C. (1995) Origin and transition of varieties of treponemal disease in the New World. *American Journal of Physical Anthropology* **20**(**Supplement**):185. (Abstract).

Rothschild, H. & Chapman, C.F. (1981) *Biocultural Aspects of Disease*. New York: Academic Press.

Rowe, J.H. (1946) Inca culture at the time of the Spanish conquest. In *Handbook of the South American Indians*, ed. J.H. Steward, vol. 2, pp. 188–330. Washington, DC: Bureau of American Ethnology, Smithsonian Institution.

Rowling, J.T. (1961) Pathological changes in mummies. *Proceedings of the Royal Society of Medicine, Section on the History of Medicine* **54**:409–15.

Rowling, J.T. (1967) Hernia in Egypt. In *Diseases in Antiquity*, ed. D. Brothwell & A.T. Sandison, pp. 444–6. Springfield, IL: C.C. Thomas.

Royal, W. & Clark, E. (1960) Natural preservation of human brain at Warm Mineral Springs, Florida. *American Antiquity* **26**(2):285–7.

Rubin, E. & Farber, J.L. (eds) (1994a) *Pathology*, 2nd edn. Philadelphia: Lippincott.

Rubin, E. & Farber, J. L. (1994b) Neoplasia. In *Pathology*, ed. E. Rubin & J.L. Farber, 2nd edn, pp. 142–98. Philadelphia: Lippincott.

Rubin, E. & Farber, J.L. (1994c). Developmental and genetic diseases. In *Pathology*, ed. E. Rubin & J.L. Farber, 2nd edn, pp. 201–61. Philadelphia: Lippincott.

Rubin, E. & Farber, J.L. (1994d). The endocrine system. In *Pathology*, ed. E. Rubin & J.L. Farber, 2nd edn, pp. 1099–147. Philadelphia: Lippincott.

Rudberg, R.D. (1954) Acute otitis media: Comparative therapeutic results of sulphonamide and penicillin administered in various forms. *Acta Otolaryngologica (Stockholm)* **113** (**Supplement**):9–79.

Rudenko, S.I. (1970) *Frozen Tombs of Siberia*. Translated by M.W. Thompson. Berkeley, CA: University of California Press.

Ruffer, M.A. (1910) Remarks on the histology and pathological anatomy of Egyptian mummies. *The Cairo Scientific Journal* **10**:3–7.

Ruffer, M.A. ([1911a] 1921) On dwarfs and other deformed persons in ancient Egypt. In *Studies in the Paleopathology of Egypt by Sir Marc Armand Ruffer Kt, C.M.G., M.D.*, ed. R.L. Moodie, pp. 35–48. Chicago: University of Chicago Press.

Ruffer, M.A. (1911b) On arterial lesions found in Egyptian mummies (1580 B.C.–525 A.D.). *Journal of Pathology and Bacteriology* **15**:453–62.

Ruffer, M.A. (1911c) Megacolon in a child of the Roman period. Mémoires Institute Égypte **6**(**3**):1–39.

Ruffer, M.A. (1913) On pathological lesions found in Coptic bodies. *Journal of Pathology and Bacteriology* **18**:149–62.

Ruffer, M.A. (1918) Arthritis deformans and spondylitis in ancient Egypt. *Journal of Pathology and Bacteriology* **22**:152–96.

Ruffer, M.A. (1920) Note on the presence of *Bilharzia haematobia* in Egyptian mummies of the twentieth dynasty (1250–1000 B.C.). *British Medical Journal* **1**:16.

Ruffer, M.A. (1921a) *Studies in the Paleopathology of Egypt by Sir Marc Armand Ruffer Kt, C.M.G., M.D.*, ed. R.L. Moodie. Chicago: University of Chicago Press.

Ruffer, M.A. (1921b) Pathological notes on the royal mummies of the Cairo museum. In *Studies in the Paleopathology of Egypt by Sir Marc Armand Ruffer Kt, C.M.G., M.D.*, ed. R.L. Moodie, pp. 166–78. Chicago: University of Chicago Press.

Ruffer, M.A. & Ferguson, A.R. (1911) Note on an eruption resembling that of variola in the skin of a mummy from the twentieth dynasty (1200–1100 B.C.). *Journal of Pathology and Bacteriology* **15**:1–3.

Ruffer, M.A. & Willmore, J.G. (1914) A tumour of the pelvis dating from Roman times (250 A.D.) and found in Egypt. *Journal of Pathology and Bacteriology* **18**:480–4.

Russell, P.F., West, L.S., Manwell, R.D. & MacDonald, G. (1963) *Practical Malariology*, 2nd edn. London: Oxford University Press.

Russell, W.M.S. (1983) The paleodemographic view. In *Disease in Ancient Man*, ed. G. Hart, pp.217–53. Toronto: Clarke Irwin.

Sager, P., Schmalzer M. & Møller-Christensen, V. (1972) A case of spondylitis tuberculosa in the Danish Neolithic Age. *Danish Medical Bulletin* **19**(**5**):176–80.

Saggs, H.W.F. (1962) *The Greatness That Was Babylon*. New York: Hawthorne Books.

Salo, W., Aufderheide, A.C., Buikstra, J. & Holcomb, T. (1994) Identification of *Mycobacterium tuberculosis* in a pre-Columbian Peruvian mummy. *Proceedings of the National Academy of Sciences of the USA* **91**:2091–4.

Salvador, J. & Carrera, J.M. (1995) *Síndromes Congénitos Malformativos (Congenital Malformation Syndromes)*. Barcelona: Masson.

Sánchez Sánchez, J.A. & Gómez Bellard, F. (1988) Renal and biliary calculi: A paleopathological analysis. In *Papers on Paleopathology Presented at the VIIIth European Members Meeting of the Paleopathology Association in Cambridge, England on September 19–22, 1990. Paleopathology Newsletter* **72** (**Supplement**):19–22. (Abstract).

Sandison, A.T. (1957) The eye in the Egyptian mummy. *Medical History* **1**:336–9.

Sandison, A.T. (1958) Autopsy findings in a case of pituitary dwarfism. *Archives of Childhood* **33**(**171**):469–72.

Sandison, A.T. (1962) Degenerative vascular disease in the Egyptian mummy. *Medical History* **6**:77–81.

Sandison, A.T. (1967a) Sir Marc Armand Ruffer (1859–1917). Pioneer of palaeopathology. *Medical History* **11**:150–6.

Sandison, A.T. (1967b) Parasitic diseases. In *Diseases in Antiquity*, ed. D. Brothwell & A.T. Sandison, pp. 178–83. Springfield, IL: C.C. Thomas.

Sandison, A.T. (1967c) Diseases of the skin. In *Diseases in Antiquity*, ed. D. Brothwell & A.T. Sandison, pp. 449–63. Springfield, IL: C.C. Thomas.

Sandison, A.T. (1967d) Degenerative vascular disease. In *Diseases in Antiquity*, ed. D. Brothwell & A.T. Sandison, pp. 474–88. Springfield, IL: C.C. Thomas.

Sandison, A.T. & Wells, C. (1967) Diseases of the reproductive system. In *Diseases in Antiquity*, ed. D. Brothwell & A.T. Sandison, pp. 498–520. Springfield, IL: C.C. Thomas.

Sandritter, W. & Thomas, C. (1981) *Macropatología. Manual y Atlas para Médicos y Estudiantes (Gross pathology. Manual and Atlas for Physicians and Students)*. Barcelona: Reverté.

Sarma, P.J. (1939) The art of healing in Rigveda. *Annals of Medical History (Series 3)* **1**:538–41.

Sarnat, B. & Schour, I. (1941) Enamel hypoplasia in relation to systemic disease. Part 1. *Journal of the American Dental Association* **28**:1989–2000.

Sartoris, D.J. & Ogden, J.A. (1989) Congenital dysplasia of the hip. In *Bone and Joint Imaging*, ed. D. Resnick, pp. 1000–14. Philadelphia: W.B. Saunders.

Saskin, H. (1984) Case No. 20: Vasculitis. (Department of Pathology, Medical College of Virginia, Richmond, VA) *Paleopathology Club Newsletter* **20**:1.

Saul, F.P., Christoforidis, A.J., Saul, J.M., Cook, D.C. & Benitez, J.T. (1981) The antiquity of Paget's disease in the Maya area. In *Papers on Paleopathology Presented at the 8th Annual Meeting of the Paleopathology Association in Detroit, Michigan, 22 April 1981. Paleopathology Newsletter* **84** (**Supplement**):3. (Abstract).

Savitt, T. L. (1993) Filariasis. In *The Cambridge World History of Human Disease*, ed. K.F. Kiple, pp. 726–30. New York: Cambridge University Press.

Savory, J. & Sedor, F.A. (1977) Arsenic poisoning. In *Clinical Chemistry and Chemical Toxicology of Metals*, ed. S.S. Brown, pp.271–86. New York: Elsevier/North Holland.

Sawicki, V.A., Allison, M.J., Dalton, H.P. & Pezzia, A. (1976) Presence of *Salmonella* antigens in feces from a Peruvian mummy. *Bulletin of the New York Academy of Medicine* **52**(**7**):805–13.

Sawin, C.T. (1993) Goitre. In *The Cambridge World History of Human Disease*, ed. K.F. Kiple, pp. 750–6. New York: Cambridge University Press.

Scaife, R.G. (1986) Pollen in human palaeofaeces; and a preliminary investigation of the stomach and gut contents of Lindow Man. In *Lindow Man: The Body In the Bog*, ed. I.M. Stead, J.B. Bourke & D. Brothwell, pp. 126–35, Ithaca, NY: Cornell University Press.

Schaberg, D.R. & Turck, M. (1991) Klebsiella-Enterobacter-Serratia infections. In *Harrison's Principles of Internal Medicine*, ed. J.D. Wilson, E. Braunwald, K.J. Isselbacher, *et al.*, 12th edn, pp. 601–2. New York: McGraw-Hill.

Schafritz, A.B., Shore, E.M., Gannon, F.H., Zasloff, M.A., Taub, R., Muenke, M. & Kaplan, F.S. (1996) Overexpression of an osteogenic morphogen in fibrodysplasia ossificans progressiva. *New England Journal of Medicine* **335**(**8**):555–61.

Schechter, D.C. (1962) Breast mutilation in the Amazons. *Surgery* **51**(**4**):554–60.

Schereschewsky, N.A. (1926) Gigantism. *Endocrinology* **10**:17–28.

Schiller, A. (1994) Bones and joints. In *Pathology*, ed. E. Rubin & J.L. Farber, 2nd edn, pp. 1273–346. Philadelphia: Lippincott.

Schinz, H.R., Baensch, W.E., Friedl, E. & Uehlinger, E. (1953) Enfermedades Inflamatorias de los Huesos (Inflammatory diseases of bone). In *Röntgen-Diagnóstico (Diagnostic Roentgenology)*, ed. H.R. Schinz, W.E. Baensch, E. Friedl & E. Uehlinger, vol. 1, pp. 487–636. Barcelona: Salvat.

Schipani, E., Langman, C.B., Parfitt, A.M., Jensen, G.S., Kikochi, S., Kooh, S.W., Cole, W.G. & Jüppner, H. (1996) Constitutively activated receptors for parathyroid hormone and parathyroid hormone-related peptide in Jansen's metaphyseal chondrodysplasia. *New England Journal of Medicine* **335**:708–14.

Schmerling, P.C. (1835) Description des ossements fossiles, a l'etat pathologique, provenant des cavernes de la province de Liége (Description of fossil remains and their pathological state, from caves in Liége province). *Bulletin de la Société Géologique de France* **2**(**7**):51–61.

Schmid, F.R. (1987) Artritis Bacteriana (Bacterial arthritis). In *Artritis y Otras Patologías Relacionadas (Arthritis and Other Allied Pathological Conditions)*, ed. D.J. McCarty, 10th edn, vol. 4, pp. 1674–97. Madrid: Panamericana.

Schmorl, G. (1909) Die pathologische Anatomie der rachitischen Knochenerkrankung mit besonderer Berücksichtigung ihrer Histologie und Pathogenese (The pathological anatomy of rachitic bone disease with emphasis on a review of its histology and pathogenesis). *Ergebnisse der inneren Medizin und Kinderheilkunde* **4**:403–54.

Schobinger, J. (ed.) (1966) *La "Momia" del Cerro el Torro (The "Mummy" of Cerro el Toro)*. Supplement to vol. 21 of *Anales de Arqueología y Etnología*. Argentina: Mendoza.

Scholtens, R.G. (1975) Filarial infections – with a note on dracunculiasis. In *Diseases Transmitted from Animals to Man*, ed. W.T. Hubbert, W.F. McCulloch & P.R. Schnurrenberger, 6th edn, pp. 572–83. Springfield, IL: C.C. Thomas.

Schultz, A.H. (1967) Notes on diseases and healed fractures of wild apes. In *Diseases in Antiquity*, ed. D. Brothwell & A.T. Sandison, pp. 47–55. Springfield, IL: C.C. Thomas.

Schultz, M. (1981) Aseptic bone necrosis found in the skeletal material from the Merovingian cemetery of Kleinjangheim, southern Germany. *Paleopathology Newsletter* **34**:7–9.

Schwabe, C.W. (1978) *Cattle, Priests and Progress in Medicine*. Minneapolis, MN: University of Minnesota Press.

Schwartz, J.H., Brauer, J. & Gordon-Larsen, P. (1995) Brief communication: Tigaran (Point Hope, Alaska) tooth drilling. *American Journal of Physical Anthropology* **97**:77–82.

Sciulli, P.W., Pacheco, P.J. & Wymer, D.A. (1988) Traumatic pathology in a Late Prehistoric individual from central Ohio. *Journal of Paleopathology* **1**(**2**):3–8.

Scoggin, C.H., Schwarz, M. I., Dixon, B. W. & Durrance, J. R. (1976) Tuberculosis of the skull. *Archives of Internal Medicine* **136**:1154–6.

Scully, R.E, Mark, E.J., McNeely, W.F. & McNeely, B.U. (1995) Case records of the Massachusetts General Hospital: Xanthogranulomatous pyelonephritis. *New England Journal of Medicine* **332**:174–9.

Seligman, C.G. (1912) A cretinous skull of the 18th dynasty. *Man (London)* **12**:17–18.

Seligman, R. (1870) Über Exostosen an Peruanaschädeln (Concerning exostoses in Peruvian skulls). *Archiv für Anthropologie, Volkerforschung und Kolonialen Kulturinandel (Braunschweig)* **4**:147–8.

Sendrail, M. (1983) *Historia Cultural de la Enfermedad (A Cultural History of Disease)*. Madrid: Espasa-Calpe.

Sevastikoglou, J. & Wernereim, B. (1953) Some views on skeletal tuberculosis (a statistical report). *Acta Orthopedica Scandinavia* **23**:67–85.

Shaaban, M. M. (1984) Trephination in ancient Egypt and the report of a new case from Dakleh Oasis. *Ossa* **9–11**:135–42.

Shadomy, H.J. (1981) The differential diagnosis of various fungal pathogens and tuberculosis in the prehistoric Indians. In *Prehistoric Tuberculosis in the Americas*, ed. J.E. Buikstra, pp. 25–34. Evanston, IL: Northwestern University Archeological Program.

Shafer, W.G., Hine, M.K. & Levy, B.M. (1983) *A Textbook of Oral Pathology*, 4th edn. Philadelphia: W.B. Saunders.

Shapiro, L. & Stallard, R.E. (1977) Etiology of periodontal disease. In *A Textbook of Preventive Dentistry*, ed. R.C. Caldwell & R.E. Stallard, pp. 74–8. Philadelphia: W.B. Saunders.

Shattock, S.G. (1909) A report upon the pathological condition of the aorta of King Menephtah, traditionally regarded as the Pharaoh of the Exodus. *Proceedings of the Royal Society of Medicine* **2**:122–7.

Shaw, A.B. (1981) Knapper's rot: Silicosis in East Anglian flint-knappers. *Medical History* **25**:151–68.

Shaw, A.F.B.(1938) A histological study of the mummy of Har-mose, the singer of the eighteenth dynasty (circa 1490 B.C.). *Journal of Pathology and Bacteriology* **47**:115–23.

Sheehy, J.L. (1958) Osteoma of the external auditory canal. *Laryngoscope* **68**:1667–73.

Shepard, C.C. (1982) Leprosy today. *New England Journal of Medicine* **307**:1640–1. (Editorial).

Shepard, C.C., Walker, L.L., Van Landingham, R.M. & Ye, S.-Z. (1982) Sensitization or tolerance to *Mycobacterium leprae* antigen by route of injection. *Infection and Immunology* **38**:673–80.

Sheridan, S.G., Mittler, D.M., Van Gerven, D.P. & Covert, H.H. (1991) Biomechanical association of dental and temporomandibular pathology in a medieval Nubian population. *American Journal of Physical Anthropology* **85**:201–5.

Sherwin, R.P., Barman, M.C. & Abraham, J.L. (1979) Silicate pneumoconiosis of farm workers. *Laboratory Investigation* **40**(**5**):576–82.

Shore, N.A. (1959) *Occlusal Equilibration and Temporomandibular Joint Dysfunction*. Philadelphia: J.B. Lippincott.

Short, C.L. (1974) The antiquity of rheumatoid arthritis. *Arthritis and Rheumatism* **17**(**3**):193–205.

Shortt, H.E. & Garnham, P.C.C. (1948) The preerythrocytic development of *Plasmodium cynomolgi* and *Plasmodium vivax*. *Transactions of the Royal Society of Tropical Medicine and Hygiene* **41**:785–95.

Shortt, H.E., Fairley, N.H., Covell, G., Shute, P.G. & Garnham, P.C.C. (1951) The pre-erythrocytic stages of *Plasmodium falciparum*. *Transactions of the Royal Society of Tropical Medicine and Hygiene* **44**:405–19.

Shufeldt, R.W. (1892–93) Notes on palaeopathology. *Popular Science Monthly* **42**:679–84.

Sievers, M.L. & Fisher, J.R. (1981) Diseases of North American Indians. In *Biocultural Aspects of Disease*, ed. H.R. Rothchild, pp. 191–252. New York: Academic Press.

Sigerist, H.E. (1951) *A History of Medicine. Volume 1. Primitive and Archaic Medicine*. New York: Oxford University Press.

Sigerist, H.E. (1961) *A History of Medicine. Volume 2*. Oxford: Oxford University Press.

Silence, D. (1981) Osteogenesis imperfecta: An expanding panorama of variants. *Clinical Orthopedics* **159**:11–25.

Silence, D.O., Horton, W.A. & Rimoin, D.L. (1979) Morphologic studies in skeletal dysplasias. *American Journal of Pathology* **96**(**3**):811–70.

Sim, B.K.L., Chitnis, C., Wasniowska, K., Hadley, T.J. & Miller, L.H. (1994) Receptor and ligand domains for invasion of erythrocytes by *Plasmodium falciparum*. *Science* **264**:1941–4.

Simandl, I. (1928) A contribution to the history of the skin. *Anthropologie (Prague)* **6**:56–60.

Simon, G. & Zorab, P.A. (1961) The radiographic changes in alkaptonuric arthritis. A report on three cases (one an Egyptian mummy). *British Journal of Radiology* **34**:384–6.

Sims, R.V. (1992) Pneumococcal vaccine: A continuing controversy. *Hospital Practice*, **April 30**:11–14.

Singh, A. & Jolly, S.S. (1961) Endemic fluorosis. *Quarterly Journal of Medicine, New Series* **30**(**120**):357–72.

Singh, A., Jolly, S.S. & Bansal, B.C. (1961) Skeletal fluorosis and its neurological complications. *Lancet* **i** (**7170**):197–200.

Singh, A., Dass, R., Hayreh, S.S. & Jolly, S.S. (1962) Skeletal changes in endemic fluorosis. *Journal of Bone and Joint Surgery* **44B(4)**:806–15.

Singh, M., Nagrath, A.R. & Maini, M.S. (1970) Changes in trabecular pattern of the upper end of the femur as an index of osteoporosis. *Journal of Bone and Joint Surgery* **52A(3)**:457–67.

Sissons, H.A. (1976) Osteoporosis and osteomalacia. In *Bones and Joints*, ed. L.V. Ackerman, H.J. Spjut and M.R. Abell, pp. 25–38. Baltimore: Williams and Wilkins.

Sjovold, T., Swedborg, I. & Diener, L. (1974) *A Pregnant Woman from the Middle Ages with Exostosis Multiplex*. Sonona, Sweden: Osteological Research Laboratory, University of Stockholm.

Skinsnes, O.K. (1973) Notes from the history of leprosy. *International Journal of Leprosy* **41**:220–37.

Skinsnes, O.K. (1980) Leprosy in archeologically recovered bamboo book in China. *International Journal of Leprosy* **48**:33.

Slatkin, D.N., Friedman, L., Irsa, A.P. & Gaffney, J.S. (1978) The ¹³C/¹²C ratio in black pulmonary pigment: A mass spectrometry study. *Human Pathology* **9**:259–67.

Smith, D.C. (1976) Quinine and fever: The development of the effective dosage. *Journal of the History of Medicine* **31**:343–67.

Smith, D.H. (1983) *Haemophilus* infections. In *Harrison's Principles of Internal Medicine*, ed. R.G. Petersdorf, R.D. Adams, E. Braunwald, K.J. Isselbacher, J. Martin & J.D. Wilson, 10th edn, pp. 967–72. New York: McGraw-Hill.

Smith, G.E. (1902) On the natural preservation of the brain in ancient Egyptians. *Journal of Anatomy and Physiology* **36**:375–81.

Smith, G.E. (1906) *A Contribution to the Study of Mummification in Egypt*. Mémoires L'Institut Égyptien, Tome V, Fascicule I, pp. 3–46 and Plates I–XIX. Cairo: National Printing Office.

Smith, G.E. (1912) *The Royal Mummies*. Cairo: Cairo Museum.

Smith, G.E. (1927) Report of the bones found in the sarcophagus of Pa-Rá messu (Tomb 5). In *British School of Archaeology in Egypt and Egyptian Research Account, Twenty-Fourth Year 1918*, ed. G. Bronton & R. Engelsbath, pp. 24–5. Publication V.41. London: Gurub.

Smith, G.E. & Dawson, W.R. (1924) *Egyptian Mummies*. London: George Allen and Unwin. (Reprinted in 1991 by Kegan Paul International, London).

Smith, G.E. & Ruffer, M.A. (1910). Pott'sche Krankheit an einer Ägyptischen Mumie aus der Zeit der 21 Dynastie (um 1000 v. Chr.) (Pott's disease in an Egyptian mummy from the 21st Dynasty (about 1000 B.C.)). In *Zur Historischen Biologie Der Krankheitserreger (Concerning the Historical Biology of the Pathogenic Agent)*, ed. Sudhoff & Sticker, vol. 3, pp. 9–16. Giessen, Germany.

Smith, G.E. & Wood Jones, F. (1910) Report on the human remains. In *The Archaeological Survey of Nubia. Report for 1907–1908. Volume II,* ed. G.A. Reisner, pp. 7–367. Cairo: National Printing Department.

Smith, G.S. & Zimmerman, M.R. (1975) Tattooing found on a 1600 year old frozen, mummified body from St. Lawrence Island, Alaska. *American Antiquity* **40**:434–7.

Smith, G.S., Bradley, Z.A., Kreher, R.E. & Dickey, T.P. (1978) *The Kialegek Site, St. Lawrence Island, Alaska*. Anthropology and Historical Preservation Cooperative Parks Unit, University of Alaska, Fairbanks Occasional Paper no. 10, April, 1978.

Smith, H., Forshufvud, S. & Wassén, A. (1962) Distribution of arsenic in Napoleon's hair. *Nature* **194**:725–6.

Smith, M. S. (1986) The diagnosis and treatment of scurvy. An historical perspective. *Journal of the Royal Naval Medical Service* **72**:104–6.

Smith, W., Andrewes, C.H. & Laidlaw, R.P. (1933) A virus obtained from influenza patients. *Lancet* **ii**:66–8.

Snider, D.E. & Roper, B.L. (1992) The new tuberculosis. *New England Journal of Medicine* **326** **(10)**:703–5. (Editorial).

Snorrason, E. (1946) Cranial deformation in the reign of Akhenaton. *Bulletin of the History of Medicine* **20**:601–10.

Snow, C.E. (1943) Two prehistoric Indian dwarf skeletons from Moundville. *Alabama Museum of Natural History Paper* **21**:1–90.

Sobotta, J. & McMurrich, J. P. (1939) *Atlas of Human Anatomy*, 5th revised English edn, vol. 1. New York: G.E. Stechert.

Söderström, J. (1938) Die rituellen Fingerstümmelungen in der Südsee und in Australia (Ritual finger amputation in the South Seas and in Australia). *Zeitschrift für Ethnologie* **70**:24–47.

Somerville, E.W. & Wilkinson, M.C. (1965) *Girdlestone's Tuberculosis of Bone and Joints,* 3rd edn. London: Oxford University Press.

Sorrel, E. & Sorrel-Dejerine, Mme. (1932) *Tuberculose Osseuse et Osteo-Articulare (Tuberculosis of Bones and Joints)*. Paris: Masson et Cie.

Soto-Heim, P. (1987) Evolucion de deformaciones intentionales, peinados, tocados y practicas funerarias en la prehistoria de Arica (Evolution of intentional deformation, hair dressings, coiffures and funerary practices in the prehistory of Arica). *Chungará (Arica, Chile)* **19**:129–214.

Soulié, R. (1982) Brucellosis: A case report dating from 650–700 A.D. *Paleopathology Newsletter* **38**:7–10.

Spanier, S.S., Enneking, W.F. & Enriquez, P. (1975) Primary malignant fibrous histiocytoma of bone. *Cancer* **36**:2084–98.

Spencer, R.F. (1976) *The North Alaskan Eskimo*. New York: Dover Publications. (First published in 1957).

Sperduti, A. & Manzi, G. (1990) Hyperostosis frontalis interna in a cranial sample from the Roman population. *Rivista di Antropologia* **68**:279–86.

Spigelman, M. & Lemma, E. (1993) The use of polymerase chain reaction (PCR) to detect *Mycobacterium tuberculosis* in ancient skeletons. *International Journal of Osteoarchaeology* **3**:137–43.

Spindler, K. (1994) *The Man in the Ice*. London: Weidenfeld and Nicolson.

Spirtos, N.M., Einsenkop, S.M. & Mishell, D.R., Jr (1987) Lithokelyphos. *Journal of Reproductive Medicine* **32**:43–6.

Spitery, E. (1983) *La Paléontologie des Maladies Osseuses Constitutionelles (The Paleontology of Constitutional Bone Diseases)*. Paris: Editions du CNRS.

Spitz, W.U. (1973) Thermal injuries. In *Medicolegal Investigation of Death*, ed. W.U. Spitz & R.S. Fisher, 2nd edn, pp. 295–319. Springfield, IL: C.C. Thomas.

Spitznagel, J. (1989) Mycobacteria: Tuberculosis and leprosy. In *Mechanism of Microbial Disease*, ed. M. Schaechter, G. Medoff & D. Schlessinger, pp.303–19. Baltimore: Williams and Wilkins.

Spjut, H.J., Dorfman, H.D., Fechner, R.E. & Ackerman, L.V. (1971) *Tumors of Bone and Cartilage*. Washington, DC: Armed Forces Institute of Pathology.

Stafne, E.C. (1963) *Oral Rentgenographic Diagnosis,* 2nd edn. Philadelphia: W.B. Saunders.

Stamp, J.T. (1961) The pathology of tuberculosis in farm animals. In *Tuberculosis in Animals*, ed. J.N. Ritchie & W.D. Macrae, pp. 1–10. London: Zoological Society of London, Symposium no. 4.

Standen, V., Arriaza, B. & Santoro, C. (1995) Una hipótesis ambiental para un marcador óseo: La exostosis auditiva externa en las poblaciones humanas prehistóricas del desierto del norte de Chile (An environmental hypothesis for an osseous marker: The external auditory canal exostosis in prehistoric human populations of northern Chile's desert). *Chungará (Arica, Chile)* **27**:99–116.

Stead, I.M., Bourke, J.B. & Brothwell, D. (1986) *Lindow Man: The Body in the Bog*. Ithaca, NY: Cornell University Press.

Stead, W.W., Senner, J.W., Reddick, W.T. & Lofgren, J.P. (1990) Racial differences in susceptibility to infection by *Mycobacterium tuberculosis*. *New England Journal of Medicine* **433**:422–7.

Steere, A.C. & Malawista S.E. (1989) Artritis Virales (Viral arthritis). In *Artritis y Otras Patologías Relacionadas (Arthritis and Allied Pathological Conditions)*, ed. D.J. McCarty, 10th edn, vol. 4, pp. 1709–25. Madrid: Panamericana.

Steinbock, R.T. (1976) *Paleopathological Diagnosis and Interpretation*. Springfield, IL: C.C. Thomas.

Steinbock, R.T. (1985) The history, epidemiology and paleopathology of kidney and bladder stone disease. *Arizona State University Anthropological Research Paper* **34**:177–200.

Steinbock, R.T. (1989) Studies in ancient calcified soft tissues and organic concretions. II: Urolithiasis (renal and urinary bladder stone disease). *Journal of Paleopathology* **3**(**1**):35–59.

Steinbock, R.T. (1990) Studies in ancient calcified soft tissues and organic concretions. III: Gallstones. *Journal of Paleopathology* **3**(**2**):95–106.

Steinbock, R.T. (1993*a*) Gallstones (cholelithiasis).In *The Cambridge World History of Human Disease*, ed. K.F. Kiple, pp. 738–41. New York: Cambridge University Press.

Steinbock, R.T. (1993*b*) Rickets and osteomalacia.In *The Cambridge World History of Human Disease*, ed. K.F. Kiple, pp. 978–80. New York: Cambridge University Press.

Steinbock, R.T. (1993*c*) Urolithiasis (renal and urinary bladder stone disease).In *The Cambridge World History of Human Disease*, ed. K.F. Kiple, pp. 1088–92. New York: Cambridge University Press.

Stenn, F.F., Milgram, J.W., Lee, S.L., Weigand, R.J. & Veis, A. (1977) Biochemical identification of homogentisic acid pigment in an ochronotic Egyptian mummy. *Science* **3**:566–8.

Sternberg, G.M. (1881) A fatal form of septicemia in the rabbit, produced by subcutaneous injection of human saliva. *National Board of Health Bulletin* **2**:781–3.

Stewart, T.D. (1953) The age incidence of neural arch defects in Alaskan natives considered from the standpoint of etiology. *Journal of Bone and Joint Surgery* **35A**:937–50.

Stewart, T.D. (1958*a*) Stone Age skull surgery: A general review, with emphasis on the New World. In *Annual Report of the Board of Regents of the Smithsonian Institution/1957*, pp. 469–91. Publication no. 4314. Washington, DC: United States Government Printing Office.

Stewart, T.D. (1958*b*) The rate of development of vertebral osteoarthritis in American whites and its significance in skeletal age identification. *The Leech* **28** (**3–5**):144—51.

Stewart, T.D. (1975) Cranial dysraphism mistaken for trephination. *American Journal of Physical Anthropology* **42**:435–8.

Stewart, T.D. (1979) *Essentials of Forensic Anthropology*. Springfield, IL: C.C. Thomas.

Stewart, T.D. & Spoehr, A. (1967) Evidence of the palaeopathology of yaws. In *Diseases in Antiquity*, ed. D. Brothwell & A.T. Sandison, pp. 307–19. Springfield, IL: C.C. Thomas.

Stirland, A. (1990) Paget's disease (osteitis deformans): A classic case? *International Journal of Osteoarchaeology* **1**(**3–4**):173–7.

Stirland, A. (1991) Pre-Columbian treponematosis in medieval Britain. *International Journal of Osteoarchaeology* **1**(**1**):39–47.

Stirland, A. & Waldron, T. (1990) The earliest cases of tuberculosis in Britain. *Journal of Archaeological Science* **17**:221–30.

Stone, J.L. & Miles, M.L. (1990) Skull trepanation among the early Indians of Canada and the United States. *Neurosurgery* **26**(**6**):1015–20.

Storrs, E.E. (1972) The armadillo as an animal model in leprosy studies. *International Journal of Leprosy* **40**:95. (Abstract).

Stout, S.D. (1974) Histological analysis of archaeological material: The identification of osteomalacia. *American Journal of Physical Anthropology* **41**(**3**):505. (Abstract).

Strano, A.J. (1976) Smallpox. In *Pathology of Tropical and Extraordinary Diseases*, ed. C.H. Binford & D.H. Connor, pp. 65–7. Washington, DC: Armed Forces Institute of Pathology.

Strano, A.J. & Font, R. (1976) Trachoma and inclusion conjunctivitis. In *Pathology of Tropical and Extraordinary Diseases*, ed. C.H. Binford & D.H. Connor, vol. 1, pp. 79–81. Washington, DC: Armed Forces Institute of Pathology.

Streitz, J.M., Aufderheide A.C., el-Najjar, M. & Ortner, D. (1981) A 1,500-year-old bladder stone. *Journal of Urology* **126**:452–3.

Strong, J.P. (1981) Pathology. In *Rypin's Medical Licensure Examinations*, ed. E.D. Frohlich, 13th edn, pp. 449–531. Philadelphia: Lippincott.

Stroppiana, L. (1973) Paleopatologia Oggi (Today's paleopathology). *Rivista di Storia della Medicina* **XVII**(**1**):140–50.

Strouhal, E. (1978) Ancient Egyptian case of carcinoma (nasopharyngeal). *Bulletin of the New York Academy of Medicine* **54**:290–2.

Strouhal, E. (1986) Embalming excerebration in the Middle Kingdom. In *Science in Egyptology*, ed. R.A. David, pp. 141–54. Manchester: Manchester University Press.

Strouhal, E. (1991*a*) A case of primary carcinoma from Christian Sayala (Egyptian Nubia). *Journal of Paleopathology* **3**(**3**):151–66.

Strouhal, E. (1991*b*) Myeloma multiplex versus osteolytic metastatic carcinoma: Differential diagnosis in dry bones. *International Journal of Osteoarchaeology* **1**:219–24.

Strouhal, E. (1991*c*) Vertebral tuberculosis in ancient Egypt and Nubia. In *Human Paleopathology. Current Syntheses and Future Options*, ed. D.J. Ortner & A.C. Aufderheide, pp. 181–94. Washington and London: Smithsonian Institution Press.

Strouhal, E. (1992) *Life of the Ancient Egyptians*. Norman, OK: University of Oklahoma Press.

Strouhal, E. (1994) Malignant tumors in the Old World. *Paleopathology Newsletter* **85** (**Mar, Supplement**):1–6.

Strouhal, E. & Jungwirth, J. (1977) Ein Verkalktes Myoma Uteri aus der Späte Römerzeit in Egyptisch-Nubien (A calcified uterine myoma from the Late Roman period in Egyptian Nubia). *Mitteilungen der Anthropologischen Gesellschaft in Wien* **107**:215–21.

Strouhal, E. & Jungwirth, J. (1980) Paleopathology of the Late Roman–Early Byzantine cemeteries at Sayala, Egyptian Nubia. *Journal of Human Evolution* **9**:61–70.

Strouhal, E. & Vyhnánek, L. (1979) Egyptian Mummies in Czechoslovak Collections. *Acta Musei Nationalis Pragae* **35B**:1–195.

Stuart-Macadam, P.L. (1989*a*) Nutritional deficiency diseases: A survey of scurvy, rickets and iron-deficiency anemia. In *Reconstruction of Life From the Skeleton*, ed. M.Y. Iscan & K.A.R. Kennedy, pp. 201–22. New York: Alan Liss.

Stuart-Macadam, P.L. (1989*b*) Porotic hyperostosis: Relationship between vault and orbital lesions. *American Journal of Physical Anthropology* **74**:511–20.

Stuart-Macadam, P.L. & Kent, S. (eds) (1992) *Diet, Demography and Disease*. New York: Aldine de Gruyter.

Suckling, G., Elliott, D.C. & Thurley, D.C. (1983) The production of developmental defects of enamel in the incisor teeth of penned sheep resulting from induced parasitism. *Archives of Oral Biology* **28**:393–9.

Suckling, G., Elliott, D.C. & Thurley, D.C. (1986) The macroscopic appearance and associated histological changes in the enamel organ of hypoplastic lesions of sheep incisor teeth resulting from induced parasitism. *Archives of Oral Biology* **31**:427–39.

Sudhoff, K. (1911) Ägyptischer Mumienmacher-Instrumente (Egyptian mummy—making instruments). *Archiv für Geschichte der Medizin* **5**:161–71.

Sudre P., Ten Dam, G. & Kochi, A. (1992) Tuberculosis: A global overview of the situation today. *Bulletin of the World Health Organization* **70**(**2**):149–59.

Suga, S. (1982) Progressive mineralization pattern of developing enamel during the maturation stage. *Journal of Dental Resarch* **61**:1532–42.

Sulzer, A.J., Cantella, R., Colichon, A., Gleason, N.N. & Walls, K.W. (1975) A focus of hyperendemic *Plasmodium malariae-P.vivax* with no *P. falciparum* in a primitive population in the Peruvian Amazon Jungle. Studies by means of immunofluorescence and blood smear. *Bulletin of the World Health Organization* **52**:273–8.

Suraiya, J.N. (1973) Medicine in ancient India with special reference to cancer. *Indian Journal of Cancer* **10**:391–402.

Susanne, C. (1970) L'Achondroplasie de la Population d'Age Franc de Coxyde (Belgique) (Achondroplasia of the Frankish period population from Coxyde (Belgium)). *Bulletin de Institute Sciences Naturels Belgique* **46**(**10**):1–52.

Suzuki, T. (1991) Paleopathological study on infectious diseases in Japan. In *Human Pale-*

opathology. *Current Syntheses and Future Options*, ed. D.J. Ortner & A.C. Aufderheide, pp. 128–39. Washington and London: Smithsonian Institution Press.

Swales, J.D. (1973) Tutankhamun's breasts. *Lancet* i(**7796**):201.

Swoboda, W. (1972) *Osteología Infantil. Osteogénesis, Malformaciones, Osteopatías (Infantile Osteology: Osteogenesis, Malformations and Osteopathies)*. Barcelona: Toray.

Symes, S.A. (1983) Harris lines as indicators of stress: An analysis of tibiae from the Crow Creek Massacre victims. Thesis on file in the Department of Anthropology at the University of Tennessee at Knoxville, TN.

Szathmary, E.J.E. (1990) Diabetes in Amerind population: Dogrib studies. In *Diabetes as a Disease of Civilization: The Impact of Culture Change on Indigenous Peoples*, ed. J.E. Joe & R.S. Young, pp. 407–34. New Babylon Studies in The Social Sciences no. 50. New York: Mouton de Gruyter.

Szent-Gyorgyi, A. (1928) Observations on the function of peroxidase systems and the chemistry of the adrenal cortex. Description of a new carbohydrate derivative. *Biochemistry Journal (London)* 22:1387–96.

Szidat, L. (1944) Über die Erhaltungsfähigkeit von Helmintheneiern in Vor- und Frühgeschichtlichen Moorleichen (On the preservation of helminth eggs in pre- and early historical bog corpses). *Zeitschrift für Parasitenkunde* **13**:265–74.

Taitz, L.S. (1973) Tutankhamun's breasts. *Lancet* i(**7795**):149.

Tapp, E. (1986) Histology and histopathology of the Manchester mummies. In *Science in Egyptology*, ed. R.A. David, pp. 347–50. Manchester: Manchester University Press.

Tapp, E., Curry, A. & Anfield, C. (1975) Sand pneumoconiosis in an Egyptian mummy. *Lancet* ii(**5965**):276.

Taylor, D.W. & Voller, A. (1993) The development and validation of a simple antigen detection ELISA for *Plasmodium falciparum* malaria. *Transactions of the Royal Society of Tropical Medicine and Hygiene* **87**:29–31.

Taylor, E.L. (1955) Parasitic helminths in medieval remains. *Veterinary Record* **67**:216–18.

Taylor, R.M. (1949) Studies on survival of influenza virus between epidemics and antigenic variants of the virus. *American Journal of Public Health* **39** (**February**):171–8.

Taylor, T.E. & Molyneux, M.E. (1995) Something new out of Africa. *New England Journal of Medicine* **332**(**21**):1441–2.

Teegen, W.R. & Schultz, M. (1994) Epidural hematoma in fetuses, newborns and infants from the early medieval settlements of Elisenhof and Starigard-Oldenburg (Germany). In *Papers on Paleopathology Presented at the Xth European Members Meeting of the Paleopathology Association in Göttingen, Germany on 29 August– 3 September 1994. Paleopathology Newsletter* **88** (**Supplement**):26. (Abstract).

Teitelbaum, L. (1980) The histopathology of osteomalacia. In *Bone Histomorphometry: Third International Workshop held at Sun Valley, May 28–June 2, 1980*, ed. W.S.S. Jee & A.M. Parfitt, pp. 475–82. Paris: Société Nouvelle de Publications Medicales Etentaires.

Tello, J.C. (1909) *La Antigüedad de la Sifilis en el Perú (The Antiquity of Syphilis in Peru)*. M.D. Dissertation, University of Lima. Lima: Ministerio de Fomento.

Tencate, A.R. (1989) *Oral Histology,* 3rd edn. St. Louis-Baltimore: C.V. Mosby Co.

Thienes, C. & Haley, T. (1972) *Clinical Toxicology.* Philadelphia: Lea and Febiger.

Thillaud, P.L. (1996) *Paléopathologie Humaine (Human Paleopathology)*. Sceaux Cedex: Kronos.

Thoma, K.H. (1944) *Oral Pathology,* 2nd edn. St. Louis-Baltimore: C.V. Mosby Co.

Thomas, H.W. (1933) Acropachy. *Archives of Internal Medicine* **51**:571–88.

Thompson, G.H. & Salter, R.B. (1992) Enfermedad de Legg-Calvé-Perthes (Legg-Calvé-Perthes disease). In *Sistema Musculoesquelético. Parte 2. Trastornos del Desarrollo, Tumores, Enfermedades Reumáticas y Reemplazamiento Articular, de F.H. Netter (Colección Ciba de Ilustraciones Médicas) (Musculoskeletal System. Part 2: Developmental Disorders, Tumors, Rheumatic Diseases and Joint Replacement of F.H. Netter (Ciba Collection of Medical Illustrations))*, ed. R.H. Freyberg & R.N. Hensinger, pp. 59–69. Barcelona: Salvat.

Thompson, P., Lynch, P.G. & Tapp, E. (1986) Neuropathological studies on the Manchester mummies. In *Science in Egyptology*, ed. R.A. David, pp. 375–8. Manchester: Manchester University Press.

Thornton, F. (1988) Extraordinary human teeth. *Journal of Paleopathology* **2**(**3**):173–6.

Thornton, R., Warren, J. & Miller, T. (1992) Depopulation in the Southeast after 1492. In *Disease and Demography in the Americas*, ed. J.W.Verano & D.H. Ubelaker, pp. 187–95. Washington, DC: Smithsonian Institution Press.

Tilghman, R.C. (1980) Captain James Scott (1728–1779): Explorations and the conquest of scurvy. *Transactions of the American Clinical and Climatological Society* **82**:1–15.

Time-Life Books (1992) *Incas: Lords of Gold and Glory*. Alexandria, VA. Time Life Inc.

Tkocz, I. & Bierring, F. (1984) A medieval case of metastasizing carcinoma with multiple osteosclerotic bone lesions. *American Journal of Physical Anthropology* **65**:373–80.

Tkocz, I., Bytzer, P. & Bierring, F. (1979) Preserved brains in medieval skulls. *American Journal of Physical Anthropology* **51**:197–202.

Todd, W. (1914) Paleolithic giants and dwarfs. *Cleveland Medical Journal* **13**:533–9.

Tonkelaar, D, Henkes, H.E. & Van Leersum, G.K. (1991) Herman Snellen (1834–1908) and Müller's "Reform-Auge." A short history of the artificial eye. *Documenta Ophthalmologica* **77**:349–54.

Torbenson, M., Aufderheide, A. & Johnson, E. (1992) Punctured human bones of the Laurel Culture from Smith Mound Four, Minnesota. *American Antiquity* **57**(**3**):506–14.

Torrella, G. (1497) Tractatus cum Consilis contra Pudendragum seu morbum Gallicum (Treatise including Treatment Suggestions for the Pudendal Condition called the French Disease). Rome. (Reprinted in Sudhoff, K. (1912) *Graphische und Typographische Erstlinge der Syphilisliteratur aus dem Jahren 1495 und 1496 (Graphic and Typographic Initial Presentations of the Syphilis Literature from the Years 1495 and 1496)*). Munich: Sudhoff.

Toynbee, J. (1849) Osseous tumours growing from the walls of the meatus externus and on the enlargement of the walls themselves; with cases. *Provincial Medical and Surgical Journal* **14**:533–7.

Trager, W. & Jensen, J.B. (1976) Human malaria parasites in continuous culture. *Science* **193**:673–5.

Trembly, D. (1994) On the antiquity of leprosy in western Micronesia. In *Papers on Paleopathology Presented at the 21st Annual Meeting of the Paleopathology Association in Denver, Colorado. Paleopathology Newsletter* **86**(**Supplement**):11. (Abstract).

Trimble, M.K. (1992) The 1832 inoculation program on the Missouri River. In *Disease and Demography in the Americas*, ed. J.W. Verano & D.H. Ubelaker, pp. 257–64. Washington, DC: Smithsonian Institution Press.

Trinkaus, E. (1983) *The Shanidar Neanderthals*. New York: Academic Press.

Trinkaus, E. (1985) Pathology and posture of the La Chapelle aux Saints Neandertal. *American Journal of Physical Anthropology* **67**:19–41.

Trueta, J. (1957) The normal anatomy of the human femoral head during growth. *Journal of Bone and Joint Surgery* **39B** (**2**):358–94.

Trueta, J. (1968) *Studies of the Development and Decay of the Human Frame*. Philadelphia: W.B. Saunders.

Tseng, W.D., Chu, H.M., How, S.W., Fong, J.M., Lin, C.S. & Yeh, Shu (1968) Prevalence of skin cancer in an endemic area of chronic arsenicism in Taiwan. *Journal of the National Cancer Institute* **40**:453–63.

Tuli, S.M. (1975) *Tuberculosis of the Spine*. New Delhi, India: Amerind Publishing Co.

Turek, S. L. (1982) *Ortopedia. Principios y Aplicaciones (Orthopedics: Principles and Applications)*. Barcelona: Salvat.

Turkel, S.J. (1989) Congenital abnormalities in skeletal populations. In *Reconstruction of Life from the Skeleton*, ed. M.Y. Iscan & K.A.R. Kennedy, pp. 109–27. New York: A.R. Liss.

Turner, C.G. & Cadien, J.D. (1969) Dental chipping in Aleuts, Eskimos and Indians. *American Journal of Physical Anthropology* **31**:303–10.

Tzaferis, V. (1985) Crucifixion – the archaeological evidence. *Biblical Archaeology Review* **11**:44–53.

Ubelaker, D.H. (1982) The development of American paleopathology. In *A History of American Physical Anthropology. 1930–1980*, ed. F. Spencer, pp. 337–56. New York: Academic Press.

Uhle, M. (1903) *Pachacamac. Report of the William Pepper, M.D., L.L.D. Peruvian Expedition of 1896*. Philadelphia: Department of Archaeology, University of Pennsylvania.

Ulrich-Bochsler, S., Schäublin, E., Zeltner, Th.B. & Glowatzki, G. (1982) Invalidisierende Wirbelsäulenverkrümmung an einem Skelettfund aus dem Frühmittelalter (7./8. bis Anfang 9. Jh.) (Disabling spinal curvature in an archaeological skeleton from the early Middle Ages (seventh, eighth or early ninth century)). *Schweizerische Medizinische Wochenschrift* **112**:1318–23.

Uribarri Murillo, G. & Palacios y Carvajal, J. (1990) *Atlas de Reumatología (Atlas of Rheumatology)*. Madrid: EMISA-Pfizer.

Urteaga, O. & Moseley, J.E. (1967) Craniometaphyseal dysplasia (Pyle's disease) in an ancient skeleton from the Mochica culture of Peru. *American Journal of Roentgenology* **99(3)**:713–16.

Urteaga, O. & Pack, G.T. (1966) On the antiquity of melanoma. *Cancer* **19**:607–10.

Uruñuela, G. & Alvarez, R. (1994) A report of Klippel-Feil syndrome in pre-Hispanic remains from Cholula, Puebla, Mexico. *Journal of Paleopathology* **6(2)**63–7.

van Gerven, D.P. (1981) Nubia's last Christians: The cemeteries of Kulunarti. *Archaeology* **34(3)**:22–30.

van Gilse, P.H.G. (1938) Des observation últerieures sur la gènese des oxostoses du donduit externe par l'irritation d'eau froid. (Recent observations on the origin of external auditory canal exostoses by cold water). *Otolaryngology (Stockholm)* **26**:243–52.

van Rippen, B.V. (1917) Precolumbian operative dentistry of the Indians of Middle and South America. *Dental Cosmos* **59(9)**:861–73.

van Tilburg, J. (1994) *Easter Island*. Washington, DC: Smithsonian Institution Press.

Vandier, J. (1964) *Manuel D'Archaeologie Égyptienne (Manual of Egyptian Archaeology)*. Paris: Editions A. et J. Picard et Cie.

Veale, H. (1866) History of an epidemic of Röteln, with observations on its pathology. *Edinburgh Medical Journal* **12**:404–14.

Verano, J.W. (1986) A mass burial of mutilated individuals at Pacatnamu. In *The Pacatnamu Papers*, ed. C.B. Donnan & G.A. Cock, vol. 1, pp. 117–38. Los Angeles: Museum of Cultural History.

Verano, J.W. (1995) Where do they rest? The treatment of human offerings and trophies in ancient Peru. In *Tombs for the Living: Andean Mortuary Practices*, ed. T. Dillehay, pp. 1–45. Washington, DC: Dumbarton Oaks.

Verger Garau, G. (1983) Sarampión (Measles). In *Patología Infecciosa Básica. Enfermedades Víricas (Basic Infectious Pathology: Viral Diseases)*, ed. F. Gudiol Munté, pp. 75–81. Madrid: IDEPSA-Antibióticos.

Verneau, R. (1879) *De la Pluralité des Races Anciennes de l'Archipes Canarien (On the Plurality of Ancient Races in the Canarian Archipelago)*. Paris: Extrait des Bulletin Société de Anthropologie. Typographie A. Hennuyer.

Vhnanek, L. & Strouhal, E. (1975) Arteriosclerosis in Egyptian mummies. *Anthropologie (Brno, Czech)* **13**:219–21.

Vilaplana, J. (1992) *Diccionario de Dermatología JIMS (JIMS' Dictionary of Dermatology)*. Barcelona: JIMS.

Villemin, J.A. (1865) De la Virulence et de la Spéceficité de la tuberculose (Concerning the virulence and specificity of tuberculosis). *Gazette Hebdomadaire de Médecine et De Chirurgie* **5**:537.

Virchow, R. (1866) Ein fall von allgemeiner Ochronose der Knorpel und Knorpelähnlichen Theile (A case of ochronosis of cartilage and cartilage-like tissues). *Archiv für Pathologische Anatomie und Physiologie und für Klinische Medizin* **37**:212–19.

Virchow, R. (1895) Knochen vom Höhlenbären mit krankhaften Veränderungen (Cave bear bones with diseased alterations). *Zeitschrift für Ethnologie (Berlin)* **27**:706–8.

Virchow, R. (1896) Beitrag zur Geschichte der Lues (Discussion of the history of syphilis). *Dermatologische Zeitschrift* **3**:1–9.

Virel, A. (1980) *Decorated Man: The Human Body as Art*. New York: Harry N. Abrams.

Vital Statistics of U.S.A. (1989) Washington, DC: Government Printing Office.

von Luschan, F. (1896a) Die Trepanirte von Tenerife (Trephined skulls from Tenerife). *Verhandlungen der Berliner Gesellschaft für Anthropologie* **28**:63–5.

von Luschan, F. (1896b) Über eine Schädelsammlung von den Canarischen Inseln (The cranial collection of the Canary Islands). In *Die Insel Tenerife (The Island Tenerife)*, ed. H. Meyer, pp. 285–319. Leipzig: Hirzel.

Vreeland, J.M. (1978) Prehistoric Andean mortuary practice: Preliminary report from Peru. *Current Anthropology* **19**:212–14.

Vreeland, J.M. & Cockburn, A. (1980) Mummies of Peru. In *Mummies, Disease and Ancient Cultures*, ed. A. Cockburn & E. Cockburn, pp. 135–74. Cambridge: Cambridge University Press.

Vyhnánek, L. (1971) Eine aus dem frühmittelalterichen Skelletmaterial (An example of casuistry from early medieval skeletal material). *Zeitschrift für Orthopaedie und ihre Grenzgebiete* **109**:922–3.

Vyhnánek, L. & Stloukal, M. (1991) Harris lines in adults: An open problem. In *Human Paleopathology. Current Syntheses and Future Options*, ed. D.J. Ortner & A.C. Aufderheide, pp. 92–4. Washington and London: Smithsonian Institution Press.

Wade, H.W. & Ledowsky, V. (1952) The leprosy epidemic at Nauru: A review. *International Journal of Leprosy* **20(1)**:1–29.

Wagner-Jauregg, J. (1922) The treatment of general paralysis by inoculation of malaria. *Journal of Nervous and Mental Diseases* **55**:369–75.

Wakely, J. (1993) Bilateral congenital dislocation of the hip, spina bifida occulta and spondylolysis in a female skeleton from the medieval cemetery at Abingdon, England. *Journal of Paleopathology* **5(1)**:37–45.

Waldron, H.A. (1993) The health of the adults. In *The Spitalsfield Project. Volume 2. The Anthropology: The Middling Sort*, ed. T. Molleson & M. Cox with H.A. Waldron & D.K. Whittaker, pp. 67–87. Council for British Archaeology Research Report no. 86. York: Council for British Archaeology.

Waldron, T. (1987a) Lytic lesions in a skull: A problem in diagnosis. *Journal of Paleopathology* **1(1)**:5–14.

Waldron, T. (1987b) The relative survival of the human skeleton: Implications for paleopathology. In *Death, Decay and Reconstruction: Approaches to Archaeology and Forensic Science*, ed. A. Boddington, A.N. Garland & R.C. Janaway, pp.55–64. Manchester: Manchester University Press.

Waldron, T., Cox, M. & Molleson, T. (1989) Osteopetrosis in an eighteenth century English family. Paper presented at the 16th Annual meeting of the Paleopathology Association held in San Diego, CA on 4–5 April, 1989. *Paleopathology Newsletter* **66 (June:Supplement)**:4. (Abstract).

Walker, A., Zimmerman, M.R. & Leakey, R.E.F. (1982) A possible case of hypervitaminosis A in *Homo erectus*. *Nature* **296**:248–50.

Walker, E.L. (1931) Experimental entamoebic dysentery. *Philippine Journal of Science* **8**:253–371.

Walker, P.L. (1989) Cranial injuries as evidence of violence in prehistoric Southern California. *American Journal of Physical Anthropology* **80**:313–23.

Walker, R., Parsche, F., Bierbrier, M. & McKerrow, J.H. (1987) Tissue identification and histologic study of six lung specimens from Egyptian mummies. *American Journal of Physical Anthropology* **72**:43–8.

Wallgren, J.E., Caple, R. & Aufderheide, A.C. (1986) Contributions of nuclear magnetic resonance studies to the question of alkaptonuria (ochronosis) in an Egyptian mummy. In *Science in Egyptology*, ed. R. A. David, pp. 321–7. Manchester: Manchester University Press.

Walsche, J.M. (1973) Tutankhamun: Klinefelter's or Wilson's? *Lancet* **i**(**7794**):109–10.

Walter, P. (1929) Fossilized human brains found. *El Palacio* **27**(**13–18**):203–4.

Walther, P.F. von (1825) Über das Alterthum der Knochenkrankheiten (On the antiquity of bone diseases). *Journal der Chirurgie und Augenheilkunst (Bonn)* **8**:16.

Warren, J.C. (1822) *A Comparative View of the Sensorial and Nervous System in Man and Animals*. Boston, MA: Ingraham.

Watrous, A.C., Anton, S.C. & Plourde, A.M. (1993) Hyperostosis frontalis interna in ancient Egyptians. *American Journal of Physical Anthropology* **16** (**Supplement**):205. (Abstract).

Watson-Jones, R. (1980) Reparación de Fracturas (Fracture repair). In *Fracturas y Heridas Articulares, de Watson-Jones (Watson-Jones – Fractures and Joint Injuries)*, ed. J.N. Wilson, vol. 1, pp. 11–47. Barcelona: Salvat.

Way, A.B. (1981) Diseases in Latin America. In *Biocultural Aspects of Disease*, ed. H.R. Rothschild, pp. 253–91. New York: Academic Press.

Weatherell, J.A. & Weidmann, S.M. (1959) The skeletal changes of chronic experimental fluorosis. *Journal of Pathology and Bacteriology* **78**:233–41.

Webb, S. (1990) Prehistoric eye disease (trachoma?) in Australian aborigines. *American Journal of Physical Anthropology* **81**:91–100.

Weber, M. (1927) Schliff con mazerierten Rohrknochen und ihre Bedeutung für die Unterscheidung der Syphilis und Osteomyelitis von der Osteodystrophia, fibrosa, sowie für die Untersuchung fraglich syphilitischer prähistorischer Knochen (Sectioning of macerated long bones and their interpretation for the differentiation of syphilis and osteomyelitis from osteodystrophy and osteofibrosis as well as examination of questionably syphilitic prehistoric bones). *Beitrage zur Pathologischen Anatomie und zur Allgemeine Pathologie* **78**:441–511.

Wedeen, R.P. (1984) *Poison in the Pot*. Carbondale, IL: Southern Illinois University Press.

Wei, O. (1973) Internal organs of a 2100 year old female corpse. *Lancet* **ii**(**7839**):1198.

Weisman, A. (1965) *The Weisman Collection of pre-Columbian Medical Sculpture*. Arlington, VA: American Anthropological Society.

Weiss, D.L. & Møller-Christensen, V. (1971) Leprosy, echinococcosis and amulets: A study of a medieval Danish inhumation. *Medical History (London)* **15**:260–7.

Weiss, K. M., Ulbrecht, Jan, S., Cavanagh, Peter R. & Buchanan, A.V. (1989) Diabetes mellitus in American Indians: Characteristics, origins and preventive health care implications. *Medical Anthropology* **11**:283–304.

Weiss, P. (1958) *Osteología Cultural. Prácticas Cefálicas. 1ª parte. Cabeza Trofeos-Trepanaciones-Cauterizaciones (Cultural Osteology. Cephalic Practices. Part 1: Trophy Heads, Trepanation and Cauterization)*. Lima: Universidad Nacional Mayor de San Marcos.

Welcker, H. (1888) Cribra orbitalia, ein etiologischdiagnostisches Merkmal am Schädel mehrerer Menschrassen (Cribra orbitalia, an etiologic and diagnostic feature in the skull of multiple human races). *Archiv Anthropologie* **17**:1–18.

Weller, M. (1972) Tutankhamun: An adrenal tumor? *Lancet* **ii**(**7790**):1312.

Weller, T.H. & Neva, F.A. (1962) Propagation in tissue culture of cytopathic agents from patients with rubella-like illnesses. *Proceedings of the Society for Experimental Biology and Medicine* **111**:215–25.

Wells, C. (1962) Joint pathology in ancient Anglo-Saxons. *Journal of Bone and Joint Surgery* **44** (**B-4**):948–9.

Wells, C. (1963a) Ancient Egyptian pathology. *Journal of Laryngology and Otology* **77**:261–5.

Wells, C. (1963b) Polyostotic fibrous dysplasia in a seventh century Anglo-Saxon. *British Journal of Radiology* **36**:925–6.

Wells, C. (1964) *Bones, Bodies and Disease*. London: Thames and Hudson.

Wells, C. (1965a) A pathological Anglo-Saxon femur. *British Journal of Radiology* **38**:393–4.

Wells, C. (1965b) Osteogenesis imperfecta from an Anglo-Saxon burial ground at Burgh Castle, Suffolk. *Medical History* **9**:88–9.

Wells, C. (1967a) Pseudopathology. In *Diseases in Antiquity*, ed. D. Brothwell & A.T. Sandison, pp. 5–19. Springfield, IL: C.C. Thomas.

Wells, C. (1967b) A new approach to palaeopathology: Harris's lines. In *Diseases in Antiquity*, ed. D. Brothwell & A.T. Sandison, pp. 390–404. Springfield, IL: C.C. Thomas.

Wells, C. (1968a) Goitre in two African sculptures. *Medical History* **12**(**1**):89–91.

Wells, C. (1968b) Osgood-Schlatter's disease in the ninth century? *British Medical Journal* **2**:623–4.

Wells, C. (1973a) A paleopathological rarity in a skeleton of Roman date. *Medical History* **17**:399–400.

Wells, C. (1973b) The palaeopathology of bone disease. *Practitioner* **210**:384–91.

Wells, C. (1974) Osteochondritis dissecans in ancient British skeletal material. *Medical History* **18**(**4**):365–9.

Wells, C. (1975) Prehistoric and historical changes in nutritional disease and associated conditions. *Progress in Food Nutrition Science* **1**(**2**):729–79.

Wells, C. & Dallas, C. (1976) Romano-British pathology. *Antiquity* **50**:53–5.

Wells, C. & Maxwell, B.M. (1962) Alkaptonuria in an Egyptian mummy. *British Journal of Radiology* **35** (**418**):679–82.

Wells, C. & Woodhouse, N. (1975) Paget's disease in an Anglo-Saxon. *Medical History* **19**(**4**):396–400.

Wendorf, M. (1989) Diabetes, the ice-free corridor, and the Indian paleosettlement of North America. *American Journal of Physical Anthropology* **79**:503–20.

West, I.E. (1986) Forensic aspects of Lindow man. In *Lindow Man. The Body in the Bog*, ed. I.M. Stead, J.B. Bourke & D. Brothwell, pp. 77–80. Ithaca, NY: Cornell University Press.

Westermark, N. & Forssman, G. (1938) The roentgen diagnosis of tuberculous spondylitis. *Acta Radiologia* **19**:207–14.

Whistler, D. (1645) Demorbo Puerili Anglorum, Quem Patrio Idiomate Indiginae Vocant The Rickets (Of a Disease of Children that the English call The Rickets). London: Lugduni Batavorum. (Cited in Clarke, 1962).

White, C. (1996) Sutural effects of fronto-occipital cranial modification. *American Journal of Physical Anthropology* **100**:397–410.

White, N. & Plorde, J.J. (1991) Malaria. In *Harrison's Principles of Internal Medicine*, ed. J.D. Wilson, E. Braunwald, K.J. Isselbacher, *et al.*, 12th edn, pp. 782–8. New York: McGraw-Hill.

White, T.D. & Folkens, P.A. (1991) *Human Osteology*. New York: Academic Press.

White, T.D. & Toth, N.(1991) The question of ritual cannibalism at Grotta Guattari. *Current Anthropology* **32**(**2**):118–24.

Whitney, W. F. (1886) Notes on the anomalies, injuries and diseases of the bones of the native races of North America. *Annual Reports of the Peabody Museum of American Archaeology and Ethnology* **3**(**5&6**):433–8.

WHO (World Health Organization) (1960a) Cretinism and endemic goitre. *WHO Chronicle* **13**(**9**):353–5.

WHO (World Health Organization) (1960b) Endemic goitre. *WHO Chronicle* **14**(**9**):337–65.

WHO (World Health Organization) (1980) *A Guide to Leprosy Control*. Geneva: World Health Organization.

WHO (World Health Organization) (1985) *Epidemiology of Leprosy in Relation to Control*. Technical Report 716. Geneva: World Health Organization.

WHO (World Health Organization) (1992) *Leprosy Situation in the World and Multidrug Therapy Coverage*. Weekly Epidemiological Record, 22 May, 1992. Geneva: World Health Organization.

Whyte, M.P. (1993) Osteogenesis imperfecta. In *Primer on the Metabolic Bone Diseases and Disorders of Mineral Metabolism*, ed. M.J. Favus, 2nd edn, pp.346–50. New York: Raven Press.

Widmer, L. & Perzigian, A.J. (1981) The ecology and etiology of skeletal lesions in Late Prehistoric populations from eastern North America. In *Prehistoric Tuberculosis in the Americas*, ed. J.E. Buikstra, pp. 99–113. Evanston, IL: Northwestern University Archeological Program.

Wilder, H.H. (1904) The restoration of dried tissues with special reference to human remains. *American Anthropologist* **6**:1–17.

Wilkins, L. (1941) Epiphyseal dysgenesis associated with hypothyroidism. *American Journal of Diseases of Children* **61**:13–34.

Wilkins, L. & Fleischman, W. (1941) The diagnosis of hypothyroidism in children. *Journal of the American Medical Association* **1116**(**22**):2459–65.

Williams, C.S. & Riordan, D.C. (1973) *Mycobacterium marinum* (atypical acid-fast bacillus) infections of the hand. *Journal of Bone and Joint Surgery* **55A**:1042–50.

Williams, H.U. (1927) Gross and microscopic anatomy of two Peruvian mummies. *Archives of Pathology and Laboratory Medicine* **4**:26–33.

Williams, H.U. (1929) Human paleopathology. *Archives of Pathology* **7**:839–902.

Williams, J.A. (1985) Evidence of hydatid disease in a Plains Woodland burial. *Plains Anthropologist (Lincoln, NE)* **30**:25–8.

Williams, N. (1996) Phage transfer: A new player turns up in cholera infection. *Science* **272**:1869–70.

Williams, R.C. (1990) Periodontal disease. *New England Journal of Medicine* **322**(**6**):373–82.

Willman, C.L., Busque, L., Griffith, B.B., Favara, B.E., McClain, K.L., Duncan, M.H. & Gilliland, D.G. (1994) Langerhans' – cell histiocytosis (histiocytosis X) – a clonal proliferative disease. *New England Journal of Medicine* **331**:154–60.

Wilson, J.D. (1991*a*) Vitamin deficiency and excess. In *Harrison's Principles of Internal Medicine*, ed. J.D. Wilson, E. Braunwald, K.J. Isselbacher, *et al.*, 12th edn, pp. 434–43. New York: McGraw-Hill.

Wilson, J. (1991*b*) Hormones and hormone action. In *Harrison's Principles of Internal Medicine*, ed. J.D. Wilson, E. Braunwald, K.J. Isselbacher, *et al.*, 12th edn, pp. 1647–52. New York: McGraw-Hill.

Wilson, J.D. (1991*c*) Endocrine disorders of the breast. In *Harrison's Principles of Internal Medicine*, ed. J.D. Wilson, E. Braunwald, K.J. Isselbacher, *et al.*, 12th edn, pp. 1795–8. New York: McGraw-Hill.

Wilson, R.R. (1972) Artificial eyes in ancient Egypt. *Survey of Ophthalmology* **16**(**5**):322–31.

Wimberger, H. (1923*a*) Zur Diagnose des Säuglingskorbuts (On the diagnosis of infantile scurvy). *Zeitschrift für Kinderheilkunde* **36**:279–85.

Wimberger, H. (1923*b*) A study of developing, florid and healing rickets as demonstrated by x-ray photography. Studies of rickets in Vienna 1919–1922. In *Medical Research Council Special Report Series, No. 77*, pp. 95–114. London: Medical Research Council.

Winlock, H.E. (1942) *Excavations at Deir el Bahari 1911–1931*. New York: McMillan.

Winlock, H.E. (1945) *The Slain Soldiers of Neb-Hepet-Re Mentu-Hotpe*. Vol. 16. New York: The Metropolitan Museum of Art Publications of Egyptian Expedition.

Witenberg, G. (1961) Human parasites in archaeological findings. *Israel Exploration Society Bulletin Jerusalem* **25**:86. (In Hebrew. English Summary In: P. Wilke & H.J. Hall (1975) *Analysis of Ancient Feces. A Discussion and Annotated Bibliography*, p. 46. Berkeley, CA: Department of Anthropology, University of California, Berkeley.)

Wittmers, L.E., Jr, Alich, A. & Aufderheide, A.C. (1981) Lead in bone I. Direct analysis for lead in milligram quantities of bone ash by graphite furnace atomic absorption spectroscopy. *American Journal of Clinical Pathology* **75**(**1**):80–5.

Woo, D. (1995) Apoptosis and loss of renal tissue in polycystic kidney diseases. *New England Journal of Medicine* **333**:18–25.

Wood, C.S. (1975) New evidence for a late introduction of malaria into the New World. *Current Anthropology* **16**(**1**):93–104.

Wood, C.S. (1979) *Human Sickness and Health: A Biocultural View*. Palo Alto, CA: Mayfield Publishing Co.

Wright, A.D., Hill, D.M., Lowy, C. & Fraser, T.R. (1970) Mortality in acromegaly. *Quarterly Journal of Medicine* **39**:1–16.

Wright, J. (1923) The dawn of surgery: The ritual mutilations of primitive magic and circumcision. *New York Medical Journal* **117**:103–5.

Wrobelewski, C. (1987) *Pigments of Imagination*. New York: Albert van der Marck Editions.

Wu, K., Schubeck, K.E., Frost, H.M. & Villanueva, A. (1970) Haversian bone formation rates determined by a new method in a mastodon, and in human diabetes mellitus and osteoporosis. *Calcified Tissue Research* **6**:204–19.

Wucherer, O. (1868) Preliminary report on a species of worm, as yet undescribed, found in the urine of patients with tropical hematuria in Brazil. *Gazeta Medica de Bahia* **3**:97–9.

Wyatt, H.V. (1976) James Lind and the prevention of scurvy. *Medical History* **20**:433–8.

Wyatt, H.V. (1993) Poliomyelitis. In *The Cambridge World History of Human Disease*, ed. K.F. Kiple, pp. 942–50. New York: Cambridge University Press.

Wyler, D.J. (1983*a*) Malaria-resurgence, resistance and research. Part 1. *New England Journal of Medicine* **308**:875–8.

Wyler, D.J. (1983*b*) Malaria-resurgence, resistance and research. Part 2. *New England Journal of Medicine* **308**:934–40.

Wyler, D.J. (1993) Malaria chemoprophylaxis for the traveler. *New England Journal of Medicine* **329**:31–7.

Wynne-Davies, R. & Fairbank, T.J. (1982) *Fairbank. Atlas de Enfermedades Generalizadas del Esqueleto (Fairbank's Atlas of Generalized Skeletal Diseases)*. Barcelona: Salvat.

Yamada, K.A. & Sherman, I.W. (1979) *Plasmodium lophurae*: Composition and properties of hemozoin, the malarial pigment. *Experimental Parasitology* **48**:61–71.

Yoe, S. (1963) *The Burman: His Life and Notions*. New York: W.W. Norton & Co., Inc. (Schway Yoe was the pseudonym of J.G. Scott).

Yoeli, M. (1955) "Facies leontina" of leprosy on an ancient Canaanite jar. *Journal of the History of Medicine* **10**:331–5.

Yoldi, A., Manzanares, J. & du Souich, Ph. (1996) Estudio de un Caso de Espondiloartritis Anquilopoyética en un Indivíduo del Siglo XVIII (Study of a case of ankylosing spondylitis in an individual from the eighteenth century). In *Salud, Enfermedad y Muerte en el Pasado. Actas del III Congreso Nacional de Palaeopatología (Health, Disease and Death in the Past. Proceedings of the Third National Paleopathology Congress)*, ed. A. Pérez-Pérez, pp. 215–23. Barcelona: Fundación Uriach 1838.

Yu, V.L. (1993) Legionnaire's disease: New understanding of community-acquired pneumonia. *Hospital Practice* (October 30) **28** (**10A**):63–70.

Zaino, E.C. (1967) Symmetrical osteoporosis, a sign of severe anemia in the prehistoric Pueblo Indians of the southwest. In *Technical Series Number 7. Miscellaneous Papers in Paleopathology: 1. Museum of Northern Arizona*, ed. W.D. Wade, pp. 40–7. Flagstaff, AZ: Northern Arizona Society of Science and Art.

Zaldívar, R. (1974) Arsenic contamination of drinking water and foodstuffs causing endemic chronic poisoning. *Beitrage zur Pathologie* **151**:384–400.

Zaldívar, R. & Ghai, G. (1980) Clinical epidemiological studies on endemic, chronic arsenic poisoning in children and adults, including observations on children with high and low intake of dietary arsenic. *Zentralblatt für Bakteriologie, Parasitenkunde, Infektionskrakheiten und Hygiene* **170**:409–21.

Zaldívar, R., Villar, I., Robinson, H., Wetterstrand, W.H., Ghai, G.L. & Brain, C. (1978) Intoxicacion arsenical crónica. Datos epidemiológicos, clínicos, patlógicos, toxicológicos y nutricionales (Chronic arsenic intoxication. Epidemiological, clinical, pathological, toxicological and nutritional data). *Revista Médica de Chile* **106**:1027–30.

Zambaco-Pachá (1897) *L'antiquité de la Syphilis (The Antiquity of Syphilis)*. Paris Medical no. 52.

Zambaco-Pachá (1914) *La lepre a Travers de les Siècles et les Contrées (Leprosy Through the Centuries and the Regions)*. Paris: Masson.

Zheng, L., Collins, F.H., Kumar, V. & Kafatos, F.C. (1993) A detailed genetic map for the X-chromosome of the malaria vector, *Anopheles gambiae*. *Science* **261**:605–8.

Zias, J. (1985) Leprosy in the Byzantine monasteries of the Judean Desert. *Koroth* **9**:242–7.

Zias, J. (1991) Death and disease in ancient Israel. *Biblical Archeologist* **54** (**Sept**):147–59.

Zias, J. & Mitchell, P.D. (1995) Psoriatic arthritis in a fifth century Judean desert monastery. *Journal of Paleopathology* **7**(**2**):151. (Abstract).

Zias, J. & Mumcuoglu, K. (1991) Prepottery Neolithic B head lice from Na'hal Hemar cave. *Atiqot* **26**:167–8.

Zias, J. & Pomeranz, S. (1992) Serial craniectomies for intracranial infection 5.5 millennia ago. *International Journal of Osteoarchaeology* **2**:183–6.

Zias, J. & Sekeles, E. (1985) The crucified man from Giv'at ha-Mivtar: A reappraisal. *Israel Exploration Journal* **35**:22–7.

Zimmerman, M.R. (1977) The mummies of the tomb of Nebwenenef: Paleopathology and archaeology. *Journal of the American Research Center in Egypt* **14**:33–6.

Zimmerman, M.R. (1978) The mummified heart: A problem in medicological diagnosis. *Journal of Forensic Sciences* **23**:750–3..

Zimmerman, M.R. (1979) Pulmonary and osseous tuberculosis in an Egyptian mummy. *Bulletin of the New York Academy of Medicine (Second Series)* **55**(**6**):604–8.

Zimmerman, M.R. (1981) A possible histiocytoma in an Egyptian mummy. *Archives of Dermatology* **117**:364–5.

Zimmerman, M.R. (1985) Paleopathology in Alaskan mummies. *American Scientist* **73**:20–5.

Zimmerman, M.R. (1986) Case No. 22: Anthracosis and fibrosis. (Department of Pathology, Medical College of Virginia, Richmond, VA) *Paleopathology Club Newsletter* **26**:1.

Zimmerman, M.R. (1990) The paleopathology of the liver. *Annals of Clinical and Laboratory Science* **20**(**5**):301–6.

Zimmerman, M.R. (1993*a*) The paleopathology of the cardiovascular system. *Texas Heart Institute Journal* **20**(**4**):252–7.

Zimmerman, M.R. (1993*b*) Curios, African Art and Paleopathology. *Paleopathology Newsletter* **84**:9–12.

Zimmerman, M.R. (1994) Case No. 52: Osteoporosis in an Alaskan mummy. (Department of Pathology, Medical College of Virginia, Richmond, VA) *Paleopathology Club Newsletter* **56**:2.

Zimmerman, M.R. (1995) Paleohistology of ancient soft tissue tumors. Paper presented at the 22nd Annual Meeting of the Paleopathology Association held in Oakland, CA, on 28–29 March, 1995. *Paleopathology Newsletter* **90** (**June**) (**Supplement**):14–15. (Abstract).

Zimmerman, M.R. & Aufderheide, A.C. (1984) The frozen family of Utqiagvik: The autopsy findings. *Arctic Anthropology* **21**:53–64.

Zimmerman, M.R. & Clark, W.H. (1976) A possible case of subcorneal pustular dermatosis in an Egyptian mummy. *Archives of Dermatology* **117**:364–5.

Zimmerman, M.R. & Hart Hansen, J.P. (1986) Tattoos and the dating of mummies. In *Dating and Age Determination of Biological Materials*, ed. M.R. Zimmerman & J.L. Angel, pp. 170–5. London: Croom Helm.

Zimmerman, M.R. & Kelley, M.A. (1982) *Atlas of Human Paleopathology*. New York: Praeger.

Zimmerman, M.R. & Smith, G.S. (1975) A probable case of accidental inhumation of 1600 years ago. *Bulletin of the New York Academy of Medicine* **51**:828–37.

Zimmerman, M.R., Yeatman, G.W., Sprinz, H. (1971) Examination of an Aleutian mummy. *Bulletin of the New York Academy of Medicine* **47**:80–103.

Zimmerman, M.R., Trinkaus, E., Lemay, M., Aufderheide, A.C., Reyman, T.A., Marrocco, G.R., Shultes, R.E. & Coughlin, E.A. (1981) Trauma and trephination in a Peruvian mummy. *American Journal of Physical Anthropology* **55**:497–501.

Zivanovic, S. (1982) *Ancient Diseases*. New York: Pica.

Zubigwe, F.T. (1982) *The Cross and the Shroud*. Smithtown, NY: Angelus Books.

Zuckerman, A.J. (1984) Paleontology of smallpox. *Lancet* **ii**(**8417–18**):1454.

Zumwalt, R.E. & Fierro, M.F. (1990) Postmortem changes. In *Handbook of Forensic Pathology*, ed. R.C. Froede, pp. 78–84. Northfield, IL: College of American Pathologists.

Zuppinger, A. (1954) Condensaciones Patológicas en la Sombra de Partes Blandas (Pathological condensations in soft tissue shadows). In *Röntgen-Diagnóstico (Diagnostic Roentgenology)*, ed. H.R. Schinz, W.E. Baensch, E. Friedl & E. Uehlinger, vol. 2, pp. 1826–905. Barcelona: Salvat.

Index